everything's an argument/with readings

Fifth Edition

EVERYTHING'S AN argument

with readings

Andrea A. Lunsford
STANFORD UNIVERSITY

John J. Ruszkiewicz
UNIVERSITY OF TEXAS AT AUSTIN

Keith Walters
PORTLAND STATE UNIVERSITY

BEDFORD / ST. MARTIN'S
BOSTON   ◆   NEW YORK

For Bedford/St. Martin's

Senior Developmental Editor: John Elliott
Production Editor: Jessica Skrocki Gould
Senior Production Supervisor: Nancy Myers
Marketing Manager: Molly Parke
Art Director: Lucy Krikorian
Text Design: Anna Palchik
Copy Editor: Rosemary Winfield
Photo Research: Sue McDermott Barlow
Cover Design: Donna Dennison
Cover Photos: (clockwise from top) Veer, Collection: Photodisc Photography;
    Veer, Collection: Digital Vision Photography; Everett Kennedy Brown/epa/
    Corbis; Veer, Collection: Brand X Photography; Original image by Matt
    Krueger at DVICE; Courtesy of Lexus; Getty Images, Inc., Photographer/
    Artist: Tom Schierlitz
Composition: Six Red Marbles
Printing and Binding: R.R. Donnelley & Sons Company

President: Joan E. Feinberg
Editorial Director: Denise B. Wydra
Editor in Chief: Karen S. Henry
Director of Development: Erica T. Appel
Director of Marketing: Karen R. Soeltz
Director of Editing, Design, and Production: Marcia Cohen
Assistant Director of Editing, Design, and Production: Elise S. Kaiser
Managing Editor: Shuli Traub

Library of Congress Control Number: 2009939558

Manufactured in the United States of America.

5 6   14 13 12 11

For information, write: Bedford/St. Martin's, 75 Arlington Street,
Boston, MA 02116   (617-399-4000)

ISBN 10: 0-312-53861-8   ISBN 13: 978-0-312-53861-3 (paperback)
ISBN 10: 0-312-61233-8   ISBN 13: 978-0-312-61233-7 (hardcover)

Acknowledgments

PREFACE

In each previous edition, we have described *Everything's an Argument* as a labor of love for us, and it remains so. Our affection for the book derives in part from knowing that it helps students to make persuasive and ethical arguments in a world where that ability grows ever more essential. *Everything's an Argument* was conceived and published (first as a brief rhetoric and then in this longer version with an anthology of readings) just as new technologies were beginning to reshape the ways persuasive writing could be framed and shared, and we have enjoyed tracking those developments—offering fresh arguments and provocative visual images in each new edition to illuminate the ways we all use language to assert our presence in the world. A best-seller in its field since its debut, *Everything's an Argument* apparently strikes a chord with students and instructors who expect a book on persuasion to be candid, balanced, and attuned to everyday events. We now offer a fifth edition, carefully revised to meet those standards and to offer writers and instructors important new tools for reading and making arguments.

The purposefully controversial title of this text sums up three key assumptions we share. First, language provides the most powerful means of understanding the world and of using that understanding to help shape lives. Second, arguments seldom if ever have only two sides: rather, they present a dizzying array of perspectives, often with as many "takes" on a subject as there are arguers. Understanding arguments, then, calls for carefully considering a full range of perspectives before coming to judgment. Finally, and most important, all language—including that of sounds and images or of symbol systems other than writing—is in some way persuasive, pointing in a direction and asking for a response. Texts of every kind beckon for reactions, from the dyed finger of a voter in Zimbabwe to the latest Twitter feed, from the American flag to Sarah Palin's shoes, from the latest reggaeton hit to the brand identity of the new Tata Nano. People walk, talk, and breathe persuasion very much as they breathe the air: everything is a potential argument.

So our purpose in *Everything's an Argument with Readings* is to present argument as something that's as everyday as an old sweater, as something we do almost from the moment we are born (in fact, an infant's first cry is as poignant a claim as we can imagine), and as something worthy of careful attention and practice. In pursuing this goal, we try to use ordinary language whenever possible and keep specialized terminology to a minimum. But we also see argument, and want students to see it, as a craft both delicate and powerful. So we have designed the book to be itself an argument for civil persuasion, with a voice that aims to appeal to readers cordially but that doesn't hesitate to make demands on them when appropriate.

To that end (and in response to numerous requests), we have written a new chapter, "Academic Arguments," to explain precisely how the arguments students encounter and write in school might differ from those they meet in other arenas of life. The chapter examines the special demands and conventions of scholarly writing and provides two extended examples, one by a student and one by a faculty member. In addition, because academic writing crosses all genres, we highlight its variety with a box in each chapter of Part 2 that illustrates how it's used in the chapter's genre, such as a definition or proposal.

The new essays in the "Academic Arguments" chapter are among six new full-length arguments—on topics ranging from Chris Rock to what to do with the International Space Station to the role music has played in U.S.-China diplomacy—that provide engaging, topical new readings for students. All of the essays in the book that use MLA documentation style have been updated to conform to the newest (2009) edition of the *MLA Handbook for Writers of Research Papers*, and Chapter 20, "Documenting Sources," has been thoroughly revised to offer guidelines and examples reflecting those in both the new *MLA Handbook* and (for APA style) the new 2010 edition of the *Publication Manual of the American Psychological Association*.

In another major improvement, and again in response to users' requests, we have expanded our chapter "Structuring Arguments" to better show how assumptions embedded within the structures of arguments shape what makers of arguments are likely to say. We use the classical oration to represent traditional thesis-driven patterns of organization and introduce Rogerian argument as a less-oppositional alternative. The chapter concludes with our thorough presentation of Toulmin argument, but now that familiar strategy is set into a fuller context. We are confident that the revised chapter offers writers better-considered choices for organizing a piece of writing.

As always, in the new edition we aim to balance attention to the critical reading of arguments (analysis) with attention to the writing of arguments (production). Once again, we have tried to demonstrate both activities with lively—and realistic—examples, on the principle that the best way to appreciate an argument may be to see it in action. We have kept the best materials from previous editions, but we have also found many new examples and arguments—including visual ones—that we believe capture the spirit of the times, a period of rapid, sometimes frightening, and yet exciting change. As always, we want students to page through the book to find the next intriguing argument or to discover one of their own.

In selecting themes and arguments for the anthology, we've tried to choose topics of interest and concern to the students we teach as well as issues and texts worth arguing about. In choosing new selections, we've sought readings that will challenge students to consider new perspectives on topics they may feel they already understand and, in particular, to contextualize themselves in a world characterized by increasing globalization. We have retained several of the chapter topics that have worked especially well in earlier editions—stereotypes in popular culture, bilingualism in America, religion in public life, and the meaning of diversity on college campuses. In revising these chapters, we have sought to find a balance between including texts that students and teachers reported finding provocative, instructive, and useful, and adding new ones that treat contemporary issues while leading us to think about argumentation and our world in novel, timely ways. For example, how do media representations of people with disabilities contribute to the further misunderstanding of this group? What can an obituary for a refugee teach us about bilingualism in the United States and about the nature of argument? How is the growth of evangelicalism among Christians and members of other faiths on U.S. campuses influencing campus life and discourse? How does such knowledge help us understand both ourselves and the debates that constitute this society at this moment in human history?

In addition to updating these chapters from the fourth edition, we have added three new chapters on topics of particular interest to college students. Certainly one of the major technological and social changes of the past few years has been the rise of social networking sites. In

"How Many Friends Have You Made Today?" we have assembled a series of readings that challenge students to look at such sites not as participants, but through the eyes of journalists and researchers. We expect many students will be surprised to find that social scientists take such sites very seriously for a range of reasons. A second new chapter grew out of our realization that Americans are now interested, to a degree that they never have been before, in what they eat and drink. In "Why Worry about Food and Water?" we present a group of readings that examines this fascination (if not obsession) and the ways that it is linked to contemporary concern with the environment. The third new chapter, "What Are You Working For?" challenges students to begin examining in earnest the links between the world of higher education they are now part of and the world of work that awaits them—or perhaps not, in an increasingly uncertain economic climate.

In choosing new selections for the anthology, in addition to looking for new genres that bring home to students the message conveyed by the book's title, we have tried to reflect the added attention to academic argument in the earlier part of the book. We have searched for examples of research writing that use a range of methodologies, including case studies, quantitative research, and ethnography, with the goal of giving students practice for analyzing the sorts of arguments they will be assigned in their various courses. We have often paired these selections with discussions of the research in the press or other media to encourage students to begin thinking about how knowledge is disseminated and how it moves from books or journal articles to everyday conversation. Finally, we have sought arguments, whether written or visual, that will help students see themselves "among others," to use Clifford Geertz's memorable turn of phrase.

Here is a summary of the key features that continue to characterize *Everything's an Argument with Readings* and of the major new features in this edition:

Key Features

Two books in one, neatly linked. Up front is a brief guide to argument; in back is a thematically organized anthology of readings. The two parts of the book are linked by cross-references in the margins, leading students from the argument chapters to specific examples in the readings and from the readings to appropriate rhetorical instruction.

A uniquely wide-ranging scope that supports the argument made by the book's title by showing students how argument is found not just in essays but in rap lyrics, news articles, scholarly writing, poems, advertisements, cartoons, posters, bumper stickers, billboards, Web sites, blogs, text messages, and other electronic environments.

Student-friendly explanations in simple, everyday language, with many brief examples and a minimum of technical terminology.

Fresh and important chapter themes that encourage students to take up complex positions. Readings on topics such as "How Does Popular Culture Stereotype You?", "What Role Should Religion Play in Public Life?", and "What Should 'Diversity on Campus' Mean?" demand that students explore the many sides of an issue, not just pro or con.

A real-world, full-color design, with readings presented in the style of the original publication. Different formats for newspaper articles, magazine articles, essays, writing from the Web, and other media help students recognize and think about the effect that design and visuals have on written arguments, and the full-color design helps bring the many images in the text to life.

New to This Edition

Three timely new chapter topics of high interest to students—social networking sites, food and water, and the world of work and its relation (or lack thereof) to higher education.

Forty-six new selections that treat provocative topics on a range of subjects. A sampling:

- "Indoctrination U.? Faculty Ideology and Changes in Student Political Orientation" presents data examining whether liberal faculty influence students' political perspective.

- "The Veterans Are Coming! The Veterans Are Coming!" offers faculty and students advice about a new demographic on campus—veterans who've returned from fighting in Iraq or Afghanistan.

- "Study Finds Teenagers' Internet Socializing Isn't Such a Bad Thing" argues that contrary to the complaints of many adults, spending time on the Internet may actually have advantages for today's youth.

- "Education Pays, but Perhaps Less Than You Thought" uses quantitative evidence to question how much higher education really pays off.
- A recipe for thick and chewy chocolate chip cookies tries to persuade students that recipes are arguments of the best kind.

A new chapter on "Academic Arguments" that defines the genre, explains its conventions, and provides full-length examples, along with a box in each chapter of Part II highlighting the use of academic argument in that chapter's genre.

Six new full-length examples of specific kinds of arguments, such as arguments of fact and proposals, that provide engaging, topical new models for students.

New material on the classical oration and Rogerian argument in Chapter 7, "Structuring Arguments."

Guidelines and examples for the latest versions of MLA (2009) and APA (2010) styles in Chapter 20, "Documenting Sources."

You Get More Digital Choices for *Everything's an Argument with Readings*

Everything's an Argument with Readings doesn't stop with a book. Online, you'll find both free and affordable premium resources to help students get even more out of the book and your course. You'll also find convenient instructor resources, such as downloadable sample syllabi, classroom activities, and a nationwide community of teachers. To learn more about or order any of the products described on the following pages, contact your Bedford/St. Martin's sales representative, email sales support (sales_support@bfwpub.com), or visit the Web site at bedfordstmartins.com/everythingsanargument/catalog.

Everything's an Argument with Readings Student Center at bedfordstmartins.com/everythingsanargument

Send students to free and open resources, provide them with an online chapter of readings that include multimedia, or upgrade to an expanding collection of innovative digital content—all in one place.

Free and open resources provide students with easy-to-access reference materials, exercises, and downloadable content.

- *TopLinks* gives links to reliable online sources that students can use to further explore topics introduced in the book.
- *Bedford Bibliographer* helps students with the process of collecting source information and making a bibliography in MLA, APA, and *Chicago* styles.
- *Exercise Central* offers over eight thousand grammar and writing exercises with immediate scoring, linked to a gradebook that you can access from the Instructor's Resources tab at the *Everything's an Argument with Readings Student Center*.

An e-chapter of readings, updated each fall, provides students with an opportunity to analyze arguments in dynamic electronic formats, including audio, video, and hypertext. The initial e-chapter includes such multimedia selections as well as traditional verbal and visual arguments on the topic of foreign attitudes toward the United States and Americans. The e-chapter is available for free only when packaged with the book. An activation code is required. To order the e-chapter packaged with the book, use ISBN-10: 0-312-64250-4 or ISBN-13: 978-0-312-64250-1.

Re:Writing Plus, now with *VideoCentral*, gathers all of Bedford/ St. Martin's premium digital content for composition into one online collection. It includes hundreds of model documents, the first ever peer-review game, and *VideoCentral*, with more than fifty brief videos for the writing classroom. *Re:Writing Plus* can be purchased separately at the *Student Center* or packaged with the book at a significant discount. An activation code is required. To order *Re:Writing Plus* packaged with the book, use ISBN-10: 0-312-62450-6 or ISBN-13: 978-0-312-62450-7.

Instructor Resources at bedfordstmartins.com/ everythingsanargument/catalog

You have a lot to do in your course. Bedford/St. Martin's wants to make it easy for you to find the support you need—and to get it quickly.

Instructor's Notes for Everything's an Argument with Readings is available in PDF format that can be downloaded from the Bedford/St. Martin's online catalog or the *Student Center*. For each chapter in the text, the *Instructor's Notes* outlines some of the challenges you might face while teaching the chapter, suggests solutions, and provides answers and teaching suggestions for the chapter exercises, ending with ideas for extending those exercises beyond the text.

TeachingCentral offers the entire list of Bedford/St. Martin's print and online professional resources in one place. You'll find landmark reference works, sourcebooks on pedagogical issues, award-winning collections, and practical advice for the classroom—all free for instructors.

Bits collects creative ideas for teaching a range of composition topics in an easily searchable blog. A community of teachers—leading scholars, authors, and editors—discuss revision, research, grammar and style, technology, peer review, and much more. Take, use, adapt, and pass the ideas around. Then, come back to the site to comment or share your own suggestion.

Content cartridges for the most common course management systems—Blackboard, WebCT, Angel, and Desire2Learn—allow you to easily download Bedford/St. Martin's digital materials for your course.

Even More Options for Students

Add more value and flexibility to your textbook with one of the following resources, free when packaged with *Everything's an Argument with Readings*. To learn more about package options or any of the products below, contact your Bedford/St. Martin's sales representative or visit the Web site at bedfordstmartins.com/everythingsanargument/catalog.

i•series on CD-ROM includes multimedia tutorials in a flexible CD-ROM format—because there are things you can't do in a book.

- **ix visual exercises** helps students visualize and put into practice key rhetorical and visual concepts. To order *ix visual exercises* packaged with the book, use ISBN-10: 0-312-62449-2 or ISBN-13: 978-0-312-62449-1.

- **i•claim visualizing argument** offers a new way to see argument—with six tutorials, an illustrated glossary, and over seventy multimedia arguments. To order *i•claim visualizing argument* packaged with the book, use ISBN-10: 0-312-62448-4 or ISBN-13: 978-0-312-62448-4.

- **i•cite visualizing sources** brings research to life through an animated introduction, four tutorials, and hands-on source practice. To order *i•cite visualizing sources* packaged with the book, use ISBN-10: 0-312-62439-5 or ISBN-13: 978-0-312-62439-2.

Acknowledgments

We owe a debt of gratitude to many people for making *Everything's an Argument* possible. Our first thanks must go to the students we have taught in our writing courses for nearly four decades, particularly students at the Ohio State University, Portland State University, Stanford University, and the University of Texas at Austin. Almost every chapter in this book has been informed by a classroom encounter with a student whose shrewd observation or perceptive question sent an ambitious lesson plan spiraling to the ground. (Anyone who has tried to teach claims and warrants on the fly to skeptical first-year students will surely appreciate why we have qualified our claims in the Toulmin chapter so carefully.) But students have also provided the motive for writing this book. More than ever, they need to know how to read and write arguments effectively if they are to secure a place in a world growing ever smaller and more rhetorically challenging.

We are grateful to our editors at Bedford/St. Martin's who contributed their talents to our book, beginning with Joan Feinberg, who has enthusiastically supported the project and provided us with the resources and feedback needed to keep us on track. Most of the day-to-day work on the project has been handled by the ever patient, perceptive, and good-humored John Elliott. We said this in the last edition, but the claim remains as true as ever: he prevented more than a few lapses of judgment yet understands the spirit of this book—which involves, occasionally, taking risks to make a memorable point. We have appreciated, too, his meticulous line editing as well as his ability to find just the right example when we were struggling to do so.

We are similarly grateful to others at Bedford/St. Martin's who contributed their talents to our book: Jessica Skrocki Gould, project editor; Nancy Myers, senior production supervisor; Lucy Krikorian, art director; Molly Parke, marketing manager; and Cecilia Seiter, associate editor. Thanks also to Kristin Bowen and Maura Shea, who assisted with the art program, as well as Sue McDermott Barlow, Naomi Kornhauser, and Linda Finigan, the art researchers.

We'd also like to thank the astute instructors and students who reviewed the fourth edition: Anthony Baker, Tennessee Technological University; Ron Brooks, Oklahoma State University; Linda Casola, Kennesaw State University; Jeff Chan, St. Edward's University and Austin Community College; Linsey Cuti, Kankakee Community College;

Stephanie Denny, Kennesaw State University; Luisa Forrest, El Centro College; Beth Gehring, Lakeland Community College; Jasara Lee Hing-Hines, Oak Ridge High School; Ellen Johnson, Arizona State University; Ginny Jones, University of North Carolina, Pembroke; Daniel L. Keegan, University of Alabama; Christy L. Kinnion, Wake Technical Community College; Lisa Kirby, North Carolina Wesleyan College; Wendy L. Lym, Austin Community College; David Moutray, Kankakee Community College; Lana Myers, Northeast Lakeview College; Andrea Neptune, Sierra College; Kristie-Ann Opaleski, Monmouth University; Abha Patel, Monmouth University; Nancy Fioritto Patete, Lakeland Community College; Samantha Ruckman, Arizona State University; Jenny Sadre-Orafai, Kennesaw State University; Shital Shah, Boston Latin Academy; Tonisha Smith, Wake Technical Community College; Paul Stevenson, Edison Preparatory School; Patty Strandquist, Eastview High School; Marianna Vieira, Southern Connecticut State University; Linda Walvoord, University of Cincinnati and Clermont College; Deborah Weaver, University of Central Florida; Lori Weber, Lakeland Community College; Erik Wennermark, University of Alabama; Stephen Wilhoit, University of Dayton.

Thanks, too, to John Kinkade, who once again revised the instructor's notes for the rhetoric chapters and for this edition also took on the notes for the readings anthology and the marginal cross-references between the front and back sections of the book. Finally, we are grateful to the students whose fine argumentative essays appear in our chapters: Milena Ateya, Claire Liu, Michael Osofsky, Sayoh Mansaray, Jack Chung, Lia Hardin, and Manasi Deshpande.

We hope that *Everything's an Argument* responds to what students and instructors have said they want and need. And we hope readers of this text will let us know how we've done: please share your opinions and suggestions with us at bedfordstmartins.com/everythingsanargument.

Andrea A. Lunsford
John J. Ruszkiewicz
Keith Walters

CONTENTS

Part 2:
Writing Arguments 131

Part 3:
Style and Presentation in Arguments   415

Part 4:
Conventions of Argument 491

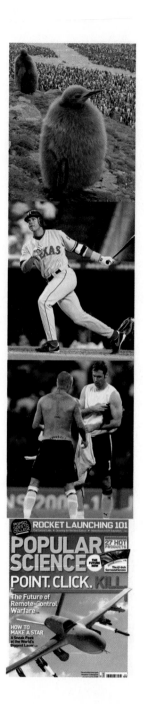

25. What Role Should Religion Play in Public Life? 849

25. What Role Should Religion Play in Public Life? 849

27. What Are You Working For? 970

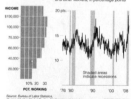

Teenage Workers
Teenagers in middle-class families are the most likely to be working. But unemployment among young workers is high.

Teens in the work force
By family income, 2005-7

Gap in unemployment rates
Difference between 16- and 17-year-olds and other workers, in percentage points

Source: Bureau of Labor Statistics, Center of Labor Market Studies, Northeastern University   THE NEW YORK TIMES

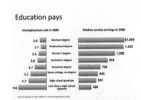

Education pays

PART 1

READING
arguments

1
Everything Is
an Argument

On January 30, 2005, when Iraqis voted for the first time following the fall of Saddam Hussein, photographs of proud citizens brandishing fingers dyed purple to prevent double-balloting flashed around the world. The raised purple digits were variously interpreted as gestures of support for democracy, defiance to terrorist threats, or even resistance to U.S. occupation.

On June 27, 2008, voters in Zimbabwe went to the polls to vote for a single candidate on a run-off ballot for president—the incumbent Robert Mugabe, who was widely regarded as the loser of the initial balloting. Now Mugabe was forcing his way into yet another term by a corrupt and violent election. If Zimbabweans voted, their fingers were dyed red. If they dared to resist, they faced consequences at the hands of government agents. So when photographs of fingers were again sent around the world, this time they made different and more somber arguments from those of the Iraqis in 2005. But they did make arguments, some of which could be spoken only outside the African dictatorship.

The caption to this image from the *New York Times* made a clear claim about the Zimbabwean election: "Some people said they feared punishment or even death unless they could produce a finger colored by red ink as evidence they had cast their ballot."

You already know that raised fingers can make statements. But so can many other images, gestures, and activities that you take for granted. There may be an argument on the T-shirt you don in the morning, in the sports column you read on the bus, in the prayers you utter before a quiz, in the off-the-cuff political remarks of a teacher lecturing, even in the assurances of a health center nurse that "this won't hurt one bit."

The clothes you wear, the foods you eat, and the groups you join are everyday things that make nuanced, sometimes unspoken arguments about who you are and what you value. So an argument can be any text—written, spoken, or visual—that expresses a point of view. Sometimes arguments can be blunt and aggressive and are composed deliberately to change what people believe, think, or do. At other times, your goals may be subtler, and your writing is designed to convince yourself or others that specific facts are reliable or that certain views should be considered—or at least tolerated.

In fact, some theorists claim that language is itself inherently persuasive and hence that every text is also an argument that is designed to influence readers. (When you say "Hi, how's it going?," for instance, in one sense you're arguing that your hello deserves a response.) Even humor makes an argument when it causes readers to recognize—through bursts of laughter or just a faint smile—how things are and how they might be different.

More obvious as arguments are those that make a direct claim based on or drawn from evidence. Such writing often moves readers to recognize problems and to consider solutions. Persuasion of this kind is usually easy to recognize:

> A country that displays an almost ruthless commitment to efficiency and performance in every aspect of its economy—a country that switched to Japanese cars the moment they were more reliable, and to Chinese T-shirts the moment they were five cents cheaper—has loyally stuck with a health-care system that leaves its citizenry pulling out their teeth with pliers.
>
> —Malcolm Gladwell, "The Moral Hazard Myth"

> [W]omen unhappy in their marriages often enter full-time employment as an escape. But although a woman's entrance into the workplace does tend to increase the stability of her marriage, it does not increase her happiness.
>
> —The Popular Research Institute, Penn State University

> We will become a society of a million pictures without much memory, a society that looks forward every second to an immediate replication of what it has just done, but one that does not sustain the difficult labor of transmitting culture from one generation to the next.
>
> —Christine Rosen, "The Image Culture"

Purposes of Argument

Although in some ways all language has an argumentative edge that aims to make a point, not all language use aims to win out over others. In contrast to the traditional Western concept of argument as being about disputation or combat, communication theorists such as Sonja Foss, Cindy Griffin, and Josina Makau describe an invitational argument, the kind that aims not to defeat another person or group but to invite others to enter a space of mutual regard and exploration. In fact, as you'll see, writers and speakers have as many purposes for arguing as for using language, including—in addition to winning—to inform, to convince, to explore, to make decisions, and even to meditate or pray.

Not Just Words

Can something as innocuous as a hoodie branded with your school's logo be an argument? And would it make a difference if that apparel were being sold by Victoria's Secret—as is the Arizona State item shown here? Spend some time working with one other student in your class to analyze the argument that a branded piece of clothing like this might make. Then write a paragraph that elaborates on that claim.

Of course, many arguments *are* aimed at winning. Such is the purpose of much writing and speaking in the political arena, business world, and law courts. Two candidates for office, for example, vie for a majority of votes; the makers of one soft drink try to outsell their competitors by appealing to public tastes; and two lawyers try to outwit each other in pleading to a judge and jury. In your college writing, you may also be called on to make an argument that appeals to a "judge" and "jury" (your instructor and classmates). You might, for instance, argue that peer-to-peer music file sharing is legal because of the established legal precedent of fair use. In doing so, you may need to defeat your unseen opponents—those who regard such file sharing as theft.

At this point, it may help to acknowledge a common academic distinction between argument and persuasion. In this view, the point of *argument* is to use evidence and reason to discover some version of the truth. Argument of this sort leads audiences toward conviction—an agreement that a claim is true or reasonable or that a course of action is desirable. The aim of *persuasion* is to change a point of view or to move others from conviction to action. In other words, writers or speakers argue to discover some truth; they persuade when they think they already know it.

In practice, this distinction between argument and persuasion can be hard to maintain. It's unnatural for writers or readers to imagine their minds divided between a part that pursues truth and a part that seeks to persuade. And yet you may want to reserve the term *persuasion* for writing that's aggressively designed to change opinions through the use of reason and other appropriate techniques. For writing that sets out to persuade at all costs—abandoning reason, fairness, and truth altogether—the term *propaganda* (with all its negative connotations) is often used. Some suggest that the term *advertising* often works just as well.

As we've already suggested, arguing isn't always about winning or even about changing others' views. In addition to invitational argument, another school of argument—called *Rogerian argument* (after the psychotherapist Carl Rogers)—is based on approaching audiences in nonthreatening ways and on finding common ground and establishing trust among those who disagree about issues. Writers who follow Rogerian approaches seek to understand the perspectives of those with whom they disagree, looking for "both/and" or "win/win" solutions (rather than "either/or" or "win/lose" ones) whenever possible. Many writers of successful arguments today follow such principles, whether consciously or not (for more on Rogerian strategies, see Chapter 7).

The risks of Rogerian argument.

"You say it's a win-win, but what if you're wrong-wrong and it all goes bad-bad?"

Some other purposes or goals of argument are worth considering in more detail.

Arguments to Inform

The Wikipedia entry titled "Local Food" provides an example of an argument to inform.

LINK TO P. 817

Many arguments—including street signs, notices of meetings, and newspaper headlines—may not seem especially "argumentative" because their main purpose is to tell members of an audience something they didn't know. Other informative arguments are more obviously designed to persuade. For example, an essential step in selling anything, especially something new, is to advise customers that it exists. The classic poster announcing the first *Batman* film in 1989 carried only two words: *June 23*. Political campaigns can be comparably blunt. Think of all the bumper stickers you've seen that merely identify a candidate, an office, and maybe a year: "Obama '08," "Jindal 2012." Such simple arguments give a candidate "name recognition" by telling voters who is available for an office.

Arguments to Convince

As a form of argument, many reports, white papers, and academic articles typically aim to convince readers rather than win out over opponents. For instance, if you are writing a report on the safety record of nuclear plants for a college course, you would likely present evidence to demonstrate to general readers (including an instructor and fellow students) that the issue merited their attention. You would not likely expect to win over activist partisans

A visual argument to inform in Key West, Florida

who already reject atomic power as an energy alternative. Yet the presence of those who might disagree is always implied in an argument, and it inevitably shapes a writer's strategies. In the following passage, for example, controversial political scientist Charles Murray uses intelligence quotient (IQ) correlations to raise questions about higher education that many readers of the *Wall Street Journal*, where his article appeared, may find troubling:

> There is no magic point at which a genuine college-level education becomes an option, but anything below an IQ of 110 is problematic. If you want to do well, you should have an IQ of 115 or higher. Put another way, it makes sense for only about 15% of the population, 25% if one stretches it, to get a college education.
>
> —Charles Murray, "What's Wrong with Vocational School?"

Murray uses numbers to draw a seemingly objective conclusion about who should attend college, hoping to convince some readers to consider

In his article on the world food crisis, Solomon H. Katz intends to convince his fellow anthropologists of the importance of understanding and shaping attitudes toward food.

LINK TO P. 794

In an argument to convince, opponents' viewpoints aren't addressed directly, but they are always implied ("Hold the electricity." "No toaster.").

RUDY PARK   *BY DARRIN BELL & THERON HEIR*

RUDY PARK: © Darrin Bell and Theron Heir/Dist. by United Feature Syndicate, Inc.

his point. But he's also arguing against those—perhaps a majority of his audience—who prefer to believe that higher education should be encouraged for all.

Arguments to Persuade

In many situations, writers unabashedly want to move audiences enough to provoke action, whether that involves buying a product, voting for a candidate, or supporting a policy. Advertisements, political blogs, and newspaper editorials use all the devices of rhetoric to motivate action, produce change, or win a point. Here Daniel Ben-Ami drives home his argument at the conclusion of a long essay on the London-based Web site Spike examining "Why people hate fat Americans":

> By focusing on fat Americans the critics of consumption are saying, implicitly at least, that people should consume less. They are arguing for a world in which Americans become more like those who live in the poorer countries of the world. From such a perspective equality means levelling everyone down rather than raising the living standards of the poor. It means giving up on the battle to resist hurricanes or to reclaim land from the sea.
>
>   Yet implementing such a viewpoint is a super-size mistake. Our aspiration for the world should be to give the poor the advantages of

affluence enjoyed by those in the West. Living standards in countries such as Ethiopia and Niger should be, at the very least, as high as those in America today. In that sense we should all aim to be fat Americans.

In these two paragraphs, Ben-Ami dramatizes his point by balance and repetition in the structure of his sentences, by reminders in the final paragraph of poverty in Ethiopia and Niger, and by a final ironic call for others to grow as fat as Americans. With these rhetorical moves, he pushes the lengthy article from analysis toward action, which is typical of most persuasive writing.

Arguments to Explore

Many important subjects call for arguments that take the form of exploration. If there's an "opponent" in such a situation at all (often there is not), it's likely the status quo or a current trend that—for one reason or another—is puzzling. Exploratory arguments may be deeply personal, such as E. B. White's often reprinted essay "Once More to the Lake," in which the author's return with his young son to a vacation spot from his own childhood leads him to reflect on time, memory, and mortality. Or the exploration may be aimed at addressing serious problems in society. Writing in 2005, James Fallows presciently explored what he saw as "America's coming economic crisis" by projecting himself forward to the election of 2016—and then looking back to speculate on what might happen between 2005 and 2016. Along the way, he considered changes that might occur in education:

> . . . we could have shored up our universities. True, the big change came as early as 2002, in the wake of 9/11, when tighter visa rules . . . cut off the flow of foreign talent that American universities had channeled to American ends. In the summer of 2007 China applied the name "twenty Harvards" to its ambition, announced in the early 2000s, to build major research institutions that would attract international talent. It seemed preposterous (too much political control, too great a language barrier), but no one is laughing now. . . . The Historic Campus of our best-known university, Harvard, is still prestigious worldwide. But its role is increasingly that of the theme park, like Oxford or Heidelberg, while the most ambitious students compete for fellowships at the Har-Bai and Har-Bei campuses in Mumbai and Beijing.
>
> —James Fallows, "Countdown to a Meltdown"

Amy Martinez Starke's obituary for Sao Yee Cha explores the Hmong woman's experience as an immigrant to the United States.

LINK TO P. 773 ....

A student from India chats with one from Romania at the University of Nottingham, England. Since 9/11, the United States has been issuing fewer visas to international students; as a result, these students are increasingly enrolling in non-American universities.

Perhaps the essential argument in any such piece is the writer's assertion that a problem exists (in this case, the damage that tighter visa rules do to American economic competitiveness) and that the writer or reader needs to solve it.

Arguments to Make Decisions

Closely allied to argument that explores is argument that aims at making good, sound decisions. In fact, the result of many exploratory arguments may be to argue for a particular decision, whether that decision relates to the best career path to follow in a tight economy or the "right" person to choose as your life partner. For college students, choosing a major is a momentous decision, and one way to go about making that decision is to argue your way through several alternatives in your own mind as well as with friends, colleagues, and even your parents. By the time you've examined the pros and cons of each alternative, you should be a little closer to a good decision.

Arguments to make decisions occur all the time in the public arena, as well. In a college essay, Elizabeth Wong explored the pros and cons of extending copyright protection to designers of apparel who wanted protection from fashion pirates and knock-off artists. But Wong came down on the opposing side, deciding that the 2007 legislation would do more harm than good. Here's a passage from her paper that makes that point:

> If this act is passed, it opens the floor for legal battles of designer against designer. The larger names, like Chanel or Louis Vuitton, will be able to hire endless lawyers and consultants to take care of these cases for them. But what is the young and struggling designer to do? If someone were to sue him, he would not likely have the resources to hire a legal team and fight the suit. Money aside, young designers simply do not have the time for lawsuits. While more established designers often have teams of design assistants doing the work, a new designer has to keep up with the grueling fashion cycle almost completely alone. With younger designers put in jeopardy by the threat of lawsuits, the field of design would narrow, and fashion itself would suffer. In this situation, the industry doesn't profit; the lawyers do.
>
> —Elizabeth Wong, "Unnecessary Precaution: Extending Copyright to Fashion Design"

You probably know that people make and sell cheap knock-offs of Louis Vuitton's high-fashion handbags, shoes, and accesssories. But a designer pretending to be a knock-off artist? Model Eva Herzigova and designer Marc Jacobs examine real Vuitton bags at a party space made up to look like a stall selling counterfeit luxury goods. What argument might this peculiar shopping space make?

Arguments to Meditate or Pray

Sometimes arguments can take the form of prayer or intense meditations on a theme. In such cases, the writer or speaker is most often hoping to transform something in him- or herself or to reach a state of equilibrium or peace of mind. If you know a familiar prayer or mantra, think for a moment of what it "argues" for and how it uses quiet meditation to accomplish that goal. Such meditations don't have to be formal prayers, however. Look, for example, at an excerpt from Michael Lassell's poem "How to Watch Your Brother Die." This poem, which evokes the confusing emotions of a man during the death of his gay brother, uses a kind of meditative language that allows the reader to reach an understanding of the speaker and to evoke meditative thought in others:

> Feel how it feels to hold a man in your arms
> whose arms are used to holding men.
> Offer God anything to bring your brother back.
> Know you have nothing God could possibly want.
> Curse God, but do not
> abandon Him.
>
> —Michael Lassell, "How to Watch Your Brother Die"

The Tree of Jesse window in France's Chartres Cathedral

Another sort of meditative argument can be found in the stained-glass windows of churches and other public buildings. Dazzled by a spectacle of light, people pause to consider a window's message longer than they might if the same idea were conveyed on paper. The window engages viewers with a power not unlike that of poetry.

Academic Arguments

To the public, describing an argument as "academic" usually means it's pointless, endless, arcane, or silly. If you've written one too many research papers, you may feel the same. But an academic argument is simply one that is held to the standards of a professional field or discipline, such as psychology, engineering, political science, or English. It is an argument presented to knowledgeable people by writers who are striving to make an honest case that is based on the best information and research available, with all of its sources carefully documented. Though we'll examine all types of arguments in this book, we'll focus on the kinds that you'll make in professional and academic situations. Such arguments typically follow patterns that are defined by their disciplines (consider the research paper again or journal articles you have read) and adhere to precise standards for handling evidence. As you'll see, the style of academic writing also tends to be more formal and impersonal than arguments in the public arena, but there are exceptions. For more about academic writing, see Chapter 6.

Occasions for Argument

Another way of thinking about arguments is to identify the public occasions that call for them. In an ancient textbook of *rhetoric* (the art of persuasion), the philosopher Aristotle provides an elegant scheme for classifying the purposes of arguments. His formula is based on issues of time—past, future, and present. It is easy to remember and helpful in its strategies for making convincing cases. But because all classifications overlap with others to a certain extent, don't be surprised to encounter many arguments that span more than one category—arguments about the past with implications for the future, arguments about the future with bearings on the present, and so on.

Arguments about the Past

Debates about what has happened in the past are called *forensic arguments*; such controversies are common in business, government, and academia. For example, in many criminal and civil cases, lawyers interrogate witnesses to establish exactly what happened at an earlier time: *Did the defendant sexually harass her employee? Did the company deliberately ignore evidence that its product was deficient? Was the contract properly enforced?* The contentious nature of some forensic arguments is evident in this excerpt from a letter to the editor of the *Atlantic Monthly*:

> Robert Bryce's article on the U.S. military's gas consumption in Iraq ("Gas Pains," May *Atlantic*) is factually inaccurate, tactically misguided, and a classic case of a red herring.
>
> —Captain David J. Morris

In replying to this letter, the author of the article, Robert Bryce, disputes Morris's statements, introducing more evidence in support of his original claim. Forensic arguments rely on evidence and testimony to recreate what can be known about events that have already occurred.

Forensic arguments also rely heavily on precedents—actions or decisions in the past that influence policies or decisions in the present—and on analyses of cause and effect. Consider the ongoing controversy over Christopher Columbus: are his expeditions to the Americas events worth celebrating, or are they unhappy chapters in human history—or a mixture of both? No simple exchange of evidence will suffice to still this debate; the effects of Columbus's actions beginning in 1492 may be studied and debated for the next five hundred years. As you might suspect from this example, arguments about history are typically forensic.

Forensic cases may also be arguments about character, such as when someone's reputation is studied in a historical context to enrich current perspectives on the person. Allusions to the past can make present arguments more vivid, as in the following selection from an essay about the reputation of Ernesto ("Che") Guevara, an Argentinian Marxist who aided several Latin American revolutions in the 1960s and whose image still appears across the globe:

> Rebels and activists the world over still take inspiration from Guevara. But the image has lost something; Che's face on a poster in 1968 isn't quite the same thing as it is on a mousepad 40 years later. Perhaps it is precisely that loss—the shedding of Che's radicalism and ideological rigor—that renders him so supremely marketable today. Things

Theodor de Bry's 1594 engraving tells one version of the Christopher Columbus story.

are not going well these days. Kids don't want revolution so much as, um, something different.

—Ben Ehrenreich, "Capitalizing on Che Guevara's Image"

Such writing can be exploratory and open-ended, the point of argument being to enhance and sharpen knowledge, not just to generate heat or score points.

Arguments about the Future

Debates about what will or should happen in the future are called *deliberative arguments*. Legislatures, congresses, and parliaments are called *deliberative bodies* because they establish policies for the future: *Should two people of the same sex be allowed to marry? Should the U.S. Treasury Department bail out failing banks and businesses in times of economic chaos?* Because what has happened in the past influences the future, deliberative judgments often rely on prior forensic arguments. Thus, deliberative arguments routinely draw on data and testimony, as in this passage from a college essay using precedents from the United Kingdom to argue for a system of national health care in the United States:

> Studies have long proven preventive health care to be more cost-effective than simply treating illnesses as they appear. According to Andrew Light, "starting in 1990, the [British] government added a new element to the [general practitioner] contract—lump sums or bonuses for carrying out preventive measures on a high percentage of the patient panel" (26). This policy has resulted in a high number of preventive measures being taken in the UK and a reduction in overall illness. So in addition to the cost benefits, more UK citizens do not have to be treated for cancer, heart-conditions, and any number of illnesses that can be prevented with vaccines.
>
> —Ryan Thomas, "The Critical Condition of Health Care"

But since no one has a blueprint for what's to come, deliberative arguments also advance by means of projections, extrapolations, and reasoned guesses (If X is true, then Y may be true; if X happens, then so may Y; if X continues, then Y may occur):

> In 2000, according to a World Health Organization assessment, 1.1 billion people worldwide had no regular access to safe drinking water, and 2.4 billion had no regular access to sanitation systems. Lack of access to clean water leads to four billion cases of diarrhea each year. Peter Gleick, an expert on global freshwater resources, reveals that even if we reach the United Nations' stated goal of halving the number of people without access to safe drinking water by 2015, as many as 76 million people will die from water-borne diseases before 2020.
>
> —Pacific Institute for Studies in Development, Environment, and Security

Arguments about the Present

Arguments about the present are often arguments about contemporary values—that is, the beliefs and assumptions that are widely held (or debated) within a society. Sometimes called *epideictic arguments* or *ceremonial arguments* because they tend to be heard at public occasions, they include inaugural addresses, sermons, eulogies, graduation speeches, and civic remarks of all kinds. Ceremonial arguments can be passionate and eloquent, rich in anecdotes and metaphor. President Ronald Reagan was a master of ceremonial discourse, and he was particularly adept at defining the core values of the American way of life:

A woman carries drums of water from a well that has been a major source of cholera in Harare, Zimbabwe. Proposals to protect and clean up the world's water supply are a common form of deliberative argument by international organizations like the United Nations.

> Ours was the first revolution in the history of mankind that truly reversed the course of government, and with three little words: "We the people." "We the people" tell the government what to do, it doesn't tell us. "We the people" are the driver, the government is the car. And we decide where it should go, and by what route, and how fast. Almost all the world's constitutions are documents in which governments tell the people what their privileges are. Our Constitution is a document in which "We the people" tell the government what it is allowed to do.
> —Ronald Reagan, "Farewell Address"

Reagan directs the American people to the founding documents of the nation to find their values. But not all ceremonial arguments reach quite this far. More typical are values arguments that explore contemporary culture, praising what's admirable and blaming what's not. In the following argument, student Latisha Chisholm looks at rap after Tupac Shakur—and doesn't like what she sees:

When I think about how rap music has changed, I generally associate the demise of my appreciation for the industry with the death of Tupac. With his death, not only did one of the most intriguing rap rivalries of all time die, but the motivation for rapping seems to have changed. Where money had always been a plus, now it is obviously more important than wanting to express the hardships of Black communities. With current rappers, the positive power that came from the desire to represent Black people is lost. One of the biggest rappers now got his big break while talking about sneakers. Others announce retirement without really having done much for the soul or for Black people's morale. I equate new rappers to NFL players that don't love the game anymore. They're only in it for the money. . . . It looks like the voice of a people has lost its heart.

—Latisha Chisholm, "Has Rap Lost Its Soul?"

As in many ceremonial arguments, Chisholm here reinforces common values such as representing one's community honorably and fairly.

Are rappers since Tupac Shakur only in it for the money? Many epideictic arguments find fault with contemporary culture.

Kinds of Argument

Yet another way of categorizing arguments is to consider their status or stasis—that is, the kinds of issues they address. This categorization system is called *stasis theory*. In ancient Greek and Roman civilizations, rhetoricians defined a series of questions by which to examine legal cases. The questions would be posed in sequence because each depended on the question(s) preceding it. Together, the questions helped determine the point of contention in an argument, the place where disputants could focus their energy, and hence the kind of argument they should make. A modern version of those questions might look like the following:

- Did something happen?
- What is its nature?
- What is its quality or cause?
- What actions should be taken?

As you can see, each stasis question explores a different aspect of a problem and uses different evidence or techniques to reach conclusions. You can use stasis theory to explore the aspects of any topic you're considering. We use the stasis issues to define key types of argument in Part 2.

Did Something Happen? Arguments of Fact

An argument of fact usually involves a statement that can be proved or disproved with specific evidence or testimony. Although relatively simple to define, such arguments are often quite subtle, involving layers of complexity that are not apparent when the question is initially posed.

For example, the question of pollution of the oceans—is it really occurring?—might seem relatively easy to settle. Either scientific data prove that the oceans are being polluted as a result of human activity, or they don't. But to settle the matter, writers and readers first have to agree on a number of points, each of which has to be studied and debated: How will pollution be defined and measured? Over what period of time? Are current deviations in water quality unprecedented? Can any deviations be attributable to human action? Nevertheless, questions of this sort can be argued primarily on the facts, complicated and contentious as they may be. (For more on arguments based on facts, see Chapter 4.)

Mark Cadena and Stuart Hata in San Francisco's City Hall after their wedding on November 3, 2008, the day before a California ballot referendum ended several months of legalized marriage ceremonies between same-sex couples in the state. The debate over this issue involves arguments of fact (does a "civil union" or "domestic partnership" provide the same benefits as a "marriage"?) as well as more basic arguments of definition (are these forms of legal recognition the same thing? must "marriage" involve two people of the opposite sex?).

What Is the Nature of the Thing? Arguments of Definition

Just as contentious as arguments based on facts are questions of definition. An argument of definition often involves determining whether one known object or action belongs in a second—and more highly contested—category. One of the most hotly debated issues in American life today involves a question of definition: is a human fetus a human being? If one argues that it is, then a second issue of definition arises: is abortion murder? As you can see, issues of definition can have mighty consequences—and decades of debate may leave the matter unresolved.

Bob Costas used an important definitional distinction to eulogize Mickey Mantle, a great New York Yankee baseball player who had many human faults:

> In the last year, Mickey Mantle, always so hard upon himself, finally came to accept and appreciate the distinction between a role model and a hero. The first he often was not, the second he always will be.
> —Bob Costas, "Eulogy for Mickey Mantle"

But arguments of definition can be less weighty than these, though still hotly contested: Is playing video games a sport? Is Batman a tragic figure? Is President Obama a liberal or a moderate? (For more about arguments of definition, see Chapter 9.)

What Is the Quality or Cause of the Thing?
Arguments of Evaluation and Causality

Arguments of definition lead naturally into arguments of quality—that is, to questions *about* quality. Most auto enthusiasts, for example, wouldn't be content merely to inquire whether the Corvette is a sports car. They'd prefer to argue whether it's a *good* sports car or a better sports car than, say, the Nissan GT-R. Or they might want to assert that it's the best sports car in the world, perhaps qualifying their claim with the caveat *for the price*.

Arguments of evaluation move forward typically by presenting criteria and then measuring individual people, ideas, or things against those standards. Both the standards and the measurement can be explored argumentatively, or they can be implied by the sheer weight of evidence. For instance, writer Molly Ivins praises Barbara Jordan by making explicit the qualities and achievements that make the woman a "great spirit":

> Barbara Jordan, whose name was so often preceded by the words "the first black woman to . . ." that they seemed like a permanent title, died Wednesday in Austin. A great spirit is gone. The first black woman to serve in the Texas Senate, the first black woman in Congress (she and Yvonne Brathwaite Burke of California were both elected in 1972, but Jordan had no Republican opposition), the first black elected to Congress from the South since Reconstruction, the first black woman to sit on major corporate boards, and so on. Were it not for the disease

that slowly crippled her, she probably would have been the first black woman on the Supreme Court—it is known that Jimmy Carter had her on his short list.

And long before she became "the first and only black woman to . . ." there was that astounding string of achievements going back to high school valedictorian, honors at Texas Southern University, law degree from Boston University. Both her famous diction and her enormous dignity were present from the beginning, her high school teachers recalled. Her precise enunciation was a legacy from her father, a Baptist minister, and characteristic of educated blacks of his day. Her great baritone voice was so impressive that her colleagues in the Legislature used to joke that if Hollywood ever needed someone to be the voice of the Lord Almighty, only Jordan would do.

—Molly Ivins, "Barbara Jordan: A Great Spirit"

In examining a circumstance or situation, we are often led to wonder what accounts for it: *how did Barbara Jordan achieve what she did, or what happened as a result of her work?* Though not strictly one of the classical stases, the question of *causality* certainly plays a role in many political, social, and scientific controversies. We want to know why something has happened, what factors have shaped the situation we are in, or what

Barbara Jordan addressing fellow members of Congress in 1978

might happen in the future as the result of actions we take now. For instance, nailing down the causes of global warming would certainly make a difference in how we define, evaluate, or act on the problem. Consider the reactions of bloggers at *Popular Science* reading yet another causal examination of the phenomenon:

> Wait, now pollution is preventing global warming? That's the conclusion of a recent study in the journal *Geophysical Research Letters*, which says rising temperatures seen in Europe over the last few years result as much from the reduction of air pollution as from the creation of it. The research, which looked at the effects of aerosols on climate, confirms an older concept known as global dimming, and complicates our understanding of how mankind affects the climate.
>
> According to the study, temperatures in Europe have risen over the past 28 years far faster than could be explained by the greenhouse effect alone. After looking at the aerosol concentrations in the atmosphere in six spots, the authors of the paper realized the temperature rise was assisted by more sunlight penetrating the newly pollution free skies. It seems that the stricter pollution standards, adopted in part to slow global warming, may have sped it up.
>
> —Stuart Fox, "Is Pollution Slowing Global Warming?"

Consider, too, how many different implications this study of causality raises and how many ways its findings can be interpreted. (For more about arguments of evaluation, see Chapter 10; for causal arguments, see Chapter 11.)

What Actions Should Be Taken? Proposal Arguments

In arguments that propose action, writers first have to describe a problem so well that readers ask: *What can we do?* So a proposal argument typically begins by proving that there is a problem. For example, in developing an argument about rising tuition at your college, you might use all the prior stasis questions to study the issue and establish how much and for what reasons tuition is rising. But the final question—*What actions should be taken?*—will be the most important, since it will lead you to develop proposals for action. In examining a nationwide move to eliminate remedial education in four-year colleges, John Cloud offers a moderate proposal:

> Students age 22 and over account for 43% of those in remedial classrooms, according to the National Center for Developmental Education.

[. . . But] 55% of those needing remediation must take just one course. Is it too much to ask them to pay extra for that class or take it at a community college?

—John Cloud, "Who's Ready for College?"

Americans tend to see the world in terms of problems and solutions. Indeed, many expect that almost any difficulty can be overcome by the proper infusion of technology and money. So proposal arguments seem especially appealing to Americans, even though quick-fix attitudes may themselves constitute a problem. (For more about proposal arguments, see Chapter 12.)

STASIS QUESTIONS AT WORK

Suppose that you have an opportunity to speak at a student conference on the issue of global warming. The Campus Young Republicans are sponsoring the conference, but they've made a point of inviting speakers with varying perspectives. You are tentatively in favor of strengthening industrial pollution standards aimed at reducing global warming trends. But you decide that you'd like to learn more about the issue. So you use the stasis questions to get started.

- **Did something happen?** Does global warming exist? Many in the oil and gas industry and some reputable scientists insist that global warming isn't a worldwide phenomenon or that evidence for its existence remains inconclusive. But most scientists who've studied the issue and most governments argue that the phenomenon is real and that it has reached serious proportions. In coming to your own conclusion about global warming, you'll weigh the factual evidence carefully. When you reach your conclusion, whatever it is, you should be able to identify problems with opposing arguments.

- **What is the nature of the thing?** Looking for definitions of global warming also reveals great disagreement. Global warming skeptics tend to define it in terms of naturally occurring events (such as periodic long-term fluctuations in climate), while most scientists and governments base their definition on human causes (emissions of carbon dioxide and methane). Thus, you begin to consider competing definitions very carefully: *How do the definitions these groups use foster the goals of each group? What's at stake for skeptics in the oil industry in promoting their definition of global warming? What's at stake*

(continued)

for the scientists and governments who put forth the opposing definition? Exploring this stasis question should help you understand how the contexts of an argument shape the claims people and groups make.

- **What is the quality of the thing?** This question will lead you to examine claims that global warming is—or is not—causing harm to the environment. Again, you quickly find that these charges are hotly contested. Exploring these differing assessments of damage done by climate change should lead you to ask who stands to gain in these analyses. *Do oil executives want to protect their investments? Do scientists want government money for grants? Where does evidence for the dangers of global warming come from? Who benefits if the dangers are accepted as real and present, and who loses?*

- **What actions should be taken?** Once again, you find wide disagreement. If global warming is occurring naturally or causing little harm, then arguably nothing needs or can be done. Or perhaps those who have made such arguments ought to sponsor a new study of global warming to prove once and for all that their assessment is correct. If, on the other hand, global warming is caused mainly by human activity and poses a clear threat to the environment, then the government and industry are bound to respond to such danger (although not everyone may agree on what such responses should be). As you investigate the proposals being made and the reasons behind them, you come closer to developing your own argument.

Audiences for Arguments

No argument, even one that engages stasis questions thoroughly, can be effective unless it speaks well to others—to what we describe as the *audiences* for arguments. Audiences cross a full range of possibilities—including the flesh-and-blood person sitting across a desk when you negotiate a student loan, the "friends" who join you in a social network, and the ideal readers that you imagine for a paper or editorial you write.

The figure on the following page may help you appreciate how many dimensions an audience can have as writers and readers negotiate their relationship to a verbal or visual text.

Readers and writers in context

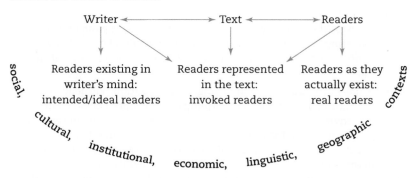

As a writer, you'll almost always be addressing an *intended* reader who exists in your own mind. As we write this textbook, we're certainly thinking of those who will read it: you are our intended reader, and ideally you know something and might even care about the subject of this book. Though we don't know you personally, we see you in our minds, for we *intend* to write for you. In the same way, the editors of *Rego: The Latino College Magazine* have a clear sense of whom they want to reach with their publication, even providing a graphic to define that audience:

Mission and Vision

- The leading lifestyle publication for the Latino collegiate, postcollegiate, and college-bound demographic
- Expand the minds of the college-age demographic

Rego, a campus magazine

- Cover the best and most pertinent issues affecting our culturally diverse target audience
- Exposure to positive role models; American, world, and popular culture; self-improvement tools; and poignant political issues

So texts have intended readers whom the writer consciously wants to address. But texts, whether visual or verbal, also have *invoked* readers—those who are represented in the text. Later in this chapter, for example, "you" (our audience) are invoked as people who recognize the importance of respecting readers. For another example, look at the second and third paragraphs of this chapter; they call on readers who should be interested in the goals of argument, whether overt or subtle. Even the cover of *Rego* invokes an audience—hip Latinos and Latinas who are intrigued by music, travel, and romance.

Writers often establish their relationships to intended and evoked audiences through their choice of pronouns, sometimes addressing favored readers as *you*, *we*, or *us*. Although such personal pronouns can help readers connect with a writer, using them can be dicey: if readers don't fit into the *us*, they may feel excluded from a text and thus less receptive to its argument. Such is the risk that writer bell hooks takes in the passage below:

> **The most powerful resource any of us can have as we study and teach in university settings is full understanding and appreciation of the richness, beauty, and primacy of our familial and community backgrounds.**
>
> —bell hooks, "Keeping Close to Home: Class and Education"

This sentence reflects hooks's intention of talking to a certain *us*—"we [who] study and teach in university settings." Readers who don't fit into such an *us* may feel excluded from this group and thus from hooks's essay. Such readers have suddenly become *they* or *them*.

In addition to intended and invoked readers, an argument will also have "real" readers—who may not be among those a writer originally imagined or called forth. You might pick up a letter written to a sibling, for instance, and read it even though it's not intended for you. Even more likely, you may read email not sent to you but rather forwarded (sometimes unwittingly) from someone else. Or you may read a legal brief prepared for a lawyer and struggle to understand it, since you're neither the intended reader nor the knowledgeable legal expert invoked in the text. As these examples suggest, writers can't always (or even usually) control who the real readers of any argument will be. As a writer, you want to think carefully about these real readers and to summon up what you do know about them, even if that knowledge is limited.

Considering Contexts

No consideration of audiences can be complete without understanding how *context* shapes and colors the perspectives readers bring to an argument. Reading always takes place in a series of contexts that move outward like concentric circles from the most immediate situation (the specific circumstance in which the reading occurs) to broader environments (including local and community contexts; institutional contexts such as school, church, or profession; and economic, cultural, and linguistic contexts).

When reporter Louise Story of the *New York Times* wrote a front-page story in 2006 saying that many women attending prestigious colleges planned to abandon their professional careers when they had children, she set off a firestorm of controversy that provoked different responses from various audiences. Some journalists challenged the integrity of Story's article and the prominence the paper gave it. Jack Schafer of Slate.com, for example, found it full of slippery and evasive qualifying terms, such as *many* and *seems*, that made its claims meaningless:

> While bogus, "Many Women at Elite Colleges Set Career Path to Motherhood" isn't false: It can't be false because it never says anything sturdy enough to be tested. So, how did it get to Page One? Is there a *New York Times* conspiracy afoot to drive feminists crazy and persuade young women that their place is in the home?
>
> —Jack Schafer, "Weasel-Words Rip My Flesh!"

Faculty members at the schools Story examined brought a different perspective to the piece. Some, like Deborah Belle, a professor of psychology at Boston University, depicted it to an interviewer for the campus newspaper, *BU Today*, as sadly emblematic of the dilemma professional women still face:

> I think the thing that resonates so badly with me about the *New York Times* article is that the onus is always on the woman, and that's not where it should be. . . . Of course there are superheroes who can do it all, but that's not the point. The point is that none of us should be forced to be in these positions.
>
> —Deborah Belle, qtd. in "The Do-It-All Dilemma"

And female students themselves—from a different generation than their professors—placed the story in their own contexts, thinking about the careers they faced. Here's Alana Steinhardt from that same *BU Today* article, bringing personal values to bear on the controversy:

> Why have kids if you can't see them grow up, and be there for the experience? . . . At BU, I'm preparing myself to be a more well-rounded person. That doesn't necessarily mean I have to work.

As you can see, arguments are created and read in complicated environments. As you compose arguments of your own, you need to think carefully about the contexts that surround your readers—and to place your topic in its context as well.

Yale student Emily Lechner, left, is one of the subjects of a controversial *New York Times* article on young women attending prestigious colleges who say their career plans will take a backseat to raising children. A variety of readers—journalists, older professional women, and other female college students—found fault with the article when viewing it in the context of their own experiences.

CULTURAL CONTEXTS FOR ARGUMENT

Considering What's "Normal"

If you want to communicate effectively with people across cultures, then learn something about the traditions in those cultures—and examine the norms guiding your own behavior:

- Explore the assumptions that guide your ways of making a point. Most of us regard our ways of thinking as "normal" or "right." Such assumptions also guide our judgments about what works in persuasive situations. But just because it may seem natural to take aggressive stands or speak bluntly in arguments, consider that others may find such aggression startling or even alarming.

(continued)

- Remember that ways of arguing are influenced by contexts that differ widely across cultures. Pay attention to how people from groups or cultures other than your own argue, and be open to the different paths of thinking you'll no doubt encounter. And be sensitive to differences in language.
- Don't assume that all people share your cultural values, ethical principles, or political assumptions. People across the world have different ways of defining *family*, *work*, or *happiness*. And as you present arguments to them, consider that they may be content with their different ways of organizing their lives and societies.
- Respect the differences among individuals *within* a given culture or group. Don't expect that every member of a community behaves—or argues—in the same way or shares the same beliefs. Avoid thinking, for instance, that there is a single Asian, African, or Hispanic culture or that Europeans are any less diverse or more predictable than Americans or Canadians in their thinking. In other words, be skeptical of stereotypes.

Appealing to Audiences

Twenty-five hundred years ago, Aristotle identified three key ways that writers can appeal to their audiences in arguments; he labeled these appeals *pathos*, *ethos*, and *logos*. These general appeals are as effective today as they were in Aristotle's time, though we usually think of them in slightly different terms.

Emotional Appeals: Pathos

Human beings often respond strongly to emotional appeals, or *pathos*. Such arguments generate emotions (such as anger, fear, jealousy, empathy, pity, and love) in readers to shape their responses and dispose them to accept a claim. For instance, while facts and figures (or logical appeals) may convince us that the AIDS epidemic in Africa is real and serious, what elicits an outpouring of support is the emotional power of televised images and newspaper accounts of suffering people. Concrete and descriptive language can similarly paint pictures in readers' minds, thus building an emotional appeal and perhaps a bond between writer and readers. For more about emotional appeals, see Chapter 2.

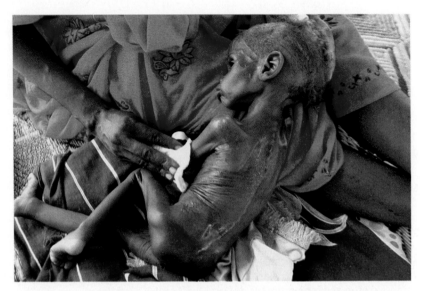

A starkly visual emotional appeal: a mother holds her ill daughter at a Doctors Without Borders clinic in Sudan, where violence and disease are killing tens of thousands.

Ethical Appeals: Ethos

Equally important to an argument's success is the writer's *ethos*, or presentation of self. When writers or speakers seem trustworthy, audiences are likely to listen to their arguments and accept them. You can make an ethical appeal to an audience simply by proving that you know what you're talking about. Or you can build credibility by emphasizing that you share values with your audience, by demonstrating that you're even-handed, and by showing that you respect both your audience and your opponents. Even visual items can make ethical appeals: consider how flags, logos, or badges convey respectability and authority. For more about ethical appeals, see Chapter 3.

Logical Appeals: Logos

Appeals to logic, or *logos*, are often given prominence and authority in U.S. culture: "Just the facts, ma'am," a famous early television detective used to say. Indeed, audiences respond well to the use of reasons and evidence—to the presentation of facts, statistics, credible testimony, cogent examples, or even a narrative or story that embodies a sound reason in support of an argument. For more about logical appeals, see Chapters 4 and 7.

Arguments and Their Rhetorical Situations

In this chapter, we've been examining elements of argument one at a time, identifying the purposes and kinds of arguments, the crux of any argument (its stasis), and ways to formulate arguments that appeal to audiences. This discussion has emphasized the social nature of argument: even if we're arguing with ourselves, there's some give-and-take involved, and the argument exists in a particular context that influences how it can be shaped and how others will receive it. The *rhetorical situation* is a shorthand phrase for this entire set of concerns, and it can be depicted as a simple triangle. (See the figure below.)

It's important to regard any rhetorical situation as dynamic, since each element of it has the potential to affect all the other elements. A change of audience in a project, for example, can lead you to reconsider all of your appeals; a change in topic may require rethinking your audience. If you begin to think in this critical way, you'll be developing a rhetorical turn of mind. You'll find yourself habitually viewing any topic from a number of perspectives and hence develop greater critical engagement with the issues and ideas important to you. Such a rhetorical frame of mind might even lead you to challenge the title of this textbook: is everything *really* an argument?

The rhetorical triangle

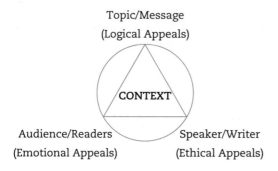

Topic/Message
(Logical Appeals)

CONTEXT

Audience/Readers
(Emotional Appeals)

Speaker/Writer
(Ethical Appeals)

RESPOND●

1. Can an argument really be any text that expresses a point of view? What kinds of arguments—if any—might be made by the following items?

    the embossed leather cover of a prayer book

    a Boston Red Sox cap

    a Livestrong bracelet

    the "explicit lyrics" label on a best-selling rock CD

    the health warning on a package of cigarettes

    a belated birthday card

    the nutrition label on a can of soup

    the cover of a science fiction novel

    a colored ribbon pinned to a shirt lapel

    a Rolex watch

2. Write six short paragraphs describing times in the recent past when you've used language to inform, to convince, to persuade, to explore, to make decisions, and to meditate or pray. Be sure to write at least one paragraph for each of these six purposes. In class, trade paragraphs with a partner, and decide whether his or her descriptions accurately fit the categories to which they've been assigned. If they don't, work with your partner to figure out why. Is the problem with the descriptions? The categories? Both? Neither?

3. In a recent newspaper or periodical, find three editorials—one that makes a forensic argument, one a deliberative argument, and one a ceremonial argument. Analyze the arguments by asking these questions: *Who is arguing? What purposes are the writers trying to achieve? To whom are they directing their arguments?* Then consider whether the arguments' purposes have been achieved in each case. If they have, offer some reasons for the arguments' success.

4. What common experiences—if any—do the following objects, brand names, and symbols evoke and for what audiences in particular?

    a USDA organic label

    the Nike swoosh

    the golden arches

    the Sean John label as seen on its Web site

    a can of Coca-Cola

    Sleeping Beauty's castle on the Disney logo

Oprah Winfrey

the Vietnam Veterans Memorial

Ground Zero at the World Trade Center site

a dollar bill

5. Read the main editorial in three or four issues of your campus news-paper. Then choose the most interesting one, and consider how the editor creates credibility, or ethos, in the editorial.

6. Take a look at the bumper sticker below, and then analyze it. What is its purpose? What kind of argument is it? Which of the stasis ques-tions does it most appropriately respond to? What appeals does it make to its readers, and how?

www.guerillastickers.com

2
Arguments Based on Emotion: Pathos

What makes you glance at a magazine ad long enough to notice a product? These days, it's probably an image or boldfaced words promising pleasure (a Caribbean beach), excitement (extreme diving on Maui), beauty (a model in low-rise jeans), technology (a glossy high-tech phone), or good health (more models). In the blink of an eye, ads can appeal to your emotions, intrigue you, and perhaps even seduce you. Look closer, and you might find logical reasons given for buying a product or service. But would you have even gotten there without an emotional tug to pull you into the page?

Emotional appeals (sometimes called *appeals to pathos*) are powerful tools for influencing what people think and believe. We all make decisions—even important ones—based on our feelings. We rent funky apartments or buy worn-out cars because we fall in love with some

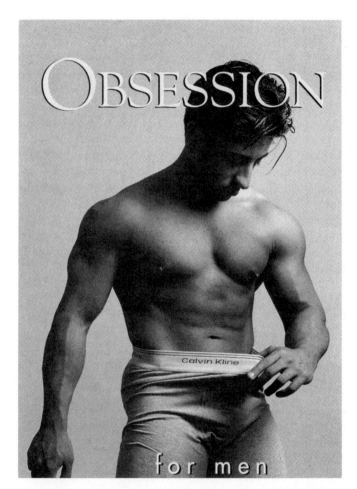

This image parodies ads that exploit one of the most powerful of emotional appeals.

small detail. On impulse, we collect whole racks of shirts or shoes that we're later too embarrassed to wear. We date and maybe even marry people that everyone else seemed to know are wrong for us—and sometimes it works out just fine.

That may be because we're not computers that use cost-and-benefit analyses to choose our friends or make our political decisions. Feelings belong in our lives. There's a powerful moment in Shakespeare's *Macbeth* when the soldier Macduff learns that his wife and children have been executed by the power-mad king. A well-meaning friend urges Macduff to "dispute it like a man." Macduff responds gruffly, "But I must also feel it as a man" (*Mac.* 4.3.219–21). As a writer, you must learn like Macduff to appreciate legitimate emotions, particularly when you want to influence the public. When you hear that formal or academic arguments should rely solely on facts, remember that facts alone often won't carry the day, even for a worthy cause. The civil rights struggle of the 1960s is a particularly good example of a movement that persuaded people equally by means of the reasonableness and the passion of its claims.

You don't have to look hard for less noble campaigns that are fueled with emotions such as hatred, envy, and greed. Democracies suffer when people use emotional arguments (and related fallacies such as personal attacks and name-calling) to drive wedges between groups, making them fearful or hateful. For that reason alone, writers should not use emotional appeals casually. (For more about emotional fallacies, see Chapter 17.)

Understanding How Emotional Arguments Work

You already know that words, images, and sounds can arouse emotions. In fact, the stirrings they generate are often physical. You've likely had the clichéd "chill down the spine" or felt something in the "pit of the stomach" when a speaker (or photograph or event) hits precisely the right note. On such occasions, it's likely that the speaker has you and people like you in mind and is seeking to rouse an emotion that will make you well disposed toward a particular message.

But sometimes speakers are called on to address not a particular group (such as a gathering of political supporters) but an entire nation or even the entire world. Such was the case during World War II when Prime Minister Winston Churchill spoke to the British House of Commons on June 4, 1940, seeking to raise British spirits and strengthen the country's resolve in resisting the German attacks:

> We shall not flag or fail. We shall go on to the end. We shall fight in France, we shall fight on the seas and oceans, we shall fight with

Hearing Barack Obama speak following a primary victory in Wisconsin, journalist Chris Matthews declared, "My, I felt this thrill going up my leg. I mean, I don't have that too often." Even some professionals can't resist a good emotional appeal.

> growing confidence and growing strength in the air, we shall defend our island, whatever the cost may be, we shall fight on the beaches, we shall fight on the landing grounds, we shall fight in the fields and in the streets, we shall fight in the hills. We shall never surrender.
> —Winston Churchill, "We Shall Fight on the Beaches"

When writers and speakers find the words and images that evoke certain emotions in people, they might also move their audiences to sympathize with ideas that they connect to those feelings and even to act on them. Make people be aware of how much they owe to others, and they'll acknowledge that debt; persuade people to hate an enemy, and they'll rally against it; help people to imagine suffering, and they'll strive to relieve it; make people feel secure or happy (or insecure or unhappy), and they'll buy products that promise such good feelings. In 2008, Barack Obama jump-started an entire presidential campaign by appealing to a single emotion—hope.

Arguments based on emotion probably count more when you're persuading than when you're arguing. When arguing, you might use reasons and evidence to convince readers something is true—for instance, that preserving wetlands is a worthy environmental goal. When persuading, however, you want people to take action—to join an environmental boycott, contribute money to an organization dedicated to wetlands protection, or write a well-researched op-ed piece for the local paper about a local marsh that is threatened by development.

The practical differences between being convinced and acting on a conviction can be enormous. Your readers may agree that contributing to charity is a noble act, but this conviction may not be enough to persuade them to part with their spare change. You need a spur that is sharper than logic, and that's when emotion might kick in. You can embarrass readers into contributing to a good cause (*Change a child's life for the price of a pizza*), make them feel the impact of their gift (*Imagine the smile on that little child's face*), or tell them a moving story (*In a tiny village in Central America . . .*). We've all seen such techniques work.

When Nancy from Ann Arbor, Michigan, called into NPR's *Talk of the Nation*, she used emotional appeals to persuade others to treat online harassment as a serious issue.

LINK TO P. 699

A March 20, 2008, cover of *Rolling Stone* presented Barack Obama as an emblem of hope, even giving him an aura. Later that election year (July 21, 2008), a *New Yorker* cover presented him and his wife, Michelle, in a different light, suggesting how his opponents would depict the Obamas to evoke the politics of another emotion—fear.

Not Just Words

Take a look at this image, which at first glance depicts the familiar stars and stripes of the American flag. But a second glance reveals corporate logos rather than stars. Study the picture carefully and write for two or three minutes about the emotions that the image arouses in you. Do you respond first to the flag and then to the logos? What clash of emotional appeals do you see here, and how do you feel about that conflict? Try your hand at creating one or two possible titles or captions for this image.

Using Emotions to Build Bridges

Kathy Freston appeals to her readers' feelings about the environment and their responsibility to it to build bridges to her audience.

LINK TO P. 800

You may sometimes want to use emotions to connect with readers to assure them that you understand their experiences or, to use President Bill Clinton's famous line, "feel their pain." Such a bridge is especially important when you're writing about matters that readers regard as sensitive. Before they'll trust you, they'll want assurances that you understand the issues in depth. If you strike the right emotional note, you'll establish an important connection. That's what Apple founder Steve Jobs does in a 2005 commencement address in which he tells the audience that he doesn't have a fancy speech, just three stories from his life:

> My second story is about love and loss. I was lucky. I found what I loved to do early in life. Woz [Steve Wozniak] and I started Apple in my parents' garage when I was twenty. We worked hard and in ten years, Apple had grown from just the two of us in a garage into a $2 billion company with over 4,000 employees. We'd just released our finest creation, the Macintosh, a year earlier, and I'd just turned thirty, and then I got fired. How can you get fired from a company you started? Well, as Apple grew, we hired someone who I thought was very talented to run the company with me, and for the first year or so, things went well. But then our visions of the future began to diverge, and eventually we had a falling out. When we did, our board of directors sided with him, and so at thirty, I was out, and very publicly out. . . .
>
> I didn't see it then, but it turned out that getting fired from Apple was the best thing that could have ever happened to me. The heaviness of being successful was replaced by the lightness of being a beginner again, less sure about everything. It freed me to enter one of the most creative periods in my life. During the next five years I started a company named NeXT, another company named Pixar and fell in love with an amazing woman who would become my wife. Pixar went on to create the world's first computer-animated feature film, *Toy Story*, and is now the most successful animation studio in the world.
>
> —Steve Jobs, "You've Got to Find What You Love, Jobs Says"

In no obvious way is Jobs's recollection a formal argument. But it prepares his audience to accept the advice he'll give later in his speech, at least partly because he's speaking from meaningful personal experiences.

A more obvious way to build an emotional tie is simply to help readers identify with your experiences. If, like Georgina Kleege, you were blind and wanted to argue for more sensible attitudes toward blind people, you might ask readers in the first paragraph of your argument to confront their prejudices. Here Kleege, a writer and college instructor, makes an emotional point by telling a story:

> I tell the class, "I am legally blind." There is a pause, a collective intake of breath. I feel them look away uncertainly and then look back. After all, I just said I couldn't see. Or did I? I had managed to get there on my own—no cane, no dog, none of the usual trappings of blindness. Eyeing me askance now, they might detect that my gaze is not quite focused. . . . They watch me glance down, or towards the door where someone's coming in late. I'm just like anyone else.
> —Georgina Kleege, "Call It Blindness"

Given that the way she narrates the first day of class, readers are as likely to identify with the students as with Kleege, imagining themselves sitting in a classroom, facing a sightless instructor, confronting their own prejudices about the blind. Kleege wants to put them on edge emotionally.

Let's consider another rhetorical situation: how do you win over an audience when the logical claims that you're making are likely to go against what many in the audience believe? Once again, a slightly risky appeal to emotions on a personal level may work. That's the tack that Michael Pollan takes in bringing readers to consider that "the great moral struggle of our time will be for the rights of animals." In introducing his lengthy exploratory argument, Pollan uses personal experience to appeal to his audience:

> The first time I opened Peter Singer's *Animal Liberation*, I was dining alone at the Palm, trying to enjoy a rib-eye steak cooked medium-rare. If this sounds like a good recipe for cognitive dissonance (if not indigestion), that was sort of the idea. Preposterous as it might seem to supporters of animal rights, what I was doing was tantamount to reading *Uncle Tom's Cabin* on a plantation in the Deep South in 1852.
> —Michael Pollan, "An Animal's Place"

In creating a vivid image of his first encounter with Singer's book, Pollan's opening builds a bridge between himself as a person trying to enter into the animal rights debate in a fair and open-minded, if still skeptical, way and readers who might be passionate about either side of this argument.

A visual version of Michael Pollan's rhetorical situation

THE BIRTH OF A VEGETARIAN

Using Emotions to Sustain an Argument

You can also use emotional appeals to make logical claims stronger or more memorable. That is the way that photographs and other images add power to arguments. In a TV attack ad, the scowling black-and-white photograph of a political opponent may do as much damage as the claim that he bought his home on the cheap from a financier convicted of fraud. Or the attractive skier in a spot for lip balm may make us yearn for brisk, snowy winter days. The technique is tricky, however. Lay on too much emotion—especially those like outrage, pity, or shame, which make people uncomfortable—and you may offend the very audiences you hoped to convince.

But sometimes a strong emotion such as anger adds energy to a passage, as it does when writer Stuart Taylor and history professor K. C. Johnson react in outrage when Mike Nifong, a prosecutor charged with deliberately lying about evidence in an emotionally charged rape case at Duke University, received only a twenty-four-hour sentence for his misconduct. In an op-ed in the *Washington Post*, the authors review the wider dimensions of the biased prosecution and turn their ire especially on faculty who were too eager to pillory three white student athletes at Duke for an alleged crime against a minority woman that subsequent investigations proved never occurred. As you read the following excerpt, notice how the authors' use of emotional language might lead some readers to share their anger and others to resent it.

> To be sure, it was natural to assume at first that Nifong had a case. Why else would he confidently declare the players guilty? But many academics and journalists continued to presume guilt months after

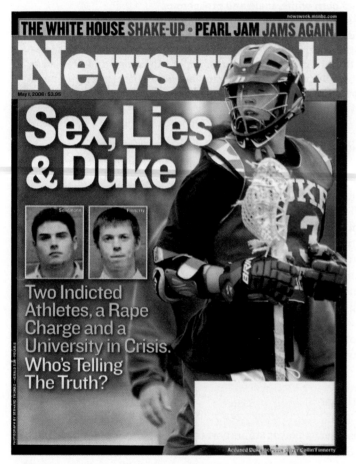

What is the emotional impact of a *Newsweek* cover like this one, which appeared on May 1, 2006, following initial indictments in what became known as the Duke University rape case? Does the magazine seem to be taking sides?

massive evidence of innocence poured into the public record. Indeed, some professors persisted in attacks even after the three defendants were declared innocent in April by North Carolina Attorney General Roy Cooper—an almost unheard-of event.

Brushing aside concern with "the 'truth' . . . about the incident," as one put it, these faculty ideologues just changed their indictments from rape to drunkenness (hardly a rarity in college); exploiting poor black women (the players had expected white and Hispanic strippers); and being born white, male and prosperous.

This shameful conduct was rooted in a broader trend toward subordinating facts and evidence to faith-based ideological posturing. Worse, the ascendant ideology, especially in academia, is an obsession with the fantasy that oppression of minorities and women by "privileged" white men remains rampant in America. Its crude stereotyping of white men, especially athletes, resembles old-fashioned racism and sexism.

—Stuart Taylor and K. C. Johnson, "Guilty in the Duke Case"

In using language this way, writers can generate emotions by presenting arguments in their starkest terms, stripped of qualifications or subtleties. Readers or listeners are confronted with core issues or important choices and asked to consider the consequences.

It's difficult to gauge how much emotion will work in a given argument. Some issues—such as racism, rape, abortion, and gun control—provoke strong feelings and, as a result, are often argued on emotional terms. But even issues that seem deadly dull—such as funding for Medicare and Social Security—can be argued passionately when proposed changes in these programs are set in human terms: cut benefits and Grandma will have to eat cat food; don't cut benefits and Social Security will surely go broke, leaving nothing for later generations of seniors. Both alternatives might scare people into paying enough attention to take political action.

Using Humor

Humor has always played an important role in argument, sometimes as the sugar that makes the medicine go down. You can slip humor into an argument to put readers at ease, thereby making them more open to a proposal you have to offer. It's hard to say no when you're laughing. Humor also makes otherwise sober people suspend their judgment and even their prejudices, perhaps because the surprise and naughtiness of wit are combustive: they provoke laughter or smiles, not reflection. That may be why TV sitcoms like *Sex and the City* and *Will & Grace* became popular with mainstream audiences, despite their sometimes controversial subjects. Similarly, it's possible to make a point through humor that might not work in more sober writing. Consider the gross stereotypes about men that humorist Dave Barry presents here, tongue in cheek, as he explains why people don't read the instructions that come with the products they buy:

> The third reason why consumers don't read manuals is that many consumers are men, and we men would no more read a manual than we would ask directions, because this would be an admission that the person who wrote the manual has a bigger . . . OK, a bigger grasp of technology than we do. We men would rather hook up our new DVD player in such a way that it ignites the DVDs and shoots them across the room—like small flaming UFOs—than admit that the manual-writer possesses a more manly technological manhood than we do.
>
> —Dave Barry, "Owners' Manual Step No. 1:
> Bang Head against the Wall"

Our laughter testifies to a kernel of truth in Barry's observations and makes us more likely to agree with his conclusions.

A writer or speaker can use humor to deal with especially sensitive issues. For example, sports commentator Bob Costas, given the honor of eulogizing the great baseball player Mickey Mantle, couldn't ignore problems in Mantle's life. So he argues for Mantle's greatness by admitting the man's weaknesses indirectly through humor:

> It brings to mind a story Mickey liked to tell on himself and maybe some of you have heard it. He pictured himself at the pearly gates, met by St. Peter who shook his head and said, "Mick, we checked the record. We know some of what went on. Sorry, we can't let you in. But before you go, God wants to know if you'd sign these six dozen baseballs."
>
> —Bob Costas, "Eulogy for Mickey Mantle"

Similarly, politicians use humor to admit problems or mistakes they couldn't acknowledge in any other way. Here, for example, is President George W. Bush at the 2004 Radio and TV Correspondents Dinner discussing his much-mocked intellect:

> Those stories about my intellectual capacity do get under my skin. You know, for a while I even thought my staff believed it. There on my schedule first thing every morning it said, "Intelligence briefing."
>
> —George W. Bush

Charles M. Blow begins his ⌐ posting about who posts on so⌐ networking sites with a joke abou⌐ how old his kids think he is—a move that will build bridges with many parents who might read the blog.

LINK TO P. 715 ....

Not all humor is well intentioned. In fact, among the most powerful forms of emotional argument is ridicule—humor aimed at a particular target. Eighteenth-century poet and critic Samuel Johnson was known for his stinging and humorous put-downs, such as this comment to an aspiring writer: "Your manuscript is both good and original, but the part that is good is not original and the part that is original is not good." Today, even bumper stickers can be vehicles for succinct arguments:

But ridicule is a two-edged sword that requires a deft hand to wield it. Humor that reflects bad taste discredits a writer completely, as does ridicule that misses its mark. Unless your target deserves assault and you can be very funny, it's usually better to steer clear of humor.

Using Arguments Based on Emotion

You don't want to play puppetmaster with people's emotions when you write arguments, but it's a good idea to spend some time early in your writing or designing process thinking about how you want readers to feel as they consider your persuasive claims. For example, would readers of your editorial about campus traffic policies be more inclined to agree with you if you made them envy faculty privileges, or would arousing their sense of fairness work better? What emotional appeals might persuade meat eaters to consider a vegan diet—or vice versa? Would sketches of stage props on a Web site persuade people to buy a season ticket to the theater, or would you spark more interest by featuring pictures of costumed performers?

Consider, too, the effect that a story can have on readers. Writers and journalists routinely use what are called *human-interest stories* to give presence to issues or arguments. You can do the same, using a particular incident to evoke sympathy, understanding, outrage, or amusement. Take care, though, to tell an honest story.

RESPOND●

1. To what specific emotions do the following slogans, sales pitches, and maxims appeal?

   "Just do it." (ad for Nike)

   "Think different." (ad for Apple Computers)

   "Reach out and touch someone." (ad for AT&T)

   "Yes we can!" (2008 presidential campaign slogan for Barack Obama)

   "Country first." (2008 presidential campaign slogan for John McCain)

   "By any means necessary." (rallying cry from Malcolm X)

   "Have it your way." (slogan for Burger King)

   "You can trust your car to the man who wears the star." (slogan for Texaco)

   "It's everywhere you want to be." (slogan for Visa)

   "Know what comes between me and my Calvins? Nothing!" (tag line for Calvin Klein jeans)

   "Don't mess with Texas!" (antilitter campaign slogan)

2. Bring a magazine to class, and analyze the emotional appeals in as many full-page ads as you can. Then classify those ads by types of emotional appeal, and see whether you can connect the appeals to the subject or target audience of the magazine. Compare your results with those of your classmates, and discuss your findings. For instance, do the ads in newsmagazines like *Time* and *Newsweek* appeal to different emotions and desires from the ads in publications such as *Cosmopolitan*, *Spin*, *Sports Illustrated*, *Automobile*, and *National Geographic*?

3. How do arguments based on emotion work in different media? Are such arguments more or less effective in books, articles, television (both news and entertainment shows), films, brochures, magazines, email, Web sites, the theater, street protests, and so on? You might explore how a single medium handles emotional appeals or compare different media. For example, why do Internet newsgroups seem to encourage angry outbursts? Are newspapers an emotionally colder source of information than television news programs? If so, why?

4. Spend some time looking for arguments that use ridicule or humor to make their point: check out your favorite Web sites; watch for bumper stickers, posters, or advertisements; and listen to popular song lyrics. Bring one or two examples to class, and be ready to explain how the humor makes an emotional appeal and whether it's effective.

3
Arguments Based on Character: Ethos

It was a moment many had been waiting for: on January 10, 2008, Ratan N. Tata, head of India's Tata Motors, unveiled Nano, "the people's car" designed to be affordable for those who had never dreamed of owning an automobile. Saying he hoped the Nano will bring "pride and joy" to millions of new owners, Tata stood aside to showcase the tiny car, reputed to sell for $2,500.

In describing the Nano, Tata Motors focuses not simply on its low cost but on what you might think of as its character: this people's car will be dependable, safe, fuel efficient, and low on emissions. In short, it is a car for everyone and can be counted on to serve its owners as well as its country's environment.

To be successful in selling the Nano, Tata Motors depends to a large extent on the character or ethos of the company itself. Writers and speakers (and companies) create ethos in at least two ways—through the reputation they bring to the table and through the language, evidence, and images they use. Tata Motors's homepage, for example, focuses on

The Tata Nano, said to be the world's cheapest car

its ethos, beginning with its carefully worded motto "Green matters" and then drawing on its reputation in its opening statement:

> True to the tradition of the Tata Group, Tata Motors is committed in letter and spirit to Corporate Social Responsibility. It is a signatory to the United Nations Global Compact, and is engaged in community and social initiatives on labour and environment standards in compliance with the principles of the Global Compact. In accordance with this, it plays an active role in community development, serving rural communities around its manufacturing locations.

In making an argument based on the character of the company, Tata Motors is also creating an ethos that it promises the Nano will live up to, perhaps even exceed, as the company works to improve the car's performance, durability, and green qualities. In doing so, Tata is appealing to the values of many today who believe that humans must reduce our carbon footprints and save energy if we are to avoid irrevocable damage to our shared planet.

Audiences pay attention to ethos and to the values that it represents. Before we accept the words (or image) of others, we must usually respect

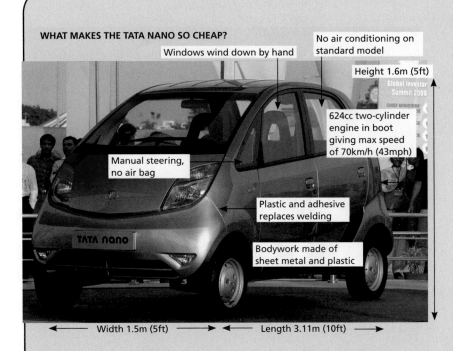

WHAT MAKES THE TATA NANO SO CHEAP?

Windows wind down by hand

No air conditioning on standard model

Height 1.6m (5ft)

624cc two-cylinder engine in boot giving max speed of 70km/h (43mph)

Manual steering, no air bag

Plastic and adhesive replaces welding

Bodywork made of sheet metal and plastic

Width 1.5m (5ft)

Length 3.11m (10ft)

Not Just Words

Someone browsing the Web for information about the Tata Nano will quickly come across images like the one on page 53—and also like the one above. This second, annotated image points out that the company can build and sell the Nano cheaply for good reasons. Some reasons, like the use of plastic, might worry those who have concerns about safety. Others may be disappointed at the lack of air conditioning or the hand-crank windows. This annotated image therefore can raise questions about some of the claims made for the Nano.

Others investigating the car and the company that produces it might note the home page claim that Tata is a "signatory to the United Nations Global Compact" and decide to find out what that means. They would soon find the logo of this UN group, which has strong suggestions of global harmony and peace:

The logo image is reinforced on the homepage of the United Nations Global Compact, which focuses on the organization's "ten principles in the areas of human rights, labour, the environment and anti-corruption [that] enjoy universal consensus." Together, the logo and images of the natural world featured on the Web site create an ethos of responsibility, openness, and trust. But readers and writers must examine issues of ethos carefully. If you looked further, for example, you would likely identify some critics of the ethos of the Global Compact. In fact, a group called Global Compact Critics uses another powerful symbol to do just that—by superimposing a big question mark on the Global Compact logo:

Look at the Web site for Tata Motors (http://www.tatamotors .com) or the Web site for the United Nations Global Compact (http://www.unglobalcompact.org):

- What specific issues of ethos can you find addressed on the homepage for either group? How is ethos created through the use of images as well as words?

- Now look at the Web site for Global Compact Critics (http:// globalcompactcritics.blogspot.com), noting the way that this group uses images to question the ethos of the UN Global Compact.

- Working with a group, create some images that could help build a positive ethos for either the Tata Nano, the UN Global Compact, or Global Compact Critics.

their authority, admire their integrity and motives, or at least acknowledge what they stand for. Potential buyers of the Nano will know something of the ethos of Tata Motors since it is the largest manufacturer of automobiles in India and one of the country's ten top corporations. But Tata's advertising campaign will also make sure that buyers know a great deal about the way that the new Nano reflects the ethos of Tata's "Green matters": its very low cost, very high mileage ratio (fifty-four miles to the U.S. gallon), and high safety standards all help to build trust and a strong consumer base.

Character alone may not carry an argument, however, and the character of Tata Motors and its Nano probably won't speak to everyone. In fact, soon after its launch, several prospective customers interviewed by the news media said the Nano's low price could backfire on the company, driving away customers who look for status rather than fuel efficiency in an automobile. As one person said, "I still like big cars." In creating arguments based on character or ethos, writers must remember that a particular character will not appeal to every kind of audience.

Nevertheless, establishing ethos is important in arguments, whether the argument is made by a company (like Tata Motors), a person (such as a presidential candidate), a group (like the American Civil Liberties Union or Students for Academic Freedom), or an institution (such as a corporation, newspaper, or college). We observe people, groups, or institutions making and defending claims all the time and ask ourselves: *Should we pay attention to them? Can we trust them?* But establishing a persuasive ethos requires not simply seeming honest or likable but also affirming an identity and sharing parts or all of it with an intended audience. For example, while Tata, Porsche, and Tesla all hope to sell lots of automobiles, they are attempting to reach different audiences. Tata, as we've seen, is targeting the millions of everyday Indians who today are riding bicycles or motorscooters; Porsche aims for drivers who want the status of a beautifully designed, powerful, and expensive car; while Tesla wants to sell to those willing to pay big bucks for a zero-emissions electric car.

If a company (or anyone building an argument from character) is well known, liked, and respected, that reputation will contribute to its persuasive power. If its character is problematic in any respect, it may have to use argument to reshape an audience's perception. The fact that Tata Motors also produces heavy trucks, for example, could call into question some of its "Green matters" claim, leading consumers to question its ethos.

Understanding How Arguments Based on Character Work

Because life is complicated, we often need shortcuts to help us make choices. We can't weigh every claim to its last milligram or trace every fragment of evidence to its original source. And we have to make such decisions daily: *Which brand of clothing should I buy? Whom should I vote for in the next election? Which reviews of an Academy Award nominee for best film should I believe? What are the real risks in taking prescription painkillers?* To answer serious questions, people typically turn to professionals— doctors, lawyers, teachers, pastors—for wise, well-informed, and frank advice. But people look to equally knowledgeable individuals to guide them in less momentous matters as well. An expert can be anyone with knowledge and experience, from a professor of nuclear physics at an Ivy League college to a short-order cook at the local diner.

Readers give the people (or institutions) they know a hearing they might not automatically grant to a stranger or someone who hasn't earned their respect or affection. That trust indicates the power of arguments based on ethos or character and accounts for why people will often take the word of the "car guy" in their neighborhood more seriously than the reviews in *Consumer Reports*. And they'll believe *Consumer Reports* more readily than the SUV ads in *People*. Appeals or arguments about character often turn on claims such as the following:

- A person (or group) does or does not have the authority to speak to this issue.
- A person (or group) is or is not trustworthy or credible on this issue.
- A person (or group) does or does not have good motives for addressing this subject.

Claiming Authority

When you read an argument, especially one that makes an aggressive claim, you have every right to wonder about the writer's authority: *What does he know about the subject? What experiences does she have that make her especially knowledgeable? Why should I pay attention to this writer?*

When you offer an argument, you have to anticipate pointed questions like these and be able to answer them, directly or indirectly. Sometimes the claim of authority will be bold and personal, as it is when writer and activist Terry Tempest Williams attacks those who poisoned the Utah deserts with nuclear radiation. What gives her the right to speak on this subject? Not scientific expertise, but gut-wrenching personal experience:

> I belong to the Clan of One-Breasted Women. My mother, my grand-mothers, and six aunts have all had mastectomies. Seven are dead. The two who survive have just completed rounds of chemotherapy and radiation.
> I've had my own problems: two biopsies for breast cancer and a small tumor between my ribs diagnosed as a "borderline malignancy."
> —Terry Tempest Williams, "The Clan of One-Breasted Women"

We are willing to listen to Williams's claims because she has lived with the nuclear peril she will deal with in the remainder of her essay.

Writers usually establish their authority in other and less striking ways. When they attach academic and professional titles to their names, for example, they're subtly building their authority by saying "this is how I've earned the right to be heard"—they are medical doctors, have law degrees, or have been state certified to work as psychotherapists. Similarly, writers can assert authority by mentioning their employers (their institutional affiliations) and the number of years that they've worked in a given field. Bureaucrats often identify themselves with their agencies, and professors with their schools. As a reader, you'll likely pay more attention to an argument about global warming if it's offered by someone who identifies herself as a professor of atmospheric and oceanic science at the University of Wisconsin–Madison, than by your Uncle Sid, who sells tools at Sears. But you'll prefer your uncle to the professor when you need advice about a reliable rotary saw.

In the opening paragraph of "Why Take Food Seriously?" Mark Bittman calls attention to his credentials—a long history of working with food and contact with many others who cook—to build his ethos.

LINK TO P. 779

When your readers are apt to be skeptical of both you and your claim, you may have to be even more specific about your credentials. That's exactly the strategy Richard Bernstein uses to establish his right to speak on the subject of teaching multiculturalism in American colleges and universities. At one point in a lengthy argument, he challenges those who make simplistic pronouncements about non-Western cultures, specifically "Asian culture." But what gives a New York writer named Bernstein the authority to write about Asian peoples? Bernstein tells us in a sparkling example of an argument based on character:

> The Asian culture, as it happens, is something I know a bit about, having spent five years at Harvard striving for a Ph.D. in a joint program called History and East Asian Languages and, after that, living either

as a student (for one year) or a journalist (six years) in China and Southeast Asia. At least I know enough to know there is no such thing as the "Asian culture."

—Richard Bernstein, *Dictatorship of Virtue*

Bernstein understates the case when he says he knows "a bit" about Asian culture and then mentions a Ph.D. program at Harvard and years of living in Asia. But the false modesty may be part of his argumentative strategy, too.

When you write for readers who trust you and your work, you may not have to make an open claim to authority. But you should know that making this type of appeal is always an option. A second lesson is that it certainly helps to know your subject when you're making a claim.

Even if an author doesn't make an explicit effort to assert it, authority can be conveyed through fairly small signals that readers may pick up almost subconsciously. On his blog, educator and writer Mike Rose responds to "In the Basement of the Ivory Tower," an *Atlantic Monthly* article that he says "offers a disheartening portrait of the 'non-traditional' (or 'remedial' or just run-of-the-mill) college student, a portrait common in mass media, and in high-brow media particularly." In the passage below, we've italicized self-assured prose that Rose uses in criticizing this essay:

It is *certainly accurate* that a number of people do enter higher education poorly prepared. And *we do need to think hard* about what the current push for "college for all" truly means, how it can be enacted in an effective way, and whether or not it offers the best remedy for past educational inequality. These are *important questions*. Articles like "In the Basement of the Ivory Tower" *don't help us answer them.*

—Mike Rose, Mike Rose's Blog

Establishing Credibility

Whereas authority is a measure of how much command a writer has over a subject, credibility speaks to a writer's honesty, respect for an audience and its values, and plain old likeability. Sometimes a sense of humor can play an important role in getting an audience to listen to you: it's no accident that all but the most serious speeches begin with a few jokes or stories. The humor puts listeners at ease and helps them identify with the speaker. In fact, a little self-deprecation can endear writers or speakers to the toughest audiences. We'll often listen to people confident enough to make fun of themselves, because they seem clever and yet aware of their own limitations.

Take, for example, the opening scene of *An Inconvenient Truth*, the documentary on the dangers of global warming. Al Gore, who later won an Academy Award for this film, takes the stage dressed in a dark suit, holding a PowerPoint clicker, and looking urgent. The Global Warming Slideshow for which he has become so well known occupies the huge screen behind him as he prepares to address a large group of students. There's a pause, and then Gore says, "Hello, my name is Al Gore, and I used to be the next president of the United States." The students erupt with roars of laughter, cheers, and whistles at this very effective piece of self-deprecating humor.

But humor alone can't establish credibility. Although a funny anecdote may help dispose an audience to listen to you, you will need to move quickly to make reasonable claims and then back them up with evidence and documentation—or, in electronic environments, to link your claims to sites with reliable information. That is, showing your authority on a topic is itself a good way to build credibility.

But there's even more to it than that. Consider that a number of studies over the years have shown that tall, slender, good-looking people have an advantage in getting a job or getting a raise. Apparently, employers make assumptions about such people's competence based on nothing more than good looks. You probably act the same way in some circumstances, even if you resent the practice.

You might recall these studies when you make an argument, knowing that like it or not, readers and audiences are going to respond to how you present yourself as a person. In other words, be sure that your writing visually conveys your message as effectively as possible. Choose a medium that shows you at your best. Some writers love a written text garnished with quotations, footnotes, charts, graphs, and a bibliography. Others can make a better case online or in some purely visual form. Choosing a medium carefully will help you design arguments that assure readers they can trust you.

You can also establish credibility by connecting your own beliefs to core principles that are well established and widely respected. This strategy is particularly effective when your position seems to be—at first glance, at least—a threat to traditional values. For example, when author Andrew Sullivan (who is himself a conservative) argues in favor of

The National Institute of Mental Health boosts its credibility by having a spokesperson acknowledge how difficult it is for an immigrant to admit to suffering from depression.

LINK TO P. 769

By far the most terrifying film
you will ever see.

aninconvenient**truth**

A GLOBAL WARNING

The movie poster for *An Inconvenient Truth*

legalizing same-sex marriages, he does so in language that echoes the
themes of family-values conservatives:

> Legalizing gay marriage would offer homosexuals the same deal soci-
> ety now offers heterosexuals: general social approval and specific
> legal advantages in exchange for a deeper and harder-to-extract-
> youself-from commitment to another human being. Like straight

marriage, it would foster social cohesion, emotional security, and economic prudence. Since there's no reason gays should not be allowed to adopt or be foster parents, it could also help nurture children. And its introduction would not be some sort of radical break with social custom. As it has become more acceptable for gay people to acknowledge their loves publicly, more and more have committed themselves to one another for life in full view of their families and their friends. A law institutionalizing gay marriage would merely reinforce a healthy social trend. It would also, in the wake of AIDS, qualify as a genuine public health measure. Those conservatives who deplore promiscuity among some homosexuals should be among the first to support it.

—Andrew Sullivan, "Here Comes the Groom"

Yet another way to affirm your credibility as a writer is to use language that shows your respect for readers, addressing them neither above nor below their capabilities. Citing trustworthy sources and acknowledging them properly prove, too, that you've done your homework (another sign of respect) and suggest that you know your subject. So does presenting ideas clearly and fairly. Details matter: helpful graphs, tables, charts, or illustrations may carry weight with readers, as will the visual attractiveness of your work (or your Web site, for that matter). Again, even correct spelling counts.

Writers who establish their credibility in this way seem trustworthy. But sometimes, to be credible, you have to admit limitations, too: *This is what I know; I won't pretend to understand more.* It's a tactic used by people as respected in their fields as the late biologist Lewis Thomas, who in this example ponders whether scientists have overstepped their bounds in exploring the limits of DNA research:

Should we stop short of learning some things, for fear of what we, or someone, will do with the knowledge? My own answer is a flat no, but I must confess that this is an intuitive response and I am neither inclined nor trained to reason my way through it.

—Lewis Thomas, "The Hazards of Science"

When making an argument, many people would be reluctant to write "I suppose" or "I must confess," but those are the very concessions that might increase a reader's confidence in a scientist and writer like Lewis Thomas.

In fact, a powerful technique for building credibility is to acknowledge outright any exceptions, qualifications, or even weaknesses in your argument. For example, a Volkswagen ad with the headline "They said it couldn't be done. It couldn't," shows pro basketball star Wilt Chamberlain, who at seven feet, one inch, tall just can't fit inside the bug. This ad is one of a classic series in which Volkswagen pokes fun at itself and admits to limitations while also promoting the good points about the car, gaining credibility in the bargain.

Making such concessions to objections that readers might raise, called *conditions of rebuttal*, sends a strong signal to the audience that you've scrutinized your own position and can therefore be trusted when you turn to arguing its merits. Speaking to readers directly, using *I* or *you*, for instance, also enables you to come closer to them when that strategy is appropriate. Using contractions and everyday or colloquial language can have the same effect. In a 2008 commencement address, Oprah Winfrey argues that the graduates need to consider how they can serve others. To build her case, she draws on her own experience—forthrightly noting some mistakes and problems that she has faced in trying to live a life of service:

> I started this school in Africa . . . where I'm trying to give South African girls a shot at a future like yours. And I spent five years making sure

Oprah Winfrey in South Africa

that school would be as beautiful as the students. . . . And yet, last fall, I was faced with a crisis I had never anticipated. I was told that one of the dorm matrons was suspected of sexual abuse.

That was, as you can imagine, devastating news. First, I cried—actually, I sobbed. . . . And the whole time I kept asking that question: What is this here to teach me? And, as difficult as that experience has been, I got a lot of lessons. I understand now the mistakes I made, because I had been paying attention to all of the wrong things. I'd built that school from the outside in, when what really mattered was the inside out.

—Oprah Winfrey, Stanford University Commencement Address

In some situations, however, you may find that a more formal tone gives your claims greater authority. Choices like these are yours to make as you search for the ethos that best represents you in a given argument.

CULTURAL CONTEXTS FOR ARGUMENT

Ethos

In the United States, students writing arguments are often asked to establish authority by drawing on personal experiences, by reporting on research that they or others have conducted, and by taking a position for which they can offer strong evidence and support. But this expectation about student authority is by no means universal.

Some cultures regard student writers as novices who can most effectively make arguments by reflecting on what they've learned from their teachers and elders—those who are believed to hold the most important knowledge, wisdom, and, hence, authority. Whenever you're arguing a point with people from cultures other than your own, therefore, you need to think about what kind of authority you're expected to have:

- Whom are you addressing, and what is your relationship with that person?

- What knowledge are you expected to have? Is it appropriate or expected for you to demonstrate that knowledge—and if so, how?

- What tone is appropriate? If in doubt, always show respect: politeness is rarely if ever inappropriate.

Coming Clean about Motives

When people are trying to sell you something, it's important (and natural) to ask: *Whose interests are they serving? How will they profit from their proposal?* Such suspicions go to the heart of ethical arguments. It's no accident that Jonathan Swift ends his satirical *A Modest Proposal* with his narrator claiming he will benefit in no way from what he suggests—that the people of eighteenth-century Ireland end their poverty by selling their infant children to be used for food:

> I profess, in the sincerity of my heart, that I have not the least personal interest in endeavoring to promote this necessary work, having no other motive than the public good of my country, by advancing our trade, providing for infants, relieving the poor, and giving some pleasure to the rich. I have no children by which I can propose to get a single penny; the youngest being nine years old, and my wife past child-bearing.
>
> —Jonathan Swift, *A Modest Proposal*

Even this monster of a narrator appreciates that his idea will gain no traction if his motives are suspect in the least. He's also smart enough to discuss his potential conflicts of interest (his own children and his wife). This is always a sensible strategy whenever your motives for offering an idea might seem driven by its potential advantage to yourself or by your attachment to a particular class, gender, faction, or other group.

Here, for example, someone posting on the Web site Serious Eats, which is "focused on celebrating and sharing food enthusiasm" online, acknowledges—in a footnote—that his attention to Martha Stewart, her Web site, and a *Martha Stewart Living* cookbook may be influenced by his employment history:

> Martha Stewart* has been blipping up on the Serious Eats radar lately.
>
> First it was this astronaut meal she chose for her longtime Microsoft billionaire friend Charles Simonyi, "a gourmet space meal of duck breast confit and semolina cake with dried apricots." Talk about going above and beyond.
>
> Then official word comes that marthastewart.com has relaunched with a fresh new look and new features. The site, which went live in its new form a few weeks before this announcement, is quite an improvement. It seems to load faster, information is easier to find, and the recipes are easier to read—although there are so many brands,

magazines, and "omnimedia" on offer that the homepage is a little dizzying at first.

Third, while reading Apartment Therapy's Kitchen blog, I ran across a review of the *Everyday Food* cookbook, which was released recently by Martha Stewart Living Omnimedia: "Guests said that the dinner cooked from this book tasted like 'restaurant food' and we'll take the compliment. There is a fullness of flavor in these recipes that is not found in other quick fix recipes. . . ."

* Full disclosure: I used to work at Martha Stewart Living magazine.

—Adam Kuban, "Martha, Martha, Martha"

Especially in online venues like the one Kuban uses here, writers have to expect that readers will hold diverse views and will be quick to point out unmentioned affiliations as serious drawbacks to credibility. In fact, attacks on such loyalties are common in political circles, where it's almost a sport to assume the worst about an opponent's motives and associations. But we all have connections and interests that represent the ties that bind us to other human beings. It makes sense that a woman might be concerned with women's issues or that investors might look out for their investments. So it can be good strategy to let your audiences know where your loyalties lie when such information does, in fact, shape your work.

There are other ways, too, to invite readers to regard you as trustworthy. Nancy Mairs, in an essay entitled "On Being a Cripple," wins the attention and respect of her readers by facing her situation with a riveting directness:

> First, the matter of semantics. I am a cripple. I choose this word to name me. I choose from among several possibilities, the most common of which are "handicapped" and "disabled." I made the choice a number of years ago, without thinking, unaware of my motives for doing so. Even now, I am not sure what those motives are, but I recognize that they are complex and not entirely flattering. People—crippled or not—wince at the word "cripple," as they do not at "handicapped" or "disabled." Perhaps I want them to wince. I want them to see me as a tough customer, one to whom the fates/gods/viruses have not been kind, but who can face the brutal truth of her existence squarely. As a cripple, I swagger.
>
> —Nancy Mairs, "On Being a Cripple"

The paragraph takes some risks because the writer is expressing feelings that may make readers unsure how to react. Indeed, Mairs herself admits that she doesn't completely understand her own feelings and motives. Yet the very admission of uncertainty helps her to build a bridge to readers.

RESPOND•

1. Consider the ethos of each of the following public figures. Then describe one or two public arguments, campaigns, or products that might benefit from their endorsements as well as several that would not.

   Oprah Winfrey—TV celebrity

   Margaret Cho—comedian

   Kate Winslet—actress

   Colin Powell—former chair of the Joint Chiefs of Staff and Secretary of State in the George W. Bush administration

   Sarah Palin—former governor of Alaska and Republican vice-presidential candidate

   Dave Chappelle—humorist and columnist

   Jeff Gordon—NASCAR champion

   Nancy Pelosi—speaker of the U.S. House of Representatives

   Bill O'Reilly—TV news commentator

   Marge Simpson—sensible wife and mother on *The Simpsons*

   Jon Stewart—host of *The Daily Show* on Comedy Central

2. Voice is a choice. That is, writers modify the tone and style of their language depending on whom they want to seem to be. In the excerpts from this chapter, Mike Rose wants to appear fair yet confident; his language aims to convince us of his expertise. Andrew Sullivan wants to seem mature, objective, and unthreatening to traditional family values. Nancy Mairs wants to come across as frank and brutally honest about herself and her situation. In different situations, even when writing about the same topics, Rose, Sullivan, and Mairs would likely adopt different voices. Rethink and then rewrite the Sullivan passage on pp. 61–62 from a more personal, subjective viewpoint, taking on the voice (the character) of someone who is gay or has gay friends or family members and using the pronoun *I* if appropriate. Or rethink and rewrite the Mairs passage on p. 66, taking on the voice of someone, either "crippled" or not, who uses *I* much less frequently than Mairs does—perhaps not at all. You may also need to change the way that

Public figures try to control their images for obvious reasons. Would you buy a used car from any of these distinguished men and women?

you claim authority, establish credibility, and demonstrate competence as you try to present a different and a more personal or a less personal ethos.

3. Opponents of Richard Nixon, the thirty-seventh president of the United States, once raised doubts about his integrity by asking a single ruinous question: *Would you buy a used car from this man?* Create your own version of the argument of character. Begin by choosing an intriguing or controversial person or group and finding an image online. Then download the image into a word-processing file. Create a caption for the photo that is modeled after the question asked about Nixon: *Would you give this woman your email password? Would you share a campsite with this couple? Would you eat lasagna that this guy fixed?* Finally, write a serious 300-word argument that explores the character flaws or strengths of your subject(s).

4. A well-known television advertisement from the 1980s featured a soap-opera actor promoting a pain-relief medication. "I'm not a doctor," he said, "but I play one on TV." Today, many celebrities—from athletes like Venus Williams to actors like Leonardo DiCaprio—use their fame in promoting products or causes. One way or another, each case of celebrity endorsement relies on arguments based on character. Develop a one-page print advertisement for a product or service you use often—anything from soap to auto repair to cell-phone service— or a political position. There's one catch: your advertisement should rely on arguments based on character, and you should choose a spokesperson who seems the *least* likely to use or endorse your product or service. The challenge is to turn an apparent disadvantage into an advantage by exploiting character.

4
Arguments Based on Facts and Reason: Logos

SPOCK: Logic and practical information do not seem to apply here.

McCOY: You admit that?

SPOCK: To deny the facts would be illogical, Doctor.

> —from *Star Trek* episode "A Piece of the Action"

When writers need to persuade, they usually try their best to provide readers with good reasons to believe them. When the choice is between logic and emotion, many of us will side with *Star Trek*'s Dr. McCoy rather than the stern Mr. Spock. Most of us respect *appeals to logos*—arguments based on facts, evidence, and reason—but like the good doctor, we're inclined to test the facts against our feelings and against the ethos of those making the appeal. Aristotle, among the first philosophers to write about persuasion, gives us a place to begin. He divided proofs based on facts and reason into two kinds—those derived from what we call *hard evidence* (Aristotle described these as *inartistic appeals*—facts, clues, statistics, testimonies, witnesses) and those based on *reason and common sense* (what Aristotle termed *artistic appeals*). These categories overlap and leak (what, after all, is *common sense?*), but they remain useful even today.

The differences can be observed in two arguments presented forty years apart at the United Nations when American representatives charged other nations with harboring weapons of mass destruction. On October 25, 1962, Adlai Stevenson, U.S. ambassador to the UN, asked, "Do you, Ambassador Zorin, deny that the U.S.S.R. has placed and is placing medium and intermediate range missiles and sites in Cuba?"—knowing that he had the hard evidence of spy photographs to prove his claim. The images showed the alleged construction beyond a reasonable doubt in an era when doctoring photographs was not an easy process.

Forty years later, on February 5, 2003, U.S. Secretary of State Colin Powell did not have the same kind of open-and-shut case when he argued to the UN Security Council that Iraq was harboring weapons of mass destruction in contravention to UN resolutions. Instead, he had to assure his worldwide audience that "what you will see is an accumulation of facts and disturbing patterns of behavior." None of his materials—including some photographs—had the immediacy or transparency

Colin Powell lost some credibility after his claim that Iraq had weapons of mass destruction proved untrue.

QUALITY

THE RACE FOR QUALITY HAS NO FINISH LINE-
SO TECHNICALLY, IT'S MORE LIKE A DEATH MARCH.

© Despair, Inc.

Not Just Words

Sometimes the difference between appeals isn't immediately self-evident. What one person considers an appeal to reason may look like an emotional or ethical argument to another. Add in the element of irony or parody, and the categories scramble even more. Take a look at the image above. At first glance, this may look like a serious poster, one that uses pathos and ethos (the title "Quality" and the picture, which implies that the poster's creator is committed to the long, lonely journey necessary to achieve this admirable goal) to argue that high standards are worth the effort. But the (logical?) caption cleverly undercuts that message. What do you think this poster's overall point is? How do words and image work together to make that point? Who is the intended audience? Finally, working within a group, discuss whether the poster represents an appeal to logic and reason, and why.

As the storylines on *CSI* suggest, hard evidence almost always makes the strongest logical argument.

of the 1962 Cuban missile crisis images. So Powell had to hope that the pattern and weight of evidence offered in a lengthy presentation would make his claim—"that Saddam Hussein and his regime are concealing their efforts to produce more weapons of mass destruction"—seem compelling. Since no such weapons were found after Western troops invaded Iraq, one might infer (logically) that hard evidence is superior to reasoning aided by less-than-compelling inferences and probabilities. In fact, Powell came to regret his dependence on the assortment of reasons he had been offered by other members of the Bush administration to back up the claims he made. Eighteen months later, he called his presentation a "blot" on his record and said that he felt "truly terrible" about being misinformed by the less-than-hard evidence he had been given.

As this example shows, hard evidence won't always be available, nor will it always be as overwhelming as the photographs that Adlai Stevenson displayed. And even when hard evidence is available, it must be carefully tested. While Stevenson could trust the veracity of the photographs that he displayed nearly fifty years ago, he probably would be more skeptical today. On July 9, 2008, a photo of Iranian missile tests was published in newspapers around the world. The photo showed four missiles being fired, but it was called into question when other photos of the tests showed only three missiles. Where had the fourth missile come from? Even after extensive examination, experts disagreed about whether the three-missile image had simply been digitally changed or whether a fourth missile had actually been fired at a later time and then composited into the original photo. In short, even the hardest of evidence needs to be scrutinized with great care before being accepted as clear and compelling proof.

Providing Hard Evidence

As the Stevenson and Powell examples suggest, even when hard evidence is contested or hard to come by, people usually prefer arguments based on facts and testimony to those grounded in reasoning alone. In a

Iranian missile test: Where did the fourth missile (second from right in the top photo) come from? Does this photo constitute "hard evidence"?

courtroom as well as in the popular media, for example, lawyers or reporters look for the "smoking gun"—the piece of hard evidence that ties a defendant to a crime. It might be an audiotape, a fingerprint, an email, or, increasingly, DNA evidence. Popular crime shows such as *CSI: Crime Scene Investigation* focus intensely on gathering this sort of "scientific" support for a prosecution. Less dramatically, the factual evidence in an argument might be columns of data carefully collected over time to prove a point about racial profiling or the effects of climate change on populations of fish and other wildlife. If you live in a state where you can be ticketed after a camera catches you running a red light, you know what hard evidence means.

Factual evidence, however, takes many forms. The ones that you use will depend on the kind of argument you're making. In fact, providing appropriate evidence ought to become a habit whenever you write an argument. The evidence makes your case plausible; it may also supply the details that make writing interesting. Consider Aristotle's claim that all arguments can be reduced to just two components:

Statement + Proof

Here's another way of naming those parts:

Claim + Supporting Evidence

In a scholarly article, you can see this connection between statements and proof in the text and the notes. As an example, we reprint a single page from a much-cited review of Michael Bellesiles's *Arming America: The Making of America's Gun Culture* by James Lindgren published in the *Yale Law Review* (see facing page). Bellesiles used evidence gathered from eighteenth-century documents to argue that gun ownership in frontier America was much rarer than advocates of the right to bear arms believed. After publication, *Arming America* was hailed by gun critics for weakening the claim of gun advocates today that the ownership of weapons has always been a part of American culture. But Lindgren, as well as many other critics and historians, found so many evidentiary flaws in Bellesiles's arguments that questions were soon raised about his scholastic integrity. Lindgren's review of *Arming America* runs for more than fifty meticulous pages (including an appendix of errors in Bellesiles's work) and contains 212 footnotes. You can see a factual argument in action just by looking at how Lindgren handles evidence on a single page. You may never write an argument as detailed as Lindgren's review, but you should develop the same respect for evidence.

This selection from James Lindgren's review of Michael Bellesiles's *Arming America: The Making of America's Gun Culture* first appeared in the *Yale Law Review*, volume 111 (2002).

LindgrenFINAL.doc   April 26, 2002 4/26/02 12:34 PM

2002]   *Arming America*   2203

B.   *How Common Was Gun Ownership?*

The most contested portions of *Arming America* involve the book's most surprising claim, that guns were infrequently owned before the mid-1800s. As I show below, the claim that colonial America did not have a gun culture is questionable on the evidence of gun ownership alone. Compared to the seventeenth and eighteenth centuries, it appears that guns are not as commonly owned today. Whereas individual gun ownership in every published (and unpublished) study of early probate records that I have located (except Bellesiles's) ranges from 40% to 79%; only 32.5% of households today own a gun.[44] This appears to be a much smaller percentage than in early America—in part because the mean household size in the late eighteenth century was six people,[45] while today it is just under two people.[46] The prevailing estimate of 40% to 79% ownership differs markedly from Bellesiles's claim that only about 15% owned guns.[47] In the remainder of this Section, I explain why.

1.   *The Gun Censuses*

Bellesiles bases his claims of low gun ownership primarily on probate records and counts of guns at militia musters.[48] He also discusses censuses of all guns in private and public hands, but on closer examination, none of these turns out to be a general census of all guns.

The trend is set in Bellesiles's first count of guns in an American community—the 1630 count of all the guns in the Massachusetts Bay Colony of about 1000 people. Bellesiles's account is quite specific: "In 1630 the Massachusetts Bay Company reported in their possession: '80 bastard musketts, . . . [10] Fowlinge peeces, . . . 10 Full musketts . . . .' There were thus exactly one hundred firearms for use among seven towns

---

44. This results from my analysis of the March 2001 release of the National Opinion Research Center's *General Social Survey, 2000* [hereinafter 2000 NORC GSS]. The data are also available at Nat'l Opinion Research Ctr., General Social Survey, *at* http://www.icpsr.umich.edu/GSS/ (last visited Apr. 8, 2002). According to the survey, 32.5% of households owned any gun, 19.7% owned a rifle, 18.6% owned a shotgun, and 19.7% owned a pistol or revolver. 2000 NORC GSS, *supra*. Only 1.2% of respondents refused to respond to the question. *Id.*

45. Inter-Univ. Consortium for Political & Soc. Research (ICPSR), Census Data for the Year 1790, http://fisher.lib.virginia.edu/cgi-local/censusbin/census.pl?year=790 (last visited Aug. 10, 2001).

46. 2000 NORC GSS, *supra* note 44.

47. BELLESILES, *supra* note 3, at 445 tbl.1.

Facts

"Facts," said John Adams, "are stubborn things," and so they make strong arguments, especially when readers believe they come from honest sources. Gathering such information and transmitting it faithfully practically define what we mean by professional journalism in one realm and scholarship in another. We'll even listen to people that we don't agree with if they can overwhelm us with evidence. Below, for example, a reviewer for the conservative magazine *National Review* praises the work of William Julius Wilson, a well-known liberal sociologist, because of how well he presents his case:

> In his eagerly awaited new book, Wilson argues that ghetto blacks are worse off than ever, victimized by a near-total loss of low-skill jobs in and around inner-city neighborhoods. In support of this thesis, he *musters mountains of data, plus excerpts from some of the thousands of surveys and face-to-face interviews that he and his research team conducted among inner-city Chicagoans.* It is a book that deserves a wide audience among thinking conservatives.
> —John J. Dilulio Jr., "When Decency Disappears" (emphasis added)

In this instance, the facts are respected even when the reviewer (Dilulio) has a very different political stance from that of the author of the book (Wilson).

When your facts are compelling, they may stand on their own in a low-stakes argument, supported by little more saying where they come from. Consider the power of phrases such as "reported by the *Wall Street Journal*," "according to MSNBC," or "in a book published by Cambridge University Press." Such sources gain credibility if they have, in readers' experience, reported facts accurately and reliably over time. In fact, one reason that you document the sources you use in an argument is to let the credibility of those sources reflect positively on you.

But arguing with facts also sometimes involves challenging the biases of even the most reputable sources if they lead to unfair or selective reporting. You don't have to search hard to find critics of the *Wall Street Journal* or MSNBC these days. In recent years, bloggers and other online critics have enjoyed pointing out the biases or factual mistakes of what conservatives like to call "mainstream media" (MSM) outlets (some liberals prefer "corporate media" or "traditional media"). These criticisms often deal not just with specific facts and coverage but with the overall way that an issue is presented or "framed."

In the following passage, for example, blogger Andrew Sullivan, who unlike many of his fellow conservatives strongly opposes using waterboarding and other extreme interrogation techniques against suspected terrorists, takes on the *New York Times*. Conservatives often accuse the *Times* of having a liberal bias in its news coverage, but in this case Sullivan attacks the newspaper for framing the issue in what he considers an unjustifiably *neutral* way:

> The front-page piece in the NYT today on Obama's thorny task in staffing the CIA, after seven years of its violation of the Geneva Conventions, is revealing in many ways. Like many in the MSM, the NYT cannot bring itself to describe the techniques that the CIA has used as "torture." And yet we *know* that the CIA has tortured prisoners under the plain legal definition of torture, and we *know* that this was the whole point of giving the CIA explicit legislative permission for this in 2006. [Yet], the only time the word "torture" is used in the NYT piece is to describe techniques practiced by other countries. This is an important point because it shows how the NYT is now actively *deceiving* its readers about this matter. Here is the NYT's locution on waterboarding, a torture technique used for centuries:
>
> > the near-drowning tactic considered by many legal authorities
> > to be torture.
>
> Can the NYT cite *one* legal authority . . . that says waterboarding is *not* torture? Can they cite one instance in American legal history in which is was *not* so defined? If not, why this absurd avoidance of *the truth* in the paper of record? . . .
>
> This is the strategy of the torture defenders: render this debate once again a red-blue, right-left ding-dong, culture war struggle. It isn't. It's a foundational, moral and constitutional issue that transcends all those categories. And the NYT does its readers a disservice in occluding that.
>
> —Andrew Sullivan, "The NYT and the T-Word"

In an ideal world, good information would always drive out bad. But you already know that we don't live in an ideal world, so sometimes bad information gets repeated in an echo chamber that amplifies the errors: if reputable media say that waterboarding or similar techniques may not constitute torture, how long will it take for people to begin to believe this?

And many media have no pretenses at all about being reputable. During the 2008 presidential campaign, the Internet buzzed with statements proclaiming that Barack Obama was Muslim, even after dozens of sources, including many people with whom Obama had worshipped, testified to his Christianity. As a reader and researcher, you should look beyond headlines, bylines, reputations, and especially rumors that fly about the Internet. Scrutinize any facts you collect before passing them on yourself. Test their reliability, and admit any problems at the start.

Statistics

Let's deal with a cliché right up front: figures lie and liars figure. Like most clichés, it contains a grain of truth. It's possible to lie with numbers, even those that are accurate, because numbers rarely speak for themselves. They need to be interpreted by writers—and writers almost always have agendas that shape the interpretations.

For example, suppose the crime rate in the city where you live has fallen from one hundred crimes per thousand residents four years ago to fifty per thousand this year. The mayor and the police chief, who are running for reelection, crow *The crime rate has been cut in half during our time in office!* But their opponents spin the figure another way—*One out of every twenty citizens of Springfield will be a crime victim this year!*—and point out that the crime rate in a nearby city has fallen by two-thirds over the same period. Suddenly that fifty per thousand looks like a sobering number. Sometimes the same statistic can be cited as a cause for celebration or for alarm.

We're not suggesting that numbers are meaningless or that you have license to use them in any way that serves your purposes. Quite the contrary. But you do have to understand the role you play in giving numbers a voice and a presence. Consider the way Armen Keteyian, writing for the *Sporting News*, raises serious questions about the safety of aluminum bats in high school and college sports, despite the insistence by many sports officials that they're safe. Keteyian makes his case by focusing on statistics and numbers—which we've italicized—suggesting otherwise:

> Bat companies point to the NCAA's *annual injury report* ranking baseball as one of the safest collegiate sports. The report also shows "there is *no . . . significant increase in batted ball injuries.*" But last December, after an 18-month study, the U.S. Consumer Product Safety Commission released a report that called the *NCAA's injury statistics* "inconclusive . . . and not complete enough" to determine whether current aluminum bats are more dangerous than wood.

The *New York Times* suggests an argument about bottled water consumption when it offers visual representations of statistical data.

LINK TO P. 840

"Let's be honest," says Anderson. "Bat manufacturers have been wonderful for college baseball. So you get caught up in that, the free product, the fact it's saving you money. But all of a sudden I see my young man lying on the ground, and I'm going, 'Is this the right thing?'"

[Many college players have been] struck—and in some cases nearly killed—by balls hit off aluminum bats certified by the NCAA and the national high school federation. To be approved, an aluminum bat must not cause *a batted ball to travel any faster than the best wood bat does.* But there's a catch: Bats are tested in a laboratory on a machine set at a *70 mph pitch speed and a 66 mph swing speed.* Why not test at far more realistic numbers, say, *85 mph pitches and 80 mph swings?*

Simple, says MacKay: "It would scare people to death."

Why? Reaction time. Experts say *the fastest batted ball a pitcher can defend against is about 97 mph.* Translation: *Less than four-tenths of a second.*

Ninety-seven mph also is the fastest a ball can be hit by a certified bat in the lab test. Sounds safe, right? But what about on the field? Well, it turns out nobody officially tests balls hit by aluminum bats under game conditions.

"We've seen some things on our radar gun—*108 miles per hour, 110 at different times,*" says Anderson. "*I've witnessed 114 myself.* Makes you question whether we are doing the right thing."

—Armen Keteyian, "Bats Should Crack, Not Skulls" (emphasis added)

This is hardly the last word on aluminum bats. In fact, since Keteyian's article was published, the Little League has pronounced that aluminum bats are as safe as wooden bats even as high school leagues across the country were banning them. Nor is the controversy likely to end any time soon, unless a persistent spike in injuries brings about consensus.

Surveys and Polls

Some of the most influential forms of statistics are those produced by surveys and polls. These measures play so large a role in people's social and political lives that writers, whether interpreting them or fashioning surveys themselves, need to give them special attention.

When they verify the popularity of an idea or proposal, surveys and polls provide persuasive appeals because, in a democracy, majority opinion offers a compelling warrant: a government should do what most people want. Polls come as close to expressing the will of the people as anything short of an election—the most decisive poll of all. (For more on

Cook's Country's taste test for chocolate chip cookies gave the surveyors a result they did not expect—homemade cookies didn't place first.

LINK TO P. 843

Fathers are more likely than mothers (33% vs. 26%) to say they sometimes play video games with their teens ages 12 to 17.

How often parents join their teens in a video game

Always **2%**
Sometimes **29%**
Never **43%**
Rarely **26%**

By Michelle Healy and Sam Ward, USA TODAY
Source: Pew Internet & American Life Project

USA Today is famous for the tables, pie charts, and graphs it creates to present statistics and poll results. What claims might the evidence in this graph support? How does the design of the item influence your reading of it?

warrants, see Chapter 7, pp. 186–92.) However, surveys and polls can do much more than help politicians make decisions. They can also provide persuasive reasons for action or intervention. When surveys show, for example, that most American sixth-graders can't locate France or Wyoming on a map—not to mention Turkey or Afghanistan—that's an appeal for better instruction in geography. When polls suggest that consumer confidence is declining, businesses may have reason to worry about their bulging inventories.

It always makes sense, however, to push back against any poll numbers reported—especially when they support your own point of view. Ask who commissioned the poll, who is publishing its outcome, who was surveyed (and in what proportions), and what stakes these parties might have in its outcome.

Are we being too suspicious? No. In fact, this sort of scrutiny is exactly what you should anticipate from your readers whenever you do surveys of your own to explore an issue. You should be confident that you've surveyed enough people to be accurate, that the people you chose for the study were representative of the selected population as a whole, and that you chose them randomly—not selecting those most likely to say what you hoped to hear.

On the other hand, as with other kinds of factual evidence, don't make the opposite mistake by discounting or ignoring polls whose findings are *not* what you had hoped for. In the following excerpts from a column in the *Dallas News*, conservative Rod Dreher forthrightly faces up to the results from a poll of registered Texas voters after the 2008 election—results that he finds ominous for his Texas Republican Party:

> The full report, which will be released today, knocks the legs out from under two principles cherished by the party's grassroots: staunch social conservatism and hard-line immigration policies. At the state level, few voters care much about abortion, school prayer and other hot-button issues. Immigration is the only conservative stand-by that rates much mention – and by hitting it too hard, Republicans lose both the Hispanics and independents that make up what the pollster defines as the "Critical Middle." . . .
>
> This is not going to go down well with the activist core of the Texas GOP, especially people like me: a social conservative with firm views on illegal immigration. But reality has a way of focusing the mind, forcing one to realize that political parties are not dogma-driven churches, but coalitions that unavoidably shift over time.
>
> —Rod Dreher, "Poll's Shocking SOS for Texas GOP"

Dreher's frank acknowledgment of findings that were unpleasant to him—which included his pointing out that the poll was conducted by a Republican polling firm—also helps him to create a positive ethos, presenting himself as a trustworthy, credible writer who follows the facts wherever they lead.

The meaning of polls and surveys is also affected by the way that questions are asked. Recent research has shown, for example, that questions about same-sex unions get differing responses according to how they are worded. When people are asked whether gay and lesbian couples should be eligible for the same inheritance and partner health benefits that heterosexual couples receive, a majority of those polled give positive responses—unless the word *marriage* appears in the question; then the responses are primarily negative. As a result, you need to be careful in constructing questions for any poll or survey you want to conduct.

You often also need to read beyond headlines and journalists' (or pollsters') summaries of poll results to be sure that you understand all the details of the findings and the ways that they are being interpreted. In a blog posting in which Dreher discusses the column excerpted above, for example, he notes:

> The news is actually even worse for Republicans than I was able to indicate in the space constrictions of a newspaper column. The

support Democrats have is strong, according to the poll, whereas those who back the GOP are lukewarm.

—Rod Dreher, "Is Texas Going Democratic?"

Finally, always keep in mind that the date of a poll may strongly affect the results—and their usefulness in an argument. On July 31, 2008, for example, the *Orange County* (California) *Registrar* carried an article with the headline "Poll: Californians Now Favor Offshore Drilling." The article reported that 51 percent of those polled favored offshore drilling for oil, which a majority of California residents had previously opposed, and noted that this was an increase of ten percentage points from a survey done a year earlier. But it also noted that the poll was conducted at a time of sharply rising gasoline prices. Within a few months, prices were falling dramatically amid the global economic recession, so an argument in favor of drilling would have to take into account the possibility that public sentiment might have shifted significantly again.

Testimonies and Narratives

Numbers and statistics are not the only good evidence that writers need. You can support arguments with all kinds of human experiences, particularly those that you or others have undergone or reported. In a court,

A drilling platform off the California coast. Polls on allowing offshore drilling tend to track fluctuations in oil prices.

for example, decisions are often based on detailed descriptions of what happened. Following is a reporter's account of a court case in which a panel of judges decided, based on the testimony presented, that a man had been sexually harassed by another man. The narrative, in this case, supplies the evidence:

> The Seventh Circuit, in a 1997 case known as *Doe v. City of Belleville*, drew a sweeping conclusion allowing for same-sex harassment cases of many kinds. Title VII was sex-neutral, the court ruled; it didn't specifically prohibit discrimination against men or women. Moreover, the judges argued, there was such a thing as gender stereotyping, and if someone was harassed on that basis, it was unlawful. This case, for example, centered on teenage twin brothers working a summer job cutting grass in the city cemetery of Belleville, Ill. One boy wore an earring, which caused him no end of grief that particular summer— including a lot of menacing talk among his co-workers about sexually assaulting him in the woods and sending him "back to San Francisco." One of his harassers, identified in court documents as a large former marine, culminated a verbal campaign by backing the earring-wearer against a wall and grabbing him by the testicles to see "if he was a girl or a guy." The teenager had been "singled out for this abuse," the court ruled, "because the way in which he projected the sexual aspect of his personality"—meaning his gender—"did not conform to his co-workers' view of appropriate masculine behavior."
> —Margaret Talbot, "Men Behaving Badly"

Personal experience carefully reported can also support a claim convincingly, especially if a writer has earned the trust of readers. In the following excerpt, Christian Zawodniak describes his experiences as a student in a first-year college writing course. Not impressed by his instructor's performance, Zawodniak provides specific evidence of the instructor's failings:

> My most vivid memory of Jeff's rigidness was the day he responded to our criticisms of the class. Students were given a chance anonymously to write our biggest criticisms one Monday, and the following Wednesday Jeff responded, staunchly answering all criticisms of his teaching: "Some of you complained that I didn't come to class prepared. It took me five years to learn all this." Then he pointed to the blackboard on which he had written all the concepts we had discussed that quarter. His responses didn't seem genuine or aimed at improving

his teaching or helping students to understand him. He thought he
was always right. Jeff's position gave him responsibilities that he
officially met. But he didn't take responsibility in all the ways he had
led us to expect.
—Christian Zawodniak, "Teacher Power, Student Pedagogy"

This portrait of a defensive instructor gives readers details by which to
assess the argument. If readers believe Zawodniak, they learn something
about teaching. (For more on establishing credibility with readers, see
Chapter 3.)

Using Reason and Common Sense

In the absence of hard facts, claims may be supported with other kinds
of compelling reasons. The formal study of principles of reasoning is
called *logic*, but few people (except perhaps mathematicians and philosophers) use formal logic to present their arguments. Many people might
recognize the most famous of all *syllogisms* (a vehicle of deductive reasoning), but that's about the extent of what they know about formal
logic:

All human beings are mortal.

Socrates is a human being.

Therefore, Socrates is mortal.

In valid syllogisms, the conclusion follows logically—and technically—
from the premises that lead up to it. Many have criticized syllogistic reasoning for being limited, and some say that the conclusion of a syllogism
is really only a restatement of the premises. Others have poked fun at
the syllogism, as in the cartoon on the facing page, which demonstrates
an error in reasoning known as the *undistributed middle term* (in this case,
the term is "black and white").

Even as gifted a logician as Aristotle recognized that most people
argue perfectly well using informal rather than formal logic. Consciously
or not, we are constantly stating claims, drawing conclusions, and making and questioning assumptions whenever we read or write. People
mostly rely on the habits of mind and cultural assumptions that they
share with their readers or listeners.

Logic: another thing that penguins aren't very good at.

© Randy Glasbergen

In Chapter 7, we describe a system of informal logic that you may find useful in shaping credible arguments—Toulmin argument. Here, we briefly examine some ways that people use informal logic in their daily lives. Once again, we begin with Aristotle, who used the term *enthymeme* to describe an ordinary kind of sentence that includes both a claim and a reason but depends on the audience's agreement with an assumption that is left implicit rather than spelled out. The following sentences are all enthymemes:

We'd better cancel the picnic because it's going to rain.

Flat taxes are fair because they treat everyone the same.

I'll buy a PC laptop instead of a Mac because it's cheaper.

NCAA football needs a real play-off to crown a real national champion.

On their own, enthymemes can be persuasive statements when most readers agree with the assumptions on which they're based. Perhaps that's why enthymemes lie at the heart of many humorous statements, like this one from Will Rogers:

> **I am not a member of any organized political party. I am a Democrat.**

Rogers is counting here on his audience filling in what is implicit: because historically the Democrats have been diverse and given to fighting among themselves, they are a "disorganized" rather than an "organized" party.

Sometimes enthymemes seem so obvious that readers don't realize that they're drawing inferences when they agree with them. Consider the first example on p. 85:

> **We'd better cancel the picnic because it's going to rain.**

Let's expand the enthymeme a bit to say more of what the speaker may mean:

> **We'd better cancel the picnic this afternoon because the weather bureau is predicting a 70 percent chance of rain for the remainder of the day.**

Embedded in this brief argument are all sorts of assumptions and fragments of cultural information that are left implicit but that help to make it persuasive:

> **Picnics are ordinarily held outdoors.**
>
> **When the weather is bad, it's best to cancel picnics.**
>
> **Rain is bad weather for picnics.**
>
> **A 70 percent chance of rain means that rain is more likely to occur than not.**
>
> **When rain is more likely to occur than not, it makes sense to cancel picnics.**
>
> **The weather bureau's predictions are reliable enough to warrant action.**

For most people, the original statement carries all this information on its own; it's a compressed argument, based on what audiences know and will accept.

But sometimes enthymemes aren't self-evident:

> **Be wary of environmentalism because it's religion disguised as science.**

iPods are undermining civil society by making us even more focused on ourselves.

It's time to make all public toilets unisex because to do otherwise is discriminatory.

In those cases, you'll have to work much harder to defend both the claim and the implicit assumptions that it's based on by drawing out the inferences that seem self-evident in other enthymemes. And you'll likely also have to supply credible evidence. A simple declaration of fact won't suffice.

Cultural Assumptions and Values

Some of the assumptions in an argument will be based on shared values derived from culture and history. In the United States, for example, few arguments work better than those based on principles of fairness and equity. Since the Declaration of Independence announces these principles, they are deeply inscribed in U.S. culture and represent a cherished value. As a result, most Americans will say that they believe all people should be treated the same way, no matter who they are or where they come from.

Because fairness is so deeply endorsed in American culture, enthymemes that rely on principles of fairness and equity need less formal support than those that challenge them. That's why, for example, both sides in debates over affirmative-action programs seek the high ground of fairness: proponents claim that affirmative action is needed to correct enduring inequities from the past; opponents suggest that the preferential policies should be overturned because they cause inequity today. Here, Linda Chavez assumes that her audience will value principles of equity:

> Ultimately, entitlements based on their status as "victims" rob Hispanics of real power. The history of American ethnic groups is one of overcoming disadvantage, of competing with those who were already here and proving themselves as competent as any who came before. Their fight was always to be treated the same as other Americans, never to be treated as special, certainly not to turn the temporary disadvantages they suffered into permanent entitlement. Anyone who thinks this fight was easier in the earlier part of this century when it was waged by other ethnic groups does not know history.
> —Linda Chavez, "Towards a New Politics of Hispanic Assimilation"

Chavez expects Hispanics to accept her claims because she believes that they don't wish to be treated differently from other ethnic groups in the society.

Societies in other times and places have held their own cultural values and principles derived from them. Medieval Europe, for example, valued aristocratic birth, and the effectiveness of many arguments in that time and place counted on widespread consensus on that principle. Other cultures, including some in Africa, have valued cooperation and community rather than individualism and based arguments on such a value.

Writers need to understand the values and cultural assumptions held by their audiences, but even an assumption that seems pervasive—like that of equity and fairness—will still be open to interpretation. In the case of Linda Chavez's argument, for instance, many citizens—whether Hispanic or not—disagreed vehemently with her arguments against affirmative action because they held different definitions of what *fair* and *equal* mean.

Providing Logical Structures for Argument

Some arguments are not tied to cultural assumptions but rather depend on particular logical structures to make their points. In the following pages, we identify a few of these logical structures.

Degree

Kathy Freston's "Vegetarian Is the New Prius" depends on arguments based on degree as she compares the environmental damage created by livestock with that created by cars.

LINK TO P. 800

Arguments based on degree are so common that people barely notice them. Nor do people pay much attention to how they work because they seem self-evident. Most audiences will readily accept that *more of a good thing or less of a bad thing is good.* In her novel *The Fountainhead*, Ayn Rand asks: "If physical slavery is repulsive, how much more repulsive is the concept of servility of the spirit?" Most readers immediately comprehend the point Rand intends to make about slavery of the spirit because they already know that physical slavery is cruel and would reject any forms of slavery that were even crueler on the principle that *more of a bad thing is bad.* Rand still needs to offer evidence that "servility of the spirit" is, in fact, worse than bodily servitude, but she has begun with a

A demonstrator at an immigrant-rights rally in New York City in 2007. Arguments based on values that are widely shared within a society—such as the idea of equal rights in American culture— have an automatic advantage with audiences.

logical structure readers can grasp. Here are other arguments that work similarly:

> If I can get a ten-year warranty on a humble Kia, shouldn't I get the same or better warranty from Lexus?
>
> The health benefits from using stem cells in research will surely outweigh the ethical risks.
>
> Better a conventional war now than a nuclear confrontation later.

Analogies

Analogies explain one idea or concept by comparing it to something else. People understand comparisons intuitively. Indeed, people habitually think in comparative terms, through similes and metaphors: *he is as slow as molasses; love is never having to say you're sorry; war is hell*. An analogy is typically a complex or extended comparison. Following is an excerpt from an extended analogy in a *New York Times* op-ed column by Thomas Friedman, entitled "9/11 and 4/11" (the 4/11 refers to the price of gas, then at $4.11):

> We don't have a "gasoline price problem." We have an addiction problem. We are addicted to dirty fossil fuels, and this addiction is driving a whole set of toxic trends that are harming our nation in different ways. . . .
>
> When a person is addicted to crack cocaine, his problem is not that the price of crack is going up. His problem is what that crack addiction is doing to his whole body. The cure is not cheaper crack, which would only perpetuate the addiction and all the problems it is creating. The cure is to break the addiction.
>
> Ditto for us. Our cure is not cheaper gasoline, but a clean energy system. And the key to building that is to keep the price of gasoline and coal—our crack—higher, not lower, so consumers are moved to break their addiction to these dirty fuels and inventors are moved to create clean alternatives.
>
> —Thomas L. Friedman, "9/11 and 4/11"

Many would resist Friedman's analogy here, perhaps arguing that it oversimplifies a complex issue and challenging his details of the analogy. And analogies of argument are routinely abused, so much so that faulty analogy (see p. 533) is one of the most familiar fallacies of argument.

Precedent

Arguments from precedent are related to arguments of analogy in that they both involve comparisons. Sometimes an argument of precedent focuses on comparable institutions. Consider an assertion like the following:

> If motorists in most other states can pump their own gas safely, surely the state of Oregon can trust its own drivers to be as capable. It's time for Oregon to permit self-service gas stations.

You could pull a lot of inferences out of this claim to explain its reasonableness: people in Oregon are as capable as people in other states, people with equivalent capabilities can do the same thing, pumping gas is not hard, and so forth. But you don't have to because most readers get the argument simply because of the way it is put together.

Here's an excerpt from an extended argument by a columnist for the student newspaper of the University of Massachusetts at Amherst calling for "bathroom reform." Note the ways in which this student calls on a number of precedents in making her case:

> Several semesters ago, transgender students began to protest the bathroom situation at UMass, demanding gender-neutral bathrooms in many dorms. This was so students who do not identify with their assigned gender at birth or with either gender could feel comfortable entering the bathrooms without going into the "wrong" bathroom. This movement filled *The Massachusetts Daily Collegian* with many columns for and against doing so, along with a table that was always manned by someone in the Campus Center. Since then, the movement for a "restroom revolution" to transform the way we think about bathrooms has died down, either due to the UMass administration's unwillingness to bend or lack of energy and time.
>
> Often I find male bathrooms to be empty while a long line stretched out the door from female bathrooms. This is due to the evident fact that males are quicker than females at relieving themselves; yet, whenever bathrooms are built, both the female and male bathrooms are built of an equal size. . . .
>
> Just several decades ago, UMass dorms were either all-female or all-male, and females could attend a male dorm only one Sunday a month, in which case the dormitory room door had to stay open and three feet had to be on the ground at all time. Today's co-ed dorms are an idea that was unheard of at that time, an idea as strange as co-ed bathrooms are today. Today, schools such as Harvard University and

As more and more restrooms go gender-neutral, they provide precedents for future arguments. This one, at Kent State University in Ohio, accommodates transgendered people, designated by the symbol at the bottom right.

the University of New Hampshire, as well as many others, have co-ed bathrooms with no problems.

At UMass, sexual assault does remain a problem and an issue that needs to be dealt with. The fact is that gender-specific bathrooms have not shown in the past to prevent sexual assaults and a perpetrator is not prevented from entering such a bathroom simply by a "no men allowed" sign. Statistically, most assaults on women are not done by complete strangers, but rather by someone that the victim already knew. By creating gender-neutral bathrooms, a greater number of people would be allowed to enter these facilities, making them less empty and isolated. . . .

Fifty years ago, women wearing men's clothing, such as pants, was taboo and unthinkable, and co-ed gym classes was an inconceivable concept. Imagine how ridiculous a notion those ideas must have been then. I don't think society will crumble now if we allow all genders to use the same bathrooms in college. Gender-segregated bathrooms are an example of an attempt to hold onto the past, but we are in a new age of equality. Why not create some equally accessible bathrooms?

—Gilad Skolnick, "A Plea for Bathroom Reform"

Other precedents deal with issues of time. For example, what courts have decided in the past often determines how courts will rule on a similar or related issue. The near avalanche of lawsuits brought by the Recording Industry Association of America (RIAA) in an attempt to stop online file sharing has over the last decade aimed at establishing a set of legal precedents that would make it harder for consumers to share music, films, and so on. In this case, opponents of the RIAA are working to establish their own legal precedents, and experts expect this argument to go on for years.

You'll encounter additional kinds of logical structures as you create your own arguments. You'll find some of them in Chapter 7 on Toulmin argument and still more in Chapter 17, "Fallacies of Argument."

RESPOND.

1. Discuss whether the following statements are examples of hard evidence or rational appeals. Not all cases are clear-cut.

   The bigger they are, the harder they fall.

   Drunk drivers are involved in more than 50 percent of traffic deaths.

   DNA tests of skin found under the victim's fingernails suggest that the defendant was responsible for the assault.

   Polls suggest that a slim majority of Americans favor a constitutional amendment to ban same-sex marriage.

   A psychologist testified that teenage violence could not be blamed on video games.

   An apple a day keeps the doctor away.

   History proves that cutting tax rates increases government revenues because people work harder when they can keep more of what they earn.

   "The only thing we have to fear is fear itself."

   Air bags ought to be removed from vehicles because they can kill young children and small-frame adults.

2. Take a look at comedian Rita Rudner's fairly complicated enthymematic argument:

   I was going to have cosmetic surgery until I noticed that the doctor's office was full of portraits by Picasso.

Working with two other students, analyze this enthymeme. What information is left implicit? What inference or conclusion does Rudner ask us to draw from this enthymeme? What causes the humor in this statement?

3. We suggest in this chapter that statistical evidence becomes useful only when responsible authors interpret the data fairly and reasonably. As an exercise, go to the *USA Today* Web site or to the newspaper itself and look for the daily graph, chart, or table called the *USA Today* snapshot. (On the Web site, you'll have a series of these items to choose from.) Pick a snapshot, and use the information in it to support at least three different claims. See if you can get at least two of the claims to make opposing or very different points. Share your claims with classmates. (The point is not to learn to use data dishonestly but to see firsthand how the same statistics can serve a variety of arguments.)

4. Testimony can be as suspect as statistics. For example, check out the newspaper ads for some recent movies. How lengthy are the quotes from reviewers? A reviewer's stinging indictment of a violent action film—"this blockbuster may prove to be a great success at the box office, but it stinks as filmmaking"—could be reduced to "A great success." Bring to class a full review of a recent film that you enjoyed. (If you haven't enjoyed any films lately, select a review of one you disliked.) Using testimony from that review, write a brief argument to your classmates explaining why they should see that movie (or why they should avoid it). Be sure to use the evidence from the review fairly and reasonably, as support for a claim that you're making. Then exchange arguments with a classmate, and decide whether the evidence in your peer's argument helps to change your opinion about the movie. What's convincing about the evidence? If it doesn't convince you, why not?

5. Choose an issue of some consequence, locally or nationally, and then create a series of questions designed to poll public opinion on the issue. But design the questions to evoke a range of responses. See if you can design a reasonable question that would make people strongly inclined to favor or approve an issue, a second question that would lead them to oppose the same proposition just as intensely, a third that tries to be more neutral, and additional questions that provoke different degrees of approval or disapproval. If possible, try out your questions on your classmates.

5
Rhetorical Analysis

When the thirty-second spot first aired in late March 2004, many viewers reacted with disbelief: What the . . . ?! The guy with the mustache . . . and a sexy underwear model . . . it couldn't be . . . could it?

But it was—counterculture folk legend pop icon Bob Dylan crooning "Love Sick" in a TV ad for Victoria's Secret, a purveyor of women's underclothes. Dylan, who had never before pitched a product other than his own recordings, now traded glances with an alluring young woman in wings and high heels. The bard who'd penned "The Times They Are A-Changin'" and "Blowin' in the Wind" had sold his birthright, disillusioned critics charged, for—yikes—a bra and blue panties. (Check YouTube for a series of related ads and videos.)

Media critic Seth Stevenson, writing in *Slate*, devoted a full column to analyzing this particular pitch, trying first to figure out why an artist of Dylan's stature would do a commercial: For money? Whimsy? Exposure?

Pitchman Bob Dylan and Victoria's Secret model Adriana Lima

But then he turns to another intriguing question—how ads manage to work their persuasive magic:

> Why would a brand that's about sexiness, youth, and glamour want any connection at all with a decrepit, sixtysomething folksinger? The answer, my friend, is totally unclear. The answer is totally unclear.
>
> Even if Victoria's Secret hopes to bring in more boomer women, do those women want their underwear to exude the spirit and essence of Bob Dylan? Or, conversely, is Bob Dylan the sort of man they're hoping to attract? Even if you're of the belief that men frequently shop at VS for their ladies, I still don't see the appeal of this ad. I, for instance, am a man, and I can assure you that Bob Dylan is not what I'm looking for in a woman's undergarment. (And if I found him there—man, would that be disturbing.)
>
> Victoria's Secret wouldn't return my calls, but media reports say the idea of putting Dylan's face in the ad (they'd been using his song— "Love Sick"—in ads for the past year or so) came straight from corporate chief Les Wexner. To the company's surprise, Dylan accepted their offer. It's at this point that someone at Victoria's Secret should have stopped the madness. Just because you can hire Bob Dylan as the figurehead for your lingerie line, doesn't mean you should. Perhaps

no one was willing to say no to the big boss, or perhaps they fully expected Dylan to say no. Joke's on them.

—Seth Stevenson, "Tangled Up in Boobs"

To pose the sort of questions that Stevenson asks here is to perform a brief rhetorical analysis—a close reading of a text to find how and whether it works to persuade. In these few paragraphs from a longer piece, Stevenson considers some of the basic strategies of argument that are explored in this book's preceding chapters. He first identifies the ethos of the company making the appeal ("sexiness, youth, and glamour") and finds it hard to reconcile it with the ethos of the celebrity that he sees in the ad ("decrepit, sixtysomething"). He considers the emotional pull that the TV commercial might have (maybe enticing older men to buy expensive underwear for women) but then rejects the logic of that approach: even men who shop for underwear at Victoria's Secret certainly don't want to think about Dylan when they do.

Then Stevenson takes a step beyond the ad itself to consider the rhetorical world in which it might have been created—one in which it would seem so cool to have a superstar spokesperson like Bob Dylan that you don't think about the messages you might be sending. Stevenson's conclusion? "Joke's on them."

Whenever you encounter a similarly puzzling, troubling, or even successful appeal, try subjecting it to a rhetorical analysis of your own. Ask yourself what strategies the piece employs to move your heart, win your trust, and change your mind—and why it does or doesn't do so. Here's how.

Composing a Rhetorical Analysis

Exactly how does a Bose ad make you want to buy new speakers, or how does an op-ed piece in the *Washington Post* suddenly change your thinking about school vouchers? A rhetorical analysis might help you understand. You perform a rhetorical analysis by analyzing how well the components of an argument work together to persuade or move an audience. You can study arguments of any kind—advertisements (as we've seen), editorials, political cartoons, and perhaps even movies or photographs. Because arguments have many aspects, you will need to focus your rhetorical analysis on elements that stand out or make the piece intriguing or problematic. You could begin by exploring issues such as the following:

- What is the purpose of this argument? What does it hope to achieve?
- Who is the audience for this argument?
- What appeals or techniques does the argument use—emotional, logical, ethical?
- What type or genre of argument is it, and how does the genre affect the argument? (You'd have every right to challenge an argument in an editorial if it lacked sufficient evidence; you'd look foolish making the same complaint about a bumper sticker.)
- Who is making the argument? What ethos does it create, and exactly how does it do so? What values attach to the ethos? How does it try to make the writer or creator seem trustworthy?
- What authorities does the argument rely on or appeal to?
- What facts are used in the argument? What logic? What evidence? How is the evidence arranged and presented?
- What claims are advanced in the argument? What issues are raised, and which ones are ignored or, perhaps, evaded?
- What are the contexts—social, political, historical, cultural—for this argument? Whose interests does it serve? Who gains or loses by it?
- What shape does the argument take? How is the argument organized or arranged? What media does the argument use?
- How does the language or style of the argument work to persuade an audience?

Questions like these should get you thinking. But don't just describe techniques and strategies in your rhetorical analysis. Instead, show how the key devices in an argument actually make it succeed or fail. Quote language freely from a written piece, or describe the elements in a visual argument. (Annotating a visual text is one option.) Show readers where and why an argument makes sense and where it seems to fall apart (just as Stevenson does in the Victoria's Secret ad). If you believe that an argument startles audiences, challenges them, insults them, or lulls them into complacency, explain precisely why that's so, and provide evidence. Don't be surprised when your rhetorical analysis itself becomes an argument. That's what it should be.

Understanding the Purpose of Arguments You Are Analyzing

To understand how well any argument works, ask what its purpose might be: To sell shoes? To advocate Social Security reform? To push a political agenda? In many cases, that purpose may be obvious. A conservative newspaper will likely advance right-wing causes on its editorial page; ads from a baby food company will show happy infants delighted with stewed prunes and squash.

But some projects may be coy about their persuasive intentions or blur the lines between types of argument. Perhaps you've responded to a mail survey or telephone poll only to discover that the questions are leading you to switch your cell-phone service. Does such a stealthy argument succeed? That may depend on whether you're more intrigued by the promise of cheaper phone rates than offended by the bait-and-switch. The deception could provide material for a thoughtful rhetorical analysis in which you measure the strengths, risks, and ethics of such strategies.

Understanding Who Makes an Argument

Knowing *who* is claiming *what* is key to any rhetorical analysis. That's why you'll usually find the name of a person or an institution attached to an argument or persuasive appeal. Do you remember the statements included in TV ads during the last federal election campaign: "Hello, I'm Candidate X—and I approve this ad"? Federal law requires such statements so that viewers can tell the difference between ads endorsed by candidates and those sponsored by groups that are not affiliated with the campaigns. Their interests and motives might be very different.

Funny, offensive, or both?

Knowing an author's name is just a starting place for a serious analysis. You need to dig deeper whenever you don't recognize the author of an argument or the institution sponsoring it—and sometimes even when you do. You could do worse than to Google the Internet to discover more about such people or groups. What else have they produced? By whom have they been published—the *Wall Street Journal*, the blog Daily Kos, *Spin*, or even 4chan? If a group has a Web site, what can you learn about its goals, policies, contributors, and funding?

The blogger bio: required reading for rhetorical analysis

Contact

Email Address: **Email Me**

One-Line Bio

I am a citizen journalist, public policy consultant and political commentator.

Biography

I am a citizen journalist, public policy consultant, and political commentator. I am particularly interested in the intersection of technology and civic engagement.

I share my insights, as well as news and information that resonate with African American voters, political influentials and thought leaders.

My blog is included in the Harvard University Web Archiving Collection, "Capturing Women's Voices," a project of the Schlesinger Library at the Radcliffe Institute for Advanced Study.

During the 2008 presidential election, posts to Anderson@Large were cross-posted to "The Ruckus," a collaboration between Newsweek.com and the Media Bloggers Association.

Identifying and Appealing to Audiences

Most arguments are composed with specific audiences in mind, and their success depends, in part, on how well their strategies, content, tone, and language meet the expectations of readers or viewers. In analyzing an argument, you must first identify its target audience(s), remembering how complex that notion can be (see Audiences for Arguments on pp. 27–33). But you can usually make an educated judgment because most arguments have contexts that, one way or another, describe whom they intend to reach and in what ways.

Both a photocopied sheet stapled to a bulletin board in a college dorm ("Why You Should Be a Socialist") and a forty-foot billboard for Bud Lite might be aimed at the same general population—college students. But each will adjust its appeals for the different moods of that group in different moments. The political screed will likely be deliberately simple in layout and full of earnest language ("We live in a world of obscene inequality") to appeal to students in a serious vein, while the liquor ad will be visually stunning and virtually text-free to connect with students when they aren't worried about uniting the workers of the world. Your rhetorical analysis might make a case for the success or failure of such audience-based strategies.

You might also examine how a writer or an argument establishes credibility with an audience. One effective means of building credibility, you will discover, comes through a seven-letter word made famous by Aretha Franklin—*respect*. Respect is crucial in arguments that invoke audiences who don't agree on critical issues or who may not have thought carefully about the issues presented. In introducing an article on problems facing African American women in the workplace, editor in chief of *Essence* Diane Weathers considers the problems that she faced with respecting all her potential readers:

> We spent more than a minute agonizing over the provocative cover line for our feature "White Women at Work." The countless stories we had heard from women across the country told us that this was a workplace issue we had to address. From my own experience at several major magazines, it was painfully obvious to me that Black and White women are not on the same track. Sure, we might all start out in the same place. But early in the game, most sisters I know become stuck—and the reasons have little to do with intelligence or drive. At some point we bump our heads against that ceiling. And while White women may complain of a glass ceiling, for us, the ceiling is concrete.

So how do we tell this story without sounding whiny and paranoid, or turning off our White-female readers, staff members, advertisers and girlfriends? Our solution: Bring together real women (several of them highly successful senior corporate executives), put them in a room, promise them anonymity and let them speak their truth.
—Diane Weathers, "Speaking Our Truth"

Both paragraphs affirm Weathers's determination to treat audiences fairly *and* to deal honestly with a difficult subject. The strategy would merit attention in any rhetorical analysis.

Look, too, for signals that writers share values with readers or at least understand an audience. In the following passage, writer Jack Solomon is clear about one value that he hopes readers have in common—a preference for "straight talk":

There are some signs in the advertising world that Americans are getting fed up with fantasy advertisements and want to hear some straight talk. Weary of extravagant product claims and irrelevant associations, consumers trained by years of advertising to distrust what they hear seem to be developing an immunity to commercials.
—Jack Solomon, "Masters of Desire: The Culture of American Advertising"

Retailers like Walmart build their credibility by simple "straight talk" to shoppers: our low prices make your life better.

It's a pretty safe assumption that consumers don't like doubletalk or duplicity, isn't it? But writers or advertisers can manage even more complex appeals to values by targeting specific groups and their experiences, values, and perceptions. Here's media critic Seth Stevenson again, first summarizing ads in a new antismoking campaign directed at teens:

> The spots: *They appear to be episodes of a sitcom called* Fair Enough. *In this series of 30-second segments, a team of tobacco executives brainstorms new ways to market to teens. Among their ideas: fruit-flavored chewing tobacco, tobacco in the form of a gum ball, and an effort to win influence with the "hipster" crowd by giving them free packs of smokes.*
> —Seth Stevenson, "How to Get Teens Not to Smoke"

Then he does a rhetorical analysis, explaining why the particular TV spot will resonate with its target audience. The creators of the ad clearly knew what might motivate teens to give up cigarettes—insecurity:

> In fact, the ultimate adolescent nightmare is to appear in any way unsavvy—like an out-of-it rookie who doesn't know the score. These *Fair Enough* ads isolate and prey on that insecurity, and they do a great job. With a dead-on, rerun sitcom parody (jumpy establishing shot; upbeat horn-section theme song ending on a slightly unresolved note; three-wall, two-camera set; canned laugh track), the ads first establish their own savvy, knowing coolness before inviting us to join them in ridiculing big tobacco's schemes. The spots are darkly comic, just the way teens like it. And rather than serving up yet more boring evidence that smoking is deadly (something that all teens, including the ones who smoke, already know) the ads move on to the far more satisfying step: kicking big tobacco in the groin.

Examining Arguments Based on Emotion: Pathos

Some emotional appeals are just ploys to win over readers with a pretty face, figurative or real. You've seen ads promising an exciting life and attractive friends if only you drink the right soda or wear a particular brand of clothes. Are you fooled by such claims? Probably not, if you pause to think about them. But that's the strategy—to distract you from thought just long enough to make a bad choice. It's a move worth commenting on in a rhetorical analysis.

Yet emotions can add real muscle to arguments, too, and that's worth noting. For example, persuading people not to drink and drive by making them fear death, injury, or arrest seems like a fair use of an emotional appeal. That's exactly what the Texas Department of Transportation did when it created a memorable ad campaign (see the figure below) featuring the image of a formerly beautiful young woman who has been horribly scarred in a fiery accident caused by a drunk driver. In a rhetorical analysis, you might note the effect of the headline right above the gut-wrenching image: "Not everyone who gets hit by a drunk driver dies."

Images and words combine to create an unforgettable emotional appeal.

In analyzing emotional appeals, judge whether the emotions raised—anger, sympathy, fear, envy, joy, or love—advance the claims offered. For example, consider how British newspaper columnist and novelist Lionel Shriver (who changed her first name from Margaret Ann when she decided men had easier lives than women) uses concrete and graphic language to evoke disgust with SUVs—and anyone who owns one—at a time of soaring gas prices:

> Filling the tank of an SUV in the U.S. has now crossed the psychologically traumatizing $100 mark. The resale value of these monsters is plummeting, and many owners are getting stuck with the things, like holding the Old Maid in cards. I greet this news with sadistic glee. People who bought SUVs were fools and I want them to suffer. Not just because I'm a sanctimonious greenie, but because I'm an aesthete. Sure, SUVs are petro-pigs, and they side-swipe cyclists into the curb. Yes, they emblemize everything about Americans the rest of the world detests: greedy, wasteful, and oblivious to the future. But on top of all that, they're ugly.
>
> —Lionel Shriver, "If the U.S. Election Were a Novel"

Does the use of pathos ("monsters," "petro-pigs") convince you, or does it distract from or undermine the claim that SUVs are ugly? Your task in a rhetorical analysis is to study an author's words, the emotions they evoke, and the claims they support and then to make such a judgment.

Examining Arguments Based on Character: Ethos

It should come as no surprise: readers believe writers who seem honest, wise, and trustworthy. So in examining the effectiveness of an argument, look for evidence of these traits. Does the writer have the experience or authority to write on this subject? Are all claims qualified reasonably? Is evidence presented in full, not tailored to the writer's agenda? Are important objections to the author's position acknowledged and addressed? Are sources documented? Above all, does the writer sound trustworthy?

Take a look at the following paragraph from a blog posting by Timothy Burke, a teacher at Swarthmore College and parent of a preschool child who is trying to think through the issue of homework for elementary school kids:

The Privacy Commissioner of Canada analyzes the legal language of social networking sites and then calls the ethos of such sites into question by telling readers that the sites are most interested in making money off the information that users put onto them.

LINK TO P. 669

So I've been reading a bit about homework, and comparing notes with parents. There is a lot of variation across districts, not just in the amount of homework that kids are being asked to do, but in the kind of homework. Some districts give kids a lot of time-consuming busywork, other districts try to concentrate on having homework assignments be substantive work that is best accomplished independently. Some give a lot from a very early point in K–12 education, some give relatively little. As both a professional educator and an individual with personal convictions, I'd tend to argue against excessive amounts of homework and against assigning busywork. But what has ultimately interested me more about reading various discussions of homework is how intense the feelings are swirling around the topic, and how much that intensity strikes me as a problem in and of itself. Not just as a symptom of a kind of civic illness, an inability to collectively and democratically work through complex issues, but also in some cases as evidence of an educational failure in its own right.

Burke establishes his ethos by citing his reading and his talks with other parents.

Burke shows that he is considering alternatives (though he then states his tentative preference).

He criticizes immoderate arguments as "a kind of civic illness" (and suggests that he will demonstrate the opposite of such an approach).

In considering the role that ethos plays in rhetorical analyses, you need to pay attention to the details, right down to the choice of words or, in a visual argument, the shapes and colors. The modest, tentative tone that Burke uses in his blog is an example of the kind of choice that can shape an audience's perception of ethos. But these details need your interpretation. Language that's hot and extreme can mark a writer as either passionate or loony. Work that's sober and carefully organized might suggest that an institution is either competent or excessively cautious. Technical terms and abstract phrases can make a writer seem either knowledgeable or pompous.

Examining Arguments Based on Facts and Reason: Logos

In analyzing most arguments, you'll have to decide whether an argument makes a plausible claim and offers good reasons for you to believe it. Not all arguments will package such claims in a single neat sentence, or *thesis*—nor should they. A writer may tell a story from which you have to infer the claim. Think of the way that many films make a social or political statement by dramatizing an issue like political corruption, government censorship, or economic injustice. Visual arguments may work the same way: viewers have to assemble the parts and draw inferences before they get the point.

In some conventional arguments (like those that you might find on an editorial page), arguments may be perfectly obvious. Writers may first stake out a claim and then present reasons that you should consider, or they may first present reasons and lay out a case that leads you toward a conclusion. Consider the following examples. The first comes from the conclusion of an August 22, 2008, editorial in the *New York Times*; the second is the lead paragraph of a July 1, 2008, editorial in the *St. Petersburg* (Florida) *Times*.

> To win the right to host [the Olympic] Games, China promised to honor the Olympic ideals of nonviolence, openness to the world and individual expression. Those promises were systematically broken, starting with this spring's brutal repression in Tibet and continuing on to the ugly farce of inviting its citizens to apply for legal protest permits and then arresting them if they actually tried to do so. . . .
>
> Surely one of the signature events of these Games was the sentencing of two women in their late 70s to "re-education through labor." Their crime? Applying for permission to protest the inadequate compensation they felt they had received when the government seized their homes years ago for urban redevelopment.
>
> A year ago, the I.O.C. predicted that these Games would be "a force for good" and a spur to human-rights progress. Instead, as Human Rights Watch has reported, they became a catalyst for intensified human-rights abuse.
>
> Mr. Bush has taken some note of China's appalling human-rights record this summer—privately meeting with Chinese dissidents in Washington just before his visit to the Games and gently nudging his hosts on religious freedom while in Beijing. With these repression-

scarred Olympics now drawing to a close, Mr. Bush and other world leaders must tell Beijing that its failure to live up to its Olympic commitments will neither be ignored nor forgotten.

The medal count and DVD sales cannot be the last word on the Beijing Games.

—"Beijing's Bad Faith Olympics," *New York Times*

Tibetans opposed to holding the 2008 Summer Olympic Games in Beijing demonstrate in front of the International Olympic Committee headquarters in Lausanne, Switzerland. In contrast to newspaper editorials, protest signs usually concentrate on emotional rather than logical arguments.

Florida's congressional delegation should stand firm against President Bush's increased pressure to allow offshore oil drilling. That would not immediately lower the price of gasoline or produce more oil, as even the president acknowledged Tuesday. It would jeopardize the foundation of Florida's economy, no matter how many assurances the oil companies make about better drilling techniques and safety.
—"Hold the Line on Offshore Drilling," St. Petersburg Times

When you encounter explicit claims like these, rhetorical analysis calls for you to look at how they are supported by good reasons and reliable evidence. A lengthy essay may, in fact, contain a series of claims, each developed to support an even larger point. Indeed, every paragraph in an argument may develop a specific and related idea. In a rhetorical analysis, you need to identify all these separate propositions and examine the relationships among them. Are they solidly linked? Are there inconsistencies that the writer should acknowledge? Does the end of the piece support what the writer said (and promised) at the beginning?

Since many logical appeals rely heavily on data and information from sources, you'll also need to examine the quality of the information presented in an argument, assessing how accurately such information is reported, how conveniently it's displayed (in charts or graphs, for example), and how well the sources cited represent a range of *respected* opinion on a topic. (For more information on the use of evidence, see Chapter 16.)

Knowing how to judge the quality of sources is more important now than ever before because the electronic pathways are clogged with junk. In some ways, the computer terminal has become the equivalent of a library reference room, but the sources available online vary widely in quality and have not been evaluated by a library professional. As a consequence, you must know the difference between reliable, firsthand, or fully documented sources and those that don't meet such standards. (For more on using and documenting sources, see Chapters 19 and 20.)

Examining the Arrangement and Media of Arguments

Arguments have a structure. Aristotle carved the structure of logical argument to its bare bones when he observed that it had only two parts:

- statement
- proof

What argument does this editorial cartoon make? What elements come together to constitute the claim? What good reasons would be needed to support it?

© Mike Lester/The Mike Lester Studio

You could do worse, in examining an argument, than to make sure that every claim a writer makes is backed by sufficient evidence. Most arguments that you read and write, however, will be more than mere statements followed by proofs. Some writers will lay their cards on the table immediately; others may lead you carefully through a chain of claims toward a conclusion. Writers may even interrupt their arguments to offer background information or cultural contexts for readers. Sometimes they'll tell stories or provide anecdotes that make an argumentative point. They'll qualify the arguments they make, too, and often pause to admit that other points of view are plausible.

In other words, there are no formulas or acceptable patterns that fit all successful arguments. Many are written on the fly in the heat of the moment. In writing a rhetorical analysis, you'll have to assess the organization of a persuasive text on its own merits.

It's fair, however, to complain about what may be *absent* from an argument. Most arguments of proposal (see Chapter 12), for example, include

In claiming that "Indian" logos and mascots perpetuate racism, Barbara Munson presents a rhetorical analysis of the logos. In the rest of her article, she challenges the logic and evidence of those who believe that these logos are not troubling or insulting.

LINK TO P. 624

a section that defends the feasibility of a new idea, explaining how it might be funded or managed. In a rhetorical analysis, you might fault an editorial that supports a new stadium for a city without addressing feasibility issues. Similarly, analyzing a movie review that reads like off-the-top-of-the-head opinion, you might legitimately ask what criteria of evaluation are in play (see Chapter 10).

Rhetorical analysis also calls for you to look carefully at an argument's transitions, headings and subheadings, documentation of sources, and overall tone or voice. Don't take such details for granted, since they all contribute to the strength—or weakness—of an argument.

Nor should you ignore the way a writer or an institution uses media. Would an argument originally made in a print editorial, for instance, work better as a spoken presentation (or vice versa)? Would a lengthy paper have more power if it included more images? Or do you find that images distract from a written argument and diminish its substance? These are important issues that you might comment on or connect to other aspects of an argument, such as its style, as you work toward a rhetorical analysis.

Finally, be open to the possibility of new or nontraditional structures of arguments. The visual arguments that you analyze may defy conventional principles of logic or arrangement—for example, making juxtapositions rather than logical transitions between elements or using quick cuts, fades, or other devices to link ideas. Quite often, these nontraditional structures will also resist the neatness of a thesis, leaving readers to construct at least a part of the argument in their heads. Advertisers are growing fond of these sorts of soft-sell multimedia productions that can seem more like games or entertainments than what they really are—product pitches. We're asked not just to buy a product but also to live its lifestyle. Is that a reasonable or workable strategy for an argument? Your analysis might entertain such possibilities.

Looking at Style

Even a coherent argument flush with evidence may not connect with readers if it's dull, off-key, or offensive. Readers naturally judge the credibility of arguments in part by how stylishly the case is made—even when they don't know exactly what style is. Consider how these simple, blunt sentences from the opening of an argument shape your image of

Not Just Words

Web sites and blogs now practically make a sport out of critiquing the stories and other arguments in older media such as newspapers, magazines, and TV news shows. It's no surprise that traditional mainstream media have pushed back, providing readers with lively examples of rhetorical analyses as part of the daily news.

In September 2005, the *San Francisco Chronicle,* regarded by conservatives as a liberal news source, included in its coverage of an anti–Iraq War demonstration the photograph above, with the following caption: "Jasmine Williams, 17, a student with the leadership group Youth Together, joins the Iraq war protest in San Francisco." The image provoked the ire of a presumably more conservative blogger at zombietime.com. Zombie, who had also photographed the event and even the same girl, but at a wider angle, found the *Chronicle's* shot disingenuous because it omitted details such as Palestinian flags in the background. Here are some of Zombie's photographs and commentary:

Now we can see that the girl is just one of several teenagers, all wearing terrorist-style bandannas covering their faces. But, as you'll notice, the bandannas are all printed with the same design. Was this a grassroots protest statement the teenagers had come up with all by themselves? To find out, let's take a look at another photo in the series, taken at the same time:

Oops—it looks like they're actually being stage-managed by an adult, who is giving them directions and guiding them toward the front of the march. But who is she? The last picture in the series reveals all. It turns out that the woman giving directions belongs to one of the Communist groups organizing the rally—if her T-shirt is to be believed, since it depicts the flag of Communist Vietnam, which has been frequently displayed by such groups at protest rallies in the United States for decades. The *San Francisco Chronicle* featured the original photograph on its front Web page in order to convey a positive message about the rally—perhaps that even politically aware teenagers were inspired to show up and rally for peace, sporting the message, "People of Color say 'No to War!'" And that served the *Chronicle*'s agenda. But this simple analysis reveals the very subtle but insidious type of bias that occurs in the media all the time. The *Chronicle* did not print an inaccuracy, nor did it doctor a photograph to misrepresent the facts. Instead, the *Chronicle* committed the sin of omission: it told you the truth, but it didn't tell you the *whole* truth.

Shortly after Zombie's photos and observations made their way around the Web, the *Chronicle* offered a rebuttal. Here's a brief portion of that newspaper's rhetorical analysis of the situation, offered by "readers' representative" Dick Rogers:

So the *Chronicle* photo didn't exactly shout "Middle America." It was far more dramatic and displayed the protester in far more detail. If the newspaper was setting out to "de-radicalize" the scene, it did a pretty

lame job. If the paper wants to sanitize a protest, it should forget tight shots of radicals in disguise and go for pictures of suburban moms with young children. Now that's centrist.

The accompanying story, by the way, noted the Palestinian angle, the arrests of members of an anarchist group and the presence of counter-demonstrators, one of whom called for "patriotism instead of a socialist revolution."

Readers should ponder what they don't see in pictures, just as they should critically judge what they do see. Photographs are representations of reality, and small slices of it at that.

But a wide-angle view isn't necessarily a bigger slice of reality. It's true that, in some cases, a story is told in more detail by stepping back. In other cases, an image is more powerful and vivid by coming in close.

—Dick Rogers, "Picturing the Debate"

Study the photographs and the contrary rhetorical analyses here. Might one of Zombie's images more accurately represent the protest than the one published in the *Chronicle*? Can you make such a judgment without more information? How could you find out more about this controversy?

Apply what you learn from this exercise to your own analysis of several news photographs selected from current newspapers, newsmagazines, or Web sites. Do the images you've chosen provide the facts you need to make a judgment about a story, or do you suspect something may have been left out of them? Do the images provoke strong emotional responses because of their careful composition, or do they manipulate your feelings? Do you have reason to trust the source offering the images, or might the ethos of that source be suspect? Select one or two of the images, and present your rhetorical analysis of them to your class.

the author and probably determine whether you're willing to continue to read the whole piece:

> We are young, urban and professional. We are literate, respectable, intelligent and charming. But foremost and above all, we know what it's like to be unemployed.
> —Julia Carlisle, "Young, Privileged and Unemployed"

Now consider how you'd approach an argument that begins like the following, responding to a botched primary election in Florida following the electoral disaster of 2000:

> The question you're asking yourself is: Does South Florida contain the highest concentration of morons in the entire world? Or just in the United States? The reason you're asking this, of course, is South Florida's performance in Tuesday's election.
> —Dave Barry, "How to Vote in One Easy Step"

Both styles probably work, but they signal that the writers are about to make very different kinds of cases. In this case, style alone tells readers what to expect.

Manipulating style also enables writers to shape readers' responses to their ideas. Devices as simple as repetition and parallelism can give sentences remarkable power. Consider this passage from liberal blogger Kevin Drum, who argues that both major U.S. political parties share in the blame for the 2008 financial meltdown:

> I haven't been able to work up quite the level of partisan outrage over the fall of Wall Street that some people have. You see, when it comes to environmental regulation, Democrats are mostly on the side of the angels. When it comes to workplace regulation, they're on the side of workers. When it comes to consumer regulation, they're on the side of consumers. But when it comes to financial regulation, they're. . . . um— well, they've been mostly on about the same side as Republicans.
> —Kevin Drum, "Bipartisan"

Or look at this sentence from a profile of Chief Justice John Roberts of the U.S. Supreme Court in the *New Yorker*:

> In every major case since he became the nation's seventeenth Chief Justice, Roberts has sided with the prosecution over the defendant, the state over the condemned, the executive branch over the legislative, and the corporate defendant over the individual plaintiff.
> —Jeffery Toobin, "No More Mr. Nice Guy: The Supreme Court's Stealth Hard-Liner"

In a rhetorical analysis, you can explore many stylistic choices. Why does a formal style work for discussing one type of subject matter but not for another? How does a writer use humor or irony to underscore an important point or to manage a difficult concession? Do stylistic choices, even something as simple as the use of contractions or personal pronouns, bring readers comfortably close to a writer, or do a highly technical vocabulary and an impersonal voice signal that an argument is for experts only?

To describe the stylistic effects of visual arguments, you may use a different vocabulary and talk about colors, camera angles, editing, balance, proportion, fonts, perspective, and so on. But the basic principle is this: the look of an item—whether a poster, an editorial cartoon, or a film documentary—can support the message that it carries, undermine it, or muddle it. In some cases, the look will *be* the message. In a rhetorical analysis, you can't ignore style.

Examining a Rhetorical Analysis

On the following pages is an argument in defense of free speech that was written by Derek Bok, a distinguished scholar and past president of Harvard University—credentials that certainly add to his ethos. Responding to it with a detailed analysis is Milena Ateya, a college student who reveals in her piece that she, too, brings unique credentials to this case.

Protecting Freedom of Expression at Harvard

DEREK BOK

For several years, universities have been struggling with the problem of trying to reconcile the rights of free speech with the desire to avoid racial tension. In recent weeks, such a controversy has sprung up at Harvard. Two students hung Confederate flags in public view, upsetting students who equate the Confederacy with slavery. A third student tried to protest the flags by displaying a swastika.

These incidents have provoked much discussion and disagreement. Some students have urged that Harvard require the removal of symbols that offend many members of the community. Others reply that such symbols are a form of free speech and should be protected.

Different universities have resolved similar conflicts in different ways. Some have enacted codes to protect their communities from forms of speech that are deemed to be insensitive to the feelings of other groups. Some have refused to impose such restrictions.

It is important to distinguish between the appropriateness of such communications and their status under the First Amendment. The fact that speech is protected by the First Amendment does not necessarily mean that it is right, proper, or civil. I am sure that the vast majority of Harvard students believe that hanging a Confederate flag in public view— or displaying a swastika in response—is insensitive and unwise because any satisfaction it gives to the students who display these symbols is far outweighed by the discomfort it causes to many others.

I share this view and regret that the students involved saw fit to behave in this fashion. Whether or not they merely wished to manifest their pride in the South—or to demonstrate the insensitivity of hanging Confederate flags, by mounting another offensive symbol in return—they must have known that they would upset many fellow students and ignore the decent regard for the feelings of others so essential to building and preserving a strong and harmonious community.

To disapprove of a particular form of communication, however, is not enough to justify prohibiting it. We are faced with a clear example of the conflict between our commitment to free speech and our desire to foster a community founded on mutual respect. Our society has wrestled with this problem for many years. Interpreting the First Amendment, the Supreme Court has clearly struck the balance in favor of free speech.

While communities do have the right to regulate speech in order to uphold aesthetic standards (avoiding defacement of buildings) or to protect the public from disturbing noise, rules of this kind must be applied across the board and cannot be enforced selectively to prohibit certain kinds of messages but not others.

Under the Supreme Court's rulings, as I read them, the display of swastikas or Confederate flags clearly falls within the protection of the free speech clause of the First Amendment and cannot be forbidden simply because it offends the feelings of many members of the community. These rulings apply to all agencies of government, including public universities.

Although it is unclear to what extent the First Amendment is enforceable against private institutions, I have difficulty understanding why a university such as Harvard should have less free speech than the surrounding society—or than a public university.

One reason why the power of censorship is so dangerous is that it is extremely difficult to decide when a particular communication is offensive enough to warrant prohibition or to weigh the degree of offensiveness against the potential value of the communication. If we begin to forbid flags, it is only a short step to prohibiting offensive speakers.

I suspect that no community will become humane and caring by restricting what its members can say. The worst offenders will simply find other ways to irritate and insult.

In addition, once we start to declare certain things "offensive," with all the excitement and attention that will follow, I fear that much ingenuity will be exerted trying to test the limits, much time will be expended trying to draw tenuous distinctions, and the resulting publicity will eventually attract more attention to the offensive material than would ever have occurred otherwise.

Rather than prohibit such communications, with all the resulting risks, it would be better to ignore them, since students would then have little reason to create such displays and would soon abandon them. If this response is not possible—and one can understand why—the wisest course is to speak with those who perform insensitive acts and try to help them understand the effects of their actions on others.

Appropriate officials and faculty members should take the lead, as the Harvard House Masters have already done in this case. In talking with students, they should seek to educate and persuade, rather than resort to ridicule or intimidation, recognizing that only persuasion is likely to produce a lasting, beneficial effect. Through such effects, I believe that we act in the manner most consistent with our ideals as an educational institution and most calculated to help us create a truly understanding, supportive community.

A Curse and a Blessing

MILENA ATEYA

Connects article to personal experience to create ethical appeal.

Provides brief overview of Bok's argument.

States Bok's central claim.

Transition sentence.

Examines the emotional appeal the author establishes through description.

Links author's credibility to use of logical appeals.

In 1991, when Derek Bok's essay "Protecting Freedom of Expression at Harvard" was first published in the *Boston Globe*, I had just come to America to escape the oppressive Communist regime in Bulgaria. Perhaps my background explains why I support Bok's argument that we should not put arbitrary limits on freedom of expression. Bok wrote the essay in response to a public display of Confederate flags and a swastika at Harvard, a situation that created a heated controversy among the students. As Bok notes, universities have struggled to achieve a balance between maintaining students' right of free speech and avoiding racist attacks. When choices must be made, however, Bok argues for preserving freedom of expression.

In order to support his claim and bridge the controversy, Bok uses a variety of rhetorical strategies. The author first immerses the reader in the controversy by vividly describing the incident: two Harvard students had hung Confederate flags in public view, thereby "upsetting students who equate the Confederacy with slavery" (51). Another student, protesting the flags, decided to display an even more offensive symbol—the swastika. These actions provoked heated discussions among students. Some students believed that school officials should remove the offensive symbols, whereas others suggested that the symbols "are a form of free speech and should be protected" (51). Bok establishes common ground between the factions: he regrets the actions of the offenders but does not believe we should prohibit such actions just because we disagree with them.

The author earns the reader's respect because of his knowledge and through his logical presentation of the issue. In partial support of his position, Bok refers to U.S.

Supreme Court rulings, which remind us that "the display of swastikas or Confederate flags clearly falls within the protection of the free speech clause of the First Amendment" (52). The author also emphasizes the danger of the slippery slope of censorship when he warns the reader, "If we begin to forbid flags, it is only a short step to prohibiting offensive speakers" (52). Overall, however, Bok's work lacks the kinds of evidence that statistics, interviews with students, and other representative examples of controversial conduct could provide. Thus, his essay may not be strong enough to persuade all readers to make the leap from this specific situation to his general conclusion.

Throughout, Bok's personal feelings are implied but not stated directly. As a lawyer who was president of Harvard for twenty years, Bok knows how to present his opinions respectfully without offending the feelings of the students. However, qualifying phrases like "I suspect that," and "Under the Supreme Court's rulings, as I read them" could weaken the effectiveness of his position. Furthermore, Bok's attempt to be fair to all seems to dilute the strength of his proposed solution. He suggests that one should either ignore the insensitive deeds in the hope that students might change their behavior, or talk to the offending students to help them comprehend how their behavior is affecting other students.

Nevertheless, although Bok's proposed solution to the controversy does not appear at first reading to be very strong, it may ultimately be effective. There is enough flexibility in his approach to withstand various tests, and Bok's solution is general enough that it can change with the times and adapt to community standards.

In writing this essay, Bok faced a challenging task: to write a short response to a specific situation that represents a very broad and controversial issue. Some people may find that freedom of expression is both a curse and a blessing because of the difficulties it creates. As one who has lived under a regime that permitted very limited,

Reference to First Amendment serves as warrant for Bok's claim.

Comments critically on author's evidence.

Examines how Bok establishes ethical appeal.

Identifies qualifying phrases that may weaken claim.

Analyzes author's solution.

Raises points that suggest Bok's solution may work.

Returns to personal experience in conclusion.

censored expression, I am all too aware that I could not have written this response in 1991 in Bulgaria. As a result, I feel, like Derek Bok, that freedom of expression is a blessing, in spite of any temporary problems associated with it.

Work Cited

Bok, Derek. "Protecting Freedom of Expression on the Campus." *Current Issues and Enduring Questions.* Ed. Sylvan Barnet and Hugo Bedau. 6th ed. Boston: Bedford, 2002. 51–52. Print. Rpt. of "Protecting Freedom of Expression at Harvard." *Boston Globe* 25 May 1991.

GUIDE to writing a rhetorical analysis

● Finding a Topic

A rhetorical analysis is usually assigned work: you're asked to describe how an argument works and to assess its effectiveness. When you're free to choose your own subject for analysis, look for one or more of the following qualities:

- a verbal or visual argument that challenges you—or disturbs, excites, amazes, or impresses
- a verbal or visual argument with lots to analyze
- a text that raises current or enduring issues of substance
- a text that you believe should be taken more seriously

Obvious places to look for arguments to analyze include the editorial and op-ed pages of any newspaper, political magazines such as *The Nation* or *National Review*, Web sites of organizations and interest groups, political blogs such as DailyKos.com or Powerline.com, corporate Web sites that post their TV ad spots, videos and statements posted to YouTube, and so on.

● Researching Your Topic

Once you've selected a text to analyze, find out all you can about it. Use the library or resources of the Web to explore

- who the author is and what his or her credentials are
- if the author is an institution, what it does, what its sources of funding are, who its members are, and so on
- who is publishing or sponsoring the piece, and what the organization typically publishes
- what the leanings or biases of the author and publisher might be
- what the context of the argument is—what preceded or provoked it and how others have responded to it

● Formulating a Claim

Begin a rhetorical analysis with a hypothesis in mind. A full thesis might not become evident until you're well into your analysis, but your final thesis should reflect the complexity of the piece that you're studying, not just state that "the editorial has good pathos and ethos but lousy logos." In developing a thesis, consider questions such as the following:

- How can I describe what this argument achieves?
- What is the purpose, and is it accomplished?
- What audiences does the argument seem to address?
- For what audiences does it work or not work?
- Which of its rhetorical features will likely influence readers most: Audience connections? Emotional appeals? Style?
- What aspects of the argument work better than others?
- How do the rhetorical elements interact?

Here's the hardest part for most writers of rhetorical analyses: whether you agree or disagree with an argument doesn't matter in a rhetorical analysis. You've got to stay out of the fray and pay attention only to how—and to how well—the argument works. That's tough to do, but keep your distance!

Examples of Possible Claims for a Rhetorical Analysis

- Many people who admire the inspiring language and elevated style of Barack Obama's speeches might be uneasy with some of the claims that he makes.
- Today's editorial in the *Daily Collegian* about campus crimes may scare first-year students, but its anecdotal reporting doesn't get down to hard numbers—and for a good reason. Those statistics don't back the position taken by the editors.
- The imageboard 4chan has been called an "Internet hate machine," yet others claim it as a great boon to creativity. A close analysis of its homepage can help to settle this debate.
- The original design of New York's Freedom Tower, with its torqued surfaces and evocative spire, made a stronger argument about American values than its replacement, a fortress-like skyscraper stripped of imagination and unable to make any statement except "I'm 1,776 feet tall."

Preparing a Proposal

If your instructor asks you to prepare a proposal for your rhetorical analysis, here's a format you might use:

- Provide a copy of the work that you intend to analyze, whether it's a printed text or something available in another medium. You might have to furnish a photograph, digital image, or URL, for instance.

- Offer a working hypothesis or tentative thesis.

- Indicate which rhetorical components seem especially compelling and worthy of detailed study. Also note where you see potential connections between elements. For example, does the piece seem to emphasize facts and logic so much that it becomes disconnected from potential audiences? If so, hint at that possibility in your proposal.

- Indicate the background information—about the author, institution, and contexts (political, economic, social, and religious) of the argument—that you intend to research.

- Define the audience that you imagine for the analysis. If you're responding to an assignment, you may be writing primarily for a teacher and classmates. But they make up a complex audience in themselves. If you can do so within the spirit of the assignment, imagine that your analysis will be published in a local newspaper, on a Web site, or in a blog.

- Suggest the media that you might use in your analysis. Will a traditional paper work? Could you use highlighting or other word-processing tools to focus attention on stylistic details? Would it be possible to use balloons or other callouts to annotate a visual argument?

- Conclude by briefly discussing the key challenges you anticipate in preparing your analysis.

● Thinking about Content and Organization

Your rhetorical analysis may take various forms, but it's likely to include the following:

- Facts about the text you're analyzing: Provide the author's name; the title or name of the work; its place of publication or its location; the date it was published or viewed.

- Contexts for the argument: Readers need to know where the text is coming from, to what it may be responding, in what controversies it might be embroiled, and so on. Don't assume that they can infer the important contextual elements.

- A synopsis of the text that you're analyzing: If you can't attach the original argument, you must summarize it in enough detail so that a reader can imagine it. Even if you attach a copy of the piece, the analysis should include a summary.

- Some claim about the rhetorical effectiveness of the work: It might be a straightforward evaluative claim or something more complex. The claim can come early in the paper, or you might work toward it steadily, providing the evidence that leads toward the conclusion you've reached.

- A detailed analysis of how the argument works: Although you'll probably analyze rhetorical components separately, don't let your analysis become a dull roster of emotional, ethical, and logical appeals. Your rhetorical analysis should be an argument itself that supports a claim; a simple list of rhetorical appeals won't make much of a point.

- Evidence for every part of the analysis.

- An assessment of alternative views and counterarguments to your own analysis.

● Getting and Giving Response

If you have access to a writing center, discuss the text that you intend to analyze with a writing consultant before you write the paper. Try to find people who agree with the argument and others who disagree, and take notes on their observations. Your instructor may assign you to a peer group for the purpose of reading and responding to one another's drafts; if not, share your draft with someone on your own. You can use the following questions to evaluate a draft. If you're evaluating someone else's draft, be sure to illustrate your points with examples. Specific comments are always more helpful than general observations.

The Claim

- Does the claim address the rhetorical effectiveness of the argument itself and not the opinion or position that it takes?

- Is the claim significant enough to interest readers?

- Does the claim indicate important relationships between various rhetorical components?

- Would the claim be one that the author or creator of the piece might regard as serious criticism?

Evidence for the Claim

- Is enough evidence furnished to explain or support all claims you make? If not, what kinds of additional evidence are needed?

- Is the evidence in support of the claim simply announced, or are its significance and appropriateness analyzed? Is a more detailed discussion needed?

- Do you use the right kind of evidence, drawn either from the argument itself or from other materials?

- Do you address any objections that readers might have to the claim, criteria, or evidence or to the way the analysis is conducted?

- What kinds of sources might you use to explain the context of the argument? Do you need to use sources to check factual claims made in the argument?

- Are all quotations introduced with appropriate signal phrases (such as "As Peggy Noonan points out"), and do they merge smoothly into your sentences?

Organization and Style

- How are the parts of the argument organized? How effective is this organization? Would some other structure work better?

- Will readers understand the relationships among the original text, your claims, your supporting reasons, and the evidence you've gathered (from the original text and any other sources you've used)? If not, what could be done to make those connections clearer? Are more transitional words and phrases needed? Would headings or graphic devices help?

- Are the transitions or links from point to point, paragraph to paragraph, and sentence to sentence clear and effective? If not, how could they be improved?

- Is the style suited to the subject and appropriate to your audience? Is it too formal? Too casual? Too technical? Too bland?

- Which sentences seem particularly effective? Which ones seem weakest, and how could they be improved? Should some short sentences be combined, or should any long ones be separated into two or more sentences?

- How effective are the paragraphs? Do any seem too skimpy or too long? Do they break the analysis at strategic points?

- Which words or phrases seem particularly effective, accurate, and powerful? Do any seem dull, vague, unclear, or inappropriate for the audience or your purpose? Are definitions provided for technical or other terms that readers might not know?

Spelling, Punctuation, Mechanics, Documentation, and Format

- Check the spelling of the author's name, and make sure that the name of any institution involved with the work is correct. Note that the names of many corporations and institutions use distinctive spelling and punctuation.

- Get the name of the text you're analyzing right.

- Are there any errors in spelling, punctuation, capitalization, and the like?

- Does the assignment require a specific format? Check the original assignment sheet to be sure.

RESPOND•

1. Describe a persuasive moment that you can recall from a speech, an article, an editorial, an advertisement, a video clip, or your personal experiences. Alternatively, research one of the following famous moments of persuasion, and describe the circumstances of the appeal—the historical situation, the issues at stake, the purpose of the argument, and the reasons it is memorable:

   Abraham Lincoln's "Gettysburg Address" (1863)

   Elizabeth Cady Stanton's draft of the "Declaration of Sentiments" for the Seneca Falls Convention (1848)

   Franklin Roosevelt's first inaugural address (1933)

   Winston Churchill's addresses to the British people during the early stages of World War II (1940)

   Martin Luther King Jr.'s "Letter from Birmingham Jail" (1963)

   Ronald Reagan's tribute to the *Challenger* astronauts (1986)

   Toni Morrison's speech accepting the Nobel Prize (1993)

   Barack Obama's "A More Perfect Union" speech on race (2008)

2. Find a written argument on the editorial page or op-ed page in a recent newspaper. Analyze this argument rhetorically, drawing on the principles discussed in this chapter. Analyze the elements of the argument that best explain why it succeeds, fails, or does something else entirely. Perhaps you can show that the author is unusually successful in connecting with readers but then has nothing to say. Or perhaps you discover that the strong logical appeal is undercut by a contradictory emotional argument. Be sure that the analysis includes a summary of the original essay and basic publication information about it (its author, place of publication, and publisher).

3. Browse YouTube or another Web site to find an example of a powerful emotional argument that's made visually, either alone or using words as well. In a paragraph, defend a claim about how the argument works. For example, does an image itself make a claim, or does it draw you in to consider a verbal claim? What emotion does the argument generate? How does that emotion work to persuade you?

4. Find a recent example of a visual argument, either in print or on the Internet. Even though you may have a copy of the image, describe it carefully in your paper on the assumption that your description is all readers may have to go on. Then make a judgment about its effectiveness, supporting your claim with clear evidence from the "text."

PART 2

WRITING
arguments

6

Academic Arguments

Much of the writing you will do in college (and some of what you may do later in your professional work) is called *academic discourse* or *academic argument*. Although this kind of writing has many distinctive characteristics that we explore in this chapter, in general terms this writing is addressed to an audience that is well informed about the topic, that attempts to convey a clear and compelling point in a somewhat formal style, and that follows agreed-upon conventions of usage, punctuation, formats, and so on. Milena Ateya's rhetorical analysis in Chapter 5 is an example of a brief academic argument, and you will find many other examples of academic arguments throughout this book.

Understanding What Academic Argument Is

As this definition suggests, *academic argument* covers a wide range of writing. Take a look at the following statements about migraine, the subject of a great deal of academic (especially medical) writing.

An advertisement for a drug, Weleda Migraine Remedy:

An excerpt from an article in the magazine *Body + Soul*: Hillarie Dowdle, "Fighting Migraines"

> For me, it's like this: I catch a whiff of perfume, or the weather shifts, or I get overtired—and boom. My fingers and toes start to burn and my vision blurs, while my hearing and sense of smell become painfully sharp. Dizzy and nauseated, I feel myself telescoping inward as the entirety of my consciousness shrinks to a hot dot of agony that takes up residence behind my right eyeball for 72 hours, never more, never less. Migraine.

A cartoon from the Web site http://www.migraine-aura.org:

© Linda Causey

An excerpt from an article in *Scientific American* (August 2008): David W. Dodick and J. Jay Gargus, "Why Migraines Strike"

At the moment, only a few drugs can prevent migraine. All of them were developed for other diseases, including hypertension, depression and epilepsy. Because they are not specific to migraine, it will come as no surprise that they work in only 50 percent of patients—and, in them, only 50 percent of the time—and induce a range of side effects, some potentially serious.

Recent research on the mechanism of these antihypertensive, anti-epileptic and antidepressant drugs has demonstrated that one of their effects is to inhibit cortical spreading depression. The drugs' ability to prevent migraine with and without aura therefore supports the school of thought that cortical spreading depression contributes to both kinds of attacks. Using this observation as a starting point, investigators have come up with novel drugs that specifically inhibit cortical spreading depression. Those drugs are now being tested in migraine sufferers with and without aura. They work by preventing gap junctions, a form of ion channel, from opening, thereby halting the flow of calcium between brain cells.

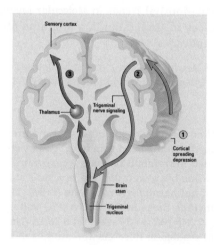

Infographic: The root of migraine pain

MORE TO EXPLORE

Migraine. Oliver Sacks. Vintage, 1999.

"Migraine—New Molecular Mechanisms." Daniela Pietrobon in *Neuroscientist*, Vol. 11, No. 4, pages 373–386; 2005.

Receptor, Transporter, and Ion Channel Diseases. J. Jay Gargus in *Encyclopedia of Molecular Cell Biology and Molecular Medicine.* Edited by Robert A. Myers. Wiley, 2005.

Chronic Daily Headache. David W. Dodick in *New England Journal of Medicine,* Vol. 354, No. 2, pages 158–165; January 12, 2006.

Recent Advances in Understanding Migraine Mechanisms, Molecules and Therapeutics. Peter J. Goadsby in *Trends in Molecular Medicine,* Vol. 13, No. 1, pages 39–44; January 2007.

ABOUT THE AUTHOR(S)

David W. Dodick and J. Jay Gargus share a deep interest in understanding and ameliorating migraine. Dodick, a professor of neurology at the Mayo Clinic in Arizona, received his medical degree at Dalhousie University in Halifax, Nova Scotia. He studies the central nervous system abnormalities behind migraine and other forms of headache. Gargus, a professor of physiology, biophysics and human genetics at the University of California, Irvine, received his medical degree and doctorate at Yale University. He is studying the genetic underpinnings of migraine and other ion channel disorders.

An excerpt from an article in the journal *Trends in Molecular Medicine*: Peter Goadsby, "Recent Advances in Understanding Migraine Mechanisms, Molecules and Therapeutics."

Peter J. Goadsby, Institute of Neurology, The National Hospital for Neurology and Neurosurgery, Queen Square, London, UK WC1N 3B

Abstract

Migraine is a complex, disabling disorder of the brain that manifests itself as attacks of often severe, throbbing head pain with sensory sensitivity to light, sound and head movement. There is a clear familial tendency to migraine, which has been well defined in a rare autosomal dominant form of familial hemiplegic migraine (FHM). FHM mutations so far identified include those in CACNA1A (P/Q voltage-gated Ca(2+) channel), ATP1A2 (N(+)-K(+)-ATPase) and SCN1A (Na(+) channel) genes. Physiological studies in humans and studies of the experimental correlate—cortical spreading depression (CSD)—provide understanding of aura, and have explored in recent years the effect of migraine preventives in CSD. Therapeutic developments in migraine have come by targeting the trigeminovascular system, with the most recent being the proof-of-principle study of calcitonin gene-related peptide (CGRP) receptor antagonists in acute migraine. To understand the basic pathophysiology of migraine, brain imaging studies have firmly established reproducible changes in the brainstem in regions that include areas that are involved in sensory modulation. These data lead to the view that migraine is a form of sensory dysmodulation—a system failure of normal sensory processing.

Introduction

Migraine is an episodic brain disorder that affects ~15% of the population [1]; it can be highly disabling, and has been estimated to be the most costly neurological disorder in the European Community at >27 billion per year [2]. Migraine is a familial episodic disorder, the key marker of which is headache with certain associated features (Table 1). By studying its component parts, one can gain insights into potential molecular mechanisms that might direct the development of new therapies. For a more-general clinical account of the disorder and its treatments, texts are available [3, 4 and 5].

Table 1. International Headache Society features of migraine [18]

Repeated episodic headache (4–72 hrs) with the following features:

Any two of:	*Any one of:*
• Unilateral	• Nausea and/or vomiting
• Throbbing	• Photophobia and phonophobia
• Worsened by movement	
• Moderate or severe	

References

1 R.B. Lipton *et al.*, Prevalence and burden of migraine in the United States: data from the American Migraine Study II, *Headache* **41** (2001), pp. 646–657.

2 P. Andlin-Sobocki *et al.*, Cost of disorders of the brain in Europe, *Eur. J. Neurol.* **12** (2005) (Suppl 1), pp. 1–27.

3 J. Olesen *et al.*, The Headaches, Lippincott, Williams & Wilkins (2005).

4 J.W. Lance and P.J. Goadsby, Mechanism and Management of Headache (7th ed.), Elsevier (2005).

5 P.J. Goadsby *et al.*, Migraine—current understanding and treatment, *N. Engl. J. Med.* **346** (2002), pp. 257–270.

It's pretty easy to tell that the article in *Trends in Molecular Medicine* is the "most academic" of these examples. But the essay from *Scientific American* also qualifies as academic argument, and the other examples (an ad, a cartoon, and an article in a popular magazine) might be used as illustration or evidence in such an argument. Each of these texts presents an argument, but the differences among them are striking.

The two visuals—the cartoon and the advertisement—use few words and rely on the image to carry a large part of the message: they are short and to the point, make implicit claims without offering support for them, and draw on emotional appeals. The article from *Body & Soul* is easy to read and to follow: it uses a narrative structure grounded in personal experience (again, note the use of pathos) that testifies to the claim. Also note its dramatic opening, fairly short sentences with simple structure, and tone of urgency and immediacy. While you might use one or more of these features in some of your college writing, especially on informal assignments, this is not an example of an academic argument.

Now compare this excerpt with the one from the end of the article in *Scientific American*. Here, we find a more nuanced and cautious tone ("At the moment, only a few drugs can prevent migraine"). The article carefully establishes the ethos of the authors to demonstrate that they are responsible and credible ("About the Authors") and provides a brief review of what is known about the topic (an overview of prior research and background information on migraine).

In addition, note that the authors' clear, direct style uses somewhat longer sentences than the popular article, with more complex structure and some technical vocabulary ("induce," "antihypertensive"), and it avoids personal information or use of first person. Finally, the article features careful presentation of evidence (the "infographic") and a focus on logical appeals (because drugs were developed for treating diseases other than migraine, they work in only 50 percent of the cases), along with references for further reading ("More to Explore").

This article, which argues that migraine is "imaginary" no longer, is written in academic style, with one major exception. Because it is intended for the broad audience that reads *Scientific American*, including many people who are not scientists but have a general interest in scientific topics, and because it adheres to the style of that particular magazine, it does not contain traditional academic citations and a list of works cited.

The final example on migraine, from a scientific journal, establishes the credentials of the author (his ethos) at the very beginning of the article by giving his institutional affiliation. It contains many citations and a long list of references, the first five of which we show here along with part of the introduction. This is a full-blown academic argument that is addressed to other physicians and scientists. In addition to the extensive citations and references, all of which contribute to the logical appeals of the article, note the review of earlier research about migraine and the use of a table, clearly labeled.

This article also features precise and sometimes highly technical language ("a rare autosomal dominant form of familial hemiplegic migraine (FHM)") and a clear, direct style that takes an authoritative stance while highlighting the importance of the topic ("Migraine is an episodic brain disorder that affects ~15% of the population [1]"). The author uses *one* rather than the more personal *I* except when he gives an overview of what he does in the article. And the careful, evenhanded tone he establishes ("These data lead to the view that migraine is a form of sensory dysmodulation") makes clear that the author's data (and not his feelings about the topic) are what are intended to convince his audience. These are all key features of academic argument.

One professor we know defines *academic argument* as "carefully structured research," and that seems to us to be a pretty good definition. In addition, we can sum up the characteristics of academic argument in a brief list. Academic argument

- is authoritative (written by experts who are addressing an audience of their peers and therefore need to establish a strong ethos)

- reviews what is known about a topic and creates new knowledge about it

- focuses on issues (facts, definitions, evaluations, or causes and effects) that are important to the writer's academic peers

- includes logical appeals based on careful research (such as field, lab, and library research)

- cites every source carefully and provides full bibliographical references so that others can find the sources

- is written in a clear and formal style

- has an evenhanded tone, deals fairly with any opposing points of view, and avoids appeals to emotion

Hyon B. Shin and Rosalind Bruno's report on the 2000 U.S. census meets all of the criteria for academic argument listed here and provides a potential model for your own writing.

LINK TO P. 724

Not Just Words

You've already seen that academic arguments often include visuals, such as the table on page 137. (The article from *Trends in Molecular Medicine* includes a second important table that we do not show here.) In *Scientific American*, which is printed in color and aims for a highly engaging design, readers see many visuals at work. In addition to the "infographic," the article excerpted on pages 135–36 includes eight other visuals, some of them as large as a full page. Charts, photographs, and drawings are included, such as this page from a twelfth-century illuminated manuscript.

The drawings help readers who have never suffered from migraine experience a few symptoms of this kind of headache. Here, the intense blues and deep reds seem to bore inward, while the aura surrounds the pain and intensifies it.

Take a look at a piece of academic writing that you are working on or have recently done, and find a passage that would be enhanced considerably by the addition of a strong visual image. What do you gain by adding the image?

Developing an Academic Argument

This chapter intends to get you thinking about academic arguments and to describe the features of these arguments in general. Not all academic arguments are similar, however, and not every academic argument includes each of the features we've presented here. Indeed, academic arguments cover a broad range—a brief note in a journal like *Nature* that announces a major breakthrough and promises more to come, short papers on important topics featured in *Physical Review Letters*, a poster presentation given at a conference on linguistics, a full research report in biology, or an undergraduate honors thesis in history. In addition, scholars today are pushing the envelope of traditional academic discourse in a number of fields. The use of narrative in medicine, for example, is on the rise as physicians try to communicate more effectively with other medical personnel.

In your first couple of years of college, the academic arguments you make may take a number of forms, but most will probably include the features we've discussed above. You'll see plenty of examples of academic argument throughout this book (including the two sample academic arguments at the end of this chapter), so keep these in mind when you get assignments in your classes; you may be able to use some of these examples as models. In addition, you can work toward making a good strong academic argument by following some time-tested techniques.

Choose a topic you want to explore in depth. Unless you are assigned a topic (and remember that even assigned topics can be tweaked to match your own interests), look for a subject you have been intrigued by—one you want to know a lot more about. In college writing, one of the hardest parts of producing an academic argument is finding a topic that can sustain your interest over a period of time but that can be narrowed enough to be manageable in the time you have to work on it. Begin by talking with friends about possible topics and explaining to them why you'd like to pursue research on this issue. Browse through books and articles that interest you, make a list of potential topics, and then zero in on one or two top choices.

Get to know the conversation surrounding your topic. Once you've chosen a topic, you need to do a lot more browsing. Start by searching on the Internet using key terms that are associated with your topic, but remember that you have access to a number of databases through your library that are not available to you on Google or other search engines. You're trying to familiarize yourself with what's been said about this topic and especially with what controversies surround it. Where do scholars agree, and where do they disagree? What key issues seem to be at stake?

Assess what you know and what you need to know. As you read and talk with others about your topic, begin to keep notes on what you have learned, including what you already know about the topic. Such notes should soon reveal where the gaps in your knowledge are. You may find that you need to read about relevant legal issues and thus end up in a law school library doing research there. Or you may find that you need to consult some experts about your topic. Instructors on your campus may have such expertise, so do some browsing on your college Web site to find faculty you might want to talk with. You can then make an appointment to visit during office hours, bringing along specific questions with you. You also may find that you need to conduct some field research—a survey, for example, or a set of observations. (See Chapter 19 for information on conducting field research.)

Begin formulating a claim about your topic. Chapter 5 provides a lot of guidance in formulating a claim, which every academic argument must have. Remember that good claims are debatable. After all, you can't argue effectively about something that everyone agrees on or accepts. In addition, your claim needs to be significant and say something meaningful about an important or controversial topic. Good claims can be supported with strong evidence and good reasons (see Chapter 16 for more information on the use of evidence). Here's the claim that the authors of the *Scientific American* article make: "Scientists and physicians are finally coming to see migraine for the complex, biologically fascinating process it is and to recognize its powerfully debilitating effects. The disorder is 'imaginary' no longer." Each piece of evidence that they present works to support that claim.

Consider your rhetorical stance and purpose. Begin by asking yourself where you are coming from in terms of this topic and how you want to represent yourself to those reading your academic argument. You may find that your stance is primarily that of a critic: you want to point out the problems and mistakes associated with some view of your topic. Or you may take the stance of a reporter—reviewing what has been said about your topic, analyzing and evaluating contributions to the conversation surrounding it, coming up with a synthesis of the most important strands of the conversation, and drawing conclusions based on them. On other occasions, your stance might be that of an advocate—one whose research strongly supports a particular view on your topic. Whatever your stance, remember that in academic arguments you want to be especially careful to come across as fair and evenhanded. In each case, your stance will be closely related to your purpose. In most of your college writing of academic arguments, your purpose will be at least two-fold—to do the best job you can in fulfilling an assignment for one of your courses and to introduce, establish, and support the claim you are making to the fullest extent possible. Luckily, these two purposes work well together.

Think about your audience(s). Here again, you will often find that you have at least a dual audience. First, you will be writing to the instructor who gave you this assignment, so make sure to take careful notes in class when the assignment is given and, if possible, set up a conference with your instructor so that you can know as much as possible about his or her expectations: what will it take to convince this audience that you have done a terrific job of writing an academic argument? Beyond your instructor, you should think of your classmates as members of your audience—informed, intelligent peers who will be interested in what you have to say. Again, what do you know about this audience, and what will they expect from your academic argument? Finally, consider yet another audience—people who are already engaged in discussing your topic. These will include the authors whose work you have read and the larger academic community of which they are a part.

Concentrate on the material you are gathering. Any academic argument is only as good as the material it presents in its support, so you need to be careful as you search for evidence. With each major piece of evidence (a lengthy article, say, that addresses your topic directly), take the time to summarize the main points, to analyze how those points are made, to evaluate their effectiveness, to synthesize the results of your analysis and evaluation, and to articulate what you think about this article. In this way, you are testing each piece of evidence and deciding which to keep—and which to throw out. In doing so, remember that you do not want to gather only material that favors your take on the topic. You want to look at all legitimate perspectives on the topic, and in doing so, you may even change your mind. That's what good research for an academic argument can do, so keep yourself open to change.

Remember that you will probably be gathering or creating visual materials as well as text materials. You may find a drawing that perfectly illustrates an aspect of your topic, or you may create a pie chart that shows the results of a questionnaire you distributed. Whether you find or create visuals for your academic argument, you need to give them the same careful scrutiny you give to articles, books, and so on. Remember that the graphic representation of data always involves an interpretation of the data: numbers can lie and pictures distort. (For more information on evaluating visuals, see Chapter 14.)

In *Fighting over Food*, Wynne Wright and Gerad Middendorf carefully provide citations for the popular headlines that show how often their topic is discussed in our culture.

LINK TO P. 784

Take special care with documentation. As you gather material for your academic argument, be scrupulous in recording where you found each source so that you can cite it accurately. Remember that different academic fields use different systems of documentation, so if your instructor has not recommended a style of documentation to you, ask in class about it. Scholars have developed these systems over a long period of time. Using them carefully and accurately shows that you understand the conventions of your field of study and that you have done your homework, and this helps to establish your credibility as a knowledgeable member of the academy. (For more detailed information on documentation, see Chapter 20.)

Think about organization. As you work on design and survey the materials that you have gathered, you are beginning the work of drafting your academic argument. At this point, look at the organization of some of the articles you have gathered. The article in *Trends in Molecular Medicine* begins with an abstract that is followed by a formal introduction. The author then organizes the rest of his article by using a series of ten subheadings (such as "The Genetics of Migraine" and "Familial Hemiplegic Migraine"). The *Scientific American* article does not have an abstract, though a box on the first page announces "Key Concepts":

Key Concepts

- Migraine is more than a headache: it is intensely painful and has distinct phases.
- The disorder used to be considered a vascular one, but recent research reveals it to be neurological, related to a wave of nerve cell activity that sweeps across the brain.
- The root of migraine may reside in brain stem malfunctioning.
- Although debate swirls about the precise cause of migraine, discoveries are already permitting the development of new treatments.

The authors of this article also make effective use of subheadings (such as "Aura's Origin," "From Aura to Ache," and "What the Future May Hold") to guide readers. Sometimes, a field will use an established set of headings for organization—abstract, introduction, materials and methods, results, discussion, conclusion, references. As you organize your academic argument, check with your instructor to see if there is a recommended pattern to follow—or create a scratch outline or storyboard for how your essay will proceed. And remember that your organization needs to take into account the placement of visuals—charts, tables, photographs, and so on.

Consider style and tone. The examples from *Scientific American* and *Trends in Molecular Medicine* demonstrate traditional academic style, which strives for clarity and directness. Such a style leans toward the formal, using the third person and avoiding a focus on *I*; avoiding colloquialisms, slang, or contractions; and using technical vocabulary where necessary. Most academic argument adopts the tone of a reasonable, fair-minded, careful thinker who is interested in coming as close to the truth about a topic as possible.

Anne E. Becker's study of body image and identity in Fiji exemplifies a clear, direct academic style. Even though she makes a complex argument, her writing remains straightforward and readable.

LINK TO P. 611

Consider design and visuals. Most college academic arguments look more like the article in *Trends in Molecular Medicine* than the one in *Scientific American*—that is, they are usually black on white, use a traditional font size and type (like 11-point Times New Roman), and lack any conscious design other than inserted tables or figures. But such conventions are changing as more and more students have access to sophisticated software that allows for the kind of design elements on display in the *Scientific American* piece. In addition to columns and boxed sidebars, the authors use a number of powerful visuals, including this one on the left that accompanies the opening of the article.

danah m. boyd and Nicole B. Ellison help readers understand the history of social network sites with a timeline that illustrates when different sites were founded. The list contains so much information that it might overwhelming to place it in a paragraph.

LINK TO P. 653

Indeed, student writers today may now go well beyond print, creating digital documents that include sound and video to go along with visuals such as photographs, charts, and so on. Writers of academic arguments need to consider what kind of design is most appropriate for their topic, their purpose, and their audience and then act accordingly. As you think about the design of your academic argument, you may want to consult your instructor—and to try out your design on friends or classmates.

Reflect on your draft and get responses. As with any important piece of writing you do, an academic argument calls for careful reflection on your draft. Now may be the time to do a formal outline so that you can "see" whether you establish the logical links you intended. In addition, you will want to judge the effectiveness of your argument, assessing what each paragraph adds and what may be missing. Turning a critical eye to your own work now can save a lot of grief in the long run. In addition to your own critique, make sure to get some response from classmates and friends. To make sure that they give you helpful responses, come up with a set of questions you have about the draft, and ask them to refer to the questions as they read. Now's the time to find out what is confusing or unclear to others, what needs further support, and so on.

Edit and proofread your text. If you are writing for publication, you will almost always get responses from a copyeditor and a proofreader, who go through your text and question you about any discrepancies, including missing references, typos, wrong words, and so on. Students don't usually get the benefit of such experts, however, so you need to be prepared to do these jobs for yourself. Proofread the piece at least three times—one time to make sure that all your ideas and main points make sense (that you haven't left out a key word, for instance); another time word for word (some people like to read backwards since that focuses attention at the word level); and a final time to check that every source mentioned in the academic argument appears in the references list and that every citation is correct. This is also the time to make any final touch-ups to your design. Remember that how the document looks is part of what establishes its credibility.

RESPOND●

1. Working with another student in your class, find examples of academic arguments from two or three different fields that strike you as being well written and effective. Spend some time looking closely at them. Do they exemplify the key features of academic arguments discussed in this chapter? What other features do they use? How are they organized? What kind of tone do the writers use? What use do they make of visuals? Draw up a brief report on your findings (a list will do), and bring it to class for discussion.

2. Look closely at the following five passages, each of which is from an opening of a published work, and decide which ones provide examples of academic argument. How would you describe each one, and what are its key features? Which is the most formal and academic? Which is the least? How might you revise them to make them more— or less—academic?

During the Old Stone Age, between thirty-seven thousand and eleven thousand years ago, some of the most remarkable art ever conceived was etched or painted on the walls of caves in southern France and northern Spain. After a visit to Lascaux, in the Dordogne, which was discovered in 1940, Picasso reportedly said to his guide, "They've invented everything." What those first artists invented was a language of signs for which there will never be a Rosetta stone; perspective, a technique that was not rediscovered until the Athenian Golden Age; and a bestiary of such vitality and finesse that, by the flicker of torchlight, the animals seem to surge from the walls, and move across them like figures in a magic-lantern show (in that sense, the artists invented animation). They also thought up the grease lamp—a lump of fat, with a plant wick, placed in a hollow stone—to light their workplace; scaffolds to reach high places; the principles of stenciling and Pointillism; powdered colors, brushes, and stumping cloths; and, more to the point of Picasso's insight, the very concept of an image. A true artist reimagines that concept with every blank canvas—but not from a void.

—Judith Thurman, "First Impressions," *The New Yorker*

I stepped over the curb and into the street to hitchhike. At the age of ten I'd put some pretty serious mileage on my thumb. And I knew how it was done. Hold your thumb up, not down by your hip as though you didn't much give a damn whether you got a ride or not. Always hitch at a place where a driver could pull out of traffic and give you time to get in without risking somebody tailgating him.

—Harry Crews, "On Hitchhiking," *Harper's*

Coral reef ecosystems are essential marine environments around the world. Host to thousands (and perhaps millions) of diverse organisms, they are also vital to the economic well-being of an estimated 0.5 billion people, or 8% of the world's population who live on tropical coasts (Hoegh-Guldberg 1999). Income from tourism and fishing industries, for instance, is essential to the economic prosperity of many countries, and the various plant and animal species present in reef ecosystems are sources for different natural products and medicines. The degradation of coral reefs can therefore have a devastating impact on coastal populations, and it is estimated that between 50% and 70% of all reefs around the world are currently threatened (Hoegh-Guldberg). Anthropogenic influences are cited as the major cause of this degradation, including sewage, sedimentation, direct trampling of reefs, over-fishing of herbivorous fish, and even global warming (Umezawa et al. 2002; Jones et al. 2001; Smith et al. 2001).

—Elizabeth Derse, "Identifying the Sources of Nitrogen to Hanalei Bay, Kauai, Utilizing the Nitrogen Isotope Signature of Macroalgae," *Stanford Undergraduate Research Journal*

Some of my best friends are women—heck, I am a woman—but I've come to the conclusion that we've seen too much of the fairer sex. For me, the final straw came last month when Britney Spears jauntily revealed her waxed nether regions to waiting photographers as she exited her limo. Britney's stunt made her the Internet smash of the season. But in providing America's workers with this cubicle distraction, Britney was doing a lot more than making her own privates public.

—Kay S. Hymowitz, "Scenes from the Exhibitionists," *Wall Street Journal*

From the richest high school to the poorest high school in America, students are being told that employment in the computer industry is nothing less than salvation from the indignities of the jobs those others have to do to survive. If you don't learn your computer skills well, if by some chance you're bored sitting in front of that screen, day after day under buzzing fluorescents, pecking at a vanilla keyboard, clicking a mouse, it's your problem, and there will be no excuse for your fate in this new economy: you will be doomed to menial, manual labor. That dirty, anybody-can-do-that work. Poor income, low prestige. Pues, así va la vida, compa, that's life if you don't get your stuff right.

—Dagoberto Gilb, "Work Union," *Gritos* [a book]

3. Read the following paragraphs, and then list changes that the writer might make to convert them into an academic argument:

Every well-traveled cosmopolite knows that America is mind-numbingly monotonous—"the most boring country to tour, because everywhere looks like everywhere else," as the columnist Thomas Friedman once told Charlie Rose. Boston has the same stores as Denver, which has the same stores as Charlotte or Seattle or Chicago. We live in a "Stepford world," says Rachel Dresbeck, the author of *Insiders' Guide to Portland, Oregon*. Even Boston's historic Faneuil Hall, she complains, is "dominated by the Gap, Anthropologie, Starbucks, and all the other usual suspects. Why go anywhere? Every place looks the same." This complaint is more than the old worry, dating back to the 1920s, that the big guys are putting Mom and Pop out of business. Today's critics focus less on what isn't there—Mom and Pop—than on what is. Faneuil Hall actually has plenty of locally owned businesses, from the Geoclassics store selling minerals and jewelry, to Pizzeria Regina ("since 1926"). But you do find the same chains everywhere.

The suburbs are the worst. Take Chandler, Arizona, just south of Phoenix. At Chandler Fashion Center, the area's big shopping mall, you'll find P. F. Chang's, California Pizza Kitchen, Chipotle Mexican Grill, and the Cheesecake Factory. Drive along Chandler's straight, flat boulevards, and you'll see Bed Bath & Beyond and Linens-n-Things; Barnes & Noble and Borders; PetSmart and Petco; Circuit City and Best Buy; Lowe's and Home Depot; CVS and Walgreens. Chandler has the Apple Store and Pottery Barn, the Gap and Ann Taylor, Banana Republic and DSW, and, of course, Target and Wal-Mart, Starbucks and McDonald's. For people allergic to brands, Chandler must be hell—even without the 110-degree days.

—Virginia Postrel, "In Praise of Chain Stores"

4. Choose two pieces of your college writing, and examine them closely. Are they examples of strong academic writing? How do they use the key features that this chapter identifies as characteristic of academic arguments? How do they use and document sources? What kind of tone do you establish in each? After studying the examples in this chapter, what might you change about these pieces of writing, and why?

5. Go to a blog that you follow, or check out one like the *Daily Kos*. Spend some time reading the articles or postings on the blog, and look for ones that you think are the best written and the most interesting. What features or characteristics of academic argument do they use, and which ones do they avoid?

Music in U.S.-China Diplomacy

CLAIRE LIU*

The introduction to the general topic stresses the importance of the power of music.

Music is often referred to as a universal language. Humans express their thoughts, emotions, and aspirations through various media of music, which can manifest individual and collective identities and can unite people. But music can also express the differences that separate people. The power of music to unify and divide is nowhere more apparent than between the peoples of two countries that have striven to understand each other for over a century.

The author provides an overview of U.S.-Chinese musical interactions.

China and the United States have a lengthy history of musical interactions accompanying their diplomatic history. One could even argue that for most Chinese, exposure to Western music preceded encounters with Americans themselves. China's introduction to American music stems from a general introduction to Western culture and music by Roman Catholic Jesuit missionaries during the sixteenth and seventeenth centuries, since music was fundamental to missionary education. After foreign powers defeated China in the first of three Opium Wars, the Treaty of Nanjing in 1842 forced China to surrender control of select "treaty ports," one of which was Shanghai.[1] Having a unique geographic status and

---

Chicago style is followed for footnotes and bibliography.

*Claire Liu wrote this essay for a course at Stanford University on the history of U.S.-China relations. A major in international relations, Liu also is studying at the Shanghai Conservatory of Music. Note that she uses her interest in music to help create a strong academic argument about U.S.-China relations. She introduces the three-part structure of her essay in a thesis paragraph on p. 151 and then uses subheadings to guide readers through the three major episodes she traces in this relationship. This essay is documented using the style recommended in *The Chicago Manual of Style*, which is widely used in the field of history.

1. Sheila Nelson and Jindong Cai, *Rhapsody in Red: How Western Classical Music Became Chinese* (New York: Angora, 2004), 26.

exemption from domestic Chinese policies, Shanghai became a hub for foreign economies, cultures, and music. In fact, Shanghai developed a reputation for being the "Paris of the East."

In the early twentieth century, the fall of the Qing dynasty marked the end of the imperial form of government in China and widespread social ferment led to the May Fourth Movement to reform society and build a renewed nation-state.[2] At the same time, another reform effort was started by a new generation of musicians and educators, many of whom were trained in music schools in Europe and Japan or had listened to Western music. They aimed to build a modern infrastructure in China, complete with Western music education. This movement was shaped by influential figures such as Xiao Youmei, Li Delun, and Li Jinhui.

This essay seeks to identify interactions between Americans and Chinese through music during the twentieth century, interactions that carry significance for U.S.-China relations. Three episodes are worth examining to highlight the function that music played in this exchange—the Chinese jazz age of the 1920s and 1930s; Chinese-American diplomacy through Western music during the time of President Richard Nixon and Secretary of State Henry Kissinger; and cultural exchanges after the United States officially recognized Beijing. Although music and politics are very different means of discourse, these episodes reveal that they may be used for similar purposes. Moreover, as China and the United States grow politically and economically more interdependent, music has increasingly been used as an agent for promoting relations between the two nations.

Note the use of an evenhanded, serious tone that characterizes academic argument.

Fairly formal language is used throughout, another characteristic of much academic argument.

A thesis paragraph announces the three-part focus for the essay.

---

2. Andrew F. Jones, *Yellow Music: Media Culture and Colonial Modernity in the Chinese Jazz Age* (Durham: Duke University Press, 2001), 101.

A subheading signals the first part: a major U.S.-Chinese musical encounter through jazz.

THE ROAD TO JAZZ

One of the first direct musical encounters between Americans and Chinese came through the advent of a quintessential American musical form—jazz. The Chinese jazz age resulted from internal and external influences on Shanghai musicians to modernize that coincided with the political, intellectual, and social revolution spawned by the May Fourth Movement. Many elite musicians preferred Western culture to what they viewed as the obsolete traditions of Chinese society. Among this elite was Xiao Youmei. A native of Guangdong province, he was the son of a respected Confucian scholar, grew up in the Portuguese colony of Macao, and was educated in Germany. He was also influenced by friends and neighbors, including a Portuguese minister who introduced him to classical music and Sun Yat-Sen, the revolutionary who introduced him to politics and nationalism.[3] With Sun's help, Xiao received a scholarship to study piano and composition at the Leipzig Music Academy in Germany beginning in 1912. He returned to China in 1921, where he supported the May Fourth Movement.

The author creates an academic ethos with evidence of her careful research on Youmei and the May Fourth Movement and uses logical appeals to argue her points.

Xiao Youmei believed that Chinese music was a stale product of "a thousand years of stagnation," a tradition "at a standstill."[4] He defined Chinese music in terms of what it lacked, which included a tempered scale, functional harmony, counterpoint, orchestration, standardized notation, and engineered instruments such as the piano.[5] These were all qualities of Western music that Xiao found worthy of emulation. Western music, according to Xiao and his supporters, was the result of superior technology, better institutions, and higher standards for practice and performance. A select population in China,

---

3. Nelson and Cai, *Rhapsody in Red*, 93.
4. Jones, *Yellow Music*, 25.
5. Ibid.

he felt certain, was ready to embrace new sounds—especially foreign ones.

At the same time, the musicians and intellectuals of the May Fourth Movement, including Xiao himself, desired to preserve Chinese culture. For example, the musicians modernized traditional Chinese instruments using Western technologies, rather than replacing them with new instruments altogether. Xiao believed that music should help construct a modern, national identity for China. Even Liang Qichao, a cautious intellectual, considered music a means of "aesthetic education, a method by which the intellectual and moral quality of citizenry could be elevated to advance the nationalistic cause."[6]

When Chinese musicians listened to foreign music, they observed and favored polyphonies, functional harmonies, and orchestration of particular genres because these represented what the musicians saw as "forward thinking." This is how American jazz became popular in China in the 1920s and 1930s.

This popularity first developed in Shanghai, the treaty port where Russians, French, Germans, Italians, Japanese, and Americans had carved out colonial territories and established businesses. A Frenchman named Labansat introduced the gramophone to the streets of Shanghai, earning money from passersby who paid to listen to a sampling from this curious machine. In 1908, Labansat set up a recording company called Pathé Orient, which initially manufactured and sold recordings of Peking opera, a traditional Chinese musical genre. The company began recording and selling a new genre of music in the form of popular songs.[7] By turning music into a portable, material object, the success of Pathé Orient created an alternative context for music and musicians that was

Additional evidence from a scholarly book is introduced to support the popularity of jazz in China and help establish the author's credibility or ethos.

---

6. Ibid., 34.
7. Ibid., 53–54.

perfect for the rich sounds of jazz. Soon, major recording companies such as RCA Victor began recording and manufacturing in Shanghai. Mass music culture evolved as department stores and street retailers played a wide range of music, including jazz. The private enterprises and symbols of upward class mobility that were widely despised elsewhere in China were highly popular in Shanghai, and thus they played a crucial role in exposing Chinese people to new ideas embedded in music.

Li Jinhui, an icon of modern Chinese popular music, is widely credited for bringing jazz to China. Born in 1891, Li loved Western music from an early age. In addition to studying and teaching music, he listened to jazz on the gramophone, or "talking box" (*hua xiazi*). Experimenting with blending sounds from jazz with traditional folk tunes, he recorded hundreds of "modern songs" between 1927 and 1936. He also composed songs for fifteen popular films and led the first all-Chinese jazz band at a posh Shanghai nightclub that had traditionally employed only foreigners. He had great ambitions—to enlighten the masses with this nonelitist music, which he likened to the literature of the common people.[8]

In pursuing these goals, Li was working within a larger setting of early multicultural encounters. The Chinese jazz age in Shanghai resulted from two unconventional populations—jazz musicians and Shanghai residents—that attracted one another. Shanghai was a mosaic of many cultures assembled from the shards of colonialism, and its residents manifested their dynamic, multicultural, capitalist qualities through their affinity for progressive music, literature, and lifestyles.

The author summarizes China's encounter with jazz.

Jazz responded perfectly to these needs. At upscale nightclubs and dance halls, American bands frequently performed live for audiences, who included foreigners, Chinese people involved in the city's modern commercial economy, and traditional Chinese. Created by African

---

8. Ibid., 73–79.

A Shanghai dance club in 1926. (Photograph courtesy of Bettman/CORBIS.)

Americans, jazz was an active form of music that liberated its performers and listeners both physically and emotionally. Jazz represented creation, improvisation, and the individual voice. And just as jazz fed the desires of newer Shanghai residents, older Chinese audiences also appreciated an inherent cultural diversity in jazz, a quality that Hollywood and conservative Americans often disregarded. It's no surprise that James Stanley, an American musician, lauded Shanghai for being a "Seventh Heaven for the jazz musician."[9]

REAL MUSIC DIPLOMACY

Social unrest caused by World War II changed the Shanghai music scene significantly, making it difficult for conservatories and other music institutions to function. Security deteriorated in Shanghai, and Xiao Youmei moved his school every few months to a new sanctuary. Many students and faculty fled Shanghai for safer areas

A subheading signals a second stage in U.S-Chinese musical encounters and helps to provide clear structure for the essay.

---

9. Ibid., 148.

Chronological order is used to trace cultural events from the 1940s to the 1960s.

at the request of worried families. But at a sad and troubling time for the country and for the music institutions, a young man named Li Delun enrolled at the Shanghai Conservatory in 1940. He came from a well-to-do Muslim family plagued by social scandal. Taking solace in Western classical music, Li began taking piano lessons in Beijing when he was a teenager. At the same time, he seized every opportunity to attend concerts, take in Hollywood movies, and listen to music shows on the radio that were intended for foreigners. After entering the Shanghai Conservatory, he attended Shanghai Municipal Orchestra concerts and studied conducting.

While Li Delun fortified his cultural education, China followed a different path. In 1949, Mao Zedong led his Communist followers to power over the Nationalists. Ensuing policy disasters (like the Great Leap Forward) and hardline leaders (like those later labeled the Gang of Four) resulted in political turmoil and international isolation for China. During the 1960s, Mao claimed it was time to get rid of the "liberal bourgeoisie" who he believed contaminated Communist thought and class struggle. He launched the Cultural Revolution, during which intellectuals, revolutionary elders, and artists—including musicians—were officially denounced and purged from leadership positions.[10]

A strong topic sentence helps guide readers.

The impact of the Cultural Revolution on music institutions in China was certainly negative. However, in an attempt to control the arts without completely destroying them, the Communist Party, largely influenced by Mao's wife Jiang Qing, established the so-called Hundred Flowers movement (based on the notion that the party should "let a hundred flowers bloom"—allow different ideas to exist—so long as each was compatible with Communist thought). Thus, the government created the Central Philharmonic Society in 1965 in response to Jiang

---

10. Warren I. Cohen, *America's Response to China* (New York: Columbia University Press, 2000), 34.

Qing's call for cultural and arts education through the Party. Li Delun was appointed its conductor.[11] Li was, as I have indicated above, strategically poised for music diplomacy, but for more than two decades after 1949, communication between China and the United States ceased. Not until the early 1970s did the leaders of both nations envision rebuilding a relationship, one in which music would again play a role.

Henry Kissinger and Richard Nixon began establishing a diplomatic dialogue with Mao Zedong and Chinese premier Zhou Enlai in 1971. In an October 5, 1970, article in *Time*, Nixon said that he wanted to improve relations with Beijing: "Maybe that role won't be possible for five years, maybe not even ten years. But in 20 years it had better be, or the world is in mortal danger. If there is anything I want to do before I die, it is go to China. If I don't, I want my children to."[12] Zhou Enlai's warm reception of the American team at the World Table Tennis championship in Japan marked the beginning of "ping-pong diplomacy." Receiving a surprising invitation from the premier for a paid visit to the People's Republic, the U.S. ping-pong team became the first American group allowed into the country since 1949.

But if sports paved the way for the first visit by an American president to Beijing, music also had a role to play. Zhou Enlai suggested to Li Delun that the Central Philharmonic should perform for Henry Kissinger during an October 1971 visit and even suggested that because "Kissinger's German[, y]ou should play Beethoven."[13] Zhou was eager to appeal to Kissinger's tastes and hoped that playing a German composer's work for the German American Secretary of State would do the trick. He believed that music could help represent the common

Sources are used to stress the role of music in bringing U.S. and Chinese leaders together.

---

11. Nelson and Cai, *Rhapsody in Red*, 215.

12. "I Did Not Want the Hot Words of TV," *Time*, October 5, 1970, http://www.time.com/time/magazine/article/0,9171,904333,00.html#.

13. Nelson and Cai, *Rhapsody in Red*, 266.

interests and values of American and Chinese leaders. But while the Central Philharmonic excelled at Beethoven's Fifth Symphony, Jiang Qing and her musical adviser were opposed to the idea of its performance. According to the adviser, Yu Huiyong, the doomed fatalist theme of the Fifth seemed inappropriate for Communist China. Eventually, the Central Philharmonic settled on Beethoven's Sixth Symphony, since it was reportedly about land and nature, though Maestro Li understood that it was actually about a landlord's property.

Nixon's visit in 1972 also called for a personalized repertoire, which included a unique version of none other than "Home on the Range." And like Kissinger, who had been treated to a Peking opera performance that he later described as "an art form of truly stupefying boredom,"[14] Nixon was taken by Jiang Qing to an opera, *The Red Detachment of Women*. While Nixon reported being impressed by its "dazzling technical and theatrical virtuosity," he was also well aware of its propagandistic ambitions.[15] Together, these interactions suggest that though diplomatic exchange occurred cordially and with good intentions, Americans and Chinese still had much to learn about each other.

In the long run, however, these visits laid the foundation for furthering what a joint U.S.-Chinese communiqué called "people-to-people contacts and exchanges in such fields as science, technology, culture, sports, and journalism" that were mutually beneficial.[16] And once again, music would be part of this effort of opening up to the West, as Zhou Enlai advocated a series of measures promoting musical discourse.

Quotations provide vivid detail.

The author uses a logical appeal: music helped lay the foundation for many later U.S.-Chinese exchanges.

---

14. Henry Kissinger, *White House Years* (Boston: Little, Brown, 1979), 779.

15. Richard Nixon, *The Memoirs of Richard Nixon* (New York: Grosset & Dunlap, 1978), 570.

16. "Joint Communiqué of the United States of America and the People's Republic of China," China Through a Lens, China.org.cn, February 28, 1972, http://www.china.org.cn/english/china-us/26012.htm.

The Music of Cultural Exchange

Following the signing of the 1972 communiqué, Zhou invited the American pianists Frances and Richard Hadden, who had lived in the city of Wuhan for some time, to perform in Beijing. Though the concert was not open to the public, it was the first classical music performance by foreigners since the beginning of the Cultural Revolution. A few months later, Premier Zhou granted permission to radio stations to play foreign music. These actions proved to be controversial and met with harsh criticism from Jiang Qing, who argued that no one should assume that such decadent sounds could be played on Chinese radio.[17]

Such events continued, however, and foreign musical ensembles began visiting Chinese concert halls. The London Philharmonic and the Vienna Philharmonic toured the country and collaborated with Chinese music circles. These international orchestra visits paved a path for Zhou's ultimate goal, which was to improve diplomatic relations with the United States. The pinnacle of these encounters took place in September 1973, when the Philadelphia Orchestra, led by the legendary Eugene Ormandy, visited China. Zhou and Jiang Qing had remembered that Ormandy helped to raise money for the medical service of China's Eighth Route Army in a 1940 benefit.[18]

Li Delun planned a warm welcome for the American group. With the approval of Zhou Enlai, the Central Philharmonic Chorus sang "America the Beautiful"—in English—a momentous symbol of camaraderie that moved many of the Americans to tears and eased lingering fears about visiting Communist China.[19]

The tour included six sold-out performances—four

> Another subheading signals the third major section of the essay: the aftermath of the diplomatic rapprochement of the early 1970s.

> Further evidence of U.S.-Chinese musical exchanges is presented. Chronological order continues to organize the essay.

> Sources are introduced in support of the claim of goodwill created by the Philadelphia Orchestra's 1973 visit to China.

17. Nelson and Cai, *Rhapsody in Red*, 268.
18. Ibid.
19. Ibid.

concerts in Beijing and two in Shanghai—and a chance for the Philadelphia musicians to sit in during one of the Central Philharmonic's rehearsals. The repertoire for the first two Beijing concerts comprised symphonies by Mozart, Brahms, and American composer Roy Harris. Tactfully chosen encores included "March of the Workers and Peasants," a popular Chinese revolutionary song and a favorite of Zhou Enlai, and John Philip Sousa's "Stars and Stripes Forever."[20] The visit was heralded as a success by the U.S. media. Harold Schonberg, who chronicled the tour for the *New York Times*, wrote favorably of banquets and warm receptions after every concert.[21] Much publicity was given to the "continual development of better understanding between China and the United States,"[22] as quoted by Ling Ling, the vice president of the Friendship Association, and toasts "to friendship with China" over lavish eleven-course meals featuring Peking duck. Boris Sokoloff, the orchestra's manager, said, "The response has been overwhelming. The hospitality and friendship are unbelievable. The Chinese went all out for us. They are a warm, friendly, delightful people, no question about it."[23] Conductor Ormandy added that this was "the most significant trip that the Philadelphia Orchestra has ever made."[24]

A counterargument is acknowledged: not everyone was impressed with the visits of Western orchestras.

Although the visit was very well received in China, Jiang Qing was less enthusiastic than her fellow citizens were about the music. She was extremely critical of what she considered "bourgeois" music and refused to listen to it or learn about composers who lived in eras when the bourgeoisie rose to power. Great composers such as Tchaikovsky, Schumann, and Debussy were ruled out. At

---

20. Ibid., 269.

21. Harold C. Schonberg, "Philadelphians a 'Big Success' in Their First Concert in China," *New York Times*, September 15, 1973, Sec. A.

22. Nelson and Cai, *Rhapsody in Red*, 270.

23. Harold C. Schonberg, "Philadelphians End China Visit," *New York Times*, September 23, 1973, Sec. A.

24. Ibid.

the root of Jiang Qing's objections was, perhaps, her unwillingness to defer to Zhou Enlai, who had invited three major Western orchestras to China against her wishes. She decided to punish him for his music diplomacy initiatives by proclaiming that from now on China should receive minimal visits from arts groups of capitalist countries. This decision broadened into a campaign against all "bourgeois" music.

When Mao died in 1976, however, Jiang Qing's power faded, she and the other members of the Gang of Four were arrested, and the Cultural Revolution came to an end. Li Delun began rebuilding his Central Philharmonic, and the orchestra performed Beethoven's Fifth on March 26, 1977. The rapturous performance ushered in a new movement with new instruments, new educational outreach activities, and new foreign exchanges. In May 1978, for example, the Boston Symphony Orchestra's conductor Seiji Ozawa accepted an invitation to guest conduct Li Delun's Central Philharmonic. The repertoire featured Chinese, Japanese, and Western music.

The end of the Cultural Revolution allows for more musical exchanges.

Soon after, violinist Isaac Stern, who had been interested in making a trip to China since the rapprochement, wrote to Kissinger asking for help in arranging a visit.[25] In 1979, a delighted Stern received an invitation to make a China tour. Bringing along a film crew to shoot a documentary called *From Mao to Mozart: Isaac Stern in China*, Stern thanked the welcoming committee in Beijing by saying, "We have come here to meet with the Chinese people, to say hello through music, and as musicians, then friends."[26] In his memoir, published twenty years later, he wrote, "I was using music as a kind of passport into the country."[27]

---

25. Isaac Stern, *My First Seventy-nine Years* (New York: Knopf, 1999), 212.

26. *From Mao to Mozart: Isaac Stern in China*, directed by Murray Lerner, performed by Isaac Stern and David Golub (New York: New Video Group, 2001), DVD.

27. Stern, *My First Seventy-nine Years*, 246.

Footage of the trip includes clips of a Chinese orchestra playing "Oh, Susanna!" with traditional Chinese instruments such as the *erhu* and *pipa* as well as Western instruments like percussion drums. Chinese musicians worked to make their guests welcome by playing American tunes—but with Chinese instruments.[28]

Quotations sum up the role of music in the rapprochement between the two countries.

In his memoir, Stern writes, "To have visited China was to have experienced an entirely different world from the one we knew. But it was a world of human beings, toward whom we came to feel great warmth and with whom we ultimately shared a common language—the humanity of music."[29] Stern describes the Chinese as inquisitive, eager, and willing to use musical exchanges to express their desires for identity as well as for friendship.

As Stern suggests, music and culture are always entwined. Music embodies cultural values and directions of thought through sound and performance. Domestic politics and foreign relations are also intimately related, as those in power exercise both in interrelated ways. But the two spheres—music and politics—are also often isolated from each other; we do not usually consider them mutually inclusive. My investigation began as a search for perception of the other through music but led me to realize that music has played a larger and more active role in politics than I thought possible.

The conclusion summarizes the author's findings and reinforces her thesis.

Moreover, the role that music has played in connecting Americans and Chinese people has grown. In the twentieth century, music said what politics and economics often could not say. History has shown that musical relations and political relations can and do benefit one another in significant ways, and the legacies of Xiao Youmei, Li Jinhui, the jazz musicians, Li Delun, and Isaac Stern live on. Orchestras regularly tour both countries, scholars exchange ideas, and young musicians have

---

28. *From Mao to Mozart.*
29. Stern, *My First Seventy-nine Years,* 252.

joined the next generation of cultural ambassadors. As music plays a greater role in U.S.-China relations, Chinese and Americans will fulfill the dreams of the pioneers who believed in the power of music.

BIBLIOGRAPHY

Cohen, Warren I. *America's Response to China*. New York: Columbia University Press, 2000.

From Mao to Mozart: Isaac Stern in China. Directed by Murray Lerner. Performed by Isaac Stern and David Golub. New York: New Video Group, 2001, DVD.

"I Did Not Want the Hot Words of TV." *Time*, October 5, 1970. http://www.time.com/time/magazine/article/0,9171,904333,00.html#.

"Joint Communiqué of the United States of America and the People's Republic of China." China Through a Lens, China .org.cn, February 28, 1972, http://www.china.org.cn/english/china-us/26012.htm.

Jones, Andrew F. *Yellow Music: Media Culture and Colonial Modernity in the Chinese Jazz Age*. Durham: Duke University Press, 2001.

Kissinger, Henry. *White House Years*. Boston: Little, Brown, 1979.

Nelson, Sheila, and Jindong Cai. *Rhapsody in Red: How Western Classical Music Became Chinese*. New York: Angora, 2004.

Nixon, Richard. *The Memoirs of Richard Nixon*. New York: Grosset & Dunlap, 1978.

Schonberg, Harold C. "Philadelphians a 'Big Success' in Their First Concert in China." *New York Times*, September 15, 1973.

———. "Philadelphians End China Visit." *New York Times*, September 23, 1973.

Stern, Isaac. *My First Seventy-nine Years*. New York: Knopf, 1999.

China: The Prizes and Pitfalls of Progress

LAN XUE

ABSTRACT

Pushes to globalize science must not threaten local innovations in developing countries, argues Lan Xue.

Developing countries such as China and India have emerged both as significant players in the production of high-tech products and as important contributors to the production of ideas and global knowledge. China's rapid ascent as a broker rather than simply a consumer of ideas and innovation has made those in the "developed" world anxious. A 2007 report by UK think tank Demos says that "U.S. and European pre-eminence in science-based innovation cannot be taken for granted. The centre of gravity for innovation is starting to shift from west to east."[1]

But the rapid increase in research and development spending in China—of the order of 20% per year since 1999—does not guarantee a place as an innovation leader. Participation in global science in developing countries such as China is certainly good news for the global scientific

This article was written by Lan Xue, a faculty member in the School of Public Policy and Management and the director of the China Institute for Science and Technology Policy, both at Tsinghua University in Beijing, China. It was published in the online edition of *Nature* in July 2008.

Illustrations by D. Parkins.

community. It offers new opportunities for collaboration, fresh perspectives, and a new market for ideas. It also presents serious challenges for the management of innovation in those countries. A major discovery in the lab does not guarantee a star product in the market. And for a country in development, the application of knowledge in productive activities and the related social transformations are probably more important than the production of the knowledge itself. By gumming the works in information dissemination, by misplacing priorities, and by disavowing research that, although valuable, doesn't fit the tenets of modern Western science, developing countries may falter in their efforts to become innovation leaders.

VICIOUS CIRCLE

China's scientific publications (measured by articles recorded in the Web of Science) in 1994 were around 10,000, accounting for a little more than 1% of the world total. By 2006, the publications from China rose to more than 70,000, increasing sevenfold in 12 years and accounting for almost 6% of the world total (see graph, next page). In certain technical areas, the growth has been more dramatic. China has been among the leading countries in nanotechnology research, for example, producing a volume of publications second only to that of the United States.

The publish-or-perish mentality that has arisen in China, with its focus on Western journals, has unintended implications that threaten to obviate the roughly 8,000 national scientific journals published in Chinese. Scientists in developing countries such as China and India pride themselves on publishing articles in journals listed in the Science Citation Index (SCI) and the Social Science Citation Index (SSCI) lists. In some top-tier research institutions in China, SCI journals have become the required outlet for research.

A biologist who recently returned to China from the United States was told by her colleague at the research institute in the prestigious Chinese Academy of Sciences (CAS) that publications in Chinese journals don't really count toward tenure or promotion. Moreover, the institute values only those SCI journals with high impact factors. Unfortunately, the overwhelming majority of the journals in SCI and SSCI lists are published in developed countries in English or other European languages. The language requirement and the high costs of these journals mean that few researchers in China will have regular access to the content. Thus as China spends

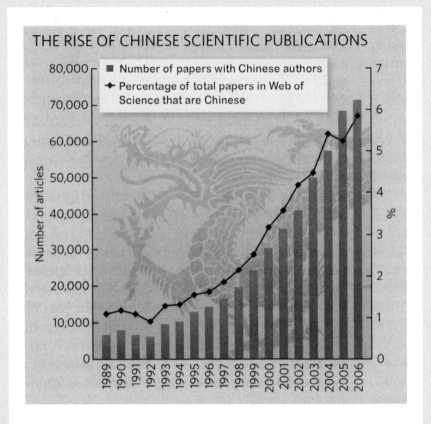

THE RISE OF CHINESE SCIENTIFIC PUBLICATIONS

more and publishes more, the results will become harder to find for Chinese users. This trend could have a devastating impact on the local scientific publications and hurt China's ability to apply newly developed knowledge in an economically useful way.

Several members of the CAS expressed their concerns on this issue recently at the 14th CAS conference in Beijing. According to Molin Ge, a theoretical physicist at the Chern Institute of Mathematics, Nankai University, Tianjin, as more high-quality submissions are sent to overseas journals, the quality of submissions to local Chinese journals declines, which lowers the impact of the local Chinese journals. This becomes a vicious circle because the lower the impact, the less likely these local jour-nals are to get high-quality submissions.[2]

SETTING AGENDAS

Research priorities in developing countries may be very different from those in developed nations, but as science becomes more globalized, so too do priorities. At the national level, developing countries' research pri-orities increasingly resemble those of the developed nations, partly as a result of international competitive pressures. For example, after the United States announced its National Nanotechnology Initiative (NNI) in 2001, Japan and nations in Europe followed suit, as did South Korea, China, India, and Singapore. According to a 2004 report by the European Union,[3] public investment in nanotechnology had increased from €400 million (U.S.$630 million) in 1997 to more than €3 billion in 2004.

Part of the pressure to jump on the international bandwagon comes from researchers themselves. Scientists in the developing world maintain communications with those elsewhere. It is only natural that they want to share the attention that their colleagues in the developed Western world and Japan are receiving by pursuing the same hot topics. The research is exciting, fast-moving, and often easier to publish. At the same time, there are many other crucial challenges to be met in developing countries. For example, public health, water and food security, and environmental pro-tection all beg for attention and resources. If people perceive these research areas as less intellectually challenging and rewarding, the issues will fail to receive the resources, support, and recognition they require. Without better agenda-setting practices, the scientific community will continue to face stinging criticism. It can send a satellite to Mars but not solve the most basic problems that threaten millions of lives in the devel-oping world.

The introduction of Western scientific ideals to the developing world can generate an environment that is hostile to the indigenous research that prima facie does not fit those ideals. The confrontation between Western medicine and traditional Chinese medicine dates back to the early days of the twentieth century when Western medicine was first introduced in China. The debate reached a peak last year when a famous actress, Xiaoxu Chen, died from breast cancer. She allegedly insisted on treatment by Chinese traditional medicine, raising the hackles of some who claimed it to be worthless. Many Chinese still support traditional medicine and say that the dominance of Western medicine risks endangering China's scientific and cultural legacy.

A similar row erupted around earthquake prediction. In the 1960s and 1970s, China set up a network of popular earthquake-prediction stations, using simple instruments and local knowledge. For the most part, the network was decommissioned as China built the modern earthquake-monitoring system run by the China Earthquake Administration. When the system failed to predict the recent Sichuan earthquake, several people claimed that non-mainstream approaches had predicted its imminence. Scientists in the agency have tended to brush off such unofficial and individual predictions. To many this seems arrogant and bureaucratic.

It would be foolish and impossible to stop the globalization of science. There are tremendous benefits to science enterprises in different countries being integrated into a global whole. One should never think of turning back the clock. At the same time, it is possible to take some practical steps to minimize the harmful effects of this trend on local innovation.

PRIORITIZING FOR THE PEOPLE

First of all, there is a need to re-examine the governance of global science in recognition of the changing international geography of science. Many international norms and standards should be more open and accommodating to the changing environment in developing countries. For example, there is a need to re-evaluate the SCI and SSCI list of journals to include quality journals in the developing countries. In the long run, the relevant scientific community could also think about establishing an international panel to make decisions on the selection of journals for these indices, given their important influence. The recent move by Thomson Reuters, the parent company of ISI, to expand its coverage of the SCI list by adding 700 regional academic journals, is a step in the right direction.[4]

English has become the de facto global language of science. Developing countries should invest in public institutions to provide translation services so that global scientific progress can be disseminated quickly. Developing countries can learn from Japan, a world leader in collecting scientific information and making it available to the public in the local language. At the same time, there should also be international institutions to provide similar services to the global science community so that "results and the knowledge generated through research should be freely accessible to all," as advocated by Nobel Laureates John Sulston and Joseph Stiglitz.[5]

When setting agendas, governments in developing countries must be careful in allocating their resources for science to achieve a balance between following the science frontier globally and addressing crucial domestic needs. A balance should also be struck between generating knowledge and disseminating and using knowledge. In addition, the global science community has a responsibility to help those developing countries that do not have adequate resources to solve problems themselves.

Finally, special efforts should be made to differentiate between pseudo-science and genuine scientific research. For the latter, one should tolerate or even encourage such indigenous research efforts in developing countries even if they do not fit the recognized international science paradigm. After all, the real advantage of a globalized scientific enterprise is not just doing the same research at a global scale, but doing new and exciting research in an enriched fashion.

REFERENCES

1. Leadbeater, C. & Wilsdon, J. *The Atlas of Ideas: How Asian Innovation Can Benefit Us All* (Demos, 2007).
2. Xie, Y. et al. *Good submissions went overseas—Chinese S&T journals could not keep up with their overseas peers*, Chinese Youth Daily, 25 June 2008.
3. http://ec.europa.eu/nanotechnology/pdf/nano_com_en_new.pdf
4. http://scientific.thomsonreuters.com/press/2008/8455931/
5. Sulston, J. & Stiglitz, J. *Science is being held back by outdated laws, The Times* (5 July 2008).

7
Structuring Arguments

Structure in arguments defines which parts go where. But as you might imagine, people don't always agree about what parts an argument should include or what their arrangement might be. Traditionally, logical arguments have been described as using either an *inductive* or *deductive* structure, but in practice the two almost always work together.

● ● ●

Inductive reasoning is the process of generalizing on the basis of a number of specific examples: if you usually become sick after eating shellfish, for instance, you'll likely draw the inductive conclusion that you're allergic to such food. In making inductive arguments, you first present the evidence you have gathered and then present your inductive conclusion:

I get hives after eating crawdads.

My mouth swells up when I eat clams.

Shrimp triggers my asthma.

↓

Shellfish makes me ill.

Deductive reasoning, on the other hand, reaches a conclusion by assuming a general principle (called the *major premise*) and then applying that principle to a specific case (called the *minor premise*). The inductive generalization "Shellfish makes me ill," for example, could serve as the major premise for a deductive chain of reasoning that you may recognize from a logic class as a *syllogism*:

Shellfish makes me ill.

Lobster is a type of shellfish.

↓

Lobster will make me ill.

Most of us shorten syllogisms by leaving out the middle term when it seems obvious: "Since all shellfish makes me ill, I shouldn't eat the lobster on this buffet." Aristotle called syllogisms shortened this way *enthymemes* and thought that such concise, self-evident claims played a key role in persuasion. If you can construct sound inductive or deductive arguments and present them clearly in words or images, you will influence most audiences.

But arguments involve more than just the tight reasoning offered within syllogisms and enthymemes. In most rhetorical situations (see Chapter 1), you will also need to define claims, explain the contexts in which you are offering them, defend your assumptions, offer convincing evidence, deal with people who disagree with you, and more. That's a lot of parts to juggle and perspectives to keep in mind. In this chapter, we present three influential ways of thinking about how to structure arguments. Chances are you'll find yourself borrowing from all of them.

The Classical Oration

Nothing may seem more pointless to you than a structure of argument that was devised by Greek and Roman rhetoricians two thousand years ago for presenting cases in courts or making speeches to a senate. Yet the elements of *the classical oration* still influence our attitudes toward persuasion (especially of the political variety) because the oration taught speakers and writers to think of arguments as debates that have winners and losers. The oration has the following sequence of six parts, most of which will seem familiar to you, despite their Latin names:

> *Exordium:* The speaker/writer tries to win the attention and goodwill of an audience while introducing a subject or problem.
>
> *Narratio:* The speaker/writer presents the facts of the case, explaining what happened when, who is involved, and so on. The *narratio* puts an argument in context.
>
> *Partitio:* The speaker/writer divides up the subject, explaining what the claim is, what the key issues are, and in what order the subject will be treated.

Mark Bittman provides a *narratio* that establishes the context for his argument when he follows the changes in American eating over several decades in his article "Why Take Food Seriously?"

LINK TO P. 779

Cicero, considered the greatest of ancient Roman orators

Confirmatio: The speaker/writer offers detailed support for the claim, using both logical reasoning and factual evidence.

Refutatio: The speaker/writer acknowledges and then refutes opposing claims or evidence.

Peroratio: The speaker/writer summarizes the case and moves the audience to action.

If you have ever written a paper in which you introduced a subject, stated a thesis, made a series of supporting arguments (often three, leading up to your best point), and drawn a conclusion, you've shown the influence of the classical oration. And you probably were expected in that paper to anticipate opposing arguments and deal with them.

The structure is powerful because it covers all the bases: readers or listeners want to know what your subject is, how you intend to cover it, and what evidence you have to offer. And you probably need a reminder to present a pleasing *ethos* when beginning a presentation and to conclude with enough *pathos* to win an audience over completely. Here, in outline form, is a five-part updated version of the classical pattern, which you may find useful on many occasions:

Introduction

- gains readers' interest and willingness to listen
- establishes your qualifications to write about your topic
- establishes some common ground with your audience
- demonstrates that you're fair and evenhanded
- states your claim

Background

- presents any necessary information, including personal narrative, that's important to your argument

Lines of argument

- presents good reasons, including logical and emotional appeals, in support of your claim

Alternative arguments

- examines alternative points of view and opposing arguments
- notes the advantages and disadvantages of these views
- explains why your view is better than others

Conclusion

- summarizes the argument
- elaborates on the implications of your claim
- makes clear what you want the audience to think or do
- reinforces your credibility and perhaps offers an emotional appeal

You may notice that the oration (and its contemporary variations) is composed with lines already drawn and the opinions of writers and speakers hardened. Greek lawyers or Roman senators knew what they had to do to prevail in a legal case or win an election. The oration gave orators on both sides of an issue a structure to achieve that success, generating material both in favor of an argument and against an opponent's point of view.

Not every piece of rhetoric, past or present, follows the structure of the oration or includes all its components. But you can likely identify some of its elements in successful arguments if you pay attention to their design. You no doubt recognize the words of the 1776 Declaration of Independence proclaiming the sovereignty of the United States:

> When in the Course of human events, it becomes necessary for one people to dissolve the political bands which have connected them with another, and to assume among the powers of the earth, the separate and equal station to which the Laws of Nature and of Nature's God entitle them, a decent respect to the opinions of mankind requires that they should declare the causes which impel them to the separation.
>
> We hold these truths to be self-evident, that all men are created equal, that they are endowed by their Creator with certain unalienable Rights, that among these are Life, Liberty, and the pursuit of Happiness—that to secure these rights, Governments are instituted among Men, deriving their just powers from the consent of the governed—That whenever any Form of Government becomes destructive to these ends, it is the Right of the People to alter or to abolish it and to institute new Government, laying its Foundation on such principles and organizing its powers in such form, as to them shall seem most likely to effect their Safety and Happiness. Prudence, indeed, will dictate that Governments long established should not be changed for light and transient causes; and accordingly all experience hath shewn that mankind are more disposed to suffer, while evils are sufferable, than to right themselves by abolishing the forms to which they are accustomed. But when a long train of abuses and usurpations, pursuing

invariably the same Object evinces a design to reduce them under absolute Despotism, it is their right, it is their duty, to throw off such Government and to provide new Guards for their future security.—Such has been the patient sufferance of these Colonies; and such is now the necessity which constrains them to alter their former Systems of Government. The history of the present King of Great Britain is a history of repeated injuries and usurpations, all having in direct object the establishment of an absolute Tyranny over these States. To prove this, let Facts be submitted to a candid world.

—Declaration of Independence, July 4, 1776

The Declaration opens with a brief *exordium* explaining to readers why the document is necessary, invoking a broad audience in acknowledging a need to show "a decent respect to the opinions of mankind." Important in this case, it also explains the assumptions on which the document rests. A *narratio* follows, offering background on the situation: because the government of George III has become destructive, the framers of the Declaration are obligated to abolish their allegiance to him. Arguably, the *partitio* begins with "The history of the present King of Great Britain is a history of repeated injuries and usurpations," followed by the longest part of the document (not reprinted here), a *confirmatio* that lists the "long train of abuses and usurpations" by George III.

This section is followed by a briefer *refutatio* addressed to the British people in which the signers argue that they have done all they could to address the crisis more conventionally: "We have warned them ["our British brethren"] . . . We have reminded them. . . . We have appealed to their native justice." All this was to no avail, of course. Not until the very end, however, do the signers assert their central claim, which amounts to a powerful *peroratio*: "That these United Colonies are, and of Right ought to be FREE AND INDEPENDENT STATES."

The authors might have organized this argument even more conventionally—for example, by beginning with the last two sentences of the excerpt and then listing the facts intended to prove the king's abuse and tyranny. But by choosing first to explain the purpose and "self-evident" assumptions behind their argument and only then moving on to demonstrate how these "truths" have been denied by the British, the authors forge an immediate connection with readers and build up to the memorable conclusion. The structure is both familiar and inventive—as your own use of key elements of the oration should be in the arguments you compose.

Rogerian Argument

During the first season of *Saturday Night Live* in 1975, comedian Gilda Radner introduced the character of Emily Litella, a feisty, public-spirited woman who aired her editorial opinions during Chevy Chase's "Weekend Update." Here's a transcript of such an episode, in which Litella objects to "busting" schoolchildren (her mishearing of the term *busing*, which referred to a controversial policy for integrating schools in the 1970s and 1980s):

> *Chevy Chase:* Weekend Update recognizes its obligation to present responsible opposing viewpoints to our editorials. Here to reply to a recent editorial is Emily Litella.
>
> *Emily Litella:* I'm here tonight to speak out against busting schoolchildren. Busting schoolchildren is a terrible, terrible thing. I hear this is going on all over the country. Mean policemen arrest little children and put them in jail in the wrong neighborhood, so they can't even play with their little friends. Imagine, busting schoolchildren! The food in jail isn't good, and even though they get bread, I don't believe they can get toast. Or nice cake. Now, who will tuck them in? Where will they hang their leggings? Where will they set up their little lemonade stands? Well, they don't have toys in jail, except maybe . . .
>
> *Chevy Chase:* [interrupting] Miss Litella?
>
> *Emily Litella:* Yes?
>
> *Chevy Chase:* I'm sorry. The editorial was on *busing* schoolchildren. Busing. Not busting.
>
> *Emily Litella:* Oh. I'm sorry. Never mind.
> —*Saturday Night Live* transcript, season 1, episode 7

Elizabeth Royte employs Rogerian argument as she sorts through the many possible answers to the question of what water we should choose to drink in *Bottlemania*.

LINK TO P. 834

What Emily embodied, week after week, was the inclination of even well-meaning citizens to misrepresent the positions of people with whom they disagree. Most of us probably don't mistake *canker* for *cancer* and *erection* for *election* as Ms. Litella hilariously did, but we may share her tendency to rush into arguments we don't entirely grasp, eager to score points against those we imagine to be opponents. At times, we may lack Emily's willingness to disengage when we're proven wrong.

The ease with which discussions of serious issues can turn into shouting matches moved scholars and teachers of rhetoric to consider whether the nonconfrontational principles applied by psychologist Carl Rogers in personal therapy sessions might also work in public situations.

Gilda Radner's Emily Litella character spoofed an earnest and concerned citizen.

In simple terms, Rogers believed that people involved in disputes should not respond to each other until they could fully, fairly, and even sympathetically state the other person's position. Scholars of rhetoric Richard E. Young, Alton L. Becker, and Kenneth L. Pike gave Rogers's approach this four-part structure when applied to rhetorical situations:

Introduction: The writer describes an issue, a problem, or a conflict. The description is rich enough to demonstrate that the writer fully understands and respects any alternative position or positions.

Contexts: The writer describes the contexts in which the alternative positions may be valid or legitimate.

Writer's position: The writer states his or her position on the issue and presents the circumstances in which that opinion would be valid.

Benefits to opponent: The writer explains to opponents how they would benefit from adopting his or her position.

The key to Rogerian argumentation is a willingness to think about opposing positions and to describe them fairly. In this respect, Rogerian argument differs significantly from the oration, which focuses on the conflicts between positions. In moving through a Rogerian structure, you have to acknowledge that alternatives to your claims exist and that they might be reasonable under certain circumstances. In admitting that your opponents deserve to be at the table, you are (at least theoretically) more likely to search for compromise. In tone, Rogerian arguments steer clear of heated and stereotypical language, emphasizing instead how all parties in a dispute might gain from working together.

Living in a society that encourages individualism and competition, you may find it hard to accept the Rogerian method as practical or even attractive. And don't hold your breath waiting for guests on *Hardball or The O'Reilly Factor* to start restating the opinions of their opponents accurately or to pay more than lip service to bipartisan compromise.

Rogerian-style moves toward understanding and cooperation are not always ineffectual or even new. Consider how Frederick Douglass tried to broaden the outlook of American audiences when he delivered a Fourth of July oration in 1852. Most nineteenth-century Fourth of July speeches followed a pattern of praising the Revolutionary War heroes and emphasizing freedom, democracy, and justice. Douglass, a former slave, had that tradition in mind as he delivered his address, praising the "great principles" that the "glorious anniversary" celebrates. But he also asked his (white) listeners to see the occasion from another point of view:

> Fellow-citizens, pardon me, allow me to ask, why am I called upon to speak here today? What have I, or those I represent, to do with your national independence? Are the great principles of political freedom and natural justice, embodied in the Declaration of Independence, extended to us? And am I, therefore, called upon to bring our humble offering to the national altar, and to confess the benefits and express devout gratitude for the blessings resulting from your independence to us? . . . I say it with a sad sense of the disparity between us. I am not included within the pale of this glorious anniversary! Your high independence only reveals the immeasurable distance between us. The blessings in which you, this day, rejoice, are not enjoyed in common. The rich inheritance of justice, liberty, prosperity and independence, bequeathed by your fathers, is shared by you, not by me. The sunlight that brought life and healing to you, has brought stripes and death to me. This Fourth of July is yours, not mine. You may rejoice, I must mourn.
>
> —Frederick Douglass, "What to the Slave Is the Fourth of July?"

Although his speech may seem confrontational, Douglass is inviting his audience to acknowledge a version of reality that they could have discovered on their own had they dared to imagine the lives of African Americans living in the shadows of American liberty. But the solution to the conflict between slavery and freedom, black and white, oppression and justice, was a long time in coming.

It arrived through the arguments of another African American orator. Speaking at the foot of the Lincoln Memorial in Washington, D.C., on August 28, 1963, Martin Luther King Jr. clearly had Douglass's address (and Abraham Lincoln's Emancipation Proclamation) in mind in the opening of his "I Have a Dream" speech, which bluntly describes the condition of blacks in the United States:

> Five score years ago, a great American, in whose symbolic shadow we stand today, signed the Emancipation Proclamation. This momentous decree came as a great beacon light of hope to millions of Negro slaves who had been seared in the flames of withering injustice. It came as a joyous daybreak to end the long night of their captivity.
>
> But one hundred years later, the Negro still is not free. One hundred years later, the life of the Negro is still sadly crippled by the manacles of segregation and the chains of discrimination. One hundred years later, the Negro lives on a lonely island of poverty in the midst of a vast ocean of material prosperity. One hundred years later, the Negro is still languished in the corners of American society and finds himself an exile in his own land.
>
> —Martin Luther King Jr., "I Have a Dream"

Martin Luther King Jr. on the steps of the Lincoln Memorial

King goes on to delineate the many injustices that were still characteristic of U.S. society. Then, in one of the most brilliant perorations in the history of speechmaking, he invokes a dream of a future in which the United States would live up to its highest ideals, such as those articulated in the Declaration of Independence. The outcome he imagines is a Rogerian-style win/win deliverance for all:

> ... when we allow freedom to ring, when we let it ring from every village and every hamlet, from every state and every city, we will be able

> to speed up that day when all of God's children, black men and white men, Jews and Gentiles, Protestants and Catholics, will be able to join hands and sing in the words of the old Negro spiritual: "Free at last! Free at last! Thank God Almighty, we are free at last!"
>
> —Martin Luther King Jr., "I Have a Dream"

Such moments in political life are rare, but the public claims to prefer nonpartisan and cooperative rhetoric to one-on-one, winner-take-all battles. Indeed, every election cycle includes pleas for a more civil national discourse—though sometimes we have to wait until the end of the campaigns for the true Rogerian notes to be sounded. Here, John McCain in his concession speech following the presidential election on November 5, 2008, urges his supporters to seek common ground with Barack Obama, the new president-elect:

> I urge all Americans who supported me to join me in not just congratulating him, but offering our next president our goodwill and earnest effort to find ways to come together to find the necessary compromises to bridge our differences and help restore our prosperity, defend our security in a dangerous world, and leave our children and grandchildren a stronger, better country than we inherited.

In his victory speech that same night, Obama appeals directly to his opponents by endorsing the sentiments of the first Republican to win the White House, Abraham Lincoln:

> As Lincoln said to a nation far more divided than ours, "We are not enemies, but friends. . . . Though passion may have strained, it must not break our bonds of affection." And, to those Americans whose support I have yet to earn, I may not have won your vote, but I hear your voices, I need your help, and I will be your president, too.

Perhaps such sentiments are just posturing and hypocrisy—the homage that vice pays to virtue. But they also hint that Rogerian rhetoric strikes a chord in many people, especially in a world that is ever more uneasy with confrontational rhetoric and increasingly open to issues of diversity.

It makes sense in structuring your own arguments to learn opposing positions well enough to state them accurately and honestly, to strive to understand the points of view of your opponents, to acknowledge those views fairly in your own work, and to look for solutions that benefit as many people as possible.

Not Just Words

Retired politicians Al Gore, a Democrat, and Newt Gingrich, a Republican, have both been associated with organizations that are seemingly designed to reach across partisan lines to solve problems. Gore's "We" focuses on issues of global warming, while Gingrich's "American Solutions" targets a host of problems, including the need to drill for more oil in the United States. Study the Web sites of these groups, and decide whether either can be described as Rogerian in its approach to argument. Do the sites persuade Americans to solve problems by working together, or do they merely use the language of bipartisanship to advance Democratic and Republican political agendas? Look for language that echoes the Rogerian emphasis on mutual understanding, cooperation, and compromise.

Toulmin Argument

Both the classical oration and Rogerian rhetoric provide general structures for argument, but a system of reasoning that was developed by British philosopher Stephen Toulmin offers advice for building convincing cases. In *The Uses of Argument* (1958), Toulmin presented structures to describe the way that ordinary people make reasonable arguments. Because Toulmin's system acknowledges the complications of life—those situations when people qualify their thoughts with words such as *sometimes, often, presumably, unless,* and *almost*—his method isn't as airtight as formal logic, the kind that uses syllogisms (see p. 171 in this chapter and p. 84 in Chapter 4). But for that reason, Toulmin logic has become a powerful and, for the most part, practical tool for understanding and shaping arguments in the real world. We use his concepts and terminology in subsequent chapters in Part 2.

You'll find Toulmin argument to be especially helpful as a way to come up with ideas and then to test them. Moreover, it will help you understand what goes where in many kinds of arguments. Perhaps most important, you'll acquire solid habits of analysis when you learn to think in Toulmin's terms.

Making Claims

In the Toulmin model, arguments begin with *claims*, which are debatable and controversial statements or assertions that you hope to prove. Notice that in this model the arguments depend on conditions set by others—your audience or readers. *It's raining* might be an innocent statement of fact in one situation; in another, it might provoke a debate: *No, it's not. That's sleet.* And so an argument begins, involving a question of definition.

Claims that are worth arguing tend to be controversial; there's no point worrying about points on which most people agree. For example, there are assertions in the statements *Twelve inches make a foot* and *Earth is the third planet from the sun.* But except in unusual circumstances, such claims aren't worth the time that it takes to argue over them.

Claims should also be debatable; they can be demonstrated using logic or evidence, the raw material for building arguments. Sometimes the line between what's debatable and what isn't can be thin. You push back your chair from the table in a restaurant and declare, *That was delicious!* A debatable point? Not really. If you thought the meal was out of sight, who can challenge your taste, particularly when your verdict affects no one but yourself?

But now imagine that you're a restaurant critic working for the local newspaper, leaning back from the same table and making the same observation. Because of your job, your claim about the restaurant's cannelloni has a different status and wider implications. People's jobs—including your own—might be at stake. *That was delicious!* suddenly becomes a claim that you have to support, bite by bite.

Many writers stumble when it comes to making claims because facing issues squarely takes thought and guts. A claim answers the question *So what's your point?* Some writers would rather ignore the question and avoid taking a stand. But when you make a claim worth writing about, you move slightly apart from the crowd and ask that it notice you.

Is there a danger that you might oversimplify an issue by making too bold a claim? Of course. But making that sweeping claim is a logical first step toward eventually saying something more reasonable and subtle. Here are some fairly simple, undeveloped claims:

> The filibuster tactic in the legislatures of both the United States and Canada ought to be abolished.
>
> It's time to legalize the medical use of marijuana.
>
> NASA should launch a human expedition to Mars.
>
> Vegetarianism is the best choice of diet.
>
> Same-sex unions deserve the same protections as those granted to marriage between a man and a woman.

Note that these claims are statements, not questions. There's nothing wrong with questions per se; in fact, they're often what you ask to reach a claim:

> Questions   What should NASA's next goal be? Should the space agency establish a permanent moon base? Should NASA launch more robotic interstellar probes? Can NASA even afford to send people to Mars?
>
> Statement   NASA should launch a human expedition to Mars.

Don't mistake one for the other.

Good claims often spring from personal experiences. Almost all of us know enough about something to merit the label *expert*—though we don't always realize it. If you're a typical first-year college student, for example, you're probably an expert about high school. You could make trustworthy claims (or complaints) about a range of consequential issues, including competency testing and the administration of athletic programs. And if you aren't a typical college student, the things that make you different—perhaps your experiences at work, in the military, or with a family—could make claims leap to mind. Whether you're a typical or nontypical college student, you might also know a lot about music, urban living, retail merchandising, inequities in government services, and so on—all fertile ground for authoritative, debatable, and personally relevant claims.

Offering Evidence and Good Reasons

A claim is just a lonely statement hanging in the wind—until it teams up with some evidence and good reasons. You can begin developing a claim by drawing up a list of reasons to support it or finding evidence that backs up the point. In doing so, you'll likely generate still more claims that are in need of more support; that's the way that arguments work.

Evidence and Reason(s) ────────▶ So Claim

One student writer, for instance, wanted to gather good reasons in support of an assertion that his college campus needed more officially designated spaces for parking bicycles. He did some research—gathering statistics about parking-space allocation, numbers of people using particular designated slots, and numbers of bicycles registered on campus. Before he went any further with this argument, however, he listed his primary reasons for wanting to increase bicycle parking:

- **Personal experience:** At least twice a week for two terms, he was unable to find a designated parking space for his bike.
- **Anecdotes:** Several of his friends told similar stories. One even sold her bike as a result.
- **Facts:** He found out that the ratio of car to bike parking spaces was 100 to 1, whereas the ratio of cars to bikes registered on campus was 25 to 1.
- **Authorities:** The campus police chief had indicated in an interview with the college newspaper that she believed a problem existed for students who tried to park bicycles legally.

On the basis of his preliminary listing of possible reasons in support of the claim, this student decided that his subject was worth more research. He was on the way to amassing a set of good reasons that were sufficient to support his claim.

In some arguments that you read, claims might be widely separated from the reasons offered to support them. In shaping your own arguments, try putting claims and reasons together early in the writing process to create enthymemes. Think of these enthymemes as test cases or even as topic sentences:

> **Bicycle parking spaces should be expanded because the number of bikes on campus far exceeds the available spots.**

> **It's time to lower the drinking age because I've been drinking since I was fourteen and it hasn't hurt me.**

> **Legalization of the medical use of marijuana is long overdue since it has been proven an effective treatment for symptoms associated with cancer.**

> **Violent video games should be carefully evaluated and their use monitored by the industry, the government, and parents because these games cause addiction and psychological harm to players.**

As you can see, attaching a reason to a claim often spells out the major terms of an argument. In rare cases, the full statement is all the argument you'll need:

> **Don't eat that mushroom: it's poisonous.**

> **We'd better stop for gas because the gauge has been reading empty for more than thirty miles.**

More often, your work is just beginning when you've put a claim together with its supporting reasons and evidence. If your readers are capable (and you should always assume that they are), then they'll begin to question your statement. They might ask whether the reasons and evidence that you're offering really do support the claim: Should the drinking age be changed simply because you've managed to drink since you were fourteen? Should the whole state base its laws on what's worked for you? They might ask pointed questions about your evidence: Exactly how do you know that the number of bikes on campus far exceeds the number of spaces available? Eventually, you've got to address both issues—quality of assumptions and quality of evidence. The connection between claim and reason(s) is a concern at the next level in Toulmin argument. (For more on enthymemes, see Chapter 4, pp. 85–87.)

Anticipate challenges to your claims.

"I know your type, you're the type who'll make me prove every claim I make."

Determining Warrants

Crucial to Toulmin argument is appreciating that there must be a logical and persuasive connection between a claim and the reasons and data supporting it. Toulmin calls this connection the *warrant*. It answers the question *How exactly do I get from the data to the claim?* Like the warrant in legal situations (a search warrant, for example), a sound warrant in an argument gives you authority to proceed with your case.

The warrant tells readers what your (often unstated) assumptions are—for example, that any practice that causes serious disease should be banned by the government. If readers accept your warrant, you can then present specific evidence to develop your claim. But if readers dispute your warrant, you'll have to defend it before you can move on to the claim itself.

When you state a warrant accurately, you sometimes expose a fatal flaw in an argument. However, stating warrants can be tricky because they can be phrased in various ways. What you're looking for is the general principle that enables you to justify the move from a reason to a specific claim—the bridge connecting them. The warrant is the assumption that makes the claim seem plausible. It's often a value or principle that you share with your readers. Let's demonstrate this logical movement with an easy example:

Don't eat that mushroom: it's poisonous.

The warrant supporting this enthymeme can be stated in several ways, always moving from the reason (*it's poisonous*) to the claim (*Don't eat that mushroom*):

Anything that is poisonous shouldn't be eaten.

If something is poisonous, it's dangerous to eat.

Here's the relationship, diagrammed:

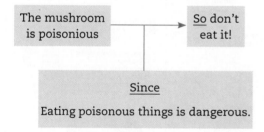

Perfectly obvious, you say? Exactly—and that's why the statement is so convincing. If the mushroom in question is a death cap or destroying angel (and you might still need expert testimony to prove that it is), the warrant does the rest of the work, making the claim that it supports seem logical and persuasive.

Let's look at a similar example, beginning with the argument in its basic form:

We'd better stop for gas because the gauge has been reading empty for more than thirty miles.

In this case, you have evidence that is so clear (a gas gauge reading empty) that the reason for getting gas doesn't even have to be stated: the

The Privacy Commissioner of Canada claims that the information we put onto social networking sites creates our online identities and that we have little control over how companies use or sell those identities. What warrants lie behind these claims?

LINK TO P. 669

POCKET NATURALIST™

MUSHROOMS

AN INTRODUCTION TO FAMILIAR NORTH AMERICAN SPECIES

Ravenel's Stinkhorn

Fading Scarlet Waxy Cap

Parasol Mushroom

Chanterelle

Turkey Tail

WATERFORD PRESS

Fly Agaric
Amanita muscaria
To 7 in. (18 cm)
Cap: Yellow to red-orange cap has white warts
Stalk: Whitish, frilled collar
Gills: Free, white to yellow
Spore Print: White
Habitat: Oak and coniferous forests. Was once used, mixed with milk, to poison house flies.

Destroying Angel
Amanita virosa
To 10 in. (25 cm)
Cap: White, smooth
Stalk: Basal bulb, collar
Gills: Free
Spore Print: White
Habitat: Mixed forests. Young caps resemble edible *Agaricus* mushrooms.

Death Cap
Amanita phalloides
To 5 in. (13 cm)
Cap: Smooth, greenish-yellow
Stalk: Widest at base, collar near top
Gills: Free
Spore Print: White
Habitat: All woods, especially under oaks and conifers.

In a pocket field guide, a simple icon—a skull and crossbones—makes a visual argument that implies a claim, a reason, and a warrant.

tank is almost empty. The warrant connecting the evidence to the claim is also compelling and pretty obvious:

> **If the fuel gauge of a car has been reading empty for more than thirty miles, then that car is about to run out of gas.**

Since most readers would accept this warrant as reasonable, they would also likely accept the statement the warrant supports.

Naturally, factual information might undermine the whole argument: the fuel gauge might be broken, or the driver might know from previous experience that the car will go another fifty miles even though the fuel gauge reads empty. But in most cases, readers would accept the warrant.

Let's look at a third easy case, one in which stating the warrant confirms the weakness of an enthymeme that doesn't seem convincing on its own merits:

> **Grades in college should be abolished because I don't like them!**

Moving from stated reason to claim, we see that the warrant is a silly and selfish principle:

> **What I don't like should be abolished.**

Most readers won't accept this assumption as a principle that is worth applying generally. It would produce a chaotic or arbitrary world, like that of the Queen of Hearts in *Alice's Adventures in Wonderland* ("Off with the heads of anyone I don't like!"). So far, so good. But how does understanding warrants make you better at writing arguments? The answer is simple: warrants tell you what arguments you have to make and at what level you have to make them. If your warrant isn't controversial, you can immediately begin to defend your claim. But if your warrant is controversial, you must first defend the warrant—or modify it or look for better assumptions on which to support the claim. Building an argument on a weak warrant is like building a house on a questionable foundation. Sooner or later, the structure will crack.

Let's consider how stating and then examining a warrant can help you determine the grounds on which you want to make a case. Here's a political enthymeme of a familiar sort:

> **Flat taxes are fairer than progressive taxes because they treat all taxpayers in the same way.**

Warrants that follow from this enthymeme have power because they appeal to a core American value—equal treatment under the law:

> **Treating people equitably is the American way.**
>
> **All people should be treated in the same way.**

You certainly could make an argument on these grounds. But stating the warrant should also raise a flag if you know anything about tax policy. If the principle is obvious and universal, then why are federal and many state income taxes progressive, requiring people at higher levels of income to pay at higher tax rates than people at lower income levels? Could the warrant not be as universally popular as it seems at first glance? To explore the argument further, try stating the contrary claim and warrants:

> **Progressive taxes are fairer than flat taxes because people with more income can afford to pay more, benefit more from government, and can shelter more of their income from taxes.**
>
> **People should be taxed according to their ability to pay.**
>
> **People who benefit more from government and can shelter more of their income from taxes should be taxed at higher rates.**

Now you see how different the assumptions behind opposing positions really are. In a small way, we've stated one basic difference between political right and political left, between Republicans and Democrats. If you decided to argue in favor of flat taxes, you'd be smart to recognize that some members of your audience might have fundamental reservations about your position. Or you might even decide to shift your entire argument to an alternative rationale for flat taxes:

> **Flat taxes are preferable to progressive taxes because they simplify the tax code and reduce the likelihood of fraud.**

Here, you have two stated reasons that are supported by two new warrants:

> **Taxes that simplify the tax code are desirable.**
>
> **Taxes that reduce the likelihood of fraud are preferable.**

Whenever possible, you'll choose your warrant knowing your audience, the context of your argument, and your own feelings. Moreover, understanding how to state a warrant and how to assess its potential makes subsequent choices better informed.

Examples of Claims, Reasons, and Warrants

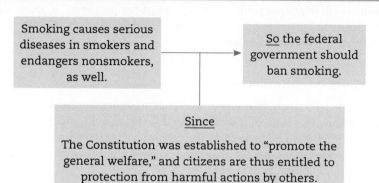

Smoking causes serious diseases in smokers and endangers nonsmokers, as well.

So the federal government should ban smoking.

Since

The Constitution was established to "promote the general welfare," and citizens are thus entitled to protection from harmful actions by others.

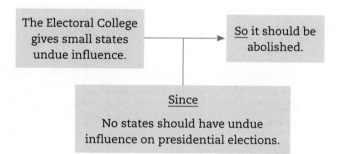

The Electoral College gives small states undue influence.

So it should be abolished.

Since

No states should have undue influence on presidential elections.

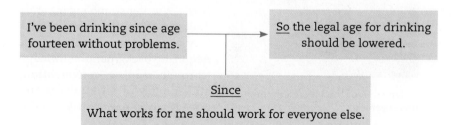

I've been drinking since age fourteen without problems.

So the legal age for drinking should be lowered.

Since

What works for me should work for everyone else.

Be careful, though, that you don't give your audience the impression that you're appealing to whatever warrants work to your advantage. If your readers suspect that your argument for progressive taxes really amounts to *I want to stick it to people who work harder than me*, your credibility may suffer a fatal blow.

Offering Evidence: Backing

As you might guess, claims and warrants provide only the skeleton of an argument. The bulk of a writer's work—the richest, most interesting part—remains to be done after the argument has been outlined. Claims and warrants that are clearly stated suggest the scope of the evidence that you now have to assemble.

An example will illustrate the point. Here's an argument in brief—suitably debatable and controversial, especially in tough times:

> **NASA should launch a human expedition to Mars because Americans need a unifying national goal.**

Here's one version of the warrant that supports the enthymeme:

> **What unifies the nation ought to be a national priority.**

To run with this claim and warrant, a writer first needs to place both in context because most points worth arguing have a rich history. Entering an argument can be like walking into a conversation that is already in progress. In the case of the politics of space exploration, the conversation has been a lively one that has been debated with varying intensity since the 1957 launch of the Soviet Union's *Sputnik* satellite (the first man-made object to orbit the earth) and sparked again after the losses of the U.S. space shuttles *Challenger* (1986) and *Columbia* (2003). A writer stumbling into this dialogue without a sense of history or economics won't get far. Acquiring background knowledge (through reading, conversation, and inquiry of all kinds) is the price that you have to pay to write

A depiction of the Mars Exploration Rover vehicle

on the subject. Without a minimum amount of information on this (or any comparable) subject, all the moves of Toulmin argument won't do you much good. You've got to do the legwork before you're ready to make a case. (See Chapter 3 for more on gaining authority.)

If you want examples of premature argument, listen to talk radio or C-SPAN phone-ins for a day or two. You'll soon learn that the better callers can hold a conversation with the host or guests, fleshing out their basic claims with facts, personal experience, and evidence. The weaker callers usually offer a claim that is supported by a morsel of data. Then such callers begin to repeat themselves, as if saying over and over again that "Republicans are fascists" or "Democrats are socialists" will make the statement true.

As noted earlier, there's no point in defending any claim until you've satisfied readers that any questionable warrants (like those about Republicans and Democrats above) on which the claim is based are defensible. In Toulmin argument, evidence you offer to support a warrant is called *backing*.

Warrant

What unifies the nation ought to be a national priority.

Backing

On a personal level, Americans want to be part of something bigger than themselves. (Emotional appeal as evidence)

In a country as regionally, racially, and culturally diverse as the United States, common purposes and values help make the nation stronger. (Ethical appeal as evidence)

In the past, big government investments such as the Tennessee Valley Authority, Hoover Dam, and *Apollo* moon program enabled many—though not all—Americans to work toward common goals. (Logical appeal as evidence)

In addition to evidence to support your warrant (backing), you'll need evidence to support your claim:

Argument in brief (enthymeme/claim)

NASA should launch a human expedition to Mars because Americans now need a unifying national goal.

Evidence

The American people are politically divided along lines of race, ethnicity, religion, gender, and class. (Fact as evidence)

A common challenge or problem often unites people to accomplish great things. (Emotional appeal as evidence)

Successfully managing a Mars mission would require the cooperation of the entire nation—and generate tens of thousands of jobs. (Logical appeal as evidence)

A human expedition to Mars would be a valuable scientific project for the nation to pursue. (Appeal to values as evidence)

As these examples show, you can draw from the full range of argumentative appeals to provide support for your claims. Appeals to values and emotions might be just as appropriate as appeals to logic and facts, and all such claims will be stronger if a writer presents a convincing ethos. Although it's possible to study such appeals separately, they work together in arguments, reinforcing each other. (See Chapter 3 for more on ethos.)

Finally, arguments can quickly shift downward from an original set of claims and warrants to deeper, more basic claims and reasons. In a philosophy course, for example, you might dig through many layers to reach what seem to be first principles. In general, however, you need to pursue an argument only as far as your audience demands, always presenting readers with adequate warrants and convincing evidence. There comes a point, as Toulmin himself acknowledges, at which readers have to agree to some basic principles, or else the argument becomes pointless.

Using Qualifiers

Toulmin's system works well in the real world because it acknowledges that *qualifiers*—words and phrases that place limits on claims, such as *usually, sometimes,* and *in many cases*—play an essential role in arguments. By contrast, formal logic requires universal premises (*All humans are mortal,* for example). Unfortunately, life doesn't lend itself well to many such sturdy truths. If we could argue only about these types of sweeping claims, we'd be silent most of the time.

Toulmin logic encourages you to limit your responsibilities in an argument through the effective use of qualifiers. You can save time if you qualify a claim early in the writing process. But you might not figure out how to limit a claim effectively until after you've explored your subject or discussed it with others.

Experienced writers cherish qualifying expressions because they make writing more precise and honest:

Qualifiers

few	more or less	often
it is possible	in some cases	perhaps
rarely	many	under these conditions
it seems	in the main	possibly
some	routinely	for the most part
it may be	most	if it were so
sometimes	one might argue	in general

Never assume that readers understand the limits you have in mind. By spelling out the terms of the claim as precisely as possible, you'll have less work to do, and your argument will seem more reasonable. In the following examples, the first claim in each pair is much harder to argue convincingly and responsibly—and tougher to research—than the second claim. (Notice that the second qualified claim doesn't use terms from the list above but instead specifies and limits the actions proposed.)

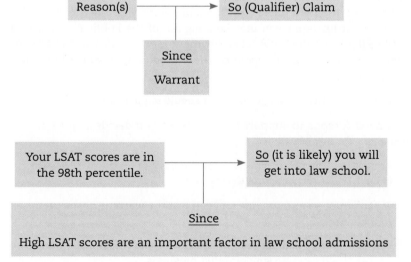

Even though she finds compelling evidence that television helps cause eating disorders in Fiji, Ellen Goodman qualifies her argument by acknowledging that no one can prove a direct causal link.

LINK TO P. 608

Unqualified Claim	People who don't go to college earn less than those who do.
Qualified Claim	*In most cases,* people who don't go to college earn less than those who do.
Unqualified Claim	Welfare programs should be cut.
Qualified Claim	*Ineffective federal* welfare programs should be *identified, modified,* and, *if necessary, eliminated.*

Understanding Conditions of Rebuttal

In *The Reader over Your Shoulder*, Robert Graves and Alan Hodge advise writers to imagine a crowd of "prospective readers" hovering over their shoulders, asking hard questions. At every stage in Toulmin argument (making a claim, offering a reason, or studying a warrant), you might consider conversing with those nosy readers, imagining them as skeptical, demanding, even a bit testy. They may well get on your nerves. But they'll likely help you foresee the objections and reservations that real readers will have regarding your arguments.

In the Toulmin system, potential objections to an argument are called *conditions of rebuttal.* Understanding and reacting to these conditions are essential to buttress your own claims where they're weak and also to understand the reasonable objections of people who see the world differently. For example, you may be a big fan of the Public Broadcasting Service (PBS) and the National Endowment for the Arts (NEA) and prefer that federal tax dollars be spent on these programs. So you offer the following claim:

Claim	The federal government should support the arts.

You need reasons to support this thesis, so you decide to present the issue as a matter of values:

Argument in Brief	The federal government should support the arts because it also supports the military.

Now you've got an enthymeme and can test the warrant, or the premises of your claim:

Warrant	If the federal government can support the military, then it can also support other programs.

But the warrant seems frail: something's missing to make a convincing case. Over your shoulder, you hear your skeptical friends wondering what wouldn't be fundable according to your very broad principle. They restate your warrant in their own mocking fashion: *Because we pay for a military, we should pay for everything!* You could deal with their objection in the body of your paper, but revising your claim might be a better way to parry the objections. You give it a try:

Revised Argument	**If the federal government can spend huge amounts of money on the military, then it can afford to spend moderate amounts on arts programs.**

Now you've got a new warrant, too:

Revised Warrant	**A country that can fund expensive programs can also afford less expensive programs.**

This is a premise that you feel more able to defend because you believe strongly that the arts are just as essential as a strong military is to the well-being of the country. (In fact, you believe that the arts are more important, but remembering those readers over your shoulder, you decide not to complicate your case by possibly overstating it.) To provide backing for this new and more defensible warrant, you plan to illustrate the huge size of the federal budget and the proportion of it that goes to various programs.

Although the warrant seems solid, you still have to offer strong grounds to support your specific and controversial claim. Once again, you cite statistics from reputable sources, this time comparing the federal budgets for the military and the arts. You break them down in ways that readers can visualize, demonstrating that much less than a penny of every tax dollar goes to support the arts.

But once more, you hear those voices over your shoulder, pointing out that the "common defense" is a federal mandate; the government is constitutionally obligated to support a military. Support for public television or local dance troupes is hardly in the same league. And the nation has run up so much debt bailing out banks and corporations that taxpayers won't be eager to subsidize *Swan Lake*, too.

Hmmm. You'd better spend a paragraph explaining all the benefits that the arts provide for the very few dollars spent, and maybe you should also suggest that such funding falls under the constitutional mandate to "promote the general welfare." Though not all readers will accept these grounds, they'll at least appreciate that you haven't ignored

Caroline Kennedy introduces Michelle Obama at the American Ballet Theatre's 2009 opening night spring gala at the Metropolitan Opera House in New York. Advocates of federal funding for the arts have often received political influential support from First Ladies.

their point of view. You gain credibility and authority by anticipating a reasonable objection.

As you can see, dealing with conditions of rebuttal is a natural part of argument. But it's important to understand rebuttal as more than mere opposition. Anticipating objections broadens your horizons and likely makes you more open to change. Recall the earlier section on Rogerian rhetoric: one of the best exercises for you or for any writer is to learn to state the views of others in your own favorable words. If you can do that, you're more apt to grasp the warrants at issue and the commonalities that you may share with others, despite differences.

Fortunately, today's wired world is making it harder to argue in isolation. Newsgroups and blogs on the Internet provide quick and potent responses to positions offered by participants in discussions. Email and instant messaging make cross-country connections feel almost like face-to-face conversations. Even the links on Web sites encourage people to think of communication as a network that is infinitely variable and open to many voices and different perspectives. Within the Toulmin system, conditions of rebuttal—the voices over the shoulder—remind us that we're part of this bigger world. (For more on arguments in electronic environments, see Chapters 14 and 15.)

Outline of a Toulmin Argument

Consider the claim that was mentioned on p. 191:

Claim	The federal government should ban smoking.
Qualifier	The ban would be limited to public spaces.
Good Reasons	Smoking causes serious diseases in smokers. Nonsmokers are endangered by secondhand smoke.
Warrants	The Constitution promises to "promote the general welfare." Citizens are entitled to protection from harmful actions by others.
Backing	The United States is based on a political system that is supposed to serve the basic needs of its people, including their health.
Evidence	Numbers of deaths attributed to secondhand smoke Lawsuits recently won against large tobacco companies, citing the need for reparation for smoking-related health care costs Examples of bans already imposed in many public places
Authority	Cite the surgeon general.
Conditions of Rebuttal	Smokers have rights, too. Smoking laws should be left to the states. Such a ban could not be enforced.
Response	The ban applies to public places; smokers can smoke in private. The power of the federal government to impose other restrictions on smoking (such as warning labels on cigarettes and bans on cigarette advertisements on television) has survived legal challenges. The experience of New York City, which has imposed such a ban, suggests that enforcement would not be a significant problem.

A Toulmin Analysis

You might wonder how Toulmin's method holds up when applied to an argument that is longer than a few sentences. Do such arguments really work the way that Toulmin predicts? After all, knowledgeable readers often don't agree on the core claim in a piece, let alone on its warrants. Yet such an analysis can be rewarding because it raises basic questions about purpose, structure, quality of evidence, and rhetorical strategy. In the following short argument, Alan Dershowitz, a professor at Harvard Law School, responds to a proposal by the school in late 2002 to impose a speech code on its students. Dershowitz's piece, originally published in the *Boston Globe* newspaper, is followed by an analysis of it in Toulmin's terms. Keep in mind what you've learned about analyzing arguments as you read this article.

Testing Speech Codes

ALAN M. DERSHOWITZ

We need not resort to hypothetical cases in testing the limits of a proposed speech code or harassment policy of the kind that some students and faculty members of Harvard Law School are proposing. We are currently experiencing two perfect test cases.

The first involves Harvard's invitation to Tom Paulin to deliver a distinguished lecture for which it is paying him an honorarium. Paulin believes that poetry cannot be separated from politics, and his politics is hateful and bigoted.

He has urged that American Jews who make aliya to the Jewish homeland and move into the ancient Jewish quarters of Jerusalem or Hebron "should be shot dead." He has called these Jews "Nazis" and has expressed "hatred" toward "them." "Them" is many of our students and graduates who currently live on land captured by Israel during the defensive war in 1967 or who plan to move there after graduation.

The Jewish quarters of Jerusalem and Hebron have been populated by Jews since well before the birth of Jesus. The only period in which they were Judenrein was between 1948 and 1967, when it was under Jordanian control, and the Jordanian government destroyed all the synagogues and ethnically cleansed the entire Jewish populations.

Though I (along with a majority of Israelis) oppose the building of Jewish settlements in Arab areas of the West Bank and Gaza, the existence of these settlements—which Israel has offered to end as part of an overall peace—does not justify the murder of those who believe they have a religious right to live in traditional Jewish towns such as Hebron.

Paulin's advocacy of murder of innocent civilians, even if it falls short of incitement, is a paradigm of hate speech. It would certainly make me uncomfortable to sit in a classroom or lecture hall listening to him spew his murderous hatred. Yet I would not want to empower Harvard to censor his speech or include it within a speech code or harassment policy.

Or consider the case of the anti-Semitic poet Amiri Baraka, who claims that "neo-fascist" Israel had advance knowledge of the terrorist attack on the World Trade Center and warned Israelis to stay away. This lie received a standing ovation, according to *The Boston Globe*, from "black students" at

Wellesley last week. Baraka had been invited to deliver his hate speech by Nubian, a black student organization, and [was] paid an honorarium with funds provided by several black organizations. Would those who are advocating restrictions on speech include these hateful and offensive lies in their prohibitions? If not, would they seek to distinguish them from other words that should be prohibited?

These are fair questions that need to be answered before anyone goes further down the dangerous road to selective censorship based on perceived offensiveness. Clever people can always come up with distinctions that put their cases on the permitted side of the line and other people's cases on the prohibited side of the line.

For example, Paulin's and Baraka's speeches were political, whereas the use of the "N-word" is simply racist. But much of what generated controversy at Harvard Law School last spring can also be deemed political. After all, racism is a political issue, and the attitudes of bigots toward a particular race is a political issue. Paulin's and Baraka's poetry purports to be "art," but the "N-word" and other equally offensive expressions can also be dressed up as art.

The real problem is that offensiveness is often in the eyes and experiences of the beholder. To many African Americans, there is nothing more offensive than the "N-word." To many Jews, there is nothing more offensive than comparing Jews to Nazis. (Ever notice that bigots never compare Sharon to Pinochet, Mussolini, or even Stalin, only to Hitler!)

It would be wrong for a great university to get into the business of comparing historic grievances or experiences. If speech that is deeply offensive to many African Americans is prohibited, then speech that is deeply offensive to many Jews, gays, women, Asians, Muslims, Christians, atheists, etc. must also be prohibited. Result-oriented distinctions will not suffice in an area so dominated by passion and historical experience.

Unless Paulin's and Baraka's statements were to be banned at Harvard—which they should not be—we should stay out of the business of trying to pick and choose among types and degrees of offensive, harassing, or discriminatory speech. Nor can we remain silent in the face of such hate speech. Every decent person should go out of his or her way to condemn what Tom Paulin and Amiri Baraka have said, just as we should condemn racist statements made last spring at Harvard Law School.

The proper response to offensive speech is to criticize and answer it, not to censor it.

ANALYSIS

Dershowitz uses an inverted structure for his argument, beginning with his evidence—two extended examples—and then extracting lessons from it. Indeed, his basic claim occurs, arguably, in the final sentence of the piece, and it's supported by three major reasons—although the third reason might be seen as an extension of the second:

> **The proper response to offensive speech is to criticize and answer it, not to censor it,** [because]
>
> - Clever people can always come up with distinctions that put their cases on the permitted side of the line and other people's cases on the prohibited side of the line.
> - It would be wrong for a great university to get into the business of comparing historic grievances or experiences.
> - [W]e should stay out of the business of trying to pick and choose among types and degrees of offensive, harassing, or discriminatory speech.

As Dershowitz presents them, the cases of Tom Paulin and Amiri Baraka suggest that smart people can always find reasons for defending the legitimacy of their offensive speech.

The closest that Dershowitz gets to stating a warrant for his argument may be in the following sentence:

> **The real problem is that offensiveness is often in the eyes and experiences of the beholder.**

He doesn't want individuals dictating the limits of free speech because if they did, freedom would likely be restrained by the "eyes and experiences" of specific people and groups and not protected by an absolute and unwavering principle. Dershowitz doesn't actually offer such a warrant, perhaps because he assumes that most readers will understand that protecting free speech is a primary value in American society.

Dershowitz establishes his ethos by making it clear that although he's offended by the speech of both Paulin and Baraka, he wouldn't censor them—even though Paulin says things that are especially offensive to him. An implicit ethical appeal is that if Dershowitz is willing to experience hate speech on his own campus, then surely the law school should be able to show such tolerance toward its students.

What Toulmin Teaches

Just as few of the arguments that you read are expressed in perfectly sequenced claims or clearly agreed-upon warrants, you might not think of Toulmin's terms as you build your own arguments. Once you're into your subject, you'll be too eager to make a point to worry about whether you're qualifying a claim or finessing a warrant. That's not a problem if you appreciate Toulmin argument for what it teaches:

- Claims should be stated clearly and qualified carefully. Arguments in magazines or newspapers often develop a single point, but to make that point they may run through a complex series of claims. They may open with an anecdote, use the story to raise the issue that concerns them, examine alternative perspectives on the subject, and then make a half-dozen related claims only as they move toward a conclusion. You have the same freedom to develop your own arguments, as long as you make sure that your claims are clear and reasonable.

- Claims should be supported with evidence and good reasons. Remember that a Toulmin structure provides the framework of an argument. Most successful arguments are thick with ideas and different kinds of evidence. You may not think of photographs or graphs as evidence, but they can serve that purpose. So can stories that may go on for many paragraphs or pages. Once you acquire the habit of looking for reasons and evidence, you'll be able to separate real supportive evidence from filler, even in arguments offered by professional writers. When you write arguments, you'll discover that it's far easier to make claims than to back them up.

- Claims and reasons should be based on assumptions that readers will likely accept. Toulmin's focus on warrants confuses a lot of people because it forces readers and writers to think about their assumptions—something that they would often prefer to avoid doing. It's tough for a writer, particularly in a lengthy argument, to stay consistent about warrants. At one point, a writer might offer a claim based on the warrant that makes "free speech" an absolute principle. But later, he might rail against those who criticize the president in wartime, making national morale a higher value than free speech. Because most people read at the surface, they may not consciously detect the discrepancy—although they may nonetheless sense at some level that something's wrong with the argument. Toulmin pushes you to

CULTURAL CONTEXTS FOR ARGUMENT

Organization

As you think about how to organize your writing, remember that cultural factors are at work: the patterns that you find satisfying and persuasive are probably ones that are deeply embedded in your culture. In the United States, many people (especially those in the academic and business worlds) expect a writer to "get to the point" as directly as possible and to articulate that point efficiently and unambiguously. The organizational patterns that are favored by U.S. engineers in their writing, for example, hold many similarities to the classical oration described some two thousand years ago. It's a highly explicit pattern that leaves little or nothing unexplained—introduction and thesis, background, overview of the parts that follow, evidence, other viewpoints, and conclusion. If a piece of writing follows this pattern, American readers ordinarily find it "well organized."

Predictably, student writers in the United States are expected to make their structures direct and their claims explicit, leaving little unspoken. Their claims usually appear early in an argument, often in the first paragraph.

But not all cultures take such an approach. Some expect any claim or thesis to be introduced subtly, indirectly, and perhaps at the end of a work, assuming that audiences will "read between the lines" to understand what's being said. Consequently, the preferred structure of arguments (and face-to-face negotiations, as well) may be elaborate, repetitive, and full of digressions. Those accustomed to such writing may find more direct Western styles overly simple, childish, or even rude.

When arguing across cultures, look for cues to determine how to structure your presentations effectively. Here are several points to consider:

- Do members of your audience tend to be very direct, saying explicitly what they mean? Or are they restrained, less likely to call a spade a spade? Consider adjusting your work to the expectations of the audience.
- Do members of your audience tend to respect authority or show consideration for the opinion of a group? They may find blunt approaches disrespectful or contrary to their expectations.
- Consider when to state your thesis: At the beginning? At the end? Somewhere else? Not at all?
- Consider whether digressions are a good idea, a requirement, or an element that's best avoided.

probe into the values that support any argument and to think of those values as belonging to particular audiences. You can't go wrong if you're both thoughtful and aware of your readers when you craft an argument.

• Effective arguments respectfully anticipate objections readers might offer. In the United States, public argument seems more partisan than ever today. Yet there's still plenty of respect for people who can make a powerful, even passionate case for what they believe without dismissing the objections of others as absurd or idiotic. They're also willing to admit the limits of their own knowledge. Toulmin argument appreciates that any claim can crumble under certain conditions, so it encourages a complex view of argument that doesn't demand absolute or unqualified positions. It's a principle that works for many kinds of successful and responsible arguments.

It takes considerable experience to write arguments that meet all these conditions. Using Toulmin's framework brings them into play automatically. If you learn it well enough, constructing good arguments can become a habit.

RESPOND •

1. Choose a controversial topic that is frequently in the news, and decide how you might structure an argument on the subject, using the general principles of the classical oration. Then look at the same subject from a Rogerian perspective. How might your argument differ? Which approach would work better for your topic? For the audiences you might want to address?

2. Following is a claim with five possible supporting reasons. State the warrant that would support each of the arguments in brief. Which of the warrants would need to be defended? Which one would a college audience likely accept without significant backing?

   We should amend the Constitution to abolish the Electoral College

   • because a true democracy is based on the popular vote, not the votes of the virtually unknown electors.

   • because under the Electoral College system the votes of people who have minority opinions in some states end up not counting.

   • because then Al Gore would have won the 2000 election.

- because the Electoral College is an outdated relic of an age when the political leaders didn't trust the people.

- because the Electoral College skews power toward small and midsize states for no good reason.

3. Claims aren't always easy to find. Sometimes they're buried deep within an argument, and sometimes they're not present at all. An important skill in reading and writing arguments is the ability to identify claims, even when they aren't obvious.

   Collect a sample of eight to ten letters to the editor of a daily newspaper (or a similar number of argumentative postings from a political blog). Read each item, and then identify every claim that the writer makes. When you've compiled your list of claims, look carefully at the words that the writer or writers use when stating their positions. Is there a common vocabulary? Can you find words or phrases that signal an impending claim? Which of these seem most effective? Which ones seem least effective? Why?

4. At their simplest, warrants can be stated as *X is good* or *X is bad*. Return to the letters to the editor or blog postings that you analyzed in exercise 3, this time looking for the warrant that is behind each claim. As a way to start, ask yourself these questions: If I find myself agreeing with the letter writer, what assumptions about the subject matter do I share with the letter writer? If I disagree, what assumptions are at the heart of that disagreement? The list of warrants you generate will likely come from these assumptions.

5. Using a paper that you're writing for this class (it doesn't matter how far along you are in the process), do a Toulmin analysis of the argument. At first, you may struggle to identify the key elements, and you might not find all the categories easy to fill. When you're done, see which elements of the Toulmin scheme are represented. Are you short of evidence to support the warrant? Have you considered the conditions of rebuttal? Next, write a brief revision plan: How will you buttress the argument in the places where it is weakest? What additional evidence will you offer for the warrant? How can you qualify your claim to meet the conditions of rebuttal? Having a clearer sense of the logical structure of your argument will help you revise more efficiently.

   It might be instructive to show your paper to a classmate and have him or her do a Toulmin analysis, too. A new reader will probably see your argument in a very different way and suggest revisions that may not have occurred to you.

8
Arguments of Fact

One roommate to another at the dorm cafeteria: "Stay away from trans fats: they're all artificial and toxic!" "Oh really?" says the other. "After dinner, let's check the facts on that."

For the umpteenth time, the *Times* is carrying a feature story about the real authorship of Shakespeare's plays. All the familiar claimants are mentioned—Francis Bacon, Christopher Marlowe, Ben Jonson, even Edward de Vere, seventeenth Earl of Oxford. But isn't it more likely that the author of *Hamlet*, *Macbeth*, and *Twelfth Night* was the person that audiences who first saw those plays thought wrote them—William Shakespeare of Stratford-upon-Avon?

Members of the faculty council are outraged to learn that the Athletic Department aims to raise $100 million to build an addition to the football stadium. The chair of the council complains in an editorial in the campus paper that the professionalization of college sports—football, in particular—is not consistent with the educational mission of the university as stated in its charter.

When an instructor announces a tough new attendance policy for her course, a student objects on the grounds that there is no evidence that students who regularly attend their lecture classes perform any better than those who do not. The instructor begs to differ.

A nutritionist notes that many people think that taking vitamin E daily will prevent colon cancer, heart attacks, cataracts, impotence in men, and wrinkles. The evidence available in many scientific studies suggests that they are probably wrong.

Understanding Arguments of Fact

Given the pressure on natural environments throughout the world, it's a triumph whenever a threatened plant or animal, such as the Peregrine falcon or the gray wolf, recovers enough to be removed from the endangered species list. Far more typically, species depart the list because they have become extinct. So imagine the excitement in April 2005 when an article in *Science* magazine carried the good news that the ivory-billed woodpecker, a strikingly hand-

some bird not seen for more than sixty years in American forests, had been spotted in Arkansas. The *Science* article staked its claim on the evidence of at least seven sightings by searchers and a brief, blurry videotape of a bird resembling the ivory-billed woodpecker flying away from a naturalist's canoe.

Was the argument sound? At least a few ornithologists remained doubtful, worried that eager colleagues may have mistaken a pileated

The ivory-billed woodpecker by John James Audubon, American naturalist and painter (1785–1851)

Cartoonist Bob Englehard of the *Hartford Courant* takes a jaundiced bird's-eye view of the ivory-billed's "rediscovery."

© 2005 Bob Englehart, The Hartford Courant, and PoliticalCartoons.com

woodpecker, a common bird with similar markings, for the extinct species. And cartoonists predictably had a field day with this elusive bird.

Some skeptics withdrew their objections to the claim after hearing audiotapes recorded in an Arkansas bottomland forest carrying the distinctive call and double-rap sound of the ivory-billed. But blue jays or nuthatches might have made the noises, experts also admitted. What would it take to seal the deal—to assure scientists and birders alike that the ivory-billed woodpecker really did survive in the wilds of Arkansas?

Researchers in Cornell University's computer-graphics program decided to try answering that question by spending more than two years developing a virtual version of the bird, based on hundreds of CAT scans of the only preserved ivory-billed woodpecker left in the world. After painstakingly tracking the virtual bird's flight and simulating the details of the original camera image, the researchers found that the wing patches in the videotape appeared to match those of an ivory-billed rather than a pileated woodpecker. But even this evidence is only enough for scientists to say "there's a good chance" that the ivory-billed is back.

"What we need is a photo," said Russell Chariff of the Cornell Lab of Ornithology to the *New York Times*, discussing the burden of proof as it existed in late 2005. True, a photograph might be faked, especially a digital image. But a clear shot of the woodpecker by a reputable researcher could indeed be the clincher—given all the other tantalizing but not quite conclusive evidence in this case.

In the meantime, bird enthusiasts are still out there in the Arkansas woods, hoping to bring this argument to a conclusion by confirming the bird's existence. Their dilemma will be like that of anyone trying to make a factual argument—to find sufficient evidence for a claim to satisfy a reasonably skeptical audience (in this case, of scientists, naturalists, and birders).

Factual arguments come in many varieties with different standards of proof. What they have in common is an attempt to establish whether something is or is not so—that is, whether a thing exists (*the ivory-billed*) or whether claims made about something are true (*The poverty rate is higher in Mississippi than in Texas*). At first glance, you might object that these aren't arguments at all but just a matter of looking things up and writing a report. And you'd be right to an extent: people don't ordinarily argue factual matters that are settled or agreed upon (*The earth orbits the sun*) or that might be decided with simple research (*Nelson Mandela was South Africa's first black president*) or the equivalent of a rule (*One foot equals 0.3048 meters*).

Transmitting facts, it would seem, should be free of the pressures and biases of argument. Yet facts become arguments when they're controversial in themselves or when they're used to challenge or change people's beliefs. A factual argument about the existence of a woodpecker has a kind of clean scientific logic to it, but there's passion in the debate because so many researchers want the bird to survive. And there's resistance among those who don't want to rush to judgment until the evidence is definitive—as it might one day be in this case.

Arguments of fact do much of the heavy lifting in our world. They report on what has been recently discovered or explore the implications of that new information and the conflicts it may engender. In recent years, for instance, we've seen plenty of contrary medical reports that raise questions about the safety or efficacy of prescription drugs, vitamin regimens, or surgical procedures. Such news has become so routine that the public is asking increasingly sophisticated questions about the studies, such as who sponsored them, who or what exactly was studied, over how many years, and among which populations. Healthy skepticism is the common attitude now, rather than simple acceptance of what the scientific community reports.

Mizuko Ito is the lead author of a study of the culture of "geeking out," which argues that a complex and intellectually engaged online culture exists among kids and teenagers; it thus counters those who believe that the young only waste time online.

LINK TO P. 686

Some factual arguments make the public aware of information that's already available to anyone who is willing to do the work of finding it and studying its implications. Malcolm Gladwell, author of *The Tipping Point*, *Blink*, and *Outliers*, has exposed patterns in our cultural behavior that seem obvious after he's pointed them out. *Blink*, for example, argues that people routinely use gut feelings to make sound (as well as dubious) judgments, an argument that has important repercussions for business, education, and the military—if Gladwell is right.

But serious factual arguments—especially those that touch on public issues—almost always have consequences. *Can we rely on wind and solar power to solve our energy needs? Will the Social Security trust fund really go broke? Should you heed the latest warnings about salmonella in tomatoes?* Various publics, national or local, need well-reasoned factual arguments on subjects of this kind to make well-informed decisions. Such arguments educate audiences.

For the same reason, we need arguments that correct or challenge beliefs and assumptions that are held widely within a society on the basis of inadequate or incomplete information. Corrective arguments appear daily in the national media, often based on detailed studies that are written by scientists, researchers, or thinkers and that the public may not encounter. Many people, for example, believe that talking on a cell phone while driving is just like listening to the radio. But their intuition is not based on hard information: more and more scientific studies suggest that using a cell phone in a car is comparable to driving under the influence of alcohol. As a result, some states have banned the use of handheld cell phones in cars.

Factual arguments also routinely address broad questions about the history or myths that societies want to believe about themselves. For example, are the accounts that we have of the American founding—or the Civil War, Reconstruction, or the heroics of the "Greatest Generation" in World War II—indeed accurate? Or do the "facts" that we believe today sometimes reflect the perspectives and prejudices of earlier times or ideologies? Scholars and historians frequently claim to be completing the historical record or looking for new information and new ways of interpreting evidence. Such revisionist history is almost always controversial and rarely settled: the British and Americans will always tell different versions of what happened in North America in 1776.

It's especially important to have factual arguments that flesh out or correct what's narrowly or mistakenly reported—whether by news media, corporations, or branches of government. For good or ill, the words of public figures and the actions of institutions, from churches to news organizations, are now always on record and searchable. When, for example, the *New York Times* criticized federal officials for cutting money for flood-control measures in the Mississippi Delta prior to the New Orleans hurricane of 2005, critics of the *Times* quickly located editorials from the same paper in 1993 and 1997 criticizing spending proposals for flood control. Corrective arguments can sometimes play like a game of "Gotcha!" but they broaden readers' perspectives and help them make judgments on the basis of better information. (They also suggest that our institutions are often just as inconsistent, fallible, and petty as the rest of us.)

As you probably suspect, factual arguments have a way of adding interest and complexity to our lives, taking what might seem simple and adding new dimensions to it. In many situations, they're the precursors to other forms of analysis, especially causal and proposal arguments. Before we can explore causes or solve problems, we need to know the facts on the ground.

Heath Ledger's powerful embodiment of the Joker in *The Dark Knight* was the last role played by this talented actor, who died suddenly six months before the film was released in the summer of 2008. Amid a swirl of rumors and gossip, even meticulous medical work couldn't determine all the "facts" of his death.

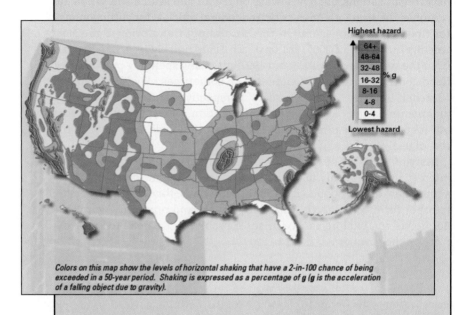

Colors on this map show the levels of horizontal shaking that have a 2-in-100 chance of being exceeded in a 50-year period. Shaking is expressed as a percentage of g (g is the acceleration of a falling object due to gravity).

Legend:
Highest hazard
64+
48-64
32-48
16-32 %g
8-16
4-8
0-4
Lowest hazard

Not Just Words

Above is a National Seismic-Hazard Map, which was created by the U.S. Geological Survey from data collected over the last hundred years. Look closely at this map, and then offer several different factual claims that might be supported by the evidence you find there. Or go to the Web site of the Geological Survey at http://neic.usgs.gov/neis/eqlists/eqstats.html, and study some of its other data for earthquakes in the United States and worldwide.

Characterizing Factual Arguments

Factual arguments tend to be driven by perceptions and evidence. A writer first notes something new or different or mistaken and wants to draw attention to that fact. Or researchers notice a pattern that leads them to look more closely at some phenomenon or behavior, exploring questions such as *What if?* or *How come?* They're also motivated by simple human curiosity or suspicion: *If being fat is so unhealthy, why aren't mortality rates rising? Just how different are the attitudes of people in so-called red and blue states?*

Such observations can lead quickly toward *hypotheses*—that is, toward tentative and plausible statements of fact whose merits need to be examined more closely. *Maybe being a little overweight isn't as bad for people as we've been told. Maybe the differences between blue and red staters have been exaggerated by media types looking for a story.* To support such hypotheses, writers then have to uncover evidence that reaches well beyond the casual observations that triggered the initial interest—like a news reporter motivated to see whether there's a verifiable story behind a source's tip.

For instance, the authors of *Freakonomics*, Stephen J. Dubner and Steven Levitt, were intrigued by the National Highway Traffic Safety Administration's claim that car seats for children were 54 percent effective in preventing deaths in auto crashes for children below the age of four. In a *New York Times* op-ed column entitled "The Seat Belt Solution," they posed an important question about that factual claim:

> But 54 percent effective compared with what? The answer, it turns out, is this: Compared with a child's riding completely unrestrained.

Their initial question about that claim led them to a more focused inquiry, then to a database on auto crashes, and then to a surprising conclusion: for kids above age twenty-four months, those in car seats were statistically safer than those without any protection but weren't safer than those confined by seat belts (which are much simpler, cheaper, and more readily available devices). Looking at the statistics every which way, the authors wonder if children older than two years would be just as well off physically—and their parents less stressed and better off financially—if the government mandated seat belts rather than car seats for them.

What kinds of evidence typically appear in sound factual arguments? The simple answer might be "all sorts," but a case can be made that

Safer than a seat belt?

factual arguments try to rely on "hard evidence" more than on logic and reason (see Chapter 4). Even so, some pieces of evidence are harder and more convincing than others.

During the 2008 election campaign, the Republican vice presidential nominee, Alaska governor Sarah Palin, offered a number of facts to support her claims that she was a strong reformer who rejected earmarks—"pork-barrel" spending projects that members of Congress sponsor primarily to benefit their own districts or states. Palin insisted on numerous occasions, for example, that she had said "no thanks to that bridge to nowhere" (a proposal to build an expensive bridge to a sparsely populated island off the Alaska coast), but little hard evidence backed her up. In fact, journalists found considerable hard evidence—such as quotations from interviews and news photos and videos—showing that Palin had actually supported the project up until 2006, when support for it in Congress began to wane. Persistent attention to the facts of this case showed that what was being presented as "hard evidence" was very soft indeed. Eventually, Palin dropped this claim from her stump speech.

Fudging the facts? The Gravina Island bridge project proved a campaign issue to nowhere for Alaska governor Sarah Palin when she ran for vice president.

Developing a Factual Argument

Factual arguments on the same subject can bubble with outrage and anger or speak with the dispassionate drone of science. The following two claims circulated in the media shortly after Hurricane Katrina struck the Gulf Coast, and they suggest the range of factual argument in both substance and style. The first, by Ross Gelbspan, shows the sweeping claims and pithy style of fact-based editorial commentary. It's angry and speculative:

> The hurricane that struck Louisiana and Mississippi on Monday was nicknamed Katrina by the National Weather Service. Its real name is global warming. . . .
> Although Katrina began as a relatively small hurricane that glanced off southern Florida, it was supercharged with extraordinary intensity by the high sea surface temperatures in the Gulf of Mexico.
> The consequences are as heartbreaking as they are terrifying.

Unfortunately, few people in America know the real name of Hurricane Katrina because the coal and oil industries have spent millions of dollars to keep the public in doubt about the issue.

The reason is simple: To allow the climate to stabilize requires humanity to cut its use of coal and oil by 70 percent. That, of course, threatens the survival of one of the largest commercial enterprises in history.

—Ross Gelbspan, "Hurricane Katrina's Real Name"

The second claim, by William M. Gray and Philip J. Klotzback writing for the Department of Atmospheric Science at Colorado State University, addresses the same issue but provides its answers in a different style:

Many individuals have queried whether the unprecedented landfall of four destructive hurricanes in a seven-week period during August–September 2004 and the landfall of two more major hurricanes in the early part of the 2005 season is related in any way to human-induced climate changes. There is no evidence that this is the case. If global warming were the cause of the increase in United States hurricane landfalls in 2004 and 2005 and the overall increase in Atlantic basin major hurricane activity of the past eleven years (1995–2005), one would expect to see an increase in tropical cyclone activity in the other storm basins as well (i.e., West Pacific, East Pacific, Indian Ocean, etc.). This has not occurred. When tropical cyclones worldwide are summed, there has actually been a slight decrease since 1995. In addition, it has been well documented that the measured global warming during the 25-year period of 1970–1994 was accompanied by a downturn in Atlantic basin major hurricane activity over what was experienced during the 1930s through the 1960s.

—William M. Gray and Philip J. Klotzback, "Forecast of Atlantic Hurricane Activity for September and October 2005 and Seasonal Update through August"

Any factual argument that you might compose—from how you state your claim to how you present evidence and the language you use—will be shaped by the occasion for the argument and the audiences that you intend to reach. But we can offer some general advice to help you get started.

Identifying an Issue

Before you can offer a factual argument, you need to identify an issue or problem that will interest (or that you believe should interest) readers.

You might look, for example, for apparent contradictions or tensions in local or national communities—situations or phenomena that are out of the ordinary in the expected order of things. You might have read that the trailers given to victims of the Katrina disaster in 2006 turned out to contain toxic chemicals: what is the latest information on this issue, and what has happened to those who were living in the trailers? Or you might notice that many people you know are deciding not to attend college. How widespread is this change, and who are the people making this choice? Or you might explore questions that many people have already formulated but haven't yet examined in detail or that have been hotly contested for some time (such as whether cell phones are really as safe as claimed or whether we'll discover twenty years from now that a generation of Americans has slow-cooked its gray matter).

Whole books are written when authors decide to pursue factual questions, even those that have been explored before. But you want to be careful not to argue matters that pose no challenge to you or your audiences. You're not offering anything new if you try to persuade readers that smoking is harmful to their health. But perhaps knowing that Microsoft founder Bill Gates and New York mayor Michael Bloomberg together pledged millions to conduct antismoking campaigns around the world might lead you to uncover information about smoking on your own campus that might provoke thoughtful examinations of the issue. Perhaps you suspect that smoking is correlated in interesting ways to academic majors, gender, or ethnic identity. Would it be important to recognize these facts—if you could prove them?

Some quick preliminary research and reading might allow you to move from an intuition, a hunch, or mere interest to a hypothesis (a tentative statement of your claim): *Women in the liberal arts are the heaviest smokers on campus.* As noted earlier, factual arguments often provoke other kinds of analysis. Where might such a claim lead if you could find evidence to support it? You might find yourself moving irresistibly toward arguments about the cause of the phenomenon, but don't do this until you establish its basis in fact.

On the other hand, the large number of cigarette butts on the ground outside the business school might suggest that your hypothesis is questionable. It may be that men studying accounting and marketing blacken their lungs as thoroughly as do women in philosophy classes. What do you do now? Abandon your hypothesis or modify it. That's what hypotheses are for. They are works in progress.

In her article "Professors' Liberalism Contagious? Maybe Not," Patricia Cohen offers an argument of fact when she presents the results of recent studies finding that professors do not affect students' political opinions.

LINK TO P. 936

Facts and Academic Arguments

As you might expect, facts play an instrumental role in academic arguments, whether for an essay in art history, a presentation in electrical engineering, or a proposal in human biology. Look how a communication scholar uses facts in an academic argument about privacy and social networking in the United States:

> According to three 2005 Pew Reports (Lenhart, 2005; Lenhart, et al., 2005; Lenhart and Madden, 2005), 87 percent of American teens aged 12–17 are using the Internet. Fifty-one percent of these teenagers state that they go online on a daily basis. Approximately four million teenagers or 19 percent say that they create their own weblogs (personal online journals) and 22 percent report that they maintain a personal Web page (Lenhart and Madden, 2005). In blogs and on personal Web sites, teenagers are providing so much personal information about themselves that it has become a concern. Today, content creation is not only sharing music and videos; it involves personal diaries.
>
> —Susan B. Barnes, "A Privacy Paradox: Social Networking in the United States"

Note that this researcher uses facts drawn from reports produced by the Pew Research Center, a well-known and respected organization. In each case, she tells readers exactly where she got her facts, and she provides a list of references at the end of the article to help readers locate the specific sources. Choose an assignment that you are working on now or have completed in the past that calls for the use of facts. Then examine your writing with an eye to how effective your facts are: Do you let readers know the sources of your facts? Are all the sources credible? What additional facts might improve this piece of writing?

What kinds of research does Libby Sanders depend upon in developing her argument of fact about the increasing number of blue-collar workers returning to college? Could you use similar research in crafting your own factual argument?

LINK TO P. 949

Researching Your Hypothesis

How and where you research your subject will depend, naturally, on your subject. You'll certainly want to review Chapter 16, "What Counts as Evidence," and Chapter 19, "Evaluating and Using Sources," before constructing an argument of fact. Libraries and the Web will provide you deep resources on almost every subject. Your task will typically be to separate the best sources from all the rest. The word *best* here has many connotations: some reputable sources may be too technical for your audiences; some accessible sources may be pitched too low or be too far removed from the actual facts.

You'll be making judgments like this routinely. But don't hesitate to go to primary sources whenever you can. For example, when gathering a comment from a source on the Web, trace it whenever possible to its original site, and read the comment in its full context. When statistics are quoted, follow them back to the source that originally offered them to be sure that they're recent and reputable. Instructors and librarians can help you appreciate the differences. Understand that even sources with pronounced biases can furnish useful information, provided that you know how to use them, take their limitations into account, and then share what you know about the sources with your readers.

Sometimes, you'll be able to do primary research on your own, especially when your subject is local and you have the resources to do it. You might be able to conduct a competent survey of campus opinions and attitudes, for example, or you could study budget records to determine trends in faculty salaries, tuition, student fees, and so on. Primary research of this sort can be challenging because even the simplest surveys or polls have to be intelligently designed and executed in a way that samples a representative population (see Chapter 4). But the work could pay off in an argument that brings new information to readers.

Refining Your Claim

As you learn more about your subject, you might revise your hypothesis to reflect what you've discovered. In many cases, these revised hypotheses will grow increasingly complex and specific. Following are three versions of essentially the same claim, with each iteration offering more information to help readers assess its merit:

> **Americans really did land on the moon, despite what some people think!**

> **Since 1969, when the *Eagle* supposedly landed on the moon, some people have been skeptical about the success of the USA's *Apollo* program.**

New details about a subject often lead to new ways to support or refute a claim about it. Conspiracy theorists claim that the absence of visible stars in photographs of the moon landing is evidence that it was staged, but photographers know that the camera exposure needed to capture the foreground—astronauts in their bright space suits—would have made the stars in the background too dim to see.

> Despite plentiful hard evidence to the contrary—from *Saturn V* launch-es witnessed by thousands to actual moon rocks tested by indepen-dent labs worldwide—some people persist in believing that NASA's moon landings were actually filmed on deserts in the American south-west as part of a massive propaganda fraud.

As you advance in your research, your hypothesis or thesis will likely pick up even more qualifying words and expressions, which help you to make reasonable claims. Qualifiers—words and phrases such as *some, most, few, for most people, for a few users, under specific conditions, usually, occasionally, seldom,* and so on—will be among your most valuable tools.

It sometimes is important to set your claim into a context that helps explain it to others who may find it untenable or hostile. For instance, professor of English Vincent Carretta anticipated strong objections after he uncovered evidence that Olaudah Equiano—the author of *The Interesting Narrative* (1789), a much-cited autobiographical account of his Middle Passage voyage and subsequent life as a slave—may have been born in South Carolina and not in western Africa. Speaking to the *Chronicle of Higher Education*, Carretta explains why Equiano may have made up African origins to serve a larger cause—a growing antipathy to slavery and slave markets:

> "Whether [Equiano] invented his African birth or not, he knew that what that movement needed was a first-person account. And because they were going after the slave trade, it had to be an account of some-one who had been born in Africa and was brought across the Middle Passage. An African-American voice wouldn't have done it."
>
> —Jennifer Howard, "Unraveling the Narrative"

Carretta asks readers to see that the new facts that he has discovered about *The Interesting Narrative* do not diminish the work's historical significance. If anything, his work has added new dimensions to its meaning and interpretation.

Deciding Which Evidence to Use

In this chapter, we've blurred the distinction between factual arguments for scientific and technical audiences and those for the general public (in media such as magazines, blogs, and television documentaries). In the former, you might find exhaustive appendices of information, including charts, graphs, and full databases. Scientific claims themselves are usually stated with great economy and precision, followed by a thorough account of methods and results. The article reporting the discovery of the ivory-billed woodpecker makes its point in two sentences: "The ivory-billed woodpecker (*Campephilus principalis*), long suspected to be extinct, has been rediscovered in the Big Woods region of eastern Arkansas. Visual encounters during 2004 and 2005, and analysis of a video clip from April 2004, confirm the existence of at least one male." The evidence then follows.

Less scientific factual arguments—claims about our society, institutions, behaviors, habits, and so on—are seldom this clean and draw on evidence from a great many different sources. For example, when the National Endowment for the Arts (NEA) published a study entitled "Reading at Risk" in June 2004 to report "the declining importance of literature to our populace," it drew its conclusion by studying a variety of phenomena in a large population:

> This survey investigated the percentage and number of adults, age 18 and over, who attended artistic performances, visited museums, watched broadcasts of arts programs, or read literature. The survey sample numbered more than 17,000 individuals, which makes it one of the most comprehensive polls of art and literature consumption ever conducted.
>
> —National Endowment for the Arts, "Reading at Risk"

Still, you could imagine other ways to measure an interest in literature, some of which might include nontraditional (graphic novels, for instance) or electronic forms not examined in the NEA study. A phenomenon as broad as "literature" is difficult to define factually because few people can agree on its dimensions. So for any study, you'll have to make choices about what evidence to draw from and be prepared to defend those choices.

Alison Bechdel's *Fun Home,* a graphic novel, is considered literature by many but a "mere comic" by others.

By contrast, a factual argument about a specific literary work (rather than the larger phenomenon of reading) might be a significantly easier task to manage because you can find much of your evidence in the poem, play, or novel itself, supplemented by historical and biographical information on the life and times of the author. For instance, is *Frankenstein* (1831) really a story about the growing impact of science and industrialism on Europe? To answer the question, you could refer to passages in Mary Shelley's novel itself and to information from histories of the period during which it was written showing a society experiencing rapid technological change.

Often, you may have only a limited number of words or pages in which to make a factual argument. What do you do then? You need to present your best evidence as powerfully as possible. But that's not difficult. You can make a persuasive factual case with just a few examples: three or four often suffice to make a point. Indeed, going on too long or presenting even good data in a way that makes it seem uninteresting or pointless can undermine a claim.

Presenting Your Evidence

In *Hard Times* (1854), British author Charles Dickens poked fun at a pedagogue he named Thomas Gradgrind, who preferred hard facts before all things human or humane. When poor Sissy Jupe (designated "girl number twenty" in his classroom) is unable at his command to define *horse*, Gradgrind turns to his star pupil:

> "Bitzer," said Thomas Gradgrind. "Your definition of a horse."
>
> "Quadruped. Graminivorous. Forty teeth, namely twenty-four grinders, four eyeteeth, and twelve incisive. Sheds coat in the spring; in marshy countries, sheds hoofs, too. Hoofs hard, but requiring to be shod with iron. Age known by marks in mouth." Thus (and much more) Bitzer.
>
> "Now girl number twenty," said Mr. Gradgrind. "You know what a horse is."
>
> —Charles Dickens, *Hard Times*

But does Bitzer? Rattling off facts about a subject isn't quite the same thing as knowing it, especially when your goal is, as it is in an argument of fact, to educate and persuade audiences. So you must take care how you present your evidence.

Factual arguments, like any others, take many forms. They can be as simple and pithy as a letter to the editor (or Bitzer's definition of a horse) or as comprehensive and formal as a senior thesis or even a dissertation. The National Commission on Adult Literacy's 2008 report, "Reach Higher, America: Overcoming Crisis in the U.S. Workforce," has the design of a formal scientific report, with sixty-five references, ten appendices, and a dozen figures and tables. Like many such studies, it also includes a foreword, an executive summary, and a detailed table of contents. All these elements help establish the ethos of the work, making it seem serious, credible, well conceived, and thorough.

For an example of how to use design and visuals in factual arguments, see the *New York Times* graphic entitled "Satisfying the National Thirst." What are the implications of such an argument?

.... **LINK TO P. 840**

Considering Design and Visuals

Precisely because factual arguments often rely on evidence that can be measured, counted, computed, or illustrated, they benefit from thoughtful, even artful presentation of data. When you prepare a factual argument, consider how its design can enhance the evidence you have to offer. If you have an argument that can be translated into a table, chart, or graph (see Chapter 14), try it. If you have lots of examples, you might present them in a list (bulleted or otherwise) and keep the language in each item roughly parallel.

Photos and images have many uses in factual arguments, from technical illustration to imaginative re-creation. Today, even amateurs can manipulate digital images in the way that only spy agencies could in the not-so-distant past, erasing people from photographs, for example. But images retain their power to illustrate what readers might otherwise have to imagine—whether actual conditions of drought, poverty, or

Figure 1

88 Million Adults Have At Least One Education Barrier

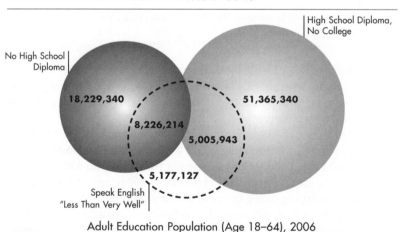

Adult Education Population (Age 18–64), 2006

<u>Source</u>: *U.S. Census Bureau, 2006 American Community Survey (Public Use Microdata Samples); prepared by National Center for Higher Education Management Systems (NCHEMS). Unduplicated population = 88,003,964.*

This figure from the National Commission on Adult Literacy's report "Reach Higher, America: Overcoming Crisis in the U.S. Workforce" illustrates the report's use of visual elements to make information accessible.

Soldiers rescue a survivor from the rubble after an earthquake in Beichuan, China, on May 13, 2008. Photos help readers understand the details of factual arguments.

disaster like the earthquake that hit China in 2008, or the dimensions of the Roman forum as it existed in the time of Julius Caesar. Readers expect the arguments they read to include visual elements, and there's little reason not to offer this assistance.

Finally, consider how your opportunities for presenting information increase when you take an argument to the Web or use presentation software such as PowerPoint or Keynote. Not only can you use still images and illustrations, but you have access to video and audio resources as well. Readers interested in the ivory-billed woodpecker controversy, for example, could download both the video that purported to show the bird in flight and the audios of its call and knock.

Key Features of Factual Arguments

In drafting a factual argument, make sure you do the following:

- Describe a situation that leads you to raise questions about what the facts in a given situation might be.

- Make a claim that addresses the status of the facts as they're known. You'll usually be establishing, challenging, or correcting them. Your claim can be presented tentatively as a hypothesis or more boldly as a thesis.

- Offer substantial and authoritative evidence to support your claims.

In academic situations, a claim typically comes first, and the evidence trails after. But it's not unusual for arguments of fact to present evidence first and then build toward a claim or thesis. Such a structure invites readers to participate in the process by which a factual claim is made (or challenged). The argument unfolds with the narrative drive of a mystery story, with readers eager to know what point the evidence is leading to.

GUIDE | to writing an argument of fact

● Finding a Topic

You're entering an argument of fact when you

- make a claim about fact or existence that's controversial or surprising: *Global warming is threatening Arctic species, especially polar bears.*
- correct an error of fact: *The overall abortion rate is not increasing in the United States, though rates are increasing in some states.*
- challenge societal myths: *Many Mexicans fought alongside Anglos in battles that won Texas its independence from Mexico.*

● Researching Your Topic

Solid research is the basis for most factual arguments. Use both a library and the Web to locate the information you need. One of your most valuable resources may be a research librarian. Take advantage of other human resources, too: don't hesitate to call experts or talk with eyewitnesses who may have special knowledge. For many factual arguments, you can begin research by consulting the following types of sources:

- newspapers, magazines, reviews, and journals (online and print)
- online databases
- government documents and reports
- Web sites, blogs, social networking sites, and listservs or newsgroups
- books
- experts in the field, some of whom might be right on your campus

In addition, your topic may require field research—a survey, a poll, or systematic observation. And whatever the sources, you will want to evaluate them carefully, making sure that each one is legitimate and credible.

● Formulating a Hypothesis

Don't rush into a thesis when you're developing a factual argument. Instead, begin with a hypothesis that expresses your beliefs at the beginning of the project but that may change as your work proceeds. You might even begin with a question to which you don't have an answer or with a broad, general interest in a subject:

- **Question:** Have higher admissions standards at BSU reduced the numbers of entering first-year students from small, rural high schools?
- **Hypothesis:** Higher admissions standards at BSU are reducing the number of students admitted from rural high schools, which tend to be smaller and less well funded than those in suburban and urban areas.

- **Question:** Have the iPod, the convenience of its iTunes, and comparable music sites reduced the amount of illegal downloading of music?
- **Hypothesis:** The iPod and its iTunes Web site may have done more than lawsuits by record companies to discourage illegal downloads of music.

- **Question:** How are prison guards who work on death row affected by their jobs?
- **Hypothesis:** A death-row assignment will desensitize prison guards to the prisoners held there.

Examples of Arguable Factual Claims

- A campus survey that shows that far more students have read *Harry Potter and the Prisoner of Azkaban* than *Hamlet* indicates that our current core curriculum lacks depth.

- Evidence suggests that the European conquest of the Americas may have had more to do with infectious diseases than any superiority in technology or weaponry.

- In the long run, dieting may be more harmful than moderate overeating.

Preparing a Proposal

If your instructor asks you to prepare a proposal for your project, here's a format that may help:

State your thesis completely. If you are having trouble doing so, try outlining it in Toulmin terms:

Claim:

Reason(s):

Warrant(s):

- Explain why the issue you're examining is important, and provide the context for raising the issue. Are you introducing new information, making available information better known, correcting what has been reported incorrectly, or complicating what has been understood more simply?

- Identify and describe those readers you most hope to reach with your proposal. Why is this group of readers most appropriate for your proposal? What are their interests in the subject?

- Discuss the kinds of evidence you expect to use in the project and the research the paper will require.

- Briefly identify the major difficulties you foresee in researching your argument.

- Describe the format or genre you expect to use: An academic essay? A formal report? A Web site? A wiki? Will you need charts, tables, graphs, other illustrations?

● Thinking about Organization

Factual arguments can be arranged many different ways. The simplest structure is to make a claim and then prove it. But even a basic approach needs an introductory section that provides a context for the claim and a concluding section that assesses the implications of the argument. A factual argument that corrects an error or provides an alternative view of some familiar concept or historical event will also need a section early on explaining what the error or the common belief is. Don't be stingy with details: be sure your opening answers the *who, what, where, when, how,* and (maybe) *why* questions that readers will bring to the case.

Some factual arguments offered in academic fields follow formulas and templates. For example, a typical paper in psychology will include an abstract, a review of literature, a discussion of method, an analysis, and a references list. You may be expected to follow a preexisting pattern for factual arguments or reports in many fields.

When you have more flexibility in the structure of your argument, pay attention to the arrangement of evidence and the transitions between key points. In many cases, it makes sense to lead with a strong piece of evidence or a striking example to interest readers in your subject and then to conclude with your strongest evidence.

Even if your argument isn't correcting an error or challenging a common belief, anticipate objections to it and find a place for them in the body of your argument. Ordinarily, you wouldn't want a factual argument in a public venue (in an op-ed piece or letter to the editor, for example) to end with your concessions or refutations. Such a strategy leaves readers thinking about the potential problems with your claim at the point when they should be impressed with its strengths. But if placed early in an argument, an acknowledgment of any problems in your analysis will usually enhance your ethos.

● Getting and Giving Response

All arguments benefit from the scrutiny of others. Your instructor may assign you to a peer group for the purpose of reading and responding to each other's drafts. If not, ask for responses from serious readers or consultants at a writing center. You can use the following questions to evaluate a draft. If you're evaluating someone else's draft, illustrate your points with examples. Specific comments are always more helpful than general observations.

The Claim

- Does the claim clearly raise a serious and arguable factual issue?
- Is the claim as clear and specific as possible?
- Is the claim qualified? If so, how?

Evidence for the Claim

- Is enough evidence provided to persuade the audience to believe the claim? If not, what kind of additional evidence is needed? Does any of the evidence provided seem inappropriate or otherwise ineffective? Why?
- Is the evidence in support of the claim simply announced, or are its significance and appropriateness analyzed? Is a more detailed discussion needed?
- Are any objections that readers might have to the claim or evidence adequately addressed?
- What kinds of sources are cited? How credible and persuasive will they be to readers? What other kinds of sources might be more credible and persuasive?
- Are all quotations introduced with appropriate signal phrases (such as "As Barbara Ehrenreich argues, . . .") and blended smoothly into the writer's sentences?
- Are all visuals titled and labeled appropriately? Have you introduced them and commented on their significance?

Organization and Style

- How are the parts of the argument organized? Is this organization effective, or would some other structure work better?

- Will readers understand the relationships among the claims, supporting reasons, warrants, and evidence? If not, what could be done to make those connections clearer? Are more transitional words and phrases needed? Would headings or graphic devices help?

- How might you use visual design elements to make your proposal more effective?

- Are there clear and effective transitions or links from point to point, paragraph to paragraph, and sentence to sentence? If not, how could they be improved?

- Is the style suited to the subject? Is it too formal? Too casual? Too technical? Too bland? How can it be improved?

- Which sentences seem particularly effective? Which ones seem weakest, and how could they be improved? Should some short sentences be combined, or should any long ones be separated into two or more sentences?

- How effective are the paragraphs? Do any seem too skimpy or too long? How can they be improved?

- Which words or phrases seem particularly effective, vivid, and memorable? Do any seem dull, vague, unclear, or inappropriate for the audience or the writer's purpose? Are definitions provided for technical or other terms that readers might not know?

Spelling, Punctuation, Mechanics, Documentation, Format

- Are there any errors in spelling, punctuation, capitalization, and the like?

- Is an appropriate and consistent style of documentation used for parenthetical citations and the list of works cited or references? (See Chapter 20.)

- Does the paper or project follow an appropriate format? Is it appropriately designed and attractively presented? How could it be improved? If it's a Web site, do all the links work?

RESPOND●

1. For each topic in the following list, decide whether the claim is worth arguing to a college audience, and explain why or why not:

   Hurricanes are increasing in number and ferocity.

   Many people die annually of cancer.

   Fewer people would die of heart disease each year if more of them paid attention to their diets.

   Japan might have come to terms more readily in 1945 if the Allies hadn't demanded unconditional surrender.

   Boys would do better in school if there were more men teaching in elementary and secondary classrooms.

   The economic recession will lead drivers to give up their gas-guzzling SUVs for more energy-efficient vehicles.

   There aren't enough high-paying jobs for college graduates these days.

   Hydrogen may never be a viable alternative to fossil fuels because it takes too much energy to change hydrogen into a usable form.

   Its opponents have grossly exaggerated the effects of the USA Patriot Act on free expression.

2. Working with a group of colleagues, generate a list of twenty favorite "mysteries" explored on cable TV shows, blogs, or tabloid newspapers. Here are three to get you started—the alien crash landing at Roswell, the existence of Atlantis, and the uses of Area 51. Then decide which— if any—of these mysteries might be resolved or explained in a reasonable factual argument and which ones remain eternally mysterious and improbable. Why are people attracted to such topics?

3. The Annenberg Public Policy Center at the University of Pennsylvania hosts FactCheck.org, a Web site that is dedicated to separating facts from opinion or falsehood in the area of politics. It claims to be politically neutral. Analyze one of its cases, either a recent controversial item listed on its homepage or another from its archives. Carefully study the FactCheck case you've chosen. Pay attention to the devices that FactCheck uses to suggest or ensure objectivity and the way that it handles facts and statistics. Then offer your own brief factual argument about the site's objectivity. A full case from FactCheck.org appears at the end of this chapter as a sample reading.

4. Because digital and electronic technologies have made still and video cameras cheap, small, and durable, they're being increasingly used in many situations to provide factual evidence. Security cameras survey

Police in New Orleans were videotaped arresting and beating a man they accused of being disorderly and drunk, a charge that the former teacher strongly disputed. The police were subsequently charged with battery.

more and more public spaces, from convenience stores to subway stations, to deter assaults or catch criminals in the act. Video recorders on police cars routinely tape encounters between officers and the public, putting both groups under scrutiny. Drivers can now get tickets in some states from cameras that catch them speeding or entering intersections after traffic lights have turned red. And the National Football League and some college leagues rely on instant replay to check calls by the officials that are disputed or questionable.

In all these circumstances, the cameras record what individuals on their own may not see or not remember well, presumably providing a better—though far from perfect—account of an event. (Overturning a call in a Big 10 football game, for example, requires "indisputable video evidence"; otherwise, the call by the referee stands.)

Does all this surveillance enhance our society or undermine it in some ways? Study just one type of surveillance, including any others you think of not mentioned here (baby monitors? cameras on cell phones?). Read up on the subject in the library or on the Web, and then make a factual argument based on what you uncover. For example, you might show whether and how people benefit from the technology, how it's being abused, or both.

The Psychological Experience of Security Officers Who Work with Executions

MICHAEL OSOFSKY

An abstract summarizes Osofsky's research. Abstracts are usually required in journal articles.

The Louisiana and Alabama "Execution Teams" were interviewed in order to understand the roles, experiences, and effects of carrying out the death penalty. One hundred twenty out of a possible one hundred twenty-four correctional officers were interviewed. Of those questioned, one hundred fifteen completed mental health inventories. The subjects were grouped based on their roles in order to gain a broader picture of the steps and their impact in carrying out the death penalty. Our results show that participants in the execution process stress "caring professionalism." There is an overwhelming emphasis on carrying out one's job at a high level. At the same time, officers are neither dehumanized nor callous, describing acting with respect and decency toward all involved. While their job is their prima facie duty, they experience stress and emotional reactions, frequently having a hard time carrying out society's "ultimate punishment."

Working with Professor Philip G. Zimbardo, Michael Osofsky wrote "The Psychological Experience of Security Officers Who Work with Executions" while he was a junior at Stanford University. His essay was published in the spring 2002 edition of the *Stanford Undergraduate Research Journal*. The paper provides an example of a factual argument with an indirect thesis: the study produces surprising insights into the lives and attitudes of officers who work with prisoners on death row. But it doesn't open with a thesis or even a hypothesis about the security officers. If the piece has a point of view to defend, it may lie in its opening account of arguments for and against the death penalty. Osofsky offers one rationale and a single sentence for the majority position in favor of the death penalty; he provides four arguments and a full paragraph to explicating the position of those who oppose the death penalty. Note that the documentation style in the paper does not conform to conventional MLA or APA style.

The topic of state-ordered executions invokes strong emotions from many people throughout the United States and around the world. In the past decade alone, dozens of countries have either placed a moratorium on executions or abolished the death penalty altogether.[1] Simultaneously, ambivalence is the term that best describes the overall attitude towards the death penalty.[2] On the one hand, the majority of the American public believes that serious offenders should be punished to the extent that they inflicted pain and suffering, namely retributive justice or the biblical concept of "an eye for an eye."[3]

Alternatively, a growing minority is horrified by the idea of state-ordered killing, regardless of the heinous nature of the crimes committed. In fact, an ABC Poll conducted in early 2001 found that public support for the death penalty had declined to 63%, a drop from 77% in 1996.[4] Many question whether the death penalty has any positive deterrent effect, citing evidence comparing states with and without capital punishment.[5] Others worry about the economic discrimination against the poor and even racist tendencies associated with the death penalty.[6] Additional opponents of capital punishment feel the punishment to be appalling, arguing that innocent individuals can be put to death.[7] Finally, many individuals question the lengthy appeals process that allows inmates to be executed years after their convictions. Over the course of ten, fifteen, or even twenty years on Death Row, inmates can be rehabilitated, the family of the victim(s) receive no closure, and prison guards can form a relationship with the inmate.[8–9]

A great deal of intrigue surrounds the members of an execution team. From stereotypes of a hooded executioner to the notion of multiple executioners with only one possessing the deadly bullet, little knowledge exists about the actual nature of how executions are carried out.[10–11]

The research essay opens by briefly examining arguments for and against the death penalty—setting the context for Osofsky's study of correctional officers involved in executions.

Our interviews of execution team members at the Louisiana State Penitentiary at Angola and Holman State Prison in Alabama utilize an unprecedented number of subjects through full and uninhibited access to the staff involved. The current study was undertaken in order to gain more understanding about the unusual responsibilities and experiences of those who are directly involved with the legal termination of the lives of others.

One hundred and twenty correctional officers at the Louisiana State Penitentiary at Angola and Holman State Prison in Alabama were interviewed anonymously in order to understand broad areas of the execution process. The one to two hour interviews were conducted over the summers of 2000 and 2001. During 2000, interviews were conducted of fifty of fifty-two members of the Louisiana execution team. During 2001, fifty interviews were conducted of security officers who either work on Death Row or are a part of the execution process in Louisiana. An additional twenty interviews were carried out involving correctional officers who have worked with executions in Alabama. In addition to gathering demographic and background information, a number of

questions were asked about the following topics: (1) The execution experience, including roles, reactions, preparation, emotions experienced, and changes over time; (2) Stresses related to their job and methods to cope with stress; (3) Support network and influence of work on relationships; (4) Aftermath of execution experience for the officer. Based on our interviews, we were able to re-create the step-by-step process of carrying out an execution. The process was largely similar in the two states, but differed due to both situational factors with the two facilities as well as the mode of execution employed in each state. (Louisiana uses lethal injection, while Alabama is one of two remaining states still employing the electric chair as its sole means of execution.)

The security officers were asked to complete three separate measures. During 2000, subjects completed the Beck Depression Inventory (BDI) and the first page of a Clinician Administered Post Traumatic Stress Disorder Scale (CAPS 1) for the DSM-IV, a life events checklist. The reported results from these two measures are primarily descriptive due to our desire to understand the execution process and psychological impacts of carrying out the death penalty. During 2001, we asked the officers to complete a questionnaire pertaining to issues of moral disengagement employed throughout the process. Interviews were tape recorded (without their names on the tapes) in order to guarantee that quotes, reactions, and attributed material were accurate.

After completing the interviews, we classified subjects into one of twelve roles: Wardens, classifications personnel, Death Row guards, death house/front gate security, liaisons to the press, mental health professionals, spiritual advisors, officers who sit with the victim's family, officers who sit with the inmate's family, the strapdown team, emergency medical technicians, and the Executioner.

Interview responses conveyed an interesting perspective on the death penalty relative to the existing literature on the subject. Consistent with current national polls, approximately two-thirds of officers indicate general support for the death penalty, stressing the heinous nature of the inmates' crimes and the impact on the victims and their families.

> Responses to the interviews suggest that guards reflect majority opinion about the death penalty in the United States.

All but three do not believe the death penalty is racially motivated. However, an equal number raised concerns that social class and poverty play major roles in determining who is executed.

"I've never seen a rich man executed," Death Row guard Willie W. asserted. The inmates on Death Row tend to come from poor, underprivileged backgrounds in which they had little access to basic necessities. Sarah S.,

> Officers do question the equity of the punishment.

the deputy warden, pointed out, "If they had educational opportunities, they wouldn't be here."

The execution team also noted that certain districts within the state are more likely to hand down a death sentence. This variation by district is a function of the District Attorneys, judges, and juries—standards that vary by city and state. A considerable number of the officers discussed their concern that many "lifers" have committed crimes that are as horrific as those committed by the inmates on Death Row. For this reason alone, several members of the execution team argued that either the sentences of those on Death Row should be commuted to life in prison or others should be on Death Row.

Further, we repeatedly heard that the death penalty simply takes too long to be carried out. Some described their identification with the inmates' pain in living and awaiting execution. Others discussed the high monetary cost to the state of the lengthy appeals process. Some worried that the victims cannot receive closure until the inmate is dead.

Ultimately, nearly every person we interviewed echoed two main components of the execution process. On the one hand, and most importantly, the security officers stressed their professionalism. Their duty is to carry out the laws of the United States, whatever those may be. They believe in their jobs, and try to do them as well as they possibly can. On the other hand, they act with decency and humanity toward the inmates. In their efforts to adjust and function successfully, they struggle internally. Although most attempt to suppress painful feelings, they state that if it ever becomes easy to participate in an execution, they would worry about themselves and their loss of humanity. Some deal with their stress by disassociative mechanisms. Some overtly exhibit their distress through transient or persistent stress, guilt, and even depression. Although many officers view Death Row inmates as the

Osofsky gives ample attention to a critical view of the death penalty expressed by "several" execution team members.

The study is not specific here about numbers. No charts or graphs summarize responses to interview questions.

Factual results here might furnish material for subsequent arguments: guards support implementation of the law yet struggle with the nature of their work.

"worst of the worst," all describe treating the inmates with decency. Death Row guard Charles S. said, "I treat them as I would want to be treated. I help them when I can and when my job permits." Strapdown team member Robert A. concurred, "They are people and deserve to be treated as such." While some prisoners do not repent or do so only superficially, the officers describe how many change, becoming cooperative in the process.

Certainly there are exceptions to the almost universal decency of the officers in this study; wrongful emotional and physical abuse can occur in a maximum-security penitentiary. Some guards have inappropriate motives for working at a prison. From our discussions it appears that most voluntarily leave or are weeded out over time. However, the officers we interviewed did not display hostility toward the inmates, but were concerned with maximizing humanity and dignity. Within the constraints needed to maintain security, they describe being kind to the inmates. Some describe feeling good about a number of inmates who shortly before their execution thank them for their compassion. If anything, after being involved on the death team, correctional officers become more reflective and take their job more seriously than ever.

> Osofsky finds that most officials approach their stressful work with death row inmates humanely and reflectively.

WORKS CITED

Osofsky provides notes keyed to the text rather than the alphabetical bibliography more typical of a works cited page.

1. Prokosch E. *Human Rights v. The Death Penalty: Abolition and Restriction in Law and Practice.* New York: Amnesty International, 1998.

2. Finckenauer JO. Public Support for the Death Penalty: Retribution as Just Deserts or Retribution as Revenge? *Justice Quarterly* 1988; 5:81–100.

3. Gale ME. Retribution, Punishment and Death. *UC Davis Law Review* 1985; 18:973–1035.

4. Ellsworth P, Ross L. Public Opinion and Capital Punishment: A Close Examination of the Views of Abolitionists and Retentionists. *Crime and Delinquency* 1983; 29:116–169.

5. Reiman JH. *The Rich Get Richer and the Poor Get Prison,* 4th ed. Boston: Allyn and Bacon, 1985.

6. Jackson J. *Legal Lynching: Racism, Injustice and the Death Penalty.* New York: Marlowe, 1996.

7. Radelet ML, Bedau HA, Putnam CE. *In Spite of Innocence: Erroneous Convictions in Capital Cases.* Boston: Northeastern University Press, 1992.

8. Radelet ML, Vandiver M, Berardo F. Families, Prisons, and Men with Death Sentences: The Human Impact of Structured Uncertainty. *J of Family Issues* 1983; 4:595–596.

9. Goldhammer GE. *Dead End.* Brunswick: Biddle Publishing Company, 1994.

10. Mailer N. *The Executioner's Song.* Boston: Little, Brown, 1979.

11. Elliot RG. *Agent of Death: The Memoirs of an Executioner.* New York: Dutton, 1940.

What Is a Civil Union?

JESS HENIG AND LORI ROBERTSON

August 9, 2007

SUMMARY

When politicians say they support civil unions but not marriage for people of the same sex, what do they mean? We find three main differences between civil unions and marriage as it's traditionally viewed:

- **The right to federal benefits.** States that allow some type of same-sex union are able to grant only state rights. The Defense of Marriage Act passed in 1996 prohibits same-sex couples from receiving federal marriage rights and benefits.
- **Portability.** Because civil unions are not recognized by all states, such agreements are not always valid when couples cross state lines.
- **Terminology.** "Marriage" is a term that conveys societal and cultural meaning, important to both gay rights activists and those who don't believe gays should marry.

"What Is a Civil Union?" was written by Jess Henig and Lori Robertson, a staff writer and managing editor, respectively, of *Annenberg Political Fact Check*. It was originally published on FactCheck.org, whose mission statement says, "We are a nonpartisan, nonprofit, 'consumer advocate' for voters that aims to reduce the level of deception and confusion in U.S. politics. We monitor the factual accuracy of what is said by major U.S. political players in the form of TV ads, debates, speeches, interviews, and news releases. Our goal is to apply the best practices of both journalism and scholarship, and to increase public knowledge and understanding." The site is sponsored by the Annenberg Public Policy Center at the University of Pennsylvania and is not funded by corporations or political groups of any kind. Note that this article does include a list of sources, but they are not listed or cited within the text in any conventional way, such as MLA or APA style.

Since this article was published in 2007, additional states have legalized civil unions, domestic partnerships, or marriages between people of the same sex. In addition, in 2009 the Obama administration announced that certain federal benefits would be extended to same-sex couples, such as allowing same-sex partners to be added to the long-term-care insurance program for federal employees.

ANALYSIS

On Aug. 9, the Democratic presidential candidates will debate issues important to gay, lesbian, bisexual and transgender individuals. The forum in Los Angeles is sponsored by the Human Rights Campaign Foundation and the MTV Networks' Logo Channel. We expect the candidates will be asked about gay marriage and civil unions—a major issue that has sparked political passions on both the right and the left.

In a questionnaire that Human Rights Campaign, a gay rights advocacy group, sent to presidential candidates, all of the Democrats said they were in favor of civil unions for gay couples—a solution that is often touted as being functionally equivalent to marriage. Only Rep. Dennis Kucinich and former Sen. Mike Gravel said they would support gay marriage. But what exactly is the difference? FactCheck.org offers this primer on the subject.

Federal Recognition

The Defense of Marriage Act (DOMA), signed into law by President Bill Clinton in 1996, stipulated that for all federal legal purposes "marriage" is a union between one man and one woman. Because of that legislation, all federal laws pertaining to married couples apply exclusively to opposite-sex couples. States that have made civil unions legal, including Connecticut, New Hampshire, New Jersey, and Vermont, have granted state benefits to same-sex couples. These include state tax benefits, better access to family health plans, co-parenting privileges, automatic preference for guardianship and decision-making authority for a medically incapacitated partner, as well as protection under state divorce and separation laws. While each state law is somewhat different, they are similar in that they convey these state rights to gay couples; they do not and cannot grant federal rights and benefits.

California, Hawaii, Maine, Oregon, Washington, and the District of Columbia have domestic partnership laws, which are fundamentally similar to civil unions. Massachusetts is the only state in which gays can legally marry, due to the 2003 Massachusetts Supreme Judicial Court ruling that said the state constitution didn't support discriminating against same-sex couples that wanted to wed. Like states that grant civil unions, Massachusetts extends all the state benefits of marriage to same-sex couples; unlike in other states, gay couples also can be issued a marriage license. However, married gay couples still are not eligible for federal benefits.

The Government Accountability Office lists 1,138 federal laws that pertain to married couples. Many in that long list may be minor or only relevant to small groups of citizens. However, a number of provisions are key to what constitutes a marriage legally in the United States:

- **Taxes.** Couples in a civil union may file a joint state tax return, but they must file federal tax returns as single persons. This may be advantageous to some couples, not so for others. One advantage for married couples is the ability to transfer assets and wealth without incurring tax penalties. Partners in a civil union aren't permitted to do that and thus may be liable for estate and gift taxes on such transfers.

- **Health insurance.** The state-federal divide is even more complicated in this arena. In the wake of the Massachusetts high court ruling, the group Gay & Lesbian Advocates & Defenders put together a guide to spousal health care benefits. GLAD's document is Massachusetts-specific but provides insight into how health insurance laws would apply to those in a civil union in other states. In general, GLAD says, it comes down to what's governed by state law and what's subject to federal oversight. If a private employer's health plans are subject to Massachusetts state insurance laws, benefits must be extended to a same-sex spouse. If the health plan is governed by federal law, the employer can choose whether or not to extend such benefits.

- **Social Security survivor benefits.** If a spouse or divorced spouse dies, the survivor may have a right to Social Security payments based on the earnings of the married couple, rather than only the survivor's earnings. Same-sex couples are not eligible for such benefits.

Other federal areas in which couples in civil unions don't have the same rights as married couples include immigration (a partner who's a foreign national can't become an American by entering into a civil union with someone) and veterans' and military benefits (only opposite-sex spouses have a right to pensions, compensation for service-related deaths, medical care, housing, and the right to burial in veterans' cemeteries). Gay couples, however, may actually benefit when applying for programs such as Medicaid or government housing that require low-income eligibility. A spouse's income is included in such applications, but a same-sex partner's income is not. One change has been made in federal law: A provision in the Pension Protection Act of 2006 allows same-sex couples to transfer 401(k) and IRA earnings to partners without penalty.

Brad Luna, director of communications at Human Rights Campaign, says there have been several unsuccessful lawsuits filed by same-sex couples who wish to receive federal benefits. "It's going to have to take the repeal of DOMA or a federal civil union law that would grant them that kind of federal recognition," he says.

Portable Unions

Since civil unions are legal only in certain states, they also can't be taken across state lines. If a couple gets married in Vermont, they can reasonably expect to still be married if they move to California; the same is not true for same-sex unions. While New Jersey law specifies that the state will recognize civil unions and domestic partnerships performed elsewhere, this is not true for all states that allow some form of same-sex partnership. And if civil partners move to a state that disallows all same-sex unions, they may find themselves with no legal standing whatsoever as a couple.

Most states have enacted DOMA legislation or passed constitutional amendments stipulating that marriage is a union exclusively between one man and one woman. In fact, only five states do not have laws on the books that prohibit same-sex marriage: Massachusetts, New Jersey, New Mexico, New York, and Rhode Island. The District of Columbia also does not have such a law. Both HRC and DOMAwatch.org, a project of the Alliance Defense Fund, which opposes gay marriage, have U.S. maps showing the breakdown of legislation by state.

The Meaning of "Marriage"

The least concrete difference between civil unions and marriage is also perhaps the most polarizing: the term "marriage" and the social and cultural weight it bears. For many, this is not just a semantic issue. Opponents are concerned that allowing gays to marry will dilute the term "marriage," threatening the institution it stands for. Supporters, meanwhile, feel that setting up a marriage-like institution for gays (such as civil unions) while defining marriage as fundamentally heterosexual is an example of flawed "separate but equal" legislation.

In an interview with FactCheck.org, Paul Cates of the Lesbian Gay Bisexual Transgender Project at the American Civil Liberties Union stressed the cultural significance of marriage: "You're not a little kid dreaming about your civil union day. It's your wedding day." When you want to commit to a partner, "you're not really thinking about the [legal] protections," he says. "It's the significance and what it means to be married and hold yourself out as married."

Opponents of gay marriage also recognize the social importance of the word. Jenny Tyree, associate analyst for marriage at Focus on the Family, a Christian organization headed by James C. Dobson, says her group "does not believe that marriage has to be redefined to care for all the people in society. We understand that every person has needs and people they want to care for. But these are pretty bold attempts to undermine the marriage institution."

Focus on the Family and other groups that oppose same-sex marriage are not just concerned with terminology. "Marriage is important because it's a time-honored enduring social institution that serves women, men and children," Tyree says. "And civil unions undermine marriage by reducing it to a bundle of rights and benefits." Despite difficulties like divorce, marriage "is still an institution that does what we need it to do for children," she adds.

Such views seem to be in the majority. A 2003 Pew Research Center survey showed that 56 percent of respondents agreed that gay marriage would undermine the traditional family.

As previously noted, even states that allow for same-sex civil unions or domestic partnerships—including California, Connecticut, Maine, Vermont, and Washington—have passed laws defining marriage as something that occurs between a man and a woman. Liberal-leaning politicians have made that distinction as well: Most of the Democratic candidates set to debate these issues support extending all the federal legal rights of married couples to same-sex couples—but they don't want to call that "marriage."

Update Aug. 9: Our article originally said that Jenny Tyree of Focus on the Family cited studies showing that children do better when raised by a married mother and father. Better than what, though? When we had a chance to do a little more checking, we found that research does seem to show that children raised by married biological parents are better off on average than those raised by cohabiting biological parents. In addition, other studies show that children raised by both parents fare better than children raised by one. Studies have also shown, though, that children raised by homosexual parents are just as emotionally and socially healthy as those raised by heterosexual parents. The Child Welfare League of America says of its position on same-sex parenting: "Studies using diverse samples and methodologies in the last decade have persuasively demonstrated that there are no systematic differences between gay or lesbian and non-gay or lesbian parents in emotional health, parenting skills, and attitudes toward parenting."

SOURCES

Connecticut General Assembly. Substitute Senate Bill No. 963. 14 Apr. 2005.

DOMAwatch.org, Alliance Defense Fund. Issues by State. 8 Aug. 2007.

Government Accountability Office. Defense of Marriage Act: Update to Prior Report. GAO.gov. 23 Jan. 2004.

Human Rights Campaign. State-by-State Information, national maps of marriage-related laws. HRC.org. 8 Aug. 2007.

New Hampshire General Court. House Bill 437-FN-LOCAL. 4 Apr. 2007.

New Jersey Legislature. Bill A3787. 21 Dec. 2006.

Vermont General Assembly. Act No. 91: An Act Relating to Civil Unions. 26 Apr. 2000.

9
Arguments of Definition

A traffic committee must define *small car* to enforce parking restrictions in a campus lot where certain spaces are marked "Small Car Only!" Owners of compact luxury vehicles, light trucks, and motorcycles have complained that their vehicles are being unfairly ticketed.

A panel of judges must decide whether computer-enhanced images will be eligible in a contest for landscape photography. At what point is an electronically manipulated image no longer a photograph?

A scholarship committee must determine whether the daughter of two European American diplomats, born while her parents were assigned to the U.S. embassy in Nigeria, will be eligible to apply for grants designated specifically for "African American students."

A young man hears a classmate describe hunting as a "blood sport." He disagrees and argues that hunting for sport has little in common with "genuine blood sports" such as cockfighting.

A committee of the student union is accused of bias by a conservative student group, which claims that the committee has brought a disproportionate share of left-wing speakers to campus. The committee defends its program by challenging the definition of *left wing* used to classify its speakers.

Understanding Arguments of Definition

Definitions matter. Just ask a scientist, a mathematician, an engineer, a lawyer, or maybe a politician.

During the early stages of the 2008 presidential campaign, some conservatives accused Barack Obama of a lack of patriotism. On one occasion, he was photographed standing a bit too casually during the national anthem, and on another a reporter noticed that he'd stopped wearing an American flag lapel pin. When questioned about the pin, he responded with a narrow definition of *patriotism*: "Shortly after 9/11 . . .

You may recall the argument started during the 2008 presidential primary season by this *Time* magazine photograph of Barack Obama, Bill Richardson, and Hillary Clinton standing for the national anthem.

that [pin] became a substitute for I think true patriotism, which is speaking out on issues that are of importance to our national security."

After hearing much criticism and perhaps realizing that his initial characterization of the term, with its emphasis on dissent, had omitted much that his fellow citizens understood by *patriotism*, Obama decided to try again. In Independence, Missouri, on June 30, 2008, he delivered a speech entitled "The America We Love," which proved to be an extended definition of the term. Among the definitions of *patriotism* that Obama offered were the following:

> For me, as for most Americans, patriotism starts as a gut instinct, a loyalty and love for country rooted in my earliest memories. I'm not just talking about the recitations of the Pledge of Allegiance or the Thanksgiving pageants at school or the fireworks on the Fourth of July, as wonderful as those things may be. Rather, I'm referring to the way the American ideal wove its way throughout the lessons my family taught me as a child.
>
> . . . That is why, for me, patriotism is always more than just loyalty to a place on a map or a certain kind of people. Instead, it is also loyalty to America's ideals—ideals for which anyone can sacrifice, or defend, or give their last full measure of devotion. I believe it is this loyalty that allows a country teeming with different races and ethnicities, religions and customs, to come together as one.
>
> . . . Of course, precisely because America isn't perfect, precisely because our ideals constantly demand more from us, patriotism can never be defined as loyalty to any particular leader or government or policy. As Mark Twain, that greatest of American satirists and proud son of Missouri, once wrote, "Patriotism is supporting your country all the time, and your government when it deserves it." We may hope that our leaders and our government stand up for our ideals, and there are many times in our history when that's occurred. But when our laws, our leaders or our government are out of alignment with our ideals, then the dissent of ordinary Americans may prove to be one of the truest expressions of patriotism.
>
> . . . In the end, it may be this quality that best describes patriotism in my mind—not just a love of America in the abstract, but a very particular love for, and faith in, the American people. That is why our heart swells with pride at the sight of our flag; why we shed a tear as the lonely notes of Taps sound. For we know that the greatness of this country—its victories in war, its enormous wealth, its scientific and cultural achievements—all result from the energy and imagination of the American people; their toil, drive, struggle, restlessness, humor and quiet heroism.

As you can see from these excerpts from Obama's much longer address, a term can be defined in many ways—by what it is, by what it isn't, by what it includes, by specific examples, by what authorities (such as Mark Twain) observe, and in this case, by feelings. And note that the expanded definition also preserves the more limited meaning that got Obama into trouble initially: "the dissent of ordinary Americans may prove to be one of the truest expressions of patriotism."

As Obama discovered, definitions matter because they are, in fact, arguments that define the concepts by which we live and operate. In the wake of Hurricane Katrina in 2005, for instance, the media were full of reports about the thousands of New Orleans residents who had fled their homes to escape the storm's horrors. In some early reports, those who had left New Orleans were labeled *refugees*. But that term rankled many native-born American citizens who were still in their home country and asked how they could be refugees, a term that was commonly used for people who were legally admitted to the United States from other countries.

As the media hastened to change its terminology to *evacuees*, however, some foreign refugees began voicing outrage at the implication that *refugee* was a derogatory term. The matter got more complicated when reporters pointed out that any legally designated foreign refugees who were affected by the hurricane would be eligible for benefits that were not available to other Katrina victims. In this case, the definition of one word meant a great deal for thousands of displaced people.

Arguments of definition can be important and contentious. They wield the power to say what someone or something is or can be. As such, these arguments can also include or exclude: a creature is an endangered species or it isn't; an act was harassment or it wasn't; a person deserves official refugee status or doesn't. Another way of approaching definitional arguments, however, is to think of what falls between *is* and *is not* in a definitional claim. In fact, some dynamic definitional disputes occur in this murky realm.

Consider the controversy over how to define *human intelligence*. Some argue that human intelligence is a capacity that is measured by tests of verbal and mathematical reasoning. In other words, it's defined by IQ and SAT scores. Others define *intelligence* as the ability to perform specific practical tasks. Still others interpret intelligence in emotional terms as a competence in relating to other people. Any of these positions could be defended reasonably, but perhaps the wisest approach would be to construct a definition of *intelligence* that is rich enough to incorporate all these perspectives—and maybe more.

Does the death penalty for juveniles like this one amount to "cruel and unusual punishment"?

Crucial political, social, and scientific terms—such as *intelligence* or *social justice*—are constantly "under construction" and are reargued and reshaped whenever they need to be updated for the times. In recent years, the Supreme Court has decided what the framers of the Constitution meant by phrases such as "cruel and unusual punishment" and "a well regulated militia." And astronomers have debated whether distant Pluto still fits the traditional definition of *planet*. (It doesn't.)

In case you're wondering, important arguments of definition can't be decided simply by running to a dictionary. Dictionaries themselves reflect the way that particular groups of people use words at a specified time and place. And like any form of writing, these reference books mirror the prejudices of their makers—as shown, perhaps most famously, in the entries of lexicographer Samuel Johnson (1709–1784), who gave the English language its first great dictionary. Johnson, no friend of the Scots, defined *oats* as "a grain which in England is generally given to horses, but in Scotland supports the people." (To be fair, he also defined *lexicographer* as "a writer of dictionaries, a harmless drudge.") Thus, it's possible to disagree with dictionary definitions or to regard them merely as starting points for arguments.

Not Just Words

Take a look at the images on this page and the facing one. What definition of *patriotism* can you infer from each one?

Kinds of Definition

Because there are different kinds of definitions, there are also different ways to make a definition argument. Fortunately, identifying a particular type of definition is less important than appreciating when an issue of definition is at stake. Let's explore some common definitional issues.

Formal Definitions

Laurie Goodstein's argument in "More Religion, But Not the Old-Time Kind" carefully sets out formal definitions for various versions of Christianity, especially *fundamentalism* and *evangelicalism*.

⸬⸬⸬⸬⸬⸬⸬⸬⸬⸬⸬⸬⸬⸬⸬⸬⸬⸬⸬ LINK TO P. 858

Formal definitions are what you find in dictionaries. Such definitions place a term in its proper genus and species—first determining its class and then identifying the features that distinguish it from other members of that class. That sounds complicated, but a definition will help you see the principle. To define *hybrid car*, you might first place it in a general class—*passenger vehicles*. Then the formal definition would distinguish hybrid cars from other passenger vehicles: *they can move using two or more sources of power, either separately or in combination*. So the full definition might look like this: *a hybrid car is a passenger vehicle* (genus) *that can operate using two or more sources of power, separately or in combination* (species).

Many arguments involve deciding whether an object meets the criteria set by a formal definition. For instance, suppose that you are considering whether a Toyota Prius and a Chevrolet Malibu are actually hybrid cars. Both are clearly passenger cars, so the genus raises no questions. But not all vehicles that claim to be hybrids are powered by two sources: some of them are just electrically assisted versions of a regular gasoline car. That's the species question. Looking closely, you discover that a Prius can run on either gas or electric power alone. But does the Malibu have that flexibility? If not, should it be labeled something other than *hybrid*—perhaps, *mild hybrid*? This real definitional question has consequences for consumers who are concerned about gas prices.

Chevrolet Malibu: full hybrid or poseur? New York City mayor Michael Bloomberg (right) was convinced, ordering Malibus in 2008 for the city's fleets of taxis and official vehicles.

Prince Charming considers whether an action would fulfill the conditions for an operational definition.

Operational Definitions

Operational definitions identify an object or idea by what it does or by what conditions create it. For example, someone's offensive sexual imposition on another person may not meet the technical definition of *harassment* unless it is considered *unwanted*, *unsolicited*, and *repeated*. These three conditions then define what makes an act that might be acceptable in some situations turn into harassment. But they might also

Melanie Springer Mock offers an operational definition when she points out that government-sponsored Nativity scenes might be considered evangelism.

LINK TO P. 877 ....

then become part of a highly contentious debate: were the conditions actually present in a given case? For example, could an offensive act really be harassment if the accused believed sexual interest was mutual and therefore solicited?

Sometimes operational definitions may sound like descriptions or even narratives. In an article called "Moms Know . . . All about Operational Definitions," Kathy Parker gives this example: "From the age of six on, I knew the essence of an operational definition, even if the term itself was not known to me. I knew that chores were not considered 'complete' until I had taken the linens off my bed and put them in the laundry hamper, picked up toys and vacuumed my room. I also knew that there would be consequences if I ignored the definition of 'complete.'"

As you might imagine, arguments arise from operational definitions whenever people disagree about what the conditions define or whether these conditions have been fulfilled. Here are some examples of those types of questions:

Questions Related to Conditions

- Can institutional racism occur in the absence of specific and individual acts of racism?
- Can someone who is paid for their community service still be called a volunteer?
- Does someone who uses steroids to enhance home-run-hitting performance deserve the title Hall of Famer?

Questions Related to Fulfillment of Conditions

- Has an institution supported traditions or policies that have led to widespread racial inequities?
- Was the compensation given to a volunteer really "pay" or simply "reimbursement" for expenses?
- Should Player X, who used steroids prescribed for a medical reason, be ineligible for the Hall of Fame?

Definitions by Example

Resembling operational definitions are definitions by example, which define a class by listing its individual members. For example, one might define *smart phones* by describing the major examples of these products or define *heirloom tomatoes* by listing all those available at the local farmers' market.

A definition of *heirloom tomatoes* would include the Speckled Roman, the Olena Ukrainian, and the Yellow Brandywine.

Arguments of this sort focus on who or what may be included in a list that defines a category—*classic movies, worst natural disasters, groundbreaking painters*. Such arguments often involve comparisons and contrasts with the items that most readers would agree belong in this list. One might, for example, wonder why the status of planet is denied to asteroids, when both planets and asteroids are bodies that orbit the sun. A comparison between planets and asteroids might suggest that size is one essential feature of the eight recognized planets that asteroids don't meet. Or one might ask why Washington, D.C., is denied the status of a state. How does it differ from the fifty recognized American states?

Other Issues of Definition

Many issues of definition cross the line among the types described here and other forms of argument. For example, if you decided to explore whether banning pornography on the Internet violates First Amendment guarantees of free speech, you'd first have to establish definitions of *pornography* and *free speech*. You could refer either to legal definitions settled by, let's say, the Supreme Court or to other definitions closer to your own beliefs, perhaps offered by experts in Internet law. Then you'd have to argue that types of pornography on the Internet are or are not in the same class or that they share or do not share the characteristics of speech protected by the First Amendment. In doing so, you'd certainly find yourself slipping into an evaluative mode because matters of definition are often also questions of value. (See Chapter 10.)

When exploring an idea, don't worry about such slippage: it's a natural part of writing. But focus an argument on a central issue or question, and be honest in examining any definition you care to defend.

Developing a Definitional Argument

For an example of the complexity that establishing definitions entails, see danah m. boyd and Nicole B. Ellison's definition of social network sites.

LINK TO P. 653

Definitional arguments don't just appear out of the blue; they evolve out of the occasions and conversations of daily life, both public and private. You might get into an argument over the definition of *ordinary wear and tear* when you return a rental car with some battered upholstery. Or you might be asked to write a job description for a new position to be created in your office: you have to define the position in a way that doesn't step on anyone else's turf on the job. Or maybe employees on your campus object to being defined as *temporary workers* when they've held their same jobs for years. Or someone derides one of your best friends as *just a nerd*. In a dozen ways every day, you encounter situations that are issues of definition. They're so frequent and indispensable that you barely notice them for what they are.

Formulating Claims

In addressing a question of definition, you'll likely formulate a *tentative claim*—a declarative statement that represents your first response to such situations. Note that such initial claims usually don't follow a single definitional formula.

Claims of Definition

A person paid to do public service is not a *volunteer*.

Institutional racism can exist—maybe even thrive—in the absence of overt civil rights violations.

Political bias has been consistently practiced by the mainstream media.

A *municipal fee* is often the same darn thing as a tax.

Napoleon Dynamite is one of many independent films to achieve *cult status*.

None of the claims listed here could stand on its own. Such claims often reflect first impressions and gut reactions. That's because stating a claim of definition is typically a starting point, a moment of bravura that doesn't last much beyond the first serious rebuttal or challenge. Statements of this sort aren't arguments until they're attached to reasons, data, warrants, and evidence. (See Chapter 7.)

Finding good reasons to support a claim of definition usually requires formulating a general definition by which to explore the subject. To be persuasive, the definition must be broad and not tailored to the specific controversy:

A volunteer is . . .

Institutional racism is . . .

Political bias is . . .

A tax is . . .

A cult film is . . .

Definitions and Academic Arguments

People within an academic field typically share a common and often highly technical vocabulary. Newcomers to any discipline (or major) have to understand how these key terms are defined: for instance, *affect* in psychology, *tort* in law, *persona* in literature, or *entropy* in engineering.

Scholars and researchers may spend considerable energy and time refining the definitions of technical items. But academics also create wholly new words to convey fresh observations and discoveries. Australian philosopher Glenn Albrecht, for example, recently

(continued)

(continued)

coined the term "solastalgia" to describe "a form of homesickness one gets when one is still at home" because familiar environments are being altered by global warming, war, terrorism, strip mining, urban gentrification, or other forces that alter a built environment. Here is Albrecht's academic definition of the term, as offered on his own blog:

> I suggest 'solastalgia' to describe the pain or sickness caused by the loss of, or inability to derive, solace connected to the present state of one's home environment. Solastalgia exists when there is recognition that the place where one resides and that one loves is under assault (physical desolation). It can be contrasted to the spatial and temporal dislocation and dispossession experienced as nostalgia. Solastalgia is the 'lived experience' of the loss of the value of the present as manifest in a feeling of dislocation; of being undermined by forces that destroy the potential for solace to be derived from the immediate and given. In brief, solastalgia is a form of homesickness one experiences when one is still at 'home'.
>
> —Glenn Albrecht, "Solastalgia: A New Psychoterratic Illness"

Clive Thompson, writing for *Wired* (January 2008), explains the newly defined term in language that is less academic:

> People are feeling displaced. They are suffering symptoms eerily similar to those of indigenous populations that are removed from their traditional homelands. But nobody is being relocated; they haven't moved anywhere. It's just that familiar markers of their area, the physical and sensory signals that define *home*, are vanishing. Their environment is moving away from them, and they miss it terribly.
>
> —Clive Thompson, "How the Next Victim of Climate Change Will Be Our Minds"

How does Albrecht's scholarly definition of solastalgia differ in style from Thompson's explanation of the phenomenon, which is aimed at the more general readership of *Wired*? Point to specific features of Albrecht's definition that mark it as academic writing.

Now consider how the following claims might be expanded with a general definition to become full-fledged definitional arguments:

Arguments of Definition

Someone paid to do public service is not a volunteer because volunteers are people who . . .

Institutional racism can exist even in the absence of overt violations of civil rights because, by definition, institutional racism is . . .

Political bias in the media is evident when . . .

A municipal fee is the same darn thing as a tax. Both fees and taxes are . . .

Napoleon Dynamite has achieved all the criteria of cult status: . . .

Notice, too, that some of the issues can involve comparisons between things—such as taxes and fees.

Crafting Definitions

Imagine that you decide to tackle the concept of paid volunteer in the following way:

> Participants in the federal AmeriCorps program are not really volunteers because they receive "education awards" for their public service. Volunteers are people who work for a cause without receiving compensation.

In Toulmin terms, the argument looks like this:

Claim	Participants in AmeriCorps aren't volunteers . . .
Reason	. . . because they are paid for their service.
Warrant	People who are compensated for their services are, ordinarily, employees.

As you can see, the definition of *volunteers* will be crucial to the shape of the argument. In fact, you might think you've settled the matter with this tight little formulation. But now it's time to listen to the readers over your shoulder (see Chapter 7), who are pushing you further. Do the terms of your definition account for all pertinent cases of volunteerism—in particular, any related to the types of public service AmeriCorps members might be involved in? Consider, too, the word *cause* in your original statement of the definition:

> **Volunteers are people who work for a cause without receiving compensation.**

Cause has political connotations that you may or may not intend. You'd better clarify what you mean by *cause* when you discuss its definition in your paper. Might a phrase such as *the public good* be a more comprehensive or appropriate substitute for a *cause*? And then there's the matter of *compensation* in the second half of your definition:

> **Volunteers are people who work for a cause without receiving compensation.**

Aren't people who volunteer to serve on boards, committees, and commissions sometimes paid, especially for their expenses? What about members of the so-called all-volunteer military? They're financially compensated for their years of service, and they enjoy benefits after they complete their tour of duty.

As you can see, you can't just offer up a definition as part of your argument and assume that readers will understand or accept it. Every part of the definition has to be weighed, critiqued, and defended. That means you'll want to investigate your subject in the library, on the Internet, and in conversation with others, including experts on your term. You might then be able to present your definition in a single paragraph, or you may have to spend several pages coming to terms with the complexity of the core issue.

After conducting research of this kind, you'll be in a better position to write an extended definition that explains to your readers what you believe makes a volunteer a volunteer, a tax a tax, and so on. At the end of this chapter, writer Lynn Peril provides just such a definition of the attitude that she claims is imposed on women in this country—what she calls "Pink Think."

Matching Claims to Definitions

Once you've formulated a definition that readers will accept—a demanding task in itself—you might need to look at your subject to see if it fits your general definition. It should provide evidence of one of the following:

- It is a clear example of the class defined.
- It clearly falls outside the defined class.

- It falls between two closely related classes or fulfills some conditions of the defined class but not others.

- It defies existing classes and categories and requires an entirely new definition.

It's possible that you might have to change your original claim at this point if the evidence you've gathered suggests that qualifications are necessary. It's amazing how often seemingly cut-and-dry issues of definition become blurry—and open to compromise and accommodation—when you learn more about them. That has proved to be the case as various campuses across the country have tried to define *hate speech* or *sexual harassment*—tricky matters. And even the Supreme Court has never said exactly what *pornography* is. Just when matters seem settled, new legal twists develop. Should virtual child pornography that is created with software be illegal, as is the real thing? Is a virtual image—even a lewd one—an artistic expression that is protected (as other works of art are) by the First Amendment?

Considering Design and Visuals

In thinking about how to present your argument of definition, don't forget that design—such as boldface and italics, headings, or links in online text—can contribute to (or detract from) its credibility and persuasiveness. Remember, too, that visuals like photographs, charts, and graphs can also help you make your case. Such items might demonstrate that the conditions for a definition have been met—as the widely circulated and horrific photographs from Abu Ghraib prison in 2004 helped to define *torture*. Or if you're working with a definitional claim about media bias, a chart might help to identify a characteristic of such prejudice, like a tendency among reporters to treat candidates in a political campaign differently. Note that such an item could also serve as evidence that the concept you are defining exists—often a matter of contention in arguments of definition.

Key Features of Definitional Arguments

In writing an argument of definition of your own, consider that it's likely to include the following parts:

- a claim involving a question of definition
- a general definition of some key concept

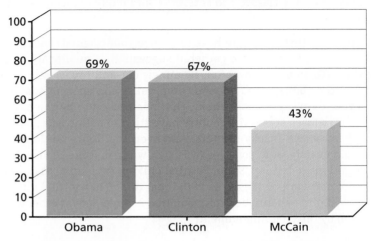

Positive Narratives in the Press
Percent of all assertions studied

A chart from a study entitled "Character and the Primaries" might be used to define a characteristic of media bias. From Journalism.org, May 29, 2008, and the Project for Excellence in Journalism of the Pew Research Center

Where can you locate the key features of a definitional argument in the Wikipedia entry on *local food*? What features are most effective? Which are least effective?

LINK TO P. 817

- a careful look at your subject in terms of that general definition
- evidence for every part of the argument, including visual evidence if appropriate
- a consideration of alternative views and counterarguments
- a conclusion drawing out the implications of the argument

It's impossible, however, to predict what emphasis each of those parts might receive or what the ultimate shape of an argument of definition will be.

Whatever form your definitional argument takes, be sure to share your draft with others who can examine its claims, evidence, and connections. Writers in isolation find it easy to think narrowly—and not to imagine that others might define *volunteer* or *institutional racism* in a completely different way. Be open to criticism and suggestions and look carefully at the terms of any definitions you offer. Do they really help readers distinguish one concept from another? Are the conditions offered sufficient or essential? Have you mistaken accidental features of a concept or object for more important features?

Don't hesitate to look to other sources for comparisons with your definitions. You can't depend on dictionaries to offer the last word about any disputed term, but you can begin with them, check encyclopedias and other reference works, and search the Web to find how your key terms are presented there. (In searching for the definition of *wetland*, for example, you could type *wetland definition* into a search engine like Google and get a limited number of useful hits.)

Finally, be prepared for surprises in writing arguments of definition. That's part of the delight in expanding the way you see the world. "I'm not a pig, I'm a sheepdog," thinks Babe in the 1995 film of the same name. Babe then goes right on to win a sheepdog competition. Such is the power of definition.

GUIDE to writing an argument of definition

● **Finding a Topic**

You're entering an argument of definition when you

- formulate a controversial or provocative definition: *In recent years, the American Dream meant a McMansion in a gated community with a deferential maid, gardener, and personal chef.*

- challenge a definition: *For most Americans today, the American Dream involves not luxury but the secure pensions, cheap energy costs, and health insurance that workers in the 1950s and 1960s enjoyed.*

- try to determine whether something fits an existing definition: *Expanding opportunity is (or is not) central to the American Dream.*

Look for issues of definition in your everyday affairs—for instance, in the way that jobs are classified at work, that key terms are described in your academic major, that politicians characterize the social issues that concern you, that you define yourself, or that others try to define you. Be alert to definitional arguments that may arise whenever you or others deploy adjectives such as *true, real, actual,* or *genuine: a true Texan, genuine environmental degradation, actual budget projections, authentic Mexican food.*

● **Researching Your Topic**

You can research issues of definition by using the following sources:

- college dictionaries and encyclopedias
- unabridged dictionaries
- specialized reference works and handbooks, such as legal and medical dictionaries
- your textbooks (check their glossaries)
- newsgroups and listservs that focus on particular topics

Be sure to browse in your library reference room. Also, use the search tools of electronic indexes and databases to determine whether or how often controversial phrases or expressions are occurring in influential materials—major online newspapers, journals, and Web sites.

When dealing with definitions, ask librarians to direct you to the most appropriate and reliable sources. For instance, in some cases, you may need to know what the legal definition of a term or concept is. A work such as *Black's Law Dictionary* or a database such as FindLaw may help. How the government defines terms may be important, too: you might check USA.gov.

● Formulating a Claim

After exploring your subject, begin to formulate a full and specific claim, a thesis that lets readers know where you stand and what issues are at stake. In moving toward this thesis, begin with the following types of questions of definition:

- questions related to genus: *Is assisting in suicide a crime?*
- questions related to species: *Is marijuana a harmful addictive drug or a useful medical treatment?*
- questions related to conditions: *Must the imposition of sexual attention be both unwanted and unsolicited to be considered sexual harassment?*
- questions related to fulfillment of conditions: *Has our college kept in place traditions or policies that might constitute racial discrimination?*
- questions related to membership in a named class: *Is any pop artist today in a class with Bob Dylan, the Beatles, Aretha Franklin, or the Rolling Stones?*

Your thesis should be a complete statement. In one sentence, you need to make a claim of definition and state the reasons that support your claim. In your paper or project itself, you may later decide to separate the claim from the reasons supporting it. But your working thesis should be a fully expressed thought. That means spelling out the details and the qualifications: *Who? What? Where? When? How many? How regularly? How completely?* Don't expect readers to fill in the blanks for you.

● Examples of Definitional Claims

- Assisting a gravely ill person in committing suicide should not be considered *murder* when the motive behind the act is to ease a person's suffering and not to do harm or to benefit from the death.
- Although marijuana is somewhat addictive, it should not be classified as a *dangerous drug* because it is less damaging to the individual and society

than heroin or cocaine and because it helps people live more comfortably with life-threatening diseases.

- Flirting with the waitstaff in a restaurant should be considered *sexual harassment* when the activity is repeated, unsolicited, and obviously unappreciated.

- Giving college admission preference to all racial minorities can be an example of *class discrimination* because such policies may favor middle- and upper-class students who are already advantaged.

● Preparing a Proposal

If your instructor asks you to prepare a proposal for your project, here's a format that may help:

State your thesis completely. If you're having trouble doing so, try outlining it in Toulmin terms:

    Claim:

    Reason(s):

    Warrant(s):

- **Explain why this argument of definition deserves attention. What's at stake? Why is it important for your readers to consider?**

- **Specify whom you hope to reach through your argument and why this group of readers would be interested in it.**

- **Briefly discuss the key challenges that you anticipate in preparing your argument: Defining a key term? Establishing the essential and sufficient elements of your definition? Demonstrating that your subject will meet those conditions?**

- **Determine what strategies you'll use in researching your definitional argument. What sources do you expect to consult: Dictionaries? Encyclopedias? Periodicals? The Internet?**

- **Determine what visuals you will include in your definitional argument. How will each one be used?**

- **Consider what format you expect to use for your project: A conventional research essay? A letter to the editor? A Web page?**

● Thinking about Organization

Your argument of definition may take various forms, but it's likely to include elements such as the following:

- a claim involving a matter of definition: *Labeling Al Qaeda and similar groups as representatives of "Islamic fascism" is understandable but misleading.*

- an attempt to establish a definition of a key term: *Genuine fascism is a mass movement within a nation resulting from democracy gone wrong.*

- an explanation or defense of the terms of the definition: *Scholars agree that fascism is a modern mass movement distinguished by the primacy of the nation over the individual, the elimination of dissent, the creation of a single-party state, and the glorification of violence on behalf of a national cause.*

- an examination of the claim in terms of the definition and all its criteria: *Fascism is highly nationalistic, but Islam is hostile to nationalism; Islam is a religious movement, but fascism is a secular movement that is usually hostile to religion.*

- a consideration of alternative views and counterarguments: *It is true that Osama bin Laden appeals to violence on behalf of his cause of restoring the medieval Islamic empire and that some fascist regimes (like Franco's Spain) were closely allied to religious authorities. . . .*

● Getting and Giving Response

All arguments benefit from the scrutiny of others. Your instructor may assign you to a peer group for the purpose of reading and responding to each other's drafts. If not, ask for responses from serious readers or consultants at a writing center. You can use the following questions to evaluate a draft. If you're evaluating someone else's draft, be sure to illustrate your points with examples. Specific comments are always more helpful than general observations.

The Claim

- Is the claim clearly an issue of definition?
- Is the claim significant enough to interest readers?
- Are clear and specific criteria established for the concept being defined? Do the criteria define the term adequately? Using this definition, could most readers identify what's being defined and distinguish it from other related concepts?

Evidence for the Claim

- Is enough evidence furnished to explain or support the definition? If not, what kind of additional evidence is needed?

- Is the evidence in support of the claim simply announced, or are its significance and appropriateness analyzed? Is a more detailed discussion needed?

- Are all the conditions of the definition met in the concept being examined?

- Are any objections readers might have to the claim, criteria, evidence, or way the definition is formulated adequately addressed?

- What kinds of sources, including visual sources, are cited? How credible and persuasive will they be to readers? What other kinds of sources might be more credible and persuasive?

- Are all quotations introduced with appropriate signal phrases (such as "As Himmelfarb argues, . . .") and blended smoothly into the writer's sentences?

Organization and Style

- How are the parts of the argument organized? Is this organization effective, or would another structure work better?

- Will readers understand the relationships among the claims, supporting reasons, warrants, and evidence? If not, what could be done to make those connections clearer? Is the function of every visual clear? Have you related each visual to a particular point in your essay and explained its significance? Are more transitional words and phrases needed? Would headings or graphic devices help?

- Are the transitions or links from point to point, paragraph to paragraph, and sentence to sentence clear and effective? If not, how could they be improved?

- Is the style suited to the subject? Is it too formal? Too casual? Too technical? Too bland? How can it be improved?

- Which sentences seem particularly effective? Which ones seem weakest, and how could they be improved? Should some short sentences be combined, or should any long ones be separated into two or more sentences?

- How effective are the paragraphs? Do any seem too skimpy or too long? How can they be improved?

- Which words or phrases seem particularly effective, vivid, and memorable? Do any seem dull, vague, unclear, or inappropriate for the audience or the writer's purpose? Are definitions provided for technical or other terms that readers might not know?

Spelling, Punctuation, Mechanics, Documentation, Format

- Are there any errors in spelling, punctuation, capitalization, and the like?

- Is an appropriate and consistent style of documentation used for parenthetical citations and the list of works cited or references? (See Chapter 20.)

- Does the paper or project follow an appropriate format? Is it appropriately designed and attractively presented? How could it be improved? If it's a Web site, do all the links work?

RESPOND•

1. Briefly discuss the criteria that you might use to define the italicized terms in the following controversial claims of definition. Compare your definitions of the terms with those of your classmates.

    Graphic novels are *serious literature*.

    Burning a nation's flag is a *hate crime*.

    Conor Oberst defines *emo*.

    Matt Drudge and Arianna Huffington are *legitimate journalists*.

    College sports programs have become *big businesses*.

    Plagiarism can be an act of civil *disobedience*.

    Satanism is a *religion* properly protected by the First Amendment.

    Campaign contributions are acts of *free speech* that should not be regulated.

    The District of Columbia should not have all the privileges of an American *state*.

    Gay and lesbian couples should have the legal privileges of *marriage*.

2. This chapter opens with sketches of five rhetorical situations that center on definitional issues. Select one of these situations, and write definitional criteria using the strategy of formal definition. For example, identify the features of a photograph that make it part of a larger class (*art, communication method, journalistic technique*). Next, identify the features of a photograph that make it distinct from other members of that larger class. Then use the strategy of operational definition to establish criteria for the same object: what does it do? Remember to ask questions related to conditions (*Is a computer-scanned photograph still a photograph?*) and questions related to fulfillment of conditions (*Does a good photocopy of a photograph achieve the same effect as the photograph itself?*).

3. In an essay at the end of this chapter, Lynn Peril makes a variety of claims about a concept she identifies as *pink think*, which she defines in part as "a set of ideas and attitudes about what constitutes proper female behavior." After reading this selection, consider whether Peril has defined a concept that operates today. If you think "pink think" still exists, prove it by showing how some activities, behaviors, products, or institutions meet the definition of the concept. Write, too, about the power that this concept has to define behavior.

    Alternatively, define a concept of your own that applies to a similar kind of stereotypical behavior—for example, *dude think* or *surfer think* or *geek think*. Then argue that your newly defined concept does, in fact, influence people today. Be sure to provide clear and compelling examples of the concept in action as it shapes the way that people think and behave.

Are little girls who play the latest version of Mystery Date still buying into Lynn Peril's concept of "pink think"?

The Offbeat Allure of Cult Films

SAYOH MANSARAY

On a Saturday afternoon in February junior Clare Marshall and her family sit in her living room watching a film that Marshall is an avid fan of: *Napoleon Dynamite*. Marshall and her family say quotes along with the movie and laugh aloud at the hilarious parts. "Girls only want boyfriends who have great skills," Clare says, imitating Napoleon's trademark throaty drawl. "You know, like nun chuck skills, bow hunting skills . . . computer hacking skills."

Opening paragraph includes a parodic definition of "great skills."

Marshall is not the only teenager who likes films that are completely different from most movies in theaters. The teen followings of nonmainstream films like *Napoleon Dynamite* and *Donnie Darko* show that today's teens are looking for films that are "off the beaten path," according to English and Literature as Film teacher Mike Horne. Teens are gravitating toward these quirky movies, raising some of them to a cult-like status.

A tentative definition of "cult film" is offered.

The consensus among Blazers is that a cult movie is a quirky, different film that did not do well in theaters but has since gained a strong and faithful following on DVD or video. In recent years the definition of cult films has begun to evolve and broaden to include films that did not actually flop in theaters. Regardless of the specific definition, recent cult films are attracting teen fans.

Sayoh Mansaray wrote this article for *Silver Chips Online*, the online newspaper of Montgomery Blair High School in Silver Spring, Maryland, where she served as public relations codirector and factcheck supervisor. *Silver Chips Online*, which has won a number of awards, is all student-run and is partially sponsored by the *Washington Post*. Note that the article, like most pieces published in newspapers, does not document sources in any formal way.

A still from *Donnie Darko*, starring Jake Gyllenhaal (left)

"IT FEELS REAL"

As Marshall continues to watch the film, a scene plays in which Napoleon talks to a girl on the phone. The girl has been forced by her mother to thank Napoleon for a picture he drew of her in hopes of getting a date. "It took me like three hours to finish the shading on your upper lip," Napoleon says to the girl, as Marshall quotes along with him.

Many teens, Marshall included, like cult films because they differ from other films in theaters. Horne says that teens gravitate to cult movies because they are not formulaic. "They are a little bit different, and they require some thought or interpretation," he says.

Junior Katrina Jabonete likes *Donnie Darko*, a film about a teen who is teetering on the edge of schizophrenia, because it is so beautifully twisted and darkly weird that the film opens itself to a thousand different interpretations. She believes that teens are drawn to cult movies because they aren't as clean or processed as mainstream flicks and because cult films are less likely to offer a concrete conclusion. Basically, they are more like real life. "[They] deal with problems and emotions in

Another characteristic of cult films is offered: they are "not formulaic" and they "require thought."

Reasons for the popularity of cult films are given.

a different, real way," she explains. "Teens relate to [these movies] because it feels real to them."

TIME WARP

While recent movies are gaining cult status, some students remain exclusively faithful to the classics, becoming part of groups that view their cult favorites over and over again.

Junior Linda Dye fits into this category. She thinks a cult movie is a film that is "so bad it's good." Take her favorite cult film, *The Rocky Horror Picture Show*, a 1975 musical about a group of gender-bending, quasi-alien, quasi-vampire, raving-lunatics-in-drag. "Ever since I first saw it, I've been completely in love with it," she gushes.

Dye is drawn to the film partially because the close-knit following allows her to interact with people she might never have known before. When Dye attended the annual *Rocky Horror* screening at the University of Maryland, she dressed up as one of the film's characters. In a bustier, a feather boa, and heels, Dye, along with the rest of the audience, yelled dialogue to the screen and made up her own lines as the movie played.

For Dye, this energy is what keeps her love for the film and its following alive. "You're sitting with these people you've never met, [but] by the end of the movie there's an energy—you're a community," she says.

"IF I HAD A TUMOR, I'D NAME IT MARLA"

Regardless of whether a movie is a classic or a recent hit, movie fans often display their love of films by quoting them. On snowy days, senior Robin Weiss likes to write one-liners from *Fight Club* like, "If I had a tumor, I'd name it Marla" and "We are a generation of men raised by women" on the icy windshields of random cars.

Marshall likes to answer questions with *Napoleon Dynamite* quotes. If a friend asks, "What are you doing today, Clare?" she might respond with a Napoleon line: "Whatever I feel like doing—gosh!"

An example of a classic cult film is provided.

Horne says that a major component of cult films is quotable dialogue. "Half the fun is reliving it with your friends," he says, smiling. Some fans can quote most of a movie, he adds. Senior Walker Davis, for example, knows most of the lines from *The Big Lebowski*.

According to Davis, cult films are never big budget productions, and no movie studio ever sets out to create a cult film—it just happens.

Many teens, like Marshall, just can't get enough of these films. Horne says that cult films are often bizarre, random, and edgy, which adds to their appeal. He says that people who watch cult films may have different motives than other moviegoers. "Many people look to film as an escape, [but] others are looking to find different thoughts," he says.

Quotable dialogue is a defining characteristic of a cult film.

Low-budget aspect of cult films, first mentioned in third paragraph, is reiterated here.

Pink Think

LYNN PERIL

From the moment she's wrapped in a pink blanket, long past the trau-matic birthday when she realizes her age is greater than her bust mea-surement, the human female is bombarded with advice on how to wield those feminine wiles. This advice ranges from rather vague proscriptions along the lines of "nice girls don't chew gum/swear/wear pants/fill-in-the-blank," to obsessively elaborate instructions for daily living. How many women's lives, for example, were enriched by former Miss America Jacque Mercer's positively baroque description of the proper way to put on a bathing suit, as it appeared in her guide *How to Win a Beauty Contest* (1960)?

> [F]irst, roll it as you would a girdle. Pull the suit over the hips to the waist, then, holding the top away from your body, bend over from the waist. Ease the suit up to the bustline and with one hand, lift one breast up and in and ease the suit bra over it. Repeat on the other side. Stand up and fasten the straps.

Instructions like these made me bristle. I formed an early aversion to all things pink and girly. It didn't take me long to figure out that many things young girls were supposed to enjoy, not to mention ways they were supposed to behave, left me feeling funny—as if I was expected to pound my square peg self into the round hole of designated girliness. I didn't know it at the time, but the butterflies in my tummy meant I had crested the first of many hills on the roller coaster ride of femininity—or, as I soon referred to it, the other f-word. Before I knew what was happening, I was hurtling down its track, seemingly out of control, and screaming at the top of my lungs.

After all, look what I was up against. The following factoids of feminin-ity date from the year of my birth (hey, it wasn't *that* long ago):

- In May of 1961, Betsy Martin McKinney told readers of *Ladies' Home Journal* that, for women, sexual activity commenced with intercourse

Lynn Peril is the publisher of the 'zine *Mystery Date*. This essay is excerpted from the introduction to *Pink Think,* a book that examines the influence of the feminine ideal.

and was completed with pregnancy and childbirth. Therefore, a woman who used contraceptives denied "her own creativity, her own sexual role, her very femininity." Furthermore, McKinney asserted that "one of the most stimulating predisposers to orgasm in a woman may be childbirth followed by several months of lactation." (Mmm, yes, must be the combination of episiotomy and sleep deprivation that does it.) Politely avoiding personal examples, she neglected to mention how many little McKinneys there were.

- During the competition for the title of Miss America 1961, five finalists were given two questions to answer. First they were asked what they would do if "you were walking down the runway in the swimsuit competition, and a heel came off one of your shoes?" The second question, however, was a bit more esoteric: "Are American women usurping males in the world, and are they too dominant?" Eighteen-year-old Nancy Fleming, of Montague, Michigan, agreed that "there are too many women working in the world. A woman's place is in the home with her husband and children." This, along with her pragmatic answer to the first question ("I would kick off both shoes and walk barefooted") and her twenty-three-inch waist (tied for the smallest in pageant history), helped Nancy win the crown.

- In 1961, toymaker Transogram introduced a new game for girls called Miss Popularity ("The True American Teen"), in which players competed to see who could accrue the most votes from four pageant judges—three of whom were male. Points were awarded for such attributes as nice legs, and if the judges liked a contestant's figure, voice, and "type." The prize? A special "loving" cup, of course! Who, after all, could love an unpopular girl?

These are all prime examples of "pink think." Pink think is a set of ideas and attitudes about what constitutes proper female behavior; a group-think that was consciously or not adhered to by advice writers, manufacturers of toys and other consumer products, experts in many walks of life, and the public at large, particularly during the years spanning the mid-twentieth century—but enduring even into the twenty-first century. Pink think assumes there is a standard of behavior to which all women, no matter their age, race, or body type, must aspire.

"Femininity" is sometimes used as a code word for this mythical standard, which suggests that women and girls are always gentle, soft, delicate, nurturing beings made of "sugar and spice and everything nice." But pink think is more than a stereotyped vision of girls and women as poor drivers who are afraid of mice and snakes, adore babies and small dogs, talk incessantly on the phone, and are incapable of keeping secrets. Integral to pink think is the belief that one's success as a woman is grounded in one's allegiance to such behavior. For example, a woman who fears mice isn't necessarily following the dictates of pink think. On the other hand, a woman who isn't afraid of mice but pretends to be because she thinks such helplessness adds to her appearance of femininity is toeing the pink think party line. When you hear the words "charm" or "personality" in the context of successful womanhood, you can almost always be sure you're in the presence of pink think.

While various self-styled "experts" have been advising women on their "proper" conduct since the invention of the printing press, the phenomenon defined here as pink think was particularly pervasive from the 1940s to the 1970s. These were fertile years for pink think, a cultural mindset and consumer behavior rooted in New Deal prosperity yet culminating with the birth of women's liberation. During this time, pink think permeated popular books and magazines aimed at adult women, while little girls absorbed rules of feminine behavior while playing games like the aforementioned Miss Popularity. Meanwhile, prescriptions for ladylike dress, deportment, and mindset seeped into child-rearing manuals, high school home economics textbooks, and guides for bride, homemaker, and career girl alike.

It was almost as if the men and women who wrote such books viewed proper feminine behavior as a panacea for the ills of a rapidly changing modern world. For example, myriad articles in the popular press devoted to the joys of housewifery helped coerce Rosie the Riveter back into the kitchen when her hubby came home from the war and expected his factory job back. During the early cold war years, some home economics texts seemed to suggest that knowing how to make hospital corners and a good tuna casserole were the only things between Our Way of Life and communist incursion. It was patriotic to be an exemplary housewife. And pink-thinking experts of the sixties and seventies, trying to maintain this ideal, churned out reams of pages that countered the onrushing tide of both the sexual revolution and the women's movement. If only all women behaved like our Ideal Woman, the experts seemed to say through the years, then everything would be fine.

You might even say that the "problem with no name" that Betty Friedan wrote about in *The Feminine Mystique* (1963) was a virulent strain of pink-thinkitis. After all, according to Friedan, "the problem" was in part engendered by the experts' insistence that women "could desire no greater destiny than to glory in their own femininity"—a pink think credo.

The pink think of the 1940s to 1970s held that femininity was necessary for catching and marrying a man, which was in turn a prerequisite for childbearing—the ultimate feminine fulfillment. This resulted in little girls playing games like Mystery Date long before they were ever interested in boys. It made home economics a high school course and college major, and suggested a teen girl's focus should be on dating and getting a boyfriend. It made beauty, charm, and submissive behavior of mandatory importance to women of all ages in order to win a man's attention and hold his interest after marriage. It promoted motherhood and housewifery as women's only meaningful career, and made sure that women who worked outside the home brought "feminine charm" to their workplaces lest a career make them too masculine.

Not that pink think resides exclusively alongside antimacassars and 14.4 modems in the graveyard of outdated popular culture: Shoes, clothing, and movie stars may go in and out of style with astounding rapidity, but attitudes have an unnerving way of hanging around long after they've outlived their usefulness—even if they never had any use to begin with.

10
Evaluations

"We don't want to go there for coffee. It's full of chemicals, it's not fair trade, and it's way overpriced."

The campus Labor Action Committee has been cochaired for four years by three students whose leadership has led to significant improvements in the way the university treats its workers. They're all graduating at once, leaving a leadership vacuum, so the group calls a special meeting to talk about what qualities it needs in its next leaders.

You've just seen *Citizen Kane* for the first time and want to share the experience with your roommate. Orson Welles's masterpiece is playing at the Student Union for only one more night, but the new *Incredible Hulk* is featured across the street in THX sound. Guess which movie your roomie wants to see? You intend to set him straight.

A senior is frustrated by the C she received on an essay written for a history class, so she makes an appointment to talk with the teaching assistant who graded the paper. "Be sure to review the assignment sheet first," the TA warns. Whoops: *now* the student notices that the back side of the sheet includes a checklist of requirements for the paper; she hadn't turned it over before.

"We have a lousy homepage," a sales representative observes at a district meeting. "What's wrong with it?" the marketing manager asks. "Everything," the sales rep replies, then quickly changes the subject when she notices the manager's furrowed brow. But the manager decides to investigate the issue. Who knows what an effective Web site looks like these days?

Understanding Evaluations

Here's the scene: you're going to be in New York City for only one night, and you want to indulge your love of musicals. You consult the *New Yorker* and find several possibilities, so you turn next to reviews, checking first with the *New York Times*. You don't have to read far before you come on a musical that sounds pretty fabulous: Lin-Manuel Miranda's *In the Heights*. "If you like the bubbly or sultry sounds of Latin music," the reviewer says, this one is for you. Since you are a big fan of Latin music, you read on:

> Under the enthusiastic guidance of the music director, Alex Lacamoire, the orchestra—band is really a better word—plays with a sense of excitement almost never heard emanating from a Broadway pit. (The standard amplification is less flattening to this music than to traditional scores.) Bright, piping fanfares from the trumpets punctuate the dance numbers; the merry tinkle of a steel drum laughs along with the jokes. The players below seem to be having as much fun as the performers onstage.
>
> That is saying plenty, for when this musical erupts in one of its expressions of collective joy, the energy it gives off could light up the George Washington Bridge for a year or two. The title song, for instance, is among the most galvanizing opening numbers in recent Broadway memory, as Usnavi gives the audience a guided tour, in briskly flowing rap, of the troubles that nip at the heels and the hopes that feed the imaginations of the neighborhood's inhabitants. . . .
>
> You could easily be cynical about the show's heartfelt belief in the possibility of a little love and a big lottery win making all things right. But then Mr. Miranda bounces back onstage, throwing down rhymes

A scene from *In the Heights*

and throwing his arms open wide as if to embrace the whole mezza-
nine. He seems to embody music's ability to make the trite seem true
again. And after all, this scrappy little musical about chasing your
dreams and finding your true home is Mr. Miranda's own dream come
true. He couldn't look more at home.

—Charles Isherwood, "The View from Uptown:
American Dreaming to a Latin Beat"

This reviewer offers you a number of reasons for choosing this particular musical—the quality of the sound ("bright, piping fanfares from
the trumpets" and "the merry tinkle of a steel drum"), the lead actor's
embodiment of "music's ability to make the trite seem true again," and
the collective joy of the dance ("the energy it gives off could light up the
George Washington Bridge for a year or two"). So you grab a ticket—and
months later see that the reviewer's evaluation of this show was matched
by the Tony Awards Committee.

Evaluations are everyday arguments. By the time you leave home in
the morning, you've likely made a dozen informal evaluations: you've
selected dressy clothes because you have a job interview in the afternoon

Lin-Manuel Miranda celebrating his Tony Award for best musical for *In the Heights*

with a law firm; you've chosen low-fat yogurt and fruit over the pancakes, butter, and syrup you really love; you've queued up the perfect playlist on your iPod for your hike to campus. In each case, you've applied criteria to a particular problem and then made a decision.

Some professional evaluations require more elaborate standards, evidence, and paperwork (imagine an aircraft manufacturer certifying a new jet for passenger service), but they don't differ structurally from the simpler choices that people make routinely. People love to voice their opinions, and they always have. In fact, a mode of ancient rhetoric—called the ceremonial, or *epideictic*—was devoted entirely to speeches of praise and blame. (See Chapter 1.)

Today, rituals of praise and blame are a significant part of American life. Adults who would choke at the notion of debating causal or definitional claims will happily spend hours appraising the Oakland Raiders, Boston Red Sox, or Detroit Pistons. Other evaluative spectacles in our culture include awards shows, beauty pageants, most-valuable-player presentations, lists of best-dressed or worst-dressed celebrities, "sexiest people" magazine covers, literary prizes, political opinion polls, consumer product magazines, and—the ultimate formal public gesture of evaluation—elections. Indeed, making evaluations is a form of entertainment in America and generates big audiences (think of *American Idol*) and revenues.

Evaluations and Academic Arguments

Evaluation is a hallmark of academic argument. You may already be familiar with two important forms of evaluation— postpublication book reviews and peer reviews of articles submitted to scholarly journals for publication (such reviews are most often "blind," in that the reviewer does not know the author's identity).

Take a look at part of one such evaluation, a book review by David Cole, a law professor at Georgetown University, of *Torture Team: Rumsfeld's Memo and the Betrayal of American Values* by Philippe Sands.

America's experiment with torture presents the Obama administration with one of its most difficult challenges: how should the nation account for the abuses that have occurred in the past, what are the appropriate remedies, and how can we ensure that such abuses not happen again? *Torture Team* offers new insight into what will surely be one of the leading human rights issues of the next several years. . . .

Because so many of the facts surrounding the torture policy are now well known, Sands's book is illuminating not so much for breaking new factual ground as for the human insight he brings to the events. Through his interviews, he tells a story about how ordinary human beings, all working within an institution designed to fight by the rules, felt tremendous pressure to bend the rules—and in most cases did so without apparent concern or self-doubt. A narrowly pragmatic ethos guided virtually all actors. The real arguments were for the most part not about whether coercive tactics were legally or morally acceptable, but about whether they worked. Some, especially those in the FBI, felt strongly that they were counterproductive, and that building rapport through noncoercive questioning was the only way to

(continued)

gain credible intelligence from captives. Others thought the idea of building rapport with al-Qaeda suspects was foolish; it could not be done. But with the courageous exception of Navy General Counsel Alberto Mora, few argued that coercive tactics were wrong because they were immoral and illegal, whether or not they worked. In America after September 11, idealists were few and far between, and an amoral, blinkered pragmatism ruled the day.

Sands is an unabashed idealist. He considers it the government lawyer's obligation to be the guardian of legality, even (and especially) where one's clients, the politically elected and appointed decision-makers, have decided that the law and the rules are inconvenient. Sands argues that torture is ineffective, and that building rapport with suspects is the better course. Indeed, he demonstrates in his own interviews the power of rapport to get subjects talking candidly. But in the end, his argument is not a pragmatic one—it is an argument of principle. The prohibition against torture is absolute, and expresses a fundamental norm about human decency, not a practical judgment about what produces results in interrogation.

—David Cole, "What to Do about Torturers"

Even an excerpt from this lengthy review in the *New York Review of Books* reveals the evaluative stance Cole takes: although the book does not add much to previously known facts about "America's experiment with torture," author Sands's compelling human insights and idealist principles make *Torture Team* worthy of careful consideration.

Criteria of Evaluation

Arguments of evaluation can produce simple rankings and winners or can lead to profound decisions about our lives, but they always involve standards. The particular standards we establish for judging anything— whether an idea, a work of art, a person, or a product—are called *criteria of evaluation.* Sometimes criteria are self-evident: an SUV that gets ten miles per gallon is a gas hog, and a piece of fish that smells even a little off shouldn't be eaten. But criteria are often complex when a potential subject is abstract: *What makes a professional referee effective? What features make a song a classic? What constitutes a living wage? How do we measure a successful foreign policy or college career?* Struggling to identify such difficult criteria of evaluation can lead to important insights into your values, motives, and preferences.

Why make such a big deal about criteria when many acts of evaluation seem effortless? We should be suspicious of our judgments even when we make them carelessly. It's irresponsible simply to think that stupid and uninformed opinions should carry the same weight as well-informed and well-reasoned opinions. Evaluations always require reflection, and when we look deeply into our judgments, we sometimes discover important *why* questions that typically go unasked:

- You challenge the grade you received in a course, but you don't question the practice of grading.

- You argue that buying a hybrid car makes more sense than keeping an SUV, but you don't ask whether taking alternative forms of transportation (like the bus or a bike) makes the most sense of all.

- You argue passionately that a Republican Congress is better for America than a Democratic alternative, but you fail to ask why voters get only two choices.

Push an argument of evaluation hard enough, and even simple judgments become challenging and intriguing.

In fact, for many writers, grappling with criteria is the toughest step in producing an evaluation. They've got an opinion about a movie or book or city policy, but they also think that their point is self-evident and widely shared by others. So they don't do the necessary work to specify the criteria for their judgments. If you know a subject well enough to evaluate it, your readers should learn something from you when you offer an opinion.

Do you think, for instance, that you could explain what (if anything) makes a veggie burger good? Though many people have eaten veggie burgers, they probably haven't spent much time thinking about them. But to evaluate them convincingly, it's not enough to claim merely that a good veggie burger is juicy or tasty. Such a claim is also not very interesting. The following criteria offered on the *Cook's Illustrated* Web site show that the writers have given the question quite a bit of thought:

> Store-bought veggie burgers border on inedible, but most homemade renditions are a lot of work. Could we develop a recipe that was really worth the effort? We wanted to create veggie burgers that even meat eaters would love. We didn't want them to taste like hamburgers, but we did want them to act like hamburgers, having a modicum of chew, a harmonious blend of savory ingredients, and the ability to go from grill to bun without falling apart.
>
> —*Cook's Illustrated*

After a lot of experimenting, *Cook's Illustrated* came up with a recipe that met these criteria.

Criteria of evaluation aren't static, either. They differ according to time and audience. Much market research, for example, is designed to find out what particular consumers want now and will want in the future—what their criteria are for buying a product. For a long time, such research indicated that consumers felt that TV was their major source of home entertainment and relegated computers to second place (and to the workplace). But that ranking began to change when online content became readily available. According to a *Los Angeles Times* article, researchers have concluded that "viewers want online video, and studios have decided they'd better give it to them, traditional corporate strategy be damned." This conclusion quickly led to some high-stakes ventures, including Hulu, an Internet video site: it's free, requires no registration or downloads, and gives viewers access to high-resolution top TV shows like Jon Stewart's *The Daily Show*.

One of Hulu's rivals, Veoh, reasons that the criteria of evaluation for such online video are still not completely understood. That is, while providers know that "viewers want online video," they don't yet know what the most *desirable* online video will be. In contrast to Hulu, which offers only a closed system of commercially produced video, Veoh is betting that viewers will continue to want the kind of user-generated content found on YouTube. So it provides both user-generated content and commercially produced shows like *CSI*. Only time will tell which of the new online video sites will better meet the criteria that users demand.

Characterizing Evaluation

One way of understanding evaluative arguments is to consider the types of evidence they use. A distinction we explored in Chapter 4 between hard evidence and arguments based on reason is helpful here. You may recall that we defined *hard evidence* as facts, statistics, testimony, and other kinds of arguments that can be measured, recorded, or even found—the so-called smoking gun in a criminal investigation. We defined *arguments based on reason* as those that are shaped by language, using various kinds of logic.

We can study arguments of evaluation the same way, looking at some as quantitative and others as qualitative. *Quantitative arguments* of evaluation rely on criteria that can be measured, counted, or demonstrated in some mechanical fashion (something is taller, faster, smoother, quieter, or more powerful than something else). In contrast, *qualitative arguments* rely on criteria that must be explained through words, relying on such matters as values, traditions, and emotions (something is more ethical, more beneficial, more handsome, or more noble than something else). A claim of evaluation might be supported by arguments of both sorts.

Fans can watch *Family Guy* on the Internet video site Hulu—but do their ideal criteria for online video also include user-generated content like YouTube?

Quantitative Evaluations

At first glance, quantitative evaluations seem to hold all the cards, especially in a society that is as enamored of science and technology as our own is. After you've defined a quantitative standard, making judgments should be as easy as measuring and counting—and in a few cases, that's the way things work out. *Who's the tallest or heaviest or loudest person in your class?* If your classmates allow themselves to be measured, you could find out easily enough, using the right equipment and internationally sanctioned standards of measurement—the meter, the kilo, or the decibel.

But what if you were to ask, *Who's the smartest person in class?* You could answer this more complex question quantitatively, using IQ tests or college entrance examinations that report results numerically. In fact, almost all college-bound students in the United States submit to this kind of evaluation, taking either the SAT or ACT to demonstrate their verbal and mathematical prowess. Such measures are widely accepted by educators and institutions, but they are also vigorously challenged. What do they actually measure? They predict likely academic success only in college, which is one kind of intelligence.

Quantitative measures of evaluation can be enormously useful, but even the most objective measures have limits. They've been devised by fallible people who look at the world from their own inevitably limited perspectives.

Qualitative Evaluations

Many issues of evaluation that are closest to people's hearts aren't subject to quantification. What makes a movie great? If you suggested a quantitative measure like length, your friends would probably hoot, "Get serious!" But what about box-office receipts, especially if they could be adjusted to reflect inflation? Would films that made the most money—an easily quantifiable measure—be the "best pictures"? That select group would include movies such as *Star Wars, The Sound of Music, Gone with the Wind, Titanic,* and *The Dark Knight.* An interesting group of films—but the best?

Or perhaps you want to argue that the Rotten Tomatoes Web site—with its ratings of films by the Rotten Tomatoes Community, by Top Critics, and by Approved Tomatometer Critics—offers a perfect way to

Not Just Words

Even what looks like totally objective counting can make a powerful evaluative argument. Look at this simple chart kept by the group Iraq Coalition Casualty Count. It offers a measure of U.S., British, and other coalition military fatalities in Iraq from March 20, 2003, when counting began, to July 8, 2009, when this chart was downloaded. What arguments of evaluation could be made based on these purely quantitative data?

MILITARY FATALITIES BY TIME PERIOD: IRAQ COALITION CASUALTY COUNT

Military Fatalities

Period	US	UK	Other*	Total	Days	Avg
7	195	3	0	198	353	0.56
6	1040	46	14	1100	534	2.06
5	933	32	21	986	412	2.39
4	715	13	18	746	318	2.35
3	580	25	27	632	216	2.93
2	718	27	59	804	424	1.90
1	140	33	0	173	43	4.02
Total	4321	179	139	4639	2300	2.02

*Other coalition countries.

Time Periods

Period 7: July 20, 2008–July 8, 2009
Period 6: February 1, 2007–July 19, 2008
Period 5: December 15, 2005–January 31, 2007
Period 4: January 31–December 14, 2005
Period 3: June 29, 2004–January 30, 2005
Period 2: May 2, 2003–June 28, 2004
Period 1: March 20, 2003–May 1, 2003

evaluate films. In the case of *Slumdog Millionaire*, Rotten Tomatoes Community members gave the film a "Tomatometer" score of 92 percent, while the Approved Critics and Top Critics both gave scores of 94 percent.

To argue for online ratings or box-office revenue as a criterion of film greatness, though, you'd have to offer a vigorous defense because many people in the audience would express serious doubts about either criterion. To define the criteria for "great movie," you'd probably look for the standards that serious critics use. You might consider the qualities that are shared by respected movies, such as their societal impact, cinematic technique, dramatic structures, casting, and so on. Most of these markers of quality could be defined with some precision but not measured or counted. Lacking hard numbers, you'd have to make your case rhetorically and convince the audience to accept your standards. A writer using qualitative measures could spend as much time defending criteria of evaluation as providing evidence that these standards are present in a particular film.

But establishing subtle criteria can make arguments of evaluation interesting. They require you, time and again, to challenge conventional wisdom. Look at the way Nick Gillespie in *Reasononline* reviews the last *Star Wars* movie, *Revenge of the Sith*:

> What might be called the continuing cultural hegemony of *Star Wars* is no small matter. With the possible exception of *The Lord of the Rings*, no other franchise has maintained a similar hold on the public imagination for so long a period of time. In a curious way, the first two installments in *The Godfather* saga did (as evidenced by the appropriation of its themes and motifs in everything from countless lesser mob movies to standup comedy to rap music). But it's undeniable that *Star Wars* is in the warp and woof of American culture, ranging from politics to toys to, of course, movies, novels, and comic books. It very much provides a backdrop, a framework, a system of reference for the ways we talk about things, whether we're talking about missile defense systems, visions of the future and technology, good vs. evil, you name it.
>
> This is all the more stunning given the generally acknowledged mediocrity of the *Star Wars* movies themselves. Indeed, it's a given that if *Star Wars* didn't start to go downhill sometime during the "Cantina Band" sequence in the very first flick, then the series actively started to suck wind harder than Billy Dee Williams in an action sequence by the start of the third release, *Return of the Jedi*, a film so bad that it may well be the space opera equivalent of *The Day the Clown*

Cried. (Personally, I lay in with those who peg the beginning of the end, if not the actual end of the end—or perhaps the high point—of the whole series to 1978's little-remembered yet still nightmare-inducing *The Star Wars Holiday Special*, which comes as close to the death-inducing video in *The Ring* as anything ever shown on non-premium cable.)

And yet, despite the craptacular nature of at least four out of six *Star Wars* movies, there's little doubt that no film event has been more anticipated than *Revenge of the Sith* (with the possible exception—and in France only—of the next *Asterix et Obelix* extravaganza).

—Nick Gillespie, "*Star Wars*, Nothing but *Star Wars*"

As Gillespie acknowledges, the *Star Wars* saga is full of flaws, some of them of a "craptacular" nature. And yet he goes on to make a much more subtle argument:

The enormous *Star Wars* industry—the movies, the cartoons, the toys, the pop-cult references—still generates interest, excitement, pleasure (this last is something that most critics, whether liberal or conservative

Does *Star Wars: The Clone Wars*, which premiered in August 2008, meet Nick Gillespie's criteria for continuing what he calls "a cultural conversation worth having"?

find absolutely terrifying), and, most important, a cultural conversation worth having. The series may well be crap—and a grave disappointment to critics who know so much better than the rest of us—but surely that's the least interesting thing about it.

Gillespie certainly knows that not everyone will agree with his assessment of the *Star Wars* saga, but his lengthy review makes clear to readers why he has come to the qualitative decision that the movies have nurtured "a cultural conversation worth having." Fans of the series are wondering whether that conversation will continue to be important in the animated continuation, *Star Wars: The Clone Wars.*

Developing an Evaluative Argument

Developing an argument of evaluation can seem like a simple process, especially if you already know what your claim is likely to be:

> *Citizen Kane* is the finest film ever made by an American director.

Having established a claim, you would then explore the implications of your belief, drawing out the reasons, warrants, and evidence that might support it:

Claim	*Citizen Kane* is the finest film ever made by an American director . . .
Reason	. . . because it revolutionizes the way we see the world.
Warrant	Great films change viewers in fundamental ways.
Evidence	Shot after shot, *Citizen Kane* presents the life of its protagonist through cinematic images that viewers can never forget.

The warrant here is, in effect, a statement of criteria—in this case, the quality that defines "great film" for the writer.

In developing an evaluative argument, you'll want to pay special attention to criteria, claims, and evidence.

Formulating Criteria

Often neglected in evaluations is the discussion of criteria. Although even casual evaluations (*The band sucks!*) might be traced to reasonable criteria, most people don't bother defending their positions until they

Notice how specific the editors of *Cook's Illustrated* magazine are in establishing their criteria for the ideal chewy chocolate chip cookie.

LINK TO P. 845 ....

are challenged (*Oh yeah?*). Yet when writers address readers whom they understand or with whom they share core values, they don't defend most of their criteria in detail. A film critic like Roger Ebert isn't expected to restate all his principles every time he writes a movie review. Ebert assumes that his readers will—over time—come to appreciate his standards.

Still, the criteria can make or break a piece. In an essay from Salon .com's series of evaluative arguments called "Masterpieces," writer Stephanie Zacharek can barely contain her enthusiasm for the Chrysler Building in midtown Manhattan:

Why does this building make people happy?

> Architects, who have both intuition and training on their side, have some very good reasons for loving the Chrysler Building. The rest of us love it beyond reason, for its streamlined majesty and its inherent sense of optimism and promise for the future, but mostly for its shimmery, welcoming beauty—a beauty that speaks of humor and elegance in equal measures, like a Noel Coward play.
>
> How can a mere building make so many people so happy—particularly so many ornery New Yorkers, who often pretend, as part of their act, not to like anything? There may be New Yorkers who dislike the Chrysler Building, but they rarely step forward in public. To do so would only invite derision and disbelief.
>
> —Stephanie Zacharek, "The Chrysler Building"

It may seem odd to suggest that one measure of a great building is that it makes people happy. And so the writer has a lot to prove. She's got to provide evidence that a building can, in fact, be delightful. And she seems to do precisely that later in the same essay when she gives life even to the windows in the skyscraper:

> Looking at the Chrysler Building now, though, it's hard to argue against its stylish ebullience, or its special brand of sophisticated cheerfulness. . . . Particularly at night, the crown's triangular windows—lit up, fanned out and stacked high into the sky—suggest a sense of movement that has more in common with dance than with architecture: Those rows of windows are as joyous and seductive as a chorus line of Jazz Age cuties, a bit of sexy night life rising up boldly from an otherwise businesslike skyline.

The criteria that Zacharek uses lead to an inventive and memorable evaluation that perhaps teaches readers to look at buildings in a whole new way.

The iPhone 3GS

So don't take criteria of evaluation for granted. If you offer vague, dull, or unsupportable principles, expect to be challenged. You're most likely to be vague about your beliefs when you haven't thought enough about your subject. Push yourself at least as far as you imagine readers will. Imagine readers looking over your shoulder, asking difficult questions. Say, for example, that you intend to argue that anyone who wants to stay on the cutting edge of personal technology will obviously prefer Apple's iPhone 3GS because it's not only a great phone but a great handheld computer. But what does that mean? What makes the device "great"? Is it that it gives access to email and the wireless Web, has a widescreen iPod, has a hybrid GPS-Wi-Fi-cell tower triangulator that pinpoints your location on the iPhone's Google, and has an astonishing number of applications? These provide some criteria that you could defend. But should you get more—or less—technical? Do you need to assert very sophisticated criteria to establish your authority to write about the subject? These are appropriate questions to ask.

Making Claims

Claims can be stated directly or, in rare instances, strongly implied. For most writers, a direct evaluative claim with the statement carefully qualified works best. Consider the differences between the following three claims and how much greater the burden of proof for the first claim would be than the burden for the second and third ones:

Margaret Cho is the most outrageous comedian around today.

Margaret Cho is one of the three or four most outrageous comedians around today.

Margaret Cho may come to be regarded as one of the most outrageous comedians of her time.

The most outrageous of them all? Margaret Cho in 2008 lamé mode.

The point of qualifying a statement isn't to make evaluative claims bland but to make them responsible and reasonable. Consider how *Pitchfork* critic Mary Pytlik evaluates a recent album, M.I.A.'s *Kala*:

> In contrast to her comparatively sparkly and streamlined debut, *Kala* is clattering, buzzy, and sonically audacious. While it still sounds, for lack of a better word, as *digital* as its predecessor, the primarily Switch-produced album paradoxically reaches further than the produced-by-committee *Arular* in terms of its overall palette of sounds. From the disco bassline and gloopy Eurovision strings of the swimmy Bollywood cover "Jimmy" to the hairy didgeridoos and pitched-up elementary school raps (courtesy of Aboriginal schoolboy crew Wilcannia Mob) of "Mango Pickle Down River" to the bubbling synths of the gloriously woozy "20 Dollar," this represents a significant expansion of M.I.A.'s already big tent of sounds. It also signifies her expansion as a performer. Where *Arular* saw her make the best of her fairly limited vocal

Ken Kobus tells the story of his life working with steel. What claims— either stated or implied—can you find in this story about the pleasures of hard work?

LINK TO P. 973

Sri Lankan–British rapper M.I.A. has won critical praise for her genre-bending hip-hop music.

abilities, *Kala* finds her reaching further outward, either by singing sweetly, as she does capably on "Jimmy," by peppering her chatter with sudden, free-floating melodies ("20 Dollar"), or by simply putting even more emphasis on the elastic qualities of her usual sing-songy delivery, as she does on the pinched-nose baile funk of "World Town" and the celebratory first single "Boyz"—a triumph of her rhythmic patter if there ever was one.

—Mary Pytlik, "M.I.A.: *Kala*"

Pytlik offers evidence to prove the claim that M.I.A.'s new album is in many ways a "triumph," but she also qualifies that claim by noting that in *Kala* the singer has had to overcome some inherent weaknesses ("her fairly limited vocal abilities," "her usual sing-songy delivery"). Pointing to flaws as well as to successes is an easier task than trying to argue that this set of songs is flawless.

Presenting Evidence

The more evidence in an evaluation the better, provided that the evidence is relevant. For example, in evaluating the performance of two computers, the speed of their processors would be important, but the quality of their keyboards or the availability of service might be less crucial.

Just as important as relevance in selecting evidence is presentation. Not all pieces of evidence are equally convincing, nor should they be treated as such. Select the evidence that is most likely to impress your readers, and arrange the argument to build toward your best material. In most cases, that best material will be evidence that's specific, detailed, and derived from credible sources. Look at the details in these paragraphs of Sean Wilsey's review of *Fun Home: A Family Tragicomic*, a graphic novel by Alison Bechdel:

> If the theoretical value of a picture is still holding steady at a thousand words, then Alison Bechdel's slim yet Proustian graphic memoir, *Fun*

Note that Stanley Fish includes a great deal of textual evidence—which he analyzes extremely carefully—in evaluating David Horowitz's Academic Bill of Rights.

LINK TO P. 929

Home, must be the most ingeniously compact, hyper-verbose example of autobiography to have been produced. It is a pioneering work, pushing two genres (comics and memoir) in multiple new directions, with panels that combine the detail and technical proficiency of R. Crumb with a seriousness, emotional complexity and innovation completely its own. Then there are the actual words. Generally this is where graphic narratives stumble. Very few cartoonists can also write—or, if they can, they manage only to hit a few familiar notes. But *Fun Home* quietly succeeds in telling a story, not only through well-crafted images but through words that are equally revealing and well chosen. Big words, too! In 232 pages this memoir sent me to the dictionary five separate times (to look up "bargeboard," "buss," "scutwork," "humectant" and "perseverated").

A comic book for lovers of words! Bechdel's rich language and precise images combine to create a lush piece of work — a memoir where concision and detail are melded for maximum, obsessive density. She has obviously spent years getting this memoir right, and it shows. You can read *Fun Home* in a sitting, or get lost in the pictures within the pictures on its pages. The artist's work is so absorbing you feel you are living in her world.

—Sean Wilsey, "The Things They Buried"

The details in this passage are rich enough to make the case that Alison Bechdel's novel is one that pushes both comics and memoirs in new directions.

In evaluation arguments, don't be afraid to concede a point when evidence goes contrary to the overall claim you wish to make. If you're really skillful, you can even turn a problem into an argumentative asset, as Bob Costas does in acknowledging the flaws of baseball great Mickey Mantle in the process of praising him:

None of us, Mickey included, would want to be held to account for every moment of our lives. But how many of us could say that our best moments were as magnificent as his?

—Bob Costas, "Eulogy for Mickey Mantle"

Considering Design and Visuals

In thinking about how to present your evidence, don't forget to consider the visual aspects of doing so. Design features—such as headings for the

A direct visual representation of what you are evaluating, such as this page from Alison Bechdel's *Fun Home*, can be critical to an evaluation's success.

different criteria you're using or, in online evaluations, links to material related to your subject—can enhance your authority, credibility, and persuasiveness. Think, too, about how you might use visual evidence to good effect. For example, you might use a bar graph to show how your subject measures up to a similar one. In a review of *Fun Home*, Sean Wilsey might have used the page shown above from the book to illustrate his point that "*Fun Home* quietly succeeds in telling a story, not only through well-crafted images but through words that are equally revealing and well chosen. Big words, too!"

Key Features of Evaluations

In drafting an evaluation, you should consider three basic elements:

- an evaluative claim that makes a judgment about a person, an idea, or an object
- the criterion or criteria by which you'll measure your subject
- evidence that the particular subject meets or falls short of the stated criteria

All these elements will be present in arguments of evaluation, but they won't follow a specific order. In addition, you'll often need an opening paragraph to explain what you're evaluating and why. Tell readers why they should care about your subject and take your opinion seriously.

Nothing adds more depth to an opinion than letting others challenge it. When you can, use the resources of the Internet or more local online networks to get responses to your opinions. It can be eye-opening to realize how strongly people react to ideas or points of view that you regard as perfectly normal. When you're ready, share your draft with friends and classmates, asking them to identify places where your ideas need additional support, either in the discussion of criteria or in the presentation of evidence.

GUIDE to writing an evaluation

● Finding a Topic

You're entering an argument of evaluation when you

- make a judgment about quality: Citizen Kane *is probably the finest film ever made by an American director.*
- challenge such a judgment: Citizen Kane *is vastly overrated by most film critics.*
- construct a ranking or comparison: Citizen Kane *is a more intellectually challenging movie than* Casablanca.

Issues of evaluation arise daily—in the judgments you make about public figures or policies; in the choices you make about instructors and courses; in the recommendations you make about books, films, or television programs; in the preferences you exercise in choosing products, activities, or charities. Be alert to evaluative arguments whenever you read or use terms that indicate value or rank—*good/bad, effective/ineffective, best/worst, competent/incompetent, successful/unsuccessful.* Finally, be aware of your own areas of expertise. Write about subjects or topics about which others regularly ask your opinion or advice.

● Researching Your Topic

You can research issues of evaluation by using the following sources:

- journals, reviews, and magazines (for current political and social issues)
- books (for assessing judgments about history, policy, etc.)
- biographies (for assessing people)
- research reports and scientific studies
- books, magazines, and Web sites for consumers
- periodicals and Web sites that cover entertainment and sports
- blogs for exploring current affairs

Surveys and polls can be useful in uncovering public attitudes: *What books are people reading? Who are the most admired people in the country? What activities or businesses are thriving or waning?* You'll discover that Web sites, newsgroups, and blogs thrive on evaluation. Browse these public forums for ideas, and, when possible, explore your own topic ideas there. But remember that all sources need to be evaluated—especially those you plan to use in an evaluation argument. So examine each source carefully, making sure that it is legitimate and credible.

● Formulating a Claim

After exploring your subject, begin to formulate a full and specific claim, a thesis that lets readers know where you stand and on what criteria you'll base your judgments. Look for a thesis that's challenging enough to attract readers' attention, not one that merely repeats views already widely held. In moving toward this thesis, you might begin with questions like these:

- What exactly is my opinion? Where do I stand?
- Can I make my judgment more specific?
- Do I need to qualify my claim?
- According to what standards am I making my judgment?
- Will readers accept my criteria, or will I have to defend them, too?
- What major reasons can I offer in support of my evaluation?

Your thesis should be a complete statement. In one sentence, you need to make a claim of evaluation and state the reasons that support your claim. Be sure your claim is specific. Anticipate the questions readers might have: *Who? What? Where? Under what conditions? With what exceptions? In all cases?* Don't expect readers to guess where you stand.

● Examples of Evaluative Claims

- Though they may never receive Oscars for their work, Sandra Bullock and Keanu Reeves deserve credit as actors who have succeeded in a wider range of film roles than most of their contemporaries.
- Many computer users are discovering that Microsoft's Vista is more trouble than it is worth.
- Barack Obama's speech on race, delivered in Philadelphia on March 18, 2008, is the most honest presentation of this issue we have heard since Martin Luther King's time.

- Jimmy Carter has been highly praised for his work as a former president of the United States, but history may show that even his much-derided term in office laid the groundwork for the foreign policy and economic successes now attributed to later administrations.

- Because knowledge changes so quickly and people switch careers so often, an effective education today is one that trains people how to learn more than it teaches them what to know.

Preparing a Proposal

If your instructor asks you to prepare a proposal for your project, here's a format that may help:

State your thesis completely. If you're having trouble doing so, try outlining it in Toulmin terms:

   Claim:

   Reason(s):

   Warrant(s):

- **Explain why this issue deserves attention. What's at stake?**
- **Specify whom you hope to reach through your argument and why this group of readers would be interested in it.**
- **Briefly discuss the key challenges you anticipate: Defining criteria? Defending them? Finding quantitative evidence to support your claim? Developing qualitative arguments to bolster your judgment?**
- **Determine what research strategies you'll use. What sources do you expect to consult?**
- **Consider what format you expect to use for your project: A conventional research essay? A letter to the editor? A Web page?**

Thinking about Organization

Your evaluation may take various forms, but it's likely to include elements such as the following:

- a specific claim: *Most trucks are unsuitable for the kind of driving Americans do.*
- an explanation or defense of the criteria (if necessary): *The overcrowding and pollution of American cities and suburbs might be relieved if more Americans*

drove small, fuel-efficient cars. Cars do less damage in accidents than heavy trucks and are also less likely to roll over.

- an examination of the claim in terms of the stated criteria: *Most trucks are unsuitable for the kind of driving Americans do because they are not designed for contemporary urban driving conditions.*

- evidence for every part of the argument: *Trucks get very poor gas mileage; they are statistically more likely than cars to roll over in accidents; . . .*

- consideration of alternative views and counterarguments: *It is true, perhaps, that trucks make drivers feel safer on the roads and give them a better view of traffic conditions. . . .*

● Getting and Giving Response

All arguments benefit from the scrutiny of others. Your instructor may assign you to a peer group for the purpose of reading and responding to each other's drafts. If not, ask for responses from some serious readers or consultants at a writing center. You can use the following questions to evaluate a draft. If you're evaluating someone else's draft, be sure to illustrate your points with examples. Specific comments are always more helpful than general observations.

The Claim

- Is the claim clearly an argument of evaluation? Does it make a judgment about something?
- Does the claim establish clearly what's being evaluated?
- Is the claim too sweeping? Does it need to be qualified?
- Will the criteria used in the evaluation be clear to readers? Do the criteria need to be defined more explicitly or precisely?
- Are the criteria appropriate ones to use for this evaluation? Are they controversial? Does evidence of their validity need to be added?

Evidence for the Claim

- Is enough evidence furnished to ensure that what's being evaluated meets the criteria established for the evaluation? If not, what kind of additional evidence is needed?
- Is the evidence in support of the claim simply announced, or are its significance and appropriateness analyzed? Is a more detailed discussion needed?

- Are any objections readers might have to the claim, criteria, or evidence adequately addressed?

- What kinds of sources, including visual sources, are cited? How credible and persuasive will they be to readers? What other kinds of sources might be more credible and persuasive?

- Are all quotations introduced with appropriate signal phrases (such as "As Will argues, . . .") and blended smoothly into the writer's sentences?

Organization and Style

- How are the parts of the argument organized? Is this organization effective, or would some other structure work better?

- Will readers understand the relationships among the claims, supporting reasons, warrants, and evidence? If not, what could be done to make those connections clearer? Are more transitional words and phrases needed? Would headings or graphic devices help?

- Are the transitions or links from point to point, paragraph to paragraph, and sentence to sentence clear and effective? If not, how could they be improved?

- Are all visuals carefully integrated into the text? Is each visual introduced and commented on to point out its significance? Is each visual labeled as a figure or a table and given a caption as well as a citation?

- Is the style suited to the subject? Is it too formal? Too casual? Too technical? Too bland? How can it be improved?

- Which sentences seem particularly effective? Which ones seem weakest, and how could they be improved? Should some short sentences be combined, or should any long ones be separated into two or more sentences?

- How effective are the paragraphs? Do any seem too skimpy or too long? How can they be improved?

- Which words or phrases seem particularly effective, vivid, and memorable? Do any seem dull, vague, unclear, or inappropriate for the audience or the writer's purpose? Are definitions provided for technical or other terms that readers might not know?

Spelling, Punctuation, Mechanics, Documentation, Format

- Are there any errors in spelling, punctuation, capitalization, and the like?

- Is an appropriate and consistent style of documentation used for parenthetical citations and the list of works cited or references? (See Chapter 20.)
- Does the paper or project follow an appropriate format? Is it appropriately designed and attractively presented? How could it be improved? If it's a Web site, do all the links work?

RESPOND •

1. Choose one item from the following list that you understand well enough to evaluate. Develop several criteria of evaluation that you could defend to distinguish excellence from mediocrity in the area. Then choose an item that you don't know much about and explain the research you might do to discover reasonable criteria of evaluation for it.

   fashion designers

   Navajo rugs

   musicals

   spoken word poetry

   UN secretaries-general

   NFL quarterbacks

   social networking sites

   TV journalists

   video games

   organic vegetables

   animated films

   universal health care plans

2. In the last ten years, there has been a proliferation of awards programs for movies, musicians, sports figures, and other categories. For example, before the Academy of Motion Picture Arts and Sciences hands out the Oscars, a half-dozen other organizations have given prizes to the annual crop of films. Write a short opinion piece assessing the merits of a particular awards show or a feature such as *People*'s annual "sexiest man" issue. What should a proper event of this kind accomplish? Does the event you're reviewing do so?

3. Local news and entertainment magazines often publish "best of" issues or articles that list readers' and editors' favorites in such categories as "best place to go on a first date," "best ice cream sundae," and "best dentist." Sometimes the categories are specific: "best places to say 'I was retro before retro was cool'" or "best movie theater seats." Imagine that you're the editor of your own local magazine and that you want to put out a "best of" issue tailored to your hometown. Develop ten categories for evaluation. For each category, list the evaluative criteria that you would use to make your judgment. Next, consider that because your criteria are warrants, they're especially tied to audience. (The criteria for "best dentist," for example, might be

tailored to people whose major concern is avoiding pain, to those whose children will be regular clients, or to those who want the cheapest possible dental care.) For several of the evaluative categories, imagine that you have to justify your judgments to a completely different audience. Write a new set of criteria for that audience.

4. Develop an argument using (or challenging) one of the criteria of evaluation presented in this chapter. You might explore one of the following topics:

> Immigrant workers deserve a fair wage and minimal benefits.
>
> A car should be energy efficient.
>
> Good songs remain in people's memories.
>
> Great films change viewers in fundamental ways.
>
> Good pets need not have fur and four legs.
>
> Great veggie burgers need just the right shape and texture.

5. For examples of powerful evaluation arguments, search the Web or your library for obituaries of famous, recently deceased individuals. Try to locate at least one such item, and analyze the types of claims it makes about the deceased. What criteria of evaluation are employed? What kinds of evidence does it present?

The Burden of Laughter: Chris Rock Fights Ignorance His Way

JACK CHUNG

Adorned in an expensive black leather jacket, the skinny comedian with the well-trimmed goatee spits out controversial insights in his angry, signature shrill voice. The hoots and hollers of the sold-out audience are intermingled with frenzied applause. The man of the hour, Chris Rock, is performing at the Apollo Theater in Harlem, only a few blocks away from where he grew up. This particular stand-up routine, entitled *Bigger and Blacker*, is Rock's third HBO special and it comes after the years of performing in smoky comic clubs, after his unfruitful years at *SNL*, after his landmark HBO special *Bring the Pain*, and after the two Emmy wins. It is 1999, and Chris Rock is on top of the comedic world.

Chris Rock! Chris Rock! Chris Rock! The comedian has become a household name in America, and he is seen everywhere from movies to talk shows to TV commercials to the documentary *Good Hair* that he presented at Sundance in 2009. More importantly, he has become arguably the most talked-about comedian of today, and he has intellectual defenders and critics who both agree

Evaluative claim stated and elaborated on

Jack Chung wrote "The Burden of Laughter: Chris Rock Fights Ignorance His Way" when he was a student in Alyssa O'Brien's first-year writing class at Stanford University. The essay (which has been shortened for use in this book) was later published in *The Boothe Prize Essays*, a volume devoted to outstanding undergraduate student writing. In commenting on this essay, O'Brien notes that it is "structured as a series of miniature performances" and that it "delves deep into the complicated history of Blackface minstrelsy, 'coon' stereotypes, and 'Jim Crow' humor" to evaluate Rock's use of humor and to argue forcefully for its effectiveness in "carrying on the tradition of a painful yet treasured humor that has long been intricately woven into the fabric of African American culture." Chung uses many sources for his essay and follows MLA style in citing them.

that the man holds a significant role in the debate over sociopolitical issues of race that rage across the nation. Interestingly, throughout the discussion of Rock's importance in affecting the public's perspective of race relations, the comedian himself has noticeably downplayed his role. He has persistently answered to both admirers and critics that he is nothing more than a "Jokeman," and that his only concern is to be funny (Rock, "Rock on a Roll" 3). However, whether or not Rock is sincere in devaluing his position as a social commentator, his comic material and activities off the stage suggest that he is indeed one of the forerunners in shaping Americans' perception of African Americans as a race, and he is a leader, though an unwilling one, in tearing down the stereotypes that both whites and black have of each other.

Evidence of claim that Rock's humor is painfully honest and often angry— a criterion by which it can be evaluated.

With his painfully honest and often angry humor, Rock upholds the traditional African-American humor that originates from the days of slavery, and he pioneers that humor to a new direction with his conscious efforts to portray the diversity of Black America. *Nothing more racist than an old black man. Because old black men went through real racism. He didn't go through that "I can't get a cab" shit. He was the cab. The white man would jump on his back and say, "Main Street." "Left, nigga! Left, you fuckin nigga!"* (Rock, *Bigger and Blacker*)

Forty minutes into his special *Bigger and Blacker*, Rock introduces this bit on the injustices that blacks suffered during the heyday of the civil rights era, and now there is a twinge of discomfort among the audience members, a discomfort echoed in Harvard psychologist A. Poussaint's assertion that such "street" comedy surely encourages the acceptance of white superiority rather than challenging it. *The New Republic* goes further by deriding it as humor that is "attempting to shuck, jive, grin, shout, and bulge [its] eyes all the way back to the days of minstrelsy" (Driver 29). Such criticism is not light, for it charges Rock's comedy with reverting to the Jim Crow humor of the nineteenth and early twentieth centuries, therefore

Counter-argument: Rock's humor does not tear down but rather perpetuates stereotypes.

undermining the progress that blacks have made in challenging such prejudiced images of themselves.

To support his argument that Chris Rock is reminiscent of the "coons" of the minstrel shows of the nineteenth century, Justin Driver gives a short history lesson of the blackface minstrels in his *New Republic* article. The minstrel shows were popularized in the 1830s by white performers who mimicked blacks by wearing black face paint, and eventually by the 1850s blacks had formed their own troupes of minstrels through which they presented the ignorant "coon" that shucked and jived (Driver 29). In this sense, Rock's buffoonish gestures can be seen as reminiscent of the minstrels, and his voice—"a high-pitched, piercing shrill that seems to work most effectively when shouted through a grotesquely enormous grin" (29)—is nothing more than a device to convey the profanity that is crucial to Rock's angry delivery (30).

Evidence in support of counter-argument

Driver is not the only critic who finds Rock's profanity irrelevant; legendary comedian Bill Cosby, offended by the vulgar language in Rock's comedy, asked Rock to remove his comedy album from Rock's opening act of the *Bring the Pain* special (Kamp 9). However, another legendary comedian, Jerry Seinfeld, defends Rock's rhetorical usage of his voice by claiming, "It's the yelling that makes it special" (qtd. in Farley 67). Indeed, when Rock shouts out the vulgar words in his routine, it is almost as if they are *meant* to grate against the ear and create the caustic pain and laughter that Rock seeks. An exasperated Rock points this out to those who cannot comprehend his use of foul language in an interview by yelling, "You ignorant people, grow up. Cursing is used for emphasis; it's never the joke" (qtd. in Nelson 2).

A counter to the counter-argument introduced

Paradoxically, even with his supposed "reactionary" comedic style that conjures up images of the "coons" past, Chris Rock is extremely popular with black audiences. Justin Driver dismisses this popularity by stating that African Americans have come to enjoy such politically incorrect gestures of minstrelsy because they have endured "coon" comedy for such a long time (32). Dexter B. Gordon, author of the article "Humor in African American Discourse: Speaking of Oppression" in *Journal of Black Studies*, disagrees with Driver, and, although he never alludes to Chris Rock in his article, his analysis of African comic traditions makes the best argument in defense of Rock's rhetorical strategies on stage. Gordon argues that at its core, African-American humor is a diverse product that ranges from the quaint and delightful to the most often obscene, bitter, and sardonic (2). He goes on to claim that much of what Driver finds offensive in Rock's presentation—the jiving, the shouting, and the shuckin—are actually distinctive "games" of African-American culture (Gordon 3). And whereas Driver sees these characteristics as traits used to "assuage white concerns about the moral propriety of slavery" (Driver 30), Gordon sees them as "part of the humor that continues to fulfill the need for a sense of power in the midst of misery, the need for both a morale booster and amusement in Black culture" (Gordon 3). His assertion that "shuckin" and "jiving" is part of African-American lore supports the idea that Chris Rock's rhetorical strategies are not a return to "coon comedy"— rather they are part of a continuation of African-American humor that keeps intact its unique methods of delivering humor.

Evidence in support of the claim that Rock's humor reflects distinct African American culture and style

One of the reasons that Rock is so successful in transforming the boundless rage of his material into a product of uproarious laughter is his keen understanding that his humor carries the seriousness and shame that Gordon links to African-American humor. Gordon says, "At its base, then, African American humor is very serious" (2), and Rock reveals this insight when he reflects on his own work: "I don't think anything I ever said onstage isn't something I first said in a conversation being perfectly serious" (qtd. in Nelson 3). Gordon also mentions that an important aspect of African-American humor is self-deprecation (2), and Rock uses this tool in a sophisticated manner that is developed through various aspects

Another criterion introduced: self-deprecating humor with a distinct edge is characteristic of Rock's humor.

of his comedy. For instance, in his book, Rock tackles the controversial subject of the word "nigger" that both blacks and whites would prefer to shy away from, and he says, "Of course, 'nigger' is just a word. White people could call us anything, like 'butter.' 'Hey you fucking butter! Pick that cotton, butter!'" By discussing the "N" word in the comedic form of the word "butter," he reduces the dignity of blacks as the "N" word is originally meant to, but he does it in a way so that readers are able to comprehend that he mocks the word and not black people. He doesn't stop there, however; he carries that joke further in his TV show, *The Chris Rock Show*, by playing a pseudo-commercial in which blacks rave about a cereal called "Nigga Please." At first glance, the casual use of the word in the parody seems derogatory to black people, but Rock uses self-degradation and even extends it to social degradation to derail the vulgarity of the word "nigger." Of course, not all of the audience gets the complex joke, and some come away offended by the coarse satire, but Rock accepts this as part of his ongoing attempt to stray from the "good-natured" humor of Aristotle and Plato: "Somebody should always be offended. Somebody in your life should always be like, 'Why did you do that?' Always. That's just being a real artist. That's the difference between Scorsese and Disney" (qtd. in Farley 68). The quote by itself is a memorable sound bite, but when Rock says on stage that a white busboy would not change positions with even a rich black man, the quote becomes the centerpiece of a philosophy of a man who has dedicated his life to bring out the wincing grimace of his spectators.

The question then arises as to why Rock turns to potentially controversial humor in his comedic acts. Why is it that he's not afraid of the angry beehive he might stir up when he says on stage, "There ain't a white man in this room who'd change places with me"? Much of his bold and perhaps even reckless courage in choosing his subject matters comes from his own personal experience.

Use of controversial humor discussed: another characteristic of Rock's style

As a teenager growing up in Brooklyn, New York, in the post–civil rights 1970s, Rock was sent to an all-white school in Bensonhurst by a mother who wanted a better education for her son (Farley 68). At the high school Rock claims that he was beaten regularly and called "nigger" every day by "white toxic waste" (Hammer 1, 3), and it is from such hellish torture that "he came away with a kind of sad wisdom that will never leave him and thoroughly inhibits his humor" (Schruers 40). Friend and actor Joe Pesci explains that Chris Rock feels entitled to poke fun of both blacks and whites because he experienced racism directly (qtd. in Nelson 2), and the result is a comedian who sounds off incisive remarks to both races. In *Rock This*, Rock says of white people, "Broke-ass white people have it bad. I'll bet you a set of black satin sheets that 80 percent of the Ku Klux Klan makes less than $13,000 a year" (29). It is debatable whether Rock truly has the liberty to denigrate another race based on his past school experience, but it is an unimportant debate; in answering the original question of the source of Rock's fearlessness, the point is that he feels he has the right to show the failings of both white and black people.

While Rock's schooling definitely led him to find humor in all groups of people, it did not affect his work as much as the loss of his father, who died in 1989 from a ruptured ulcer after spending 55 years of his life holding two jobs as a union trucker and a cab driver (Schruers 42). At the time of his father's death, Rock was a struggling comedian trying to make a name for himself: with his father's death, something changed. Looking back, Rock says, "The only time I ever wanted to give it up is when my dad died" (qtd. in Chappell 168). Rock, however, did not give up; instead, he came away from the experience with a new sense of urgency to take risks in his comedy before he had to face his own death. In a *Rolling Stone* interview with Fred Schruers, Rock shares some of his thoughts: "You could be played out tomorrow and it's no fault of your own. . . . Work as hard as you can . . . and go out swinging. If you're going to make mistakes, make aggressive mistakes" (qtd. in Schruers 64). This epiphany freed Rock to produce the edgy comedic sketches that paved his way to fame. In an ironic and cruel twist of fate, the death of Rock's father may have been a great gift; Rock was now finally ready to unleash his most insightful fury.

Another criterion—risk taking—is central to Rock's humor.

> *There's, like, a civil war going on with black people, and there's two sides: there's black people . . . and there's niggas. And niggas have got to go! Every time black people want to have a good time, ign'ant-ass niggas fuck it up! Can't do shit without some ign'ant-ass niggas fuckin it up!*
> (Rock, *Bring the Pain*)

"Niggas vs. Black People." The notorious comic sketch from his 1996 HBO special remains his most divisive and brilliant piece of work, and it is repeated and discussed to this day. When Chris Rock proclaimed this manifesto in front of a large viewing audience, he floored everyone, blacks and whites, by unveiling thoughts that blacks had of each other. *Can't do nothing! Can't keep a disco open more than three weeks. Grand opening closing!* The white media was amazed by this revelation that blacks were critical of some members of their own community, and they praised Rock for his daring monologue (Farley 69). Blacks, on the other hand, were divided on the piece; some loved it for what they saw as an honest portrayal while others hated it for the possibility that it could lead to even more stereotypical thinking among white people. The opinions on "Niggas vs. Black People" varied greatly, but no one could deny the importance of the piece in explaining Rock's views on race.

The 1996 HBO sketch noted as meeting the evaluative criteria discussed

When Chris Rock presented "Niggas vs. Black People" in *Bring the Pain*, he believed that he was speaking to a mostly African-American audience about the "gangsta" blacks that other blacks despised for the negative image they portrayed to the media. Even after the backlash Rock received for the routine, he held steadfastly to his notion that there were a minority of "Niggas" in the black community who undermine much of the positive values that the majority of black hold. Fellow comedian Mario Joiner agrees with Rock's perspective by commenting on the sketch, "Every black person can relate to it—hell, you got cousins you don't want to be around" (Kamp 6). Support also came in the form of Rock's mother in a 1998 *60 Minutes* interview with Ed Bradley when she defended her son's monologue by saying, "I love my people. I don't want to live next door to niggers either" ("Chris Rock: Comedy").

However, Ed Bradley, a black man himself, was unsatisfied by Ms. Rock's input on the matter and demanded to know the difference between "niggers" and black people. His grilling of the comedian's mother seemed to imply that he disapproved of Rock's performance because it fails to divide a clear line between the supposed two distinct groups of people, and the confusion may lead to racial stereotypical thinking in which all blacks are regarded as having some "nigga" characteristics.

Indeed, Justin Driver argues that Rock's well-intentioned but unconvincing separation of "niggas" from black people "legitimates [certain whites'] racist view of the world" (31). He then concludes his article by saying that Rock belongs to a group of comedians and rappers who feed stereotypes of blacks by "extolling negative behavior among African Americans as the only genuine blackness" and that his work "obscures the rich and varied truth about black life in America today" (33).

As adamant as some critics are in their belief that Rock tarnishes the image of blacks in the eyes of the rest of America, there are those who would counter that such bits as "Niggas vs. Black People" shed light on the elasticity of the black experience. In response to *The New Republic*'s searing criticism, *Time* writer Bruce Handy defends Rock by saying, "I would wager that Rock is making a point about how street culture celebrates boorish behavior, and how that can feed racist stereotypes, and

Critics take aim at Rock once again.

Evidence in support of the critics' position considered

The critics' points are challenged by other Rock supporters.

how dispiriting that is" (67). With this statement, Handy directly contradicts Driver with his opinion that Rock does not perpetrate stereotypes with his comedy but rather seeks to help the black majority discard the negative labels brought on by the "gangsta" nihilism of a handful of blacks who are overly represented in television and music. Jill Nelson echoes similar sentiments when she says that the black majority that Rock supposedly wants to reveal to the public is a broad range of working-class people who seek to move forward, not backwards (1). In one particular segment of *Rock This*, Rock is especially apparent as the frustrated voice of the "silent black majority" when he exclaims, "White people don't know how to tell the difference between one black man and another. If they could, we'd all get along. . . . To white people, even Ed Bradley and Bryant Gumbel hanging out, waiting to cross the street together, is potentially scary" (11).

The debate continues, as critics charge Rock with encouraging stereotypes.

Even if Rock fights rather than encourages stereotyping, there remains the criticism of his "Niggas vs. Black People" riff that it exposes the taboo subjects spoken amongst only blacks to the public for full disclosure. In his interview with *60 Minutes*, Rock deduces that much of his criticism from black people on the use of the "N" word comes because he says it where white people could hear it ("Chris Rock: Comedy"). Professor and cultural critic Michael Eric Dyson registers his disapproval of Rock's revelation of black thought to white audiences when he says: "Rock signifies an unwillingness among the younger black generation to abide by the dirty-laundry theory. That theory suggests you don't say anything self-critical or negative about black people where white people can hear it. But the hip-hop generation believes in making money off the publication of private pain and agony" (qtd. in Farley 69).

Another critic disagrees, offering evidence in support of Rock.

Dyson's concerns seem legitimate, but *Time* writer Chris Farley contends that it is precisely because Rock refuses to uphold the "dirty-laundry theory" that his comedy becomes a powerful agent to advance blacks. He argues that although *Bring the Pain* was aired on HBO and not on BET, it was a comedy routine made about blacks, for blacks (Farley 69). It was a momentous event, for it was one of the first times that whites were ignored in the scheme of the situation, and Farley predicts that more undisclosed aspects of the black community will be revealed on the national stage because blacks no longer care about the image they may relay to white people (Farley 70).

Return to central claims of the essay

In the larger context of the history of African-American humor, Rock's "Niggas vs. Black People" follows the formula of bitter self-denigrating humor, but it is elevated to something African-American humor had not been before. Whereas in the past such humor had served as a quiet venting of anger and aggression for blacks who acknowledged white superiority, Rock shared that humor with his fellow African Americans in a medium that white audiences could observe but not play a role in, and the result was that much of the black inferiority complex associated with African-American culture was absolved. In speaking of the long range effects of such an emancipation, hip-hop mogul Russell Simmons chuckles, "Now [members of the mainstream media] have to live with [Rock] even though he makes them uncomfortable, and I think that's fabulous" (qtd. in Farley 70). For the first time, African-American humor disassociated itself from any kind of white involvement, and the pieces of such a shake-up are still falling today as African-American humor continually reshapes its role in black culture.

The breadth of passionate debate that Rock's comedy elicits from intellectuals is evidence enough that he is advancing discussion of the foibles of black America, but Rock continually insists that he has no political aims: "Really, really at the end of the day, the only important thing is being funny. I don't go out of my way to be political" (qtd. in Bogosian 58). His unwillingness to view himself as a black leader triggers Justin Driver to say, "[Rock] wants to be caustic and he wants to be loved" (32). Even supporters wistfully sigh, "One wishes Rock would own up to the fact that he's a damned astute social critic" (Kamp 7).

Rock's ultimate goals probed: is he only a jokeman, or is he a leader?

Although Rock would at first seem merely content to let his comic material speak for itself, his activities have shown him to be carrying out his mission to increase black diversity in the entertainment industry. In the fall of 1998, he started a college humor magazine entitled the *Illtop Journal* at Howard University to create an "infrastructure" through which young black talent could hone their humorous writing skills (Rock, "Rock on a Roll" 2; Kamp 3). He has also used *The Chris Rock Show* as a political forum for notable black leaders such as Jesse Jackson and Marion Barry to voice their opinions. When the show ended its run in year 2000, activist Reverend Al Sharpton remarked that there should be "a national day of mourning," for the show "provided a forum where people like

Evidence introduced to support view of Rock as a leader

me could talk to a different part of America that did not necessarily get exposure to us" ("Chris Rock Pulls Plug"). Regarding the purpose of the show, Rock himself has been proud of the way it broadened the range of black humor, and in the *Vanity Fair* interview, he boasts, "One thing we do well is, it's the only time in history you've seen a black guy do something dry" (qtd. in Kamp 9). Even though Rock may never admit that he is more than a comedian, he uses the *Illtop Journal* and *The Chris Rock Show* to reveal to America of the multiple dimensions of black life. Perhaps, then, Rock is not an unwilling leader as originally stated in one of the opening paragraphs but a leader in the disguise of a comedian.

Summation of argument

I think we need a new leader. We haven't had a leader in awhile. Someone to move you (Rock, *Bigger and Blacker*). With these words, Rock slowly works his way to the closing remarks of his race sketch in *Bigger and Blacker*. As he peers into the dark of the Apollo Theater, he must realize that the invisible faces staring back at him regard him as one such leader. He is not the leader in the mold of Martin Luther King Jr. or Barack Obama, but he is a leader nonetheless, for he carries with him the burden of carrying on the tradition of a painful yet treasured humor that has long been woven into the fabric of African-American culture. As the curtains draw down at the end of the show to drown out the standing ovation, Rock knows that his work for the day is done, but tomorrow he will arrive at his office of *The Chris Rock Show* to continue his work of portraying the eclectic characteristics of black people. The teaching never stops, and he does it under the façade of humor because he understands that the purpose of his humor, African-American humor, is to make "visible the invisible while masking its own anger and rage" (Gordon 11). Rock gives the adoring crowd one last crooked grin, and the audience is unsure whether the grin is a smile or a smirk as they watch his shadow trail off the stage.

WORKS CITED

Bogosian, Eric. "Chris Rock Has No Time for Your Ignorance." *New York Times Magazine* 5 Oct. 1997: 56–59. Print.

Chappell, Kevin. "Bigger, Better, and Hotter! Chris Rock Talks about Fame, Controversy, and the Challenge of Being No. 1." *Ebony* Oct. 1999: 162–70. Print.

"Chris Rock: Comedy, Life, and Career of Entertainer Chris Rock." *Sixty Minutes.* CBS, WCBS, New York, 6 Sept. 1998. Web. Transcript. 24 Feb. 2002.

"Chris Rock Pulls Plug on His HBO Show." *CNN.com.* Cable News Network, 8 Dec. 2000. Web. 26 Feb. 2002.

Driver, Justin. "The Mirth of a Nation: Black Comedy's Reactionary Hipness." *New Republic* 4 June 2001: 29–33. Print.

Farley, Christopher John. "Seriously Funny." *Time* 13 Sept. 1999: 66–70. Print.

Gordon, Dexter B. "Humor in African American Discourse: Speaking of Oppression." *Journal of Black Studies* 29 (Nov. 1998): 254–76. Web. 22 Feb. 2002.

Hammer, Steve. Interview. *NUVO Newsweekly.* Aug. 1994. Web. 22 Feb. 2002.

Handy, Bruce. "Chris Rock: Even When Cracking Jokes That Make Us Cringe, He Shows Us That Laughter Can Be the Best Revenge." *Time* 9 July 2001: 67. Print.

Kamp, D. "The Color of Truth." *Vanity Fair* Aug. 1999. Web. 19 Feb. 2002.

Nelson, Jill. "Alternative Rock." *US News* 10–12 July 1998. Web. 22 Feb. 2002.

Poussaint, Alvin F. Foreword. *African American Viewers and the Black Situation Comedy: Situating Racial Humor.* By Robin R. Means Coleman. New York: Garland, 2000. xi–xiv. Web. 22 Feb. 2002.

Rock, Chris, perf. *The Best of the Chris Rock Show.* Warner Home Video, 1999. DVD.

——, perf. *Bigger and Blacker.* HBO, 1999. DVD.

——, perf. *Bring the Pain.* HBO, 1996. DVD.

——. *Rock This!* Darby, PA: Diane, 1997. 6–31. Print.

——. "Rock on a Roll: Chris Rock Takes His Comedy Very Seriously." Interview by Keven Powell. *Papermag* Aug. 2000. Web. 23 Feb. 2002.

Schruers, Fred. "Chris Rock Star." *Rolling Stone* 2 Oct. 1997: 38–42, 64–65. Print.

With Friends Like These . . .

TOM HODGKINSON

I despise Facebook. This enormously successful American business describes itself as "a social utility that connects you with the people around you." But hang on. Why on God's earth would I need a computer to connect with the people around me? Why should my relationships be mediated through the imagination of a bunch of supergeeks in California? What was wrong with the pub?

And does Facebook really connect people? Doesn't it rather disconnect us, since instead of doing something enjoyable such as talking and eating and dancing and drinking with my friends, I am merely sending them little ungrammatical notes and amusing photos in cyberspace, while chained to my desk? A friend of mine recently told me that he had spent a Saturday night at home alone on Facebook, drinking at his desk. What a gloomy image. Far from connecting us, Facebook actually isolates us at our workstations.

Facebook appeals to a kind of vanity and self-importance in us, too. If I put up a flattering picture of myself with a list of my favorite things, I can construct an artificial representation of who I am in order to get sex or approval. ("I like Facebook," said another friend. "I got a shag out of it.") It also encourages a disturbing competitiveness around friendship: it seems that with friends today, quality counts for nothing and quantity is king. The more friends you have, the better you are. You are "popular," in the sense much loved in American high schools. Witness the cover line on Dennis Publishing's new *Facebook* magazine: "How to Double Your Friends List."

It seems, though, that I am very much alone in my hostility. At the time of writing Facebook claims 59 million active users, including 7 million in the UK, Facebook's third-biggest customer after the U.S. and Canada. That's 59 million suckers, all of whom have volunteered their ID card information and consumer preferences to an American business they

---

Tom Hodgkinson, author of *How to Be Idle* and *How to Be Free*, writes for *The Guardian*, the *Sunday Times*, and other British publications. "With Friends Like These" was published in January 2008 in *The Guardian*. (The correction on p. 334 appeared two days later.)

know nothing about. Right now, 2 million new people join each week. At the present rate of growth, Facebook will have more than 200 million active users by this time next year. And I would predict that, if anything, its rate of growth will accelerate over the coming months. As its spokesman Chris Hughes says: "It's embedded itself to an extent where it's hard to get rid of."

All of the above would have been enough to make me reject Facebook forever. But there are more reasons to hate it. Many more.

Facebook is a well-funded project, and the people behind the funding, a group of Silicon Valley venture capitalists, have a clearly thought out ideology that they are hoping to spread around the world. Facebook is one manifestation of this ideology. Like PayPal before it, it is a social experiment, an expression of a particular kind of neoconservative libertarianism. On Facebook, you can be free to be who you want to be, as long as you don't mind being bombarded by adverts for the world's biggest brands. As with PayPal, national boundaries are a thing of the past.

Although the project was initially conceived by media cover star Mark Zuckerberg, the real face behind Facebook is the forty-year-old Silicon Valley venture capitalist and futurist philosopher Peter Thiel. There are only three board members on Facebook, and they are Thiel, Zuckerberg and a third investor called Jim Breyer from a venture capital firm called Accel Partners (more on him later). Thiel invested $500,000 in Facebook when Harvard students Zuckerberg, Chris Hughes and Dustin Moskowitz went to meet him in San Francisco in June 2004, soon after they had launched the site. Thiel now reportedly owns 7 percent of Facebook, which, at Facebook's current valuation of $15 billion, would be worth more than $1 billion. There is much debate on who exactly were the original co-founders of Facebook, but whoever they were, Zuckerberg is the only one left on the board, although Hughes and Moskowitz still work for the company.

Thiel is widely regarded in Silicon Valley and in the U.S. venture capital scene as a libertarian genius. He is the co-founder and CEO of the virtual banking system PayPal, which he sold to eBay for $1.5 billion, taking $55 million for himself. He also runs a £3 billion hedge fund called Clarium Capital Management and a venture capital fund called Founders Fund. *Bloomberg Markets* magazine recently called him "one of the most successful hedge fund managers in the country." He has made money by betting on rising oil prices and by correctly predicting that the dollar would weaken. He and his absurdly wealthy Silicon Valley mates have recently been labeled "The PayPal Mafia" by *Fortune* magazine, whose reporter also observed that Thiel has a uniformed butler and a $500,000 McLaren supercar. Thiel is also a chess master and intensely competitive. He has been known to sweep the chessmen off the table in a fury when losing. And he does not apologize for this hypercompetitiveness, saying: "Show me a good loser and I'll show you a loser."

But Thiel is more than just a clever and avaricious capitalist. He is a futurist philosopher and neocon activist. A philosophy graduate from Stanford, in 1998 he cowrote a book called *The Diversity Myth*, which is a detailed attack on liberalism and the multiculturalist ideology that dominated Stanford. He claimed that the "multiculture" led to a lessening of individual freedoms. While a student at Stanford, Thiel founded a right-wing journal, still up and running, called *The Stanford Review*—motto: *Fiat Lux* ("Let there be light"). Thiel is a member of TheVanguard.org, an Internet-based neoconservative pressure group that was set up to attack MoveOn.org, a liberal pressure group that works on the Web. Thiel calls himself "way libertarian."

TheVanguard is run by one Rod D. Martin, a philosopher-capitalist whom Thiel greatly admires. On the site, Thiel says: "Rod is one of our nation's leading minds in the creation of new and needed ideas for public policy. He possesses a more complete understanding of America than most executives have of their own businesses."

This little taster from their Web site will give you an idea of their vision for the world: "TheVanguard.org is an online community of Americans who believe in conservative values, the free market and limited government as the best means to bring hope and ever-increasing opportunity to everyone, especially the poorest among us." Their aim is to promote policies that will "reshape America and the globe." TheVanguard describes its politics as "Reaganite/Thatcherite." The chairman's message says: "Today we'll teach MoveOn [the liberal Web site], Hillary and the leftwing media some lessons they never imagined."

So Thiel's politics are not in doubt. What about his philosophy? I listened to a podcast of an address Thiel gave about his ideas for the future. His philosophy, briefly, is this: since the seventeenth century, certain enlightened thinkers have been taking the world away from the old-fashioned nature-bound life, and here he quotes Thomas Hobbes' famous characterization of life as "nasty, brutish and short," and towards a new virtual world where we have conquered nature. Value now exists in imaginary things. Thiel says that PayPal was motivated by this belief: that you can find value not in real manufactured objects, but in the relations between human beings. PayPal was a way of moving money around the world with no restriction. *Bloomberg Markets* puts it like this: "For Thiel, PayPal was all about freedom: it would enable people to skirt currency controls and move money around the globe." Clearly, Facebook is another uber-capitalist experiment: can you make money out of friendship? Can you create communities free of national boundaries—and then sell Coca-Cola to them? Facebook is profoundly uncreative. It makes nothing at all. It simply mediates in relationships that were happening anyway.

Thiel's philosophical mentor is one René Girard of Stanford University, proponent of a theory of human behavior called *mimetic desire*. Girard reckons that people are essentially sheeplike and will copy one another without much reflection. The theory would also seem to be proved correct in the case of Thiel's virtual worlds: the desired object is irrelevant; all you need to know is that human beings will tend to move in flocks. Hence financial bubbles. Hence the enormous popularity of Facebook. Girard is a regular at Thiel's intellectual soirees. What you don't hear about in Thiel's philosophy, by the way, are old-fashioned real-world concepts such as art, beauty, love, pleasure and truth.

The Internet is immensely appealing to neocons such as Thiel because it promises a certain sort of freedom in human relations and in business, freedom from pesky national laws, national boundaries and suchlike. The Internet opens up a world of free trade and laissez-faire expansion. Thiel also seems to approve of offshore tax havens, and claims that 40 percent of the world's wealth resides in places such as Vanuatu, the Cayman Islands, Monaco and Barbados. I think it's fair to say that Thiel, like Rupert Murdoch, is against tax. He also likes the globalization of digital culture because it makes the banking overlords hard to attack: "You can't have a workers' revolution to take over a bank if the bank is in Vanuatu," he says.

If life in the past was nasty, brutish and short, then in the future Thiel wants to make it much longer, and to this end he has also invested in a firm that is exploring life-extension technologies. He has pledged £3.5 million to a Cambridge-based gerontologist called Aubrey de Grey, who is searching for the key to immortality. Thiel is also on the board of advisers of something called the Singularity Institute for Artificial Intelligence. From its fantastical Web site, the following: "The Singularity is the technological creation of smarter-than-human intelligence. There are several technologies . . . heading in this direction . . . Artificial Intelligence . . . direct brain-computer interfaces . . . genetic engineering . . . different technologies which, if they reached a threshold level of sophistication, would enable the creation of smarter-than-human intelligence."

So by his own admission, Thiel is trying to destroy the real world, which he also calls "nature," and install a virtual world in its place, and it is in this context that we must view the rise of Facebook. Facebook is a deliberate experiment in global manipulation, and Thiel is a bright young thing in the neoconservative pantheon, with a penchant for far-out techno-utopian fantasies. Not someone I want to help get any richer.

The third board member of Facebook is Jim Breyer. He is a partner in the venture capital firm Accel Partners, who put $12.7 million into Facebook in April 2005. On the board of such U.S. giants as Wal-Mart and Marvel Entertainment, he is also a former chairman of the National Venture Capital Association (NVCA). Now these are the people who are really making things happen in America, because they invest in the new young talent, the Zuckerbergs and the like. Facebook's most recent round of funding was led by a company called Greylock Venture Capital, who put in the sum of $27.5 million. One of Greylock's senior partners is called Howard Cox, another former chairman of the NVCA, who is also on the board of In-Q-Tel. What's In-Q-Tel? Well, believe it or not (and check out their Web site), this is the venture-capital wing of the CIA. After 9/11, the U.S. intelligence community became so excited by the possibilities of new technology and the innovations being made in the private sector that in 1999 they set up their own venture capital fund, In-Q-Tel, which "identifies and partners with companies developing cutting-edge technologies to help deliver these solutions to the Central Intelligence Agency and the broader U.S. Intelligence Community (IC) to further their missions."

The U.S. defense department and the CIA love technology because it makes spying easier. "We need to find new ways to deter new adversaries," defense secretary Donald Rumsfeld said in 2003. "We need to make the leap into the information age, which is the critical foundation of our transformation efforts." In-Q-Tel's first chairman was Gilman Louie, who served on the board of the NVCA with Breyer. Another key figure in the In-Q-Tel team is Anita K. Jones, former director of defense research and engineering for the U.S. department of defense, and—with Breyer—board member of BBN Technologies. When she left the U.S. department of defense, Senator Chuck Robb paid her the following tribute: "She brought the technology and operational military communities together to design detailed plans to sustain U.S. dominance on the battlefield into the next century."

Now even if you don't buy the idea that Facebook is some kind of extension of the American imperialist program crossed with a massive information-gathering tool, there is no way of denying that as a business, it is pure megagenius. Some Net nerds have suggested that its $15 billion valuation is excessive, but I would argue that if anything that is too modest. Its scale really is dizzying, and the potential for growth is virtually limitless. "We want everyone to be able to use Facebook," says the impersonal voice of Big Brother on the Web site. I'll bet they do. It is Facebook's enormous potential that led Microsoft to buy 1.6 percent for $240 million. A recent rumor says that Asian investor Lee Ka-Shing, said to be the ninth richest man in the world, has bought 0.4 percent of Facebook for $60 million.

The creators of the site need do very little bar fiddle with the program. In the main, they simply sit back and watch as millions of Facebook addicts voluntarily upload their ID details, photographs and lists of their favorite consumer objects. Once in receipt of this vast database of human beings, Facebook then simply has to sell the information back to advertisers, or, as Zuckerberg puts it in a recent blog post, "to try to help people share information with their friends about things they do on the Web." And indeed, this is precisely what's happening. On November 6 last year, Facebook announced that twelve global brands had climbed on board. They included Coca-Cola, Blockbuster, Verizon, Sony Pictures and Condé Nast. All trained in marketing bullshit of the highest order, their representatives made excited comments along the following lines:

"With Facebook Ads, our brands can become a part of the way users communicate and interact on Facebook," said Carol Kruse, vice president, global interactive marketing, the Coca-Cola Company.

"We view this as an innovative way to cultivate relationships with millions of Facebook users by enabling them to interact with Blockbuster in convenient, relevant and entertaining ways," said Jim Keyes, Blockbuster chairman and CEO. "This is beyond creating advertising impressions. This is about Blockbuster participating in the community of the consumer so that, in return, consumers feel motivated to share the benefits of our brand with their friends."

"Share" is Facebookspeak for "advertise." Sign up to Facebook and you become a free walking, talking advert for Blockbuster or Coke, extolling the virtues of these brands to your friends. We are seeing the commodification of human relationships, the extraction of capitalistic value from friendships.

Now, by comparison with Facebook, newspapers, for example, begin to look hopelessly outdated as a business model. A newspaper sells advertising space to businesses looking to sell stuff to their readers. But the system is far less sophisticated than Facebook for two reasons. One is that newspapers have to put up with the irksome expense of paying journalists to provide the content. Facebook gets its content for free. The other is that Facebook can target advertising with far greater precision than a newspaper. Admit on Facebook that your favorite film is *This Is Spinal Tap*, and when a *Spinal Tap*-esque movie comes out, you can be sure that they'll be sending ads your way.

It's true that Facebook recently got into hot water with its Beacon advertising program. Users were notified that one of their friends had made a purchase at certain online shops; 46,000 users felt that this level

of advertising was intrusive, and signed a petition called "Facebook! Stop invading my privacy!" to say so. Zuckerberg apologized on his company blog. He has written that they have now changed the system from "opt-out" to "opt-in." But I suspect that this little rebellion about being so ruthlessly commodified will soon be forgotten: after all, there was a national outcry by the civil liberties movement when the idea of a police force was mooted in the UK in the mid-nineteeth century.

Furthermore, have you Facebook users ever actually read the privacy policy? It tells you that you don't have much privacy. Facebook pretends to be about freedom, but isn't it really more like an ideologically motivated virtual totalitarian regime with a population that will very soon exceed the UK's? Thiel and the rest have created their own country, a country of consumers.

Now, you may, like Thiel and the other new masters of the cyberverse, find this social experiment tremendously exciting. Here at last is the Enlightenment state longed for since the Puritans of the seventeenth century sailed away to North America, a world where everyone is free to express themselves as they please, according to who is watching. National boundaries are a thing of the past and everyone cavorts together in free-wheeling virtual space. Nature has been conquered through man's boundless ingenuity. Yes, and you may decide to send genius investor Thiel all your money, and certainly you'll be waiting impatiently for the public flotation of the unstoppable Facebook.

Or you might reflect that you don't really want to be part of this heavily funded program to create an arid global virtual republic, where your own self and your relationships with your friends are converted into commodities on sale to giant global brands. You may decide that you don't want to be part of this takeover bid for the world.

For my own part, I am going to retreat from the whole thing, remain as unplugged as possible, and spend the time I save by not going on Facebook doing something useful, such as reading books. Why would I want to waste my time on Facebook when I still haven't read Keats' "Endymion"? And when there are seeds to be sown in my own back yard? I don't want to retreat from nature, I want to reconnect with it. Damn air-conditioning! And if I want to connect with the people around me, I will revert to an old piece of technology. It's free, it's easy and it delivers a uniquely individual experience in sharing information: it's called talking.

The following correction was printed in the *Guardian's* Corrections and Clarifications column, Wednesday, January 16, 2008

The U.S. intelligence community's enthusiasm for hi-tech innovation after 9/11 and the creation of the In-Q-Tel, its venture capital fund, in 1999 were anachronistically linked in the article below. Since 9/11 happened in 2001 it could not have led to the setting up of In-Q-Tel two years earlier.

11
Causal Arguments

Concerned that middle-school students are consuming too much junk food and soda pop at lunch, a principal considers banning vending machines on her campus. But then she discovers how much revenue those machines generate for her school, and she quickly has second thoughts.

An experienced columnist tours Greenland with the minister of climate and energy and sees firsthand evidence of the effects of climate change on Greenland's ice sheet. He concludes that "we've added so many greenhouse gases to the atmosphere . . . that our kids are likely going to spend a good part of their adulthood . . . just dealing with the climate implications of our profligacy."

Researchers in Marin County, California, discover that the occurrence of breast cancer cases is significantly higher there than in any other urban area in California. They immediately begin work to investigate possible causes.

A large soft-drink manufacturer wants to increase its worldwide market share among teenage buyers. Its executives know that another company has been the overwhelming market leader for years—and they set out to learn exactly why.

Convinced of the strong and compelling causal link between second-hand smoke and lung cancer—as well as other diseases—New York mayor Michael Bloomberg and Microsoft's Bill Gates team up to contribute $375 million to support projects around the world that will raise tobacco taxes, help smokers quit, and ban advertising of tobacco products.

A state legislator notes that gasoline prices are consistently between twenty-five and fifty cents higher in one large city in the state than elsewhere. After some preliminary investigation, the legislator decides to bring a class action lawsuit on behalf of the people of this city, arguing that price fixing and insider deals are responsible for the price difference.

Understanding Causal Arguments

The eye-catching title image of a *National Geographic* story poses a simple question: "Why Are We So Fat?" You can probably guess that simple questions like this rarely have simple answers. But in this case, the author, Cathy Newman, argues that there are no real surprises:

> [I]n one sense, the obesity crisis is the result of simple math. It's a calories in, calories out calculation. The First Law of Fat says that anything you eat beyond your immediate need for energy, from avocados to ziti, converts to fat. . . . The Second Law of Fat: The line between being in and out of energy balance is slight. Suppose you consume a mere 5 percent over a 2,000-calorie-a-day average. "That's just one hundred calories; it's a glass of apple juice," says Rudolph Leibel, head of molecular genetics at Columbia University College of Physicians and Surgeons. "But those few extra calories can mean a huge weight gain." Since one pound of body weight is roughly equivalent to 3,500 calories, that glass of juice adds up to an extra 10 pounds over a year.
> —Cathy Newman, "Why Are We So Fat?"

And yet you know that there's more to it than that—as Newman's full story reveals. "Calories in, calories out" may explain the physics of weight

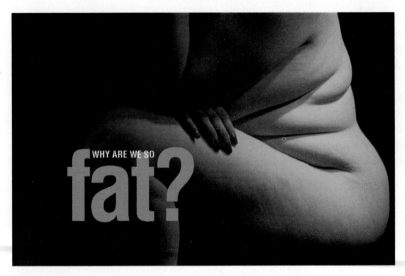

And the answer is . . . ?

gain. But why in recent years have we so drastically shifted the equation from out to in? Because people instinctually crave fatty foods? Because we've grown addicted to fast food? Because fast-food restaurants and junk-food corner stores are the only ones available in some neighborhoods? Because we walk less? Because we've become Internet (or video game) addicts? Whatever the reasons for our increased tonnage, the consequences can be measured by everything from the width of airliner seats to the rise of diabetes in the general population. Many explanations are offered by scientists, social critics, and health gurus, and many are refuted. Figuring out what's going on is an importance exercise in cause-and-effect argument.

Causal arguments—from the consequences of poverty in Africa to the causes of terrorism around the globe—are at the heart of many major policy decisions, both national and international. But arguments about causes and effects also inform many choices that people make every day. Suppose that you need to petition for a grade change because you were unable to turn in a final project on time. You'd probably enumerate the reasons for your failure—the death of your cat, followed by an attack of the hives, followed by a crash of your computer—hoping that a committee reading the petition might see these explanations as tragic enough to change your grade. In identifying the causes of the situation, you're implicitly arguing that the effect (your failure to submit the project on time) should be considered in a new light. Unfortunately, the committee might accuse you of faulty causality (see pp. 527–29) and judge that your failure to complete the project is due more to procrastination than to the reasons you offer.

Causal arguments exist in many forms and frequently appear as part of other arguments (such as evaluations or proposals). It may help focus your work on causal arguments to separate them into three major categories:

- arguments that state a cause and then examine its effects

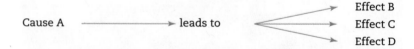

- arguments that state an effect and then trace the effect back to its causes

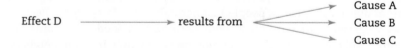

- arguments that move through a series of links: A causes B, which leads to C and perhaps to D

Cause A → leads to Cause B → leads to Cause C → leads to Effect D

ARGUMENTS THAT STATE A CAUSE AND THEN EXAMINE ITS EFFECTS

What would happen if openly homosexual men and women were allowed to join (or stay in) the American military? The possible effects of this "cause" could be examined in detail and argued powerfully. You could imagine very different cases (and consequences) presented by people on various sides of this hot-button issue. In such an argument, you'd be successful if you could show compellingly that the cause would indeed lead to the effects you describe. Or you could challenge the causal assumptions made by people you don't agree with.

Before he explains how we can better think about our lives, Stewart Friedman argues that the metaphor of "work-life balance" causes people to believe that they have to give up too much in their lives.

LINK TO P. 1024

Unfortunately, causes and effects are rarely this easy to determine.

©bobseal'09. www.bobseal.com

Take a look at the opening of an article from the *Christian Science Monitor* on the increased production of ethanol from corn:

> Policymakers and legislators often fail to consider the law of unintended consequences. The latest example is their attempt to reduce the United States' dependence on imported oil by shifting a big share of the nation's largest crop—corn—to the production of ethanol for fueling automobiles.
>
> Good goal, bad policy. In fact, ethanol will do little to reduce the large percentage of our fuel that is imported (more than 60 percent),

and the ethanol policy will have ripple effects on other markets. Corn farmers and ethanol refiners are ecstatic about the ethanol boom and are enjoying the windfall of artificially enhanced demand. But it will be an expensive and dangerous experiment for the rest of us.

—Colin A. Carter and Henry I. Miller, "Hidden Costs of Corn-based Ethanol"

Note that the researchers here begin with a cause—raising the percentage of the corn crop used for ethanol—and then point to several effects of that cause that they will later explore. In this case, they say, some of these effects are clearly "unintended consequences."

ARGUMENTS THAT STATE AN EFFECT AND THEN TRACE ITS CAUSES

This type of argument might begin with a certain effect (for example, Hollywood's record-breaking slump in movie attendance in 2007) and then trace the effect or effects to the most likely causes (a rise in DVD sales, the increase in large-screen home theaters, the growing tendency

Cartoonist Mark Alan Stamaty portrays an effect and three of its causes.

© Mark Alan Stamaty

to stay home for entertainment because of the rise in gasoline prices, increasingly noisy cell-phone–using audiences, mediocre movies, and unimaginative remakes). Or you might examine the reasons that Hollywood executives offer for their industry's dip and decide whether their causal analyses pass muster.

Like other kinds of causal arguments, those tracing effects to a cause can have far-reaching significance. In 1962, for example, the scientist Rachel Carson seized the attention of millions with a famous causal argument about the effects that the overuse of chemical pesticides might have on the environment. Here's an excerpt from the beginning of her book-length study of this subject. Note how she begins with the effects before saying she'll go on to explore the causes:

> [A] strange blight crept over the area and everything began to change. Some evil spell had settled on the community: mysterious maladies swept the flocks of chickens; the cattle and sheep sickened and died. Everywhere was a shadow of death. The farmers spoke of much illness among their families. . . . There had been several sudden and unexplained deaths, not only among adults but even among children, who would be stricken suddenly while at play and die within a few hours. The roadsides, once so attractive, were now lined with browned and withered vegetation as though swept by fire. These, too, were silent, deserted by all living things. Even the streams were now lifeless. Anglers no longer visited them, for all the fish had died.
>
> In the gutters under the eaves and between the shingles of the roofs, a white granular powder still showed a few patches; some weeks before it had fallen like snow upon the roofs and lawns, the fields and streams. No witchcraft, no enemy action had silenced the rebirth of new life in this stricken world. The people had done it themselves. . . . What has silenced the voices of spring in countless towns in America? This book is an attempt to explain.
>
> —Rachel Carson, *Silent Spring*

Today, one could easily write a causal argument of the first type about *Silent Spring* and the environmental movement that it spawned.

ARGUMENTS THAT MOVE THROUGH A SERIES OF LINKS: A CAUSES B, WHICH LEADS TO C AND PERHAPS TO D

In an environmental science class, for example, you might decide to argue that a national law regulating smokestack emissions from utility plants is needed because of the following reasons:

1. Emissions from utility plants in the Midwest cause acid rain.

2. Acid rain causes the death of trees and other vegetation in eastern forests.

3. Powerful lobbyists have prevented midwestern states from passing strict laws to control emissions from these plants.

4. As a result, acid rain will destroy most eastern forests by 2020.

In this case, the first link is that emissions cause acid rain; the second, that acid rain causes destruction in eastern forests; and the third, that states have not acted to break the cause-and-effect relationship that is established by the first two points. These links set the scene for the fourth link, which ties the previous points together to argue from effect: unless X, then Y.

Characterizing Causal Arguments

Causal arguments tend to share several characteristics.

THEY ARE OFTEN PART OF OTHER ARGUMENTS.

Many causal arguments stand alone and address questions that are fundamental to our well-being: *Why are juvenile asthma and diabetes increasing so dramatically in the United States? What are the causes of the rise in cases of malaria in Africa, and what can we do to counter this rise? What will happen to Europe if its birthrate continues to decline?*

But causal analyses often work to further other arguments—especially proposals. For example, a proposal to limit the time that children spend playing video games might first draw on a causal analysis to establish that playing video games can have bad results—such as violent behavior, short attention spans, and decreased social skills. The causal analysis provides a rationale that motivates the proposal. In this way, causal analyses can be useful in establishing good reasons for arguments in general.

THEY ARE ALMOST ALWAYS COMPLEX.

The complexity of most causal relationships makes it difficult to establish causes and effects. For example, scientists and politicians continue to disagree over the extent to which acid rain is actually responsible for

Causal Claims and Academic Arguments

As this chapter demonstrates, making causal claims stick is almost always a delicate and difficult matter. Yet causal reasoning is important to academic arguments across the disciplines. Here, professor of communications Fred Turner looks at the relationship between the Burning Man phenomenon and forms of new media production emerging in Silicon Valley. Here is the abstract of Turner's article:

> Every August for more than a decade, thousands of information technologists and other knowledge workers have trekked out into a barren stretch of alkali desert and built a temporary city devoted to art, technology and communal living: Burning Man. Drawing on extensive archival research, participant observation, and interviews, this paper explores the ways that Burning Man's bohemian ethos supports new forms of production emerging in Silicon Valley and especially at Google. It shows how elements of the Burning Man world—including the building of a socio-technical commons, participation in project-based artistic labor, and the fusion of social and professional interaction—help shape and legitimate the collaborative manufacturing processes driving the growth of Google and other firms. The paper thus develops the notion that Burning Man serves as a key cultural infrastructure for the Bay area's new media industries.
>
> —Fred Turner, "Burning Man at Google: A Cultural Infrastructure for New Media Production"

Note the care with which Turner states his case. He is not arguing for a simple or direct cause-and-effect relationship. Rather, he says that he will argue that Burning Man is part of a web of events that have helped to shape certain processes. In academic arguments, writers treat causal relationships with special care.

the death of many eastern forests. Or consider the complexity of analyzing the causes of some kinds of food poisoning: in 2008, investigators spent months trying to discover whether tomatoes, cilantro, or jalapeno peppers were the cause of a nationwide outbreak of food poisoning.

Sarah Karnasiewicz's "Campus Crusade for Guys" reveals the complexity of causal arguments as she sifts through possible causes of the gender gap in higher education.

·············· **LINK TO P. 909**

Likewise, those trying to untangle the causes leading to a rise in teenage pregnancy are faced with a complex web of potential causes rather than a clear causal relationship. But when you can show that X definitely causes Y, you'll have a powerful argument at your disposal because causal arguments must take into account an enormous number of factors, conditions, and alternative possibilities. That's why, for example, great effort went into establishing an indisputable link between smoking and lung cancer. Once proven, decisive legal action could finally be taken to warn smokers.

THEY ARE OFTEN DEFINITION BASED.

One reason that causal arguments are complex is that they often depend on careful definitions. Recent figures from the U.S. Department of Education, for example, show that the number of high school dropouts is rising and that this rise has caused an increase in youth unemployment. But exactly how does the study define *dropout*? A closer look may suggest that some students (perhaps a lot) who drop out "drop back in" and complete high school or that some who drop out become successful business owners. Further, how does the study define *employment*? Until you can provide definitions that answer such questions, you should proceed cautiously with a causal argument.

THEY USUALLY YIELD PROBABLE RATHER THAN ABSOLUTE CONCLUSIONS.

In examining the effects of a down economy on teenagers from well-off families, Lisa W. Forderaro acknowledges the difficulty of coming to absolute conclusions but still argues for the importance of her findings.

·············· **LINK TO P. 977**

Because causal relationships are almost always complex, they seldom can yield more than a high degree of probability and are almost always subject to critique or charges of false causality. (We all know smokers who defy the odds to live long, cancer-free lives.) Scientists in particular are wary of making causal claims—such as environmental factors cause infertility, for example, because it's highly unlikely that a condition as variable as infertility can be linked to any one single cause.

Even after an event, proving what caused it can be hard. During the campus riots of the late 1960s, for example, a commission was charged with determining the causes of riots on a particular campus. After two years of work and almost a thousand pages of evidence and reports, the commission was unable to pinpoint anything but a broad network of contributing causes and related conditions.

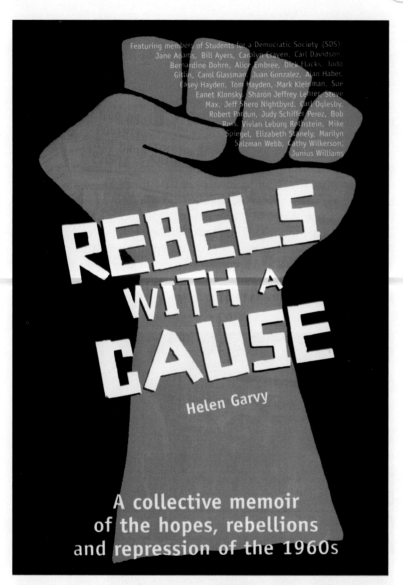

The poster for a documentary film based on this book features an interesting comment on causality: "It isn't the rebels who cause the troubles of the world; it's the troubles that cause the rebels." Some forty years after the campus riots of the late 1960s, scholars are still arguing over their causes.

Not Just Words

When Rachel Carson wrote *Silent Spring* to warn of the environmental dangers of pesticides (see p. 341), one of her targets was the widespread use of DDT in American agriculture. DDT was an effective pesticide, but used indiscriminately it had harmful long-term side effects for birds and other animals. Environmentalists succeeded in virtually banning the use of DDT in the rich industrialized countries. But now some developing nations are interested in restoring its use. Why? DDT kills or repels the mosquitoes responsible for malaria, one of the most insidious diseases in some African and Asian countries. As you might imagine, this controversy is a heated one, and arguments on either side go well beyond words. Look at the accompanying two images, and think about the argument that each one is making.

© Cox & Forkum Editorial Cartoons

Each of these images makes at least one complex argument about causes and effects relating to the use of pesticides such as DDT. Working with one or two classmates, study these images, and then make a list of the possible causal arguments that each one makes.

To demonstrate that A caused B, you must find the strongest possible evidence and subject it to the toughest scrutiny. But a causal argument doesn't fail just because you can't find a single compelling cause. In fact, causal arguments are often most effective when they help readers appreciate how tangled our lives and landscapes really are.

Developing Causal Arguments

Formulating a Claim

You might decide to write a wildly exaggerated or parodic causal argument for humorous purposes. Humorist Dave Barry does this when he explains the causes of El Niño and other weather phenomena: "So we see that the true cause of bad weather, contrary to what they have been claiming all these years, is TV weather forecasters, who have also single-handedly destroyed the ozone layer via overuse of hair spray." Most of the causal reasoning you do, however, will take a serious approach to subjects that you, your family, and your friends care about.

To begin creating a strong causal claim, try listing some of the effects—events or phenomena—that you'd like to know the causes of:

- What causes led to the decreasing numbers of salmon along the northwest coast?
- What's really responsible for rises and falls in gasoline prices?
- What has led to warnings of contamination along your favorite creek?
- Why has the divorce rate leveled off in recent decades?
- Why do so few young Americans vote, even in major elections?

Or try moving in the opposite direction, listing some phenomena or causes you're interested in and then hypothesizing what kinds of effects they may produce:

- What will happen if your campus institutes a coed policy on all dorm bathrooms?
- What will be the effects of a total crackdown on peer-to-peer file sharing?

You probably know that people make and sell cheap imitations of Prada's high-fashion handbags, shoes, and accessories. But what would cause someone to make a fake Prada store? A group of German artists built one outside the small west Texas town of Marfa. What effects do you imagine have resulted?

- What will happen if more liberal (or conservative) judges are appointed to the U.S. Supreme Court?
- What will happen if China and India become thriving industrialized nations?

Read a little about the causal issues that interest you most, and then try them out on friends and colleagues. Can they suggest ways to refocus or clarify what you want to do? Can they offer leads to finding information about your subject? If you've already asserted some cause-and-effect relationships, can they offer counterexamples or refutations? Finally, map out a rough statement about the causal relationship you want to explore:

A might cause (or might be caused by) B for the following reasons:

1.

2.

3.

Such a statement should be tentative because writing a causal argument will often be a research exercise in which you uncover facts, not assume them to be true. Often, your early assumptions (*Tuition was raised to renovate the stadium*) might be undermined by the facts you later discover (*Tuition doesn't fund the construction or maintenance of campus buildings*).

Developing the Argument

Penn Jillette traces several effects of not believing in God in his essay "This I Believe." What claims and warrants can you identify in his argument?

LINK TO P. 898

Once you've drafted a claim, you can explore cause-and-effect relationships, drawing out the reasons, warrants, and evidence that can support the claim most effectively:

Claim	Losing seasons caused the football coach to lose his job.
Reason	The team lost more than half its games for three seasons in a row.
Warrant	Winning is the key to success for major-team college coaches.
Evidence	For the last ten years, coaches with more than two losing seasons in a row have lost their jobs.

Claim	Certain career patterns cause women to be paid less than men.
Reason	Women's career patterns differ from men's, and in spite of changes in the relative pay of other groups, women's pay still lags behind that of men.
Warrant	Successful careers are made during the period between ages twenty-five and thirty-five.
Evidence	Women often drop out of or reduce work during the decade between ages twenty-five and thirty-five to raise families.

In further developing a causal argument, you can draw on many strategies that we've already touched on. In the article that the following passage is excerpted from, Stephen King uses dozens of examples—from *The Texas Chainsaw Massacre*, *The Gory Ones*, and *Invasion of the Body Snatchers* to *Night of the Living Dead*, *Psycho*, *The Amityville Horror*, and *The Thing*—to answer a causal question: why do people love horror movies?

> The mythic horror movie, like the sick joke, has a dirty job to do. It deliberately appeals to all that is worst in us. It is morbidity unchained, our most base instincts let free, our nastiest fantasies realized . . . and it all happens, fittingly enough, in the dark. For those reasons, good liberals often shy away from horror films. For myself, I like to see the most aggressive of them—*Dawn of the Dead*, for instance—as lifting a trap door in the civilized forebrain and throwing a basket of raw meat

Dawn of the Dead—satisfying uncivilized cravings since 1978

to the hungry alligators swimming around in that subterranean river beneath.

Why bother? Because it keeps them from getting out, man. It keeps them down there and me up here.

—Stephen King, "Why We Crave Horror Movies"

Another way to support (or undermine) a causal argument is through the use of analogies. The strength of such an argument lies in how closely you can relate the two phenomena being compared. In exploring why women consistently earn less pay than men even when they're performing the same jobs, Sarah Banda Purvis draws an analogy between working women and sports:

An analogy I use when describing my experiences as a female manager in corporate America is that I was allowed to sit on the bench but never given a chance to get on the field and play in the game.

—Sarah Banda Purvis, "What Do Working Women Want in the Twenty-first Century?"

She goes on to trace the effects that constantly being relegated to the "bench" has on earning power. If you find this analogy unsatisfactory, you might suggest that it falsely portrays the causal relationship of women and promotion. After all, benchwarmers are usually players who don't perform as well as those on the field. Surely Purvis doesn't want to suggest that women aren't moving up in the business world because they don't play the game as well as men.

Establishing causes for physical effects (like diseases) often calls for another means of support—testing *hypotheses*, or theories about possible causes. This kind of reasoning, which is often highly technical, helped researchers to identify a mystery disease that struck nearly fifty people in Quebec City. Puzzled by cases involving the same effects (nausea, shortness of breath, cough, stomach pain, weight loss, and a marked blue-gray skin coloration), doctors at first hypothesized that the common cause was severe vitamin deficiency. But the large number of cases within a short time made this explanation unlikely; after all, sudden epidemics of vitamin deficiency are rare. In addition, postmortem examinations of the twenty people who died revealed severe damage to the heart muscle and the liver, features inconsistent with the vitamin-deficiency hypothesis. So the doctors sought a clue to the mysterious disease in something the victims shared: all fifty had been beer lovers and had drunk a particular brew.

It seemed possible that the illness was connected to that brand, which was brewed in both Quebec City and Montreal. But Montreal had no outbreak of the disease. The hypothesis, then, was further refined: could the brewing processes be different in the two cities? Bingo. The Quebec brewery added a cobalt compound to its product to enhance the beer's foaminess; the Montreal brewery did not. Furthermore, the compound was first added only a month before the first victims became ill. Yet doctors in this case were still cautious about the causal connection because the cobalt hadn't been present in sufficient quantities to kill a normal person. Yet twenty had died. After persistent scientific analysis, the doctors decided that this fact must be related to the victims' drinking habits, which in some way reduced their resistance to the chemical. For those twenty people, a normally nonlethal dose of cobalt had proven fatal.

Not all the evidence in compelling causal arguments needs to be strictly scientific. Many causal arguments rely on *ethnographic observations*—the systematic study of ordinary people in their daily routines. How would you explain, for example, why some people step aside when they encounter someone head-on and others do not? In an argument that attempts to account for such behavior, investigators Frank Willis, Joseph Gier, and David Smith observed "1,038 displacements involving 3,141 persons" at a Kansas City shopping mall. In results that surprised the investigators, "gallantry" seemed to play a significant role in causing people to step aside for one another—more so than other causes that the investigators had anticipated (such as deferring to someone who's physically stronger or higher in status). Doubtless you've read of other such studies, perhaps in psychology courses.

Finally, you may want to consider using personal experiences in support of a causal argument. Indeed, people's experiences generally lead them to seek out or to avoid various causes and effects. If you're consistently praised for your prowess at ultimate Frisbee, you'll probably look for opportunities to produce that pleasant effect. If three times in a row you get sick after eating shrimp, you'll almost certainly identify the shellfish as the cause of your difficulties and stop eating it. Personal experience can also help build your credibility as a writer, gain the empathy of your listeners, and thus support your causal claim. Although one person's experiences cannot ordinarily be universalized, they can still argue eloquently for causal relationships. Leslie Marmon Silko uses personal experience to explain her shift from studying to become a lawyer to becoming a writer, photographer, and activist, arguing that the best way to seek justice isn't through the law but through the power of stories:

> When I was a sophomore in high school I decided law school was the place to seek justice. . . . I should have paid more attention to the lesson of the Laguna Pueblo land claims lawsuit from my childhood: The lawsuit was not settled until I was in law school. The U.S. Court of Indian Claims found in favor of the Pueblo of Laguna, but the Indian Claims Court never gives back land wrongfully taken; the court only pays tribes for the land. . . . The Laguna people wanted the land they cherished; instead, they got twenty-five cents for each of the six million acres stolen by the state. The lawsuit had lasted twenty years, so the lawyers' fees amounted to nearly $2 million.
>
> I completed three semesters in the American Indian Law School Fellowship Program before I realized that injustice is built into the Anglo-American legal system. . . . But I continued in law school until our criminal law class read an appeal to the U.S. Supreme Court to stop the execution of a retarded black man convicted of strangling a white librarian in Washington, D.C., in 1949. The majority on the Court refused to stop the execution, though it was clear that the man was so retarded that he had no comprehension of his crime. That case was the breaking point for me. I wanted nothing to do with such a barbaric legal system.
>
> My time in law school was not wasted: I had gained invaluable insights into the power structure of mainstream society, and I continue to follow developments in the law to calculate prevailing political

winds. It seems to me there is no better way to uncover the deepest values of a culture than to observe the operation of that culture's system of justice.

[But] I decided the only way to seek justice was through the power of stories.

—Leslie Marmon Silko, *Yellow Woman and a Beauty of Spirit:*
Essays on Native American Life Today

All these strategies—the use of examples, analogies, testing hypotheses, experimental evidence, and personal experience—can help you support a causal argument or undermine a causal claim you regard as faulty. However, you may still have to convince readers that the reasons you offer are indeed compelling. In terms of causal arguments, this may mean distinguishing among immediate, necessary, and sufficient reasons. In the case of the mysterious illness in Quebec City, the immediate reasons for illness were the symptoms themselves—nausea, shortness of breath, and so on. But they weren't the root causes of the disease. Drinking the particular beer in question served as a necessary reason: without the tainted beer, the illness wouldn't have occurred. However, the researchers had to search harder for the sufficient reason—the reason that causes the effect (the illness) if it's present. In the case of the Quebec City beer, that reason turned out to be the addition of cobalt.

Even everyday causal analysis can draw on this distinction among reasons. What caused you, for instance, to choose the college you wanted to attend? Immediate reasons might be the proximity of the school to your home or the college's rich curriculum in your major interest. But what are the necessary reasons—the ones without which your choice of that college could not occur? Adequate funds? Good test scores and academic record? The expectations of your family? You might even explore possible sufficient reasons, those that—if present—will guarantee the effect of your attending that college. In such a case, you may be the only person with enough information to determine what the sufficient reasons might be.

Considering Design and Visuals

You may find that the best way to illustrate a causal relationship is to present it visually. Consider the way that even a simple bar graph like the one on the facing page can make a point clearly and emphatically—in this case, showing the dramatic effects of lowered birthrates. The report that uses this figure explores the effects that such a change would

Figure 1. The comparative size of successive generations across time when fertility is constant at 1.3 births per woman

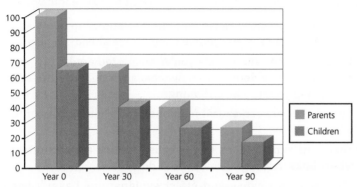

A simple graph can provide dramatic evidence for a causal claim—in this case, the effect of reduced fertility rates on a population.

have on the economies of the world. Or you might study the intriguing ways that editorial cartoonists embed causal relationships in some of their pieces, inviting readers to find causal connections as they interpret the images, as in the cartoon below.

Cartoonist Lisa Benson suggests that the push to develop alternative fuels has a serious effect on the world's supply of food.

Used with the permission of Lisa Benson and the Washington Post Writers Group in conjunction with the Cartoonist Group. All rights reserved.

Key Features of Causal Arguments

In drafting your own causal argument, you'll want to do the following:

- Thoroughly question every cause-and-effect relationship in the argument, both those you suggest yourself and others already in play.

- Show that the causes and effects you've suggested are highly probable and backed by evidence, or show what's wrong with the faulty causal reasoning you may be critiquing.

- Assess any links between causal relationships (what leads to or follows from what).

- Show that your explanations of any causal chains are accurate, or show where links in a causal chain break down.

- Show that plausible cause-and-effect explanations haven't been ignored or that the possibility of multiple causes or effects has been given due consideration.

In developing a causal argument, you'll address many of these items, though their order may vary. You may open an essay dramatically by describing an effect and then "flash back" to its multiple causes. Or you might open with a well-known phenomenon, identify it as a cause, and then trace its effects. Or you might begin by suggesting plausible explanations for an event that have been ignored for one reason or another. In any case, you should sketch an organizational plan and get reactions to it from your instructor, writing center consultants, and colleagues before proceeding to a full draft. When the draft is complete, you should again look for critical readers who are willing to test the strength of your causal argument.

GUIDE to writing a causal argument

● Finding a Topic

A little time spent brainstorming will turn up some good possibilities for causal arguments of several kinds, including those that grow out of your personal experiences. *Just exactly what led to the slump in my grades last term?* Beyond your own personal concerns, many public issues lend themselves to causal analysis and argument: *What factors have led to the near bankruptcy of the nation's major airlines? What will happen if the United States takes the lead in reducing greenhouse gas emissions? What effects have been caused by the ban on the use of trans fats in many cities' restaurants?* As you're brainstorming possibilities for your causal argument, don't ignore important current campus issues: *What have been the effects of the decision to admit a larger number of students each year? What are the likely outcomes of shifting the academic calendar from a quarter to a semester system? If, as some argue, there has been a significant increase of racism and homophobia on campus, what has caused that increase? What are its consequences?*

Finally, remember that it's fair game to question existing assumptions about causality for being inaccurate or not probing deeply enough into the reasons for a phenomenon. You can raise doubts about the facts or assumptions that others have made and perhaps offer a better causal connection. For example, some writers have argued that obsessive playing of violent video games leads to antisocial or violent behavior. Others have challenged this causal argument, noting that a large percentage of youth crime is carried out by those who play very few video games. What's going on here? Perhaps your research can provide an answer.

● Researching Your Topic

Causal arguments will lead you to many different resources:

- current news media—especially magazines and newspapers (online or in print)
- online databases
- scholarly journals

- books written on your subject (here you can do a keyword search, either in your library or online)

- blogs, Web sites, listservs, social networking sites, or newsgroups devoted to your subject

In addition, why not carry out some field research of your own? Conduct interviews with appropriate authorities on your subject, or create a questionnaire aimed at establishing a range of opinion on your subject. The information you get from interviews or from analyzing responses to a questionnaire can provide evidence to back up your claims.

● Formulating a Claim

First, identify the kind of causal argument that you expect to make—one moving from cause(s) to effect(s); one moving from effect(s) to cause(s); or one involving a series of links, with cause A leading to B, which then leads to C. (See pp. 337–42 for a review of these kinds of arguments.) Or you might be debunking an existing cause-and-effect claim.

Your next move may be to explore your own relationship to your subject. What do you know about the subject and its causes and effects? Why do you favor (or disagree with) the claim? What significant reasons can you offer in support of your position? In short, you should end this process of exploration by formulating a brief claim or thesis about a particular causal relationship. It should include (1) a statement that says, in effect, *A causes (or does not cause or is caused by) B*, and (2) a summary of the reasons supporting this causal relationship. Remember to make sure that your thesis is as specific as possible and that it's sufficiently controversial or interesting to hold your readers' interest. Recognize, too, that any such claim is tentative and is subject to change as your project develops and you learn more about your subject.

● Examples of Causal Claims

- Right-to-carry gun laws are, in part, responsible for increased rates of violent crimes in states that have approved such legislation.

- Sophisticated use of the Internet is now a must for any presidential candidate who hopes to win.

- The proliferation of images in film, television, and computer-generated texts is changing the way we read and process information.

- The many extensions of the copyright laws to protect and provide incentives to creators have diminished the right of the public to information, severely limited the fair-use doctrine, and added billions of dollars to the coffers of Disney and other huge entertainment conglomerates.

- Grade inflation is lowering the value of a college education.

● Preparing a Proposal

If your instructor asks you to prepare a proposal for your project, here's a format that may help:

State the thesis of your argument completely. If you're having trouble doing so, try outlining it in Toulmin terms:

Claim:

Reason(s):

Warrant(s):

- Explain why this argument deserves attention. Why is it important for your readers to consider?

- Specify whom you hope to reach through your argument and why this group of readers is an appropriate audience. What interest or investment do they have in the issue? Why will they (or should they) be concerned?

- Briefly identify and explore the major challenges you expect to face in supporting your argument. Will demonstrating a clear causal link between A and B be particularly difficult? Will the data that you need to support the claim be hard to obtain?

- List the strategies that you expect to use in researching your argument. Will you be interviewing? Surveying opinion? Conducting library and online searches? Other?

- Briefly identify and explore the major counterarguments that you might expect in response to your argument.

- Consider what format, genre, or media will work best for your argument. Will you be preparing a Web site? A press release? An editorial for the local newspaper? A report for an organization you belong to?

● Thinking about Organization

Whatever genre or format you decide to use, your causal argument should address the following elements:

- a specific causal claim somewhere in the paper: *Devastating flash floods associated with El Niño were responsible for the dramatic loss of homes in central California in early 2003.*

- an explanation of the claim's significance or importance: *Claims for damage from flooding put some big insurance companies out of business; as a result, homeowners couldn't get coverage, and many who lost their homes had to declare bankruptcy.*

- evidence sufficient to support each cause or effect—or, in an argument based on a series of causal links, evidence to support the relationships among the links: *The amount of rain that fell in central California in early 2008 was 25 percent below normal, leading inexorably to drought conditions.*

- a consideration of alternative causes and effects and evidence that you understand these alternatives and have thought carefully about them before rejecting them: *Although some say that excessive and sloppy logging and poor building codes were responsible for the loss of homes, the evidence supporting these alternative causes is not convincing.*

● Getting and Giving Response

All arguments can benefit from the scrutiny of others. Your instructor may assign you to a peer group for the purpose of reading and responding to each other's drafts. If not, ask for responses from some serious readers or consultants at a writing center. You can use the following questions to evaluate a draft. If you're evaluating someone else's draft, be sure to illustrate your points with examples. Specific comments are always more helpful than general observations.

The Claim

- What's most effective about the claim? What are its strengths?
- Is the claim sufficiently qualified?
- Is the claim specific enough to be clear? How could it be narrowed and focused?
- How strong is the relationship between the claim and the reasons given to support it? How could that relationship be made more explicit?

- Is it immediately evident why the claim is important? How could it be rephrased in a way that more forcefully and clearly suggests its significance?

- Does the claim reveal a causal connection? How could it be revised to make the causal links clearer?

Evidence for the Claim

- What's the strongest evidence offered for the claim? What, if any, evidence needs to be strengthened?

- Is enough evidence offered that these particular causes are responsible for the effect that has been identified, that these particular effects result from the identified cause, or that a series of causes and effects are linked? If not, what kind of additional evidence is needed? What kinds of sources might provide this evidence?

- How credible and persuasive will the sources likely be to potential readers? What other kinds of sources might be more credible and persuasive?

- Is the evidence in support of the claim simply announced, or are its appropriateness and significance analyzed? Is a more detailed discussion needed?

- Have all the major alternative causes and effects as well as objections to the claim been considered? What support is offered for rejecting these alternatives? Where is additional support needed?

Organization and Style

- How are the parts of the argument organized? Is this organization effective, or would some other structure work better?

- Will readers understand the relationships among the claims, supporting reasons, warrants, and evidence? If not, what could be done to make those connections clearer? Are more transitional words and phrases needed? Would headings or graphic devices (diagrams, flowcharts, illustrations) help?

- Are the transitions or links from point to point, paragraph to paragraph, and sentence to sentence clear and effective? If not, how could they be improved?

- Is the style suited to the subject? Is it too formal? Too casual? Too technical? Too bland? Too geeky? How can it be improved?

- Which sentences seem particularly effective? Which ones seem weakest, and how could they be improved? Should some short sentences be combined, or should any long ones be separated into two or more sentences?

- How effective are the paragraphs? Do any seem too skimpy or too long? How can they be improved?

- Which words or phrases seem particularly effective, vivid, and memorable? Do any seem dull, unclear, or inappropriate for the audience or the writer's purpose? Are definitions provided for technical or other terms that readers might not know?

Spelling, Punctuation, Mechanics, Documentation, Format

- Are there any errors in spelling, punctuation, capitalization, and the like?

- Is an appropriate and consistent style of documentation used for parenthetical citations and the list of works cited or references? (See Chapter 20.)

- Does the paper or project follow an appropriate format? Is it appropriately designed and attractively presented? How could it be improved? If it's a Web site, do all the links work?

RESPOND •

1. The causes of some of the following events and phenomena are well
   known and frequently discussed. But do you understand them well
   enough to spell out the causes to someone else? Working in a group,
   see how well (and in how much detail) you can explain each of the following events or phenomena. Which explanations are relatively clear,
   and which seem more open to debate?

   earthquakes

   the Burning Man festival

   the collapse of communism in Eastern Europe in 1989

   arroyos

   the AIDS pandemic in Africa

   the popularity of the *Batman* films

   the swelling caused by a bee sting

   the mortgage crisis of 2008 and 2009

   the rise in cases of autism

   the destruction of the space shuttle *Columbia*

2. One of the fallacies of argument discussed in Chapter 17 is the *post
   hoc, ergo propter hoc* ("after this, therefore because of this") fallacy.
   Causal arguments are particularly prone to this kind of fallacious reasoning, in which a writer asserts a causal relationship between two
   entirely unconnected events. When Angelina Jolie gave birth to twins,
   for instance, the stock market rallied by nearly 600 points, but it would
   be difficult to argue that one caused the other.

   Because causal arguments can easily fall prey to this fallacy, you
   might find it useful to try to create and defend an absurd connection
   of this kind. Begin by asserting a causal link between two events or
   phenomena that likely have no relationship: *The enormous popularity of
   the iPhone is partially due to global warming.* Then spend a page or so
   spinning out an imaginative argument to defend the claim. It's OK to
   have fun with this exercise, but see how convincing you can be at generating plausible arguments.

3. Working with a group, write a big *Why?* on a sheet of paper or computer screen, and then generate a list of *why* questions. Don't be too
   critical of the initial list:

   Why?

   — do people laugh?

   — do some animals form monogamous relationships?

— do college students binge drink?

— do teenagers drive fast?

— do babies cry?

Generate as long a list as you can in fifteen minutes. Then decide which of the questions might make plausible starting points for intriguing causal arguments.

4. Here's a schematic causal analysis of one event, exploring the difference among immediate, necessary, and sufficient causes. Critique and revise the analysis as you see fit. Then create another of your own, beginning with a different event, phenomenon, incident, fad, or effect.

Event: Traffic fatality at an intersection

Immediate cause: An SUV that runs a red light, totals a Miata, and kills its driver

Necessary cause: Two drivers who are navigating Friday rush-hour traffic (if no driving, then no accident)

Sufficient cause: An SUV driver who is distracted by a cell-phone conversation

Cultural Stress Linked to Suicide

LIA HARDIN

May 31, 2007

Asian American women demonstrate a high rate of suicide when compared with women of other ethnicities, California State–Fullerton researcher Eliza Noh found in a recent empirical study.

The causal claim is introduced: several factors lead to mental health problems. Credentials of researchers are established.

Noh and Stanford mental health professionals Alejandro Martinez, the director of Counseling and Psychological Services (CAPS), and Rona Hu, director of the Acute Inpatient Unit at Stanford Hospital, told *The Daily* that parental pressure, cultural differences between the United States and Asian countries, and avoidance of mental health issues in Asian American families can contribute to the prevalence of mental health problems.

Examples of deaths attributed to the identified factors are given.

Following the death of graduate student Mengyao "May" Zhou earlier this year and the recent revelation that Azia Kim had been squatting in Stanford dorms for eight months despite the fact that she was not a student, suicide and mental health issues in the Asian American community have become widely discussed on the Stanford campus.

Citing the ongoing study, Noh said that the tendency of Asian American women to ignore or deny stress, depression, and other mental health problems can cause the larger anxieties that lead to suicide.

Expert testimony in support of claim is introduced.

"There are multiple factors that contribute to suicidality," Noh said. "[For Asian American women] there is this pressure to do well in school and that pressure comes

---

Lia Hardin wrote this article as a staff writer for her campus newspaper, the *Stanford Daily*. In it, she explores the factors that contribute to the relatively high rate of suicide among Asian American women. Because she is writing for a newspaper, Hardin does not provide any formal documentation of her sources but simply identifies the three authorities who supplied most of her information.

from their family members. There is a miscommunication or a lack of communication with their parents. There is a cultural division between them and their parents."

"They are expected to listen to their parents," she said, "to do well in school, not to ask questions and not to talk back."

All those cultural pressures can lead Asian American women to treat mental health issues like an elephant in the room, exacerbating existing problems and generating others.

A second expert researcher is cited.

Hu argued that, for many Asian American women, culturally related issues can contribute directly to mental health problems. She cited young women she knew who had been disowned by their families because of circumstances that parents interpreted as failures.

"The whole concept in the Asian family is that the family is not a democracy," Hu said. "Parents feel entitled to make decisions for their children, including what major or career to choose, or whom to marry. There's a line from a movie where they say, 'There's no word for *privacy* in Chinese.'"

"The sense of shame can be a big part of Asian American culture and that's something that Americans don't understand so much," she added. "If Hugh Grant is caught doing something [shameful,] he apologizes and goes on with his movie career. In Asia, shame can endure for generations. The default Asian coping mechanism is denial."

A third researcher is cited.

Martinez added that differences between education systems in America and Asian countries can lead to misunderstandings within families.

"Specifically in some Asian countries, people have to make career decisions almost when they get to high school," Martinez said. Coming from such a background, parents often misinterpret their children's decision to explore different fields in college.

"If someone did that in their country of origin, it would be a dramatic setback," he said. "They may not be familiar with how much flexibility is possible in the United States."

Martinez cited Korea's suicide rate, which is far higher than the United States.

"The consequences of someone getting a 'B' in a class at Stanford really aren't that great in the context of career decisions and career opportunities," he said. "In other cultures they can be significant."

Noh said that open discussion of mental health issues in the community, along with the availability of resources that can cater specifically to Asian Americans, can be used to counter the problem.

Ways to address the problem are introduced.

"There has to be some serious commitment on the part of the community," Noh said. "[Resources] need to be appropriate for Asian American students. Councilors should be trained in the languages that they speak and have some level of cultural awareness of [students'] backgrounds."

Without those specially tailored resources, she said, Asian American women in her study often chose to reject counseling and therapy altogether.

"The big fear was that they didn't want to go to strangers who didn't know about their situation," she said. "Asian Americans have the lowest rates of utilization of mental health services. There is something about traditional mental health services that doesn't appeal to Asian Americans."

Hu and Martinez said that Stanford has resources for Asian Americans available at campus mental health facilities.

Campus resources for addressing the problem are reviewed.

"We address this in two ways," Martinez said. "An important one is to have diversity on our staff. In addition to that, we do commit some of our resources to making sure that all of our staff have sensitivity to the communities that make up Stanford students."

Hu said that at the Stanford Hospital, some of the attending physicians and residents in psychiatry are Asian and that staff members fluent in Mandarin are available.

Hu and Noh both said that in addition to providing ethnicity-specific resources, fostering discussion of suicide and mental health is important because avoidance of the issue is pervasive in the Asian American community.

"Helping to de-stigmatize things is very helpful," Hu said. "I don't see people disowned so frequently in other cultures."

A final contributing factor to suicide: feeling alone and helpless.

"The number one factor that [study participants] felt in terms of contributing to suicide is that they felt alone and helpless and that they didn't have any place to turn," Noh said. "I've received lots of emails of thanks . . . from people happy that there is dialogue taking place."

Stinging Tentacles Offer Hint of Oceans' Decline

ELISABETH ROSENTHAL

BARCELONA, Spain—Blue patrol boats crisscross the swimming areas of beaches here with their huge nets skimming the water's surface. The yellow flags that urge caution and the red flags that prohibit swimming because of risky currents are sometimes topped now with blue ones warning of a new danger: swarms of jellyfish.

In a period of hours during a day a couple of weeks ago, 300 people on Barcelona's bustling beaches were treated for stings, and 11 were taken to hospitals.

From Spain to New York, to Australia, Japan and Hawaii, jellyfish are becoming more numerous and more widespread, and they are showing up in places where they have rarely been seen before, scientists say. The faceless marauders are stinging children blithely bathing on summer vacations, forcing beaches to close and clogging fishing nets.

But while jellyfish invasions are a nuisance to tourists and a hardship to fishermen, for scientists they are a source of more profound alarm, a signal of the declining health of the world's oceans.

Elisabeth Rosenthal is a physician as well as an award-winning journalist. She writes on energy, climate change, and other science-related topics, often for the *New York Times*, where this article was published in August 2008.

"These jellyfish near shore are a message the sea is sending us saying, 'Look how badly you are treating me,'" said Dr. Josep-María Gili, a leading jellyfish expert, who has studied them at the Institute of Marine Sciences of the Spanish National Research Council in Barcelona for more than 20 years.

The explosion of jellyfish populations, scientists say, reflects a combination of severe overfishing of natural predators, like tuna, sharks and swordfish; rising sea temperatures caused in part by global warming; and pollution that has depleted oxygen levels in coastal shallows.

These problems are pronounced in the Mediterranean, a sea bounded by more than a dozen countries that rely on it for business and pleasure. Left unchecked in the Mediterranean and elsewhere, these problems could make the swarms of jellyfish menacing coastlines a grim vision of seas to come.

"The problem on the beach is a social problem," said Dr. Gili, who talks with admiration of the "beauty" of the globular jellyfish. "We need to take care of it for our tourism industry. But the big problem is not on the beach. It's what's happening in the seas."

Jellyfish, relatives of the sea anemone and coral that for the most part are relatively harmless, in fact are the cockroaches of the open waters, the ultimate maritime survivors who thrive in damaged environments, and that is what they are doing.

Within the past year, there have been beach closings because of jellyfish swarms on the Côte d'Azur in France, the Great Barrier Reef of Australia, and at Waikiki and Virginia Beach in the United States.

In Australia, more than 30,000 people were treated for stings last year, double the number in 2005. The rare but deadly Irukandji jellyfish is expanding its range in Australia's warming waters, marine scientists say.

While no good global database exists on jellyfish populations, the increasing reports from around the world have convinced scientists that the trend is real, serious and climate-related, although they caution that jellyfish populations in any one place undergo year-to-year variation.

"Human-caused stresses, including global warming and overfishing, are encouraging jellyfish surpluses in many tourist destinations and productive fisheries," according to the National Science Foundation, which is issuing a report on the phenomenon this fall and lists as problem areas Australia, the Gulf of Mexico, Hawaii, the Black Sea, Namibia, Britain, the Mediterranean, the Sea of Japan and the Yangtze estuary.

In Barcelona, one of Spain's most vibrant tourist destinations, city officials and the Catalan Water Agency have started fighting back, trying desperately to ensure that it is safe for swimmers to go back in the water.

Each morning, with the help of Dr. Gili's team, boats monitor offshore jellyfish swarms, winds and currents to see if beaches are threatened and if closings are needed. They also check if jellyfish collection in the waters near the beaches is needed. Nearly 100 boats stand ready to help in an emergency, said Xavier Duran of the water agency. The constant squeal of Dr. Gili's cellphone reflected his de facto role as Spain's jellyfish control and command center. Calls came from all over.

Officials in Santander and the Basque country were concerned about frequent sightings this year on the Atlantic coast of the Portuguese man-of-war, a sometimes lethal warm-water species not previously seen regularly in those regions.

Farther south, a fishing boat from the Murcia region called to report an off-shore swarm of *Pelagia noctiluca*—an iridescent purplish jellyfish that issues a nasty sting—more than a mile long. A chef, presumably trying to find some advantage in the declining oceans, wanted to know if the local species were safe to eat if cooked. Much is unknown about the jellyfish, and Dr. Gili was unsure.

In previous decades there were jellyfish problems for only a couple of days every few years; now the threat of jellyfish is a daily headache for local officials and is featured on the evening news. "In the past few years the dynamic has changed completely—the temperature is a little warmer," Dr. Gili said.

Though the stuff of horror B-movies, jellyfish are hardly aggressors. They float haplessly with the currents. They discharge their venom automatically when they bump into something warm—a human body, for example—from poison-containing stingers on mantles, arms or long, threadlike tendrils, which can grow to be yards long.

Some, like the Portuguese man-of-war or the giant box jellyfish, can be deadly on contact. *Pelagia noctiluca*, common in the Mediterranean, delivers a painful sting producing a wound that lasts weeks, months or years, depending on the person and the amount of contact.

In the Mediterranean, overfishing of both large and small fish has left jellyfish with little competition for plankton, their food, and fewer predators. Unlike in Asia, where some jellyfish are eaten by people, here they have no economic or epicurean value.

The warmer seas and drier climate caused by global warming work to the jellyfish's advantage, since nearly all jellyfish breed better and faster in warmer waters, according to Dr. Jennifer Purcell, a jellyfish expert at the Shannon Point Marine Center of Western Washington University.

Global warming has also reduced rainfall in temperate zones, researchers say, allowing the jellyfish to better approach the beaches. Rain runoff from land would normally slightly decrease the salinity of coastal waters, "creating a natural barrier that keeps the jellies from the coast," Dr. Gili said.

Then there is pollution, which reduces oxygen levels and visibility in coastal waters. While other fish die in or avoid waters with low oxygen levels, many jellyfish can thrive in them. And while most fish have to see to catch their food, jellyfish, which filter food passively from the water, can dine in total darkness, according to Dr. Purcell's research.

Residents in Barcelona have forged a prickly coexistence with their new neighbors.

Last month, Mirela Gómez, 8, ran out of the water crying with her first jellyfish sting, clutching a leg that had suddenly become painful and itchy. Her grandparents rushed her to a nearby Red Cross stand. "I'm a little afraid to go back in the water," she said, displaying a row of angry red welts on her shin.

Francisco Antonio Padrós, a 77-year-old fisherman, swore mightily as he unloaded his catch one morning last weekend, pulling off dozens of jellyfish clinging to his nets and tossing them onto a dock. Removing a few shrimp, he said his nets were often "filled with more jellyfish than fish."

By the end of the exercise his calloused hands were bright red and swollen to twice their normal size. "Right now I can't tell if I have hands or not—they hurt, they're numb, they itch," he said.

Dr. Santiago Nogué, head of the toxicology unit at the largest hospital here, said that although 90 percent of stings healed in a week or two, many people's still hurt and itched for months. He said he was now seeing 20 patients a year whose symptoms did not respond to any treatment at all, sometimes requiring surgery to remove the affected area.

The sea, however, has long been central to life in Barcelona, and that is unlikely to change. Recently when the beaches were closed, children on a breakwater collected jellyfish in a bucket. The next day, Antonio López, a diver, emerged from the water. "There are more every year—we saw hundreds offshore today," he said. "You just have to learn how to handle the stings."

12
Proposals

A student looking forward to spring break proposes to two friends that they join a group that will spend the vacation helping to build a school in a Guatemalan village.

The members of a club for undergrad business majors talk about their common need to create informative, appealing résumés. After much talk, three members suggest that the club develop a Web site that will guide members in building such résumés and provide links to other resources.

A project team at a large architectural firm works for three months developing a response to an RFP (request for proposal) to convert a university library into a digital learning center.

The undergraduate student organization at a large state university asks the administration for information about how long it takes to complete a degree in each academic major. After analyzing this information, the group recommends a reduction in the number of hours needed to graduate.

Understanding and Categorizing Proposals

Think big, and be patient. You might be amazed by what you accomplish. Executive director of the Sierra Club Foundation and renowned environmentalist David Brower (1912–2000) long blamed himself for not standing firm against the Glen Canyon Dam project in northern Arizona—which in 1963 began holding back the waters of the Colorado River, flooding some of the most wild and beautiful canyons in the world to create a reservoir more than 100 miles long, Lake Powell. "I have worn sackcloth and ashes ever since, convinced that I could have saved the place if I had simply got off my duff," he wrote.

But he did more than penance. In a 1997 article entitled "Let the River Run through It," Brower made a blunt proposal:

> But as surely as we made a mistake years ago, we can reverse it now. We can drain Lake Powell and let the Colorado River run through the dam that created it, bringing Glen Canyon and the wonder of its side canyons back to life. We can let the river do what it needs to do downstream in the Grand Canyon itself.
>
> We don't need to tear the dam down, however much some people would like to see it go. Together the dam's two diversion tunnels can send 200,000 cubic feet of water per second downstream, twice as much as the Colorado's highest flows. Once again Grand Canyon would make its own sounds and, if you listened carefully, you would hear it sighing with relief. The dam itself would be left as a tourist attraction, like the Pyramids, with passers-by wondering how humanity ever built it, and why.
>
> —David Brower, "Let the River Run through It"

Droughts have shrunk Lake Powell dramatically in the years since Brower wrote this article, and the concrete arch of Glen Canyon Dam still holds fast against the Colorado River. But the logic of Brower's proposal has persisted. In 2008, film director Greg MacGillivray recalled Brower's proposal in his documentary film *Grand Canyon Adventure: River at Risk*, which followed author and photographer Wade Davis, environmentalist Robert Kennedy Jr., and their daughters Tara and Kick as they traveled down the Colorado. With voiceover by Robert Redford, this film defends Brower's proposal and demonstrates how the regulated flow of the Colorado relates to the current world water crisis.

Pointing out that the creation of the Glen Canyon Dam changed the flow of the Colorado forever, the film shows that the river, once a source of water and power for 25 million Americans, continues to suffer from the severe drought and overregulation. As MacGillivray says, "In our film, the Colorado becomes a metaphor for global water issues, revealing how interconnected our rivers, water supply, and human actions really are." This film ends with a proposal that is broader than Brower's—that every viewer take action to protect water now, from installing low-flow shower heads, to voting in ways that will help protect the Colorado, to thinking about water in completely new and much more serious ways.

Not all proposals are as dramatic or far-reaching as those made by Brower and *Grand Canyon Adventure*, but such arguments, whether casual

Glen Canyon Dam with a power plant at its base

Lake Powell, created by the dam, now stands at only 46 percent capacity: should it be drained?

Cracks five feet deep scar lakebeds that were formerly fed by the Colorado River.

or formal, are important in all of our lives. How many proposals do you make or respond to in one day? Your neighbor might suggest that you work together to clean up a park down the street, you and a colleague might collaborate on a project to save time and effort, you could call your best friend to check out a new movie, or you might approach your boss about implementing an idea you've just had. In each case, the proposal implies that some action should take place and suggests that there are sound reasons why it should.

In their simplest form, proposal arguments look something like this:

A should do B because of C.

┌──────── A ────────┐ ┌──────────── B ────────────┐
Our student government should endorse the Academic Bill of Rights
┌──────────────────── C ────────────────────┐
because students should not be punished in their courses for their reasonable political views.

Proposals come at us so routinely that it's not surprising that they cover a dizzyingly wide range of possibilities, from local and concrete

Existing suicide-prevention barriers on the Golden Gate Bridge often prove ineffective.

practices (*A student should switch dorms immediately; A company should switch from one supplier of paper to another*) to broad matters of policy (*The U.S. Congress should act to reform immigration rules*). So it may help to think of proposal arguments as divided roughly into two kinds—those that focus on practices and those that focus on policies.

Here are several examples:

Proposals about Practices

- The college should allow students to pay tuition on a month-by-month basis.

- The NCAA should implement a playoff system to determine its Division I football champion.

- San Francisco should erect a more effective suicide-prevention barrier on the Golden Gate Bridge.

Proposals about Policies

- The college should adopt a policy guaranteeing a "living wage" to all campus workers.

- The state should repeal all English-only legislation.

- The police department should institute a policy to train officers in intercultural communication.

Characterizing Proposals

Edward F. Palm offers five proposals about how professors should treat veterans returning to campus. What details in Palm's explanation show how carefully he has tailored his proposals to a specific audience?

LINK TO P. 955

Proposals have three main characteristics:

- They call for action or response, often in response to a problem.

- They focus on the future.

- They center on the audience.

Proposals always call for some kind of action. They aim at getting something done—or sometimes at *preventing* something from being done. Proposals marshal evidence and arguments to persuade people to choose a course of action: *Let's build a completely green home; Let's oppose the latest Supreme Court ruling; Let's create a campus organization for first-generation college students.* But you know the old saying, "You can lead a horse to water, but you can't make it drink." It's usually easier to *convince* audiences what a good course of action is than to *persuade* them to take it (or pay for it). You can present a proposal as cogently as possible—but usually you can't make an audience take the action you propose.

Proposal arguments must appeal to more than good sense—as David Brower and Greg MacGillivray do. Ethos matters, too. It helps if a writer carries a certain gravitas (Brower was one of the great environmentalists of the twentieth century, and MacGillivray is well known for his searing environmental documentaries). If your word and experience are credible, then an audience is more likely to do what you propose.

In addition, proposal arguments focus on the future—what people, institutions, or governments should do over the upcoming weeks, months, or even decades. This orientation toward the future presents special challenges, since few of us have crystal balls. Proposal arguments must therefore offer the best evidence available to suggest that actions we recommend will achieve what they promise.

In 2008, for example, oil magnate T. Boone Pickens appeared in a series of television commercials presenting evidence that the United States must move beyond an unsustainable reliance on fossil fuel. In these TV spots, Pickens drew on his ethos, presenting himself as one who had been an "oilman all my life" but who now understood from the weight of evidence that he and the country had to move beyond oil. He asked viewers to watch for a proposal he would be making, and within a month, additional advertisements appeared in which Pickens proposed his own energy plan (the United States should move aggressively to harvest power from the wind) and offered evidence to suggest that doing so would provide major help in curing the "oil addiction." Putting his money where his mouth is, Pickens—a billionaire many times over—immediately ordered $2 billion worth of wind turbines.

It will take years, however, to see whether Pickens's crystal ball provided the best answer to America's dependence on oil. By mid-2009, technical problems had already forced him to cancel plans for a single huge "wind farm" in the Texas Panhandle and to explore other options in the Midwest and Canada.

T. Boone Pickens defending his wind-power proposal

Finally, proposals have to focus on particular audiences, especially on people who can get something done. Sometimes, proposal arguments are written to general audiences. You can find these arguments, for example, in newspaper editorials and letters to the editor. And such appeals to a broad group make sense when a proposal—say, to finance new toll roads or build an art museum—must surf on waves of community support and financing. But such grand proposals also need to influence individuals (such as financiers, developers, public officials, and legislators) who have the power to make change actually happen. On your own campus, for example, a plan to alter admissions policies might be directed both to students in general and (perhaps in a different form) to the university president, members of the faculty council, and admissions officers. Identifying your potential audiences is critical to the success of any proposal.

An effective proposal also has to be compatible with the values of the audience. Some ideas may make good sense but cannot be enacted. For example, many American towns and cities have a problem with expanding deer populations. Without natural predators, the deer are moving closer to homes, dining on gardens and shrubbery, and endangering traffic. Yet one obvious and feasible solution—culling the herds through hunting—is usually not acceptable to the communities (perhaps too many people remember *Bambi*).

Proposals have to take audience values into account. Shooting deer, even when they're munching on garden flowers, is unacceptable to most suburbanites.

Developing Proposals

How do you develop an effective proposal? Start by showing that a problem needs a solution or that some need is not being met. Then make a proposal that addresses the problem or meets the need. Explain in detail why adopting your proposal will address the need or problem better than other solutions, and finally, show that the proposal is both feasible and acceptable. This might sound easy, but writing a proposal argument can be a process of discovery. At the outset, you think you know exactly what ought to be done, but by the end, you may see (and even recommend) other options.

Defining a Need or Problem

To make a proposal to solve a problem or meet a need, first establish that a need or problem exists. You'll typically describe the problem that you intend to address at the beginning of your project as a way to lead up to a specific claim. But in some cases, you could put the need or problem right after your claim as the major reason for adopting the proposal: *Let's ban cell phones on campus now. Why? Because we've become a school of walking zombies. No one speaks or even acknowledges the people they meet or pass on campus. Half of our students are so busy chattering to people that they don't participate in the community around them.*

The task of establishing a need or problem calls on you to do the following:

- Paint a picture of the need or problem in concrete and memorable ways.
- Show how the need or problem affects the audience for the argument as well as the larger society.
- Explain why the need or problem is significant.
- Explain why other attempts to address the issue may have failed.

In proposing that community service be required for students enrolled in state colleges, for example, you might begin by painting a picture of a self-absorbed "me first and only" society that values instant gratification. After evoking this dismal scene, you might trace the consequences of such behavior for your campus and community, arguing, for instance, that it fosters excessive competition, leaves many of society's most vulnerable members without helping hands, and puts the responsibility of assisting people solely in the hands of government—thereby adding to its size and cost and raising taxes for all. You might have to cite some authorities and statistics to prove that the problem you're diagnosing is real and that it touches everyone likely to read your argument. Then readers will be ready to hear your proposal.

Look at how Craig R. Dean, a lawyer and executive director of the Equal Marriage Rights Fund, prepares his claim—that the United States should legalize same-sex marriage—by explaining the significant problems that the existing ban on gay marriages creates:

> In November 1990, my lover, Patrick Gill, and I were denied a marriage license because we are gay. In a memorandum explaining the District's decision, the clerk of the court wrote that "the sections of the District of Columbia code governing marriage do not authorize marriage between persons of the same sex." By refusing to give us the same legal recognition that is given to heterosexual couples, the District has degraded our relationship as well as that of every other gay and lesbian couple.
>
> At one time, interracial couples were not allowed to marry. Gays and lesbians are still denied this basic civil right in the U.S.—and around the world. Can you imagine the outcry if any other minority group was denied the right to legally marry today? Marriage is more than a piece of paper. It gives societal recognition and legal protection to a relationship. It confers numerous benefits to spouses; in the District alone, there are more than 100 automatic marriage-based rights. In every state in the nation, married couples have the right to be on each other's health, disability, life insurance and pension plans. Married couples receive special tax exemptions, deductions and refunds. Spouses may automatically inherit property and have rights of survivorship that avoid inheritance tax. Though unmarried couples—both gay and heterosexual—are entitled to some of these rights, they are by no means guaranteed.
>
> For married couples, the spouse is legally the next of kin in case of death, medical emergency or mental incapacity. In stark contrast, the family is generally the next of kin for same-sex couples. In the shadow of AIDS, the denial of marriage rights can be even more ominous. . . .
>
> Some argue that gay marriage is too radical for society. We disagree. According to a 1989 study by the American Bar Association, eight to 10 million children are currently being reared in three million gay households. Therefore, approximately 6 percent of the U.S. population is made up of gay and lesbian families with children. Why should these families be denied the protection granted to other families? Allowing gay marriage would strengthen society by increasing tolerance. It is paradoxical that mainstream America perceives gays and lesbians as unable to maintain long-term relationships while at the same time denying them the very institutions that stabilize such relationships.
>
> —Craig R. Dean, "Legalize Gay Marriage"

Notice, too, that Dean indicates that the problems faced by gays who seek to marry have consequences for all members of the potential audience—who also might face problems stemming from intolerance. Although homosexuals might benefit most directly from solving the problem he describes, ultimately everyone in society gains.

In describing the problem that your proposal argument intends to solve, you may also need to review earlier attempts to address it. Many issues have a long history that you can't afford to ignore. For example, if you were arguing for a college football play-off, you might point out that the current bowl championship series represents an attempt—largely unsuccessful—to crown a widely recognized national champion. Some problems seem to grow worse every time someone tinkers with them. You might pause before proposing any additional attempt at reform of the current system of financing federal election campaigns when you discover that previous reforms have resulted in more bureaucracy, more restrictions on political expression, and more unregulated money flowing into the system. *Enough is enough* is a potent argument when faced with such a mess.

Making a Strong and Clear Claim

After you've described and analyzed a problem or state of affairs, you're prepared to make a claim. Begin with your claim (a proposal of what X or Y should do) followed by the reason(s) that X or Y should act and the effects of adopting the proposal:

Claim	Communities should encourage the development of charter schools.
Reason	Charter schools are not burdened by the bureaucracy that is associated with most public schooling.
Effects	Instituting such schools will bring more effective education to communities and offer an incentive to the public schools to improve their programs.

Having established a claim, you can explore its implications by drawing out the reasons, warrants, and evidence that can support it most effectively:

Claim	In light of a recent U.S. Supreme Court decision that ruled that federal drug laws cannot be used to prosecute doctors who prescribe drugs for use in suicide, our state should immediately pass a bill legalizing physician-assisted suicide for patients who are terminally ill.

Before she proposes vegetarianism as a solution, Kathy Freston first argues to establish the threat of serious environmental problems that result from meat consumption.

LINK TO P. 800

Reason	Physician-assisted suicide can relieve the suffering of those who are terminally ill and will die soon.
Warrant	The relief of suffering is desirable.
Evidence	Oregon voters have twice approved the state's Death with Dignity Act, which has been in effect since 1997, and to date the suicide rate has not risen sharply nor have doctors given out a large number of prescriptions for death-inducing drugs. Several other states are considering ballot initiatives in favor of doctor-assisted suicide.

In this proposal argument, the *reason* sets up the need for the proposal, whereas the *warrant* and *evidence* demonstrate that the proposal is just and could meet its objective. Your actual argument would develop each point in detail.

Showing That the Proposal Addresses the Need or Problem

An important but tricky part of making a successful proposal lies in relating the claim to the need or problem that it addresses. When gasoline prices soared in the summer of 2008, John McCain, then the Republican nominee for president, proposed to end the long-standing U.S. ban on offshore drilling for oil, a move that he had earlier opposed. McCain could certainly show that a problem existed: the economic effects of the highest-ever gas prices were being exacerbated by the spiraling cost of food and the housing and mortgage crisis. He and other advocates of dropping the ban had a harder time, however, showing that the action they proposed would actually address the problem. Indeed, experts from the Bush administration's Department of Energy said that adopting such a proposal would have little effect on the price of oil for at least twenty years. Later, McCain admitted that such drilling would have only "psychological effects," which, he said, would be "beneficial."

Sometimes a proposal calls for audiences to dream a little about how it fulfills a need or solves a problem that might not be immediately recognizable. That strategy was taken by President John F. Kennedy in a famous speech that he gave on September 12, 1962, explaining his proposal that the United States land a man on the moon by the end of the 1960s. Here are three paragraphs from his speech at Rice University, explaining why:

> We set sail on this new sea because there is new knowledge to be gained, and new rights to be won, and they must be won and used for

John and Cindy McCain promoting offshore oil drilling.

the progress of all people. For space science, like nuclear science and all technology, has no conscience of its own. Whether it will become a force for good or ill depends on man, and only if the United States occupies a position of pre-eminence can we help decide whether this new ocean will be a sea of peace or a new terrifying theater of war. I do not say that we should or will go unprotected against the hostile mis-use of space any more than we go unprotected against the hostile use of land or sea, but I do say that space can be explored and mastered without feeding the fires of war, without repeating the mistakes that man has made in extending his writ around this globe of ours.

There is no strife, no prejudice, no national conflict in outer space as yet. Its hazards are hostile to us all. Its conquest deserves the best of all mankind, and its opportunity for peaceful cooperation may never come again. But why, some say, the moon? Why choose this as our goal? And they may well ask why climb the highest mountain? Why, 35 years ago, fly the Atlantic? Why does Rice play Texas?

We choose to go to the moon. We choose to go to the moon in this decade and do the other things, not because they are easy, but because they are hard, because that goal will serve to organize and measure the best of our energies and skills, because that challenge is one that we are willing to accept, one we are unwilling to postpone, and one which we intend to win, and the others, too.

—John F. Kennedy

Proposals and Academic Argument

Academic writers are often called to present proposals in the form of applications for grants. In fact, you may have an opportunity to write a grant proposal during your undergraduate years to secure funding from a campus organization for a favorite project. Here is the introduction to a grant proposal that was submitted to the National Science Foundation:

Integrative Approaches to Bilingual Cognition and Interaction

This project proposes a new initiative to integrate doctoral education and research in Computer Science and Psychology, with extension planned to Linguistics and Education. The project's specific focus will be the connections between cognitive models of language and cognitive models in human-computer interaction, with a particular emphasis on bilingualism. The principal research efforts will involve understanding (1) the nature of bilingual language processing, combining cognitive and computational methods, and (2) how to develop real-time conversational systems based on cognitively accurate models for bilingual populations, especially at time scales of 300 milliseconds and below. The project will play a major part in a university-wide initiative on research and education in the interdisciplinary field of language and cognition. The project will also serve as a model for integrating doctoral programs across college and departmental boundaries. Students served by this project will include significant numbers of Hispanics; over 70 percent of the University's 19,000 students are Mexican American, and another 12 percent are Mexican nationals. The project's full proposal provides a list of project participants, detailed rationale, description of methods, step by step outcomes, and an itemized budget.

Note that this introduction sets out the major research questions to be answered, connects the proposal to larger university efforts, identifies the population to be served by the project, and provides an overview of what is to come in the full proposal.

Showing That the Proposal Is Feasible

To be effective, proposals must be *feasible*—that is, the action proposed can be carried out in a reasonable way. Demonstrating feasibility calls on you to present evidence—from similar cases, from personal experience, from observational data, from interview or survey data, from Internet research, or from any other sources—showing that what you propose can indeed be done with the resources available. "Resources available" is key: if the proposal calls for funds, personnel, or skills beyond reach or reason, your audience is unlikely to accept it. When that's the case, it's time to reassess your proposal, modify it, and test any new ideas against these revised criteria. This is also when you can reconsider proposals that others might suggest are better, more effective, or more workable than yours. There's no shame in admitting that you may have been wrong. When drafting a proposal, ask friends to think of counterproposals. If your own proposal can stand up to such challenges, it's likely a strong one.

When Charles Murray proposes that certification tests replace the college degree as the new requirement for jobs, he must explain to his readers how and why his proposal is feasible for both employers and job seekers.

LINK TO P. 982

Using Personal Experience

If your own experience backs up your claim or demonstrates the need or problem that your proposal aims to address, then consider using it to develop your proposal (as Craig R. Dean does in the opening of his proposal to legalize gay marriage). Consider the following questions in deciding when to include your own experiences in making a proposal:

Eboo Patel relates a personal experience of ignoring religious discrimination as a way of encouraging his readers to take a stand in favor of religious pluralism.

LINK TO P. 897

- Is your experience directly related to the need or problem that you seek to address or to your proposal about it?

- Will your experience be appropriate and speak convincingly to the audience? Will the audience immediately understand its significance, or will it require explanation?

- Does your personal experience fit logically with the other reasons that you're using to support your claim?

Be careful. If a proposal seems crafted to serve mainly your own interests, you won't get far.

Considering Design and Visuals

Because proposals often address specific audiences, they can take a number of forms—a letter, memo, Web page, feasibility report, brochure, or prospectus. Each form has different design requirements. Indeed, the

Richard Branson with a model of Virgin Galactic's *Mothership*

design may add powerfully to—or detract significantly from—the effectiveness of the proposal. Even in a college essay that is written on a computer, its headings and subheadings, variations in type (such as boldface or italics), and white space and margins can guide readers through the proposal and enhance its persuasiveness. So before you produce a final copy of any proposal, plan its design.

A related issue to consider is whether a graphic image might help readers understand key elements of the proposal—what the challenge is, why it demands action, and what exactly you're suggesting—and help make the idea more attractive. That strategy is routinely used in professional proposals by architects, engineers, and government agencies. When British businessman Richard Branson updated his proposal to take people on (very expensive) trips into space, he presented an animated video explaining the concept of space tourism and showing what such a trip would be like. The brief animation made the proposal seem exciting, attractive, and possible and appeared on YouTube and other sites (you can check it out at http://www.virgingalactic.com).

Key Features of Proposals

In drafting a proposal, make sure you include:

- a description of a problem that needs a solution
- a claim that proposes a practice or policy that addresses a problem or need, is oriented toward action, is directed at the future, and is appropriate to your audience
- statements that clearly relate the claim to the problem or need
- evidence that the proposal will effectively address the need or solve the problem and that it's workable

To fully develop your proposal, you will need to address all these elements, though you may choose to arrange them in several ways. A proposal might open with a vivid description of a problem and even an image (such as photographs of beautiful canyons that were destroyed by the Glen Canyon Dam). Or it might open with your proposal itself, which perhaps is stunning or unexpected in its directness.

Organize your proposal carefully, and ask for responses to your organizational plan from your instructor and classmates.

Not Just Words

Every day, groups make proposals that need to be approved by community or government groups, which often wind up paying for them. Such proposals are typically presented in the most flattering and appealing way possible.

Take a look at the images associated with a proposed project, a huge sports, entertainment, and shopping complex planned for New Jersey.

The Meadowlands Xanadu Complex as it was planned to look on completion

The site plan for Meadowlands Xanadu

These and a number of other images on the Web site for Meadowlands Xanadu support the proposed project by showing how traffic will flow in and around it, how it will serve its customers in five different venues, and how it will enhance the surrounding neighborhood and skyline. Look for similar examples of planned complexes or developments online. Is your community considering a new museum, library, stadium, or park, or is a local developer planning to turn a warehouse district into a shopping mall? Collect as much information as you can find about the proposal, and ask what it will offer to your community. Then design a brochure, poster, or Web site that would support or oppose the proposal. Be creative—and remember that design involves more than just images and photos.

GUIDE to writing a proposal

● Finding a Topic or Identifying a Problem

Your everyday experience often calls on you to consider problems and to make proposals—to change your academic major for important reasons, to add to the family income by starting a home-based business, or to oppose restricting new scholarships to specific student groups. In addition, your work or your job may require you to solve problems or make proposals to a boss, a board of directors, the local school board, someone you want to impress: the list could go on and on. You also can make proposals to online groups; with email one click away, the whole world can be the audience for your proposal.

In all these cases, you'll be calling for action or critiquing an action. Why not make an informal list of proposals that you'd like to explore in a number of different areas? Or do some freewriting on a subject of great interest to you, and see if it leads to a proposal. Either method of exploration is likely to turn up several possibilities for a good proposal argument.

● Researching Your Topic

Proposals often call for research. Even a simple one like *Let's start painting the house this weekend* raises questions that require some investigation: *Who has the time for the job? What sort of paint will be the best? How much will the job cost?* A proposal for adopting block scheduling at your local high school calls for careful research into evidence that supports the use of such a system. *Where has it been effective, and why?* And for proposals about social issues (for example, that information on the Internet should be freely accessible to everyone, even minors), extensive research would be necessary to provide adequate support.

For many proposals, you can begin your research by consulting the following types of sources:

- newspapers, magazines, reviews, and journals (online and print)
- online databases
- government documents and reports

- Web sites, blogs, social networking sites, listservs, or newsgroups
- books
- experts in the field, some of whom might be right on your campus

In addition, you might decide to carry out some field research—a survey of student opinions on Internet accessibility, for example, or interviews with people who are well informed about your subject.

Finally, remember that your proposal's success can depend on the credibility of the sources you use in support of it. As a result, you need to evaluate each source carefully (see Chapter 19).

● Formulating a Claim

As you think about and explore your topic, begin formulating a claim about it. To do so, come up with a clear and complete thesis that makes a proposal and states the reasons that this proposal should be followed. To start formulating a claim, explore and respond to the following questions:

- What do I know about the proposal that I'm making?
- What reasons can I offer to support my proposal?
- What evidence do I have that implementing my proposal will lead to the results I want?

● Examples of Proposal Claims

- Because we are in an economic crisis, because many people need help, and because President Obama's National Day of Service (January 19, 2009) was a success, schools and colleges should develop and implement service programs that all students can participate in.
- Every home should be equipped with a well-stocked emergency kit that can sustain inhabitants for at least three days in a natural disaster.
- Congress should repeal the Copyright Extension Act, since it disrupts the balance between incentives for creators and the right of the public to information as set forth in the U.S. Constitution.
- The Environmental Protection Agency must allow California and other states to establish tighter controls on greenhouse gases.

● Preparing a Proposal

If your instructor asks you to prepare a proposal for your project, here's a format that may help:

State the thesis of your proposal completely. If you're having trouble doing so, try outlining it in Toulmin terms:

Claim:

Reason(s):

Warrant(s):

- Explain the problem you intend to address and why your proposal is important. What's at stake in taking or not taking the action that you propose?

- Identify and describe those readers that you hope to reach with your proposal. Why is this group of readers most appropriate for your proposal? What are their interests in the subject?

- Briefly discuss the major difficulties that you foresee for your argument: Demonstrating that the action you propose is necessary? Demonstrating that it's workable? Moving the audience beyond agreement to action? Something else?

- List the research that you need to do. What kinds of sources do you need to consult?

- Note down the format or genre that you expect to use: An academic essay? A formal report? A Web site?

● Thinking about Organization

Proposals can take many different forms but generally include the following elements:

- a description of the problem you intend to address or the state of affairs that leads you to propose the action: *Our neighborhood has recently experienced a rash of break-ins and burglaries. Neighbors feel like captives in their homes, and property values are threatened.*

- a clear and strong proposal, including the reasons for taking the proposed action and the effects that taking this action will have: *Our neighborhood should establish a Block Watch program to reduce break-ins and vandalism and involve our kids in building neighborhood pride.*

- a clear connection between the proposal and a significant need or problem: *Break-ins and vandalism have been on the rise in our neighborhood for the last three years in part because neighbors have lost contact with one another.*

- a demonstration of ways in which the proposal addresses the need: *A Block Watch program establishes a rotating monitor system for the streets in a neighborhood and a voluntary plan to watch homes.*

- evidence that the proposal will achieve the desired outcome: *Block Watch programs in three other local areas have significantly reduced break-ins and vandalism.*

- a consideration of alternative ways to achieve the desired outcome and a discussion of why these are not feasible: *We could ask for additional police presence, but funding would be hard to get.*

- a demonstration that the proposal is workable and practical: *Because Block Watch is voluntary, our own determination and commitment are all we need to make it work.*

● Getting and Giving Response

All arguments can benefit from the scrutiny of others. Your instructor may assign you to a peer group for the purpose of reading and responding to each other's drafts. If not, ask for responses from some serious readers or consultants at a writing center. You can use the following questions to evaluate a draft. If you're evaluating someone else's draft, be sure to illustrate your points with examples. Specific comments are always more helpful than general observations.

The Claim

- Does the claim clearly call for action? Is the proposal as clear and specific as possible?

- Is the proposal too sweeping? Does it need to be qualified? If so, how?

- Does the proposal clearly address the problem that it intends to solve? If not, how could the connection be strengthened?

- Is the claim likely to get the audience to act rather than just to agree? If not, how could it be revised to do so?

Evidence for the Claim

- Is enough evidence furnished to get the audience to support the proposal? If not, what kind of additional evidence is needed? Does any of the evidence provided seem inappropriate or otherwise ineffective? Why?

- Is the evidence in support of the claim simply announced, or are its significance and appropriateness analyzed? Is a more detailed discussion needed?

- Are any objections that readers might have to the claim or evidence adequately addressed?

- What kinds of sources are cited? How credible and persuasive will they be to readers? What other kinds of sources might be more credible and persuasive?

- Are all quotations introduced with appropriate signal phrases (such as "As Ehrenreich argues, . . .") and blended smoothly into the writer's sentences?

- Are all visuals titled and labeled appropriately? Have you introduced them and commented on their significance?

Organization and Style

- How are the parts of the argument organized? Is this organization effective, or would some other structure work better?

- Will readers understand the relationships among the claims, supporting reasons, warrants, and evidence? If not, what could be done to make those connections clearer? Are more transitional words and phrases needed? Would headings or graphic devices help?

- How have you used visual design elements to make your proposal more effective?

- Are the transitions or links—from point to point, paragraph to paragraph, and sentence to sentence—clear and effective? If not, how could they be improved?

- Is the style suited to the subject? Is it too formal? Too casual? Too technical? Too bland? How can it be improved?

- Which sentences seem particularly effective? Which ones seem weakest, and how could they be improved? Should some short sentences be combined, or should any long ones be separated into two or more sentences?

- How effective are the paragraphs? Do any seem too skimpy or too long? How can they be improved?

- Which words or phrases seem particularly effective, vivid, and memorable? Do any seem dull, vague, unclear, or inappropriate for the audience or the writer's purpose? Are definitions provided for technical or other terms that readers might not know?

Spelling, Punctuation, Mechanics, Documentation, Format

- Are there any errors in spelling, punctuation, capitalization, and the like?

- Is an appropriate and consistent style of documentation used for parenthetical citations and the list of works cited or references? (See Chapter 20.)

- Does the paper or project follow an appropriate format? Is it appropriately designed and attractively presented? How could it be improved? If it's a Web site, do all the links work?

RESPOND●

1. For each problem and solution, make a list of readers' likely objections to the solution offered. Then propose a more defensible solution of your own, and explain why you think it's more workable than the original solution.

Problem	Future shortfalls in the Social Security system
Solution	Raise the age of retirement to seventy-five.
Problem	Extended drought that has killed flowers in the city's parks
Solution	Ration the use of water throughout the city.
Problem	Increasing rates of obesity in the general population
Solution	Ban the sale of high-fat items in fast-food restaurants.
Problem	Increasing school violence
Solution	Authorize teachers and students to carry concealed handguns.
Problem	Increases in sexual assaults on and around campus
Solution	Establish an 8:00 p.m. curfew on weekends.

2. People write proposal arguments to solve problems and to change the way things are. But problems aren't always obvious: what troubles some people might be no big deal to others. To get an idea of the range of problems people face on your campus (some of which you may not even have thought of as problems), divide into groups, and brainstorm about things that annoy you on and around campus, including wastefulness in the cafeterias, 8:00 a.m. classes, and long lines for football or concert tickets. Ask each group to aim for at least twenty gripes. Then choose one problem, and as a group, discuss how you'd prepare a proposal to deal with it. Remember that you'll need to (a) make a strong and clear claim, (b) show that the proposal meets a clear need or solves a significant problem, (c) present good reasons that adopting the proposal will effectively address the need or problem, and (d) show that the proposal is workable and should be adopted.

3. In the essay "Send It Somewhere Special" (p. 411), Michael Benson proposes that we convert the International Space Station into an interplanetary spacecraft, turning it from "an Earth-orbiting caterpillar into an interplanetary butterfly." Using the Toulmin model discussed in Chapter 7, analyze the proposal's structure. What claim does Benson make, and what reasons does he give to support the claim? What warrants connect the reasons to the claim? What evidence does he provide? Alternatively, make up a rough outline of Benson's proposal, and track the reasons that he presents to support his claim.

A Call to Improve Campus Accessibility for the Mobility Impaired

MANASI DESHPANDE

INTRODUCTION

The paper opens with a personal example and dramatizes the issue of campus accessibility.

Wes Holloway, a sophomore at the University of Texas at Austin, never considered the issue of campus accessibility during his first year on campus. But when an injury his freshman year left him wheelchair-bound, he was astonished to realize that he faced an unexpected challenge: maneuvering around the UT campus. Hills that he had effortlessly traversed became mountains; doors that he had easily opened became anvils; and streets that he had mindlessly crossed became treacherous terrain. Says Wes: "I didn't think about accessibility until I had to deal with it, and I think most people are the same way."

Both problem and solution are previewed here, with more details provided in subsequent sections of the paper.

For the ambulatory individual, access for the mobility impaired on the UT campus is easy to overlook. Automatic door entrances and bathrooms with the universal handicapped symbol make the campus seem sufficiently accessible. But for many students and faculty at UT, including me, maneuvering the UT campus in a wheelchair is a daily experience of stress and frustration. Although the University has made a concerted and continuing effort to improve access, students and faculty with physical disabilities still suffer from discriminatory

---

Manasi Deshpande wrote this formidable essay for a course preparing her to work as a consultant in the Writing Center at the University of Texas at Austin. Note how she reaches out to a general audience to make an argument that might seem to have a narrow constituency. She also effectively uses headings to guide readers through the complexities of her proposal. This essay is documented using MLA style.

The details in these proposals make them seem plausible and feasible.

The level of detail bolsters the author's personal ethos: she has carefully thought about these ideas and has earned a serious hearing.

The introduction's conclusion summarizes the argument and rallies support for its proposals.

This section examines the bureaucratic dimensions of the campus accessibility problem. The author's fieldwork (mainly interviews) enhances her authority and credibility.

hardship, unequal opportunity to succeed, and lack of independence.

The University must make campus accessibility a higher priority and take more seriously the hardship that the campus at present imposes on people with mobility impairments. Administrators should devote more resources to creating a user-friendly campus rather than simply conforming to legal requirements for accessibility. The University should also enhance the transparency and approachability of its services for members with mobility impairments. Individuals with permanent physical disabilities would undoubtedly benefit from a stronger resolve to improve campus accessibility. Better accessibility would also benefit the more numerous students and faculty with temporary disabilities and help the University recruit a more diverse body of students and faculty.

ASSESSMENT OF CURRENT EFFORTS

The current state of campus accessibility leaves substantial room for improvement. There are approximately 150 academic and administrative buildings on campus (Grant). Eduardo Gardea, intern architect at the Physical Plant, estimates that only about nineteen buildings comply fully with the Americans with Disabilities Act (ADA). According to Penny Seay, Ph.D., director of the Center for Disability Studies at UT Austin, the ADA in theory "requires every building on campus to be accessible." However, as Bill Throop, associate director of the Physical Plant, explains, there is "no legal deadline to make the entire campus accessible"; neither the ADA nor any other law mandates that certain buildings be made compliant by a certain time. Though not bound by specific legal obligation, the University should strive to fulfill the spirit of the law and recognize campus accessibility as a pressing moral obligation.

While the University has made substantial progress in accessibility improvements, it has failed to make campus accessibility a priority. For example, the Campus Master Plan, published in 1999 by the University, does not include improvements in campus accessibility as one of its major goals for the design and architecture of the University. It mentions accessibility only once to recommend that signs for wayfinding comply with the ADA. The signs should provide "direction to accessible building entrances and routes" and "clear identification of special facilities" (Gleeson et al. 90). Nowhere does the Master Plan discuss the need to design these accessible building entrances, routes, and special facilities or how to fit accessibility improvements into the larger renovation of the campus.

THE BENEFITS OF CHANGE
Benefits for People with Permanent Mobility Impairments

Improving campus accessibility would significantly enhance the quality of life of students and faculty with mobility impairments. The campus at present poses discriminatory hardship on these individuals by making daily activities such as getting to class and using the bathroom unreasonably difficult. Before Wes Holloway leaves home, he must plan his route carefully to avoid hills, use ramps that are easy to maneuver, and enter the side of the building with the accessible entrance. As he goes to class, Wes must go out of his way to avoid poorly paved sidewalks and roads. Sometimes he cannot avoid them and must take an uncomfortable and bumpy ride across potholes and uneven pavement. If his destination does not have an automatic door, he must wait for someone to open the door for him because it is too heavy for him to open himself. To get into Burdine Hall, he has to ask a stranger to push him through the heavy narrow doors because his fingers would get crushed if he pushed himself. Once in the classroom, Wes must find a suitable place to sit, often far away from his classmates because stairs block him from the center of the room.

Other members of the UT community with mobility impairments suffer the same daily hardships as Wes.

The paper uses several layers of headings to organize its diverse materials.

The author outlines the challenges faced by a student with mobility impairment.

Accessibility problems are given a human face with numerous examples of the problems that mobility-impaired people face on campus.

According to Mike Gerhardt, student affairs administrator of Services for Students with Disabilities (SSD), approximately eighty students with physical disabilities, including twenty to twenty-five students using wheelchairs, are registered with SSD. However, the actual number of students with mobility impairments is probably higher because some students choose not to seek services from SSD. The current state of campus accessibility discriminates against all individuals with physical disabilities in the unnecessary hardship it imposes.

Beyond inflicting daily stress on people with mobility impairments, the poor accessibility on campus denies these individuals their independence. Students with physical disabilities must often ask for help from others, especially in opening doors without functional automatic door entrances. Bathrooms without access also deny these individuals their independence. Once when I needed to use a bathroom in Burdine Hall, I found that none of the stalls was accessible. To be able to use the bathroom in privacy, I had to ask a stranger to stand outside the bathroom and make sure no one entered.

The author offers her personal perspective on the subject—a factual appeal that has an emotional dimension.

The state of campus accessibility also denies people with physical disabilities an equal opportunity to succeed. In the summer of 2004, I registered for CH 204, a chemistry lab, because I planned to be a Human Biology major. The major requires students to take four labs. When I got to the lab on the first day of class, I found that I could not perform any tasks independently. The supposedly accessible lab bench was just as high as the other benches, so I could not write, take proper measurements, or handle equipment on the bench. I could not reach the sink. The lab was so cramped that I could hardly fit through the aisles, and I wheeled around in fear of bumping into someone carrying glass equipment. Services for Students with Disabilities informed me that it would not be able to provide me with an assistant. Though I was fully capable of performing the labs myself, the lack of accessibility made me unable to complete even the simplest tasks.

Even with an assistant, I would have lacked independence and felt unequal to my classmates. After this experience, I dropped both the class and the major.

Benefits for People with Temporary Mobility Impairments

In addition to helping the few members of the UT campus with permanent mobility impairments, a faster rate of accessibility improvement would also benefit the much larger population of people with temporary physical disabilities. Many students and faculty will become temporarily disabled from injury at some point during their time at the University. Sprained ankles, torn ACLs, and fractured legs all require use of crutches or a wheelchair. Judy Lu, a second-year Business Honors Program/Plan II/ Pre-med major, used crutches for two weeks when she sprained her ankle playing volleyball. She encountered difficulties similar to those facing people with permanent disabilities, including finding accessible entrances, opening doors without automatic entrances, and finding convenient classroom seating. Getting around campus on crutches "was not convenient at all," and her temporary disability required her to "plan ahead a whole lot more" to find accessible routes and entrances.

The author broadens the appeal of her proposal by showing how improved accessibility will benefit everyone on campus.

All members of the UT community face the risk of enduring an injury that could leave them with a temporary physical disability. According to Dr. Jennifer Maedgen, assistant dean of students and director of SSD, about 5 to 10 percent of the approximately 1,000 students registered with SSD at any given time have temporary disabilities. The number of students with temporary physical disabilities is largely underreported because many students do not know about SSD or do not feel the need for temporary academic accommodations. By improving campus accessibility, the University would reach out not only to its few members with permanent physical disabilities but in fact to all of its members, even those who have never considered the possibility of mobility impairment or the state of campus accessibility.

Numbers provide hard evidence for an important claim.

Benefits for the University

The author offers a new but related argument: enhanced accessibility could bolster recruitment efforts.

Better accessibility would also benefit the University as a whole by increasing recruitment of handicapped individuals and thus promoting a more diverse campus. When prospective students and faculty with disabilities visit the University, they might decide not to join the UT community because of poor access. On average, about 1,000 students, or 2 percent of the student population, are registered with SSD. Mike Gerhardt reports that SSD would have about 1,500 to 3,000 registered students if the University reflected the community at large with respect to disability. These numbers suggest that the University can recruit more students with disabilities by taking steps to ensure that they have an equal opportunity to succeed. Improving accessibility is one way to achieve a more diverse campus.

COUNTERARGUMENTS

The paper examines and refutes two specific objections to the proposal.

Arguments against devoting more effort and resources to campus accessibility have some validity but ultimately prove inadequate. Some argue that accelerating the rate of accessibility improvements and creating more efficient services require too much spending on too few people. However, this spending actually enhances the expected quality of life of all UT community members rather than just the few with permanent physical disabilities. Unforeseen injury can leave anyone with a permanent or temporary disability at any time. In making decisions about campus accessibility, administrators must realize that having a disability is not a choice and that bad luck does not discriminate well. They should consider how their decisions would affect their campus experience if they became disabled. Despite the additional cost, the University should make accessibility a priority and accommodate more accessibility projects in its budget.

Others argue that more money would not accelerate change because the physical constraints of the campus limit the amount of construction that can take place. Mr. Gerhardt, for example, argues that "more money wouldn't make a difference" because ADA projects must be spaced over the long term to minimize disruption from construction. Other administrators, architects, and engineers, however, feel that money does play a significant role in the rate of ADA improvements. Although Mr. Throop of the Physical Plant acknowledges that the campus only has the capacity to absorb a certain amount of construction, he nonetheless feels that the Physical Plant "could do more if [it] had more monetary resources" and argues that the University "should fund [the Plant] more." Dr. Maedgen of SSD agrees, saying that the main constraint to making the campus more accessible more quickly is "mostly money." Even though there is "a real desire to do it," the problem "tends to be fiscally oriented in nature."

RECOMMENDATIONS

Foster Empathy and Understanding for Long-Term Planning

The University should make campus accessibility a higher priority and work toward a campus that not only fulfills legal requirements but also provides a user-friendly environment for the mobility impaired. Increased effort and resources must be accompanied by a sincere desire to understand and improve the campus experience of people with mobility impairments. It is difficult for the ambulatory person to empathize with the difficulties faced by these individuals. Recognizing this problem, the University should require the administrators who allocate money to ADA projects to use wheelchairs around the campus once a year. This program would help them understand the needs of people using wheelchairs. It would also allow them to assess the progress of campus accessibility as afforded by their allocation of resources. Administrators must realize that people with physical disabilities are not a small, distant, irrelevant group; anyone can join their ranks at any time. Administrators

After establishing a case for enhanced campus accessibility, the author offers several suggestions for action.

should ask themselves if they would find the current state of campus accessibility acceptable if an injury forced them to use a wheelchair on a permanent basis.

In addition, the University should actively seek student input for long-term improvements to accessibility. The University is in the process of creating the ADA Accessibility Committee, which, according to the office of the Dean of Students' Web site, will "address institutionwide, systemic issues that fall under the scope of the Americans with Disabilities Act." This committee will replace the larger President's Committee on Students with Disabilities. Linda Millstone, the University's ADA coordinator, reports that the three student representatives on the President's Committee "were not engaged" and that even now she is "not hearing a groundswell of interest from students." The University should not take this apparent lack of interest to mean that its members with mobility impairments face no problems. According to Ms. Millstone, a survey done about two years ago indicated that students were "clueless" that the President's Committee even existed. This ignorance is not the fault of students but rather a failure of the University to make its accessibility efforts open and transparent. Students should play a prominent and powerful role in the new ADA Accessibility Committee. Since students with mobility impairments traverse the campus more frequently than most administrators, they understand the structural problems of the campus. The Committee should select its student representatives carefully to make sure that they are driven individuals committed to working for progress and representing the interests of students with disabilities. The University should consider making Committee positions paid so that student representatives can devote sufficient time to their responsibilities.

Improve Services for the Mobility Impaired

The University should also work toward creating more useful, transparent, and approachable services for its members with physical disabilities by making better use of online technology and helping students take control of their own experiences. Usefulness of services would decrease the dependence of people with physical disabilities on others and mitigate the stress of using a wheelchair on campus. Approachability would help these individuals take control of their campus experience by allowing more freedom of expression and encouraging self-advocacy. Transparency would allow people with mobility impairments to understand and appreciate the University's efforts at improving campus accessibility.

First, SSD can make its Web site more useful by updating it frequently with detailed information on construction sites that will affect accessible routes. The site should delineate alternative accessible routes and approximate the extra time required to use the detour. This information would help people with mobility impairments to plan ahead and avoid delays, mitigating the stress of maneuvering around construction sites.

The University should also develop software for an interactive campus map. The software would work like Mapquest or Google Maps but would provide detailed descriptions of accessible routes on campus from one building to another. It would be updated frequently with new ADA improvements and information on construction sites that impede accessible routes. In addition, the interactive map would rate building features such as entrances, bathrooms, and elevators on their level of accessibility. It would also report complaints received by SSD and the Physical Plant regarding access around and inside buildings. The software would undoubtedly ease the frustration of finding accessible routes to and from buildings.

Since usefulness and approachability of services are most important for students during their first encounters with the campus, SSD should hold formal one-on-one orientations for new students with mobility impairments. SSD should inform students in both oral and written format of their rights and responsibilities and make them aware of problems that they will encounter on the campus. For example, counselors should advise students to look at their classrooms well in advance and assess potential problems such as poor building access, the need for an elevator key, and the design of the classroom. Beyond making services more useful, these orientations would give students the impression of University services as open and responsive, encouraging students to report problems that they encounter and assume the responsibility of self-advocacy.

As a continuing resource for people with physical disabilities, the SSD Web site should include an anonymous forum for both general questions and specific complaints and needs. The forum should be restricted by the University of Texas Electronic Identification (UTEID) to students registered with SSD. Obviously, if a student has an urgent problem, he or she should visit or call SSD as soon as possible. However, for less pressing problems such as a nonfunctional automatic door button or the need for a curb cut, an anonymous forum would allow for an easy way to let administrators know of a problem. By looking at the forum, administrators and the Physical Plant can get a good idea of the most pressing accessibility issues on campus and notify students of when they will fix the reported problems. Many times, students notice problems but do not report them because they find visiting or calling SSD time-consuming or because they do not wish to be a burden. The anonymity and immediate feedback provided by the forum would allow for more freedom of expression and provide students an easier way to solve the problems they face.

Services for the mobility impaired should also increase their transparency by actively advertising current accessibility projects on their Web sites. My research has given me the strong impression that the administrators, architects, and engineers on the front lines of ADA improvements are devoted and hard-working. To a person with a mobility impairment, however, improvements to campus accessibility seem sluggish at best. In addition to actually devoting more resources to accessibility, then, the University should give its members with mobility impairments a clearer idea of its ongoing efforts to improve campus accessibility. Detailed online descriptions of ADA projects, including the cost of each project, would affirm its resolve to create a better environment for its members with physical disabilities.

Conclusion

Although the University has made good progress in accessibility improvements on an old campus, it must take bold steps to improve the experience of its members with mobility impairments. At present, people with permanent mobility impairments face unreasonable hardship, unequal opportunity to succeed, and lack of independence. The larger number of people with temporary disabilities faces similar hardships, and the University as a whole suffers from lack of diversity with respect to disability. To enhance the quality of life of all of its members and increase recruitment of disabled individuals, the University should focus its resources on increasing the rate of accessibility improvements and improving the quality of its services for the mobility impaired. Administrators must learn not to view people with disabilities as a "them" distinct from "us," instead recognizing that the threat of mobility impairment faces everyone.

As a public institution, the University has an obligation to make the campus more inclusive and serve as an example for disability rights. With careful planning and a genuine desire to respond to special needs, practical and cost-effective changes to the University campus can significantly improve the quality of life of many of its members and prove beneficial to the future of the University as a whole.

WORKS CITED

Gardea, Eduardo. Personal interview. 24 Mar. 2005.

Gerhardt, Michael. Personal interview. 8 Apr. 2005.

Gleeson, Austin, et al. *The University of Texas at Austin Campus Master Plan*. Austin: U of Texas, 1999. Print.

Grant, Angela. "Making Campus More Accessible." *Daily Texan Online*. 14 Oct. 2003. Web. 1 Mar. 2005.

Holloway, Wesley Reed. Personal interview. 5 Mar. 2005.

Lu, Judy Yien. Personal interview. 5 Mar. 2005.

Maedgen, Jennifer. Personal interview. 25 Mar. 2005.

Office of the Dean of Students, University of Texas at Austin. "ADA Student Forum." 6 Apr. 2005. Web. 23 Apr. 2005.

Seay, Penny. Personal interview. 11 Mar. 2005.

Throop, William. Personal interview. 6 Apr. 2005.

Send It Somewhere Special

MICHAEL BENSON

Consider the International Space Station, that marvel of incremental engineering. It has close to 15,000 cubic feet of livable space; 10 modules, or living and working areas; a Canadian robot arm that can repair the station from outside; and the capacity to keep five astronauts (including the occasional wealthy rubbernecking space tourist) in good health for long periods. It has gleaming, underused laboratories; its bathroom is fully repaired; and its exercycle is ready for vigorous mandatory workouts.

The only problem with this $156 billion manifestation of human genius—a project as large as a football field that has been called the single most expensive thing ever built—is that it's still going nowhere at a very high rate of speed. And as a scientific research platform, it still has virtually no purpose and is accomplishing nothing.

I try not to write this cavalierly. But if the station's goal is to conduct yet more research into the effects of zero gravity on human beings, well, there's more than enough of that already salted away in Russian archives, based on the many years of weightlessness that cosmonauts heroically logged in a series of space stations throughout the 1970s, '80s and '90s. By now, ISS crews have also spent serious time in zero gravity. We know exactly what weightlessness does and how to counter some of its atrophying effects. (Cue shot of exercycle.)

And if the station's purpose is to act as a "stepping stone" to places beyond—well, that metaphor, most recently used by NASA Administrator Michael Griffin, is pure propaganda. As any student of celestial mechanics can tell you, if you want to go somewhere in space, the best policy is to go directly there and not stop along the way, because stopping is a waste of precious fuel, time and treasure. Which is a pretty good description of the ISS, parked as it is in constant low Earth orbit.

Michael Benson, the author of *Beyond: Visions of the Interplanetary Probes*, writes frequently about space science. On July 13, 2008, "Send It Somewhere Special" appeared in the *Washington Post*'s weekend Outlook section. Benson's proposal to retrofit the International Space Station as an interplanetary spacecraft proved to be highly controversial.

This is no doubt why, after the horrifying disintegration of the space shuttle *Columbia* in 2003, the Bush administration belatedly recognized that, if we're going to spend all that money on manned spaceflight, we should justify the risks by actually sending our astronauts somewhere. So NASA is now developing a new generation of rockets and manned space-craft. By 2020, the Constellation program is supposed to take astronauts beyond low Earth orbit for the first time since *Apollo 17* returned from the moon in 1972. Yes, that'll be almost 50 years. Where will they go? To the moon—the only place humans have already visited.

Which leads us right back to the expensively orbiting ISS. It hasn't a fig-leaf's role left. The moon is the new "stepping stone," with Mars bruited as a next destination. Although NASA officials will never quite say so, their current attitude seems to be that the station is essentially a high-maintenance distraction, even a mistake. Their plan is to finish assem-bling the thing ASAP and hand the keys over to the Russians, Canadians, Europeans and Japanese, with minimal continuing U.S. involvement. This should happen by the shuttle's mandatory retirement in 2010. Meanwhile, we're still writing a lot of high-denomination checks and preparing the two remaining shuttles for risky flights to finish something we then plan to be largely rid of. This seems absurd. I have an alternative proposal:

Send the ISS somewhere.

The ISS, you see, is already an interplanetary spacecraft—at least potentially. It's missing a drive system and a steerage module, but those are technicalities. Although it's ungainly in appearance, it's designed to be boosted periodically to a higher altitude by a shuttle, a Russian *Soyuz* or one of the upcoming new Constellation program *Orion* spacecraft. It could fairly easily be retrofitted for operations beyond low-Earth orbit. In prin-ciple, we could fly it almost anywhere within the inner solar system—to any place where it could still receive enough solar power to keep all its systems running.

It's easy to predict what skeptics both inside and outside NASA will say to this idea. They'll point out that the new Constellation program is already supposed to have at least the beginnings of interplanetary ability. They'll say that the ISS needs to be resupplied too frequently for long missions. They'll worry about the amount of propellant needed to push the ISS's 1,040,000 pounds anywhere—not to mention bringing them all back.

There are good answers to all these objections. We'll still need the new Constellation *Ares* boosters and *Orion* capsules—fortuitously, they can easily be adapted to a scenario in which the ISS becomes the living-area and lab core of an interplanetary spacecraft. The *Ares* V heavy-lift booster could easily send aloft the additional supplies and storage and drive modules necessary to make the ISS truly deep-space-worthy.

The *Orion* crew exploration module is designed to be ISS-compatible. It could serve as a guidance system and also use its own rocket engine to help boost and orient the interplanetary ISS. After remaining dormant for much of the one-year journey to, say, Mars, it could then be available to conduct independent operations while the ISS core orbited the Red Planet, or to investigate an asteroid near Earth, for instance.

But, the skeptics will say, the new *Orion* capsule's engines wouldn't be nearly enough; a spacecraft as large as the ISS would need its own drive system. Here, too, we're in surprisingly good shape. The ISS is already in space; the amount of thrust it needs to go farther is a lot less than you might think. Moreover, a drive system doesn't have to be based on chemical rockets. Over the past two decades, both the U.S. and Japanese programs have conducted highly successful tests in space of ion-drive systems. Unlike the necessarily impatient rockets we use to escape Earth's gravity and reach orbit, these long-duration, low-thrust engines produce the kind of methodical acceleration (and deceleration) appropriate for travel once a spacecraft is already floating in zero gravity. They would be a perfect way to send the ISS on its way and bring it back to Earth again.

This leaves a lander. A lunar lander substantially larger than the spidery *Apollo*-era LEMs is currently on the drawing board. It's not nearly as far along in development as the *Ares* booster and *Orion* spacecraft components of the Constellation program—which is a good thing. While I question the need to return to the moon in the first place, I wouldn't exclude it as a possible destination, so I think we should modify the lander's design to make it capable of touching down on either the moon or Mars and then returning to the ISS with samples for study in its laboratories. Such landers could also investigate the moon's poles, where we think water may be present, or one of the near-Earth asteroids—which may have raw materials suitable for use by future generations of space explorers.

But, our skeptics will sputter, this will all cost far more money than the Constellation program. Who'll pay for it?

Actually, it will in effect save all the money we've already spent on the ISS. And the station is already an international project, with substantial financial and technological input from the Russians, Canadians, Europeans and Japanese. In recent years, the Chinese, who have developed their own human spaceflight capabilities, have made repeated overtures to NASA, hoping to be let in on the ISS project. They've been unceremoniously rebuffed by the Bush administration, but a new administration may be more welcoming. An interplanetary ISS—the acronym now standing for International Space Ship—would be a truly international endeavor, with expenses shared among all participating nations.

How likely is any of this to happen? Not very. A lot depends on the flexibility of a NASA that hasn't always been particularly welcoming to outside ideas. On the other hand, the agency also collaborates with outsiders all the time. So it's not impossible. The reason the ISS went from being a purely American, Reagan-era project ("Space Station Freedom") to one including the Russians and many other nations was a political decision by the Clinton administration. A similar political vision will be necessary here.

All the billions already spent on the space station would pay off—spectacularly—if this product of human ingenuity actually went somewhere and did something. But it would also serve as a compelling demonstration that we're one species, living on one planet, and that we're as capable of cooperating peacefully as we are at competing militaristically. Let's begin the process of turning the ISS from an Earth-orbiting caterpillar into an interplanetary butterfly.

PART 3

STYLE AND PRESENTATION IN arguments

13
Style in Arguments

A classmate sitting with you in the library throws down a journal article that he has been reading. "Dry as dust," he complains. You know exactly what he means.

A person you know only slightly objects strenuously when you characterize her in-class comments as laced with irony, saying, "Sorry, you're wrong *again*. Irony's not my style." Since you'd meant this as a compliment, you decide to apologize and ask her how she would describe her style.

An architectural team working to design a new fast-food restaurant studies the most successful franchises of the last twenty-five years. What they find suggests that each franchise has a trademark architectural style, so they go to work seeking something new and distinctive— and something as unlike McDonald's design as possible.

A photographer looking to land the cover photo on *Vogue* takes a tour of college campuses. At each school, he sits patiently in the student union, watching as students pass by. He's looking for a face with "fresh new style."

A researcher trying to describe teen style crafted a questionnaire and distributed it to five hundred teens in three different cities. Why was she not surprised when the style mentioned favorably most often was "hip-hop style"?

● ● ●

Arguments have their own styles. One classical orator and statesman outlined three basic styles of communication, identifying them as *high* (formal or ornate), *middle* (understated and very clear), and *low* (everyday or humorous). High style in argument is generally formal, serious, even high-minded—an argument wearing its best tuxedo. Middle style marks most ordinary arguments, from the commonplace to the professional: these arguments have sturdy work clothes on. And low style is informal, colloquial, humorous—an argument with its shoes off and feet propped up. Even choice of font can help to convey a style: you could think of French Script, for example, as ornate or high, Garamond as understated or middle, and Comic Sans as everyday or low.

Such broad characterizations can give only a very general sense of an argument's style, however. To think more carefully about style in argument, consider the relationship among style and word choice, sentence structure, punctuation, and what we call special effects.

Style and Word Choice

The vocabulary that you choose for an argument helps to define its style, so your words should match the tone that you want to establish as well as the subject and purpose of your piece. For most academic arguments, formal language is appropriate. In an article that urges every member of society to care about energy issues, Chevron CEO Dave O'Reilly adopts a formal and serious tone: "We call upon scientists and educators, politicians and policy-makers, environmentalists, leaders of industry, and each one of you to be part of reshaping the next era of energy." Had he written "How 'bout everybody rallyin' round to mix up a new energy plan?," the effect would have been quite different.

Slang and colloquial terms can sometimes enliven an argument, but they also can bewilder readers. An article about arms-control negotiations that uses terms like *nukes* and *boomers* to refer to nuclear weaponry might confuse some readers and irritate others who assume that the shorthand betrays a callous attitude toward a serious subject. Be alert, too, to the use of jargon in arguments. Although *jargon* (the special vocabulary of members of a profession, trade, or field) serves as shorthand for experts, it can alienate readers who don't recognize technical words or acronyms.

Another key to an argument's style is its control of *connotation*, the unspoken associations that surround many words. Note, for example, the differences in connotation among the following three statements:

> Students from the Labor Action Committee (LAC) carried out a hunger strike to call attention to the below-minimum wages that are being paid to campus temporary workers, saying, "The university must pay a living wage to all its workers."

> Left-wing agitators and radicals tried to use self-induced starvation to stampede the university into caving in to their demands.

> Champions of human rights put their bodies on the line to protest the university's tightfisted policy of paying temporary workers scandalously low wages.

Here, the first sentence is the most neutral. It presents the facts and offers a quotation from one of the students. The second sentence uses loaded terms like "agitators," "radicals," and "stampede" to create a negative image of this event, while the final sentence uses other loaded words to create a positive view. As these examples demonstrate, words matter.

Finally, arguments that use concrete and specific words rather than abstract and general ones will make a more vivid impact on readers and listeners. Responding to a claim that American students are falling behind their counterparts in Asia and Europe, Jay Mathews uses memorable language to depict the stereotype:

> Most commentary on the subject leaves the impression that China and India are going to bury the United States in an avalanche of new technology. Consider, for example, a much-cited 2005 *Fortune* article that included the claim that China turned out 600,000 engineers in the previous year, India graduated 350,000, and poor, declining America could manage only 70,000. The cover of *Fortune* showed a buff Chinese

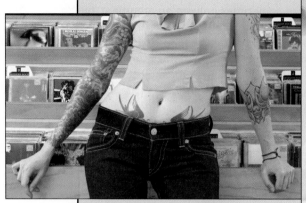

Not Just Words

Choose one of the images above, and study it for a few minutes.
How would you describe the style of the person depicted—just by
thinking about choice of pants, stance, and so on? How does the
photograph help to convey that style? Consider the composition,
the use of color, and so on.

beach bully looming over a skinny Uncle Sam. The headline said, "Is the U.S. a 97-Pound Weakling?"

—Jay Mathews, "Bad Rap on the Schools"

Mathews could have used more general language (such as "Most commentators imply that foreign countries are going to produce much more new technology than the United States"), but his concrete language ("bury," "avalanche," and "buff Chinese beach bully looming over a skinny Uncle Sam") makes this passage more memorable and creates a style that moves readers along.

Sentence Structure and Argument

Choices about sentence structure also can define the style of an argument. A series of sentences needs variety to keep readers involved. Writers of effective arguments take this maxim to heart, working to vary sentence patterns and lengths.

Varying sentence length can be especially effective. Here's George Orwell in a famous passage from his essay "Politics and the English Language," moving easily between sentences of varying length to make an upbeat point:

> A man may take to drink because he feels himself to be a failure, and then fail all the more completely because he drinks. It is rather the same thing that is happening to the English language. It becomes ugly and inaccurate because our thoughts are foolish, but the slovenliness of our language makes it easier for us to have foolish thoughts. The point is that the process is reversible.
>
> —George Orwell, "Politics and the English Language"

Here is Ronald Reagan on July 12, 1987, standing at Berlin's Brandenburg Gate before the wall that still separated Western and Soviet sectors in the city and delivering a strong appeal that leads to three short, powerful imperatives:

> There is one sign the Soviets can make that would be unmistakable, that would advance dramatically the cause of freedom and peace. General Secretary Gorbachev, if you seek peace, if you seek prosperity for the Soviet Union and Eastern Europe, if you seek liberalization: Come here to this gate! Mr. Gorbachev, open this gate! Mr. Gorbachev, tear down this wall!
>
> —Ronald Reagan

Paying attention to the way that sentences begin can similarly help to build an argument's effectiveness. In the article by Chevron CEO O'Reilly mentioned on page 418, we find the following paragraph:

> Demand is soaring like never before. As populations grow and economies take off, millions in the developing world are enjoying the benefits of a lifestyle that requires increasing amounts of energy. In fact, some say that in 20 years the world will consume 40% more oil than it does today. At the same time, many of the world's oil and gas fields are maturing. And new energy discoveries are mainly occurring in places where resources are difficult to extract, physically, economically, and even politically. When growing demand meets tighter supplies, the result is more competition for the same resources.
>
> —Dave O'Reilly

Look at how much less effective this passage becomes when the sentences all begin in the same way—that is, with the subject first:

> Demand is soaring like never before. Millions in the rapidly developing world are enjoying the benefits of a lifestyle that requires increasing amounts of energy. Some say that in 20 years the world will consume 40% more oil than it does today. Many of the world's oil and gas fields are maturing. New energy discoveries are mainly occurring in places where resources are difficult to extract, physically, economically, and even politically. Growing demand and tighter supplies result in more competition for the same resources.

The second version omits all transitions ("In fact," "At the same time") and openings that vary the subject-first order ("As populations grow," "When growing demand meets tighter supplies"), which makes the passage much less interesting to read, harder to understand, and less persuasive as an argument.

Effective arguments can also make good use of parallel structures in sentences. In a review of a biography of writer Henry Roth, Jonathan Rosen includes the following description:

> His hands were warped by rheumatoid arthritis; the very touch of his computer keyboard was excruciating. But he still put in five hours a day, helped by Percocet, beer, a ferocious will, and the ministrations of several young assistants.
>
> —Jonathan Rosen, "Writer, Interrupted"

In the first sentence, Rosen chooses a coordinate structure, with the first clause about Roth's arthritic hands perfectly balanced by the following clause describing the results of putting those hands on a keyboard. In the second sentence, Rosen uses a series of parallel specific nouns and noun phrases ("Percocet," "beer," "the ministrations") to build up a picture of Roth as extremely persistent.

Punctuation and Argument

In a memorable comment, actor and director Clint Eastwood said, "You can show a lot with a look. . . . It's punctuation." Eastwood is right about punctuation's effect, either in acting or in arguing. As you read and write arguments, consider choices of punctuation closely. Here are some ways in which punctuation helps to enhance style.

The semicolon is a handy punctuation mark since it signals a pause that is stronger than a comma but not as strong as a period. Here, Mary Gordon uses a semicolon in an argument about "the ghosts of Ellis Island":

> Immigration acts were passed; newcomers had to prove, besides moral correctness and financial solvency, their ability to read.
> —Mary Gordon, "More than Just a Shrine"

"You can show a lot with a look. . . . It's punctuation."

Gordon could have put a period after "passed," separating this passage into two sentences. But she chooses a semicolon instead, giving the sentence an abrupt rhythm that suits her topic—laws that imposed strict requirements on immigrants.

Semicolons can also make passages easier to read, as in the following example:

> Every year, whether the Republican or the Democratic party is in office, more and more power drains away from the individual to feed vast reservoirs in far-off places; and we have less and less say about the shape of events which shape our future.
> —William F. Buckley Jr., "Why Don't We Complain?"

Writers also use end punctuation to good effect. Although the exclamation point can be distracting and irritating if overused (think of those email messages you get from friends that fairly bristle with them), it can be helpful if used infrequently. Exclamation points are especially good for indicating a speaker's tone. For example, in an argument about the treatment of prisoners at Guantánamo, consider how Jane Mayer evokes the sense of desperation in some of the suspected terrorists:

> As we reached the end of the cell-block, hysterical shouts, in broken English, erupted from a caged exercise area nearby. "Come here!" a man screamed. "See here! They are liars! . . . No sleep!" he yelled. "No food! No medicine! No doctor! Everybody sick here!"
> —Jane Mayer, "The Experiment"

The question mark is another handy mark of punctuation. In a fairly negative review of Steven Spielberg's *War of the Worlds*, David Denby uses a series of questions to drive home the point he's been making:

> As the scenes of destruction cease, one has to ponder the oddity of a science-fiction movie without science, or even routine curiosity. Who are the aliens? What is their chemical makeup and how might they be vulnerable? What does the attack mean? Nobody raises any of these issues.
> —David Denby, "Stayin' Alive"

Two other punctuation marks are often important in establishing the style of an argument. While sometimes used interchangeably, the colon and the dash have different effects. The colon often introduces explanations or examples and separates elements from one another. Alison Lurie uses a colon in this way:

> The men may also wear the getup known as Sun Belt Cool: a pale beige suit, open-collared shirt (often in a darker shade than the suit), cream-colored loafers and aviator sunglasses.
> —Alison Lurie, "The Language of Clothes"

A dash or a pair of dashes, on the other hand, is often used to insert comments or highlight material within a sentence. Notice how columnist Maureen Dowd uses dashes to set off her point about the Bush administration's claim that it doesn't need search warrants to spy on individuals suspected of terrorist connections:

> Even when [Vice President Dick Cheney] can easily—and retroactively—get snooping warrants, he doesn't want their stinking warrants. Warrants are for sissies.
> —Maureen Dowd, "Looking for a Democratic Tough Guy, or Girl"

In the following example, *New York Times Book Review* critic Joel Conarroe uses dashes to mock their overuse by sportswriter Roger Angell and to show how they can slow the pace of the prose:

> Mr. Angell is addicted to dashes and parentheses—small pauses or digressions in the narrative like those moments when the umpire dusts off home plate or a pitcher rubs up a new ball—that serve to slow an already deliberate movement almost to a standstill.
> —Joel Conarroe, "Ode on a Rainbow Slider"

As these examples suggest, punctuation is often key to creating the rhythm of an argument. Take a look at how Maya Angelou uses a dash along with another punctuation mark—ellipsis points—to indicate a pause or hesitation, in this case one that builds anticipation:

> Then the voice, husky and familiar, came to wash over us—"The winnah, and still heavyweight champeen of the world . . . Joe Louis."
> —Maya Angelou, "Champion of the World"

Creating rhythms can be especially important in online communication when writers are trying to invest their arguments with emotion or emphasis. Some writers still use asterisks in online communication to

Charles Murray includes two pairs of dashes in his essay questioning the necessity of a college education. How would you describe the function of each pair in his argument?

LINK TO P. 982

convey the sense that italic type creates in print texts: "You *must* respond to this email today!" Others use emoticons or other new characters (from the ubiquitous smiley face ☺ to combinations like g2g for "got to go") to establish a particular rhythm, tone, and style. In some online writing, experimentation is acceptable, but in an argument where the stakes are high, writers use conventional style to avoid alienating their audiences.

Special Effects: Figurative Language and Argument

Look at any magazine or Web site, and you'll see how figurative language works on behalf of arguments. When a writer says that "the digital revolution is whipping through our lives like a Bengali typhoon," she's making an implicit argument about the speed and strength of the digital revolution. When another writer calls Disney World a "smile factory," she begins a stinging critique of the way pleasure is "manufactured" there.

Just what is figurative language? Traditionally, the terms *figurative language* and *figures of speech* refer to language that differs from the ordinary—language that calls up, or "figures," something else. But all language could be said to call up something else. The words *table* and *war*, for example, aren't themselves a table or a war; rather, they call up these concepts in our imaginations in different forms. Thus, just as all language is by nature argumentative, so are all figures of speech. Far from being mere decoration or embellishment (something like icing on the cake of thought), figures of speech are indispensable to language use.

Figurative language brings two major strengths to arguments. First, it aids understanding by drawing parallels between an unknown and a known. For example, to describe DNA as they had identified it, scientists Watson and Crick used two familiar examples—a helix (spiral) and a zipper. Today, arguments about computer technologies are filled with similar uses of figurative language. Indeed, Microsoft likens its entire word processing system to an office (as in Microsoft Office) to make its software features understandable and familiar to users. Second, figurative language makes arguments memorable. A person argued that slang should be used in formal writing because "slang is language that takes off its coat, spits on its hands, and gets to work." In a brief poem that carries a powerful argument, Langston Hughes uses figurative language to explore the consequences of unfulfilled dreams:

What happens to a dream deferred?

Does it dry up
Like a raisin in the sun?
Or fester like a sore—
And then run?
Does it stink like rotten meat?
Or crust and sugar over—
Like a syrupy sweet?

Maybe it just sags
Like a heavy load.

Or does it explode?
—Langston Hughes, "Harlem—A Dream Deferred"

You may be surprised to learn that during the European Renaissance, schoolchildren sometimes learned and practiced using as many as 180 figures of speech. Such practice seems unnecessary today, especially because figures of speech come naturally to native speakers of the English language. People speak of "chilling out," "taking flak," "nipping a plot in the bud," "getting our act together," "blowing your cover," "marching to a different drummer," "seeing red," "smelling a rat," "being on cloud nine," "throwing in the towel," "tightening our belts," "rolling in the aisles," and "turning the screws": you get the picture. In fact, you and your friends probably have favorite figures of speech that you use every day. Try taking a quick inventory. Listen to everything that's said around you for one day, and jot down any figurative language you hear.

Figures of speech have traditionally been classified into two main types: *tropes* involve a change in the ordinary signification, or meaning, of a word or phrase, and *schemes* involve a special arrangement of words. We can't provide a complete catalog of figures and their special effects in this chapter, but here is a brief listing—with examples—of some of the most familiar kinds. They can be used to very good effect in the arguments you write.

Tropes

METAPHOR

Marjorie Agosín acknowledges the power of metaphor by replacing the proverbial phrase "translators are traitors" with the metaphor of translators as "splendid friends" in the last sentence of her essay. What other metaphors can you find in her essay?

LINK TO P. 745

One of the most pervasive uses of figurative language, *metaphor* implies a comparison between two things and thereby clarifies and enlivens many arguments. In the following passage, novelist and poet Benjamin Saenz uses several metaphors to describe his relationship to the southern border of the United States:

> It seems obvious to me now that I remained always a son of the border, a boy never quite comfortable in an American skin, and certainly not comfortable in a Mexican one. My entire life, I have lived in a liminal space, and that space has both defined and confined me. That liminal space wrote and invented me. It has been my prison, and it has also been my only piece of sky.
>
> —Benjamin Saenz, "Notes from Another Country"

In another example, Ron Rosenbaum uses an artful series of comparisons to describe how much he dislikes Billy Joel in an unambiguously titled article from *Slate*:

> Which brings me to Billy Joel—the Andrew Wyeth of contemporary pop music—and the continuing *irritation* I feel whenever I hear his

Billy Joel: schlock 'n' roll?

tunes, whether in the original or in the multitude of elevator-Muzak versions. It is a kind of mystery: Why does his music make my skin crawl in a way that other bad music doesn't? Why is it that so many of us feel it is possible to say Billy Joel is—well—just *bad*, a blight upon pop music, a plague upon the airwaves more contagious than West Nile virus, a dire threat to the peacefulness of any given elevator ride, not rock 'n' roll but schlock 'n' roll?

—Ron Rosenbaum, "The Worst Pop Singer Ever"

Language use is so filled with metaphors that these powerful, persuasive tools often zip by unnoticed, so be on the lookout for effective metaphors in everything you read. For example, when a reviewer of new software that promises complete filtering of advertisements on the World Wide Web refers to the product as "a weedwhacker for the Web," he's using a metaphor to advance an argument about the nature and function of that product. Enjoy the metaphor, but think about it, too.

SIMILE

A *simile* is a figure of speech that uses *like* or *as* to compare two things. The device is pervasive in both written and spoken language. Eminem's song "Like Toy Soldiers," for example, compares human beings to toy soldiers who "all fall down," are "torn apart," and "never win" but fight on anyway. A radio announcer says that the UCLA men's basketball team is so eager for the NCAA playoffs that its players are "like pit bulls on pork chops." One of our grandmothers used to say, "Prices are high as a cat's back" or, as a special compliment, "You look as pretty as red shoes." Here's a formal written example from an article in the *New Yorker* magazine:

You can tell the graphic-novels section in a bookstore from afar, by the young bodies sprawled around it like casualties of a localized disaster.
—Peter Schjeldahl, "Words and Pictures: Graphic Novels Come of Age"

And here's a carefully crafted zinger by John McCain, playing off Barack Obama's celebrity status during the 2008 presidential campaign:

Taking in my opponent's performances is a little like watching a big summer blockbuster, and an hour in, realizing that all the best scenes were in the trailer you saw last fall.

Similes play a major part in many arguments, as you can see in this excerpt from a brief *Wired* magazine review of a new magazine for women:

> Women's magazines occupy a special niche in the cluttered infoscape of modern media. Ask any *Vogue* junkie: no girl-themed Web site or CNN segment on women's health can replace the guilty pleasure of slipping a glossy fashion rag into your shopping cart. Smooth as a pint of chocolate Häagen-Dazs, feckless as a thousand-dollar slip dress, women's magazines wrap culture, trends, health, and trash in a single, decadent package. But like the diet dessert recipes they print, these slick publications can leave a bad taste in your mouth.
>
> —Tiffany Lee Brown, "En Vogue"

Here, three similes are in prominent display—"smooth as a pint of chocolate Häagen-Dazs" and "feckless as a thousand-dollar slip dress" in the third sentence and "like the diet dessert recipes" in the fourth. Together, the similes add to the writer's image of mass-market women's magazines as a mishmash of "trash" and "trends."

ANALOGY

Analogies compare two things, often point by point, to show similarity (as in *Many are tempted to draw an analogy between the computer and the human brain*) or to argue that if two things are alike in one way they are probably alike in other ways as well. Often extended to several sentences, paragraphs, or even whole essays, analogies can clarify and emphasize points of comparison. In considering the movie *Hustle and Flow*, a reviewer draws an analogy between the character DJay and the late, great musician, composer, and bandleader Duke Ellington:

> As [actor] Howard develops DJay's frustration and rue, he avoids the obvious, the overemphatic. His self-mocking performance is so ironically refined and allusive that one might think that Duke Ellington himself had slipped into an old undershirt and hit the fetid streets of Memphis.
>
> —David Denby, "Stayin' Alive"

And in an argument about the failures of the aircraft industry, another writer uses an analogy for potent contrast:

> If the aircraft industry had evolved as spectacularly as the computer industry over the past twenty-five years, a Boeing 767 would cost five

hundred dollars today, and it would circle the globe in twenty minutes on five gallons of fuel.

—*Scientific American*

Analogies applied to politics are so common that *The New Republic* writer Michael Schaffer poked fun of them in a piece that shows how such comparisons work structurally. Here are examples for both Barack Obama and John McCain:

Obama is: John F. Kennedy in 1960

Evidence: Appeal to new generation; first member of long-discriminated group to win; glamorous wife; support of Ted and Caroline Kennedy.

Representative media quote: "Today, for a brief shining hour, the young got to see what we saw—not the gauzy images of 'Camelot,' but the living spirit of The New Frontier." —Chris Matthews, *Hardball*

Political cartoonist Michael Ramirez demonstrates how analogies work visually in arguing in favor of drilling in the Arctic National Wildlife Refuge (ANWR).

By permission of Michael Ramirez and Creators Syndicate, Inc.

McCain is: Theodore Roosevelt in 1904

Evidence: Reformist history; past quarrels with party insiders.

Representative media quote: "Apart from their superficial similarities—the wreathing, weather-beaten face, the stocky build, the cowboy affectations—they do have some important traits in common. An obsession with things military, great personal courage, a genial way with reporters and an almost gravitational instinct toward the center of any political controversy." —Roosevelt biographer Edmund Morris, *Chicago Tribune*

—Michael Schaffer, "Political Analogies Are Like Toothbrushes"

CULTURAL CONTEXTS FOR ARGUMENT

Formality and Other Style Issues

Style is always affected by language, culture, and rhetorical tradition. Effective style therefore varies broadly across cultures and depends on the rhetorical situation—purpose, audience, and so on.

At least one important style question needs to be considered when arguing across cultures: what level of formality is most appropriate? In the United States, a fairly informal style is often acceptable and even appreciated. Many cultures, however, tend to value formality.

If you're in doubt, it's wise to err on the side of formality, especially in communicating with elders or with those in authority:

- Take care to use proper titles as appropriate (*Ms.*, *Mr.*, *Dr.*, and so on).
- Don't use first names unless you've been invited to do so.
- Steer clear of slang, jargon, and hip expressions. When you're communicating with members of other cultures, slang may not be understood, or it may be seen as disrespectful.
- Avoid potentially puzzling cultural allusions, such as sports analogies or musical references.

Beyond formality, stylistic preferences vary widely. When arguing across cultures or languages, the most important stylistic issue might be clarity. When you're communicating with people whose native languages are different from your own, analogies and similes almost always aid in understanding. Likening something unknown to something familiar can help make your argument forceful—and understandable.

OTHER TROPES

Several other tropes deserve special mention.

Signifying, in which a speaker cleverly and often humorously needles the listener, is a distinctive trope that is found extensively in African American English. In the following passage, two African American men (Grave Digger and Coffin Ed) signify on their white supervisor (Anderson), who has ordered them to discover the originators of a riot:

> "I take it you've discovered who started the riot," Anderson said.
> "We knew who he was all along," Grave Digger said.
> "It's just nothing we can do to him," Coffin Ed echoed.
> "Why not, for God's sake?"
> "He's dead," Coffin Ed said.
> "Who?"
> "Lincoln," Grave Digger said.
> "He hadn't ought to have freed us if he didn't want to make provisions to feed us," Coffin Ed said. "Anyone could have told him that."
>
> —Chester Himes, *Hot Day, Hot Night*

In these *Boondocks* strips, Huey signifies on Jazmine, using indirection, ironic humor, and two surprising twists.

Coffin Ed and Grave Digger demonstrate the major characteristics of effective signifying—indirection, ironic humor, fluid rhythm, and a surprising twist at the end. Rather than insulting Anderson directly by pointing out that he's asked a dumb question, they criticize the question indirectly by ultimately blaming a white man (and not just any white man but one they're supposed to revere). This twist leaves the supervisor speechless, teaching him something and giving Grave Digger and Coffin Ed the last word—and the last laugh.

You'll find examples of signifying in the work of many African American writers. You may also hear signifying in NBA basketball, where it's an important element of trash talking. What Grave Digger and Coffin Ed do to Anderson, Allen Iverson regularly does to his opponents on the court.

Take a look at the example of signifying from a *Boondocks* cartoon (see the figure on p. 433). Note how Huey seems to be sympathizing with Jazmine and then, in two surprising twists, reveals that he has been needling her all along.

Hyperbole is the use of overstatement for special effect, a kind of pyrotechnics in prose. The tabloid papers and gossip magazines whose headlines scream at shoppers in the grocery checkout line are champions of hyperbole. (Journalist Tom Wolfe once wrote a satirical review of a *National Enquirer* writers' convention that he titled "Keeps His Mom-in-Law in Chains Meets Kills Son and Feeds Corpse to Pigs.") Everyone has seen these overstated arguments and perhaps marveled at the way they sell.

Hyperbole is also the trademark of serious writers. In a column arguing that men's magazines fuel the same kind of neurotic anxieties about appearance that have long plagued women, Michelle Cottle uses hyperbole and humor to make her point:

> What self-respecting '90s woman could embrace a publication that runs such enlightened articles as "Turn Your Good Girl Bad" and "How to Wake Up Next to a One-Night Stand"? Or maybe you'll smile and wink knowingly: What red-blooded hetero chick wouldn't love all those glossy photo spreads of buff young beefcake in various states of undress, ripped abs and glutes flexed so tightly you could bounce a check on them? Either way you've got the wrong idea. My affection for *Men's Health* is driven by pure gender politics. . . . With page after page of bulging biceps and Gillette jaws, robust hairlines and silken skin, *Men's Health* is peddling a standard of male beauty as unforgiving and

unrealistic as the female version sold by those dewy-eyed pre-teen waifs draped across covers of *Glamour* and *Elle*.

—Michelle Cottle, "Turning Boys into Girls"

As you might imagine, hyperbole can easily backfire, so it pays to use it sparingly and for an audience whose reactions you can predict with confidence. American journalist H. L. Mencken ignored this advice in 1921 when he used relentless hyperbole to savage the literary style of President Warren Harding. Note that in doing so, he says that he's offering a "small tribute," making the irony even more notable:

> I rise to pay my small tribute to Dr. Harding. Setting aside a college professor or two and half a dozen dipsomaniacal newspaper reporters, he takes the first place in my Valhalla of literati. That is to say, he writes the worst English that I have ever encountered. It reminds me of a string of wet sponges; it reminds me of tattered washing on the line; it reminds me of stale bean-soup, of college yells, of dogs barking idiotically through endless nights. It is so bad that a sort of grandeur creeps into it. It drags itself out of the dark abysm (I was about to write abscess!) of pish, and crawls insanely up the topmost pinnacle of posh. It is rumble and bumble. It is flap and doodle. It is balder and dash.
>
> —H. L. Mencken, "Gamalielese"

Understatement, on the other hand, requires a quiet, muted message to make its point effectively. In her memoir, Rosa Parks—the civil rights activist who made history in 1955 by refusing to give up her bus seat to a white passenger—uses understatement so often that it becomes a characteristic of her writing and a mark of her ethos. She refers to Martin Luther King Jr. simply as "a true leader," to Malcolm X as a person of "strong conviction," and to her own lifelong efforts as simply a small way of "carrying on."

Understatement can be particularly effective in arguments that might seem to call for its opposite. When Watson and Crick published their first article on the structure of DNA (p. 426), they felt that they had discovered the secret of life. (Imagine what the *National Enquirer*'s headlines might have been for this story.) Yet in an atmosphere of extreme scientific competitiveness, they closed their article with a vast understatement that emphasizes the importance of their discovery: "It has not escaped our notice that the specific pairing we have postulated immediately suggests a possible copying mechanism for the genetic material." A half century later, considering the profound developments that have taken place in genetics, including the cloning of animals, the power of this understatement still resonates strongly.

Rhetorical questions don't really require answers. Rather, they help assert or deny something about an argument. Most of us use rhetorical questions frequently. Think of the times that you've said, "Who cares?" or "Why me?" or "How should I know?" These are all rhetorical questions. Rhetorical questions also show up in written arguments. In a review of a book-length argument about the use and misuse of power in the Disney dynasty, Linda Watts uses a series of rhetorical questions to introduce part of the book's argument:

> If you have ever visited one of the Disney theme parks, though, you have likely wondered at the labor—both seen and unseen—necessary to maintain these fanciful environments. How and when are the grounds tended so painstakingly? How are the signs of high traffic erased from public facilities? What keeps employees so poised, meticulously groomed, and endlessly cheerful?
> —Linda S. Watts, review of *Inside the Mouse*

And Debra Saunders opens her argument for the legalization of medical marijuana with a rhetorical question:

> If the federal government were right that medical marijuana has no medicinal value, why have so many doctors risked their practices by recommending its use for patients with cancer or AIDS?
> —Debra Saunders, "Feds Should Respect Court's Ruling for Docs"

Antonomasia is probably most familiar to you from sports coverage: "His Airness" means Michael Jordan; "The Great One," Wayne Gretzky; "The Sultan of Swat," Babe Ruth. But it's also used in fields like politics, sometimes neutrally (Arnold Schwarzenegger as "The Governator"), sometimes as a

Baseball player Roger Clemens became know as "The Rocket" because of his powerful pitching.

David Horowitz relies on numerous rhetorical questions—and even offers an answer to one—in his essay "In Defense of Intellectual Diversity." How do you think the rhetorical questions contribute to his argument?

LINK TO P. 922

compliment (Ronald Reagan as "The Great Communicator"), and sometimes as a crude and sexist put-down (Sarah Palin as "Caribou Barbie"). Such shorthand substitutions of a descriptive word or phrase for a proper name can pack arguments into just one phrase. What does calling Jordan "His Airness" argue about him?

Irony, the use of words to convey a meaning in tension with or opposite to their literal meanings, also works powerfully in arguments. One of the most famous sustained uses of irony in literature occurs in Shakespeare's *Julius Caesar* as Marc Antony punctuates his condemnation of Brutus with the repeated ironic phrase "But Brutus is an *honourable* man." Publications such as *The Onion* and the online *Ironic Times* are noted for their satiric treatment of politics and popular culture, scoring points while provoking a chuckle.

Schemes

Schemes, figures that depend on word order, can add syntactic "zing" to arguments. Here, we present the ones that you're likely to see most often.

Parallelism involves the use of grammatically similar phrases or clauses for special effect:

> For African Americans, the progress toward racial equality over the last half century was summed up in a widely quoted sequence: "Rosa sat so that Martin could walk. Martin walked so that Obama could run. Obama ran so that our children could fly."

> Current government programs don't protect poor people very well against the cost of becoming sick. They do much better at protecting sick people against the risk of becoming poor.
> —Michael Kinsley, "To Your Health"

> The laws of our land are said to be "by the people, of the people, and for the people."

Antithesis is the use of parallel structures to mark contrast or opposition:

> That's one small step for a man, one giant leap for mankind.
> —Neil Armstrong

> Marriage has many pains, but celibacy has no pleasures.
> —Samuel Johnson

Those who kill people are called murderers; those who kill animals, sportsmen.

Inverted word order, in which the parts of a sentence or clause are not in the usual subject-verb-object order, can help make arguments particularly memorable:

Into this grey lake plopped the thought, I know this man, don't I?

—Doris Lessing

Hard to see, the dark side is.

—Yoda

Good looking he was not; wealthy he was not; but brilliant—he was.

As with anything else, however, too much of such a figure can quickly become, well, too much.

Anaphora, or effective repetition, can act like a drumbeat in an argument, bringing the point home. Here is an emotional section from Ronald Reagan's June 6, 1984, address to the aging World War II veterans who assembled in Normandy, France, for the fortieth anniversary of D-Day:

Behind me is a memorial that symbolizes the Ranger daggers that were thrust into the top of these cliffs. And before me are the men who put them there.

These are the boys of Pointe du Hoc. These are the men who took the cliffs. These are the champions who helped free a continent. These are the heroes who helped end a war.

—Ronald Reagan

In an argument about the future of Chicago, Lerone Bennett Jr. similarly uses repetition to link Chicago to innovation and creativity:

[Chicago]'s the place where organized Black history was born, where gospel music was born, where jazz and the blues were reborn, where the Beatles and the Rolling Stones went up to the mountaintop to get the new musical commandments from Chuck Berry and the rock'n'roll apostles.

—Lerone Bennett Jr., "Blacks in Chicago"

And speaking of the Rolling Stones, here's Dave Barry using repetition comically in his comments on their 2002 tour:

Recently I attended a Rolling Stones concert. This is something I do every two decades. I saw the Stones in the 1960s, and then again in the 1980s. I plan to see them next in the 2020s, then the 2040s, then the 2060s, at their 100th anniversary concert.

—Dave Barry, "OK, What Will Stones Do for 100th Anniversary?"

Penn Jillette uses anaphora when he begins the last four paragraphs of his essay with the same opening phrase. How does this repetition affect your reaction to his argument?

LINK TO P. 898

Reversed structures for special effect have been used widely in political argumentation. President John F. Kennedy's inaugural address in 1961 charged citizens to "ask not what your country can do for you; ask what you can do for your country." Like the other figures we've listed here, this one can help make arguments memorable:

> **The Democrats won't get elected unless things get worse, and things won't get worse until the Democrats get elected.**
>
> —Jeane Kirkpatrick

> **Your manuscript is both good and original. But the part that is good is not original, and the part that is original is not good.**
>
> —Samuel Johnson

RESPOND.

1. Turn to something you read frequently—a blog, a sports or news magazine, or a friend's page on Twitter—and look closely at the sentences. What seems distinctive about them? Do they vary in terms of their length and the way that they begin? If so, how? Do they use parallel structures or other structural devices to good effect? How easy to read are they, and what accounts for that ease?

2. Try your hand at writing a brief movie review for your campus newspaper, experimenting with punctuation as one way to create an effective style. Consider whether a series of questions might have a strong effect, whether exclamation points would add or detract from the message you want to send, and so on. When you've finished the review, compare it to one written by a classmate, and look for similarities and differences in your choices of punctuation.

3. In the following advertising slogans, identify the types of figurative language used—metaphor, simile, analogy, hyperbole, understatement, rhetorical question, antonomasia, irony, parallelism, antithesis, inverted word order, anaphora, or reversed structure.

    "Good to the last drop." (Maxwell House coffee)

    "It's the real thing." (Coca-Cola)

    "Melts in your mouth, not in your hands." (M&M's)

    "Be all that you can be." (U.S. Army)

    "Breakfast of champions." (Wheaties)

    "Double your pleasure; double your fun." (Doublemint gum)

"Got milk?" (America's Milk Processors)

"Let your fingers do the walking." (the Yellow Pages)

"Think small." (Volkswagen)

"Like a Rock." (Chevy trucks)

"Real bonding, real popcorn, real butter, real good times." (Pop-Secret Popcorn)

4. Some writers or public speakers are well known for their use of tropes and schemes. (Tom Wolfe and Jesse Jackson come to mind.) Using the Internet, find the text of an essay or a speech by someone who uses figures of speech liberally. Pick a paragraph that seems particularly rich in figures, and rewrite it, eliminating every trace of figurative language. Then read the two paragraphs—the original and your revised version—aloud to your class. With your classmates' help, imagine rhetorical situations in which the figure-free version would be most appropriate.

5. Now find an example of prose that seems dry and nonfigurative (such as a technical manual, instructions for operating appliances, or a legal document). Rewrite part of the piece in the most figurative language that you can come up with. Then try to list rhetorical situations in which this newly figured language might be most appropriate.

14
Visual Arguments

You know that you shouldn't buy camping gear just because you see it advertised in a magazine. But what's the harm in imagining yourself in Yosemite National Park with the sun setting, the camp stove open, and the tent up? That could be *you* there in Mariposa Grove, just like the tanned campers in the ad. What was the brand name of that gear again, and what's the company's URL?

A student government committee is meeting to talk about campus safety. One member has prepared a graph showing a steady increase in on-campus robberies over the last five years and has brought several photographs that bring these crimes vividly to life.

A photographer is banned from accompanying U.S. Marines in an Afghan war zone because he has posted photographs on a Web site showing dead American soldiers who were killed by a suicide bomber. Supporters of the photographer believe that his images provide a visual argument against the conflict. Those who oppose his act believe that he is exploiting dead heroes for a political purpose.

You've never heard of the sponsoring time-share resort. But its impressive letter is printed on thick bond paper with smart color graphics, and hey, the company's CEO is offering you a free weekend at its Palm Beach facility just to consider investing in a time-share. In addition, the firm's Web site seems professional: it's quick-loading and easy to navigate. Somebody's on the ball. Perhaps you should take the firm up on its offer.

A shiny silver convertible passes you effortlessly on a steep slope along a curving mountain interstate highway. It's moving too fast for you to read the nameplate, but on the grill you see a three-pointed star. Maybe after you graduate from law school and your student loans are paid off?

The Power of Visual Arguments

We don't need to be reminded that visual images have clout. Just think for a moment about where you were on September 11, 2001, when you first saw images of the hijacked planes that slammed into the World Trade Center towers. Or remember the images of the August 2005 floodwaters in New Orleans and the desperate citizens who were driven to rooftops in the wake of Hurricane Katrina. Or maybe you recall the dramatic opening ceremonies of the 2008 Summer Olympics in Beijing. Images like these stick in our memories.

Yet even in mundane moments, visual images—from T-shirts to billboards to movie and computer screens—influence us. Everyone seems to be trying to get our attention with images as well as words. Some argue that images today pack more punch than words, especially for the "millennial" generation that has grown up doing much of its reading onscreen. As technology makes it easier for people to create and transmit images, images become more compelling than ever, brought to us via Blu-ray and high-definition television on our smartphones and computers, on our walls, in our pockets, and even in our cars.

But visual arguments weren't invented by YouTube, and they've always had power. The pharaohs of Egypt lined the banks of the Nile River with statues of themselves to assert their authority, and Roman emperors had their portraits stamped on coins for the same reason.

What arguments does an image of *Air Force One* in flight usually make? What arguments were provoked by the scene above, a low-altitude pass over New York City by an identical backup plane—with no public notice in advance—on April 27, 2009?

Some thirty thousand years ago, people in the south of France created magnificent cave paintings, suggesting that people have long used images to celebrate and to communicate.

For the authors of this book, two events marked turning points in the growing power of media images. The first occurred in 1960 when presidential candidates John F. Kennedy and Richard M. Nixon met in a nationally televised debate. Kennedy, robust and confident in a dark suit, faced a pale and haggard Nixon who had recently recovered from an illness. Kennedy looked cool and "presidential"; Nixon did not. Many viewers believe that the contrasting images that Kennedy and Nixon presented on that evening changed the direction of the 1960 election campaign and led to Kennedy's narrow victory. The debate also established television as the chief medium for political communication in the United States until the rise of the Internet.

Richard M. Nixon and John F. Kennedy in a televised debate, 1960

The second event is more recent—the introduction in the early 1980s of personal computers with graphic interfaces. These machines, which initially seemed strange and toylike, operated with easy-to-use icons and pictures rather than through complicated commands made up of letters, numbers, and symbols. Subtly at first and then with the force of a tsunami, graphic computers (the only kind that people use now) moved society further away from an age of print into an era of electronic, image-saturated communications.

At the end of the opening decade of a new millennium, people have adjusted to a world of seamless, multichannel, multimedia communications. The prophet of this time was Marshall McLuhan, who over forty years ago proclaimed that "the medium is the massage," with the play on *message* and *massage* intentional. Certainly images massage us all the time, and anyone reading and writing today has to be prepared to deal with arguments that shuffle more than words.

Not Just Words

One of the best-known photographs that appeared after the September 11, 2001, terrorist attacks was shot by Thomas Franklin. It shows three firefighters hoisting the American flag in the wreckage of the World Trade Center as dust settles around them. In 2002, the image was used on a fund-raising stamp that sold for forty-five cents, with proceeds going to the Federal Emergency Management Agency. Part of the picture's appeal was its resemblance to another famous American image—Joe Rosenthal's photo of U.S. Marines raising the flag on Iwo Jima in 1945. That image was made into a three-cent stamp that became the best-selling U.S. stamp for many years.

Take a look at the two images, and consider how they're composed. What attracts your attention? How do your eyes move over the images? What immediate impression do they create? Also notice other features of the stamps—tinting, text placement, font, and wording. What argument do these stamps make about America?

Shaping the Message

Images make arguments of their own. A photograph, for example, isn't a faithful representation of reality; it's reality shaped by the photographer's point of view. You can see photographic and video arguments at work everywhere, particularly during political campaigns. Staff photographers place candidates in settings that show them in the best possible light (shirtsleeves rolled up and surrounded by smiling children and red-white-and-blue bunting), and their opponents look for opportunities to present the other side's candidates in a bad way. Closer to home, you may well have selected photographs that show you at your best to include on MySpace or Facebook.

Those who produce images shape the messages that those images convey, but those who "read" those images are by no means passive. Human vision is selective. To some extent, we actively shape what we see and have learned to see things according to their meanings within our culture. People don't always see things the same way, which explains why eyewitnesses to the same event often report it differently. Even instant replays don't always solve disputed calls on football fields. The visual images that surround us today and argue forcefully for our attention, time, and money are constructed to invite, perhaps even coerce, us into seeing them in just one way. But since we all have our own frames of reference, we resist such pressures. So visual arguments might best be described as a give-and-take, a dialogue, or even a tussle.

Analyzing Visual Elements of Arguments

Analyzing the visual elements of arguments is a challenge, especially when you encounter multimedia appeals on the Web. Here are some questions that can help you recognize and analyze visual and multimedia arguments:

About the Creators and Distributors

- Who created this visual text? Who distributed it?
- What can you find out about these people and other work that they have they done?

- What does the creator's attitude seem to be toward the image?
- What do the creator and the distributor intend its effects to be? Do they have the same intentions?

About the Medium

- Which media are used for this visual text? Images only? Words and images? Sound, video, graphs, or charts?
- How are the media used to communicate words and images? How do various media work together?

Big Tobacco's latest double talk

3,000 kids a day get hooked on tobacco. 1 in 3 will die from it. The best way to prevent these deaths is pretty obvious: stop tobacco marketing that hooks kids. But America's rogue tobacco companies don't want that. Bad for sales. So watch out for more deadly double talk in a new blitz of ads from Big Tobacco starting this week. They want policymakers to believe they're all about prevention...while they spend **$15.5 million a day** on marketing that attracts kids. These companies know almost **9 out of 10** adults hooked on cigarettes started as kids. Without children, Big Tobacco has no future.

ain't pretty

Don't believe Big Tobacco
They're still addicting kids

CAMPAIGN for TOBACCO-FREE Kids
www.tobaccofreekids.org

Analyzing Visual Elements: The Creators and Distributors

"Ain't Pretty" is one of a series of print ads created and distributed by the Campaign for Tobacco-Free Kids, which the *New York Times Magazine* describes as "the country's leading anti-tobacco lobby." The campaign itself represents a coalition of more than one hundred organizations (listed on its Web site) working together to discourage and prevent smoking, from the Academy of General Dentistry and the American Federation of Teachers to the Church of Jesus Christ of Latter-Day Saints and the Sierra Club. But whose view of Big Tobacco does the image in the ad represent? Only that of the Campaign for Tobacco-Free Kids, or that of all the individual members of the coalition? What sorts of reactions might the image evoke?

**Analyzing Visual
Elements:
The Medium**

In summer 2008, Democratic Speaker Nancy Pelosi recessed the House of Representatives rather than allow an up or down vote on an energy bill that authorized drilling for oil off American coastlines. She also ordered the lights and C-SPAN cameras turned off in the chamber as she headed off on a five-week vacation. Republican representatives remained in the darkened chamber and responded with a multimedia protest. As they argued about energy issues, they used cell phone and video cameras to record the shutdown and then communicated with constituents via podcasts, blogs, and a Twitter feed. These online media allowed the protesters to gain public attention, despite a lack of coverage by mainstream news outlets. Protesters for democracy in Iran later used similar techniques.

- What effect does the medium have on the message of the visual text? How would the message be altered if different media were used?
- What role is played by the words that accompany the visual text? How do they clarify, reinforce, blur, or contradict the image's message?

About Viewers and Readers

- What does the visual text assume about its viewers and about what they know and agree with?
- What overall impression does the visual text create in you?

**Analyzing Visual Elements:
The Viewers and Readers**

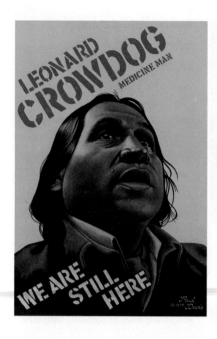

In 1977, Paul Davis created this poster celebrating Native American political activist Leonard Crowdog. The poster uses simple language and a strong image to express solidarity among Native Americans (and their political allies) and to affirm Crowdog's call for renewal of Native American traditions. In what ways can visual arguments invoke their audiences or even become a part of their cultural histories? With what visual items (such as posters or CD art) do you identify?

- What positive or negative feelings about individuals, scenes, or ideas does the visual intend to evoke in viewers?

About Content and Purpose

- What argumentative purpose does the visual text convey? What is it designed to convey?

- What cultural values does the visual evoke? The good life? Love and harmony? Sex appeal? Youth? Adventure? Economic power or dominance? Freedom? Does the visual reinforce these values or question them? What does the visual do to strengthen the argument?

- What emotions does the visual evoke? Are these the emotions that it intends to evoke?

About Design

- How is the visual text composed? What's your eye drawn to first? Why?

- What's in the foreground? In the background? What's in or out of focus? What's moving? What's placed high, and what's placed low?

**Analyzing Visual Elements:
The Content and Purpose**

An Associated Press photograph of Republican vice-presidential candidate Sarah Palin at a campaign rally in Bethlehem, Pennsylvania, started a controversy in October 2008, as news organizations and commentators raised questions about the content and purpose of the image. Some found it sexist and prurient, but others called it upbeat or emblematic of a new kind of feminism. Did the photographer and AP (which has been accused of both left- and right-wing bias in its overall political coverage) have a political agenda in taking and distributing the shot? Or did people read their own arguments into it?

What's to the left, in the center, and to the right? What effect do these placements have on the message?

- Is any information (such as a name, face, or scene) highlighted or stressed to attract your attention?

- How are light and color used? What effects are they intended to have on you? What about video? Sound?

- What details are included or emphasized? What details are omitted or deemphasized? To what effect? Is anything downplayed, ambiguous, confusing, distracting, or obviously omitted? To what end?

- What, if anything, is surprising about the design of the visual text? What do you think is the purpose of that surprise?

- Is anything in the visual repeated, intensified, or exaggerated? Is anything presented as "supernormal" or idealistic? What effects are intended by these strategies, and what effects do they have on you as a viewer? How do they clarify or reinforce (or blur or contradict) the message?

Analyzing Visual Elements: The Design

For years, United Colors of Benetton has launched memorable advertising campaigns with themes of political and social justice. Controversial in both content and design, its ads—like this one from a series that supports African economic development—compel audiences to think about issues not directly related to the fashions sold by Benetton. How does your eye construct this ad? What do you notice first? Do the parts make sense when you put them together?

- How are you directed to move within the argument? Are you encouraged to read further? Click on a link? Scroll down? Fill out a form? Provide your email address? Place an order?

Using Visuals in Your Own Arguments

You can and sometimes should use visuals in your writing. Many college classes now call for projects to be posted on the Web, which almost always involves the use of images. Other courses invite or require students to make multimedia presentations using software such as PowerPoint or even old-fashioned overhead projectors with transparencies.

On the following pages, we sketch out some basic principles of visual rhetoric. To help you appreciate the argumentative character of visual texts, we examine them under some of the same categories that we use for written and oral arguments earlier in this book (Chapters 2, 3, and 4).

You may be surprised by some of the similarities that you'll see between visual and verbal arguments.

Visual Arguments That Appeal to Emotion

Antonin Scalia's article "God's Justice and Ours" includes images that make powerful emotional claims, but the images weren't chosen by him. Do these images help support his argument, or do they work against it? Why?

LINK TO P. 881

People tend to be suspicious of arguments supported by multimedia elements because they can be used to manipulate our senses. In fact, many advertisements, political documentaries, rallies, marches, and even church services do use visuals to trigger emotions. Who hasn't teared up at a funeral when members of a veteran's family are presented with an American flag and a bugler plays "Taps" in the distance? Who hasn't been moved emotionally by a powerful film performance that is accompanied by a heart-wrenching musical score? You might also have seen or heard about *Triumph of the Will*, a 1935 propaganda film authorized by the National Socialists that powerfully depicts Hitler as the benign savior of the German people and a hero of superhuman dimensions. It's a chilling reminder of how images can be manipulated and abused.

You can't flip through a magazine without being cajoled or seduced by images of all kinds—most of them designed in some way to attract your eye and attention. Sometimes emotions can support the legitimate claims that you hope to advance. Emotions certainly run high at sporting events or ceremonies that honor human achievements, such as high school and college graduations.

APPRECIATE THE EMOTIONAL POWER OF IMAGES

Images can bring a text or presentation to life. Sometimes images have the power to persuade by sheer pathos. This was the case with photographs that showed 1960s civil rights demonstrators being assaulted by police dogs and water hoses and that showed the 2005 victims of Hurricane Katrina, which led many people to contribute to relief campaigns. You have an advantage if you can present images that make arguments almost entirely on their own.

But images you select for a presentation may be equally effective if the visual text works well with other components of the argument. Indeed, a given image might support many different kinds of arguments. Consider the famous *Apollo 8* photograph of our planet as a big blue marble hanging above the horizon of the moon. You might use this image to introduce an argument about the need for additional investment in the space program. Or it might become part of an argument about the need

A striking image, like this *Apollo 8* photograph of the earth shining over the moon, can support many different kinds of arguments.

to preserve our frail natural environment or an argument against nationalism: *From space, we are one world.* You could make any of these claims without the image, but the photograph—like most images—might touch members of your audience more powerfully than words alone could.

APPRECIATE THE EMOTIONAL POWER OF COLOR

Color has great power. Consider the color red. It attracts hummingbirds—and traffic cops. It excites the human eye in ways that other colors don't. You can make a powerful statement with a red dress or a red car because the color evokes emotions—but so do black, green, pink, and even brown. Our response to color is part of our biological and cultural makeup. So it makes sense to consider what colors are compatible with the kinds of arguments you're making. You might find that the best choice is black on a white background.

In most situations, you can be guided in your selection of colors by your own good taste, by designs you admire, or by the advice of friends or helpful professionals. Some design and presentation software will even help you choose colors by offering dependable "default" shades or an array of preexisting designs and compatible colors (for example, of presentation slides).

The colors that you choose for a design should follow certain commonsense principles. If you're using background colors on a political poster, Web site, or slide, the contrast between words and background should be vivid enough to make reading easy. For example, white letters on a yellow background are not usually legible. Similarly, any bright background color should be avoided for a long document because reading is easiest with dark letters against a light or white background. Avoid complex patterns, even though they might look interesting and be easy

The ancient statues that you see in museums are usually white or pale gray. But evidence suggests that the Greeks and Romans painted these figures brightly, as you can see in this original (right) and painted copy (left) in an Athens museum. Buildings, too, were far more colorful than the white marble facades that we see in Hollywood re-creations of Athens or Rome. How might your appreciation of these buildings change if you imagined them in color?

to create. Often, they interfere with other more important elements of a presentation.

When you use visuals in your college projects, test them on prospective readers. That's what professionals do because they appreciate how delicate the choices about visual and multimedia texts can be. These responses will help you analyze your own arguments and improve your success with them.

Visual Arguments Based on Character

What does visual argument have to do with ethos or character? Consider two argumentative essays submitted to an instructor. One is scrawled in thick pencil on pages ripped from a spiral notebook, and little curls of paper dangle from the left margin. The other is neatly typed on bond paper and in a form that the professor likely regards as "professional." Is there much doubt about which argument will (at least initially) get the more sympathetic reading?

You might object that appearances shouldn't count for so much, and you would have a point. The argument scratched in pencil could be the stronger piece, but it is at a disadvantage because its author has sent the wrong signals. Visually, the writer seems to be saying, "I don't much care about this message or the people I'm sending it to." At times, you might want to send exactly such a signal to an audience, but the visual rhetoric of your piece ought to be a deliberate choice and not an accident. Also

Near the end of her campaign for the 2008 presidential nomination of her party, Hillary Clinton loosened up a bit with reporters. Many thought that images such as this one enhanced her ethos by making her seem down to earth and likable.

These three images are used to convey authority and credibility. Do the Obama pre-presidential seal, the corporate logo of McDonald's, and the state seal of Louisiana accomplish their goals? Why or why not?

keep control of your own visual image. In most cases, when you present an argument, you want to appear authoritative and credible.

LOOK FOR IMAGES THAT REINFORCE YOUR AUTHORITY AND CREDIBILITY

How does the image of Kenneth Cole's model make an argument about that company's ethos? What kind of authority does Cole's company seek from this image and the others (described in the headnote) that were part of the "We All Walk in Different Shoes" campaign?

LINK TO P. 621

For a brochure about your new small business, for instance, you might be considering images of your office, state-of-the-art equipment, and competent staff to reassure consumers that your company has the resources to do its job. Similarly, for a Web site about a company or organization that you represent, you would include its logo or emblem because such images provide credibility. That's why university Web sites often include the seal of the institution somewhere on the homepage or why the president of the United States travels with a presidential seal to hang on the speaker's podium. An emblem or a logo can convey a wealth of cultural and historical implications.

CONSIDER HOW DESIGN REFLECTS YOUR CHARACTER

Almost every design element sends signals about character and ethos, so be sure to think carefully about them. For example, the type fonts that you select for a document can mark you as warm and inviting or as efficient and contemporary. The warm and inviting fonts often belong to a family called *serif*. The serifs are those little flourishes at the ends of the strokes that make the fonts seem handcrafted and artful:

warm and inviting (Bookman Old Style)

warm and inviting (Times New Roman)

warm and inviting (Bookman)

Cleaner, modern fonts go without those little flourishes and are called *sans serif*. These fonts are cooler, simpler, and, some argue, more readable on a computer screen (depending on screen resolution):

efficient and contemporary (Helvetica)

efficient and contemporary (Arial Black)

efficient and contemporary (Lucida Sans)

You may also be able to use decorative fonts. These are appropriate for special uses but not for long texts:

decorative and special uses (Zapf Chancery)

decorative and special uses (Goudy Handtooled BT)

Other typographic elements shape your ethos as well. The size of type can make a difference. If your text or headings are boldfaced and too large, you'll seem to be shouting. Tiny type, on the other hand, might make you seem evasive:

Lose weight! Pay nothing!*

*Excludes the costs of enrollment and required meal purchases. Minimum contract: 12 months.

Similarly, your choice of color—especially for backgrounds—can make a statement about your taste, personality, and common sense. For instance, you'll create a bad impression with a Web page whose dark background colors or busy patterns make reading difficult. If you want to be noticed, you might use bright colors—the same sort that would make an impression in clothing or cars. But subtle background shades are a better choice in most situations.

Don't ignore the power of illustrations and photographs. Because they reveal what you visualize, images can communicate your preferences, sensitivities, and inclusiveness. Conference planners, for example, are careful to create brochures that represent all participants, and they make sure that the brochure photos don't show only women, only men, or only members of one racial or ethnic group.

Even your choice of medium says something important about you. Making an appeal on a Web site sends signals about your technical skills, contemporary orientation, and personality. If you direct people to a

Olympic champion Michael Phelps learned a quick lesson about ethos when a drug-related incident tarnished his reputation, costing him an endorsement deal with Kellogg's. His photograph had already appeared on boxes of Kellogg's Corn Flakes and Wheaties.

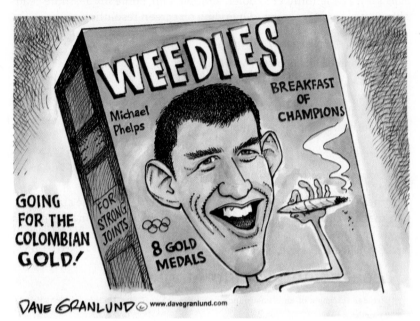

© Dave Granlund/Cagle Cartoons, Inc.

Facebook or Flickr page, be sure that the images and items there present you in a favorable light.

Presentations that rely on an overhead projector, an LCD projector with software, or photocopied handouts give different impressions about the presenters. When reporting on a children's story that you're writing, the most effective medium of presentation might be cardboard and paper made into an oversized book and illustrated by hand.

FOLLOW DESIGN CONVENTIONS

Many kinds of writing have required design conventions. When that's the case, follow them to the letter. It's no accident that lab reports for science courses are sober and unembellished. Visually, they reinforce the professional ethos of scientific work. The same is true of a college research paper. You might resent the tediousness of placing page numbers in the right place or aligning long quotations just so, but these visual details help convey your competence. So whether you're composing a term paper, résumé, screenplay, or Web site, look for authoritative models and follow them.

Visual Arguments Based on Facts and Reason

People tend to associate facts and reason with verbal arguments, but here, too, visual elements play an essential role. Indeed, it's hard to imagine a compelling presentation these days that doesn't rely, to some degree, on visual elements to enhance or even make the case.

Many readers and listeners now expect ideas to be represented graphically. Not long ago, media critics ridiculed the colorful charts and graphs in newspapers like *USA Today*. Now, comparable features appear in even the most traditional publications because they work: they convey information efficiently. And viewers have adjusted to the multiple data streams that cable news, weather, and finance channels routinely broadcast around talking heads on split screens.

The *New York Times* offers an argument about bottled water that is based on facts and reason and created mostly by visual elements.

LINK TO P. 840

ORGANIZE INFORMATION VISUALLY

A design works well when readers can look at an item and understand what it does. A brilliant, much-copied example of such an intuitive design is a seat adjuster invented many years ago by Mercedes-Benz (see below). It's shaped like a tiny seat. Push any element of the control, and the real seat moves the same way—back and forth, up and down. No instructions are necessary.

Good visual design can work the same way in an argument by conveying information without elaborate instructions. Titles, headings, subheadings, enlarged quotations, running heads, and boxes are some common visual signals.

When you present headings in the same type font, size, and color, you're showing that the information under these headings is in some way related. Use headings when they'll guide your readers through your document. For

Mercedes-Benz's seat adjuster

complex and very long pieces, you may use both headings and subheadings. So in a conventional term paper, headings and subheadings group information that's connected or parallel. Similarly, on a Web site, two or three types of headings might group chunks of related information.

You should also decide how text should be arranged on a page by searching for relationships among items that should look alike. In this book, for example, bulleted lists are used to offer specific guidelines, and boxes titled "Not Just Words" have colored backgrounds and present visual arguments. You might use a list or a box to set off information that should be treated differently from the rest of the presentation, or you might visually mark it in other ways—by shading, color, or typography.

An item presented in large type or under a large headline should be more important than one that gets less visual attention. Place illustrations carefully: what you position front and center will appear more important than items in less conspicuous places. On a Web site, key headings should usually lead to subsequent pages on the site.

You take a risk if you violate the expectations of your audience or if you present a visual text without coherent signals. Particularly for Web-based materials, which may be accessible to people around the world, you can't make many assumptions about what seems coherent in diverse cultures. So you need to think about the roadmap that you're giving viewers whenever you present them with a visual text.

Remember, too, that design principles evolve and change from medium to medium. A printed text or an overhead slide, for example, ordinarily works best when its elements are easy to read, simply organized, and surrounded by restful white space. But some types of Web pages seem to thrive on visual clutter. They attract and hold their audiences' attention by packing a wide variety of information onto a relatively limited screen. Look closely, and you'll probably find the logic in these designs.

USE VISUALS TO CONVEY DATA EFFICIENTLY

Words are powerful and capable of precision and subtlety. But some information is conveyed more efficiently by charts, graphs, drawings, maps, or photos than by words. When making an argument, especially to a large group, consider what information should be delivered in nonverbal form.

Cable television news shows, like many Web pages, seem to thrive on visual clutter, packing a lot of information into a relatively small place. Split screens, news "crawls" across the bottom, and sports scores (or electoral votes) in small type at the top make for a busy look but let viewers with varied interests (and limited patience and attention spans) see at a glance the information they want.

A **pie chart** is an effective way of comparing parts to the whole. You might use a pie chart to illustrate the ethnic composition of your school, the percentage of taxes paid by people at different income levels, or the consumption of energy by different nations. Pie charts depict such information memorably, as those on p. 462 show.

A **graph** is an efficient device for comparing items over time or according to other variables. You could use a graph to trace the rise and fall of test scores over several decades or to show college enrollment by sex, race, and Hispanic origin, as in the bar graph on p. 462.

Diagrams or **drawings** are useful for drawing attention to details. You can use drawings to illustrate complex physical processes or designs of all sorts. After the 2001 attack on the World Trade Center, for example, engineers used drawings and diagrams to help citizens understand precisely what led to the total collapse of the buildings.

You can use **maps** to illustrate location and spatial relationships—something as simple as the distribution of office space in your student union or as complex as the topography of Utah. Such information would be far more difficult to explain using words alone.

The U.S. Census Bureau organizes its information in graphs and maps to help readers make sense of the large amount of data that it is presenting.

LINK TO P. 724

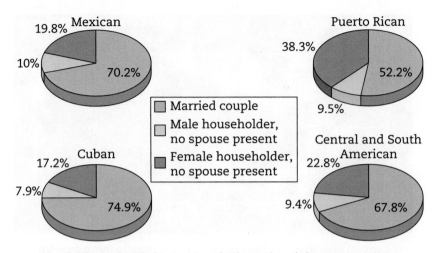

Family households by type and Hispanic origin group, 2002

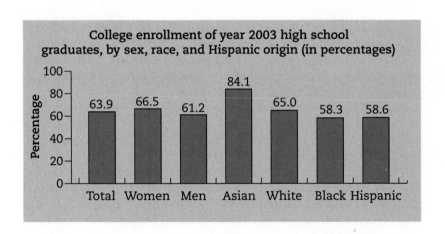

FOLLOW PROFESSIONAL GUIDELINES FOR PRESENTING VISUALS

Charts, graphs, tables, and illustrations play such an important role in many fields that professional groups have come up with guidelines for labeling and formatting these items. You need to become familiar with those conventions as you advance in a field. A guide such as the *Publication Manual of the American Psychological Association* (6th edition) or the *MLA Handbook for Writers of Research Papers* (7th edition) describes these rules in detail.

REMEMBER TO CHECK FOR COPYRIGHTED MATERIAL

You also must be careful to respect copyright rules when using visual items that were created by someone else. It's relatively easy these days to download visual texts of all kinds from the Web. Some of these items— such as clip art or government documents—may be in the *public domain*, meaning that you're free to use them without requesting permission or paying a royalty. But other visual texts may require permission, especially if you intend to publish your work or use the item commercially. And remember: anything you place on a Web site is considered "published." (See Chapter 18 for more on intellectual property.)

RESPOND.

1. The December 2002 issue of the *Atlantic Monthly* included the following poem and the photograph that may have inspired it (shown on p. 464). Look carefully at the image, read the poem several times, at least once aloud. Working with another person in your class, discuss how the words of the poem and the image interact with one another. What difference would it make if you hadn't seen the photo before reading this text? Write a brief report of your findings, and bring it to class for discussion.

   > A waterfall of black chains
   > looms behind the man in the stovepipe hat.
   > Cigar. Wrinkled clothes. This is
   > Isambard Kingdom Brunel.
   > Who could not stop working. Slept
   > and ate at the shipyard.
   > The largest ship in the world.
   > Driven to outdo himself.

This photograph of the engineer Isambard Kingdom Brunel was taken by Robert Howlett in 1857 and is included in the National Portrait Gallery's collection in London.

Fashioned from iron plate and
powered by three separate means.
Able to sail to Ceylon and back
without refueling. Fated
to lay the Atlantic cable, the India cable.
Untouched in size for forty years.
The Great Leviathan. The Little Giant,
Isambard Kingdom Brunel.
Builder of tunnels, ships, railroads, bridges.
Engineer and Genius of England.
He should have built churches, you know.
Everything he prayed for came true.

—John Spaulding, "The Launching Chains of the *Great Eastern*"

2. Find an advertisement that has both verbal and visual elements. Analyze the ad's visual argument by answering some of the questions

on pp. 446–51, taking care to "reread" its visual elements as carefully as you would its words. After you've answered each question as thoroughly as possible, switch ads with a classmate, and analyze the new argument in the same way. Then compare your own and your classmate's responses to the two advertisements. If they're different—and there's every reason to expect that they will be—how do you account for the differences? What effect does the audience have on the argument's reception? What differences appear between your own active reading and your classmate's?

3. You've no doubt noticed how visual design and textual material are presented on the Web. In the best Web pages, text and images work together rather than simply compete for space. Even if you've never used the Web, you still know a great deal about graphic design from newspapers and magazines. Your own college papers use design principles to create effective texts.

   Find three or four Web pages or magazine pages that you think exemplify good visual design—and then find three or four that don't. When you've picked the good and bad designs, draw a rough sketch of each page's physical layout. Where are the graphics? Where is the text? What are the size and position of text blocks relative to graphics? How is color used? Can you discern common design principles among the pages, or does each good page work well in its own way? Write a brief explanation of what you find, focusing on the way that the visual arguments influence audiences.

4. Go to the Web page for the Pulitzer Prize archives at http://pulitzer.org. Pick a year to review, and then study the images of the winners in three categories—editorial cartooning, spot news photography, and feature photography. (Click on "Works" to see the images.) Choose one image that you believe makes a strong argument, and write one paragraph that describes the image and the argument that it makes.

15
Presenting Arguments

In the wake of a devastating earthquake, political leaders take to the airwaves to promise quick action and material support for survivors. Local church leaders search for words to console their congregations and give them hope.

To protest the installation of more traffic cameras at intersections, an activist distributes a PowerPoint presentation online detailing just how little revenue the devices generate for cities that use them and how much they earn for the companies that operate them.

At a campus rally, a spoken-word poet performs a piece against racism and homophobia.

For a course on Elizabethan drama, a student creates a multimedia presentation to demonstrate that Shakespeare's strong female characters reflect the power wielded by Elizabeth I.

During their wedding in Vancouver, a couple exchanges special vows that they've worked together to create.

Sometimes the choice of how to deliver an argument to an audience is made for you: the boss says, "Write a report," or an instructor says, "Build a Web site." But often, you'll need to decide on your own the form of presentation that best fits your topic, purpose, and audience. The following advice can help you make good choices.

Print Presentations

For many arguments that you make in college, print remains the best medium of delivery. Print texts are more permanent than most Web-based materials, they're inexpensive and easy to produce, and they offer a precise way to express abstract ideas or to set down complicated chains of reasoning. But in making an argument in print, writers face an embarrassment of riches. Printed documents used to be created in standard formats—black print on 8½ x 11 white paper read left to right, top to bottom—but today's print texts come in a dizzying array of shapes, sizes, and colors.

As you think about presenting textual arguments, here are some issues to consider:

- What overall tone do you want to create in this written argument? What's the purpose of your argument, and to whom is it addressed?

- What format will get your message across most effectively? A formal report with a table of contents and an executive summary? A newsletter? A triple-fold brochure?

- What fonts will make your argument most readable? Will varying the font or type size help guide readers through your text? Will it draw attention to what's most important?

- Will you use subheads as another guide to readers? If so, what size type will you select for them? Will you use all caps, boldface, or italics? In any case, be consistent in the style and the structure of subheads (all nouns, for example, or all questions).

- Should you use colors other than black ink and white paper in presenting your argument? If so, what colors best evoke your tone and purpose? What colors will be most appealing to your audience?

- How will you use white or blank space in your argument? To give readers time to pause? To establish a sense of openness or orderliness?
- Will you use visuals in your print argument? If so, how will you integrate them smoothly into the text? (For more on the role of visuals in arguments, see Chapter 14.)

Oral and Multimedia Presentations

Students tell us that they're frequently being asked to make oral presentations in their classes these days—but also complain that they're rarely given instructions about how to do so. And students returning from summer internships in a range of fields from engineering to the arts report that their employers simply expect them to be proficient at delivering arguments orally and to accompany such presentations with the appropriate illustrative materials.

It's hard to generalize here, but capable presenters attribute their success to several crucial elements:

- They have thorough knowledge of their subjects.
- They pay attention to the values, ideas, and needs of their listeners.
- They use structures and styles that make their spoken arguments easy to follow.
- They realize that oral arguments are interactive (live audiences can argue back!).
- They appreciate that most oral presentations involve visuals, and they plan accordingly.
- They practice, practice—and then practice some more.

Oral Arguments in Discussions

Most of the oral arguments that you'll make in college will occur in ordinary discussions. You are arguing all the time, whether in exploring the meaning of a poem in English class, arguing against a textbook's interpretation of an economic phenomenon, or trying to reform a student government policy on funding political organizations. In such

Not Just Words

The figures above illustrate three different modes of presentation—an informative blog, a printed report, and an oral or multimedia presentation for a live audience. Spend time talking with a classmate about the choices that were involved in selecting each of these methods of presentation, and then report your findings to the class.

everyday contexts, many people automatically choose a tone of voice, kind of evidence, and length of speaking time that suit the situation.

You can improve your performance in such situations by observing effective speakers and by joining conversations whenever you can. The more that you participate in lively discussions, the more comfortable you'll be with speaking your mind. To make sure that your in-class comments count, follow these tips:

- Do the required reading so that you know what you're talking about.
- Listen with a purpose, and jot down important points.
- Speak to the point under discussion so that your comments are relevant.
- Ask questions about issues that matter to you: others probably have the same thoughts.
- Occasionally offer brief summaries of points that have already been made to make sure that everyone is "on the same page."
- Respond to questions or comments by others in specific rather than vague terms.
- Try to learn the names of people in the discussion, and then use them.
- When you are already part of a discussion, invite others to join in.

CULTURAL CONTEXTS FOR ARGUMENT

Speaking Up in Class

Speaking up in class is viewed as inappropriate or even rude in some cultures. In the United States, however, doing so is expected and encouraged. Some instructors even assign credit for such class participation.

Formal Oral and Multimedia Presentations

When asked to make a formal presentation in class or on the job, consider the context carefully. Note how much time you have to prepare and how long the presentation should be. You want to use your slot effectively and not infringe on the time of others. Consider also what visual aids, handouts, or other materials might make the presentation success-ful. Will you have to use an overhead projector or just a blackboard? Or can you use PowerPoint or other presentation software?

Check out where your presentation will take place. In a classroom with fixed chairs? A lecture or assembly hall? An informal sitting area? Will you have a lectern? Other equipment? Will you sit or stand? Remain in one place or move around? What will the lighting be, and can you adjust it? Sometimes oral presentations are group efforts. When that's the case, plan and practice accordingly. The work will need to be divvied up, and you will need to work out who speaks when. Finally, note any criteria for evaluation: how will your live oral argument be assessed?

In addition to these logistical matters, consider these rhetorical ele-ments whenever you make a formal presentation:

Amy Tan's "Mother Tongue" is a speech that is a fully written-out script. What features can you identify that establish this text as an argument to be heard?

LINK TO P. 763

Purpose

- Determine your major argumentative purpose. Is it to inform? To con-vince or persuade? To explore? To make a decision? To entertain? Something else?

Audience

- Who is your audience? An interested observer? A familiar face? A stranger? What will be the mix of age groups, men and women, and so on? Are you a peer of the audience members? Think carefully about what they already know about your topic and what opinions they're likely to hold.

Structure

- Structure your presentation so that it's easy to follow, and plan an introduction that gets the audience's attention and a conclusion that makes your argument memorable. You'll find more help with struc-ture on p. 473.

Arguments to Be Heard

Even if you deliver a live presentation from a printed text, be sure to compose a script that is to be *heard* rather than *read*. Such a text—whether in the form of note cards, an overhead list, or a fully written-out script—should feature a strong introduction and conclusion, an unambiguous structure with helpful transitions and signposts, concrete diction, and straightforward syntax.

STRONG INTRODUCTIONS AND CONCLUSIONS

Like readers, listeners remember beginnings and endings best. Work hard, therefore, to make these elements of your spoken argument especially memorable. Consider including a provocative or puzzling statement, opinion, or question; a memorable anecdote; a powerful quotation; or a vivid visual image. If you can refer to the interests or experiences of your listeners in the introduction or conclusion, then do so.

Look at the introduction to Toni Morrison's acceptance speech to the Nobel Academy when she won the Nobel Prize for Literature:

> "Once upon a time there was an old woman. Blind but wise." Or was it an old man? A guru, perhaps. Or a griot soothing restless children. I have heard this story, or one exactly like it, in the lore of several cultures. "Once upon a time there was an old woman. Blind. Wise."
>
> —Toni Morrison

Here, Morrison uses a storytelling strategy, calling on the traditional "Once upon a time" to signal to her audience that she's doing so. Note also the use of repetition and questioning. These strategies raise interest and anticipation in her audience: how will she use this story in accepting the Nobel Prize?

Toni Morrison accepting the Nobel Prize for Literature in 1993

CLEAR STRUCTURES AND SIGNPOSTS

For a spoken argument, you want your organizational structure to be crystal clear. So offer an overview of your main points toward the beginning of the presentation, and make sure that you have a clearly delineated beginning, middle, and end. Throughout the report or lecture, remember to pause between major points and to offer signposts to mark your movement from one topic to the next. They can be transitions as obvious as *next, on the contrary,* or *finally.* Such words act as memory points in your spoken argument and thus should be explicit and concrete: *The second crisis point in the breakup of the Soviet Union occurred hard on the heels of the first,* rather than *The breakup of the Soviet Union came to another crisis.* You can also keep listeners on track by repeating key words and concepts and by using unambiguous topic sentences to introduce each new idea.

STRAIGHTFORWARD SYNTAX AND CONCRETE DICTION

Avoid long, complicated sentences, and as much as possible, use straightforward syntax (subject-verb-object, for instance, rather than an inversion of that order). Remember, too, that listeners can hold onto concrete verbs and nouns more easily than they can grasp a steady stream of abstractions. So when you need to deal with abstract ideas, try to illustrate them with concrete examples.

Take a look at the following text that student Ben McCorkle wrote about *The Simpsons,* first as he prepared it for an essay and then as he adapted it for a live oral and multimedia presentation:

Neal Conan introduces a complex legal case in clear language as the host of the radio show *Talk of the Nation.* What tactics does he employ to make his opening easy for listeners to understand?

LINK TO P. 699

Print Version

The Simpson family has occasionally been described as a "nuclear" family, which obviously has a double meaning: first, the family consists of two parents and three children, and, second, Homer works at a nuclear power plant with very relaxed safety codes. The overused label *dysfunctional,* when applied to the Simpsons, suddenly takes on new meaning. Every episode seems to include a scene in which son Bart is being choked by his father, the baby is being neglected, or Homer is sitting in a drunken stupor transfixed by the television screen. The comedy in these scenes comes from the exaggeration of commonplace household events (although some talk shows and news programs would have us believe that these exaggerations are not confined to the madcap world of cartoons).

—Ben McCorkle, "The Simpsons: A Mirror of Society"

Oral Version (with a visual illustration)

What does it mean to describe the Simpsons as a *nuclear* family? Clearly, a double meaning is at work. First, the Simpsons fit the dictionary meaning—a family unit consisting of two parents and some children. The second meaning, however, packs more of a punch. You see, Homer works at a nuclear power plant [pause here] with *very* relaxed safety codes!

Still another overused family label describes the Simpsons. Did everyone guess I was going to say *dysfunctional*? And like "nuclear,"

Homer Simpson in a typical pose

when it comes to the Simpsons, "dysfunctional" takes on a whole new meaning.

Remember the scene when Bart is being choked by his father?

How about the many times the baby is being neglected?

Or the classic view—Homer sitting in a stupor transfixed by the TV screen!

My point here is that the comedy in these scenes often comes from double meanings—and from a lot of exaggeration of everyday household events.

Note that the revised version presents the same information as the original, but this time it's written to be *heard*. The revision uses helpful signposts, some repetition, a list, italicized words to prompt the speaker to give special emphasis, and simple syntax so that it's easy to listen to.

Arguments to Be Remembered

You can probably think of oral and multimedia arguments that still stick in your memory—a song like Bruce Springsteen's "Born in the USA," for instance, or Paris Hilton's hilarious riff on a 2008 John McCain campaign ad. Such arguments are memorable in part because they offer us intriguing ideas (Hilton's energy policy!) that are reinforced by figures of speech and devices of language (her reference to a "wrinkly, white-haired guy"). One especially powerful strategy in oral arguments is deliberate repetition, especially when linked with parallelism and climactic order. (See Chapter 13 for more on using figurative language to make arguments more vivid and memorable.)

REPETITION, PARALLELISM, AND CLIMACTIC ORDER

Whether they're used alone or in combination, repetition, parallelism, and climactic order are especially appropriate for spoken arguments that sound a call to arms or that seek passionate engagement from the audience. Perhaps no person in the twentieth century used them more effectively than Martin Luther King Jr., whose sermons and speeches helped to spearhead the civil rights movement. Standing on the steps of the Lincoln Memorial in Washington, D.C., on August 23, 1963, with hundreds of thousands of marchers before him, King called on the nation to make good on the "promissory note" represented by the Emancipation Proclamation.

For an example of how repetition and parallelism can help make an argument memorable, check out Eboo Patel's essay "We Are Each Others' Business."

LINK TO P. 897

Look at the way that King uses repetition, parallelism, and climactic order in the following paragraph to invoke a nation to action:

> It is obvious today that America has defaulted on this promissory note insofar as her citizens of color are concerned. Instead of honoring this sacred obligation, America has given the Negro people a bad *check* which has come back marked "*insufficient funds.*" But *we* refuse to believe that the bank of justice is bankrupt. *We* refuse to believe that there are *insufficient funds* in the great vaults of opportunity of this nation. So *we have come* to cash this *check*—a *check* that will give us upon demand the riches of freedom and the security of justice. *We have also come* to this hallowed spot to remind America of the fierce urgency of now. This is no *time* to engage in the luxury of cooling off or to take the tranquilizing drug of gradualism. *Now is the time to* rise from the dark and desolate valley of segregation to the sunlit path of racial justice. *Now is the time to* open the doors of opportunity to all of God's children. *Now is the time to* lift our nation from the quicksands of racial injustice to the solid rock of brotherhood.
>
> —Martin Luther King Jr., "I Have a Dream" (emphasis added)

The italicized words highlight the way that King uses repetition to drum home his theme. But along with that repetition, he sets up a powerful set of parallel verb phrases, calling on all "to rise" from the "dark and desolate valley of segregation" to the "sunlit path of racial justice" and "to open the doors of opportunity" for all. The final verb phrase ("to lift") leads to a strong climax as King moves from what each individual should do to what the entire nation should do: "to lift our nation from the quicksands of racial injustice to the solid rock of brotherhood." These stylistic choices, together with the vivid image of the "bad check," help to make King's speech powerful, persuasive—and memorable.

You don't have to be as highly skilled as King to take advantage of the power of repetition and parallelism. Simply repeating a key word in your argument can impress it on your audience, as can arranging parts of sentences or items in a list in parallel order.

The Role of Visuals in Oral and Multimedia Arguments

Visual materials—chart, graphs, posters, slides, and PowerPoint screens—often figure prominently in oral arguments and should be carefully prepared. Don't think of them as add-ons but rather as major tools for conveying your message and supporting your claims. In many cases, a picture can truly be worth a thousand words.

Be certain that any visuals that you use are large enough to be seen by all members of your audience. If you use slides or overhead projections, the information on each frame should be simple, clear, and easy to process. For audience members to read information on a transparency, this means using 36 point type for major headings, 24 point for subheadings, and at least 18 point for all other text. For slides, use 24 point for major headings, 18 point for subheadings, and at least 14 point for other text.

The same rule of clarity and simplicity holds true for posters, flip charts, and chalkboards. And remember not to turn your back on your audience while you refer to these visuals. If you prepare supplementary materials (such as bibliographies or other handouts) for the audience, don't distribute them until the audience actually needs them. Or wait until the end of the presentation so that they don't distract listeners from your spoken argument.

If you've watched many PowerPoint presentations, you're sure to have seen some bad ones. But nothing is more deadly than a speaker who stands up and reads from each screen. It is fine to use presentation slides to furnish an overview for a presentation and to give visual signposts to listeners. But never read the slides word for word—or even put much prose on a screen. You'll just put your audience to sleep.

For an oral and multimedia presentation, one student used the PowerPoint slides shown on pp. 478, 480, and 482 to compare Frank Miller's graphic novel *Sin City* and its movie adaptation. Notice that the student uses text throughout, but in moderation. Next take a look at the written script (written to be heard) that the student developed for this presentation. The student does not read from the slides; rather, the slides illustrate the points that he's making orally. The text on the slides sums up—and occasionally supplements—his oral presentation. This careful use of text makes the student's argument clear and easy to follow.

His choices in layout and font size also aim for clarity but without sacrificing visual appeal. The choice of white and red text on a black background is appropriate for the topic—a stark black-and-white graphic novel and its shades-of-gray movie version. But be aware that light writing on a dark background can be hard to read and that dark writing on a white or cream-colored background is almost always a safer choice.

(Note that if your presentation shows or is based on source materials—either text or images—your instructor may want you to include a slide that lists the sources at the end of the presentation.)

The Office of the Privacy Commissioner of Canada balances text and audio effectively in the YouTube clip warning about threats to Internet privacy.

LINK TO P. 669

From Frames to Film:
Graphic Novels on the Big Screen

Presentation by Sach Wickramasekara
PWR 2-06, Professor Lunsford
Wallenberg Hall Room 329
March 8, 2006

Introduction

A frame from the *Sin City* graphic novel.

"Instead of trying to make it [*Sin City*] into a movie which would be terrible, I wanted to take cinema and try and make it into this book."

- Robert Rodriguez, DVD Interview

The same scene from the *Sin City* movie.

[Opening Slide: Title]

Hi, my name is Sach.

[Change Slide: Introduction]

Take a look at this pair of scenes. Can you tell which one's from a movie and which one's from a graphic novel? How can two completely different media produce such similar results? Stay tuned; you're about to hear how.

[Pause]

Today I'll be analyzing *Sin City's* transition from a graphic novel to the big screen. The past decade has seen an increasing trend of comic books and graphic novels morphing into big-budget movies, with superhero flicks such as *Spider-Man* and *X-Men* headlining this list. However, until recently, movies borrowed from their comic book licenses but never stuck fully to their scripts. That all changed with *Sin City,* and I'll show you how dedication to preserving the look and feel of the graphic novel is what makes the screen version of *Sin City* neither a conventional graphic novel nor a conventional movie, but a new, innovative art form that's a combination of the two.

[Body]

[Change Slide—Technology]

Part of what makes *Sin City* so innovative is the technology powering it. The movie captures the look of the graphic novel so

Technology

Right: The original scene from the graphic novel.

Left: The scene is filmed with live actors on a green screen set.

Right: The final version of the scene, after the colors have been changed to shades of black and white. Notice the sapphire shade of the convertible, and how it stands out from the background.

Audio and Voice

"When I read the books, I felt that they were fantastic exactly as they were . . . I loved that the dialogue didn't sound like movie dialogue." - Robert Rodriguez

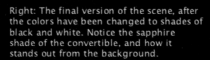

"*Just one hour to go. My last day on the job. Early retirement. Not my idea. Doctor's orders. Heart condition. Angina, he calls it.*"

- *Sin City* movie

well by filming actors on a green screen and using digital imagery to put detailed backdrops behind them. Computer technology also turns the movie's visuals into shades of black and white with rare dashes of color splashed in, reproducing the noir feel of the original novels. Thus, scenes in *Sin City* have a photorealistic yet stylized quality that differentiates them from both the plain black-and-white images of the comics and the real sets used in other movies.

[Change Slide—Audio and Voice]

Pretty pictures are all well and good, but everyone knows that voice is just as important in a movie, especially because the media of comics and film use words so differently. The *Sin City* movie reproduces many sections of the novel that have a first-person narrator as monologues, and the script is lifted word for word from Miller's originals. This gives the dialogue an exaggerated quality that is more fantastic than realistic, which is exactly what director Robert Rodriguez intended. Here is an example from the film. "*Just one hour to go. My last day on the job. Early retirement. Not my idea. Doctor's orders. Heart condition. Angina, he calls it.*" A text box monologue fits perfectly in comics, where you read it and hear the character's voice in your head, but you wouldn't expect to hear it within an actual film. This contrast in narrative styles between the spoken word and how it is used is another factor that makes *Sin City* such an original work.

[Change Slide—Time and Structure]

Films are based on movement and sound, but comics divide movement into a series of "freeze-frame" images and represent

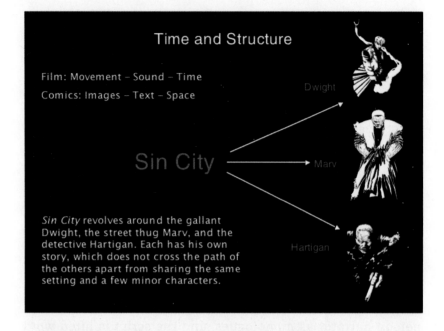

Time and Structure

Film: Movement – Sound – Time
Comics: Images – Text – Space

Sin City

Dwight

Marv

Hartigan

Sin City revolves around the gallant Dwight, the street thug Marv, and the detective Hartigan. Each has his own story, which does not cross the path of the others apart from sharing the same setting and a few minor characters.

Works Consulted

Goldstein, Hillary. "Five Days of Sin." *IGN.com.* 1 Apr. 2006. IGN Entertainment. Web. 12 Feb. 2006.

"The Making of *Sin City*." *Sin City* DVD preview page. Buena Vista Online Entertainment. Web. 4 Feb. 2006.

Miller, Frank. *The Big Fat Kill*. Milwaukie: Dark Horse Books, 1994. Print.

---.*The Hard Goodbye*. Milwaukie: Dark Horse Books, 1991. Print.

---.*That Yellow Bastard*. Milwaukie: Dark Horse Books, 1996. Print.

Otto, Jeff. "*Sin City* Review." *IGN.com: Filmforce.* 29 Mar. 2005. IGN Entertainment. Web. 10 Feb. 2006.

Robertson, Barbara. "The Devil's in the Details." *Computer Graphics World.* Apr. 2005: 18. *Expanded Academic ASAP.* Web. 11 Feb. 2006.

Sin City. Dir. Robert Rodriguez. Perf. Bruce Willis, Jessica Alba, Mickey Rourke, and Clive Owen. Dimension, 2005. DVD.

sound as text. If you freeze the *Sin City* movie at certain frames, the scene might look identical to what is portrayed in the graphic novel. Press the play button again, and the characters appear to jump to life and begin moving within the frame. Thus, it's easy to view *Sin City* as a beautifully depicted, real-time graphic novel, where time is the factor that makes the story move forward, instead of space separating the different panels of the graphic novel.

[Pause]

Like the graphic novel by Frank Miller that it's based on, the *Sin City* movie is composed of a series of stories with different protagonists such as Marv, Dwight, and the detective Hartigan. These separate tales share only their settings and several secondary characters. Therefore, the movie feels episodic, rather than continuous like a feature-length film. Just as Miller's originals were a compilation of short stories linked by their setting, *Sin City* has the unique feel of being three short films linked by Miller's vision of an alternate universe.

[Change Slide—Works Consulted]

[Pause]

Sin City has opened the doors for future comic adaptations, none more anticipated than *Sin City 2* itself. There hasn't been a lot of info. on this movie, but apparently it'll be based on a brand new story that Frank Miller is writing. It'll be intriguing to see director Rodriguez adapt a graphic novel that hasn't even been written yet, so keep an eye out for this one. Any questions?

The best way to test the effectiveness of your visuals is to try them out on friends, family members, classmates, or roommates. If they don't get the meaning of the visuals right away, revise and try again.

Remember, finally, that visuals and accompanying media tools can help make your presentation accessible but that some members of your audience may not be able to see your presentation or may have trouble seeing or hearing them. Here are a few key rules to remember:

- Use words to describe projected images. Something as simple as *That's Franklin Roosevelt in 1944* can help even sight-impaired audience members appreciate what's on a screen.

- Consider providing a written handout that summarizes your presentation or putting the text on an overhead projector—for those who learn better by reading *and* listening.

- If you use video, take the time to label sounds that might not be audible to audience members who are hearing impaired. (Be sure your equipment is caption capable and use the captions; they can be helpful to everyone when audio quality is poor.)

Some Oral and Multimedia Presentation Strategies

In spite of your best preparation, you may feel some anxiety before a live presentation. This is natural. (According to one Gallup poll, Americans often identify public speaking as a major fear and as scarier than possible attacks from outer space.) Experienced speakers say that they have strategies for dealing with anxiety—and even that a little anxiety (and accompanying adrenaline) can act to a speaker's advantage.

The most effective strategy seems to be thoroughly knowing your topic and material. Confidence in your own knowledge goes a long way toward making you a confident speaker. In addition to being well prepared, you may want to try some of the following strategies:

- Practice a number of times, running through every part of the presentation. Leave nothing out, even audio or visual clips. Work with the equipment that you intend to use so that you are familiar with it. It also may help to visualize your presentation, imagining the scene in your mind as you run through your materials.

- Time your presentation to make sure you stay within your allotted slot.

- Tape yourself (video, if possible) at least once so that you can listen to your voice. Tone of voice and body language can dispose audiences for—or against—speakers. For most oral arguments, you want to develop a tone that conveys commitment to your position as well as respect for your audience.

- Think about how you'll dress for your presentation, remembering that audience members usually notice how a speaker looks. Dressing for an effective presentation depends on what's appropriate for your topic, audience, and setting, but most experienced speakers choose clothes that are comfortable, allow easy movement, and aren't overly casual. Dressing up a little indicates that you take pride in your appearance, have confidence in your argument, and respect your audience.

- Get some rest before the presentation, and avoid consuming too much caffeine.

- Relax! Consider doing some deep-breathing exercises. Then pause just before you begin, concentrating on your opening lines.

- Maintain eye contact with members of your audience. Speak to them, not to your text or to the floor.

- Most speakers make a stronger impression standing than sitting, so stand if you have that option. Moving around a bit may help you maintain good eye contact.

- When using presentation slides, stand to the side so that you don't block the view. Look at the audience rather than the slide.

- Interact with the audience whenever possible; doing so will often help you relax and even have some fun.

Finally, remember to allow time for audience responses and questions. Keep your answers brief so that others may join the conversation. And at the very end of your presentation, thank the audience for its attention to your arguments.

A Note about Webcasts: Live Presentations over the Web

This discussion of live oral and multimedia presentations has assumed that you'll be speaking before an audience that's in the same room with you. Increasingly, though—especially in business, industry, and science—the presentations you make will be live, but you won't be in the same physical space as the audience. Instead, you might be in front of a camera that will capture your voice and image and relay them via the Web to attendees who might be anywhere in the world. In another type of Webcast, participants can see only your slides or the software that you're demonstrating, using a screen-capture relay without cameras, and you're not visible but still speaking live.

In either case, as you learn to adapt to Webcast environments, most of the strategies that work in oral and multimedia presentations for an audience that's physically present will continue to serve you well. But there are some significant differences:

- Practice is even more important in Webcasts, since you need to be able to access online any slides, documents, video clips, names, dates, and sources that you provide during the Webcast.

- Because you can't make eye contact with audience members, it's important to remember to look into the camera (if you are using one), at least from time to time. If you're using a stationary Webcam, perhaps one mounted on your computer, practice standing or sitting without moving out of the frame and yet without looking stiff.

- Even though your audience may not be visible to you, assume that if you're on camera, the Web-based audience can see you. If you slouch, they'll notice. Also assume that your microphone is always live. Don't mutter under your breath, for example, when someone else is speaking or asking a question.

Web-Based Presentations

Even without the interactivity of Webcasts, most students have enough access to the Web to use its powers for effective presentations, especially in Web sites and blogs.

Web Sites

Students are increasingly creating Web sites for themselves, working hard at their self-presentation and showcasing their talents and accomplishments. They are also creating Web sites for extracurricular organizations, for work, or for class assignments and creating pages for themselves on MySpace or Facebook.

In planning any Web site, you'll need to pay careful attention to your rhetorical situation—the purpose of your site, its intended audience, and the overall impression that you want to make. To get started, you may want to visit several sites that you admire, looking for effective design ideas and ways of organizing navigation and information. Creating a map or storyboard for your site will help you to think through the links from page to page.

Experienced Web designers cite several important principles for Web-based presentations. The first of these is *contrast*, which is achieved through the use of color, icons, boldface, and so on; contrast helps guide readers through the site. The second principle, *proximity*, calls on you to keep together the parts of a page that are closely related, again for ease of reading. *Repetition* means using a consistent design throughout the site for the elements (such as headings and links) that help readers move smoothly through the site. Finally, designers concentrate on an *overall impression* or mood for the site, which means that the site's colors and visuals should help to create that impression rather than challenge or undermine it.

Here are some additional tips that may help you design your site:

- The homepage of your site should be eye-catching, inviting, and informative. Use titles and illustrations to make clear what the site is about.

- Think carefully about two parts of every page—the navigation area (menus or links) and the content areas. You want to make these two areas clearly distinct from one another. And make sure you *have* a navigation area for every page, including links to the key sections of the site and a link back to the homepage. Ease of navigation is one key to a successful Web site.

- Either choose a design template that is provided by Web-writing tools (like DreamWeaver), or create a template of your own that ensures that the elements of each page are consistent.

- Remember that some readers may not have the capacity to download heavy visuals or to access elements like Flash. If you want to reach a wide audience, stick with visuals that can be downloaded easily.

- Remember to include Web contact information on every page, but not your personal address or phone number.

Blogs

No Web texts have captured the public imagination more swiftly than blogs, which are now too numerous to count. Blogs take the idea of a personal Web page and give it the interactivity of a listserv, allowing readers to make comments and respond both to the blogger and to one another. Many if not most blogs contain primarily the writer's ideas and musings, but others have become prominent sources of news and opinion in politics, entertainment, and other fields.

In many ways, these blogs offer an alternative to traditional newspapers, TV networks, and periodicals, now somewhat derisively described by bloggers as the mainstream media (MSM). Blogs have broken important news stories and given more breadth to the political spectrum. As such, blogs create an ideal space for building communities, engaging in arguments, and giving voice to views and opinions of ordinary, everyday folks. We seldom see these people writing or being written about in major print media—many of which now sponsor blogs themselves as part of their electronic versions.

Blogs also have downsides. They're idiosyncratic, can be self-indulgent and egoistic, and can distort issues by spreading misinformation very quickly.

Blogs appear to be changing the ways that people communicate and redistributing power in ways that we still don't fully understand. If you're a reader of blogs, be sure to read carefully. The information on blogs

Political blogs get plenty of attention, but many of the most popular sites focus on technology, social networks, and cultural phenomena.

hasn't been critically reviewed in the way that traditional print sources review their stories. Nevertheless, blogs have reported many instances of the mainstream media's failure to live up to their own standards.

If you're a blogger, you know that the rules of etiquette for blogging and conventions for blogs are still evolving. In the meantime, you'll be wise to join the spirit of any blog that you contribute to, be respectful in your comments (even very critical ones), and think carefully about the audience that you want to reach in every entry you make.

RESPOND •

1. Take three or four paragraphs from an essay that you've recently written. Then, following the guidelines in this chapter, rewrite the passage to be heard by a live audience. Finally, make a list of every change that you made.

2. Find a print presentation that you find particularly effective. Study it carefully, noting how its various elements—format, type sizes, typefaces, color, white space, visuals, and overall layout—work to deliver its message. If you find a particularly ineffective print presentation, carry out the same analysis to figure out why it's bad. Finally, prepare a five-minute presentation of your findings to deliver in class.

3. Attend a lecture or presentation on your campus, and observe the speaker's delivery. Note the strategies that the speaker uses to capture and hold your attention (or not). What signpost language and other guides to listening can you detect? How well are visuals integrated into the presentation? What aspects of the speaker's tone, dress, eye contact, and movement affect your understanding and appreciation (or lack of it)? What's most memorable about the presentation, and why? Finally, write up an analysis of this presentation's effectiveness.

4. Go to a Web site that you admire or consult frequently. Then answer the following questions: Why is a Web site—a digital presentation—the best way to present this material? What advantages over a print text or a live oral and multimedia presentation does the Web site have? What would you have to do to "translate" the argument(s) of this site into print or live oral format? What might be gained or lost in the process?

PART 4

CONVENTIONS OF argument

16
What Counts as Evidence

A person who cycles from home to work thinks that she notices some animosity from drivers of cars along her route. She decides to conduct some careful observations to test her hypothesis, and if it proves to be accurate, she'll design a survey to find out how other cyclists respond to and manage such animosity.

A business consultant wants to identify characteristics of effective teamwork so that he can convince his partners to adopt these characteristics as part of their training program. To begin gathering evidence for this argument, the consultant decides to survey members of three effective teams and then conduct in-depth interviews with each member.

To support his contention that people are basically honest, an economist points to the detailed records kept by a vendor who sells muffins on the honor system in downtown offices. The merchant discovers that only a small percentage of people take advantage of him. The numbers also show that executives cheat more than middle-management employees.

For an argument aimed at showing that people still often unconsciously think of occupations as either masculine or feminine, a student decides to carry out an experiment. She will ask fifty people chosen at random to draw pictures of a doctor, a police officer, a nurse, a CEO, a lawyer, and a secretary—and see which are depicted as men and which as women. The results of this experiment will become evidence for (or against) the argument.

Trying to convince her younger brother to give up his out-of-date Mac in favor of a PC laptop, a college student mentions her three years of personal experience using a PC for her college coursework.

In arguing that Wikipedia is a reliable source of information, a student writer provides evidence for this claim by citing sixteen library sources that review and critique "the people's encyclopedia."

● ● ●

Evidence and the Rhetorical Situation

As the examples above demonstrate, people use all kinds of evidence in making and supporting claims. But this evidence doesn't exist in a vacuum. Instead, the quality of evidence—how it was collected, by whom, and for what purposes—may become part of the argument itself. Evidence may be persuasive in one time and place but not in another; it may convince one kind of audience but not another; it may work with one type of argument but not the kind you are writing.

To be most persuasive, evidence should match the time and place in which you make your argument. For example, arguing that a twenty-first-century Marine general should employ tactics of delay and strategic retreat because that strategy worked effectively for George Washington is likely to fail if Washington's use of the tactic is the only evidence provided. After all, a military maneuver that was effective in 1776 for an outnumbered band of revolutionaries is likely to be irrelevant today for a much different fighting force. In the same way, a writer may achieve excellent results by citing her own experiences and an extensive survey of local teenagers as evidence to support a new teen center for her small-town community, but she may have less success in using the same

The need for evidence depends a lot on the rhetorical situation.

Global warming...

GLOBAL WARMING
SCEPTICS SOCIETY

WEATHER
STATISTICS

Someone who needs
more evidence.

Someone who needs
less evidence.

© John Ditchburn/INKCINCT Cartoons

evidence in arguing for a teen center in a distant, large inner-city area where her personal authority may count for less.

College writers also need to consider the fields that they're working in. In disciplines such as experimental psychology or economics, *quantitative data*—the sort that can be observed and counted—may be the best evidence. In many historical or literary or philosophical studies, however, the same kind of data may be less appropriate or persuasive, or even impossible to come by. As you become more familiar with a particular discipline, you'll gain a sense of what it takes to prove a point or support a claim. The following questions will help you understand the rhetorical situation of a particular discipline:

- How do other writers in the field use *precedence*—examples of actions or decisions that are very similar—and authority as evidence? What or who counts as an authority in this field? How are the credentials of authorities established?

- What kinds of data are preferred as evidence? How are such data gathered and presented?
- How are statistics or other numerical information used and presented as evidence? Are tables, charts, or graphs commonly used? How much weight do they carry?
- How are definitions, causal analyses, evaluations, analogies, and examples used as evidence?
- How does the field use firsthand and secondhand sources as evidence?
- Is personal experience allowed as evidence?
- How are quotations used as part of evidence?
- How are images used as part of evidence, and how closely are they related to the verbal parts of the argument being presented?

As these questions suggest, evidence may not always travel well from one field to another.

Firsthand Evidence and Research

Firsthand evidence comes from research that you have carried out or been closely involved with, and much of this kind of research requires you to collect and examine data. Here, we discuss the kinds of firsthand research that are most commonly conducted by student writers.

Observations

"What," you may wonder, "could be easier than observing something?" You just choose a subject, look at it closely, and record what you see and hear. If observing were easy, however, all eyewitnesses would provide reliable accounts. Yet experience shows that several people who have observed the same phenomenon generally offer different, sometimes even contradictory, evidence on the basis of those observations. (When TWA Flight 800 exploded off the coast of New Jersey in 1996, eyewitnesses gave various accounts, some claiming that they saw what might have been a missile streaking toward the passenger jet. The official report found that an internal electrical short likely ignited vapors in a fuel tank.) Trained observers say that recording an observation accurately requires intense concentration and mental agility.

Before you begin an observation, decide exactly what you want to find out, and anticipate what you're likely to see. Do you want to observe an action that is repeated by many people (such as people at the checkout line in a grocery store for an argument that the store should install a new software program that automates pricing)? A sequence of actions (such as the stages that are involved in student registration, which you want to argue is far too complicated)? The interactions of a group (such as meetings of the campus interfaith group, which you hope will create a code of principles to guide difficult discussions)? Once you have a clear sense of what you'll observe and what questions you'll try to answer through the observation, use the following guidelines to achieve the best results:

- Make sure that the observation relates directly to your claim.
- Brainstorm about what you're looking for, but don't be rigidly bound to your expectations.
- Develop an appropriate system for collecting data. Consider using a split notebook or page: on one side, record the minute details of your observations; on the other, record your thoughts or impressions.
- Be aware that the way you record data will affect the outcome, if only in respect to what you decide to include in your observational notes and what you leave out.
- Record the precise date, time, and place of the observation.

In the following excerpt, *New York Times* media critic Virginia Heffernan uses information that she has drawn from careful study and observation to argue that Kanye West has created "a masterpiece blog" and an "online gallery of art and design" in a stunning "Web site that would improbably cross memoir and mall":

> The site looks nothing like the Web forays of other rap figures: Nas, Lil Wayne and 50 Cent use shadowy photographs of themselves in dark-alley spaces leavened mostly by sparkling Champagne bottles and fist-size diamonds.
>
> By contrast, the conceit of Kanye UniverseCity is a crayon-colored cartoon cityscape—an ever-expanding metropolis on the order of Shanghai. Click on features of the city, and up come chances to live the Kanye life, which is stylish, roguish, worldly, tech-savvy and socially responsible. Naturally you can buy its trappings and contribute to its causes. (West has recently turned his attention to traumatized veterans of the war in Iraq.) . . .

Kanye West's kanyeuniversecity.com—evidence that's easy to observe

West's site is also just fun. On the blog, West serves as an all-seeing coolhunter, turning up a range of favorite things—German art installations, limited-edition Parisian fashion, an iPod remote control worn like a wedding ring. ("Avant garde" is a category on the site.) For now, West styles himself as a hip and male answer to Oprah Winfrey, a cultural curator with incalculable influence over an audience that he alone has united. And if Oprah, whose O *Magazine* pushes cashmere sweaters and melamine bowls, is the Smithsonian, West is the Whitney.

—Virginia Heffernan, "Kanye on Keyboards"

The authors of *Living and Learning with New Media* make extensive use of interviews in their exploration of geek culture. Why do you think the authors opt to rely on this kind of evidence?

LINK TO P. 681

Interviews

Some evidence is best obtained through direct interviews. If you can talk with an expert—in person, on the phone, or online—you might obtain information you couldn't have gotten through any other type of research. In addition to an expert opinion, you might ask for firsthand accounts, biographical information, or suggestions of other places to look or other people to consult. The following guidelines will help you conduct effective interviews:

- Determine the exact purpose of the interview, and be sure it's directly related to your claim.

- Set up the interview well in advance. Specify how long it'll take, and if you wish to tape-record the session, ask permission to do so.

- Prepare a written list of both factual and open-ended questions. (Brainstorming with friends can help you come up with good questions.) Leave plenty of space for notes after each question. If the interview proceeds in a direction that you hadn't expected but that seems promising, don't feel that you have to cover every one of your questions.

- Record the subject's full name and title, as well as the date, time, and place of the interview.

- Be sure to thank those people whom you interview, either in person or with a follow-up letter or email message.

Newspapers often use interviews to add perspective to stories or to check the authenticity of claims. Steve Fainuru, a reporter for the *Washington Post*, uses that technique to weigh the validity of an internal U.S. Army report that found flaws in the Stryker, a military transport vehicle used in Iraq:

> But in more than a dozen interviews, commanders, soldiers and mechanics who use the Stryker fleet daily in one of Iraq's most dangerous areas unanimously praised the vehicle. The defects outlined in the report were either wrong or relatively minor and did little to hamper the Stryker's effectiveness, they said.
>
> "I would tell you that at least 100 soldiers' lives have been saved because of the Stryker," said Col. Robert B. Brown, commander of the 1st Brigade, 25th Infantry Division, Stryker Brigade Combat Team, which uses about 225 Strykers for combat operations throughout northern Iraq. "That's being conservative," he said.
>
> —Steve Fainuru, "Soldiers Defend Faulted Strykers"

Note how the story uses a dramatic quotation to represent the opinion expressed in the interviews. A more academic study might include the full transcript of the interviews to give readers access to more firsthand data.

Surveys and Questionnaires

The Pew Global Attitudes Project explains how complex and wide-ranging a survey must be to produce useful data.

LINK TO P. 851

Surveys usually require the use of questionnaires. Questions should be clear, easy to understand, and designed so that respondents' answers can be easily analyzed. Questions that ask respondents to say "yes" or "no" or to rank items on a scale (1 to 5, for example, or "most helpful" to "least helpful") are particularly easy to tabulate. Because tabulation can take time and effort, limit the number of questions you ask. Note also that people often resent being asked to answer more than about twenty questions, especially online.

Here are some other guidelines to help you prepare for and carry out a survey:

- Write out your purpose in conducting the survey, and make sure that its results will be directly related to your purpose.

- Brainstorm potential questions to include in the survey, and ask how each relates to your purpose and claim.

- Figure out how many people you want to contact, what the demographics of your sample should be (for example, men in their twenties or an equal number of men and women), and how you plan to reach these people.

- Draft questions that are as free of bias as possible, making sure that each calls for a short, specific answer.

- Think about possible ways that respondents could misunderstand you or your questions, and revise with these points in mind.

- Test the questions on several people, and revise those questions that are ambiguous, hard to answer, or too time-consuming to answer.

- If your questionnaire is to be sent by mail or email or posted on the Web, draft a cover letter explaining your purpose and giving a clear deadline. For mail, provide an addressed, stamped return envelope.

- On the final draft of the questionnaire, leave plenty of space for answers.

- Proofread the final draft carefully. Typos will make a bad impression on those whose help you're seeking.

- After you've done your tabulations, set out your findings in clear and easily readable form, using a chart or spreadsheet if possible.

In arguing that the effects of Hurricane Katrina are still being felt by New Orleans residents more than three years after the event, the Kaiser

A key requirement of survey questions is that they be easy to understand.

"*Next question: I believe that life is a constant striving for balance, requiring frequent tradeoffs between morality and necessity, within a cyclic pattern of joy and sadness, forging a trail of bittersweet memories until one slips, inevitably, into the jaws of death. Agree or disagree?*"

Family Foundation drew on data from an extensive survey that revealed a "still struggling population" that feels "forgotten by the nation and its leaders":

> Overall, the study finds about four in 10 residents who lived through the storm report that their lives are still very or somewhat disrupted—only marginally better than the share who reported this level of disruption in Fall 2006.

A photo taken in New Orleans in January 2008. A visual can provide evidence for a statistical survey.

Designed and analyzed by Foundation researchers, the survey was fielded house-to-house and by telephone in Spring 2008 among 1,294 residents of Orleans Parish. The survey is the second of at least three that the Foundation will conduct to track residents' experiences and views as the city rebuilds after Hurricane Katrina and the subsequent levee breaches that devastated huge sections in August 2005. By providing an over-time assessment of residents' experiences, priorities, goals and concerns, the Foundation hopes to give people a continuing chance to report on how the recovery effort is affecting them, to inform leaders of the public's priorities and to maintain national attention on the efforts to rebuild New Orleans.

—Kaiser Family Foundation, "New Orleans Three Years after the Storm: The Second Kaiser Post-Katrina Survey, 2008"

Experiments

Some arguments can be supported by evidence that is gathered through experiments. In the sciences, data from experiments conducted under rigorously controlled conditions are highly valued. For other kinds of writing, more informal experiments may be acceptable, especially if they're intended to provide only part of the support for an argument.

If you want to argue, for instance, that the recipes in *Gourmet* magazine are impossibly tedious to follow and take far more time than the average person wishes to spend preparing food, you might ask five or six people to conduct an experiment—following two recipes from a recent issue and recording and timing every step. The evidence that you gather from this informal experiment could provide some concrete support—by way of specific examples—for your contention.

But such experiments should be taken with a grain of salt (maybe organic in this case). They may not be effective with certain audiences, and if they can easily be attacked as skewed or sloppily done ("The people you asked to make these recipes couldn't cook a Pop-Tart"), then they may do more harm than good.

In a blog entry (with accompanying video) on TheNextWeb.com, Joop Dorresteijn reports on an experiment that he and a colleague carried out:

> **Established blogs like ReadWriteWeb and Techcrunch proudly show a Feedburner chicklet that displays the site's popularity. But beware— since people are more likely to subscribe to a site with a larger number of readers, some sites manipulate the counter.**
>
> **Every once and a while co-editor Patrick and I stumble on a shady looking website with a ton of readers. That made us wonder whether Feedburner is hackable. I've sacrificed my personal blog for a hacking experiment and the result; *faking your subscriber count IS possible!***
>
> **We found an easy way to hack Feedburner (not the obvious hack that simply steals a chicklet from a popular site). Looking at the subscriber count at some sites, we see we're not the first ones who found out, but we are the first ones to write it down. All it takes is an OPML file, a Netvibes Universe, and a good night's sleep.**
>
> —Joop Dorresteijn, "Feedburner Hack: How to Get 2500 Subscribers Overnight"

The author goes on to explain that this experiment has gotten swift results: as of this posting, Google is working on a solution to the problem. In the meantime, Dorresteijn says, "the hack still works."

Personal Experience

Personal experience can serve as powerful evidence when it's appropriate to the subject, to your purpose, and to the audience. If it's your only

Edward F. Palm relates his personal experiences as a veteran to explain how academia sometimes sends mixed messages about having veterans on campus. How does his evidence help build his argument?

LINK TO P. 955

evidence, however, personal experience usually won't be sufficient to carry the argument. Nevertheless, it can be effective for drawing in listeners or readers, as N'Gai Croal does in arguing that the video games with the greatest potential are those that appeal to the nongeek:

> I still get questions every now and then from people looking for advice on how to get their hands on a Nintendo Wii. But more and more, I'm hearing stories from people who've already scored one and are still rhapsodizing about it months after taking possession of the slim white console. The gushing comes from some of the most unexpected people. The grill man at my favorite New York burger joint told me last week that in his household, he mows down zombies in Resident Evil 4, his wife works out using Wii Fit, and he's introducing his son to the classic games of his youth via the Wii's download service. Similarly, a cardiologist friend of mine and his medical-resident girlfriend use Wii Golf to unwind; when they have friends over on the weekends, the same relaxing game turns into a fierce competition.
>
> As someone who covers videogames for *Newsweek*, I've marveled at how quickly the tastes of nontraditional players have moved from the margins of the industry toward the center. This is happening at the same time that geek tastes have taken center stage in other areas of pop culture: witness the summer movie schedule, which looks like new-release Wednesdays at your local comic-book shop.
>
> —N'Gai Croal, "You Don't Have to Be a Nerd"

CULTURAL CONTEXTS FOR ARGUMENT

Using Personal Experience

Personal experience counts in making academic arguments in some but not all cultures. Showing that you have personal experience with a topic can carry strong persuasive appeal with many English-speaking audiences, however, so it will probably be a useful way to argue a point in the United States. As with all evidence used to make a point, evidence based on your own experience must be pertinent to the topic, understandable to the audience, and clearly related to your purpose and claim.

Personal experience provides evidence for the popularity of Wii bowling (at least among humans).

Secondhand Evidence and Research

Secondhand evidence comes from sources beyond yourself—books, articles, films, online documents, photographs, and so on.

Library Sources

Your college library has printed materials (books, periodicals, reference works) as well as computer terminals that provide access to electronic catalogs, indexes, and other libraries' catalogs via the Internet. Although this book isn't designed to give a complete overview of library resources, we can make some important distinctions and pose a few key questions that can help you use the library most efficiently.

Two Important Distinctions

- Remember the distinction between *library databases* and the *Internet/ Web.* Your library's computers hold important resources that aren't on the Web or aren't available to you except through the library's system. The most important of these resources is the library's catalog of its

Not Just Words

Images often play a role in providing evidence for arguments. In documenting human-rights abuses in the conflict in Darfur province in Sudan, researchers with Human Rights Watch gave paper and crayons to hundreds of children and invited them to draw while the researchers interviewed the children's parents and neighbors. The children's drawings were published in *The Smallest Witnesses: The Conflict in Darfur through Children's Eyes*, a moving argument that claims that the government of Sudan is guilty of ethnic cleansing and crimes against humanity. The children's powerful drawings also led to many exhibitions and a series of videotaped presentations. Take a look at the drawings below, and then talk with classmates about what would be lost if the authors had offered only verbal descriptions of what the children drew.

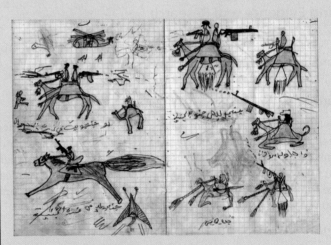

Picture of janjaweed and their weapons

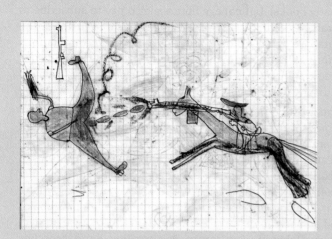

A drawing of a typical execution

Bombing by government forces

holdings (mostly books), but college libraries also pay to subscribe to scholarly databases—guides to journal and magazine articles, the *Lexis/Nexis* database of news stories and legal cases, and compilations of statistics, for example—that you can use for free. You should consult these electronic sources through your college library, perhaps even before turning to the Web.

- Remember the distinction between *subject headings* and *keywords*. The *Library of Congress Subject Headings* (LCSH) are standardized words and phrases that are used to classify the subject matter of books and articles. Library catalogs and databases usually use the LCSH headings to index their contents by author, title, publication date, and subject headings. When you do a subject search of the library's catalog, you're searching only one part of the electronic record of the library's books, and you need to use the exact wording of the LCSH. These subject headings are available in your library. On the other hand, searches with keywords use the computer's ability to look for any term in any field of the electronic record. Keyword searching is less restrictive than searching by subject headings, but it requires you to think carefully about your search terms to get good results. In addition, you need to use certain techniques to limit (or expand) your search. These include combining keywords with *and*, *or*, *not*, parentheses, and quotation marks or using similar procedures that are built into the catalog's or database's search mechanism.

Some Questions for Beginning Research

- What kinds of sources do you need to consult? Check your assignment to see whether you're required to consult different kinds of sources. If you'll use print sources, find out whether they're readily available in your library or whether you must make special arrangements (such as an interlibrary loan) to use them. If you need to locate nonprint sources (such as audiotapes, videotapes, artwork, or photos), find out where those are kept and whether you need special permission to examine them.

- How current do your sources need to be? If you must investigate the latest findings about, say, a new treatment for HIV/AIDS, you'll probably want to check periodicals, medical journals, and the Web. If you want broader, more detailed coverage and background information, you may need to depend more on books. If your argument deals with a specific time period, you may need to examine newspapers, magazines, and books written during that period.

- How many sources should you consult? Expect to look over many more sources than you'll end up using, and be sure to cover all major perspectives on your subject. The best guideline is to make sure you have enough sources to support your claim.

- Do you know your way around the library? If not, ask a librarian to help you locate the following resources in the library—general and specialized encyclopedias; biographical resources; almanacs, yearbooks, and atlases; book and periodical indexes; specialized indexes and abstracts; the circulation computer or library catalog; special collections; audio, video, and art collections; and the interlibrary loan office.

Online Sources

Many important resources for argument are now available in databases, either online or on CD-ROM, and many libraries now share the resources of their electronic catalogs through *WorldCat*. Like library catalogs and databases, the Internet and Web offer two ways to search for sources related to your argument—one using subject categories and one using keywords.

A subject directory organized by categories (such as you might find at http://dir.yahoo.com) allows you to choose a broad category like "Entertainment" or "Science" and then click on increasingly narrow categories like "Movies" or "Astronomy" and then "Thrillers" or "The Solar System" until you reach a point where you're given a list of Web sites or the opportunity to do a keyword search.

With the second kind of Internet search option, a search engine, you start right off with a keyword search—filling in a blank, for example, on the opening page of http://www.google.com. Because the Internet contains vastly more material than even the largest library catalog or database, exploring it with a search engine requires careful choices and combinations of keywords. For an argument about the fate of the antihero in contemporary films, for example, you might find that *film* and *hero* produce far too many possible matches, or hits. You might further narrow the search by adding a third keyword—say, *American* or *current*. In doing such searches, you'll need to observe the search logic that is followed by a particular database. Using *and* between keywords (*movies and heroes*) usually indicates that both terms must appear in a file for it to be called up. Using *or* between keywords usually instructs the computer to locate every file in which either one word or the other shows up, and using *not* tells the computer to exclude files containing a particular word from the search results (*movies not heroes*).

Using Evidence Effectively

You may gather an impressive amount of evidence on your topic—from firsthand interviews, from careful observations, and from intensive library and online research. But until that evidence is woven into the fabric of your own argument, it's just a pile of data. You still have to turn that data into information that will be persuasive to your intended audiences.

CULTURAL CONTEXTS FOR ARGUMENT

Defining Evidence

How do you decide what evidence will best support your claims? The answer depends, in large part, on how you define *evidence*. Differing notions of what counts as evidence can lead to arguments that go nowhere fast.

Journalists are often called on to interview those whose view of what constitutes effective evidence differs markedly from their own. When Italian journalist Oriana Fallaci interviewed the Ayatollah Khomeini, Iran's supreme leader, in 1971, she argued in a way that's common in North American and Western European cultures: she presented claims that she considered to be adequately backed up with facts ("Iran denies freedom to people.... Many people have been put in prison and even executed, just for speaking out in opposition"). In response, Khomeini relied on very different kinds of evidence—analogies ("Just as a finger with gangrene should be cut off so that it will not destroy the whole body, so should people who corrupt others be pulled out like weeds so they will not infect the whole field") and, above all, the authority of the Qur'an. Partly because of these differing

(continued)

beliefs about what counts as evidence, the interview ended unsuccessfully.

People in Western nations tend to give great weight to factual evidence, but even in those countries, what constitutes evidence can differ radically. This is so, for example, in debates in the United States between proponents of evolutionary theory and supporters of what is termed "intelligent design." In arguing across cultural divides, whether international or otherwise, you need to think carefully about how you're accustomed to using evidence—and about what counts as evidence to other people (without surrendering your own intellectual principles).

Here are some questions to help you review the types of evidence on which you're building your argument:

- Do you rely on facts? Examples? Firsthand experience?

- Do you include testimony from experts? Which experts are valued most (and why)?

- Do you cite religious or philosophical texts? Proverbs or everyday wisdom?

- Do you use analogies and metaphors as evidence? How much do they count?

Once you've determined what counts as evidence in your own arguments, ask the same questions about the use of evidence by members of other cultures.

Considering Audiences

The ethos that you bring to an argument (see Chapter 3) is crucial to your success in connecting with your audience. You want to present yourself as reliable and credible, but you also need to think about the way that your evidence relates to your audience. Is it appropriate to this particular group of readers or listeners? Does it speak to them in ways that they'll understand and respond to? Does it acknowledge their concerns?

It's hard to give definite advice for making sure that your evidence fits an audience. But in general, timeliness is important to audiences: the more up-to-date your evidence, the better. In addition, evidence that represents typical rather than extreme circumstances usually is more convincing. For example, in arguing for a campuswide security escort service after 10 p.m., a writer who cites the actual number of students who have recently been threatened or attacked on their way across campus after dark will be in a stronger position than one who cites only one sensational attack that occurred four years ago.

Building a Critical Mass

Throughout this chapter, we've stressed the need to discover as much evidence as possible in support of your claim. If you can find only one or two pieces of evidence—only one or two reasons or illustrations to back up your contention—then you may be on weak ground. Although there's no definite way of saying how much evidence is enough, you should build toward a critical mass by having several pieces of evidence all pulling in the direction of your claim.

And remember that *circumstantial evidence* (that is, indirect evidence that suggests that something occurred but doesn't prove it directly) may not be enough if it is the only evidence that you have. After seven years of intensive investigation into the anthrax killings that came shortly after September 11, 2001, the FBI was set to bring a case against scientist

In their study of college teachers' influence on their students, Mack D. Mariani and Gordon J. Hewitt attempt to build a critical mass of evidence that faculty political ideology does not affect student political ideology. Do you think they offer enough evidence?

LINK TO P. 941

Police removing mail suspected of containing anthrax from a box in New York City in October 2001

Bruce Ivins. But the evidence was all circumstantial: there was no "smoking gun," no direct, firsthand evidence of Ivins's guilt. After he committed suicide, the FBI closed the case, even though many critics demanded a trial to test whether a critical mass of evidence had been obtained.

If your evidence for a claim relies solely on circumstantial evidence, on personal experience, or on one major example, you should extend your search for additional sources and good reasons to back up your claim—or modify the claim. Your initial position may have been wrong. For example, if your claim that violent video games are leading young people to violent acts rests only on your personal experience or on indirect, circumstantial evidence (that several young people who had committed violent acts also had video games in their homes), then you don't have very strong support for your claim.

Arranging Evidence

Review your evidence, deciding which pieces support specific points in the argument. In general, try to position your strongest pieces of evidence in key places—near the beginning of paragraphs, at the end of the introduction, or toward a powerful conclusion. In addition, try to achieve a balance between, on the one hand, your own argument and your own words, and on the other hand, the sources that you use or quote in support of the argument. The sources of evidence are important props in the structure, but they shouldn't overpower the structure (your argument) itself.

RESPOND.

1. What counts as evidence depends in large part on the rhetorical situation. One audience might find personal testimony compelling in a given case, whereas another might require data that only experimental studies can provide. Imagine that you want to argue that advertisements should not include demeaning representations of chimpanzees and that the use of primates in advertising should be banned. You're encouraged to find out that a number of companies such as Honda and Puma have already agreed to such a ban, so you decide to present your argument to other companies' CEOs and advertising officials. What kind of evidence would be most compelling to this group? How would you rethink your use of evidence if you were writing for the campus newspaper, for middle schoolers, or for animal-rights group

members? What can you learn about what sort of evidence each of these groups might value—and why?

2. Finding, evaluating, and arranging evidence in an argument is often a discovery process. Sometimes you're concerned not only with digging up support for an already established claim but also with creating and revising tentative claims. Surveys and interviews can help you figure out what to argue, as well as provide evidence for a claim.

   Interview a classmate with the goal of writing a brief proposal argument about the career that he or she should pursue. The claim should be something like *My classmate should be doing X in five years from now.* Limit yourself to ten questions. Write them ahead of time, and don't deviate from them. Record the results of the interview (written notes are fine; you don't need a tape recorder). Then interview another classmate with the same goal in mind. Ask the same first question, but this time let the answer dictate the next nine questions. You still get only ten questions.

   Which interview gave you more information? Which one helped you learn more about your classmate's goals? Which one better helped you develop claims about his or her future?

3. Imagine that you're trying to decide whether to take a class with a particular professor but you don't know if he or she is a good teacher. You might already have an opinion, based on some vaguely defined criteria and dormitory gossip, but you're not sure if that evidence is reliable. You do some digging on RateMyProfessor.com and then decide to observe a class before you make your final decision.

   Visit a class in which you aren't currently enrolled, and make notes on your observations following the guidelines given in this chapter (pp. 496–97). You probably need only a single visit to take the notes, though you would probably take longer to write a thorough evaluation of the professor.

   Write a short evaluation of the professor's teaching abilities on the basis of your observations. Then write an analysis of your evaluation. Is it honest? Fair? What other kinds of evidence might you need if you wanted to make an informed decision about the class and the teacher? What evidence is available to you in terms of local files of teaching evaluations, online teaching evaluation sites, and so on?

17
Fallacies of Argument

"Just what you'd expect an eco-alarmist like that to say."

"If you don't give me an A in this class, I won't get into medical school!"

"Ask not what your country can do for you; ask what you can do for your country."

"No blood for oil!"

"All my friends have iPhones."

"9/11 changed everything."

• • •

Certain types of argumentative moves are so controversial that they're traditionally classified as *fallacies*—arguments that are flawed by their very nature or structure. But you might find it more interesting to think of them as *flashpoints* or *hotspots* because they instantly raise questions about the ethics of argument—that is, whether a particular strategy of argument is fair, honest, or principled. You should avoid fallacies in your own writing and challenge them in arguments that you hear or read. But it's important to appreciate that one person's fallacy may well be another person's perceptive insight.

Consider, for example, the fallacy termed *ad hominem* ("to the man") argument. It describes a strategy of attacking the character of people that you disagree with rather than the substance of their arguments: *So you think that Reverend Jeremiah Wright is a racist, a radical, and an anti-Semite? Well, you're just a white-bread, redneck bigot yourself.* Many people have blurted out such insults at some time in their lives and later regretted them.

In some situations, however, a person's moral fiber actually *is* central to an argument. The problem arises in deciding when such arguments are legitimate and when they are fallacious. You're very likely to think of personal attacks on people that you admire as *ad hominem* slurs and those on people that you disagree with as reasonable criticisms. As you can imagine, debates about character can become polarizing. Consider 50 Cent and Kanye West or maybe MSNBC's Keith Olbermann and all the people that he labels as "the worst person in the world." (For more on arguments based on character, see Chapter 3.)

Sometimes fallacies are errors that you can detect and expose in someone else's work, but often they are strategies that hurt everyone (including the person using them) because they make productive argument more difficult. Fallacies muck up the frank but civil conversations that people should be able to have—regardless of their differences.

To help you understand fallacies of argument, we've classified them according to three rhetorical appeals discussed in earlier chapters—emotional arguments, ethical arguments, and logical arguments (see Chapters 2, 3, and 4).

Fallacies of Emotional Argument

Emotional arguments can be powerful and suitable in many circumstances, and most writers use them frequently. However, writers who pull on their readers' heartstrings or raise their blood pressure too often can violate the good faith on which legitimate argument depends.

Readers won't trust a writer who can't make a point without frightening someone, provoking tears, or stirring up hatred.

Scare Tactics

Scare tactics are common in everything ranging from ads for life insurance to threats of audits by the Internal Revenue Service. Politicians, advertisers, and public figures sometimes peddle their ideas by scaring people and exaggerating possible dangers well beyond their statistical likelihood. Such ploys work because it's usually easier to imagine something terrible happening than to appreciate its statistical rarity. Why do many people fear flying more than they fear driving? More people die from auto accidents every year, but such accidents don't fire up our imaginations as spectacularly as air disasters do.

Scare tactics can also be used to stampede legitimate fears into panic or prejudice. People who genuinely fear losing their jobs can be persuaded to fear that immigrants might work for less money. People who are living on fixed incomes can be convinced that minor modifications of entitlement programs represent dire threats to their standard of living. Such tactics have the effect of closing off thinking because people who are scared often act irrationally. Even well-intended fear campaigns—like those directed against the use of illegal drugs, smoking, or unprotected sex—can misfire if their warnings prove too shrill. People just stop listening.

Either-Or Choices

One way to simplify arguments and give them power is to reduce the options for action to only two choices. One option (or the preferred existing policy) might be drawn in warm, favorable terms, whereas the other is cast as a dangerous alternative. That's the nature of the choices that President George W. Bush offered in an August 20, 2005, radio address to the nation:

> Our troops know that they're fighting in Iraq, Afghanistan, and elsewhere to protect their fellow Americans from a savage enemy. They know that if we do not confront these evil men abroad, we will have to face them one day in our own cities and streets, and they know that the safety and security of every American is at stake in this war, and they know we will prevail.

The Privacy Commissioner of Canada offers a warning about the dangers of entering personal information online. What is your assessment of the warning? Does it verge on scare tactics or address the issue responsibly?

LINK TO P. 669

The parental ultimatum—a classic form of the *either-or* argument

"They say we can go there for Thanksgiving or they can cut us out of the will. Our choice."

Sometimes neither alternative is pleasant: that's the nature of many ultimatums. For instance, the Allies in World War II offered the Axis powers only two choices as the conflict drew to a close—either continued war and destruction or unconditional surrender. No third option was available.

Either-or choices can be well-intentioned strategies to get something accomplished. Parents use them all the time ("Eat your broccoli, or you won't get dessert"). But they become fallacious arguments when they reduce a complicated issue to excessively simple terms or when they're designed to obscure legitimate alternatives.

For instance, to suggest that renewable power sources such as wind and solar represent the only long-term solution to our energy needs may have rhetorical power, but the choice is too simple. Energy shortages can be fixed in any number of ways, *including* wind and solar power. But to

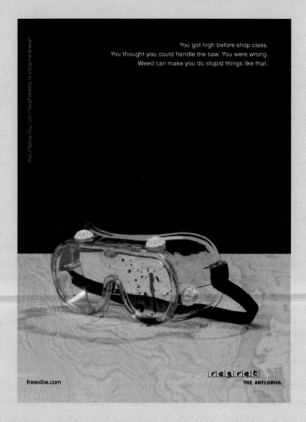

You got high before shop class.
You thought you could handle the saw. You were wrong.
Weed can make you do stupid things like that.

freevibe.com

r|e|g|r|e|t
THE ANTI-DRUG.

Not Just Words

Look at the advertisement above. Is it a scare tactic? A legitimate warning? Something in between? How effective do you think this ad would be for college students or for people who use marijuana or might be tempted to? What effect does the text in the upper right-hand corner have on your answers to these questions? What about the text at the bottom? Do graphic images like this and sponsor labels like "Partnership for a Drug-Free America" make the campaign against marijuana and other illegal drugs more effective—or less so? How does this ad compare with the one about drunk driving on p. 104?

promote such renewable resources as the *only* reasonable option risks losing the support of people who know better.

But *either-or* arguments—like most scare tactics—are often purposefully designed to seduce those who don't know much about a subject. That's another reason that the tactic violates principles of civil discourse. Argument should enlighten people by making them more knowledgeable and more capable of acting intelligently and independently. We usually don't have to choose one side over the other. Here, Paris Hilton pokes fun at opposing political camps for debating energy issues in *either-or* terms by offering her own alternative:

> Ok, so here's my energy policy. Barack wants to focus on new technologies to cut foreign oil dependency and McCain wants offshore drilling. Well, why don't we do a hybrid of both candidates' ideas? We can do limited offshore drilling with strict environmental oversight, while creating tax incentives to get Detroit making hybrid and electric cars. That way, the offshore drilling carries us until the new technologies kick in, which will then create new jobs and energy independence. Energy crisis solved.
>
> —Paris Hilton, funnyordie.com

Slippery Slope

The slippery-slope fallacy describes an argument that portrays today's tiny misstep as tomorrow's slide into disaster. Some arguments that aim at preventing dire consequences do not take the slippery-slope approach (for example, the parent who corrects a child for misbehavior now is acting sensibly to prevent more serious problems as the child grows older). A slippery-slope argument becomes wrongheaded when a writer exaggerates the likely consequences of an action, usually to frighten readers. As such, slippery-slope arguments are also scare tactics. For instance, defenders of civil liberties often depict any action by Western democracies to use eavesdropping technologies domestically to track terrorists as assaults on freedom of speech reminiscent of those of the KGB.

In recent years, the issue of same-sex marriage has similarly encouraged slippery-slope arguments:

> Anyone else bored to tears with the "slippery slope" arguments against gay marriage? Since few opponents of homosexual unions are brave enough to admit that gay weddings just freak them out, they hide behind the claim that it's an inexorable slide from legalizing gay

marriage to having sex with penguins outside JC Penney's. The problem is it's virtually impossible to debate against a slippery slope.
—Dahlia Lithwick, "Slippery Slop"

Ideas and actions do have consequences, but they aren't always as dire as writers fond of slippery-slope tactics would have you believe.

Sentimental Appeals

Sentimental appeals are arguments that use tender emotions excessively to distract readers from facts. Often, such appeals are highly personal

WORLD WILDLIFE FUND
2009 CALENDAR

Baby Animals

This calendar is designed to elicit sympathy for the penguins on its cover and inspire donations to the wildlife organization that protects them. But sometimes sentimental images of threatened species are attached to much less worthy sales pitches—for soda or camping gear, for example.

and individual and focus attention on heartwarming or heart-wrenching situations that make readers feel guilty if they challenge an idea, a policy, or a proposal. Emotions become an impediment to civil discourse when they keep people from thinking clearly.

Yet sentimental appeals are a major vehicle of television news, where tugging at viewers' heartstrings can mean high ratings. For example, when a camera documents the day-to-day sacrifices of parents who are trying to meet their mortgage payments in a tough economy, their on-screen struggles can represent the spirit of an entire class of people threatened by callous bankers. Another family, also behind in its mortgage payments, might be shown living large in an oversized house while legislators ask for public funds to bail such people out. In either case, the conclusion the reporter wants you to reach is supported by powerful images that evoke emotions in support of that conclusion. But though the individual stories presented may stir genuine emotions, they seldom give a complete picture of a complex social or economic issue.

Bandwagon Appeals

Kathy Freston mentions several celebrities who have advocated vegetarianism. Would you consider this a bandwagon appeal? An appeal to false authority? A legitimate argument?

LINK TO P. 800

Bandwagon appeals are arguments that urge people to follow the same path that everyone else is taking. Many American parents seem to have an innate ability to refute bandwagon appeals. When their kids whine, *Everyone else is going camping overnight without chaperones,* the parents reply, *And if everyone else jumps off a cliff (or a railroad bridge or the Empire State Building), you will too?* The children stomp and groan—and then try a different line of argument.

Unfortunately, not all bandwagon approaches are transparent. Although people like to imagine themselves as independent thinkers, they can be seduced by ideas that are repeated obsessively in the mass media—the intellectual equivalent of a feeding frenzy. Even legitimate issues that are raised by a news event may be transformed into a bandwagon when powerful media and political voices all shout the same thing. In recent decades, bandwagon issues have included the war on drugs, the nuclear freeze movement, the campaign against drunk driving, campaign finance reform, illegal immigration, the defense of marriage, and bailouts for banks and businesses. These issues are all too complex to permit the suspension of judgment that bandwagon tactics require.

Rather than think independently about where to go, it's often easier to get on board the bandwagon with everyone else.

Fallacies of Ethical Argument

Not surprisingly, readers give their closest attention to authors whom they respect or trust. So writers usually want to present themselves as honest, well informed, likable, or sympathetic in some way. But *trust me* is a scary warrant. Not all the devices that writers use to gain the attention and confidence of readers are admirable. (For more on appeals based on character, see Chapter 3.)

Appeals to False Authority

One effective strategy for supporting an idea is to draw on the authority of widely respected people, institutions, and texts. In fact, many academic research papers find and reflect on the work of reputable authorities and introduce these authorities through direct quotations, citations (such as footnotes), or allusions. (For more on assessing the reliability of sources, see Chapter 19.) False authority, however, occurs when writers offer themselves or other authorities as sufficient warrant for believing a claim:

Claim	**X is true because I say so.**
Warrant	**What I say must be true.**
Claim	**X is true because Y says so.**
Warrant	**What Y says must be true.**

Few readers would accept a claim that states authority quite so baldly as in these formulas. Nonetheless, claims of authority drive many persuasive campaigns. American pundits and politicians are fond of citing the U. S. Constitution and its Bill of Rights (Canadians have their Charter of Rights and Freedoms) as ultimate authorities, a reasonable practice when the documents are interpreted respectfully. However, the rights and liberties claimed sometimes aren't in the texts themselves or don't mean what the speakers think they do. And most constitutional matters are debatable—as volumes of court records prove.

Likewise, religious believers often base arguments on books or traditions that wield great authority within a particular religious community. However, the power of these texts is usually limited outside that group and less capable of persuading others solely on the grounds of their authority.

Institutions can be cited as authorities, too. Serious attention should be paid to claims that are supported by respected authorities—such as the Centers for Disease Control, the National Science Foundation, the *Wall Street Journal*, and the *Globe and Mail*. But information and opinions should not be accepted simply because they are put forth by such offices and agencies. To quote a Russian proverb made famous by Ronald Reagan, "Trust, but verify."

Dogmatism

Barbara Munson expresses strong opinions about the use of Native American mascots and logos. Is any part of her argument dogmatic? If so, where? If not, why not?

LINK TO P. 624

A writer who asserts or assumes that a particular position is the only one that is conceivably acceptable within a community is expressing dogmatism. Indeed, dogmatism is a fallacy of character because the tactic undermines the trust that must exist between those who make and listen to arguments. When people speak or write dogmatically, they imply that no arguments are necessary: the truth is self-evident. You're probably listening to a dogmatic opinion when someone begins a sentence with *No rational person would disagree that . . .* or *It's clear to anyone who has thought about it that. . . .*

Even so, some arguments present positions and claims that are so outrageous or absurd that they're beyond civil discourse and are unworthy of serious attention. For example, attacks on the historical reality of the Holocaust fall into this category. But few subjects that can be defended with facts, testimony, and good reasons ought to be off the table in a free society. In general, whenever someone suggests that raising an issue for debate is somehow "unacceptable," "inappropriate," or "outrageous"—whether on the grounds that it's racist, sexist, unpatriotic, blasphemous, insensitive, or offensive in some other way—you should be suspicious.

Ad Hominem Arguments

As explained earlier, *ad hominem* (from the Latin for "to the man") arguments are attacks directed at the character of a person rather than at the claims he or she makes. The theory is simple: when you destroy the credibility of your opponents, you either destroy their ability to present reasonable appeals or distract from the successful arguments they may be offering. Here, for example, Christopher Hitchens questions whether former secretary of state Henry Kissinger should be appointed to head an important government commission in 2002:

> But can Congress and the media be expected to swallow the appointment of a proven coverup artist, a discredited historian, a busted liar, and a man who is wanted in many jurisdictions for the vilest of offenses?
>
> —Christopher Hitchens, "The Case against Henry Kissinger"

There's not much doubt about where Hitchens stands. Liberal critics of Rush Limbaugh's politics rarely fail to note his problems with the drug OxyContin; conservative detractors of Speaker of the House Nancy Pelosi can't resist mentioning that the district she represents is that far-left haven San Francisco.

In such cases, *ad hominem* tactics turn arguments into two-sided affairs with good guys and bad guys, and that's unfortunate, since character often *does* matter in argument. People expect the proponent of peace to be civil, a secretary of the treasury to pay his taxes, and the

David Horowitz accuses some of those who disagree with his proposed Academic Bill of Rights of having engaged in *ad hominem* attacks directed at him and not at the content or merit of his Bill of Rights.

LINK TO P. 922

champion of family values to be a faithful spouse. But it's fallacious to attack an idea by uncovering the foibles of its advocates or by attacking their motives, backgrounds, or unchangeable traits.

Fallacies of Logical Argument

You'll encounter a problem in any argument when the claims, warrants, or pieces of evidence in it are invalid, insufficient, or disconnected. In theory, such problems seem easy enough to spot, but in practice, they can be camouflaged by a skillful use of words or images. Indeed, logical fallacies pose a challenge to civil argument because they often seem reasonable and natural, especially when they appeal to people's self-interests. Whole industries (such as online psychics) depend on one or more of the logical fallacies for their existence. Political campaigns, too, rely on them to prop up the current staple of democratic advertising—the fifteen-second TV spot.

Hasty Generalization

Among logical fallacies, only faulty causality might be as prevalent as hasty generalization. A hasty generalization is an inference drawn from insufficient evidence: *Because* my *Honda broke down, then* all *Hondas must be junk*. It also forms the basis for most stereotypes about people or institutions: because *a few* people in a large group are observed to act in a certain way, *all* members of that group are inferred to behave similarly. The resulting conclusions are usually sweeping claims of little merit: *Women are bad drivers; men are slobs; Scots are stingy; Italians are lecherous; English teachers are nitpicky; scientists are nerds*. You could, no doubt, expand this roster of stereotypes by the hundreds.

To draw valid inferences, you must always have sufficient evidence—a random sample of a population, a selection large enough to represent fully the subjects of your study, an objective methodology for sampling the population or evidence, and so on (see Chapter 16). And you must qualify your claims appropriately. After all, people do need generalizations to make reasonable decisions in life. Such claims can be offered legitimately if placed in context and tagged with appropriate qualifiers—*some, a few, many, most, occasionally, rarely, possibly, in some cases, under certain circumstances, in my limited experience*.

"Google must be anti-American because the company decorates its famous logo for occasions such as the anniversary of *Sputnik*, Earth Day, and Persian New Year but not Memorial Day in the United States." A hasty generalization? Check "holiday logos" at Google, and decide for yourself.

You should be especially alert to the fallacy of hasty generalization when you read reports and studies of any kind, especially case studies that are based on carefully selected populations. Be alert for the fallacy in the interpretation of poll numbers, too. Everything from the number of people selected to the time the poll was taken to the exact wording of the questions may affect its outcome.

Faulty Causality

In Latin, the fallacy of faulty causality is described by the expression *post hoc, ergo propter hoc*, which translates as "after this, therefore because of this." Odd as the translation may sound, it accurately describes what faulty causality is—the fallacious assumption that because one event or

Chapter 26 includes several editorial cartoons that comment on affirmative action. Notice that several rely on accusations of faulty causality to make their case.

LINK TO P. 917

action follows another, the first causes the second. Consider a lawsuit commented on in the *Wall Street Journal* in which a writer sued Coors (unsuccessfully), claiming that drinking copious amounts of the company's beer had kept him from writing a novel.

Some actions do produce reactions. Step on the brake pedal in your car, and you move hydraulic fluid that pushes calipers against disks to create friction that stops the vehicle. If you are the chair of the Federal Reserve Board, you drop interest rates to lower the cost of borrowing to increase the growth of the economy in order to reduce unemployment—you hope. Causal relationships of this kind are reasonably convincing because one can provide evidence of relationships between the events sufficient to convince most people that an initial action did, indeed, cause subsequent actions.

In other cases, however, a supposed connection between cause and effect turns out to be completely wrong. For example, doctors now believe that when an elderly person falls and is found to have a broken leg or hip, the break usually caused the fall rather than the other way around. And as the Federal Reserve example suggests, causality can be especially difficult to control or determine when complex economic, political, or social relationships are involved.

That's why suspiciously simple or politically convenient causal claims should always be subject to scrutiny. By mid-2008, it was apparent that the military situation in the long-running Iraq War had changed significantly, with American casualties down dramatically and violence throughout the still-occupied country significantly reduced. The Bush administration credited that improvement to a military strategy called the surge—which involved a change in counterinsurgency tactics of American troops and a temporary increase in their numbers. Critics of the war, however, claimed that the surge only appeared to work because it had occurred just as Sunni tribal leaders decided to turn against Al Qaeda and support the Iraqi government. Whose causal claim was right? Perhaps that of both camps, as a writer for the *Washington Post* explains:

> The arrival of additional U.S. forces signaled renewed resolve. Sunni tribal leaders, having glimpsed the dismal future in store for their people under a regime controlled by al-Qaeda in Iraq and fearful of abandonment, were ready to throw in their lot with the coalition. The surge did not create the first of the tribal "awakenings," but it was the catalyst for their expansion and eventual success. The tribal revolt took off

after the arrival of reinforcements and as U.S. and Iraqi units fought to make the Iraqi people secure.

— Peter Mansoor, "How the Surge Worked"

The final word on this complicated causal relationship will probably be written by military historians decades from now when more facts are known and can be interpreted with fewer partisan pressures.

Begging the Question

There's probably not a teacher in the country who hasn't heard the following argument: *You can't give me a C in this course; I'm an A student.* For a member of Congress accused of taking kickbacks, a press secretary makes a version of the same argument: *Representative X can't be guilty of accepting such bribes; she's an honest person.* In both cases, the problem with the claim is that it's made on grounds that cannot be accepted as true because those grounds are in doubt. How can the student claim to be an A student when he just earned a C? How can the accused bribe taker defend herself on the grounds of honesty when that honesty is now suspect? Setting such arguments in Toulmin terms helps to expose the fallacy:

Claim	You can't give me a C in this course . . .
Reason	. . . because I'm an A student.
Warrant	An A student is someone who can't receive Cs.

Claim	Representative X can't be guilty of accepting bribes . . .
Reason	. . . because she's an honest person.
Warrant	An honest person cannot be guilty of accepting bribes.

With the warrants stated, you can see why begging the question— assuming as true the very claim that's disputed—is a form of circular argument that is divorced from reality. If you assume that an A student can't receive Cs, then the first argument stands. But no one is an A student *by definition*; that standing is earned by performance in individual courses. Likewise, even though someone with a record of honesty is unlikely to accept bribes, a claim of honesty isn't an adequate defense against specific charges. An honest person won't accept bribes, but merely claiming that someone is honest doesn't make her so. (For more on Toulmin argument, see Chapter 7.)

A wannabe resists believing "I'm a writer because I say I am." Begging the question can deceive ourselves as well as others.

"I don't usually tell people I'm a writer because
I've never actually written anything."

Equivocation

The finest definition of *equivocation* and its most famous literary examples come from Shakespeare's tragedy *Macbeth*. In the drama, three witches, representing the fates, make prophecies that favor the ambitious Macbeth but that prove disastrous when understood more fully. He's told, for example, that he has nothing to fear from his enemies "till Birnam wood / Do come to Dunsinane" (*Mac.* 5.5.44–45). Although it seems impossible that trees could move, they indeed appear to move when enemy soldiers cut down branches from the forest of Birnam for camouflage and march on Macbeth's fortress. Catching on to the game, Macbeth starts "to doubt the equivocation of the fiend / That lies like truth" (5.5.43–44). An equivocation is an argument that gives a lie an honest appearance; it's a half-truth.

Equivocations are usually juvenile tricks of language. Consider the plagiarist who copies a paper word for word from a source and then declares (honestly, she thinks) that "I wrote the entire paper myself"— meaning that she physically copied the piece on her own. But the plagiarist is using *wrote* equivocally—in a limited sense—and knows that most people understand the word to mean both composing as well as mere copying of words. Many public figures are fond of parsing their words carefully so that no certain meaning emerges. In the 1990s, Bill Clinton's "I never had sex with that woman" claim became notorious when the then-president defined *sex* in a narrow way. In the first decade of the twenty-first century, critics of the Bush administration said its many denials that *torture* was being used on U.S. prisoners abroad amounted to a long series of equivocations.

Baseball star Alex Rodriguez admitted that he had taken performance-enhancing drugs during the 2003 season, but said that "I don't know exactly what" and hinted that they may have been legal substances. Some expert observers think that's an equivocation—a dishonest play on the word *know*—since he tested positive for drugs that can't be obtained legally in the United States.

Non Sequitur

A non sequitur is an argument in which claims, reasons, or warrants fail to connect logically; one point doesn't follow from another. As with other fallacies, children are notably adept at framing non sequiturs. Consider this familiar form: *You don't love me or you'd buy me that bicycle!* It might be more evident to harassed parents that no connection exists between love and Huffys if they were to consider the implied warrant:

Claim   **You must not love me . . .**
Reason   **. . . because you haven't bought me that bicycle.**
Warrant   **Buying bicycles for children is essential to loving them.**

A five-year-old might endorse that warrant, but no responsible adult would because love doesn't depend on buying bicycles. Activities more logically related to love might include feeding and clothing children, taking care of them when they're sick, providing shelter and education, and so on.

Non sequiturs occur when writers omit a step in an otherwise logical chain of reasoning, assuming that readers agree with what may be a highly contestable claim. For example, it's a non sequitur simply to argue that the comparatively poor performance of American students on international mathematics examinations means that the country should spend more money on math education. Such a conclusion might be justified if a correlation were known or found to exist between mathematical ability and money spent on education. But the students' performance might be poor for reasons other than education funding, so a writer should first establish the nature of the problem before offering a solution.

The Straw Man

Those who resort to the "straw-man" fallacy attack an argument that isn't really there. It's much weaker or more extreme than the one that the opponent is actually making. The speaker or writer "sets up a straw man" in this way to create an argument that's easy to knock down, proceeds to do so, and then claims victory over the opponent—whose real argument was quite different. In a February 20, 2009, *Weekly Standard* column, Republican political commentator Fred Barnes suggests that President Obama is fond of the device:

> Obama may not be eloquent, but he is glib and clever and at times persuasive. One of his favorite rhetorical devices is setting up a straw man, then knocking it down. He invoked this classic ploy subtly in his inaugural address, crudely in his press conference. "We will restore science to its rightful place," Obama said at his inauguration. Really? Where had science been? "We are ready to lead once more," he said, as if we—America—hadn't been. He may have disapproved of the prior administration's policies in the world, but that doesn't mean it wasn't

leading. Also in his inaugural speech, Obama said, "we can no longer afford indifference to suffering outside our borders." When were we indifferent? Not in Obama's lifetime.

—Fred Barnes, "Obama's First Month"

A lot of "straw-man" arguments have been advanced in the recent debates over evolution and intelligent design. Some who argue against intelligent design say that its advocates attribute life to the actions of a white-haired deity in the sky. Some who argue against evolutionary theory allege that its adherents hold that evolution is all chance—implying that a structure as complicated as the human eye came into existence randomly. But in both instances, such speakers are refuting arguments that their opponents haven't actually made. At least in their public political or legal statements, supporters of intelligent design don't make claims about who or what the "intelligent designer" is. And supporters of evolution contend that the process is driven by random mutations in genes but that organisms evolve only if such mutations make them better adapted to their environment (such as by increasing their ability to detect light) and thus more likely to reproduce. Both sides are attacking weak arguments that their opponents aren't actually making. As a result, both sides are ignoring the tougher issues.

Faulty Analogy

Comparisons give ideas greater presence; they also may help to clarify one concept by measuring it against another that is more familiar. Consider how quickly you make a judgment about Britney Spears after reading this comparison with Madonna:

> [R]egardless of how hard she tries, Britney's not Madonna. To be fair, Madonna wasn't Madonna at first either, but emulating someone else—even if they're as successful as Madonna—usually doesn't work in the end.
>
> —Erik J. Barzeski

When comparisons are extended, they become *analogies*—ways of understanding unfamiliar ideas by comparing them with something that's already known. People understand the world around them largely through comparisons, metaphors, and analogies. But useful as such comparisons are, they may prove false either taken on their own and pushed too far, or taken too seriously. At this point, they become *faulty analogies*—inaccurate or inconsequential comparisons between objects or concepts. For instance,

Russian deputy foreign minister Sergei Ivanov startled observers on August 13, 2008, when he justified his country's military incursion into the tiny neighboring country of Georgia by claiming a comparison to the 9/11 terrorist attacks:

> We just reacted because we didn't have any other option. Any civilized country would act the same way. I may remind you, September the 11th, the reaction was similar. American citizens were killed. You know the reaction.
>
> —Sergei Ivanov

RESPOND●

1. The following list of political slogans or phrases may be examples of logical fallacies. Discuss each item to determine what you may know about the slogan. Then decide which, if any, fallacy might be used to describe it.

    "Leave no child behind." (George Bush policy and slogan)

    "It's the economy, stupid." (sign on the wall at Bill Clinton's campaign headquarters)

    "Nixon's the one." (campaign slogan)

    "Remember the Alamo." (battle cry)

    "Make love, not war." (antiwar slogan during the Vietnam War)

    "A chicken in every pot." (campaign slogan)

    "No taxation without representation." (American colonial slogan)

    "Loose lips sink ships." (slogan from World War II)

    "Guns don't kill, people do." (NRA slogan)

    "If you can't stand the heat, get out of the kitchen." (attributed to Harry S. Truman)

    "We are the ones we've been waiting for. We are the change that we seek." (Obama campaign statement)

2. We don't want you to argue fallaciously, but it's fun and good practice to frame argumentative fallacies in your own language. Pick an argumentative topic—maybe one that you've used for a paper in this class—and write a few paragraphs making nothing but fallacious arguments in each sentence. Try to include all the fallacies of emotional, ethical, and logical argument that are discussed in this chapter.

3. Choose a paper you've written for this or another class, and analyze it carefully for signs of fallacious reasoning. Once you've tried analyzing your own prose, find an editorial, a syndicated column, and a political speech, and look for the fallacies in them. Which fallacies are most common in the four arguments? How do you account for their prevalence? Which are the least common? How do you account for their absence? What seems to be the role of audience in determining what's a fallacy and what isn't?

4. Arguments on the Web are no more likely to contain fallacies than are arguments in any other medium, but the fallacies can take on different forms. The hypertextual nature of Web arguments and the ease of including visuals with text make certain fallacies more likely to occur there. Find a Web site that is sponsored by an organization (the Future of Music Coalition, perhaps), business (Coca-Cola, Pepsi), or other group (the Democratic or Republican National Committee), and analyze the site for fallacious reasoning. Among other considerations, look at the relationship between text and graphics and between individual pages and the pages that surround or are linked to them. How does the technique of separating information into discrete pages affect the argument? Then consider sending an e-mail message to the site's creators, explaining what you found and proposing ways the arguments in the site could be improved.

5. Political blogs such as wonkette.com, andrewsullivan.com, DailyKos .com, and InstaPundit.com typically provide quick responses to daily events and detailed critiques of material in other media sites, including national newspapers. Study one active political blog for a few days to determine whether and how the blogger critiques the material he or she links to. Does the blogger point to fallacies in arguments? If so, does he or she explain them or just assume readers understand them or will figure them out? Summarize your findings in an oral report to your class.

18

Intellectual Property, Academic Integrity, and Avoiding Plagiarism

On a college campus, a student receives a warning: she has been detected using peer-to-peer music file-sharing software. Has she been practicing fair use, or is she guilty of copyright infringement?

A student writing an essay about the effect of Title IX of the Education Amendments of 1972 on college athletic programs finds some powerful supporting evidence for his argument on a Web site. Can he use this information without gaining permission?

Day-care centers around the country receive letters arguing that they'll be liable to lawsuit if they use representations of Disney characters without explicit permission or show Disney films "outside the home."

A tattoo artist claims ownership of the butterfly design on a movie star's arm and protests when his work appears in an advertisement without permission. The actor argues that it's her arm.

Haute couture houses—angered by the prevalence of cheap knockoffs of their dresses, handbags, and shoes—ask Congress to pass legislation protecting their apparel designs for three years.

Musicians argue against other musicians, saying that the popular use of "sampling" in songs amounts to a form of musical plagiarism.

● ● ●

In agricultural and industrial eras, products that could provide a livelihood were likely to be concrete things—crops, tools, machines. But in our current age of information, intellectual property is one of society's most important products—hence the importance of and controversies surrounding what counts as "property" in an information age.

Perhaps the framers of the U.S. Constitution foresaw that the bases of the nation's economy would shift. To accommodate these kinds of changes, they expressed in the Constitution a delicate balance between the public's need for information and the worker's need to be encouraged to create products—both material and intellectual. Thus, the Constitution (in article 1, section 8, clause 8), empowers Congress

> [t]o promote the progress of Science and useful Arts, by securing for limited Times to Authors and Inventors the exclusive Right to their respective Writings and Discoveries.

This passage allows for limited protection (copyright) of the expression of ideas ("Writings and Discoveries"), and over time that limit has been extended to lifetime plus seventy years.

Why is this historical information important to student writers? First, writers need to know that ideas cannot be copyrighted: only the expression of those ideas is protected. Second, some works fall out of copyright and can be used without paying a fee. Third, the current debates over who owns online materials—materials that may never take any concrete form—will be resolved in ways that will directly affect students and teachers. For up-to-date information about copyright law, see the U.S. Copyright Office site (http://copyright.gov).

Crediting Sources in Arguments

Giving full credit to your sources enhances your ethos in argumentative writing. In the first place, saying "thanks" to those who've helped you suggests gratitude and candidness, qualities that audiences like. Second,

Who owns the guardian angel on David Beckham's back—the athlete or the tattoo artist, Louis Molloy, who created it?

Wikipedia is commonly attacked as an unreliable source. Take a look at the entry for *Local food,* paying special attention to how the article acknowledges sources. Do you think the material is adequately sourced and cited?

LINK TO P. 817

acknowledging your sources demonstrates that you have "done your homework," understand what others have written about the topic, and encourage others to join the conversation as well. Finally, citing sources reminds you to think critically about how well you've used them. Are they timely and reliable? Have you referenced them in a biased or overly selective way? Have you used them accurately, double-checking all quotations and paraphrases? Thinking through such questions will improve your work.

Citing Sources and Recognizing Plagiarism

In many ways, "nothing new under the sun" is more than just a cliché. Most of what you think or write is built on what you've previously read or experienced. And trying to recall every source of influence, even for just one day, would leave you little time to say anything. Luckily, you'll seldom, if ever, be called on to list every influence on your life. But you do have responsibilities in school and professional situations to acknowledge any intellectual property you've borrowed to create arguments. If you don't, you may be accused of *plagiarism*—claiming as your own the words or intellectual work of others.

Avoiding plagiarism is important because in Western culture using someone else's language and ideas without acknowledgment is considered dishonest. Plagiarism can have devastating consequences—especially, though not only, in school.

Inaccurate or Incomplete Citation of Sources

You may be accused of plagiarism if you use a paraphrase that's too close to the original wording or sentence structure of your source material (*even* if you cite the source), if you leave out the parenthetical reference for a quotation (*even* if you include the quotation marks themselves), or if you don't indicate clearly the source of an idea you obviously didn't come up with on your own. And the accusation can be made even if you didn't intend to plagiarize. This kind of inaccurate or incomplete citation of sources often results either from carelessness or from not learning how to use citations accurately and fully.

Here, for example, is the first paragraph from an essay by Russell Platt published in the *Nation* (http://www.thenation.com/doc/20051003/platt):

> **Classical music in America, we are frequently told, is in its death throes: its orchestras bled dry by expensive guest soloists and greedy musicians unions, its media presence shrinking, its prestige diminished, its educational role ignored, its big record labels dying out or merging into faceless corporate entities. We seem to have too many well-trained musicians in need of work, too many good composers going without commissions, too many concerts to offer an already satiated public.**
>
> **—Russell Platt, "New World Symphony"**

To cite this passage correctly in MLA style, you could quote directly from it, using both quotation marks and some form of attribution. Either of the following versions would be acceptable:

> Russell Platt has doubts about claims that classical music is "in its death throes: its orchestras bled dry by expensive guest soloists and greedy musicians unions" ("New World").

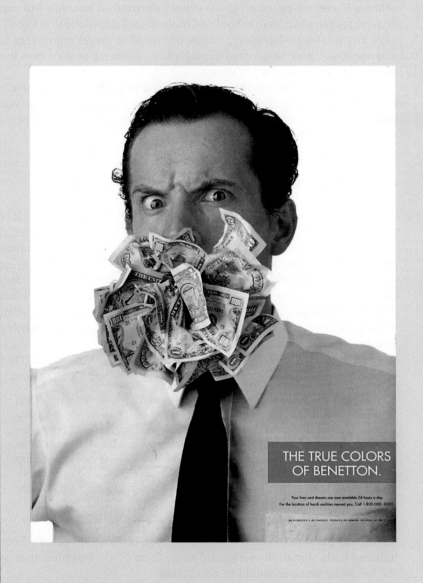

THE TRUE COLORS
OF BENETTON.

Your lives and dreams are now available 24 hours a day
For the location of harsh realities nearest you, Call 1-800-000-0000

Not Just Words

Like words, images and designs can also be claimed as intellectual property. As we explain in this chapter, you can download a photograph you find on the Web and use it, with appropriate documentation, in an academic paper. But you'd probably need permission from the copyright holder to use it online, even for an academic Web project.

Logos and other visual designs are similarly protected. The T-shirts and ball caps with your school's symbol and colors likely have a royalty cost built in, with the money going back to the institution. For commercial and artistic reasons, institutions and corporations protect their designs, logos, symbols, and signs.

How, then, can the *Onion, Saturday Night Live,* or Adbusters.org take familiar designs and logos and use them in their publications, shows, or Web sites? It's unlikely that Benetton approved a spoof (see facing page) suggesting that its famous series of socially conscious ads are just about making money. Yet there it is on Adbusters.org, along with dozens of other like-minded parodies.

The answer is in the word *parody*. The U.S. Supreme Court has decided that parody falls within fair-use provisions of copyright law and that satire is protected by the First Amendment's protection of free speech, at least when such a lampoon targets public figures. You can explore these decisions easily on the Web (search for "Parody" and "Supreme Court").

Working in a small group, create a parody of a familiar visual item or advertising campaign, perhaps beginning with an image from the Web. Be sure to take advantage of any skills people in your group may have with software such as Photoshop, which will enable you to change or manipulate images. Or use paper: cutting and pasting still works. Design a parody that makes a thoughtful point.

But is classical music in the United States really "in its death throes," as some critics of the music scene suggest (Platt)?

You might also paraphrase Platt's paragraph, putting his ideas entirely in your own words but giving him due credit:

A familiar story told by critics is that classical music faces a bleak future in the United States, with grasping soloists and unions bankrupting orchestras and classical works vanishing from radio and television, school curricula, and the labels of recording conglomerates. The public may not be able or willing to support all the talented musicians and composers we have today (Platt).

All of these sentences with citations would be keyed to a works-cited entry at the end of the paper that would look like the following in MLA style:

Platt, Russell. "New World Symphony." *The Nation*. The Nation, 3 Oct. 2005.
    Web. 15 Oct. 2009.

How might a citation go wrong? As we indicated, omitting either the quotation marks around a borrowed passage or an acknowledgment of the source is grounds for complaint. Neither of the following sentences provides enough information for a correct citation:

But is classical music in the United States really in its death throes, as some critics of the music scene suggest (Platt)?

But is classical music in the United States really "in its death throes," as some critics of the music scene suggest?

Just as faulty is a paraphrase such as the following, which borrows the words or ideas of the source too closely. It represents plagiarism, though it identifies the source from which almost all the ideas—and a good many words—are borrowed:

In "New World Symphony," Russell Platt observes that classical music is thought by many to be in bad shape in America. Its orchestras are being sucked dry by costly guest artists and insatiable unionized musicians, its place on TV and radio is shrinking, its stature is diminished, its role in education is largely ignored, and its big record contracts are declining too. The problem may also be that we have too many well-trained musicians who need employment, too many good composers going without jobs, too many concerts for a public that prefers *Desperate Housewives*.

Even the original observation at the end of the paragraph isn't enough to change the fact that the paraphrase is just Platt's original, lightly stirred.

Because the consequences of even unintentional plagiarism can be severe, it's important to understand how it can happen and how you can guard against it. In a January 2002 article published in *Time* magazine, historian Doris Kearns Goodwin explains how someone else's writing wound up unacknowledged in her book. The book in question, nine hundred pages long and with 3,500 footnotes, took Goodwin ten years to write.

A Doonesbury cartoon on intellectual property pokes fun at best-selling historian and presidential biographer Stephen Ambrose, who was found to have plagiarized passages from at least twelve authors in at least six of his books—and in his doctoral dissertation.

DOONESBURY   *BY GARRY TRUDEAU*

During these ten years, she says, she took most of her notes by hand, organized the notes into boxes, and—after the draft was completed—returned to her sources to check that all the material from them was correctly cited. "Somehow in this process," Goodwin claims, "a few books were not fully rechecked," and so she omitted some necessary quotation marks in material she didn't acknowledge. Reflecting back on this experience, Goodwin says that discovering such carelessness in her own work was troubling—so troubling that in the storm of criticism that ensued over the discovery of these failures to cite properly, she resigned from her position as a member of the Pulitzer Prize Committee.

Acknowledging Your Use of Sources

Proper acknowledgement of sources is crucial in academic writing. Check out Mack D. Mariani and Gordon J. Hewitt's extensive notes for an example of how to do it right.

LINK TO P. 941

The safest way to avoid charges of plagiarism is to acknowledge all of your sources, with the following three exceptions:

- common knowledge, which is a specific piece of information most readers will know (that Barack Obama won the 2008 presidential election, for instance)
- facts available from a wide variety of sources (that the Japanese bombed Pearl Harbor on December 7, 1941, for example)
- your own findings from field research (observations, interviews, experiments, or surveys you have conducted), which should be presented as your own

For all other source material, you should give full credit: place quotation marks around any quoted material, cite your sources according to the documentation style you're using, and include them in a list of references or works cited. Material to be credited includes all of the following:

- direct quotations
- facts that are not widely known
- arguable statements
- judgments, opinions, and claims that have been made by others
- images, statistics, charts, tables, graphs, or other illustrations that appear in any source
- collaboration—that is, the help provided by friends, colleagues, instructors, supervisors, or others

For more on using and documenting sources, see Chapters 19 and 20.

Using Copyrighted Internet Sources

If you've done any surfing on the Internet, you know that it opens the door to worldwide collaborations: you can contact individuals and groups around the globe and have access to whole libraries of information. As a result, writing (especially online writing) often is made up of a patchwork of materials that are woven from many sources. But when you gather information from Internet sources and use it in your own work, it's subject to the same rules that govern information gathered from other types of sources.

Even if the material does not include a copyright notice or symbol ("© 2009 by John J. Ruszkiewicz and Andrea A. Lunsford," for example), it's likely to be protected by copyright laws, and you may need to request permission to use part or all of it. Although they're currently in flux, "fair-use" legal precedents still allow writers to quote brief passages from published works without permission from the copyright holder if the use is for educational or personal, noncommercial reasons and if full

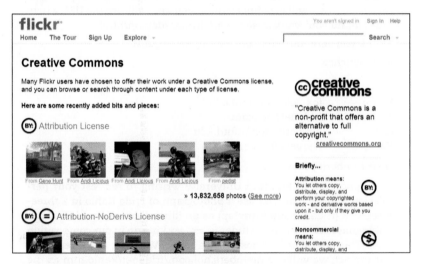

A growing number of works such as photographs, music, and video are published online under so-called Creative Commons license that often eliminates the need to request permission. These works—marked with a Creative Commons license at Flickr, for example—are made available to the public under this alternative to copyright, which grants blanket permission to reuse or remix work under certain terms if credit is given to the work's creator.

credit is given to the source. For personal communications (such as email) or for listserv postings, however, you should ask permission of the writer before you include any of his or her material in your own argument. For graphics, photos, or other images that you wish to reproduce in your text, you should also request permission from the creator or owner if the text is going to be disseminated beyond your classroom—especially if it's going to be published online.

Here are some examples of student requests for permission:

From:	sanchez.32@stanford.edu
To:	litman@mindspring.com
CC:	lunsford.2@stanford.edu
Subject:	Request for permission

Dear Professor Litman:

I am writing to request permission to quote from your essay "Copyright, Owners' Rights and Users' Privileges on the Internet: Implied Licences, Caching, Linking, Fair Use, and Sign-on Licences." I want to quote some of your work as part of an article I am writing for the *Stanford Daily* to explain the complex debates over ownership on the Internet and to argue that students at my school should be participating in these debates. I will give full credit to you and will cite the URL where I first found your work (msen.com/~litman/dayton/htm).

Thank you very much for considering my request.

Raul Sanchez

From:	fox.360@stanford.edu
To:	fridanet@aol.com
CC:	lunsford.2@stanford.edu
Subject:	Request for permission

Dear Kimberley Masters:

I am a student at Stanford University writing to request your permission to download and use a photograph of Frida Kahlo in a three-piece suit (fridanet/suit.htm#top) as an illustration in a project about Kahlo that I and two other students are working on in our composition class. This project will be posted on a school Web site. In the report on our project, we will cite members.aol.com/fridanet/kahlo.htm as the URL, unless you wish for us to use a different source.

Thank you very much for considering our request.

Jennifer Fox

CULTURAL CONTEXTS FOR ARGUMENT

Understanding Plagiarism

Not all cultures accept Western notions of plagiarism, which rest on a societal agreement that language can be owned by writers. Indeed, in many countries and in some communities within the United States, using the words of others is considered a sign of respect and an indication of knowledge—and attribution is not expected or required. In writing arguments in the United States, however, you should credit all materials except those that are common knowledge, that are available in a wide variety of sources, or that are your own findings from field research.

Acknowledging Collaboration

We've already noted the importance of acknowledging the inspirations and ideas you derive from talking with others. Such help counts as one form of collaboration, and you may also be involved in more formal kinds of collaborative work—preparing for a group presentation to a class, for example, or writing a group report. Writers generally acknowledge all participants in collaborative projects at the beginning of the presentation, report, or essay. In print texts, the acknowledgment is often placed in a footnote or brief prefatory note.

The seventh edition of the *MLA Handbook for Writers of Research Papers* (2009) calls attention to the growing importance of collaborative work and gives the following advice on how to deal with issues of assigning fair credit all around:

> Joint participation in research and writing is common and, in fact, encouraged in many courses and in many professions. It does not constitute plagiarism provided that credit is given for all contributions. One way to give credit, if roles were clearly demarcated or were unequal, is to state exactly who did what. Another way, especially if roles and contributions were merged and shared, is to acknowledge all concerned equally. Ask your instructor for advice if you are not certain how to acknowledge collaboration.

In a selection from the *Digital Youth Project,* the authors generously acknowledge the collaboration that went into their study. Note how often they introduce the contributions of individual researchers and the role that each individual played in creating the whole study.

LINK TO P. 686

RESPOND•

1. Not everyone agrees that intellectual material is property that should be protected. The slogan "information wants to be free" has been showing up in popular magazines and on the Internet, often with a call to readers to take action against protection such as data encryption and further extension of copyright.

   Using a Web search engine, look for pages where the phrase "free information" appears. Find several sites that make arguments in favor of free information, and analyze them in terms of their rhetorical appeals. What claims do the authors make? How do they appeal to their audience? What's the site's ethos, and how is it created? After you've read some arguments in favor of free information, return to this chapter's arguments about intellectual property. Which arguments do you find most persuasive? Why?

2. Although this text is concerned principally with ideas and their written expression, other forms of intellectual property are also legally protected. For example, scientific and technological developments are protectable under patent law, which differs in some significant ways from copyright law.

   Find the standards for protection under U.S. copyright law and U.S. patent law. You might begin by visiting the U.S. copyright Web site (http://copyright.gov). Then imagine that you're the president of a small, high-tech corporation and are trying to inform your employees of the legal protections available to them and their work. Write a paragraph or two explaining the differences between copyright and patent, and suggest a policy that balances employees' rights to intellectual property with the business's needs to develop new products.

3. Define *plagiarism* in your own terms, making your definition as clear and explicit as possible. Then compare your definition with those of two or three other classmates, and write a brief report on the similarities and differences you noted in the definitions. You might research terms such as *plagiarism*, *academic honesty*, and *academic integrity* on the Web.

4. Spend fifteen or twenty minutes jotting down your ideas about intellectual property and plagiarism. Where do you stand, for example, on the issue of music file sharing? On downloading movies free of charge? Do you think these forms of intellectual property should be protected under copyright law? How do you define your own intellectual property, and in what ways and under what conditions are you willing to share it? Finally, come up with your own definition of *academic integrity*.

19
Evaluating and Using Sources

As many examples in this text have shown, the effectiveness of an argument often depends on the quality of the sources that support or prove it. You'll need to carefully evaluate and assess all your sources, including those that you gather in libraries, from other print sources, in online searches, or in your own field research.

Remember that different sources can contribute in different ways to your work. In most cases, you'll be looking for reliable sources that provide accurate information or that clearly and persuasively express opinions that might serve as evidence for a case you're making. At other times, you may be looking for material that expresses ideas or attitudes—how people are thinking and feeling at a given time. You might need to use a graphic image, a sample of avant-garde music, or a controversial YouTube clip that doesn't fit neatly into categories such as "reliable" or "accurate" yet is central to your argument. With any and all such sources and evidence, your goals are to be as knowledgeable about them and as

When might a tattle-tale actually be a reliable source—and how would you know?

"I'm *not* being a tattle-tale! — I'm being a reliable source!"

© www.cartoonstock.com

responsible in their use as you can be and to share honestly what you learn about them with readers.

You don't want to be naïve in your use of any source material. Most of the evidence that is used in arguments on public issues—even material from influential and well-known sources—comes with considerable baggage. Scientists and humanists alike have axes to grind, corporations have products to sell, bureaucracies have power to maintain, politicians have policies and candidacies to promote, journalists have reputations to make, media owners and editors have readers, listeners, viewers, and advertisers to attract and to avoid offending. All of these groups produce and use information to their own benefit, and it's not (usually) a bad thing that they do so. You just have to be aware that when you take information from a given source, it will often carry with it at least some of the enthusiasms, assumptions, and biases (conscious or not) of the people who produce and disseminate it. Teachers and librarians are not exempted from this caution.

To correct for these biases, draw on as many reliable sources as you can manage when you're preparing to write. You shouldn't assume that

CNN's Nancy Grace, a former prosecutor, has been accused of allowing her pro-prosecution bias to influence her commentary.

all arguments are equally good or that all the sides in a controversy can be supported by the same weight of evidence and good reasons. But you want to avoid treading so narrowly among sources that you miss essential issues and perspectives. That's easy to do when you read only sources that agree with you or when the sources that you read all seem to carry the same message.

Especially when writing on political subjects, you should be aware that the sources you're reading or viewing almost always support particular beliefs and goals. That fact has been made apparent in recent years by bloggers—from all parts of the political spectrum—who put the traditional news media under daily scrutiny, exposing errors, biases, and omissions. Even so, political bloggers (mostly amateur journalists, although many are professionals in their own fields) have their own agendas, but unlike most writers in mainstream news outlets, they often admit their biases openly and frankly.

Evaluating Sources

Print Sources

Since you want information to be reliable and persuasive, it pays to evaluate each potential source thoroughly. The following principles can help you evaluate print sources:

- *Relevance.* Begin by asking what a particular source will add to your argument and how closely the source is related to your argumentative claim. For a book, the table of contents and the index may help you decide. For an article, look for an abstract that summarizes the contents. If you can't think of a good reason for using the source, set it aside. You can almost certainly find something better.

- *Credentials of the author.* Sometimes the author's credentials are set forth in an article, in a book, or on a Web site, so be sure to look for them. Is the author an expert on the topic? To find out, you can gather information about the person on the Internet using a search engine like Yahoo! or Ask.com. Another way to learn about the credibility of an author is to search Google Groups for postings that mention the author or to check the Citation Index to find out how others refer to this author. If you see your source cited by other sources you're using, look at how they cite it and what they say about it that could provide clues to the author's credibility.

- *Stance of the author.* What's the author's position on the issue(s) involved, and how does this stance influence the information in the source? Does the author's stance support or challenge your own views?

- *Credentials of the publisher or sponsor.* If your source is from a newspaper, is it a major one (such as the *Wall Street Journal* or the *Washington Post*) that has historical credentials in reporting, or is it a tabloid? Is it a popular magazine like *O: The Oprah Magazine* or a journal sponsored by a professional group, such as the *Journal of the American Medical Association*? If your source is a book, is the publisher one you recognize or has its own Web site?

- *Stance of the publisher or sponsor.* Sometimes this stance will be obvious: a magazine called *Save the Planet!* will take a pro-environmental stance, whereas one called *America First!* will probably take a conservative stance. But other times, you need to read carefully between the lines to identify particular positions and see how the stance affects the message the source presents. Start by asking what the source's goals are: what does the publisher or sponsoring group want to make happen?

- *Currency.* Check the date of publication of every book and article. Recent sources are often more useful than older ones, particularly in the sciences. However, in some fields (such as history and literature), the most authoritative works are often the older ones.

- *Accuracy.* Check to see whether the author cites any sources for the information or opinions in the article and, if so, how credible and current they are.

Note the differences between the cover of *Popular Science* and that of a physics journal.

- *Level of specialization.* General sources can be helpful as you begin your research, but later in the project you may need the authority or currency of more specialized sources. Keep in mind that highly specialized works on your topic may be difficult for your audience to understand.

- *Audience.* Was the source written for a general readership? For specialists? For advocates or opponents?

- *Length.* Is the source long enough to provide adequate details in support of your claim?

- *Availability.* Do you have access to the source? If it isn't readily accessible, your time might be better spent looking elsewhere.

- *Omissions.* What's missing or omitted from the source? Might such exclusions affect whether or how you can use the source as evidence?

Electronic Sources

You'll probably find working on the Internet both exciting and frustrating, for even though this tool is enormously useful, it contains information of widely varying quality. Because it is a source that's mostly open and unregulated, careful researchers look for corroboration before accepting evidence they find online, especially if it comes from a site whose sponsor's identity is unclear.

In such an environment, you must be the judge of the accuracy and trustworthiness of particular electronic sources. In making these judgments, you can rely on the same criteria and careful thinking that you use to assess print sources. In addition, you may find the following questions helpful in evaluating online sources:

- Who has posted the document or message or created the site? An individual? An interest group? A company? A government agency? Does the URL offer any clues? Note especially the final suffix in a domain name—*.com* (commercial), *.org* (nonprofit organization), *.edu* (educational institution), *.gov* (government agency), *.mil* (military), or *.net* (network). Also note the geographical domains that indicate country of origin—as in *.ca* (Canada) or *.ar* (Argentina). The homepage or first page of a site should tell you something about the sponsorship of the source, letting you know who can be held accountable for its information. (You may need to click on an "About Us" button.) Finally, links may help you learn how credible and useful the source is. Click on some links to see if they lead to legitimate and helpful sites.

- What can you determine about the credibility of the author or sponsor? Can the information in the document or site be verified in other sources? How accurate and complete is it? On a blog, for example, look for a link that identifies the creator of the site (some blogs are managed by multiple authors). Also review the links the blog offers. They'll often help you understand both the perspective of the site and its purposes.

- Who can be held accountable for the information in the document or site? How well and thoroughly does it credit its own sources?

- How current is the document or site? Be especially cautious of undated materials. Most reliable sites are updated regularly.

- What perspectives are represented? If only one perspective is represented, how can you balance or expand this point of view? Is it a straightforward presentation, or could it be a parody or satire?

Several years ago, the Stanford Persuasive Technology Lab argued that Google News might become the "most credible Web site of them all." The lab listed twenty-five reasons in support of this conclusion, including the timeliness of the information, the lack of a single viewpoint or ideology, and the ad-free policy. Since then, however, liberals have charged that Google News gives more coverage to conservative stories than it should, and conservatives have claimed that it excludes some important right-leaning sources. And yet computer algorithms, not human editors, select the stories in Google News. For readers who are sensitive to media perspectives, even machines have biases. But humans do create the machines and the algorithms.

Field Research

If you've conducted experiments, surveys, interviews, observations, or any other field research in developing and supporting an argument, make sure to review your results with a critical eye. The following questions can help you evaluate your own field research:

- Have you rechecked all data and all conclusions to make sure they're accurate and warranted?

- Have you identified the exact time, place, and participants in all your field research?

- Have you made clear what part you played in the research and how, if at all, your role could have influenced the results or findings?

- If your research involved other people, have you gotten their permission to use their words or other materials in your argument? Have you asked whether you can use their names or whether the names should be kept confidential?

In the Afterword to her ethnographic study of a family trying to balance home and office, Alesia Montgomery reviews the process and the results of her field research with a critical eye.

LINK TO P. 1008

Using Sources

As you locate, examine, and evaluate sources in support of an argument, remember to keep a careful record of where you've found them. For print sources, you should keep a working bibliography either on your computer or in a notebook you can carry with you. For each book, write the name of the author, the title of the book, the city of publication, the publisher, the date of publication, and the place that you found it (the section of the library, for example, and the call number for the book). For each article, write the name of the author, the title of the article, the title of the periodical, and the volume, issue, and exact page numbers. Include any other information you may later need in preparing a works-cited list or references list.

For electronic sources, keep a careful record of the information you'll need in a works-cited list or references list. Write the author and title information, the name of the database or other online site where you found the source, the full electronic address (URL), the date the document was first produced, the date it was published on the Web or most recently updated, and the date you accessed and examined it. The simplest way to ensure that you have this information is to print a copy of the source, highlight source information, and write down any other pertinent information.

Signal Words and Introductions

Because your sources are crucial to the success of your arguments, you need to introduce them carefully to your readers. Doing so usually calls for using a signal phrase of some kind in the sentence to introduce the source. Typically (but not always), the signal phrase precedes the quotation:

> According to noted primatologist Jane Goodall, the more we learn about the nature of nonhuman animals, the more ethical questions we face about their use in the service of humans.

> The more we learn about the nature of nonhuman animals, the more ethical questions we face about their use in the service of humans, according to noted primatologist Jane Goodall.

> The more we learn about the nature of nonhuman animals, according to noted primatologist Jane Goodall, the more ethical questions we face about their use in the service of humans.

In each of these sentences, the signal phrase tells readers that you're drawing on the work of a person named Jane Goodall and that this person is a "noted primatologist."

Now look at an example that uses a quotation from a source in more than one sentence:

> In *Job Shift*, consultant William Bridges worries about "dejobbing and about what a future shaped by it is going to be like." Even more worrisome, Bridges argues, is

the possibility that "the sense of craft and of professional vocation . . . will break down under the need to earn a fee" (228).

The signal verbs "worries" and "argues" add a sense of urgency to the message Bridges offers and suggest that the writer either agrees with—or is neutral about—Bridges's points. Other signal verbs have a more negative slant, indicating that the point being introduced in the quotation is open to debate and that others (including the writer) might disagree with it. If the writer of the passage above had said, for instance, that Bridges "unreasonably contends" or that he "fantasizes," these signal verbs would carry quite different connotations from those associated with "argues."

In some cases, a signal verb may require more complex phrasing to get the writer's full meaning across:

> Bridges recognizes the dangers of changes in work yet refuses to be overcome by them: "The real issue is not how to stop the change but how to provide the necessary knowledge and skills to equip people to operate successfully in this New World" (229).

As these examples illustrate, the signal verb is important because it allows you to characterize the author's or source's viewpoint as well as your own—so choose these verbs with care.

Some Frequently Used Signal Verbs

acknowledges	claims	emphasizes	remarks
admits	concludes	expresses	replies
advises	concurs	hypothesizes	reports
agrees	confirms	interprets	responds
allows	criticizes	lists	reveals
argues	declares	objects	states
asserts	disagrees	observes	suggests
believes	discusses	offers	thinks
charges	disputes	opposes	writes

Quotations

To support your argumentative claims, you'll want to quote (that is, to reproduce an author's precise words) in at least three kinds of situations—when the wording is so memorable or expresses a point so well

Sarah Karnasiewicz depends heavily on quotations in her article "The Campus Crusade for Guys." How many different signal verbs can you find? How do these choices help shape her argument?

LINK TO P. 909

JACQUES STEINBERG
ATTACK DOG

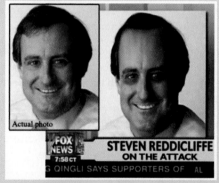

STEVEN REDDICLIFFE
ON THE ATTACK

Decontamination Vehicle

Security

10 Nov 2002

Chemical Munitions Bunker

Delivery Service Truck

SUV

10 Nov 2002

International House of Pancakes

Not Just Words

What's wrong with these pictures? During a segment of *Fox & Friends*, a television news and opinion show, hosts Steve Doocy and Brian Kilmeade called *New York Times* reporter Jacques Steinberg and editor Steven Reddicliffe "attack dogs" and displayed photos of the two men. When Media Matters for America (http://mediamatters.org/index), the progressive research and information Web site, took a closer look, it found that the photos of the two journalists seemed to have been digitally altered. Take a look at the photos: What differences do you see between the before and after pictures? How do they affect your perception of the reporters? How could you determine how the photos were altered and who was responsible for doing so? To what degree does the digital alteration undermine the authority of *Fox & Friends* as a source? How trustworthy do you find Media Matters for America to be?

Of course, anyone with a computer and Photoshop software can alter images or create fabrications. But as filmmaker Errol Morris demonstrates in an argument entitled "Photography as a Weapon," sometimes you don't even need to alter an image: all you have to do is change the caption. As an example, Morris shows grainy photos displayed in 2002 as part of the Bush administration's "proof" that Iraq had weapons of mass destruction. Different captions, he says, would have been just as credible as the "real" ones since viewers couldn't really tell what they were looking at anyway.

Morris sums up by asking whether photographs "provide illustration of a text or an idea of evidence of some underlying reality or both? And if they are evidence, don't we have to know that the evidence is *reliable*, that it can be trusted?" These are questions you should ask yourself about any photographs you want to use in your writing.

that you cannot improve it or shorten it without weakening it, when the author is a respected authority whose opinion supports your own ideas particularly well, and when an author challenges or disagrees with others in the field.

Direct quotations (such as a memorable phrase in your introduction or a detailed eyewitness account) can be effective in capturing your readers' attention. In an argument, quotations from respected authorities can help build your ethos as someone who has sought out experts in the field. Finally, carefully chosen quotations can broaden the appeal of your argument by drawing on emotion as well as logic, appealing to the reader's mind and heart. A student who is writing on the ethical issues of bullfighting, for example, might introduce an argument that bullfighting is not a sport by quoting Ernest Hemingway's comment that "the formal bull-fight is a tragedy, not a sport, and the bull is certain to be killed" and might accompany the quotation with an image such as the one below.

Stanley Fish incorporates numerous quotations from David Horowitz's Academic Bill of Rights as a way of arguing against Horowitz's position. Fish is careful to quote accurately so that he can then explain how his views on intellectual diversity differ from Horowitz's.

LINK TO P. 929

A tragedy, not a sport?

The following guidelines can help you make sure that you quote accurately:

- If the quotation extends over more than one page in the original source, note the placement of page breaks in case you decide to use only part of the quotation in your argument.
- Label the quotation with a note that tells you where and how you think you'll use it.
- Make sure you have all the information necessary to create an in-text citation as well as an item in your works-cited list or references list.
- When using a quotation in your argument, introduce the author(s) of the quotation, and follow the quotation with commentary of your own that points out the significance of the quotation.
- Copy quotations carefully, reproducing the punctuation, capitalization, and spelling exactly as they are in the original.
- Enclose the quotation in quotation marks (don't rely on your memory to distinguish your own words from those of your source). If in doubt, recheck all quotations for accuracy.
- Use square brackets if you introduce words of your own into the quotation or make changes to it ("And [more] brain research isn't going to define further the matter of 'mind'").
- Use ellipsis marks if you omit material ("And brain research isn't going to define . . . the matter of 'mind'").
- If you're quoting a short passage (four lines or less in MLA style; forty words or less in APA style), it should be worked into your text, enclosed by quotation marks. Long quotations should be set off from the regular text. Begin such a quotation on a new line, indenting every line one inch or ten spaces (MLA) or a half inch or five to seven spaces (APA). Set-off quotations do not need to be enclosed in quotation marks.

Paraphrases

Paraphrases involve putting an author's material (including major and minor points, usually in the order they're presented in the original) into your own words and sentence structures. Here are guidelines that can help you paraphrase accurately:

- When using a paraphrase in your argument, identify the source of the paraphrase, and comment on its significance.

- Collect all the information necessary to create an in-text citation as well as an item in your works-cited list or references list. For online sources without page numbers, record the paragraph, screen, or other section number(s) if indicated.
- If you're paraphrasing material that extends over more than one page in the original source, note the placement of page breaks in case you decide to use only part of the paraphrase in your argument.
- Label the paraphrase with a note suggesting where and how you intend to use it in your argument.
- Include all main points and any important details from the original source, in the same order in which the author presents them.
- Leave out your own comments, elaborations, or reactions.
- State the meaning in your own words and sentence structures. If you want to include especially memorable or powerful language from the original source, enclose it in quotation marks.
- Recheck to make sure that the words and sentence structures are your own and that they express the author's meaning accurately.

Summaries

A summary is a significantly shortened version of a passage or a whole chapter of a work that captures the main ideas in your own words. Unlike a paraphrase, a summary uses just enough information to record the points you want to emphasize. Summaries can be extremely valuable in supporting arguments. Here are some guidelines to help you prepare accurate and helpful summaries:

Though she is not writing an academic argument, Tamar Lewin effectively summarizes a lengthy and complex study in her article on teenagers' online socializing. Compare her summary to the excerpt from the study itself, which follows Lewin's article.

············· LINK TO P. 676

- When using a summary in an argument, identify the source, and add your own comments about why the material in the summary is significant for the argument that you're making.
- Collect all the information necessary to create an in-text citation as well as an item in your works-cited list or references list. For online sources without page numbers, record the paragraph, screen, or other section number(s) if available.
- If you're summarizing material that extends over more than one page, indicate page breaks in case you decide to use only part of the summary in your argument.

- Label the summary with a note that suggests where and how you intend to use it in your argument.

- Include just enough information to recount the main points you want to cite. A summary is usually much shorter than the original.

- Use your own words. If you include any language from the original, enclose it in quotation marks.

- Recheck to make sure that you've captured the author's meaning accurately and that the wording is entirely your own.

CULTURAL CONTEXTS FOR ARGUMENT

Identifying Sources

Although some language communities and cultures expect audiences to recognize the sources of important documents and texts, thereby eliminating the need to cite them directly, conventions for writing in North America call for careful attribution of any quoted, paraphrased, or summarized material. When in doubt, explicitly identify your sources.

Visuals

If a picture is worth a thousand words, then using pictures calls for caution: one picture might overwhelm or undermine the message you're trying to send in your argument. However, as you've seen in Chapter 14, visuals can powerfully affect audiences and help them to understand or accept your arguments. In choosing visuals to include in your argument, each one needs to make a strong contribution to your message and be appropriate and fair to your subject or topic and your audience.

When you use visuals in your written arguments, treat them as you would any other sources you integrate into your text. Like quotations, paraphrases, and summaries, visuals need to be introduced and commented on in some way. In addition, label (as "Figure" or as "Table") and number ("Figure 1," "Figure 2," and so on) all visuals, provide a caption that includes source information and describes the visual, and cite the source in your references list or works-cited list. Even if you create a visual (such as a bar graph) by using information from a source (the results, say, of a Gallup Poll), you must cite the source. If you use a photograph you took yourself, cite it as a personal photograph.

Below is a visual that accompanied the introduction to an article entitled "An S.U.V. Traffic Jam" that appeared in the business section of the *New York Times* on August 13, 2008. Note that the caption indicates the way the visual is related to the argument (the bunch of car keys hanging from a salesman's neck indicates the many sport-utility vehicles that are sitting on sales lots throughout the country) and that a credit line identifies the source of the visual (this photograph was taken by Fabrizio Costantini for the *Times*). If you were going to use this as the first visual in an essay, you would include the source, describe the image in relationship to your topic, and label it "Figure 1." As long as you use this image only in a print text for your instructor and classmates, you're allowed fair use of it. Before you can post your argument and this image on the Web or otherwise publish the image for a wider audience, however, you need to request permission from the copyright owner (see Chapter 18, pp. 545–46).

Fabrizio Costantini for The New York Times
Kevin Whims, an account representative for Dealer Specialties shown at Matthews-Hargreaves Chevrolet in Royal Oak, Mich., had more ignition keys than customers Friday.

RESPOND●

1. Select one of the essays at the end of Chapters 8 to 12. Write a brief summary of the essay that includes both direct quotations and paraphrases. Be careful to attribute the ideas properly, even when you paraphrase, and to use signal phrases to introduce quotations. Then trade summaries with a partner, comparing the passages you selected to quote and paraphrase and the signal phrases you used to introduce them. How do your choices create an ethos for the original author that differs from the one your partner has created? How do the signal phrases shape a reader's sense of the author's position? Which summary best represents the author's argument? Why?

2. Return to the Internet sites you found in exercise 1 of Chapter 18 (p. 548) that discuss free information. Using this chapter's criteria for evaluating electronic sources, judge each of those sites. Select three that you think are most trustworthy, and write a paragraph summarizing their arguments and recommending them to an audience unfamiliar with the debate.

3. Choose a news Web site that you have visited. Then, using the guidelines discussed in this chapter, spend some time evaluating its credibility. You might begin by comparing it with Google News or another site that has a reputation for being reliable.

20
Documenting Sources

What does documenting sources have to do with argument? First, the sources that a writer chooses form part of any argument, showing that he or she has done some homework, knows what others have said about the topic, and understands how to use these items as support for a claim. Similarly, the list of works cited or references makes a statement, saying, "Look at how thoroughly this essay has been researched" or "Note how up-to-date I am!"

Even the choice of documentation style makes an argument in a subtle way. You'll note in the instructions that follow, for example, that the Modern Language Association (MLA) style requires putting the date of publication of a print source at or near the end of a works-cited list entry, whereas the American Psychological Association (APA) style places that date near the beginning of a reference-list citation. Pay attention to such fine points of documentation style, always asking what these choices suggest about the values of scholars and researchers who use a particular system of documentation.

MLA Style

Documentation styles vary from discipline to discipline, with one format favored in the social sciences and another in the natural sciences, for example. Widely used in the humanities, MLA style is fully described in the *MLA Handbook for Writers of Research Papers* (7th edition, 2009). In this discussion, we provide guidelines drawn from the *MLA Handbook* for in-text citations, notes, and entries in the list of works cited.

In-Text Citations

MLA style calls for in-text citations in the body of an argument to document sources of quotations, paraphrases, summaries, and so on. For in-text citations, use a signal phrase to introduce the material, often with the author's name *(As LaDoris Cordell explains, . . .)*. Keep an in-text citation short, but include enough information for readers to locate the source in the list of works cited. Place the parenthetical citation as near to the relevant material as possible without disrupting the flow of the sentence, as in the following examples.

1. Author Named in a Signal Phrase

Ordinarily, use the author's name in a signal phrase to introduce the material, and cite the page number(s) in parentheses.

Loomba argues that Caliban's "political colour" is black, given his stage representations, which have varied from animalistic to a kind of missing link (143).

2. Author Named in Parentheses

When you don't mention the author in a signal phrase, include the author's last name before the page number(s) in the parentheses.

Oil from shale in the western states, if it could be extracted, would be equivalent to six hundred billion barrels, more than all the crude so far produced in the world (McPhee 413).

3. Two or Three Authors

Use all authors' last names.

Gortner, Hebrun, and Nicolson maintain that "opinion leaders" influence other people in an organization because they are respected, not because they hold high positions (175).

4. Four or More Authors

The MLA allows you to use all authors' last names or to use only the first author's name with *et al.* (in regular type, not italicized). Although either format is acceptable when applied consistently throughout a paper, in an argument it is better to name all authors who contributed to the work.

> Similarly, as Goldberger, Tarule, Clinchy, and Belenky note, their new book builds on their collaborative experiences (xii).

5. Organization as Author

Give the full name of a corporate author if it's brief or a shortened form if it's long.

> In fact, one of the leading foundations in the field of higher education supports the recent proposals for community-run public schools (Carnegie Corporation 45).

6. Unknown Author

Use the full title of the work if it's brief or a shortened form if it's long.

> "Hype," by one analysis, is "an artificially engendered atmosphere of hysteria" ("Today's Marketplace" 51).

7. Author of Two or More Works

When you use two or more works by the same author, include the title of the work or a shortened version of it in the citation.

> Gardner presents readers with their own silliness through his description of a "pointless, ridiculous monster, crouched in the shadows, stinking of dead men, murdered children, and martyred cows" (*Grendel* 2).

8. Authors with the Same Last Name

When you use works by two or more authors with the same last name, include each author's first initial in the in-text citation.

> Father Divine's teachings focused on eternal life, salvation, and socioeconomic progress (R. Washington 17).

9. Multivolume Work

Note the volume number first and then the page number(s), with a colon and one space between them.

> Aristotle's "On Plants" is now available in a new translation edited by Barnes (2: 1252).

10. Literary Work

Because literary works are often available in many different editions, you need to include enough information for readers to locate the passage in any edition. For a prose work such as a novel or play, first cite the page number from the edition you used, followed by a semicolon; then indicate the part or chapter number (114; ch. 3) or act or scene in a play (42; sc. 2).

> In *The Madonnas of Leningrad*, Marina says "she could see into the future" (7; ch. 1).

For a poem, cite the stanza and line numbers. If the poem has only line numbers, use the word *line(s)* in the first reference (lines 33–34) and the number(s) alone in subsequent references.

> On dying, Whitman speculates "All that goes onward and outward, nothing collapses, / And to die is different from what any one supposed, and luckier" (6.129-30).

For a verse play, omit the page number, and give only the act, scene, and line numbers, separated by periods.

> Before he takes his own life, Othello says he is "one that loved not wisely but too well" (5.2.348).

> As *Macbeth* begins, the witches greet Banquo as "Lesser than Macbeth, and greater" (1.3.65).

11. Works in an Anthology

For an essay, short story, or other short work within an anthology, use the name of the author of the work, not the editor of the anthology; but use the page number(s) from the anthology.

> In the end, if the black artist accepts any duties at all, that duty is to express the beauty of blackness (Hughes 1271).

12. Sacred Text

To cite a sacred text, such as the Qur'an or the Bible, give the title of the edition you used, the book, and the chapter and verse (or their equivalent), separated by a period. In your text, spell out the names of books. In a parenthetical reference, use an abbreviation for books with names of five or more letters (for example, *Gen.* for Genesis).

> He ignored the admonition "Pride goes before destruction, and a haughty spirit before a fall" (*New Oxford Annotated Bible,* Prov. 16.18).

13. Indirect Source

Use the abbreviation *qtd. in* to indicate that what you're quoting or paraphrasing is quoted (as part of a conversation, interview, letter, or excerpt) in the source you're using.

> As Catherine Belsey states, "to speak is to have access to the language which defines, delimits and locates power" (qtd. in Bartels 453).

14. Two or More Sources in the Same Citation

Separate the information for each source with a semicolon.

> Adefunmi was able to patch up the subsequent holes left in worship by substituting various Yoruba, Dahomean, or Fon customs made available to him through research (Brandon 115-17; Hunt 27).

15. Entire Work or One-Page Article

Include the citation in the text without any page numbers or parentheses.

> The relationship between revolutionary innocence and the preservation of an oppressive postrevolutionary regime is one theme Milan Kundera explores in *The Book of Laughter and Forgetting.*

16. Work without Page Numbers

If the work isn't numbered by page but has numbered sections, parts, or paragraphs, include the name and number(s) of the section(s) you're citing. (For *paragraphs*, use the abbreviation *par.* or *pars.*; for *section*, use *sec.*; for *part*, use *pt.*)

> Zora Neale Hurston is one of the great anthropologists of the twentieth century, according to Kip Hinton (par. 2).

17. Electronic or Nonprint Source

Give enough information in a signal phrase or parenthetical citation for readers to locate the source in the list of works cited. Usually give the author or title under which you list the source.

> In his film version of *Hamlet*, Zeffirelli highlights the sexual tension between the prince and his mother.

> Describing children's language acquisition, Pinker explains that "what's innate about language is just a way of paying attention to parental speech" (Johnson, sec. 1).

Explanatory and Bibliographic Notes

The MLA recommends using explanatory notes for information or commentary that doesn't readily fit into your text but is needed for clarification, further explanation, or justification. In addition, the MLA allows bibliographic notes for citing several sources for one point and for offering thanks to, information about, or evaluation of a source. Use a superscript number in your text at the end of a sentence to refer readers to the notes, which usually appear as endnotes (with the heading *Notes*, not underlined or italicized) on a separate page before the list of works cited. Indent the first line of each note five spaces, and double-space all entries.

TEXT WITH SUPERSCRIPT INDICATING A NOTE

> Stewart emphasizes the existence of social contacts in Hawthorne's life so that the audience will accept a different Hawthorne, one more attuned to modern times than the figure in Woodberry.[3]

NOTE

> [3] Woodberry does, however, show that Hawthorne was often unsociable. He emphasizes the seclusion of Hawthorne's mother, who separated herself from her family after the death of her husband, often even taking meals alone (28). Woodberry seems to imply that Mrs. Hawthorne's isolation rubbed off on her son.

List of Works Cited

A list of works cited is an alphabetical listing of the sources you cite in your essay. The list appears on a separate page at the end of your argument, after any notes, with the heading *Works Cited* centered an inch from the top of the page; don't underline or italicize it or enclose it in quotation marks. Double-space between the heading and the first entry, and double-space the entire list. (If you're asked to list everything you've read as background—not just the sources you cite—call the list *Works Consulted*.) The first line of each entry should align on the left; subsequent lines indent one-half inch or five spaces. See p. 585 for a sample works-cited page.

BOOKS

The basic information for a book includes four elements, each followed by a period:

- the author's name, last name first
- the title and subtitle, italicized
- the publication information, including the city, a shortened form of the publisher's name (such as Harvard UP), and the publication date
- the medium of publication (*Print*)

For a book with multiple authors, only the first author's name is inverted.

1. One Author

Castle, Terry. *Boss Ladies, Watch Out: Essays on Women, Sex, and Writing*. New York: Routledge, 2002. Print.

2. Two or More Authors

Jacobson, Sid, and Ernie Colón. *The 9/11 Report: A Graphic Adaptation*. New York: Hill, 2006. Print.

3. Organization as Author

American Horticultural Society. *The Fully Illustrated Plant-by-Plant Manual of Practical Techniques*. New York: American Horticultural Society and DK Publishing, 1999. Print.

4. Unknown Author

National Geographic Atlas of the World. New York: National Geographic, 1999. Print.

5. Two or More Books by the Same Author

List the works alphabetically by title. Use three hyphens for the author's name for the second and subsequent works by that author.

Lorde, Audre. *A Burst of Light.* Ithaca: Firebrand, 1988. Print.

---. *Sister Outsider.* Trumansburg: Crossing, 1984. Print.

6. Editor

Rorty, Amelie Oksenberg, ed. *Essays on Aristotle's Poetics.* Princeton: Princeton UP, 1992. Print.

7. Author and Editor

Shakespeare, William. *The Tempest.* Ed. Frank Kermode. London: Routledge, 1994. Print.

8. Selection in an Anthology or Chapter in an Edited Book

List the author(s) of the selection or chapter; its title; the title of the book in which the selection or chapter appears; *Ed.* and the name(s) of the editor(s); the publication information; and the inclusive page numbers of the selection or chapter.

Brown, Paul. "'This thing of darkness I acknowledge mine': *The Tempest* and the Discourse of Colonialism." *Political Shakespeare: Essays in Cultural Materialism.* Ed. Jonathan Dillimore and Alan Sinfield. Ithaca: Cornell UP, 1985. 48–71. Print.

9. Two or More Works from the Same Anthology

Include the anthology itself in the list of works cited.

Gates, Henry Louis, Jr., and Nellie McKay, eds. *The Norton Anthology of African American Literature.* New York: Norton, 1997. Print.

Then list each selection separately by its author and title, followed by a cross-reference to the anthology.

Karenga, Maulana. "Black Art: Mute Matter Given Force and Function." Gates and McKay 1973–77.

Neal, Larry. "The Black Arts Movement." Gates and McKay 1960–72.

10. Translation

Hietamies, Laila. *Red Moon over White Sea.* Trans. Borje Vahamaki. Beaverton, ON: Aspasia, 2000. Print.

11. Edition Other Than the First

Lunsford, Andrea A., and John J. Ruszkiewicz, and Keith Walters. *Everything's an Argument with Readings.* 5th ed. Boston: Bedford, 2010. Print.

12. One Volume of a Multivolume Work

Byron, Lord George. *Byron's Letters and Journals.* Ed. Leslie A. Marchand. Vol. 2. London: Murray, 1973–82. Print. 12 vols.

13. Two or More Volumes of a Multivolume Work

Byron, Lord George. *Byron's Letters and Journals.* Ed. Leslie A. Marchand. 12 vols. London: Murray, 1973–82. Print.

14. Preface, Foreword, Introduction, or Afterword

Kean, Thomas H., and Lee H. Hamilton. Foreword. *The 9/11 Report: A Graphic Adaptation.* By Sid Jacobson and Ernie Colón. New York: Hill, 2006. ix-x. Print.

15. Article in a Reference Work

Kettering, Alison McNeil. "Art Nouveau." *World Book Encyclopedia.* 2002 ed. Print.

16. Book That Is Part of a Series

Include the series title and number after the publication information.

Moss, Beverly J. *A Community Text Arises.* Cresskill: Hampton, 2003. Print. Language and Social Processes Ser. 8.

17. Republication

Scott, Walter. *Kenilworth.* 1821. New York: Dodd, 1996. Print.

18. Government Document

United States. Cong. House Committee on the Judiciary. *Impeachment of the President.* 40th Cong., 1st sess. H. Rept. 7. Washington: GPO, 1867. Print.

19. Pamphlet

An Answer to the President's Message to the Fiftieth Congress. Philadelphia: Manufacturer's Club of Philadelphia, 1887. Print.

20. Published Proceedings of a Conference

Edwards, Ron, ed. *Proceedings of the Third National Folklore Conference.* 26-27 Nov. 1988. Canberra, Austral.: Australian Folk Trust, 1988. Print.

21. Title within a Title

Tauernier-Courbin, Jacqueline. *Ernest Hemingway's* A Moveable Feast: *The Making of a Myth.* Boston: Northeastern UP, 1991. Print.

PERIODICALS

The basic entry for a periodical includes four elements, each followed by a period:

- the author's name, last name first
- the article title, in quotation marks
- the publication information, including the periodical title (italicized), the volume and issue numbers (if any), the date of publication, and the page number(s)
- the medium of publication (*Print*)

For works with multiple authors, only the first author's name is inverted. Note that the period following the article title goes inside the closing quotation mark. Finally, note that the MLA omits *the* in titles such as *The New Yorker*.

22. Article in a Journal

Give the issue number, if available.

Anderson, Virginia. "'The Perfect Enemy': Clinton, the Contradictions of Capitalism, and Slaying the Sin Within." *Rhetoric Review* 21 (2002): 384-400. Print.

Radavich, David. "Man among Men: David Mamet's Homosocial Order." *American Drama* 1.1 (1991): 46-66. Print.

23. Article That Skips Pages

Seabrook, John. "Renaissance Pears." *New Yorker* 5 Sept. 2005: 102+. Print.

24. Article in a Monthly Magazine

Wallraff, Barbara. "Word Count." *Atlantic* Nov. 2002: 144-45. Print.

25. Article in a Weekly Magazine

Reed, Julia. "Hope in the Ruins." *Newsweek* 12 Sept. 2005: 58-59. Print.

26. Article in a Newspaper

Friend, Tim. "Scientists Map the Mouse Genome." *USA Today* 2 Dec. 2002: A1. Print.

27. Editorial or Letter to the Editor

Posner, Alan. "Colin Powell's Regret." Editorial. *New York Times* 9 Sept. 2005: A20. Print.

28. Unsigned Article

"Court Rejects the Sale of Medical Marijuana." *New York Times* 26 Feb. 1998, late ed.: A21. Print.

29. Review

Ali, Lorraine. "The Rap on Kanye." Rev. of *Late Registration,* by Kanye West. *Newsweek* 5 Sept. 2005: 72-73. Print.

ELECTRONIC SOURCES

Most of the following models are based on the MLA's guidelines for citing electronic sources in the *MLA Handbook* (7th edition, 2009), as well as on up-to-date information available at its Web site (http://mla.org). The MLA no longer requires the use of URLs but assumes that readers can locate a source by searching using the author, title, and other publication information given in the citation. The basic MLA entry for most electronic sources should include the following elements:

- name of the author, editor, or compiler
- title of the work, document, or posting
- information for print publication, if any

- information for electronic publication
- medium of publication (e.g., *Web*, CD-ROM, etc.)
- date of access

30. Document from a Professional Web Site

When possible, include the author's name; the title of the document, in quotations; the name of the Web site, italicized; the sponsor or publisher; the date of publication; the medium consulted (*Web*); and the date you accessed the site.

"A History of Women's Writing." *The Orlando Project: An Integrated History of Women's Writing in the British Isles.* U of Alberta, 2000. Web. 14 Mar. 2006.

31. Entire Web Site

Include the name of the person or group who created the site, if relevant; the title of the site, italicized, or (if there is no title) a description such as *Home page*, not italicized; the publisher or sponsor of the site; the date of publication or last update; the medium consulted (*Web*); and the date of access.

Bowman, Laurel. *Classical Myth: The Ancient Source.* U of Victoria, 7 Mar. 2007. Web. 12 Sept. 2008.

Mitten, Lisa. *Native American Sites.* Lisa A. Mitten, 16 Sept. 2008. Web. 3 Dec. 2008.

32. Course, Department, or Personal Web Site

For a course Web site, include the instructor's name; the title of the site, italicized; a description of the site (such as *Course home page*, *Dept. home page*, or *Home page*—not italicized); the sponsor of the site (academic department and institution); dates of the course or last update to the page; the medium; and date of access. For an academic department, list the name of the department; a description; the academic institution; the date the page was last updated (use *n.d.* for no date, not italicized); the medium (*Web*); and the date of access.

Dept. of English. Home page. Amherst Coll., n.d. Web. 5 Apr. 2007.

Lunsford, Andrea A. Home page. Stanford U, 27 Mar. 2003. Web. 17 May 2008.

Lunsford, Andrea A. *Memory and Media.* Course home page. Dept. of English, Stanford U, Sept.–Dec. 2002. Web. 13 Mar. 2006.

33. Online Book

Cite an online book as you would a print book. After the print publication information (if any), give the title of the Web site or database in which the book appears, italicized; the medium (*Web*); and the date of access.

> Riis, Jacob A. *How the Other Half Lives: Studies among the Tenements of New York.* Ed. David Phillips. New York: Scribner's, 1890. *The Authentic History Center.* Web. 26 Mar. 2009.

Treat a poem, essay, or other short work within an online book as you would a part of a print book. After the print publication information (if any), give the title of the Web site or database, italicized; the medium (*Web*); and the date of access.

> Dickinson, Emily. "The Grass." *Poems: Emily Dickinson.* Boston: Roberts Brothers, 1891. *Humanities Text Initiative American Verse Project.* Web. 6 Jan. 2008.

34. Article in an Online Journal

For an article in an online journal, cite the same information that you would for a print journal. If the online article does not have page numbers, use *n. pag.* (not italicized). Then add the medium consulted (*Web*) and the date of access.

> Johnson, Eric. "The 10,000-Word Question: Using Images on the World-Wide Web." *Kairos* 4.1 (1999): n. pag. Web. 20 Mar. 2007.

35. Article in an Online Magazine or Newspaper

For an article in an online magazine or newspaper, cite the author; the title of the article, in quotation marks; the name of the magazine or newspaper, italicized; the sponsor of the Web site; the date of publication; the medium (*Web*); and the date you accessed the article.

> Broad, William J. "In Ancient Fossils, Seeds of a New Debate on Warming." *New York Times.* New York Times, 7 Nov. 2006. Web. 12 Jan. 2009.

> McIntosh, Jill. "Test Drive: 2009 Subaru Forester 2.5X Touring." *Canadian Driver.* CanadianDriver Communications, 23 July 2008. Web. 30 Aug. 2008.

36. Posting to a Discussion Group

Begin with the author's name; the title of the posting, in quotation marks (if there is no title, use the description *Online posting*, not italicized); the name of the Web site, italicized; the sponsor or publisher of the site (use *N.p.*, not italicized, if there is no sponsor); the date of the posting; the medium; and the date of access.

> Kent, Robert. "Computers Legalized, Net Still Banned for Cubans." *Freenet Chat.*
> The Free Network Project, 5 May 2008. Web. 15 Nov. 2008.

37. Work from an Online Database or a Subscription Service

For a work from an online database, list the author's name; the title of the work, in quotation marks; any print publication information; the name of the database, italicized; the medium consulted (*Web*); and the date of access.

> "Bolivia: Elecciones Presidenciales de 2002." *Political Database of the Americas.*
> Web. 12 Nov. 2006.

> Penn, Sean, and Jon Krakauer. "*Into the Wild* Script." *Internet Movie Script
> Database.* Web. 12 June 2008.

For a work from an online service to which your library subscribes, include the same information as for an online database. After the information about the work, give the name of the database, italicized; the medium; and the date you accessed the work.

> "Breaking the Dieting Habit: Drug Therapy for Eating Disorders." *Psychology Today*
> Mar. 1995: 12+. *ProQuest.* Web. 30 Nov. 2008.

If you're citing an article from a subscription service to which you subscribe (such as AOL), use the following model:

> Weeks, W. William. "Beyond the Ark." *Nature Conservancy* Mar.-Apr. 1999. *America
> Online.* Web. 30 Nov. 2008.

38. Email Message

Include the writer's name; the subject line, in quotation marks; *Message to [recipient's name]* (not italicized); the date of the message; and the medium of delivery (*E-mail*). (Note that MLA style is to hyphenate *e-mail*.)

> Moller, Marilyn. "Seeing Crowns." Message to Beverly Moss. 3 Jan. 2003. E-mail.

39. Computer Software or Video Game

Include the title, italicized; the version number (if given); publication information; and the medium. If you are citing material downloaded from a Web site, include the title and version number (if given), but instead of publication information, add the publisher or sponsor of the Web site; the date; the medium (*Web*); and the date of access.

The Sims 2. Redwood City: Electronic Arts, 2004. CD-ROM.

Web Cache Illuminator. Vers. 4.02. NorthStar Solutions, n.d. Web. 12 Nov. 2007.

40. CD-ROM, Diskette, or Magnetic Tape, Single Issue

McPherson, James M., ed. *The American Heritage New History of the Civil War.* New York: Viking, 1996. CD-ROM.

41. Periodically Revised CD-ROM

Include the author's name; publication information for the print version of the text (including its title and date of publication); the medium (*CD-ROM*); the title of the database (italicized); the name of the company producing it; and the publication date of the database (month and year, if possible).

Heyman, Steven. "The Dangerously Exciting Client." *Psychotherapy Patient* 9.1 (1994): 37–46. CD-ROM. *PsycLIT.* SilverPlatter. Nov. 2006.

42. Multidisc CD-ROM

The 1998 Grolier Multimedia Encyclopedia. Danbury: Grolier Interactive, 1998. CD-ROM. 2 discs.

OTHER SOURCES (INCLUDING ONLINE VERSIONS)

43. Unpublished Dissertation

Fishman, Jenn. "'The Active Republic of Literature': Performance and Literary Culture in Britain, 1656–1790." Diss. Stanford U, 2003. Print.

44. Published Dissertation

Baum, Bernard. *Decentralization of Authority in a Bureaucracy.* Diss. U of Chicago, 1959. Englewood Cliffs: Prentice, 1961. Print.

45. Article from a Microform

Sharpe, Lora. "A Quilter's Tribute." *Boston Globe* 25 Mar. 1989: 13. Microform. *NewsBank: Social Relations* 12 (1989): fiche 6, grids B4–6.

46. Personal, Published, or Broadcast Interview

For a personal interview, list the name of the person interviewed, the label *Personal interview* (not italicized), and the date of the interview.

> Mullin, Joan. Personal interview. 2 Sept. 2008.

For a published interview, list the name of the person interviewed; the title (if any) or if there is no title, use the label *Interview by [interviewer's name]* (not italicized); then add the publication information, including the medium.

> Marshall, Andrew. "The Marshall Plan." Interview by Douglas McGray. *Wired.*
>   CondéNet, Feb. 2003. Web. 17 Mar. 2007.

> Taylor, Max. "Max Taylor on Winning." *Time* 13 Nov. 2000: 66. Print.

For a broadcast interview, list the name of the person interviewed, the label *Interview* (not italicized), and the name of the interviewer (if relevant); then list information about the program, the date of the interview, and the medium.

> Fairey, Shepard. "Spreading the Hope: Street Artist Shepard Fairey." Interview by
>   Terry Gross. *Fresh Air.* Natl. Public Radio. WBUR, Boston. 20 Jan. 2009. Radio.

If you listened to an archived version online, after the site's sponsor (if known), add the date of the interview, the medium (*Web*), and the date of access.

> Fairey, Shepard. "Spreading the Hope: Street Artist Shepard Fairey." Interview by
>   Terry Gross. *Fresh Air.* Natl. Public Radio. 20 Jan. 2009. Web. 13 Feb. 2009.

47. Letter

Treat a published letter like a work in an anthology, but include the date of the letter.

> Jacobs, Harriet. "To Amy Post." 4 Apr. 1853. *Incidents in the Life of a Slave Girl.*
>   Ed. Jean Fagan Yellin. Cambridge: Harvard UP, 1987. 234-35. Print.

48. Film

> Jenkins, Tamara, dir. *The Savages.* Perf. Laura Linney and Philip Seymour Hoffman.
>   2007. Fox Searchlight. Web. 4 Mar. 2008.

> *The Lord of the Rings: The Return of the King.* Dir. Peter Jackson. Perf. Elijah
>   Wood, Ian McKellen. New Line Cinema, 2003. Film.

49. Television or Radio Program

"Box Office Bombshell: Marilyn Monroe." *A&E Biography.* Narr. Peter Graves. Writ.
Andy Thomas, Jeff Schefel, and Kevin Burns. Dir. Bill Harris. Arts and
Entertainment Network. 23 Oct. 2002. Television.

Schorr, Daniel. "Week in Review with Daniel Schorr." *Weekend Edition.* Natl. Public
Radio. KQED, San Francisco. 20 Dec. 2008. Radio.

50. Sound Recording

Black Rebel Motorcycle Club. "Howl." *Howl.* RCA Records, 2005. CD.

Massive Attack. "Future Proof." *100th Window.* Virgin, 2003. CD.

51. Work of Art or Photograph

List the artist or photographer; the work's title, italicized; the date of
composition (if unknown, use *n.d.*); and the medium of composition (*Oil
on canvas, Bronze, Photograph*). Then cite the name of the museum or other
location and the city. To cite a reproduction in a book, add the publication information. To cite artwork found online, omit the medium of composition, and after the location add the title of the database or Web site,
italicized; the medium consulted (*Web*); and the date of access.

Chagall, Marc. *The Poet with the Birds.* 1911. Minneapolis Inst. of Arts.
Artsmia.org. Web. 6 Oct. 2003.

General William Palmer in Old Age. 1810. Oil on canvas. National Army Museum,
London. *White Mughals: Love and Betrayal in Eighteenth-Century India.*
William Dalrymple. New York: Penguin, 2002. 270. Print.

Ulmann, Doris. *Man Leaning against a Wall.* 1930. Photograph. Smithsonian
American Art Museum, Washington, DC.

52. Lecture or Speech

Jobs, Steve. Baccalaureate Address. Stanford University, Stanford, CA. 18 June
2005. Address.

53. Performance

Anything Goes. By Cole Porter. Perf. Klea Blackhurst. Shubert Theatre, New Haven.
7 Oct. 2003. Performance.

54. Map or Chart

The Political and Physical World. Map. Washington: Natl. Geographic, 1975. Print.

55. Cartoon

Brodner, Steve. Cartoon. *Nation* 31 Mar. 2003: 2. Print.

56. Advertisement

Chevy Avalanche. Advertisement. *Time* 14 Oct. 2002: 104. Print.

On p. 584, note the formatting of the first page of a sample essay written in MLA style. On p. 585, you'll find a sample works-cited page written for the same student essay.

Sample First Page for an Essay in MLA Style

Lesk 1

Emily Lesk

Professor Arraéz

Electric Rhetoric

15 November 2008

Red, White, and Everywhere

America, I have a confession to make: I don't drink Coke. But don't call me a hypocrite just because I am still the proud owner of a bright red shirt that advertises it. Just call me an American. Even before setting foot in Israel three years ago, I knew exactly where I could find one. The tiny T-shirt shop in the central block of Jerusalem's Ben Yehuda Street did offer other designs, but the one with a bright white "Drink Coca-Cola Classic" written in Hebrew cursive across the chest was what drew in most of the dollar-carrying tourists. While waiting almost twenty minutes for my shirt (depicted in Fig. 1), I watched nearly every customer ahead of me ask for "the Coke shirt, *todah rabah* [thank you very much]."

At the time, I never thought it strange that I wanted one, too. After having absorbed sixteen years of Coca-Cola propaganda through everything from NBC's Saturday morning cartoon lineup to the concession stand at Camden Yards (the Baltimore Orioles' ballpark), I associated the shirt with singing along to the "Just for the Taste of It" jingle and with America's favorite pastime, not with a brown fizzy beverage I refused to consume. When I later realized the immensity of Coke's

Fig. 1. *Hebrew Coca-Cola T-shirt.* Personal photograph. Despite my dislike for the beverage, I bought this Coca-Cola T-shirt in Israel.

Sample List of Works Cited for an Essay In MLA Style

Works Cited

Coca-Cola Santa pin. Personal photograph by the author. 9 Nov. 2008.

"The Fabulous Fifties." *Beverage Industry* 87.6 (1996): 16. *General OneFile*. Web. 2 Nov. 2008.

"Fifty Years of Coca-Cola Television Advertisements." *American Memory*. Motion Picture, Broadcasting and Recorded Sound Division, Lib. of Cong. 29 Nov. 2000. Web. 5 Nov. 2008.

"Haddon Sundblom and Coca-Cola." *Thehistoryofchristmas.com*. 10 Holidays, 2004. Web. 2 Nov. 2008.

Hebrew Coca-Cola T-shirt. Personal photograph by the author. 8 Nov. 2008.

Ikuta, Yasutoshi, ed. *'50s American Magazine Ads*. Tokyo: Graphic-Sha, 1987. Print.

Pendergrast, Mark. *For God, Country, and Coca-Cola: The Definitive History of the Great American Soft Drink and the Company That Makes It*. 2nd ed. New York: Basic, 2000. Print.

I Need a Hero

Seeking a bomb-throwing, passionate, visionary, liberal Scalia for a seat on the Supreme Court.

By Dahlia Lithwick
Posted Tuesday, Feb. 3, 2009, at 7:04 PM ET

Folks are wondering what kind of thumbprint Barack Obama should be leaving on the U.S. Supreme Court. It's hardly a theoretical question. Justice John Paul Stevens will soon be 89. Justice Ruth Bader Ginsburg is 75. And while both have insisted they aren't going anyplace anytime soon, the rumor mill continues to whisper that Justice David Souter (a mere 'tween at 69) is also thinking about packing it in.

The prospect of a liberal slot on the court being filled by a liberal president has some liberals dreaming big—as was evidenced in a piece last weekend, by Adam Liptak, asking whether President Obama should appoint someone "who by historical standards is a full-throated liberal, a lion like Justice William J. Brennan Jr. or Justice Thurgood Marshall?"

Today's high court is balanced between four conservatives and four moderate liberals. Moderate-conservative Anthony Kennedy remains the deciding vote in hotly contested cases. But liberals have long fussed that despite this 4-1-4 lineup, the court has still lurched far to the right of mainstream American thinking. One of the most vocal proponents of this view is

Not Just Words

Like the article from Slate.com shown above, many online texts acknowledge their sources not with parenthetical citations or lists of references but with direct electronic links to the sources themselves. What are the implications of documenting sources in this nonverbal way? Links make it easy to check what a source actually says and the context in which it occurs. But is there a downside for the writer or the reader in not having the source's name appear within the text and a list of sources at the end? Might the colors and underlining used to indicate links distract the reader from the writer's point or emphasize the source more than the writer's own ideas? What happens if the source is revised or deleted after it is linked in a text?

APA Style

The Publication Manual of the American Psychological Association (6th edition, 2010) provides comprehensive advice to student and professional writers in the social sciences. Here we draw on the *Publication Manual*'s guidelines to provide an overview of APA style for in-text citations, content notes, and entries in the list of references.

For an example of APA style in academic writing, see Wynne Wright and Gerad Middendorf's introduction to "Fighting Over Food: Change in the Agrifood System."

LINK TO P. 784

In-Text Citations

APA style calls for in-text citations in the body of an argument to document sources of quotations, paraphrases, summaries, and so on. These in-text citations correspond to full bibliographic entries in the list of references at the end of the text.

1. Author Named in a Signal Phrase

Generally, use the author's name in a signal phrase to introduce the cited material, and place the date, in parentheses, immediately after the author's name. For a quotation, the page number, preceded by *p.* (neither underlined nor italicized), appears in parentheses after the quotation. For electronic texts or other works without page numbers, paragraph numbers may be used instead, preceded by the abbreviation *para.* For a long, set-off quotation, position the page reference in parentheses one space after the punctuation at the end of the quotation.

According to Brandon (1993), Adefunmi opposed all forms of racism and believed that black nationalism should not be a destructive force.

As Johnson (2005) demonstrates, contemporary television dramas such as *ER* and *Lost* are not only more complex than earlier programs but "possess a quality that can only be described as subtlety and discretion" (p. 83).

2. Author Named in Parentheses

When you don't mention the author in a signal phrase, give the name and the date, separated by a comma, in parentheses at the end of the cited material.

The Sopranos has achieved a much wider viewing audience than ever expected, spawning a cookbook and several serious scholarly studies (Franklin, 2002).

3. Two Authors

Use both names in all citations. Use *and* in a signal phrase, but use an ampersand (&) in parentheses.

> Associated with purity and wisdom, Obatala is the creator of human beings, whom he is said to have formed out of clay (Edwards & Mason, 1985).

4. Three to Five Authors

List all the authors' names for the first reference. In subsequent references, use just the first author's name followed by *et al.* (in regular type, not underlined or italicized).

> Lenhoff, Wang, Greenberg, and Bellugi (1997) cite tests that indicate that segments of the left brain hemisphere are not affected by Williams syndrome whereas the right hemisphere is significantly affected.

> Shackelford (1999) drew on the study by Lenhoff et al. (1997).

5. Six or More Authors

Use only the first author's name and *et al.* (in regular type, not underlined or italicized) in every citation, including the first.

> As Flower et al. (2003) demonstrate, reading and writing involve both cognitive and social processes.

6. Organization as Author

If the name of an organization or a corporation is long, spell it out the first time, followed by an abbreviation in brackets. In later citations, use the abbreviation only.

> *First Citation:* (Federal Bureau of Investigation [FBI], 2002)

> *Subsequent Citations:* (FBI, 2002)

7. Unknown Author

Use the title or its first few words in a signal phrase or in parentheses (in the example below, a book's title is italicized).

> The school profiles for the county substantiate this trend (*Guide to secondary schools*, 2003).

8. Authors with the Same Last Name

If your list of references includes works by different authors with the same last name, include the authors' initials in each citation.

> G. Jones (1998) conducted the groundbreaking study of retroviruses, whereas P. Jones (2000) replicated the initial trials two years later.

9. Two or More Sources in the Same Citation

List sources by the same author chronologically by publication year. List sources by different authors in alphabetical order by the authors' last names, separated by semicolons.

> While traditional forms of argument are warlike and agonistic, alternative models do exist (Foss & Foss, 1997; Makau, 1999).

10. Specific Parts of a Source

Use abbreviations (*p.*, *pt.*, and so on) in a parenthetical citation to name the part of a work you're citing. However, *chapter* is not abbreviated.

> Pinker (2003, p. 6) argued that his research yielded the opposite results.

> Pinker (2003, Chapter 6) argued that his research yielded the opposite results.

11. Online Document

To cite a source found on the Internet, use the author's name and date as you would for a print source, and indicate the chapter or figure of the document, as appropriate. If the source's publication date is unknown, use *n.d.* ("no date"). To document a quotation, include paragraph numbers if page numbers are unavailable. If an online document has no page or paragraph numbers, provide the heading of the section and the number of the paragraph that follows.

> Werbach argued convincingly that "despite the best efforts of legislators, lawyers, and computer programmers, spam has won. Spam is killing email" (2002, p. 1).

12. Email and Other Personal Communication

Cite any personal letters, email messages, electronic postings, telephone conversations, or personal interviews by giving the person's initial(s) and last name, the identification, and the date. Do not list email in the references list, and note that APA style uses a hyphen in the word *e-mail*.

> E. Ashdown (personal communication, March 9, 2003) supported these claims.

Content Notes

The APA recommends using content notes for material that will expand or supplement your argument but otherwise would interrupt the text. Indicate such notes in your text by inserting superscript numerals. Type the notes themselves on a separate page headed *Footnotes* (not underlined, italicized, or in quotation marks) centered at the top of the page. Double-space all entries. Indent the first line of each note five to seven spaces, and begin subsequent lines at the left margin.

TEXT WITH SUPERSCRIPT INDICATING A NOTE

Data related to children's preferences in books were instrumental in designing the questionnaire.[1]

NOTE

[1]Rudine Sims Bishop and members of the Reading Readiness Research Group provided helpful data.

List of References

The alphabetical list of sources cited in your text is called *References*. (If your instructor asks you to list everything you've read as background—not just the sources you cite—call the list *Bibliography*.) The list of references appears on a separate page or pages at the end of your paper, with the heading *References* (not underlined, italicized, or in quotation marks) centered one inch from the top of the page. Double-space after the heading, and begin your first entry. Double-space the entire list. For print sources, APA style specifies the treatment and placement of four basic elements—author, publication date, title, and publication information. Each element is followed by a period.

- *Author:* List all authors with last name first, and use only initials for first and middle names. Separate the names of multiple authors with commas, and use an ampersand (&) before the last author's name.
- *Publication date:* Enclose the publication date in parentheses. Use only the year for books and journals; use the year, a comma, and the month or month and day for magazines and newspapers. Do not abbreviate

the month. If a date is not given, put *n.d.* ("no date," not italicized) in the parentheses. Put a period after the parentheses.

- *Title:* Italicize titles and subtitles of books and periodicals. Do not enclose titles of articles in quotation marks. For books and articles, capitalize only the first word of the title and subtitle and any proper nouns or proper adjectives. Capitalize all major words in the title of a periodical.

- *Publication information:* For a book published in the United States, list the city of publication and state abbreviation. For books published outside the United States, identify city and country. Provide the publisher's name, dropping *Inc., Co.,* or *Publishers.* If the state is already included within the publisher's name, do not include the postal abbreviation for the state. For a periodical, follow the periodical title with a comma, the volume number (italicized), the issue number (if provided) in parentheses and followed by a comma, and the inclusive page numbers of the article. For newspaper articles and for articles or chapters in books, include the abbreviation *p.* ("page") or *pp.* ("pages").

The following APA-style examples appear in a "hanging indent" format, in which the first line aligns on the left and the subsequent lines indent one-half inch or five spaces.

BOOKS

1. One Author

Jones, L. H. (2004). *William Clark and the shaping of the West.* New York, NY: Hill and Wang.

2. Two or More Authors

Steininger, M., Newell, J. D., & Garcia, L. (1984). *Ethical issues in psychology.* Homewood, IL: Dow Jones-Irwin.

3. Organization as Author

Use the word *Author* (neither underlined nor italicized) as the publisher when the organization is both the author and the publisher.

Linguistics Society of America. (2002). *Guidelines for using sign language interpreters.* Washington, DC: Author.

4. Unknown Author

National Geographic atlas of the world. (1999). Washington, DC: National
Geographic Society.

5. Book Prepared by an Editor

Hardy, H. H. (Ed.). (1998). *The proper study of mankind.* New York, NY: Farrar,
Straus.

6. Selection in a Book with an Editor

Villanueva, V. (1999). An introduction to social scientific discussions on class. In
A. Shepard, J. McMillan, & G. Tate (Eds.), *Coming to class: Pedagogy and
the social class of teachers* (pp. 262-277). Portsmouth, NH: Heinemann.

7. Translation

Perez-Reverte, A. (2002). *The nautical chart* (M. S. Peaden, Trans.). New York, NY:
Harvest. (Original work published 2000)

8. Edition Other Than the First

Wrightsman, L. (1998). *Psychology and the legal system* (3rd ed.). Newbury Park,
CA: Sage.

9. One Volume of a Multivolume Work

Will, J. S. (1921). *Protestantism in France* (Vol. 2). Toronto, Ontario, Canada:
University of Toronto Press.

10. Article in a Reference Work

Chernow, B., & Vattasi, G. (Eds.). (1993). Psychomimetic drug. In *The Columbia
encyclopedia* (5th ed., p. 2238). New York, NY: Columbia University Press.

If no author is listed, begin with the title.

11. Republication

Sharp, C. (1978). *History of Hartlepool.* Hartlepool, United Kingdom: Hartlepool
Borough Council. (Original work published 1816)

12. Government Document

U.S. Bureau of the Census. (2001). *Survey of women-owned business enterprises.*
    Washington, DC: Government Printing Office.

13. Two or More Works by the Same Author

List the works in chronological order of publication. Repeat the
author's name in each entry.

Rose, M. (1984). *Writer's block: The cognitive dimension.* Carbondale: Southern
    Illinois University Press.

Rose, M. (1995). *Possible lives: The promise of public education in America.*
    Boston, MA: Houghton Mifflin.

PERIODICALS

14. Article in a Journal Paginated by Volume

Kirsch, G. E. (2002). Toward an engaged rhetoric of professional practice. *Journal
    of Advanced Composition, 22,* 414-423.

15. Article in a Journal Paginated by Issue

Carr, S. (2002). The circulation of Blair's Lectures. *Rhetoric Society Quarterly,
    32*(4), 75-104.

16. Article in a Monthly Magazine

Baker, C. (2008, September). Master of the universe. *Wired, 16*(9), 134-141.

17. Article in a Newspaper

Nagourney, A. (2002, December 16). Gore rules out running in '04. *The New York
    Times,* pp. A1, A8.

18. Letter to the Editor or Editorial

Erbeta, R. (2008, December). Swiftboating George [Letter to the editor].
    Smithsonian, 39(9), 10.

19. Unsigned Article

Guidelines issued on assisted suicide. (1998, March 4). *The New York Times*, p. A15.

20. Review

Avalona, A. (2008, August). [Review of the book *Weaving women's lives: Three generations in a Navajo family*, by L. Lamphere]. New Mexico, *86*(8), 40.

21. Published Interview

Shor, I. (1997). [Interview with A. Greenbaum]. *Writing on the Edge, 8*(2), 7-20.

22. Two or More Works by the Same Author in the Same Year

List two or more works by the same author published in the same year alphabetically by title (excluding *A*, *An*, or *The*), and place lowercase letters (*a*, *b*, etc.) after the dates.

Murray, F. B. (1983a). Equilibration as cognitive conflict. *Developmental Review*, 3, 54-61.

Murray, F. B. (1983b). Learning and development through social interaction. In L. Liben (Ed.), *Piaget and the foundations of knowledge* (pp. 176-201). Hillsdale, NJ: Erlbaum.

ELECTRONIC SOURCES

The following models are based on the APA's *Publication Manual* (6th edition). A change for handling electronic sources involves the use of a digital object identifier (DOI) when available (instead of a URL) to locate an electronic source. The DOI is a unique number assigned to an electronic text (article, book, or other item) and intended to give reliable access to it. A second change is that a date of retrieval is no longer necessary unless a source changes very frequently. The basic APA entry for most electronic sources should include the following elements:

- name of the author, editor, or compiler
- date of electronic publication or most recent update
- title of the work, document, or posting
- publication information, including the title, volume or issue number, and page numbers

- the DOI (digital object identifier—see above) of the document, if one is available
- a URL, only if a DOI is not available, with no angle brackets and no closing punctuation.

23. World Wide Web Site

To cite a whole site, give the address in a parenthetical reference. To cite a document from a Web site, include information as you would for a print document, followed by a note on its retrieval. Provide a date of retrieval only if the information is likely to change frequently.

American Psychological Association. (2000). DotComSense: Commonsense ways to protect your privacy and assess online mental health information. Retrieved from http://helping.apa.org/dotcomsense

Mullins, B. (1995). Introduction to Robert Hass. Readings in contemporary poetry at Dia Center for the Arts. Retrieved from http://www.diacenter.org/prg/poetry/95_96/intrhass.html

24. Article from an Online Periodical

For an article you read online, provide either a DOI or the URL of the periodical's home page preceded by *Retrieved from.*

Lambert, N. M., Graham, S. M., & Fincham, F. D. (2009). A prototype analysis of gratitude: Varieties of gratitude experiences. *Personality and Social Psychology Bulletin, 35,* 1193-1207. doi:10.1177/0146167209338071

Palmer, K. S. (2000, September 12). In academia, males under a microscope. *The Washington Post.* Retrieved from http://www.washingtonpost.com

25. Article or Abstract from a Database

For an article you find on a database, provide a DOI if one is available. If the online article does not have a DOI, locate the home page for the journal in which the article appears and provide that URL. You need not identify the database you have used.

Kennedy, C., & Covell, K. (2009). Violating the rights of the child through inadequate sexual health education. *International Journal of Children's Rights, 17*(1), 143-154. doi:10.1163/092755608X278939

Hayhoe, G. (2001). The long and winding road: Technology's future. *Technical Communication, 48*(2), 133-145. Retrieved from http://www.stc.org/pubs/techcommGeneral01.asp

26. Software or Computer Program

McAfee Office 2000. (Version 2.0) [Computer software]. (1999). Santa Clara, CA: Network Associates.

27. Online Government Document

Cite an online government document as you would a printed government work, adding the date of access and the URL. If you don't find a date, use *n. d.*

Finn, J. D. (1998, April). *Class size and students at risk: What is known? What is next?* Retrieved from United States Department of Education website http://www.ed.gov/pubs/ClassSize/title.html

28. Posting to a Discussion Group

Include an online posting in the references list only if you're able to retrieve the message from a mailing list's archive. Provide the author's name; the date of posting, in parentheses; and the subject line from the posting. Include any information that further identifies the message in square brackets. For a Listserv message, end with the retrieval statement, including the name of the list and the URL of the archived message.

Troike, R. C. (2001, June 21). Buttercups and primroses [Msg 8]. Message posted to the American Dialect Society's ADS-L electronic mailing list, archived at http://listserv.linguistlist.org/archives/ads-1.html

29. Newsgroup Posting

Include the author's name, the date and subject line of the posting, the access date, and the name of the newsgroup.

Wittenberg, E. (2001, July 11). Gender and the Internet [Msg 4]. Retrieved from news://comp.edu.composition

30. Email Message or Synchronous Communication

Because the APA stresses that any sources cited in your list of references must be retrievable by your readers, you shouldn't include entries for email messages or synchronous communications (MOOs, MUDs); instead, cite these sources in your text as forms of personal communication (see p. 589). And remember that you shouldn't quote from other people's email without asking their permission to do so.

OTHER SOURCES

31. Technical or Research Reports and Working Papers

Wilson, K. S. (1986). Palenque: *An interactive multimedia optical disc prototype for children* (Working Paper No. 2). New York: Center for Children and Technology, Bank Street College of Education.

32. Unpublished Paper Presented at a Meeting or Symposium

Welch, K. (2002, March). *Electric rhetoric and screen literacy.* Paper presented at the meeting of the Conference on College Composition and Communication, Chicago.

33. Unpublished Dissertation

Seward, D. E. (2008). *Civil voice in Elizabethan parliamentary oratory: The rhetoric and composition of speeches delivered at Westminster in 1566* (Unpublished doctoral dissertation). University of Texas at Austin, Austin, TX.

34. Poster Session

Mensching, G. (2002, May). *A simple, effective one-shot for disinterested students.* Poster session presented at the National LOEX Library Instruction Conference, Ann Arbor, MI.

35. Motion Picture, Video, or DVD

Jackson, P. (Director). (2003). *The lord of the rings: The return of the king.* [Motion picture]. Los Angeles: New Line Cinema.

36. Television Program, Single Episode

Imperioli, M. (Writer), & Buscemi, S. (Director). (2002, October 20). Everybody hurts [Television series episode]. In D. Chase (Executive producer), *The Sopranos.* New York: Home Box Office.

37. Sound Recording

Begin with the writer's name, followed by the date of copyright. Give the recording date at the end of the entry (in parentheses, after the period) if it's different from the copyright date.

> Ivey, A., Jr., & Sall, R. (1995). Rollin' with my homies [Recorded by Coolio]. On *Clueless* [CD]. Hollywood, CA: Capitol Records.

RESPOND●

1. The MLA and APA styles differ in several important ways, both for in-text citations and for lists of sources. You've probably noticed a few: the APA lowercases most words in titles and lists the publication date right after the author's name, whereas the MLA capitalizes most words and puts the publication date at the end of the works cited entry. More interesting than the details, though, is the reasoning behind the differences. Placing the publication date near the front of a citation, for instance, reveals a special concern for that information in the APA style. Similarly, the MLA's decision to capitalize titles isn't arbitrary: that style is preferred in the humanities for a reason. Find as many consistent differences between the MLA and APA styles as you can. Then, for each difference, try to discover the reasons these groups organize or present information in that way. The MLA and APA style manuals themselves may be of help. You might also begin by determining which academic disciplines subscribe to the APA style and which to the MLA.

2. Working with another person in your class, look for examples of the following sources: an article in a journal, a book, a film, a song, and a TV show. Then make a references page or works-cited entry for each one, using either MLA or APA style.

arguments

21
How Does Popular Culture Stereotype *You?*

If you check the dictionary, you'll learn that the term *stereotype* originally referred to a printing plate that was cast in metal from a mold of a page of set type. English borrowed the word from French, but its parts are ultimately of Greek origin: *stereo* means "solid" or "three-dimensional," and *type* means "model." By extension, the word has come to mean a widely held image that is fixed and allows for little individuality among a group's members. Ironic, isn't it, that a term that originally referred to a three-dimensional printing plate has come to refer to a one-dimensional representation of a group?

The selections in this chapter focus on stereotyping in popular culture, challenging you to analyze what many would consider to be unsavory or unfair stereotypes of various groups from a range of perspectives. The chapter opens with a news article from 2007 about evictions at a DePauw University sorority. Many of campus, including some of the sorority's members, noticed that those who were evicted did not fit most Americans' stereotype of a sorority sister.

Next are a pair of readings on the same topic—an op-ed piece (an essay that appears on the page opposite a newspaper's editorial page) by syndicated columnist Ellen Goodman, "The Culture of Thin Bites Fiji," and an excerpt from a scholarly research article by medical anthropologist and physician Anne E. Becker, "Television, Disordered Eating, and Young Women in Fiji." Both authors explore the arrival of American television on the South Pacific island of Fiji and its consequences for young women and their changing body image. (Becker's presentation of her research at an academic conference sparked Goodman's original article.) Not only do young Fijian women reject traditional local notions of beauty by striving to be thin, but they also have specific reasons for desiring to be so.

An image that was part of an advertising insert from clothing designer Kenneth Cole challenges stereotypes as it reminds us that "We All Walk in Different Shoes." You may have noticed that Cole has long seen advertising of his products as a public space for sparking discussion about cultural stereotypes.

The next two selections examine the long-standing controversy about American Indian mascots and imagery in sports. Barbara Munson's online text "Common Themes and Questions about the Use of 'Indian' Logos" and Joe Lapointe's new article "Bonding over a Mascot" present very different perspectives on this topic. Munson writes as an American Indian answering frequently asked questions about a phenomenon that she finds offensive while Lapointe offers a journalist's view of a state university where Indians are proud of their campus's logo.

Stuart Elliott's "Uncle Ben, Board Chairman" reports on corporate efforts to reclaim and rehabilitate a controversial image that has long been associated with a particular brand of rice. You'll get to decide how well the Mars Corporation has succeeded in this challenging task.

Closing the chapter, Charles A. Riley II's book preface focuses passionately on how people with disabilities are—and aren't—represented in the media and popular culture. In addition to his take on the problem, we include a set of guidelines from the National Center on Disability and Journalism that offers advice about how the media might do a better job than they currently do in this regard.

Originally, stereotypes were part of a printer's trade, enabling the printer to disseminate information quickly and cheaply. No less a part of popular culture today, stereotypes of a different sort still disseminate information. You'll have to evaluate how much that information is worth.

▼ *Sam Dillon currently works as a national correspondent for the New York Times, writing often on issues relating to education in the United States. Earlier in his career, he reported from various Latin American countries. His journalistic writing has garnered several prestigious awards, including two Pulitzer Prizes. The New York Times broke this story about the Delta Zeta sorority at DePauw University in its February 25, 2007, edition, setting off a widely discussed controversy that eventually led to the closure of the sorority on the university's campus. As you read this article, consider the ways in which stereotyping might have played a role in what happened—and what didn't.*

Evictions at Sorority Raise Issue of Bias

SAM DILLON

GREENCASTLE, Ind.—When a psychology professor at DePauw University here surveyed students, they described one sorority as a group of "daddy's little princesses" and another as "offbeat hippies." The sisters of Delta Zeta were seen as "socially awkward."

Worried that a negative stereotype of the sorority was contributing to a decline in membership that had left its Greek-columned house here half empty, Delta Zeta's national officers interviewed 35 DePauw members in November, quizzing them about their dedication to recruitment. They judged 23 of the women insufficiently committed and later told them to vacate the sorority house.

The 23 members included every woman who was overweight. They also included the only Korean and Vietnamese members. The dozen students allowed to stay were slender and popular with fraternity

Women at DePauw University who either were asked to leave the Delta Zeta house or resigned in protest hold a sorority photo.

men—conventionally pretty women the sorority hoped could attract new recruits. Six of the 12 were so infuriated they quit.

"Virtually everyone who didn't fit a certain sorority member archetype° was told to leave," said Kate Holloway, a senior who withdrew from the chapter during its reorganization.

"I sensed the disrespect with which 5 this was to be carried out and got fed up," Ms. Holloway added. "I didn't have room in my life for these women to come in and tell my sisters of three years that they weren't needed."

Ms. Holloway is not the only angry one. The reorganization has left a messy aftermath of recrimination and tears on this rural campus of 2,400 students, 50 miles southwest of Indianapolis.

The mass eviction battered the self-esteem of many of the former sorority members, and some withdrew from classes in depression. There have been student protests, outraged letters from alumni° and parents, and a faculty petition calling the sorority's action unethical.

DePauw's president, Robert G. Bottoms, issued a two-page letter of reprimand to the sorority. In an interview in his office, Dr. Bottoms said he had been stunned by the sorority's insensitivity.

"I had no hint they were going to disrupt the chapter with a membership reduction of this proportion in the middle of the year," he said. "It's been very upsetting."

The president of Delta Zeta, which 10 has its headquarters in Oxford, Ohio, and its other national officers declined to be interviewed. Responding by e-mail to questions, Cynthia Winslow Menges, the executive director, said the sorority had not evicted the 23 women, even though the national officers sent those women form letters that said: "The membership review team has recommended you for alumna status. Chapter members receiving alumnae status should plan to relocate from the chapter house no later than Jan. 29, 2007."

Ms. Menges asserted that the women themselves had, in effect, made their own decisions to leave by demonstrating a lack of commitment to meet recruitment goals. The sorority paid each woman who left $300 to cover the difference between sorority and campus housing.

The sorority "is saddened that the isolated incident at DePauw has been mischaracterized," Ms. Menges wrote. Asked for clarification, the sorority's public relations representative e-mailed a statement saying its actions were aimed at the "enrichment of student life at DePauw."

This is not the first time that the DePauw chapter of Delta Zeta has stirred controversy. In 1982, it attracted national attention when a black student was not allowed to join, provoking accusations of racial discrimination.

Earlier this month, an Alabama lawyer and several other DePauw alumni who graduated in 1970 described in a letter to *The DePauw*, the student newspaper, how Delta Zeta's national leadership had tried unsuccessfully to block a young woman with a black father and a white mother from joining its DePauw chapter in 1967.

Despite those incidents, the chap- 15 ter appears to have been home to a diverse community over the years, partly because it has attracted brainy women, including many science and math majors, as well as talented disabled women, without focusing as

---

archetype: here, a model or perfect example.

alumni: the masculine plural form of *alumnus*, a (male) graduate. The feminine singular form is *alumna*, and the feminine plural is *alumnae*. These plural forms are retained from Latin, their language of origin.

exclusively as some sororities on potential recruits' sex appeal, former sorority members said.

"I had a sister I could go to a bar with if I had boy problems," said Erin Swisshelm, a junior biochemistry major who withdrew from the sorority in October. "I had a sister I could talk about religion with. I had a sister I could be nerdy about science with. That's why I liked Delta Zeta, because I had all these amazing women around me."

But over the years DePauw students had attached a negative stereotype to the chapter, as evidenced by the survey that Pam Propsom, a psychology professor, conducts each year in her class. That image had hurt recruitment, and the national officers had repeatedly warned the chapter that unless its membership increased, the chapter could close.

At the start of the fall term the national office was especially determined to raise recruitment because 2009 is the 100th anniversary of the DePauw chapter's founding. In September, Ms. Menges and Kathi Heatherly, a national vice president of the sorority, visited the chapter to announce a reorganization plan they said would include an interview with each woman about her commitment. The women were urged to look their best for the interviews.

The tone left four women so unsettled that they withdrew from the chapter almost immediately.

Robin Lamkin, a junior who is an **20** editor at *The DePauw* and was one of the 23 women evicted, said many of her sisters bought new outfits and

Elizabeth Haneline, who was among those evicted, said, "The Greek system hasn't changed at all, but instead of racism, it's image now."

modeled them for each other before the interviews. Many women declared their willingness to recruit diligently, Ms. Lamkin said.

A few days after the interviews, national representatives took over the house to hold a recruiting event. They asked most members to stay upstairs in their rooms. To welcome freshmen downstairs, they assembled a team that included several of the women eventually asked to stay in the sorority, along with some slender women invited from the sorority's chapter at Indiana University, Ms. Holloway said.

"They had these unassuming freshman girls downstairs with these plastic women from Indiana University, and 25 of my sisters hiding upstairs," she said. "It was so fake, so completely

dehumanized. I said, 'This calls for a little joke.'"

Ms. Holloway put on a wig and some John Lennon rose-colored glasses, burst through the front door and skipped around singing, "Ooooh! Delta Zeta!" and other chants.

The face of one of the national representatives, she recalled, "was like I'd run over her puppy with my car."

At least part of the disagreement behind this conflict lies in different criteria for evaluating who makes a good member of a sorority. See Chapter 10 for more on how to develop criteria for evaluation arguments.

LINK TO P. 289

The national representatives announced their decisions in the form letters, delivered on Dec. 2, which said that Delta Zeta intended to increase membership to 95 by the 2009 anniversary, and that it would recruit using a "core group of women."

Elizabeth Haneline, a senior computer science major who was among those evicted, returned to the house that afternoon and found some women in tears. Even the chapter's president had been kicked out, Ms. Haneline said, while "other women who had done almost nothing for the chapter were asked to stay."

Six of the 12 women who were asked to stay left the sorority, including Joanna Kieschnick, a sophomore majoring in English literature. "They said, 'You're not good enough' to so many people who have put their heart and soul into this chapter that I can't stay," she said.

In the months since, Cynthia Babington, DePauw's dean of students, has fielded angry calls from parents, she said. Robert Hershberger, chairman of the modern languages department, circulated the faculty petition; 55 professors signed it.

"We were especially troubled that the women they expelled were less about image and more about academic achievement and social service," Dr. Hershberger said.

During rush activities this month, 11 first-year students accepted invitations to join Delta Zeta, but only three have sought membership.

On Feb. 2, Rachel Pappas, a junior who is the chapter's former secretary, printed 200 posters calling on students to gather that afternoon at the student union. About 50 students showed up and heard Ms. Pappas say the sorority's national leaders had misrepresented the truth when they asserted they had evicted women for lack of commitment.

"The injustice of the lies," she said, "is contemptible."

Correction: March 2, 2007

An article on Sunday about the eviction at DePauw University of members of the Delta Zeta sorority by the national organization referred incorrectly to a woman identified only as a black member of the sorority. Although the woman, Leah Souder, was not in fact one of 35 sorority members interviewed by the national organization, nor was she among the 23 of those 35 who received eviction letters, she says she has not heard from the national office since its reorganization of the DePauw chapter and assumes she is no longer a member.

RESPOND●

1. What examples of stereotyping do you find in this article? Who is being stereotyped? What or who, do you believe, are the sources of the stereotypes? What evidence is there in the article of people who are criticizing or contesting stereotypes? Who are they, and how are they calling stereotypes into question?

2. Paragraphs 13–14 provide historical background about the Delta Zeta sorority on the DePauw campus. Is this information necessary to the article? If so, how? If not, why not? What is the relationship between paragraphs 13–14 and paragraphs 15–16? What is the role of these two latter paragraphs in the article?

3. In printed newspapers, corrections appear several days after the original article is printed, but someone doing research might well not notice them. In contrast, a correction posted on an electronic source will always be available to future readers. In some cases, the correction is incorporated into the original article rather than being noted separately at the end of the article. The correction that appears at the end of this article reminds us that even award-winning journalists sometimes make errors. How serious, in your opinion, was the error in Dillon's original article? Does this correction influence how you read or evaluate the article? Does it influence how you evaluate the ethos of the writer? (For a discussion of ethos, see Chapter 3.)

4. As the headnote on p. 603 implies, this article set off a national controversy. For information about what happened, read the entry entitled "DePauw University Delta Zeta Controversy" on Wikipedia. As is common with Wikipedia entries, especially those about fairly recent events, all the references cited are electronic sources. Thus, you can inspect the sources that were used in writing the article. Choose three of the articles used as sources, and **write an evaluative argument** focusing on the support that they provide for the claims they make. (For a discussion of evaluative arguments, see Chapter 10.)

5. One way to analyze the situation at DePauw is to consider it as an argument of definition: Did stereotyping occur in the Delta Zeta sorority? **Write an argument of definition** considering the situation described in this article and the Wikipedia entry on the "DePauw University Delta Zeta Controversy." You'll need to formulate a definition of stereotyping and demonstrate why the events at DePauw did or did not constitute stereotyping.

▼ Ellen Goodman, an award-winning columnist, writes regularly for the Boston Globe, where this article first appeared in May 1999, a few days after many newspapers had featured a news story about how adolescent Fijian girls' self-image was affected by watching American TV. Goodman's column generally appears on the op-ed pages of newspapers across the country. As you read, consider how she uses a discussion of a scientific study and the evidence it cites to make a claim about what she sees as a larger social problem. Keep in mind that Goodman is writing shortly after the shootings at Columbine High School in Colorado, where two male students killed and wounded a number of other students and teachers.

The Culture of Thin Bites Fiji

ELLEN GOODMAN

First of all, imagine a place women greet one another at the market with open arms, loving smiles, and a cheerful exchange of ritual compliments:

"You look wonderful! You've put on weight!"

Does that sound like dialogue from Fat Fantasyland? Or a skit from fat-is-a-feminist-issue satire? Well, this Western fantasy was a South Pacific fact of life. In Fiji, before 1995, big was beautiful and bigger was more beautiful—and people really did flatter one another with exclamations about weight gain.

In this island paradise, food was not only love, it was a cultural imperative. Eating and overeating were rites of mutual hospitality. Everyone worried about losing weight—but not the way we do. "Going thin" was considered to be a sign of some social problem, a worrisome indication the person wasn't getting enough to eat.

The Fijians were, to be sure, a bit 5 obsessed with food; they prescribed herbs to stimulate the appetite. They were a reverse image of our culture. And that turns out to be the point.

Something happened in 1995. A Western mirror was shoved into the face of the Fijians. Television came to the island. Suddenly, the girls of rural coastal villages were watching the girls of *Melrose Place* and *Beverly Hills 90210*, not to mention *Seinfeld* and *E.R.*

Within 38 months, the number of teenagers at risk for eating disorders more than doubled to 29 percent. The number of high school girls who vomited for weight control went up five times to 15 percent. Worse yet, 74 percent of the Fiji teens in the study said they felt "too big or fat" at least some of the time and 62 percent said they had dieted in the past month.

This before-and-after television portrait of a body image takeover was drawn by Anne Becker, an anthropologist and psychiatrist who directs research at the Harvard Eating Disorders Center. She presented her research at the American Psychiatric Association last week with all the usual caveats. No, you cannot prove a direct causal link between television and eating disorders. Heather Locklear doesn't cause anorexia. Nor does Tori Spelling cause bulimia.

Fiji is not just a Fat Paradise Lost. It's an economy in transition from subsistence agriculture to tourism and its entry into the global economy has threatened many old values.

Nevertheless, you don't get a much 10 better lab experiment than this. In just 38 months, and with only one channel, a television-free culture that defined a fat person as robust has become a television culture that sees robust as, well, repulsive.

All that and these islanders didn't even get *Ally McBeal.*

"Going thin" is no longer a social disease but the perceived requirement for getting a good job, nice clothes, and fancy cars. As Becker says carefully, "The acute and constant bombardment of certain images in the media are apparently quite influential in how teens experience their bodies."

Speaking of Fiji teenagers in a way that sounds all too familiar, she adds, "We have a set of vulnerable teens consuming television. There's a huge disparity between what they see on television and what they look like themselves—that goes not only to clothing, hairstyles, and skin color, but size of bodies."

In short, the sum of Western culture, the big success story of our entertainment industry, is our ability to export insecurity: We can make any woman anywhere feel perfectly rotten about her shape. At this rate, we owe

Calista Flockhart in 1998

the islanders at least one year of the ample lawyer Camryn Manheim in *The Practice* for free.

I'm not surprised by research 15 showing that eating disorders are a cultural byproduct. We've watched the female image shrink down to Calista Flockhart at the same time we've seen eating problems grow. But Hollywood hasn't been exactly eager to acknowledge the connection between image and illness.

Over the past few weeks since the Columbine High massacre, we've broken through some denial about violence as a teaching tool. It's pretty clear that boys are literally learning how to hate and harm others.

Maybe we ought to worry a little more about what girls learn: To hate and harm themselves.

Chapter 11 notes that causal arguments are often included as part of other arguments. Goodman's article reports on Anne Becker's research (an excerpt of which is reprinted in the following selection, beginning on page 611) to support a larger argument.

LINK TO P. 336

RESPOND●

1. What is Goodman's argument? How does she build it around Becker's study while not limiting herself to that evidence alone? (Consider, especially, paragraphs 15–17.)

2. What knowledge of popular American culture does Goodman assume that her *Boston Globe* audience has? How does she use allusions to American TV programs to build her argument? Note, for example, that she sometimes uses such allusions as conversational asides—"All that and these islanders didn't even get *Ally McBeal*," and "At this rate, we owe the islanders at least one year of the ample lawyer Camryn Manheim in *The Practice* for free"—to establish her ethos. (For a discussion of ethos, see Chapter 3.) In what other ways do allusions to TV programs contribute to Goodman's argument? Do you understand her

allusions to 1995's TV programs or popular culture? If not, how are you in the same situation as the islanders? If you do understand, offer to explain the allusions to your classmates who don't.

3. At least by implication, if not in fact, Goodman makes a causal argument about the entertainment industry, women's body image, and the consequences of such an image. What sort of causal argument does she set up? (For a discussion of causal arguments, see Chapter 11.) How effective do you find it? Why?

4. Many professors would find Goodman's conversational style inappropriate for most academic writing assignments. Choose several paragraphs of the text that contain information appropriate for an argumentative academic paper. Then **write a few well-developed paragraphs** on the topic. (Paragraphs 4–8 could be revised in this way, though you would put the information contained in these five paragraphs into only two or three longer paragraphs. Newspaper articles often feature short paragraphs of one or two sentences, which is generally an inappropriate length for paragraphs in academic writing.)

A Fijian woman—before 1995

▼ Anne E. Becker received her MD and PhD in anthropology as well as her ScM in epidemiology from Harvard University. Currently, she serves as an associate professor of medical anthropology and of psychiatry at the Harvard Medical School, where she directs the Social Sciences MD-PhD Program. As this book goes to press, she is writing a book-length study based on her long-term research in Fiji on teenage girls, eating disorders, and suicidal behavior. This selection presents three sections of one of Becker's articles, "Television, Disordered Eating, and Young Women in Fiji," which originally appeared in a special 2004 issue of the academic journal Culture, Medicine and Psychiatry that was devoted to global eating disorders. As you read these sections—"Abstract," "Discussion," and "Conclusions"—consider how writing about research for other researchers (as Becker has done here) differs from writing about research for a popular audience (as Ellen Goodman does in the previous selection, "The Culture of Thin Bites Fiji," which relies on an earlier oral presentation of Becker's research as a starting point for Goodman's discussion).

Television, Disordered Eating, and Young Women in Fiji: Negotiating Body Image and Identity during Rapid Social Change

ABSTRACT. Although the relationship between media exposure and risk behavior among youth is established at a population level, the specific psychological and social mechanisms mediating the adverse effects of media on youth remain poorly understood. This study reports on an investigation of the impact of the introduction of television to a rural community in Western Fiji on adolescent ethnic Fijian girls in a setting of rapid social and economic change. Narrative data were collected from 30 purposively selected ethnic Fijian secondary school girls via semi-structured, open-ended interviews. Interviews were conducted in 1998, 3 years after television was first broadcast to this region of Fiji. Narrative data were analyzed for content relating to response to television and mechanisms that mediate self and body image in Fijian adolescents. Data in this sample suggest that media imagery is used in both creative and destructive ways by adolescent Fijian girls to navigate opportunities and conflicts posed by the rapidly changing social environment. Study respondents indicated their explicit modeling of the perceived positive attributes of characters presented in television dramas, but also the beginnings of weight and body shape preoccupation, purging behavior to control weight, and body disparagement.° Response to television appeared to be shaped by a desire for competitive social positioning during a period of rapid social transition. Understanding vulnerability to images and values imported with media will be critical to preventing disordered eating and, potentially, other youth risk behaviors in this population, as well as other populations at risk.

disparagement: speaking about something in a negative way.

KEY WORDS: body image, eating disorders, Fiji, modernization

DISCUSSION

Minimally, and at the most superficial level, narrative data reflect a shift in fashion among the adolescent ethnic Fijian population studied. A shift in aesthetic ideals is remarkable in and of itself given the numerous social mechanisms that have long supported the preference for large bodies. Moreover, this change reflects a disruption of both apparently stable traditional preference for a robust body shape and the traditional disinterest in reshaping the body (Becker 1995).

Subjects' responses to television in this study also reflect a more complicated reshaping of personal and cultural identities inherent in their endeavors to reshape their bodies. Traditionally for Fijians, identity had been fixed not so much in the body as in family, community, and relationships with others, in contrast to Western-cultural models that firmly fix identity in the body/self. Comparatively speaking, social identity is manipulated and projected through personal, visual props in many Western social contexts, whereas this was less true in Fiji. Instead, Fijians have traditionally invested themselves in nurturing others—efforts that are then concretized in the bodies that one cares for and feeds. Hence, identity is represented (and experienced) individually and collectively through the well-fed bodies of others, not through one's own body (again, comparatively speaking) (Becker 1995). In addition, since Fiji's economy has until recently been based in subsistence agriculture, and since multiple cultural practices encourage distribution of material resources, traditional Fijian identity has also not been represented through the ability to purchase and accumulate material goods.

More broadly than interest in body shape, however, the qualitative data demonstrate a rather concrete identification with television characters as role models of successful engagement in Western, consumeristic lifestyles. Admiration and emulation of television characters appears to stem from recognition that traditional channels are ill-equipped to assist Fijian adolescents in navigating the landscape of rapid social change in Fiji. Unfortunately, while affording an opportunity to develop identities syntonic° with the shifting social context, the behavioral modeling on Western appearance and customs appears to have undercut traditional cultural resources for identity-making (Becker et al. 2002). Specifically, narrative data reveal here that traditional sources of information about self-presentation and public comportment have been supplanted by captivating and convincing role models depicted in televised programming and commercials.

syntonic: emotionally responsive to one's environment.

It is noteworthy that the interest in reshaping the body differs in subtle but important ways from the drive for thinness observed in other social contexts. The discourse on reshaping the body is, indeed, quite explicitly and pragmatically focused on competitive social positioning—for both employment opportunities and peer approval. This discourse on weight and body shape is suffused with moral as well as material associations (i.e., that appear to be commentary on the social body). That is, repeatedly expressed sentiment that excessive weight results in laziness and undermines domestic productivity may reflect a concern about how Fijians will "measure up" in the global economy. The juxtaposition of extreme affluence depicted on most television programs against the materially impoverished Fijians associates the nearly uniformly thin bodies and restrained appetites of television characters with the (illusory) promise of economic opportunity and success. Each child's future, as well as the fitness of the social body, seems to be at stake. 5

In this sense, disordered eating among the Fijian schoolgirls in this study appears to be primarily an instrumental means of reshaping body and identity to enhance social and economic opportunities. From this perspective, it may be premature to comment on whether or not disordered eating behaviors share the same meaning as similar behaviors in other cultural contexts. It is also premature to say whether these behaviors correspond well to Western nosologic° categories describing eating disorders. Regardless of any differences in psychological significance of the behaviors, however, physiologic risks will be the same. Quite possibly—and this remains to be studied in further detail—disordered eating may also be a symbolic embodiment of the anxiety and conflict the youth experience on the threshold of rapid social change in Fiji and during their personal and collective navigation through it.

nosologic: relating to diseases.

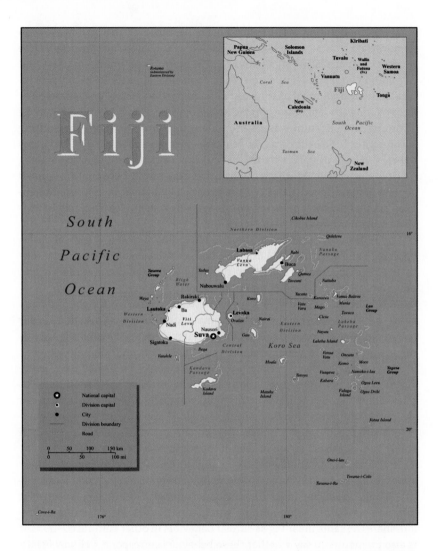

Moreover, there is some preliminary evidence that the disordered eating is accompanied by clinical features associated with the illnesses elsewhere and eating disorders may be emerging in this context. Finally, television has certainly imported more than just images associating appearance with material success; it has arguably enhanced reflexivity about the possibility of reshaping one's body and life trajectory and popularized the notion of competitive social positioning.

The impact of imported media in societies undergoing transition on local values has been demonstrated in multiple societies (e.g., Cheung and Chan 1996; Granzberg 1985; Miller 1998; Reis 1998; Tan et al. 1987; Wu 1990). As others have argued in other contexts, ideas from imported media can be used to negotiate "hybrid identities" (Barker 1997) and otherwise incorporated into various strategies for social positioning (Mazzarella 2003) and coping with modernization (Varan 1998). Likewise and ironically, here as elsewhere in the world (see Anderson-Fye 2004), Fijian youth must craft an identity which adopts Western values about productivity and efficiency in the workplace while simultaneously selling their Fijian-ness (an essential asset to their role in the tourist industry). Self-presentation is thus carefully constructed so as to bridge and integrate dual identities. That these identities are not consistently smoothly fused is evidenced in the ambivalence in the narratives about how thin a body is actually ideal.

The source of the emerging disordered eating among ethnic Fijian girls thus appears multifactorial and multidetermined. Media images that associate thinness with material success and marketing that promotes the possibility of reshaping the body have supported a perceived nexus° between diligence (work on the body), appearance (thinness), and social and material success (material possessions, economic opportunities, and popularity with peers). Fijian self-presentation has absorbed new dimensions related to buying into Western styles of appearance and the ethos of work on the body. A less articulated parallel to admiration for characters, bodies, and lifestyles portrayed on imported television is the demoralizing perception of not comparing favorably as a population. It is as though a mirror was held up to these girls in which they perhaps saw themselves as poor and overweight. The eagerness they express in grooming themselves to be hard workers or perhaps obtain competitive jobs perhaps reflects their collective energy and anxiety about how they, as individuals, and as a Fijian people, are going to fare in a globalizing world. Thus preoccupation with weight loss and the restrictive eating and purging certainly reflect pragmatic strategies to optimize social and economic success. At the same time, they surely contribute to body- and self-disparagement and reflect an embodied distress about the uncertainty of personal future and the social body.

Epidemiologic data° from other populations confirm an association between social transition (e.g., transnational migration, modernization, urbanization) and disordered eating among vulnerable groups (Anderson-Fye and Becker 2004). In particular, the association between upward mobility and disordered eating across diverse populations has relevance here (Anderson-Fye 2000; Buchan and Gregory 1984; Silber 1986; Soomro et al. 1995; Yates

Becker uses survey and interview data to support her argument about eating disorders in Fiji. Chapter 4 offers examples of "hard evidence" used in arguments based on fact.

LINK TO P. 73

nexus: a point of convergence or intersection.

epidemiologic data: data, likely quantitative, concerning the cause, spread, and control of diseases.

1989). Exposure to Western media images and ideas may further contribute to disordered eating by first promoting comparisons that result in perceived economic and social disadvantage and then promoting the notion that efforts to reshape the body will enhance social status. It can be argued that girls and young women undergoing social transition may perceive that social status is enhanced by positioning oneself competitively through the informed use of cultural symbols—e.g., by bodily appearance and thinness (Becker and Hamburg 1996). This is comparable to observations that children of immigrants to the U.S. (for whom the usual parental "map of experience" is lacking) substitute alternative "cultural guides" from the media as resources for negotiating successful social strategies (Suarez-Orozco and Suarez-Orozco 2001). In both scenarios, adolescent girls and young women assimilating to new cultural standards encounter a ready cultural script for comportment and appearance in the media.

Conclusions

> "I've wondered how television is made and how the actress and actors,
> I always wondered how television, how people acted on it, and I'm kind
> of wondering whether it's true or not." (S-48)

The increased prevalence of disordered eating in ethnic Fijian schoolgirls 10 is not the only story—or even the most important one—that can be pieced together from the respondents' narratives on television and its impact.[1] Nor are images and values transmitted through televised media singular forces in the chain of events that has led to an apparent increase in disordered eating attitudes and behaviors. The impact of media coupled with other sweeping economic and social change is likely to affect Fijian youth and adults in many ways. On the other hand, this particular story allows a window into the powerful impact and vulnerability of this adolescent female population. This story also allows a frame for exploring resilience and suggesting interventions for future research.

In some important ways, Fiji is a unique context for investigating the impact of media imagery on adolescents. In Fiji in particular, the evolving and multiple—and potentially overlapping or dissonant—social terrain presents novel challenges and opportunities for adolescents navigating their way in the absence of guidance from "conventional" wisdom and social hierarchies that may have grown obsolete in some respects. Doubtless the profound ways in which adolescent girls are influenced by media imagery extend beyond the borders of Fiji and the ways in which young women in Fiji consume and reflect on televised media may suggest mechanisms for its impact on youth in other social contexts. This study, therefore, allows insight into the ways in which social change intersects with the developmental tasks of adolescence to pose the risk of eating disorders and other youth risk behaviors.

Adolescent girls and young women in this and other indigenous, small-scale societies may also be especially vulnerable to the effects of media exposure for several key reasons. For example, in the context of rapid social change, these girls and young women may lack traditional role models for how to successfully maneuver in a shifting economic and political environment. Moreover, in societies in which status is traditionally ascribed° rather than achieved,° girls and women may feel more compelled to secure their social position through a mastery of self-presentation that draws heavily from imported media. It is a logical and frightening conclusion that vulnerable girls and women across diverse populations who feel marginalized from the locally dominant culture's sources of prestige and status may anchor their identities in widely recognized cultural symbols of prestige popularized by media-imported ideas, values, and images. Further, these girls and women have no reference for comparison of the televised images to the "realities" they portray and thus to critique and deconstruct the images they see compared with girls and women who are "socialized" into a culture of viewership. Without thoughtful interventions[2]—yet to be explored with the affected communities—the unfortunate outcome is likely to be continued increasing rates of disordered eating and other youth risk behaviors in vulnerable populations undergoing rapid modernization and social transition.

ascribed status: status that one is granted by others, often on the basis of external qualities (for example, being a firstborn son in a society that values male children and pays attention to birth order).

achieved status: status that one somehow wins or attains (example, placing first in a competition).

Singer-songwriter Jill Scott plays Precious Ramotswe, owner of the No. 1 Ladies' Detective Agency, in the television miniseries about Alexander McCall Smith's fictional sleuth, set in Botswana. Ramotswe frequently reflects on her status as a "traditionally built" African woman in a society where standards of female attractiveness are rapidly changing.

Notes

1. For example, the increased incidence of suicide and other self-injury in Fiji (Pridmore et al. 1995) may index social distress related to rapid social change.

2. Prevention efforts that might be useful include psychoeducational information about the psychological and medical risks associated with bingeing, purging, and self-starvation as well as media literacy programs that assist youth in critical and informed viewing of televised programming and commercials.

References

Anderson-Fye, E.P.

2000 Self-Reported Eating Attitudes Among High School Girls in Belize: A Quantitative Survey. Unpublished Qualifying Paper. Department of Human Development and Psychology, Harvard University, Cambridge, MA.

Anderson-Fye, E.

2004 A "Coca-Cola" Shape: Cultural Change, Body Image, and Eating Disorders in San Andrés, Belize. Culture, Medicine and Society 28: 561–595.

Anderson-Fye, E., and A.E. Becker

2004 Socio-Cultural Aspects of Eating Disorders. *In* Handbook of Eating Disorders and Obesity. J.K. Thompson, ed., pp. 565–589. Wiley.

Barker, C.

1997 Television and the Reflexive Project of the Self: Soaps, Teenage Talk and Hybrid Identities. British Journal of Sociology 48: 611–628.

Becker, A.E.

1995 Body, Self, Society: The View from Fiji. Philadelphia: University of Pennsylvania Press.

Becker, A.E., and P. Hamburg

1996 Culture, the Media, and Eating Disorders. Harvard Review of Psychiatry 4: 163–167.

Becker, A.E., R.A. Burwell, S.E. Gilman, D.B. Herzog, and P. Hamburg

2002 Eating Behaviors and Attitudes Following Prolonged Television Exposure Among Ethnic Fijian Adolescent Girls. British Journal of Psychiatry 180: 509–514.

Buchan, T., and L.D. Gregory

1984 Anorexia Nervosa in a Black Zimbabwean. British Journal of Psychiatry 145: 326–330.

Cheung, C.K., and C.F. Chan

1996 Television Viewing and Mean World Value in Hong Kong's Adolescents. Social Behavior and Personality 24: 351–364.

Granzberg, G.

1985 Television and Self-Concept Formation in Developing Areas. Journal of Cross-Cultural Psychology 16: 313–328.

Mazzarella, W.
  2003 Shoveling Smoke: Advertising and Globalization in Contemporary India.
       Durham, NC: Duke University Press.
Miller, C.J.
  1998 The Social Impacts of Televised Media Among the Yucatec Maya. Human
       Organization 57: 307–314.
Pridmore, S., K. Ryan, and L. Blizzard
  1995 Victims of Violence in Fiji. Australian and New Zealand Journal of Psychiatry
       29: 666–670.
Reis, R.
  1998 The Impact of Television Viewing in the Brazilian Amazon. Human
       Organization 57: 300–306.
Silber, T.J.
  1986 Anorexia Nervosa in Blacks and Hispanics. International Journal of Eating
       Disorders 5: 121–128.
Soomro, G.M., A.H. Crisp, D. Lynch, D. Tran, and N. Joughin
  1995 Anorexia Nervosa in 'Non-White' Populations. British Journal of Psychiatry
       167: 385–389.
Suarez-Orozco, C., and M.M. Suarez-Orozco
  2001 Children of Immigration. Cambridge, MA: Harvard University Press.
Tan, A.S., G.K. Tan, and A.S. Tan
  1987 American TV in the Philippines: A Test of Cultural Impact. Journalism
       Quarterly 64: 65–72, 144.
Varan, D.
  1998 The Cultural Erosion Metaphor and the Transcultural Impact of Media
       Systems. Journal of Communication 48: 58–85.
Wu, Y.K.
  1990 Television and the Value Systems of Taiwan's Adolescents: A Cultivation
       Analysis. Dissertation Abstracts International 50: 3783A.
Yates, A.
  1989 Current Perspectives on the Eating Disorders: I. History, Psychological
       and Biological Aspects. Journal of the American Academy of Child and
       Adolescent Psychiatry 28(6): 813–828.

RESPOND

1. How does Becker link exposure to Western media to the changing
   notions young Fijian women have of their own bodies? Why does
   Becker claim these women now want to be thin? How are these
   changes linked to other social changes occurring in Fiji, to adolescence, and to gender, especially in small-scale societies?

2. As Becker notes, she relies on qualitative data—specifically, interview data—to support her arguments. Why are such data especially appropriate, given her goals of understanding the changing social meanings of body image for young Fijian women as part of other rapid social changes taking place in Fiji? (For a discussion of firsthand evidence, see Chapter 16.)

3. Throughout the Discussion and Conclusions sections, Becker repeatedly qualifies her arguments to discourage readers from extending them further than she believes her data warrant. Find two cases where she does so, and explain the specific ways that she reminds readers of the limits of her claims. (For a discussion on qualifying claims and arguments, see Chapter 7.)

4. These excerpts from Becker's article represent research writing for an academic audience. What functions does each of the reprinted sections serve for the article's readers, and why is each located where it is? Why, for example, is an abstract placed at the beginning of an article? Why are key words a valuable part of an abstract?

5. In paragraph 3, in the "Discussion" section of her article, Becker compares and contrasts how Westerners (which would include Americans) and Fijians understand identity, especially as it relates to the body. **Write an essay** in which you evaluate Becker's characterization of Western notions of identity. (For a discussion of evaluative arguments, see Chapter 10.) Unless you have detailed knowledge of a culture very different from Western cultures (Fiji, for example), you may want to begin by trying to demonstrate that Becker's assessment is correct, at least to some degree, rather than claiming that she misunderstands the West. Once you've conceded that there's at least some truth in her assessment, you may be able to cite cases of American subcultures that don't "firmly fix identity in the body/self."

Making a Visual Argument:
We All Walk in Different Shoes
KennethCole.com

Kenneth Cole

Kenneth Cole, a popular American clothing designer, has long used socially conscious advertising to challenge consumers to examine their assumptions. In fact, he was among the first U.S. advertisers to have done so. Since the mid-1980s, when his company began sponsoring ads about AIDS, it has developed a reputation for controversial advertising campaigns and related products. For example, as part of World AIDS Day in 2005, Cole produced T-shirts reading "We all have AIDS." You can view this and other ads in the "Ad Archive" section of the Kenneth Cole Web site (kennethcole.com/content/popUp.jsp?page=archive&h=650&w=820). Cole is also the author of Awearness: Inspiring Stories about How to Make a Difference (2008), a book issued to mark the twenty-fifth anniversary of his company, and he has a blog and Web site to encourage consumers to work for social change. The photograph and caption reprinted on the following page represent one page of an advertising insert distributed in Sunday newspapers during 2008. The other pages of the insert showed a transgender woman, a Hasidic Jewish reggae recording artist, an African American with albinism, and heavily tattooed "punk evangelist" Jay Bakker, founder and pastor of Revolution Church. As you study the ad, consider the subtle and not so subtle ways in which it plays with stereotypes while advertising Cole's products.

621

WE ALL
WALK IN
DIFFERENT
SHOES.

SHARON BLYNN, OVARIAN CANCER SURVIVOR.
Writer, actor, and founder of baldisbeautiful.org.

KENNETHCOLE.COM

RESPOND●

1. What is your initial response to this ad? How does it fit into the series in which it appears, as described in the headnote to this selection? How have the designers of the ads played with stereotypes? How does the choice of individuals who are included (none is a professional model) further the claim that "We all walk in different shoes"?

2. Advertising focuses heavily on emotional arguments, although it often presents ethical and logical arguments as well. Where do you find evidence of each in this ad? (For a discussion of emotional, ethical, and logical arguments, see Chapters 2, 3, and 4, respectively.)

3. Visit the "Ad Archive" Web site that is mentioned in the headnote to this selection, and browse through the ads there. Which do you find especially effective? Why? Choose three ads that you find especially successful, and **write an evaluative essay** in which you explain their effectiveness. If you do not find any of the ads successful, **write an evaluative essay** in which you explain their failings. (In either case, you will need to consider the issue of audience: for whom would this ad be successful and why?) Be sure to attach copies of the ads to your essay. (For a discussion of evaluative essays, see Chapter 10, and for a discussion of visual arguments, see Chapter 14.)

Chapter 14 discusses the power of visual arguments, and this ad is, of course, primarily visual. But what does the text add to the power of the image?

LINK TO P. 442

Common Themes and Questions about the Use of "Indian" Logos

BARBARA MUNSON

"Indian" logos and nicknames create, support and maintain stereotypes of a race of people. When such cultural abuse is supported by one or many of society's institutions, it constitutes institutional racism. **It is not conscionable that public schools be the vehicle of institutional racism.** The logos, along with other societal abuses and stereotypes, separate, marginalize, confuse, intimidate and harm Native American children and create barriers to their learning throughout their school experience. Additionally, the logos teach non-Indian children that it's all right to participate in culturally abusive behavior. Children spend a great deal of their time in school, and schools have a very significant impact on their emotional, spiritual, physical and intellectual development. As long as such logos remain, both Native American and non-Indian children are learning to tolerate racism in our schools. The following illustrate the common questions and statements that I have encountered in trying to provide education about the "Indian" logo issue.

"We have always been proud of our 'Indians'." People are proud of their high school athletic teams, even in communities where the team name and symbolism do not stereotype a race of people. In developing high school athletic traditions, schools have borrowed from Native American cultures the

The logo of the Alliance Against Racial Mascots organization

sacred objects, ceremonial traditions and components of traditional dress that were most obvious, without understanding their deep meaning or appropriate use. High school traditions were created without in-depth knowledge of Native traditions; they are replete with inaccurate depictions of Indian people, and promote and maintain stereotypes of rich and varied cultures. High school athletic traditions have taken the trappings of Native cultures onto the playing field where young people have played at being "Indian." Over time, and with practice, generations of children in these schools have come to believe that the pretended "Indian" identity is more than what it is.

"We are honoring Indians; you should feel honored." Native people are saying that they don't feel honored by this symbolism. We experience it as no less than a mockery of our cultures. We see objects sacred to us—such as the drum, eagle feathers, face painting and traditional dress—being used, not in sacred ceremony, or in any cultural setting, but in another culture's **game.** We are asking that the public schools stop demeaning, insulting, harassing and misrepresenting Native peoples, their cultures and religions, for the sake of school athletics. Why must some schools insist on using symbols of a **race** of people? Other schools are happy with their logos which offend no human being. Why do some schools insist on categorizing Indian people along with animals and objects? If your team name were the Pollacks, Niggers, Gooks, Spics, Honkies or Krauts, and someone from the community found the name and symbols associated with it offensive and asked that it be changed, would you not change the name? If not, why not? I apologize for using this example but have found no way to get this point across without using similar derogatory names for other racial and ethnic groups.

"Why is the term 'Indian' offensive?" The term "Indian" was given to indigenous people on this continent by an explorer who was looking for India, a man who was lost and who subsequently exploited the indigenous people. "Indian" is a designation we have learned to tolerate, it is not the name we call ourselves. We are known by the names of our Nations—Oneida (On ^ yoteaka), Hochunk, Stockbridge-Munsee, Menominee (Omaeqnomenew), Chippewa (Anishanabe), Potawatomi, etc. There are many different nations with different languages and different cultural practices among the Native American peoples—as in Europe there are French, Swiss, Italian, German, Polish, English, Irish, Yugoslavs, Swedes, Portuguese, Latvians, etc.

"Why is an attractive depiction of an Indian warrior just as offensive as an ugly caricature?" Both depictions present and maintain stereotypes.   5

The bolded statements and questions that Munson uses to organize this argument are common rebuttals to arguments made against Native American mascots. For more on anticipating rebuttals and structuring arguments, see Chapter 7.

LINK TO P. 170

Both firmly place Indian people in the past, separate from our contemporary cultural experience. It is difficult, at best, to be heard in the present when someone is always suggesting that your real culture only exists in museums. The logos keep us marginalized and are a barrier to our contributing here and now. Depictions of mighty warriors of the past emphasize a tragic part of our history; focusing on wartime survival, they ignore the strength and beauty of our cultures during times of peace. Many Indian cultures view life as a spiritual journey filled with lessons to be learned from every experience and from every living being. Many cultures put high value on peace, right action and sharing.

Indian men are not limited to the role of warrior; in many of our cultures a good man is learned, gentle, patient, wise and deeply spiritual. In present time as in the past, our men are also sons and brothers, husbands, uncles, fathers and grandfathers. Contemporary Indian men work in a broad spectrum of occupations, wear contemporary clothes and live and love just as men do from other cultural backgrounds.

The depictions of Indian "braves," "warriors" and "chiefs" also ignore the roles of women and children. Although there are patrilineal Native cultures, many Indian nations are both matrilineal and child centered. Indian cultures identify women with the Creator because of their ability to bear children, and with the Earth which is Mother to us all. In most Indian cultures the highest value

is given to children; they are closest to the Creator and they embody the future. In many Native traditions, each generation is responsible for the children of the seventh generation in the future.

"We never intended the logo to cause harm." That no harm was intended when the logos were adopted may be true. It is also true that we Indian people are saying that the logos are harmful to our cultures, and especially to our children, in the present. When someone says you are hurting them by your action, if you persist, then the harm becomes intentional.

"We are paying tribute to Indians." Indian people do not pay tribute to one another by the use of logos, portraits or statues. The following are some ways that we exhibit honor:

In most cultures to receive an eagle feather is a great honor, and often such a feather also carries great responsibility.

An honor song at a Pow-Wow or other ceremony is a way of honoring a person or a group.

We honor our elders and leaders by asking them to share knowledge and experience with us or to lead us in prayer. We defer to elders. They go first in many ways in our cultures.

We honor our young by not doing things to them that would keep them from becoming who and what they are intended to be.

We honor one another by listening and not interrupting.

We honor those we love by giving them our time and attention.

Sometimes we honor people through gentle joking.

We honor others by giving to them freely what they need or what belongs to them already because they love it more or could use it better than we do.

"Aren't you proud of your warriors?" Yes, we are proud of the warriors who   10
fought to protect our cultures and preserve our lands. We are proud and we don't want them demeaned by being "honored" in a sports activity on a **playing** field. Our people died tragically in wars motivated by greed for our lands. Our peoples have experienced forced removal and systematic genocide. Our warriors gave their sacred lives in often vain attempts to protect the land and preserve the culture for future generations. Football is a game.

"This is not an important issue." If it is not important, then why are school boards willing to tie up their time and risk potential law suits rather than simply change the logos? I, as an Indian person, have never said it is unimportant. Most Indian adults have lived through the pain of prejudice and harassment in schools when they were growing up, and they don't want their children to experience more of the same. The National Council of American Indians, the Great Lakes InterTribal Council, the Oneida Tribe, and the Wisconsin Indian Education Association have all adopted formal position statements because this is a very important issue to Indian people. This issue speaks to our children being able to form a positive Indian identity and to develop appropriate levels of self-esteem. In addition, it has legal ramifications in regard to pupil harassment and equal access to education. If it's not important to people of differing ethnic and racial backgrounds within the community, then change the logos because they are hurting the community's Native American population.

"What if we drop derogatory comments and clip art and adopt pieces of REAL Indian culturally significant ceremony, like Pow-Wows and sacred songs?" Though well intended, these solutions are culturally naive and would exchange one pseudo-culture for another. Pow-Wows are gatherings of Native people which give us the opportunity to express our various cultures and strengthen our sense of Native American community. Pow-Wows have religious, as well as social, significance. To parodize such ceremonial gatherings for the purpose of cheering on the team at homecoming would multiply exponentially the current pseudo-cultural offensiveness. Bringing Native religions onto the playing field through songs of tribute to the "Great Spirit"

or Mother Earth would increase the mockery of Native religions even more than the current use of drums and feathers. High school football games are secular; The Creator and Mother Earth are sacred.

"We are helping you preserve your culture." The responsibility for the continuance of our cultures falls to Native people. We accomplish this by surviving, living and thriving; and, in so doing, we pass on to our children our stories, traditions, religions, values, arts and our languages. We sometimes do this important work with people from other cultural backgrounds, but they do not and cannot continue our cultures for us. Our ancestors did this work for us, and we continue to carry the culture for the generations to come. Our cultures are living cultures—they are passed on, not "preserved."

"This logo issue is just about political correctness." Using the term "political correctness" to describe the attempts of concerned Native American parents, educators and leaders to remove stereotypes from the public schools trivializes a survival issue. A history of systematic genocide has decimated over 95% of the indigenous population of the Americas. Today, the average life expectancy of Native American males is age 45. The teen suicide rate among Native people is several times higher than the national average. Stereotypes, ignorance, silent inaction and even naive innocence damage and destroy individual lives and whole cultures. Racism kills.

"What do you mean, there is hypocrisy involved in retaining an 'Indian' logo?" Imagine that you are a child in a society where your people are variously depicted as stoic, brave, honest, a mighty warrior, fierce, savage, stupid, dirty, drunken and only good when dead. Imagine going to a school where many of your classmates refer to your people as "Dirty Squaws" and "Timber Niggers." Imagine hearing your peers freely, loudly and frequently say such things as "Spear an Indian, Save a Walleye," or more picturesquely proclaim "Spear a Pregnant Squaw, Save a Walleye." Imagine that the teachers and administration do not forbid this kind of behavior. Imagine that this same school holds aloft an attractive depiction of a Plains Indian Chieftain and cheers on its "Indian" team. Imagine that in homecoming displays, cheers and artwork you see your people depicted inaccurately in ways that demean your cultural and religious practices. Imagine that when you bring your experiences to the attention of your school board and request change, they simply ignore you and decide to continue business as usual. Imagine that the same school board states publicly that it opposes discriminatory practices, provides equal educational opportunity and supports respect for cultural differences.

"Why don't community members understand the need to change; isn't it a simple matter of respect?" On one level, yes. But in some communities, people have bought into local myths and folklore presented as accurate historical facts. Sometimes these myths are created or preserved by local industry. Also, over the years, athletic and school traditions grow up around the logos. These athletic traditions can be hard to change when much of a community's ceremonial and ritual life, as well as its pride, becomes tied to high school athletic activities. Finally, many people find it difficult to grasp a different cultural perspective. Not being from an Indian culture, they find it hard to understand that things which are not offensive to themselves might be offensive or even harmful to someone who is from a Native culture. Respecting a culture different from the one you were raised in requires some effort. Even if a person lives in a different culture, insight and understanding of that culture will require interaction, listening, observing and a willingness to learn.

The Native American population, in most school districts displaying "Indian" logos, is proportionally very small. When one of us confronts the logo issue, that person, his or her children and other family members, and anyone else in the district who is Native American become targets of insults and threats; we are shunned and further marginalized—our voices become even harder to hear from behind barriers of fear and anger. We appreciate the courage, support, and sometimes the sacrifice, of all who stand with us by speaking out against the continued use of "Indian" logos. When you advocate for the removal of these logos, you are strengthening the spirit of tolerance and justice in your community; you are modeling for all our children— thoughtfulness, courage and respect for self and others.

RESPOND•

1. What's Munson's argument? Why is it stated where and as it is? How might her purpose in writing have led her to present her material in this way? Would the selection have been more or less effective if she'd formatted her argument as a "regular" essay, consisting of an intro- duction that leads to her thesis statement, several paragraphs of a body, and a conclusion? Why?

2. Examine the "common questions and statements" to which Munson replies, and try to determine why she arranged them in this order. Would her argument be strengthened or weakened if these paragraphs were in a different order? Are there advantages and disadvantages to such implicit organization of an argument?

3. How would you characterize Munson's tone in this selection? Her ethos? What evidence would you cite for your conclusions? How do her tone and ethos contribute to or detract from her argument? Would you characterize this argument as Rogerian? (For a discussion of Rogerian argumentation, see Chapter 1.) Why or why not?

4. One of Munson's concerns is the influence of "Indian" logos on children, both Native American and non-Indian. Do you agree with her argument? Why or why not? How does her mention of children early in the argument add to the weight or gravity of her topic as she defines it?

5. Although American Indian logos, names, mascots, and symbols show up in many places in popular culture, Munson is concerned specifically with athletics and sports events. Why? In what sense does her article demonstrate that these logos, names, mascots, and symbols have become part of larger political debates? (For a discussion of evaluative arguments, see Chapter 10.)

6. One way to understand Munson's argument is to claim that racism of any sort isn't a matter of intention but of effect and that the effects of racism are pernicious both for those who belong to the group that's the target of the racism and for those who don't, especially those who perpetrate the racism. Part of her argument is also that members of the targeted group are best positioned to determine whether racism has occurred. **Write an essay** in which you evaluate either or both of these claims, using examples relating to another group.

In 2005, the National Collegiate Athletic Association (NCAA) enacted *new rules governing "mascots, nicknames, or images deemed hostile or abusive in terms of race, ethnicity, or national origin." These rules address the issues that were raised in the previous selection by Barbara Munson, "Common Themes and Questions about the Use of 'Indian' Logos." In this New York Times article from December 29, 2006, Joe Lapointe, who writes about sports and sports-related issues for the newspaper, investigates the situation at Florida State University, one of several schools that received NCAA permission to retain an Indian-themed mascot, in its case because of an arrangement with the Seminole Tribe of Florida. As you read this selection, look for evidence of the "complex relationship" that exists between Florida State athletics and the Seminole Tribe and the ways in which, even now, stereotypes are part of that complexity.*

Bonding over a Mascot

JOE LAPOINTE

A few new statues of a Seminole family in 19th-century clothing stand outside the football stadium at Florida State University. The father holds a long gun, the son a bow and arrow, and the mother an infant in her arms as she looks warily to her right.

The statues represent the era when the Seminoles and the United States were at war. The public art is part of a complex relationship between Seminole culture and sports at Florida State. This bond has strengthened since a crackdown by the National Collegiate Athletic Association last year against American Indian mascots, nicknames and imagery among sports teams.

Not every university enjoys a harmonious relationship with Indians. But a sense of cooperation seems to permeate the Florida State campus in Tallahassee, Fla., where Toni Sanchez was among 21 students to complete a new course this month called History of the Seminoles and Southeastern Tribes.

Sanchez, a senior majoring in English, called the N.C.A.A. edict "beyond idiotic" and offensive. She described the new statues as beautiful.

"I know what a real Seminole is," 5 she said. "This Anglo guilt and regret don't affect me."

Sanchez is from a family with Seminole and Hispanic ancestry. Her father, once a farm worker, is now a casino operator. Her mother is a teacher. Sanchez also plays trumpet at football games in a marching band that wears arrowheads on the back of its uniforms.

Of the tribal flag near the new statues, another recent addition, she said, "Every time I look at it, I get really giddy inside." Of the use of the Seminole imagery for the university's sports, she said, "I'm so proud of it."

Florida State was one of 18 institutions cited by the N.C.A.A. in August 2005 for "mascots, nicknames or images deemed hostile or abusive in terms of race, ethnicity or national origin." The institutions were forbidden to use the symbols in postseason events controlled by the N.C.A.A., like the national championship basketball tournament that begins in March.

Five programs have since received permission to continue using their imagery because they received approval from specific Indian groups, in Florida State's case the 3,200-member Seminole Tribe of Florida. Five others have changed or are in the process of

Toni Sanchez, a student from a family with Seminole and Hispanic ancestry, is proud of the use of Seminole imagery at Florida State.

sity might "gradually let certain things fade."

He said he told the Seminole Tribe of Florida's council, "If you don't want Florida State to be the Seminoles, we ain't Seminoles anymore." Wetherell said the tribe approved the use partly because the campus is in the capital and tribal leaders "are not only good businessmen, they are great politicians."

He said the new history course was proposed before the N.C.A.A. edict.

But Neil Jumonville, the chairman of the history department, said the N.C.A.A. resolution accelerated the creation of the class and that his staff received advice from local Seminole leaders.

"These are people who are savvy about their place in the American myth," Jumonville said. "And they are smart enough to manipulate the myth for their own good."

The first class was taught by 20 Christopher R. Versen, who recently earned his doctorate in American history.

"I wanted to challenge students to think about identity," Versen said. "What is it inside us that makes us identify ourselves one way or another? What external factors play into identity?"

How would you compare the ethos of Myles Brand and that of T. K. Wetherell, both leaders of large institutions, as they appear in this article? For help in thinking about your ideas, see Chapter 3.

LINK TO P. 52 ....

changing, said Bob Williams, an N.C.A.A. spokesman. The other eight, he said, remain on the list and are subject to the policy, including the Illinois Fighting Illini and the North Dakota Fighting Sioux.

Myles Brand, the president of the 10 N.C.A.A., said in a telephone interview last week that his organization made the right decision but witnessed more negative reaction to the ruling than expected.

"What we've accomplished in part is to raise the level of awareness nationally about how we treat Native Americans," Brand said. "If we don't stand by our values, we lose our integrity."

At times, Indians are reduced to casual caricature that would not be tolerated by other groups, he said,

adding that the N.C.A.A. had been honored for its stance by Indian groups in Oklahoma and Indiana.

Less complimentary is T. K. Wetherell, the president of Florida State, who said the N.C.A.A. was "more interested in being politically correct" and did not consult the Seminole tribe before making its decision.

"The way they weaseled out was to say, 'O.K., as long as the tribe continues to support it,' " he said.

Wetherell, a former Florida State 15 football player who also teaches history, wore a hunting outfit when interviewed recently in his office. He pointed to a team logo of an Indian's face that he said had elements of caricature. "That's not really a Seminole-looking deal," Wetherell said. "This is a marketing tool." He said the univer-

The Seminoles are an amalgam of several tribes, predominantly Creek, that included escaped slaves. They migrated south to the Everglades in retreat from the United States Army. Some were driven out during the Trail of Tears period under President Andrew Jackson.

Those descendants live as the Seminole Nation of Oklahoma. The Seminoles in Florida once had a commercial hunting economy. Since 1979, their economic status has improved because of casino gambling.

Earlier this month, the Seminoles acquired Hard Rock International—the music-themed chain of restaurants, hotels and casinos—for $965 million.

Versen said he did not discuss 25 sports identity with his students because he was afraid it would become a distraction. But a guest speaker who raised the mascot issue was Max Osceola, one of three councilmen for the Seminole Tribe of Florida.

"If I had a child and named it after you, would you consider it an honor?" Osceola said he asked the students. He also reflected on a former mascot, Sammy Seminole, who was retired in 1972.

"He had a big nose and he lived in a teepee," Osceola said. "He looked like a buffoon."

The current mascot is named, coincidentally, Osceola, after a 19th-

A Florida State student dressed as the Seminole leader Osceola rides a horse onto the field at home football games.

century warrior. A student dressed as Osceola rides a horse named Renegade onto the football field and throws a flaming spear. This mascot's clothing was designed by the tribe.

Tina Osceola, who is the executive director of the tribe's historical resources department and is a cousin of Max Osceola's, said, "We've given them license to be theatrical."

A statue of the warrior riding atop 30 Renegade stands outside the stadium above the word "Unconquered,"

because the Seminoles never surrendered to the United States.

When the Seminoles announced in New York the purchase of Hard Rock, Max Osceola joked that Indians once sold Manhattan for trinkets but were now "going to buy Manhattan back, one burger at a time."

Not everyone outside the tribe approves of all of the Indian trappings at sporting events, including the tomahawk chop hand gesture and a droning cheer that sounds like background music heard in old western movies.

Joe Quetone, the executive director of the nonprofit Florida Governor's Council on Indian Affairs Inc., said, "Things fans do are outrageous and ridiculous."

Bobby Bowden, the head football coach, did not respond to four recent requests for comment on the issue placed with the university's sports information department.

From a student's perspective, 35 Sanchez said that people who were genuinely concerned with the circumstances of Indians should concentrate less on sports iconography and more on alcoholism, suicide, teen pregnancy and high school dropout rates.

"After all those years of diseases, occupation and war, we're still here," she said. "I refuse to believe that a silly mascot will take us down."

RESPOND●

1. The selection offers some insights into how and why Florida State University has been able to retain its mascot, the Seminole, despite the 2005 NCAA rules. Based on this article, how and why has the discussion at Florida State moved past an argument over stereotypes? What problems has bonding over the mascot solved for the various parties involved? Which problems has it not solved?

2. This article carries the title "Bonding over a Mascot." (As you may be aware, journalists rarely, if ever, title their own articles.) We might also read the article as an analysis of the ways in which Florida State and the Seminole Tribe have bonded against the NCAA. What are the advantages for each group of bonding against the NCAA over the mascot? How has such cooperation worked, at least in the eyes of some, to reduce demeaning stereotypes?

3. Like most writers, Lapointe relies on ethical appeals in constructing his argument—his own ethos and the ethos of those he quotes. Whom does he choose to quote in this article? How does the identity of these individuals—who they are or the role that they play—influence their credibility with you as a reader? How would the article have been different if Lapointe had begun it by focusing on Seminole students who were unhappy with their tribe's decision?

4. How might Barbara Munson, author of the previous selection, "Common Themes and Questions about the Use of 'Indian' Logos," respond to Toni Sanchez's position as expressed in this article? Why?

5. Using the Internet, investigate subsequent developments in response to the 2005 NCAA rules. You may wish to **write an essay** in which you present an argument of fact or in which you use the available facts to construct an argument of definition involving stereotypes and their consequences. (For a discussion of arguments of fact, see Chapter 8; for a discussion of arguments of definition, see Chapter 9.)

▼ *This feature article from the March 30, 2007, business section of the New York Times raises an interesting question about stereotypes: can an image that has become a marketing liability be salvaged and transformed into an asset? Its author, Stuart Elliott, has been writing for over twenty years about issues related to advertising and media in a number of publications, including the Times. (By the time you finish this selection, you won't be surprised to learn that his interests include old advertising.) As you read this article, reflect on your own experience with the character of Uncle Ben and other characters that are associated with various products, asking yourself whether they might have been teaching you covert lessons.*

Uncle Ben, Board Chairman

STUART ELLIOTT

A racially charged advertising character, who for decades has been relegated to a minor role in the marketing of the products that still carry his name, is taking center stage in a campaign that gives him a makeover—Madison Avenue style—by promoting him to chairman of the company.

The character is Uncle Ben, the symbol for more than 60 years of the Uncle Ben's line of rices and side dishes now sold by the food giant Mars. The challenges confronting Mars in reviving a character as racially fraught as Uncle Ben were evidenced in the reactions of experts to a redesigned Web site (unclebens.com), which went live this week.

"This is an interesting idea, but for me it still has a very high cringe factor," said Luke Visconti, partner at Diversity Inc. Media in Newark, which publishes a magazine and Web site devoted to diversity in the workplace.

"There's a lot of baggage associated with the image," Mr. Visconti said, which the makeover "is glossing over."

Uncle Ben, who first appeared in 5 ads in 1946, is being reborn as Ben, an accomplished businessman with an opulent office, a busy schedule, an extensive travel itinerary and a penchant for sharing what the company calls his "grains of wisdom" about rice and life. A crucial aspect of his biography remains the same, though: He has no last name.

Vincent Howell, president for the food division of the Masterfoods USA unit of Mars, said that because consumers described Uncle Ben as having "a timeless element to him, we didn't want to significantly change him."

"What's powerful to me is to show an African-American icon in a position of prominence and authority,"

An Uncle Ben's–sponsored event

Mr. Howell said. "As an African-American, he makes me feel so proud."

The previous reluctance to feature Uncle Ben prominently in ads stood in stark contrast to the way other human

636

The longtime image of Aunt Jemima, in a photo taken between 1933 and 1951; a number of women, including Anna Robinson, shown here, portrayed the character at events like state fairs.

How do the images reproduced with this article—especially the one of the woman who portrayed Aunt Jemima in the early twentieth century and the ones on the boxes she's holding—affect your responses to the claims made by the advertisers, spokespeople, and critics in the article? For more on how images affect arguments, see Chapter 14.

LINK TO P. 442

Before the civil rights movement took hold, marketers of food and household products often used racial and ethnic stereotypes in creating brand characters and mascots.

In addition to Uncle Ben, there 10 was Aunt Jemima, who sold pancake mix in ads that sometimes had her exclaiming, "Tempt yo' appetite;" a grinning black chef named Rastus, who represented Cream of Wheat hot cereal; the Gold Dust Twins, a pair of black urchins who peddled a soap powder for Lever Brothers; the Frito Bandito, who spoke in an exaggerated Mexican accent; and characters selling powdered drink mixes for Pillsbury

characters like Orville Redenbacher and Colonel Sanders personify their products. That reticence can be traced to the contentious history of Uncle Ben as the black face of a white company, wearing a bow tie evocative of servants and Pullman porters° and bearing a title reflecting how white Southerners once used "uncle" and "aunt" as honorifics for older blacks because they refused to say "Mr." and "Mrs."

Pullman porter: from the 1860s to the 1960s, Pullman was the most common brand of sleeping car on American trains. The Pullman Palace Car Company hired African American men to serve as porters—employees who helped travelers with their bags. Although the job was demeaning in certain ways, it offered more job security and higher wages than many other options at the time. Pullman porters were all addressed as "George," probably both because of the company's founder, George Pullman, and because of racial attitudes discussed in this article.

under names like Injun Orange and Chinese Cherry—the latter baring buck teeth.

"The only time blacks were put into ads was when they were athletic, subservient or entertainers," said Marilyn Kern Foxworth, the author of *Aunt Jemima, Uncle Ben and Rastus: Blacks in Advertising Yesterday, Today and Tomorrow.*

After the start of the civil rights movement, such characters became "lightning rods" in a period when consumers started to want "images our children could look up to and emulate," Ms. Kern Foxworth said.

As a result, most of those polarizing ad characters were banished when marketers—becoming more sensitive to the changing attitudes of consumers—realized they were no longer appropriate. A handful like Uncle Ben, Aunt Jemima and the Cream of Wheat chef were redesigned and kept on, but in the unusual status of silent spokescharacters, removed from ads and reduced to staring mutely from packages.

Times, however, change, as evidenced by real-life figures as disparate as Wally Amos, the founder of Famous Amos cookies; Oprah Winfrey; and Senator Barack Obama, the Illinois Democrat who is running for president. In advertising, there are now black authority figures serving as spokesmen in multimillion-dollar campaigns, like Dennis Haysbert,° for Allstate, and James Earl Jones,° for Verizon.

That helped executives at 15 Masterfoods and its advertising agency, TBWA/Chiat/Day, consider the risky step of reviving the character.

"There's no doubt we realized we had a very powerful asset we were not using strongly enough," Mr. Howell said.

So about 18 months ago, the company and agency decided "to reach out to our consumers" and gauge attitudes toward Uncle Ben, Mr. Howell said. There were no negative responses or references to the stereotyped aspects of the character, he said. Rather, the consumers "focused on positive images, quality, warmth, timelessness," he added, and "the legend of Uncle Ben."

That encouraged the idea that "we could bring him to life," Mr. Howell said, sensitive to "the sorts of concerns that are important to me as an African-American."

Joe Shands, a creative director at the Playa del Rey, Calif., office of TBWA/Chiat/Day, said the freedom to use the character to sell the Uncle Ben's brand was a welcome change from the years when "all we've had to work with is a portrait." "We wanted to know if there was something there we could utilize to talk about new products, existing products, the values of the company," Mr. Shands said, adding that both black and white consumers described the character as someone "they know and love."

"Through the magic of marketing, 20 we've made him the chairman," Mr. Shands said. Uncle Ben's office, he said, is "reflective of a man with great wisdom who has done great things."

Magazine ads in the campaign, which carries the theme "Ben knows best," present a painting of the character in a gold frame with the chairman's title affixed on a plaque.

The painting is also on display on the home page of the redesigned Web site, which offers a virtual tour of Ben's office. Visitors can browse through his e-mail messages, examine

---

Dennis Haysbert (b. 1954): an American actor.

James Earl Jones (b. 1931): an American actor known for his melodious bass voice.

his datebook and read his executive memorandums.

"It's important consumers begin to hear from Uncle Ben," said Mr. Howell of Masterfoods, who is based in Los Angeles.

Despite the character's impressive new credentials, some advertising executives expressed skepticism that the campaign could avoid negative overtones.

The ads are "asking us to make the 25 leap from Uncle Ben being someone who looks like a butler to overnight being a chairman of the board," Ms. Kern Foxworth said. "It does not work for me."

"I applaud them for the effort and trying to move forward," she added, but the decision to keep the same portrait of Uncle Ben, bow tie and all, also dismayed her because "they're trying so hard to hold onto something I'm trying so hard to get rid of."

Howard Buford, chief executive at Prime Access in New York, an agency specializing in multicultural campaigns, said he gave the campaign's creators some credit. "It's potentially a very creative way to handle the baggage of old racial stereotypes as advertising icons," he said, but "it's going to take a lot of work to get it right and make it ring true."

For instance, Mr. Buford said, noting all the "Ben" references in the ads, "Rarely do you have someone of that stature addressed by his first name"— and minus any signs of a surname.

Mr. Buford, who is a real-life black leader of a company, likened the promotion of Uncle Ben to the abrupt plot twists on TV series like *Benson* and *Designing Women*, when black characters in subservient roles one season became professionals the next.

"It's nice that now, for the 21st 30 century, they're saying this icon can 'own' a company," Mr. Buford said, "but they're going to have to make him a whole person."

Mr. Visconti of Diversity Inc. Media struck a similar chord. He said he would have turned Ben's office into "a learning experience," furnishing it with, for example, books by Frederick Douglass and the Rev. Dr. Martin Luther King Jr.

"I've never been in the office of African-Americans of this era who didn't have something in their office showing what it took to get them there," Mr. Visconti said.

The actual biography of Uncle Ben is at variance with his fanciful new identity. According to Ms. Kern Foxworth's book and other reference materials, there was a Ben—no surname survives—who was a Houston rice farmer renowned for the quality of his crops. During World War II, Gordon L. Harwell, a Texas food broker, supplied to the armed forces a special kind of white rice, cooked to preserve the nutrients, under the brand name Converted Rice.

In 1946, Mr. Harwell had dinner with a friend (or business partner) in Chicago (or Houston) and decided that a portrait of the maitre d'hotel of the restaurant, Frank Brown, could represent the brand, which was renamed Uncle Ben's Converted Rice as it was being introduced to the consumer market.

In coming months, visitors to the 35 Uncle Ben's Web site will be able to discover new elements of the character, Mr. Howell said, like full-body digital versions of Uncle Ben and voice mail messages. The Web site was designed by an agency, Tequila, that is a sibling of TBWA/Chiat/Day, and the budget for the campaign, print and online, is estimated at $20 million. TBWA/Chiat/Day is part of the TBWA Worldwide unit of the Omnicom Group.

If the makeover for Uncle Ben is deemed successful, could there be similar changes in store for other racially charged characters?

Last month, the Cream of Wheat chef got a new owner when B&G Foods completed a $200 million deal to buy his brand, and its companion, Cream of Rice, from Kraft Foods.

"We're doing consumer focus work right now to understand how important the character is," said David L. Wenner, chief executive at B&G in Parsippany, N.J.

If any changes were to be made, "you would need to be very careful," he added, "and you would want to do it with dignity."

RESPOND●

1. Are you convinced? How successful has Mars been in reclaiming the image of Uncle Ben? To what extent do you find that your responses to Mars's efforts are based on fact and reason? On your emotional response? On your willingness to trust the arguments made by Mars about why it is doing what it has done? Once you have responded to this question, visit the Uncle Ben's Web site (http://unclebens.com) and see whether your response changes.

2. Increasingly, public figures, especially women in the world of entertainment, are referred to by their first name alone (such is the case with Oprah Winfrey, Martha Stewart, Tyra Banks, Madonna Ciccone, and the late Diana, Princess of Wales). Why is the issue of Uncle Ben's lack of a last name an important one for many people? How does an understanding of the history of the African American experience help account for this concern?

3. Paragraph 13 of this selection explains that many early ad characters fell into disuse and those that were retained were rendered silent, "removed from ads and reduced to staring mutely from packages." Why do you imagine that these characters were no longer allowed to speak? In other words, in what ways can an ad character's speech contribute to, encourage, or call into question negative stereotypes?

4. Paragraph 10 of this selection gives a list of created characters that were used to sell products during certain times in twentieth-century North America. Investigate one or more of these characters, finding out what you can about its origin, use, and demise. **Write a factual argument** in which you present your findings. (For a discussion of factual arguments, see Chapter 8.)

5. Return to question 1 above. **Write an evaluative essay** in response to this question, making explicit your criteria for evaluation. Your essay may focus on the selection, the Web site, or both of them. (For a discussion of evaluative arguments, see Chapter 10.)

▼ Charles A. Riley II is a professor of journalism at Baruch College, part of the City University of New York. He also served as editor in chief of WE, a now-defunct national bimonthly magazine that focused on disability issues. During his career, he has received several awards for his writing on issues relating to disability. (Riley is able-bodied, a fact that he believes has important consequences for his writing on these issues.) Among his books are Aristocracy and the Modern Imagination *(1980);* Disability and Business: Best Practices and Strategies for Inclusion *(1980);* Color Codes: Modern Theories of Color in Philosophy, Painting and Architecture, Literature, Music, and Psychology *(1995);* Small Business, Big Politics: What Entrepreneurs Need to Know to Use Their Growing Political Power *(1996); and* The Jazz Age in France *(2004). The selections featured here come from* Disability and the Media: Prescriptions for Change *(2005). These selections include the opening pages of Riley's "Preface" as well as an appendix created by the National Center on Disability and Journalism in 2002 that offers guidelines for portraying people with disabilities in the media. As you read, note ways in which Riley marshals evidence to demonstrate a need for change and the appendix constitutes a set of proposals to create that change.*

Disability and the Media: Prescriptions for Change

CHARLES A. RILEY II

Every time Aimee Mullins sees her name in the papers she braces herself for some predictable version of the same headline followed by the same old story. Paralympian, actress, and fashion model, Mullins is a bilateral, below-the-knee amputee, who sprints a hundred meters in less than sixteen seconds on a set of running prostheses called Cheetahs because they were fashioned after the leg form of the world's fastest animal. First, there are the headlines: "Overcoming All Hurdles" (she is not a hurdler, although she is a long jumper) or "Running Her Own Race," "Nothing Stops Her," or the dreaded overused "Profile in Courage." Then come the clichés and stock scenes, from the prosthetist's office to the winner's podium. Many of the articles dwell on her success as the triumph of biomechanics, a "miracle of modern medicine,"

Aimee Mullins competing in the 1996 Atlanta Paralympics

641

Coppélia: a nineteenth-century French comic and sentimental opera in which Dr. Coppélius creates a dancing doll that is so lifelike that a young man falls in love with her.

Six Million Dollar Woman: an allusion to *Six Million Dollar Man*, a late 1970s ABC television program about an astronaut who was "rebuilt" after a crash to become a cyborg, part human and part machine.

ur-narrative: the prefix *ur-* refers to the earliest, original, or most primitive or basic. It is the source narrative on which all others are based.

Warholian: a reference to Andy Warhol (1928–1987), American avant-garde artist who commented in 1968, "In the future, everyone will be famous for fifteen minutes," a critique of how modern media create instant celebrities.

Before he offers his proposal, Riley first explains how stereotyping causes problems for the disabled. For more on causal arguments, see Chapter 11.

LINK TO P. 335

turning her fairy tale into a Coppelia° narrative (or a *Six Million Dollar Woman*° movie sequel). From the local paper where she grew up (Allentown, Pennsylvania), to national exposure in *Esquire* and *People* and guest spots on *Oprah*, Mullins's "inspiring" saga is recycled almost verbatim by well-meaning journalists for audiences who never seem to get enough of its feel-good message even if they never actually find out who Mullins is.

This is the patronizing, trivializing, and marginalizing ur-narrative° of disability in the media today. The mainstream press finds it irresistible, but this steady diet of sugar has its dangers. The cliché has excluded the mature, fully realized coverage that people with disabilities have long deserved. For Mullins, it has translated into well over her Warholian° fifteen minutes of fame, bringing her the financial rewards of sponsorships, motivational speaking gigs, and modeling contracts at the expense of being turned into a latter-day poster child.° Stories about her rarely get around to mentioning that she was a Pentagon intern while making the dean's list as an academic star in history and diplomacy at Georgetown, or that she is one of the actresses in Matthew Barney's avant-garde *Cremaster* film series.

Mullins is not the only celebrity with a disability to be steamrolled out of three-dimensional humanity into allegorical° flatness. All the branches of

Early examples of poster children

poster child: a perfect representative. The source of the phrase is the image of a disabled child or one with a visible disease whose photo is used on posters to elicit sympathy and donations.

allegorical: the adjectival form of *allegory*, a moral story in which the characters, always one-dimensional in nature, suggest a meaning beyond the story. Thus, in Aesop's fable about the ant and the grasshopper, listeners are to understand that the wise person prepares for future needs, as the ant did, rather than wasting time, as did the grasshopper.

the media considered here, from print to television, radio and the movies (including advertisements) to multimedia and the Internet, are guilty of the same distillation of stories to meet their own, usually fiscal, ends. For example, even though her autobiography is remarkably ahead of its time in its anticipation of disability culture, by the time Helen Keller° had been sweetened for movie audiences in Patti Duke's° version of her life, little was left out of the fiery trailblazer. In much the same way, Christopher Reeve° and Michael J. Fox° have been pigeonholed by print and television hagiographers° as lab experiments and tragic heroes. Packaged to raise philanthropic or advertising dollars, they perform roles no less constrained than the pretty-boy parts they played on screen earlier in their lives.

What is wrong with this picture? By jamming Mullins and the others into prefabricated stories—the supercrip, the medical miracle, the object of pity—writers and producers have outfitted them with the narrative equivalent of an ill-fitting set of prostheses. Each of these archetypal narratives has its way of reaching mass audiences, selling products (including magazines and movie tickets), and financially rewarding both the media outlet and the featured subject. In some ways, as optimists point out, this represents an improvement. We have had millennia of fiction and nonfiction depicting angry people

Helen Keller (1880–1968): the first American who was both deaf and blind to graduate from college, Keller was an author and activist for progressive causes.

Patti Duke (b. 1946): an American actress who played Helen Keller in the 1959 play *The Miracle Worker* and in the 1962 film version of the story.

Christopher Reeve (1952–2004): an American actor who is best known for his four Superman films. In 1995, he was paralyzed in a riding accident and used a wheelchair for the rest of his life. After his accident, he became an activist for public issues related to spinal-cord injuries and stem-cell research.

Michael J. Fox (b. 1961): an award-winning Canadian-born actor. Diagnosed with Parkinson's disease in 1991, he revealed the condition to the public in 1998 and partially retired in 2000.

hagiographer: technically, one who studies saints. Here, hagiography is used to refer to the ways in which able-bodied individuals often portray people with disabilities as saints, thereby refusing to let them be fully human.

Patti Duke (center) as Helen Keller in The Miracle Worker

Michael J. Fox

Oedipus: the mythical Greek king who unknowingly fulfills a prophecy that he will kill his father and marry his mother. After realizing what he has done, he blinds himself.

Ahab: the captain of the whaling ship in Herman Melville's 1851 novel *Moby Dick*. After losing a leg in an earlier effort to kill the whale Moby Dick, Ahab is obsessed with harpooning the creature. His actions lead to the loss of the ship and the lives of all onboard with the exception of Ishmael, whose narrative opens the novel.

with disabilities as villains, from Oedipus° to Ahab° to Dr. Strangelove.° The vestigial traces of that syndrome still occasionally recur, although with far less frequency, in current movies or television series and in journalists' fixation on the mental instability of violent criminals. However, today's storytellers, including those in the disability media, are more likely to make people with disabilities into "heroes of assimilation," to borrow a phrase from Erving Goffman's° seminal work on disability, *Stigma: Notes on the Management of Spoiled Identity.*

As Goffman knew too well, just as the stigmatization of the villain had its 5 dilatory effects on societal attitudes, so too does relentless hagiography, particularly by transforming individuals into symbols and by playing on an audience's sympathy and sense of superiority. Those who labor in the field of disability studies point out that disability culture and its unique strengths are absent from this story of normalization. Others would simply note that the individual is lost in the fable, an all-American morality tale that strikes one of the most resonant chords in the repertoire: redemption. Like the deathless Horatio Alger° tale, the story of the hero of assimilation emphasizes many of the deepest values and beliefs of the Puritan tradition, especially the notion that suffering makes us stronger and better. An able-bodied person falls from grace (often literally falling or crashing, as in the case of many spinal cord

Dr. Strangelove: the title character in the 1964 film comedy *Dr. Strangelove or: How I Learned to Stop Worrying and Love the Bomb*. Strangelove, played by Peter Sellers, used a wheelchair and suffered from alien hand syndrome. He is often used to represent the stereotype of a "mad scientist."

Erving Goffman (1922–1982): a highly influential Canadian-born sociologist who taught in the United States. His work was much concerned with the nature of the

social organization of everyday life.

Horatio Alger Jr. (1832–1899): the prolific author of popular "rags to riches" tales in which hardworking, virtuous poor boys rise to stable and productive lives at the lower edges of the middle class.

injuries), progresses through the shadows of rehabilitation and depression, and by force of willpower along with religious belief pulls through to attain a quality of life that is less disabled, more normal, basking in the glow of recognition for beating the odds.

This pervasive narrative can be found in print, on television, in movies, in advertisements, and on the Web. Its corrosive effect on understanding and attitudes is as yet unnoticed. It is impossible to know the full degree of damage wreaked by the demeaning and wildly inaccurate portrayal of people with disabilities, nor is it altogether clear whether much current progress is being made. Painful as it is for me as an advocate to report the bad news, I cannot help but point out that the "movement" has slowed to a crawl in terms of political and economic advancement for 54 million Americans. The stasis° that threatens is at least partly to be blamed on a reassuring, recurring image projected by the media that numbs nondisabled readers and viewers into thinking that all is well.

stasis: here, inactivity or lack of movement.

This study aims to expose the extent of the problem while pinpointing how writers, editors, photographers, filmmakers, advertisers, and the executives who give them their marching orders go wrong, or occasionally get it right. Through a close analysis of the technical means of representation, in conjunction with the commentary of leading voices in the disability community, I hope to guide future coverage to a more fair and accurate way of putting the disability story on screen or paper. Far from another stab at the political correctness target, the aim of this content analysis of journalism, film, advertising, and Web publishing is to cut through the accumulated clichés and condescension to find an adequate vocabulary that will finally represent the disability community in all its vibrant and fascinating diversity. Nothing like that will ever happen if the press and advertisers continue to think, write, and design as they have in the past.

Appendix A

Guidelines for Portraying People with Disabilities in the Media

Fear of the unknown. Inadequate experience. Incorrect or distorted information. Lack of knowledge. These shape some of the attitudinal barriers that people with disabilities face as they become involved in their communities.

People working in the media exert a powerful influence over the way people with disabilities are perceived. It's important to the 54 million Americans with disabilities that they be portrayed realistically and that their disabilities are explained accurately.

Awareness is the first step toward change.   10

TIPS FOR REPORTING ON PEOPLE WITH DISABILITIES

- When referring to individuals with disabilities use "disability," not "handicapped."
- Emphasize the person, not the disability or condition. Use "people with disabilities" rather than "disabled persons," and "people with epilepsy" rather than "epileptics."
- Omit mention of an individual's disability unless it is pertinent to the story.
- Depict the typical achiever with a disability, not just the super-achiever.
- Choose words that are accurate descriptions and have non-judgmental connotations.
- People with disabilities live everyday lives and should be portrayed as contributing members of the community. These portrayals should:

    Depict people with disabilities experiencing the same pain/pleasure that others derive from everyday life, e.g., work, parenting, education, sports and community involvement.

    Feature a variety of people with disabilities when possible, not just someone easily recognized by the general public.

    Depict employees/employers with disabilities working together.
- Ask people with disabilities to provide correct information and assistance to avoid stereotypes in the media.
- Portray people with disabilities as people, with both strengths and weaknesses.

APPROPRIATE WORDS WHEN PORTRAYING PEOPLE WITH DISABILITIES

Never Use

victim—use: person who has/experienced/with.

[the] cripple[d]—use: person with a disability.

afflicted by/with—use: person has.

invalid—use: a person with a disability.

normal—most people, including people with disabilities, think they are.

patient—connotes sickness. Use: person with a disability.

Avoid Using
wheelchair bound/confined—use: uses a wheelchair or wheelchair user.
homebound employment—use: employed in the home.

Use with Care
courageous, brave, inspirational and similar words routinely used to describe persons with disabilities. Adaption to a disability does not necessarily mean someone acquires these traits.

INTERVIEWING PEOPLE WITH DISABILITIES

When interviewing a person with a disability, relax! Conduct your interview as you would with anyone. Be clear and candid in your questioning and ask for clarification of terms or issues when necessary. Be upfront about deadlines, the focus of your story, and when and where it will appear.

Interviewing Etiquette

- Shake hands when introduced to someone with a disability. People with limited hand use or artificial limbs do shake hands.
- Speak directly to people with disabilities, not through their companions.
- Don't be embarrassed using such phrases as "See you soon," "Walk this way" or "Got to run." These are common expressions, and are unlikely to offend.
- If you offer to help, wait until the offer is accepted.
- Consider the needs of people with disabilities when planning events.
- Conduct interviews in a manner that emphasizes abilities, achievements and individual qualities.
- Don't emphasize differences by putting people with disabilities on a pedestal.

When Interviewing People with Hearing Disabilities

- Attract the person's attention by tapping on his or her shoulder or waving.
- If you are interviewing someone with a partial hearing loss, ask where it would be most comfortable for you to sit.

This Appendix offers a set of clear guidelines but sometimes does not explain the reasoning behind particular guidelines. Practice identifying the warrants, as described in Chapter 7, that lie behind these claims.

LINK TO P. 186

- If the person is lip-reading, look directly at him/her and speak slowly and clearly. Do not exaggerate lip movements or shout. Do speak expressively, as facial expressions, gestures and body movements will help him/her understand you.

- Position yourself facing the light source and keep hands and food away from your mouth when speaking.

When Interviewing People with Vision Disabilities

- Always identify yourself and anyone else who might be present.
- When offering a handshake, say, "Shall we shake hands?"
- When offering seating, place the person's hand on the back or arm of the seat.
- Let the person know if you move or need to end the conversation.

When Interviewing People with Speech Disabilities

- Ask short questions that require short answers when possible.
- Do not feign understanding. Try rephrasing your questions, if necessary.

When Interviewing People Using a Wheelchair or Crutches

- Do not lean on a person's wheelchair. The chair is part of his/her body space.
- Sit or kneel to place yourself at eye level with the person you are interviewing.
- Make sure the interview site is accessible. Check for:
  Reserved parking for people with disabilities
  A ramp or step-free entrance
  Accessible restrooms
  An elevator if the interview is not on the first floor
  Water fountains and telephones low enough for wheelchair use

Be sure to notify the interviewee if there are problems with the location. Discuss what to do and make alternate plans.

WRITING ABOUT DISABILITY

One of the first and most significant steps to changing negative stereotypes and attitudes toward people with disabilities begins when we rethink the way written and spoken images are used to portray people with disabilities.

The following is a brief, but important, list of suggestions for portraying people with disabilities in the media.

People with disabilities are not "handicapped," unless there are physical or attitudinal barriers that make it difficult for them to participate in everyday activities. An office building with steps and no entry ramp creates a "handicapping" barrier for people who use wheelchairs. In the same way, a hotel that does not have a TTY/telephone (teletypewri ter) creates a barrier for someone who is hearing disabled. It is important to focus on the person, not necessarily the disability. In writing, name the person first and then, if necessary, explain his or her disability. The same rule applies when speaking. Don't focus on someone's disability unless it's crucial to the point being made.

In long, written materials, when many references have been made to persons with disabilities or someone who is disabled, it is acceptable for later references to refer to "disabled persons" or "disabled individuals."

Because a person is not a condition or a disease, avoid referring to some- 15 one with a disability by his or her disability alone. For example, don't say someone is a "post-polio" or a "C.P." or an "epileptic." Refer instead to someone who has post-polio syndrome, or has cerebral palsy, or has epilepsy.

Don't use "disabled" as a noun because it implies a state of separateness. "The disabled" are not a group apart from the rest of society. When writing or speaking about people with disabilities, choose descriptive words and portray people in a positive light.

Avoid words with negative connotations:

- Avoid calling someone a "victim."

- Avoid referring to people with disabilities as "cripples" or "crippled." This is negative and demeaning language.

- Don't write or say that someone is "afflicted."

- Avoid the word "invalid" as it means, quite literally, "not valid."

- Write or speak about people who use wheelchairs. Wheelchair users are not "wheelchair-bound."

- Refer to people who are not disabled as "non-disabled" or "able-bodied." When you call non-disabled people "normal," the implication is that people with disabilities are not normal.

- Someone who is disabled is only a patient to his or her physician or in a reference to medical treatment.

- Avoid cliches. Don't use "unfortunate," "pitiful," "poor," "dumb," "crip," "deformed," "retard," "blind as a bat" or other patronizing and demeaning words.

- In the same vein, don't glamorize or make heroes of people with disabilities simply because they have adapted to their disabilities.

Your concerted efforts to use positive, non-judgmental respectful language when referring to people with disabilities in writing and in everyday speaking can go a long way toward helping to change negative stereotypes.

These guidelines are used by permission. Copyright © 2002, National Center on Disability and Journalism.

Aimee Mullins practices her jumps.

RESPOND •

1. In what ways does Riley contend that the media and popular culture wrongly stereotype people with disabilities? What negative consequences follow from this stereotyping for such people? For those who do not have disabilities? Why?

2. How convincingly has Riley defined a problem or need, which is the first step in a proposal argument? (For a discussion of proposal arguments, see Chapter 12.)

3. What is your response to "Appendix A: Guidelines for Portraying People with Disabilities in the Media"? Are you familiar with the practices that these guidelines seek to prevent? Do you find the guidelines useful or necessary? Why or why not? What justification might be offered for why specific guidelines are important? (Here, you will want to choose three or four of the guidelines and make explicit the arguments in support of each of them.)

4. Look for some specific representations of people with disabilities in current media and popular culture—in advertisements, television programs, or movies. To what extent do these representations perpetuate the stereotypes that Riley discusses, "the supercrip, the medical miracle, the object of pity" (paragraph 4)? **Write an argument of fact** in which you present your findings. (For a discussion of arguments of fact, see Chapter 8.) If you do not find representations of people with disabilities in various media or in popular culture, that absence is significant and merits discussion and analysis.

5. **Write an evaluative essay** in which you assess the value of these guidelines. In other words, if the media follow these guidelines, what will the consequences be for the media? For society at large? To what extent will following these guidelines likely influence negative stereotypes about people with disabilities? (For a discussion of evaluative arguments, see Chapter 10.)

22
How Many Friends Have You Made Today?

Perhaps no phenomenon defines popular culture among young people in the United States and around the world at this moment as much as social network sites (SNSs) do. They shape daily life for their users in ways that nonusers can scarcely imagine or appreciate. In this chapter, the selections will provide you with new ways of thinking about and evaluating SNSs and the roles that they play for their users. As you'll see, social scientists are currently devoting a great deal of effort and time to understanding these questions.

The chapter opens with a selection from the research article "Social Network Sites: Definition, History, and Scholarship" in which danah m. boyd and Nicole B. Ellison survey the existing research on and academic discussions of SNSs. The second selection, a YouTube video and transcript from the Privacy Commissioner of Canada, describes how SNSs work from the perspective of marketers and what the consequences might be for users. (It is interesting to consider why governments feel the need to educate their citizens about these issues.) Next, journalist

Heather Havenstein reminds SNS users of an uncomfortable truth that many apparently keep forgetting. The title of her *Computerworld* article delivers the message clearly and succinctly: "One in Five Employers Uses Social Networks in Hiring Process."

The next three selections are closely related. Tamar Lewin's newspaper article on the Digital Youth Project, "Study Finds Teenagers' Internet Socializing Isn't Such a Bad Thing," examines the findings of Mizuko Ito's research team on how teenagers are using digital media. It provoked comments, often impassioned, from nearly sixty readers, and we include the four comments selected by the papers' editors as most interesting.

We then present two sections of the report by Ito and her team that sparked the discussion. In investigating teenagers' online habits, these researchers delineated three categories of participation—hanging out, messing around, and geeking out (the terms are those used by the teenagers studied). The selections reprinted here include the "Executive Summary" of the major findings of the study as well as "Geeking Out," a description of the patterns of participation among the teenagers most heavily involved in digital media.

The next selection, a transcript from the National Public Radio program *Talk of the Nation*, hosted by Neal Conan, considers the legal aftermath of Megan Meier's suicide. Meier was a thirteen-year-old who took her life after receiving hurtful messages on MySpace, supposedly from a teenage boy; in fact, the teenage boy was nonexistent, and the MySpace account had been set up by someone associated with the mother of one of Megan's female classmates. The legal question became whether creating a fake online profile was a criminal act. Conan's discussion with two experts, Kim Zetter and Andy Carvin, and callers reminds us of the potential legal, ethical, and social implications of SNSs.

The chapter closes with Charles M. Blow's analysis of the findings of research on network profiles, particularly their honesty. Blow often writes for the *New York Times*, and this essay, like many of his blog postings, examines how quantitative data (numbers) are presented and the effect that such visual arguments have on readers.

For many, if not most, readers of this book, social network sites help define reality as you know it. The selections in this chapter may help you understand that reality in new ways.

▼ *Among the people who are most interested in social network sites are researchers—especially marketing researchers and younger social scientists. The authors of this selection, an excerpt from "Social Network Sites: Definition, History, and Scholarship," are two researchers who take these sites seriously. danah m. boyd is finishing her doctorate at the School (School of Information) at the University of California at Berkeley; she is also a fellow at the Berkman Center for Internet and Society at Harvard Law School. Nicole B. Ellison is an assistant professor in the Department of Telecommunication, Information Studies, and Media at Michigan State University. The article excerpted here was published in 2007 as the lead article in a special issue of* Journal of Computer-Mediated Communication *that was dedicated to research on social networking sites. We reproduce approximately the first half of their paper—the abstract, the introduction, a definition selection, and a history of these sites. As you read, consider how well these last two sections succeed in fulfilling their stated functions as an argument of definition and an argument of fact.*

Social Network Sites: Definition, History, and Scholarship (Excerpt)

DANAH M. BOYD AND NICOLE B. ELLISON

ABSTRACT.   Social network sites (SNSs) are increasingly attracting the attention of academic and industry researchers intrigued by their affordances and reach. This special theme section of the *Journal of Computer-Mediated Communication* brings together scholarship on these emergent phenomena. In this introductory article, we describe features of SNSs and propose a comprehensive definition. We then present one perspective on the history of such sites, discussing key changes and developments. After briefly summarizing existing scholarship concerning SNSs, we discuss the articles in this special section and conclude with considerations for future research.

INTRODUCTION

Since their introduction, social network sites (SNSs) such as MySpace, Facebook, Cyworld, and Bebo have attracted millions of users, many of whom have integrated these sites into their daily practices.° As of this writing, there

practices: here, behaviors.

affordances: easily discoverable characteristics of a thing that enable a person to perform an action.

social networks: social groups that focus on an individual and all of the people connected to her or him in any way (as family member, friend, coworker, etc.).

are hundreds of SNSs, with various technological affordances,° supporting a wide range of interests and practices. While their key technological features are fairly consistent, the cultures that emerge around SNSs are varied. Most sites support the maintenance of pre-existing social networks,° but others help strangers connect based on shared interests, political views, or activities. Some sites cater to diverse audiences, while others attract people based on common language or shared racial, sexual, religious, or nationality-based identities. Sites also vary in the extent to which they incorporate new information and communication tools, such as mobile connectivity, blogging, and photo/video-sharing.

Scholars from disparate fields have examined SNSs in order to understand the practices, implications, culture, and meaning of the sites, as well as users' engagement with them. This special theme section of the *Journal of Computer-Mediated Communication* brings together a unique collection of articles that analyze a wide spectrum of social network sites using various methodological techniques, theoretical traditions, and analytic approaches. By collecting these articles in this issue, our goal is to showcase some of the interdisciplinary scholarship around these sites.

The purpose of this introduction is to provide a conceptual, historical, and scholarly context for the articles in this collection. We begin by defining what constitutes a social network site and then present one perspective on the historical development of SNSs, drawing from personal interviews and public accounts of sites and their changes over time. Following this, we review recent scholarship on SNSs and attempt to contextualize and highlight key works. We conclude with a description of the articles included in this special section and suggestions for future research.

Social Network Sites: A Definition

We define social network sites as web-based services that allow individuals 5 to (1) construct a public or semi-public profile within a bounded system, (2) articulate a list of other users with whom they share a connection, and (3) view and traverse their list of connections and those made by others within the system. The nature and nomenclature of these connections may vary from site to site.

While we use the term "social network site" to describe this phenomenon, the term "social networking sites" also appears in public discourse, and the two terms are often used interchangeably. We chose not to employ the term "networking" for two reasons: emphasis and scope. "Networking" emphasizes relationship initiation, often between strangers. While networking is

Note how carefully boyd and Ellison distinguish between the terms "social network site" and "social networking sites." As Chapter 9 explains, definitional arguments are powerful because they make important distinctions.

LINK TO P. 249

possible on these sites, it is not the primary practice on many of them, nor is it what differentiates them from other forms of computer-mediated communication (CMC).

What makes social network sites unique is not that they allow individuals to meet strangers, but rather that they enable users to articulate and make visible their social networks. This can result in connections between individuals that would not otherwise be made, but that is often not the goal, and these meetings are frequently between "latent° ties" (Haythornthwaite, 2005) who share some offline connection. On many of the large SNSs, participants are not necessarily "networking" or looking to meet new people; instead, they are primarily communicating with people who are already a part of their extended social network. To emphasize this articulated social network as a critical organizing feature of these sites, we label them "social network sites."

latent: potentially able to be activated.

While SNSs have implemented a wide variety of technical features, their backbone consists of visible profiles that display an articulated list of Friends[1] who are also users of the system. Profiles are unique pages where one can "type oneself into being" (Sundén, 2003, p. 3). After joining an SNS, an individual is asked to fill out forms containing a series of questions. The profile is generated using the answers to these questions, which typically include descriptors such as age, location, interests, and an "about me" section. Most sites also encourage users to upload a profile photo. Some sites allow users to enhance their profiles by adding multimedia content or modifying their profile's look and feel. Others, such as Facebook, allow users to add modules ("Applications") that enhance their profile.

The visibility of a profile varies by site and according to user discretion. By default, profiles on Friendster and Tribe.net are crawled by search engines, making them visible to anyone, regardless of whether or not the viewer has an account. Alternatively, LinkedIn controls what a viewer may see based on whether she or he has a paid account. Sites like MySpace allow users to choose whether they want their profile to be public or "Friends only." Facebook takes a different approach—by default, users who are part of the same "network" can view each other's profiles, unless a profile owner has decided to deny permission to those in their network. Structural variations around visibility and access are one of the primary ways that SNSs differentiate themselves from each other.

After joining a social network site, users are prompted to identify others 10 in the system with whom they have a relationship. The label for these relationships differs depending on the site—popular terms include "Friends," "Contacts," and "Fans." Most SNSs require bi-directional confirmation for

Facebook lets users enhance their profiles with applications.

Friendship, but some do not. These one-directional ties are sometimes labeled as "Fans" or "Followers," but many sites call these Friends as well. The term "Friends" can be misleading, because the connection does not necessarily mean friendship in the everyday vernacular sense, and the reasons people connect are varied (boyd, 2006a).

The public display of connections is a crucial component of SNSs. The Friends list contains links to each Friend's profile, enabling viewers to traverse the network graph by clicking through the Friends lists. On most sites, the list of Friends is visible to anyone who is permitted to view the profile, although there are exceptions. For instance, some MySpace users have hacked their profiles to hide the Friends display, and LinkedIn allows users to opt out of displaying their network.

Most SNSs also provide a mechanism for users to leave messages on their Friends' profiles. This feature typically involves leaving "comments," although sites employ various labels for this feature. In addition, SNSs often have a private messaging feature similar to webmail. While both private messages and comments are popular on most of the major SNSs, they are not universally available.

Not all social network sites began as such. QQ started as a Chinese instant messaging service, LunarStorm as a community site, Cyworld as a Korean discussion forum tool, and Skyrock (formerly Skyblog) was a French blogging service before adding SNS features. Classmates.com, a directory of school affiliates launched in 1995, began supporting articulated lists of Friends after SNSs became popular. AsianAvenue, MiGente, and BlackPlanet were early

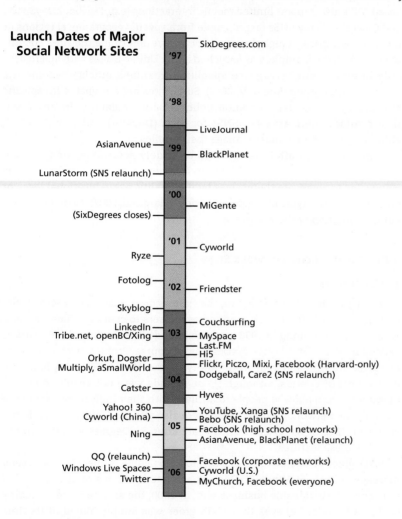

Launch Dates of Major Social Network Sites

'97	SixDegrees.com
'98	
'99	LiveJournal; AsianAvenue; BlackPlanet
	LunarStorm (SNS relaunch)
'00	MiGente; (SixDegrees closes)
'01	Cyworld; Ryze
'02	Friendster; Fotolog
	Skyblog
'03	Couchsurfing; LinkedIn; Tribe.net, openBC/Xing; MySpace; Last.FM; Hi5
'04	Orkut, Dogster; Multiply, aSmallWorld; Flickr, Piczo, Mixi, Facebook (Harvard-only); Dodgeball, Care2 (SNS relaunch); Catster; Hyves
'05	Yahoo! 360; Cyworld (China); YouTube, Xanga (SNS relaunch); Bebo (SNS relaunch); Facebook (high school networks); Ning; AsianAvenue, BlackPlanet (relaunch)
'06	QQ (relaunch); Windows Live Spaces; Facebook (corporate networks); Cyworld (U.S.); Twitter; MyChurch, Facebook (everyone)

Figure 1. Timeline of the launch dates of many major SNSs and dates when community sites relaunched with SNS features.

SixDegrees.com alludes not only to the general idea of "six degrees of separation" between any two human beings but also to Six Degrees of Kevin Bacon, the popular game that applies this concept to the actor considered a center of the Hollywood universe.

SixDegrees.com: the name is an allusion to the claim of Hungarian writer Frigyes Karinthy in the late 1920s that "if a person is one step away from each person they know and two steps away from each person who is known by one of the people they know, then everyone is an average of six 'steps' away from each person on Earth."

popular ethnic community sites with limited Friends functionality before re-launching in 2005–2006 with SNS features and structure.

Beyond profiles, Friends, comments, and private messaging, SNSs vary greatly in their features and user base. Some have photo-sharing or video-sharing capabilities; others have built-in blogging and instant messaging technology. There are mobile-specific SNSs (e.g., Dodgeball), but some web-based SNSs also support limited mobile interactions (e.g., Facebook, MySpace, and Cyworld). Many SNSs target people from specific geographical regions or linguistic groups, although this does not always determine the site's constituency. Orkut, for example, was launched in the United States with an English-only interface, but Portuguese-speaking Brazilians quickly became the dominant user group (Kopytoff, 2004). Some sites are designed with specific ethnic, religious, sexual orientation, political, or other identity-driven categories in mind. There are even SNSs for dogs (Dogster) and cats (Catster), although their owners must manage their profiles.

While SNSs are often designed to be widely accessible, many attract 15 homogeneous populations initially, so it is not uncommon to find groups using sites to segregate themselves by nationality, age, educational level, or other factors that typically segment society (Hargittai, 2007), even if that was not the intention of the designers.

A History of Social Network Sites

The Early Years

According to the definition above, the first recognizable social network site launched in 1997. SixDegrees.com° allowed users to create profiles, list their Friends and, beginning in 1998, surf the Friends lists. Each of these features existed in some form before SixDegrees, of course. Profiles existed on most major dating sites and many community sites. AIM and ICQ buddy lists supported lists of Friends, although those Friends were not visible to others. Classmates.com allowed people to affiliate with their high school or college and surf the network for others who were also affiliated, but users could not create profiles or list Friends until years later. SixDegrees was the first to combine these features.

SixDegrees promoted itself as a tool to help people connect with and send messages to others. While SixDegrees attracted millions of users, it failed to become a sustainable business and, in 2000, the service closed. Looking back, its founder believes that SixDegrees was simply ahead of its time (A. Weinreich, personal communication, July 11, 2007). While people were already flocking to the Internet, most did not have extended networks of friends who were online. Early adopters° complained that there was little to do after accepting Friend requests, and most users were not interested in meeting strangers.

From 1997 to 2001, a number of community tools began supporting various combinations of profiles and publicly articulated Friends. AsianAvenue, BlackPlanet, and MiGente allowed users to create personal, professional, and dating profiles—users could identify Friends on their personal profiles without seeking approval for those connections (O. Wasow, personal communication, August 16, 2007). Likewise, shortly after its launch in 1999, LiveJournal listed one-directional connections on user pages. LiveJournal's creator suspects that he fashioned these Friends after instant messaging buddy lists (B. Fitzpatrick, personal communication, June 15, 2007)—on LiveJournal, people mark others as Friends to follow their journals and manage privacy settings. The Korean virtual worlds site Cyworld was started in 1999 and added SNS features in 2001, independent of these other sites (see Kim & Yun, 2007). Likewise, when the Swedish web community LunarStorm refashioned itself as an SNS in 2000, it contained Friends lists, guestbooks, and diary pages (D. Skog, personal communication, September 24, 2007).

The next wave of SNSs began when Ryze.com was launched in 2001 to help people leverage their business networks. Ryze's founder reports that he first introduced the site to his friends—primarily members of the San Francisco business and technology community, including the entrepreneurs and investors behind many future SNSs (A. Scott, personal communication, June 14, 2007). In particular, the people behind Ryze, Tribe.net, LinkedIn, and Friendster were tightly entwined personally and professionally. They believed that they could support each other without competing (Festa, 2003). In the end, Ryze never acquired mass popularity, Tribe.net grew to attract a passionate niche user base, LinkedIn became a powerful business service, and Friendster became the most significant, if only as "one of the biggest disappointments in Internet history" (Chafkin, 2007, p. 1).

Like any brief history of a major phenomenon, ours is necessarily in- 20 complete. In the following section we discuss Friendster, MySpace, and Facebook, three key SNSs that shaped the business, cultural, and research landscape.

The Rise (and Fall) of Friendster

Friendster launched in 2002 as a social complement to Ryze. It was designed to compete with Match.com, a profitable online dating site (Cohen, 2003).

early adopters: those individuals within a society who are quick to take up and use new things, whether a new technology, fashion, or way of speaking. Typically social leaders, early adopters stand between innovators (the first to adopt a change) and late adopters.

friends-of-friends: in research on social networks, as in everyday conversation, people who do not know one another well but who have a friend in common.

Burning Man arts festival: an annual festival held in the Black Rock Desert in Nevada that culminates in the burning of a large wooden image of a man.

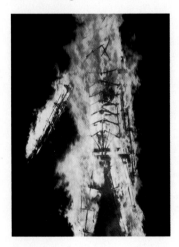

While most dating sites focused on introducing people to strangers with similar interests, Friendster was designed to help friends-of-friends° meet, based on the assumption that friends-of-friends would make better romantic partners than would strangers (J. Abrams, personal communication, March 27, 2003). Friendster gained traction among three groups of early adopters who shaped the site—bloggers, attendees of the Burning Man arts festival,° and gay men (boyd, 2004)—and grew to 300,000 users through word of mouth before traditional press coverage began in May 2003 (O'Shea, 2003).

As Friendster's popularity surged, the site encountered technical and social difficulties (boyd, 2006b). Friendster's servers and databases were ill-equipped to handle its rapid growth, and the site faltered regularly, frustrating users who replaced email with Friendster. Because organic growth had been critical to creating a coherent community, the onslaught of new users who learned about the site from media coverage upset the cultural balance. Furthermore, exponential growth meant a collapse in social contexts: Users had to face their bosses and former classmates alongside their close friends. To complicate matters, Friendster began restricting the activities of its most passionate users.

The initial design of Friendster restricted users from viewing profiles of people who were more than four degrees away (friends-of-friends-of-friends-of-friends). In order to view additional profiles, users began adding acquaintances and interesting-looking strangers to expand their reach. Some began massively collecting Friends, an activity that was implicitly encouraged through a "most popular" feature. The ultimate collectors were fake profiles representing iconic fictional characters: celebrities, concepts, and other such entities. These "Fakesters" outraged the company, who banished fake profiles and eliminated the "most popular" feature (boyd, in press-b). While few people actually created Fakesters, many more enjoyed surfing Fakesters for entertainment or using functional Fakesters (e.g., "Brown University") to find people they knew.

The active deletion of Fakesters (and genuine users who chose non-realistic photos) signaled to some that the company did not share users' interests. Many early adopters left because of the combination of technical difficulties, social collisions, and a rupture of trust between users and the site (boyd, 2006b). However, at the same time that it was fading in the U.S., its popularity skyrocketed in the Philippines, Singapore, Malaysia, and Indonesia (Goldberg, 2007).

SNSs Hit the Mainstream

From 2003 onward, many new SNSs were launched, prompting social soft- 25
ware analyst Clay Shirky (2003) to coin the term YASNS: "Yet Another Social
Networking Service." Most took the form of profile-centric sites, trying to
replicate the early success of Friendster or target specific demographics.
While socially-organized SNSs solicit broad audiences, professional sites
such as LinkedIn, Visible Path, and Xing (formerly openBC) focus on business
people. "Passion-centric" SNSs like Dogster (T. Rheingold, personal communication, August 2, 2007) help strangers connect based on shared interests.
Care2 helps activists meet, Couchsurfing connects travelers to people with
couches, and MyChurch joins Christian churches and their members.
Furthermore, as the social media and user-generated content phenomena
grew, websites focused on media sharing began implementing SNS features
and becoming SNSs themselves. Examples include Flickr (photo sharing),
Last.FM (music listening habits), and YouTube (video sharing).

With the plethora° of venture-backed startups launching in Silicon Valley,
few people paid attention to SNSs that gained popularity elsewhere, even
those built by major corporations. For example, Google's Orkut failed to build
a sustainable U.S. user base, but a "Brazilian invasion" (Fragoso, 2006) made
Orkut the national SNS of Brazil. Microsoft's Windows Live Spaces (a.k.a. MSN
Spaces) also launched to lukewarm U.S. reception but became extremely
popular elsewhere.

Few analysts or journalists noticed when MySpace launched in Santa
Monica, California, hundreds of miles from Silicon Valley. MySpace was begun
in 2003 to compete with sites like Friendster, Xanga, and AsianAvenue,
according to co-founder Tom Anderson (personal communication, August 2,
2007); the founders wanted to attract estranged Friendster users (T. Anderson,
personal communication, February 2, 2006). After rumors emerged that
Friendster would adopt a fee-based system, users posted Friendster messages encouraging people to join alternate SNSs, including Tribe.net and
MySpace (T. Anderson, personal communication, August 2, 2007). Because of
this, MySpace was able to grow rapidly by capitalizing on Friendster's alien-
ation of its early adopters. One particularly notable group that encouraged
others to switch were indie-rock bands who were expelled from Friendster
for failing to comply with profile regulations.

While MySpace was not launched with bands in mind, they were welcomed. Indie-rock bands from the Los Angeles region began creating profiles,
and local promoters used MySpace to advertise VIP passes for popular clubs.

plethora: large number, often
with the connotation of excess.

MySpace founder Tom Anderson

Intrigued, MySpace contacted local musicians to see how they could support them (T. Anderson, personal communication, September 28, 2006). Bands were not the sole source of MySpace growth, but the symbiotic relationship between bands and fans helped MySpace expand beyond former Friendster users. The bands-and-fans dynamic was mutually beneficial: Bands wanted to be able to contact fans, while fans desired attention from their favorite bands and used Friend connections to signal identity and affiliation.

Furthermore, MySpace differentiated itself by regularly adding features based on user demand (boyd, 2006b) and by allowing users to personalize their pages. This "feature" emerged because MySpace did not restrict users from adding HTML into the forms that framed their profiles; a copy/paste code culture emerged on the web to support users in generating unique MySpace backgrounds and layouts (Perkel, in press).

Teenagers began joining MySpace *en masse* in 2004. Unlike older users, most teens were never on Friendster—some joined because they wanted to connect with their favorite bands; others were introduced to the site through older family members. As teens began signing up, they encouraged their friends to join. Rather than rejecting underage users, MySpace changed its user policy to allow minors. As the site grew, three distinct populations began to form: musicians/artists, teenagers, and the post-college urban social crowd. By and large, the latter two groups did not interact with one another

A Rutgers University student explaining Facebook to a newbie

except through bands. Because of the lack of mainstream press coverage during 2004, few others noticed the site's growing popularity.

Then, in July 2005, News Corporation purchased MySpace for $580 million (BBC, 2005), attracting massive media attention. Afterwards, safety issues plagued MySpace. The site was implicated in a series of sexual interactions between adults and minors, prompting legal action (Consumer Affairs, 2006). A moral panic concerning sexual predators quickly spread (Bahney, 2006), although research suggests that the concerns were exaggerated.[2]

A Global Phenomenon

While MySpace attracted the majority of media attention in the U.S. and abroad, SNSs were proliferating and growing in popularity worldwide. Friendster gained traction in the Pacific Islands, Orkut became the premier SNS in Brazil before growing rapidly in India (Madhavan, 2007), Mixi attained widespread adoption in Japan, LunarStorm took off in Sweden, Dutch users embraced Hyves, Grono captured Poland, Hi5 was adopted in smaller countries in Latin America, South America, and Europe, and Bebo became very popular in the United Kingdom, New Zealand, and Australia. Additionally, previously popular communication and community services began implementing SNS features. The Chinese QQ instant messaging service instantly became the largest SNS worldwide when it added profiles and made friends visible (McLeod, 2006), while the forum tool Cyworld cornered the Korean market by introducing homepages and buddies (Ewers, 2006).

Blogging services with complete SNS features also became popular. In the U.S., blogging tools with SNS features, such as Xanga, LiveJournal, and Vox, attracted broad audiences. Skyrock reigns in France, and Windows Live Spaces dominates numerous markets worldwide, including in Mexico, Italy, and Spain. Although SNSs like QQ, Orkut, and Live Spaces are just as large as, if not larger than, MySpace, they receive little coverage in U.S. and English-speaking media, making it difficult to track their trajectories.

Expanding Niche Communities

Alongside these open services, other SNSs launched to support niche demographics before expanding to a broader audience. Unlike previous SNSs, Facebook was designed to support distinct college networks only. Facebook began in early 2004 as a Harvard-only SNS (Cassidy, 2006). To join, a user had to have a harvard.edu email address. As Facebook began supporting other schools, those users were also required to have university email addresses associated with those institutions, a requirement that kept the site relatively

As this cartoon from Slate.com suggests, social networking can quickly get out of hand.

closed and contributed to users' perceptions of the site as an intimate, private community.

Beginning in September 2005, Facebook expanded to include high school 35 students, professionals inside corporate networks, and, eventually, everyone. The change to open signup did not mean that new users could easily access users in closed networks—gaining access to corporate networks still required the appropriate .com address, while gaining access to high school networks required administrator approval. (As of this writing, only membership in regional networks requires no permission.) Unlike other SNSs, Facebook users are unable to make their full profiles public to all users. Another feature that differentiates Facebook is the ability for outside developers to build "Applications" which allow users to personalize their profiles and perform other tasks, such as compare movie preferences and chart travel histories.

While most SNSs focus on growing broadly and exponentially, others explicitly seek narrower audiences. Some, like aSmallWorld and Beautiful-People, intentionally restrict access to appear selective and elite. Others—activity-centered sites like Couchsurfing, identity-driven sites like BlackPlanet, and affiliation-focused sites like MyChurch—are limited by their target demographic and thus tend to be smaller. Finally, anyone who wishes to create a niche social network site can do so on Ning, a platform and hosting service that encourages users to create their own SNSs.

Currently, there are no reliable data regarding how many people use SNSs, although marketing research indicates that SNSs are growing in popularity worldwide (comScore, 2007). This growth has prompted many corporations to invest time and money in creating, purchasing, promoting, and advertising

SNSs. At the same time, other companies are blocking their employees from accessing the sites. Additionally, the U.S. military banned soldiers from accessing MySpace (Frosch, 2007) and the Canadian government prohibited employees from Facebook (Benzie, 2007), while the U.S. Congress has proposed legislation to ban youth from accessing SNSs in schools and libraries (H.R. 5319, 2006; S. 49, 2007).

The rise of SNSs indicates a shift in the organization of online communities. While websites dedicated to communities of interest still exist and prosper, SNSs are primarily organized around people, not interests. Early public online communities such as Usenet and public discussion forums were structured by topics or according to topical hierarchies, but social network sites are structured as personal (or "egocentric") networks, with the individual at the center of their own community. This more accurately mirrors unmediated social structures, where "the world is composed of networks, not groups" (Wellman, 1988, p. 37). The introduction of SNS features has introduced a new organizational framework for online communities, and with it, a vibrant new research context.

NOTES

1. To differentiate the articulated list of Friends on SNSs from the colloquial term "friends," we capitalize the former.
2. Although one out of seven teenagers received unwanted sexual solicitations online, only 9% came from people over the age of 25 (Wolak, Mitchell, & Finkelhor, 2006). Research suggests that popular narratives around sexual predators on SNSs are misleading—cases of unsuspecting teens being lured by sexual predators are rare (Finkelhor, Ybarra, Lenhart, boyd, & Lordan, 2007). Furthermore, only .08% of students surveyed by the National School Boards Association (2007) met someone in person from an online encounter without permission from a parent.

REFERENCES

Bahney, A. (2006, March 9). Don't talk to invisible strangers. *New York Times*. Retrieved July 21, 2007 from http://www.nytimes.com/2006/03/09/fashion/thursdaystyles/09parents.html

BBC. (2005, July 19). *News Corp in $580m Internet buy*. Retrieved July 21, 2007 from http://news.bbc.co.uk/2/hi/business/4695495.stm

Benzie, R. (2007, May 3). Facebook banned for Ontario staffers. *The Star*. Retrieved July 21, 2007 from http://www.thestar.com/News/article/210014

boyd, d. (2004). Friendster and publicly articulated social networks. *Proceedings of ACM Conference on Human Factors in Computing Systems* (pp. 1279–1282). New York: ACM Press.

Boyd and Ellison rely on numerous types of sources, all carefully cited, in constructing their argument. For more on the varieties of evidence that can build an argument, see Chapter 19, Evaluating and Using Sources.

LINK TO P. 549

Friendster founder Jonathan Abrams

boyd, d. (2006a). Friends, Friendsters, and MySpace Top 8: Writing community into being on social network sites. *First Monday, 11* (12). Retrieved July 21, 2007 from http://www.firstmonday.org/issues/issue11_12/boyd/

boyd, d. (2006b, March 21). Friendster lost steam. Is MySpace just a fad? *Apophenia Blog.* Retrieved July 21, 2007 from http://www.danah.org/papers/FriendsterMySpaceEssay.html

boyd, d. (in press-b). None of this is real. In J. Karaganis (Ed.), *Structures of Participation.* New York: Social Science Research Council.

Cassidy, J. (2006, May 15). Me media: How hanging out on the Internet became big business. *The New Yorker, 82* (13), 50.

Chafkin, M. (2007, June). How to kill a great idea! *Inc. Magazine.* Retrieved August 27, 2007 from http://www.inc.com/magazine/20070601/features-how-to-kill-a-great-idea.html

Cohen, R. (2003, July 5). Livewire: Web sites try to make Internet dating less creepy. Reuters. Retrieved July 5, 2003 from http://asia.reuters.com/newsArticle.jhtml?type=internetNews&storyID=3041934

comScore. (2007). *Social networking goes global.* Reston, VA. Retrieved September 9, 2007 from http://www.comscore.com/press/release.asp?press=1555

Consumer Affairs. (2006, February 5). Connecticut opens MySpace.com probe. *Consumer Affairs.* Retrieved July 21, 2007 from http://www.consumeraffairs.com/news04/2006/02/myspace.html

Ewers, J. (2006, November 9). Cyworld: Bigger Than YouTube? *U.S. News & World Report.* Retrieved July 30, 2007 from LexisNexis.

Festa, P. (2003, November 11). Investors snub Friendster in patent grab. *CNet News.* Retrieved August 26, 2007 from http://news.com.com/2100-1032_3-5106136.html

Finkelhor, D., Ybarra, M., Lenhart, A., boyd, d., Lordan, T. (2007, May 3). Just the facts about online youth victimization: Researchers present the facts and debunk myths. *Internet Caucus Advisory Committee Event.* Retrieved July 21, 2007 from http://www.netcaucus.org/events/2007/youth/20070503transcript.pdf

Fragoso, S. (2006). WTF a crazy Brazilian invasion. In F. Sudweeks & H. Hrachovec (Eds.), *Proceedings of CATaC 2006* (pp. 255–274). Murdoch, Australia: Murdoch University.

Frosch, D. (2007, May 15). Pentagon blocks 13 web sites from military computers. *New York Times.* Retrieved July 21, 2007 from http://www.nytimes.com/2007/05/15/washington/15block.html

Goldberg, S. (2007, May 13). Analysis: Friendster is doing just fine. *Digital Media Wire.* Retrieved July 30, 2007 from http://www.dmwmedia.com/news/2007/05/14/analysis-friendster-is-doing-just-fine

Hargittai, E. (2007). Whose space? Differences among users and non-users of social network sites. *Journal of Computer-Mediated Communication, 13* (1), article 14. http://jcmc.indiana.edu/vol13/issue1/hargittai.html

Haythornthwaite, C. (2005). Social networks and Internet connectivity effects. *Information, Communication, & Society, 8* (2), 125–147.

H.R. 5319. (2006, May 9). *Deleting Online Predators Act of 2006.* H.R. 5319, 109th Congress. Retrieved July 21, 2007 from http://www.govtrack.us/congress/billtext.xpd?bill=h109-5319

Kim, K.-H. & H. Yun. (2007). Cying for me, Cying for us: Relational dialectics in a Korean social network site. *Journal of Computer-Mediated Communication, 13* (1), article 15. http://jcmc.indiana.edu/vol13/issue1/kim.yun.html

Kopytoff, V. (2004, November 29). Google's Orkut puzzles experts. *San Francisco Chronicle.* Retrieved July 30, 2007 from http://www.sfgate.com/cgi-bin/article.cgi?f=/c/a/2004/11/29/BUGU9A0BH441.DTL

Madhavan, N. (2007, July 6). India gets more Net Cool. *Hindustan Times.* Retrieved July 30, 2007 from http://www.hindustantimes.com/StoryPage/StoryPage.aspx?id=f2565bb8-663e-48c1-94ee-d99567577bdd

McLeod, D. (2006, October 6). QQ Attracting eyeballs. *Financial Mail* (South Africa), p. 36. Retrieved July 30, 2007 from *LexisNexis.*

National School Boards Association. (2007, July). *Creating and connecting: Research and guidelines on online social—and educational—networking.* Alexandria, VA. Retrieved September 23, 2007 from http://www.nsba.org/site/docs/41400/41340.pdf

O'Shea, W. (2003, July 4–10). Six Degrees of sexual frustration: Connecting the dates with Friendster.com. *Village Voice.* Retrieved July 21, 2007 from http://www.villagevoice.com/news/0323,oshea,44576,1.html

Perkel, D. (in press). Copy and paste literacy? Literacy practices in the production of a MySpace profile. In K. Drotner, H. S. Jensen, & K. Schroeder (Eds.), *Informal Learning and Digital Media: Constructions, Contexts, Consequences.* Newcastle, UK: Cambridge Scholars Press.

S. 49 (2007, January 4). *Protecting Children in the 21st Century Act of 2007.* S. 49, 110th Congress. Retrieved July 27, 2007 from http://www.govtrack.us/congress/bill.xpd?bill=s110-49

Shirky, C. (2003, May 13). People on page: YASNS . . . *Corante's Many-to-Many.* Retrieved July 21, 2007 from http://many.corante.com/archives/2003/05/12/people_on_page_yasns.php

Sundén, J. (2003). *Material Virtualities.* New York: Peter Lang.

Wellman, B. (1988). Structural analysis: From method and metaphor to theory and substance. In B. Wellman & S. D. Berkowitz (Eds.), *Social Structures: A Network Approach* (pp. 19–61). Cambridge, UK: Cambridge University Press.

Wolak, J., Mitchell, K., & Findelhor, D. (2006). Online victimization of youth: Five years later. *Report from Crimes Against Children Research Center,* University of New Hampshire. Retrieved July 21, 2007 from http://www.unh.edu/ccrc/pdf/CV138.pdf

RESPOND•

1. How much of the information in this selection is new to you? Were you aware of any, some, most, or all of the developments that boyd and Ellison discuss? Why is it useful for researchers to write articles that lay out criteria for defining a social phenomenon and trace its history?

2. Evaluate the section of the article entitled "Social Network Sites: A Definition" as an argument of definition. What kind(s) of definition do the authors offer? Why do they prefer the term "social network site" to "social networking site" (paragraph 6)? How persuasive are their arguments for this choice? How effective is their definition of this category of Web sites? (For a discussion of arguments of definition, see Chapter 9.)

3. Evaluate the section of the article entitled "A History of Social Network Sites" as a factual argument. Why does the subsection "The Early Years" begin with the statement, "According to the definition above, . . ." (paragraph 16)? In other words, why did the authors provide a definitional argument before an argument of fact about the history of social network sites? What sorts of evidence do the authors cite in constructing this argument? Why do they frequently cite personal communications? (For a discussion of arguments of fact, see Chapter 8.)

4. What role(s) does Figure 1 play in the authors' argument? Would the article have been weaker without it? Why or why not? (For a discussion of visual arguments, see Chapter 14.)

5. A common genre of academic writing, especially in the social sciences, is a "review of the literature," which presents earlier research on a topic. Imagine that you are writing a paper about research on social network sites. **Write a one- to two-paragraph summary** of the portion of this article that you have read. This will be an argument of fact. (For a discussion of arguments of fact, see Chapter 8.)

A Friend of a Friend of a Friend Knows You're on Vacation

OFFICE OF THE PRIVACY COMMISSIONER OF CANADA/COMMISSARIAT À LA PROTECTION DE LA VIE PRIVÉE DU CANADA

As part of the Office of the Privacy Commissioner's outreach effort, we are exploring other vehicles for communicating important privacy issues. We have already begun this blog, are experimenting with videos on YouTube and Google Video, and now have finished a Flash presentation.

The Flash presentation found below asks "what would you want a friend of a friend of a friend to know about you?" From our point of view as privacy advocates, a lot of online users do not take the time to really read and understand the user agreements required by all social networks. As online media consumers, we are used to "clicking" a box and ignoring the text inside.

It's becoming obvious that a lot of Canadians—and others—are signing over their privacy rights to these companies in exchange for access to increasingly popular social networks.

This is a choice they can make, but we would hope that people would take a minute to think about their choices—and how much information they end up handing over to corporations, advertisers and marketing companies.

You need a flashplayer enabled browser to view this YouTube video. View the 5 presentation: What does a friend of a friend of a friend need to know about you?

This entry was posted on Monday, November 5th, 2007 at 12:25 pm and is filed under Privacy Online, Social Networks. You can follow any responses to this entry through the RSS 2.0 feed. You can leave a response, or trackback from your own site.

Transcript of "What Does a Friend of a Friend of a Friend Need to Know about You?"

Online, you really are who you say you are. The things you say or write take on a life of their own. **They form your identity.**

We found this transcript of a YouTube video and the video itself on a blog hosted by the Office of the Privacy Commissioner of Canada (http://blog.privcom.gc.ca, accessed November 2007). The blog entry explains the purpose of the video. As you read the blog posting and the transcript and watch the video, pay attention to the ways in which the Internet enables users to embed arguments within one another. Also focus on the visual information contained in the video that is not contained in the transcript.

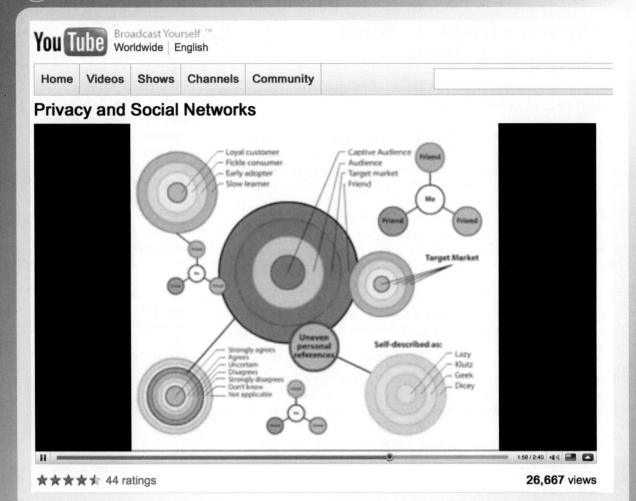

A scene from the YouTube video "What Does a Friend of a Friend of a Friend Need to Know about You?"

But the social networking sites where we express ourselves don't just focus on individuals. Instead, they make money repackaging user data into **trends** and **patterns.**

Personal data has become a hot commodity and social sites are the public face of a much larger commercial operation.

Knowing your hometown, favourite TV show or politics is **where the money is.**   10

And once information is added to the database, **users have little control.** Check out one such user agreement . . .

"By posting User Content to any part of the Site, you automatically grant . . . the Company an irrevocable, perpetual, non-exclusive, transferable, fully paid, worldwide license . . . to use, copy, publicly perform, display, reformat, translate, excerpt . . . such User Content . . . for any purpose . . ."

On social sites, it really isn't all about you but your data. Businesses trade in the information we enter: what we like, where we live, what our interests are.

Then advertisers can target us for products. Today's technology makes social sites **a gold mine of information for marketing companies**, or political interest groups, or **potential employers.**

As data about you is shared, what will it mean? More catalogs on your door-   15
step? More email adverts in your inbox? More questions during your next job interview?

The ways personal information can be used, repackaged and sold are virtually limitless.

As social sites become more popular, every time you add more data about yourself, it's as though you've answered a survey.

And on the basis of that information, others may make decisions about you. About your employability? About your work ethic? About your preferences?

All without your knowledge, or consent, or ever actually having been asked . . . so next time you update your information online, ask yourself some tough questions first.

For more information, visit the website of the Office of the Privacy   20
Commissioner of Canada—privcom.gc.ca.

> Are the concerns brought up in this presentation justified or overblown? Chapter 17 discusses potential fallacies of argument, including scare tactics. Does this presentation rely on scare tactics or is it a responsible warning? Explain your reasoning.
>
> LINK TO P. 517

RESPOND •

1. What are the purposes of and occasions for these arguments? How would you characterize these arguments in terms of stasis theory? (For a discussion of the purposes of and occasions for arguments as well as stasis theory, see Chapter 1.) How effective are these arguments? Why?

2. Focus on the written and read-aloud versions of the transcript of the YouTube video. How effective is the reader of the transcript in presenting the argument that he is reading? How does he use intonation rhetorically as he performs the transcript? In what ways does the video represent an argument to be heard? (For a discussion of presenting arguments, see Chapter 15.)

3. Focus on the visual information that is presented in the video. What information and what kinds of information are presented? You might want to make a list of all of the visual images that are presented in the video and then categorize these images according to type and function. How relevant or necessary is this information to the overall argument made by the video? (For a discussion of visual arguments, see Chapter 14.)

4. **Write an essay** in which you analyze the relationship between the spoken and visual arguments that are presented by the video "What Does a Friend of a Friend of a Friend Need to Know about You? Privacy on Social Networks." In your rhetorical analysis, be sure to consider the ways in which the spoken and visual arguments work together— that is, how they complement and support one another. (For a discussion of rhetorical analyses, see Chapter 5.)

One in Five Employers Uses Social Networks in Hiring Process

HEATHER HAVENSTEIN

More than one in five employers search social networking sites to screen job candidates, according to a survey of more than 31,000 employers released by CareerBuilder.com this week.

Of the hiring managers who use social networks, one-third said they found information on such sites that caused them to toss the candidate out of consideration for a job, the survey said.

The study found that the number of hiring managers that are turning to social networks like MySpace and Facebook to delve into candidates' online behavior is increasing quickly: Some 22% of employers said they already peruse social networks to screen candidates, while an additional 9% said they are planning to do so. Only 11% of managers used the technology in 2006.

The top areas of concern found on social networking sites include:

- Information about alcohol or drug use (41% of managers said this was a top concern)
- Inappropriate photos or information posted on a candidate's page (40%)
- Poor communication skills (29%)
- Bad-mouthing of former employers or fellow employees (28%)
- Inaccurate qualifications (27%)
- Unprofessional screen names (22%)
- Notes showing links to criminal behavior (21%)
- Confidential information about past employers (19%)

The study did find that 24% of hiring managers found content on social networks that helped convince them to hire a candidate. Hiring managers said that profiles showing a professional image and solid references can boost a candidate's chances for a job.

5

◀ Heather Havenstein, who has had a long career as a journalist focusing on information technology (IT), is a senior reporter at Computerworld, a publication and electronic resource for IT professionals. We found this article, dated September 12, 2008, on the Internet. As you read it, consider the way that Havenstein uses statistics to support her claims.

Havenstein opens her article with an argument of fact, establishing that employers use social networking sites to screen candidates. Chapter 8 explains how arguments of fact work.

LINK TO P. 208

"Hiring managers are using the Internet to get a more well-rounded view of job candidates in terms of their skills, accomplishments and overall fit within the company," said Rosemary Haefner, vice president of human resources at CareerBuilder.com, in a statement. "As a result, more job seekers are taking action to make their social networking profiles employer-friendly. Sixteen percent of workers who have social networking pages said they modified the content on their profile to convey a more professional image to potential employers."

CareerBuilder recommends that job seekers:

- Remove pictures, content and links that can send the wrong message to potential employers.
- Update social networking profiles regularly to highlight latest accomplishments.
- Consider blocking comments to avoid questionable posts; avoid joining groups whose names could turn off potential employers.
- Consider setting profile to private so only designated friends can view it.

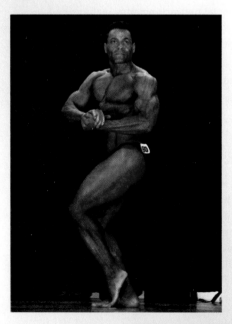

Exposing yourself to risk: Boston firefighter Alberto Arroyo posted his photo from a body-building competition held two weeks after he had filed for permanent disability status due to back injuries.

RESPOND

1. Statistics play an important role in Havenstein's argument. How would the article be different if she had not used statistics? How effective would it be? Why? (To think about this question, you might mentally remove the statistics in the list in paragraph 4 while substituting more general statements for statistically based claims in the text so that "one in five" in the first paragraph becomes "a few.")

2. Havenstein's article is brief and to the point. Why do you think that brevity and directness characterize much of the writing for *Computerworld* and other sources of information about technology on the Internet?

3. Analyze Havenstein's article as a proposal argument. What problem is addressed? The claim? The proposal? (For a discussion of proposal arguments, see Chapter 12.)

4. In many ways, Havenstein's article can be seen as a logical follow-up to the previous selection, "A Friend of a Friend of a Friend Knows You're on Vacation." It provides a case study on issues of privacy and social network sites, one dealing with the specific situation of job seekers. Based on the information in the previous selection or your own experience, how likely is it that following the suggestions of CareerBuilder will remove all evidence of potentially objectionable behavior from a social network site?

5. In college writing, students are frequently asked to synthesize information from multiple sources. **Write three to five paragraphs** that might be part of a larger research paper, for example, in which you combine information from the previous selection and this one to offer a factual or definitional argument about the nature of a problem along with a set of proposals for dealing with that problem. You may wish to supplement the proposals that are offered in Havenstein's article with suggestions of your own. (For information about arguments of fact, arguments of definition, and proposal arguments, see Chapters 8, 9, and 12, respectively. For information about paraphrasing and citing sources, see Chapter 18.)

6. Issues relating to privacy, social network sites, and employability continue to evolve as SNSs, laws about technology, and theories about privacy develop. Using the Internet, investigate one or more of these topics, and **create an argument**—either a traditional essay or a multimedia argument. You might wish to consider creating an evaluative argument or a causal argument that focuses on these topics. (For information on evaluative arguments and causal arguments, see Chapters 10 and 11, respectively.)

▼ *Like several other readings in this book, this article by Tamar Lewin
from the November 20, 2008,* New York Times *represents a common kind
of journalistic writing—reporting on academic research for a broad audience. Lewin has written for the* Times *since 1982, often about issues
relating to social policy. As part of this selection, we also include four of the
fifty-nine comments about the article that were posted by readers on the*
Times *Web site. These four comments are the Editors' Selections—the ones
that the paper's editors consider the most perceptive and representative of a
range of opinion. (Each posted comment indicates the number of readers
who recommended the comment to others.) As you read Lewin's article, try
to anticipate the sorts of comments that readers made about it, and as you
study the comments, evaluate the evidence that readers use to support their
claims. Following this two-part selection, we present two excerpts from the
research study that Lewin cites in her article.*

Study Finds Teenagers' Internet
Socializing Isn't Such a Bad Thing

TAMAR LEWIN

Good news for worried parents: All
those hours their teenagers spend
socializing on the Internet are not a
bad thing, according to a new study
by the MacArthur Foundation.

"It may look as though kids are
wasting a lot of time hanging out with
new media, whether it's on MySpace
or sending instant messages," said
Mizuko Ito, lead researcher on the
study, *Living and Learning with New
Media.* "But their participation is giving them the technological skills and
literacy they need to succeed in the
contemporary world. They're learning
how to get along with others, how to
manage a public identity, how to create a home page."

The study, conducted from 2005
to last summer, describes new-media
usage but does not measure its effects.

"It certainly rings true that new
media are inextricably woven into
young people's lives," said Vicki
Rideout, vice president of the Kaiser
Family Foundation and director of its
program for the study of media and
health. "Ethnographic studies° like
this are good at describing how young
people fit social media into their lives.
What they can't do is document
effects. This highlights the need for

---

ethnographic studies:
studies based on the use of
ethnographic methods,
traditionally associated
with the discipline of
anthropology. Researchers
conduct long-term participant observation to
describe in rich detail the
world as it is experienced
by the group or groups
studied (here, teenagers
using technology). Their
goal is not to make claims
about all members of a
social group (for example,
all teenagers) but to offer
"thick descriptions" of
those members whose
behavior is documented.

larger, nationally representative studies."°

Ms. Ito, a research scientist in the department of informatics at the University of California, Irvine, said that some parental concern about the dangers of Internet socializing might result from a misperception. 5

"Those concerns about predators and stranger danger have been overblown," she said. "There's been some confusion about what kids are actually doing online. Mostly, they're socializing with their friends, people they've met at school or camp or sports."

The study, part of a $50 million project on digital and media learning, used several teams of researchers to interview more than 800 young people and their parents and to observe teenagers online for more than 5,000 hours. Because of the adult sense that socializing on the Internet is a waste of time, the study said, teenagers reported many rules and restrictions on their electronic hanging out, but most found ways to work around such barriers that let them stay in touch with their friends steadily throughout the day.

"Teens usually have a 'full-time intimate community' with whom they communicate in an always-on mode

via mobile phones and instant messaging," the study said.

This is not news to a cluster of Bronx teenagers, gathered after school on Wednesday to tell a reporter about their social routines. All of them used MySpace and instant messaging to stay in touch with a dozen or two of their closest friends every evening. "As soon as I get home, I turn on my computer," said a 15-year-old boy who started his MySpace page four years ago. "My MySpace is always on, and

when I get a message on MySpace, it sends a text message to my phone. It's not an obsession; it's a necessity." (School rules did not permit using students' names without written parental permission, which could not be immediately obtained.)

Only one student, a 14-year-old girl, had ever opted out—and she lasted only a week. 10

"It didn't work," she said. "You become addicted. You can't live without it."

---

representative studies: here, research based on random samples (in which every teenager would have an equal chance of being chosen for the study). Such studies permit researchers to generalize from the sample studied to the population at large (here, all U.S. teenagers). Depending on their design, the studies could also permit researchers to make claims about the effects of technology use on different groups of teens.

Compare a couple of paragraphs from this article with the two excerpts from the study that follows. Using what you've learned about academic arguments in Chapter 6, detail some of the difference between the news story and the academic studies.

LINK TO P. 133

In a situation familiar to many parents, the study describes two 17-year-olds, dating for more than a year, who wake up and log on to their computers between taking showers and doing their hair, talk on their cell-phones as they travel to school, exchange text messages through the school day, then get together after school to do homework—during which time they also play a video game—talk on the phone during the evening, perhaps ending the night with a text-messaged "I love you."

Teenagers also use new media to explore new romantic relationships, through interactions casual enough to ensure no loss of face if the other party is not interested.

The study describes two early Facebook messages, or "wall posts," by teenagers who eventually started dating. First, the girl posted a message saying, "hey . . . hm. wut to say? iono lol/well I left you a comment . . . u sud feel SPECIAL haha." (Translation: Hmm . . . what to say? I don't know. Laugh out loud. Well I left you a comment . . . You should feel special.)

A day later, the boy replied, "hello 15 there . . . umm I don't know what to say, but at least I wrote something . . ."

While online socializing is ubiquitous, many young people move on to a period of tinkering and exploration, as they look for information online, customize games or experiment with digital media production, the study found.

For example, a Brooklyn teenager did a Google image search to look at a video card and find out where in a computer such cards are, then installed his own.

What the study calls "geeking out" is the most intense Internet use, in which young people delve deeply into a particular area of interest, often through a connection to an online interest group.

"New media allow for a degree of freedom and autonomy for youth that is less apparent in a classroom setting," the study said. "Youth respect one another's authority online, and they are often more motivated to learn from peers than from adults."

READERS' COMMENTS ON THE ARTICLE, EDITORS' SELECTIONS

2.   20
November 20, 2008 11:37 am
This type of interaction has become especially significant in cultures and countries where public socializing is limited. It allows younger people to circumvent social norms that frown upon young people of the opposite sex mixing.

—Pete, New York City

6.
November 20, 2008 11:37 am
I'll agree it helps their tech skills, but literacy?

—Joe, Chicago Suburbs

Are social media providing a solution for "an impoverished public sphere"—or perpetuating the problem?

9.
November 20, 2008 11:37 am
Great, so they have technological skills. But they are not getting outside, getting exercise, connecting with nature. Nor are they truly developing social skills—e-communicating is a far cry from navigating face to face interactions.

—KPod, Wisconsin

22.
November 20, 2008 1:20 pm
To us who are part of this generation, grown-up talk of "literacy" and "skills" sound like the same cheery, contrarian rationalization that brought us "hand-eye coordination." If you think these are the benefits—and non-standard English is the threat—you are missing nearly everything.

Social media clearly speaks to deep needs in us. We need a public life and common space. We crave a sense of participation in each other's lives. We are eager to make the boundaries between stranger, acquaintance and friend more fluid, more full of possibilities. We thrill at the chance to create a common experience, rather than just watch one.

As far as we can tell, our parents' 25 (grandparents'?) generation abandoned public space. We grew up in suburbs, begging for rides to the mall. We grew up in cities on supposedly risky streets. Our parents were obsessed with child abductions. We went to universities where video games and alcohol concerns pushed socializing behind closed doors. We visited Europe and saw picnics, plazas, squares, piazzas, biergartens, joined the evening passegiatta, korso and paseo, and we swooned. After college, everyone we knew spread to the four corners of the Earth, and meeting people became much harder.

Social media is our solution for an impoverished public sphere. The downside? It will certainly perpetuate it. The real danger is not our spelling. It is this: the brighter the mirage—and it is, without a doubt, a mirage—the less motivation we will have to actually build the world we desire and deserve.

—Elliot Cole, La Honda, CA

RESPOND.

1. Who is likely the intended audience for this article? The invoked audience? What evidence can you cite? (For a discussion of audience, see Chapter 1.)

2. Is any of this information news to you? Why might it be news to the readers of the *New York Times*?

3. How does Lewin move between the findings of the study and interviews with adolescents at a Bronx school? How does the information gathered from interviews contribute to Lewin's argument? How would the article be different without this information? (For a discussion of interviewing, see Chapter 16.)

4. How well did you anticipate the topics of the reader comments that were chosen by the *Times*'s editors? To what extent to do you agree with the comments? The most developed of the comments was written by Elliot Cole. What is his argument? What evidence does he give? In what ways does he believe that the "older generation" is missing the point in many of its complaints about younger people's uses of technology?

5. Visit the *New York Times* Web site (http://www.nytimes.com) and read all of the comments on Lewin's article. (One way to find them is to locate the Lewin article based on the information given in the head-note, and then click on "Read all comments" when you get the article.) Choose several comments that you find most interesting—perhaps a series of comments on a single topic—and **write an analysis** of them. You may wish to evaluate the evidence that the comment writers use to support their claims, or you may wish to illustrate and explain fallacies that you find. This assignment gives you a great deal of freedom in choosing your focus. (For a discussion of evidence and of fallacies, see Chapters 16 and 17, respectively.)

▼ *This selection and the following one are taken from* Living and Learning with New Media: Summary of Findings from the Digital Youth Project, *the 2008 research report that Tamar Lewin discusses in the previous selection, "Study Finds Teenagers' Internet Socializing Isn't Such a Bad Thing." (The entire report can be found at digitalyouth.ischool.berkeley.edu/files/ report/digitalyouth-WhitePaper.pdf.) Here, we present the report's executive summary, which is a common genre in professional writing. Much like an abstract in a research article, an executive summary highlights the major findings that are discussed in the report.*

The study that this report provides information about is Digital Youth Research: Kids' Informal Learning with Digital Media *(http://digitalyouth .ischool.berkeley.edu/report), a three-year collaborative project that was conducted by researchers at the University of Southern California (USC) and the University of California at Berkeley. It was funded by the John D. and Catherine T. MacArthur Foundation's five-year, $50 million initiative "to help determine how digital media are changing the way young people learn, play, socialize, and participate in civic life." The project involved a team of twenty-eight researchers led by Mizuko Ito, a Japanese-born cultural anthropologist who is the research director of the Digital Media and Learning Hub at the University of California at Irvine.*

As you read this executive summary, notice how the findings are stated in a way that questions many common assumptions that those who did not grow up with digital technologies have about technology and young people. Notice, too, how the summary points out the implications of the findings much in the way that a proposal argument does.

"Executive Summary," Living and Learning with New Media

MIZUKO ITO ET AL.*

Social network sites, online games, video-sharing sites, and gadgets such as iPods and mobile phones are now fixtures of youth culture. They have so permeated young lives that it is hard to believe that less than a decade ago these

---

* The other authors were Heather A. Horst, Matteo Bittanti, danah boyd, Becky Herr-Stephenson, Patricia G. Lange, C. J. Pascoe, and Laura Robinson.

The homepage of the Digital Youth Project

white paper: an authoritative report that is issued by an institution (such as a government, a foundation, or a research or policy institute).

ethnographic study: a study that is based on ethnographic methods, traditionally associated with the discipline of anthropology. Researchers conduct long-term observation and participation to describe in rich detail the world as it is experienced by the group or groups studied (here, teenagers using technology). Their goal is not to make claims about all members of a social group (for example, all teenagers) but to offer "thick descriptions" of those members whose behavior is documented.

ecology: here, relationships that exist between young people and their media-saturated environment, including interactions with other people via these media.

technologies barely existed. Today's youth may be coming of age and struggling for autonomy and identity as did their predecessors, but they are doing so amid new worlds for communication, friendship, play, and self-expression.

This white paper° summarizes the results of a three-year ethnographic study,° funded by the John D. and Catherine T. MacArthur Foundation, examining young people's participation in the new media ecology.° It represents a condensed version of a longer treatment of the project findings. The study was motivated by two primary research questions: How are new media being integrated into youth practices and agendas? How do these practices change the dynamics of youth-adult negotiations over literacy, learning, and authoritative knowledge?

EXTENDING FRIENDSHIPS AND INTERESTS

Online spaces enable youth to connect with peers in new ways. Most youth use online networks to extend the friendships that they navigate in the familiar contexts of school, religious organizations, sports, and other local activities. They can be "always on," in constant contact with their friends via texting, instant messaging, mobile phones, and Internet connections. This continuous presence requires ongoing maintenance and negotiation, through private communications like instant messaging or mobile phones, as well as in public ways through social network sites such as MySpace and Facebook. With these "friendship-driven" practices, youth are almost always associating with people they already know in their offline lives. The majority of youth use new media to "hang out" and extend existing friendships in these ways.

A smaller number of youth also use the online world to explore interests and find information that goes beyond what they have access to at school or in their local community. Online groups enable youth to connect to peers who share specialized and niche interests of various kinds, whether that is online gaming, creative writing, video editing, or other artistic endeavors. In these "interest-driven" networks, youth may find new peers outside the boundaries of their local community. They can also find opportunities to publicize and distribute their work to online audiences and to gain new forms of visibility and reputation.

Self-Directed, Peer-Based Learning

In both friendship-driven and interest-driven online activity, youth create   5 and navigate new forms of expression and rules for social behavior. In the process, young people acquire various forms of technical and media literacy by exploring new interests, tinkering, and "messing around" with new forms of media. They may start with a Google search or "lurk" in chat rooms to learn more about their burgeoning interest. Through trial and error, youth add new media skills to their repertoire, such as how to create a video or customize games or their MySpace page. Teens then share their creations and receive feedback from others online. By its immediacy and breadth of information, the digital world lowers barriers to self-directed° learning.

Others "geek out" and dive into a topic or talent. Contrary to popular images, geeking out is highly social and engaged, although usually not driven primarily by local friendships. Youth turn instead to specialized knowledge groups of both teens and adults from around the country or world, with the goal of improving their craft and gaining reputation among expert peers. What makes these groups unique is that while adults participate, they are not automatically the resident experts by virtue of their age. Geeking out in many respects erases the traditional markers of status and authority.

self-directed: directed or controlled by the self. (*Other-directed* implies that someone else, perhaps a parent or teacher, is making the decisions.)

New media allow for a degree of freedom and autonomy for youth that is less apparent in a classroom setting. Youth respect one another's authority online, and they are often more motivated to learn from peers than from adults. Their efforts are also largely self-directed, and the outcome emerges through exploration, in contrast to classroom learning that is oriented toward set, predefined goals.

How do the implications of this study suggest different proposal arguments? See Chapter 12 for more on proposal arguments.

LINK TO P. 373

IMPLICATIONS FOR EDUCATORS, PARENTS, AND POLICYMAKERS

New media forms have altered how youth socialize and learn, and this raises a new set of issues that educators, parents, and policymakers should consider.

Social and recreational new media use as a site of learning. Contrary to adult perceptions, while hanging out online, youth are picking up basic social and technological skills they need to fully participate in contemporary society. Erecting barriers to participation deprives teens of access to these forms of learning. Participation in the digital age means more than being able to access "serious" online information and culture. Youth could benefit from educators being more open to forms of experimentation and social exploration that are generally not characteristic of educational institutions.

Recognizing important distinctions in youth culture and literacy. 10 Friendship-driven and interest-driven online participation have very different kinds of social connotations. For example, whereas friendship-driven activities center on peer culture, adult participation is more welcome in the latter, more "geeky," forms of learning. In addition, the content, ways of relating, and skills that youth value are highly variable depending on what kinds of social groups they associate with. This diversity in forms of literacy means that it is problematic to develop a standardized set of benchmarks to measure levels of new media and technical literacy.

Capitalizing on peer-based learning. Youth using new media often learn from their peers, not teachers or adults, and notions of expertise and authority have been turned on their heads. Such learning differs fundamentally from traditional instruction and is often framed negatively by adults as a means of "peer pressure." Yet adults can still have tremendous influence in setting "learning goals," particularly on the interest-driven side, where adult hobbyists function as role models and more experienced peers.

New role for education? Youths' participation in this networked world suggests new ways of thinking about the role of education. What would it mean to really exploit the potential of the learning opportunities available through online resources and networks? Rather than assuming that education is primarily about preparing for jobs and careers, what would it mean to think of it as a process guiding youths' participation in public life more generally? Finally, what would it mean to enlist help in this endeavor from engaged and diverse publics that are broader than what we traditionally think of as educational and civic institutions?

RESPOND •

1. What research questions did the Digital Youth Project seek to answer? Based on this summary, what answers have the researchers found?

2. The summary and accompanying report identify three genres of participation in the new media—hanging out, messing around, and geeking out—each in some sense building on the previous one. (Ethnographers generally label social phenomena with the terms that are used by those they study, so we can assume that the young people in the study used these terms in talking about their experiences and those of others.) How does each stage represent a deepening and more complex relationship with technology? In what ways does each stage assume different sorts of interpersonal relationships that are mediated by technology, that is, that depend on technology in some way?

3. In what ways is the section titled "Implications for Educators, Parents, and Policymakers" (paragraphs 8–12) a proposal argument? In what ways could this section serve as the basis for more specific proposals? (For a discussion of proposal arguments, see Chapter 12.)

4. Building on your response to question 3, choose one of the implications listed, and **write a proposal argument** in which you take one of the researchers' suggestions as a starting point. In other words, take the suggestion as a statement of the need or problem, and propose an appropriate, feasible response. You will likely want to skim the "Conclusions and Implications" section of the actual report (digital youth.ischool.berkeley.edu/files/report/digitalyouth-WhitePaper.pdf) before choosing which implication to pursue. (For a discussion of proposal arguments, see Chapter 12.)

▼ *This selection and the previous one are taken from* Living and Learning with New Media: Summary of Findings from the Digital Youth Project, *the 2008 research report that Tamar Lewin discusses in an earlier selection,* "Study Finds Teenagers' Internet Socializing Isn't Such a Bad Thing." *(The entire report can be found at digitalyouth.ischool.berkeley.edu/files/report/ digitalyouth-WhitePaper.pdf.) Here, we present the section on "geeking out," the third and most intense form of participation with new media that the study found among young people, the first two being "hanging out" and "messing around." This selection should give you insight into how researchers use observations and interviews to construct arguments, specifically descriptions and analyses of cultures and the ways they work.*

Like the preceding selection, the study that this report provides information about is Digital Youth Research: Kids' Informal Learning with Digital Media *(http://digitalyouth.ischool.berkeley.edu/report), a three-year collaborative project that was conducted by researchers at the University of Southern California (USC) and the University of California at Berkeley. It was funded by the John D. and Catherine T. MacArthur Foundation's five-year, $50 million initiative "to help determine how digital technologies are changing the way young people learn, play, socialize, and participate in civic life." The project involved a team of twenty-eight researchers led by Mizuko Ito, a Japanese-born cultural anthropologist who is the research director of the Digital Media and Learning Hub at the University of California at Irvine.*

As you read this selection on geeking out, notice how the researchers compare and contrast different groups of young people who geek out while drawing generalizations about the use of new media. Also note how different the descriptions offered here are from familiar stereotypes about geeks.

Geeking Out

MIZUKO ITO ET AL.*

The ability to engage with media and technology in an intense, autonomous, and interest-driven way is a unique feature of today's media environment. Particularly for kids with newer technology and high-speed Internet at home,

---

* The other authors were Heather A. Horst, Matteo Bittanti, danah boyd, Becky Herr-Stephenson, Patricia G. Lange, C. J. Pascoe, and Laura Robinson.

the Internet can provide access to an immense amount of information related to their particular interests, and it can support various forms of "geeking out"—an intense commitment to or engagement with media or technology, often one particular media property, genre, or type of technology. Geeking out involves learning to navigate esoteric° domains of knowledge and practice and participating in communities that traffic in these forms of expertise. It is a mode of learning that is peer-driven, but focused on gaining deep knowledge and expertise in specific areas of interest.

esoteric: understood by only a small number of people.

Ongoing access to digital media is a requirement of geeking out. Often, however, such access is just part of what makes participation possible. Family, friends, and other peers in on- and offline spaces are particularly important in facilitating access to the technology, knowledge, and social connections required to geek out. Just as in the case of messing around, geeking out requires the time, space, and resources to experiment and follow interests in a self-directed° way.

self-directed: directed or controlled by the self. (*Other-directed* implies that someone else, perhaps a parent or teacher, is making the decisions.)

Furthermore, it requires access to specialized communities of expertise. Contrary to popular images of the socially isolated geek, almost all geeking out practices we observed are highly social and engaged, although not necessarily expressed as friendship-driven social practices. Instead, the social worlds center on specialized knowledge networks and communities that are driven by specific interests and a range of social practices for sharing work and opinions. The online world has made these kinds of specialized hobby and knowledge networks more widely available to youth. Although generally considered marginal to both local, school-based friendship networks and to academic achievement, the activities of geeking out provide important spaces of self-directed learning that is driven by passionate interests.

SPECIALIZED KNOWLEDGE NETWORKS

When young people geek out, they are delving into areas of interest that exceed common knowledge; this generally involves seeking expert knowledge networks outside of given friendship-driven networks. Rather than simply messing around with local friends, geeking out involves developing an identity and pride as an expert and seeking fellow experts in far-flung networks. Geeking out is usually supported by interest-based groups, either local or online, or some hybrid of the two, where fellow geeks will both produce and exchange knowledge on their subjects of interest. Rather than purely "consuming" knowledge produced by authoritative sources, geeked out engagement involves accessing as well as producing knowledge to contribute to the knowledge network.

In her study of anime music video (AMV)^{xlvii} creators ("Anime Fans"),   5
Mizuko Ito interviewed Gepetto, an 18-year-old Brazilian fan. He was first
introduced to AMVs through a local friend and started messing around creating AMVs on his own. As his skills developed, however, he sought out the
online community of AMV creators on animemusicvideos.org to sharpen his
skills. Although he managed to interest a few of his local friends in AMV
making, none of them took to it to the extent that he did. He relies heavily on
the networked community of editors as sources of knowledge and expertise
and as models to aspire to. In his local community, he is now known as a
video expert by both his peers and adults. After seeing his AMV work, one of
his high-school teachers asked him to teach a video workshop to younger
students. He jokes that "even though I know nothing," to his local community
"I am the Greater God of video editing." In other words, his engagement with
the online interest group helped develop his identity and competence as a
video editor well beyond what is typical in his local community.

In the geeked-out gaming world, players and game designers now expect
that game play will be supported by an online knowledge network that provides tips, cheats,° walk-throughs,° mods,° and reviews that are generated by
both fellow players and commercial publishers. Personal knowledge exchange
among local gamer friends, as well as this broader knowledge network, is a

cheat: a tool that allows someone to be more successful at a computer or video game.

walk-through: in computer and video gaming, a document that helps a player play a game successfully.

mod (< modification): a modification of software that changes the appearance of a computer game or how it operates.

Anime fans at a convention, dressed as their favorite characters

vital part of more sophisticated forms of game play that are in the geeking out genre of engagement. Although more casual players mess around by accessing cheats and hints online, more geeked out players will consume, debate, and produce this knowledge for other players. Rachel Cody notes that the players in her study of *Final Fantasy XI* routinely used guides produced both commercially and by fellow players. The guides assisted players in streamlining some parts of the game that otherwise took a great deal of time or resources. Cody observed that a few members of the linkshell° in her study kept Microsoft Excel files with detailed notes on all their crafting in order to postulate theories on the most efficient ways of producing goods. As Wurlpin, a 26-year-old male from California, told Rachel Cody, the guides are an essential part of playing the game. He commented, "I couldn't imagine [playing while] not knowing how to do half the things, how to go, who to talk to."

linkshell: a guild, or group of players, in a multiplayer computer or video game who often play together.

INTEREST-BASED COMMUNITIES AND ORGANIZATIONS

Interest-based geeking-out activities can be supported by a wide range of organizations and online infrastructures. Most interest groups surrounding fandom, gaming, and amateur media production are loosely aggregated through online sites such as YouTube, LiveJournal, or DeviantArt, or more specialized sites such as animemusicvideos.org, fanfiction.net, and gaming sites such as Allakhazam or pojo.com. In addition, core participants in specific interest communities will often take a central role in organizing events and administering sites that cater to their hobbies and interests. Fan sites that cater to specific games, game guilds, and media series are proliferating on the Internet, as are specialized networks within larger sites such as LiveJournal or DeviantArt. Real-life meetings such as conventions, competitions, meet-ups, and gaming parties are also part of these kinds of distributed, player- and fan-driven forms of organization that support the ongoing life and social exchange of interest-driven groups.

As part of Mizuko Ito's case study on "Anime Fans," she researched the practices of amateur subtitlers, or "fansubbers," who translate and subtitle anime and release it through Internet distribution. In our book *Hanging Out, Messing Around, and Geeking Out*, we describe some of the ways in which fansubbers form tight-knit work teams with jobs that include translators, timers, editors, typesetters, encoders, quality checkers, and distributors.[xlviii] Fansub groups often work faster and more effectively than professional localization industries, and their work is viewed by millions of anime fans around the world. They often work on tight deadlines, and the fastest groups will turn around an episode within 24 hours of release in Japan. For this, fansubbers

Players use weapons and magic to battle their human and monster enemies in a scene from Final Fantasy XI.

receive no monetary rewards, and they say that they pursue this work for the satisfaction of making anime available to fans overseas and for the pleasure they get in working with a close-knit production team that keeps in touch primarily on online chat channels and web forums. Fansubbing is just one example of the many forms of volunteer labor and organizations that are run by fans. In addition to producing a wide range of creative works, fans also organize anime clubs, conventions, web sites, and competitions as part of their interest-driven activities.

The issue of leadership and team organization was a topic that was central to Rachel Cody's study of *Final Fantasy XI*. Cody spent seven months participant-observing in a high-level "linkshell," or guild. Although many purely social linkshells do populate FFXI, Cody's linkshell was an "endgame" linkshell, meaning that the group aimed to defeat the high-level monsters in the game. The participants organized the linkshell in a hierarchical system, with a leader and officers who had decision-making authority, and new members needed to be approved by the officers. Often the process of joining the linkshell involved a formal application and interview, and members were expected to conform to the standards of the group and perform effectively in battle as a team. The linkshell would organize "camps" where sometimes more than 150 people would wait for a high-level monster to appear and then attack with a well-planned battle strategy. Gaming can function as a site for organizing collective action, which can vary from the more lightweight arrangements of kids getting together to play competitively to the more formal arrangements that we see in a group such as Cody's linkshell.

In all of these cases, players are engaging in a complex social organization 10 that operates under different sets of hierarchies and politics than those that occupy them in the offline world. These online groups provide an opportunity for youth to exercise adult-like agency° and leadership that is not otherwise available to them. Although the relationships they foster in these settings are initially motivated by media-related interests, these collaborative arrangements and ongoing social exchange often result in deep and lasting friendships with new networks of like-minded peers.

agency: here, the ablility to make choices and determine courses of action.

FEEDBACK AND LEARNING

Interest-based communities that support geeking out have important learning properties that are grounded in peer-based sharing and feedback. The mechanisms for getting input on one's work and performance can vary from ongoing exchange on online chat and forums to more formal forms of rankings, critiques, and competition. Unlike what young people experience in school, where they are graded by a teacher in a position of authority, feedback in interest-driven groups is from peers and audiences who have a personal interest in their work and opinions. Among fellow creators and community members, the context is one of peer-based reciprocity, where participants can gain status and reputation but do not hold evaluative authority over one another.

Not all creative groups we examined have a tight-knit community with established standards. YouTube, for example, functions more as an open aggregator° of a wide range of video-production genres and communities, and the standards for participation and commentary differ according to the goals of particular video makers and social groups. Critique and feedback can take many forms, including posted comments on a site that displays works, private message exchanges, offers to collaborate, invitations to join other creators' social groups, and promotion from other members of an interest-oriented group. Study participants did not value simple five-star rating schemes as mechanisms for improving their craft, although they considered them useful in boosting ranking and visibility. Fansubbers generally thought

aggregator: here, a Web application that collects and stores online content for easy access.

that their audience had little understanding of what constituted a quality fansub and would take seriously only the evaluation of fellow producers. Similarly, AMV creators play down rankings and competition results based on "viewer's choice." The perception among creators is that many videos win if they use popular anime as source material, regardless of the merits of the editing. Fan fiction writers also felt that the general readership, while often providing encouragement, offered little in the way of substantive feedback.

In contrast to these attitudes toward audience feedback, a comment from a respected fellow creator carries a great deal of weight. Creators across different communities often described an inspiring moment when they received positive feedback and suggestions from a fellow creator whom they respected.

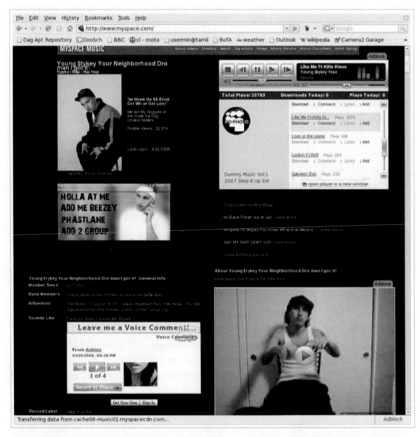

An example of a MySpace Music profile (screen capture by Dilan Mahendran, 2006)

In Dilan Mahendran's study ("Hip-Hop Music Production"), Edric, a 19-year-old Puerto Rican rapper, described his nervousness at his first recording session and the moment when he stepped out of the booth. "And everyone was like, 'Man, that was nice. I liked that.' And I was like, 'For real?' I was like, 'I appreciate that.' And ever since then I've just been stuck to writing, developing my style." Receiving positive feedback from peers who shared his interest in hip-hop was tremendously validating and gave him motivation to continue with his interests. Some communities have specific mechanisms for receiving informed feedback from expert peers. Animemusicvideos.org has extended reviewer forms that can be submitted for videos, and it hosts a variety of competitions in which editors can enter their videos. All major anime conventions also have AMV competitions in which the best videos are selected by audiences as well as by fellow editors.

Young people participating in online writing communities can get substantive feedback from fellow writers. In fan fiction, critical feedback is provided by "beta readers," who read "fics" before they are published and give suggestions on style, plot, and grammar. Clarissa (17 years old, white), an aspiring writer and one of the participants in C. J. Pascoe's study "Living Digital," participates in an online role-playing board, *Faraway Lands* (a pseudonym). Aspiring members must write lengthy character descriptions to apply, and these are evaluated by the site administrators. Since receiving glowing reviews of her application, Clarissa has been a regular participant on the site, and she has developed friendships with many of the writers there. She has been doing a joint role play with another participant from Spain, and she has a friend from Oregon who critiques her work and vice versa. She explains how this feedback from fellow writers feels more authentic to her than the evaluations she receives in school. "It's something I can do in my spare time, be creative and write and not have to be graded," because, "you know how in school you're creative, but you're doing it for a grade so it doesn't really count?"[xlix]

> This argument introduces sources using signal phrases so that the audience has a better understanding of each source's authority. Take a look at Chapter 19 for more on how to incorporate sources successfully.
>
> LINK TO P. 549

RECOGNITION AND REPUTATION

In addition to providing opportunities for young people to learn and improve 15 their craft, interest-driven groups also offer a way to gain recognition and reputation as well as an audience for creative work. Although participants do not always value audience feedback as the best mechanism for improving their work, most participants in interest-driven communities are nevertheless motivated by knowing that their work will be viewed by others or by being part of an appreciative community.

For example, zalas, a Chinese American in his early 20s and a participant in Mizuko Ito's study of "Anime Fans," is an active participant in the anime fandom. zalas is an officer at his university anime club, a frequent presenter at local anime conventions, and a well-known participant in online anime forums and IRC (Internet Relay Chat), where he is connected to fellow fans 24/7. He will often scour the Japanese anime and game-related sites to get news that English-speaking fans do not have access to. "It's kinda like a race to see who can post the first tidbit about it." He estimates that he spends about eight hours a day online keeping up with his hobby. "I think pretty much all the time that's not school, eating, or sleeping." He is a well-respected expert in the anime scene because of this commitment to pursuing and sharing knowledge.

Specialized video communities, such as AMVs or live-action "vidding,"[1] will often avoid general-purpose video-sharing sites such as YouTube because they are not targeted to audiences who are well informed about their genres of media. In fact, on one of the forums dedicated to AMVs, any instance of the term "YouTube" is automatically censored. Even within these specialized groups, however, creators do seek visibility. Most major anime conventions now will include an AMV competition in which the winning works are showcased, in addition to venues for fan artists to display and sell their work. The young hip-hop artists Dilan Mahendran spoke to also participated in musical competitions that gave them visibility, particularly if they went home with awards. Even fansubbers who insist that quality and respect among peers are more important than download numbers will admit that they do track the numbers. As one fansubber in Ito's study of "Anime Fans" put it, "Deep down inside, every fansubber wants to have their work watched, and a high amount of viewers causes them some kind of joy whether they express it or not." Fansub groups generally make their "trackers," which record the number of downloads, public on their sites.

Young people can use large sites such as MySpace and YouTube as ways of disseminating their work to broader audiences. In Dilan Mahendran's "Hip-Hop Music Production" study, the more ambitious musicians would use a MySpace Music template as a way to develop profiles that situated them as musicians rather than a standard teen personal profile. The style of these kinds of MySpace pages differs fundamentally from the more common profiles that center on social communication and the display of friendships. Similarly, video makers who seek broader audiences gravitate toward YouTube as a site to gain visibility. YouTube creators monitor their play counts and comments for audience feedback. Frank, a white 15-year-old male from Ohio who posts on YouTube, stated, "But then even when you get one good comment, that makes up for 50 mean comments, 'cause it's just the fact of knowing that someone else out there liked your videos and stuff, and it doesn't really matter about everyone else that's criticized you" (Patricia Lange, "YouTube and Video Bloggers").

In some cases, young people parlayed their interests into income and even a sustained career. Max, a 14-year-old boy in Patricia Lange's "YouTube and Video Bloggers" study, turned into a YouTube sensation when he recorded his mother, unaware that people around her could hear her and had started to laugh, singing along to the Boyz II Men song playing in her headphones. Max posted the video on YouTube and it attracted the attention of the ABC television show *Good Morning America*, on which the video eventually aired. In the two years since it was posted, the video received more than 2 million views and more than 5,000 text comments, many of them expressing support. Max's work also attracted attention from another media company, which approached him about the possibility of buying another of his videos for an online advertisement. We also found cases of hip-hop artists who market their music, fan artists who sell their work at conventions, and

Wizard Rock band Harry and the Potters. For a lucky few, social networking can lead to fame and fortune.

youth who freelance as web designers. Among the case studies of anime and Harry Potter fans, a handful of youth successfully capitalized on their creative talents. Becky Herr-Stephenson's study of Harry Potter fans ("Harry Potter Fandom") focuses in part on podcasters who comment on the franchise. Although most podcasters are clearly hobbyists, a small number have become celebrities in the fandom who go on tours, perform "Wizard Rock," and in some cases, have gained financial rewards.

By linking niche audiences,[li] online media-sharing sites make amateur- 20 and youth-created content visible to other creators and audiences. Aspiring creators do not need to look exclusively to professional and commercial works for models of how to pursue their craft. Young people can begin by modeling more accessible and amateur forms of creative production. Even if they end there, with practices that never turn toward professionalism, youth can still gain status, validation, and reputation among specific creative communities and smaller audiences. The ability to specialize, tailor one's message and voice, and communicate with small publics is facilitated by the growing availability of diverse and niche networked publics. Gaining reputation as a rapper within the exclusive community of Bay Area Hyphy-genre hip-hop,[lii] being recognized as a great character writer on a particular role-playing board, or being known as the best comedic AMV editor for a particular anime series are all examples of fame and reputation within specialized communities of interest. These aspirational trajectories do not necessarily resolve into a vision of "making it big" or becoming famous in established commercial media production. Yet these aspirations still enable young people to gain validation, recognition, and audience for their creative works and to hone their craft within groups of like-minded and expert peers. Gaining recognition in these niche and amateur groups means validation of creative work in the here and now without having to wait for rewards in a far-flung and uncertain future in creative production.

NOTES*

xlvii. Anime music videos (AMVs) are remix fan videos, in which editors combine footage from anime with other soundtracks. Most commonly, editors use popular Euro-American music, but some also edit to movie trailer or TV ad soundtracks or to pieces of dialogue from movies and TV. ["Anime Fans" is the title of a study by Mizuko Ito of transnational anime fandom and amateur cultural production, part of this research.]

* This list does not include the works cited parenthetically within the text. These are all small studies, apparently unpublished, that were themselves part of the Digital Youth Research project.

xlviii. See Patricia G. Lange and Mizuko Ito, "Creative Production," in Mizuko Ito and others, *Hanging Out, Messing Around, and Geeking Out: Living and Learning with New Media* (Cambridge, MA: MIT Press, forthcoming).

xlix. C. J. Pascoe, "'You Have Another World to Create': Teens and Online Hangouts," in Ito et al., *Hanging Out.*

l. Vidding, like AMVs, is a process of remixing footage from TV shows and movies to soundtracks of an editor's choosing. Unlike AMVs, however, the live-action vidding community has been dominated by women.

li. Chris Anderson, *The Long Tail: Why the Future of Business Is Selling Less of More* (New York: Hyperion, 2006).

lii. Hyphy is a rap genre that originated in the San Francisco Bay Area and is closely associated with the late rapper Marc Dre and with Fabby Davis Junior. Hyphy music is often categorized as rhythmically up-tempo with a focus on eclectic instrumental beat arrangements, and it is also tightly coupled with particular dance styles.

RESPOND.

1. In what ways does the researchers' description of geeking out contrast sharply with stereotypes of geeks in popular culture? What kinds of evidence do the researchers provide for their claims? How convincing do you find their argument? (For a discussion of evaluating evidence, see Chapter 16.)

2. Readers expect arguments that are based on ethnographic methods to be characterized by detailed descriptions of specific cases, events, or situations because such descriptions constitute much of the support for the claims that the arguments make. Choose two such descriptions in this selection that you find especially effective, and explain why you find them successful.

3. Select one of the subsections of this selection (for example, "Specialized Knowledge Networks" or "Interest-Based Communities and Organizations"), and use Toulmin argumentation (see Chapter 7) to analyze its claims. Pay attention to issues of evidence (as in question 1 above), warrants, backing, and qualifiers. In this case, you will be treating the subsection that you choose to analyze like a stand-alone essay whose argument can be isolated and analyzed.

4. Based on the description given here, **write two definitions** of *geeking out.* One should be a short double-spaced paragraph and the second should be at least one double-spaced page in length. The definitions may contain elements of formal definition, operational definition, and definition by example, and the longer definition will likely build on the first one. (For a discussion of arguments of definition, see Chapter 9.)

5. As the headnote to this selection explains, the researchers distinguish among three genres of young people's participation in new media—hanging out, messing around, and geeking out. To what extent does your participation with the new media fit into the categories that are delineated in this report and discussed briefly in the previous selection (the "Executive Summary" to *Living and Learning with New Media: Summary of Findings from the Digital Youth Project*)? **Write an essay** in which you evaluate the characterization of it that is offered by the researchers. Your evaluation should be based on your own experiences, those of people you know well, and artistic appeals (the internal logic and consistency of the claims made by the researchers). You will likely want to skim the "Genres of Participation with the New Media" section of the actual report (digitalyouth.ischool.berkeley.edu/files/report/digitalyouth-WhitePaper.pdf) before making your decision about which category to evaluate—that is, which category most closely matches your own experience. (For a discussion of artistic appeals, see the opening of Chapter 4; for a discussion of evaluative arguments, see Chapter 10.)

▼ *This transcript comes from the December 4, 2008, Talk of the Nation—a weekday call-in program on National Public Radio (NPR) that promotes a national conversation on issues in the news. It is hosted by award-winning journalist Neal Conan, who has been affiliated with NPR for over a quarter of a century. Although the general topic of the day's program is whether creating a fake online profile is (or should be) a criminal act, the program was a response to one of the most emotional U.S. news stories of 2008. A Missouri woman named Lori Drew, with the assistance of a young employee, created a MySpace account in the name of Josh Evans, a nonexistent teenage boy. "Josh" then began flirting online with thirteen-year-old Megan Meier, a classmate of Drew's daughter. Shortly afterward, "Josh" sent her a message that said "the world would be a better place without you," and Meier took her own life.*

In November 2008, Drew was convicted of three misdemeanor criminal charges as a result of her actions. In July 2009, however, a federal judge in Los Angeles overturned the verdict on the grounds that the federal statute used to convict her was too vague and that if the conviction were allowed to stand, "one could literally prosecute anyone who violates a terms of service agreement." It was not clear whether an appeal would be filed by the U.S. attorney who initially brought the case.

As noted in the transcript, Kim Zetter reports for Wired.com, and Andy Carvin is senior strategist for online communities at NPR, where he has worked since 2006 to find ways of using new media (including social networking and user-generated content) to keep the radio network relevant to its listeners. As you read this transcript, consider how call-in programs represent complex multilayered arguments that emerge and shift across the program. Likewise, note the many perspectives from which the discussion on the program analyzed Lori Drew's actions on MySpace. (You can listen to this program at http://www.npr.org/templates/story/story.php?storyId=97819135.)

Is Creating a Fake Online Profile a Criminal Act?

NEAL CONAN, KIM ZETTER, ANDY CARVIN, AND CALLERS

NEAL CONAN (Host): This is *Talk of the Nation*. I am Neal Conan in Washington. Last week, Lori Drew was convicted of three misdemeanors° in a widely publicized cyber-bullying case. The charges involved violations of the Federal

Neal Conan broadcasting

misdemeanor: a lesser criminal offense (in contrast to a felony).

Lori Drew leaves the U.S. Federal Courthouse in Los Angeles after her conviction.

Computer Fraud and Abuse Act. A jury found Drew illegally accessed computers without authorization and violated the terms of service for the social networking site, MySpace, but that hardly explains the emotional worldwide interest in this trial. Drew is the woman who along with a young employee created a fake MySpace account and then posed as a non-existent teenage boy named Josh Evans.

The fake account was used to flirt with 13-year-old Megan Meier and siphoned gossip about Drew's daughter, a classmate. At the end, the online relationship turned ugly. The last message to Megan Meier read, "the world would be a better place without you." She committed suicide shortly afterwards. Some believe the jury let Lori off too lightly. She was found not guilty on felony° counts. Others worry that a federal prosecutor° has now criminalized anyone who violates the terms of service of any website. Now later this hour, we'll talk about another Internet controversy, the audience that watched a man kill himself, with Ayelet Waldman, a writer whose cyberfriends intervened to help her through her lowest moment.

But first, the Lori Drew verdict: does the punishment fit the crime? 800-989-8255 is our phone number. Email us, talk@npr.org You can join the conversation on our website, as well. Go to npr.org, click on *Talk of the Nation.* And we begin with Kim Zetter, a reporter who has covered this story for Wired.com

felony: a serious crime, especially one that may result in a prison sentence of greater than a year.

prosecutor: the public official who argues on behalf of the prosecution (the government) in a criminal trial.

*Megan Meier's mother holding
photos of her daughter*

with us today from the Youth Radio Studios in Oakland, California. Nice to
have you on the program.

Ms. KIM ZETTER (Reporter, Wired.com): Thanks for having me.

CONAN: And, I guess, there is not too much doubt that Lori Drew did something   5
that was reprehensible. The question is, was it criminal?

Ms. ZETTER: Right. And you know, the jurors found a lesser charge in this case.
She was charged with felonies, and the distinction between the felony and
the misdemeanor verdict that the jury came out with was whether or not
she intended to inflict emotional distress on Megan Meier, who killed herself. And the jury found that they did find her guilty of the misdemeanor
charge of unauthorized access, but they found that that wasn't—her intent
wasn't to inflict emotional distress. The testimony had indicated that the
intent of creating the account was to solicit information from Megan about
what Megan might have been saying about Lori Drew's daughter, Sarah.

CONAN: So intent, as in a lot of crimes, is crucial to the verdict here?

Ms. ZETTER: Yes.

CONAN: And the other question that a lot of people have: how come this was tried in Los Angeles?

Ms. ZETTER: The MySpace servers are based in Los Angeles County in Beverly 10 Hills. So the charges—the felony charges or misdemeanor charges, either way—have to involve interstate communication. So the communications that were sent from Lori Drew's computer in Missouri had to pass through the MySpace servers in Los Angeles, and so that's why the charges were brought there.

CONAN: And because it was interstate,° it comes under federal jurisdiction.°

Ms. ZETTER: Yes. And it was brought in Los Angeles because authorities in Missouri didn't bring charges, and so the Los Angeles County prosecutors decided to find some way of bringing justice in this case. And they were able to determine that they could have jurisdiction in Los Angeles.

CONAN: Was the prosecutor satisfied with this verdict?

Ms. ZETTER: I believe he was. I mean, he didn't call it a victory, but he said he was pleased with it. He felt that the jury held Lori Drew responsible for her actions. So yeah.

CONAN: And is her legal team planning to appeal the sentence? 15

Ms. ZETTER: Well, there is one step before that. They are planning to appeal, but there is a motion° that is still pending from U.S. District Judge George Wu at the—when the prosecution rested its case, the defense° filed a motion for direct acquittal.° And this is kind of standard in cases for defense attorneys to do this, but in this case, Judge Wu is seriously entertaining the motion, and he asked for briefs from both sides. The defense motion is based on the view that the prosecution failed to prove that Drew both was aware of the terms of service, that she read them, and that she intended to violate them. So they've ask Judge Wu to essentially acquit her, and that would override the jury's verdict of guilty on the misdemeanor. If Judge Wu decides to let the verdict stand, then the defense attorneys have indicated that they do plan to appeal at the Ninth Circuit Court.

CONAN: On the grounds of what?

Ms. ZETTER: On grounds that the prosecutors overstepped in using a Computer Fraud and Abuse Act for something that normally would be considered a civil° action, which is a breach of contract.°

interstate: involving more than one state and, hence, triggering the application of federal law rather than state law.

jurisdiction: here, the area or region over which a court has power.

motion: in legal contexts, a request to a judge for a ruling, an order, and so on.

defense: the attorneys representing the defendant, or the person against whom criminal charges have been brought (here, Lori Drew).

direct acquittal: a ruling that the accused (here, Lori Drew) is not guilty.

civil: relating to relationships between private citizens of the same country and laws governing such relationships, in contrast to laws governing criminal, international, or military situations.

breach of contract: failure to carry out the terms of a contract or agreement.

CONAN: These terms of service, by the way—I mean, that's these little questions that come up when every time you enter a website or join a website, and they have all of these very fine print things, and does anybody ever read them?

Ms. ZETTER: Well, there were two people that I spoke with or—one of the jurors, 20 the jury foreman claims that she does read them. Megan Meier's mother, Tina Meier, testified in court that she always reads the terms of service, you know, top to bottom before she signs on to any site. And she explained that she used to be employed by a law firm, and so it was drilled into her to read everything before she signs it. So she claims that she did, and the jury fore-woman that I interviewed after the case was over indicated that she also reads these before she signs them. I don't personally read them, and I don't personally know anyone who reads them, but there may be people out there who do.

CONAN: We're talking about the verdict in the Megan Meier case and whether it criminalizes activities that a lot of people would consider—well, maybe rep-rehensible but questions of free speech on the Web. And Kim Zetter, that's, I guess, where this goes next?

Ms. ZETTER: I, well, there is a free-speech issue in terms of the precedent that this could set. It's important to remember that this case in itself wasn't a free-speech issue because, of course, the charge that was made against her was for computer access. So they used what was considered reprehensible speech as the excuse to bring the charges, but it's not technically a free-speech case.

CONAN: Well, with us here in Studio 3A is Andy Carvin, NPR's senior strategist for online communities. Nice to have you back on the show, Andy.

ANDY CARVIN: Thanks for having me here.

CONAN: And I know that you'd been writing about this and the implications of 25 this. So does this raise free-speech issues for some people?

CARVIN: I think for some people, it does raise free-speech issues, because people have debated even though clearly what she did was reprehensible in many people's minds, there wasn't a specific law that she broke in terms of the kind language and the way she'd led her on when talking to Megan pre-tending to be this young boy. But when you look at the actual case that was brought against her, it wasn't a free-speech case as Kim just mentioned. In some ways, you may want to look at this as a privacy case because she was specifically found guilty for violating terms of service using this law that Kim mentioned is called the Computer Fraud and Abuse Act, which was written specifically for going after hackers doing really malicious things on computer servers.

But the way the prosecutors framed the case, they use that same law to go after Lori Drew by saying when she went and accepted the terms of service, she ignored some of the aspects of the terms of service. Now, what's gotten so many people upset about this is people do that every single day. The vast majority of people I've asked in the last few days about this they've said that they don't bother reading terms of service. I just talked a couple of hours ago with a woman who specializes in doing web accessibility testing and of the more than a thousand tests she has done, almost no one ever bothers to click that box to actually read it. They just click the check mark and keep going.

So I think it's human nature that, to just gloss over this legalese and not pay attention to it. But if the way the prosecution took place, if that were taken to an extreme, cases such as people under the age of 18 using Google—technically that's violation in their terms of service. People signing for the NPR website to be a part of our community: If a 17-year-old student did that for one of their classes, that's a violation. If you don't keep your Facebook page up-to-date, that's a violation. The list goes on and on.

CONAN: Are those crimes, is, I guess, the question?

CARVIN: Precisely. And, you know, I've lost track of the number of times, per- 30 sonally, when I've come to create accounts on new websites, if I don't really trust the site, because I really don't know the people behind it, sometimes, I'll purposely go and not put my real birth date because frankly, I don't trust them to handle my private information. They have to earn that trust.

CONAN: But that's a violation of terms of service.

CARVIN: It is exactly. So put the shackles on me right now. OK.

CONAN: Let's see if we can get some callers in on this conversation, 800-989-8255. Email is talk@npr.org. Cathy is on the line with us from St. Louis in Missouri.

CATHY (Caller): Hi. Thank you for taking my call.

CONAN: Sure.   35

Does violating terms of service really constitute a *crime*? Think about how powerful and important this argument of definition is. For more on how definitional arguments work, see Chapter 9.

LINK TO P. 249

CATHY: I'm coming from a more emotional place than a terms of services place with this comment. I'm in St. Louis. I live pretty close to where this all happened, and I think that the energy and outrage was generated about this, and it broke here first because an adult behaved so—in such a reprehensible way. And I don't think that our reactions in the Midwest or in St. Louis or St. Charles are any different than anywhere else. What she did was wrong, and the legalese part of it in some ways is baffling, because there are lots of people who behave badly on the Internet, and I personally am very glad that they were able to prosecute in California. It was very frustrating to all of us who are parents, and who live around here to think that this could go on again. And she deserved—again, I'm saying this emotionally—she deserved way more punishment than she got. She did not act like an adult, and bullying isn't tolerated in our schools; why should bullying be tolerated on the Internet?

CONAN: Kim Zetter, that was the feeling that a lot of people had was this federal prosecutor was saying, "Well, she must be guilty of something. Let's find out what."

Ms. ZETTER: Yeah, that's definitely the opinion of people who've been opposed to this. It's interesting. This definitely was a verdict based on emotion, and the jury foreman woman that I spoke with said that the—if she had been able to, she would have gladly given Drew the full extent of 20 years in federal prison for this. But what's interesting about this, if you—when you dig down into all the details of this, there were three people involved in this account, and it was Lori Drew, her 13-year-old daughter, and an 18-year-old employee.

In the testimony, it was uncovered that Lori Drew actually had very little direct role in the activities of that account. It was Ashley Grills, the 18-year-old employee, who came up with the idea for the account. It was her who opened the account, and Ashley Grills clicked on the terms of services agreement, and she testified that she did not read them. She testified that both Lori Drew and Sarah Drew were in the room when she opened the account, but Sarah Drew's daughter contradicted that and said that neither of them were home when Ashley Grills created the account.

Ashley Grills also testified that she was the one that sent the majority of the 40 messages to Josh, and that she was the one who sent the last that sent messages to—I'm sorry—that sent the messages as Josh to Megan, and she was the one that sent the last message to Megan that said "the world would be a better place without you." So when it comes to the direct activity of what Lori Drew engaged in, there was very little. She was involved in the conspiracy— which by the way, she didn't get convicted of. So it's interesting in terms of if you break it down, what she was fully responsible for and why she was prosecuted instead of Ashley Grills.

CONAN: Cathy, thank you very much for the call. We're going to continue on this point when we come back from a short break, so stay with us if you would, OK? We're talking with Kim Zetter of Wired.com and Andy Carvin who works on online communities here for us at NPR about this verdict in this very emotional case about cyber bullying. You're listening to *Talk of the Nation* from NPR News.

CONAN: This is *Talk of the Nation*. I'm Neal Conan in Washington. We're talking about the verdict in the first federal cyber-bullying case. It's been called the MySpace suicide trial. Some legal experts criticize the verdict for setting a scary precedent for anybody using the Web, while others complain the defendant, Lori Drew, was not punished harshly enough. What do you think? 800-989-8255. Email us, talk@npr.org. You can also join the conversation on our website at npr.org. Just click on *Talk of the Nation*. We're talking with Wired.com reporter Kim Zetter. You can find a link to her in-depth reporting on the case on our blog and with NPR senior strategist for online communities, Andy Carvin, and there's a (unintelligible) on our blog as well. Again, that's all at npr.org/blogofthenation.

Here's an email from Jamie in St. Charles, Missouri. Again, this is near where this happened. "I live in Waynesville, Missouri. I have a six-year-old daughter and a seven-year-old son. As a mother, I find what this woman did absolutely awful. Putting that aside, there is a difference between free speech and attacking an individual. There are laws in Missouri and I assume, nationally, regarding phone harassment and physical harassment. I don't believe this is any different. Free speech is not the freedom to attack someone or impersonate someone. Allowing this behavior opens the door to so many negative people attacking others. Ms. Drew did not attack a belief or a system or religion or even express her beliefs. She absolutely intended to emotionally harm the recipient and individual of her messages." Andy, this is similar to the call we had just before the break.

CARVIN: I think there's no doubt that people, especially in Missouri, are outraged and disgusted about this whole situation, and it became a national story as well even though it did take a while for the story to break nationally. I think people have a visceral reaction when they hear the name "mother was involved" in a case like this. You hear cases all the time of cyber bullying that are young person on young person, if you will, but the fact that supposedly a mature adult, and a mother at that, was involved really sticks on people really, really hard. So people were quite disgusted when local authorities weren't able to come up with something on the law books that was appropriate for an online incident such as this.

And so it wasn't that surprising that when federal prosecutors started look- 45 ing at the case, they looked at everything available in their entire arsenal. It just so happens though that they picked a particular way of attacking the case that has raised the ire of Internet advocates on both the left and the right because it raises these very complex issues of what it means to participate in the online sites and what kind of protection you have to protect your own rights.

CONAN: And Kim Zetter, again, from a legal aspect, and I know this has been discussed in the periphery of this case, the Supreme Court has repeatedly found that outrageous behavior is entirely constitutional. You may not like it. Nevertheless, that's what free speech means.

Ms. ZETTER: Well, yeah, but there is the element of tortious act here, and if your intent is to inflict emotional distress, which is what she was charged with in this case, there are laws that do indeed cover that. So yes, you can have a protection of speech, but you can also have actions that intend to create harm, and in that case, this is what she was charged with. I mean, it was the whole of the actions. The ruse of posing as a 16-year-old boy, of not revealing who they were, of drawing her into a relationship with him so that she fell in love with him essentially, and then turning on her. So it wasn't just speech in this case. It was a whole—as she was charged with a conspiracy in this matter.

CONAN: Let's get Scott on the line. Scott with us from Kansas City, Missouri.

SCOTT (Caller): Hey, how are you guys doing today?

CONAN: Good. Thanks. 50

SCOTT: So I'm a little frustrated in how to talk about this, but the woman, OK, she's was in wrong, she shouldn't have—she should not—definitely not have not done what she had done. But I'm sure that the prosecuting attorney could have found a way better way to go about it than to take and twist user guidelines for a website and make a criminal case out of it. I mean, I'm sorry, I just don't believe in taking Google user agreement and Gmail user agreements, and you know, so a person want to spam out some email out of Gmail. So we're going to turn around and throw criminal charges on him. A

RPG: role-playing games, a type of online games.

A fan of World of Warcraft, *one of the most popular role-playing games, dressed as a game character.*

slippery slope: an action or situation that may lead to a series of unwanted consequences, much as losing one's footing at the top of a hill may lead to a terrible fall. (Chapter 17 discusses the related notion of slippery-slope fallacies.)

leavenworth.com: an allusion to Leavenworth, a U.S. federal penitentiary for men located in Leavenworth, Kansas.

Leavenworth Federal Penitentiary

user account for some of these RPG° games, you know, they turn around and say they want to list this stuff, which is against the user agreements for the video game.

CONAN: Right. Andy Carvin, the perception is that these user agreements on the Web are there for liability, to protect the company.

CARVIN: Absolutely. They're there to make sure that the company doesn't find users doing things that aren't acceptable to them and puts them in legal jeopardy, which is why they're written in these very dense legalese. In fact, there was this study done by a couple of researchers at Carnegie Mellon University, and they looked at terms of service agreements as they're called on some of the major online community sites, and the average one was about 2,500 words long, and it took about 10 minutes for a person to read properly.

So they calculated if you took the amount of time for everyone to read, if everyone actually read all this stuff, there would be a loss of approximately $365 billion in productivity. Now, of course, I'm pretty sure the vast majority of people don't bother to spend the time to read these things, but that's what has gotten so many people upset about this case is because even though it's very, very unlikely that any of us are going to get charged for violating a term of service for one of these sites, people are concerned that this is a slippery slope.°

SCOTT: And regardless of you even reading these terms agreements, when somebody clicks this I Agree button and they click Submit, the worse that they're expecting if they violate these terms of service is their accounts are going to get banned. You know, slap on the wrist. They may have to move on to the next Facebook or MySpace or whatever.   55

CONAN: Nobody really expects to log in to leavenworth.com,° you know?

CARVIN: No one gives it a second thought.

CONAN: *Dot gov*, I guess.

SCOTT: I don't think anybody even after this is going to realize that they just put a cornerstone on prosecuting people criminally for going against user agreements on websites. I mean, that's completely insane.

CONAN: All right. Thanks very much for the call, Scott.   60

SCOTT: All right.

CONAN: Let's see if we can go now to Nancy. Nancy is calling us from Ann Arbor in Michigan.

NANCY (Caller): Hi. I just want to state that 14 to 15 years ago I was harassed on the Internet before it was even the World Wide Web on a religious alt group that was out there. And I had lost a child, and I'd mentioned in the group I lost a child. And one of the people in the group who I thought was my friend for some reason began to blame me for the loss of my child, and called me on the phone, posted my home address and my phone number. We'd get hang-up calls in the middle of the night.

To this day, I don't guard my identity online, but I have a private phone number, and I'm very careful what information I give out. The day before we got the call that we were able to adopt a child, this person had driven me to the point where I was seriously considering a suicide. They blamed me for the death of my child. They would email "Your son will never play horsey with your husband. He's dead. He's buried in the ground, and you probably could have stopped it." That was not the case, but when you get this day after day, after day, after day.

CONAN: It could be overwhelming, Nancy. Did you report this to the police?   65

NANCY: Yeah, but there weren't any laws there that could protect me. They referred me to the FBI, and the FBI said there is nothing they could to. This was over the Internet, and they weren't personal attacks. It wasn't "We're going to come and get you." It was "If you had done this instead of that, then your child would be alive."

CONAN: Given that experience, what do you think of the verdict in this case?

NANCY: I'm horrified, because I was lucky. We've adopted two children. We have birthed two children since then, but the day before we got the call to adopt our oldest child, all of my son's stuff fell out on me in the closet, and I was— I'm horrified, because I was so close to just ending my life, because I felt so responsible. And I hadn't felt that way until this person started saying what they did. I'd been ensured by the doctors that there is nothing I could have done, but when you're being worn down and worn down and the email addresses would change, so I didn't know who it was coming from.

So I'd open the emails. It wasn't a matter of simply blocking this person or their ISP. They change ISPs three times to avoid being caught. And the FBI said there was nothing they can do. There were no laws on the books, because they did not threaten me personally. They just were harassing me.

How does Andy Carvin's use of the research from Carnegie Mellon affect his authority? Do you trust his statistics? For more on what counts as evidence, see Chapter 16.

LINK TO P. 493

CONAN: Nancy, we are so glad—I know, you can still hear the emotion in your 70 voice—but I'm really glad that you made it through.

NANCY: I'm a little nervous that by being on the radio, these people are going to figure where I am and how badly they hurt me, because I tried very hard to hide that. But it worked out well, but it's still something I'm working through almost 15 years later. So, you know . . .

CONAN: Yeah.

NANCY: I understand why a young woman, a very young girl in her teenage years, being hurt like that, knowing she was unstable. This woman knew she had problems. Lori knew that she had problems, and she pushed all those buttons anyway. And not only that, but she probably encouraged her child to do it too. And over what was being said about her in school? Girls can be so cruel at that age. And . . .

CONAN: Regrettably it's not just girls but . . .

NANCY: Yeah, I know it's not. I know it's not. But you know, I don't blame her 75 parents. I don't blame her parents one bit. She probably felt so ashamed and embarrassed that—or that she never even said a word to them.

CONAN: Nancy, again. We've been through this, and thank you for sharing the story.

NANCY: Well, thank you for having me. Thank you.

CONAN: OK. Bye-bye. And Kim Zetter, that raises the question—obviously that kind of pain is very real and it's long-lasting and emotional distress. You know, it may not be the legal definition, but I think we just heard it. Is there anything in the works that—legally—that would allow prosecutors to go after such people and still with it be in the realm of the First Amendment?

Ms. ZETTER: Well, curiously, there was a law passed in 2006, and I've asked the Los Angeles prosecutors why they didn't use this law. Let me just explain a bit what it is. In 2005, the Department of Justice Appropriations Bill includes something buried in it about cyber bullying, and it specifically states that if you use an interactive Internet service, computer service in order to harass someone, and you do so under a false identity, you can be charged and the punishment is up to two years in prison.

Now, the bill was signed by President Bush in January 2006. The incidences 80 that occurred in the Drew case occurred in September and October of 2006. So it's unclear to me if there was some kind of—if there was something in the statute of—I've gone through the statute, and I don't find anything that says that it didn't go into place until perhaps January 2007 or something. As far as I know, it was in place when these incidents occurred, and I don't know why prosecutors in L.A., whether or not they were even aware of the statute or why they didn't use it, or if there's some reason that they couldn't have used it. So it appears that there is something that can be used in a case like this. I understand that there is also a bill that has been introduced in Congress regarding cyber bullying. I don't know where it is at this point, and I don't recall who's actually introduced it yet.

CONAN: And whether or if it's in Congress now and has not been approved, it's going to be—it would have to be reintroduced in the next session of Congress, which is when the next Congress comes back in January. So, well anyway.

Ms. ZETTER: Right.

CONAN: Kim Zetter is a reporter with Wired.com, also with us Andy Carvin, a senior strategist for online communities here at NPR. You're listening to *Talk of the Nation* from NPR News. And Josh is on the line. Josh calling us from Tulsa, Oklahoma.

JOSH (Caller): Hi. I don't have an opinion on the verdict or anything. I just was wondering how the prosecution was able to go after the defendant for a violation of terms of service when the—I believe the victim herself was violating terms of service. I can't remember for sure but MySpace, I thought, was—the minimum age was 14. And that's simply my question is how was the prosecution able to go after?

CONAN: Kim Zetter, did that come up in the trial?   85

Ms. ZETTER: It did actually. I think the MySpace age limit now is 13. I think it was lowered earlier this year. But at the time in 2006, it was 14. And Tina Meier, Megan's mother, had allowed her to open an account about a month and a half before she turned 14. So it did come up. The defense brought it up and, you know, the issue was, you know, how do you charge Lori Drew with something when the victim was guilty of at least part of the same thing of what she's been charged with. You know, prosecutors decide, you know, who to prosecute and why to prosecute. I mean, Megan Meier didn't create an account in order to harass other people and that's, you know, this is the whole basis of the prosecution here. Again, I want to come back to the idea of the role that Ashley Grills played in all of this. And it's probably more appropriate to ask why she wasn't charged in this . . .

CONAN: I was just about to ask why she wasn't charged. Did you ask the prosecutors?

Ms. ZETTER: She was granted immunity,° because they needed her to testify against the defendant. So, you know—and again the emotional element of this case, the whole reason that this grabbed, you know, the public such as our St. Charles caller explained. You know, she was absolutely right that it was Missouri that was affected by this case. It was nationally, even internationally. The whole reason this grabbed people was the role of an adult woman. Had this been just perhaps an activity with an 18-year-old girl and a 13-year-old girl, we probably wouldn't have had this case at all. So it is the outrage over an adult who should have known better of why one person is prosecuted and another one isn't.

immunity: freedom from prosecution under certain conditions, often in exchange for testimony in a court case.

CONAN: This email from Selene (ph),° Jupiter, Florida. The pundits are going to say the decision opens up huge concerns for anyone who registers and uses an online account or a social networking site or anything else, because that violation of a site's terms of use can lead to a similar fate. I don't agree. I don't think this case will be used as a precedent towards those ends. Rather, I believe the jury made their decision based on the fact that intentional psychological harm was inflicted by Drew and her accomplices on Megan, but they could not hang their hats on a law that prohibits such an act because none exists. Therefore, they hung their hats on the violation of MySpace service and accordingly the Computer Fraud and Abuse Act. That's it. That's what it comes down to. So Andy, I guess the question I know people are worried about is if this is a precedent. Are they right to be?

ph: "phonetic," an indication that the transcriber was unsure of how a word, most often a name, is spelled and has therefore spelled it the way that it sounds.

CARVIN: It's a valid point. It's quite possible that no one will ever be charged the same way again, and it was done for a very unique circumstance. But at the same time that's the nature of slippery slopes when people complain about them. The concern is what if it began a process in which other people could be tried in such a way that their rights are violated. Again, I think it's largely because people were so disgusted in this particular circumstance. They felt they had to do something. So unless a similar situation arises, it's possible that maybe it won't happen again, but we just don't know.

CONAN: And Kim Zetter, was that part of the prosecution's argument here? This is a deterrent. We should be able to prosecute in such cases?

Ms. ZETTER: Yeah, they were very clear especially after the verdict came down in the press conference that, you know, they weren't going to make a plan of bringing prosecutions like this. They were very clear that this was special circumstances that's—you know, called for action and in the absence of another law that they could use, this is what they had to go on. So if another law is passed and, you know, soon, then they wouldn't have to use this law again.

CONAN: Kim Zetter, thanks very much for your time today.

Ms. ZETTER: Thank you.

CONAN: Kim Zetter, a reporter for Wired.com with us today from Youth Radio in 95
Oakland, California. Our thanks as well to Andy Carvin, NPR's senior strategist for online communities with us here in the Studio 3A. Thanks, Andy.

CARVIN: Thanks for having me, Neal.

CONAN: Coming up, the online suicide of 19-year-old Abraham Briggs watched by at least a 100 cyber voyeurs via webcam prompted Ayelet Waldman to consider the actions of her own web community in some of her darkest days. We'll talk with her next. Stay with us. I'm Neal Conan. It's the *Talk of the Nation* from NPR News.

RESPOND.

1. The discussion in this transcript reminds us that stasis theory is alive and well in contemporary America. (For a discussion of stasis theory, see Chapter 1.) In fact, U.S. legal argumentation is based on stasis the-ory: one must establish that something indeed happened, one must be able to define the events in terms of categories of the law, one must then be able to evaluate the events in light of the categories set up by the law, and finally one must propose a course of action—a judge-ment. There is general agreement—at least among the public—that "Lori Drew did something that was reprehensible" (paragraph 5), a question of fact, but there was and is no agreement about the exact nature of what she did in light of existing categories of the law. According to the transcript, why are laws relating to free speech not applicable in this case? How did this fact lead federal prosecutors in Los Angeles to charge Drew with violations of the Federal Computer Fraud and Abuse Act? What was the outcome? Why did that outcome leave so many people disappointed?

2. Andy Carvin notes that the federal prosecutors chose to frame the questions at issue in the case in such a way that "Internet advocates on both the left and the right" were angered "because it raises these very complex issues of what it means to participate in the online sites

and what kind of protection you have to protect your own rights" (paragraph 45). What might he have in mind? In other words, why would conservatives and/or libertarians be unhappy with this case? And liberals?

3. Perhaps the most interesting caller is Nancy (paragraphs 63–77). Read the portion of the transcript that reports her comments. Now listen to the radio program, if you have not done so, at http://www.npr.org/templates/story/story.php?storyId=97819135. Does your response to Nancy's comments change after having heard her make them? What accounts for the difference? What might this example teach us about the potential power of spoken argument?

4. Do you regularly read the terms of service agreement for social networking sites or other sites you visit? Why or why not? Do you feel that you are taking risks if you do not?

5. Should creating a fake online profile be a criminal act? Why or why not? **Write an essay** in which you argue for one side of this question or the other. In so doing, you may wish to discuss the case of Megan Meier. Although this transcript provides a great deal of factual information about the details of the case, you may wish to do additional research about it. If you do, be sure to document any sources you use. (For a discussion of documenting sources, see Chapter 20.)

6. Research current debates about cyber bullying on social networking sites, and **write a proposal argument** in which you make a proposal about how to limit cyber bullying and its consequences on these sites. (For a discussion of proposal arguments, see Chapter 12.)

A Profile of Online Profiles

CHARLES M. BLOW

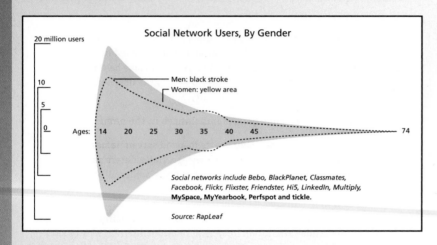

Social Network Users, By Gender

20 million users

10
5
0

Men: black stroke
Women: yellow area

Ages: 14 20 25 30 35 40 45   74

Social networks include Bebo, BlackPlanet, Classmates,
Facebook, Flickr, Flixster, Friendster, Hi5, LinkedIn, Multiply,
MySpace, MyYearbook, Perfspot and tickle.

Source: RapLeaf

◀ In this blog posting from September 9, 2008, Charles M. Blow, visual op-ed columnist at the New York Times and art director of National Geographic magazine, examines research on online profiles and their truthfulness—or lack thereof. (The original posting can be found at http://blow.blogs.nytimes .com/2008/09/09/a-profile-of -online-profiles.) As you read this posting, note the work that the graphics do in supporting, or even making, the argument.

I recently created a Facebook account. My kids thought it was hysterical. They said that I was too old. I'm only 38, but as far as they are concerned, Moses was my best friend in kindergarten.

Being a numbers guy, this got me interested in procuring hard data on social network users . . . and their behavioral traits while logged on. Here is some of what I found:

1. GENDER: According to a RapLeaf study released in July of 49.3 million people, 20 percent more females used social networks than men (this surprised me). The biggest disparity was for people under 25. In my age range, 35 to 40, men outnumbered women (see chart above).

    According to an April study by RapLeaf, men use social networking more for business and women more for socializing. From the report:

    "Men tend to be more transactional° and less relationship building when it comes to their friends on social networks. Women tend to have slightly more friends on average."

5   *transactional:* concerned with getting things done (that is, transactions).

715

2. BEST "HANDLES": When it came to dating sites, things really got interesting. In April, *The Times* of London reported on a study by Dr. Monica Whitty, "a lecturer in cyber-psychology," which revealed the names or "handles" that garnered the most numerous responses among online daters. Here's what it said:

"Playful and flirtatious names such as 'fun2bwith' or 'imsweet' were ranked top by both men and women daters as those they would most like to contact. Physical descriptors such as 'cutie' or 'blueeyes' were close behind. 'These names suggest an outgoing or fun nature, or clarify the user's positive physical appearance,' said Dr. Monica Whitty."

But there seemed to be some gender imbalances in the names:

"However she advised female lonely hearts to avoid screen names which attempt to be classy, or show how clever they are. Males daters said they would be less likely to contact screen names such as 'wellread' or 'well-educated,' although the study found women were more drawn to names that suggested men were cultured. 'Less flirtatious names may be more appealing to women because they are wary of men who might be using the site to find one-night stands rather than long-term relationships,' Dr. Whitty said."

3. LYING: According to a study entitled "Separating Fact from Fiction: An Examination of Deceptive Self-Presentation in Online Dating Profiles" that was published this year in the *Personality and Social Psychology Bulletin*, there is quite a bit of lying going on in online profiles. And, men lie more than women. Shocker!   10

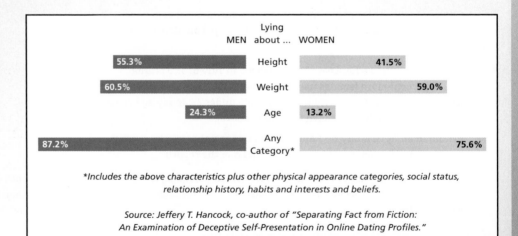

| | Lying | |
MEN	about ...	WOMEN
55.3%	Height	41.5%
60.5%	Weight	59.0%
24.3%	Age	13.2%
87.2%	Any Category*	75.6%

*Includes the above characteristics plus other physical appearance categories, social status, relationship history, habits and interests and beliefs.

Source: Jeffery T. Hancock, co-author of "Separating Fact from Fiction: An Examination of Deceptive Self-Presentation in Online Dating Profiles."

It also turns out that people online are more accepting of some lies than others. From the study:

"Participants believed that lying about relationship information is less socially acceptable than lying about any other category. . . . Men considered it more acceptable than women to lie about their social status . . . [and] found it more acceptable than women to lie about their occupation, education and marginally about their relationship status."

Below are some graphs from his report. Note how almost all women understate their weight and most men overstate their height. Typical.

Who is Blow's intended audience? What might a reader hope to learn from this argument? For more on how authors and audiences relate and interact, see Chapter 1.

LINK TO P. 3

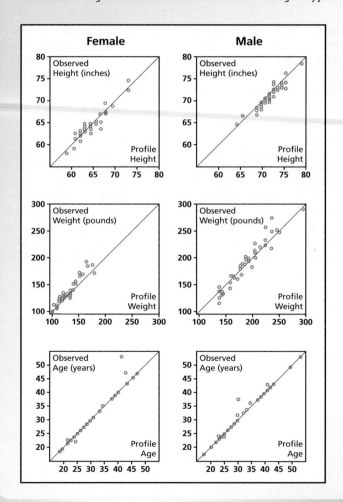

RESPOND ●

1. Do the findings of the research that Blow cites surprise you? Why or why not?

2. In what ways is a "handle" an argument? What kind of argument might it be? Why might an email address like "2Hot2Handl@ . . . com" not be an appropriate address for a student to use in academic or business contexts?

3. According to the research that Blow cites, how are social network sites gendered—that is, how do males and females behave differently on them?

4. A comment posted on the blog by someone who signed herself (him-self?) "Mom" noted that at least some of the midteen bulge in the chart may be due to underage teens lying about their age to partici-pate in these sites. What does this observation suggest about the chal-lenges of interpreting data, especially quantitative data?

5. A major challenge of using graphics to accompany a verbal text is finding appropriate ways to incorporate them into the text, since a figure is often not self-explanatory. Ideally, a writer describes the fig-ure in sufficient detail that the reader is able to understand the mean-ing of the figure and why it is being used. **Write a paragraph of description** about two of the figures that are featured in this article. The best choices will likely be the first two, which treat different phe-nomena, or one of the pairs of charts giving data on females and males. A good way to think about this assignment is to imagine describing the figures to someone who cannot see them. Thinking about them that way should help you decide what information is important and what the argument of each figure is.

23
What's It Like
to Be Bilingual
in the United States?

The title of Rochelle Sharpe's newspaper article "English Loses Ground," the first reading selection in this chapter, expresses a sentiment that is common among many Americans: English is endangered in the United States. Yet is the truth of the matter so simple? The remaining selections in this chapter consider the question through the eyes (and ears) of Americans who are bilingual or who study bilingualism professionally.

Hyon B. Shin and Rosalind Bruno, demographers for the U.S. Census Bureau, give an overview of information from the 2000 census about the use of languages other than English in the United States. Although nearly one in five people in the United States speaks a language other than English at home, over 92 percent of the population reported speaking English very well.

The next several selections present much more individual and personal views on bilingualism. The protagonist in a short story by Sandra Cisneros, "Bien Pretty," argues that if you haven't made love in Spanish with a native speaker of the language, you can't imagine what you've missed. Marjorie Agosín, a professor, writer, human rights activist, and political refugee from Chile, explains in prose and poetry why she "writes in Spanish and lives in translation."

In "The 'F Word,'" Firoozeh Dumas, an immigrant from Iran who married someone with a French family name, examines how Americans deal and don't deal with foreign names. The protagonist in a chapter from *Monkey Bridge*, a novel by law professor Lan Cao, describes the situation of another refugee, an adolescent Vietnamese girl who, because she absorbs English quickly and comes to understand U.S. culture easily, must parent her mother, who finds things like supermarkets disorientingly foreign. Award-winning novelist Amy Tan frames the question a bit differently: in "Mother Tongue," her concern is not just bilingualism but more directly the varieties of English that she and her immigrant mother speak.

The final two selections illustrate other aspects of bilingualism in America. Two public service announcements in Spanish—and our English translations of the text—ask you to reflect on issues of language choice and intended audience. The chapter closes with an obituary written by Amy Martinez Starke for Sao Yee Cha, a Hmong woman who moved to Portland, Oregon, in 1978 after two years spent living in a refugee camp in Thailand following the aftermath of the Vietnam War. In describing her life, it also comments on her struggles with English and reminds us that Americans who speak languages other than English came to be here in any number of ways.

If you grew up bilingual (or multilingual), these readings give you a chance to think about how your experiences compare with those of other Americans who know and use more than one language. If you don't already speak a language besides English, there's still time: monolingualism isn't a terminal disease, a favorite bumper sticker argues. Even as English plays an increasingly important role in the world, learning another language changes the way you understand yourself and the world. In the meantime, these readings offer you the chance to learn things about the lives of a growing number of Americans—even people sitting in your classroom—that you might otherwise never know.

▼ *This selection originally appeared on November 16, 2008, in USA Weekend, a weekly magazine that appears on Sunday in over six hundred newspapers weekly. Reporter Rochelle Sharpe, who shared the Pulitzer Prize in 1991, has written for the* Wall Street Journal, Business Week, *and the Gannett News Service, which publishes* USA Weekend, *among other publications. Sharpe often contributes short, fact-filled articles for the magazine in a feature entitled "By the Numbers." This selection focuses on a recent U.S. Census Bureau report about language issues; the data were drawn from the 2005–2007 American Community Survey, which collected information from a subset of the American population (in contrast to the more comprehensive national census that is conducted every ten years, which seeks to gather information on everyone living in the United States and its possessions and territories). As do all census reports, it relies on "report data": someone in the household reports on the behavior of all household members. As you might imagine, report data are not always an accurate representation of actual behavior. For many reasons, people are not able or willing to report what they actually do. In reading this article, try to identify the arguments that Sharpe is making and the relationships between those arguments and the article's title, "English Loses Ground." (As you likely are aware, journalists rarely compose the titles or headlines under which their articles appear.)*

English Loses Ground

ROCHELLE SHARPE

Listen to conversations around America's dinner tables these days and the voices you hear may well be holding forth in Spanish, Russian or Chinese.

Nationally, nearly one of every five people over the age of 5 spoke a foreign language at home in 2007, the Census Bureau says. That is a dramatic change since 1990, when just 13.8% of people spoke a foreign language at home.

The changes are due, in part, to the burgeoning growth of the Latino population, which has doubled in size since 1990.

More than 34.5 million people older than 5 spoke Spanish at home in 2007; another 8.3 million spoke Chinese or another Asian language at home.

California is the state with the 5 highest concentration of foreign-language speakers, 42.6%. And in some pockets of the country, it's rare to hear English at all. In Hialeah, Fla., just 7.5% of its residents spoke English at home in 2000.

The nation has started to see a growing number of linguistically

Sharpe's article relies heavily on facts and reason, especially statistics. Chapter 4 offers other examples of how to use logos in presenting your arguments.

LINK TO P. 69

isolated households, in which no one over 14 years old speaks English well. More than 5.5 million households were linguistically isolated in 2007, including about one of every four Spanish-speaking households. It's a serious barrier for them, hampering not only their job prospects, but also their ability to get emergency help from doctors, police or firefighters.

"There's a tremendous hunger to learn English," says John Trasvina, president and general counsel of the Mexican American Legal Defense and Educational Fund. But there aren't enough places that teach the language.

Gone are the old night schools that once taught English to immigrants. Now, there are year-long waiting lists for English classes in some areas of the country, Trasvina says.

Recent lawmaking exacerbates the situation. Last year, Arizona banned undocumented people from paying in-state rates for community college classes. A decade ago, California passed a law restricting bilingual education in public schools. And today, more than half of U.S. states have laws mandating English as their official language.

RESPOND•

1. What argument(s) does Sharpe seem to be making? Does she have an explicit thesis? Does she believe that the changes she documents are for the better or the worse, or is it impossible to tell? Is the title appropriate for this article? Why or why not?

2. How does the information in the two final paragraphs complicate efforts to answer question 1? In what ways do these paragraphs seem to be functioning as causal arguments? From this perspective, what forces or situations are cast as causes and which as results? (For a discussion of causal arguments, see Chapter 11.)

3. Not surprisingly in an article from a series entitled "By the Numbers," Sharpe uses many statistics. How effectively has she used them? (For a discussion of the use of statistics, see Chapter 4.)

4. Sharpe appears to make some interesting assumptions about language knowledge and language use. In paragraph 5, for example, she writes: "And in some pockets of the country, it's rare to hear English at all. In Hialeah, Fla., just 7.5% of its residents spoke English at home in 2000." Should we assume that those who report speaking a language other than English at home are unable to speak English at all? That they do not speak it in public at least on some occasions? For those who report speaking English and another language, why might their home be the context in which they are most likely to report using

their heritage language? The context in which they are most likely to *actually* use the heritage language?

5. Part of the data on which Sharpe bases this article almost surely come from what was at the time a recent census report concerning the 2005–2007 American Community Survey. (Because Sharpe did not give the source of her statistics, we had to do our best to locate it.) You may view these data at http://factfinder.census.gov/servlet/STTable?_bm=y&-geo_id=01000US&-qr_name=ACS_2007_3YR_G00_S1601&-ds_name=ACS_2007_3YR_G00, the URL for "S1601. Language Spoken at Home, 2005–2007 American Community Survey Three-Year Estimates." You can find the statistic with which Sharpe begins the article under "Total" in the third row down (19.5 percent). Looking along the same row, "Speaks a language other than English," you will note that 55.7 percent of those who report speaking a language other than English at home also report speaking English "very well." Might this have been a relevant piece of data to include in Sharpe's article? Why or why not? How does this latter statistic present a more complicated picture than the overall impression given by Sharpe's article or its title? (If you are interested, the sources of data for most, if not all, of her other statistics are almost assuredly those available at http://factfinder.census.gov/servlet/ACSSAFFPeople?submenuId=people_8&_sse=on under "Language.")

6. **Write a short essay** in which you evaluate the effectiveness of Sharpe's argument, including her use of statistics. (For a discussion of evaluative arguments, see Chapter 10.)

▼ *This selection, "Language Use and English-Speaking Ability: 2000," is a 2003 U.S. Census Bureau report written by Hyon B. Shin with Rosalind Bruno, both of whom are demographic statisticians employed by the Census Bureau. (A demographer is someone who studies the characteristics of populations—matters like population size and density, birth and death rates, and changes over time—using quantitative data; hence, a demographic statistician is a statistician who specializes in analyzing demographic data.) Like reports from the Census Bureau generally, this document provides the most complete and readily accessible presentation of data from specific sets of questions on the 2000 census. (The census in America is conducted each decade, and the last comprehensive one at the time of publication was conducted in 2000.) The relevant questions here are those that deal with the reported use of a language other than English at home and the reported ability of individuals to speak English. As you read this report, seek to determine the kind of argument it is—factual, definitional, evaluative, causal, or proposal—and why. Likewise, pay attention to the information that is provided about the area in which you live or areas in which you have lived. After all, the report is documenting social changes that have occurred during your lifetime.*

Language Use and English-Speaking Ability: 2000

HYON B. SHIN with ROSALIND BRUNO

The ability to communicate with government and private service providers, schools, businesses, emergency personnel, and many other people in the United States depends greatly on the ability to speak English.[1] In Census 2000, as in the two previous censuses, the U.S. Census Bureau asked people aged 5 and over if they spoke a language other than English at home. Among the 262.4 million people aged 5 and over, 47.0 million (18 percent) spoke a language other than English at home.

This report, part of a series that presents population and housing data collected in Census 2000, presents data on language spoken at home and the ability to speak English of people aged 5 and over. It describes population distributions and characteristics for the United States, including regions, states, counties, and selected places with populations of 100,000 or more.

Figure 1.
Reproduction of the Questions on Language From Census 2000

11 a. Does this person speak a language other than English at home?

☐ Yes
☐ No → *Skip to 12*

b. What is this language?

(For example: Korean, Italian, Spanish, Vietnamese)

c. How well does this person speak English?

☐ Very well
☐ Well
☐ Not well
☐ Not at all

Source: U.S. Census Bureau, Census 2000 questionnaire.

The questions illustrated in Figure 1 were asked in the census in 1980, 1990, and 2000. Various questions on language were asked in the censuses from 1890 to 1970, including a question on "mother tongue" (the language spoken in the person's home when he or she was a child.)

The first language question in Census 2000 asked respondents whether they spoke a language other than English at home. Those who responded "Yes" to Question 11a were asked what language they spoke. The write-in answers to Question 11b (specific language spoken) were optically scanned and coded. Although linguists recognize several thousand languages in the world, the coding operations used by the Census Bureau put the reported languages into about 380 categories of single languages or language families.[2]

For people who answered "Yes" to Question 11a, Question 11c asked   5 respondents to indicate how well they spoke English. Respondents who said they spoke English "Very well" were considered to have no difficulty with English. Those who indicated they spoke English "Well," "Not well," or "Not at all" were considered to have difficulty with English—identified also as people who spoke English less than "Very well."

The number and percentage of people in the United States who spoke a language other than English at home increased between 1990 and 2000.

In 2000, 18 percent of the total population aged 5 and over, or 47.0 million people, reported they spoke a language other than English at home.[3] These figures were up from 14 percent (31.8 million) in 1990 and 11 percent (23.1 million) in 1980. The number of people who spoke a language other than English at home grew by 38 percent in the 1980s and by 47 percent in the 1990s. While the population aged 5 and over grew by one-fourth from 1980 to 2000, the number who spoke a language other than English at home more than doubled.

In 2000, most people who spoke a language other than English at home reported they spoke English "Very well" (55 percent or 25.6 million people). When they are combined with those who spoke only English at home, 92 percent of the population aged 5 and over had no difficulty speaking

---

Four Major Language Groups

Spanish includes those who speak Ladino.

Other Indo-European languages include most languages of Europe and the Indic languages of India. These include the Germanic languages, such as German, Yiddish, and Dutch; the Scandinavian languages, such as Swedish and Norwegian; the Romance languages, such as French, Italian, and Portuguese; the Slavic languages, such as Russian, Polish, and Serbo-Croatian; the Indic languages, such as Hindi, Gujarathi, Punjabi, and Urdu; Celtic languages; Greek; Baltic languages; and Iranian languages.

Asian and Pacific Island languages include Chinese; Korean; Japanese; Vietnamese; Hmong; Khmer; Lao; Thai; Tagalog or Pilipino; the Dravidian languages of India, such as Telegu, Tamil, and Malayalam; and other languages of Asia and the Pacific, including the Philippine, Polynesian, and Micronesian languages.

All other languages include Uralic languages, such as Hungarian; the Semitic languages, such as Arabic and Hebrew; languages of Africa; native North American languages, including the American Indian and Alaska native languages; and some indigenous languages of Central and South America.

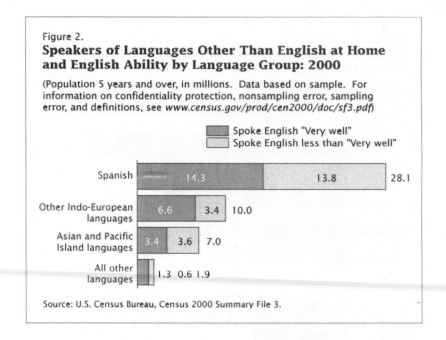

Figure 2.
Speakers of Languages Other Than English at Home and English Ability by Language Group: 2000

(Population 5 years and over, in millions. Data based on sample. For information on confidentiality protection, nonsampling error, sampling error, and definitions, see *www.census.gov/prod/cen2000/doc/sf3.pdf*)

Spoke English "Very well"
Spoke English less than "Very well"

Spanish: 14.3 | 13.8 | 28.1
Other Indo-European languages: 6.6 | 3.4 | 10.0
Asian and Pacific Island languages: 3.4 | 3.6 | 7.0
All other languages: 1.3 0.6 1.9

Source: U.S. Census Bureau, Census 2000 Summary File 3.

English. The proportion of the population aged 5 and over who spoke English less than "Very well" grew from 4.8 percent in 1980, to 6.1 percent in 1990, and to 8.1 percent in 2000.

In Figure 2, the number of speakers of the four major language groups (Spanish, Other Indo-European languages, Asian and Pacific Island languages, and All other languages) are shown by how well they spoke English (see text box on previous page). Spanish was the largest of the four major language groups, and just over half of the 28.1 million Spanish speakers spoke English "Very well."

Other Indo-European language speakers composed the second largest group, with 10.0 million speakers, almost two-thirds of whom spoke English "Very well." Slightly less than half of the 7.0 million Asian and Pacific Island-language speakers spoke English "Very well" (3.4 million). Of the 1.9 million people who composed the All other language category, 1.3 million spoke English "Very well."

After English and Spanish, Chinese was the language most commonly 10 spoken at home (2.0 million speakers), followed by French (1.6 million speakers) and German (1.4 million speakers, see Figure 3). Reflecting historical

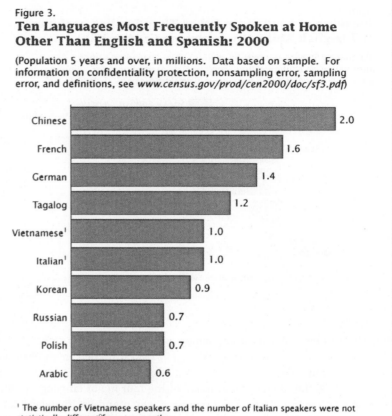

Figure 3.

Ten Languages Most Frequently Spoken at Home Other Than English and Spanish: 2000

(Population 5 years and over, in millions. Data based on sample. For information on confidentiality protection, nonsampling error, sampling error, and definitions, see *www.census.gov/prod/cen2000/doc/sf3.pdf*)

Language	Millions
Chinese	2.0
French	1.6
German	1.4
Tagalog	1.2
Vietnamese[1]	1.0
Italian[1]	1.0
Korean	0.9
Russian	0.7
Polish	0.7
Arabic	0.6

[1] The number of Vietnamese speakers and the number of Italian speakers were not statistically different from one another.

Note: The estimates in this figure vary from actual values due to sampling errors. As a result, the number of speakers of some languages shown in this figure may not be statistically different from the number of speakers of languages not shown in this figure.

Source: U.S. Census Bureau, Census 2000 Summary File 3.

statistically different: that is, any differences in actual population for the speakers of Vietnamese and Italian are not relevant from a statistical perspective.

patterns of immigration, the numbers of Italian, Polish, and German speakers fell between 1990 and 2000, while the number of speakers of many other languages increased.

Spanish speakers grew by about 60 percent and Spanish continued to be the non-English language most frequently spoken at home in the United States. The Chinese language, however, jumped from the fifth to the second most widely spoken non-English language, as the number of Chinese speakers

Table 1.
Twenty Languages Most Frequently Spoken at Home by English Ability for the Population 5 Years and Over: 1990 and 2000

(Data based on sample. For information on confidentiality protection, sampling error, nonsampling error, and definitions, see www.census.gov/prod/cen2000/doc/sf3.pdf)

Language spoken at home	1990		2000					
				Number of speakers				
					English-speaking ability			
	Rank	Number of speakers	Rank	Total	Very well	Well	Not well	Not at all
United States	(X)	230,445,777	(X)	262,375,152	(X)	(X)	(X)	(X)
English only	(X)	198,600,798	(X)	215,423,557	(X)	(X)	(X)	(X)
Total non-English	(X)	31,844,979	(X)	46,951,595	25,631,188	10,333,556	7,620,719	3,366,132
Spanish	1	17,339,172	1	28,101,052	14,349,796	5,819,408	5,130,400	2,801,448
Chinese	5	1,249,213	2	2,022,143	855,689	595,331	408,597	162,526
French	2	1,702,176	3	1,643,838	1,228,800	269,458	138,002	7,578
German	3	1,547,099	4	1,382,613	1,078,997	219,362	79,535	4,719
Tagalog	6	843,251	5	1,224,241	827,559	311,465	79,721	5,496
Vietnamese[1]	9	507,069	6	1,009,627	342,594	340,062	270,950	56,021
Italian[1]	4	1,308,648	7	1,008,370	701,220	195,901	99,270	11,979
Korean................	8	626,478	8	894,063	361,166	268,477	228,392	36,028
Russian	15	241,798	9	706,242	304,891	209,057	148,671	43,623
Polish................	7	723,483	10	667,414	387,694	167,233	95,032	17,455
Arabic................	13	355,150	11	614,582	403,397	140,057	58,595	12,533
Portuguese[2]	10	429,860	12	564,630	320,443	125,464	90,412	28,311
Japanese[2]..............	11	427,657	13	477,997	241,707	146,613	84,018	5,659
French Creole	19	187,658	14	453,368	245,857	121,913	70,961	14,637
Greek................	12	388,260	15	365,436	262,851	65,023	33,346	4,216
Hindi[3].................	14	331,484	16	317,057	245,192	51,929	16,682	3,254
Persian	18	201,865	17	312,085	198,041	70,909	32,959	10,176
Urdu[3]	(NA)	(NA)	18	262,900	180,018	56,736	20,817	5,329
Gujarathi	26	102,418	19	235,988	155,011	50,637	22,522	7,818
Armenian.............	20	149,694	20	202,708	108,554	48,469	31,868	13,817
All other languages	(X)	3,182,546	(X)	4,485,241	2,831,711	1,060,052	479,969	113,509

NA Not available.   X Not applicable.

[1] In 2000, the number of Vietnamese speakers and the number of Italian speakers were not statistically different from one another.
[2] In 1990, the number of Portuguese speakers and the number of Japanese speakers were not statistically different from one another.
[3] In 1990, Hindi included those who spoke Urdu.

Note: The estimates in this table vary from actual values due to sampling errors. As a result, the number of speakers of some languages shown in this table may not be statistically different from the number of speakers of languages not shown in this table.

Source: U.S. Census Bureau, Census 2000 Summary File 3.

rose from 1.2 to 2.0 million people (see Table 1.)[4] The number of Vietnamese speakers doubled over the decade, from about 507,000 speakers to just over 1 million speakers.

Of the 20 non-English languages most frequently spoken at home shown in Table 1, the largest proportional increase was for Russian speakers, who nearly tripled from 242,000 to 706,000. The second largest increase was for French Creole speakers (the language group that includes Haitian Creoles), whose numbers more than doubled from 188,000 to 453,000.

Table 2.
Language Use and English-Speaking Ability for the Population 5 Years and Over for the United States, Regions, and States and for Puerto Rico: 1990 and 2000

(Data based on sample. For information on confidentiality protection, sampling error, nonsampling error, and definitions, see www.census.gov/prod/cen2000/doc/sf3.pdf)

Area	1990			2000					1990 and 2000 percent change in "Spoke a language other than English at home"
	Population 5 years and over	Spoke a language other than English at home	Percent	Population 5 years and over	Spoke a language other than English at home	Percent	Spoke English less than "Very well"	Percent	
United States	230,445,777	31,844,979	13.8	262,375,152	46,951,595	17.9	21,320,407	8.1	47.4
Region									
Northeast	47,319,352	7,824,285	16.5	50,224,209	10,057,331	20.0	4,390,538	8.7	28.5
Midwest	55,272,756	3,920,660	7.1	60,054,144	5,623,538	9.4	2,398,120	4.0	43.4
South	79,248,852	8,669,631	10.9	93,431,879	14,007,396	15.0	6,149,756	6.6	61.6
West	48,604,817	11,430,403	23.5	58,664,920	17,263,330	29.4	8,381,993	14.3	51.0
State									
Alabama	3,759,802	107,866	2.9	4,152,278	162,483	3.9	63,917	1.5	50.6
Alaska	495,425	60,165	12.1	579,740	82,758	14.3	30,842	5.3	37.6
Arizona	3,374,806	700,287	20.8	4,752,724	1,229,227	25.9	539,937	11.4	75.5
Arkansas	2,186,665	60,781	2.8	2,492,205	123,755	5.0	57,709	2.3	103.6
California	27,383,547	8,619,334	31.5	31,416,629	12,401,756	39.5	6,277,779	20.0	43.9
Colorado	3,042,986	320,631	10.5	4,006,285	604,019	15.1	267,504	6.7	88.4
Connecticut	3,060,000	466,175	15.2	3,184,514	583,913	18.3	234,799	7.4	25.3
Delaware	617,720	42,327	6.9	732,378	69,533	9.5	28,380	3.9	64.3
District of Columbia	570,284	71,348	12.5	539,658	90,417	16.8	38,236	7.1	26.7
Florida	12,095,284	2,098,315	17.3	15,043,603	3,473,864	23.1	1,554,865	10.3	65.6
Georgia	5,984,188	284,546	4.8	7,594,476	751,438	9.9	374,251	4.9	164.1
Hawaii	1,026,209	254,724	24.8	1,134,351	302,125	26.6	143,505	12.7	18.6
Idaho	926,703	58,995	6.4	1,196,793	111,879	9.3	46,539	3.9	89.6
Illinois	10,585,838	1,499,112	14.2	11,547,505	2,220,719	19.2	1,054,722	9.1	48.1
Indiana	5,146,160	245,826	4.8	5,657,818	362,082	6.4	143,427	2.5	47.3
Iowa	2,583,526	100,391	3.9	2,738,499	160,022	5.8	68,108	2.5	59.4
Kansas	2,289,615	131,604	5.7	2,500,360	218,655	8.7	98,207	3.9	66.1
Kentucky	3,434,955	86,482	2.5	3,776,230	148,473	3.9	58,871	1.6	71.7
Louisiana	3,886,353	391,994	10.1	4,153,367	382,364	9.2	116,907	2.8	−2.5
Maine	1,142,122	105,441	9.2	1,204,164	93,966	7.8	24,063	2.0	−10.9
Maryland	4,425,285	395,051	8.9	4,945,043	622,714	12.6	246,287	5.0	57.6
Massachusetts	5,605,751	852,228	15.2	5,954,249	1,115,570	18.7	459,073	7.7	30.9
Michigan	8,594,737	569,807	6.6	9,268,782	781,381	8.4	294,606	3.2	37.1
Minnesota	4,038,361	227,161	5.6	4,591,491	389,988	8.5	167,511	3.6	71.7
Mississippi	2,378,805	66,516	2.8	2,641,453	95,522	3.6	36,059	1.4	43.6
Missouri	4,748,704	178,210	3.8	5,226,022	264,281	5.1	103,019	2.0	48.3
Montana	740,218	37,020	5.0	847,362	44,331	5.2	12,663	1.5	19.7
Nebraska	1,458,904	69,872	4.8	1,594,700	125,654	7.9	57,772	3.6	79.8
Nevada	1,110,450	146,152	13.2	1,853,504	427,972	23.1	207,687	11.2	192.8
New Hampshire	1,024,621	88,796	8.7	1,160,340	96,088	8.3	28,073	2.4	8.2
New Jersey	7,200,696	1,406,148	19.5	7,856,268	2,001,690	25.5	873,088	11.1	42.4
New Mexico	1,390,048	493,999	35.5	1,689,911	616,964	36.5	201,055	11.9	24.9
New York	16,743,048	3,908,720	23.3	17,749,110	4,962,921	28.0	2,310,256	13.0	27.0
North Carolina	6,172,301	240,866	3.9	7,513,165	603,517	8.0	297,858	4.0	150.6
North Dakota	590,839	46,897	7.9	603,106	37,976	6.3	11,003	1.8	−19.0
Ohio	10,063,212	546,148	5.4	10,599,968	648,493	6.1	234,459	2.2	18.7
Oklahoma	2,921,755	145,798	5.0	3,215,719	238,532	7.4	98,990	3.1	63.6
Oregon	2,640,482	191,710	7.3	3,199,323	388,669	12.1	188,958	5.9	102.7
Pennsylvania	11,085,170	806,876	7.3	11,555,538	972,484	8.4	368,257	3.2	20.5
Rhode Island	936,423	159,492	17.0	985,184	196,624	20.0	83,624	8.5	23.3
South Carolina	3,231,539	113,163	3.5	3,748,669	196,429	5.2	82,279	2.2	73.6
South Dakota	641,226	41,994	6.5	703,820	45,575	6.5	16,376	2.3	(NS)
Tennessee	4,544,743	131,550	2.9	5,315,920	256,516	4.8	108,265	2.0	95.0
Texas	15,605,822	3,970,304	25.4	19,241,518	6,010,753	31.2	2,669,603	13.9	51.4
Utah	1,553,351	120,404	7.8	2,023,875	253,249	12.5	105,691	5.2	110.3
Vermont	521,521	30,409	5.8	574,842	34,075	5.9	9,305	1.6	(NS)
Virginia	5,746,419	418,521	7.3	6,619,266	735,191	11.1	303,729	4.6	75.7
Washington	4,501,879	403,173	9.0	5,501,398	770,886	14.0	350,914	6.4	91.2
West Virginia	1,686,932	44,203	2.6	1,706,931	45,895	2.7	13,550	0.8	3.8
Wisconsin	4,531,134	263,638	5.8	5,022,073	368,712	7.3	148,910	3.0	39.9
Wyoming	418,713	23,809	5.7	462,809	29,485	6.4	8,919	1.9	23.8
Puerto Rico	3,522,037	(NA)	(NA)	3,515,228	3,008,567	85.6	2,527,156	71.9	(NA)

NA Not available.   NS Not statistically different from zero at the 90-percent confidence level.
Source: U.S. Census Bureau, Census 2000 Summary File 3 and 1990 Census Summary Tape File 3.

THE GEOGRAPHIC DISTRIBUTION OF PEOPLE WHO SPOKE A LANGUAGE OTHER THAN ENGLISH

This section discusses the geographic distribution of the population aged 5 and over who stated in Census 2000 that they spoke a language other than English at home.

The West had the greatest number and proportion of non-English-language speakers.[5]

People who spoke languages other than English at home were not distributed equally across or within regions in 2000.[6] While the West had only slightly more than one-fifth of the U.S. population aged 5 and over, it was home to more than one-third (37 percent) of all non-English-language speakers, the highest proportion of any region (see Table 2). Within regions, the proportion who spoke a non-English language at home was 29 percent in the West, 20 percent in the Northeast, 15 percent in the South, and only 9 percent in the Midwest.

Reflecting the higher proportion of speakers of non-English languages in the West, people in that region were more likely than those in the other regions to have difficulty with English. In 2000, 14 percent of all people aged 5 and over in the West spoke English less than "Very well"—compared with 9 percent in the Northeast, 7 percent in the South, and 4 percent in the Midwest.

Figure 4 illustrates the prevalence of the four major non-English-language groups spoken in each region. Spanish was spoken more than any other language group in all regions. The West and the South combined had about three times the number of Spanish speakers (21.0 million) as the Northeast and the Midwest combined (7.1 million). In the Northeast and the Midwest, Spanish speakers composed slightly less than half of all non-English-language speakers, while in the South and the West, they represented around two-thirds (71 percent and 64 percent, respectively), in large part because of the geographic proximity to Mexico and other Spanish-speaking countries.

In the Northeast, the Midwest, and the South, speakers of Other Indo-European languages made up the second largest non-English-language speaking group, while in the West, the second largest group was speakers of Asian and Pacific Island languages. Half of Asian and Pacific Island-language speakers lived in the West in 2000.

Table 3 shows the change in the number of speakers of Spanish, Other Indo-European languages, Asian and Pacific Island languages, and All other languages between 1990 and 2000. The largest percentage increase of Spanish

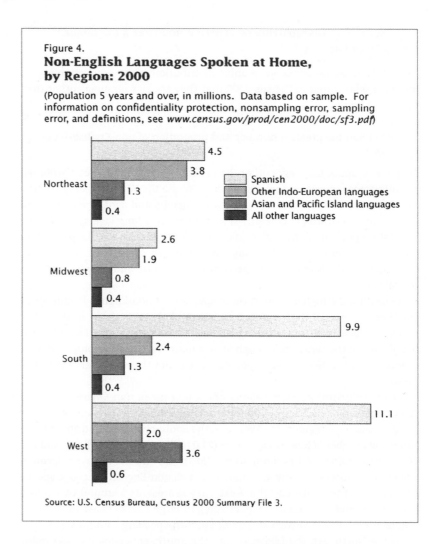

Figure 4.
Non-English Languages Spoken at Home, by Region: 2000

(Population 5 years and over, in millions. Data based on sample. For information on confidentiality protection, nonsampling error, sampling error, and definitions, see *www.census.gov/prod/cen2000/doc/sf3.pdf*)

Legend:
- Spanish
- Other Indo-European languages
- Asian and Pacific Island languages
- All other languages

Northeast: 4.5, 3.8, 1.3, 0.4
Midwest: 2.6, 1.9, 0.8, 0.4
South: 9.9, 2.4, 1.3, 0.4
West: 11.1, 2.0, 3.6, 0.6

Source: U.S. Census Bureau, Census 2000 Summary File 3.

speakers was in the Midwest. Asian Pacific Island-language speakers increased most rapidly in the South and the Midwest. Although the number of Spanish speakers grew in all regions, more than three-fourths of that growth was in the West and the South. The number of Asian and Pacific Island-language speakers grew substantially in all regions, with the greatest numerical increase in the West, which was home to more than half of all Asian and Pacific Island-language speakers in both years.

Table 3.
Language Spoken at Home for the Population 5 Years and Over Who Spoke a Language Other Than English at Home for the United States and Regions: 1990 and 2000

(Data based on sample. For information on confidentiality protection, sampling error, nonsampling error, and definitions, see www.census.gov/prod/cen2000/doc/sf3.pdf)

Area	Spanish			Other Indo-European languages			Asian and Pacific Island languages			All other languages		
	1990	2000	Percent change	1990	2000	Percent change	1990	2000	Percent change	1990	2000	Percent change
United States ..	17,345,064	28,101,052	62.0	8,790,133	10,017,989	14.0	4,471,621	6,960,065	55.6	1,238,161	1,872,489	51.2
Region												
Northeast........	3,133,043	4,492,168	43.4	3,547,154	3,778,958	6.5	845,442	1,348,621	59.5	298,646	437,584	46.5
Midwest.........	1,400,651	2,623,391	87.3	1,821,772	1,861,729	2.2	459,524	760,107	65.4	238,713	378,311	58.5
South..........	5,815,486	9,908,653	70.4	1,909,179	2,390,266	25.2	715,235	1,277,618	78.6	229,731	430,859	87.5
West...........	6,995,884	11,076,840	58.3	1,512,028	1,987,036	31.4	2,451,420	3,573,719	45.8	471,071	625,735	32.8

Source: U.S. Census Bureau, Census 2000 Summary File 3 and 1990 Census Summary Tape File 3.

More than one-quarter of the population in seven states spoke a language other than English at home in 2000.

California had the largest percentage of non-English-language speakers (39 percent), followed by New Mexico (37 percent), Texas (31 percent), New York (28 percent), Hawaii (27 percent), Arizona, and New Jersey (each about 26 percent, see Table 2). The five states with fewer than 5 percent of the population who spoke a language other than English at home were all in the South—Tennessee (4.8 percent), Alabama and Kentucky (each 3.9 percent), Mississippi (3.6 percent), and West Virginia (2.7 percent).

Eight states had over 1 million non-English-language speakers in 2000, led by California (12.4 million) with more than twice the number of any other state. Texas had the second largest number of non-English-language speakers (6.0 million), followed by New York (5.0 million), Florida (3.5 million), Illinois (2.2 million), New Jersey (2.0 million), Arizona (1.2 million), and Massachusetts (1.1 million).

During the 1990s, California surpassed New Mexico as the state with the 20 largest proportion of non-English-language speakers. While the proportion of non-English-language speakers in New Mexico increased slightly from 36 percent to 37 percent, the proportion in California jumped from 31 percent to 39 percent.

The number of non-English-language speakers at least doubled in six states from 1990 to 2000. The largest percentage increase occurred in Nevada, where the number increased by 193 percent. Nevada also had the highest rate of population increase during the decade. Georgia's non-English-language-speaking residents increased by 164 percent, followed by North Carolina (151 percent), Utah (110 percent), Arkansas (104 percent), and Oregon (103 percent).[7]

Since 1990, the proportion of people who spoke a language other than English at home decreased in three states. North Dakota had the largest decrease (19 percent), followed by Maine (11 percent) and Louisiana (2 percent). These three states also had low rates of population growth from 1990 to 2000.

Counties with a large proportion of the population who spoke a language other than English at home were concentrated in border states.

Figure 5 illustrates the high proportions of people who spoke a language other than English at home in 2000 in the states that border Mexico, the

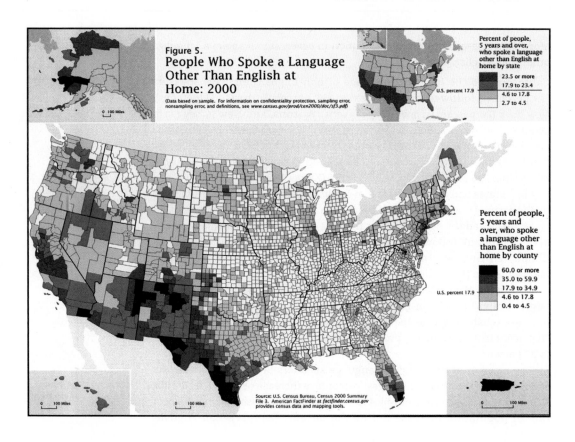

Figure 5.
People Who Spoke a Language Other Than English at Home: 2000

(Data based on sample. For information on confidentiality protection, sampling error, nonsampling error, and definitions, see *www.census.gov/prod/cen2000/doc/sf3.pdf*)

Percent of people, 5 years and over, who spoke a language other than English at home by state

- 23.5 or more
- 17.9 to 23.4
- 4.6 to 17.8
- 2.7 to 4.5

U.S. percent 17.9

Percent of people, 5 years and over, who spoke a language other than English at home by county

- 60.0 or more
- 35.0 to 59.9
- 17.9 to 34.9
- 4.6 to 17.8
- 0.4 to 4.5

U.S. percent 17.9

Source: U.S. Census Bureau, Census 2000 Summary File 3. American FactFinder at *factfinder.census.gov* provides census data and mapping tools.

Pacific Ocean, or the Atlantic Ocean. Some of the "border states" were entry points for many immigrants.

In 2000, in about 1 percent of the 3,141 counties in the United States, more than 60 percent of the population spoke a language other than English at home. In seven counties, more than 80 percent of the population spoke a non-English language at home—Maverick, Webb, Starr, Kenedy, Zavala, Presidio, and Hidalgo—all in Texas. All but one of the 20 counties with the highest proportions of non-English-language speakers were located in Texas (Santa Cruz County, Arizona, being the exception).

Figure 5 shows the high proportion of non-English-language speakers in 25 counties with large cities, such as Atlanta, Chicago, Miami, and New York City. Other counties with relatively high proportions of non-English-language speakers included concentrations of people who spoke Native American languages.[8] For example, in Bethel Census Area, Alaska, 66 percent of the population spoke a language other than English at home, and 97 percent of the non-English-language speakers spoke a Native North American language. The Navajo speakers in the Navajo Nation Indian Reservation, which spanned several counties throughout Arizona, New Mexico, and Utah, accounted for a large proportion of the population who spoke a language other than English at home in these counties.

In some counties, relatively high proportions of non-English-language speakers are found in small, rural populations. For example, the proportions of non-English-language speakers were 25 percent in Logan County and 36 percent in McIntosh County in North Dakota and 33 percent in McPherson County in South Dakota.[9] In these three counties, each with a population of fewer than 4,000, German speakers were predominant among non-English-language speakers: 95.3 percent, 98.1 percent, and 99.6 percent, respectively.[10]

Among all counties, the median percentage of the population who spoke a language other than English at home was 4.6 percent.[11] The fact that the proportion was below 4.6 percent in one-half of all counties, while the national average was 17.9 percent, reflects the large number of counties (primarily non-metropolitan counties in the Midwest and the South) with relatively small populations and with low proportions of non-English-language speakers.

Figure 5 illustrates the low proportions of non-English-language speakers in many counties in the South and the Midwest, including Alabama, Arkansas, Iowa, Kentucky, Michigan, Mississippi, Missouri, Tennessee, West Virginia, and Wisconsin. In West Virginia, all but 2 of the 55 counties had a proportion of non-English-language speakers below 4.6 percent.

Places with the highest percentages of non-English-language speakers, Spanish speakers, and people who spoke English less than "Very well" were concentrated in California, Florida, and Texas.

Of the 245 places with 100,000 or more population in 2000, Hialeah, Florida, topped the list with 93 percent of the population aged 5 and over who spoke a language other than English at home in 2000.[12] In addition, 92 percent spoke Spanish and 59 percent spoke English less than "Very well" in Hialeah (see Table 4).[13] Six additional places were included in all three categories in Table 4: Laredo and Brownsville, Texas; East Los Angeles, El Monte, and Santa Ana, California; and Miami, Florida.

McAllen and El Paso, Texas, and Elizabeth, New Jersey, were included in 30 two of three categories. Pomona, Garden Grove, and Salinas, all in California, were included in one of the three categories.

ADDITIONAL FINDINGS

How many people were linguistically isolated?

In the United States, the ability to speak English plays a large role in how well people can perform daily activities. How well a person speaks English may indicate how well he or she communicates with public officials, medical personnel, and other service providers. It could also affect other activities outside the home, such as grocery shopping or banking. People who do not have a strong command of English and who do not have someone in their household to help them on a regular basis are at even more of a disadvantage. They are defined here as "linguistically isolated" (see text box below).

Linguistically Isolated

A linguistically isolated household is one in which no person aged 14 or over speaks English at least "Very well." That is, no person aged 14 or over speaks only English at home, or speaks another language at home and speaks English "Very well."

A linguistically isolated person is any person living in a linguistically isolated household. All the members of a linguistically isolated household are tabulated as linguistically isolated, including members under 14 years old who may speak only English.

Table 4.
Ten Places of 100,000 or More Population With the Highest Percentage of People 5 Years and Over Who Spoke a Language Other Than English at Home, Who Spoke Spanish at Home, and Who Spoke English Less Than "Very Well": 2000

(Data based on sample. For information on confidentiality protection, sampling error, nonsampling error, and definitions, see *www.census.gov/prod/cen2000/doc/sf3.pdf*)

Place	Number	Percent	90-percent confidence interval
Spoke a Language Other Than English			
Hialeah, FL	197,504	92.6	92.3 - 92.9
Laredo, TX	145,510	91.8	91.4 - 92.2
East Los Angeles, CA[1]	97,645	87.4	86.8 - 88.0
Brownsville, TX	110,003	87.2	86.7 - 87.7
El Monte, CA	84,834	80.7	80.0 - 81.4
Santa Ana, CA	241,303	79.6	79.2 - 80.0
McAllen, TX	73,882	76.1	75.3 - 76.9
Miami, FL	254,536	74.6	74.2 - 75.0
El Paso, TX	369,000	71.3	70.9 - 71.7
Elizabeth, NJ	75,305	67.5	66.7 - 68.3
Spoke Spanish			
Hialeah, FL	195,884	91.9	91.6 - 92.2
Laredo, TX	144,633	91.3	90.9 - 91.7
Brownsville, TX	109,153	86.6	86.1 - 87.1
East Los Angeles, CA[1]	96,525	86.4	85.8 - 87.0
McAllen, TX	71,800	74.0	73.2 - 74.8
Santa Ana, CA	211,276	69.7	69.2 - 70.2
El Paso, TX	356,558	68.9	68.5 - 69.3
Miami, FL	227,293	66.6	66.1 - 67.1
El Monte, CA	64,889	61.8	61.0 - 62.6
Pomona, CA	74,557	55.0	54.2 - 55.8
Spoke English Less Than "Very Well"			
Hialeah, FL	126,358	59.3	58.7 - 59.9
East Los Angeles, CA[1]	57,966	51.9	51.1 - 52.7
Santa Ana, CA	156,692	51.7	51.2 - 52.2
El Monte, CA	53,662	51.1	50.2 - 52.0
Miami, FL	160,790	47.1	46.6 - 47.6
Laredo, TX	69,071	43.6	42.9 - 44.3
Brownsville, TX	52,970	42.0	41.2 - 42.8
Garden Grove, CA	57,313	37.6	36.9 - 38.3
Elizabeth, NJ	41,068	36.8	36.0 - 37.6
Salinas, CA	49,099	35.9	35.2 - 36.6

[1] East Los Angeles, CA, is a census designated place and is not legally incorporated.

Note: Because of sampling error, the estimates in this table may not be significantly different from one another or from rates for other places not listed in this table.

Source: U.S. Census Bureau, Census 2000 Summary File 3.

In 2000, 4.4 million households encompassing 11.9 million people were linguistically isolated. These numbers were significantly higher than in 1990, when 2.9 million households and 7.7 million people lived in those households.

ABOUT CENSUS 2000

Why Census 2000 Asked about Language Use and English-Speaking Ability

The question on language use and English-speaking ability provides government agencies with information for programs that serve the needs of people who have difficulty speaking English. Under the Voting Rights Act, information about language ability is needed to meet statutory requirements for making voting materials available in minority languages.

The Bilingual Education Program uses data on language to allocate grants to school districts for children with limited English proficiency. These data also are needed for local agencies developing services for the elderly under the Older Americans Act.

Accuracy of the Estimates

The data contained in this report are based on the sample of households who 35 responded to the Census 2000 long form. Nationally, approximately 1 out of every 6 housing units was included in this sample. As a result, the sample estimates may differ somewhat from the 100-percent figures that would have been obtained if all housing units, people within those housing units, and people living in group quarters had been enumerated using the same questionnaires, instructions, enumerators, and so forth. The sample estimates also differ from the values that would have been obtained from different samples of housing units, people within those housing units, and people living in group quarters. The deviation of a sample estimate from the average of all possible samples is called the sampling error.

In addition to the variability that arises from the sampling procedures, both sample data and 100-percent data are subject to nonsampling error. Nonsampling error may be introduced during any of the various complex operations used to collect and process data. Such errors may include: not enumerating every household or every person in the population, failing to obtain all required information from the respondents, obtaining incorrect or inconsistent information, and recording information incorrectly. In addition, errors can occur during field review of the enumerators' work, during

As a way of enhancing their ethos, Shin and Bruno detail the methodology of the census and acknowledge the potential for error. Chapter 3 explains other strategies for establishing credibility.

LINK TO P. 59

clerical handling of the census questionnaires, or during the electronic processing of the questionnaires.

Nonsampling error may affect the data in two ways: (1) errors that are introduced randomly will increase the variability of the data and, therefore, should be reflected in the standard errors; and (2) errors that tend to be consistent in one direction will bias both sample and 100-percent data in that direction. For example, if respondents consistently tend to underreport their incomes, then the resulting estimates of households or families by income category will tend to be understated for the higher income categories and overstated for the lower income categories. Such biases are not reflected in the standard errors.

While it is impossible to completely eliminate error from an operation as large and complex as the decennial census, the Census Bureau attempts to control the sources of such error during the data collection and processing operations. The primary sources of error and the programs instituted to control error in Census 2000 are described in detail in *Summary File 3 Technical Documentation* under Chapter 8, "Accuracy of the Data," located at www.census .gov/prod/cen2000/doc/sf3.pdf.

All statements in this Census 2000 Brief have undergone statistical testing and all comparisons are significant at the 90-percent confidence level, unless otherwise noted. The estimates in tables, maps, and other figures may vary from actual values due to sampling and nonsampling errors. As a result, estimates in one category may not be significantly different from estimates assigned to a different category. Further information on the accuracy of the data is located at www.census.gov/prod/cen2000/doc/sf3.pdf. For further information on the computation and use of standard errors, contact the Decennial Statistical Studies Division at 301-763-4242.

For More Information

The Census 2000 Summary File 3 data are available from the American 40 FactFinder on the Internet (factfinder.census.gov). They were released on a state-by-state basis during 2002. For information on confidentiality protection, nonsampling error, sampling error, and definitions, also see www .census.gov/prod/cen2000/doc/sf3.pdf or contact the Customer Services Center at 301-763-INFO (4636).

Information on population and housing topics is presented in the Census 2000 Brief series, located on the Census Bureau's Web site at www.census .gov/population/www/cen2000/briefs.html. This series presents information on race, Hispanic origin, age, sex, household type, housing tenure, and social, economic, and housing characteristics, such as ancestry, income, and housing costs.

For additional information on language use and English-speaking ability, including reports and survey data, visit the Census Bureau's Internet site at www.census.gov/population/www/socdemo/lang_use.html. To find information about the availability of data products, including reports, CD-ROMs, and DVDs, call the Customer Services Center at 301-763-INFO (4636), or e-mail webmaster@census.gov.

NOTES

1. The text of this report discusses data for the United States, including the 50 states and the District of Columbia. Data for the Commonwealth of Puerto Rico are shown in Table 2 and Figure 5.
2. More detailed information on language and language coding can be found in "Summary File 3: 2000 Census of Population and Housing Technical Documentation" issued December 2002 (www.census.gov/prod/cen2000/doc/sf3.pdf).
3. The estimates in this report are based on responses from a sample of the population. As with all surveys, estimates may vary from the actual values because of sampling variation or other factors. All statements made in this report have undergone statistical testing and are significant° at the 90-percent confidence level unless otherwise noted.
4. The changes in ranks between 1990 and 2000 have not been tested and may not be statistically significant.
5. Hereafter, this report uses the term "non-English-language speakers" to refer to people who spoke a language other than English at home, regardless of their ability to speak English (see Table 1).
6. The Northeast region includes the states of Connecticut, Maine, Massachusetts, New Hampshire, New Jersey, New York, Pennsylvania, Rhode Island, and Vermont. The Midwest region includes the states of Illinois, Indiana, Iowa, Kansas, Michigan, Minnesota, Missouri, Nebraska, North Dakota, Ohio, South Dakota, and Wisconsin. The South region includes the states of Alabama, Arkansas, Delaware, Florida,

significant: that is, statistically significant. In this case, the chances are that the statements in the report are valid (unless otherwise noted) at least nine out of ten times. (Because the data are based on a sample of the population rather than the entire population, these statistics are estimates; the issue is how accurate these estimates are.)

Georgia, Kentucky, Louisiana, Maryland, Mississippi, North Carolina, Oklahoma, South Carolina, Tennessee, Texas, Virginia, West Virginia, and the District of Columbia, a state equivalent. The West region includes the states of Alaska, Arizona, California, Colorado, Hawaii, Idaho, Montana, Nevada, New Mexico, Oregon, Utah, Washington, and Wyoming.

7. The percentage increases between Arkansas and Utah and between Arkansas and Oregon were not statistically different from one another.

8. For more detailed information on language use and English-speaking ability, see Summary File 3.

9. The proportions of non-English-language speakers in McIntosh County, North Dakota, and McPherson County, South Dakota, were not statistically different from each other.

10. The proportions of German speakers among non-English-language speakers in Logan County and McIntosh County, North Dakota, were not statistically different from each other.

11. The median percentage is a point estimate based on a sample.

12. Census 2000 showed 245 places in the United States with 100,000 or more population. They included 238 incorporated places (including 7 city-county consolidations) and 7 census designated places that were not legally incorporated. For a list of these places by state, see www.census.gov/population/www/cen2000/phc-t6.html.

13. The percentages of people who spoke English less than "Very well" in Hialeah, Florida, and Laredo, Texas, were not statistically different from each other. The percentages of people who spoke Spanish in Hialeah, Florida, and Laredo, Texas, were also not statistically different from each other.

RESPOND ●

1. What kind of argument—factual, definitional, evaluative, causal, or proposal—does this selection represent? What evidence would you offer? Why should we expect such arguments from the U.S. Census Bureau, whose logo includes the statement "Helping You Make Informed Decisions"? (For a discussion of kinds of argument, see Chapter 1.)

2. This report was produced by the U.S. Census Bureau. How does that fact itself represent an ethical appeal? For example, how might it influence your evaluation of the credibility of this report as a source you might use for constructing an academic argument? (For a discussion of ethical appeals, see Chapter 3. For a discussion of evaluating sources, see Chapter 19.)

3. Examine Figure 5 carefully. What is the value of presenting the data in two ways—by county (the larger map) and by state (the smaller map inset in the upper right-hand corner)? (The island in the lower right-hand corner is Puerto Rico.) What do these two presentations of the

same data remind us about the nature of visual arguments? (For a discussion of visual arguments, see Chapter 14.)

4. Note 5 explains the use of the term "non-English-speakers," while the shaded box on page 736 provides definitions for the terms "linguistically isolated household" and "linguistically isolated person." What kinds of definitions are these? (For a discussion of kinds of definitions, see Chapter 9.) Demographers need category labels, but these labels have received criticism from social scientists who study issues of language in society. What might their complaints be? In other words, in what ways might these labels be seen as inaccurate, unfair, and perhaps even prejudicial? Why is this question of special relevance in a report of this kind?

5. The next-to-last section of the report is entitled "Accuracy of the Estimates." Why is this information useful or even necessary to readers? How do these qualifications (that is, instances of qualifying the claims made) strengthen the argument? The credibility of the report? The ethos of the authors? (For a discussion of qualifying claims, see Chapter 7.)

6. Although you might have an impression and perhaps some experiential knowledge of the social changes going on in the communities where you've lived, we bet that you've learned something from this report. Use this information as a starting point for an investigation of your own. In all cases, you will be composing an academic argument. (For a discussion of academic arguments, see Chapter 6.) You might, for example, (a) **interview** older people in your community (or a community you have lived in) about how, based on their impressions, the demographics of the community have changed over the past ten, twenty, or thirty years with respect to people who speak a language other than English; (b) use this report and information from the references that it cites (other census reports or actual census data, all downloadable) to **provide a detailed, factual argument** about languages other than English in the community you live in (or one you have lived in); (c) **locate** earlier census data to create a factual argument about how the community you live in (or one you have lived in) has changed with respect to the presence of other languages there; or (d) **propose another topic** that uses these data as a starting point.

From "Bien Pretty"

SANDRA CISNEROS

I'd never made love in Spanish before. I mean not with anyone whose *first* language was Spanish. There was crazy Graham, the anarchist labor organizer who'd taught me to eat jalapeños and swear like a truck mechanic, but he was Welsh and had learned his Spanish running guns to Bolivia.

And Eddie, sure. But Eddie and I were products of our American education. Anything tender always came off sounding like the subtitles to a Buñuel° film.

But Flavio. When Flavio accidentally hammered his thumb, he never yelled "Ouch!" he said "¡Ay!" The true test of a native Spanish speaker.

¡Ay! To make love in Spanish, in a manner as intricate and devout as la Alhambra.°To have a lover sigh *mi vida, mi preciosa, mi chiquitita,* and whisper things in that language crooned to babies, that language murmured by grandmothers, those words that smelled like your house, like flour tortillas, and the inside of your daddy's hat, like everyone talking in the kitchen at the same time, or sleeping with the windows open, like sneaking cashews from the crumpled quarter-pound bag Mama always hid in her lingerie drawer after she went shopping with Daddy at the Sears.

That language. That sweep of palm leaves and fringed shawls. That startled 5 fluttering, like the heart of a goldfinch or a fan. Nothing sounded dirty or hurtful or corny. How could I think of making love in English again? English with its starched *r*'s and *g*'s. English with its crisp linen syllables. English crunchy as apples, resilient and stiff as sailcloth.

But Spanish whirred like silk, rolled and puckered and hissed. I held Flavio close to me, in the mouth of my heart, inside my wrists.

Incredible happiness. A sigh unfurled of its own accord, a groan heaved out from my chest so rusty and full of dust it frightened me. I was crying. It surprised us both.

"My soul, did I hurt you?" Flavio said in that other language.

I managed to bunch my mouth into a knot and shake my head "no" just as the next wave of sobs began. Flavio rocked me, and cooed, and rocked me. *Ya, ya, ya.* There, there, there.

I wanted to say so many things, but all I could think of was a line I'd read 10 in the letters of Georgia O'Keeffe years ago and had forgotten until then. Flavio . . . did you ever feel like flowers?

Born in Chicago in 1954, Sandra Cisneros is a Mexican American writer who lives and writes in a much-discussed purple house in San Antonio, Texas. The author of several books about the Mexican American experience, most recently the 2002 novel Caramelo, she's the recipient of a number of important awards, including a MacArthur Foundation fellowship. In this excerpt from the short story "Bien Pretty," which appeared in Woman Hollering Creek and Other Stories (1991), Cisneros helps readers understand how bilinguals experience the languages they know. As you read, note how Cisneros uses careful description to make her argument.

(Luis) Buñuel (1900–1983): a Spanish filmmaker, famous for his often bizarre, surrealist visual imagery.

la Alhambra: from an Arabic phrase meaning "the red palace"; a palace, citadel, and gardens in Grenada in southern Spain, home of the Nasrid sultans in the thirteenth and fourteenth centuries and famous for its detailed Islamic carving and tilework.

A doorway in the Alhambra

What tropes does Cisneros use in
her essay? See descriptions of the
different types of figurative language
in Chapter 13 to help you figure out
your answer.

LINK TO P. 426

RESPOND●

1. For Cisneros—and one can likely claim it for all bilinguals—in some sense the languages she knows aren't equal. Rather, each language is associated with different worlds of experience. What does Spanish connote for the narrator in Cisneros's text? What does English connote? Where would such connotations come from?

2. One resource that bilingual writers have is codeswitching—switching between the languages they know. In this excerpt, we see the simple noun phrase "la Alhambra" (paragraph 4) from Spanish, which we can correctly understand even if we know no Spanish. We also see the phrase "*Ya, ya, ya*" (paragraph 9), which is followed immediately by the English equivalent, "There, there, there." Yet we also find the phrases "*mi vida, mi preciosa, mi chiquitita*" (paragraph 4), which we may not be able to figure out the meanings of. (In fact, the phrases translate literally as "my life, my precious [one], my dearest little [one]"—things native speakers of English wouldn't normally say to one another, even when being intimate. Such phrases are perfectly normal among speakers of Spanish.) Why might writers purposely create texts that include parts readers may not be able to understand? Why would such a strategy be especially effective when talking about intimacies like making love?

3. All humans probably have an emotional attachment to one or more languages or language varieties, most often one associated with childhood. **Create a text** in which you explore and define the meaning of some language or language variety—a regional, social, or ethnic variety of English, for example—for you. Your text can take the form of an essay, or you may wish to create a sketch more like Cisneros's (though you needn't write about anything so intimate as love making!). In it, seek to help readers—both those who know that language variety and those who don't—understand its meanings and significance for you.

▼ *Marjorie Agosín is a professor of Spanish at Wellesley College in Massachusetts and an award-winning writer and human rights activist. She was reared in Chile, the country to which her grandparents had moved early in the twentieth century at a time when Jews faced persecution in parts of Europe. Her family moved to the United States in the 1970s, after a right-wing military coup overthrew the Chilean government. In this essay, which originally appeared in* Poets & Writers *in 1999 and was translated by Celeste Kostopulos-Cooperman, Agosín explains why she, as a political exile, "writes in Spanish and lives in translation." In the poem that follows it, "English," translated by Monica Bruno, Agosín compares and contrasts English and Spanish. As you read, consider how the experiences of an exile might differ from those of immigrants who come to the United States for other reasons, particularly with regard to language.*

Always Living in Spanish

MARJORIE AGOSÍN

RECOVERING THE FAMILIAR, THROUGH LANGUAGE

In the evenings in the northern hemisphere, I repeat the ancient ritual that I observed as a child in the southern hemisphere: going out while the night is still warm and trying to recognize the stars as it begins to grow dark silently. In the sky of my country, Chile, that long and wide stretch of land that the poets blessed and dictators abused, I could easily name the stars: the three Marias, the Southern Cross, and the three Lilies, names of beloved and courageous women.

But here in the United States, where I have lived since I was a young girl, the solitude of exile makes me feel that so little is mine, that not even the sky has the same constellations, the trees and the fauna the same names or sounds, or the rubbish the same smell. How does one recover the familiar? How does one name the unfamiliar? How can one be another or live in a foreign language? These are the dilemmas of one who writes in Spanish and lives in translation.

Since my earliest childhood in Chile I lived with the tempos and the melodies of a multiplicity of tongues: German, Yiddish,° Russian, Turkish, and many Latin songs. Because everyone was from somewhere else, my relatives

Yiddish: a Germanic language, much influenced by Hebrew and Aramaic and spoken by Ashkenazi Jews in Central and Eastern Europe and their descendants. In the nineteenth century, it was found in most of the world's countries with an Ashkenazi population, including the United States. Yiddish is written in the Hebrew alphabet.

shtetl: a small Jewish village or town in Eastern Europe (originally, a Yiddish word meaning "little town").

Ladino: a nearly extinct Romance language based on archaic Castilian Spanish and spoken by Sephardic Jews in the Balkans, North Africa and the Middle East, Turkey, and Greece. It originated in Spain (the Toledo that Agosín refers to is a city in Spain) and was carried elsewhere by the descendants of Jews exiled from there during the Inquisition.

diasporic: relating to a diaspora, or dispersion of a group of people across a large geographic area to which they aren't native.

laughed, sang, and fought in a Babylon of languages. Spanish was reserved for matters of extreme seriousness, for commercial transactions, or for illnesses, but everyone's mother tongue was always associated with the memory of spaces inhabited in the past: the shtetl,° the flowering and vast Vienna avenues, the minarets of Turkey, and the Ladino° whispers of Toledo. When my paternal grandmother sang old songs in Turkish, her voice and body assumed the passion of one who was there in the city of Istanbul, gazing by turns toward the west and the east.

Destiny and the always ambiguous nature of history continued my family's enforced migration, and because of it I, too, became one who had to live and speak in translation. The disappearances, torture, and clandestine deaths in my country in the early seventies drove us to the United States, that other America that looked with suspicion at those who did not speak English and especially those who came from the supposedly uncivilized regions of Latin America. I had left a dangerous place that was my home, only to arrive in a dangerous place that was not: a high school in the small town of Athens, Georgia, where my poor English and my accent were the cause of ridicule and insult. The only way I could recover my usurped country and my Chilean childhood was by continuing to write in Spanish, the same way my grandparents had sung in their own tongues in diasporic° sites.

The new and learned English language did not fit with the visceral emotions and themes that my poetry contained, but by writing in Spanish I could recover fragrances, spoken rhythms, and the passion of my own identity. Daily I felt the need to translate myself for the strangers living all around me, to tell them why we were in Georgia, why we ate differently, why we had fled, why my accent was so thick, and why I did not look Hispanic. Only at night, writing poems in Spanish, could I return to my senses, and soothe my own sorrow over what I had left behind.

This is how I became a Chilean poet who wrote in Spanish and lived in the southern United States. And then, one day, a poem of mine was translated and published in the English language. Finally, for the first time since I had left Chile, I felt I didn't have to explain myself. My poem, expressed in another language, spoke for itself . . . and for me.

Sometimes the austere sounds of English help me bear the solitude of knowing that I am foreign and so far away from those about whom I write. I must admit I would like more opportunities to read in Spanish to people whose language and culture is also mine, to join in our common heritage and in the feast of our sounds. I would also like readers of English to understand the beauty of the spoken word in Spanish, that constant flow of oxytonic° and

oxytonic: with the main stress on the final or single syllable of a word.

paraoxytonic° syllables (*Verde que te quiero verde*),° the joy of writing—of danc-ing—in another language. I believe that many exiles share the unresolvable torment of not being able to live in the language of their childhood.

I miss that undulating and sensuous language of mine, those baroque descriptions, the sense of being and feeling that Spanish gives me. It is per-haps for this reason that I have chosen and will always choose to write in Spanish. Nothing else from my childhood world remains. My country seems to be frozen in gestures of silence and oblivion. My relatives have died, and I have grown up not knowing a young generation of cousins and nieces and nephews. Many of my friends were disappeared,° others were tortured, and the most fortunate, like me, became guardians of memory. For us, to write in Spanish is to always be in active pursuit of memory. I seek to recapture a world lost to me on that sorrowful afternoon when the blue electric sky and the Andean cordillera° bade me farewell. On that, my last Chilean day, I car-ried under my arm my innocence recorded in a little blue notebook I kept even then. Gradually that diary filled with memoranda, poems written in free verse, descriptions of dreams and of the thresholds of my house surrounded by cherry trees and gardenias. To write in Spanish is for me a gesture of sur-vival. And because of translation, my memory has now become a part of the memory of many others.

Translators are not traitors, as the proverb says, but rather splendid friends in this great human community of language.

paraoxytonic: with the main stress on the next-to-last syllable of a word.

Vérde qué té quiéro vérde (stressed syllables marked, transla-tion, "Green. How I want you green"): the opening line of a famous poem by Federico García Lorca and an illustration of stress falling on oxytonic and paraoxy-tonic syllables.

were disappeared: although *dis-appear* is generally an intransitive verb that cannot take a direct object or be used in the passive voice, Chileans and Spanish speakers from other countries with repressive political regimes began using this "incorrect" grammatical construction to refer to individuals who disappeared and were presumed dead after being taken into custody by the authorities, often for no valid reason. The expression is now used in many languages, includ-ing English.

cordillera: mountain ranges consisting of more or less parallel chains of peaks.

To conclude her essay, Agosín defines translators as "splendid friends." What other argument of definition can you find in this piece? Chapter 9 details the variety and power of arguments of definition.

LINK TO P. 249

Cordillera in Torres del Paine National Park, Chile

English

MARJORIE AGOSÍN Translated by Monica Bruno

I discovered that English
is too skinny,
functional,
precise,
too correct,   5
meaning
only one thing.
Too much wrath,
too many lawyers and sinister policemen,
too many deans at schools for small females,   10
in the Anglo-Saxon language.

II

In contrast Spanish
has so many words to say come with me friend,
make love to me on
the *césped,* the *grama,* the *pasto.*[1]   15
Let's go party,[2]
at dusk, at night, at sunset.
Spanish
loves
the unpredictable, it is   20
dementia,
all windmills° and velvet.

III

Spanish
is simple and baroque,

Don Quijote after a failed joust with a windmill. Standing at his side is his faithful servant, Sancho Panza.

windmills: an allusion to Don Quijote (see note on next page), who tilted at windmills with his lance, imagining them to be giants.

---

[1] All three words mean "grass" in English.

[2] The Spanish version of this poem uses two phrases that mean "to party": *de juerga* and *de fiesta.*

a palace of nobles and beggars,   25
it fills itself with silences and the breaths of dragonflies.
Neruda's° verses
saying "I could write the saddest verses
tonight,"
or Federico° swimming underwater through the greenest of greens. 30

IV

Spanish
is Don Quijote° maneuvering,
Violeta Parra° grateful
spicy, tasty, fragrant
the rumba, the salsa, the cha-cha.   35
There are so many words
to say
naive dreamers
and impostors.
There are so many languages in our   40
language: Quechua,° Aymará,° Rosas chilensis,° Spanglish.°

(Pablo) Neruda (1904–1973): the pen name of the Nobel Prize–winning Chilean poet, politician, and diplomat, considered by many the finest Latin American poet of the twentieth century.

Federico (García Lorca) (1898–1936): a Spanish poet and playwright. A sympathizer with leftist causes and a homosexual, Lorca was executed by a Nationalist firing squad in the Spanish Civil War. He wrote "Verde, que te quiero verde," cited by Agosín in her essay.

Don Quijote (also spelled Quixote): the hero of Miguel de Cervantes's satiric novel of the same name, originally published in two volumes in 1605 and 1615. Quijote is a knight who, after reading too many courtly romances, goes off to find adventure. Quijote's name and the adjective *quixotic* are often applied to someone who, inspired by high (but often false) ideals, pursues an impossible task.

Violeta Parra (1917–1967): a Chilean folksinger most often associated with "La Nueva Canción," a style of Latin American popular music much influenced by folk traditions. Her best-known work is perhaps "Gracias à la vida" ("Thanks to Life").

Quechua: the language of the former Inca empire and the major indigenous language of the central Andes today.

Aymará: one of the major indigenous languages of Bolivia.

Rosas chilensis: Latin species name for a rose indigenous to Chile.

Spanglish: a popular label for the practice of switching between Spanish and English within a conversation or sentence, as many bilingual Hispanics do when they speak with other bilinguals.

V

I love the imperfections of
Spanish,
the language takes shape in my hand:
the sound of drums and waves,   45
the Caribbean in the radiant foam of the sun,
are delirious upon my lips.
English has fallen short for me,
it signifies business,
law   50
and inhibition,
never the crazy, clandestine,
clairvoyance of
love.

RESPOND.

1. Why does Agosín write only in Spanish? How do her reasons for using Spanish compare with those of Cisneros? How does she regard using Spanish as relating to her ancestry as a Jew?

2. What sort of experiences did Agosín have while trying to learn English? How typical do you think her experiences were? In other words, how do Americans who are native speakers of English treat nonnative speakers of English? How did Spanish represent a source of strength and consolation to Agosín during the period when she was learning English?

3. What does Spanish represent for Agosín? Why would it represent these things for her?

4. As the selections by Cisneros and Agosín make clear, for many Americans whose ancestors can be traced somehow to the Spanish-speaking world, to lose Spanish would be to lose a fundamental part of their identity as individuals and as members of larger groups. Using these texts, perhaps personal experience, and perhaps discussions you have with people who claim to be bilingual or bidialectal (that is, to speak a dialect of English other than Standard English, the variety expected and rewarded at school), **write an essay** in which you seek to define the role of language(s) in the creation of individual and group identity. (For a discussion of arguments of definition, see Chapter 9.)

▼ This selection, an excerpt from Funny in Farsi: A Memoir of Growing Up Iranian in America (2003), is Firoozeh Dumas's often hilarious account of what happens when language and cultures come into contact and often collide as they inevitably do in the children of immigrants. (By the way, Farsi is another name for the Persian language, which is the most widely spoken language in Iran.) In "The 'F Word,'" Dumas describes how Americans in general deal (or fail to deal) with names from languages unfamiliar to them. Dumas explains how dealing with this situation is part of the immigrant experience for those from many language backgrounds. As you read, note how she employs humor and figurative language, using the latter even as a structural device.

The "F Word"

FIROOZEH DUMAS

My cousin's name, Farbod, means "Greatness." When he moved to America, all the kids called him "Farthead." My brother Farshid ("He Who Enlightens") became "Fartshit." The name of my friend Neggar means "Beloved," although it can be more accurately translated as "She Whose Name Almost Incites Riots." Her brother Arash ("Giver") initially couldn't understand why every time he'd say his name, people would laugh and ask him if it itched.

All of us immigrants knew that moving to America would be fraught with challenges, but none of us thought that our names would be such an obstacle. How could our parents have ever imagined that someday we would end up in a country where monosyllabic names reign supreme, a land where "William" is shortened to "Bill," where "Susan" becomes "Sue," and "Richard" somehow evolves into "Dick"? America is a great country, but nobody without a mask and a cape has a z in his name. And have Americans ever realized the great scope of the guttural sounds they're missing? Okay, so it has to do with linguistic roots, but I do believe this would be a richer country if all Americans could do a little tongue aerobics and learn to pronounce "kh," a sound more commonly associated in this culture with phlegm, or "gh," the sound usually made by actors in the final moments of a choking scene. It's like adding a few new spices to the kitchen pantry. Move over, cinnamon and nutmeg, make way for cardamom° and sumac.°

cardamom: a spice commonly used in the Middle East, South Asia, and East Asia.

sumac: a dark red, sour-tasting spice used in many Middle Eastern cuisines.

751

Exotic analogies aside, having a foreign name in this land of Joes and Marys is a pain in the spice cabinet. When I was twelve, I decided to simplify my life by adding an American middle name. This decision serves as proof that sometimes simplifying one's life in the short run only complicates it in the long run.

My name, Firoozeh, chosen by my mother, means "Turquoise" in Farsi. In America, it means "Unpronounceable" or "I'm Not Going to Talk to You Because I Cannot Possibly Learn Your Name and I Just Don't Want to Have to Ask You Again and Again Because You'll Think I'm Dumb or You Might Get Upset or Something." My father, incidentally, had wanted to name me Sara. I do wish he had won that argument.

To strengthen my decision to add an American name, I had just finished 5 fifth grade in Whittier, where all the kids incessantly called me "Ferocious." That summer, my family moved to Newport Beach, where I looked forward to starting a new life. I wanted to be a kid with a name that didn't draw so much attention, a name that didn't come with a built-in inquisition as to when and why I had moved to America and how was it that I spoke English without an accent and was I planning on going back and what did I think of America?

My last name didn't help any. I can't mention my maiden name, because:

"Dad, I'm writing a memoir."

"Great! Just don't mention our name."

Suffice it to say that, with eight letters, including a z, and four syllables, my last name is as difficult and foreign as my first. My first and last name together generally served the same purpose as a high brick wall. There was one exception to this rule. In Berkeley, and only in Berkeley, my name drew people like flies to baklava. These were usually people named Amaryllis or Chrysanthemum, types who vacationed in Costa Rica and to whom lentils described a type of burger. These folks were probably not the pride of Poughkeepsie, but they were refreshingly nonjudgmental.

When I announced to my family that I wanted to add an American name, 10 they reacted with their usual laughter. Never one to let mockery or good judgment stand in my way, I proceeded to ask for suggestions. My father suggested "Fifi." Had I had a special affinity for French poodles or been considering a career in prostitution, I would've gone with that one. My mom suggested "Farah," a name easier than "Firoozeh" yet still Iranian. Her reasoning made sense, except that Farrah Fawcett was at the height of her popularity and I didn't want to be associated with somebody whose poster hung in every postpubescent boy's bedroom. We couldn't think of any American names beginning with F, so we moved on to J, the first letter of our last name. I don't know why we limited ourselves to names beginning with my initials, but it made sense at that moment, perhaps by the logic employed moments before bungee jumping. I finally chose the name "Julie" mainly for its simplicity. My brothers, Farid and Farshid, thought that adding an American name was totally stupid. They later became Fred and Sean.

That same afternoon, our doorbell rang. It was our new next-door neighbor, a friendly girl my age named Julie. She asked me my name and after a moment of hesitation, I introduced myself as Julie. "What a coincidence!" she said. I didn't mention that I had been Julie for only half an hour.

Thus I started sixth grade with my new, easy name and life became infinitely simpler. People actually remembered my name, which was an entirely refreshing new sensation. All was well until the Iranian Revolution,° when I found myself with a new set of problems. Because I spoke English without an accent and was known as Julie, people assumed I was American. This meant that I was often privy to their real feelings about those "damn I-raynians." It was like having those X-ray glasses that let you see people undressed, except that what I was seeing was far uglier than people's underwear. It dawned on me that these people would have probably never invited me to their house had they known me as Firoozeh. I felt like a fake.

When I went to college, I eventually went back to using my real name. All was well until I graduated and started looking for a job. Even though I had graduated with honors from UC–Berkeley, I couldn't get a single interview. I was guilty of being a humanities major, but I began to suspect that there was more to my problems. After three months of rejections, I added "Julie" to my résumé. Call it coincidence, but the job offers started coming in. Perhaps it's the same kind of coincidence that keeps African Americans from getting cabs in New York.

Once I got married, my name became Julie Dumas. I went from having an identifiably "ethnic" name to having ancestors who wore clogs. My family and non-American friends continued calling me Firoozeh, while my co-workers and American friends called me Julie. My life became one big knot, especially when friends who knew me as Julie met friends who knew me as Firoozeh. I felt like those characters in soap operas who have an evil twin. The two, of course, can never be in the same room, since they're played by the same person, a struggling actress who wears a wig to play one of the twins and dreams of moving on to bigger and better roles. I couldn't blame my mess on a screenwriter; it was my own doing.

Iranian Revolution: the series of events, beginning in 1979, that transformed Iran from a constitutional monarchy to a populist Islamic theocracy, first ruled by Ayatollah Khomeini. Americans associate the Revolution with the holding of 66 American hostages at the U.S. embassy in Tehran for a period of 444 days (1979–1981).

Humor unites this book excerpt. How does Dumas use humor to increase the appeal of her argument? See Chapter 2 for a discussion of how humor works in argument.

.... LINK TO P. 48

I decided to untangle the knot once and for all by going back to my real 15 name. By then, I was a stay-at-home mom, so I really didn't care whether people remembered my name or gave me job interviews. Besides, most of the people I dealt with were in diapers and were in no position to judge. I was also living in Silicon Valley, an area filled with people named Rajeev, Avishai, and Insook.

Every once in a while, though, somebody comes up with a new permutation and I am once again reminded that I am an immigrant with a foreign name. I recently went to have blood drawn for a physical exam. The waiting room for blood work at our local medical clinic is in the basement of the building, and no matter how early one arrives for an appointment, forty coughing, wheezing people have gotten there first. Apart from reading *Golf Digest* and *Popular Mechanics,* there isn't much to do except guess the number of contagious diseases represented in the windowless room. Every ten minutes, a name is called and everyone looks to see which cough matches that name. As I waited patiently, the receptionist called out, "Fritzy, Fritzy!" Everyone looked around, but no one stood up. Usually, if I'm waiting to be called by someone who doesn't know me, I will respond to just about any name starting with an F. Having been called Froozy, Frizzy, Fiorucci, and Frooz and just plain "Uhhhh . . . ," I am highly accommodating. I did not, however, respond to "Fritzy" because there is, as far as I know, no t in my name. The receptionist tried again, "Fritzy, Fritzy DumbAss." As I stood up to this most linguistically original version of my name, I could feel all eyes upon me. The room was momentarily silent as all of these sick people sat united in a moment of gratitude for their own names.

Despite a few exceptions, I have found that Americans are now far more willing to learn new names, just as they're far more willing to try new ethnic foods. Of course, some people just don't like to learn. One mom at my children's school adamantly refused to learn my "impossible" name and instead settled on calling me "F Word." She was recently transferred to New York where, from what I've heard, she might meet an immigrant or two and, who knows, she just might have to make some room in her spice cabinet.

RESPOND•

1. How might you summarize Firoozeh Dumas's argument? What's its subject—the importance of names, the ways in which Americans have traditionally responded to unfamiliar names, the immigrant experience, all of these?

2. Carefully reread paragraph 12, in which Dumas explains how having an "American" name and speaking English without a foreign accent was like having "X-ray glasses." Is Dumas's portrayal of Americans in this passage and elsewhere in the essay flattering? Humorous? Honest? In this passage, Dumas notes that "people assumed I was American." What definition of "American" must she (and those she writes about) be assuming? Is such a definition valid, given evidence she presents elsewhere in the essay and the fact that the United States is often called a nation of immigrants? At what point does an immigrant become an American?

3. How would you describe Dumas's use of humor? Find three examples that you especially like, and explain how the humor helps the author achieve her goals. In what ways does Dumas's argument represent satire, with the simultaneous goals of ridiculing and remedying a problematic situation? (For a discussion of the uses of humor in argumentation, see Chapter 2.)

4. How does Dumas use the repeated metaphor of the spice cabinet to help structure her argument? Why is this metaphor an appropriate one, given her topic? How does the metaphor permit her to critique the mother who called her "F Word" (paragraph 17)?

5. **Write a rhetorical analysis** of Dumas's argument that focuses on evaluating the contribution of humor to its overall effect. One way to think about the role of humor is to imagine what the essay might have been like if Dumas had tried to write about this subject in a straightforward, serious manner. (For a discussion of how to do a rhetorical analysis, see Chapter 5.)

The Gift of Language

LAN CAO

▶ Lan Cao is currently Boyd Fellow and professor of law at the Marshall-Wythe School of Law at the College of William and Mary. She's the author of Monkey Bridge (1997), the novel from which this excerpt comes. (A monkey bridge is a spindly bamboo bridge used by Vietnamese peasants.) The novel recounts the experiences of a young woman who, like Lan Cao, came to the United States fleeing the Vietnam War. Cao herself arrived here in 1975.

At this point in the novel the narrator, an adolescent girl, and her mother have moved to the States, having had to leave behind the girl's maternal grandfather—their only other living relative. The girl had arrived before the mother and had stayed with an American colonel her family had befriended while he was in Vietnam. He and his wife are the Uncle Michael and Aunt Mary referred to in the text. This excerpt begins with a comparison of American and Asian markets but quickly moves to more complex topics. As you read, try to put yourself in Lan Cao's position. For some readers, it will be an all too familiar one; for others, it may be an almost unimaginable one.

I discovered soon after my arrival in Falls Church that everything, even the simple business of shopping the American way, unsettled my mother's nerves. From the outside, it had been an ordinary building that held no promises or threats beyond four walls anchored to a concrete parking lot. But inside, the A&P brimmed with unexpected abundance. Built-in metal stands overflowed with giant oranges and grapefruits meticulously arranged into a pyramid. Columns of canned vegetables and fruits stood among multiple shelves as people well rehearsed to the demands of modern shopping meandered through the fluorescent aisles. I remembered the sharp chilled air against my face, the way the hydraulic door made a sucking sound as it closed behind.

My first week in Connecticut with Uncle Michael and Aunt Mary, I thought Aunt Mary was a genius shopper. She appeared to have the sixth sense of a bat and could identify, record, and register every item on sale. She was skilled in the art of coupon shopping—in the American version of Vietnamese haggling, the civil and acceptable mode of getting the customers to think they had gotten a good deal.

The day after I arrived in Farmington, Aunt Mary navigated the cart—and me—through aisles, numbered and categorized, crammed with jars and cardboard boxes, and plucked from them the precise product to match the coupons she carried. I had been astonished that day that the wide range of choices did not disrupt her plan. We had a schedule, I discovered, which Aunt Mary mapped out on a yellow pad, and which we followed, checking off item after item. She called it the science of shopping, the ability to resist the temptations of dazzling packaging. By the time we were through, our cart would be filled to the rim with cans of Coke, the kinds with flip-up caps that made can openers obsolete, in family-size cartons. We had chicken and meat sealed in tight, odorless packages, priced and weighed. We had fruits so beautifully polished and waxed they looked artificial. And for me, we had mangoes and papayas that were still hard and green but which Aunt Mary had handed to me like rare jewels from a now extinct land.

But my mother did not appreciate the exacting orderliness of the A&P. She could not give in to the precision of previously weighed and packaged food,

Bilingual outreach worker helping Vietnamese shoppers in the United States

the bloodlessness of beef slabs in translucent wrappers, the absence of carcasses and pigs' heads. In Saigon, we had only outdoor markets. "Sky markets," they were called, vast, prosperous expanses in the middle of the city where barrels of live crabs and yellow carps and booths of ducks and geese would be stacked side by side with cardboard stands of expensive silk fabric from Hong Kong. It was always noisy there—a voluptuous mix of animal and human sounds that the air itself had assimilated and held. The sharp acrid smell of gutters choked by the monsoon rain. The unambiguous odor of dried horse dung that lingered in the atmosphere, partially camouflaged by the fat, heavy scent of guavas and bananas.

My mother knew the vendors and even the shoppers by name and would 5 take me from stall to stall to expose me to her skills. They were all addicted to each other's oddities. My mother would feign indifference and they would inevitably call out to her. She would heed their call and they would immediately retreat into sudden apathy. They knew my mother's slick bargaining skills, and she, in turn, knew how to navigate with grace through their extravagant prices and rehearsed huffiness. Theirs had been a mating dance, a match of wills.

Toward the center of the market, a man with a spotted boa constrictor coiled around his neck stood and watched day after day over an unruly hodgepodge of hand-dyed cotton shirts, handkerchiefs, and swatches of white muslin; funerals were big business in Vietnam. To the side, in giant paper bags slit with round openings, were canaries and hummingbirds which my mother bought, one hundred at a time, and freed, one by one, into our garden; it was a good deed designed to generate positive karma for the family. My mother, like the country itself, was obsessed with karma. In fact, the Vietnamese word for "please," as in "could you please," means literally "to make good karma." "Could you please pass the butter" becomes "Please make good karma and pass me the butter." My mother would cup each bird in her hand and set it on my head. It was her way of immersing me in a wellspring of karmic charm, and in that swift moment of delight when the bird's wings spread over my head as it contemplated flight, I believed life itself was utterly beautiful and blessed.

Every morning, we drifted from stack to stack, vendor to vendor. There were no road maps to follow—tables full of black market Prell and Colgate were pocketed among vegetable stands one day and jars of medicinal herbs the next. The market was randomly organized, and only the mighty and experienced like my mother could navigate its patternless paths.

But with a sense of neither drama nor calamity, my mother's ability to navigate and decipher simply became undone in our new life. She preferred the improvisation of haggling to the conventional certainty of discount coupons, the primordial messiness and fishmongers' stink of the open-air market to the aroma-free order of individually wrapped fillets.

Now, a mere three and a half years or so after her last call to the sky market, the dreadful truth was simply this: we were going through life in reverse, and I was the one who would help my mother through the hard scrutiny of ordinary suburban life. I would have to forgo the luxury of adolescent experiments and temper tantrums, so that I could scoop my mother out of harm's way and give her sanctuary. Now, when we stepped into the exterior world, I was the one who told my mother what was acceptable or unacceptable behavior.

All children of immigrant parents have experienced these moments. 10 When it first occurs, when the parent first reveals the behavior of a child, is a defining moment. Of course, all children eventually watch their parents' astonishing return to the vulnerability of childhood, but for us the process begins much earlier than expected.

"We don't have to pay the moment we decide to buy the pork. We can put as much as we want in the cart and pay only once, at the checkout counter."

It took a few moments' hesitation for my mother to succumb to the peculiarity of my explanation.

And even though I hesitated to take on the responsibility, I had no other choice. It was not a simple process, the manner in which my mother relinquished motherhood. The shift in status occurred not just in the world but in the safety of our home as well, and it became most obvious when we entered the realm of language. I was like Kiki, my pet bird in Saigon, tongue untwisted and sloughed of its rough and thick exterior. According to my mother, feeding the bird crushed red peppers had caused it to shed its tongue in successive layers and allowed it to speak the language of humans.

Every morning during that month of February 1975, while my mother paced the streets of Saigon and witnessed the country's preparation for imminent defeat, I followed Aunt Mary around the house, collecting words like a beggar gathering rain with an earthen pan. She opened her mouth, and out came a constellation of gorgeous sounds. Each word she uttered was a round stone, with the smoothness of something that had been rubbed and polished by the waves of a warm summer beach. She could swim straight through her syllables. On days when we studied together, I almost convinced myself that we would continue that way forever, playing with the movement of sound itself. I would listen as she tried to inspire me into replicating the "th" sound with the seductive powers of her voice. "Slip the tip of your tongue between your front teeth and pull it back real quick," she would coax and coax. Together, she and I sketched the English language, its curious cadence and rhythm, into the receptive Farmington landscape. Only with Aunt Mary and Uncle Michael could I give myself an inheritance my parents never gave me: the gift of language. The story of English was nothing less than the poetry of sound and motion. To this day, Aunt Mary's voice remains my standard for perfection.

My superior English meant that, unlike my mother and Mrs. Bay, I knew the difference between "cough" and "enough," "bough" and "through," "trough" and "thorough," "dough" and "fought." Once I made it past the fourth or fifth week in Connecticut, the new language Uncle Michael and Aunt Mary were teaching me began gathering momentum, like tumbleweed in a storm. This was my realization: we have only to let one thing go—the language we think in, or the composition of our dream, the grass roots clinging underneath its rocks—and all at once everything goes. It had astonished me, the ease with which continents shift and planets change course, the casual way in which the earth goes about shedding the laborious folds of its memories. Suddenly, out of that difficult space between here and there, English revealed itself to me with the ease of thread unspooled. I began to understand the levity and

Cao uses the personal experience of the narrator to build her story. In what ways can this experience be considered evidence? Chapter 16 examines varieties of evidence, including personal experience.

LINK TO P. 493

Khe Sanh: a remote U.S. Marine base in Vietnam. On January 21, 1968, troops from the North Vietnamese Army attacked the base, starting an eleven-week battle that was one of the most brutal of the Vietnam War.

Tet Offensive: a surprise attack on over a hundred South Vietnamese cities and towns by the North Vietnamese Army in 1968 during the truce declared to celebrate Tet, the Vietnamese New Year. Although many of the 70,000 North Vietnamese troops died and their military was left unstable, the offensive is often considered a public relations defeat for the United States because it made North Vietnam's military seem stronger than many had believed and reduced the American public's willingness to continue the war.

Ho Chi Minh Trail: a complex network of paths, roads, and jungle trails leading from the panhandle of northern Vietnam through Laos and Cambodia and into southern Vietnam. The trail was used throughout the Vietnam War to resupply the North Vietnamese military with food and weaponry, to transport soldiers into South Vietnam, and to launch close-range attacks on South Vietnam.

weight of its sentences. First base, second base, home run. New terminologies were not difficult to master, and gradually the possibility of perfection began edging its way into my life. How did those numerous Chinatowns and Little Italys sustain the will to maintain a distance, the desire to inhabit the edge and margin of American life? A mere eight weeks into Farmington, and the American Dream was exerting a sly but seductive pull.

By the time I left Farmington to be with my mother, I had already created 15 for myself a different, more sacred tongue. Khe Sanh,° the Tet Offensive,° the Ho Chi Minh Trail°—a history as imperfect as my once obviously imperfect English—these were things that had rushed me into the American melting pot. And when I saw my mother again, I was no longer the same person she used to know. Inside my new tongue, my real tongue, was an astonishing new power. For my mother and her Vietnamese neighbors, I became the keeper of the word, the only one with access to the light-world. Like Adam, I had the God-given right to name all the fowls of the air and all the beasts of the field.

The right to name, I quickly discovered, also meant the right to stand guard over language and the right to claim unadulterated authority. Here was a language with an ocean's quiet mystery, and it would be up to me to render its vastness comprehensible to the newcomers around me. My language skill, my ability to decipher the nuances of American life, was what held us firmly in place, night after night, in our Falls Church living room. The ease with which I could fabricate wholly new plot lines from TV made the temptation to invent especially difficult to resist.

And since my mother couldn't understand half of what anyone was saying, television watching, for me, was translating and more. This, roughly, was how things went in our living room:

The Bionic Woman had just finished rescuing a young girl, approximately my age, from drowning in a lake where she'd gone swimming against her mother's wishes. Once out of harm's way, Jaime made the girl promise she'd be more careful next time and listen to her mother.

Translation: the Bionic Woman rescued the girl from drowning in the lake, but commended her for her magnificent deeds, since the girl had heroically jumped into the water to rescue a prized police dog.

"Where's the dog?" my mother would ask. "I don't see him." 20

"He's not there anymore, they took him to the vet right away. Remember?" I sighed deeply.

"Oh," my mother said. "It's strange. Strong girl, Bionic Woman."

The dog that I convinced her existed on the television screen was no more confusing than the many small reversals in logic and the new identities we experienced her first few months in America.

"I can take you in this aisle," a store clerk offered as she unlocked a new register to accommodate the long line of customers. She gestured us to "come over here" with an upturned index finger, a disdainful hook we Vietnamese use to summon dogs and other domestic creatures. My mother did not understand the ambiguity of American hand gestures. In Vietnam, we said "Come here" to humans differently, with our palm up and all four fingers waved in unison—the way people over here waved goodbye. A typical Vietnamese signal beckoning someone to "come here" would prompt, in the United States, a "goodbye," a response completely opposite from the one desired.

"Even the store clerks look down on us," my mother grumbled as we 25 walked home. This was a truth I was only beginning to realize: it was not the enormous or momentous event, but the gradual suggestion of irrevocable and protracted change that threw us off balance and made us know in no uncertain terms that we would not be returning to the familiarity of our former lives.

It was, in many ways, a lesson in what was required to sustain a new identity: it all had to do with being able to adopt a different posture, to reach deep enough into the folds of the earth to relocate one's roots and bend one's body in a new direction, pretending at the same time that the world was the same now as it had been the day before. I strove for the ability to realign my eyes, to shift with a shifting world and convince both myself and the rest of the world into thinking that, if the earth moved and I moved along with it, that motion, however agitated, would be undetectable. The process, which was as surprising as a river reversing course and flowing upstream, was easier said than done.

RESPOND ●

1. What's your initial response to this excerpt from Cao's novel? Given the mother's cultural expectations, which she has brought from Vietnam, is it logical for her to respond as she does? In what senses is Cao forced to parent her mother?

2. How does Cao construct the argument she makes here? What sorts of evidence does she rely on? How does she use language effectively to convey her ideas? (Chapters 7, 16, and 13, respectively, will help you answer these questions.)

3. The tale that Cao tells has been told many times in the writings of immigrants, especially those who arrive in the United States as chil-

dren with parents who speak little or no English. What are the consequences for family life? How does language become a source of power for the child? How does this power disrupt traditional patterns of family life?

4. Cao, like many immigrant children, lost much of her native language—Vietnamese—as well as French, another language widely spoken by educated Vietnamese at that time. (France had colonized Vietnam for many years prior to the war.) The decline in her ability to use these languages had negative repercussions for her relationship with her parents. As she commented in an interview given while she was a visiting law professor at Duke University, "The more educated I became, the more separate I was from my parents. I think that is a very immigrant story." Even native speakers of English often report similar situations in their own lives. Should such separation from one's home community be a necessary consequence of education for native or nonnative speakers of English in the United States? Why or why not? Might there be ways to prevent it? Are there benefits to preventing it? Should such efforts be made? Why? **Write an essay** in which you tackle these questions. Your essay will likely include features of evaluative, causal, and proposal arguments. (For discussions of these, see Chapters 10, 11, and 12, respectively.) If the situation described is unfamiliar to you, you might make a point of interviewing people who know about it firsthand.

Mother Tongue

AMY TAN

I am not a scholar of English or literature. I cannot give you much more than personal opinions on the English language and its variations in this country or others.

I am a writer. And by that definition, I am someone who has always loved language. I am fascinated by language in daily life. I spend a great deal of my time thinking about the power of language—the way it can evoke an emotion, a visual image, a complex idea, or a simple truth. Language is the tool of my trade. And I use them all—all the Englishes I grew up with.

Recently, I was made keenly aware of the different Englishes I do use. I was giving a talk to a large group of people, the same talk I had already given to half a dozen other groups. The nature of the talk was about my writing, my life, and my book, *The Joy Luck Club*. The talk was going along well enough, until I remembered one major difference that made the whole talk sound wrong. My mother was in the room. And it was perhaps the first time she had heard me give a lengthy speech—using the kind of English I have never used with her. I was saying things like, "The intersection of memory upon imagination" and "There is an aspect of my fiction that relates to thus-and-thus"—a speech filled with carefully wrought grammatical phrases, burdened, it suddenly seemed to me, with nominalized forms, past perfect tenses, conditional phrases—all the forms of standard English that I had learned in school and through books, the forms of English I did not use at home with my mother.

Just last week, I was walking down the street with my mother, and I again found myself conscious of the English I was using, the English I do use with her. We were talking about the price of new and used furniture and I heard myself saying this: "Not waste money that way." My husband was with us as well, and he didn't notice any switch in my English. And then I realized why. It's because over the twenty years we've been together I've often used that same kind of English with him, and sometimes he even uses it with me. It has become our language of intimacy, a different sort of English that relates to family talk, the language I grew up with.

So you'll have some idea of what this family talk I heard sounds like, I'll 5 quote what my mother said during a recent conversation which I videotaped and then transcribed. During this conversation, my mother was talking about

◀ Amy Tan, best known for her novels The Joy Luck Club (1989) and The Kitchen God's Wife (1991), writes most often about relationships between Chinese American daughters and their mothers and about each group's struggles with generational and cultural differences. Her work is often praised for its sensitive and realistic rendering of dialogue. During her adolescence, Tan lost her father and her brother to brain tumors. As she recounts, she went on to study English at San Jose State University rather than becoming a neurosurgeon, as her mother had hoped. Tan began as a technical writer but started writing fiction after reading a novel by Louise Erdrich, a Native American writer. This text is a talk Tan gave as part of a panel entitled "Englishes: Whose English Is It Anyway?" at a language symposium in San Francisco in 1989. As you read, try to imagine hearing Tan deliver this speech.

Tan's open, informal style may make you feel as if you're part of a conversation among friends, but her text is carefully prepared in ways that casual conversation is not. See Chapter 13 to learn some of the techniques that Tan uses so effectively.

LINK TO P. 415

a political gangster in Shanghai who had the same last name as her family's, Du, and how the gangster in his early years wanted to be adopted by her family which was rich by comparison. Later, the gangster became more powerful, far richer than my mother's family, and one day showed up at my mother's wedding to pay his respects. Here's what she said in part:

"Du Yusong having business like fruit stand. Like off the street kind. He is Du like Du Zong—but not Tsung-ming Island people. The local people call putong, the river east side, he belong to that side local people. That man want to ask Du Zong father take him in like become own family. Du Zong father wasn't look down on him, but didn't take seriously, until that man big like become mafia. Now important person, very hard to inviting him. Chinese way, came only to show respect, don't stay for dinner. Respect for making big celebration, he shows up. Mean gives lots of respect. Chinese custom. Chinese social life that way. If too important won't have to stay too long. He come to my wedding. I didn't see, I heard it. I gone to boy's side, they have YMCA dinner. Chinese age I was 19."

You should know that my mother's expressive command of English belies how much she actually understands. She reads the *Forbes* report, listens to *Wall Street Week*, converses daily with her stockbroker, reads all of Shirley MacLaine's books with ease—all kinds of things I can't begin to understand. Yet some of my friends tell me they understand fifty percent of what my mother says. Some say they understand eighty to ninety percent. Some say they understand none of it, as if she were speaking pure Chinese. But to me, my mother's English is perfectly clear, perfectly natural. It's my mother tongue. Her language, as I hear it, is vivid, direct, full of observation and imagery. That was the language that helped shape the way I saw things, expressed things, made sense of the world.

Lately, I've been giving more thought to the kind of English my mother speaks. Like others, I have described it to people as "broken" or "fractured" English. But I wince when I say that. It has always bothered me that I can think of no way to describe it other than "broken," as if it were damaged and needed to be fixed, as if it lacked a certain wholeness and soundness. I've heard other terms used, "limited English," for example. But they seem just as bad, as if everything is limited, including people's perception of the limited English speaker.

I know this for a fact, because when I was growing up, my mother's "limited" English limited my perception of her. I was ashamed of her English. I believed that her English reflected the quality of what she had to say. That is, because she expressed them imperfectly her thoughts were imperfect. And I had plenty of empirical evidence to support me: the fact that people in department stores, at banks, and at restaurants did not take her seriously, did not give her good service, pretended not to understand her, or even acted as if they did not hear her.

My mother has long realized the limitations of her English as well. When I 10 was fifteen, she used to have me call people on the phone to pretend I was she. In this guise, I was forced to ask for information or even to complain and yell at people who had been rude to her. One time it was a call to her stockbroker in New York. She had cashed out her small portfolio and it just so happened we were going to go to New York the next week, our very first trip outside California. I had to get on the phone and say in an adolescent voice that was not very convincing, "This is Mrs. Tan."

And my mother was standing in the back whispering loudly, "Why he don't send me check, already two weeks late. So mad he lie to me, losing me money."

And then I said in perfect English, "Yes, I'm getting rather concerned. You had agreed to send the check two weeks ago, but it hasn't arrived."

Then she began to talk more loudly, "What he want, I come to New York tell him front of his boss, you cheating me?" And I was trying to calm her down, make her be quiet, while telling the stockbroker, "I can't tolerate any more excuses. If I don't receive the check immediately, I am going to have to speak to your manager when I'm in New York next week." And sure enough, the following week there we were in front of this astonished stockbroker, and I was sitting there redfaced and quiet, and my mother, the real Mrs. Tan, was shouting at his boss in her impeccable broken English.

We used a similar routine just five days ago, for a situation that was far less humorous. My mother had gone to the hospital for an appointment, to find out about a benign brain tumor a CAT scan had revealed a month ago. She said she had spoken very good English, her best English, no mistakes. Still, she said, the hospital did not apologize when they said they had lost the CAT scan and she had come for nothing. She said they did not seem to have any sympathy when she told them she was anxious to know the exact diagnosis since her husband and son had both died of

Author Amy Tan and her mother

brain tumors. She said they would not give her any more information until the next time and she would have to make another appointment for that. So she said she would not leave until the doctor called her daughter. She wouldn't budge. And when the doctor finally called her daughter, me, who spoke in perfect English—lo and behold—we had assurances the CAT scan would be found, promises that a conference call on Monday would be held, and apologies for any suffering my mother had gone through for a most regrettable mistake.

I think my mother's English almost had an effect on limiting my possibili- 15 ties in life as well. Sociologists and linguists probably will tell you that a person's developing language skills are more influenced by peers. But I do think that the language spoken in the family, especially in immigrant families which are more insular, plays a large role in shaping the language of the child. And I believe that it affected my results on achievement tests, IQ tests, and the SAT. While my English skills were never judged as poor, compared to math, English could not be considered my strong suit. In grade school, I did moderately well, getting perhaps Bs, sometimes B+s in English, and scoring perhaps in the sixtieth or seventieth percentile on achievement tests. But those scores were not good enough to override the opinion that my true abilities lay in math and science, because in those areas I achieved As and scored in the ninetieth percentile or higher.

This was understandable. Math is precise; there is only one correct answer. Whereas, for me at least, the answers on English tests were always a judgment call, a matter of opinion and personal experience. Those tests were constructed around items like fill-in-the-blank sentence completion, such as "Even though Tom was _____, Mary thought he was _____." And the correct answer always seemed to be the most bland combinations of thoughts, for example, "Even though Tom was shy, Mary thought he was charming," with the grammatical structure "even though" limiting the correct answer to some sort of semantic opposites, so you wouldn't get answers like "Even though Tom was foolish, Mary thought he was ridiculous." Well, according to my mother, there were very few limitations as to what Tom could have been, and what Mary might have thought of him. So I never did well on tests like that.

The same was true with word analogies, pairs of words, in which you were supposed to find some sort of logical, semantic relationship—for example, "sunset" is to "nightfall" as _____ is to _____. And here, you would be presented with a list of four possible pairs, one of which showed the same kind of relationship: "red" is to "stoplight," "bus" is to "arrival," "chills" is to "fever," "yawn" is to "boring." Well, I could never think that way. I knew what the tests were asking, but I could not block out of my mind the images already created by the first pair, "sunset is to nightfall"—and I would see a burst of colors against a darkening sky, the moon rising, the lowering of a curtain of stars. And all the other pairs of words—red, bus, stoplight, boring—just threw up a mass of confusing images, making it impossible for me to sort out something as logical as saying: "A sunset precedes nightfall" is the same as "a chill precedes a fever." The only way I would have gotten that answer right would have been to imagine an associative situation, for example, my being disobedient and staying out past sunset, catching a chill at night, which turns into feverish pneumonia as punishment, which indeed did happen to me.

I have been thinking about all this lately, about my mother's English, about achievement tests. Because lately I've been asked, as a writer, why there are not more Asian-Americans represented in American literature. Why are there few Asian-Americans enrolled in creative writing programs? Why do so many Chinese students go into engineering? Well, these are broad sociological questions I can't begin to answer. But I have noticed in surveys—in fact, just last week—that Asian students, as a whole, always do significantly better on math achievement tests than in English. And this makes me think that there are other Asian-American students whose English spoken in the home might also be described as "broken" or "limited." And perhaps they also have teachers who are steering them away from writing and into math and science, which is what happened to me.

Fortunately, I happen to be rebellious in nature, and enjoy the challenge of disproving assumptions made about me. I became an English major my first year in college after being enrolled as pre-med. I started writing nonfiction as a freelancer the week after I was told by my former boss that writing was my worst skill and I should hone my talents toward account management.

But it wasn't until 1985 that I finally began to write fiction. And at first I 20 wrote using what I thought to be wittily crafted sentences, sentences that would finally prove I had mastery over the English language. Here's an example from the first draft of a story that later made its way into *The Joy Luck Club*, but without this line: "That was my mental quandary in its nascent state." A terrible line, which I can barely pronounce.

Fortunately, for reasons I won't get into today, I later decided I should envision a reader for the stories I would write. And the reader I decided upon was my mother, because these were stories about mothers. So with this reader in mind—and in fact, she did read my early drafts—I began to write stories using all the Englishes I grew up with: the English I spoke to my mother, which for lack of a better term might be described as "simple"; the English she used with me, which for lack of a better term might be described as "broken"; my translation of her Chinese, which could certainly be described as "watered down"; and what I imagined to be her translation of her Chinese if she could speak in perfect English, her internal language, and for that I sought to preserve the essence, but not either an English or a Chinese structure. I wanted to capture what language ability tests can never reveal: her intent, her passion, her imagery, the rhythms of her speech and the nature of her thoughts.

Apart from what any critic had to say about my writing, I knew I had succeeded where it counted when my mother finished reading my book and gave me her verdict: "So easy to read."

RESPOND •

1. How have Tan's attitudes toward her mother's English changed over the years? Why? In what ways does Tan describe a situation that probably is faced by most children of immigrants? In what ways is this situation like or unlike the embarrassment that children generally feel about their parents at some point in their growing up?

2. Why is Tan suspicious of language ability tests? What are her complaints? What sorts of evidence does she offer? Do you agree or disagree with her argument? Why?

3. Tan's text was written to be read aloud by the author herself. In what ways might this fact be important? (For a discussion of the features of arguments to be heard, see Chapter 15.) What would it be like, for example, to have heard Tan deliver this text? How would such an experience have been different from reading it on the page? Had Tan written the piece to be read silently by strangers—as her novels are, for example—how might she have altered it? Why?

4. What does Tan mean when she claims that she uses "all the Englishes [she] grew up with" (paragraph 2)? What are these Englishes? What are her problems in giving them labels? Do you agree with Tan's implied argument that we should use all our Englishes and use them proudly? Why or why not? Are there any limits to this position? If so, what are they? **Write an essay** evaluating Tan's position. (In preparing for this assignment, you might think about the Englishes that you know and use. Do they all have recognizable names or convenient labels? Do you associate them with certain people or places or activities? What does each represent to you? About you? Do you have ambivalent feelings about any of them? Why? For a discussion of evaluative arguments, see Chapter 10.)

Making a Visual Argument:
Public Service Announcements in Spanish

Here, we present two public service announcements in Spanish, both posters or ads for magazines, that are ultimately comments on bilingualism in the United States. The first, "En la comunidad latina tenemos una cultura de silencio," was created by the National Institute of Mental Health (NIMH), part of the U.S. Department of Health and Human Services. NIMH focuses on supporting research about mental and behavioral disorders, advocating for people who suffer from them, and raising awareness of them in the general population. This poster was part of a 2005 campaign to raise awareness about depression in men. In addition to this poster, which we found at http://nimh.nih.gov, the campaign included public service announcements for broadcast media, print publications, and a Web site.

The second ad, "No eres un superheroe," was created for the Agency for Healthcare Research and Quality (AHRQ), another part of the U.S. Department of Health and Human Services, by the Ad Council. The Council, a private, nonprofit organization, seeks to use the talents and resources of those in communication and advertising to create public service advertisements for various media. This ad campaign was launched in March 2008; information about it, including a justification for it, can be found at http://www.adcouncil.org/default.aspx?id=489.

As you study these visual arguments, consider the relationship between choice of language and intended audience.

"En la comunidad
latina tenemos una
cultura de silencio".

—Rodolfo Palma-Lulión, Estudiante Universitario

Idiomatic translation:
"In the Latino community, we have a culture of
silence."
—Rodolfo Palma-Lulión, University Student

**Real Men. Real Depression.
Estos hombres son reales.
La depresión también.**

"Nadie tiene depresión en la comunidad
latina. En la comunidad latina tenemos
una cultura de silencio en ciertos
aspectos de nuestra vida. Especialmente
como inmigrantes trabajamos duro.
Eso es lo que se espera. Y decir que
uno tiene depresión es como dejar que
la vida te gane". La depresión es una
enfermedad real que se puede tratar
con éxito. Para más información, llame al
1-866-227-6464, visite www.nimh.nih.gov,
o contacte a su médico.

**Hay que tener valor para
solicitar ayuda. Rodolfo lo hizo.**

NIMH
National Institute
of Mental Health

National Institutes of Health

These men are real. So is depression.
"No one in the Latino community suffers from
depression. In the Latino community, we have a
culture of silence about certain aspects of our life.
Especially, as immigrants, we work hard. That's
what's expected. And to say that you're depressed
is like letting life defeat you." Depression is a real
illness that can be treated successfully. For more
information, call 1-866-227-6464, visit www.nimh
.nih.gov, or contact your doctor.

You have to be brave to ask for help. Rodolfo
did it.

Think carefully about the photographs
included with this poster and the one
on the next page. What other images
might make effective arguments
here? See Chapter 14 for more on
visual arguments.

LINK TO P. 441

NO ERES UN SUPERHEROE

VISITA A TU DOCTOR
REGULARMENTE.
POR TU SALUD Y POR TU FAMILIA.

Encuentra más información en **www.ahrq.gov**

Idiomatic translation:
You're not a superhero.
Visit your doctor regularly.
For your health and for your family.
Get more information at www.ahrq.go

1. Both of these posters use Spanish, either predominantly or completely. Why? How do language choice and targeted audience interact in these advertisements? Many Hispanic Americans are highly bilingual, although some of them prefer English, some prefer Spanish, and others have no preference. On the other hand, some Hispanic Americans speak little or no English, and still others speak little or no Spanish. How does this situation complicate efforts to create advertisements that target the Hispanic community?

2. Evaluate each of these ads as an argument. In *"En la comunidad latina tenemos una cultura de silencio,"* what role does the personal testimony of Rodolfo Palma-Lulión play in the advertisement? Does it matter that he is a university student? Why or why not? Why might the designers have included the phrase "Real Men. Real Depression" in English? In *"No eres un superheroe,"* what are the links between the text and the visual images?

3. Some might criticize these U.S. government agencies or the Ad Council for producing advertisements or running programs in any language other than English. What arguments might they use for such criticisms? What costs, direct or indirect, might there be if U.S. government agencies do *not* produce advertisements or design programs in languages other than English? (If you're having trouble with this question, you might visit the Web site for the Ad Council ad for the AHRQ, which explains the need for an ad campaign focused on this topic for this audience.)

4. Bilingualism is once again a part of daily life in a growing number of public places in the United States, much as it was in many places during periods before World War I in particular. Thus, we find that billboards in many cities, signs and flyers in many neighborhoods, and ads in certain magazines are sometimes in a language other than English or are bilingual in some way. Find two advertisements (which could include public service announcements) that include a language other than English, and then **write an evaluative essay** in which you offer a rhetorical analysis of the two ads, comparing them and evaluating which is more likely to be effective for the intended audience, which you'll have to define. (It's worth remembering that billboards in Spanish advertising a particular brand of Mexican beer near many colleges may be targeted more at students who know no Spanish other than *cerveza* than they are at those who are fluent in the language.) If your skills in other languages are limited, you may need to seek a classmate's help in translating the ads. Be sure to include copies of the advertisements you analyze in or with your evaluative essay. (For discussions of rhetorical analysis and evaluative arguments, see Chapters 5 and 10, respectively.)

This selection documents the life of Sao Yee Cha, a Hmong woman who moved to Portland, Oregon, in 1978 after spending two years in a refugee camp in Thailand following the aftermath of the Vietnam War. The Hmong are a Southeast Asian ethnic group that traditionally lived as farmers in isolated mountainous regions of Laos. Early in the 1960s, the U.S. Central Intelligence Agency recruited many Hmong men to fight in what later became known as "The Secret War" against communists in neighboring Vietnam. (Between 12,000 and 40,000 Hmong are estimated to have died in these efforts. The name of the war derives from the fact that the United States did not publicly acknowledge its role in the Laotian civil war until later.) Following the U.S. withdrawal from Vietnam in 1975 and the Communist takeover of Laos, the Hmong were targeted for persecution, and many fled to refugee camps in neighboring countries. Today, the United States is home to the largest Hmong community outside of Asia.

This article appeared in September 2008 in the Portland newspaper The Oregonian *in its weekly series "Life Story," which reports on the life of an everyday person from the local community who has recently passed away. It was written by Amy Martinez Starke, a staff writer for the paper. As you read this selection, ask yourself what sort of argument an obituary represents. Also consider how Sao Yee Cha's experiences of bilingualism were similar to and different from those recounted by other writers in this chapter.*

Starke does not rely on a great deal of figurative language, but her obituary is gracefully and stylishly written. Take a look at the discussion of sentence structure and punctuation in Chapter 13 for more on how to use style in argument.

LINK TO P. 421

Hmong Elder Didn't Forget the Old Ways

AMY MARTINEZ STARKE

By 7, she was fetching water from the river. By 14, she was married, and by 21, she was raising livestock, harvesting rice, and raising three small children while her husband was off with other Hmong recruits waging guerrilla war against the Viet Cong.

For years, Sao Yee Cha cared alone for their farm and children. She considered this her duty as wife to Sua Lee as he rose through the ranks to captain.

When the Communists seized power and with her husband marked for execution, the family, now including seven surviving children, set out for a refugee camp on foot through the jungle.

They spent more than two years in a squalid north Thailand camp with thousands of other refugees. In 1978, when Sao Yee was 40 and pregnant with her last child, a church in Portland offered to sponsor the family.

Sao Yee foresaw one big problem: She had heard there was no rice in America, only bread. When the family got off the plane and Coke and sandwiches were placed in front of them, their worst fears were confirmed. "How can we live without rice?" Sao Yee cried.

She was stunned at the sight of so many blue eyes and had to learn how

5

773

Sao Yee Cha in a Thai refugee camp

to ride an escalator in her long Laotian skirt.

The woman who had been able to navigate minefields in Laos found she faced still more challenges resettling in an apartment near Roosevelt High School.

It was a cold November when they arrived. They had to learn how to turn on the stove and how to use a shower and a Western toilet.

She gave birth to her last child and named him Emanuel° for the hospital where he was born in Portland.

Fred Meyer° took the place of their 10 farm, and she was relieved to learn that there was rice in America. But learning to shop for that rice was difficult.

Then she had to sit in a classroom studying English. Sao Yee had never been to school.

Within four months of their arrival, her husband, a highly decorated veteran, clan elder, shaman° and traditional healer, got a job at the Hilton Portland. Sao Yee got a job picking strawberries, green beans and cucumbers. She sewed bags for potatoes and onions, and she made water hoses.

She saw her children through Portland public schools and through eight marriages to fellow Hmong; she paid four dowries° and collected four dowries.

She tried to learn to drive. But that ended quickly after she hit a telephone pole. She grew to like the Tri-Met° bus system, which brought her independence. Although she could barely read, she could describe the way to Value Village° by visual landmarks.

In 1984, Sao Yee insisted the family 15 buy a house on Southeast Woodstock and 57th instead of renting.

In 1997, they moved to a 10-acre farm in Woodburn.° Sao Yee—now known as Grandma—could raise cows and pigs, silkie chickens and Muscovy ducks, long green beans, hot peppers and green mustard. Grandma and her husband lived with their oldest son's family.

Each morning early, Grandma got up early to cook, pack lunches and do laundry. Men weren't allowed in her kitchen.

"This is my role; this is what I do," she insisted.

She used her cell phone to call friends. For hours, she and those friends were glued to the TV watching Hmong DVDs she bought by the dozens. They were mostly love stories and soap opera dramas, always with Hmong folk songs.

And ever since arriving in Port- 20 land, she followed pro wrestling; she got to go to Wrestlemania in Seattle

---

Emanuel: Legacy Emanuel Hospital and Health Center, a private hospital in Portland, Oregon, founded in 1912 by Lutherans.

Fred Meyer: a grocery and department store founded in 1922 in Portland, Oregon, and now a division of the Kroger Company.

shaman: in many traditional belief systems, an individual who has the knowledge and power to serve as intermediary between this world and the spirit world.

dowry: in many traditional societies, the money, property, or goods that a bride brings to her husband. The American custom of having the bride's family pay for the wedding developed from this practice.

Tri-Met: The Tri-Country Metropolitan Transportation District of Oregon, Portland's public transportation system.

Value Village: a for-profit chain of secondhand thrift stores.

Woodburn: an agricultural community 30 miles south of Portland.

Sao Yee Cha and one of her grandchildren

Sao Yee Cha in traditional Hmong dress

Sao Yee Cha at home in America

once. She liked Las Vegas and Spirit Mountain,° but would gamble no more than $30.

She flew to Minnesota to visit two daughters and took the Greyhound to California to visit another daughter, fretting about the housework left undone back home.

At first, she thought the family's stay in America might be temporary. But gradually she realized this was home and was glad to be here.

Still, 30 years in this country did not dim her dismay at seeing her young ones growing up with new ways of thinking.

The tiny woman who had borne so much now had to bear the burden of enforcing the old ways.

She lectured her daughters and 25 daughters-in-law to respect their husbands' authority. When they resisted and told her of the new ways, she cried.

It hurt her to see her grandchildren accept American culture. "Girls don't court boys!" she cried. "In our tradition, we don't do that! Don't disgrace your family!"

She lamented the loss of a world in which all knew their place, their role according to age and gender and clan.

Grandma Sao Yee, who suffered from several health problems, died suddenly at age 70, two weeks after visiting her daughters in Minneapolis, where she took in the Mall of America.

She never went back to Laos.

At the traditional Hmong mourning ritual, shamans, through ancient words and tunes, retraced her life's journey and guided her soul back to the spot where her placenta° was buried, there to be reunited with her ancestors and then to be reborn. 30

Spirit Mountain: a casino in Grande Ronde, Oregon, operated by the Confederated Tribes of the Grand Ronde Community of Oregon.

placenta: an internal organ that connects the developing fetus with its mother's body; it is expelled shortly after the birth of the child. The placenta is generally incinerated in the West, but in many of the world's cultures is thought to have special powers or value and thus may be buried or disposed of in a special, often ceremonial, fashion.

RESPOND•

1. How is Sao Yee Cha's bilingualism like and unlike that of others whose experiences have been described in this chapter?

2. What sort of occasion gives rise to an obituary—forensic, deliberative, or epideictic? (The answer may be more complex than it seems. For a discussion of occasions for argument, see Chapter 1.)

3. In what ways do the illustrations that accompany this selection form part of the argument? What do they contribute to the force of the argument? (For a discussion of visual arguments, see Chapter 14.)

4. **Write an essay** in which you compare and contrast bilingualism in America as experienced by two or more of the individuals whose lives, real or fictional, are recounted in this chapter. You may wish to compare the lives of those who were or might have been exiles or refugees, to focus on two or more individuals who discuss childhood memories tied to bilingualism or a language other than English, to examine the challenges faced by two or more as they sought to be part of life in a country that generally identifies itself as being monolingual, or to explore another topic. This essay may employ aspects of factual, definitional, evaluative, and causal arguments as well as rhetorical analysis. (For discussions of these, see Chapters 8–11 and 5, respectively.)

5. Based on what you have learned from readings in this chapter or from other experiences that you have had, interview one or more bilinguals, and **write an essay** in which you analyze their experiences. (Chapter 16 presents information on interviews, and Chapter 20 presents information on using sources from field research.) As in the previous questions, this essay may employ aspects of factual, definitional, evaluative, and causal arguments as well as rhetorical analysis. (For discussions of these, see Chapters 8–11 and 5, respectively.)

24
Why Worry about Food and Water?

A major change in American culture over the past decade or so has been an increasing interest in (and some would claim obsession with) food and water. Until the economic downturn began in 2008, at least, Americans increasingly ate meals in (or took them out from) restaurants, and they continue to be concerned with where their food comes from, whether and how it is processed, and how it is prepared. Turn on cable television at any hour of the day or night, and you can find someone demonstrating how to prepare food. During the same period, bottled water became ubiquitous in American life. Everywhere you go, people are likely to be carrying bottles of water, something that simply wasn't the case a decade ago.

How might we understand these changes? Or as award-winning cookbook author and blogger Mark Bittman asks in this chapter's first selection, "Why Take Food Seriously?" The question that serves as the title of his magazine article challenges you to find answers.

The next two selections provide academic perspectives on the issue. Wynne Wright and Gerad Middendorf's "Introduction: Fighting over Food—Change in the Agrifood System" offers an overview of how complex the food and agricultural system is and how it continues to become more so. This essay is an excerpt from the introduction to a 2008 book they edited, *The Fight over Food: Producers, Consumers, and Activists Challenge the Global Food System*. An anthropologist writing for his colleagues, Solomon H. Katz offers a global perspective on a related issue, the causes and consequences of the world food crisis. These two selections remind us of the larger context for things happening in North America.

The next three are less formal and more specific. In a blog posting, "conscious living counselor" Kathy Freston contends that "Vegetarian Is the New Prius." As you evaluate her comparison and reasoning, give some thought to why all Amercians don't drive Priuses and why they haven't all become vegetarians. In a largely visual argument, illustrator Claire Ironside compares and contrasts the carbon footprint that is associated with eating apples and oranges where she lives. Next comes Wikipedia's entry on "Local Food." Launched in 2001, Wikipedia heralded a major change in the creation and diffusion of information in a host of languages about nearly everything. The local food movement argues that food grown near where you live is better for you, the environment, and the world than is food from far away. As you'll see, not everyone agrees.

The next two selections focus on water, specifically the bottled kind. Mark Coleman's review of *Bottlemania: How Water Went on Sale and Why We Bought It* offers an evaluative argument about Elizabeth Royte's 2008 book, while the following selection comes from the concluding chapter of the book itself. As you'll see, Royte appreciates the complex reasons to buy bottled water—and to avoid it. Along with this excerpt, a visual argument from the *New York Times* helps you appreciate the number of plastic bottles created by the bottled water craze in the United States.

The final two selections in the chapter come from *Cook's Country Magazine* and *Cook's Illustrated Magazine*. The first is an evaluation of ready-to-bake dough for chocolate chip cookies, and the second is a recipe for making the real thing from scratch. After you analyze the recipe as an argument, we encourage you to try it. We did, and our students agreed that the folks at *Cook's Illustrated* know what they're talking about. Did you ever think that a chocolate chip cookie could be an argument? Think again.

Although not formally educated in the field, Mark Bittman came to food through journalism and now focuses professionally on cooking at home. He is the author of several award-winning cookbooks, including How to Cook Everything: Simple Recipes for Great Food *(1998; revised edition 2008) and* How to Cook Everything Vegetarian *(2007). He also wrote* Food Matters: A Guide to Conscious Eating with More than Seventy-five Recipes *(2008), a book that seeks to confront many of the issues that are raised by selections in this chapter while also helping people eat good food. Bittman created the weekly cooking column for the New York Times, "The Minimalist," over a decade ago, and he blogs at "Bitten: Mark Bittman on Food" (http://bitten.blogs .nytimes.com). Since 2005, he has often appeared on television talking about food and demonstrating how to cook.*

In this 2008 selection from the New York Times Sunday Magazine's series "The Way We Live Now," Bittman claims that Americans' eating habits are changing, and none too soon for our own good. As you read this selection, try to characterize Bittman's intended audience: what is life like for the audience that Bittman is writing for, what sorts of experiences and knowledge do they have, and what values do they likely hold?

Why Take Food Seriously? Because Your Life Depends on It

MARK BITTMAN

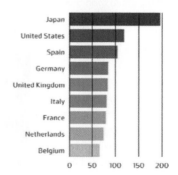

FAST-FOOD NATIONS

Meals eaten out per person, per year, 2005

Source: "The Atlas of Food," by Erik Millstone and Tim Lang.

O ur relationship with food is changing more rapidly than ever, and like many others, I've watched in awe. As a food journalist and author for 30 years, my perspective has been unusual: I've worked with influential people in the field while remaining in frequent contact with my readers, who are some unknowable percentage of the home-cooking, food-obsessed segment of the public.

I've never been more hopeful. (In fact, I was never hopeful at all until recently.) Each year, each month it sometimes seems, there are more signs that convenience, that mid-20th-century curse word, may give way to quality—even what you might call wholesomeness—just before we all turn into the shake-sucking fatties of *Wall-E.*°

We are taking food seriously again.

Until 50 years ago, of course, every household had at least one person who took food seriously every day. But from the 1950s on, the majority of the population began contentedly cooking less and less, eating out more and more and devouring food that was worse and worse, until the horrible global slop served by fast-food and "casual dining" chains came to dominate the scene. One result: an unprecedented rise in obesity levels and a not-unrelated climb in health-care costs.

Yet we would not let food go to hell permanently, 5 at least not without a fight. And even at its nadir° there were signs of awakening. Beginning in the 1960s, more Americans than ever discovered France, Italy, Mexico, Japan and other countries, where traditional cooking remained intact. Revised immigration laws gave us a new and varied influx of immigrants, whose previously rare cuisines—Tibetan, Cambodian, Ethiopian and Ecuadorean, for example—became visible in many cities. At the same time, people like Julia Child,° Marcella Hazan° and Julie Sahni° made once-exotic cuisines accessible for amateurs.

Nevertheless many Americans began applying the word "cooking" to the act of defrosting and heating mass-produced frozen food in a microwave oven. Still, by the mid-'80s there were new vistas for food lovers. There was a nascent° food-as-art scene, presaging° Ferran Adrià.° Old-style French food—the fancy stuff,

---

Wall-E: a 2008 computer-animated science fiction movie set in the twenty-second century, when humans have become unable to walk because of all the liquid food they've consumed.

nadir: lowest point.

Julia Child (1912–2004): an American cookbook author and television personality credited with introducing French cooking techniques and food to a broad American audience. Her first cookbook, written with Simone Beck

and Louisette Bertholle, was *Mastering the Art of French Cooking* (1961). In 1963, she became host of *The French Chef* on educational television, which became the best-known cooking program in the United States.

Julia Child, the doyenne of French cooking in America

Marcella Hazan (b. 1924): an Italian-born cookbook author credited with introducing Italian cooking techniques and Italian regional cuisine to a broad American audience. She emigrated to the United States in 1956. Her first cookbook was *The Classic Italian Cook Book: The Art of Italian Cooking and the Italian Art of Eating* (1973).

Julie Sahni: an Indian-born cookbook author, cooking school operator, and former chef at two Indian restaurants in New York

City. Her most famous cookbook is *Classic Indian Cooking* (1980).

nascent: developing, being born.

presage: to foreshadow or come before.

Ferran Adrià (b. 1962): a Catalonian chef and cookbook author who currently is the top-ranked chef of Europe.

with sauces—died a quick death (thank you, Paul Bocuse°). Fantastic local ingredients, treated minimally, became all the rage (thank you, Alice Waters° and friends). European chefs in the United States embraced Asian ingredients (thank you, Jean-Georges Vongerichten°).

At first these changes affected few people. But a confluence of factors—new cuisines, a cultural fixation on health, frustration with low-quality food—led to a renewed appreciation of eating and home cooking. Logically, this led to an increased awareness of industrially raised animals and overprocessed food and ultimately to an interest in local ingredients, in vegetables, in sustainability, in human health.

Then there was food television. We were ripe for the Food Network's° Emeril,° Rachael,° Mario° and Bobby,° who created a buzz based on celebrity that grabbed not only the middle-aged and the young but also the very young. And when 6-year-olds started wanting to be chefs—that was different.

The news wasn't all good. At the millennium, we knew that fish had disappeared from the seas, taste had disappeared from chickens, regulation had all but disappeared from government agencies and humanity had disappeared from the way we handle animals. Obesity and its associated lifestyle diseases became news, as did acute illnesses like salmonella and mad cow. It also became clear to everyone who took the

---

Paul Bocuse (b. 1926): a French chef, among the finest of the last century, often associated with *nouvelle cuisine* (French, "new cooking"), which emphasized light, delicate preparations in contrast to heavy, high-calorie traditional French cuisine.

Alice Waters (b. 1944): an American chef, cookbook author, and founder of the restaurant Chez Panisse. In addition to helping create "California cuisine," she was among the earliest American proponents of using locally grown, fresh ingredients.

Jean-Georges Vongerichten (b. 1956): a French-born chef now residing in the United States who owns a number of elite restaurants around the world. He is also a cookbook author.

Food Network: since 1993, an American cable television channel (now broadcast worldwide) offering instruction and entertainment. The channel has made many chefs, including those whose names follow, household names.

Emeril Lagasse on a 2005 magazine cover, a reminder that food is big business in America

Emeril (Lagasse) (b. 1959): an American celebrity chef and cookbook author perhaps best known for his Louisiana cuisine (though Lagasse was born in Massachusetts to a French

Canadian father and a Portuguese mother).

Rachael (Ray) (b. 1968): an American celebrity chef, talk-show host, and cookbook author. Her ancestry is Cajun on her father's side and Sicilian on her mother's.

Mario (Batali) (b. 1960): an American celebrity chef and cookbook author. Batali is the great-grandson of Italians on his father's side; his mother's ancestry is French Canadian and English.

Bobby (Flay) (b. 1964): an American celebrity chef and television personality. He is fourth-generation Irish American.

time to think that our overconsumption of meat was contributing to the hunger of nearly one billion fellow earthlings.

This has led many Americans to think as much 10 about food as they do about *Survivor* or the N.F.L.—which is to say a lot—and its preparation is no longer limited to what was once called a housewife. The unrelenting pressure on women to join the work force encouraged (forced?) men to at least learn how to turn on the stove; from there, many of them took to cooking enthusiastically (some, no doubt, because so many gadgets are involved). Those children who dream of being chefs share in the cooking; nearly every young person I meet cooks routinely.

Of course, food continues to be fetishized; organic food has been commodified; the federal government subsidizes almost all of the wrong kinds of food production; supermarkets peddle way too much nonreal food ("junk food" or, to use my mother's word, "dreck"°); and weight-loss diets still discourage common-sense eating. But questions like "Would you prefer a mass-produced organic grape from Chile or a nonorganic one from a backyard vine in Upstate New York?" are more common in conversation, and the dialogue about food routinely includes words like *locavore,*° *vegetarian, sustainable*° and *flexitarian.*°

The real issues—how do we grow and raise, distribute and sell, prepare and eat food? And how do our patterns of doing these things affect the rest of the world (and vice versa)?—are simply too big to ignore.

And if we are obsessing about where our food is from and how it's grown rather than whether our fries are cooked in beef fat or "cholesterol-free oil" (or, even worse, whether our gold-leaf-topped° foie gras° is good for us), this is progress.

Simply put, many more Americans are seeing food as more than a necessary fuel whose only requirement is that it can be obtained and consumed without much difficulty or cost. Perhaps just in time, we're saying, "Hold the shake," and looking for something more wholesome.

---

dreck: inferior or worthless merchandise, junk.

locavore: a person who is committed to eating locally produced food.

sustainable: here, able to continue without serious or long-term damage to the environment.

flexitarian: a vegetarian who is willing to eat

chicken (or even red meat) on occasion.

gold-leaf: here, edible, paper-thin gold used to decorate a dish.

foie gras: (French, "fatty liver") an appetizer usually made of goose liver. Because the geese are generally force fed, this food has been boycotted by people concerned with animal rights.

Chapter 17 points out that what looks like a fallacy to some might be a good argument to others. Does Bittman slide into scare tactics, the slippery slope fallacy, or bandwagon approaches in this essay? Why or why not?

LINK TO PP. 517, 520, AND 522

RESPOND•

1. In what ways is Americans' relationship with food changing, according to Bittman? What evidence does he provide? For Bittman, what is the good news about our relationship with food? The bad news?

2. You are one of the real readers of Bittman's argument. Who were his intended readers—that is, what kind of readers did Bittman assume would read this text? How do you know? Who are the invoked readers—that is, those who are represented in the text? What kinds of experience and knowledge do they have? What are their values? Provide evidence from the text for your claims. (For a discussion of categories of audiences, see Chapter 1.)

3. How have changing gender roles influenced Americans' relationship with food, according to Bittman? Do you agree? Why or why not?

4. Examine the chart labeled "Fast-Food Nations." Based on this sample of nine nations, where does the United States fall in "meals eaten out per person" (meaning meals prepared by restaurants)? What relationship, if any, is there between this chart and Bittman's argument? How representative is your behavior of the behavior of most Americans? In other words, is it likely you ate more or fewer than 120 meals or so out (or from restaurants) in 2005? How does your behavior compare with that of your classmates? What accounts for the differences? The similarities?

5. What changes have you experienced in your own lifetime with regard to thinking about food, preparing it, and consuming it? What do you think triggered those changes? **Compose an argument** in which you discuss food-related changes in your own life and in the lives of most Americans. You may choose to present a factual argument, an evaluative one, or a causal one. (For discussions of factual, evaluative, and causal arguments, see Chapters 8, 10, and 11, respectively.)

Wynne Wright is an assistant professor in the field of community, food, and agriculture at Michigan State University; her research examines local and global responses to the restructuring of the food and agriculture system. Gerad Middendorf is an associate professor of sociology at Kansas State University; his research focuses on agriculture, the environment, and international development. In this excerpt from their introduction to the 2008 collection they edited, The Fight over Food: Producers, Consumers, and Activists Challenge the Global Food System, *Wright and Middendorf review the changes in what they term the "agrifood system"—the food and agriculture system. In many ways, their argument parallels Mark Bittman's in the previous selection, "Why Take Food Seriously? Because Your Life Depends on It." You'll see that they approach the topic in a more academic way and from a different perspective than Bittman does. As you read, think about the similarities and differences in the two arguments.*

Introduction: Fighting over Food—Change in the Agrifood System

WYNNE WRIGHT AND GERAD MIDDENDORF

Time magazine recently reported the story of a man in Ann Arbor, Michigan, who had been pulled over in his pickup truck by the state police for hauling illegal cargo. This was the culmination of a sting operation that resulted in seizure of the cargo. But this was no ordinary drug bust; the driver of the mud-splattered pickup truck was a dairy farmer dealing in raw milk (Cole 2007). A growing number of consumers, often from urban locales, are seeking out the warm, white liquid straight from the udder for what they perceive as its superior nutritional value. The Food and Drug Administration (FDA) does not see it that way. The FDA line is that unpasteurized milk contains E. coli,° salmonella,° and listeria°—all risks to human health. It is illegal to transport raw milk across state lines, just as it is illegal to sell raw milk in twenty-three states. As a result, farmers and raw milk drinkers have found a creative way to circumvent this obstacle by partnering together to organize a small co-operative venture,° known as a cow-share. It is legal to drink straight from your own cow, so by organizing a cow-share co-op, consumers are effectively

E. coli: bacteria that cause diarrhea.

salmonella: bacteria that cause certain kinds of food poisoning.

listeria: bacteria that cause listeriosis, a potentially fatal disease in humans.

cooperative venture: a project (in this case, a cow) that is owned by several people or organizations.

drinking from the cow they own and partnering with the farmer to do the milking and caretaking. The confiscation of the raw milk has set off something of a maelstrom in Michigan. Raw milk drinkers are a dedicated bunch; members of the farmer's cow-share cooperative could not run fast enough to the aid of their farmer, offering support in numerous ways. It seems that this case is not so unique. People appear to be struggling over the meaning of raw milk—dubbed "real" milk by its supporters—in a number of states. New York, Maryland, Ohio, Kentucky, Indiana, Nebraska, Colorado, Arizona—the raw milk crack down is spreading, while at the same time resistance is mounting. The conflict over raw milk and the growing divide among producers, consumers, and the state° is merely the most recent example of a radically changing food system. The case of raw milk suggests that we are increasingly confronting a food and agriculture system[1] that is being restructured in both subtle and highly politicized ways.

state: here, the government at any level (such as town, county, state, or country).

In this book we probe the tremendous dynamism° of these social forces to explore the lessons they teach us for understanding the complexity of human agency.° Some of the agrifood system changes are quiet and almost slip under the radar for their ordinary, everyday properties. Other changes are constantly scrutinized and are highly politicized on the domestic and international stages, bringing a multitude of actors with divergent interests into conflict with one another. We can see the political and sociocultural nature of this process in diverse initiatives, from campaigns to prevent animal cruelty, to the now routine on-site protests against the opening of McDonald's restaurants around the world, to the rise of a new entrepreneurial ethos in producers and a heightened reflexivity among consumers. A casual observer of the media might conclude that something qualitatively new is afoot in humans' relationship to food and agriculture. Consider the following newspaper headlines: "Kinder, Gentler Food: Restaurants, Groceries, and Activists Force Farmers to Change Treatment of Their Animals" (Perkins 2004); "Monsanto Lab in Crystal Closes amid Food Protests" (*Bangor Daily News* 2000); "The Slow Food Movement: Slow Food Protests over Fast Foods and Food Safety" (*New Internationalist* 2002); "Tests Confirm 2nd Case of Mad Cow Disease in U.S." (Newman 2005). If headlines are barometers of social trends, then it appears that we are indeed witnessing an explosion of efforts aimed at reconfiguring our relationship to agriculture and food.

dynamism: energy or power.

agency: in theories of social behavior, the ability of "social actors" (individuals) to act freely without constraint.

We are experiencing the rise of an "alternative" food system that attempts to exist outside of the mainstream commodity-driven° network. This alternative network comprises a repertoire° vast in economic scale, political intentions, and cultural overhaul. Growth in interest and activity around organic foods, eco-labeled foods, direct marketing,° fair trade,° local foods,

commodity-driven: here, treating food only as something to be bought and sold.

repertoire: the total of items making up a range of things (here, the alternative network).

direct marketing: selling directly from the producer to the buyer.

fair trade: an agreement that agricultural producers will be paid a fair price, often one that enables them to earn a living wage.

food box schemes: programs whereby customers agree to purchase a box of vegetables and fruits grown by a nearby farmer on a regular basis; the contents of the box are determined by availability, not customer choice.

paradigm: here, framework or system.

antidisparagement laws: laws against public questioning of the safety of a food product without scientific evidence to support the claim.

confined animal feeding operations (CAFOs): farms that raise animals for consumption and confine them in large numbers in very small spaces (a subcategory of factory farming).

aquatic "feedlots": confined spaces where fish are farmed commercially.

mad cow disease: the popular name for bovine spongiform encephalopathy (BSE), a degenerative disease in cattle. Most scientists believe that it can be transmitted to humans who eat the brain or spinal cord of cows infected with BSE.

A food box from an organic farm

community kitchens and gardens, community-supported agriculture, food box schemes,° farmers' markets, and assorted community buying clubs collectively demonstrate the emergence of a new production/consumption paradigm° and are some of the topics taken up in this book. The resurgence of such locally embedded food networks is growing in the United States, but Americans are not alone in charting a new food course. Whatmore, Stassart, and Renting (2003, 389) conclude that such projects "represent some of the most rapidly expanding food markets in Europe over the last decade." But efforts to construct new alternatives to the existing food system are not the only subject we explore in this book. At the same time, challenges to the current commodity-driven food system by producers and consumers are growing. Struggles over the organization of the current food system are evident in food antidisparagement laws,° as well as in the backlash against confined animal feeding operations (CAFOs),° aquatic "feedlots,"° genetically engineered foods, mad cow disease,° *E. coli* contamination, biopiracy,° and dissent targeted at transnational° trade regulatory bodies such as the World Trade Organization (WTO).°

These efforts are only some of the phenomenal changes taking place in the agrifood system. A complete list might be nearly impossible to compile. Therefore, we have been somewhat selective in our account. The essays in

Chickens in a confined animal feeding operation in Oklahoma

biopiracy: the corporate-funded development of organic materials (such as plants and genetic material) gathered from a group or country that is not fairly compensated for the potential value of the material.

transnational: across national boundaries.

World Trade Organization (WTO): an international organization based in Geneva, Switzerland, that governs matters related to world trade. Over 95 percent of the world's countries are members.

this volume highlight some of the major transformations with which many readers will be familiar and, at the same time, demonstrate the arenas of contest° that are increasingly part and parcel of our food system.

It is this broad arena of contest—the aggregation° of efforts to reshape the conventional agrifood system—that frames our conceptualization of the fight over food. What do these streams of social change share in common? They signify a mounting reflexivity° and new modes of action among producers, consumers, and activists in the production and consumption of food (Fine 1995; Fine and Leopold 1993; Goodman 1999, 2004; Lockie et al. 2002; Murdoch, Marsden, and Banks 2000). Food, along with its attendant° production processes, is moving to the forefront of our consciousness. It is being reconsidered in light of changing values, norms, customs, science and technology, and institutional resources, and is no longer invisible in our culture. Many of our long-held assumptions about food—from the way it is produced to the way we eat—are now in flux.

These new configurations provide us with an opportunity for a sociological study of the various ways that agency is expressed by humans. All of these contests in the agrifood system—from the rising demand for raw milk to the segmentation° of our local supermarkets—are products of human

contest: here, a struggle, controversy, or strife.

aggregation: a collection.

reflexivity: here, reflection on one's actions and their consequences.

attendant: accompanying.

segmentation: a division into segments or parts.

social structure: the organization of society into groups (such as social classes or ethnic or religious groups), patterns of behavior (such as how food is prepared), and social institutions (such as marriage, religion, or political systems).

structuralist: here, relating to a mid-twentieth-century theory that social structures determine behavior and that humans have limited ability to act freely.

generate: to create using existing materials and patterns of behavior.

collective: group.

exponentially: as exponents versus mathematically (3×3 versus $3 + 3$).

quiescence: motionlessness, inactivity.

affluence: wealth.

postmaterialist: (literally, "after materialist") Postmaterialist theories suggest that people who have satisfied material needs (like food and lodging) can develop values like free speech and participatory democracy.

agency. We recognize that social structure° can direct, even constrain agency, yet we have avoided overly structuralist° accounts that suggest that agency can be squelched under the unbending rigor of structure. We also steer away from interpretations that seem to imply that agency is free to be realized without any constraint whatsoever. In the transformations taking place in the agrifood system we are reminded that actors exercise agency in numerous ways. They may reflexively and creatively generate° new forms of action (e.g., new markets), or they may resist the establishment of new forms of action or the continuity of activity. Finally, this volume examines the ways in which individual action and collective° activity are articulated. It links the reflexivity of consumers with the collective acts of citizens and attempts to prompt a dialogue that focuses on the synthesis of those roles along with other social roles humans play in society.

How did we get here? In the postwar era of abundance, food moved to the back burner of the consciousness of many in the industrialized world. For most, it became plentiful, inexpensive, more convenient, and perceived as relatively nutritious. Given a willingness to trust those embedded in our food-provisioning system, we relinquished our civic responsibility for food system oversight to farmers, nutritionists, food corporations, agribusinesses, and the state; in other words, we let the experts take charge. Issues of how, where, and by whom food was grown were not generally topics of conversation around the dinner table. In some circles, it might even be considered unacceptable or impolite to inquire about the social life of our dinner.

As we migrated away from the farm and the dinner table through the twentieth century, our consciousness of food likewise migrated away form the biological and social basis of production. As women moved into the workplace and those in the West generally increased the hours spent at work outside the household each week, interest increased in processed foods that provided convenience (e.g., canned, frozen, and prepared foods) (Goodman and Redclift 1991). All the while, confidence in the food system soared—we were assured that food processors were providing us with nutritious choices and that food scientists were using state-of-the art technology to resolve food safety issues. The choices available to the typical shopper appeared to multiply exponentially° on supermarket shelves. Most of us believed that our food was being produced by farm families who received a living wage for their labor. Their dependence upon healthy soil and clean water assured us that they would not compromise environmental integrity through poor production practices. Yet we now know that the story of postwar development of the agrifood system is one of both successes and failures.

Although initially it was ridiculed, Rachel Carson's *Silent Spring* (1962) shocked many out of their quiescence° over the environmental impacts of indiscriminate pesticide use in agriculture. Since that time, numerous scholars have demonstrated the role agricultural policy has played in encouraging a production treadmill that results in relatively inexpensive and abundant foods, while at the same time expelling farmers from the land, with crippling effects for rural communities (Brown 1988; Cochrane 1979; Dudley 2000; Strange 1988). And now, in the early twenty-first century, we have turned our attention to issues of health and safety (Critser 2003; Nestle 2002). As it turns out, the glorious choices that literally bulge from the shelves of grocery retailers also symbolize the price many in the advanced industrial world pay for a diet of affluence.°

These growing realizations stem, in part, from our postmaterialist° age, in which some of us have the luxury of putting quality and identity issues surrounding food front and center in our consciousness. But many in less developed countries, as well as an embarrassing number in industrialized nations, continue to combat issues of food insecurity° with unfortunate regularity. Ten years after the World Food Summit, where we pledged to tackle the problem of hunger and food insecurity, "virtually no progress has been made." The Food and Agriculture Organization of the United Nations estimates that 854 million people suffer from undernourishment worldwide, 845 million of them in developing° and transitional economies° and 9 million in the industrialized world (FAO 2006). In the United States alone, 11.9 percent of the population—or about 5.7 million—is food insecure (Nord, Andrews, and Carlson 2004). The simultaneous proliferation of food boutiques for the wealthy and food banks for the poor is a distressing paradox that defines an era of overindulgence alongside deprivation (Van Esterik 2005).

What interests us in this volume are the numerous and multifaceted° initiatives in the agrifood system that attempt to bring about change in some way, whether through an effort to address social disparities such as hunger and food insecurity or to raise health or environmental concerns, change our eating patterns, or diminish corporate influence. Food and agriculture have become public debates in transnational, national, and regional policy, in part because they offer what social movement° theorists refer to as a "consensus frame."° The desire for accessible "quality" food, a healthy environment, and regional economic development transcends the social markers of race, class, gender, and geography that divide us. We all want and need sustainable livelihoods.

Social scientists have variously referred to this distinctive impulse in food provisioning as an "alternative geography of food" (Whatmore and Thorne

10

food insecurity: in research and many government contexts, a term that has replaced *hunger.*

developing economies: the industrializing countries of Asia, Africa, and Central and South America, many of which were colonized well into the twentieth century.

transitional economies: countries that are moving from a centralized, state-controlled economy to a free-market system. Examples include China, Vietnam, much of central and eastern Europe, and nations that were formerly part of the Soviet Union.

multifaceted: many-faced or taking many forms.

social movement: an initially informal effort of individuals to change a social or political situation. Recent social movements in the United States include the civil rights movement, the women's rights movement, the gay rights movement, and the anti-abortion movement.

consensus frame: a way of defining a problem that assumes that all stakeholders (those who have something at stake in the problem) agree on some aspects of the issues.

stewardship: responsible caretaking.

reciprocity: a mutual exchange, often of rights and obligations.

incubating: here, creating slowly and carefully.

portend: to foretell or predict.

resistance: an opposition to the current way of doing things or to those in power.

atomized: broken into its smallest units or parts.

social capital: a network of relationships that can be exploited for personal gain (such as meeting people who might later help you).

productionist-centered: focused on issues of production rather than issues of consumption, ecology, and so on.

function: here, a result.

paramount: of chief importance.

1997) or an "alternative agro-food network" (Murdoch, Marsden, and Banks 2000). We find particularly useful Lyson's concept of "civic agriculture" as a way of describing this remaking of our agrifood system. Civic agriculture is an organizational production strategy "tightly linked to a community's social and economic development" (Lyson 2004, I). This approach offers an integrative vision that promotes local environmental stewardship° and rural community culture, including reciprocity° and norms of neighboring, while simultaneously incubating° engines for economic development. In this way, it liberates communities and food systems from global dependence by promoting paths of local interdependence. We feel that Lyson's concept of civic agriculture comes closest to reuniting us with our food and our social obligations to each other. We will return to this subject in the concluding chapter. In this volume, we use a case study approach to analyze the developmental processes of food system change, thereby filling a gap in the agrifood literature.

We examine many of these trends and ask whether, taken together, they portend° an "accumulation of resistance"° that may fundamentally transform the predominant agrifood system, or whether they represent rather fragmented, atomized° expressions of symbolic consumption. In other words, do these trends signify a transformative social movement or merely the emergence of "bourgeois bohemian" or "bobo" (Brooks 2001) food consumption patterns? Have the affluent classes merely reembraced food as a form of social capital° (Bourdieu 1984), or do the efforts to redesign our food system suggest the birth of a new institutional arrangement, one that could replace the conventional productionist-centered° agrifood system?

While anthropologists, economists, geographers, and agricultural sociologists have tried to present the range of new agricultural and food initiatives and explain their resonance, few have attempted to draw them together and examine their transformative potential. Seldom have we seen in the social science agrifood literature cogent attempts to grapple with these initiatives as a comprehensive form of social change. Can they be explained as a function° of new forms of human agency, or as resistance to the dominant mode of agriculture? Or both? In this volume, we explore these questions.

An exhaustive review of the literature is beyond the scope of this introduction, but we hope to provide some tools to help the reader grasp the ways in which social change is possible. We turn first to an overview of some of the changes taking place in our agrifood system. In other words, we look at what's "new" in agrifood systems. This involves the discussion of a concept of paramount° interest in this volume—human agency. We provide an overview of this concept and touch briefly on some of the conceptual debates in the literature where they relate to agrifood system change. We conclude the introduction with a brief overview of the case studies in the book.

NOTE

1. Hereafter, we abbreviate the food and agriculture system "agrifood system."

REFERENCES

Bangor Daily News. 2000. "Monsanto Lab in Crystal Closes amid Food Protests." 3 May. www.biotech-info.net/monsanto_lab.html.

Bourdieu, Pierre. 1984. *Distinction: A Social Critique of the Judgment of Taste.* Cambridge: Harvard University Press.

Brooks, David. 2001. *Bobos in Paradise: The New Upper Class and How They Got There.* New York: Simon and Schuster.

Brown, William P. 1988. *Private Interests, Public Policy, and American Agriculture.* Lawrence: University Press of Kansas.

Carson, Rachel. 1962. *Silent Spring.* Boston: Houghton Mifflin.

Cochrane, Willard W. 1979. *The Development of American Agriculture: A Historical Analysis.* Minneapolis: University of Minnesota Press.

Cole, Wendy. 2007. "Got Raw Milk? Be Very Quiet." *Time* magazine, 13 March. www.time.com/time/health/article/0,8599,1598525,00.html.

Critser, Greg. 2003. *Fat Land: How Americans Became the Fattest People in the World.* Boston: Houghton Mifflin.

Dudley, Kathryn Marie. 2000. *Debt and Dispossession: Farm Loss in America's Heartland.* Chicago: University of Chicago Press.

Fine, Ben. 1995. "From Political Economy to Consumption." In *Acknowledging Consumption: A Review of New Studies,* ed. Daniel Miller, 127–63. London: Routledge.

Fine, Ben, and Ellen Leopold. 1993. *The World of Consumption.* London: Routledge.

Food and Agriculture Organization of the United Nations (FAO). 2006. "The State of Food Insecurity in the World: Eradicating World Hunger—Taking Stock Ten Years after the World Food Summit." www.fao.org/doccrep/009/a0750e/a0750000.html.

Goodman, David. 1999. "Agro-Food Studies in the 'Age of Ecology': Nature, Corporeality, Bio-Politics." *Sociologia Ruralis* 39(1): 17–38.

———. 2004. "Rural Europe Redux: Reflections on Alternative Agro-Food Networks and Paradigm Change. *Sociologia Ruralis* 44(1): 3–16.

Goodman, David, and Michael Redclift. 1991. *Refashioning Nature: Food, Ecology, and Culture.* London: Routledge.

Lockie, Stewart, Kristin Lyons, Geoffrey Lawrence, and Kerry Mummery. 2002. "Eating 'Green': Motivations behind Organic Food Consumption in Australia." *Sociologia Ruralis* 42(1): 20–37.

Chapter 18 argues that crediting sources enhances authors' ethos by showing that they've done their homework—as these authors clearly have.

LINK TO P. 537

Lyson, Thomas A. 2004. *Civic Agriculture: Reconnecting Farm, Food, and Community.* Medford, Mass.: Tufts University Press.

Murdoch, Jonathan, Terry Marsden, and Jo Banks. 2000. "Quality, Nature and Embeddedness." *Economic Geography* 76(2): 107–25.

Nestle, Marion. 2002. *Food Politics: How the Food Industry Influences Nutrition and Health.* Berkeley and Los Angeles: University of California Press.

New Internationalist. 2002. "The Slow Food Movement: Slow Food Protests over Fast Foods and Food Safety." 1 March. www.newint.org/issue343/action.htm.

Newman, Maria. 2005. "Tests Confirm 2nd Case of Mad Cow Disease in the U.S." *New York Times*, 24 June.

Nord, Mark, Margaret Andrews, and Steven Carlson. 2004. "Household Food Security in the United States." Food Assistance and Nutrition Report (FANRR42), October. Washington, D.C.: U.S. Department of Agriculture, Economic Research Service.

Perkins, Jerry. 2004. "Kinder, Gentler Food: Restaurants, Groceries, and Activists Force Farmers to Change Treatment of Their Animals." *Des Moines Register*, 7 March, 1A.

Strange, Marty. 1988. *Family Farming: A New Economic Vision.* Lincoln: University of Nebraska Press.

Van Esterik, Penny. 2005. "No Free Lunch." *Agriculture and Human Values* 22(2): 207–8.

Whatmore, Sarah, Pierre Stassart, and Henk Renting. 2003. "What's Alternative about Alternative Food Networks?" *Environment and Planning A* 35(3): 389–91.

Whatmore, Sarah, and Lorraine Thorne. 1997. "Nourishing Networks: Alternative Geographies of Food." In *Globalising Food: Agrarian Questions and Global Restructuring*, ed. David Goodman and Michael J. Watts, 287–304. London: Routledge.

RESPOND ●

1. According to Wright and Middendorf, what social forces have led to our fights over food—that is, to the changing relationships between Americans and food? Which of these forces were you aware of before reading this selection? What might account for your awareness or lack of awareness of them?

2. Where are the areas of overlap and difference between Wright and Middendorf's analysis of our changing relationship with food and Mark Bittman's analysis in the previous selection, "Why Take Food Seriously? Because Your Life Depends on It"? What might be the sources of those differences?

3. Legal debates often involve arguments about definitions. In what ways do the raw milk, cow-share cooperatives (paragraph 1) demonstrate

how individuals and groups use definitional arguments to obey the letter of the law but avoid satisfying the intent of the law?

4. As the headnote explains, this selection is from the introductory chapter of a book of articles that were written by academic researchers about issues related to food. What cues in the text tell the reader that this selection is part of an introduction? In other words, what do readers expect the introduction of a book to do, and how does this particular selection fulfill those expectations?

5. This selection mentions many food topics—such as raw milk, fair trade, biopiracy, and confined animal feeding operations—that are subjects of controversy. Research one of these topics and **write an essay** in which you define the term and describe the complexities of the controversy surrounding the topic. (You may well learn that part of the debate is what label should be applied to the issue.) You will be creating a definitional argument about both a term and the controversies surrounding the topic. (For a discussion of definitional arguments, see Chapter 9.)

▼ Solomon H. Katz's "The World Food Crisis: An Overview of the Causes and Consequences" is the first of four articles on the world food crisis from the October 2008 issue of Anthropology News, the official newspaper of the American Anthropological Association (AAA). The box "Food Crisis Information & Resources" (p. 797) appeared as a sidebar to these articles. Thus, the intended audience for this material is clear—anthropologists of all kinds.

Katz directs the Krogman Center for Childhood Growth and Development at the University of Pennsylvania, where he is a professor of anthropology. He is also a fellow at the university's Center for Spirituality and the Mind and the Leonard Davis Institute for Health Economics; editor-in-chief of the Encyclopedia of Food and Culture (2003), and chair of the AAA's Task Force on World Food Problems. In this selection, he constructs several causal arguments. Focus on how these arguments are structured, and consider whether there are links between Katz's view of the world food crisis and the changing relationship of Americans to their food that was described in the previous two selections (Mark Bittman's "Why Take Food Seriously? Because Your Life Depends on It" and Wynne Wright and Gerad Middendorf's "Introduction: Fighting over Food—Change in the Agrifood System").

The World Food Crisis: An Overview of the Causes and Consequences

SOLOMON H. KATZ

On July 2, 2007, UN Secretary General Ban Ki-moon issued an upbeat progress report on the UN Millennium Goals° adopted in 2000. Of the eight objectives listed, addressing food and poverty by halving the number of poor and hungry people of the world (from 880 million to 440 million) by the year 2015 was the number one UN goal. A year later, with no extraordinary droughts, floods or crop pestilence,° a world food crisis of major proportions has erupted. How global food prices soared to unprecedented levels so quickly and became so devastating is the subject of this overview. It also summarizes prospects for solving the crisis and suggests how anthropologists might play an active role in increasing the stability of the world food systems.

THE MACRO PICTURE

To understand the macro factors underlying the first world food crisis

UN Millennium Goals: eight goals that the 123 members of the United Nations and at least 23 international organizations adopted to improve living conditions in the world's poorest countries.

pestilence: disease.

of the twenty-first century, it is necessary to focus on the major associated developments of the twentieth century: (1) tremendous increases in population due to public health measures that reduced infant mortality and infectious diseases and (2) vast improvements in agricultural productivity and efficiency. As a result, over the last fifty years an enormous labor surplus has emerged and economies have shifted, creating mass rural to urban migration. By 2006 over half the world's population resided in urban environments dependent on purchased food rather than subsistence farming.° Also, global food distribution, resulting from the rapid growth of world trade and the recent global trend toward capitalism, has had a major impact on food production systems.

Another significant issue is that major food crop production (e.g., rice, wheat, corn and soy) became dependent on technological advances associated with the Green Revolution° of the 1970s. This revolution used hybridized seeds,° which are bred and now genetically modified for high productivity and management of disease resistance and pest control, but which also require irrigation and heavy use of fertilizer, making them highly dependent on fossil fuels such as oil and natural gas.

These very successful global developments have shifted enormous capital resources° to take advantage of cheaper labor costs. As a result, the material standards° of Asia have risen dramatically over the last decade, along with the use of agricultural products for animal feed, the consumption° of animal protein and the depletion of world oil resources. Finally, scientific evidence over the last two decades demonstrates that irreversible global climate changes are being induced by carbon dioxide released into the atmosphere by the consumption of fossil fuels, changing weather patterns in ways that adversely° influence global agricultural productivity.

RECENT CAUSES

The proximate° triggers of the current world food crisis lie in a series of agricultural factors and related government responses. The first trigger was a global wheat shortage induced by a two-year (2006-07) wheat crop failure in Australia associated with a prolonged draught, which may have been an indicator of major climate change. Next, the price of US corn (maize) increased dramatically, coinciding with the early 2007 adoption of legislation providing financial incentives to use corn as a biofuel (ethanol) in order to reduce US dependence on foreign oil as a source of gasoline. Farmers responded to the incentives by planting more corn than ever before, with the exception of the 1944 crop planted to avoid mass starvation in Europe. The increased 2007 corn acreage was at the expense of soybean production, creating a shortage of soybeans and another price increase. Because most of the corn produced in the US is used as feed for livestock, the jump in the price of corn was felt first by livestock farmers, causing them to reduce production of animal-based products and increasing the price of meat, dairy and eggs. Finally, European Union policy shifted toward stimulating biofuel production, increasing

5

---

subsistence farming: producing crops for personal survival rather than for making a profit.

Green Revolution: the introduction in the 1960s and 1970s of improved seeds, chemical fertilizers, irrigation, and improved management techniques (especially in poorer countries) that increased agricultural productivity.

hybridized seeds: seeds bred scientifically to produce the highest yield.

material standards: material goods that are available to most people in a society.

capital resources: large investments in equipment or buildings that can be used and reused in the creation of other goods or services.

consumption: here, use.

adversely: negatively.

proximate: immediate or most recent.

competition for palm oil,° which is heavily used as cooking oil in India and China but is also an efficient source of diesel. The resulting increase in the price of palm oil produced shortages and price problems in Asia.

Competition over these basic food and fuel commodities resulted in inevitable inflation° on the global food market. Rapid price increases produced serious social unrest in parts of the world. In Mexico, Felipe Calderón° acted against his free trade philosophy by fixing corn prices to avoid further street violence over the rise in US corn prices. Similar street protests broke out in over 40 countries over the next year and a half. To quell this unrest, many Asian food-exporting countries slowed or even stopped the export of food, taking inflationary pressure off their domestic° food prices. Unfortunately, in addition to delaying price increases, such price fixing schemes also inhibit agricultural investment and productivity since profits are cut, and can

Soaring U.S. corn prices led to street protests in Mexico.

lead to dramatic global food price increases over time.

Non-agricultural factors such as hoarding and speculation appear to have also influenced food price infla-tion. For example, in the Philippines, which is heavily dependent on imported rice, hoarding by middle-men to induce further price rises became punishable by life imprison-ment at the height of the rice crisis in 2008. The food futures° commodities° markets appear to be another impor-tant factor in the volatility° in food prices. According to an April 2008 account in Canada's *The Globe and Mail*, upwards of 50% of the Chicago Board of Trade price for wheat futures has been influenced by speculative° investment.

A NEW FOCUS ON THE ENTIRE FOOD CHAIN

There have been signs this August that the market price bubble° caused by the factors outlined above is over. The US economy has slowed, reducing demand for oil, and oil and ethanol prices have decreased. World wheat prices have dropped with better pros-pects from Australia and soybeans have once again been heavily planted

---

palm oil: a vegetable oil that is derived from oil palm trees.

inflation: a progressive rise in prices without a comparable increase in the volume of available money. Thus, inflation causes the purchasing power of money to decline.

Felipe Calderón (Hinojosa) (b. 1962): the current president of Mexico.

domestic: relating to one's own country (in contrast to other countries).

futures: contracts to buy (or have the option of buy-ing) a farm product, at a specified time in the

future for a price agreed on today.

commodities: agricultural or mining products that can be bought, processed, and resold.

volatility: a rapid and unpredictable shifting or fluctuating.

speculative: characterized by chance or risk.

market price bubble: a sit-uation that occurs when people are willing to pay a price (for something such as houses or technology stocks) that is far greater than the actual value of the item. If prices suddenly fall, the bubble is said to have burst.

in the Midwest, promising further decreases in the price of this crop. Also, with recognition of the environmental damage created by the rapid increase in palm oil production in Indonesia and Malaysia, the European Union has modified its position regarding using palm oil to produce diesel, resulting in reduced competition and declining prices for this cooking oil commodity. Furthermore, Thailand and Vietnam (Asia's largest rice exporters) have experienced excellent rice harvests.

So, if major food crop prices are rapidly declining, is the world food crisis over? Should we, as we did following the early 1970s food crisis, return to business as usual? There are several compelling reasons why we should not. First, about two billion people live in poverty, many in poor urban areas, and many malnourished and even starving from high food prices. These numbers are so vast that it is difficult to grasp their significance. The toil in terms of loss of life, permanently stunted growth and loss of infectious disease resistance is a truly overwhelming challenge. If all the food that is now in the "pipeline" could reach the people in need (which it cannot), it would still take these populations time to recover. It is increasingly clear that although prices will go down they are not likely to return to the low levels of the past. No one expects energy, water, land, fertilizer or new seed costs to decrease in the near future. There is also a dangerous new threat: a wheat rust, Ug99, which has already infected wheat in Africa and has spread across the Arabian Peninsula to Iran with the possibility of devastating the highly susceptible world wheat crop. World wheat production will almost certainly become the next major threat to the world food chain.

The solution to the current world food crisis not only involves increasing food production but also demands a new focus on the efficiency and sustainability of every step of the human food chain in order to improve human diets, particularly as the Green Revolution hits limiting factors, such as water, agricultural land and fertilizer availability. We need to look beyond the Green Revolution for solutions and refocus our attention on a "food chain revolution," examining: (1) the sustainability and diversity of food production, (2) the efficiency of food storage and transportation and (3) the dietary significance and opportunities of food processing to enhance and rebalance nutrients removed or harmed by depleted and contaminated soils. We

Food Crisis Information and Resources

To stay up-to-date on the world food crisis and how anthropologists can contribute to developing solutions, please attend the upcoming AAA Annual Meeting symposium "AAA Task Force Responds to the World Food Crisis" on Friday, November 21, 2008, 4:00 pm, Union Square Rooms 23 and 24. During the meeting, the task force will announce a Hewlett Foundation-sponsored contest for student videos addressing the world food crisis.

You can also explore the Food Crisis Wiki (https://wfmo.pbwiki .com), which offers hundreds of articles and room for discussion. First time users should log in through https://wfmo.pbwiki.com/ shared.php?rph=8e5ae1679cac629e30c6e3cbac2e36875b4e83f1. Once you have entered the wiki, click "Side Bar" (upper right), which guides you through the extensive site.

For current news updates and articles also see:

Relief Web: www.reliefweb.int/rw/rwb.nsf/GlobalFoodCrisis
BBC: http://news.bbc.co.uk/2/hi/in_depth/world/2008/costoffood
NPR: www.npr.org/templates/story/story.php?storyid=90006310
Guardian: www.guardian.co.uk/environment/food
The Washington Post: www.washingtonpost.com/wp-srv/world/ globalfoodcrisis
The Economist: www.economist.com/opinion/displaystory.cfm ?story_id=11050146
Time Magazine: www.time.com/time/world/article/0,8599, 1717572,00.html
National Geographic: http://news.nationalgeographic.com/news/ food_crisis.html
The New York Times: http://topics.nytimes.com/top/news/ business/series/the_food_chain

also need to reexamine the cultural factors that lead to food waste, over-consumption and spoilage. By focusing on the entire human food chain, anthropologists can make an enormous contribution to the understanding and amelioration° of current and future food crises at both local and global levels.

We are just beginning to comprehend the rapid changes in climate and water stores threatening many parts of the globe. These problems require anthropologists to be sensitive to all aspects of the human food chain and global ecosystems. Food is one of the great links that ties us to one another as well as to our entire evolutionary history and current diversity of cultures. When a world food crisis occurs, it is thus not surprising to see it involve all aspects of human life. The challenge for us will be to bring clarity and understanding to the forces underlying the food crisis to enable policymakers to establish a sustainable, food-secure future.

---

amelioration: improvement.

RESPOND●

1. It is fairly easy to analyze this essay as a proposal argument. What is Katz proposing? Why is it appropriate for him to make such a proposal to anthropologists? If you're not sure what anthropologists study, research that topic before answering the question. (For a discussion of proposal arguments, see Chapter 12.)

2. Like all good proposal arguments, this one makes a strong case that a problem needs to be solved. In defining that problem, Katz lays out several complex causal arguments, which are often a feature of proposal arguments. What are those arguments, and how might they be characterized? To respond to this question, reread the article, listing each cause and effect that Katz discusses. After you have a list, categorize the causes and effects by representing them visually as illustrated in "Understanding Causal Arguments" in Chapter 11.

3. Why might Katz have arranged his arguments in the order he did? Would the selection have been as successful if, for example, he had begun by discussing the recent causes of the world food crisis rather than beginning with what he terms "The Macro Picture"? Why or why not?

4. Accompanying Katz's essay is a sidebar titled "Food Crisis Information and Resources." Why might the editors of *Anthropology News* have included this information in their series on the world food crisis? How would you characterize it as an argument? (Is it, for example, definitional or evaluative?) Why do you think that the editors recommended electronic rather than print resources?

5. How does Katz's essay complicate the discussions of food in the previous two selections—Mark Bittman's "Why Take Food Seriously? Because Your Life Depends on It" and Wynne Wright and Gerad Middendorf's "Introduction: Fighting over Food—Change in the Agrifood System"? What links might exist between Americans' fights over food and the world food crisis? Investigate some aspect of this issue, beginning with the sources provided by the AAA, and **write a causal essay** in which you analyze an issue related to food in the United States and the larger world. (For a discussion of causal essays, see Chapter 11. For a discussion of evaluating electronic sources, see Chapter 19.)

▶ Kathy Freston is an American "conscious living counselor," talk-show guest, and best-selling author of Quantum Wellness: A Practical and Spiritual Guide to Health and Happiness (2008), among other titles. She also contributes to The Huffington Post, a liberal news Web site billing itself as "The Internet Newspaper: News, Blogs, Video, Community," where this selection appeared in January 2007. As you read Freston's proposal argument, ask yourself why, given the arguments that she makes, all Americans have not become vegetarians.

greenhouse gases: gases in the atmosphere that, like the glass roof of a greenhouse, trap solar heat and contribute to global warming.

Vegetarian Is the New Prius

KATHY FRESTON

President Herbert Hoover promised "a chicken in every pot and a car in every garage." With warnings about global warming reaching feverish levels, many are having second thoughts about all those cars. It seems they should instead be worrying about the chickens.

Last month, the United Nations published a report on livestock and the environment with a stunning conclusion: "The livestock sector emerges as one of the top two or three most significant contributors to the most serious environmental problems, at every scale from local to global." It turns out that raising animals for food is a primary cause of land degradation, air pollution, water shortage, water pollution, loss of biodiversity, and not least of all, global warming.

That's right, global warming. You've probably heard the story: emissions of greenhouse gases° like carbon dioxide are changing our climate, and scientists warn of more extreme weather, coastal flooding, spreading disease, and mass extinctions. It seems that when you step outside and wonder what happened to winter, you might want to think about what you had for dinner last night. The U.N. report says almost a fifth of global warming emissions come from livestock (i.e., those chickens Hoover was talking about, plus pigs, cattle, and others)—that's more emissions than from all of the world's transportation combined.

For a decade now, the image of Leonardo DiCaprio cruising in his hybrid Toyota Prius has defined the gold standard for environmentalism. These gas-sipping vehicles became a veritable symbol of the consumers' power to strike a blow against global warming. Just think: a car that could cut your vehicle emissions in half—in a country responsible for 25% of the world's total greenhouse gas emissions. Federal fuel economy standards languished in Congress, and average vehicle mileage dropped to its lowest level in decades, but the Prius showed people that another way is possible. Toyota could not import the cars fast enough to meet demand.

Last year researchers at the University of Chicago took the Prius down a peg 5 when they turned their attention to another gas guzzling consumer purchase. They noted that feeding animals for meat, dairy, and egg production requires growing some ten times as much crops as we'd need if we just ate pasta primavera,° faux° chicken nuggets, and other plant foods. On top of that, we have to transport the animals to slaughterhouses, slaughter them, refrigerate their carcasses, and distribute their flesh all across the country. Producing a calorie of meat protein means burning more than ten times as much fossil fuels—and spewing more than ten times as much heat-trapping carbon dioxide—as does a calorie of plant protein. The researchers found that, when it's all added up, the average American does more to reduce global warming emissions by going vegetarian than by switching to a Prius.

pasta primavera: (Italian, "spring pasta") a dish of pasta and vegetables (such as tomatoes, onions, broccoli, carrots, and peas).

faux: (French, "false") false or fake.

According to the UN report, it gets even worse when we include the vast quantities of land needed to give us our steak and pork chops. Animal agriculture takes up an incredible 70% of all agricultural land, and 30% of the total land surface of the planet. As a result, farmed animals are probably the biggest cause of slashing and burning the world's forests. Today, 70% of former Amazon rainforest is used for pastureland, and feed crops cover much of the remainder. These forests serve as "sinks," absorbing carbon dioxide from the air, and burning these forests releases all the stored carbon dioxide, quantities that exceed by far the fossil fuel emission of animal agriculture.

As if that wasn't bad enough, the real kicker comes when looking at gases besides carbon dioxide—gases like methane and nitrous oxide, enormously effective greenhouse gases with 23 and 296 times the warming power of carbon dioxide, respectively. If carbon dioxide is responsible for about one-half of human-related greenhouse gas warming since the industrial revolution, methane and nitrous oxide are responsible for another one-third. These super-strong gases come primarily from farmed animals' digestive processes, and from their manure. In fact, while animal agriculture accounts for 9% of our carbon dioxide emissions, it emits 37% of our methane, and a whopping 65% of our nitrous oxide.

It's a little hard to take in when thinking of a small chick hatching from her fragile egg. How can an animal, so seemingly insignificant against the vastness of the earth, give off so much greenhouse gas as to change the global climate? The answer is in their sheer numbers. The United States alone slaughters more than 10 billion land animals every year, all to sustain a meat-ravenous culture that can barely conceive of a time not long ago when "a chicken in every pot" was considered a luxury. Land animals raised for food make up a staggering 20% of the entire land animal biomass° of the earth. We are eating our planet to death.

biomass: here, all living land animals.

What we're seeing is just the beginning, too. Meat consumption has increased five-fold in the past fifty years, and is expected to double again in the next fifty.

It sounds like a lot of bad news, but in fact it's quite the opposite. It means we   10 have a powerful new weapon to use in addressing the most serious environmental crisis ever to face humanity. The Prius was an important step forward, but how often are people in the market for a new car? Now that we know a greener diet is even more effective than a greener car, we can make a difference at every single meal, simply by leaving the animals off of our plates. Who would have thought: what's good for our health is also good for the health of the planet!

Going veg provides more bang for your buck than driving a Prius. Plus, that bang comes a lot faster. The Prius cuts emissions of carbon dioxide, which spreads its warming effect slowly over a century. A big chunk of the problem with farmed animals, on the other hand, is methane, a gas which cycles out of the atmosphere in just a decade. That means less meat consumption quickly translates into a cooler planet.

acid rain: rain contaminated by acids that are created by the burning of fossil fuels (like coal, natural gas, or petroleum).

prodigious: extraordinarily large.

Not just a cooler planet, also a cleaner one. Animal agriculture accounts for most of the water consumed in this country, emits two-thirds of the world's acid-rain-causing° ammonia, and is the world's largest source of water pollution—killing entire river and marine ecosystems, destroying coral reefs, and of course, making people sick. Try to imagine the prodigious° volumes of manure churned out by modern American farms: 5 million tons a day, more than a hundred times that of the human population, and far more than our land can possibly absorb. The acres and acres of cesspools stretching over much of our countryside, polluting the air and contaminating our water, make the Exxon Valdez oil spill° look minor in comparison. All of which we can fix surprisingly easily, just by putting down our chicken wings and reaching for a veggie burger.

Doing so has never been easier. Recent years have seen an explosion of environmentally-friendly vegetarian foods. Even chains like Ruby Tuesday, Johnny Rockets, and Burger King offer delicious veggie burgers and super-market refrigerators are lined with heart-healthy creamy soymilk and tasty veggie deli slices. Vegetarian foods have become staples at environmental gatherings, and garnered celebrity advocates like Bill Maher, Alec Baldwin, Paul McCartney, and of course Leonardo DiCaprio. Just as the Prius showed us that we each have in our hands the power to make a difference against a problem that endangers the future of humanity, going vegetarian gives us a new way to dramatically reduce our dangerous emissions that is even more effective, easier to do, more accessible to everyone and certainly goes better with french fries.

Ever-rising temperatures, melting ice caps, spreading tropical diseases, stronger hurricanes. . . . So, what are you doing for dinner tonight? Check out www.VegCooking.com for great ideas, free recipes, meal plans, and more! Check out the environmental section of www.GoVeg.com for a lot more information about the harmful effect of meat-eating on the environment.

Exxon **Valdez** *oil spill:* a 1989 oil spill in Prince William Sound, Alaska. It is considered among the world's worst environmental disasters because of the extensive damage that it inflicted on local wildlife.

Chapter 7 discusses the importance of understanding conditions of rebuttal. What kinds of rebuttals should this author anticipate?

LINK TO P. 196

RESPOND●

1. For Freston, why is vegetarianism the new Prius? How does she compare a diet with an automobile and use the comparison to her advantage?

2. In what ways is Freston's argument a proposal argument? An evaluative argument? Why do we expect all proposal arguments to contain evaluative elements, even if they aren't full evaluative arguments? (For a discussion of evaluative arguments, see Chapter 10. For a discussion of proposal arguments, see Chapter 12.)

3. In American journalism and in Internet postings like Freston's, writers often do not provide references or sources for their statistics. Using the Internet, try to find evidence that either supports or calls into question three of the statistics that Freston uses.

4. As is also common in such Internet postings, Freston uses informal language, including conversational sentence structures and wording that would not be appropriate in much academic writing. Working with a classmate, find at least three examples of her informal language, and revise them to convey the same information in ways that are appropriate for academic writing generally. If you're having trouble with this question, compare the language in this selection to that in the previous one, Solomon H. Katz's "The World Food Crisis: An Overview of the Causes and Consequences," which is written in a formal, academic style. (For a discussion of academic argument, see Chapter 6. For a discussion of style in argument, see Chapter 13, especially the first few sections of the chapter.)

5. Study the cartoon reprinted here, which gives three reasons a person might be or become vegetarian.

"I started my vegetarianism for health reasons, then it became a moral choice, and now it's just to annoy people."

In light of this cartoon, how would you characterize Freston's reasons for becoming and remaining vegetarian? What arguments could someone make in support of becoming vegetarian for each of the three reasons given in the cartoon? How does the fact that carnivores—people who eat meat—sometimes suspect that at least some vegetarians avoid eating meat "just to annoy people" create an extra burden for those arguing in support of vegetarianism?

6. **Write an essay** in which you evaluate Freston's argument, considering the question posed in the headnote to the selection: given Freston's proposal argument, why aren't all Americans vegetarians? In other words, evaluate both the effectiveness of Freston's presentation of the argument for vegetarianism and the more complex issue of why, in the face of such evidence (and other arguments that might be made), America is not a nation of vegetarians.

▼ *Claire Ironside is an instructor of illustration at Sheridan College School of Animation, Art, and Design in Ontario, Canada, where she teaches in the applied illustration program. With training in environmental and communication design studies, she is especially interested in issues of social engagement and activism as well as sustainability. This selection, "Apples to Oranges," uses primarily visual means to make its argument. Its title plays on an everyday expression that is used when two things are compared unfairly because they are fundamentally different in one or more ways. We found this selection in Food, a 2008 book edited by John Knechtel. It appears in the Alphabet City series, copublished by Alphabet City Media and the MIT Press. Each volume focuses on a single theme and brings together artists and writers from diverse perspectives to encourage readers to question their basic assumptions about the topic. As you study this selection, think about what it would take to translate Ironside's argument into words alone and whether doing so is even possible. (By the way, to convert kilometers to miles, multiply the number of kilometers by .62 to get a rough equivalent.)*

Making a Visual Argument: Apples to Oranges
Claire Ironside

The Big Apple
Colborne, Ontario

photo: Claire Ironside

apples
to
oranges
claire
ironside

The Orange Julep
Montreal, Quebec

Photo: Adrian Black

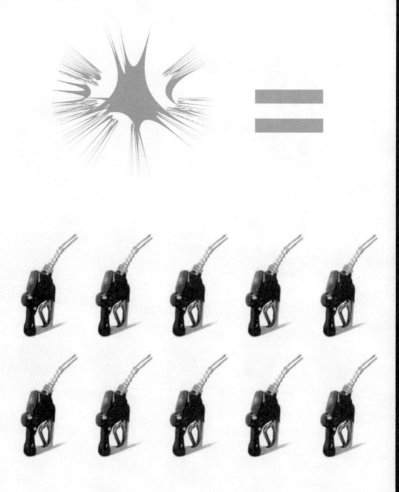

200   food

Your food travels an average distance of 2,414 kilometers to get to your plate, which is a large part of the reason every calorie you eat takes an average of 10 fossil fuel calories to produce.*

A look at the fossil fuel inputs of a locally grown, organic apple, and a California orange, both destined for the Toronto market, reveals the difference.

* Dr. Joseph Pimentel, Cornell University professor of ecology and agricultural science.

Colborne to Toronto
178 km

Colborne

Toronto

Orange County to Toronto
5,632 km

Orange County

Toronto

Fossil fuel inputs
of a local, organic apple

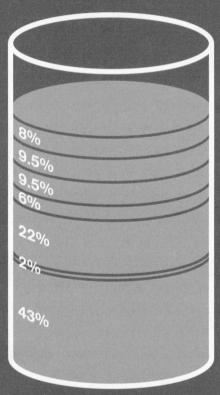

organic local
farming

8%

commercial
preparation/storage

9.5%

bulk packaging

9.5%

retail storage/
maintaining

6%

preparation/
manufacturing

22%

transportation

2%

home storage/
cooking

43%

Fossil fuel inputs
of a Californian orange

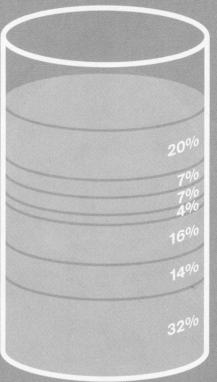

20%   industrial farming

         commercial
         preparation/storage
7%   bulk packaging
7%   retail storage/
4%   maintaining

         preparation/
16% manufacturing

14% transportation

         home storage/
32% cooking

Total fossil fuel footprint of a local, organic apple compared with average

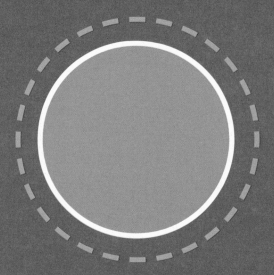

APPLE FOSSIL FUEL FOOTPRINT
1:8

Total fossil fuel footprint of a Californian orange compared with average

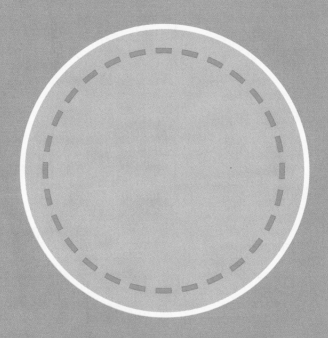

ORANGE FOSSIL FUEL FOOTPRINT
1:12

1. What is Ironside's explicit argument? What kind of argument is it (for example, of fact or definition)? Might she be making an implicit argument? What would that argument be? And what kind of argument is it?

2. Analyze each pair of pages in Ironside's argument. What does each juxtaposition contribute to her argument? How would you characterize the purpose of the comparison related to fossil-fuel inputs? What value might there be in the details given? What sorts of conclusions might we draw from this juxtaposition?

3. Evaluate the visual aspects of Ironside's argument, including her choice of colors.

4. Ironside's argument is part of a larger debate about carbon footprints. As this book goes to press, there are many Internet sites where you can calculate your own footprint. One is the Nature Conservancy's "What's My Carbon Footprint?" (http://www.nature.org/initiatives/climatechange/calculator). After you've calculated your footprint at this site, visit others, and compare the calculations you get there. Write an essay in which you report your findings and discuss the factors that might account for any discrepancies. (For a discussion of arguments of fact and definition, see Chapters 8 and 9, respectively.)

5. Ironside takes a single fact (about the relationship between each calorie you consume and the fossil-fuel calories that are required to produce it) and illustrates this fact in a complex and sophisticated way. She compares two examples and demonstrates the nature of the average by showing an example that is above average and one that is below average. Choose a single fact about food (perhaps related to the statistics that you analyzed in question 3 of the previous selection, Freston's "Vegetarian Is the New Prius"), and think of a visual argument that can illustrate it (as Ironside has here). You can either create the visual argument or describe it in words by discussing aspects of design (color, shape, images, and so on). (For a discussion of visual argument, see Chapter 14.)

Local Food

WIKIPEDIA

Local food (also **regional food** or **food patriotism**) or the **local food movement** is a "collaborative effort to build more locally based, self-reliant food economies—one in which sustainable food production, processing, distribution, and consumption is integrated to enhance the economic, environmental and social health of a particular place"[1] and is considered to be a part of the broader sustainability movement. It is part of the concept of local purchasing and local economies, a preference to buy locally produced goods and services. Those who prefer to eat locally grown/produced food sometimes call themselves "localvores" or locavores.[2]

Marylebone farmers' market

Contents   [hide]

Local food systems   [edit]

Local food systems are an alternative to the global corporate models where producers and consumers are separated through a chain of processors/manufacturers, shippers and retailers. With an increasing scale of industrial food systems the control of quality is increasingly decided by the middlemen while a local food system redevelops these relationships and encourages a return of quality control to the consumer and the producer, respectively. These quality characteristics are not only in the product but in the method of producing.[3]

Defining a movement   [edit]

During the early 20th century, the demise of the family farm and the growth of corporate farms was experienced through much of the United States. In the late 1960s and early '70s with the growth of the back to the land movement there were increasing numbers of small farms selling a variety of products to local communities. Since the 1970s the increase of multinational food companies has increased the size of not only farms but also the overall food system. During this same time period, a slow and steady movement of farmers and consumers building relationships and changing purchasing habits occurred and is still occurring.

The concept is often related to the slogan "*Think globally, act locally*," common in green politics. Those supporting development of a local food economy consider that since food is needed by everyone, everywhere, every day, a small change in the way it is produced and marketed will have a great effect on health, the ecosystem and preservation of cultural diversity. They say shopping decisions favoring local food consumption directly affect the well-being of people, improve local economies and may be more ecologically sound.

Pioneering and influential work in the area of local economies was done by   5
noted economist E. F. Schumacher.

Local food networks include community gardens, food co-ops, Community-Supported Agriculture (CSA), farmers' markets, and seed savers groups. The principal distinction between these systems and other agrifood systems is the spatial dimension. Local food networks have been described as "community-based agriculture" (e.g. Pimbert et al., 2001), "direct agricultural markets"[4], and "localist agriculture" (Hines et al., 2000). The terms "network" and "system" are sometimes used interchangeably, but there appears to be a preference for "network".

Definitions of "local"   [edit]

The definition of "local" or "regional" is flexible and is different depending on the person in question. Some local business with specific retail and production focuses, such as cheese, may take a larger view of what is 'local' while a local farm may see the area within a day's driving as local (since this is where they can efficiently move their products to). Some see "local" as being a very small area (typically, the size of a city and its surroundings), others

As Chapter 9 argues, many political, social, and scientific terms are constantly "under construction," as the word *local* is here.

LINK TO P. 253

suggest the ecoregion or bioregion size, while others refer to the borders of their nation or state.

Some proponents of "local food" consider that the term "local" has little to do with distance or with the size of a "local" area. For example, some see the American state of Texas as being "local", although it is much larger than some European countries. In this case, transporting a food product across Texas could involve a longer distance than that between northern and southern European countries. It is also argued that national borders should not be used to define what is local. For example, a cheese produced in Alsace (France) is likely to be more "local" to German people in Frankfurt than to French people in Marseille.

The concept of "local" is also seen in terms of ecology, where food production is considered from the perspective of a basic ecological unit defined by its climate, soil, watershed, species and local agrisystems, a unit also called an ecoregion or foodshed. The concept of the foodshed is similar to that of a watershed; it is an area where food is grown and eaten. The size of the foodshed varies depending on the availability of year-round foods and the variety of foods grown and processed. In a way, replacing the term 'water' with 'food' reconnects food with nature. "The term 'foodshed' thus becomes a unifying and organizing metaphor for conceptual development that starts from a premise of the unity of place and people, of nature and society."[5]

Where local food is determined by the distance it has traveled, the wholesale 10 distribution system can confuse the calculations. Fresh food that is grown very near to where it will be purchased, may still travel hundreds of miles out of the area through the industrial system before arriving back at a local store. This is seen as a labeling issue by local food advocates, who suggest that, at least in the case of fresh food, consumers should be able to see exactly how far each food item has traveled.

Often, products are grown in one area and processed in another, which may cause complications in the purchasing of local foods. In the international wine industry, much "bulk wine" is shipped to other regions or continents, to be blended with wine from other locales. It may even be marketed quite misleadingly as a product of the bottling country. This is in direct opposition to both the concept of "local food" and the concept of terroir.°

terroir: (French, "soil") a term used with certain food products (such as wine, tea, coffee, cheese) to indicate the influence of the soil and weather on the product. Thus, grapes of the same variety that are grown in different countries (or different regions of a single country) produce wines that have different characteristics because of variations in soil composition, rainfall, temperature, sunlight, and so on.

Locavore   [edit]

A **locavore** is someone who eats food grown or produced locally or within a certain radius such as 50, 100, or 150 miles. The locavore movement encourages consumers to buy from farmers' markets or even to produce their own food, with the argument that fresh, local products are more nutritious and taste better. Locally grown food is an environmentally friendly means of obtaining food, since supermarkets that import their food use more fossil fuels and non-renewable resources.

"Locavore" was coined by Jessica Prentice from the San Francisco Bay Area on the occasion of World Environment Day 2005 to describe and promote the practice of eating a diet consisting of food harvested from within an area most commonly bound by a 100-mile radius. "Localvore" is sometimes also used.

The new Oxford American Dictionary chose locavore, a person who seeks out locally produced food, as its word of the year 2007.[6] The local foods movement is gaining momentum as people discover that the best-tasting and most sustainable choices are foods that are fresh, seasonal, and grown close to home. Some locavores draw inspiration from the *The 100-Mile Diet* or from advocates of local eating like Barbara Kingsolver whose book *Animal, Vegetable, Miracle* chronicles her family's attempts to eat locally. Others just follow their taste buds to farmers' markets, community-supported agriculture programs, and community gardens.

A study in the 2007 Dewey Health Review revealed that a Locavore diet (study   15 included 100 individuals ages 18–55 eating local food grown within an 80-mile radius) resulted in a 19% increase in sturdiness of bowel movement and an overall drop in sleep apnea and night terrors.

Labelling   [edit]

Local food is, by definition, food produced locally. Whether the seed—an integral part of the "food"—was grown or procured locally as well is usually left out of this definition, leading to even greater ambiguity as to its meaning. Many local food proponents tend to equate it with food produced by local independent farmers, while equating non-local food with food produced and transformed by large agribusiness. They may support resisting globalization of food by pressing for policy changes and choosing to buy local food. They may also follow the practice of the boycott or buycott.

Non-local food is often seen as a result of corporate management policies, heavy subsidies, poor animal welfare, lack of care for the environment, and poor working conditions. This limited interpretation is likely due to the fact that the organic movement is largely responsible for renewed public interest in local and regional markets. Those subscribing to this interpretation often insist on buying food directly from local family farms, through direct channels such as farmers' markets, food cooperatives and community-supported agriculture plans. For many, local food is interpreted as unprocessed food, to be transformed by the consumer or local shop rather than by the food industry. As such, local food (as opposed to global food) reduces or eliminates the costs of transport, processing, packaging, and advertising.

As large corporations and supermarket distribution increasingly dominate the organic food market, the concept of local food, and sometimes 'sustainable food', is increasingly being used by independent farmers, food activists, and aware consumers to refine the definition of organic food and organic agriculture. By this measure, food that is certified organic but not grown locally is viewed as possibly "less organic" or not of the same overall quality or benefit, as locally grown organic products. Some consumers see the general advantages of "organic" as also invested in "locally grown", therefore local food *not* grown "organically" may trump generically "organic" in purchase decisions. Also, because local food tends to be fresh (or minimally processed, such as cheese and milk), as opposed to processed food, the bias against processed food is often at least implicit in the local food argument. The marketing phrase, *fresh, local, organic*, summarizes these arguments.

Impacts of local food systems   [edit]

Food quality   [edit]
Another effect is the increase in food quality and taste. Locally grown fresh food is consumed almost immediately after harvest, so it is sold fresher and usually riper (e.g. picked at peak maturity, as it would be from a home

garden). Also, the need for chemical preservatives and irradiation to artificially extend shelf-life is reduced or eliminated.

Gastronomy

Additionally, preserving or renewing regional foodways, including unique [20]
localized production practices, indigenous knowledge, agricultural landscapes, and local/regional landraces° of crops or livestock that may be rare or otherwise endangered. It is increasingly being tied to the movement to preserve farmland (farming) in areas where development pressures threaten these landscapes.

Polyculture° and sustainable farming [edit]

A major impact of local food systems is to encourage multiple cropping, i.e. growing multiple species and a wide variety of crops at the same time and same place, as opposed to the prevalent commercial practice of large-scale, single-crop monoculture.°

With a higher demand for a variety of agricultural products, farmers are more likely to diversify their production, thereby making it easier to farm in a sustainable way. For example, winter intercropping (e.g. coverage of leguminous° crops during winter) and crop rotation reduces pest pressure, and also the use of pesticides. Also, in an animal/crop multicultural system, the on-farm byproducts like manure and crop residues are used to replace chemical fertilizers, while on-farm produced silage° and leguminous crops feed the cattle instead of imported soya. Manure and residues being considered as byproducts rather than waste, will have reduced effects on the environment, and reduction in soya import is likely to be economically interesting for the farmer, as well as more secure (because of a decrease of market dependence on outside inputs).

In a polycultural agroecosystem, there is usually a more efficient use of labour as each crop has a different cycle of culture, hence different time of intensive care, minimization of risk (lesser effect of extreme weather as one crop can compensate for another), reduction of insect and disease incident (diseases are usually crop specific), maximization of results with low levels of technology (intensive monoculture cropping often involves very high-technology material

landraces: plants or animals that were domesticated more or less naturally in particular regions. Cumulatively, they are characterized by greater diversity than plants or animals that have been domesticated by humans.

polyculture: the practice of growing multiple crops, generally in the same field.

monoculture: the practice of growing only one crop.

leguminous: relating to legumes, a family of plants that have pods. Common examples are beans, peas, peanuts, clover, and carob.

silage: food for cows or sheep that is made of fermented crops (either the grain or the entire plant). Examples include corn, alfalfa, oats, and sorghum.

multiculture: a synonym for
polyculture.

and sometimes the use of genetically modified seeds). Multiculture° also seeks
to preserve indigenous biodiversity.

Local economies   [edit]

Local food production strengthens local economies by protecting small farms,
local jobs, and local shops, thereby increasing food security.

One example of an effort in this direction is community-supported agricul-   25
ture (CSA), where consumers purchase advance shares in a local farmer's
annual production, and pick up their shares, usually weekly, from communal
distribution points. In effect, CSA members become active participants in local
farming, by providing up-front cash to finance seasonal expenses, sharing in
the risks and rewards of the growing conditions, and taking part in the distribution system. Some CSA set-ups require members to contribute a certain
amount of labor, in a form of cooperative venture.

The popular resurgence of farmers' markets in many parts of the world,
including Europe and North America (from 1,755 in 1994 to 4,385 in 2006 in the
U.S.)[7], contributes to local economies. They are traditional in many societies,
bringing together local food and craft producers for the convenience of local
consumers. Today, some urban farmers' markets are large-scale enterprises,
attracting tens of thousands on a market day, and vendors are not always
"local". However, the majority of markets are still built around local farmers.

Another at present small but notable trend is local food as part of a barter
system. In localized economies, where a variety of common goods and
services are provided by individuals and businesses within the immediate
community (as opposed to by outlets and branches of large corporations), a
direct exchange of values is quite feasible. Some CSA projects, for example,
trade services or labor for food. Particularly in the developed nations, the
move away from local food to agribusiness over the last 100 years has had a
profound socioeconomic effect, by redistributing populations into urban
areas, and concentrating ownership of land and capital. In addition, the traditional farming skill set, which by necessity included a diverse range of
knowledge and abilities required to manage a farm, has given way to new
generations of specialists. When farming for local consumption was a cornerstone of local economies, the farmer was an integral, leading member of the
community, a far different position from today. Support for local food is seen

by some as a way to rediscover valuable community structures, values and perspectives.

Cost to consumer   [edit]

Critics also say that local food tends to be more expensive to the consumer than food bought without regard to provenance and could never provide the variety currently available (such as having summer vegetables available in winter, or having kinds of food available which can not be locally produced due to soil, climate or labor conditions).

However, proponents claim that the lower price of commodified food (which is sometimes called *cheap food*) is often due to a variety of governmental subsidies, including direct ones such as price supports, direct payments or tax breaks, and indirect ones such as subsidies for trucking via road infrastructure investment, and often does not take into account the true cost of the product. They further indicate that buying local food does not necessarily mean giving up all food coming from distant ecoregions, but rather favoring local foods when available. They also point out that local foods often represent *more* variety, not less, as obscure local delicacies (including wild foods) are rediscovered, and as more types of produce (varieties or indeed species) are grown in the garden or allotment, types that would not be acceptable in the supermarket-driven food chain.

A study published in the May 2008 issue of the *American Journal of Agricultural Economics* suggests that the average supermarket shopper is willing to pay a premium price for locally produced foods. The study also showed that shoppers at farm markets are willing to pay almost twice as much extra as retail grocery shoppers for the same locally produced foods. In 2005, the researchers surveyed shoppers at 17 Midwestern locations, including seven retail grocery stores, six on-site farm markets and four farmers' markets hosting sellers from multiple farms. The researchers used data from 477 surveys.[8]

30

Effect on exporting countries   [edit]

Some critics argue that by convincing consumers in developed nations not to buy food produced in the third world, the local food movement damages the economy of third world nations, which often rely heavily on food exports and cash crops.

Environmental impact   [edit]

Critics of the local food movement point out that transport is only one component of the total environmental impact of food production and consumption. In fact, any environmental assessment of food that consumers buy needs to take into account how the food has been produced and what energy is used in its production. For example, it is likely to be more environmentally friendly for tomatoes to be grown in Spain and transported to the UK° than for the same tomatoes to be grown in greenhouses in the UK requiring electricity to light and heat them. The solutions to this though would be either using low-impact energy sources on the greenhouses, such as solar, geothermal or wind, or to switch to eating seasonally.

the UK: the United Kingdom— England, Scotland, Wales, and Northern Ireland.

A study by Lincoln University of Christchurch, New Zealand challenges claims about food miles by comparing total energy used in food production in Europe and New Zealand, taking into account energy used to ship the food to Europe for consumers.[9]

> New Zealand has greater production efficiency in many food commodities compared to the UK. For example New Zealand agriculture tends to apply less fertilizers (which require large amounts of energy to produce and cause significant CO_2 emissions) and animals are able to graze year round outside eating grass instead of large quantities of brought-in feed such as concentrates. In the case of dairy and sheep meat production NZ is by far more energy efficient even including the transport cost than the UK, twice as efficient in the case of dairy, and four times as efficient in case of sheep meat. In the case of apples NZ is more energy efficient even though the energy embodied in capital items and other inputs data was not available for the UK.

An August 6, 2007 article in *The New York Times* gave examples of how eating locally grown food sometimes causes an increase, instead of decrease, in the carbon footprint. As one example, the article stated, ". . . lamb raised on New Zealand's clover-choked pastures and shipped 11,000 miles by boat to Britain produced 1,520 pounds of carbon dioxide emissions per ton while British lamb produced 6,280 pounds of carbon dioxide per ton, in part because poorer British pastures force farmers to use feed. In other words, it is four times more energy-efficient for Londoners to buy lamb imported from the other side of the world than to buy it from a producer in their backyard."[10]

According to a study by engineers Christopher Weber and H. Scott Matthews   35
of Carnegie Mellon University, of all the greenhouse gases emitted by the food
industry, only 4% comes from transporting the food from producers to retailers. The study also concluded that adopting a vegetarian diet, even if the
vegetarian food is transported over very long distances, does far more to
reduce greenhouse gas emissions, than does eating a locally grown diet.[11]

See also   [edit]

- Agroecology
- *Animal, Vegetable, Miracle*
- Bioregionalism
- Community-based economics
- FARMA
- Farm to fork
- Farm to School
- Food miles
- Gandhi's "Principles of Swadeshi"
- Localism (politics)
- Low carbon diet
- Permaculture
- Slow Food
- Sustainable agriculture
- Ark of Taste

References

1. Feenstra, G. (2002) Creating space for sustainable food systems: lessons
   from the field. *Agriculture and Human Values*. 19(2). 99–106.
2. Roosevelt, M. (2006) The Lure of the 100-Mile Diet. *Time Magazine*. Sunday
   June 11, 2006. Accessed at http://www.time.com/time/magazine/article/
   0,9171,1200783,00.html on Nov 1, 2007 at 10:35 am PDT.
3. Sonnino, R. & Marsden, T. (2006) Beyond the Divide: rethinking relationships between alternative and conventional food networks in Europe.
   Economic Journal of Geography. pp. 181–199.

4. Hinrichs, C. C. (2000) Embeddedness and local food systems: notes on two types of direct agricultural markets. *Journal of Rural Studies*, 16(3), 295–303.

5. Coming Into the Foodshed. *Agriculture and Human Values* 13:3 (Summer): 33–42, 1996. (http://www.cias.wisc.edu/foodshed/pubsntools/comingin .htm) Accessed on Nov 5, at 10:42 pm CST

6. Severson, Kim (22 July 2008). "A Locally Grown Diet With Fuss but No Muss" (http://www.nytimes.com/2008/07/22/dining/22local.html?ref=us), *The New York Times*. Retrieved on 4 August 2008.

7. USDA Agricultural Marketing Services (2006). Farmers Market Growth. http://www.ams.usda.gov/farmersmarkets/farmersmarketgrowth.htm accessed on Dec 6, 2006 at 10:44 pm PST

8. Newswise: Shoppers Willing to Pay Premium for Locally Grown Food (http://newswise.com/articles/view/541406/) Retrieved on June 15, 2008.

9. Food Miles: Comparative Energy/Emissions Performance of New Zealand's Agriculture Industry (http://www.regsw.org.uk/content/industryreports/ viewitem.aspx?artID=4624)

10 Food that Travels Well (http://www.nytimes.com/2007/08/06opinion/ 06mcwilliams.html?_r=1&oref=slogin), *The New York Times*, August 6, 2007

11. Food miles are less important to environment than food choices, study concludes (http://news.mongabay.com/2008/0602-ucsc_liaw_food_miles .html.), Jane Liaw, special to mongabay.com June 2, 2008

External links

- Tasting Food, Tasting Sustainability: Defining the Attributes of an Alternative Food System With Competent, Ordinary People. (http://fin-darticles.com/p/articles/mi_qu3800/is_200007/ai_n8899894) Human Organization 59:2 (July): 177–186.

- LOTRA—The Local Trade Alliance—Reviving America's local communities (http://www.lotra.org/)

- Local Fair Trade Network (http://www.localfairtrade.org/)

- Why long-haul food may be greener than local food with low air-miles (http://www.timesonline.co.uk/tol/news/environment/article3294448.ece)

- Find Local Food Producers—An Online Directory of UK Local Food Producers (http://www.farmshop.uk.com/farmshops/)

- CISA—Community Involved in Sustaining Agriculture (http://www .buylocalfood.org/), a community organization comprised of farmers, consumers and professionals working together to sustain agriculture and the unique rural character of western Massachusetts for the past 15 years.

- This page was last modified on 4 January 2009, at 16:57.
- All text is available under the terms of the GNU Free Documentation License. (See Copyrights for details.)
  Wikipedia® is a registered trademark of the Wikimedia Foundation, Inc., a U.S. registered 501(c)(3) tax-deductible nonprofit charity.

RESPOND.

1. In what ways is an encyclopedia entry an argument? What kind of argument is it? What evidence can you provide for your claims?

2. How does this Wikipedia entry contribute to your understanding of issues relating to food in the United States and the world? In what ways does it complement the previous readings in this chapter by providing new ways for thinking about the issues discussed? In what ways does it provide information that is not discussed in earlier readings? What might account for these situations?

3. Labels matter. In fact, we contend that names are often arguments. What are the differences in referring to the trends described in this selection as "local food," "regional food," "food patriotism," and "the local food movement"? To answer this question, you'll need to determine the denotations and connotations of each name. Which sorts of groups might favor or disfavor each name? Why?

4. Compare this January 17, 2009, version of Wikipedia's "Local food" entry with the version that is posted when you read this selection. What changes have been made to the selection? (If you click on the tabs labeled "Discussion," "Edit This Page," and "History" at the top of the entry, they will provide you with information about earlier versions of the page and the discussions that led to its current version.) What does studying the discussion and history of the article teach you about evaluating it? About how knowledge is constructed in Wikipedia?

5. As the headnote to the selection implies, there has been a great deal of controversy about how to evaluate Wikipedia entries, an issue that the Wikipedia entry for "Wikipedia" addresses. Read that entry, and find a Wikipedia entry on a topic that you know well. **Write an evaluative essay** in which you evaluate the Wikipedia entry on that topic in

light of the "Wikipedia" entry and the discussion of evaluating sources in Chapter 19. One issue to consider is audience: encyclopedia entries are generally written for people who do not know a great deal about a subject. In other words, ask yourself how well the entry conveys information to a reader who knows little or nothing about its subject. (Note that the blue text indicates links to other Wikipedia entries or to sources for this entry.)

Be sure to include a copy of the entry that you evaluate along with your essay. In evaluating the entry, you will likely want to quote from it, so remember the tips given in Chapters 18, 19, and 20 on crediting, using, and documenting sources.

6. Investigate the local food movement in your own town or in a nearby town or city. What forms does it take? Is it a new phenomenon, or is it part of the way that people have always eaten there? (You may need to interview some older people to gather such information.) If there is little or no evidence of a local food movement where you live, try to discover why. If you find strong evidence of such a movement, what can you discover about its origins? About how it has changed? **Write an essay** in which you report your results. The essay may be primarily factual in nature, or it may be definitional, evaluative, or causal. Similarly, it may take the form of a proposal. (For a discussion of these types of essays, see Chapters 8–12, respectively.)

▼ *The selections thus far in this chapter have focused on food, but water (particularly bottled water) also has been part of these discussions for several reasons. In this selection, which appeared in June 2008 in the Los Angeles Times, Mark Coleman reviews a book that deals with these issues,* Bottlemania: How Water Went on Sale and Why We Bought It *by Elizabeth Royte. (The next selection is an excerpt from Royte's book.) As you read Coleman's selection, consider book reviews as a subcategory of evaluative arguments, and learn as much as you can about the arguments that Royte presents about bottled water.*

Review of *Bottlemania: How Water Went on Sale and Why We Bought It*

MARK COLEMAN

In 2006, Americans consumed, per capita,° more than 25 gallons of bottled water—twice as much as in 1997 and almost five times as much as in 1987. And what ignites Elizabeth Royte's reportorial spark in *Bottlemania*—at least initially—is the ecological cost of all those plastic empties: We discard between 30 billion and 40 billion bottles of Poland Spring, the most popular brand, in a year.

Like her previous book, *Garbage Land: On the Secret Trail of Trash*, this tautly paced volume more closely resembles a travel narrative than a tree-hugging° jeremiad.° Royte doesn't traffic in platitudes,° moral certainties or oversimplification; she's unafraid of ambiguity. Seamlessly blending scientific explanation and social observation, she pursues the course of Poland Spring back to its source in Fryeburg, Maine.

"Fryeburg is tied up in fits," she writes. "Its abundance of fine water

has cast its unwitting residents into the middle of a social, economic, and environmental drama." Her mordant° wit comes in handy: "It's easier to picture kids guzzling beer out here than deer nuzzling around mossy springs," she notes. "But Fryeburg, for all its out-of-season torpor,° once bustled with economic activity: sawmills and timber operations, a shoe manufacturing plant, a couple of machine shops, corn shops, and dozens of thriving dairy farms. Now, it has the water-extraction business, which

---

per capita: (Latin, "per head") per person.

tree-hugging: strongly environmentalist, often

implying criticism of such a stance.

jeremiad: an extended complaint, usually sad or mournful in nature.

platitudes: trite, often meaningless, statements.

mordant: biting or sarcastic.

torpor: lethargy or inactivity.

contributes nothing to the town's long-term economic welfare."

What drives this obsessive thirst—this compulsion to pay for something we can essentially get for free? Royte characterizes the nationwide craving for bottled water, "in a country where more than 89 percent of tap water meets or exceeds federal health and safety regulations," as both an outrageous marketing coup° and an unparalleled social phenomenon. Beginning in the late 1970s with Orson Welles'° high-toned television pitches for Perrier, bottled water has been promoted for its snob appeal as much as its health benefits. Jennifer Aniston's° recent spots for Smartwater strike Royte as typically absurd. "Some ads depict her naked and others place her, clad, in an elegant restaurant, where her plastic water bottle looks, to someone with my peculiar mindset, like litter amid the crystal stemware."

Royte's "peculiar mindset" is that 5 of an unabashed tap-water enthusiast who savors the irony that "purified" water from municipal sources—Dasani and Aquafina, as opposed to bottled spring water or mineral water, like Perrier—accounts for 44% of U.S. bottled-water sales. If her personal disavowal of bottled water borders on the puritanical, it also comes across as pragmatic: "Foie gras° tastes better than chopped liver. That doesn't mean I'm going to buy it. I don't need to spoil myself. I don't want to get used to expensive things . . . that might . . . disrupt the social and environmental order."

Like any good travel writer, Royte possesses an intellectual curiosity that continually lures her off the beaten path. The second half of *Bottlemania* takes a sharp turn, upending many of the author's previous assumptions about tap water.

"I decide to visit Kansas City," she writes, "where the public utility sucks from the Missouri River something that resembles chocolate Yoo-Hoo° and turns it into water so good that national magazines shower it with awards and even the locals buy it in bottles." All along the Missouri and the Mississippi, cities drink from and discharge into the same river. Visiting a municipal water-treatment plant, Royte is alternately impressed and appalled: "[T]he filtering process mimics, in a supercondensed time frame, the purifying processes of nature. It's the same ecosystem service provided for free in such places as Fryeburg, Maine, by glacier-made beds of sand and gravel."

Royte knows when not to intrude, when to let a devastating quote or damning exchange stand on its own:

"What do you do with the atrazine [an herbicide] once you filter it out?"

"We put it back in the river."   10

It seems that because of oil spills, industrial discharges, agricultural runoff, animal waste and sewage (both treated and raw), tap water is far from risk-free. Suddenly, the stainless-steel extraction pipes of Poland Spring don't seem quite so redundant,° and Royte admits that after her tap-water investigations, "I'm not immune to the appeal of springwater." Yet the conclusion of *Bottlemania* is more thoughtful than despairing, even though much of what we've learned isn't comforting. If our future really

---

coup: a clever accomplishment or triumph.

Orson Welles (1915–1985): an American actor, director, producer, and writer perhaps best known for his film *Citizen Kane* (1941).

Jennifer Aniston (b. 1969): an American film and television actress perhaps best known for her role in the television series *Friends.*

foie gras: (French, "fatty liver") an appetizer that usually is made of goose liver. Because the geese are generally force fed, this food has been boycotted by those concerned with animal rights.

Yoo-Hoo: a bottled chocolate drink.

redundant: unnecessary or useless because it duplicates something that already exists.

does include drinking reclaimed or "repurified" wastewater, Royte is willing to hold her nose and remain philosophical. "As bad as toilet-to-tap sounds," she concludes, "I have to remind myself: all water is recycled."

Chapter 10 notes that evaluation arguments always depend upon evaluative criteria, such as those Coleman makes explicit when he notes how Elizabeth Royte succeeds as a writer.

LINK TO P. 289

RESPOND ●

1. How would you characterize Mark Coleman's evaluation of Elizabeth Royte's book? Do you think that he likes the book? How well? Why? What evidence can you cite for your characterization of his evaluation?

2. A review of a book (or movie or DVD or concert) is, by definition, an evaluative argument. What criteria does Coleman use in evaluating Royte's book? Do these criteria seem appropriate and sufficient to the task? Why or why not? (For a discussion of evaluative arguments, see Chapter 10.)

3. Coleman contends that as a writer, "Royte doesn't traffic in platitudes, moral certainties or oversimplification; she's unafraid of ambiguity" (paragraph 2). What evidence do you find for these claims in his review? Should you find any?

4. Examine Coleman's use of quotations from Royte's book. What functions do they serve in Coleman's own argument? (In answering this question, you may wish to make a list of all the quotations to examine their functions carefully.)

5. Using the discussion of evaluative arguments in Chapter 10, **write an evaluation** of Coleman's review of Royte's book. In other words, formulate criteria for evaluating a review, and then apply them to this review. An interesting way to complete this assignment would be to locate other reviews of this book, determine how they are similar to and different from Coleman's, and use this knowledge as you formulate your criteria. Consider the kinds of information, evaluations, and evidence that you, as a reader, would hope to find in a review.

▼ *This selection consists of two parts. The first is an excerpt from the clos-ing chapter of the book reviewed in the previous selection, Elizabeth Royte's* Bottlemania: How Water Went on Sale and Why We Bought It. *The sec-ond is a graphic from the July 2007* New York Times *that is now posted as part of a "Times Topics" Web page on "Bottled Water" (http://topics.nytimes .com/top/reference/timestopics/subjects/w/water/bottled_water/index.html).*

The selection from Royte's final chapter helps to conclude the book by responding to two of its motivating questions: what kind of water should we be drinking and why? In addition to Bottlemania, *published in 2008, Royte is also the author of* The Tapir's Morning Bath: Solving the Mysteries of the Tropical Rain Forest *(2002) and* Garbage Land: On the Secret Trail of Trash *(2005). The graphic "Satisfying the National Thirst . . . with Lots of Bottles" from the* New York Times *makes arguments about one of the controversies surrounding bottled water in overwhelmingly visual ways. As you read the excerpt from* Bottlemania, *pay attention to the ways that Royte gives us signs that she is coming to the end of her book's argu-ment. As you study the* New York Times *graphic, consider how its arguments complement those that Royte uses.*

Excerpt from *Bottlemania: How Water Went on Sale and Why We Bought It*

ELIZABETH ROYTE

EPA: the United States Environmental Protection Agency, a government agency that is charged with protecting the country's environment.

NRDC: the National Resources Defense Council, a nongovern-mental organization that contends that it is "the nation's most effective environmental action group."

For now, what should we be drinking? The EPA° tells us that the Untied States has one of the safest water supplies in the world. "I wouldn't hesitate to drink tap water anywhere in the country," Cynthia Dougherty, director of the EPA's Office of Groundwater and Drinking Water, says. Drink a glass of water in any city in the United States, Dr. Ronald B. Linsky of the National Water Research Institute said in *Avoiding Rate Shock: Making the Case for Water Rates*, a report published by the American Water Works Association, and you "have a very, very high assurance of safe, high-quality drinking water." If you fall into no risk category, says the NRDC,° you can drink most cities' tap water without a problem.

Statements like these confirm my personal bias: that water should be locally sourced, delivered by energy-efficient, publicly owned pipes, generate close to zero waste, and cost, for eight glasses a day, about forty-nine cents a year. Buy that water in bottles and you'd be spending $1,400.

But it isn't that simple: if it were, 20 percent of Americans wouldn't drink only bottled water. In 2006, 89.3 percent of the nation's nearly fifty-three thousand community water systems were in compliance with more than ninety EPA standards. That left 29.8 million people with water that missed the mark on either health or reporting standards, or both. (Many in this group live on Indian lands, and many drink from small systems, which have the most trouble meeting regulations.) Moreover, neither the EPA nor your water utility has anything to say about the condition of the pipes in your house. And then there are those risk categories.

"Right to know" reports advise the very young, the pregnant, the very old, or the immunocompromised° (for example, people who are HIV-positive or undergoing chemotherapy) to consult with their doctors before drinking tap water, even in communities where water gets high marks. Some scientists define the at-risk population even more broadly, to include not just babies but children and teens, lactating° women, and anyone over fifty-five. "Look at your annual report, then decide, based on your personal situation, if you need to do anything different," Dougherty says.

What's the big concern? It depends whom you ask; when you're a ham- 5 mer, everything looks like a nail. Scientists who study lead worry about lead. Scientists who study the connections between chemicals and cancer worry about disinfection by-products.° Microbiologists worry about tiny bugs.

Studies by epidemiologists° indicate that at least seven million Americans experience gastrointestinal° illnesses from waterborne microbes each year, of whom a thousand die. "Different people react to the same environment in different ways," says Ronnie D. Levin, a longtime EPA employee who is also a visiting scientist in the water and health program at the Harvard School of Public Health. "There is no bright golden line° that says there's no risk." Seven million is too many, Levin says. "I did a cost-benefit analysis and I think we can do better than that, without increasing the amount of disinfectants in the water."

Levin is wary of using more chlorine and other disinfectants because they generate disinfection by-products, "none of which are good." Her solution? Require utilities that rely on surface water to filter it first, to remove organic contaminants, and then to disinfect, instead of the other way around.

Until those utilities retrofit, I ask Levin, what about bottled water?

---

immunocompromised: having a compromised or not fully functional immune system to fight disease.

lactating: producing milk.

disinfection by-products: the results of chemical interactions between the organic material in the water to be treated and the chemicals used to treat the water.

epidemiologists: scientists who study how diseases are spread and controlled.

gastrointestinal: involving the stomach and intestines.

bright golden line: a clear marker distinguishing between two categories (here, with risk and without risk).

There is uncertainty about that too, she says. "It really comes down to your comfort level. Bottled water's monitoring and enforcement aren't good." Because we don't know the results of plants' inspections, "it's a crapshoot what you're getting."

So what do you drink? 10

"You've got to go with what you've got." Tap, in other words.

Do you filter?

"I do the right thing," she says, which I take to mean yes.

By this point I've spoken to enough scientists and environmental experts to believe my countertop Brita° is giving me more psychological than physical benefit, and that anyone with good reason to be suspicious of her tap water should invest in a point-of-use filter—the kind of gizmo you install on your faucet or under your sink. (Of pour-through filters, Levin says, "If there's nothing to filter out of your water, they are fine.") But not everyone is at high risk of illness, not everyone can afford a point-of-use filter and its maintenance (if they're not changed regularly, filters can put contaminants *into* water), and the money might better be spent on other preventive health measures.

To smooth out equity issues (under-the-sink filters can cost a couple hun- 15 dred dollars to buy and plumb), Robert D. Morris, the epidemiologist, suggests that utilities help pay for, install, and maintain point-of-use devices. In that way, water utilities could have confidence, he writes in *The Blue Death*, "that occasional occurrences of accidental, incidental, or intentional contamination would have little if any consequence." What would that cost? I ask him. "About a third of the utility's annual cost," he says, "but it's onetime only. You'd amortize° that cost, and you'd recycle the filters. There are economies of scale in buying a lot of them. But, yes, the consumer will ultimately pay for it."

All these caveats° beg the question: how do I know if I should be suspicious of my water? The EPA says, "Read your annual water report." But those documents—written by the utility—can be flawed, and some are essentially propaganda. (And again, they say nothing about the condition of your pipes.) They report yearly averages over time and, with some contaminants, over multiple locations within a system, which can obscure spikes. They don't necessarily list contaminants that aren't regulated (such as perchlorate,° radon,° and MTBE°), and their reporting periods close long before data reach customers. Reports may state that finished water has no cryptosporidium,° but the protozoan° parasite is notoriously difficult to detect.

When the NRDC studied the water-quality reports of nineteen cities in 2001, it gave five of them a poor or failing grade for burying, obscuring, and

---

Brita: a commercial brand of water filter.

amortize: in accounting or budgeting, to spread the cost of something over the period when it will be used rather than treating the entire cost as a one-time expense.

caveats: warnings.

perchlorate: a potentially dangerous water contaminant. The degree of danger is debated.

radon: a radioactive chemical element that occurs as a gas in the atmosphere and in some spring water.

MTBE: methyl tertiary butyl ether, a chemical compound that is used as an additive to gasoline. It easily pollutes groundwater supplies.

cryptosporidium: a protozoan that causes human diarrhea.

protozoan: relating to a single-cell microorganism.

omitting findings about health effects of contaminants in city water supplies, printing misleading statements, and violating a number of right-to-know requirements, such as the rule that says reports must identify known sources of pollutants in city water. What's a devotee of the tap to do? Read your report carefully, learn about the health effects of contaminants, call your utility with questions, then test your water yourself.

Drinking the waters of the Ashokan and other upstate reservoirs, here in New York City, my husband and I fall into no obvious risk category, but could eight-year-old Lucy fight off cryptosporidiosis?° (Treatment with ultraviolet light hasn't yet started.) And while disinfection by-products worry me a little (I live far from where the chlorine goes in, which gives trihalomethanes° a longer time to build up), do they worry me enough to spend another hundred bucks a year on filters?

To settle the question, I order my own tests. I fill four different containers with unfiltered tap water and mail them on ice to a certified lab in Ypsilanti, Michigan. When I rip open the envelope in two weeks, I'm relieved: I've got no lead, no coliform, no nitrates, and my total trihalomethanes are well within federal limits (at least on this November day: they may be higher in the heat of summer). But my manganese°—of all things—is 40 percent higher than the federal standard (though still 5.7 times lower than that tasty Gerolsteiner° I drank in Bryant Park). My Brita won't remove the mineral, but according to experts, this level presents no health risk to either children or adults. Steven Schindler, my water-testing guru at the Department of Environmental Protection, says the city never exceeded the state's limit of 0.3 parts per million in 2007. (The federal limit is 0.05 parts per million, but it's a "secondary level," which means utilities aren't required to test for it; the contaminant affects only the aesthetics of the water. At long last, the mystery of the reddish fuzz in the bottom of my Brita appears to be solved.) If manganese is my only problem, I'm happy. Like the vast majority of Americans, I can keep drinking tap water without worry.

I come away from my investigations with at least one certainty: not all tap water is perfect. But it is the devil we know,° the devil we have standing to negotiate with and to improve. Bottled-water companies don't answer to the public, they answer to shareholders. As Alan Snitow and Deborah Kaufman write in *Thirst*, "If citizens no longer control their most basic resource, their water, do they really control anything at all?"

Bottled water does have its place—it's useful in emergencies and essential for people whose health can't tolerate even filtered water. But it's often no better than tap water, its environmental and social price is high, and it lets

cryptosporidiosis: an infection caused by cryptosporidium and characterized by chronic diarrhea.

trihalomethanes: chemical compounds in solvents and refrigerants.

manganese: a chemical element that is necessary in trace levels for all life but that may destroy the central nervous system when people are overexposed to it.

Gerolsteiner: a naturally carbonated mineral water from Germany.

the devil we know: an allusion to the expression "Better the devil we do know than the one we don't." It means that something known (and possibly problematic) should be chosen over something unknown that could turn out to be much worse.

Chapter 7 explains that in classical rhetoric, the *peroratio* summarized the speaker's case and moved the audience to action. Note how Royte here begins reviewing her argument and exploring future actions her readers should take.

LINK TO P. 173

Which is the greater problem, the water or the plastic bottle it comes in?

aquifer: a permeable underground layer of soil, rock, or sand that stores and yields water.

PR: public relations.

flacks: spokespeople, especially those who can turn a potential disadvantage into an advantage.

Wendell Berry (b. 1934): a Kentucky-born writer, critic, and farmer.

our public guardians off the hook for protecting watersheds, stopping polluters, upgrading treatment and distribution infrastructure, and strengthening treatment standards.

Certainly, nearly everything humans do has an environmental impact—biking to work, recycling newspapers, and drinking tap water included. But understanding that impact is the first step toward reducing it. It's true that the impact of bottled water looks minuscule next to other water uses—growing beef, say, or manufacturing cars. But try telling that to someone who lives on a springwater truck route or who drinks from a well that shares an aquifer° with a commercial pump. As Lucy sings out when I try to tell her that some problem of hers is trivial in the larger scheme of things, "Not for me-eeee."

If someday I find myself wanting to buy bottled water, I will do it as an informed consumer, someone who knows that the images on the label may not reflect an ecological reality, that part of its sticker price may be landing in the pockets of lawyers and PR° flacks,° that profits probably aren't benefiting those who live near the source, and that the bottle and its transportation have a significant carbon footprint. And then I will try to drink with the fullest pleasure; pleasure that, to quote Wendell Berry° on the pleasure of eating, "does not depend on ignorance."

WORKS CITED

Avoiding rate shock: Making the case for water rates. 2004. Denver: American Water Works Association.

Morris, Robert D. 2007. *The blue death: Disease, disasters, and the water we drink.* New York: HarperCollins.

Snitow, Alan, Deborah Kaufman, and Michael Fox. 2007. *Thirst: Fighting the corporate theft of our water.* San Francisco: Jossey-Bass.

Satisfying the National Thirst...

Beverage Digest, which tracks trends in the industry, reports that the amount of liquid consumed by the average American holds steady at an estimated 182.5 gallons per year. Bottled water's share is growing, while almost everything else is in decline.

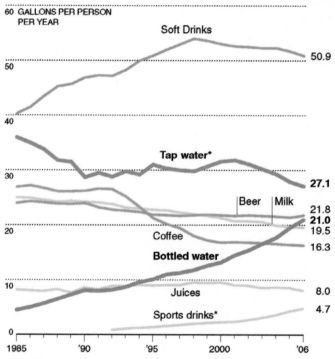

60 GALLONS PER PERSON PER YEAR

Soft Drinks — 50.9

Tap water* — 27.1

Beer | Milk — 21.8 / 21.0

Coffee — 19.5

Bottled water — 16.3

Juices — 8.0

Sports drinks* — 4.7

1985 '90 '95 2000 '06

*Tap water figures include small quantities of other beverages; they included sports drinks until 1992.

...With Lots of Bottles

This is what an average American's yearly consumption of bottled water looks like (in one of many possible combinations of bottles). It was 21 gallons — or 79.5 liters — in 2006.

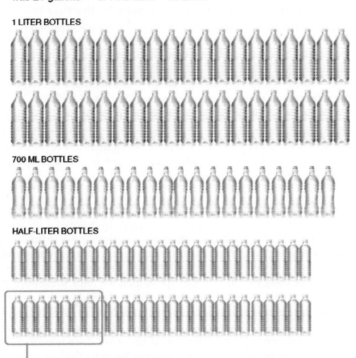

1 LITER BOTTLES

700 ML BOTTLES

HALF-LITER BOTTLES

About one gallon of bottled water per American is imported — 300 million gallons total last year.

ESTIMATING THE CARBON COST According to an analysis by the Natural Resources Defense Council, the 43 million gallons of bottled water imported from the European Union into New York area ports last year traveled 3,500 miles and created 3,800 tons of carbon dioxide — equivalent to 660 cars running for a year.

About one million gallons came from Fiji, a distance of 8,000 miles, creating an additional 190 tons of CO_2 (another 30 cars running).

EUROPE

New York

FIJI

RESPOND •

1. Briefly summarize Royte's response to the question with which she begins this excerpt. How well does she support her conclusions?

2. Summarize the arguments that are made by the *New York Times* graphic on pp. 840–41, and describe several contexts in which it could conceivably be used. Evaluate the graphic's effectiveness as a visual argument. (You may wish to locate the *Times* article with which this graphic originally appeared and use that information as part of your evaluation. For a discussion of evaluative arguments, see Chapter 10. For a discussion of visual arguments, see Chapter 14.)

3. In paragraph 2 of the previous selection, Mark Coleman's review of Royte's book, Coleman claims that "Royte doesn't traffic in platitudes, moral certainties or oversimplification; she's unafraid of ambiguity." What evidence for his evaluation do you see in this excerpt from Royte's book?

4. One of the ways that readers know that Royte is writing for a popular audience rather than an academic one is that she does not use footnotes or precise references (for example, page numbers) for quotations. She includes a list of works entitled "Selected Bibliography and Further Reading" at the end of the book, although it is not comprehensive, as we discovered tracking down the references for the three works that she cited in this excerpt (which we have presented as a Works Cited list). What are the advantages and disadvantages of using footnotes and explicit citations from a writer's point of view? A reader's? A publisher's? How does the absence of footnotes and explicit citations influence your evaluation of her text? Does it make it less formal and more inviting? Does it weaken Royte's ethos as a credible, trustworthy author? Why?

5. What is the current state of public debates about issues of water—tap versus bottled, local versus imported, natural versus flavored, plastic bottles and the carbon footprint? Investigate recent debates about water, and **construct an academic argument** that treats one of these topics. The argument may be factual, evaluative, or causal in nature. (For a discussion of academic argument, see Chapter 6. For a discussion of factual, evaluative, and causal arguments, see Chapters 8, 10, and 11, respectively.)

▼ *We end this chapter on food and water with two common genres of argument among people who take food seriously—an evaluative argument about which brand of ready-to-bake chocolate chip cookie dough is best and a recipe for homemade chocolate chip cookies. Both Cook's Country Magazine and the related Cook's Illustrated Magazine provide what they term "foolproof" recipes for home cooks as well as evaluations of cooking equipment and ingredients. Both publications pride themselves on not being glossy, advertising-laden magazines created by "food stylists"; rather, the recipes published have been tested and retested many times in the same test kitchen that is used for the public television program America's Test Kitchen. Thus, these magazines represent another aspect of the current American interest with food—cooking programs on television that are linked to magazines and cookbooks, all of which have a presence on the Internet.*

Unlike some magazines, however, these do not accept advertising, a fact that they use as an ethical appeal when they promote their "unbiased" and "objective" stance in evaluating cookware or ingredients. Rather than focusing on preparing food according to traditional recipes, these magazines try to develop recipes that take a minimum of time and effort while offering consistent high-quality results. Many cooks now subscribe to the magazines' Web sites, which grant them access to over sixteen years of recipes and videos. "Ready-to-Bake Chocolate Chip Cookies" appeared in the April 2005 issue of Cook's Country, and "Solving the Mystery of the Chewy Chocolate Chip Cookie" appeared in the January 1996 issue of Cook's Illustrated. As you read these two selections, analyze each in ways that you likely never have looked at recipes and "best of" lists—as arguments.

Ready-to-Bake Chocolate Chip Cookies

COOK'S COUNTRY MAGAZINE

LIST OF PRODUCTS TESTED
Homemade Cookies (with Nestlé Toll House Semi-
Sweet Morsels)
Nestlé Toll House Chocolate Chip Cookie Dough
Nestlé Toll House Refrigerated Chocolate Chip
Cookie Dough Bar

To determine if we could cheat and buy ready-to-bake cookie dough, we baked up cookies from homemade dough, cookie dough sold in the traditional log shape, and the new dough bars.

Nothing beats a good homemade cookie straight from the oven, right? Or can you cheat and buy ready-to-bake cookie dough? To find out if our tasters could tell the difference, we baked up three batches of cookies: one homemade recipe taken from the back of a bag of semisweet chips; one refrigerator dough sold in the traditional log shape; and one from a new product sold as a dough bar. No need to slice or measure the dough—it's already been cut into individual pieces. Just break off as many as you like and bake.

Our results were, well, surprising: The homemade batch didn't win? It seems that when it comes to chocolate chip cookies, the number of chips per cookie is what counts. Both types of ready-to-bake cookies were chock full of tiny chips, and one (the winner) had more chips than our homemade cookies. While tasters praised the homemade cookies for being light and chewy and having great butterscotch flavor, they criticized their sparse dotting of chips. Granted, the chips were larger than those in the ready-to-bake doughs, but tasters wanted more chocolate bite-for-bite. Of course, this problem can be easily remedied by adding more chips or by switching to the mini-chips used in the other doughs.

Of the two types of ready-to-bake cookies, the slice-and-bake (or more accurately, scoop and bake, from a log of dough) won not only for having the most chips but also for their more natural, craggy appearance. (Because the soft dough is hard to slice, the cookies look better if you scoop the dough.) The break-and-bake cookies were a little too flat and uniform to suggest homemade.

How much does the convenience of ready-made 5 dough cost? The break-and-bake cookies and the slice-and-bake cookies each cost $3.59 and give you between 20 and 24 cookies (made from 18 ounces of dough). The ingredients for our homemade cookies cost about $4.50, but the recipe makes at least four dozen cookies—certainly a better value.

If extra money (and artificial ingredients) are not a deterrent, the log of prepared cookie dough (not the break-and-bake variety) is your best bet. Personally, we'd rather save some money and make our own cookies. We'll just add more chips next time.

WINNER: Nestlé Toll House Chocolate Chip Cookie Dough

These cookies are "loaded with chips" and have "nice craggy top and crisp edges."

	PRODUCT TESTED	PRICE*
RECOMMENDED	Nestlé Toll House Chocolate Chip Cookie Dough "Loaded with chips," "nice craggy top and crisp edges."	$3.69 for about 2 dozen cookies
RECOMMENDED	Homemade Cookies (with Nestlé Toll House Semi-Sweet Morsels) "Crunchy and chewy with the best flavor," but "low chip-to-cookie ratio."	$4.50 for about 4 dozen cookies
NOT RECOMMENDED	Nestlé Toll House Refrigerated Chocolate Chip Cookie Dough Bar "Flat and compact," and "too uniform."	$3.69 for 20 cookies

*Prices subject to change.

What kind of argument might freshly baked chocolate chip cookies be?

Solving the Mystery of the Chewy Chocolate Chip Cookie

COOK'S ILLUSTRATED MAGAZINE

After testing 40 variations, we discover how to make a thick, chewy gourmet shop cookie at home.

THE PROBLEM

We tried innumerable published recipes claiming to produce thick, chewy cookies but were disappointed batch after batch.

THE GOAL

The quest began simply enough: We wanted to duplicate, at home, the big, delicious, chewy chocolate chip cookies bought in the trendy specialty cookie shops. For us, first and foremost, this genre of home-baked chocolate chip drop cookie had to look and taste like the ultimate, sinful cookie: thick (1/2 inch high), jumbo (3 inches in diameter), and bursting with chocolate. It also had to have a mouthwatering, uneven surface texture with rounded edges and be slightly crispy but tender on the outside and rich, buttery, soft, and chewy on the inside.

THE SOLUTION

One key element in achieving this cookie was melting the butter. According to food scientist Shirley Corriher, when butter is melted, free water and fat separate. When this melted butter is combined with flour, the proteins in the flour grab the water and each other to immediately form elastic sheets of gluten. This creates a product with a chewy texture. At the same time, the sugars and fats are working to inhibit gluten formation, which prevents the cookies from getting too tough. After numerous tests, varying the type of flour, the proportion of flour to butter, and sifting and not sifting, we decided that the best cookie resulted from unsifted, bleached, all-purpose flour, which has a lower protein content than unbleached. Also, the problem of the cookie hardening after several hours was eliminated by the addition of a single egg yolk; the added fat acts as a tenderizer.

Thick and Chewy Chocolate Chip Cookies

Makes 1 1/2 dozen 3-inch cookies.

These truly chewy chocolate chip cookies are delicious served warm from the oven or cooled. To ensure a chewy texture, leave the cookies on the cookie sheet to cool. You can substitute white, milk chocolate, or peanut butter chips for the semi- or bittersweet chips called for in the recipe. In addition to chips, you can flavor the dough with one cup of nuts, raisins, or shredded coconut.

INGREDIENTS

2 1/8	cups bleached all-purpose flour (about 10 1/2 ounces)
1/2	teaspoon table salt
1/2	teaspoon baking soda
12	tablespoons unsalted butter (1 1/2 sticks), melted and cooled slightly
1	cup brown sugar (light or dark) (7 ounces)
1/2	cup granulated sugar (3 1/2 ounces)
1	large egg
1	large egg yolk
2	teaspoons vanilla extract
1–2	cups chocolate chips or chunks (semi- or bittersweet)

INSTRUCTIONS

1. Heat oven to 325 degrees. Adjust oven racks to upper- and lower-middle positions. Mix flour, salt, and baking soda together in medium bowl; set aside.
2. Either by hand or with electric mixer, mix butter and sugars until thoroughly blended. Mix in egg, yolk, and vanilla. Add dry ingredients; mix until just combined. Stir in chips.
3. Following illustrations on the next page, form scant 1/4 cup dough into ball. Holding dough ball using fingertips of both hands, pull into two equal halves. Rotate halves ninety degrees and, with jagged surfaces exposed, join halves together at their base, again forming a single cookie, being careful not to smooth dough's uneven surface. Place formed dough onto one of two parchment paper-lined 20-by-14-inch lipless cookie sheets, about nine dough balls per sheet. Smaller cookie sheets can be used, but fewer cookies can be baked at one time and baking time may need to be adjusted. (Dough can be refrigerated up to 2 days or frozen up to 1 month—shaped or not.)

4. Bake, reversing cookie sheets' positions halfway through baking, until cookies are light golden brown and outer edges start to harden yet centers are still soft and puffy, 15 to 18 minutes (start checking at 13 minutes). (Frozen dough requires an extra 1 to 2 minutes baking time.) Cool cookies on cookie sheets. Serve or store in airtight container.

STEP-BY-STEP

Shaping Thick Chocolate Chip Cookies

  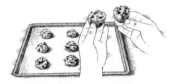

1. *Creating a jagged surface on each dough ball gives the finished cookies an attractive appearance. Start by rolling a scant 1/4 cup of dough into a smooth ball.*

2. *Holding the dough ball in the fingertips of both hands, pull the dough apart into two equal halves.*

3. *Each half will have a jagged surface where it was ripped from the other. Rotate each piece 90 degrees so that the jagged edge faces up.*

4. *Jam the halves back together into one ball so that the top surface remains jagged.*

As Chapter 3 explains, authors can increase their authority by detailing their experience with the subject and by appealing to specialized knowledge, two strategies that we can see the author of this article employing.

LINK TO P. 57

RESPOND •

1. What kind of argument is the first section of "Ready-to-Bake Chocolate Chip Cookies"? (For example, an argument of fact or of definition?) The list of recommended products? What kind of argument is "Solving the Mystery of the Chewy Chocolate Chip Cookie"? The recipe? What evidence can you provide for your claims?

2. Examine carefully the first section of "Ready-to-Bake Chocolate Chip Cookies" and the first section of "Solving the Mystery of the Chewy Chocolate Chip Cookie." What sorts of ethical appeals do you find in each? What sorts of appeal to emotion? To facts and reason? (For a discussion of kinds of appeals, see Chapters 2, 3, and 4.)

3. As described in the headnote to the selections, *Cook's Country* and *Cook's Illustrated* are distinct magazines, each with a Web site (http://www.cookscountry.com and http://www.cooksillustrated.com). Visit both of these sites to see how their intended audiences are similar and different. In making your assessment, you will want to consider all the available evidence, including visual layout, kinds of recipes given, and language used. **Write an essay** in which you describe your findings. (For a discussion of factual arguments, see Chapter 8. For a discussion of definitional arguments—and you may be defining each audience, see Chapter 9. Chapter 1 discusses intended audiences.)

4. Agree to the proposal argument that the recipe offers: bake the cookies. Or, if you don't like thick and chewy chocolate chip cookies or this particular recipe for them, find another recipe for a dish that you do like, and follow it meticulously. **Write an essay** in which you evaluate the recipe that you used and the resulting food that you prepared. This assignment will be most fun if you and friends do the cooking—or at least the tasting—together. You may even want to taste the cookies as a class. (For a discussion of evaluative arguments, see Chapter 10.)

5. If you are especially interested in food issues and in doing research, research the carbon footprint of the cookies discussed here. (As you may recall, question 4 about Claire Ironside's "Apples to Oranges" reading earlier in this chapter discusses the notion of carbon footprint.) This task will require a trip or two to the grocery store, careful reading of labels, and research on the Internet. (In fact, a group of students might take on this project together. If there are several groups, each could focus on a different cookie recipe or different category of recipe.) After you have completed the necessary research, **write a factual argument** about what you discovered. (For a discussion of arguments of fact, see Chapter 8.)

25
What Role Should Religion Play in Public Life?

One thing distinguishing the United States from other industrialized countries is the role faith and religious belief play in the public arena. On the one hand, the U.S. Constitution mandates the separation of church and state, the nation has no state religion, and Americans aren't required to pay dues or taxes to any religious institution. Most Americans—including those who are religious—are generally happy with that state of affairs: they don't want others dictating what they should believe or practice. On the other hand, Americans can't deny that the words "In God We Trust" appear on all American currency (a practice begun in 1861 and extended to all currency and coins by 1955) or that if businesses close one day each week, they generally do so on Sunday, the Christian holy day. The anxiety with which many Americans, whether believers or nonbelievers, await Supreme Court rulings that focus on religion in any way reminds us that these issues continue to be very much alive. In some sense, to be American is to have a strong stake in the proper boundary between church and state and to participate in these arguments. The selections in this chapter provide occasions for doing just that.

An excerpt from a recent Pew Global Attitudes Project report reminds us that, among economically advanced countries, the United States has the highest percentage of citizens who claim that religion is important in their daily lives. Like the Pew study, Laurie Goodstein's "More Religion, but Not the Old-Time Kind" gives a global context for thinking about religion in American public life.

The next few selections, much like case studies, focus on specific topics inside the country. In "Evangelicalism Rebounds in Academe," D. Michael Lindsay traces the growing presence of evangelical Christianity on college campuses, including many where it was absent a few decades ago. (He reminds us, however, that a number of the country's private colleges, especially its elite schools, were originally affiliated with a Christian denomination.) Michelle Bryant's "Selling Safe Sex in Public Schools" highlights Shelby Knox's struggle as a Christian in the conservative state of Texas to fight for comprehensive sex education in public schools there.

Writing as a Christian, more specifically as a Mennonite, Melanie Springer Mock in "Separation of Church and State: A War on Christmas and Other Misguided Notions" offers a stance that many readers might not predict, regardless of their own attitudes toward religion and public life. In "God's Justice and Ours," Antonin Scalia analyzes why he believes that he cannot and should not separate his Catholicism from his task as a U.S. Supreme Court justice.

Mariam Rahmani explains why "Wearing a Head Scarf Is My Choice as a Muslim" and why others should respect it. Randy Cohen, author of the *New York Times* column "The Ethicist," offers advice on dealing with offense taken in a business context when a man refuses to shake a woman's hand because of his religious convictions, and readers write to tell Cohen that they don't think he knows what he's talking about.

The chapter concludes with the transcripts of three audio essays from *This I Believe*, the popular National Public Radio program that is devoted to values and public life. They are by Nobel Prize laureate Albert Einstein (whose heritage was German and Jewish), Muslim interfaith activist Eboo Patel, and comedian Penn Jillette, who argues "There Is No God."

As national election campaigns and rounds of Supreme Court rulings remind us, religious beliefs continue to be part of American public life. For that reason alone, we owe it to ourselves to spend time evaluating how such beliefs manifest themselves in public discourse.

▼ *In quantitative studies, an outlier is a piece of data that lies outside the normal distribution—one that is in some sense extreme or unusual. As this selection demonstrates, when it comes to religiosity, the United States is an outlier with respect to the Western European and other economically advanced nations it resembles in many other ways. This excerpt comes from the Spring 2008 Survey of the Pew Global Attitudes Project, which conducts opinion surveys in countries worldwide. The Project is part of the work of the Pew Research Center, which bills itself as a "nonpartisan 'fact tank' . . . that provides information on the issues, attitudes, and trends shaping America and the world." This particular survey involved twenty-four nations in the Americas, Europe, the Middle East, Asia and the Pacific, and sub-Saharan Africa.*

Here, we reproduce only the first part of Section 2 of the report, which focuses on religiosity, or the degree to which people from various countries report that religion is an important part of their lives. (The specific question asked, Question 83, was "How important is religion in your life—very important, somewhat important, not too important, or not at all important?") The topics treated in the full report (available at http://pewglobal.org/reports/pdf/262.pdf) include attitudes toward three religious groups (Jews, Christians, and Muslims); religiosity in the countries surveyed; public opinion in countries with significant Muslim populations about extremism, about Saudi Arabia and other "important countries," and about issues related to gender; and public opinion in Pakistan with regard to Al Qaeda, the Taliban, and specific political figures there. As you read, consider the ways in which this excerpt's graphs and tables help explain the information in the text while providing information not contained there. Likewise, start thinking about the possible consequences of the information given here with respect to understanding America and our neighbors across the world.

When It Comes to Religion, the United States Is an Outlier
Spring 2008 Survey (Excerpt)

PEW GLOBAL ATTITUDES PROJECT

2. RELIGIOSITY

In most countries surveyed, majorities consider religion an essential part of their lives. However, younger people are generally less likely to say religion is very important to them. This is especially true in Western Europe, where

Relying heavily on statistical data, the Pew Global Attitudes Project constructs an argument of fact about the role of religion in countries all over the world, with a special focus on religion's place in American life. For more on arguments of fact, see Chapter 8.

LINK TO P. 208

relatively few young people say religion plays a key role in their lives, but the same pattern can be found in other countries around the world as well, including the United States.

In addition to an age gap, there is also a significant gender gap in most nations over religion's importance. Women are consistently more likely than men to describe religion as very important to them. The largest gender gap on the survey appears in the U.S., where 65% of women consider religion very important, compared with just 44% of men.

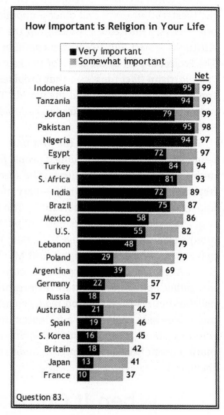

How Important is Religion in Your Life

■ Very important
▨ Somewhat important

		Net
Indonesia	95	99
Tanzania	94	99
Jordan	79	99
Pakistan	95	98
Nigeria	94	97
Egypt	72	97
Turkey	84	94
S. Africa	81	93
India	72	89
Brazil	75	87
Mexico	58	86
U.S.	55	82
Lebanon	48	79
Poland	29	79
Argentina	39	69
Germany	22	57
Russia	18	57
Australia	21	46
Spain	19	46
S. Korea	16	45
Britain	18	42
Japan	13	41
France	10	37

Question 83.

Generally, there is a clear relationship between wealth and religiosity: in rich nations fewer people view religion as important than in poor nations. In the current survey, people who live in the poorest nations almost unanimously say religion is important to them, while the citizens of Western Europe and other wealthy nations tend to say it plays a less significant role. However, Americans—who tend to be religious despite their country's wealth—continue to be a major exception to this pattern.

Muslim respondents consistently rate religion as an important part of their lives, and traditional Islamic practices—such as praying five times a day and fasting during Ramadan—are common among the Muslim publics surveyed.

IMPORTANCE OF RELIGION

Majorities say religion is very or somewhat important in their personal lives 5 in 17 of the 23 nations where the question was asked. In 14 countries, more than three-quarters of those surveyed say religion is important, and in eight countries it is more than 90%.

Moreover, in 12 nations, majorities say religion is *very* important. In Indonesia, Tanzania, Pakistan and Nigeria, more than nine-in-ten say it is very important.

Consistently, Muslim respondents say religion is central to their lives. Even in Turkey, a Muslim nation with a strong tradition of secularism, 94% say it is important. In the Arab nations of Jordan (99% important) and Egypt (97%), the numbers are even more overwhelming. Overall, Lebanese are slightly less likely to hold this view, although it is more common among the country's Sunni (98%) and Shia (82%) Muslims than among Lebanese Christians (67%).

Nearly all Indonesians (99%) and Pakistanis (98%) surveyed consider religion important. Elsewhere in the Asia and Pacific region, about nine-in-ten (89%) in predominantly Hindu India rate religion important. The picture is quite different, however, in the more economically advanced nations of Japan (41% important), South Korea (45%) and Australia (46%).

More than eight-in-ten consider religion important in the African and Latin American countries surveyed, with the exception of Argentina, where a sizeable minority (30%) says religion is not significant in their lives.

Religion is generally less central to the lives of Europeans. Poland is the 10 only European country in which more than six-in-ten consider religion important. And in three nations—France, Britain, and Spain—majorities say religion is not important in their lives.

On this measure, the United States differs considerably from Western Europe and other economically advanced nations. About eight-in-ten Americans (82%) say religion is important, and most (55%) consider it *very* important.

WEALTH AND RELIGIOSITY

The extent to which the United States differs from other wealthy nations in Europe and elsewhere can be demonstrated by examining the relationship between a country's wealth and people's views about the importance of religion.[1] Generally, religion plays a much less central role in the lives of individuals in high income countries. This can be seen in the relative unimportance of religion in Western Europe, as well as in Australia and Japan, all of which cluster near the bottom right of the chart on the following page, indicating high levels of wealth and low ratings for the importance of religion.

In contrast, nearly all respondents consider religion important in the survey's poorest countries, such as Tanzania, Nigeria, Pakistan, Indonesia, and Jordan, which tend to cluster near the upper left of the chart. Meanwhile, in "middle income" nations such as Poland, Argentina, and Russia, religion is neither as central to the lives of people as in poorer countries, nor as unimportant as in much of Western Europe. Across the 23 countries where this

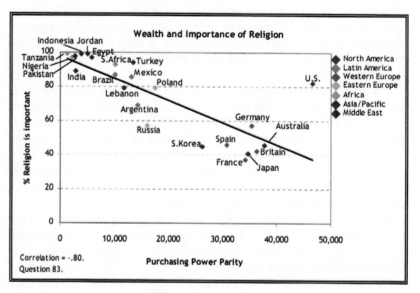

This figure, "Wealth and Importance of Religion," illustrates the correlation, or statistical relationship, between wealth (as measured in terms of purchasing power parity and graphed along the x-axis) and the importance of religion (as measured by the percentage of respondents who answered "very important" or "somewhat important," graphed along the y-axis). Purchasing power parity measures the cost of goods in several countries, corrects for price differences between countries, and permits meaningful comparisons among the standards of living in different countries. The horizontal line that slopes from the upper left to the lower right represents a perfect negative correlation for these data: as purchasing power parity goes up, religiosity goes down. The countries clustered closest to this line (like Nigeria, Pakistan, Brazil, Lebanon, Germany, and Australia) illustrate this negative correlation most strongly. Countries farther away from the line (most notably the United States) represent outliers. The figure gives a correlation coefficient of -.80, which represents a strong negative relationship. (A perfect negative correlation is -1.0, a perfect positive correlation is 1.0, and no relationship at all between wealth and religiosity would be zero.)

question was asked, there is a strong negative correlation (-.80) between the percentage of people saying religion is important and a country's wealth, measured in terms of purchasing power parity.

The clear exception to this patten is the United States, which is a much more religious country than its degree of prosperity would suggest. Despite its wealth, the United States is in the middle of the global pack when it comes to the importance of religion. Indeed, on this question, the U.S. is closer to considerably less developed nations such as India, Brazil and Lebanon than to other western nations.

YOUNGER PEOPLE LESS RELIGIOUS

In most countries surveyed, younger 15 people are less likely to say religion is central to their lives. In countries from nearly every region, persons under age 40 are generally less likely to consider religion *very* important to them.

This is true in the United States, where just under half of 18–39-year-olds (48%) say religion is very important, compared with majorities of those age 40–59 (55%) and those ages 60 and older (64%).

There are age gaps regarding the importance of religion in several European countries as well, especially Poland, which is overwhelmingly Roman Catholic. While 49% of Poles ages 60 and older say religion is very important, considerably fewer 40–59-year-olds (29%) and 18–39-year-olds (20%) express this view.

Young people are also less religious in another traditionally Catholic European nation: Spain. Just 9% of Spaniards under age 40 consider religion very important, compared with 21% of those ages 40–59 and 30% of those 60 and older.

Fewer Young People See Religion as Very Important

	% very important		
	18-39	40-59	60+
	%	%	%
U.S.	48	55	64
Britain	15	16	23
France	8	9	15
Germany	21	21	25
Spain	9	21	30
Poland	20	29	49
Russia	14	17	27
Turkey	83	84	88
Egypt	69	76	*
Jordan	77	84	*
Lebanon	46	50	*
Australia	18	19	29
India	70	77	75
Indonesia	95	95	*
Japan	7	9	22
Pakistan	95	96	*
S. Korea	11	20	*
Argentina	27	43	57
Brazil	72	75	84
Mexico	52	61	77
Nigeria	94	94	*
S. Africa	80	83	82
Tanzania	94	92	*

Question 83.
*Fewer than 100 respondents age 60 or older.

Large age gaps also exist outside of Europe and the U.S. In Latin America, a solid majority (57%) of Argentines older than 60 describe religion as a very important part of their lives, but only 43% of 40–59-year-olds and 27% of those younger than 40 do so. More than three-in-four (77%) older Mexicans say religion is very important, compared with 61% of those in the middle age category and about half (52%) of younger Mexicans.

Age differences over religion's importance do not exist everywhere, how- 20 ever. In Indonesia and Pakistan, at least 95% of people both under 40 and over 40 agree that religion is very important. The three African nations on the survey also stand out for their lack of an age gap. For instance, roughly eight-in-ten South Africans rate religion as very important in all three age groups.

THE RELIGION GENDER GAP

Women are consistently more likely than men to rate religion as very important in their lives. The gender gap is especially pronounced in the United States. Nearly two-thirds (65%) of American women consider religion very important, a view shared by only 44% of men.

Women are significantly more likely than men to consider religion very significant in all three Latin American countries on the poll: Argentina (a 16 percentage point gap), Mexico (16 points) and Brazil (11 points).

Double-digit gaps over religion's importance exist in several other countries as well: Poland (12 points), South Africa (12 points), Spain (11 points), Russia (10 points) and Lebanon (10 points).

The gender gap over religion's importance is smaller or even non-existent in some of the poorest nations in the survey: India, Pakistan, Egypt, Jordan, Nigeria, Indonesia and Tanzania.

Women More Likely to Say Religion is Very Important		
	% religion very important	Gender
	Women	Men	gap
	%	%	
U.S.	65	44	+21
Argentina	46	30	+16
Mexico	66	50	+16
Poland	35	23	+12
S. Africa	87	75	+12
Spain	24	13	+11
Brazil	80	69	+11
Russia	22	12	+10
Lebanon	53	43	+10
Australia	25	18	+7
Britain	22	15	+7
Germany	25	19	+6
Turkey	87	81	+6
S. Korea	18	13	+5
France	12	8	+4
Japan	15	11	+4
India	74	71	+3
Pakistan	97	94	+3
Egypt	73	72	+1
Jordan	80	79	+1
Nigeria	94	94	0
Indonesia	95	96	-1
Tanzania	93	96	-3

Question-83.

NOTE

1. For more on the relationship between wealth and religiosity, see "World Publics Welcome Global Trade—But Not Immigration," released October 4, 2007, which features data from the 47-nation 2007 Pew Global Attitudes survey.

RESPOND•

1. Did any of the results of this survey surprise you? Which ones? Why? Do the findings reported for countries that you are familiar with, most notably the United States, seem reasonable? If not, what does that fact teach us about the relationship between everyday opinion and claims that are based on reliable research?

2. What factors, in your opinion, might account for why the United States is such an outlier among Western and economically advanced countries?

3. How do the graphs and tables in this selection contribute to the argument being made? How clear are they? How apparent are the arguments they make? Which one is easiest to understand? Which one is the most complex? Why?

4. Odds are that this selection presents you with information about another of the world's countries that was new to you. Choose one of the countries surveyed, and research the role that religion has played in that country's history. If at all possible, try to interview one or more people from that country (perhaps using the Internet) to find information to supplement your other research. (If you are not from the United States, choose a country other than your native one to investigate.) **Write a factual essay** in which you present your findings. (For a discussion of factual essays, see Chapter 8.)

5. **Write an essay** in which you evaluate your responses to this selection. Following up on question 1, you may discuss your surprise (or lack of it) or some other emotional response you have: chagrin, dismay, or happiness. You may also wish to discuss logical or rational responses that you have to this selection. As Chapter 10 reminds us, because good evaluative arguments are based on explicit criteria, you'll need to examine your own assumptions about the United States, the larger world, and religion in public life in responding to this question.

▼ *In her January 2005 article "More Religion, but Not the Old-Time Kind,"*
Laurie Goodstein, national religion editor for the New York Times, thinks
globally about a growth of participation in religion. Although so-called fun-
damentalist religious groups here and abroad have gained attention in the
news over the past few years and especially since September 11, 2001,
many researchers contend that Pentecostalism, rather than fundamentalism,
accounts for the greatest increase in membership. As you read, pay attention
to the sorts of definitional arguments that Goodstein makes.

More Religion, but Not the Old-Time Kind

LAURIE GOODSTEIN

Almost anywhere you look around the world, with the glaring exception of Western Europe, religion is now a rising force. Former Communist countries are humming with mosque builders, Christian missionaries and freelance spiritual entrepreneurs of every possible persuasion. In China, underground "house churches"° are proliferating so quickly that neither the authorities nor Christian leaders can keep reliable count. In much of South and Central America, exuberant Pentecostal churches, where worshipers catch the Holy Spirit and speak in tongues, continue to spread, challenging the Roman Catholic tradition. And in the United States, religious conservatives, triumphant over their role in the reelection of President Bush, are increasingly asserting their power in politics, the media and culture.

The tsunami in Asia could spur religious revival as well, as victims and onlookers turn to mosques, temples and churches both to help them fathom the catastrophe and to provide humanitarian assistance.

What does all this rising religiosity add up to? It is easy to assume that a more religious world means a more fractious world, where violent conflict is fueled by violent fundamentalist movements.

But some religion experts say that while it is clear that religiosity is on the rise, it is not at all clear that fundamentalism is. Indeed, there may be a rising backlash against violent fundamentalism of any faith.

The world's fastest growing religion is not any type of fundamentalism, but the Pentecostal wing of Christianity. While Christian fundamentalists are focused on doctrine and the inerrancy° of Scripture, what is most important for Pentecostals is what they call "spirit-filled" worship, 5

---

house churches: groups of believers who meet in private homes, rather than churches; in the Chinese case, these believers choose to meet in homes instead of attending the churches monitored and controlled by the Chinese government.

inerrancy: the belief that a text, especially a sacred text, is free from error of any kind.

including speaking in tongues and miracle healing. Brazil, where American missionaries planted Pentecostalism in the early 20th century, now has a congregation with its own TV station, soccer team and political party.

Most scholars of Christianity believe that the world's largest church is a Pentecostal one—the Yoido Full Gospel Church in Seoul, South Korea, which was founded in 1958 by a converted Buddhist who held a prayer meeting in a tent he set up in a slum. More than 250,000 people show up for worship on a typical Sunday.

"If I were to buy stock in global Christianity, I would buy it in Pentecostalism," said Martin E. Marty, professor emeritus of the history of Christianity at the University of Chicago Divinity School and a coauthor of a study of fundamentalist movements. "I would not buy it in fundamentalism."

After the American presidential election in November [2004], some liberal commentators warned that the nation was on the verge of a takeover by Christian "fundamentalists."

But in the United States today, most of the Protestants who make up what some call the Christian right are not fundamentalists, who are more prone to create separatist enclaves, but evangelicals, who engage the culture and share their faith. Professor Marty defines fundamentalism as essentially a backlash against secularism and modernity.

For example, at the fundamental- 10 ist Bob Jones University, in Greenville, S.C., students are not allowed to listen to contemporary music of any kind, even Christian rock or rap. But at Wheaton College in Illinois, a leading evangelical school, contemporary Christian music is regular fare for many students.

Christian fundamentalism emerged in the United States in the 1920's, but was already in decline by the 1960's. By then, it had been superseded by evangelicalism, with its Billy Graham°-style revival meetings, radio stations and seminaries.

The word "fundamentalist" itself has fallen out of favor among conservative Christians in the United States, not least because it has come to be associated with extremism and violence overseas.

Fundamentalism in non-Christian faiths became a phenomenon in the rest of the world in the 1970's with "the failure and the bankruptcy of secular, nationalistic liberal creeds around the world," said Philip Jenkins, a professor of history and religious studies at Pennsylvania State University. Among the "creeds cracking up" were nationalism,° Marxism,° socialism,° pan-Arabism° and pan-Africanism.°

Billy Graham (b. 1918): born William Franklin Graham Jr., a Protestant evangelical minister best known for his crusades, or public revivals.

nationalism: the belief that nations (composed of ethnically or culturally defined groups of people) are the most appropriate unit for organizing political life and that loyalty to one's nation should be more important than all other loyalties.

Marxism: the school of thought associated with Karl Marx (1818–1883), a philosopher, political theorist, and economist who focused on struggles between economic classes as the major force in history.

socialism: an economic, political, and social system in which ownership of the means of production (industry, natural resources, etc.) lies in the hands of the government with the stated goal of minimizing social inequality by distributing wealth equitably; it is usually contrasted with capitalism.

pan-Arabism: various twentieth-century political movements that focused on uniting all Arab countries in a single cultural or even political entity.

pan-Africanism: various twentieth-century political movements that focused on uniting all African nations, especially those south of the Sahara, by ending all forms of colonialism and external domination, especially those of European countries.

Christians pray together at the City of David Church in the affluent Victoria Island section of Lagos.

NIGERIA

Followers of largest religions, 2005

(Pentecostals are found in most Christian traditions)

CHRISTIAN
61.4 million total

MUSLIM
54.7 million

ANIMIST°
13.6 million

Avg. yearly growth of selected faiths, 1990–2000

All Nigerian Christians
| 3% growth |

Protestant (33.4% of Nigerian Christians*)
| 4.7 |

Roman Catholic (30.5)
| 4.3 |

Anglican (31.8)
| 3.5 |

Independent (43.2)
| 2.3 |

| 2.7 | (Muslim)

| 2.9 | (Animist)

*Percentages add up to more than 100 because many people affiliate with more than one religion.

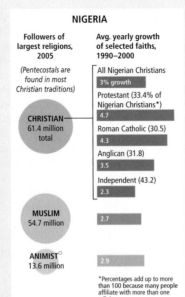

Animist: here and traditionally, a practitioner of a traditional, indigenous religion who believes that spirits inhabit some or all things.

Ganesh: among the best known and most loved representations of the divine in Hinduism, he represents wisdom and intellect, and he is seen as the remover of obstacles.

Source of statistics: Center for the Study of Global Christianity at Gordon-Conwell Theological Seminary

Hindus perform an immersion ritual with a statue of Ganesh,° one of their most revered deities.

INDIA

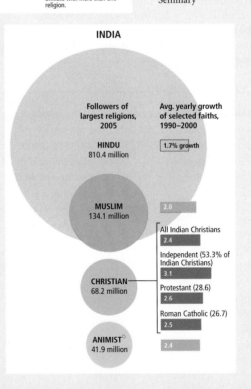

Followers of largest religions, 2005

HINDU
810.4 million

MUSLIM
134.1 million

CHRISTIAN
68.2 million

ANIMIST°
41.9 million

Avg. yearly growth of selected faiths, 1990–2000

| 1.7% growth | (Hindu)

| 2.0 | (Muslim)

All Indian Christians
| 2.4 |

Independent (53.3% of Indian Christians)
| 3.1 |

Protestant (28.6)
| 2.6 |

Roman Catholic (26.7)
| 2.5 |

| 2.4 | (Animist)

INDONESIA

Followers of largest religions, 2005

Avg. yearly growth of selected faiths, 1990–2000

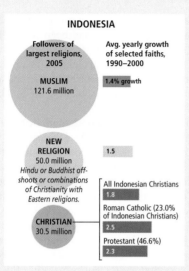

MUSLIM
121.6 million

1.4% growth

NEW RELIGION
50.0 million
Hindu or Buddhist off-shoots or combinations of Christianity with Eastern religions.

1.5

All Indonesian Christians
1.8

Roman Catholic (23.0% of Indonesian Christians)
2.5

CHRISTIAN
30.5 million

Protestant (46.6%)
2.3

In Jakarta, a celebration of Id al-Fitr marks the end of the Muslim holy month of Ramadan.°

BRAZIL

Followers of largest religions, 2005

Avg. yearly growth of selected faiths, 1990–2000

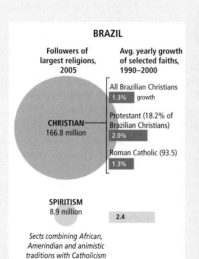

All Brazilian Christians
1.3% growth

CHRISTIAN
166.8 million

Protestant (18.2% of Brazilian Christians)
2.0%

Roman Catholic (93.5)
1.3%

SPIRITISM
8.9 million

2.4

Sects combining African, Amerindian and animistic traditions with Catholicism

Mass celebration at Igreja Brasil para Cristo, a Pentecostal church in São Paulo.

Source of statistics: Center for the Study of Global Christianity at Gordon-Conwell Theological Seminary

Ramadan: the Muslim holy month of fasting—abstaining from food, beverage, smoking, or sexual activity—observed each day from the time one cannot distinguish a black thread from a white thread before dawn until sunset.

"From the 1970's on, you get the growth of not just more conservative religion, but religion with a political bent," said Professor Jenkins, the author of *The Next Christendom: The Coming of Global Christianity.*

Now, the future of fundamental- 15 ism is murky, with several contradictory trends at work simultaneously.

There is little doubt that one fundamentalism can feed another, spurring recruitment and escalating into a sort of religious arms race. In Nigeria's central Plateau State, Muslim and Christian gangs have razed one another's villages in the last few years, leaving tens of thousands of dead and displaced. In rioting in India in 2002, more than 1,000 people, most of them Muslims, were killed by Hindus in Gujarat state—retaliation for a Muslim attack a day earlier on a train full of Hindus, which killed 59.

Husain Haqqani, a Pakistani political commentator and visiting scholar at the Carnegie Endowment for International Peace in Washington, said that insurgents in Falluja, Iraq, recruited fighters with the false rumor that Christian crusaders with the Rev.

Franklin Graham's° aid organization, Samaritan's Purse, were on the way over to convert Muslims. (Mr. Graham is known throughout the Muslim world for his statement that Islam is a "very evil and wicked religion.") Fundamentalism does not necessarily lead to intolerance, said Professor Jenkins of Pennsylvania State. "People with very convinced, traditional views can get along together for a very long time," he said. "But sometimes we get into cycles where they can't, and we seem to be in one of those cycles right now."

Analysts are also seeing signs of a backlash as religious believers grow disenchanted with movements that have produced little but bloodshed, economic stagnation and social repression.

In last year's elections in India, voters repudiated the ruling Bharatiya Janata Party,° a Hindu nationalist group whose cadres had helped stir up violence in some Indian states against Muslims and others.

And in Indonesia, the world's larg- 20 est Muslim country, mainstream Islamic groups in September helped

elect as president a secular general who had been relatively outspoken about the threat posed by the radical group Jemaah Islamiyah,° which is responsible for several acts of terrorism, including the bombing in Bali in 2002.

Fundamentalist movements also stumble because they plan for the overthrow, but not for the governing. Half the Muslim world is illiterate, Mr. Haqqani said, but the Taliban didn't make a dent in improving literacy when it ruled in Afghanistan. If Iran had a free and fair plebiscite° today, Professor Marty said, "the ayatollahs would be dumped."

For reasons like this, said R. Scott Appleby, a history professor at the University of Notre Dame and director of the Joan B. Kroc Institute for International Peace Studies, "it would be misleading to say fundamentalism is on the rise now." He added: "I would say we're just more aware of it because these people are better organized, more mobile and more vocal than ever before."

In 2003, Professor Appleby and two other scholars, Gabriel A. Almond

---

Franklin Graham (b. 1952): born William Franklin Graham III, a Protestant evangelical minister; he now serves as president of a mission organization, Samaritan's Purse, and is chief executive officer of his father's organization, the Billy Graham Evangelical Organization.

Bharatiya Janata Party: Indian People's Party, one of the largest political parties in India, seen by some as representing Hindu fundamentalism.

Jemaah Islamiyah: Islamic Community, an Islamic terrorist organization found in certain Southeast Asian countries and committed to establishing a theocracy, or state ruled according to religion or by religious leaders. It is assumed to be responsible for

several bombings in the Philippines and Indonesia.

plebiscite: a direct vote of the people to decide an important matter.

and Emmanuel Sivan, published *Strong Religion*, a book based on research done with Professor Marty for the Fundamentalism Project. The book's subtitle was *The Rise of Fundamentalisms Around the World*.

Now, Mr. Appleby said, "There is some evidence, some literature that says fundamentalism is on the decline, that it has peaked or is peaking precisely because it has a tendency toward violence and intolerance, and those ultimately don't work. They lead to bloodshed, loss of life, and no recognizable economic upturn, and there is an exhaustion with it."

That is not to say that he does not 25 foresee more bitter, sometimes violent religious clashes. By their very nature, fundamentalists endure because they are motivated by transcendent° ideas like salvation or, in some places, martyrdom. Mr. Appleby said he did not expect to see growth, but a persistence of "deadly pockets of would-be revolutionaries who are empowered to a greater degree than ever by a little technological savvy and organizational ability."

The American government is poorly prepared to make the necessary distinctions between what is merely religious fervor and what is potentially dangerous fundamentalism, said Thomas F. Farr, who left his post as director of the office of international religious freedom in the State Department about a year ago.

"Most of my foreign service friends would rather have root canal than talk to a Muslim imam about religion," said Mr. Farr, who now works with the Institute for Global Engagement, a Washington-based group working on international religious freedom.

What they need to ask, he said, is: "Do these religions have within them exclusivist tendencies in an absolutist sense, or can they be open to other human beings outside their circle? These are inevitably theological questions."

RESPOND●

1. How would you characterize Laurie Goodstein's argument in this selection? Why might it be important to contextualize her subject—religion as a "rising force"—globally? How would you characterize the ethos Goodstein creates in discussing this topic? Why might she do so? (For a discussion of how writers create their ethos and why it's important, see Chapter 3.)

2. Like many complex arguments, this selection contains arguments of several kinds, including definitional arguments. Based on the information given in the article, how would you define and distinguish among the categories "fundamentalists," "evangelicals," and "Pentecostals"? Are these definitions adequate for this context—that is, for understanding the information presented in this selection? Why or why not? (For a discussion of definitional arguments, see Chapter 9.)

3. This selection also offers a number of causal claims. List three. What sorts of causal claims are they? Who makes the claims you've listed—the author or the sources she cites? Is the origin of the claims important in how you or other readers might evaluate the strength or validity of the selection's arguments? Why or why not? How do these causal claims advance its argument(s)? (For a discussion of causal arguments, see Chapter 11.)

transcendent: beyond the limits of human thought and understanding.

If Goodstein is arguing that the current surge in religion is different from surges in the past, can we call this a definitional argument? Use Chapter 9 as a guide in considering your answer.

LINK TO P. 249

4. This selection contains a visual argument—a complex set of "country profiles" that provides several kinds of information about Nigeria, India, Indonesia, and Brazil—reproduced from the original version of the article. What do the profiles contribute to the selection? (In other words, do you think you would have read or understood the selection differently had this visual argument not been included? How so?) Study the information given in the country profiles. Make a list of the kinds of information each profile gives. Why is this information useful and appropriate, given the focus of the selection? What functions do the circles of different sizes play in communicating information? How do the photographs contribute to this visual argument?

5. Create two country profiles like the ones given in this selection, one for the United States and one for another country of your choosing (other than the four given here). Be sure to include the sources of your information. When you've completed this assignment, compare your profile for the United States with those created by two classmates. If there are differences, seek to locate the cause(s) of those differences. For example, did you rely on different sources for the basic information you used, or did you classify, combine, or represent the information you found in different ways?

6. The closing paragraphs of this selection juxtapose Thomas F. Farr's contrast between "merely religious fervor" and "potentially dangerous fundamentalism" (paragraph 26), on the one hand, and religions that are "open to other human beings outside their circle" and those having "within them exclusivist tendencies in an absolutist sense" (paragraph 28). Farr argues that the former contrast has political implications for the U.S. government, while the latter involves "theological questions." Are these two dichotomies equivalent? **Write an essay** in which you define the terms of each dichotomy and evaluate the relationships among them.

7. When Goodstein wrote this article, George W. Bush had just been reelected as president of the United States, and she links his reelection with the claim that religion is a "rising force" outside of Western Europe (paragraph 1). Has the situation changed during the Obama presidency? In other words, in what ways is religion now a force—or not—in American public life in comparison with the ways that it was during the Bush presidency? Rather than relying only on your own knowledge or experience, you may wish to interview several people, preferably people of two or more generations, as well as doing some research about this topic on the Internet. **Write an essay** in which you define the nature of the shift, if any, in the role of religion in American public life during these two presidencies. (For a discussion of definitional arguments, see Chapter 9.)

▼ *In this selection, D. Michael Lindsay, assistant professor of sociology and assistant director of the Center on Race, Religion, and Urban Life at Rice University in Houston, Texas, argues that evangelicalism is growing in importance on American college campuses. As he notes, the claims that he makes are based on research he did for a 2007 book,* Faith in the Halls of Power: How Evangelicals Joined the American Elite. *Like the scholars who were quoted in the previous selection by Laurie Goodstein, "More Religion, but Not the Old-Time Kind," Lindsay distinguishes between fundamentalism and evangelicalism. He wrote this article for the May 2008 issue of the* Chronicle of Higher Education, *a highly respected newspaper (published weekly in print and daily online on weekdays) that focuses on all aspects of postsecondary education. As background to the article, keep in mind that higher education in colonial New England was designed to train Christian ministers and that many private U.S. colleges and universities were founded by religious denominations, whether or not they have retained their denominational ties. As Lindsay notes, until the early twentieth century, religious conservatives played a dominant role in higher education in the United States. As you read this selection, consider the kinds of evidence that Lindsay offers for his thesis, and reflect on whether you see evidence of evangelicalism on the campus you attend.*

Evangelicalism Rebounds in Academe

D. MICHAEL LINDSAY

In 1993, Michael Weiskopf wrote an article for the *Washington Post* in which he described evangelicals in the United States as "poor, uneducated, and easy to command." Although the comment provoked outrage from evangelicals, Weiskopf's assertion was not without merit. At the time, only 15 percent of evangelicals held college or graduate degrees. Even though religious conservatives dominated higher education at the turn of the 20th century, by 1993 they had lost their influence within the academy.

Yet on campuses across the country, evangelicalism is rebounding. Evangelical students make up larger and larger portions of the incoming classes at Harvard, Princeton, and Stanford. They join robust campus-ministry groups that sponsor everything from debates to spring-break "mission" trips. And while they still fall slightly below the national average, the percentage of evangelicals receiving bachelor's degrees has climbed 133 percent from 1976 to 2004, according to the General Social Survey conducted by the National Opinion Research Corporation, more than doubling the change within the general population.

Nowhere has this phenomenon been more evident than on America's top campuses. In 2003, Peter Gomes, the Pusey Minister at Harvard's Memorial Church, said, "There are probably more evangelicals [on

Harvard's campus today] than at any time since the 17th century."

What is driving this seismic change in American higher education, and what does it mean? To answer those questions, I spent the last five years interviewing 360 evangelicals who are members of the nation's political, business, and cultural elites—perhaps the most comprehensive examination of religion at this level of society ever conducted.

Not surprisingly, one-third of the leaders I interviewed attended highly selective universities. The pluralistic impulse that now guides admissions policy has opened new doors for religiously committed students at such elite institutions. Colleges and universities with national outreach now recruit in the South and Midwest as vigorously as they do on the East and West Coasts.

Ethnic diversity also matters. Whereas Asian-Americans account for only 4 percent of the U.S. population, they represent 15 percent of the student enrollment at Ivy League

The Yale University chapter of Campus Crusade for Christ in 2008

institutions. Many of these students are evangelical. In fact, I found that 90 percent of the members of the Yale chapter of Campus Crusade for Christ° are Asian-American. In the 1980s, the same chapter was 100 percent white. The changing demography of incoming classes at institutions such as Duke, MIT, and Yale has played a significant role in the evangelical ascendancy.

At the same time, evangelical scholarship has become part of the intellec-

tual mainstream. Harvard Divinity School now has a privately funded chair° in evangelical theological studies. In subjects such as history and philosophy, evangelical scholars have become central figures within their fields. Alvin Plantinga, a graduate and onetime faculty member of evangelical Calvin College,° has served as president of the central division of the American Philosophical Association. The historian George M. Marsden won the Bancroft Prize° in 2004 for his

---

Campus Crusade for Christ: an international, interdenominational Christian evangelical organization that was begun on the UCLA campus in 1951 as a ministry for students.

chair: a prestigious professorship that is paid for in part or in whole by a private donor. Endowed chairs often are named for the donor, the chair's specialization, and the department or school. Lindsay is referring to the Alonzo L. McDonald Family Professor of Evangelical Theological

Studies at Harvard Divinity School.

Calvin College: a liberal arts college in Grand Rapids, Michigan. The college is named after John Calvin, the sixteenth-century French Protestant reformer, and is associated with the Christian Reformed Church.

Bancroft Prize: a prestigious annual prize that is given for a book written about the history of the Americas or diplomacy.

critically acclaimed biography of Jonathan Edwards.° Evangelical scholars have become particularly noticeable in disciplines that address religious questions, but respected scholars in other fields have been coming forward in recent years to talk about their evangelical faith. The most conspicuous example is Francis Collins, director of the National Human Genome Research Institute, who wrote the best-selling *The Language of God: A Scientist Presents Evidence for Belief* (Free Press, 2006).

The "opening of the evangelical mind,"° as Alan Wolfe has aptly called it, may be surprising to some, but it is not unprecedented. Indeed anti-intellectualism° within Christianity is

actually an anomaly° of the 20th century. For most of Christianity's history, faith and learning have been intertwined. Over the centuries, intellectuals received religious sanction for their scholarly pursuits, and the church—in both Roman Catholic and Protestant traditions—supported a range of intellectual activity, from the scientific research of Newton° to the literary contributions of Chesterton.° History is on the side of evangelical intellectual strivings.

What do those developments mean for American higher education? For a start, America's universities—notably including elite institutions—are looking more like America. Evangelicals are still underrepresented

on major university campuses compared with their size in the U.S. population, but the tide is turning.

That is energizing intellectual life. 10 Evangelicals have reinvigorated theistic° approaches to philosophy and paid attention to subjects in political science and sociology that were, for too long, overlooked by others. Those include such subjects as the religious roots of American social movements and the role of Christian missionaries in the spread of global capitalism. Although some fields are more amenable to evangelicals than others, a range of disciplines now engage religious questions. In a column for the *Chronicle*, Stanley Fish° wrote, "When Jacques Derrida° died, I was called by

Jonathan Edwards (1703–1785): an American Congregationalist minister and theologian, whose 1741 "fire and brimstone" sermon "Sinners in the Hands of an Angry God" is often included in anthologies of American literature.

"opening of the evangelical mind": an allusion to

Allan Bloom's bestselling 1987 book, *The Closing of the American Mind*, a critique of American higher education.

anti-intellectualism: a distrust of or hostility toward modern academic theories and research.

anomaly: an unusual situation or departure from what is normal.

(Sir Isaac) Newton (1643–1727): an English mathematician, philosopher, and theologian. Known for his research on gravity, motion, color, and light, he is one of two mathematicians who are

credited with developing calculus.

(G. K.) Chesterton (1874–1936): an English man of letters who wrote in many genres—journalism, philosophy, biography, detective fiction, fantasy, poetry, and Christian apologetics (works that seek to defend Christianity against its critics).

theistic: assuming and acknowledging a belief in God.

Stanley Fish (b. 1938): an influential American literary theorist and law professor.

Jacques Derrida (1930–2004): a French philosopher who was born in Algeria. He was one of the most influential thinkers of the second half of the twentieth century.

a reporter who wanted to know what would succeed high theory and the triumvirate of race, gender, and class as the center of intellectual energy in the academy. I answered like a shot: religion." In the same article, Fish contended that religion must not be simply studied at arm's length, but must be considered as a viable "candidate for the truth."

Not everyone agrees. The historian David A. Hollinger has argued that universities do not need more Christianity, because religion no longer offers a distinctive mode of proof or way of thinking. Yet in most disciplines, we recognize that scholars bring to their research interpretive frames of reference. Just as one's race and gender can illumine a scholar's work, so too can one's religious commitments. In some quarters, religious conviction grounds a sense of personal vocation for scholars, and, at the least, religion has become a vitally important area of scholarly inquiry.

Forty years ago, conventional sociological wisdom said that society would secularize as it modernized. Such predictions were dead wrong. Levels of education and development have risen sharply around the world, while at the same time religion's influence has grown. It's time for the academy to come to grips with this dynamic. Moral and religious issues will become even more prominent in all disciplines. Greater religious pluralism,° in the United States and around the world, will continue to generate new sources of conflict while also suggesting possibilities for cooperation.

Unlike fundamentalists who retreat from pluralistic environments, evangelicals relish the chance to engage people who hold different beliefs. This could present an opportunity for deeper understanding on our campuses, but it will happen only if we bring evangelicals into our classroom discussions. Just as the debate surrounding intelligent design° has forced many biologists to engage religious topics in the classroom, so will rising religious pluralism. As we make greater progress in medicine and genomics, we should expect the number of moral issues surrounding those developments to multiply. That, joined with the rising number of evangelical students on our campuses, will demand of us at least a basic understanding of what this religious community believes.

Evangelicals are the most discussed but least understood group in American society. Observers often assume that they are in lockstep with the Republican Party, but the sociologist Christian Smith has shown that 70 percent of evangelicals do not identify with the religious right. Other observers conclude that evangelicals principally serve their own interests, but Allen D. Hertzke's persuasive *Freeing God's Children: The Unlikely Alliance for Global Human Rights* (Rowman and Littlefield, 2004) shows that evangelicals work as vigorously to protect the religious freedom of Buddhists and Jews around the world as they do that of their fellow Christians. A number of journalists and pundits° have written about evangelicals since 2000, but the most interesting and helpful works have been academic studies based on empirical° research. (Pick up one of those instead of a best-selling polemic° to learn more about the subject. Hint: Avoid any work that includes "theocracy" in the title.)

---

religious pluralism: the acceptance of the value and validity of religions other than one's own.

intelligent design: the intellectual position that an external, controlling, intelligent cause—rather than the processes of evolution—best accounts for the nature and complexity of living things and the universe more broadly. Supporters of this position generally see God as that intelligent cause, though in many cases, they state their arguments without making that assumption explicit.

pundit: originally, an authority or expert. The term is now often used to mean someone who makes critical evaluations in an authoritative way.

empirical: based on evidence gained from experimentation or observation (in contrast to relying on opinion).

polemic: an argument that is characterized by a strong, direct attack.

Will evangelicals radically reshape America's institutions of higher learning? Probably not, but it will not be for lack of effort. Evangelicals are devoting enormous resources to making colleges and universities more amenable to their convictions. They are supporting scholarship programs, university research centers, and student groups. Yet the evangelical ascendancy of the last three decades demonstrates how tough it is to change major institutions. George Bennett, who served as treasurer of the Harvard Corporation from 1965 to 1973, became the highest-ranking evangelical at Harvard over the last half-century. What was the net effect of his evangelical influence? In his own words: "Not much. At Harvard, being what it is now . . . religion takes a back seat." At the end of his term on the Harvard Corporation, the institution was not much different, in terms of openness to evangelicals or their ideals, than it had been when he started. If anyone was in a position to enact cultural change for evangelicals at Harvard, it was George Bennett. The fact that he didn't shows the strength of institutional inertia.

Many colleagues ask me whether evangelicals have enough power to "take over" the country. I often tell

15 them that the evangelical movement is not even united enough to agree on what that would mean. Yet the question belies a concern felt by many about evangelicals, a group that has been bombastic° in politics. Will they bring their placards and protests with them as they join the academic establishment, or will they soften their edges?

Are the concerns that animate evangelicals in politics the same concerns of evangelicals in the academy? In some ways, yes, but there are important differences to keep in mind. Evangelical populism°—which has served the movement well in American politics—is disdained by many evangelicals in the academy, and for good reason. Populism and intolerance may not be twinborn, but they are related. Also the political conservatism of American evangelicalism is far less common among evangelical academics. On foreign policy, the environment, and care for the poor, evangelical scholars share many of the concerns of their secular colleagues.

Nearly every evangelical scholar I encountered embodies a "cosmopolitan"° evangelical faith. They are "worldly" believers, in the best sense of the term. They regularly rub shoulders

with people of different faiths and of no faith at all. They aim not to "take back" the country for their faith, but simply want their faith to be seen as reasonable, genuine, and attractive. This cosmopolitan style of faith has helped evangelicals gain a seat at the table within the arts world. Evangelicals who have succeeded, such as the visual artist Makoto Fujimura—the youngest person ever named to the National Council on the Arts—don't desire to impose their moral vision on the rest of the artistic community, but at the same time, they don't want to exclude their faith from the work they do. The same can be said of evangelicals within the groves of academe.° Their rise into the halls of power is significant, but not menacing. Cosmopolitan evangelicals will not overturn the apple cart. They want civil discourse, not a culture war.

And we can learn from them. Indeed, in our understanding of evangelicals and the evangelical movement, we could all benefit from a more cosmopolitan outlook.

---

bombastic: here, stating its stance in an exaggerated manner.

populism: a social or political movement focusing on everyday people (in contrast to elites).

cosmopolitan: "at home all over the world," as the *Random House Unabridged Dictionary* aptly states it (in contrast to *provincial,* having a view of the world that is tied to a specific place).

groves of academe: higher education. The allusion is to a line in a poem by the Roman poet Horace (65 BCE–8 BCE).

Much of Lindsay's argument is concerned with establishing the fact of the rise of evangelicals on campus, but he also makes a causal argument when he examines the effects of evangelicals on academe. See Chapter 11 for more on causal arguments.

LINK TO P. 335

RESPOND•

1. What is Lindsay's argument? What sorts of evidence does Lindsay cite to support his claims? Why is it not surprising that Lindsay relies heavily on logical arguments (that is, facts and reason) rather than, say, emotional arguments to examine a potentially controversial topic like religion on college campuses? (For a discussion of kinds of evidence, see Chapter 16; for a discussion of logical arguments, see Chapter 4.)

2. A stereotype of evangelicals (and people of faith in general) is that they are anti-intellectual, an issue that Lindsay addresses in paragraph 8. How does Lindsay seek to counter this stereotype in that paragraph? How does he seek to counter it throughout the remainder of the article?

3. Interestingly, Lindsay does not offer readers an explicit definition of *evangelicals* in this article. At the same time, the article's statements about evangelicals—both who they are and who they aren't—can help us to assemble a definition. First, consider why Lindsay might not have included an explicit definition of the category of people that he is discussing. What are the advantages and disadvantages of not offering explicit definitions in cases like this? Second, based on the information in the article, put together a definition of the term *evangelicals* as Lindsay uses it. Finally, compare your definition with those on sites like dictionary.com. How is it similar? How is it different? (For a discussion of arguments of definition, see Chapter 9.)

4. Lindsay's article can be analyzed as a causal argument or perhaps more accurately as a series of such arguments. Make a list of the causal arguments that you find in this selection, and then analyze them according to the discussion "Understanding Causal Arguments" in Chapter 11. You'll see that Lindsay frequently marks the beginning of a new causal argument syntactically—that is, by using a specific sentence form. What sentence form does he use?

5. Lindsay's intended audience for this essay is people involved directly in higher education across the United States—administrators and faculty, in particular. Consider the audience that Lindsay invokes—that is, directly addresses or represents—in the text. What values does Lindsay expect these readers might have? Do you think that he expects them to believe in any faith? To be evangelicals? Why or why not? If you find this question challenging, you may wish to ask yourself why Lindsay ends the essay as he does. In other words, why might the topics in the last four paragraphs be placed where they are? In what ways do these paragraphs represent emotional arguments as well as logical

arguments? (For a discussion of invoked audience, see Chapter 1; for a discussion of emotional arguments, see Chapter 2.)

6. What evidence is there on your campus of evangelical Christianity (which is Lindsay's focus) or other faiths? How has that presence changed over time? Why? Is it related in any way to shifts in the demographics (such as the ethnic, economic, or geographical background) of students who attend your school? **Write an essay** in which you describe the current situation, and provide causal arguments about how it came to be. Like Lindsay, you may wish to rely on several kinds of evidence—demographic information, historical information, and interviews with current and former students, faculty, and staff. Note that even if you attend a college that is associated with a particular faith, the nature and extent of the expression of that faith have likely changed over time. (For a discussion of factual and causal arguments, see Chapters 8 and 11, respectively.)

▶ In "Selling Safe Sex in Public Schools," Michelle Bryant, formerly of the Office of Public Affairs at the University of Texas at Austin, interviews Shelby Knox, then a government major at UT and the subject of the award-winning 2005 documentary film The Education of Shelby Knox, which was shown at the Sundance Film Festival and aired on PBS's P.O.V. series. According to a recent blog posting by Knox on the Huffington Post, she currently lives in New York City, where she is "a full-time speaker and organizer working with progressive organizations to promote sex education, women's rights, and youth empowerment."

This essay originally appeared as a feature article in the fall 2005 issue of Life & Letters: A Publication of the College of Liberal Arts of the University of Texas at Austin. As you read, consider why an article about someone like Knox is an appropriate subject for such a publication.

Selling Safe Sex in Public Schools

MICHELLE BRYANT

Teenagers are viewing sexual content in music videos, movies, and, thanks to Paris Hilton,° even hamburger commercials. But what do they really know or need to know about sex? Some people feel schools need to teach teenagers about abstinence only. Opponents say that withholding information about condom use and birth control will only lead to unwanted pregnancies and sexually transmitted diseases (STDs).°

The debate over sex education has intensified in recent years because of substantial increases in federal funding for abstinence-only programs. In 2005, $167 million was appropriated, up from $80 million in 2001. President George W. Bush's proposed 2006 budget includes $206 million for such programs. Schools that choose comprehensive or abstinence-plus curricula don't qualify for this funding and must pay for the programs out of their general budget, provided by local and state governments.

On the frontline of the heated sex education debate stands Shelby Knox, currently a government major at The University of Texas at Austin. Although her hometown's high schools teach abstinence as the only safe alternative, Knox was shocked to learn that Lubbock, Texas, has some of the highest rates of teen pregnancy and STDs in the nation.

At age 15, Knox, a budding opera singer and a devout Christian who has pledged abstinence until marriage, became an unlikely advocate for comprehensive sex education, attracting the attention of documentary filmmakers Rose Rosenblatt and Marion Lipschutz. They documented her efforts in the

Paris Hilton (b. 1981): an American celebrity, heiress, socialite, model, actress, and entrepreneur. Here, she attends the Weinstein Co. Golden Globe after-party on January 16, 2006, in Beverly Hills, California.

STDs: sexually transmitted diseases. They can be transmitted during sexual activity or intercourse and include chlamydia, crabs, gonorrhea, hepatitis, herpes, HIV, HPV, scabies, and syphilis.

film *The Education of Shelby Knox,* which has been broadcast nationally on the P.O.V. series on PBS and won the Excellence in Cinematography Award in the documentary category at the 2005 Sundance Film Festival.

Through her work with the Lubbock Youth Commission, a group of high 5
school students empowered by the mayor to give Lubbock's youth a voice in city government, Knox began her fight for comprehensive sex education in public schools.

"We decided sex education was going to be our issue because we all knew someone who had been touched by the high rates of STDs and teen pregnancy," Knox said.

The youth commission received extensive media coverage, but little attention from school officials. After repeated requests, the school board finally allowed them to present their recommendations, but to no avail. However, Knox refused to give up, despite being repeatedly discouraged by the pastor of her church and the conservative Southern Baptist culture of the town. She was even told that she was "going to hell," literally.

"I felt like it was my responsibility as a student to use my voice and speak out," Knox said. "I was surprised when we did that the school board didn't

Bryant's interview with Shelby Knox provides nearly all of the information and evidence to support her argument. See the guidelines in Chapter 16 to help you plan and conduct your own interviews.

··· **LINK TO P. 498**

recognize us. They didn't say 'You're students. Maybe you know what's going on.' They were really blasé about the whole thing and that was a little disconcerting.

"That's why I got certified to teach at the local health department," she added. "I became a peer educator in my high school because once I learned that the school board wasn't going to do anything I felt like I should.

"Most students were very supportive of sex education," she said. "They 10 realized that the fact that we didn't have sex education was a big problem. Once students realized that I had the information they were looking for, they would ask me questions about where they could get tested for STDs and how they could get condoms.

"If a student asks a teacher about sex," she added, "the teacher is required to answer with 'Abstinence is the only way to prevent STDs and teen pregnancy.' If they don't, they're in danger of losing their job."

During the time the youth commission led the comprehensive sex education campaign, STDs and teen pregnancy rates in Lubbock dropped. The Texas Health Department attributed this to a "rise in responsibility" because of the youth commission's advocating condom use.

By her senior year, Knox committed to working with a group of gay teens who decided to sue the Lubbock School Board because they were denied the right to form a gay-straight alliance in school. This was not a fight the other members of the youth commission, afraid of adding more controversy to their already contentious agenda, wanted to join. Soon after, the mayor of Lubbock announced that he was considering doing away with the youth commission because of a city budget shortfall. The youth commission agreed to operate without funding and, in the process, abandoned the sex education campaign. Since that time, the rates of STDs and teen pregnancy in Lubbock have gone back up. An infuriated Knox resigned from the youth commission, but continued fighting for what she felt was right.

When an organization came to Lubbock to protest the gay teenagers' lawsuit, Knox, along with her mother, joined a counter protest, carrying a sign that read "God Loves Everybody," an affirming belief that has guided Knox into adulthood.

"I think that God wants you to question," Knox said. "To do more than just 15 blindly be a follower, because he can't use blind followers. He can use people like me who realize there's more in the world that can be done."

During the Spring 2006 semester, Knox will participate in the UT in D.C. program, which offers qualified students the opportunity to study and intern in Washington, D.C. She hopes to do an internship with Advocates for Youth or the Sexuality Information and Education Council of the United States. She is

Shelby Knox at home in Lubbock, Texas, with her parents, Danny and Paula Knox

also a member of the Student Senate, University Democrats and Madrigal Choir. She continues to be an advocate for comprehensive sex education and has spoken with teen activists across the nation in conjunction with the film.

"Getting to connect with teens who can make a difference in their communities is the best part of this," Knox said. "I wish that I would have known of other teens that were doing this. When I speak I give them my e-mail and tell them we can talk because I know how hard it is to be a teenager in high school who is doing something controversial."

RESPOND •

1. What sort of ethos does Shelby Knox create for herself during the interview reported here? What role(s) does her faith play in that ethos? Would her narrative or ethos be different if Knox were an atheist? Why or why not? (For a discussion of ethos, see Chapter 3.)

2. What causal arguments do you find in the narrative of Shelby Knox's experiences? Why are these arguments crucial to the argument made by the selection? (For a discussion of causal arguments, see Chapter 11.)

3. In paragraph 15, Knox contends, "I think that God wants you to question." What does Knox want people of faith to question? Why? Why do you imagine Knox believes "he [God] can't use blind followers"? (Obviously, Knox is using "blind" metaphorically in this case.)

4. This article first appeared in *Life & Letters: A Publication of the College of Liberal Arts of the University of Texas at Austin*, a magazine that highlights the research and achievements of faculty and students in the college. It's distributed within the college and to its friends and supporters, including donors, many of whom would be politically conservative and would identify as evangelical Christians. How can you see awareness of the magazine's intended audience in the selection of Shelby Knox as the topic of an article? In the way her story is presented? How might the selection challenge readers holding various political or religious beliefs? How does the illustration on page 875, which was published with the article in *Life & Letters*, contribute to the argument?

5. This selection represents an especially popular genre in American culture, a narrative about an individual who, motivated by a set of principled beliefs—whether sacred, secular, or both—was moved to action in the public arena. Find another example of this genre that you believe to be especially effective, and **write a rhetorical analysis** of it. (For information about writing a rhetorical analysis, see Chapter 5.) In your analysis, be sure to include information about why you find the narrative you've chosen effective and perhaps moving. Be sure to include a copy of the text you analyze when you turn in your rhetorical analysis.

▼ *Melanie Springer Mock is an associate professor of writing and literature at George Fox University in Newberg, Oregon, and a Mennonite. Mennonites are a Christian denomination with sixteenth-century roots in what is today the Netherlands. The denomination began as part of what became known as the Protestant Reformation. George Fox University is named for the founder of the Religious Society of Friends (Quakers) and is affiliated with the evangelical branch of Friends in the United States. Together with the Church of the Brethren, the Mennonites and the Quakers are the denominations historically known as peace churches, which advocate a pacifism that is derived from their understanding that Jesus practiced and preached nonviolence. In this opinion piece, which appeared in December 2008 in The Oregonian newspaper, published in Portland, Oregon, Mock takes an unusual stance on a controversy that has flared over the past decade or so. As you read, pay attention to the ways in which Mock uses emotional and ethical appeals to make her claims.*

Separation of Church and State: A War on Christmas and Other Misguided Notions

MELANIE SPRINGER MOCK

Other than the hot, hot days of summer, Christmas is my favorite time of year. I love Christmas lights and decorating a tree and shopping for presents. I love celebrating Advent° in a greenery-draped church and singing carols as the Christmas lights glow bright around us. And most definitely, I love Christmas Eve services, when we gather around a Nativity° to celebrate Jesus' birth.

Yet, even though I love Christmas and all its decorating splendor, I'm convinced Christmas displays should not appear in government-owned spaces. Nativities and other Christian symbols of Christmas don't belong in state capitols, in courthouses, in city parks. More accurately, it is because I am a Christian that I am convinced the government should not be celebrating Jesus' birth.

Advent: the birth or coming of Christ or, here, the part of the church calendar leading up to Christmas, a period of expectation and anticipation.

Nativity: the birth of Jesus or a representation of this event. A Nativity, also called a crèche or manger scene, recalls the account of Jesus's birth found primarily in the Gospel of Luke in the Christian New Testament. It often includes representations of the newborn Jesus lying in a manger (the trough that held hay for the animals); Mary, his mother; Joseph, her husband; shepherds; angels; and animals such as cattle, sheep, and donkeys. Representations of the Magi (also called the "Wise Men" or "Three Kings"), who brought gifts to Jesus, according to the Gospel of Matthew, are also often part of this display.

To kick off a campaign to promote the display of Nativity scenes on public and private property across the country, Christian activists exhibit one during a news conference in front of the U.S. Supreme Court building in Washington in November 2008.

Somewhere in the country every year, though, conflicts flame about the presence of Christian-specific decorations in government spaces. Washington state is among the latest to enter the fray, with atheist and Christian groups duking it out over decorating the Capitol building. Some claim that government organizations should be free to include Nativities in their Christmas displays, while others argue that doing so violates the Constitution's First Amendment. The battles have in places become so fierce that some on the right—such as the Liberty Counsel and Fox television commentator Bill O'Reilly—have declared that there's a "War on Christmas," claiming that secularists are trying to destroy "the reason for the season."

Not only do I believe the Prince of Peace° would reject any militaristic language about "war" over his birth, I'm also convinced that Christians should not engage in crusades about Christmas decorations in the public square. For while O'Reilly and gang blame the Christmas war on secularists, it's important to remember that many Christians are also strong proponents of the separation of church and state, and believe that the government has no business endorsing Christianity, either explicitly or implicitly. Yet by placing Nativities in capitol buildings and city parks, the government is advocating for Christianity to the exclusion of other faiths embraced by its citizens.

The reasons for my own beliefs are 5 complicated, wrapped as they are in my church denomination's history of persecution by church-states, where refusing to worship as a Catholic or Lutheran sometimes meant punishment and death. The martyrdom° of Anabaptists° in Europe led them to believe wholly in the need for separation between church and state entities, and they carried this conviction with them as they fled the persecution of one church-state, and then others.

I grew up hearing this history of martyrdom, and learned—almost by osmosis, it seemed—that the U.S. Constitution ensured that which the Mennonites held dear: that the church and the state would remain separate.

Of course, there are many who believe the First Amendment has been misconstrued, and that government displays of religious symbols don't violate the church/state separation. And the U.S. Supreme Court decided

---

Prince of Peace: a name for Jesus in the Christian tradition. The name derives from the child mentioned in Isaiah 9:5 in the Hebrew Bible, which Christians call the "Old Testament." This name is an example of antonomasia, a trope. (See

Chapter 13 for a discussion of this and other tropes.)

martyrdom: the persecution suffered by Mennonites and other Anabaptists during the sixteenth century. A book dating from 1660, *Martyrs Mirror*, which documents the history of many who

died for their faith, especially Anabaptists, remains a book second in importance only to the Bible as religious reading for many Mennonites.

Anabaptists: several sixteenth century European Protestant movements (including the Amish, the

Mennonites, the Church of the Brethren, and German Baptists, among others) that opposed infant baptism (practiced by other Protestants and by Roman Catholics) and insisted instead on believer's baptism, which occurs after a person's profession of faith in Jesus Christ.

in the 1980s that government bodies could place Christian symbols alongside other secular holiday exhibits, so that Frosty the Snowman can stand beside a Nativity, or Rudolph beside a menorah.°

But I wonder why such government displays are even necessary. Putting aside arguments about the First Amendment and church/state separation, do Christians really need baby Jesus on the courthouse steps to remind them of his birth? If the answer is yes, then perhaps that says more about their faith (or faithlessness) than it does about Christmas decorations or the Constitution.

And if people want Nativities in government spaces to remind non-Christians about "the reason for the season," that seems like evangelism, an act in which the government should play no role. After all, if Christians were a minority faith—as my Mennonite ancestors were in Europe several centuries ago—I imagine they would not wish to be evangelized by those in the majority, be they Muslims or Jews or Hare Krishnas.° Purposefully, our Constitution means we'll never have to face that threat.

Mostly, though, I long to keep the 10 sacred just that: sacred. The focus of every Christian should be on the real

manger, rather than on whether Nativities should appear in the public square, pressed up next to Santa and the elves. To believe and act otherwise—that we need to fight some presumed war on Christmas by putting Christian displays in government spaces—cheapens what should be the central focus of a Christian's adoration: the birth of a savior.

---

menorah: a candelabrum that is associated with Judaism. Here, it is the eight-branched candelabrum lit nightly during the Feast of Lights (Hanukkah). This holiday continues for eight nights in December in memory of the rededication of the Temple in Jerusalem following the successful Maccabean

Revolt during the second century BCE. (The candelabrum holds eight candles as well as a "helper" candle used to light the others.)

Hare Krishnas: a popular label for those affiliated with the International Society for Krishna Consciousness, a branch of

Vaishnava Hinduism founded in New York City in 1966 but whose origins date to the sixteenth century or earlier. Hare Krishnas wear orange-yellow robes and chant in public places.

Mock repeatedly appeals to her Christian beliefs as a Mennonite to build her ethos in this argument that criticizes some of her fellow Christians. See Chapter 3 for a discussion of how to establish an authoritative ethos.

LINK TO P. 52

RESPOND

1. What stance does Mock, as a Christian, take on the issue of "the war on Christmas"? What makes her stance unusual among some Christians? How does she use that fact strategically in organizing her argument?

2. What is Mock's understanding of the notion of the separation of church and state? How well does she explain it? How well does she justify it?

3. Note the ethical appeals that Mock uses to support her position. How does she create an ethos as a Christian? As a Mennonite? As an American? (For a discussion of ethical appeals and arguments, see Chapter 3.)

4. What sorts of emotional and logical arguments does Mock use? How effective are they? (For a discussion of emotional and logical arguments, see Chapters 2 and 4, respectively.)

5. In what senses is Mock's argument a proposal? A proposal addressed specifically to Christians? To all Americans? (For a discussion of proposal arguments, see Chapter 12.).

6. Investigate debates about the so-called war on Christmas or related public debates about the display of religious symbols in public spaces. If there have been such controversies in your area, you may wish to focus on them. **Write a rhetorical analysis** of a single text—an editorial, a letter to the editor, a blog posting, a cartoon, a transcript of a media program, or a court opinion—in a specific debate about religious symbols in public contexts. You'll need to provide background information to contextualize the specific debate, and you'll want to include a copy of the text you analyze with your analysis. (For a discussion of rhetorical analyses, see Chapter 5.)

God's Justice and Ours

ANTONIN SCALIA

Before proceeding to discuss the morality of capital punishment, I want to make clear that my views on the subject have nothing to do with how I vote in capital cases that come before the Supreme Court. That statement would not be true if I subscribed to the conventional fallacy that the Constitution is a "living document"—that is, a text that means from age to age whatever the society (or perhaps the Court) thinks it ought to mean.

In recent years, that philosophy has been particularly well enshrined in our Eighth Amendment° jurisprudence, our case law dealing with the prohibition of "cruel and unusual punishments." Several of our opinions have said that what falls within this prohibition is not static, but changes from generation to generation, to comport with "the evolving standards of decency that mark the progress of a maturing society." Applying that principle, the Court came close, in 1972, to abolishing the death penalty entirely. It ultimately did not do so, but it has imposed, under color of the Constitution, procedural and substantive limitations that did not exist when the Eighth Amendment was adopted—and some of which had not even been adopted by a majority of the states at the time they were judicially decreed. For example, the Court has prohibited the death penalty for all crimes except murder, and indeed even for what might be called run-of-the-mill murders, as opposed to those that are somehow characterized by a high degree of brutality or depravity. It has prohibited the mandatory imposition of the death penalty for any crime, insisting that in all cases the jury be permitted to consider all mitigating factors and to impose, if it wishes, a lesser sentence. And it has imposed an age limit at the time of the offense (it is currently seventeen) that is well above what existed at common law.

If I subscribed to the proposition that I am authorized (indeed, I suppose compelled) to intuit and impose our "maturing" society's "evolving standards of decency," this essay would be a preview of my next vote in a death penalty case. As it is, however, the Constitution that I interpret and apply is not living but dead—or, as I prefer to put it, enduring. It means today not what current society (much less the Court) thinks it ought to mean, but what it meant when it was adopted. For me, therefore, the constitutionality of the death penalty is not a difficult, soul-wrenching question. It was clearly permitted when the Eighth Amendment was adopted (not merely for murder, by the

◀ Justice Antonin Scalia has served as a member of the U.S. Supreme Court since 1986. This article, which originally appeared in First Things: The Journal of Religion and Public Life in May 2002, is based on remarks that he had made at a forum on religion and public life at the University of Chicago's Divinity School. In it, Scalia distinguishes between two fundamentally different ways of interpreting the U.S. Constitution, discusses the changing attitude of democratic societies to the death penalty, and ends by disagreeing with a proclamation by Pope John Paul II and the most recent version of the Catholic catechism. As you read, note the care with which Scalia defines and illustrates the terms he uses, and consider the ways in which these comments were written to be read aloud.

Eighth Amendment: "Excessive bail shall not be required, nor excessive fines imposed, nor cruel and unusual punishments inflicted."

way, but for all felonies—including, for example, horse-thieving, as anyone can verify by watching a western movie). And so it is clearly permitted today. There is plenty of room within this system for "evolving standards of decency," but the instrument of evolution (or, if you are more tolerant of the Court's approach, the herald that evolution has occurred) is not the nine lawyers who sit on the Supreme Court of the United States, but the Congress of the United States and the legislatures of the fifty states, who may, within their own jurisdictions, restrict or abolish the death penalty as they wish.

But while my views on the morality of the death penalty have nothing to do with how I vote as a judge, they have a lot to do with whether I can or should be a judge at all. To put the point in the blunt terms employed by Justice Harold Blackmun towards the end of his career on the bench, when he announced that he would henceforth vote (as Justices William Brennan and Thurgood Marshall had previously done) to overturn all death sentences, when I sit on a Court that reviews and affirms capital convictions, I am part of "the machinery of death." My vote, when joined with at least four others, is, in most cases, the last step that permits an execution to proceed. I could not take part in that process if I believed what was being done to be immoral.

Capital cases are much different from the other life-and-death issues that   5 my Court sometimes faces: abortion, for example, or legalized suicide. There it is not the state (of which I am in a sense the last instrument) that is decreeing death, but rather private individuals whom the state has decided not to restrain. One may argue (as many do) that the society has a moral obligation to restrain. That moral obligation may weigh heavily upon the voter, and upon the legislator who enacts the laws; but a judge, I think, bears no moral guilt for the laws society has failed to enact. Thus, my difficulty with *Roe v. Wade* is a legal rather than a moral one: I do not believe (and, for two hundred years, no one believed) that the Constitution contains a right to abortion. And if a state were to permit abortion on demand, I would—and could in good conscience—vote against an attempt to invalidate that law for the same reason that I vote against the invalidation of laws that forbid abortion on demand: because the Constitution gives the federal government (and hence me) no power over the matter.

With the death penalty, on the other hand, I am part of the criminal-law machinery that imposes death—which extends from the indictment, to the jury conviction, to rejection of the last appeal. I am aware of the ethical principle that one can give "material cooperation" to the immoral act of another when the evil that would attend failure to cooperate is even greater (for example, helping a burglar tie up a householder where the alternative is that the burglar would kill the householder). I doubt whether that doctrine is even applicable to the trial judges and jurors who must themselves determine that the death sentence will be imposed. It seems to me these individuals are not merely engaged in "material cooperation" with someone else's action, but are themselves decreeing death on behalf of the state.

The same is true of appellate judges in those states where they are charged with "reweighing" the mitigating and aggravating factors and determining de novo° whether the death penalty should be imposed: they are themselves decreeing death. Where (as is the case in the federal system) the appellate judge merely determines that the sentence pronounced by the trial court is in accordance with law, perhaps the principle of material cooperation could be applied. But as I have said, that principle demands that the good deriving from the cooperation exceed the evil which is assisted. I find it hard to see how any appellate judge could find this condition to be met, unless he believes retaining his seat on the bench (rather than resigning) is somehow essential to preservation of the society—which is of course absurd. (As Charles de Gaulle is reputed to have remarked when his aides told him he could not resign as President of France because he was the indispensable man: "Mon ami, the cemeteries are full of indispensable men.")

I pause here to emphasize the point that in my view the choice for the judge who believes the death penalty to be immoral is resignation, rather than simply ignoring duly enacted, constitutional laws and sabotaging death penalty cases. He has, after all, taken an oath to apply the laws and has been given no power to supplant them with rules of his own. Of course if he feels strongly enough he can go beyond mere resignation and lead a political campaign to abolish the death penalty—and if that fails, lead a revolution. But rewrite the laws he cannot do. This dilemma, of course, need not be confronted by a proponent of the "living Constitution," who believes that it means what it ought to mean. If the death penalty is (in his view) immoral, then it is (hey, presto!) automatically unconstitutional, and he can continue to sit while nullifying a sanction that has been imposed, with no suggestion of its unconstitutionality, since the beginning of the Republic. (You can see why the "living Constitution" has such attraction for us judges.)

It is a matter of great consequence to me, therefore, whether the death penalty is morally acceptable. As a Roman Catholic—and being unable to jump out of my skin—I cannot discuss that issue without reference to Christian tradition and the Church's Magisterium.°

The death penalty is undoubtedly wrong unless one accords to the state a scope of moral action that goes beyond what is permitted to the individual. In my view, the major impetus behind modern aversion to the death penalty is the equation of private morality with governmental morality. This is a

de novo: Latin phrase meaning "anew, afresh"; considering the matter anew; with regard to law, the same as if a case had not been heard before and as if no decision previously had been rendered.

Magisterium: in Catholic theology, the divinely appointed authority given to the Pope and bishops of the Catholic Church to teach the truths of religion.

10

predictable (though I believe erroneous and regrettable) reaction to modern, democratic self-government.

Few doubted the morality of the death penalty in the age that believed in the divine right of kings. Or even in earlier times. St. Paul had this to say (I am quoting, as you might expect, the King James version):

> Let every soul be subject unto the higher powers. For there is no power but of God: the powers that be are ordained of God. Whosoever therefore resisteth the power, resisteth the ordinance of God: and they that resist shall receive to themselves damnation. For rulers are not a terror to good works, but to the evil. Wilt thou then not be afraid of the power? Do that which is good, and thou shalt have praise of the same: for he is the minister of God to thee for good. But if thou do that which is evil, be afraid; for he beareth not the sword in vain: for he is the minister of God, a revenger to execute wrath upon him that doeth evil. Wherefore ye must needs be subject, not only for wrath, but also for conscience sake. (Romans 13:1–5)

This is not the Old Testament, I emphasize, but St. Paul. One can understand his words as referring only to lawfully constituted authority, or even only to lawfully constituted authority that rules justly. But the core of his message is that government—however you want to limit that concept—derives its moral authority from God. It is the "minister of God" with powers to "revenge," to "execute wrath," including even wrath by the sword (which is unmistakably a reference to the death penalty). Paul of course did not believe that the individual possessed any such powers. Only a few lines before this passage, he wrote, "Dearly beloved, avenge not yourselves, but rather give place unto wrath: for it is written, Vengeance is mine; I will repay, saith the Lord." And in this world the Lord repaid—did justice—through His minister, the state.

These passages from Romans represent the consensus of Western thought until very recent times. Not just of Christian or religious thought, but of secular thought regarding the powers of the state. That consensus has been upset, I think, by the emergence of democracy. It is easy to see the hand of the Almighty behind rulers whose forebears, in the dim mists of history, were supposedly anointed by God, or who at least obtained their thrones in awful and unpredictable battles whose outcome was determined by the Lord of Hosts, that is, the Lord of Armies. It is much more difficult to see the hand of God—or any higher moral authority—behind the fools and rogues (as the losers would have it) whom we ourselves elect to do our own will. How can their power to avenge—to vindicate the "public order"—be any greater than our own?

Scalia embeds a definition argument in his article as evidence for his principal argument. See Chapter 9 for more about definition arguments and how to use them effectively.

LINK TO P. 250

So it is no accident, I think, that the modern view that the death penalty is immoral is centered in the West. That has little to do with the fact that the West has a Christian tradition, and everything to do with the fact that the West is the home of democracy. Indeed, it seems to me that the more Christian a country is, the less likely it is to regard the death penalty as immoral. Abolition has taken its firmest hold in post-Christian Europe, and has least support in the church-going United States. I attribute that to the fact that, for the believing Christian, death is no big deal. Intentionally killing an innocent person is a big deal: it is a grave sin, which causes one to lose his soul. But losing this life, in exchange for the next? The Christian attitude is reflected in the words Robert Bolt's play has Thomas More° saying to the headsman: "Friend, be not afraid of your office. You send me to God." And when Cranmer asks whether he is sure of that, More replies, "He will not refuse one who is so blithe to go to Him." For the nonbeliever, on the other hand, to deprive a man of his life is to end his existence. What a horrible act!

Besides being less likely to regard death as an utterly cataclysmic punish- 15 ment, the Christian is also more likely to regard punishment in general as deserved. The doctrine of free will—the ability of man to resist temptations to evil, which God will not permit beyond man's capacity to resist—is central to the Christian doctrine of salvation and damnation, heaven and hell. The post-Freudian secularist, on the other hand, is more inclined to think that people are what their history and circumstances have made them, and there is little sense in assigning blame.

Of course those who deny the authority of a government to exact vengeance are not entirely logical. Many crimes—for example, domestic murder in the heat of passion—are neither deterred by punishment meted out to others nor likely to be committed a second time by the same offender. Yet opponents of capital punishment do not object to sending such an offender to prison, perhaps for life. Because he deserves punishment. Because it is just.

The mistaken tendency to believe that a democratic government, being nothing more than the composite will of its individual citizens, has no more moral power or authority than they do as individuals has adverse effects in other areas as well. It fosters civil disobedience, for example, which proceeds on the assumption that what the individual citizen considers an unjust law— even if it does not compel him to act unjustly—need not be obeyed. St. Paul would not agree. "Ye must needs be subject," he said, "not only for wrath, but also for conscience sake." For conscience sake. The reaction of people of faith to this tendency of democracy to obscure the divine authority behind government should not be resignation to it, but the resolution to combat it as

Thomas More (1478–1535): English statesman, author, and lawyer who was beheaded in 1535 for refusing to take the oath of the Act of Succession, which would have passed the British throne to Elizabeth, a Protestant, rather than the Catholic Princess Mary. His final words were "The king's good servant, but God's first."

Thomas More in the Tower of London, where he was held for fifteen months before his execution

Napoleonic tradition: during his coronation as Emperor of France in 1804, Napoleon Bonaparte (1769–1821) is said to have taken the crown out of the hands of the Pope and crowned himself, a symbolic demonstration that power in his empire stemmed from the state and not the church.

Evangelium Vitae: Latin title, meaning "The Gospel of Life," of a 1995 encyclical, or papal letter, defining the Church's teachings on the value and sacredness of all stages of human life, from conception to death. Papal encyclicals are always written in Latin, and their titles are the opening words of the document. They are not considered infallible; that is, Catholics need not believe they are free of error.

recusal: disqualification.

effectively as possible. We have done that in this country (and continental Europe has not) by preserving in our public life many visible reminders that—in the words of a Supreme Court opinion from the 1940s—"we are a religious people, whose institutions pre-suppose a Supreme Being." These reminders include: "In God we trust" on our coins, "one nation, under God" in our Pledge of Allegiance, the opening of sessions of our legislatures with a prayer, the opening of sessions of my Court with "God save the United States and this Honorable Court," annual Thanksgiving proclamations issued by our President at the direction of Congress, and constant invocations of divine support in the speeches of our political leaders, which often conclude, "God bless America." All this, as I say, is most un-European, and helps explain why our people are more inclined to understand, as St. Paul did, that government carries the sword as "the minister of God," to "execute wrath" upon the evildoer.

A brief story about the aftermath of September 11 nicely illustrates how different things are in secularized Europe. I was at a conference of European and American lawyers and jurists in Rome when the planes struck the twin towers. All in attendance were transfixed by the horror of the event, and listened with rapt attention to the President's ensuing address to the nation. When the speech had concluded, one of the European conferees—a religious man—confided in me how jealous he was that the leader of my nation could conclude his address with the words "God bless the United States." Such invocation of the deity, he assured me, was absolutely unthinkable in his country, with its Napoleonic tradition° of extirpating religion from public life.

It will come as no surprise from what I have said that I do not agree with the encyclical Evangelium Vitae° and the new Catholic catechism (or the very latest version of the new Catholic catechism), according to which the death penalty can only be imposed to protect rather than avenge, and that since it is (in most modern societies) not necessary for the former purpose, it is wrong.

I have given this new position thoughtful and careful consideration—and 20
I disagree. That is not to say I favor the death penalty (I am judicially and judiciously neutral on that point); it is only to say that I do not find the death penalty immoral. I am happy to have reached that conclusion, because I like my job, and would rather not resign. And I am happy because I do not think it would be a good thing if American Catholics running for legislative office had to oppose the death penalty (most of them would not be elected); if American Catholics running for Governor had to promise commutation of all death sentences (most of them would never reach the Governor's mansion); if American Catholics were ineligible to go on the bench in all jurisdictions imposing the death penalty; or if American Catholics were subject to recusal° when called for jury duty in capital cases.

RESPOND.

1. Justice Scalia devotes the first part of this article to distinguishing between those who read the Constitution as a "living document," the meaning of which changes as society "matures," and those who see it as "enduring," with a focus on its meaning at the time it was drafted. What, for Scalia, are the characteristics and consequences of each view? Which of the two views do you prefer? Why? Does either one leave you uncomfortable? Why or why not?

2. Throughout the article, Scalia makes other important distinctions: cases in which the state (that is, the government) decrees death versus those where it does not restrain death from occurring (paragraph 5), private morality versus governmental morality (paragraph 10), European versus American attitudes toward religion in public life (paragraph 14), legal versus moral matters (paragraph 17), and Christian versus post-Freudian secularist perspectives on death (paragraph 15), among others. Choose two such distinctions, and specify the basis of the distinction (in each case, a kind of definition—see Chapter 9).

3. Scalia concludes by claiming that it's a good thing for American Catholics (and, by extension, people of any faith in America) to be involved in aspects of public and political life in the United States. Do you agree or disagree? Why?

4. Scalia argues that a justice who finds the death penalty immoral should resign from the bench (paragraph 8). Do you agree or disagree? Why? Whatever your stance, you'll need to do your best to anticipate and acknowledge potential rebuttals against your position.

5. Scalia claims that the state should be accorded "a scope of moral action that goes beyond what is permitted to the individual" (paragraph 10); in other words, he believes that it's a grave mistake to assume that "a democratic government, being nothing more than the composite will of its individual citizens, has no more moral power or authority than they do as individuals" (paragraph 17). **Write an essay** in the form of a proposal argument in which you propose and evaluate the consequences of each of these positions, arguing ultimately for the position you find more justifiable. (For a discussion of proposal arguments, see Chapter 12.)

▼ *"Wearing a Head Scarf Is My Choice as a Muslim: Please Respect It," by Mariam Rahmani, originally appeared in July 2005 in the* Austin (Texas) American Statesman. *During that summer, Rahmani, a rising high-school senior from Theodore Roosevelt High School in Kent, Ohio, was participating in the 2005 Telluride Association Summer Program at the University of Texas at Austin. (The Telluride Association sponsors several such programs for high school juniors annually at institutions around the country. The-six-week programs, which focus on various topics, are seminars much like upper-division college courses.) As you read, consider how Rahmani's proposal for dealing with differences of religion and culture in the public space anticipates and responds to potential counterarguments.*

Wearing a Head Scarf Is My Choice as a Muslim: Please Respect It

MARIAM RAHMANI

This fall, French public school students will experience their second year under a law that bans the display of all religious symbols in schools. The law has aroused immense controversy because it forbids female Muslims to wear *hijab*°—hence its nickname, "the veil law."°

---

hijab: the head covering worn by some Muslim women. It usually covers the hair and neck, but not the face. A woman's wearing the *hijab* is generally taken by Muslims to signify modesty.

"the veil law": a French law passed in March 2004 that outlaws the wearing of "conspicuous religious symbols" in public schools. Although the law named no specific articles of clothing or jewelry, it was understood as outlawing the *hijab* (or even head-scarves), yarmulkes (worn by some Jewish boys), tur-bans (as worn by Sikh boys), and large crosses (as some Christians might wear). "Discreet symbols of faith," such as hands of Fatima (worn by some Muslims), Stars of David (a symbol of Judaism), and small crosses (associated with Christianity), were permitted. To understand the law, one must appreciate that the separation of church and state has been much stron-ger in France than in the United States for quite some time. In general, the French assume that religion is a private matter and shouldn't be part of the public arena. Those sup-porting the law contend that it ensures that schools will be places where ethnic or religious identities don't become more important than the values all French people share.

In passing it, the French government argued that its public school system should be an open arena encouraging students to engage in independent thought. This is a worthy aim for any educational system. Here in the United States, we have generally kept religion out of public schools for similar reasons. The trouble is not the French law's goal, but rather the Western perception that the Islamic *hijab* can't exist in a system allowing free inquiry.

I will soon begin my senior year of high school in Kent, Ohio, and am spending my summer here in Austin. Seven years ago, I made a personal decision to begin wearing *hijab*. You might wonder why.

At the root of *hijab* is the philosophy that a woman should be regarded for her personality, mind and abilities rather than her physicality. Wearing *hijab* reminds me not to focus on the superficial and instead to channel my energies toward developing my character and intellect. To me, this encapsulates the spirit of independent thought.

Ironically, much of the Western world views the Islamic *hijab* as a symbol 5 of male oppression. But every day in the West, we are inundated with images that reduce women to sex symbols. Why do people think that my choosing to act on my own will—and without the pressure of having to physically impress the opposite sex—is "oppressive"?

Are advertisements that use scantily clothed women merely to sell a product, or that present women as mindless individuals valued only for their beauty, really "liberating"?

Hijab enables a woman to maintain her dignity. It helps her demand respect as an equal of any man rather than as an object for his pleasure.

The negative association Westerners have of *hijab* is that weak or brainwashed Muslim girls are forced by their families to wear it. The French law supposedly will liberate these girls.

My experience shows the opposite: a number of Muslim girls with *hijab* have passed through Kent's school system as dedicated and involved students who have become a part of the school community's fabric. Most females who are found with *hijab* in the Western world are strong, independently minded women who consciously and voluntarily resolve to wear it because it makes sense to them. I suspect this is why some people have grown afraid: they are intimidated by the prospect of capable young women choosing to live lives different than their own.

The issue is not oppression of women. It is about the unwillingness of two 10 ideologies to coexist in mutual respect and understanding. A female with *hijab* registers as an unknown in the common Western mind, and humans are naturally wary of the unknown. Legislation inspired by such fear only succeeds in ostracizing these women.

In December 2003, about 3,000 people attended a demonstration in Paris to protest a law forbidding Islamic veils in French schools.

Among the elements in Rahmani's article are definition arguments that explore the meanings of the *hijab* and gender oppression. See Chapter 9 for more on making definition arguments.

LINK TO P. 250

It's pointless to debate whether young women with *hijab* have excluded themselves from society or vice versa. A barrier now separates the two, making impossible the very kind of open, cooperative intellectual understanding that the French law was meant to foster.

Mainstream societies have often rejected the customs and beliefs of immigrant communities. These communities then isolate themselves to preserve their customs. No one benefits.

In an increasingly interdependent world, we must tolerate one another even when our attitudes diverge. On the issue of *hijab* in the West, both parties must first agree to disagree. Muslim women with *hijab* are not asking Western women to do the same, and likewise, Western society should respect our decisions. Furthermore, people who are ignorant of the principles behind *hijab* should seek to inform themselves, and Muslims should be patient to provide answers.

As human beings, we must realize that we all share the same basic desires for happiness and meaning in our lives. No one should suffer discrimination because we choose different paths to achieve these common goals.

RESPOND ●

1. What is Mariam Rahmani's argument? How does she define the meaning of wearing the *hijab* and justify it? How effectively does she anticipate and respond to potential counterarguments?

2. How does Rahmani call into question Western notions of "liberation" for women?

3. If women of any faith or no faith at all believe that they're regarded by men or society at large for their "physicality," should they have to take action, or should men or society change? Why? How?

4. Rahmani sets up a strong contrast between the West and Islam, yet she is, based on available evidence, a Muslim in and of the West. If we assume this statement is true, has Rahmani contradicted herself or weakened her argument? In other words, must there be a strong contrast between Islam and the West? Why or why not?

5. In paragraph 13, Rahmani contends that we must "agree to disagree." Do you agree with her position, or are there alternatives she hasn't mentioned? What might they be?

6. In the same paragraph, Rahmani issues a challenge both to those who "are ignorant of the principles behind *hijab*" and to Muslims. Whatever your background, do some research on the topic, seeking to

understand why some Muslim women wear the *hijab* and why others, including many who are very devout, choose not to. As you'll soon discover, differences are linked in complex ways to a woman's understanding of Islam and, especially for recent immigrants or their children or grandchildren, the country or region from which they've come. You'll easily be able to find information on this topic on the Web, but you may also want to try to interview several Muslim women to obtain their views on this complex topic. **Write a definitional essay** in which you seek to make explicit the principles that various women attend to in their decision to wear or not wear the *hijab* or to cover their hair in some other way. (For a discussion of definitional arguments, see Chapter 9.)

In "The Ethicist," a weekly advice column in the New York Times Magazine that is also syndicated across the United States and Canada, Randy Cohen helps readers make sense of ethical dilemmas that they encounter in their daily lives. Cohen, who describes himself as culturally Jewish but not religiously observant, is also the "freelance ethicist" for National Public Radio's All Things Considered and author of The Good, the Bad and the Difference: How to Tell Right from Wrong in Everyday Situations (2002). Since the late nineteenth century, Americans have turned to newspaper columnists for advice. From the perspective of argumentation, columnists evaluate situations (Chapter 10) and offer readers proposals about potential courses of action they might take—or should have taken (Chapter 12). In this specific case, a New Yorker asked how she might balance her opposition to what she perceived as an act of sexism committed in the name of religion with her commitment to others' right to religious expression.

Read the query, read Cohen's response, and decide whether you agree or disagree with Cohen's analysis. Then see what readers of the Times had to say about Cohen's analysis and advice. Readers continued to write letters to the editor about this column for several weeks, with readers ultimately responding to other readers' letters. The first three letters appeared three weeks after the initial column, accompanied by the editorial comment "The Ethicist was reprimanded by hundreds of Orthodox Jews, outraged at criticism of a religious rule banning a handshake between the sexes." The last three letters appeared two weeks after the initial letters were printed.

Between the Sexes

THE ETHICIST
RANDY COHEN

The courteous and competent real-estate agent I'd just hired to rent my house shocked and offended me when, after we signed our contract, he refused to shake my hand, saying that as an Orthodox Jew he did not touch women. As a feminist, I oppose sex discrimination of all sorts. However, I also support freedom of religious expression. How do I balance these conflicting values? Should I tear up our contract?

—J.L., New York

This culture clash may not allow you to reconcile the values you esteem. Though the agent dealt you only a petty slight, without ill intent, you're entitled to work with someone who will treat you with the dignity and respect he shows his male clients. If this involved only his own person—adherence to laws concerning diet or dress, for example—you should of course be tolerant. But his actions directly affect you. And sexism is sexism, even when motivated by religious convictions. I believe you should tear up your contract.

Had he declined to shake hands with everyone, there would be no problem. What he may not do, however, is render a class of people untouchable. Were he, say, an airline ticket clerk who refused to touch Asian-Americans, he would find himself in hot water and rightly so. Bias on the basis of sex is equally discreditable.

Some religions (and some civil societies) that assign men and women distinct spheres argue that while those two spheres are different, neither is inferior to the other. This sort of reasoning was rejected in 1954 in the great school desegregation case, *Brown v. Board of Education*, when the Supreme Court declared that separate is by its very nature unequal. That's a pretty good ethical guideline for ordinary life.

There's a terrific moment in *Cool Hand Luke*, when a prison guard about to put Paul Newman in the sweatbox says—I quote from memory—"Sorry, Luke, just doing my job." Newman replies, "Calling it your job don't make it right, boss." Religion, same deal. Calling an offensive action religious doesn't make it right.

Letters in Response to Cohen's Advice

As a Jew, a feminist and a future rabbi, I share the Ethicist's contempt for discriminatory religious norms and practices (Oct. 27). However, the practice of "shomer negiah"—of refraining from engaging in any physical contact with members of the opposite sex who are not family—does not fall into this category. Had the Ethicist done his research, he would have known that the laws of negiah apply equally to both sexes and do not render either women or men peculiarly "untouchable." These laws are based on the belief that platonic male-female contact can easily degenerate into sexual impropriety.

Whether or not one agrees with this logic, it does not lend itself to an accusation of sexism. The real disgrace is that the Ethicist answered this query without educating himself about the religious practice upon which it is based and without consulting Jewish authorities who could assist him in this endeavor.

—Cara Weinstein Rosenthal
South Orange, N.J.

The Orthodox Jew who refused to shake a woman's hand after signing a real-estate contract was wrongfully accused of sexism and of acting without the "dignity and respect he shows his male clients." Rather, it was out of respect to his own wife and to other women that the man did not extend his hand; his intent was to elevate and sanctify the relationship between men and women, which is all too often trivialized.

—Helen Pogrin
New York

A real-estate agent is hired to rent a house, and the woman who hires him wants to tear up the contract because his religious beliefs prevent him from shaking hands? The agent was courteous and competent. What more did she want? The prohibition of physical contact between unrelated men and women has nothing to do with sexism. Religious freedom is a constitutional and moral right. No one should understand that more than the Ethicist.

—Robert M. Gottesman
Englewood, N.J.

Randy Cohen sure unleashed the Furies (Letters, Nov. 17, responding to the Ethicist from Oct. 27). Actually, Cohen has a good point, and his critics protest too much. Orthodox Judaism hardly treats women as equal to men. Orthodox men regularly express in prayer their gratitude to God for not having made them women. I suspect that the prohibition against touch isn't all that egalitarian either. After all, it is women who are viewed as impure for large segments of their lives.

—Eva Landy
Barrington, R.I.

Our rabbi—who is modern and egalitarian—gave a sermon on the Ethicist column, and he carefully drew the distinction between a religious belief and a discriminatory act. One question I have heard frequently: had the religion in question been one less familiar to the writer—say, Islam—would Cohen have given such a glib response without checking with religious experts and without considering both parties' sensitivities?

—Paul Berman
Edison, N.J.

As a Jewish woman, respectful but nonobservant, I can understand the discomfort of the woman who was offended. As a lawyer, however, I know that discomfort is never cause for breaking a contract.

—Margaret R. Loss
New York

For his readers to trust his advice, Cohen must first convince them of his credibility as "The Ethicist." See Chapter 3 for more on how authors establish credibility with their audience.

LINK TO P. 59

RESPOND

1. Do you agree or disagree with Randy Cohen's analysis of the situation that J.L. describes? In other words, did the Orthodox Jew's refusal to shake hands with a woman who wasn't a relative by blood or marriage constitute an act of sexism in terms of the intentions of the real-estate agent or its effect on his client? Should J.L., as Cohen suggests, have torn up the contract? Why or why not?

2. Evaluate the responses to Cohen's column. What sorts of arguments—emotional, ethical, or logical—do the letter writers use? Which specific arguments do you find most persuasive? Why? (For a discussion of emotional, ethical, and logical arguments, see Chapters 2, 3, and 4, respectively.)

3. How should a pluralistic society like ours accommodate religious expression when that expression violates—or appears to violate, in the eyes of some—other principles that are important, such as gender equality? **Write a proposal argument** in which you offer criteria for balancing these two when they're in conflict. (For a discussion of proposal arguments, see Chaper 12.) Note that the case described here involves an individual's providing a contractual service to another; the range of such conflicts is, in fact, much broader. Thus, you may wish to write about the case Cohen describes, or you may prefer to research other cases, which may have involved, for example, such issues as the right of parents who are Christian Scientists to deny or limit medical care for their children. The most effective proposals will be those that demonstrate they've dealt with the case they examine in its complexity.

This I Believe describes itself as "a public dialogue about belief—one essay at a time." Broadcast since 2005 on the National Public Radio programs All Things Considered, Tell Me More, and Weekend Edition Sunday, the series challenges listeners to write and read aloud three-minute essays analyzing the core values that shape their ways of seeing the world and living in it. The program is produced by Dan Gediman and hosted by Jay Allison. (A Canadian version, hosted by Preston Manning and broadcast since 2007, can be heard on CBC Radio One.) In some cases, contributors refer directly or indirectly to their religious beliefs; in others, they do not. The program thus provides a public forum where religion can but does not necessarily play a role, a situation that reminds us of the complex relationship between religious belief and other kinds of beliefs that influence moral behavior.

This I Believe is modeled on the radio series of the same name from the 1950s. Created by journalist Edward R. Murrow, the earlier series was a response to events of the time—the U.S. propaganda battle against the Soviet Union during the Cold War and some Americans' paranoia about the spread of "godless" communism. (It was during this period that the phrase "under God" was added to the Pledge of Allegiance.)

The program's Web site (http://thisibelieve.org) provides this information about the purposes of This I Believe:

"As in the 1950s, this is a time when belief is dividing the nation and the world," says Allison about life today. "We are not listening well, not understanding each other—we are simply disagreeing, or worse. . . ." In reviving This I Believe, Allison and Gediman say their goal is not to persuade Americans to agree on the same beliefs. Rather, they hope to encourage people to begin the much more difficult task of developing respect for beliefs different from their own.

Here, we present three essays, one from the 1950s and two recent ones. All three mention God, though they are written by a Jew, a Muslim, and an atheist. Albert Einstein (1879–1955), whose essay dates from the original program in the 1950s, was a German-born American theoretical physicist whose heritage was Jewish and who won the Nobel Prize in 1921. Eboo Patel (b. 1967), whose essay was broadcast in November 2005, is the founder and executive director of the Chicago-based Interfaith Youth Core, an international nonprofit that helps young people from different faiths work together helping others. He is author of Acts of Faith: The Story of an American Muslim, the Struggle for the Soul of a Generation, *and he blogs on* The Faith Divide. *Penn Jillette (b. 1955), whose essay was also broadcast in November 2005, is half of the team Penn & Teller; he is a comedian, a juggler, an illusionist, a writer, and a fellow at the Cato Institute, a libertarian think tank. He has appeared in films, music videos, and television programs, including* Dancing with the Stars.

An Ideal of Service to Our Fellow Man

ALBERT EINSTEIN

The most beautiful thing we can experience is the mysterious—the knowledge of the existence of something unfathomable to us, the manifestation of
the most profound reason coupled with the most brilliant beauty. I cannot

imagine a god who rewards and punishes the objects of his creation, or who has a will of the kind we experience in ourselves. I am satisfied with the mystery of life's eternity and with the awareness of—and glimpse into—the marvelous construction of the existing world together with the steadfast determination to comprehend a portion, be it ever so tiny, of the reason that manifests itself in nature. This is the basis of cosmic religiosity, and it appears to me that the most important function of art and science is to awaken this feeling among the receptive and keep it alive.

State: here, government.

I sense that it is not the State° that has intrinsic value in the machinery of humankind, but rather the creative, feeling individual, the personality alone that creates the noble and sublime.

Man's ethical behavior should be effectively grounded on compassion, nurture, and social bonds. What is moral is not of the divine, but rather a purely human matter, albeit the most important of all human matters. In the course of history, the ideals pertaining to human beings' behavior toward each other and pertaining to the preferred organization of their communities have been espoused and taught by enlightened individuals. These ideals and convictions—results of historical experience, empathy, and the need for beauty and harmony—have usually been willingly recognized by human beings, at least in theory.

The highest principles for our aspirations and judgments are given to us westerners in the Jewish-Christian religious tradition. It is a very high goal: free and responsible development of the individual, so that he may place his powers freely and gladly in the service of all mankind.

The pursuit of recognition for its own sake, an almost fanatical love of   5 justice, and the quest for personal independence form the traditional themes of the Jewish people, of which I am a member.

But if one holds these high principles clearly before one's eyes and compares them with the life and spirit of our times, then it is glaringly apparent that mankind finds itself at present in grave danger. I see the nature of the current crises in the juxtaposition of the individual to society. The individual feels more than ever dependent on society, but he feels this dependence not

organic: here, living.

in the positive sense, cradled, connected as part of an organic° whole; he sees it as a threat to his natural rights and even his economic existence. His position in society, then, is such that that which drives his ego is encouraged and developed, and that which would drive him toward other men—a weak

atrophy: to waste away or decline.

impulse to begin with—is left to atrophy.°

It is my belief that there is only one way to eliminate these evils, namely, the establishment of a planned economy coupled with an education geared toward social goals. Alongside the development of individual abilities, the education of the individual aspires to revive an ideal that is geared toward the service of our fellow man, and that needs to take the place of the glorification of power and outer success.

We Are Each Other's Business

EBOO PATEL

Norman Rockwell's Freedom of Worship

I am an American Muslim. I believe in pluralism.° In the Holy Quran, God tells us, "I created you into diverse nations and tribes that you may come to know one another." I believe America is humanity's best opportunity to make God's wish that we come to know one another a reality.

In my office hangs Norman Rockwell's° illustration *Freedom of Worship*. A Muslim holding a Quran in his hands stands near a Catholic woman fingering her rosary. Other figures have their hands folded in prayer and their eyes filled with piety. They stand shoulder-to-shoulder facing the same direction, comfortable with the presence of one another and yet apart. It is a vivid depiction of a group living in peace with its diversity, yet not exploring it.

We live in a world where the forces that seek to divide us are strong. To overcome them, we must do more than simply stand next to one another in silence.

I attended high school in the western suburbs of Chicago. The group I ate lunch with included a Jew, a Mormon, a Hindu, a Catholic and a Lutheran. We were all devout to a degree, but we almost never talked about religion. Somebody would announce at the table that they couldn't eat a certain kind of food, or any food at all, for a period of time. We all knew religion hovered behind this, but nobody ever offered any explanation deeper than "my mom said," and nobody ever asked for one.

A few years after we graduated, my Jewish friend from the lunchroom   5 reminded me of an experience we both wish had never happened. A group of thugs in our high school had taken to scrawling anti-Semitic slurs on classroom desks and shouting them in the hallway.

I did not confront them. I did not comfort my Jewish friend. Instead I averted my eyes from their bigotry, and I avoided my friend because I couldn't stand to face him.

My friend told me he feared coming to school those days, and he felt abandoned as he watched his close friends do nothing. Hearing him tell me

pluralism: an acceptance of the value and validity of religions other than one's own.

Norman Rockwell (1894–1978): an American illustrator and painter. Much loved by the American public, Rockwell created magazine covers for the *Saturday Evening Post* for over four decades. The illustration mentioned by Patel, *Freedom of Worship*, is part of Rockwell's 1943 series of oil paintings; the other titles in the series are *Freedom of Speech, Freedom from Want,* and *Freedom from Fear*. This list of freedoms comes from President Franklin D. Roosevelt's 1941 State of the Union Address.

Patel subtly makes a proposal argument even though he never explicitly proposes one particular action. For help in understanding how to see this argument as a proposal, see Chapter 12.

LINK TO P. 373

Gwendolyn Brooks (1917–2000): an American poet. In 1950, she became the first African American to win a Pulitzer Prize; it was awarded for *Annie Allen,* her second book of poetry.

of his suffering and my complicity is the single most humiliating experience of my life.

My friend needed more than my silent presence at the lunch table. I realize now that to believe in pluralism means I need the courage to act on it. Action is what separates a belief from an opinion. Beliefs are imprinted through actions.

In the words of the great American poet Gwendolyn Brooks:° "We are each other's business; we are each other's harvest; we are each other's magnitude and bond."

I cannot go back in time and take away the suffering of my Jewish friend, 10 but through action I can prevent it from happening to others.

There Is No God

PENN JILLETTE

I believe that there is no God. I'm beyond atheism. Atheism is not believing in God. Not believing in God is easy—you can't prove a negative, so there's no work to do. You can't prove that there isn't an elephant inside the trunk of my car. You sure? How about now? Maybe he was just hiding before. Check again. Did I mention that my personal heartfelt definition of the word "elephant" includes mystery, order, goodness, love and a spare tire?

So, anyone with a love for truth outside of herself has to start with no belief in God and then look for evidence of God. She needs to search for some objective evidence of a supernatural power. All the people I write e-mails to often are still stuck at this searching stage. The atheism part is easy.

But, this *This I Believe* thing seems to demand something more personal, some leap of faith that helps one see life's big picture, some rules to live by. So, I'm saying, "This I believe: I believe there is no God."

Having taken that step, it informs every moment of my life. I'm not greedy. I have love, blue skies, rainbows and Hallmark cards, and that has to be enough. It has to be enough, but it's everything in the world and everything in the world is plenty for me. It seems just rude to beg the invisible for more. Just the love of my family that raised me and the family I'm raising now is enough that I don't need heaven. I won the huge genetic lottery and I get joy every day.

Believing there's no God means I can't really be forgiven except by kind-   5
ness and faulty memories. That's good; it makes me want to be more thoughtful. I have to try to treat people right the first time around.

Believing there's no God stops me from being solipsistic.° I can read ideas
from all different people from all different cultures. Without God, we can
agree on reality, and I can keep learning where I'm wrong. We can all keep
adjusting, so we can really communicate. I don't travel in circles where people say, "I have faith, I believe this in my heart and nothing you can say or do
can shake my faith." That's just a long-winded religious way to say, "shut up,"
or another two words that the FCC° likes less. But all obscenity is less insulting than, "How I was brought up and my imaginary friend means more to me
than anything you can ever say or do." So, believing there is no God lets me be
proven wrong and that's always fun. It means I'm learning something.

Believing there is no God means the suffering I've seen in my family, and
indeed all the suffering in the world, isn't caused by an omniscient, omni-
present, omnipotent force that isn't bothered to help or is just testing us, but
rather something we all may be able to help others with in the future. No God
means the possibility of less suffering in the future.

Believing there is no God gives me more room for belief in family, people,
love, truth, beauty, sex, Jell-O and all the other things I can prove and that
make this life the best life I will ever have.

Jillette knows that at least some members of his audience will be suspicious of his atheism, so he inserts humor into his argument to try to build bridges with them. For more on using the emotional argument of humor, see Chapter 2.

LINK TO P. 48

solipsistic: self-absorbed or egotistical.

FCC: the Federal Communications Commission, which among other duties enforces restrictions on the use of indecent or obscene lan-guage in the broadcast media. (Indecent, but not obscene, lan-guage can be used only between 10 p.m. and 6 a.m., when children are assumed not to be listening.)

RESPOND ●

1. Which of these three arguments do you find most effective? Why? Seeking to put aside whatever religious beliefs you might have, which writer do you think makes the strongest case for his beliefs? Why?

2. Choose the essay that you believe is strongest, and characterize it. Is it an argument of fact? Of definition? Of evaluation? Is it causal? Is it a proposal? What role does religious belief—or the lack of it—play in structuring the argument?

3. How is the essay by Einstein like the essays by Patel and Jillette? How is it different? In considering this question, pay attention to all aspects of the essays, but especially language, formality, the ways in which personal experiences are used, and the ways in which personal beliefs are expressed. What might account for the differences?

4. Visit the Web site for *This I Believe* (http://thisibelieve.org), and listen to several of the essays that you find there. You may wish to listen to essays from the 1950s or to contemporary ones. You may wish to exam-ine the most frequently viewed or listened-to essays, or you may wish

to search for essays that treat a specific topic. Choose three essays that you find especially effective (perhaps even moving), and **write a rhetorical analysis** of them, paying special attention to the kinds of arguments used. (For a discussion of rhetorical analyses, see Chapter 5.)

5. **Write an essay** for the *This I Believe* series. One section of the program's Web site (http://thisibelieve.org/essaywritingtips) provides tips for creating a successful submission. Essays are generally 350 to 500 words in length, and they need to discuss a value—motivated by religion or not—that you believe in. You will be writing an essay to be read aloud. (Recall that Chapter 15 discusses arguments to be heard.) We encourage you to submit your essay to the series if it is still being broadcast at the time you are using this textbook. If you are successful, let us know. Perhaps we'll use your essay in the sixth edition of *Everything's an Argument, with Readings.*

26
What Should "Diversity on Campus" Mean?

Visit your school's homepage, and see what you find when you click on links about diversity. If your school is like most, you might conclude that *diversity* has a meaning that is narrower than the *Oxford English Dictionary*'s definition of the term as "the condition or quality of being diverse, different, or varied; difference, unlikeness." (For linguists, cases of semantic narrowing often stand as evidence that social change of one sort of another is taking place in the community where the narrowing occurs.) The arguments in this chapter challenge you to think about the meanings of *diversity* on your own campus—what it might mean, what it should mean, and whether it's relevant at all.

The chapter opens with a portfolio of visual arguments—five award-winning posters in an annual competition with the theme of diversity at Western Washington University. In many ways, each poster is a definitional argument of sorts. Next, Sarah Karnasiewicz's "The Campus Crusade for Guys" documents the struggles of many campuses to attract and keep male students as the percentage of men in college drops. Next, we present a series of five cartoons that focus on the 2003 U.S. Supreme Court decision permitting the University of Michigan Law School to continue using some forms of affirmative action in admissions. Note how these cartoons on ethnic diversity question the way that arguments on this topic are framed.

The next four selections examine the question of intellectual diversity, a topic of recent interest to American conservatives. The issue is the brainchild of David Horowitz, whose essay defends the notion and its importance. Stanley Fish critiques the notion. In her newspaper article about empirical research on this topic, Patricia Cohen asks if professors' liberalism is contagious and reaches the conclusion that it may not be. Among the studies that she mentions is one by Mack D. Mariani and Gordon J. Hewitt, "Indoctrination U.? Faculty Ideology and Changes in Student Political Orientation," and an excerpt from that research is the fourth selection on this topic.

The following two selections focus on categories of students that are often overlooked in discussions of diversity. In "Blue-Collar Boomers Take Work Ethic to College," Libby Sander examines the potential consequences of older Americans' returning to college in times of economic downturn. Likewise, Edward F. Palm offers some advice to those already on campus about the growing numbers of students who are veterans from the wars in Afghanistan and Iraq.

The chapter closes with an excerpt from the introduction to Walter Benn Michaels's book *The Trouble with Diversity: How We Learned to Love Identity and Ignore Inequality*. Michaels argues that our discussions of diversity, especially when focused on ethnic or racial diversity, are simply on the wrong track. Such discussions may keep us occupied, he contends, but they conveniently prevent us from dealing with deeper, more serious issues that we all work hard to avoid.

The selections will require you to think about evaluating the possible competing answers to a single question: what should "diversity on campus" mean?

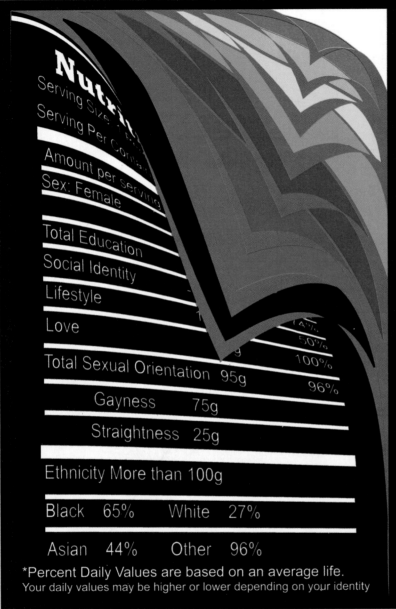

Nutrition

Serving Size

Serving Per Cont

Amount per serving

Sex: Female

Total Education

Social Identity

Lifestyle

Love

Total Sexual Orientation   95g

Gayness   75g

Straightness   25g

Ethnicity More than 100g

Black   65%   White   27%

Asian   44%   Other   96%

*Percent Daily Values are based on an average life.
Your daily values may be higher or lower depending on your identity

Joseph Wagner, *Peeling Off Labels,* **2009**

Making a Visual Argument: Student-Designed Diversity Posters

◁ Visit the Western Washington University homepage (http://wwu.edu), click on "Diversity" and you'll find this quote from the university president, Karen W. Morse: "Diversity is central to Western's mission and strategic action plan and is considered to be an integral component of a quality education. Our goals recognize the changing composition of society as a whole, and its impact on the world for which students are educated." The posters that follow were designed to promote the residence halls of Western Washington University in Bellingham, Washington. Called Residence Life, the student-run organization that oversees these on-campus dormitories holds a poster contest each year to showcase Western Washington's overall commitment to diversity. As you study these winning designs, consider the definition each offers of diversity.

Stephanie Heyman, *Everyone a Part, No One Apart*, 2003

Melanie Frost, *Embracing Diversity in University Residences,* **1998**

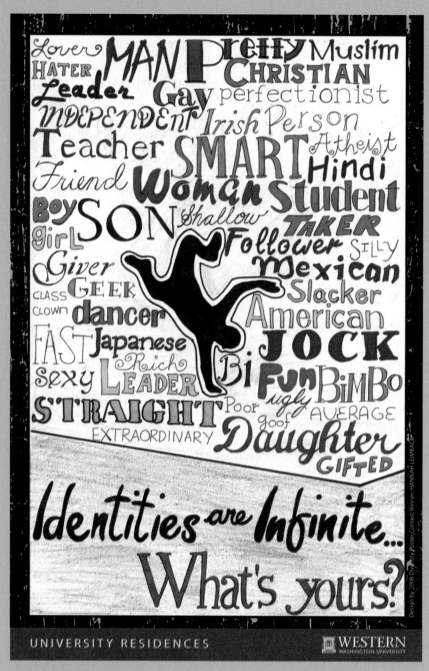

Hannah Leimback, *Identities Are Infinite . . . What's Yours?*, 2008

Megan Stampfli, *Embrace Diversity*, 2004

RESPOND●

1. Which of these visual arguments do you find most appealing? Least appealing? Why?

2. Analyze the relationship between text (the words used) and the visual images and layout in each of the posters. What's the interaction between the text, on the one hand, and the visual images and layout, on the other, in each one? Which poster is most effective in this regard? Why?

3. If you take each of these posters to be a definitional argument, defining diversity in some way, what argument is each making? In other words, how does each poster define *diversity*? (For a discussion of definitional arguments, see Chapter 9.)

4. In defining and commenting on the notion of diversity, these posters range from approaching the topic in a didactic fashion (that is, seeking to teach a moral lesson) to approaching it much more vaguely. (Note the evaluative—and potentially negative—connotations the labels "didactic" and "vague" carry.) Choose the posters that you find most explicitly didactic and those that you find most vague in their approach to the topic. Justify your choices. Which approach do you prefer? Why? Which do you believe is more effective in situations like this one? Why?

5. **Write an essay** in which you evaluate two of these posters, commenting on the definition of diversity presented or assumed (question 3); the relationship between text, on the one hand, and visual images and layout, on the other (question 2); and the artists' approach to the subject (question 4). (For a discussion of evaluative arguments, see Chapter 10.)

6. **Write a definitional essay** in which you define the notion of diversity as it might or should be understood on American college campuses today or your campus specifically. (For a discussion of definitional arguments, see Chapter 9.)

The Campus Crusade for Guys

SARAH KARNASIEWICZ

Child psychologist Michael Thompson has devoted his professional life to advocating for America's boys. As the bestselling author of "Raising Cain," he's logged thousands of hours as an educational speaker and makes frequent appearances on national television as an authority on troubled young men. But Thompson is also the father of a 20-year-old daughter. And when asked if, given their much-maligned status in schools these days, boys ought to be given a leg up in college admissions, his answer is blunt: "I'd be horrified if some lunkhead boy got accepted to a school instead of my very talented and prepared daughter," he says, "just because he happened to be a guy."

But that may be just what is happening. Amid national panic over a growing academic gender gap, educators have begun to ask, might it be time to adopt affirmative action for boys?

The statistics are revealing: Fewer men apply to colleges every year and those who do disproportionately occupy the lowest quarter of the applicant pool. Thirty-five years ago, in the early days of widespread coeducation, the gender ratio on campuses averaged 43-57, female to male. Now, uniformly, the old ratios have been inverted. Across races and classes—and to some extent, around the Western world—women are more likely to apply to college and, once enrolled, more likely to stick around through graduation.

Even in a vacuum, discussions of gender-based affirmative action would be deeply political. But the possibility of a full-fledged battle appears especially likely these days, as we find ourselves in the middle of what's popularly known as the "war on boys." If you watch the news or read the papers, you know the soldiers: Last year, Laura Bush launched a federal initiative focused on boys who have been neglected by their schools and communities; Christina Hoff Sommers, George Gilder and Michael Gurian have swarmed the talk show circuit and editorial pages, bemoaning the lack of male role models in American schools and accusing educators of alienating boys by prizing passive, "feminized" behavior such as sitting quietly, reading independently, and focusing on sedentary rather than dynamic projects. (Though Thompson, for the record, says "education has actually become more dynamic and teaching gotten better for boys"—and, I quote, "We used to have to hit them to keep

◀ Sarah Karnasiewicz, writer, editor, and photographer, is currently a deputy editor of Salon.com's Life section. She has degrees in journalism, children's literature, and fine art. Much of her work focuses on the topics of education, youth culture, food, and family. In "The Campus Crusade for Guys," which originally appeared in February 2005 on Salon.com, Karnasiewicz examines the growing practice of what seems to be affirmative action for male applicants to many of the country's colleges and universities. As you read, consider the gender balance on your campus and how it, along with your own biological sex, might influence your response to this selection.

them still."] *New York Times* Op-Ed writer John Tierney made waves in January with an essay warning that educational success will come back to haunt women as a dearth of educated, eligible husbands turns them into miserable spinsters—and in a rebuttal, *Nation* columnist Katha Pollitt asked why, years ago when she was in school and men made up the majority, no one was worrying about whether they'd find wives. Finally, a few weeks ago, *Newsweek* joined the fray with an eight-page cover story by Peg Tyre, breathlessly captioned "The Boy Crisis," and laden with oversize color photos of doleful white boys, seemingly adrift in a sea of competent, well-adjusted girls.

With all this coverage, you'd be excused for thinking the debate is a recent   5
development. But the truth is that affirmative action for men, like the gender gap itself, is simply not news. Back in 1999, a young woman filed a federal civil rights lawsuit against the University of Georgia in Athens, after it was revealed that the school had attempted to balance gender on campus by awarding preference to male applicants, much the way it might build racial diversity by assigning extra admissions "points" to minority students. At the time, the school, in its defense, told the *Christian Science Monitor* that it was trying to reverse male flight from campus (at the time the ratio was 45-55] before it "became something bad." Unfortunately for the university, the district court judge assigned to the case wasn't convinced, ruling instead that "the desire to 'help out' men who are not earning baccalaureate degrees in the same numbers as women . . . [was] far from persuasive."

Talk to admissions insiders today, though, and they'll tell you that the University of Georgia case did not so much end affirmative action for men as drive it underground. "My belief is that there are already many informal affirmative action policies," says Thompson. "It is entirely possible that a better qualified girl has not gotten into a school because admissions officers were trying to create a more even ratio." Tom Mortenson, senior policy analyst at the Pell Institute for Opportunity in Higher Education and creator of the *Postsecondary Education Opportunity Newsletter*, who in the mid-'90s was one of the first scholars to draw attention to the gender gap, agrees. "I know [affirmative action for boys] is being practiced, especially on liberal arts campuses where the gap is biggest," he explains, "because I've had administrators tell me so."

Last fall, their interest piqued by the flurry of news stories describing the growing chasm between boys and girls in higher education, Sandy Baum and Eban Goodstein, economics professors at Skidmore College and Lewis and Clark College, respectively, embarked on a close study of admissions data from 13 liberal arts schools, hunting for an unacknowledged preference for men in the admissions process. "I'd just read so many stories about the declining number of men applying to colleges," says Baum, "that it seemed inevitable that the disparity would or already had launched a campaign of affirmative action."

Baum and Goodstein's findings, while not conclusive, did carry weighty implications for the future of college admissions. At the time of their research, explains Baum, the incoming class at every school they studied was still composed of more than 50 percent girls, which made sweeping pronouncements about the prevalence of affirmative action difficult to support. And their profiles of male and female applicants were based primarily on statistical data—a standardized test score or GPA—thereby preventing them from taking into account many of the murky intangibles, like extracurricular activities, recommendations and personal essays, on which many admissions officers rely.

Still, in the case of schools where the gender imbalance was most acute—at colleges that were once single-sex, for instance—and where women consistently accounted for more than 60 percent of applicants, Baum and Goodstein *did* find compelling evidence that male students had a statistically greater probability of being accepted than female students of comparable qualifications. Their conclusion? "There seems to be a kind of affirmative action tipping point that occurs when an application pool becomes too heavily weighted toward women. But the interesting thing is that that point is by no means the 50-50 mark—it's likely closer to 40-60," explains Baum. "So while we did not find widespread gender preferencing, given the trends on campuses, with more and more schools approaching that tipping point, we could certainly see a big change."

And it's not just former women's colleges facing a 40-60 divide anymore. A quick survey of colleges and universities around the nation found that Kalamazoo College in Michigan comes in at 45-55, the University of New Mexico at 43-57, New York University at 40-60, and Howard University at 34-66 (low-income, minority men and women are most affected by the educational gender gap). Michael Barron, director of admissions at the University of Iowa, has watched his school's 44-56 ratio hold steady throughout his nearly two-decade tenure at the university. "We just have consistently had more women than men, and I know there's a lot of schools—like the University of North Carolina, Chapel Hill, for example—that have been even closer to 40-60 for quite some time," he says. As a state-supported institution that, according

10   Karnasiewicz presents convincing statistics in support of her argument that the college male population is waning. Explore other aspects of arguments of fact in Chapter 8.

LINK TO P. 208

to Barron, "has a stewardship responsibility to accept students regardless of issues of gender or race," Iowa maintains that it has no intention of "either consciously or subconsciously" differentiating between men and women in the admissions process. But, Barron admits, "I wouldn't want it said that we are unconcerned. We are watchful and mindful and will be looking to see what happens . . . and whether there is a role for colleges and universities to play as part of the solution."

Karen Parker, director of admissions at Hampshire College in Amherst, Mass., reports that for the past three years her entering classes have had an average ratio of 41-59, and that men only account for 38 percent of applicants. "I don't believe that the school needs to be exactly 50-50, but from a cultural stand-point, I do think it's important that we have men engaged," she says. "Hampshire doesn't practice affirmative action right now—but I certainly can't say we won't in the future. It's a really perplexing problem and just not a good sign of things to come."

But schools that have not gone so far as to accept male students over more qualified women are still finding ways to shift their admissions agenda toward young men. "There are things schools can and do do," says Christina Hoff Sommers, resident scholar at the American Enterprise Institute for Public Policy Research and author of "Who Stole Feminism?" and "The War against Boys." "Strengthening their engineering departments, getting a hockey team. Some schools are changing admission documents to appeal to male minds—and I know we're supposed to pretend there's no difference [between male and female minds], but anyone in advertising will tell you there is."

And for sure, many colleges are banking on these differences. "At our national conference each year we invariably have a speaker devoted specifically to recruiting boys," explains David Hawkins, the director of public policy at the National Association of College Admission Counseling. "Now most four-year colleges work with their own internal marketing department or contract out to an independent agency that tailors their marketing to young men—and they are very, very aggressive."

Since teenage boys are often crazy about technology, a number of universi-ties, including Case Western Reserve, Seton Hill and MIT (which, admittedly, at 57-43, doesn't seem to have a problem attracting men), have launched admission-oriented blogs designed to offer an intimate, uncensored look at college life. Other schools take a more subliminal approach, by packing their catalogs with pictures of smiling, confident young men and playing up dark, "masculine" color schemes in mailings.

"There is no doubt that schools are trying to market themselves to boys now, just the way they did to women 30 years ago," says Joseph Tweed, president-elect of the New York State Association of College Counselors and director of college counseling at the Trinity-Pawling School, a private all-boys school in upstate New York. "Everyone is asking, 'How do we do this? Do we change the structure of classes? Do we send out glossier materials?' But I think what worries educators the most is that boys don't seem as focused on the process as girls. [Boys] seem to feel they'll be OK, whereas with girls there's still a sense that if they don't do well, don't go to college, there'll be a consequence that will be negative."   15

Tweed's point raises a controversial question that most crusaders in the "war on boys" would rather dismiss. Despite their flagging performance in elementary and high school, men have hardly abdicated their power to women. While women may have held the majority in higher education for more than a decade, men still earn more than women, still hold the vast number of tenure-track university positions. Women possess executive positions at less than 2 percent of Fortune 500 companies. Could it be that men aren't going to college because they don't *have* to?

According to Laura Perna, assistant professor of educational policy and leadership at the University of Maryland, the gender gap is all about economics. Last fall, Perna published a paper in the *Review of Higher Education* in which she determined that young women might be more motivated to pursue higher education because, consciously or unconsciously, they sense that there are real economic advantages at stake. Her examination of a Department of Education sample of more than 9,000 high school students, interviewed over a period of eight years, revealed that women with bachelor's degrees earn 24 percent more than women without, while young men with bachelor's degrees experience no significant economic gains. For practical proof of her hypothesis, one need only consider that most well-paid, skilled, blue-collar professions continue to be dominated by men—while minimum-wage jobs in hospitality and service remain the province of women.

Tom Mortenson, of Opportunity, remains skeptical. "I've heard that story, but think of it this way—men have had a 3,000-year head start, while everything women have accomplished has largely been in the last 30 years," he says. "So yes, if you're a big, strong guy, there are jobs out there. But the fields that are growing fastest are in healthcare, education, leisure and travel, and the services—all areas that women are better at than we are. So if guys want access to that world, they'd better get an education that qualifies them. Because they won't be big and strong forever." In the future Mortenson imagines, America's changing economy leaves generations of unprepared, aimless, undereducated and emasculated men wasting away, taking the health and happiness of their wives and families with them. But as with Tierney and some of the other boy crusaders, some of Mortenson's greatest fears aren't focused on the perils facing men who lose course in school, but on the freedoms of women who don't. "On the one hand, you want to embrace the success of women," he tells me. "Yet, as more and more women substitute careers for having babies, I've come to see that we're looking at a population crisis. The most educated women have the fewest children—this is not rocket science, it's just the way things work. We need women to have 2.1 children [in order to maintain the U.S. population], but the recent Census Bureau reports show that American women with bachelor's degrees average only 1.7. You can do the math—if we continue this way the white population is headed for extinction."

Having worked for decades to increase educational opportunities across class, race and gender lines, Mortenson knows his talk about women's responsibility to preserve the species will get him in trouble—indeed, it already has. He says his daughter, age 29 and childless (but equipped with a master's degree), won't speak to him on the subject. But.even his fatherly concern ("I want my daughter to have it all, but I worry that in old age she'll be lonely") can't disguise some of the insidious implications underneath those concerns: that educated white women might single-handedly be responsible for the decline of Western civilization.

In the fall 2005 issue of *Ms.* magazine, Phyllis Rosser wrote that rather than   20
being "celebrated for [our] landmark achievements, [women] have engendered fear," and offers up this fact, conspicuously absent from most media coverage of the gender gap: "There has been no decline in bachelor's degrees awarded to men," she writes. "The numbers awarded to women have simply increased." Put simply, in the words of Jacqueline King, director of the Center of Policy Analysis at the American Council of Education, who is quoted in Rosser's piece, "The [real news] story is not one of male failure, or even lack of opportunity—but rather one of increased academic success among females and minorities."

The boy crusaders believe that the seeds of academic failure are planted in primary school, which raises the question: Why are we waiting until college to redress the problem? "I've read many reports that male middle-school students are lagging behind their female counterparts," says Michael Barron. "So it seems to me that that's where we need to look. Because the fact is, all we have available to us, once people begin applying to college, is a product of what they've done before. Our reaction has to come sooner."

Until that happens, however, and should current enrollment trends continue, it's reasonable to assume that creative forms of admissions preferencing will continue to stir debate. As our phone conversation ends, Michael Thompson's voice turns grave. "I want to make very clear that I do not subscribe to this notion of a 'war' on boys," he says. "I think we have been living in a very exciting time when we have taken the shackles off of girls in education. I loved what feminism did for girls—we got inside them and understood them. My personal mission just happens to be to get people to think about boys with the same depth."

RESPOND●

1. What argument(s) is Karnasiewicz making with respect to the nature of diversity on campus? How persuasive do you find it? Why? Should there be affirmative action for men? Why or why not? In what ways does the visual argument accompanying the article support its claims? How effective do you find it? Why?

2. Although this article is about gender, it's also about issues of race, ethnicity, and class as well as the intersection of these social variables. What sorts of observations or claims are made about each of these variables in the article? Do you agree or disagree with them? Do you find any of the claims made about these topics troubling? Why or why not?

3. How and why are females and males stigmatized by a lack of education or by the kind of job they might hold? Although it isn't mentioned, in what ways might the marriage market encourage young women to attend college (or even to succeed academically, more broadly)?

4. What's the allusion in Karnasiewicz's title? (If you need a hint, check out http://ccci.org.) How and why is it appropriate, given the subject matter of the article? Is the allusion risky in any way? Why or why not?

5. Among the kinds of evidence that Karnasiewicz uses effectively is statistics. Where and how do she and those she cites use statistics advantageously? In what ways does she qualify claims made on the basis of statistical data? How does qualifying arguments in this way contribute to Karnasiewicz's ethos? (For a discussion of using facts like statistics, see Chapter 4; for a discussion of ethos, see Chapter 3.)

6. Investigate gender and admissions at the college or university you attend, and **write an essay** in which you treat this topic in some way. Ideas might include an analysis of statistics on the sex of applicants, those accepted, and those who enroll over some period of time; an analysis of your institution's efforts to attract females, males, or both; or interviews with students about whether the school should strive to ensure that a certain percentage of students is male (or female). If you attend a college that is or was single sex, you may wish to investigate debates about admitting students of the other sex. Your essay may define something, analyze a causal relationship, evaluate something, or make a proposal.

Making a Visual Argument:
Cartoonists Take On Affirmative Action

▼ The most recent U.S. Supreme Court decision about affirmative action having a direct impact on higher education is Grutter v. Bollinger (2003). In this decision, the Court declared that the University of Michigan Law School had "a compelling interest in achieving a diverse student body" and could use considerations of race and ethnicity in questions of admissions within certain bounds. The decision was criticized by many, not least of all because it didn't draw what lawyers term "a bright line" delimiting the situations when considerations of race or ethnicity are permissible and when they aren't.

Here, we present five cartoonists' response to this decision and issues related to affirmative action more broadly. Mike Lester is a cartoonist for the Rome News-Tribune in Rome, Georgia; "It's <u>GOT</u> to Be the Shoes" appeared in June 2003. Dennis Draughon's "Supreme Irony" appeared in April 2003 in the Scranton Times of Scranton, Pennsylvania. "Daniel Lives on Detroit's Eastside . . . ," by Mike Thompson, originally appeared in the Detroit Free Press in June 2003. Signe Wilkinson's "Admissions" was first published in January 2003 in the Philadelphia Daily News in Philadelphia, Pennsylvania. Finally, "Pricey" first appeared in November 2003 in The Breeze, the student newspaper of James Madison University in Harrisonburg, Virginia; it was drawn by Dean Camp, who was a cartoonist for the paper during academic year 2003–2004.

As you study these cartoons, consider the range of ways in which the artists wed words and illustrations to create humorous arguments about a not-so-humorous issue.

Mike Lester, *It's <u>GOT</u> to Be the Shoes*

Dennis Draughon, *Supreme Irony*

Mike Thompson, *Daniel Lives on Detroit's Eastside . . .*

Signe Wilkinson, *Admissions*

Dean Camp, *Pricey*

RESPOND

1. Briefly summarize the argument being made by each cartoon. Which do you find most effective? Least effective? Why?

2. In what ways do the cartoons by Mike Lester and Dennis Draughon mock the Supreme Court? How does Lester's cartoon use gender and gender stereotypes humorously? How might Sarah Karnasiewicz, author of "The Campus Crusade for Guys," respond to this cartoon? How does each of these cartoons use irony?

3. In what ways do the cartoons by Mike Thompson and Signe Wilkinson make similar arguments? How do their arguments differ?

4. How can the cartoon by Dean Camp be read as relevant to debates about affirmative action?

5. Investigate the admissions practices at your college or university to see if you can discover the percentage of students who were admitted on the basis of so-called objective criteria like scores alone and the number who weren't. Dig a bit deeper to see whether you can get information about the cases of "discretionary admission"—that is, students who are "legacy admits" as the children of alumni, the children of donors or well-known personalities, athletes, those from out of state, and those who aren't members of the dominant ethnic group(s) on your campus. How do you evaluate what you discover? If you're unable to gather such information, why do you suppose it isn't readily available? **Write an essay** in which you make a proposal about how your school might (or should) deal with managing the competing demands for seats in the entering class. What sorts of demands are there? From whom? What are the consequences of heeding some of these demands but not others? (For a discussion of proposal arguments, see Chapter 12.)

▼ David Horowitz is *founder of the Center for the Study of Popular Culture, a nonprofit organization in Los Angeles, and editor of the popular conservative Web site FrontPageMag.com. A frequent commentator on Fox News network, he's also affiliated with Students for Academic Freedom. Always a social activist, Horowitz identified earlier in his life as a leftist and even a Marxist but later became a conservative. He's the author of numerous* books, including Uncivil Wars: The Controversy over Reparations for Slavery (2002), Left Illusions: An Intellectual Odyssey (2003), *and* The Professors: The 101 Most Dangerous Academics in America (2006).

As you read this essay, first published in the Chronicle of Higher Education *in 2004, consider how Horowitz seeks to acknowledge and rebut possible critiques of his arguments. (To examine the Academic Bill of Rights, go to http://www.studentsforacademicfreedom.org/documents/1925/abor.)*

In Defense of Intellectual Diversity

DAVID HOROWITZ

American Association of University Professors (AAUP): an organization created in 1915 "to advance academic freedom and shared governance, to define fundamental professional values and standards for higher education, and to ensure higher education's contribution to the common good." Its motto is "Academic Freedom for a Free Society," and its "Statement of Principles on Academic Freedom and Tenure" is the basis for employment practices, including the granting of tenure (the right not to be dismissed without cause after some initial probationary period), at many colleges and universities across the country.

I am the author of the Academic Bill of Rights, which many student governments, colleges and universities, education commissions, and legislatures are considering adopting. Already, the U.S. House of Representatives has introduced a version as legislation, and the Senate should soon follow suit.

State governments are also starting to rally around efforts to protect student rights and intellectual diversity on campuses: In Colorado, the State Senate president, John K. Andrews Jr., has been very concerned about the issue, and State Rep. Shawn Mitchell has just introduced legislation requiring public institutions to create and publicize processes for protecting students against political bias. Lawmakers in four other states have also expressed a strong interest in legislation of their own, based on some version of the Academic Bill of Rights. Students for Academic Freedom is working to secure the measure's adoption by student governments and university administrations on 105 member campuses across the country (http://www.studentsforacademic freedom.org).

The Academic Bill of Rights is based squarely on the almost 100-year-old tradition of academic freedom that the American Association of University Professors° has established. The bill's purposes are to codify that tradition; to emphasize the value of "intellectual diversity," already implicit in the concept of academic freedom; and, most important, to enumerate the rights of students to not be indoctrinated or otherwise assaulted by political propagandists in the classroom or any educational setting.

Although the AAUP has recognized student rights since its inception, however, most campuses have rarely given them the attention or support they deserve. In fact, it is safe to say that no college or university now adequately defends them. Especially recently, with the growing partisan activities of some faculty members and the consequent politicization of some aspects of the curriculum, that lack of support has become one of the most pressing issues in the academy.

Moreover, because I am a well-known conservative and have published studies of political bias in the hiring of college and university professors, critics have suggested that the Academic Bill of Rights is really a "right-wing plot" to stack faculties with political conservatives by imposing hiring quotas. Indeed, opponents of legislation in Colorado have exploited that fear, writing numerous op-ed pieces about alleged right-wing plans to create affirmative-action programs for conservative professors.

Nothing could be further from the truth. The actual intent of the Academic Bill of Rights is to remove partisan politics from the classroom. The bill that I'm proposing explicitly forbids political hiring or firing: "No faculty shall be hired or fired or denied promotion or tenure on the basis of his or her political or religious beliefs." The bill thus protects all faculty members—left-leaning critics of the war in Iraq as well as right-leaning proponents of it, for example—from being penalized for their political beliefs. Academic liberals should be as eager to support that principle as conservatives.

Some liberal faculty members have expressed concern about a phrase in the bill of rights that singles out the social sciences and humanities and says hiring in those areas should be based on competence and expertise and with a view toward "fostering a plurality of methodologies and perspectives." In fact, the view that there should be a diversity of methodologies is already accepted practice. Considering that truth is unsettled in these discipline areas, why should there not be an attempt to nurture a diversity of perspectives as well?

Perhaps the concern is that "fostering" would be equivalent to "mandating." The Academic Bill of Rights contains no intention, implicit or otherwise, to mandate or produce an artificial "balance" of intellectual perspectives. That would be impossible to achieve and would create more mischief than it would remedy. On the other hand, a lack of diversity is not all that difficult to detect or correct.

5 Is it wise for Horowitz to remind his readers that he's "a well-known conservative" and to point out that he's accused of pushing a "right-wing plot"? How might his frankness affect his argument? For some ideas, read the sections of Chapter 3 that deal with establishing credibility and presenting motives.

LINK TO P. 59

pragmatism: an American philosophical school dating from the later 1800s. Among its concerns—and the concerns of those who would use this label today—are the relationships among meaning, reality, and truth. Its early practitioners included Charles Sanders Peirce, William James, John Dewey, and George Herbert Mead.

postmodernism: an intellectual movement during the last quarter of the twentieth century representing a rejection of the tenets of modernism, which it characterized as emphasizing reason, rationality, "grand narratives" of progress, and the harnessing of nature through science. In contrast, discussions of postmodernism often juxtapose things that seem not to go together in some sense—for example, wearing an expensive piece of clothing with something from a thrift store or combining design features from several periods of architectural history in one building. Postmodernists point out that things that are unreal—Disneyland, Las Vegas, television crime shows, *American Idol* or *Survivor*—often seem more real to many people than everyday reality, whether poverty across town or violence around the world committed in the name of

By adopting the Academic Bill of Rights, an institution would recognize scholarship rather than ideology as an appropriate academic enterprise. It would strengthen educational values that have been eroded by the unwarranted intrusion of faculty members' political views into the classroom. That corrosive trend has caused some academics to focus merely on their own partisan agendas and to abandon their responsibilities as professional educators with obligations to students of all political persuasions. Such professors have lost sight of the vital distinction between education and indoctrination, which—as the AAUP recognized in its first report on academic freedom, in 1915—is not a legitimate educational function.

Because the intent of the Academic Bill of Rights is to restore academic 10 values, I deliberately submitted it in draft form to potential critics who did not share my political views. They included Stanley Fish, dean of the College of Liberal Arts and Sciences at the University of Illinois at Chicago; Michael Bérubé, a professor of English at Pennsylvania State University at University Park; Todd Gitlin, a professor of journalism and sociology at Columbia University; and Philip Klinkner, a professor of government at Hamilton College. While their responses differed, I tried to accommodate the criticisms I got, for example, deleting a clause in the original that would have required the deliberations of all committees in charge of hiring and promotion to be recorded and made available to a "duly constituted authority."

I even lifted wholesale one of the bill's chief tenets—that colleges and professional academic associations should remain institutionally neutral on controversial political issues—from an article that Dean Fish wrote for *The Chronicle* ("Save the World on Your Own Time," January 23, 2003). He has also written an admirable book, *Professional Correctness* (Clarendon Press, 1995), which explores the inherent conflict between ideological thinking and scholarship.

Since the Academic Bill of Rights is designed to clarify and extend existing principles of academic freedom, its opponents have generally been unable to identify specific provisions that they find objectionable. Instead, they have tried to distort the plain meaning of the text. The AAUP itself has been part of that effort, suggesting in a formal statement that the bill's intent is to introduce political criteria for judging intellectual diversity and, thus, to subvert scholarly standards. It contends that the bill of rights "proclaims that all opinions are equally valid," which "negates an essential function of university education." The AAUP singles out for attack a phrase that refers to "the uncertainty and unsettled character of all human knowledge" as the rationale for respecting diverse viewpoints in curricula and reading lists in the humanities and social sciences. The AAUP claims that "this premise . . . is anti-thetical to the basic scholarly enterprise of the university, which is to establish and transmit knowledge."

The association's statements are incomprehensible. After all, major schools of thought in the contemporary academy—pragmatism,° postmodernism,° and deconstructionism,° to name three—operate on the premise that knowledge is uncertain and, at times, relative. Even the hard sciences, which do not share such relativistic assumptions, are inspired to continue their research efforts by the incomplete state of received knowledge. The university's mission is not only to transmit knowledge but to pursue it—and from all vantage points. What could be controversial about acknowledging that? Further, the AAUP's contention that the Academic Bill of Rights threatens true academic standards by suggesting that all opinions are equally valid is a red herring,° as the bill's statement on intellectual diversity makes clear: "Exposing students to the *spectrum of significant scholarly viewpoints* on the subjects examined in their courses is a major responsibility of faculty." (Emphasis added.)

As the Academic Bill of Rights states, "Academic disciplines should welcome a diversity of approaches to unsettled questions." That is common sense. Why not make it university policy?

The only serious opposition to the Academic Bill of Rights is raised by 15 those who claim that, although its principles are valid, it duplicates academic-freedom guidelines that already exist. Elizabeth Hoffman, president of the University of Colorado System, for example, has personally told me that she takes that position.

But with all due respect, such critics are also mistaken. Most universities' academic-freedom policies generally fail to make explicit, let alone codify, the institutions' commitment to intellectual diversity or the academic rights of students. The institutions also do not make their policies readily available to students—who, therefore, are generally not even aware that such policies exist.

For example, when I met with Elizabeth Hoffman, she directed me to the University of Colorado's Web site, where its academic-freedom guidelines are posted. Even if those guidelines were adequate, posting them on an Internet site does not provide sufficient protection for students, who are unlikely to visit it. Contrast the way that institutions aggressively promote other types of diversity guidelines—often establishing special offices to organize and enforce all sorts of special diversity-related programs—to such a passive approach to intellectual diversity.

doing good. Postmodernism has adherents in disciplines as varied as literature, architecture, anthropology, philosophy, and film.

deconstructionism: a way of reading texts—whether philosophical, literary, or everyday—that was influential in academic circles in the last quarter of the twentieth century. Drawing its inspiration from the French philosopher Jacques Derrida, deconstruction focused on the ways in which all texts contain contradictions of various sorts. Since there can be no single, correct interpretation of a text, there will always be competing interpretations—a position misinterpreted by some of deconstruction's critics as arguing that all interpretations are equally valid.

red herring: a logical fallacy that introduces an irrelevant topic to shift focus from the topic at hand. The label is said to come from an early practice of using a strongly scented smoked herring to distract a dog following the scent of something else.

At Colorado's Web site, for example, one can read the following: "Sections of the AAUP's 1940 Statement of Principles on Academic Freedom and Tenure have been adopted as a statement of policy by the Board of Regents." Few people reading that article or visiting the site would suspect that the following protection for students is contained in the AAUP's 1940 statement: "Teachers are entitled to freedom in the classroom in discussing their subject, but they should be careful not to introduce into their teaching controversial matter which has no relation to their subject."

Is there a college or university in America—including the University of Colorado—where at least one professor has not introduced controversial matter on the war in Iraq or the Bush White House in a class whose subject matter is not the war in Iraq, or international relations, or presidential administrations? Yet intrusion of such subject matter, in which the professor has no academic expertise, is a breach of professional responsibility and a violation of a student's academic rights.

We do not go to our doctors' offices and expect to see partisan propaganda posted on the doors, or go to hospital operating rooms and expect to hear political lectures from our surgeons. The same should be true of our classrooms and professors, yet it is not. When I visited the political-science department at the University of Colorado at Denver this year, the office doors and bulletin boards were plastered with cartoons and statements ridiculing Republicans, and only Republicans. When I asked President Hoffman about that, she assured me that she would request that such partisan materials be removed and an appropriate educational environment restored. To the best of my knowledge, that has yet to happen.

Not everyone would agree about the need for such restraint, and it should be said that the Academic Bill of Rights makes no mention of postings and cartoons—although that does not mean that they are appropriate. I refer to them only to illustrate the problem that exists in the academic culture when it comes to fulfilling professional obligations that professors owe to all students. I would ask liberal professors who are comfortable with such partisan expressions how they would have felt as students seeking guidance from their own professors if they had to walk a gantlet of cartoons portraying Bill Clinton as a lecher, or attacking antiwar protesters as traitors.

The politicized culture of the university is the heart of the problem. At Duke University this year, a history professor welcomed his class with the warning that he had strong "liberal" opinions, and that Republican students should probably drop his course. One student did. Aided by Duke Students for Academic Freedom, the young man then complained. To his credit, the professor apologized. Although some people on the campus said the professor had been joking, the student clearly felt he faced a hostile environment. Why should the professor have thought that partisanship in the classroom was professionally acceptable in the first place?

At the University of North Carolina at Chapel Hill, a required summer-reading program for entering freshmen stirred a controversy in the state legislature last fall. The required text was Barbara Ehrenreich's socialist tract on poverty in America, *Nickel and Dimed: On (Not) Getting By in America* (Metropolitan Books, 2001). Other universities have required the identical text in similar programs, and several have invited Ehrenreich to campus to present her views under the imprimatur of the institution and without rebuttal.

That reflects an academic culture unhinged. When a university requires a single partisan text of all its students, it is a form of indoctrination, entirely inappropriate for an academic institution. If many universities had required Dinesh D'Souza's *Illiberal Education: The Politics of Race and Sex on Campus* (Vintage Books, 1992) or Ann Coulter's *Treason: Liberal Treachery from the Cold War to the War on Terrorism* (Crown Forum, 2003) as their lone freshman-reading text, there would have been a collective howl from liberal faculties, who would have immediately recognized the inappropriateness of such institutional endorsement of controversial views. Why not require two texts, or four? (My stepson, who is a high-school senior, was required to read seven texts during his summer vacation.)

The remedy is so simple. Requiring readings on more than one side of a political controversy would be appropriate educational policy and would strengthen, not weaken, the democracy that supports our educational system. Why is that not obvious to the administrators at Chapel Hill and the other universities that have instituted such required-reading programs? It's the academic culture, stupid.°

25

"It's the academic culture, stupid": an allusion to the phrase "It's the economy, stupid," used by Bill Clinton's strategists during the 1992 presidential campaign to keep him focused on his message.

RESPOND•

1. What argument(s) is David Horowitz making? How valid do you find it? Why?

2. How does Horowitz characterize the recent history of higher education in America in paragraphs 4–5 and 10? Pay special attention to his word choices—for example, "restore academic values" in paragraph 10. How do they give you insight into his understanding of the history

of higher education and the readers he's invoking? What evidence does he provide for his claims?

3. Horowitz is critical of professors who discuss "controversial matter on the war in Iraq or the Bush White House in a class whose subject matter is not the war in Iraq, or international relations, or presidential administrations," arguing that the "intrusion of such subject matter, in which the professor has no academic expertise, is a breach of professional responsibility and a violation of a student's academic rights" (paragraph 19). From Horowitz's perspective, should the arguments in Chapters 21 through 27 of this textbook be seen as breaches of the authors' professional responsibility or a violation of your academic rights? Why or why not? By what criteria can such decisions be made?

4. In his closing paragraphs, Horowitz contends that "the remedy is so simple." Do you agree or disagree? Do you feel the "problem," as he has formulated it, is a fair or correct assessment of the situation, or does it need to be defined in other terms—perhaps not as a "problem," for example? **Write an evaluative essay** in which you assess Horowitz's definition of the situation as a problem, his characterization of that problem, and his favored solution. (For a discussion of evaluative arguments, see Chapter 10.)

▼ *Since 2005, Stanley Fish has served as Davidson-Kahn Distinguished University Professor of Humanities and Law at Florida International University, teaching in the College of Law there. At the time he wrote "'Intellectual Diversity': The Trojan Horse of a Dark Design," which first appeared in the* Chronicle of Higher Education *in February 2004, he was dean of the College of Liberal Arts and Sciences at the University of Illinois at Chicago. Fish made his reputation as one of the most important literary theorists of this era with his work on the poet John Milton, the notion of interpretive communities, and issues of legal and literary texts and interpretation. He's the author of many books, including* Is There a Text in This Class? The Authority of Interpretive Communities *(1980),* Doing What Comes Naturally: Change, Rhetoric, and the Practice of Theory in Literary and Legal Studies *(1989),* There's No Such Thing As Free Speech, and It Is a Good Thing, Too *(1994), and* Save the World on Your Own Time *(2008). As you read this selection, evaluate carefully the criticisms Fish raises of David Horowitz's notion of intellectual diversity.*

"Intellectual Diversity": The Trojan Horse° of a Dark Design°

STANLEY FISH

Whenever I've been asked who won (or is winning) the culture wars in the academy, I say it depends on what you mean by winning.

If victory for the right meant turning back or retarding the growth of programs like women's studies, African-American studies, Chicano studies,

A scene with the Trojan horse in the 2004 movie Troy, *directed by Wolfgang Petersen*

Trojan horse: according to Virgil's ancient Roman epic poem *The Aeneid,* ten years into the Trojan War the Greeks besieging Troy found a strategy that broke the stalemate. They pretended to withdraw and sail away, leaving behind a large hollow wooden horse as a gift to the Trojans. The Trojans, convinced that the Greeks had given up and gone home, pulled the horse inside the city walls and got drunk in celebration. That night, Greek soldiers, who had hidden inside the horse, descended and opened the gates of the city to let in other Greek soldiers, and the Greek army destroyed Troy, murdering the men and taking the women and children as slaves.

Dark Design: possibly an allusion to *The Dark Design,* a science-fiction novel by American novelist Philip José Farmer.

Latino studies, cultural studies, gay and lesbian (and now transgender) studies, postmodern studies, and poststructuralist theory, then the left won big time, for these programs flourish (especially among the young) and are the source of much of the intellectual energy in the liberal arts.

But if the palm is to be awarded to the party that persuaded the American public to adopt its characterization of the academy, the right wins hands down, for it is now generally believed that our colleges and universities are hotbeds (what is a "hotbed" anyway?) of radicalism and pedagogical irresponsibility where dollars are wasted, nonsense is propagated, students are indoctrinated, religion is disrespected, and patriotism is scorned.

The left may have won the curricular battle, but the right won the public-relations war. The right did this in the old-fashioned way, by mastering the ancient art of rhetoric and spinning a vocabulary that, once established in the public mind, performed the work of argument all by itself. The master stroke, of course, was the appropriation from the left (where it had been used with a certain self-directed irony) of the phrase "political correctness," which in fairly short order became capitalized and transformed from an accusation to the name of a program supposedly being carried out by the very persons who were the accusation's object. That is, those who cried "political correctness" hypostatized° an entity about which they could then immediately complain. This was genius.

hypostatize: to make into a substance. In this case, by creating the label, the right had created something that they could complain about.

Now they're doing it again, this time by taking a phrase that seems positively benign and even progressive (in a fuzzy-left way) and employing it as the Trojan horse of a dark design. That phrase is "intellectual diversity," and the vehicle that is bringing it to the streets and coffee shops of your hometown is David Horowitz's Academic Bill of Rights, which has been the basis of legislation introduced in Congress, has stirred some interest in a number of states, and has been the subject of editorials (both pro and con) in leading newspapers. 5

Opponents of the Academic Bill of Rights contend that despite disclaimers of any political intention and an explicit rejection of quotas, the underlying agenda is the decidedly political one of forcing colleges and universities to hire conservative professors in order to assure ideological balance.

Horowitz replies (in print and conversation) that he has no desire to impose ideological criteria on the operations of the academy; he does not favor, he tells me, legislation that would have political bodies taking over the responsibility of making curricular and hiring decisions. His hope, he insists, is that colleges and universities will reform themselves, and he offers the Academic Bill of Rights (which is the product of consultation with academics of various persuasions) as a convenient base-line template to which they might refer for guidance.

For the record, and as one of those with whom he has consulted, I believe him, and I believe him, in part, because much of the Academic Bill of Rights is as apolitical and principled as he says it is. It begins by announcing that "the central purposes of a University are the pursuit of truth, the discovery of new knowledge through scholarship and research, the study and reasoned criticism of intellectual and cultural traditions . . . and the transmission of knowledge and learning to a society at large." (I shall return to the clause deleted by my ellipsis.)

The bill goes on to define academic freedom as the policy of "protecting the intellectual independence of professors, researchers and students in the pursuit of knowledge and the expression of ideas from interference by legislators or authorities within the institution itself."

In short, "no political, ideological or religious orthodoxy will be imposed 10 on professors." Nor shall a legislature "impose any orthodoxy through its control of the university budget," and "no faculty shall be hired or fired or denied promotion or tenure on the basis of his or her political or religious beliefs." The document ends by declaring that academic institutions "should maintain a posture of organizational neutrality with respect to the substantive disagreements that divide researchers on questions within, or outside, their fields of inquiry."

It's hard to see how anyone who believes (as I do) that academic work is distinctive in its aims and goals and that its distinctiveness must be protected from political pressures (either external or internal) could find anything to disagree with here. Everything follows from the statement that the pursuit of truth is a—I would say the—central purpose of the university. For the serious embrace of that purpose precludes deciding what the truth is in advance, or ruling out certain accounts of the truth before they have been given a hearing, or making evaluations of those accounts turn on the known or suspected political affiliations of those who present them.

While it may be, as some have said, that the line between the political and the academic is at times difficult to discern—political issues are legitimately the subject of academic analysis; the trick is to keep analysis from sliding into advocacy—it is nevertheless a line that can and must be drawn, and I would go so far as to agree with Horowitz when he criticizes professors who put posters of partisan identification on their office doors and thus announce to the students who come for advice and consultation that they have entered a political space.

But it is precisely because the pursuit of truth is the cardinal value of the academy that the value (if it is one) of intellectual diversity should be rejected.

The notion first turns up, though not by name, in the clause I elided where Horowitz lists among the purposes of a university "the teaching and general development of students to help them become creative individuals and productive citizens of a pluralistic society."

Teaching, yes—it is my job to introduce students to new materials and 15 equip them with new skills; but I haven't the slightest idea of how to help students become creative individuals. And it is decidedly not my job to produce citizens for a pluralistic society or for any other. Citizen building is a legitimate democratic activity, but it is not an academic activity. To be sure, some of what happens in the classroom may play a part in the fashioning of a citizen, but that is neither something you can count on—there is no accounting for what a student will make of something you say or assign—nor something you should aim for. As admirable a goal as it may be, fashioning citizens for a pluralistic society has nothing to do with the pursuit of truth.

For Horowitz, the link between the two is to be found in the idea of pluralism: Given the "unsettled character of all human knowledge" and the fact (which is a fact) "that there is no humanly accessible truth that is not in principle open to challenge," it follows, he thinks, that students being prepared to live in a pluralistic society should receive an education in pluralism; and it follows further, he says, that it is the obligation of teachers and administrators "to promote intellectual pluralism" and thereby "protect the principle of intellectual diversity."

But it is a mistake to go from the general assertion that no humanly accessible truth is invulnerable to challenge to the conclusion that therefore challenges must always be provided. That is to confuse a theory of truth with its pursuit and to exchange the goal of reaching it for a resolution to keep the question of it always open.

While questions of truth may be generally open, the truth of academic matters is not general but local; questions are posed and often they do have answers that can be established with certainty; and even if that certainty can theoretically be upset—one cannot rule out the future emergence of new evidence—that theoretical possibility carries with it no methodological obligation. That is, it does not mandate intellectual diversity, a condition that may attend some moments in the pursuit of truth when there is as yet no clear path, but not a condition one must actively seek or protect.

To put it simply, intellectual diversity is not a stand-alone academic value, no more than is free speech; either can be a help in the pursuit of truth, but neither should be identified with it; the (occasional) means should not be confused with the end.

Now if intellectual diversity is not an academic value, adherence to it as 20 an end in itself will not further an academic goal; but it will further some goal, and that goal will be political. It will be part of an effort to alter the academy so that it becomes an extension of some partisan vision of the way the world should be.

Such an effort will not be a perversion of intellectual diversity; intellectual diversity as a prime academic goal is already a perversion and its transformation into a political agenda, despite Horowitz's protestations and wishes to the contrary, is inevitable and assured. It is just a matter of which party seizes it and makes it its own.

For a while (ever since the *Bakke* decision°), it was the left that flew the diversity banner and put it to work in the service of affirmative action, speech codes, hostile-environment regulations, minority hiring, and more. Now it is the right's turn, and Horowitz himself has mapped out the strategy and laid bare the motives:

> "I encourage [students] to use the language that the left has deployed so effectively on behalf of its own agendas. Radical professors have created a 'hostile learning' environment for conservative students. There is a lack of 'intellectual diversity' on college faculties and in academic classrooms. The conservative viewpoint is 'under-represented' in the curriculum and on its reading lists. The university should be an 'inclusive' and intellectually 'diverse' community" ("The Campus Blacklist," April 2003).

It is obvious that for Horowitz these are debating points designed to hoist the left by its own petard;° but the trouble with debating points is that they can't be kept in bounds. Someone is going to take them seriously and advocate actions that Horowitz would probably not endorse.

Someone is going to say, let's monitor those lefty professors and keep tabs on what they're saying; and while we're at it, let's withhold federal funds from programs that do not display "ideological balance" ("balance" is also an unworthy academic goal); and let's demand that academic institutions demonstrate a commitment to hiring conservatives; and let's make sure that the material our students read is pro-American and free of the taint of relativism; and let's publish the names of those who do not comply.

This is not a hypothetical list; it is a list of actions already being taken. In 25 fact, it is a list one could pretty much glean from the Web site of State Senator John K. Andrews Jr., president of the Colorado Senate (http://www.andrewsamerica.com/), a site on which the Academic Bill of Rights is invoked frequently.

Bakke decision: a reference to the 1978 U.S. Supreme Court case *University of California Regents v. Bakke,* which outlawed racial quotas in academic admissions policies but reaffirmed the legality of affirmative action.

hoist . . . by its own petard: an allusion to a line from Shakespeare's *Hamlet.* It means literally to be blown into the air by one's own bomb—that is, to be injured figuratively by something one had planned to use to injure others.

Lynne Cheney campaigning with her husband, Dick Cheney, in Philadelphia in August 2000

Lynne Cheney: a conservative public servant who holds or has held important positions in the American Enterprise Institute for Public Policy Research, the American Council of Trustees and Alumni, and the Reader's Digest Association. Trained as a scholar of nineteenth-century British literature, she's the author of numerous books, including *American Memory: A Report on the Humanities in the Nation's Public Schools* (1987), *Academic Freedom* (1992), *America: A Patriotic Primer* (2002), *A Is for Abigail: An Almanac of Amazing American Women* (2003), *When Washington Crossed the Delaware: A Wintertime Story for Young Patriots* (2004), and *A Time for Freedom: What Happened When in America* (2005). She's also the wife of former Vice President Dick Cheney.

Andrews, like everyone else doing the intellectual diversity dance, insists that he opposes "any sort of quotas, mandated hiring or litmus test"; but then he turns around and sends a letter to Colorado's universities asking them to explain how they promote "intellectual diversity."

Anne D. Neal, of the Lynne Cheney°–inspired American Council of Trustees and Alumni, plays the same double game in a piece entitled "Intellectual Diversity Endangered" (http://www.cfif.org/htdocs/freedomline/current/guest_commentary/student_right_to_learn.htm). First she stands up for the value of academic freedom ("no more important value to the life of the mind"), but then she urges university trustees to see to it "that all faculty . . . present points of view other than their own in a balanced way" (something you might want to do but shouldn't have to do) and to "insist that their institutions offer broad-based survey courses," and "to monitor tenure decisions" for instances of "political discrimination," and to "conduct intellectual diversity reviews and to make the results public."

These are only two examples of what the mantra of "intellectual diversity" gets you. And to make the point again, these are not examples of a good idea taken too far, but of a bad idea taken in the only direction—a political direction—it is capable of going. As a genuine academic value, intellectual diversity is a nonstarter. As an imposed imperative, it is a disaster.

RESPOND ●

1. What is Stanley Fish's attitude toward the Academic Bill of Rights and the notion of intellectual diversity? Which issues do Fish and David Horowitz, author of the Academic Bill of Rights, agree about? Which issues do they disagree about? Why?

2. Fish argues that if one agrees that "the pursuit of truth is the cardinal value of the academy," then one must reject the notion of intellectual diversity (paragraph 13). What arguments does he offer for this position? Do you agree or disagree? Why?

3. In paragraphs 14–15, Fish likewise rejects the idea that the job of higher education is to produce "creative individuals" and help students become "productive citizens." What are his arguments for this position? Do you agree or disagree? Why?

4. In paragraphs 16–23, Fish contends that despite Horowitz's claims to the contrary, his goal is to "hoist the left by its own petard." What evidence does Fish provide for his claims? How do these claims compare with Horowitz's comments in his essay, "In Defense of Intellectual Diversity" (p. 922)?

5. In paragraph 24, Fish argues that the notion of balance is an unworthy academic goal. What does he mean here? Should the idea of balance mean that all possible positions are represented as being of equal value? Should it have some other meaning? Is it, as Fish contends, in contrast to Horowitz, not a useful goal in the pursuit of knowledge or truth? (In answering these questions, you'll likely want to consider several topics from different disciplines, using them as examples.)

6. Throughout this book, we've argued that images are arguments. Let's consider the photo of Lynne Cheney that appears near the end of this selection. As the caption notes, it shows Cheney campaigning with her husband, who later served as vice president from 2001 to 2009. We can imagine some readers criticizing us for using a photo of Cheney in which she is represented as acting on behalf of her husband rather than being represented in terms of her own professional achievements. Why might such readers be critical? Others might praise us for using this photo. What might their reasoning be? What is your opinion about the choice of this photo? What values led you to your conclusions?

7. Study both this selection and the previous one by David Horowitz. This selection offers an argument against intellectual diversity, and Horowitz offers an argument for it. You may wish to examine the "Academic Bill of Rights," discussed by both authors (it can be found at http://www.studentsforacademicfreedom.org/documents/1925/abor). **Write an evaluative essay** in which you consider the strengths and weaknesses of each side. You may choose either to take a strong stance or to be as objective as possible so that the reader won't know where you locate yourself in this debate. (To consider: should we expect those who align themselves with Horowitz to choose the latter alternative, working hard to demonstrate complete balance in the everyday sense of the term, while expecting those who align themselves with Fish to choose the former alternative, taking a strong stance—or vice versa? Why?) (For a discussion of evaluative arguments, see Chapter 10.)

Fish takes apart two major aspects of Horowitz's bill of rights, essentially claiming that they are undermined by their own fallacious logic. Do you agree? Use the descriptions of fallacies in Chapter 17 to support your answer.

LINK TO P. 515

▼ *Do liberals—who are overrepresented on college faculties relative to their numbers in the general population, especially at elite private and large public institutions—turn their students into liberals? Contrary to the claims of critics of American higher education like David Horowitz, author of an essay earlier in this chapter, this selection notes that the answer may well be no. (The following selection by Mack Mariani and Gordon Hewitt is an excerpt from one of the research studies cited in this selection to support that claim.) The author of this selection, Patricia Cohen, writes for the* New York Times, *often on issues related to education. As you read this article, which first appeared in the* Times *in November 2008, you'll discover that some critics of American colleges and universities argue that debates between people like Horowitz and Stanley Fish, author of the previous selection (which are labeled debates between conservatives and liberals), are on the wrong track completely. Seek to figure out what diversity on campus means for these critics.*

Professors' Liberalism Contagious? Maybe Not

PATRICIA COHEN

An article of faith among conservative critics of American universities has been that liberal professors politically indoctrinate their students. This conviction not only fueled the culture wars but has also led state lawmakers to consider requiring colleges to submit reports to the government detailing their progress in ensuring "intellectual diversity," prompted universities to establish faculty positions devoted to conservatism and spurred the creation of a network of volunteer watchdogs to monitor "political correctness" on campuses.

Just a few weeks ago Michael Barone, a fellow at the conservative American Enterprise Institute, warned in the *Washington Times* against "the liberal thugocracy," arguing that today's liberals seem to be taking "marching orders" from "college and university campuses."

But a handful of new studies have found such worries to be overwrought. Three sets of researchers recently concluded that professors have virtually no impact on the political views and ideology of their students.

If there has been a conspiracy among liberal faculty members to influence students, "they've done a pretty bad job," said A. Lee Fritschler, a professor of public policy at George Mason University and an author of the new book *Closed Minds? Politics and Ideology in American Universities* (Brookings Institution Press).

The notion that students are induced to move leftward "is a fantasy," said Jeremy D. Mayer, another of the book's authors. (Bruce L. R. Smith is the third co-author of the book.) When it comes to shaping a young person's political views, "it is really hard to change the mind of anyone over 15," said Mr. Mayer, who did extensive research on faculty and students.

"Parents and family are the most important influence," followed by the news media and peers, he said. "Professors are among the least influential."

A study of nearly 7,000 students at 38 institutions published in the current *PS: Political Science and Politics,* the journal of the American Political

Science Association, as well as a second study that has been accepted by the journal to run in April 2009, both reach similar conclusions. "There is no evidence that an instructor's views instigate political change among students," Matthew Woessner and April Kelly-Woessner, a husband-and-wife team of political scientists who have frequently conducted research on politics in higher education, write in that second study.

Their work is often cited by people on both sides of the debate, not least because Mr. Woessner describes himself as politically conservative.

No one disputes that American academia is decidedly more liberal than the rest of the population, or that there is a detectable shift to the left among students during their college years. Still, both studies in the peer-reviewed° *PS*, for example, found that changes in political ideology could not be attributed to proselytizing professors but rather to general trends among that age group. As Mack D. Mariani at Xavier University and Gordon J. Hewitt at Hamilton College write in the current issue, "Student political orientation does not change for a majority of students while in college, and for those that do change there is evidence that other factors have an effect on that change, such as gender and socioeconomic status."

That may be, said Daniel Klein, 10 an economist at George Mason, but those results don't necessarily mean there isn't a problem. Mr. Klein, whose research has shown that registered Democrats vastly outnumber Republicans among faculty in the humanities and social sciences at American colleges and universities, maintains that the focus on the liberal-conservative split is misdirected. Such terms are vague and can be used to describe everything from attitudes about religion and family to the arts and lifestyles, he said.

The real issue, said Mr. Klein, who calls himself a libertarian,° is that social democratic ideas dominate universities—ideas that play down the importance of the individual and promote government intervention.

Such "academic groupthink" means that the works of such thinkers are not offered enough, he argues. "A major tragedy is that they're not getting exposed to the good stuff," he said, citing the works of John Stuart Mill,° Adam Smith,° Friedrich Hayek° and Milton Friedman.°

---

peer-reviewed: evaluated by fellow researchers. During the process of peer review of articles being considered for publication in scholarly journals, neither the authors nor the reviewers know the identity of the other parties. This system helps to ensure that evaluation is fair because the research, rather than the person who conducted it, is evaluated. In academic fields, the most prestigious publications are those that have gone through the process of peer review.

libertarian: a political philosophy that works to minimize the role of government in order to maximize the freedom of individuals.

John Stuart Mill (1806–1873): a British philosopher and economist. As an economist, he was a supporter of free markets; as a philosopher, he is best known for his writings on the nature of liberty and on utilitarianism, the philosophy that the good is whatever creates happiness for the greatest number of people.

Adam Smith (1723–1790): a Scottish moral philosopher who is considered to be the father of modern economics. His *An Inquiry into the Nature and Causes of the Wealth of Nations* (1776) presents an argument for free markets that continues to influence economic theories.

Friedrich Hayek (1899–1992): an Austrian-born philosopher and economist who shared the Nobel Prize for economics in 1974. His work staunchly defends classical liberalism, which emphasizes individual freedom, limited government, and free-market capitalism.

Milton Friedman (1912–2006): an American economist, public intellectual, and 1976 Nobel Prize winner in economics. Friedman taught at the University of Chicago for over thirty years. A strong opponent of government control or intervention in markets, he is considered one of the most influential economists of the last half century.

"Even if we had hard, definite evidence that students weren't influenced by their professors, there is still reason for great concern about the composition of the faculty," Mr. Klein added.

K. C. Johnson, a historian at the City University of New York, characterizes the problem as pedagogical, not political. Entire fields of study, from traditional literary analysis to political and military history, are simply not widely taught anymore, Mr. Johnson contended: "Even students who want to learn don't have the opportunity because there are no specialists on the faculty to take courses from."

"The conservative critics are **15** inventing a straw man that doesn't exist and are missing the real problem that does," he added.

Anne Neal, the president of the American Council of Trustees and Alumni, which closely follows this issue, agrees that "it is not about left and right."

Many researchers and critics also agree that a better grounding in American history and politics is important. "It wasn't too long ago that schools and universities required civic education and American history," Mr. Fritschler noted. "Almost all of those requirements have evaporated."

A number of organizations that have a large base of conservative supporters, like Ms. Neal's council and the National Association of Scholars, have been promoting a return to traditional courses in western civilization and American history.

Mr. Fritschler said that perhaps the most insidious° side effect of assumptions about liberal influence has been an overall disengagement on campus from civic and political affairs, and a reluctance to promote serious debate of political issues. If anything, he added, the problem is not too much politics, but too little.

This article has been revised to reflect the following correction:

Correction: November 6, 2008

An article on Monday about research that has found that professors have virtually no impact on the political views and ideology of their students omitted the name of a co-author of the book *Closed Minds? Politics and Ideology in American Universities*, two of whose authors were quoted in the article. In addition to A. Lee Fritschler and Jeremy D. Mayer, Bruce L. R. Smith is a co-author of the book.

Milton Friedman

K. C. Johnson argues that conservative critics of academic life have employed an argument based on a fallacy. For more on the straw man argument and other fallacies, see Chapter 17.

insidious: harmful in a subtle and often almost hidden way.

LINK TO P. 515

RESPOND•

1. The first half of this article contends that an "article of faith" among certain critics of American higher education may, in fact, be false. What is the article of faith, and what arguments and evidence does Cohen cite that may undercut it?

2. The second half of this article takes a different turn, arguing that there is, indeed, a problem on American campuses but a problem of a very different nature. According to this section of the article, what is the real problem? Cohen closes this article by indirectly quoting A. Lee Fritschler: "If anything . . . the problem is not too much politics, but too little"(paragraph 19). What does Fritschler mean by this statement? What would you imagine Fritschler's own political values and commitments to be? Why?

3. In paragraph 15, Cohen quotes K. C. Johnson: "The conservative critics are inventing a straw man that doesn't exist and are missing the real problem that does." What does Johnson mean? What is a straw man, when one is discussing arguments? Does it involve ethical, emotional, or logical appeals? Why? What is the specific straw man that Johnson contends is being created in this situation? (For a discussion of fallacies of argument, including a straw-man argument, see Chapter 17.)

4. Cohen mentions the American Council of Trustees and Alumni (paragraph 16) and the National Association of Scholars (paragraph 18). Do some research on these two organizations to discover their positions and the values to which they are committed. In light of this research, evaluate Anne Neal's claim that "it is not about left and right." In other words, based on your research, would you expect that most of the members of these two organizations are politically conservative and therefore affiliated with the right or politically liberal and therefore affiliated with the left? Why? Is this information relevant to Neal's claim? Why or why not?

5. In paragraph 17, A. Lee Fritschler is quoted as claiming that "almost all" of the requirements involving civic education and American history have disappeared from college campuses. Investigate the situation on your own campus. How have the requirements for graduation shifted over the past several decades? Does your school require fewer courses in civic education and American history than it used to? Does it require different courses in these areas? Has it added new requirements? What is their nature? To answer these questions, you will have to visit your school's library. Although an electronic catalog lists the requirements for your current academic year, the catalogs from previous years probably exist only in paper format. **Write an essay** in which

you document and evaluate the changes in graduation requirements at your institution. (For a discussion of arguments of fact, see Chapter 8; for a discussion of evaluative arguments, see Chapter 10.) One way to complete this assignment would be to work in groups, with each group surveying a five- to ten-year period going back several decades. Each group would then write an essay on its findings, and then all groups together could evaluate what the changes in requirements might mean.

▼ *Earlier selections by David Horowitz ("In Defense of Intellectual Diversity") and Stanley Fish ("'Intellectual Diversity': The Trojan Horse of a Dark Design") take a theoretical or ideological perspective on the question of what influence faculty beliefs might have on students, and the previous selection, "Professors' Liberalism Contagious? Maybe Not," by Patricia Cohen reviews recent empirical research on the topic. Here, we present the introduction and discussion from one of the studies that Cohen discusses—"Indoctrination U.? Faculty Ideology and Changes in Student Political Orientation." The selection comprises two sections from the article: the introduction, or opening section of the article, and the discussion, or closing section. (Omitted are a review of previous research literature; a discussion of the research questions, data, and methodology; and the reporting of the quantitative results and analysis.) The article was published in October 2008 in PS: Political Science & Politics, a journal of the American Political Science Association that focuses on political science, teaching, and contemporary politics. Mack D. Mariani is an assistant professor of political science at Xavier University in Cincinnati, and Gordon J. Hewitt is assistant dean of the faculty for institutional research at Hamilton College in Clinton, New York. As you read this selection, consider how arguments based on quantitative evidence, like this one, differ from those of Horowitz and Fish, which are not. Likewise, consider the ways that Mariani and Hewitt seek to demonstrate that their research is unbiased.*

Indoctrination U.?
Faculty Ideology and Changes in Student Political Orientation (Excerpt)

MACK D. MARIANI AND GORDON J. HEWITT

In the provocatively titled *Indoctrination U.,*° David Horowitz argues that radical members of college faculties have "intruded a political agenda into the academic curriculum," engaging in propaganda rather than scholarship and indoctrinating students rather than teaching them (Horowitz 2007, xi). Although allegations of liberal bias in academia are nothing new, the issue has gained increased attention as the result of efforts by Horowitz and the

indoctrination: the teaching of people to accept and believe things uncritically, often with the connotation of brainwashing.

empirical: derived from observation; here, drawing conclusions based on the statistical analysis of survey data (in contrast to drawing conclusions based on a theory).

CIRP Freshman Survey: the Cooperative Institutional Research Program Freshman Survey. It is administered annually to over 40,000 freshmen at 700 two-year colleges, four-year colleges, and universities.

College Student Survey: an exit survey of college seniors at four-year institutions across the country much like the CIRP survey of freshmen. Since 2006, it has been called the College Senior Survey.

Higher Education Research Institute (HERI) Faculty Survey: a survey of faculty at two- and four-year institutions that is conducted every three years by the Higher Educational Research Institute, which is home to the Cooperative Institutional Research Program.

statistically: based on the use of tests of statistical significance. The findings represent an actual relationship between variables rather than a chance occurrence.

Center for the Study of the Popular Culture (CSPC) to promote the Academic Bill of Rights for American colleges and universities.[1]

According to Horowitz, the goal of the Academic Bill of Rights is to inspire college officials "to enforce the rules that were meant to ensure the fairness and objectivity of the college classroom" (Horowitz 2007, 2).[2] Supporters argue that an Academic Bill of Rights is needed to "protect students from one-sided liberal propaganda . . . [and] to safeguard a student's right to get an education rather than an indoctrination."[3] Opponents of the initiative, including the American Association of University Professors, have characterized the Academic Bill of Rights as an assault on academic freedom (Jacoby 2005; Schrecker 2006) that is based on exaggerated claims of anti-conservative bias (Ehrlich and Colby 2004; Wiener 2005; Jacobson 2006a; 2006d; Jaschik 2006b).[4]

Although a growing body of social science research indicates that college faculties are disproportionately liberal and Democratic, at least when compared with the population in general (Brookings 2001; HERI 2002; Klein and Western 2005; Jaschik 2005; Klein and Stern 2005a; 2005b; 2006; Rothman, Lichter, and Nevitte 2005), there has been very little systematic research on whether faculty members' political leanings actually affect the ideological views of the students they teach. If students' political views are being changed by a left-leaning professoriate, we should be able to see evidence of that influence; indeed, we would expect that changes in political orientation would be most dramatic among students at more ideologically liberal institutions.

This study utilizes empirical° evidence from the CIRP Freshman Survey,° the College Student Survey,° and the Higher Education Research Institute (HERI) Faculty Survey° to assess the effect of faculty ideology on the political attitudes of undergraduate students over the course of a four-year college career (2001–2005). Our analysis of 38 private colleges and 6,807 student respondents indicates that, consistent with a number of previous studies, faculty members are predominantly liberal and Democratic. We find little evidence, however, that faculty ideology is associated with changes in students' ideological orientation. The students at colleges with more liberal faculties were not statistically° more likely to move to the left than students at other institutions.

DISCUSSION

The goal of this study is to assess whether faculty political orientation is   5
associated with changes in student political orientation. The findings presented here suggest that faculty political orientation at the institutional level

does not significantly° influence student political orientation. The descriptive data also indicate that while faculty orientation is overwhelmingly liberal, student orientation when leaving college is not significantly different than the population at large. Our analysis did find that other institutional and personal characteristics, including institutional control, gender and socio-economic status, have an effect on changes in student political ideology. It should be noted that neither of the regression models° had a high level of predictive value (R^2 = .002, R^2 = .006),° but they did show which key variables were significantly correlated with change in student political orientation.

The finding that institutional control is correlated with change in political orientation is not surprising. Students at religiously controlled institutions were less likely to move to the left during their college career and we believe that this is most likely due to self-selection. Students with strong religious beliefs are probably more likely to attend religiously controlled institutions. Institutional culture may also play a part, as both the freshman and faculty surveys indicate higher levels of conservatism among peers and faculty members at religious institutions.

Our results show that female college students are more likely than men to move to the left during the course of their college careers. It is well established that in the general population women are more liberal than men and according to Dey (1997) and data from the ANES° that is also the case for college-aged women.[5] Our results also indicate that higher socioeconomic status (as measured by estimated parental income) is associated with changes in political orientation toward the right. The finding that more wealthy students are more likely to move to the right during the course of their college careers (and vice versa) may reflect increasing student awareness about political parties and ideologies and where they stand on issues related to wealth, taxes, and government assistance for lower-income Americans (see for instance Stonecash, Brewer, and Mariani 2002).

Though we are hopeful that this study contributes to ongoing debates about faculty ideology and indoctrination, there are some limitations to this study that should be taken into account by other researchers. We are mindful, for instance, that our finding that students move leftward during college is not, by itself, evidence of indoctrination. Students may move to the left as a result of other factors, such as shared cultural influences, a common stage in personal development, or as a reaction to peer pressure, current events, or political developments. We have tried to deal with this problem by controlling for faculty ideology; if faculty ideology has an impact on student ideology then changes in student ideology should be more pronounced at institutions with more liberal faculty members and vice versa. We find little

significantly: in quantitative studies, this word has a technical meaning, specifically, systematically in a way that is demonstrably unlikely due to chance.

regression models: statistical tools that enable researchers to predict one variable when they know the value of another variable (or variables).

R: Pearson's coefficient of regression or the coefficient of determination. It shows how statistically useful the model is in predicting what will occur in the future. As the authors note, the predictive value of the two models was low (two cases out of 1,000 and six out of 1,000), but the analysis demonstrates which variables are correlated (related) from a statistical point of view.

ANES: the American National Election Study. The reference for this 2004 study is in the list of references.

Mariani and Hewitt's review of other research done on this question is one of the hallmarks of academic writing. For more features of academic argument, check out Chapter 6.

LINK TO P. 133

evidence that this is the case. Of course, this finding does not necessarily mean that professors act fairly or without ideological bias in their teachings, subject matter, or selection of reading materials. Professors could, after all, be *failing* to indoctrinate students despite their concerted efforts to do so! Regardless of any biases (intentional or unintentional) that professors bring to their teaching, the findings presented here may help alleviate the concern that students, on a widespread basis, are adopting the political positions of their liberal professors.

Another limitation of this paper is that it focuses on institutions and, in doing so, it does not tell us much of anything about a student's individual experiences or the ideological views of the particular professors a student interacted with during their college career. While it would be preferable to take into account the ideology of the faculty members who actually taught each particular student, privacy laws make it very difficult to gather the data without running into considerable problems with regard to sample size and representativeness. In addition there are some advantages to our approach of looking at overall faculty ideology. Part of the argument is that students are being indoctrinated not just in class, but from the general climate created by faculty members that pervades their teaching, scholarship, and outside of the classroom activities. The indoctrination argument is, in large part, about what goes on in the classroom. But what goes on in the classroom is affected by the broader campus culture and vice versa. Thus, the overall faculty ideology of the institution is likely to influence all students in some way.

Though the number of students examined here is considerable (6,807), the 10 number of institutions remains relatively small (38). We were limited by the fact that relatively few institutions participate in all three of the surveys needed to account for faculty ideology and changes in student ideology over time. There are no public universities in the sample, and large percentages are selective liberal arts colleges. Though this is a limitation, many of the conservative critiques focus in particular on elite and private colleges, so it is not entirely without merit to use this sample as a test of the indoctrination argument. It should also be noted that students at these institutions who take longer than four years to complete their programs are unlikely to be included in the senior year surveys used in this study (and were therefore likely to be dropped from the dataset).

A final limitation of this study relates to the potential impact of an exogenous° shock—the September 11 terrorists attacks. The college students in our sample began college in the fall of 1999 and finished in the spring of 2003. For the students in this sample, the terrorist attacks of September 11, 2001, took place at the start of their junior year in college, roughly midway through

exogenous: outside. Here, a variable was external to the study, and its impact could not be controlled or determined.

their college careers. Clearly, the September 11 attacks have the potential to impact this cohort of students' political viewpoints. For this reason, further research is needed to assess whether similar changes occur for other groups of students whose college careers occurred under different historical circumstances.

To summarize, there are four important findings here related to questions about faculty ideology and fears that liberal faculty members are indoctrinating students to adopt a liberal ideology. First, it is very clear that faculty members tend to be liberal and are much more liberal than the general population. Second, there is evidence that there is a degree of self-selection going on among students when they choose a college. Students tend to enroll at institutions that have a faculty orientation makeup more similar to their own. This area is ripe for further research, for there may be other institutional factors at play, such as campus culture or history. Third, students whose ideology changes while in college tend to change to the left, but that movement is within the normal orientation range of 18–24-year-olds in the general population. Fourth, and most important, there is no evidence that faculty ideology at an institutional level has an impact on student political ideology. Student political orientation does not change for a majority of students while in college, and for those that do change there is evidence that other factors have an effect on that change, such as gender and socioeconomic status. Based on the data presented in this study, college students appear to be more firm in their political beliefs than conventional wisdom suggests. Though students' political ideology is not set in stone, it does not appear to change as a result of faculty ideology, at least at an institutional level.

Notes

*We wish to thank John Pryor of the Higher Education Research Institute at UCLA, Daniel Klein at GMU, and our colleagues at Hamilton College and Xavier University for their support and assistance on this project. Given that this is a study of faculty ideology, it seems reasonable to be open about our own ideological dispositions. We come from divergent political and ideological perspectives. One author is conservative and has worked extensively for Republican candidates and officeholders, while the other is liberal and active in Democratic politics at the local level.

1. The Center for the Study of Popular Culture was launched by Horowitz in 1988. In 2006, the center was renamed the David Horowitz Freedom Center. See David Horowitz Freedom Center, "About Us." www.horowitzfreedomcenter.org/FlexPage .aspx?area=aboutus (June 8, 2007).

2. The full text of the Academic Bill of Rights is available at www.studentsfor academicfreedom.org. A print version can be found in Horowitz (2007, 129–132). See also Horowitz 2004, Hegel 2004, and Klein 2004.

3. Rep. Jack Kingston (R-GA), as cited in Alyson Klein (2004). See also Horowitz 2004. Note too that there are those on the right who have voiced their opposition to the Academic Bill of Rights; see for instance Beck 2005.

4. In 2005 and 2006, the Academic Bill of Rights was introduced in Congress and at least 21 state legislatures. It resulted in a series of highly contentious state legislative hearings (Schrecker 2006; Jacobson 2006a) but little concrete legislative action. See, for instance, Jacobson 2005, 2006a, 2006b, 2006c, 2006d, and Jaschik 2006a. For a state by state roundup on the status of legislation related to the Academic Bill of Rights, see the Free Exchange Coalition's "Legislative Tracker" at www .freeexchangeoncampus.org/index.php?option=come_content&task=section&id =5&Itemid=61 (September 24, 2007). Note that the AAUP, which strongly opposes the Academic Bill of Rights, is a member of the Free Exchange Coalition.

5. According to the American National Election Study of 2004, 29.6% of females of all ages self-identified as left-of-center (slightly liberal, liberal, or extremely liberal), compared to 20.7% of males. Among 18–24-year-olds, 38.9% of females identified themselves as left-of-center, compared to 33.3% of males (ANES 2004).

REFERENCES

The American National Election Studies. 2004. Ann Arbor, MI: University of Michigan, Center for Political Studies.

Beck, Stefan. 2005. "Time in the Trenches: Campus Conservative Need to Toughen Up." *National Review Online*, April 13. www.nationalreview.com/comment/ beck200504130758.asp (June 8, 2007).

Brookings Institution. 2001. "National Survey on Government Endeavors." www .brook.edu/comm/reformwatch/rw04_surveydata.pdf (June 8, 2007).

Dey, Eric L., 1997. "Undergraduate Political Attitudes: Peer Influence in Changing Social Context." *The Journal of Higher Education* 68 (4): 398–413.

Ehrlich, Tom, and Anne Colby. 2004. "Political Bias in Undergraduate Education." *Carnegie Perspectives: The Carnegie Foundation for the Advancement of Teaching* 90 (3). www.carnegiefoundation.org/perspectives/sub.asp?key=245&subkey=1135 (June 8, 2007).

Hebel, Sara. 2004. "Patrolling Professors' Politics." *Chronicle of Higher Education*, February 13. http://chronicle.com/weekly/v50/i23/23a01801.htm (June 8, 2007).

Higher Education Research Institute (HERI). 2002. "The American College Teacher: National Norms for 2001–2002: UCLA Study Finds Growing Gap in Political Liberalism between Male and Female Faculty." Press release. www.gseis.ucla .edu/heri/act_pr_02.html (May 29, 2007).

Horowitz, David. 2007. *Indoctrination U.: The Left's War on Academic Freedom*. New York: Encounter Books.

———. 2004. "In Defense of Intellectual Diversity." *Chronicle of Higher Education*, February 13. http://chronicle.com/weekly/v50/i23/23b01201.htm (June 8, 2007).

Jacobson, Jennifer. 2006a. "Pa. Lawmakers Get Mixed Message on Fixing Perceived Liberal Bias in Academe." *Chronicle of Higher Education*, April 7. http://chronicle .com/weekly/v52/i31/31a03701.htm (June 8, 2007).

———. 2006b. "Tilting at Academe." *Chronicle of Higher Education*, March 24. http://chronicle.com/weekly/v52/i29/29a02501.htm (June 8, 2007).

———. 2006c. "Political-Bias Bill Passes S.D. House." *Chronicle of Higher Education*, February 17. http://chronicle.com/weekly/v52/i24/24a03201.htm (June 8, 2007).

———. 2006d. "Conservative Activist Admits Lack of Evidence for Some Allegations of Faculty Bias." *Chronicle of Higher Education*, January 20. http://chronicle.com/weekly/v52/i20/20a03301.htm (June 8, 2007).

———. 2005. "Pennsylvania Lawmakers Hold Hearings on Political Bias in College Classrooms." *Chronicle of Higher Education*, November 25. http://chronicle.com/weekly/v52/i14/14a03201.htm (June 8, 2007).

Jacoby, Russel. 2005. "So Universities Hire Liberal Faculty—This Is News?" History News Network, George Mason University, March 28. http://hnn.us/article/10836.html (June 8, 2007).

Jaschik, Scott. 2006a. "Grading Edge for Conservative Students." *Inside Higher Ed.*, March 30.

———. 2006b. "Retractions from David Horowitz." *Inside Higher Ed.*, January 11.

———. 2005. "Leaning to the Left." *Inside Higher Ed.*, March 30. http://insidehighered.com/news/2005/03/30/politics (June 8, 2007).

Klein, Alyson. 2004. "Worried on the Right and the Left." *Chronicle of Higher Education*, July 9. http://chronicle.com/weekly/v50/i44/44a02101.htm (June 8, 2007).

Klein, Daniel B., and Charlotta Stern. 2006. "Sociology and Classical Liberalism." *The Independent Review: A Journal of Political Economy* 11 (1): 37–52.

———. 2005a. "Political Diversity in Six Disciplines." *Academic Questions* 18 (1): 40–52.

———. 2005b. "Professors and Their Politics: The Policy Views of Social Scientists." *Critical Review: An Interdisciplinary Journal of Politics and Society* 17 (3 & 4): 257–303.

Klein, Daniel B., and Andrew Western. 2005. "Voter Registration of Berkeley and Stanford Faculty." *Academic Questions* 18 (1): 53–65.

Rothman, Stanley, S. Robert Lichter, and Neil Nevitte. 2005. "Politics and Professional Advancement among College Faculty." *The Forum* 3 (1).

Schrecker, Ellen. 2006. "Worse than McCarthy." Point of View. *Chronicle of Higher Education*, February 10. http://chronicle.com/weekly/v52/i23/23b02001.htm (June 8, 2007).

Stonecash, Jeff, Mark Brewer, and Mack Mariani. 2002. *Diverging Parties Realignment, Social Change, and Political Polarization*. Boulder, CO: Westview.

Wiener, Jon. 2005. "When Students Complain about Professors, Who Gets to Define the Controversy?" *Chronicle of Higher Education*, March 13. http://chronicle.com/weekly/v51/i36/36b01201.htm (May 25, 2006).

RESPOND●

1. One purpose of this research was to use the statistical analysis of data gathered from students to test a claim commonly made by conservative critics of American universities. What claim is being tested? State this claim as a Toulmin argument. (For a discussion of Toulmin argumentation, see Chapter 7.)

2. What did Mariani and Hewitt find when they tested the claim discussed in question 1? What is the difference between a purely logical argument (as discussed in question 1) and one based on empirical data (as is the case in this research)?

3. Briefly outline the "Discussion" section of this selection to get a clear idea of how it is structured. In outlining, you are looking for the major topic of each paragraph and the way that the paragraphs work together to conclude the article. Based on this particular "Discussion" section, how would you characterize the functions of a discussion section of a research article? In other words, how is this section structured and why?

4. A large part of the "Discussion" section describes the limitations of the research. How does this discussion contribute to the researchers' ethos? In what ways does an acknowledgment of the limitations of a research study function like qualifiers in an argument? How does the authors' note—the unnumbered footnote indicated by an asterisk—contribute to their ethos? (For a discussion of ethos, see Chapter 3. For a discussion of qualifiers, see Chapter 7.)

5. A common task in academic and professional writing is summarizing in one or two paragraphs an aspect of an empirical study like this one. **Write a summary** of the limitations of the study discussed by the authors, and **write a summary** of the findings of the study. Summaries can be seen as a category of factual arguments. (For a discussion of arguments of fact, see Chapter 8.)

▼ Unlike people in many other countries, Americans can take college classes at any point in their life (if they can pay for them), and a growing number of older Americans are going to college for the first time or returning to school for any number of reasons. In this selection, Libby Sander, a staff reporter at the Chronicle of Higher Education, a newspaper that covers all aspects of postsecondary education, examines some of the consequences of this phenomenon. Her focus in this January 2008 article is older Americans who are returning to community colleges. The economic downturn beginning late in 2008 and continuing throughout 2009 has resulted in increased unemployment, which often encourages adults to return to school to gain additional education and skills. As you read this selection, think about the extent to which students at your school represent what this article terms "the traditional student . . . fresh out of high school" and the extent to which age is part of diversity on your campus.

Blue-Collar° Boomers Take Work Ethic to College

LIBBY SANDER

For 16 years, Russell Kearney awoke at 1:30 a.m. to hoist boxes of Wonder bread and Hostess cakes onto a truck and deliver them along a 120-mile route through eastern North Carolina.

After a decade, lifting and pushing thousands of pounds of bread—sometimes as much as 10 tons a day—he ruptured a disk in his back, making it feel "like my spine was cut in half," Mr. Kearney says. But he continued to work for five more years, until finally, "I just couldn't get out of the chair," he says. "I just couldn't do it any more."

And so, at age 53, after a lifetime of working in heavy-labor jobs, Mr. Kearney took an unexpected detour from the delivery route he figured he'd be driving until retirement. This new road led straight to the classroom, a setting he hadn't seen since graduating from high school in 1968. At nearby Lenoir Community College, he trained for a new kind of job, one that did not involve such strain on his body—a job, he hoped, that would give him a steady paycheck through the rest of his 50s and well into his 60s.

Mr. Kearney's journey to college is becoming a common one among workers in the baby-boomer° generation who are old enough to feel the strain of decades of physical labor, but too young to retire.

With the help of community colleges, some baby boomers are changing gears and retraining for new jobs that are less physically taxing. In doing 5

---

blue-collar: working-class. Blue-collar jobs involve physical labor and are usually paid by the hour, in contrast to white-collar jobs, which are paid by salaries.

baby boomer: someone born between 1946 and the early 1960s. After the end of World War II, the birthrate increased rapidly as soldiers returned home, and it began dropping sharply by the mid-1960s.

"A lot of older people think they're not as useful, as productive as they used to be," Mr. Kearney says. "But I see older people who could work rings around younger people. Just because you got a few years on you, you can do it."

WORKING LONGER

The image of aging boomers as prosperous preretirees eager to repair to the golf course belies a much more complicated portrait. A sizable demographic° of people will require some sort of retraining in order to keep working and keep the paychecks coming in.

"It is a story that's just unfolding," says Susan Porter Robinson, vice president for lifelong learning at the American Council on Education. "It's really a mosaic. If you look at them proportionately, yes, baby boomers are very well educated in terms of their predecessors. . . . But you have to then dig deeper to look at those who've been disenfranchised° from those opportunities."

Of the nearly 80 million baby boomers born between 1946 and 1965 who will reach retirement age over the next 20 years, many are expected to keep working well into their 60s or even their 70s.

By 2014, 41 percent of adults aged 55 and older will still be in the

10

so, these workers are among those who are redefining the traditional notion of retirement by working much later in life. And they are also leaving their mark on community colleges, many of which are fine-tuning their programs and making them more accessible to older adults.

"There's this image that older students are only coming to college for life enrichment, to take this and that course for their own personal enjoyment," says Jan Abushakrah, a sociology professor at Portland Community College, in Oregon, and director of its gerontology program. But in a recent survey of older students at her college,

Ms. Abushakrah says, more than three-quarters said they came back to school to find a job or a new skill to keep a current job. "The older students are serious about using the college experience to get the skills that they need."

Mr. Kearney's days of loading the bread truck may be over, but his desire to work is not. Now 57, he spends his days in the operating room at Wayne Memorial Hospital, in his hometown of Goldsboro, N.C., where he is a surgical technologist. He assists surgeons in everything from routine procedures to 2 a.m. Caesarean sections, which he says he finds exciting.

Sander offers both inartistic proofs, such as statistical evidence, and artistic proofs, those based on reason and common sense, to buttress her claims. For more on using logos in arguments, see Chapter 4.

LINK TO P. 69

demographic: a group of people who are alike with respect to some social characteristic (such as age, social class, or ethnicity).

disenfranchised: not granted full rights or opportunities.

workplace, according to recent estimates by the Bureau of Labor Statistics. And in a 2005 survey of adults between the ages of 50 and 59 by the MetLife Foundation and Civic Ventures, 66 percent said they planned to keep working in some fashion during their retirement years. Of that 66 percent, 15 percent said they would never retire.

David Cox, an electrician in Soap Lake, Wash., expects to work into his 60s. He spent years crawling on his stomach to run wires through confined spaces before deciding, at age 53, that he much preferred the idea of young electricians doing the crawling while he ran the business.

"I'm getting old for this kind of stuff," says Mr. Cox, who suffered a back injury last spring that brought his wire-running days to an abrupt end. But, he says, "I refuse to sit around the house and do nothing because I can't work." So Mr. Cox, who is now 54, enrolled in the industrial electrical-technology program at Big Bend Community College, in nearby Moses Lake. There, he is studying toward an associate degree that would give him the credentials he says he needs to start such a business.

The wave of baby boomers return- 15 ing to school is expected to crest in coming years, and administrators say it will do more than just alter the typical notion of retirement. Those boomer students will further challenge the outdated notion of what constitutes a "traditional" student.

That traditional student—fresh out of high school and able to take four years or more to complete a bachelor's degree—"just doesn't exist any more," says Ms. Abushakrah. "Many colleges still assume that that's the typical student and all other people are exceptions. But the exceptions are becoming the rule."

For those workers who never finished college or skipped it altogether, the transition to a second or third career can be difficult, especially if their previous jobs involved little or no interaction with the technology that is the bedrock of many occupations. Community colleges play a key role in reaching out to these kinds of students, determining their needs, helping them decide which new career path to pursue, and giving them the proper schooling to do it.

But even community colleges, which, by definition, serve their communities, are finding that they need to revamp some of their policies to fulfill this mission.

"The colleges are going to have to adapt to serve this population," says George Boggs, president of the American Association of Community Colleges. "Community colleges have been the most adaptable institutions around. They offer classes on the weekends, in the evenings, in shopping centers and churches. They're very flexible in trying to meet the needs of students, so I think they're going to be very flexible in reaching these students as well."

READY FOR A CHANGE

As colleges adapt to older students, 20 they must consider the needs of those like Dannie Hill. Mr. Hill gave college a try decades ago after graduating from high school in Brooklyn. But taking classes while working full time at a fast-food restaurant to support his mother and two younger siblings proved to be too much, he says. So he dropped out. After a few years working as a messenger on Wall Street and in the purchasing department of a major financial-services company, he went into construction.

For the 20 or so years that Mr. Hill worked in construction, in New York City and Pennsylvania, he grew accustomed to wearing seven layers of clothing in the winter, lifting lumber or Sheetrock, framing walls, and lugging heavy materials around a work site. And though he took pride in working with his hands and seeing the buildings he helped construct, it exhausted him, and he didn't want to do it forever.

"It's hard on your back, hard on your joints, especially in the wintertime," says Mr. Hill, of Bethlehem, Pa. "It's four months of you against Mother Nature, just trying to get the job done."

Mr. Hill, who is 46, decided last year that he wanted a change—and that he needed a college education to make it happen.

"Unless I have certain training, I'm not going to be able to walk into an office," Mr. Hill says. "I want a job sitting down, at the computer, in the cubicle. Show me what papers to push. After being out in the field for so many years, I would like a sit-down job."

A single parent of a 14-year-old 25 son, Mr. Hill recently completed his first semester at Northampton

Community College, in Pennsylvania, where he took courses in philosophy and psychology two nights a week. He attends Northampton as part of Act 101, a state-funded program that assists lower-income adults going back to school.

The most difficult part of being back in school, Mr. Hill says, is the technology. "Kids are saying, 'Just download it here and put it on your MP3 player to your iPod to your flash drive.'...Oh, my goodness," he laughs, "there's just so much stuff you don't get into unless you're a student."

Despite the challenges that computers present, Mr. Hill says his most important tool still works just fine. "The most rewarding thing, I have to admit, was actually realizing that the brain has not stopped working and that you can obtain new knowledge even in this modern, technical world," he says. "And when I got my first A, that really said to me, wow, I can do this."

But the joy of high marks is tempered by a certain sense of urgency, he adds: "I don't have time to fail the class, because I don't have time to make it up. I have to get it right the first time."

Changes Ahead

Older students like Mr. Kearney, Mr. Hill, and Mr. Cox are emblematic of the no-nonsense approach that many adult students bring to their college experience, says Bernie Ronan, acting president of Mesa Community College, in Mesa, Ariz.

"They do not have the luxury nor the interest in going back to college for two or three or four years," Mr. Ronan says. "They need something they can get quick. So what that says to institutions like mine is that the traditional 16-week semester needs to be modified significantly so that individuals can come in and maximize learning in blocks that are more intense and more tailored."

Older students ask for flexible class schedules, credit for prior learning or work experience, and thorough career-placement counseling when the time comes to look for a job. They want the learning experience to create a seamless transition into a new career.

To achieve that, degree programs have to be a fair reflection of the job opportunities in a region, making partnerships between institutions, industry groups, and local economic-development agencies essential, says Mr. Ronan, whose college near Phoenix is one of the largest in the country.

Although community colleges are relatively nimble and responsive to the regions they serve, Mr. Ronan says, they have still been slow to react. But that is changing.

The sheer size of the baby-boomer cohort,° Mr. Ronan says, means that changes in curriculum and support services are mandatory. Simply tweaking a course offering here or there is not going to satisfy the demands of older students.

"The buzz that's created around this population is growing," Mr. Ronan says. "These people are just flowing out of one kind of employment and into another every day. The more that happens, the more you have to pay attention to it."

Many educators predict that the changes in curriculum and support services triggered by the baby boomers' arrival will benefit all students, regardless of their age. By responding to the needs of baby boomers now, they say, community colleges will have the opportunity to engage in institutionwide makeovers that will help them educate future generations more efficiently.

For Mr. Hill, the "honest concern" that administrators at his college have shown him makes all the difference, he says. "A person at my age has a lot of different boundaries when they start making decisions and changes in their lives," he says. "You really kind of need a program that's going to open their arms and roll out the red carpet and show them the way.

"Nobody is spoon-feeding me," he hastens to add. "But they make it accessible."

---

cohort: a group of individuals who belong to a particular demographic category. It often is used with respect to age (for example, the baby boomers).

RESPOND•

1. What argument(s) is Libby Sander making in this selection? What factors account for the situation that she is describing? To what extent are these older Americans becoming students as a matter of choice? As a matter of necessity? As Sander describes the situation, in what ways does social class intersect with the values that these students bring to school with them?

2. As noted, this article was written before the economic downturn of 2008. How has the economic situation in the United States changed since that time? Do you believe that these changes have had any influence on who is attending college or why? What evidence might you offer for your position?

3. What sorts of evidence does Sander present to support her claims? How might her article have been different if she had relied only on, let's say, statistics? How would the tone of the article, for example, have been different? (For a discussion of kinds of evidence, see Chapter 4 on logical appeals and Chapter 16 on what counts as evidence.)

4. How does the presence of older Americans on campus change the nature of college life? How might the life experiences of people like Russell Kearney, David Cox, and Dannie Hill influence their behavior as students? How might they influence the nature or content of class discussions, for example? What advantages might there be to having a student population that is not all of a single age cohort?

5. Conduct some research on the age demographics of the school you attend. You might, for example, investigate statistics about whether the average age of the student population has changed over the past few years or even decades. You might further try to determine whether the age of students is statistically related to their sex or to other demographic variables like ethnicity or social class. (All of the cases Sander discusses are men.) Another option for this assignment would be to interview two or more older students, asking what led them to come or return to school and what sorts of experiences they have had. If you are such a student, you may wish to document your own experiences or to interview similarly situated students to see how representative your experiences have been. An interesting issue with regard to this group of students is how schools refer to them; common labels are "returning students," "students older than average," or "nontraditional students." You might analyze the arguments made by each of these labels and others you collect from visiting the Web sites of various colleges and universities. Finally, you could document how your school seeks to welcome and accommodate these students. Here, you might wish to interview staff members who focus on

assisting them. Depending on what you have discovered and your own goals, in reporting your findings you may wish to **create a factual argument, an evaluation, or a proposal,** to name some possibilities. (For discussions of these categories of argument, see Chapters 8, 10, and 12, respectively.) Don't limit your options to a traditional written argument: creating a video based on interviews with several students might be an effective choice for this assignment.

▼ Edward F. Palm is dean for social sciences and humanities at Olympic College, a two-year community college in Bremerton, Washington. He served with the U.S. Marines in the Vietnam War. In this essay, posted in September 2008 on insidehighered.com, a Web site devoted to issues in postsecondary education, Palm offers advice to those who work as administrators, faculty, and staff at colleges and universities about how to help today's veterans integrate into college life and be successful students. The essay opens with two lines from "Tommy," a poem by the British writer Rudyard Kipling (1865–1936), who was awarded the Nobel Prize for Literature in 1907. "Tommy" was a term commonly used to refer to a British soldier, and the poem bitterly criticizes the way that British civilians dealt with enlisted soldiers at the time it was written. The phrase "thin red 'eroes" refers to especially heroic British soldiers from a particular battle in the Crimean War in 1854, while "blackguards," pronounced blaggards, refers to the then-common stereotype of British enlisted soldiers as vagabonds and criminals. As you read this selection, note the many ways that Palm establishes a credible and trustworthy ethos, and pay attention to how he structures this proposal argument.

The Veterans Are Coming! The Veterans Are Coming!

EDWARD F. PALM

> We aren't no thin red 'eroes, nor we aren't no blackguards too,
> But single men in barracks, most remarkable like you.
> —"Tommy," Rudyard Kipling (1892)

Picture it: Marine Corps boot camp, Parris Island,° summer, circa 1965.

Five weeks into the program, two Marine recruits find themselves on mess° duty, assigned to the pot shack, a small detached building out behind the mess hall proper. For the first time since arriving on the island, these two are out from under the watchful eyes of drill instructors and able to talk freely to one another. Up until then, a strict code of silence had been enforced, with recruits allowed to speak only to their drill instructors, and even then, only when spoken to.

Parris Island: a U.S. Marine base near Beaufort, South Carolina, that trains enlisted soldiers.

mess: military jargon referring to meals and the preparation of food.

Marines at Parris Island

955

As they dutifully scrub a never-ending series of pots large enough to cook missionaries in, they take advantage of their new-found freedom to compare notes about how they are enjoying their stay in this semi-tropical paradise.

"I'm glad I'm going to be out of here next week!" one of the recruits remarks, his voice echoing out from the bottom of the pot he was leaning into.

"Whadaya mean?" the other asks, reminding his comrade in suds that they   5
had three weeks to go until graduation.

"I know, but I'm only 16, and I turned myself in last week." [The minimum enlistment age has always been seventeen, with a parent's consent; eighteen-year-olds can enlist with or without a parent's blessing.]

"They said they'd have me out within a couple weeks," he adds, "in time to begin my senior year back at my old high school." "I got in so much trouble and was generally such a pain in the ass," he explains, "that my mother finally offered to lie about my age and sign the papers if I would go in the service. So that's what I did."

"You know," he admits, "I used to think school was the worst thing that ever happened to me. But when I get back in that classroom, they're going to have to beat me out with a stick!"

I was the other recruit, the one who was of age and who had no Get-Out-of-Parris-Island-Free card. I've often wished I had made a note of that underage recruit's name and hometown. He was almost a high school drop-out, and I would bet that he went on to become a doctor, lawyer, teacher, or some other sort of professional.

I too would emerge from the Marine Corps reborn as a serious student, but   10
my road to Damascus° lasted about four years and included a side trip to Vietnam. As one who has spent a good bit of his subsequent life in academic circles, I have often wished that we could treat many of today's high-school juniors to summer camp at Parris Island. If nothing else, these campers would certainly come back with the material for wondrous essays on how they spent their summer vacations. But, like my young friend in the pot shack, many would come back with a new-found appreciation for the opportunity to get an education.

road to Damascus: an unexpected experience that causes one's life to change course. The allusion is to the New Testament narrative of Saul, who persecuted Christians until while traveling to Damascus he had an experience that led to his sudden conversion to Christianity, after which he took the name Paul and became the faith's greatest advocate.

Former soldiers stock up on textbooks and other academic supplies in 1945. Up to $500 in tuition, fees, books, and materials for each academic year was provided free to veterans under the World War II GI Bill.

Palm offers a story about his past in the military and mentions his long-standing connection to academic life as ways of enhancing his authority to speak about how campuses should treat veterans. For more on building an ethos, see Chapter 3.

LINK TO P. 52 ....

Would that it were possible! But the good news is that today's colleges and universities are soon to enjoy a great influx of academically born-again,° highly motivated students. War, as I can personally attest, has a way of reordering one's priorities and values, and today's veterans will soon have access to the best education benefits available since the World War II GI Bill.° This new GI Bill, in fact, is even more generous than its "Good War"° predecessor. Veterans of the wars in Iraq and Afghanistan, as well as any veteran who just manages to get discharged honorably, will not only get tuition, fees, books, and a living allowance. They will also be able to transfer their educational benefits to their spouses or children. Either way, we in academe° stand to gain. The question is, are we really ready to welcome today's veterans into our midst?

We do, in fact, have an unfortunate history to overcome. Not everyone in America's ivory towers° was eager to roll out the red carpet for that first wave

born-again: having had a conversion experience (like Paul).

GI Bill: any act of Congress that provides support for veterans returning to civilian life. Such bills generally include scholarship support for vocational or higher education.

Good War: a phrase that sometimes is used to refer to World War II, an example of antonomasia (see Chapter 13).

academe: higher education.

ivory towers: a phrase that sometimes is used to refer to colleges and universities, an example of antonomasia (see Chapter 13). It often carries strong negative connotations.

of government subsidized veterans. The prevailing fear was that the democratization of higher education would inevitably result in the debasement of higher education. Academic standards have indeed slipped since World War II but for a whole host of cultural and societal reasons and not simply as a result of our efforts to accommodate returning GI's.

By the time I started college in the late '60s, the snobbery of the late '40s seemed to have been largely forgotten, but some older professors still seemed to feel the need to apologize for their predecessors. My own adviser, for instance, upon learning that I had been in Vietnam, hastened to assure me that he had been very much in favor of welcoming veterans to campus and that he felt we had "a lot to contribute." His reassurance seemed gratuitous° at the time. Vietnam veterans were facing a very different sort of suspicion. We were being repeatedly portrayed in the media as psychologically maimed and socially debilitated and, therefore, potentially dangerous. I cannot say that I directly and knowingly suffered from this stigma, but then again, I stopped volunteering the information that I had been in Vietnam.

gratuitous: uncalled for or unjustified.

Of course, popular support for the military is much stronger now than it was then, and today's veterans need not fear being viewed as objects of suspicion on campus. Or do they?

I have been concerned recently in finding promotional literature on upcoming symposia° that seem to link the need for "Threat Assessment" or "Behavior Intervention" teams with "serving" or "integrating" returning veterans. What next?   15

symposia: the plural of *symposium,* a formal word for a lecture or lecture series.

Should we expect to hear administrators sounding the alarm? *"The veterans are coming, the veterans are coming! Lock up the women and the livestock!"* Frankly, I worry that this is how certain right-wing critics of academe are going to interpret the linkage of threat assessment and veterans.

In all fairness, I have no doubt that these symposia are worthwhile, and I will take it on faith that the organizers are not viewing a potential influx of veterans as a threat to campus safety and simply want to be prepared to offer non-academic psychological counseling to any veteran who may need and want it. Most faculty and administrators, I would hope, realize that, of all the horrific campus shootings we have heard about in recent years, not one of the perpetrators was a military veteran.

This is not to dispute the need itself. In light of recent events, any campus that does not have an appropriately qualified team poised to intervene in cases of troubling or threatening behavior is putting itself at great risk. But to connect this need to the anticipated influx of veterans could prove to be a public relations nightmare and could actually provoke some of the very behavior we seek to avoid. One of the paradoxes of military history is that countries that have prepared for war have generally gotten it. Individual human nature can be equally paradoxical. People who are unjustly treated as objects of suspicion, out of anger and resentment, sometimes act out in ways that justify that suspicion. But that is the worst case scenario. *Rambo*° was only a figment of novelist David Morrell's imagination. The great majority of veteran students who feel mistrusted and misjudged will not act out violently; they will simply drop out.

Rambo: a novel by David Morrell about a Vietnam War veteran. It inspired a series of movies starring Sylvester Stallone.

This is likewise not to deny that many of today's combat veterans suffer from Post-traumatic Stress Disorder° or that campuses should not make counseling and other support services available to them. I can personally attest that a little combat goes a long way. But, again, the great majority of PTSD sufferers are not disruptive or violent and should not be viewed as such until or unless they provide reasonable cause. As for offering counseling, the advice of many a wise piano teacher regarding when to start children on lessons would seem to apply here as well: "when they ask for them."

Post-traumatic Stress Disorder (PTSD): a persistent severe anxiety following an extremely psychologically stressful experience. It often seriously disrupts a person's life.

How then should we view and treat today's returning veterans? A little sensitivity training may be in order. I am not a psychologist or a counselor myself, but as a veteran, I think I can offer five pieces of common sense advice that would go a long way toward striking the right tone as a veteran-friendly school.   20

First, treat veterans as you would any other student. Do not single them out for special attention. Individualized mailings or special meetings to explain the V.A.'s policies and the school's certification requirements may be in order, but guard against any suggestion that veterans will need any more special attention than any of today's students who may or may not be academically or culturally prepared for college. Remember that the average veteran has proven his or her ability to adapt to strange surroundings and to navigate his or her way through a more complicated bureaucracy than the average academic could endure.

Second, do not thank veterans you don't know for their service. Most people who have served had mixed motives for enlisting in the first place and complicated feelings about the experience of having served, especially in combat. If my own post-Vietnam experience is any indication—and I think it is—it takes many veterans a long time to sort out how they feel about what they've been through and whether it was worthwhile—especially if the country remains divided about whether the cause was noble and the war necessary. To thank a veteran you don't know for his or her service is to put that veteran on the spot. It assumes an ideological and political kinship that may or may not exist. I know it makes me uncomfortable. Keep in mind as well that some will doubt your sincerity, wondering if what you're really saying is, "I'm glad you went so that I [or my son or daughter] didn't have to go." Wait until you know a veteran well—including how he or she really feels about having served—before deciding to offer your thanks.

Third, do not shy away from any political or social issues appropriate to your class. While they may have conformed to military discipline long enough and well enough to earn honorable discharges, veterans are not monolithic° in their attitudes, ideals, and values. Expect them to be just as open-minded and diverse in their opinions and viewpoints as any other group of today's students. Conversely, expect them to resent unfounded assumptions about their politics and personal beliefs.

monolithic: uniform and rigid, like a large block of stone.

By the same token, if you have never been in the military, do not assume that you really know what it is like and what it is all about. Even more important, reserve judgment about whether academe really is the superior institution. Having been both a military officer and an academic, I have learned two things: First, academics are no more open-minded than anyone else; they are just better at articulating and defending their prejudices. Second, I have known Marine colonels who are more collegial and collaborative than commanding, and I have known college presidents who are more commanding than collegial and collaborative. Do not approach today's veterans as "people who were lost and now are found."

Fourth, when it comes to what they did in the war, don't ask; wait for them 25 to decide if and when they want to tell. The experience of combat is largely ineffable.° It cannot be adequately expressed or shared with people who have not experienced it, and most who have are conflicted about it. If they do choose to share, do not judge. Remember that those who have not been there

ineffable: unable to be captured or expressed in words.

do not share the same frame of reference. Hemingway° had a phrase for it: "a way you'll never be." Remember as well that a pretentious moral empathy can be just as infuriating as an uninformed disapproval. In general, veterans prefer to let other veterans do the listening. They know they'll understand.

Finally, expect veterans to do well. Just as the expectation that someone will behave badly can create a self-fulfilling prophecy, greeting someone with the expectation that he or she will excel can achieve the desired result. That same undergraduate adviser who puzzled me with his patronizing comment about supporting the first G.I. Bill more than redeemed himself later by soliciting my comments in class when we were discussing a story set in a World War II training camp, Philip Roth's° "Defender of the Faith." I was able to clarify some of the military practices and customs on which the story turns, and my professor stoked my self-confidence by telling the class that "he speaks from an interesting perspective; he was in the military himself."

Such made-to-order opportunities to bring a particular student in, admittedly, do not come along every day. And, with older students in general, instructors always need to guard against appearing to be patronizing or condescending. But, in general, we should expect veterans to be as highly motivated and appreciative of getting a second chance at an education as was that underage Marine back in the pot shack.

(Ernest) Hemingway (1899–1961): an American writer and Nobel Prize winner.

Philip Roth (b. 1933): an American writer and Pulitzer Prize winner. "Defender of the Faith" involves a Jewish military officer who tries to avoid being manipulated by another Jewish soldier into giving him special treatment because of their shared ethnicity.

RESPOND●

1. In what ways is Palm's essay a proposal argument? What does he propose? What situation leads him to offer his proposal? How appropriate do you find Palm's advice? (For a discussion of proposal arguments, see Chapter 12.)

2. The first half of Palm's essay is based on personal experiences. In what ways does Palm use these experiences to construct logical arguments? Ethical arguments? Emotional arguments? (For a discussion of these kinds of arguments, see Chapters 4, 3, and 2, respectively.) An interesting way to think about this question would be to consider what the essay would be like if it began with paragraph 15.

3. One resource that writers of arguments have is their readers' knowledge of earlier texts, events, and situations. By referring to specific things that readers know, writers communicate more than they

explicitly say. (*Intertextuality* is the technical label for this relationship, especially when it involves relationships between written texts or text-like things, such as films.) Palm takes advantage of this fact throughout this essay. How, for example, does an understanding of the allusion in the title, the poem by Kipling, the New Testament story of Paul, the *Rambo* novel and the movies it inspired, and the Roth short story strengthen and enrich Palm's argument? How does the use of such intertextuality contribute to Palm's ethos? What is missed by readers who do not have knowledge of these texts, events, or situations?

4. Giving advice to others, especially people you do not know well, is always a challenging rhetorical task. How well does Palm do? Consider the tone that he uses in the final third of the essay, where he gives "five pieces of common sense advice" (paragraph 20). How would you characterize it? Do you find the tone effective? Why or why not?

5. Track down Palm's original essay on the Internet, and read the comments that readers posted in response to it. Choose two that you find especially effective—that make clear, appropriate arguments in a concise fashion—and **write a rhetorical analysis** of them in which you explain and demonstrate why they represent effective arguments. (For a discussion of rhetorical analyses, see Chapter 5.)

6. Do research on veterans and higher education. Depending on your interest and the school that you attend, this research could take several forms—historical research into how the original GI Bill affected American society, including its class system; interviews of veterans of different generations who returned to school after completing military service or veterans from the Iraq and Afghanistan wars who currently attend your school; interviews of school staff or administrators who help veterans return to school; or research about how your school helps returning veterans. **Write an essay** in which you present your findings.

▼ *Walter Benn Michaels is currently a professor of English at the University of Illinois at Chicago, where he teaches literary theory and American literature. His influential essay "Against Theory," coauthored with Steven Knapp, was published in 1982, and his books include* The Shape of the Signifier: 1967 to the End of History *(2004). This selection is an excerpt from the introduction to his most recent book,* The Trouble with Diversity: How We Learned to Love Identity and Ignore Inequality *(2006). Michaels begins this selection with an extended discussion of a literary text, F. Scott Fitzgerald's* The Great Gatsby, *one of the most famous American novels, which was published in 1925. Its central character, Jay Gatsby, seeks to win back Daisy Buchanan, a beautiful woman whom he had met and courted years earlier when he was a poor soldier but who had married a man fron an "old money" background like her own. After meeting her, Gatsby had changed his name to cover up his German immigrant roots at a time when people of most immigrant backgrounds were not fully accepted in elite society. He had also become wealthy, but his money was "new money"; though readers never learn exactly where it comes from, its sources are clearly disreputable and likely illegal. Many scholars now see* The Great Gatsby *as one of the best literary depictions and critiques of American life and values. While you read this selection, consider why we chose to end a chapter on diversity with this selection.*

The Trouble with Diversity: How We Learned to Love Identity and Ignore Inequality

WALTER BENN MICHAELS

"The rich are different from you and me" is a famous remark supposedly made by F. Scott Fitzgerald to Ernest Hemingway,° although what made it famous—or at least made Hemingway famously repeat it—was not the remark itself but Hemingway's reply: "Yes, they have more money." In other words, the point of the story, as Hemingway told it, was that the rich really aren't very different from you and me. Fitzgerald's mistake, he thought, was that he mythologized or sentimentalized the rich, treating them as if they were a different kind of person instead of the same kind of person with more money. It

Ernest Hemingway (1899–1961): an American writer and Nobel Prize winner. His first novel was *The Sun Also Rises* (1926).

963

Robert Cohn: a Jewish character in *The Sun Also Rises* who develops an inferiority complex as a result of his outsider status.

kike: an ethnic slur referring to Jews that was widely used in the early twentieth century.

was as if, according to Fitzgerald, what made rich people different was not what they *had*—their money—but what they *were*, "a special glamorous race."

To Hemingway, this difference—between what people owned and what they were—seemed obvious, and it was also obvious that the important thing was what they were. No one cares much about Robert Cohn's° money in *The Sun Also Rises*, but everybody feels the force of the fact the he's a "race-conscious" "little kike."° And whether or not it's true that Fitzgerald sentimentalized the rich and made them more glamorous than they really were, it's certainly true that he, like Hemingway, believed that the fundamental differences—the ones that really mattered—ran deeper than the question of how much money you had. That's why in *The Great Gatsby*, the fact that Gatsby has made a great deal of money isn't quite enough to win Daisy Buchanan back. Rich as he has become, he's still "Mr. Nobody from Nowhere," not Jay Gatsby but Jimmy Gatz. The change of name is what matters. One way to look at *The Great Gatsby* is as a story about a poor boy who makes good, which is to say, a poor boy who becomes rich—the so-called American dream. But *Gatsby* is not really about someone who makes a lot of money; it is instead about someone who tries and fails to change who he is. Or, more precisely, it's about someone who pretends to be something he's not; it's about Jimmy Gatz pretending to be Jay Gatsby. If, in the end, Daisy Buchanan is very different from Jimmy Gatz, it's not because she's rich and he isn't (by the end, he is) but because Fitzgerald treats them as if they really do belong to different races, as if poor boys who made a lot of money were only "passing" as rich. "We're all white here," someone says, interrupting one of Tom Buchanan's racist outbursts. Jimmy Gatz isn't quite white enough.

Robert Redford played the lead in the 1974 film The Great Gatsby.

What's important about *The Great Gatsby*, then, is that it takes one kind of difference (the difference between the rich and the poor) and redescribes it as another kind of difference (the difference between the white and the not-so-white). To put the point more generally, books like *The Great Gatsby* (and there have been a great many of them) give us a vision of our society divided into races rather than into economic classes. And this vision has proven to be extraordinarily attractive. Indeed, it's been so attractive that the vision has survived even though what we used to think were the races have not. In the 1920s, racial science° was in its heyday; now very few scientists believe that there are any such things as races. But many of those who are quick to remind us that there are no biological entities called races are even quicker to remind us that races have not disappeared; they should just be understood as social entities instead. And these social entities have turned out to be remarkably tenacious, both in ways we know are bad and in ways we have come to think of as good. The bad ways involve racism, the inability or refusal to accept people who are different from us. The good ways involve just the opposite: embracing difference, celebrating what we have come to call diversity.

Indeed, in the United States, the commitment to appreciating diversity emerged out of the struggle against racism, and the word *diversity* itself began to have the importance it does for us today in 1978 when, in *Bakke v. Board of Regents*,° the Supreme Court ruled that taking into consideration the race of an applicant to the University of California (in this case, it was the medical school at UC Davis) was an acceptable practice if it served "the interest of diversity." The point the Court was making here was significant. It was not asserting that preference in admissions could be given, say, to black people because they had previously been discriminated against. It was saying instead that universities had a legitimate interest in taking race into account in exactly the same way they had a legitimate interest in taking into account what part of the country an applicant came from or what his or her nonacademic interests were. They had, in other words, a legitimate interest in having a "diverse student body," and racial diversity, like geographic diversity, could thus be an acceptable goal for an admissions policy.

Two things happened here. First, even though the concept of diversity was 5 not originally connected with race (universities had long sought diverse student bodies without worrying about race at all), the two now came to be firmly associated. When universities publish their diversity statistics today, they're not talking about how many kids come from Oregon. My university—the University of Illinois at Chicago—is ranked as one of the most diverse in the country, but well over half the students in it come from Chicago. What

racial science: the scientific investigation of and debate about matters related to race. The field often attracts those who are seeking to find evidence for the existence of distinct races and for ranking them in a hierarchy, though many scientists studying these issues disavow both aims.

Bakke v. Board of Regents: *Regents of the University of California v. Bakke,* a 1978 U.S. Supreme Court decision. Bakke, a white man, claimed that he had been discriminated against in violation of federal and state laws when he was not admitted to the UC-Davis medical school in 1973 and 1974 even though nonwhite candidates with significantly lower test scores were. In a 5–4 decision, the Court ruled that quota systems for admissions are illegal but that schools can consider race as one of many factors in admissions decisions. (Subsequent Supreme Court decisions have largely maintained this position.) Bakke was later admitted to and graduated from the UC-Davis medical school; his name and this case continue to be associated with the notion of reverse discrimination.

end run: a football play in which the person carrying the ball tries to run around the end of the opposing team's line. As a figure of speech, it is any action that tries to get around opponents or difficulties without confronting them directly, often through the use of trickery.

Michaels offers several different arguments, but perhaps the richest and most complex is his causal argument that traces the effects of our traditional thinking about diversity. For more on how causal arguments work, see Chapter 11.

LINK TO P. 335

the rankings measure is the number of African Americans and Asian Americans and Latinos we have, not the number of Chicagoans.

And, second, even though the concept of diversity was introduced as a kind of end run° around the historical problem of racism (the whole point was that you could argue for the desirability of a diverse student body without appealing to the history of discrimination against blacks and so without getting accused by people like Alan Bakke of reverse discrimination against whites), the commitment to diversity became deeply associated with the struggle against racism. Indeed, the goal of overcoming racism, which had sometimes been identified as the goal of creating a "color-blind" society, was now reconceived as the goal of creating a diverse, that is, a color-conscious, society.[1] Instead of trying to treat people as if their race didn't matter, we would not only recognize but celebrate racial identity. Indeed, race has turned out to be a gateway drug for all kinds of identities, cultural, religious, sexual, even medical. To take what may seem like an extreme case, advocates for the disabled now urge us to stop thinking of disability as a condition to be "cured" or "eliminated" and to start thinking of it instead on the model of race: we don't think black people should want to stop being black; why do we assume the deaf want to hear?[2]

The general principle here is that our commitment to diversity has redefined the opposition to discrimination as the appreciation (rather than the elimination) of difference. So with respect to race, the idea is not just that racism is a bad thing (which of course it is) but that race itself is a good thing. Indeed, we have become so committed to the attractions of race that (as I've already suggested above and as we'll see at greater length in chapter 1) our enthusiasm for racial identity has been utterly undiminished by scientific skepticism about whether there is any such thing. Once the students in my American literature classes have taken a course in human genetics, they just stop talking about black and white and Asian races and start talking about black and European and Asian cultures instead. We love race, and we love the identities to which it has given birth.

The fundamental point of this book is to explain why this is true. The argument, in its simplest form, will be that we love race—we love identity— because we don't love class.[3] We love thinking that the differences that divide us are not the differences between those of us who have money and those who don't but are instead the differences between those of us who are black and those who are white or Asian or Latino or whatever. A world where some of us don't have enough money is a world where the differences between us present a problem: the need to get rid of inequality or to justify it. A world where some of us are black and some of us are white—or biracial or Native American or transgendered—is a world where the differences between us present a solution: appreciating our diversity. So we like to talk about the differences we can appreciate, and we don't like to talk about the ones we can't. Indeed, we don't even like to acknowledge that they exist. As survey after survey has shown, Americans are very reluctant to identify themselves as belonging to the lower class and even more reluctant to identify themselves as belonging to the upper class. The class we like is the middle class.

But the fact that we all like to think of ourselves as belonging to the same class doesn't, of course, mean that we actually do belong to the same class. In reality, we obviously and increasingly don't. "The last few decades," as *The Economist*° puts it, "have seen a huge increase in inequality in America."[4] The rich *are* different from you and me, and one of the ways they're different is that they're getting richer and we're not. And while it's not surprising that most of the rich and their apologists on the intellectual right are unperturbed by this development, it is at least a little surprising that the intellectual left has managed to remain almost equally unperturbed. Giving priority to issues like affirmative action and committing itself to the celebration of difference, the intellectual left has responded to the increase in economic inequality by insisting on the importance of cultural identity. So for thirty years, while the gap between the rich and the poor has grown larger, we've been urged to respect people's identities—as if the problem of poverty would be solved if we just appreciated the poor. From the economic standpoint, however, what poor people want is not to contribute to diversity but to minimize their contribution to it—they want to stop being poor. Celebrating the diversity of American life has become the American left's way of accepting their poverty, of accepting inequality.

I have three goals in writing this book. The first is to show how our current notion of cultural diversity—trumpeted as the repudiation of racism and biological essentialism°—in fact grew out of and perpetuates the very concepts it congratulates itself on having escaped. The second is to show how and why the American love affair with race—especially when you can dress race up as culture—has continued and even intensified. Almost everything we say about culture (that the significant differences between us are cultural, that such differences should be respected, that our cultural heritages should be perpetuated, that there's a value in making sure that different cultures survive) seems to me mistaken, and this book will try to show why. And the third goal is—by shifting our focus from cultural diversity to economic equality—to help alter the political terrain of contemporary American intellectual life.

10

The Economist: a weekly news-magazine based in London and focusing on international affairs. Its target audience is affluent and highly educated.

essentialism: the assumption that all members of a category are alike or share similar, if not identical, characteristics. Essentialist arguments take the form of "All X's are Y" and often appear in arguments about social difference. Examples include claims that gay men aren't athletic, straight men aren't empathetic, and people from a specific ethnic group are (or are not) intelligent.

NOTES

1. Consciousness of color was, it goes without saying, always central to American society insofar as that society was a committedly racist one. The relevant change here—marked rather than produced by *Bakke*—involved (in the wake of both the successes and failures of the civil rights movement) the emergence of color consciousness as an antiracist position. The renewed black nationalism in the 1960s is one standard example of this transition, but the phenomenon is more general. You can get a striking sense of it by reading John Okada's *No-No Boy*, a novel about the Japanese Americans who answered no to the two loyalty questions on the questionnaire administered to them at the relocation centers they were sent to during World War II. The novel itself, published in 1957, is a pure product of the civil rights movement, determined to overcome race (and ignore class) in the imagination of a world in which people are utterly individualized—"only people." It began to become important, however, as an expression of what Frank Chin, in an article written in 1976 and included as an appendix to the current edition, calls "yellow soul," and when it's taught today in Asian American literature classes, reading it counts toward the fulfillment of diversity requirements that Okada himself would not have understood.

2. Simi Linton, *Claiming Disability* (New York: New York University Press, 1998), 96.

3. The relations between race and class have been an important topic in American writing at least since the 1930s, and in recent years they have, in the more general form of the relations between identity and inequality, been the subject of an ongoing academic discussion. Some of the more notable contributions include *Culture and Equality* (2000) by Brian Barry, *Redistribution or Recognition* (2003), an exchange between Nancy Fraser and Axel Honneth, and *The Debate on Classes* (1990), featuring an important essay by Erik Olin Wright and a series of exchanges about that essay. And in my particular field of specialization, American literature, Gavin Jones is about to publish an important and relevant book called *American Hunger*. I cite these texts in particular because, in quite different ways, they share at least some of my skepticism about the value of identity. And I have myself written in an academic context about these issues, most recently in *The Shape of the Signifier* (2004). *The Trouble with Diversity* is in part an effort to make some of the terms of the discussion more vivid to a more general audience. More important, however, it is meant to advance a particular position in that discussion, an argument that the concept of identity is incoherent and that its continuing success is a function of its utility to neoliberalism.

4. *The Economist*, December 29, 2004.

RESPOND •

1. What, for Walter Benn Michaels, is the real issue that American society needs to confront? How, for him, does defining *diversity* in terms of a celebration of difference, especially ethnic difference, prevent Americans from both seeing the real issue and doing anything about it? In what ways does our society's focus on ethnic and cultural diversity necessarily perpetuate racism and biological essentialism (paragraph 10)?

2. Why and how are these issues relevant to discussions of diversity on campus in general? On the campus you attend?

3. Later in this introduction, Michaels, a liberal, points out ways in which both conservatives and liberals in American public life, first, focus on racial or ethnic differences rather than issues of social inequality and, second, benefit from doing so. In a 2004 essay, "Diversity's False Solace," he notes:

   > [W]e like policies like affirmative action not so much because they solve the problem of racism but because they tell us that racism is the problem we need to solve. . . . It's not surprising that universities of the upper middle class should want their students to feel comfortable [as affirmative action programs enable and encourage them to do]. What is surprising is that diversity should have become the hallmark of liberalism.

   Analyze the argument made in this paragraph as a Toulmin argument. (For a discussion of Toulmin argumentation, see Chapter 7.)

4. How would you characterize Michaels's argument? In what ways is it an argument of fact? A definitional argument? An evaluative argument? A causal argument? A proposal? (For a discussion of these kinds of arguments, see Chapters 8–12.)

5. This chapter has provided many perspectives on an issue that is hotly debated on American campuses and in American society at large—diversity. What should a diverse campus look like, and why? Should diversity be something that schools strive for? If so, what kinds of diversity? Why? **Write a proposal essay** in which you define and justify the sort(s) of diversity, if any, that your school should aim for. Seek to draw widely on the perspectives that you've read in this chapter—in terms of topics discussed and also approaches to those or other topics that you might consider. (For a discussion of proposals, see Chapter 12.)

27
What Are You Working For?

If you're reading this introduction, odds are that you have reasons for doing so and much broader reasons for being in school in the first place. Your family and friends assume that you're working toward something—perhaps a grade or a diploma. In this chapter, the selections encourage you to engage in deliberative arguments with your classmates and yourself about your long-term motivations and expectations. You'll examine the goals that you are working to reach after you leave college and enter a world where work—in the narrow sense of making a living—will in many ways be one of your primary activities.

The chapter opens with two stories from interviews for StoryCorps, a project that records narratives from the lives of ordinary Americans; each deals with work in a different way. Next, Lisa W. Foderaro reports on the effect of the recent economic downturn on teenagers, especially those with well-to-do parents, many of whom are reducing allowances and encouraging their children to find part-time jobs. In an op-ed essay, Charles Murray asks whether members of what he terms the "Obama generation" should drop out of college because of the mismatch that he sees between what happens there and what the world of work requires; readers of the essay respond, and most of them argue for staying in school.

The following three selections consider whether education pays off in later financial rewards. The U.S. Bureau of Labor Statistics presents statistics showing that it does, but in a blog posting, Laurence Shatkin cries, "Not so fast!" and explains why the department's statistics don't tell the whole story. In contrast, an excerpt from a report by Sandy Baum and Jennifer Ma, writing for the College Board, provides what seem like endless statistics extolling the benefits of a college education for individuals and for society as well. (Did you know that college-educated people are more likely than less educated people to give blood, to vote, and not to smoke?)

An excerpt from Alesia Montgomery's ethnographic study of a family where three members work in the high-tech industry in Silicon Valley demonstrates how technology has shifted the meaning of work and home. While ethnographers tend to avoid drawing broad generalizations, her historical survey and description of this family remind us that home is no longer a shelter from the problems of the world of work. The final selection in the chapter, an excerpt from Stewart Friedman's book *Total Leadership: Be a Better Leader, Have a Richer Life* and a transcript of an Amazon.com video about it argue that folks who think in terms of a balance between work and life commit a logical fallacy. Friedman proposes a different way of defining the problem and finding a solution, one that we hope is useful to you now and in the future.

Students are in college for various reasons, and your immediate focus may not be the world of work that awaits you after graduation. Yet as the selections in this chapter remind you, many employers and researchers who study higher education see college as preparation for work. You are learning useful information, but you are also developing habits of work and mind that should serve you well in the future. With luck, these selections may help you define your own goals so that you'll know what you're working for now and later.

▼ We open this chapter on education and work with two stories that were part of the StoryCorps Project, an award-winning effort to record the stories of everyday Americans talking to someone inside the mobile StoryCorps booth. Two CDs are created for each story told, one for the storyteller and one for the American Folklife Center at the Library of Congress so that future generations will be able to hear contemporary Americans talk about things that matter to them. Some 10,000 stories had been collected by 2007, and excerpts from forty-nine of them were chosen for the 2007 volume Listening Is an Act of Love: A Celebration of American Life from the StoryCorps Project, edited by Dave Isay, the founder of StoryCorps and its parent company, Sound Portraits Productions. The two interviews included here are from the chapter "Work and Dedication." The first, recorded in July 2005 in New Town, North Dakota, is an interview with Monica Mayer, a physician who is a family practitioner on the Fort Berthold Reservation in New Town. The interviewer is Dr. Mayer's cousin, Spencer Wilkinson Jr., who is also her patient. The second interview was recorded in Pittsburgh in June 2006 and features Ken Kobus, who is telling his friend Ron Baraff about his working life in a steel mill. Both of these interviews tell stories of parents' influence on their children's choice of career. Give some thought to how your parents or caregivers have influenced the hopes that you have for your working life.

Dr. Monica Mayer, 45, Interviewed by Her Cousin and Patient, Spencer Wilkinson Jr., 39

DAVE ISAY, EDITOR

Dr. Monica Mayer and Spencer Wilkinson Jr.

half-breed: an offensive term describing someone who is of mixed ethnic heritage, especially someone with one American Indian parent and one parent of European origin.

Recorded in New Town, North Dakota

Spencer Wilkinson Jr.: What made you choose to pursue a career in medicine?

Dr. Monica Mayer: My father was full-blood German, and my mother was full-blood Indian, and it was pretty tough in the sixties growing up half-breed,° so to speak. My father didn't have any sons, so he raised us like little boys. And I must have been in about seventh grade, and I wasn't doing well in school. In fact, I was maybe getting Cs, and I'm the oldest of three girls. So my dad packed us up in his pickup truck and took us out to his old homestead land, which is about eighteen miles north of New Town, in the middle of nowhere. Well, New Town's kind of in the middle of nowhere, but, I mean, this is *really* in the middle of nowhere. And he packed us some lunches and some water. He dropped us off out there at seven or eight in the morning and said he wanted all the rocks picked up and put in the northwest corner in one big pile and that he'd come back that night to pick us up, and it had better be done.

So there we were, working hard all day, and then he comes back. And we're dirty, stinky, sweaty, sore muscles, crying. My dad pulls up, and he gets out of the pickup. And we must have been a sight to see. I looked at him and said, since I was the oldest—my two younger sisters are hiding behind me— "Dad, we don't think this is fair we have to work this hard." And I remember him saying, "Is that right? Well, do you think I like working like this everyday?" "No." He said, "You know, your mother said you girls don't like school and you're not doing very well. So I talked to Momma, and we decided that you're going to come out here and work like this so your hind ends will get used to how your life's going to be when you get older." So I said, "Well, if we got good grades, do we have to come out here and work this hard?" And he said, "No. That's the deal."

Well, he didn't have to bust my head twice up against the brick wall. My two younger sisters and I were laughing about that, because they remember that particular day exactly the way I remembered it. One day of hard labor changed everything.

July 29, 2005

Today, Monica Mayer practices family medicine on the Fort Berthold reservation in New Town, North Dakota. Her sister Holly is the Director of Public Health Nurses on the reservation, and her sister Renee is Tribal Social Services Director.

Ken Kobus, 58, Tells His Friend Ron Baraff, 42, about Making Steel

DAVE ISAY, EDITOR

RECORDED IN PITTSBURGH, PENNSYLVANIA

Ken Kobus: Both of my grandfathers worked in the mill. My father started in 1937. I started about twenty-nine years later, in 1966, at the same plant. I was always enthralled with steel from the time I was a very young person. I always wanted to go into the mill, but I was always too young to go. And finally when I turned sixteen, I told my dad that he had to take me—and I bugged him until he did.

These personal narratives about work are appealing in part because of the bridges they build through emotional arguments. For more about how pathos works in arguments, see Chapter 2.

LINK TO P. 38

Ken Kobus (l.) and Ron Baraff (r.)

You look at it from his point of view, he was a union guy. And for him to come to the mill on his day off, he had to take a bit of harassment for it: "What the heck are you doing here?" My dad had straight dark black hair; his nickname was Crow. When we finally got into the mill, they said, "Crow, what are you doing here? It's your day off! Are you crazy?" At the same time, though, he was very proud. He thought enough to bring his son into the place that he worked.

When I went into the shop, I was actually a little bit frightened. All these things were moving back and forth, and I was afraid I was going to get run over and didn't know where to move. My dad just walked straight through like nothing was going on. Steelmaking is just beautiful. It's unimaginable beauty. When you're charging a furnace, you get all these sparkles off of the iron, and so you just see thousands and thousands of sparkles.

We proceeded into the plant, and my dad went over and talked to the boss of the shop. I found out that they were going to tap a furnace. I remember it like yesterday, although it's now forty-two years later. We went over to the furnace, and I found out that they were going to let me tap the furnace. When we went over, a lot of the guys started gathering around. Even though I was sixteen, I recognized that something was strange. This probably is not the way it is normally done. But I didn't really care because I was going to get to tap the furnace, and if these guys want to watch, fine with me.

There was a battery box with a switch and a little button that you used to   5
set off the dynamite charge and the foreman said, "When I tell you to, flip the switch; and when I tell you to tap, press the button." And my dad came to me and says, "I don't care what you do," he says, "don't let go of that battery box."

So came time and they blew the siren for "all clear" and then waited a little bit just to make sure that nobody's below, because when the steel lets loose, sparks go everywhere. It came time to flip the switch, and then it came time to press the button. The dynamite blew up and made such a god-awful sound, and there was smoke and fire and sparks everywhere. And then the steel started running into the spout, and there were flames shooting up and out of the spout, and I jumped up in the air. I must have jumped three, four feet in the air, I was so scared. And then I knew why all these guys were around. They started laughing, because it was such a sight to see somebody so scared. I was the show for that day, and they had their good laugh on me.

But it was spectacular. The steel started running and went into the ladle. When it hits the bottom of the ladle, it goes *splunch* and makes all kinds of different sounds that you never expect. What do you think happens when 2,900-degree steel hits finely powdered coal that's lying in the bottom of the ladle? Well, it creates a fire that you just can't imagine. The fire almost hit the roof of the shop, and it was eighty feet above you, and you're standing right beside this ladle of running steel. And the supervisor is not telling the guys to run away; he's telling them, "Throw some bags here" and "Throw some this there." There's all these people moving around, and there's all this heat, and it's just an unforgettable experience.

Two years later I started working in the mills. I worked in the foundry. I was the third helper on the electric furnace, and I worked various jobs in the steel foundry.

Ron Baraff: If you could choose any job in the steel mill, what would it be?

Ken: Oh, I'd choose my dad's job. He was a first helper, in charge of an open-hearth furnace. To face a furnace is just—It's hard to describe because when you open a door of the furnace, it's at over 3,000 degrees, and your whole body's standing in front of a door opened to hell. It has effects on your body; it stretches your skin. And you watch cold steel, scrap metal, being put into there, and you just watch it become more and more red and red and red, and then it just sort of like disappears and falls apart. You see huge, huge boiling steel—it's not water, it's steel. And you see these bubbles and these balls flopping out and it's just like a volcano. You're looking in a volcano. 10

I know it stuck with my father for all his life. I mean, when he was dying, he couldn't talk. He had throat cancer, and so they took his voice box out— and he was in a lot of pain. I was in the hospice, and I was watching him in the bed once and the doctor came in. He saw that I was looking at my dad, and my dad was lying on his back and his hands up in the air, and he was turning and manipulating. The doctor says, "I wonder what the heck he's doing." Because, you know, he did it all the time. He would be lying on his back, and he would be doing this stuff, and they had no clue as to what he was doing. I said, "He's making steel." I could see what he was doing. He was opening furnace doors, and he was adjusting the gas on the furnace and the draft. I could see. The doctor was amazed. To the day he died that's what he lived: steelmaking. And that's quite an impression. And it's made an impression on me, too. I could always recommend to somebody to watch steel being born. It's just fantastic. It's a spectacle that is unreal.

I've been working for forty years, and it's just long, hard work. A lot of times I can't imagine how the men bear up against it. The guys knew how to work and could face up to the job and just were so strong. I was proud to be around many guys that could do that, that wanted to do that, and had pride in doing that. They took pride in what they did. And they knew that people looked at them with honor. They made steel.

June 20, 2006

RESPOND

1. Although we generally don't think of stories as arguments, they all express points of view. (In fact, everything is an argument, if we believe the title of this book.) Summarize the arguments made by each of these narratives.

2. What does each of these narratives teach us about work and dedication?

3. In her interview, does Monica Mayer sound like a doctor as she talks? Why or why not? Is her language appropriate to the context and audience? Why or why not? Would her story have been different if she had used more formal language? Would it have been as effective? Why or why not? (For a discussion of style in arguments, see Chapter 13.)

4. One of Ken Kobus's arguments is that "steelmaking is just beautiful" (paragraph 3). Was such a claim surprising for you? Why? What evidence does Kobus offer? For him, what is the nature of the beauty of steelmaking? (It is, for example, not like the beauty of flowers in spring or a child's face.) In what ways is his discussion of this issue a definitional argument? (For a discussion of definitional arguments, see Chapter 9.)

5. Interview someone you know about the job that they hold or hope to hold. One of the appendices to *Listening Is an Act of Love*, "Favorite StoryCorps Questions," lists these questions under the heading "Work":

   What do you do for a living?
   Tell me about how you got into your line of work.
   Do you like your job?
   What did you want to be when you grew up?
   What lessons has your work life taught you?
   Do you plan on retiring? If so, when? How do you feel about it?
   Do you have any favorite stories about your work life?

   These questions may help you get started. You might interview a family member or someone else who has been influential in your own thinking about your career goals, or you might interview someone who has a job that you think you'd never want. After you've completed the interview, **write an essay** in which you present what you learned, creating a portrait of the person from the perspective of her or his work life (or the goals that she or he has for work in the future). Parts of the argument will likely be factual, and others will be definitional, evaluative, or causal. The shape of the argument will depend on what you learn in the interview and your own goals in writing. Remember that Chapter 16 offers some additional tips on interviews.

▼ *The economic downturn that began in the middle of 2008 had far-reaching consequences for nearly all Americans, rich or poor, who found that their lives had changed in a very short period of time. Predictions as we write in early 2009 assume that even after the downturn ends, its consequences will be with us in many ways for a long time. This article, which appeared in the New York Times in December 2008, explores the effects of the downturn on teenagers in terms of changes in their lives at the time and in their future options. Lisa W. Foderaro has written for the Times for over two decades. She frequently writes about issues related to higher education and to the New York City metropolitan area. (This article appeared in the "New York" section of the national edition of the Times.) As you read this article, think back to late 2008, and reflect on what your life and the lives of your family and friends were like at the time, whether things have gotten better or worse, and what the consequences of the economic situation have been or will be for your working future.*

The Well-to-Do Get Less So, and Teenagers Feel the Crunch

LISA W. FODERARO

Jodi Hamilton began her senior year of high school in Woodcliff Lake, N.J., this fall on the usual prosperous footing. Her parents were providing a weekly allowance of $100 and paying for private Pilates classes, as well as a physics tutor who reported once a week to their 4,000-square-foot home.

But in October, Jodi's mother lost her job managing a huge dental practice in the Bronx, then landed one closer to home that requires more hours for less money. Pilates was dropped, along with takeout sushi dinners, and Jodi's allowance, which covers lunch during the week, slipped to $60. Instead of having a tutor, Jodi has become a tutor, earning $150 a week through that and baby-sitting.

"I just thought it would be responsible to get a job and have my own money so my parents didn't have to pay for everything," said Jodi, who is 17. "I always like to be saving up for something that I have my eye on—a ring, a necklace, a handbag."

It is impossible to quantify how many affluent parents have trimmed allowances in recent months—or how many of their offspring, in turn, have sought either formal employment or odd jobs. But interviews with dozens of teenagers, parents, educators, and employers suggest that many youngsters from well-to-do families seem to have found a new work ethic as the economic crisis that has jeopardized their parents' jobs and investments has also led to less spending money for Saturday night movies or binges at Abercrombie & Fitch.

After focusing on studies and 5 résumé-polishing extracurricular activities in recent years, these teenagers are job-seeking at the worst possible time, however, with employment of 16- to 19-year-olds at its lowest level in 61 years as out-of-work adults compete for low-paying positions.

"We have the Mall at Short Hills a stone's throw away, and there are a load of kids who applied," said Nancy Siegel, head counselor at Millburn High School in New Jersey. "But they are not finding the market welcoming."

977

Teenage Workers

Teenagers in middle-class families are the most likely to be working. But unemployment among young workers is high.

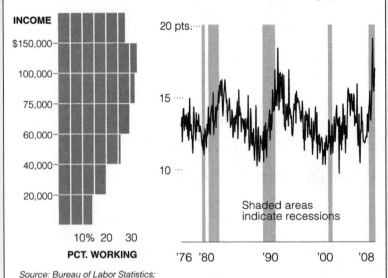

Teens in the work force
By family income, 2005-7

Gap in unemployment rates
Difference between 16- and 17-year-olds and other workers, in percentage points

Shaded areas indicate recessions

Source: Bureau of Labor Statistics;
Center of Labor Market Studies, Northeastern University

THE NEW YORK TIMES

At the marble-sheathed Westchester mall in White Plains, job applications have increased at stores including Origins, Tommy Hilfiger and the Gap, where job queries from teenagers are up 30 percent over last fall.

Julia Stark, a senior at Packer Collegiate Institute, a top private school in Brooklyn, said that this fall she and her friends are "all trying to work as much as we can" to pay for weekend restaurant dinners, a welcome break from a heavy course load and college applications.

In Greenwich, Conn., a Web-based program that connects high school students with nearby job opportunities has attracted 100 seekers each month since September, up from 40 to 60 a month last fall.

"I didn't want to bug my parents for extra cash over the long weekend," said Christian Rosier, a junior, who found a job on the Greenwich Student Employment Service the week before Thanksgiving that paid $50 for a few hours of moving furniture. "I like the one-shot jobs because I can do it on a Friday afternoon and still have time to hang out with my friends on the weekend."

Teenagers from working- and middle-class families are, of course, feeling similar—if not more acute—pressure. Sumit Pal, 17, a senior at Information Technology High School in Queens, said his parents cut his $5 weekly allowance two months ago after the deli where his father works started to lose business. Sumit was interviewed two weeks ago for a job at a company that sponsors rock bands.

"I don't mind losing my allowance," he said. "It goes toward other things, like groceries."

Teenage participation in the national labor force has fallen steadily since 1979, when 49 percent of all 16- and 17-year-olds had some kind of work; last year, the figure was 30 percent.

A recent study by the Center for Labor Market Studies at Northeastern University showed that teenage employment from 2005 to 2007 rose with household incomes that go up to $150,000 a year: 14 percent of teenagers from families earning less than $20,000 a year work, as do 26 percent of those whose families make $60,000, 32 percent of those earning $80,000, and 33 percent of those between $120,000 and $150,000.

Over $150,000, it drops to 28 per- 15 cent. "Research shows that the bigger

Since her allowance was cut to $60 a week from $100, Jodi Hamilton, 17, right, has taken up tutoring. Her pupil here is Sigourney Barman, 12.

allowance you get from Mom and Dad," explained Andrew M. Sum, director of Northeastern's center, "the less likely you are to work."

Since the 1990s, many affluent children seeking admission to selective colleges have been discouraged from paid work and steered instead toward volunteer service projects. Rebuilding homes in New Orleans or teaching English in developing countries, seemingly better résumé fodder, supplanted after-school or summer jobs scooping ice cream or answering phones.

"There's been such a push to demonstrate to colleges that they're involved with activities and charities that it's almost too pedestrian° to say that work is part of what I do," said William S. Miron, the principal at Millburn High School.

Brent A. Neiser of the National Endowment for Financial Education, a group based in Colorado that offers financial literacy programs, said parents tend to "shortchange the benefits of scut° work" but that even ho-hum employment can be valuable—and impress admissions officers.

"Dress codes, rules, punctuality, and being teachable is enrichment in itself," Mr. Neiser said. "You're contributing to the economy, you're contributing to your personal economy, and you're picking up skill sets and habits that will prepare you for your full-time employment."

Michael Pollack, a vice president 20 of CBS, said that he was happy to see his 14-year-old son, Zachary, get a job at a veterinary hospital in Scarsdale, N.Y., in September, because Zachary was learning some basic lessons about money.

"I really want him to feel it and save it and spend it so he knows that money goes away," Mr. Pollack said. "If he wants to treat all his friends to a movie, that's great. But he needs to see that it bottoms out. Where else are they going to get that experience?"

Zachary, who earns $80 a weekend for 11 hours feeding and caring for animals, said that he was glad to "help my parents with our financial situation."

"Things I need, they'll buy," he said, "and things I want, I'll buy."

---

pedestrian: here, ordinary or not worth mentioning.   *scut:* tedious, menial.

Jill Tipograph, who lives in Bergen County and owns Everything Summer, a company that advises parents on camp, travel, and work opportunities, said she sent her son to college in Boston this fall with a lump sum in his bank account that was supposed to last the semester. "But he went through the money like water," she said.

So Ms. Tipograph and her hus- 25 band decided to deposit a set amount once a week and told their son to use the prepaid meal plan more often. "We also said that if you feel you can't live on the allowance we're giving you, then please look for a part-time job," she added.

He seems to be getting the message, choosing a 10-hour bus ride over a train or plane for a recent visit to a friend in Washington.

Kat Rosier, a single mother of boys ages 12 and 17 in Greenwich, has resisted the idea of a job for her older son, Christian, who plays hockey and rows on the crew team, even as her interior design business has suffered.

"Here's my dilemma," she explained. "His time is so limited, and I would hate for his grades to fall this year so he could make $100 a week and then for him to not get into as good a college as he wants."

Still, having recently lost a job sprucing up the second home of a client who works in finance, Ms. Rosier said her family might need to adjust some habits. "The other night Christian had eight friends over and I spent $110 on pizza," she said. "I don't mind doing that, but he's got to know that the pizza budget is not $500 a month."

Christian said he was otherwise 30 cutting back: "If I'm hungry, I won't drive to McDonald's. I'll just eat something at home instead of spending $10 on lunch."

Jodi Hamilton's mother, Jill, said she had been impressed by her daughter's determination to earn, noting that "she sent out a massive e-mail for baby-sitting and tutoring, and she got so many offers there aren't enough hours in the week."

Suddenly, the tables are turned: Two weeks ago, Ms. Hamilton borrowed $640 from Jodi.

Foderaro's article explores the effects of an economic downturn on teenagers from different economic classes. For more on how causal arguments work, see Chapter 11.

LINK TO P. 335

RESPOND●

1. What challenges did the economic downturn present to the teenagers who are discussed in Lisa W. Foderaro's article? In what ways were teenagers from different social classes similarly affected? In what ways were the effects different? Were the differences purely quantitative (that is, different degrees of the same effects), or were they qualitative (that is, different kinds of effects)? How and why?

2. The article discusses the ways that high school students are expected to create a particular kind of ethos as college applicants. What consequences, if any, do you think the economic downturn might have on this application process and these expectations? Why?

3. The graphic "Teenage Workers" did not appear in the print version of this article but was included in the online version. Are there aspects of the graphic that you find surprising? These figures are for teens who did paid work outside the home. Work that is not paid officially (taxed by the government) is not included. Thus, work done around the house, on most farms, or in a family business was not shown on this

graphic. What information does the graphic contribute to the article that is not already included in the written text? The graph on the left, "Teens in the work-force," is discussed in some detail in the article, but the graph on the right, "Gap in unemployment rates," is not. **Write a paragraph** in which you describe this graphic as you would if you were using it to construct an argument of your own.

4. Not all readers were happy with the topic or content of Foderaro's article. In addition to the *Times*'s "Readers' Comments" (which you can access at community.nytimes.com/article/comments/2008/12/13/ nyregion/13teens), the article was the subject of a snarky posting on the *NYTPicker*, a blog devoted to the *Times* (which can be found at www .nytpick.com/2008/12/crisis-deepens-lisa-foderaro-reports). Check out one or more of these sources. Then **write an evaluative essay** in which you evaluate some aspects of the responses to the article. As you'll note, there are many topics worthy of investigation—for example, emotionally charged responses based on the economic status or social class of the writer or narratives about the writer's own experiences with work or money growing up. In considering the electronic replies to the article, you may wish to start by examining the Editors' Selections or the Readers' Recommendations. An interesting topic might be the relationship—or lack of a relationship—between the replies that are favored by readers and those favored by the editors. (For a discussion of evaluative arguments, see Chapter 10.)

▼ *This essay appeared on the op-ed page (the page opposite the editorial page) of the New York Times in late December 2008 as part of a series focusing on possible changes in American society as it moved from the Bush administration to the Obama presidency. The letters to the editor in response to the essay were published in January 2009. The essay was written by Charles Murray, a political scientist and libertarian who is associated with the American Enterprise Institute, a conservative think tank (research organization) in Washington, D.C. He is author of the 2008 book* Real Education: Four Simple Truths for Bringing America's Schools Back to Reality, *among others, and coauthor (with Richard Herrnstein) of the controversial 1994 book* The Bell Curve: Intelligence and Class Structure in American Life. *Murray grew up in Newton, Iowa, and attended Harvard for his undergraduate degree and the Massachusetts Institute of Technology for his doctorate. The essay treats aspects of a philosophical issue that dates back to the ancient Greeks: what does it mean to be educated, and what should an education be good for? As you read, try to determine Murray's answers to these questions with regard to American society. Then evaluate them in light of your own understanding of American society and your life.*

Should the Obama Generation Drop Out?

CHARLES MURRAY

Barack Obama has two attractive ideas for improving post-secondary education—expanding the use of community colleges and tuition tax credits—but he needs to hitch them to a broader platform. As president, Mr. Obama should use his bully pulpit° to undermine the bachelor's degree as a job qualification. Here's a suggested battle cry, to be repeated in every speech on the subject: "It's what you can do that should count when you apply for a job, not where you learned to do it."

The residential college° leading to a bachelor's degree at the end of four years works fine for the children of parents who have plenty of money. It works fine for top students from all backgrounds who are drawn toward academics. But most 18-year-olds are not from families with plenty of money, not top students, and not drawn toward academics. They want to learn how to get a satisfying job that also pays well. That almost always means education beyond high school, but it need not mean four years on a

---

bully pulpit: a position that ensures that the person holding it will be listened to, often used in reference to a political office or other highly visible position. (When

Theodore Roosevelt first used this term in reference to the U.S. presidency, *bully* was used to mean "very good" or "admirable," as in the old slang expression "Bully for you.")

residential college: a four-year institution where one lives and studies to earn an undergraduate degree.

campus nor cost a small fortune. It need not mean getting a bachelor's degree.

I am not discounting the merits of a liberal education.° Students at every level should be encouraged to explore subjects that will not be part of their vocation. It would be even better if more colleges required a rigorous core curriculum for students who seek a traditional bachelor's degree. My beef is not with liberal education but with the use of the degree as a job qualification.

For most of the nation's youths, making the bachelor's degree a job qualification means demanding a credential that is beyond their reach. It is a truth that politicians and educators cannot bring themselves to say out loud: A large majority of young people do not have the intellectual ability to do genuine college-level work.

If you doubt it, go back and look 5 through your old college textbooks, and then do a little homework on the reading ability of high school seniors. About 10 percent to 20 percent of all 18-year-olds can absorb the material in your old liberal arts textbooks. For engineering and the hard sciences, the percentage is probably not as high as 10.

No improvements in primary and secondary education will do more than tweak those percentages. The core disciplines taught at a true college level are tough, requiring high levels of linguistic and logical-mathematical ability.° Those abilities are no more malleable° than athletic or musical talent.

You think I'm too pessimistic? Too elitist? Readers who graduated with honors in English literature or Renaissance history should ask themselves if they could have gotten a B.S. in physics, no matter how hard they tried. (I wouldn't have survived freshman year.) Except for the freakishly gifted, all of us are too dumb to get through college in many majors.

But I'm not thinking just about students who are not smart enough to deal with college-level material. Many young people who have the intellectual ability to succeed in rigorous liberal arts courses don't want to. For these students, the distribution requirements of the college degree do not open up new horizons. They are bothersome time-wasters.

When Murray says that he's "not discounting the importance of a liberal education," he's qualifying his argument. Are there other places where you see Murray qualifying his claim? For more on qualifiers and other aspects of structuring arguments, see Chapter 7.

LINK TO P. 170

A century ago, these students would happily have gone to work after high school. Now they know they need to acquire additional skills, but they want to treat college as vocational training, not as a leisurely journey to well-roundedness.

As more and more students who 10 cannot get or don't want a liberal education have appeared on campuses, colleges have adapted by expanding the range of courses and adding vocationally oriented majors. That's appropriate. What's not appropriate is keeping the bachelor's degree as the measure of job preparedness, as the minimal requirement to get your foot in the door for vast numbers of jobs that don't really require a B.A. or B.S.

Discarding the bachelor's degree as a job qualification would not be

---

liberal education: an education that focuses on the development of general intellectual skills and abilities, usually requiring coursework in a wide range of subjects (in the form of general education requirements) in addition to focused study in a single area (a major), as opposed to an education that is focused narrowly on the mastery of the specific skills that are necessary for a particular profession.

linguistic and logical-mathematical ability: the abilities tested by the verbal and quantitative sections of tests like the Scholastic Achievement Test (SAT) that are required for admission to many colleges and universities.

malleable: able to be shaped or changed.

difficult. The solution is to substitute certification tests, which would provide evidence that the applicant has acquired the skills the employer needs.

Certification tests can take many forms. For some jobs, a multiple-choice test might be appropriate. But there's no reason to limit certifications to academic tests. For centuries, the crafts have used work samples to certify journeymen and master craftsmen. Today, many computer programmers without college degrees get jobs by presenting examples of their work. With a little imagination, almost any corporation can come up with analogous° work samples.

The benefits of discarding the bachelor's degree as a job qualification would be huge for both employers and job applicants. Certifications would tell employers far more about their applicants' qualifications than a B.A. does, and hundreds of thousands of young people would be able to get what they want from post-secondary education without having to twist themselves into knots to comply with the rituals of getting a bachelor's degree.

Certification tests would not eliminate the role of innate ability—the most gifted applicants would still have an edge—but they would strip away much of the unwarranted halo effect°

that goes with a degree from a prestigious university. They would put everyone under the same spotlight.

Discrediting the bachelor's degree 15 is within reach because so many employers already sense that it has become education's Wizard of Oz. All we need is someone willing to yank the curtain aside. Barack Obama is ideally positioned to do it. He just needs to say it over and over: "It's what you can do that should count when you apply for a job, not where you learned to do it."

Letters to the Editor: Should a College Degree Be Essential?

To the Editor:

Devaluing the bachelor's degree would not help students who earn it or those who don't go to college. A bachelor's degree may indeed serve as a foot in the door for a recent graduate, but that's all it does. That graduate still has to show that he or she can do the job.

The degree tells an employer that an applicant had the ability and perseverance to accomplish something.

Charles Murray suggests that instead of degrees, we use "certification tests, which would provide evidence that the applicant has acquired the skills the employer needs." This would amount to a postcollege SAT, when the precollege SAT has enough problems.

An employer takes a chance on any applicant, even one with a degree. There already are two-year colleges and technical training schools for

people who can't or won't earn a four-year degree.

The responsible thing to do is to 5 make sure that all students who have the ability to earn a degree aren't prevented from doing so by the cost.

Jeff Adler
Livingston, N.J., Dec. 28, 2008

---

analogous: comparable or similar.

halo effect: the tendency to let a single characteristic inflate one's evaluation of a person. It is an error of overgeneralization.

Here, Murray claims that graduates of prestigious universities may be judged more positively than individuals with comparable

skills or abilities who attend less prestigious schools.

To the Editor:

I recently graduated with a bachelor's degree in history and am now in law school, hoping to earn the degree that will lead to a paycheck. Though this will eventually pay my mortgage, my liberal arts education will be what sustains me emotionally, intellectually, and in my relationships with other human beings.

To say that young Americans are, for the most part, "not smart enough to deal with college-level material" and that we must scratch the bachelor's degree from our list of must-haves is to treat a symptom rather than the cause.

Employers must ask that their employees relate to one another and to the world around them; a broad, liberal education helps students to arrive at the point at which that kind of sympathy is possible.

Make college affordable, make it accessible, make it free, make it a requirement for employment. Don't accept defeat.

Lillian Hoodes
Chicago, Dec. 28, 2008

To the Editor:

Finally, someone dared to say what every college professor knows in her heart: half the students in her classroom shouldn't be there and don't want to be there.

We have created this B.A.-B.S. grail for millions of students who would be far better educated if they could focus on something that they want to learn.

For 12 years, I was a professor of English at the flagship campus of a big state university. My students were majoring in computers, nursing, landscape design, and kinesiology. They didn't care about "Beowulf" or John Milton. The university wanted them there, however, because more four-year graduates meant more money from the legislature. Now we can no longer tolerate such waste.

We should redesign college curriculums so that students can study something useful, get a job, and help redevelop the economy.

Rather than dumbing down "hard" 5 courses, so that everyone picks up a smattering of knowledge they will never use, universities should offer challenging courses in students' majors. If that major takes three instead of four years to complete, that's fine. The goal is to become productive without wasting time or money.

Sandra Sherman
New York, Dec. 28, 2008
The writer is assistant director of the Intellectual Property Law Institute, Fordham Law School.

To the Editor:

Students who have battled for a bachelor's degree will have learned a valuable skill. It is unlikely that most of them will practice only one trade throughout their career. They will have to learn a range of skills that were unheard of when they were students.

Charles Murray should bless them for having learned how to learn. If they are thus armed, our economy will have a chance.

Michel Dedina
San Francisco, Dec. 28, 2008

RESPOND●

1. Charles Murray's argument is a proposal. Summarize the argument, paying attention to what Chapter 12 says about how to develop a proposal. How well has Murray succeeded in developing a proposal based on the criteria that are given in that chapter? (In other words, evaluate Murray's argument as a proposal argument.)

2. As noted, Murray is a libertarian. Libertarians place a high premium on individual liberty and the value of individuals (in contrast to the

opinions of a group or society as a whole or the power of a government). Libertarians value both personal freedom and economic freedom. (This is in contrast to liberals, who place more value on personal freedom; conservatives, who place more value on economic freedom; and authoritarians or totalitarians, who value neither.) As the headnote states, Murray is from a small town in Iowa, and thanks to his intelligence (including his ability to do well on tests like the SAT), he was able to attend Harvard as an undergraduate. More recently, he has become critical of such standardized tests and the power that they have in American society. Although he once saw such tests as having a "democratizing" effect, he now contends that they no longer do so. Where do we see evidence of Murray's libertarian beliefs in this essay?

3. The letters to the editor that were published in response to Murray's essay demonstrate that reality is more complex than Murray portrays it. Choose a letter that you think is especially effective in responding to Murray's proposal, and explain how it demonstrates weaknesses in his position. If none of these letters appeal to you, look on the *Times* Web site for others that were published in the *Times* in response to this article or look for substantial comments that were posted on the Web site about Murray's article. (Note that your answer to this question does not depend on your response to the essay. You may agree fully with Murray's position while still acknowledging that these letters point out aspects of the situation that he fails to address.)

4. Do you find Murray's argument convincing? Why or why not? If American society were to implement Murray's proposal, what would be the consequences for colleges and universities? For teenagers thinking about their future? For employers? For society at large? For you and your friends?

5. What should be the purpose of postsecondary education in the United States? Should its primary focus be a liberal education (that is, a college diploma that indicates that a person knows certain things, has certain skills, and possesses certain abilities)—as it generally currently is? Or should Americans seek other models of the relationship among education, learning, and the knowledge and skills that are needed to get and keep a job in an increasingly globalized economy? **Write a definitional essay** in which you define the purpose of postsecondary education in the United States early in the twenty-first century. Your essay may have aspects of factual, evaluative, causal, and proposal arguments. (For a discussion of definitional essays, see Chapter 9.)

Education Pays

U.S. BUREAU OF LABOR STATISTICS

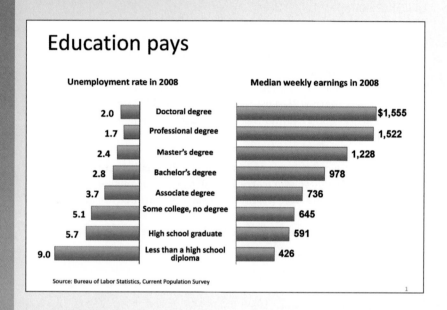

Education pays

Unemployment rate in 2008 | | **Median weekly earnings in 2008**

Unemployment rate	Degree	Median weekly earnings
2.0	Doctoral degree	$1,555
1.7	Professional degree	1,522
2.4	Master's degree	1,228
2.8	Bachelor's degree	978
3.7	Associate degree	736
5.1	Some college, no degree	645
5.7	High school graduate	591
9.0	Less than a high school diploma	426

Source: Bureau of Labor Statistics, Current Population Survey

Education pays in higher earnings and lower unemployment rates.

Note: Data are 2007 annual averages for persons age 25 and over. Earnings are for full-time wage and salary workers.

Source: Bureau of Labor Statistics, Current Population Survey.

◀ In this selection, we present first a graph, "Education Pays," that was posted on the Web site of the United States Department of Labor's Bureau of Labor Statistics (BLS). These statistics might lead to a fairly clear conclusion that represents conventional wisdom: the greater your level of education, the more money you will make and the less likely you'll end up unemployed.

To accompany this graph, we include Laurence Shatkin's "Education Pays, but Perhaps Less Than You Thought," a blog posting on FastCompany.com that explains why the BLS statistics and graph don't tell the whole story. Shatkin is an author and specialist in career information as well as a senior product developer at JIST, a publishing company that focuses on the fields of job searches, career exploration, and occupational information, among others.

As you examine the graph in light of the blog posting, consider the potential pitfalls of trusting statistics that you find on the Internet. Likewise, give some thought to Shatkin's final claim.

Education Pays, but Perhaps Less Than You Thought

LAURENCE SHATKIN

If you Google the phrase "education pays," the very first hit you'll get is a page at the Bureau of Labor Statistics that features a chart representing the median weekly earnings in 2007 of people with various levels of education. The higher the level of education, the higher the income. For example, high school graduates earned $604 per week, compared to $987 for those with a bachelor's degree and $1,497 for those with a doctoral degree. The figures are derived from the Current Population Survey.

The chart makes a compelling case and is probably popular with guidance counselors. My daughter, who teaches a GED° class for Spanish-speakers at a community college, has used the figures from this chart in a brochure aimed at recruiting students. I have used the figures in a book for JIST. A related fact that is often quoted is that the advantage of a college degree has been growing in recent years.

GED: General Education Development tests, which are given in the United States and Canada. Certificates of passing the tests are often used as the equivalent of a high school diploma.

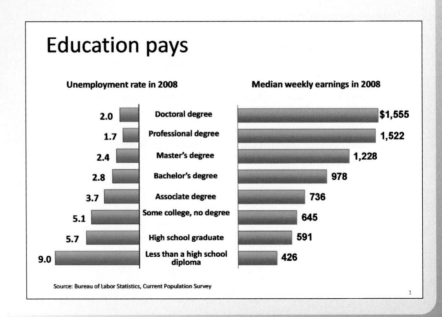

Education pays

Unemployment rate in 2008		Median weekly earnings in 2008
2.0	Doctoral degree	$1,555
1.7	Professional degree	1,522
2.4	Master's degree	1,228
2.8	Bachelor's degree	978
3.7	Associate degree	736
5.1	Some college, no degree	645
5.7	High school graduate	591
9.0	Less than a high school diploma	426

Source: Bureau of Labor Statistics, Current Population Survey

1

But this week I came across a study that qualifies the information in this chart. The article, "Real Wage Inequality," by Enrico Moretti of U.C. Berkeley, does not refute the "Education Pays" figures, but it points out that earnings are just one factor in the equation of well-being. Moretti notes that, from 1980 to 2000, college graduates have tended to concentrate in cities, especially in cities where the cost of housing is higher and has increased rapidly during this period. (The differences in housing costs do not seem to be related to housing quality. That is, college grads do not seem to live in a more expensive style of housing; rather, they live where the same kind of housing simply costs more.) As a result, the advantage of the college degree in terms of spending cash is not as great as the chart might suggest.

Specifically, Moretti found that half of the college wage advantage disappears when one accounts for the difference in housing costs. For example, in 2000 the college graduates were earning about 60% more but were enjoying an actual advantage of only 37%–43%. He also found that the increase in the advantage of a college degree between 1980 and 2000, often said to be about 20%, actually is between 8% and 10% when housing costs are factored in.

It's interesting to consider the question of *why* college graduates are concentrating in these high-rent cities. Moretti evaluates two possible explanations. The demand-pull hypothesis assumes that high-skilled workers are more productive in these cities, and therefore job opportunities are attracting college grads there. The supply-pull hypothesis assumes that college graduates are flocking to high-rent cities because they are attracted by amenities° other than employment, and their presence in these cities is driving up rents. Moretti argues for the demand-pull hypothesis, noting that as college graduates crowd into cities, their relative wages also get a boost, indicating their greater productivity. However, he does not rule out that a supply-pull phenomenon may also be occurring.

5

amenities: things that make life comfortable, enjoyable, or pleasant. Shatkin is likely thinking about the fact that urban areas, in contrast to rural areas, provide a wider range of restaurants, stores, and leisure-time opportunities.

Moretti bases his comparisons on pre-tax earnings, but he notes that taxation causes further erosion of the college advantage. Because the federal income tax is progressive, college grads in expensive cities may have higher pre-tax earnings, but this comes with a larger tax bite in addition to the rent bite already noted. Furthermore, he notes, the tax codes in California and in New England coastal states are also progressive,° meaning an additional tax bite for college grads there.

progressive: imposing higher rates of taxation on higher amounts of income.

Shatkin's analysis of the data demonstrates that statistics don't always tell the whole story. For more on arguments based on facts and reason, see Chapter 4.

LINK TO P. 69

Would these findings change my advice to a young person? Not at all. Education may not produce as great an increment in spending cash as the BLS chart suggests, but it still provides an advantage. It also provides many nonmonetary satisfactions that economists rarely measure.

RESPOND•

1. According to Laurence Shatkin, why are the statistics from the U.S. Bureau of Labor Statistics at least partially misleading? (Be careful here: there is more than one step to the argument.)

2. What might account for the concentration of college graduates in urban areas, according to Enrico Moretti? Which hypothesis does he prefer? The fact that Moretti does not rule out one of the two hypotheses likely means that he does not have adequate data to draw a conclusion. Do you favor one hypothesis over the other on the basis of your life experiences? Which one and why? Why might Moretti, as an economist, not be willing to trust his life experience in answering this question?

3. Does Moretti's study or Shatkin's discussion of taxes mean that the Bureau of Labor Statistics is wrong? Why or why not?

4. Chapter 4 discusses statistics as examples of hard evidence or what Aristotle termed "inartistic appeals." What does this selection remind us about the nature and limitations of so-called hard evidence?

5. Shatkin closes his blog posting by stating that despite the research he discusses, he would not change his advice to young people to get an education because it pays both in actual monetary terms and in "many nonmonetary satisfactions that economists rarely measure" (paragraph 7). Do you agree with this advice? If so, would you agree if there were no monetary benefit? Why or why not? What sorts of "nonmonetary satisfactions," if any, have you gotten or do you hope to get from your education? **Write an essay** in which either you define and evaluate these satisfactions or you explain why you believe that your education has not provided them. You may also wish to speculate about whether economists could find ways of measuring these satisfactions. (For a discussion of definitional and evaluative essays, see Chapters 9 and 10, respectively.)

▼ *The College Board is a not-for-profit corporation that administers stan-*
dardized tests, including the SAT, PSAT/NMSQT, and AP exams and CLEP
tests. Sandy Baum is a senior policy analyst for the College Board as well as
a professor of economics at Skidmore College in Sarasota Springs, New York.
Jennifer Ma is a consultant to the College Board. This 2007 report represents
an update of a 2004 report that was supplemented in 2005 and 2006. As
the title implies, the goal of this report of nearly fifty pages is to document
the ways in which higher education is beneficial to us as individuals and as
members of society. Baum and Ma also address the distribution of benefits
(or responses to the question "Who participates and succeeds in higher edu-
cation?")

The excerpt included here comes from the first section of the report,
although in the questions that follow, we direct you to an online version of
the report to inspect the second part of it. Throughout, we have retained the
original number of each figure so that you will have a clear idea of the num-
ber of figures that have been included and omitted. An especially interesting
feature of this report is that except for minimal introductory materials, a
page of references, and two appendices at the end, virtually the entire report
consists of single pages devoted to different topics, each with a figure and
bulleted commentary.

Education Pays: The Benefits of Higher Education for Individuals and Society (2007)

SANDY BAUM AND JENNIFER MA FOR THE COLLEGE BOARD

EXECUTIVE SUMMARY

Students who attend institutions of higher education obtain a wide range of
personal, financial, and other lifelong benefits; likewise, taxpayers and society as a whole derive a multitude of direct and indirect benefits when citizens have access to postsecondary education. Accordingly, uneven rates of
participation in higher education across different segments of U.S. society
should be a matter of urgent interest not only to the individuals directly

affected, but also to public policy-makers at the federal, state, and local levels.

This report presents detailed evidence of the private and public benefits of higher education. It also sheds light on the distribution of these benefits by examining both the progress and the persistent disparities in participation in postsecondary education.

The benefits of higher education for individuals and for society as a whole are both monetary and nonmonetary.

Benefits to Individuals

- There is a positive correlation between higher levels of education and higher earnings for all racial/ethnic groups and for both men and women.

- In addition to earning higher wages, college graduates are more likely than others to enjoy employer-provided health insurance and pension benefits.

SOME TECHNICAL NOTES FROM APPENDIX B OF THIS REPORT

high school graduate: includes those who hold a GED, or General Education Development Diploma.

education level: the highest level attained. Thus, the term "high school graduate" refers to those who have completed high school but who have not attended college.

professional degrees: degrees like an M.D. (Doctor of Medicine), held by most medical doctors; DDS (Doctor of Dental Science or Surgery), held by most dentists; DVM (Doctor of Veterinary Medicine), held by most veterinarians; LLB (Bachelor of Law), and J.D. (Doctor of Jurisprudence), held by graduates of law school.

rounding: dollar amounts are rounded to the nearest $100.

ADDITIONAL USEFUL INFORMATION

PINC: an acronym for "personal income." When listed as a source, PINC data can be found in the U.S. Census Bureau's *Current Population Survey*.

median: the middle figure, when a series of numbers is arranged from lowest to highest. When the distribution of a set of numbers—for example, the salaries for any group—does not conform to a normal distribution or Bell curve, researchers use the median (rather than the average, also called the mean) as the basis for comparison.

- The income gap between high school graduates and college graduates has increased significantly over time. The earnings benefit is large enough for the average college graduate to recoup both earnings forgone during the college years and the cost of full tuition and fees in a relatively short period of time.

- The considerable nonmonetary rewards of a college education include better health and greater opportunities for the next generation.

- Any college experience produces a measurable return when compared with none, but the benefits of completing a bachelor's degree or higher are particularly large.

Societal Benefits

- Higher levels of education correspond to lower unemployment and poverty rates. So, in addition to contributing more to tax revenues than others do, adults with higher levels of education are less likely to depend on social safety-net programs, generating decreased demand on public budgets.

- The earnings of workers with lower education levels are positively affected by the presence of college graduates in the workforce.

- College graduates have lower smoking rates, more positive perceptions of personal health, and healthier lifestyles than individuals who did not graduate from college.

- Higher levels of education are correlated with higher levels of civic participation, including volunteer work, voting, and blood donation, as well as with greater levels of openness to the opinions of others.

5

Given the extent of higher education's benefits to society, gaps in access to college are matters of great significance to the country as a whole. This report shows that despite the progress we have made in improving educational opportunities, participation in higher education differs significantly by family income, parent education level, and other demographic characteristics.

Patterns of Postsecondary Participation

- Among students with top test scores, virtually all students from the top quarter of families in terms of income and parental education enroll in postsecondary education, but about 25 percent of those in the lowest socioeconomic quartile do not continue their education after high school.

- Differences in family background generate smaller differences in postsecondary participation among students with high test scores than among those with lower levels of measured academic achievement.

- Gaps in postsecondary enrollment rates by income and race/ethnicity are persistent. Moreover, black and Hispanic students, as well as low-income students, are less likely than others to complete degrees if they do enroll. Students from rural areas and male students also have relatively lower levels of participation in higher education.

- Gaps between individuals who participate and succeed in higher education and those who don't have a major impact on the next generation. The young children of college graduates display higher levels of school readiness indicators than children of parents who did not graduate from college. For high school graduates from families with similar incomes, students whose parents went to college are significantly more likely to go to college themselves than those whose parents did not go to college.

- International comparisons indicate that the United States ranks higher in overall degree attainment than in degree attainment in science and engineering.

The story told by the indicators in this report is that higher education does pay. It yields a high rate of return for students from all racial/ethnic groups, for men and for women, and for those from all family backgrounds. It also delivers a high rate of return for society. The specific evidence of these benefits included in this report provides the basis for more informed decisions about public and private investments in higher education opportunities.

INTRODUCTION

This edition of *Education Pays: The Benefits of Higher Education for Individuals and Society* updates and adds to our 2004 publication. In 2004, we designed this report as a companion to our annual releases, *Trends in Student Aid* and *Trends in College Pricing*. Our goal was to expand the conversation about paying for college to include more concrete information about why the major investment in higher education is so important, both for individual students and for the society to which they belong. We also wanted to sharpen the focus on who participates and succeeds in higher education and who is excluded from this opportunity. In 2005 and 2006, we published brief supplements to *Education Pays*. This year, we have updated much of the information what we included in past years and have added some new indicators of both the value of higher education and how that value is distributed. We are releasing this report separately from the *Trends* reports, with the hope that the evidence provided here will help to generate conversations, policy proposals, and further research into the contribution of higher education to the well-being of our society.

People generally think of college education in personal terms. Public opin- 10 ion polls reveal a widespread understanding of the role of education in opening the door to a middle-class lifestyle. Students invest considerable time and energy, in addition to dollars, into building their futures through education. The prospect of wider opportunities and a higher standard of living leads families to save in advance, sacrifice current consumption opportunities, and go into debt in order to enable their children to continue their education after high school. Yet in recent years, questions about whether the investment is worthwhile have become more common. As the price of a college education continues to rise more rapidly than the price of other goods and services, more students and families are facing difficult choices about the sacrifices involved.

It is true that after adjusting for inflation, the earnings of male college graduates are no higher than they were in the early 1970s, and the earnings of female college graduates have increased only moderately. However, as this report documents clearly, the earnings gap between high school and college graduates has grown dramatically. The gap between the earnings of high school graduates and the earnings of four-year college graduates has for many years been larger for women than for men. Over time, this gap has continued to grow for men, almost catching up to the gap for women, which has remained close to its current high level for the past decade.

The nonmonetary benefits enjoyed by individuals who participate and succeed in higher education are much more difficult to quantify and document. Although it is not possible for us to focus on all of them in this publication, it is certainly not our intention to diminish these critical outcomes, which include many aspects of personal and intellectual growth and fulfillment.

The broader societal benefits of investment in higher education also are fundamental to the well-being of our nation. State and local governments appropriate billions of dollars each year for public colleges and universities and the federal government provides grants, loans, and work assistance, as well as tax credits and deductions, to help students finance postsecondary education. The specific information contained in this report can increase our understanding of the importance of higher education for both the equity and the efficiency of our society.

In the pages that follow, we describe a variety of differences in the earnings, choices, and behavior patterns that correspond to differences in education levels. Some of the benefits of higher education documented in this report are widely cited; others are less well-known. We have attempted to bring generally available government statistics together with less familiar academic research in order to paint a detailed and integrated picture of the benefits of higher education and how they are distributed. Where possible, we have summarized complex analyses in a manner consistent with the straightforward presentation style of this report. We provide references to more in-depth and sophisticated analyses so that readers can pursue issues of particular interest.

It is frequently difficult to determine precisely how much of the variation 15 observed in the patterns reported here is directly attributable to education and how much is actually the result of other factors. Individual characteristics that influence the probability of enrolling in and graduating from postsecondary institutions may have a direct and systematic influence on other outcomes. For example, it is likely that the skills and motivation required for college success would increase earnings even for those with little formal education. Under these circumstances, if many of the people who now go to college were to stop enrolling, they might earn more than the average high school graduate.

Sophisticated statistical analysis can help to clarify the difference between correlation and causation. We cite this type of evidence when it is available. However, many of the graphs in this report simply compare the patterns evidenced by people with different education levels. In general, while simple descriptions of correlations provide useful clues about causal effects, they do not reliably indicate the size of the effects, and instead are best interpreted as providing broad-gauged evidence of the powerful role that higher education plays in the lives of individuals and in society.

caveat: a warning.

Another caveat° necessary to the accurate interpretation of the information provided here is that, as mentioned above, not all of the benefits of higher education can be quantified. The personal satisfaction and enhanced life experiences generated by higher education are virtually impossible to measure. Moreover, the actual benefits of many of the outcomes we describe here, such as increased civic participation, cannot realistically be translated into terms that allow them to be compared to the costs of the investment. Our intent is not to minimize the importance of the less tangible or quantifiable outcomes of education. Rather, we hope that a more thorough and coherent view of the benefits on which we focus will highlight the significance of our society's investment in higher education and provide some grounding for public policy deliberations.

As was the case in 2004, the story told by the indicators in this report is that education does pay. It has a high rate of return for students from all racial/ethnic groups, for men and for women, and for those from all family backgrounds. It also has a high rate of return for society. We all benefit from the higher tax revenues, the greater productivity, the lower demands on social support programs, and the greater levels of civic participation of college-educated adults.

Once these individual and societal benefits of higher education are clear, it becomes critical to increase our understanding of the gaps we still face in patterns of participation in postsecondary education. College enrollment rates have increased significantly over the past three or four decades, both overall and for all demographic groups. However, this good news is dampened by the persistent gaps in participation in postsecondary education among people from different backgrounds. People from low-income families and those whose parents did not attend college, as well as blacks and Hispanics, are much less likely than more affluent people, those whose parents have college degrees, and whites and Asians to enroll in college and to earn degrees. Enrollment rates of recent high school graduates were higher in 2005 than they had been a decade earlier at all income levels except the most affluent 20 percent of the population, and the growth has been most rapid for students from the lowest income families. But the progress has not been consistent, and over the second half of the decade, increased participation has been almost exclusively in the upper half of the income distribution.

Many factors contribute to the variation in postsecondary participation 20 rates. Financial constraints, wide disparities in elementary and secondary educational opportunities, academic preparation, aspirations, and expectations all play a role in the differentials documented here. There is no attempt in the discussion that follows to sort out the relative weights of these different factors. The evidence does, however, clearly indicate that financial constraints create barriers. There are significant differences by family income level in college enrollment rates among high school graduates with very high test scores, and among those whose parents have similar education levels. A strong academic background is not always sufficient to allow students to overcome financial barriers. It does, however, significantly improve post-secondary opportunities. Within income groups, students with high achievement levels are significantly more likely to go to college than others, as are those whose parents have high levels of education.

Our intent is not to analyze the causes or to propose solutions for the gaps in postsecondary participation we document, but to highlight the missed opportunities for individuals and for society. If all demographic groups attained education levels similar to those who are most successful by this measure, more individuals would enjoy the benefits described in this report. Moreover, society would function more efficiently, and enjoy a variety of shared benefits.

The significant costs of the public and private investments in higher education are very visible. It is important that both the successes and the shortfalls of these investments be equally visible.

PART I: INDIVIDUAL AND SOCIETAL BENEFITS OF HIGHER EDUCATION

Individual students and their families reap much of the benefit of higher education. For members of all demographic groups, average earnings increase measurably with higher levels of education. During their working lives, typical college graduates earn over 60 percent more than typical high school graduates, and those with advanced degrees earn two to three times as much as high school graduates. Salaries are not the only form of compensation correlated with education level; college graduates are more likely than other employees to enjoy employer-provided health and pension benefits. More-educated people are less likely to be unemployed and less likely to live in poverty. These economic returns make financing a college education a good investment. Although incurring debt should always be approached with caution, even students who borrow a sizable share of the funds required to pay for college are likely to be financially better off relatively soon after graduation than they would be if they began their full-time work lives immediately after high school.

Society as a whole also enjoys a financial return on the investment in a higher education. In addition to widespread productivity increases, the higher earnings of educated workers generate higher tax payments at the local, state, and federal levels, Consistent productive employment reduces dependence on public income-transfer programs and all workers, regardless of education level, earn more when there are more college graduates in the labor force.

Because the individual outcomes affect the well-being of others, it is not 25 possible to neatly separate the benefits to individuals from those shared by society as a whole. For example, just as all workers benefit from the increased productivity of their coworkers, unemployment can result in a loss to the entire economy.

Beyond the economic return to individuals and to society as a whole, higher education improves quality of life in a variety of other ways, only some of which can be easily quantified. The economic advantages already mentioned have broader implications. For example, reduced poverty increases material standards of living and improves the overall well-being of the population; the psychological implications of unemployment are also significant. In addition to their nonmonetary benefits, poverty and unemployment affect spending on public assistance programs. Moreover, adults with higher levels of education are more likely to engage in organized volunteer work, to vote, and to donate blood; they are also more likely to live healthy lifestyles. College-educated adults are more likely than others to be open to differing views of others, and the young children of adults with higher levels of education have higher cognitive skills and engage in more extracurricular, cultural, athletic, and religious activities than other children. In other words, participation in postsecondary education improves the quality of civil society.

The indicators included here do not provide a comprehensive measure of the benefits of higher education. They do, however, provide an indication of the nature and extent of the return on our investment in educational opportunities.

Figure 1.1: Estimates of state and local tax payments are based on U.S. averages reported by the Institute for Taxation and Economic Policy (2003). Federal income taxes are based on IRS (2006) data for average 2004 tax payments based on AGI categories. Tax burdens for each income level are imputed based on the payments reported for income brackets. Social Security and Medicare taxes are based on the federal formula in effect in 2005.

Education, Earnings, and Tax Payments

Figure 1.1: Median Earnings and Tax Payments of Full-Time Year-Round Workers Ages 25 and Older, by Education Level, 2005

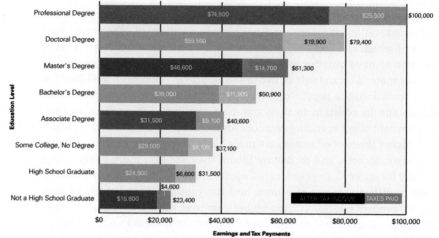

Note: Taxes paid include federal income, Social Security, and Medicare taxes, and state and local income, sales, and property taxes.
Sources: U.S. Census Bureau, 2006, PINC-03; Internal Revenue Service, 2006; McIntyre et al., 2003; calculations by the authors.

The bars in this graph show median earnings at each education level. The lighter segments represent the average federal, state, and local taxes paid at these income levels. The darker segments show after-tax income.

Higher levels of education lead to both higher levels of earnings for individuals and higher tax revenues for federal, state, and local governments.

- In 2005, the typical full-time year-round worker in the United States with a four-year college degree earned $50,900, 62 percent more than the $31,500 earned by the typical full-time year-round worker with only a high school diploma.

- Those with master's degrees earned almost twice as much, and those with professional degrees earned over three times as much per year as high school graduates.

- Median earnings for those with some college but no degree were 18 percent higher than those for high school graduates, and adults with associate degrees earned 29 percent more than high school graduates.

- The typical college graduate working full-time year-round paid 134 percent more in federal income taxes and almost 80 percent more in total federal, state, and local taxes than the typical high school graduate.

- Those who hold professional degrees paid almost $19,000 more in total taxes in 2005 than high school graduates.

Also important:

- All of the differences in earnings reported here may not be attributable to education level. Education credentials are correlated with a variety of other factors that affect earnings including, for example, parents' socioeconomic status and some personal characteristics.
- While the average high school graduate might not increase his or her earnings to the level of the average college graduate simply by earning a bachelor's degree, careful research on the subject suggests that the figures cited here do not measurably overstate the financial return of higher education (Carneiro et al., 2003; Rouse, 2005; Harmon et al., 2003).

Lifetime Earnings

Figure 1.2: Expected Lifetime Earnings Relative to High School Graduates, by Education Level

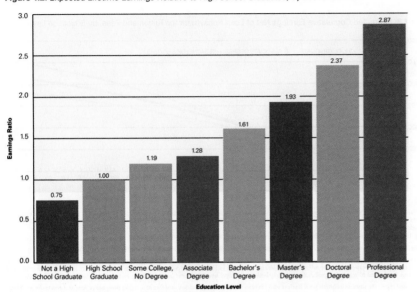

Notes: Based on the sum of median 2005 earnings from ages 25 to 64 for each education level. Future earnings are discounted using a 3 percent annual rate to account for the reality that, because of foregone interest, dollars received in the future are not worth as much as those received today.
Sources: U.S. Census Bureau, 2006, PINC-03; calculations by the authors.

The typical bachelor's degree recipient can expect to earn about 61 percent more over a 40-year working life than the typical high school graduate earns over the same period.

- Median lifetime earnings for individuals with some college but no degree are 19 percent higher than median lifetime earnings for high school graduates with no college experience.
- Median lifetime earnings for individuals with associate degrees are 28 percent higher than median lifetime earnings for high school graduates.
- Median lifetime earnings for doctoral degree recipients are between two and two and a half times as high as median lifetime earnings for high school graduates, and median lifetime earnings for professional degree recipients are even higher.

Figure 1.2: No allowance is made for the shorter work life resulting from the time spent in college and out of the labor force.

Baum and Ma offer an enormous quantity of data to argue for the benefits of higher education, but graphs and charts allow them to present that data efficiently. For more on how visual arguments work, see Chapter 14.

LINK TO P. 441

Also important:

- The typical expected earnings over the working lives of four-year college graduates add up to $800,000 more than the expected earnings of high school graduates. If college graduates who also earn higher degrees are included, the lifetime earnings premium is over $1,000,000.
- Accounting for the fact that some of the higher earnings are many years in the future, the increased earning power of a college education is worth about $450,000 in today's dollars. If college graduates who also earn higher degrees are included, the lifetime earnings premium is over $570,000.

Figure 1.3: This calculation is based on 2005 median earnings levels. It assumes the college graduate is out of the labor force for four years, at ages 18–21, and borrows the entire 2005-06 average tuition and fees of $5,492 at a public four-year college and tuition and fees for the following years, assuming a 5 percent increase each year. Annual interest of 6.8 percent is assumed to accrue while the student is in school and during repayment. Estimates are based on a standard 10-year student loan repayment plan. Tuition payments and earnings are discounted at a 3 percent rate, compounded for every year beyond age 18. This discount rate represents real interest, since all earnings are in 2005 dollars.

Earnings Premium Relative to Price of Education

Figure 1.3: Estimated Cumulative Earnings Net of Loan Repayment for Tuition and Fees, by Education Level

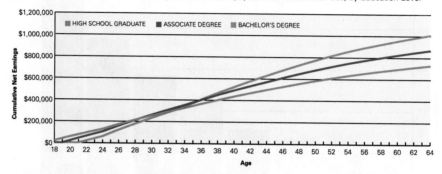

Notes: Based on median 2005 earnings for each education level at each age and discounted using a 3 percent annual rate. Earnings for bachelor's degree recipients include only those with no advanced degree. Assumes tuition and fees are financed with borrowing, and loan payments are made for 10 years after graduation.

Sources: U.S. Census Bureau, 2006, PINC-03, PINC-04; The College Board, 2005; calculations by the authors.

The green line shows the cumulative earnings at each age for the typical high school graduate who enters the workforce full-time at age 18.

The blue line shows the cumulative earnings at each age for the typical college graduate who enters the workforce at age 22, after spending four years out of the labor force and having borrowed to pay the full tuition and fees at the average public four-year college or university. Loan payments on this debt are subtracted from earnings for the first 10 years after graduation, covering both the principal and 6.8 percent interest charges incurred both during and after college.

The purple line shows the same calculation for a student who borrows to cover average tuition and fees at a public two-year college and enters the workforce at age 20.

In all cases, dollar amounts beyond age 18 are discounted by an annual rate of 3 percent to account for the reality that dollars received in the future are not worth as much as those received today, which can begin immediately to earn interest.

By age 33, the typical college graduate who enrolled at age 18 has earned enough to compensate for borrowing to pay the full tuition and fees at the average public four-year institution, including interest on student loans to cover those charges, and earnings forgone during the college years.

- For the typical student who borrows to cover tuition and fees and earns an associate degree two years after high school graduation, total earnings net of educational expenditures exceed the total earnings of high school graduates by age 29, after nine years of full-time work.
- The earnings of typical four-year college graduates exceed those of typical two-year college graduates, causing the investment in the extra two years of education to be recouped by age 36, after 14 years of earnings.
- The longer college graduates remain in the workforce, the greater the payoff to their investment in higher education.

Also important:

- If the calculation of the value of cumulative net earnings is based on average tuition and fees at a private four-year college, the earnings of college graduates without advanced degrees exceed the median earnings of high school graduates at age 40.
- If the calculation of the value of cumulative earnings is based on a simple sum of median annual earnings without taking into account the lesser value of earnings in the future, the net total earnings of the public two-year college graduate surpass those of the high school graduate at age 28 instead of 29, and the net total earnings of the public four-year college graduate surpass those of the high school graduate at age 31 instead of 33.
- According to the U.S. Census data, the average 2005 earnings for four-year college graduates between ages 25 and 34 with no advanced degree were $19,200 higher than the average earnings of high school graduates in the same age group. This earnings difference is three and a half times the annual tuition and fees at public four-year colleges in 2005-06.

Earnings by Education Level, Race/Ethnicity, and Gender

Figure 1.4: Median Earnings of Full-Time Year-Round Workers Ages 25–34, by Race/Ethnicity, Gender, and Education Level, 2005

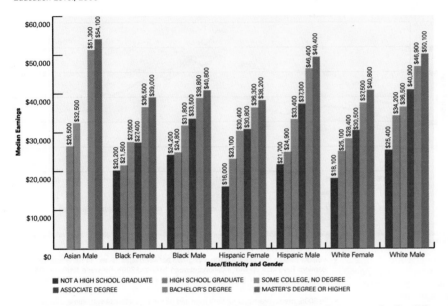

Note: Sample sizes for Asian females as well as Asian males with less than a high school diploma and associate degrees are too small to allow reliable reporting.
Source: U.S. Census Bureau, 2006, PINC-03.

Among 25- to 34-year-olds, the earnings premium for four-year college graduates is highest for Asian and Hispanic males. The premium is higher for black women than for women of other racial/ethnic groups.

- In 2005, median earnings for Hispanic male bachelor's degree recipients between ages 25 and 34 were 86 percent higher than median earnings for Hispanic male high school graduates. For Asian men, the premium was 94 percent. It was 56 percent for black men and 37 percent for white men.

- Median earnings for black female bachelor's degree recipients between ages 25 and 34 were 70 percent higher than median earnings for black female high school graduates. For Hispanic women, the earnings premium was 57 percent, and for white women it was 49 percent.

- The earnings premium for four-year college degree recipients was higher for white and black women than for men, but among Hispanics, the earnings premium was larger for males.

- Within racial/ethnic groups between ages 25 and 34, the largest gaps between median earnings for full-time male workers and full-time female workers were for whites who had not completed a four-year degree.

- The smallest gender-based earnings gap was for black college graduates, with male bachelor's degree recipients earning only 6 percent more than female bachelor's degree recipients.

Earnings Over Time by Education Level and Gender

Figure 1.6: Median Earnings of Full-Time Year-Round Workers Ages 25–34, by Gender and Education Level, 1971–2005 (in Constant 2005 Dollars)

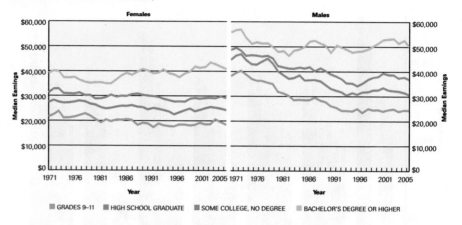

Sources: National Center for Education Statistics (NCES), 2007, Indicator 20 (based on U.S. Census Bureau, *Current Population Survey*); calculations by the authors.

Earnings differentials by level of education have increased significantly over the past 35 years. Over the past decade, the earnings premium for a college education has increased for men and has remained relatively steady for women.

- Female college graduates are the only group between ages 25 and 34 for whom median earnings have kept up with inflation between 1971 and 2005. Between 1995 and 2005, all groups except men with no more than a high school education have seen earnings increase beyond inflation.

- In 2005, median earnings for both men and women ages 25–34 with some college but no four-year degree were 20 percent higher than median earnings for high school graduates. For men, this earnings premium was at its highest level since 1971, but had been steady since 2002. For women, the earnings premium has fluctuated around this level since the early 1980s.

- Median earnings for men ages 25–34 with a bachelor's degree or higher were 64 percent higher in 2005 than median earnings for male high school graduates. The earnings premium has risen from 19 percent in 1975, 37 percent in 1985, and 56 percent in 1995.

- Median earnings for women ages 25–34 with a bachelor's degree or higher were 68 percent higher in 2005 than median earnings for female high school graduates. The earnings premium rose from 37 percent in 1975 to 47 percent in 1985, and to 71 percent in 1995.

Also important:

The overall distribution of income in the United States became more unequal during this time period. The share of total income received by families in the lowest 20 percent of the income distribution fell from 5.5 percent in 1971 to 4.6 percent in 1990 and to 4.0 percent in 2004; the share of total income received by families in the highest 20 percent of the income distribution rose from 41.1 percent in 1971 to 44.3 percent in 1990 and to 47.9 percent in 2004 (U.S. Census Bureau, 2007, Table 678).

Economic Benefits to Others

Figure 1.9: The Impact of Increases in the Proportion of College Graduates in the Workforce on Wages of All Workers, by Education Level

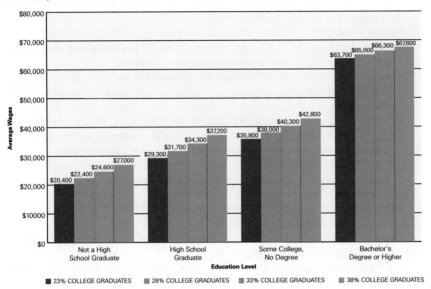

Sources: Moretti, 2004; calculations by the authors.

The green bars represent the actual circumstances in 2005 when 28 percent of the adult population held bachelor's degrees. Bars for 23 percent, 33 percent, and 38 percent college graduates illustrate hypothetical average wages that would prevail with those proportions of college graduates if wages in the United States changed in the pattern estimated by Moretti (2004) for metropolitan areas.

Workers with lower education levels earn more if others in the same metropolitan area are more educated.

- Estimates suggest that controlling for other factors, a 1 percentage point increase in the proportion of the population holding a four-year college degree leads to a 1.9 percent increase in the wages of workers without a high school diploma and a 1.6 percent increase in the wages of high school graduates.

- A 1 percentage point increase in the proportion of the population holding a four-year college degree leads to an increase of about 1.2 percent in the wages of workers with some college and an increase of 0.6 percent in the wages of college graduates.

Also important:

The findings reported on this page are from economist Enrico Moretti's study of the spillover effects of college education. Controlling for the relevant characteristics of both individuals and cities, he estimates the increase in wages resulting from increased educational attainment in the workforce.

REFERENCES

(Not all sources used are included in this list.)

Carneiro, P., Heckman, J.J., and Vytlacil E. (2003). "Understanding What Instrumental Variables Estimate: Estimating Marginal and Average Returns to Education." University of Chicago Working Paper.

College Board (2005). *Trends in College Pricing.* Washington, DC: The College Board.

Harmon, C., Oosterbeek, H., and Walker, I. (2003). "The Returns to Education: Microeconomics." *Journal of Economic Surveys.* 17, 115–56.

Internal Revenue Service (2006). *Statistics of Income Tax Stats, Number of Individual Income Tax Returns, Income, Exemptions and Deductions, Tax, and Average Tax, 2002–2004.*

McIntyer, R., Denk, R., Francis, N., Gardner, M., Gomaa, W., Hsu, F., and Sims, R. (2003). *Who Pays? A Distributional Analysis of the Tax Systems of All Fifty States.* 2nd Edition. Washington, DC: Institute on Taxation and Economic Policy.

Moretti, E. (2004). "Estimating the Social Return to Education: Evidence from Longitudinal and Repeated Cross-Sectional Data." *Journal of Econometrics,* 121:175–212.

National Center for Education Statistics (NCES) (2007). *The Condition of Education.* Washington, DC: U.S. Department of Education.

Rouse, C.E. (2005). "The Labor Market Consequences of an Inadequate Education." Princeton University Working Paper.

U.S. Census Bureau (2006). *Current Population Survey, Annual Social and Economic Supplement, Current Population Reports.*

U.S. Census Bureau (2007). *Statistical Abstract of the United States.* Washington, DC: U.S. Department of Commerce.

RESPOND●

1. What goals did the College Board have in producing this report? What goals do Sandy Baum and Jennifer Ma state that it did *not* have? (See, for example, paragraph 21.) How does this report help the College Board realize its goals? In what ways does the report represent an argument of fact? (For a discussion of arguments of fact, see Chapter 8.)

2. Who is the intended audience for the report? (Assume that there are several intended audiences. Who might they be, and why?)

3. Paragraphs 14–17 discuss the challenges of understanding and using statistical information. How does this discussion contribute to the ethos of the College Board, as publisher of the report? How does it seek to prevent misuse of the data included in the report? (A correlation is a relationship between two phenomena that, as noted, cannot be interpreted as one of cause and effect. For example, skin cancer

rates are high among tennis players in the Southwest. Thus, there is a correlation between frequently playing tennis in the Southwest and developing skin cancer. But playing tennis itself doesn't cause skin cancer anywhere, including the Southwest, so there is no cause-and-effect relationship between playing tennis and cancer. The high level of skin cancer there is linked to high levels of sun exposure.

4. What is your response to this excerpt? How aware were you of the information presented here? Does this information encourage you to think in new ways about your efforts to get a college education? Why or why not? If so, how?

5. The figures included in this selection relate to the financial benefits of higher education. Choose one figure that you find especially interesting, and **write a summary of the figure** that you might include in an essay on this topic. Your summary should be two or three paragraphs in length. It will likely be informed by the commentary included with each figure, but do not rely only on that commentary. Instead, analyze the chart yourself so that you can draw generalizations not already included in the commentary.

6. As noted, the second part of the original report focuses on the distribution of the benefits of higher education by seeking to answer the question "Who Participates and Succeeds in Higher Education?" Download the report, and study its second part. (The report is available at http://www.collegeboard.com/prod_downloads/about/news _info/trends/ed_pays_2007.) Choose at least two figures, and **write a factual argument** based on them. If you are in science or engineering, for example, you may wish to choose Figure 2.12, "Percentage of Individuals Age 24 with First University Degree in Science and Engineering and Other Fields, by Selected Region and Country/ Economy, 2002 or Most Recent Year" and Figure 2.13, "International Comparisons: Achievement Levels of 15-Year-Olds." Use these two figures to write an essay about how American youth compare to people of other countries with respect to math and sciences. (For a discussion of arguments based on fact, see Chapter 8.)

"Kitchen Conferences and Garage Cubicles: The Merger of Home and Work in the 24-7 Global Economy" originally appeared in the 2008 book The Changing Landscape of Work and Family in the American Middle Class: Reports from the Field, *edited by Elizabeth Rudd and Lara Descartes. Each of the fourteen major chapters of the book reports on a study that was conducted by a researcher affiliated with the University of Michigan's Center on the Ethnography of Everyday Life, funded during the late 1990s by the Alfred P. Sloan Foundation to provide insights into the changing nature of working families in the United States. Ethnography, a genre of writing that seeks to produce "thick descriptions" of a social group, community, or culture in context, is based on long-term participant observation: the researcher spends extended periods of time with the people who are being studied to understand how the world looks from their perspective. Alesia Montgomery, for example, explains that she spent ten to fifteen hours a week for four months observing one family and conducted interviews and follow-up visits over five years. An especially interesting feature of* The Changing Landscape *is that each chapter has an afterword in which the researcher reflects on the research process.*

Although all of the studies in the book are interesting, we chose this one for two reasons: it provides useful historical information on the shifting nature of the family, home, and work over the past few hundred years (which it uses as background for a detailed ethnographic study), and the study focuses on how the globalized economy is altering how we think about family, home, and work. In this excerpt, we present the first half of the study, its conclusion, and the afterword, in which Montgomery, currently an assistant professor of sociology at Michigan State University, provides some biographical details. Several sections providing more detail about the lives of the family are omitted. As you read, consider how Montgomery combines knowledge of history with ethnographic observations to give readers insights into the complexities of family, home, and work in early twenty-first-century America.

Kitchen Conferences and Garage Cubicles: The Merger of Home and Work in the 24-7 Global Economy (Excerpt)

ALESIA MONTGOMERY

> This is the true nature of home—it is the place of Peace; the shelter . . .
> so far as the anxieties of the outer life penetrate into it . . . it ceases to
> be home; it is then only a part of that outer world which you have
> roofed over, and lighted fire in.
>
> —John Ruskin, 1865, *Sesame and Lilies*

Silicon Valley: the southern part of the San Francisco Bay area, sometimes referred to as the "capital" or center of the high-tech industry in the United States.

As I began studying their mergers of paid work and family life in February 2000, Marjaneh and Steve—a married couple in their thirties—and Marjaneh's parents had just bought a home in an affluent Silicon Valley° neighborhood.[1]

Marjaneh and her parents were Iranian immigrants. Steve was American-born, with roots in Eastern Europe. Their new surroundings seemed idyllic. Beyond their window, squirrels played in fruit trees, birds darted from dangling feeders, and a golden retriever bounded down the quiet street to catch a Frisbee tossed by children.

The view from the family's window did not completely reveal the setting of their home lives. Email, faxes, and phone calls linked their home to high-tech firms within Silicon Valley and around the world. Although there were no parking lots or numbered suites, their pleasant neighborhood with its rose gardens and fruit trees was, in some sense, a busy industrial park. During the high-tech boom of the late 1990s, the family and some of their neighbors converted their garages and lofts into offices that enabled their homes to serve as "branches" of Silicon Valley firms. Marjaneh, her husband, and her father all had demanding high-tech jobs, and they collaborated on job tasks at home to meet these demands even though they had different employers. A business cycle (the high-tech boom and bust) and a cultural calendar (most notably, observance of the Iranian New Year, *Norouz°*) clashed in the home. Ancient seasonal celebrations organized around the cycles of agricultural work are not easily sustained in a 24-7 work world. Marjaneh's mother, a

Montgomery relies on multiple forms of evidence, both firsthand and secondhand, to build her argument. How many different forms of evidence can you find? For more on the wide variety of evidence you can use to build an argument, see Chapter 16.

LINK TO P. 493 ....

Norouz: the New Year celebration in Iran and Central Asia. It occurs on the first day of spring and dates to the pre-Christian era.

High-density housing has become popular as the population of Silicon Valley exploded, making affordable housing scarce.

store manager, was the only family member who did not work in high-tech. She struggled to get the family to maintain "normal" patterns of family time, room use, and guest entertainment.

Does opening the home to job demands and work anxieties threaten the "true nature of the home," as nineteenth-century writer John Ruskin warned? In this chapter I argue that contemporary gender relations, management strategies, and technological practices enable diverse family and work forms—including work collaborations at home between husbands and wives and among parents and their adult children. Far from weakening family bonds, these mergers of home and work foster family cohesion. Unlike relations in the old middle class of shopkeepers, these mergers are not necessarily male-dominated—in Marjaneh's home, *she* led work collaborations. Yet similar to shopkeeping, the collaborations of Marjaneh and her family increased family togetherness and interdependence. Paid work and family life often are described as competing for time—an accurate description of time conflicts when work and home are separate spheres (Hochschild 1989, 1997, Perlow 1997). However, for Marjaneh's family and similar households in which work and home merge, the problem is not so much that job demands usurp family time, but rather that the home does not buffer job pressures.

THE TRANSFORMATION OF FAMILY LABOR FROM AGRARIAN TO HIGH-TECH WORK

The separation of family life and paid work has not always been the norm. The industrial transformations of the eighteenth and nineteenth centuries in the United States and Europe increasingly removed production from the home, while cultural transformations valorized the home as a haven from the harsh work world. John Ruskin (1865) and other writers encouraged the rising middle class to embrace this new domestic ideal, but the separation of spheres was neither decisive nor abrupt. Employers relied upon fathers to discipline family work units in some early factories (Tilly and Scott 1989), and kin were sources of capital and labor for big industrialists and small shopkeepers (Segalan 1996). The baker's wife iced cakes a few steps from her husband, the butcher and his son chopped meat on the same counter, and for the family of grocers who lived in their shop, work and home merged. Until the early twentieth century, even scientists drew their households into their work (Pycior, Slack, and Abir-Am 1996). To gain access to their fields, the few women in science collaborated at home with their male relatives.

In the early twentieth century, corporations supplanted many family firms (Winder 1995), credentialed engineers replaced informally trained mechanics 5

(Noble 1977), and "big science"—large projects that required numerous researchers and massive facilities—rose to prominence (Galison and Hevly 1992). Paid work became increasingly impersonal in its staffing and site. Based on his study of engineering firms in the 1970s, Robert Zussman (1987) describes engineering as the "prototypical occupation" of the "new middle class." The men in his study did not draw their wives into their work lives, and their wives did not involve them in family care. At the time of Zussman's study, some stay-at-home wives did "invisible work" such as typing that helped their husbands' careers (Kanter 1977, Papanek 1973, Smith 1987), but few wives of engineers had sufficient technical skills to help their husbands with work.

A move toward egalitarian marriages (Scanzoni, Polonko, Teachman, and Thompson 1989) and an easing of barriers to women's education and employment have expanded the possibilities for spousal collaboration in technical professions. Over the past few decades, women in the United States have increased their education in science and technology. For example, women held 17.9 percent of bachelor's degrees in engineering by 1996, compared to only 0.4 percent in 1966 (National Science Foundation 2000). In those years, the percentages of women with bachelor's degrees in the physical sciences and computer science also rose (from 14 percent to 37 percent and from 14.6 percent to 27.6 percent, respectively).

As the possibilities for spouses to collaborate increase, new management strategies encourage collaborations across firms. Compared to firms in the 1950s, employers today offer less job security and fewer job ladders; professionals use their personal ties to update their skills, find jobs, and advance their "boundaryless careers" across firms (Arthur and Rousseau 1996). Firms also have become less bounded. To deal with increased competition in the global economy, business is increasingly organized as a "network enterprise" that comprises shifting project alliances within and across firms and nations (Castells 1996).

The high-tech industry exemplifies trends toward boundaryless careers and firms. Researchers note the challenges of job insecurity, long work hours, and transnational work processes in high-tech (Barley and Kunda 2004, Benner 2002, Ó Riáin 2000), and they trace the inter-firm and personal ties that enhance careers and the bottom line of high-tech firms (Saxenian 1994, 1996). Employers sometimes demand that managers and professionals make themselves available twenty-four hours a day, seven days a week, to collaborate with distant colleagues on far-flung projects.

New communication tools facilitate these 24-7 work flows. Economic historian Joel Mokyr (2001) speculates that the benefits of moving production from households to centralized workplaces during the Industrial Revolution may be changing today with the advent of new technologies. The barriers to organizing workers and information across different places and times have decreased. Mokyr predicts that centralized workplaces will continue to exist for aspects of production that require face-to-face coordination, but many workers increasingly will work from home.

In 2002, approximately 61 percent of U.S. employees reportedly used 10 email on the job, and almost half of these work emailers also reportedly checked their work email from home (Fallows 2002). Between 2001 and 2002, more than a third of workers (38 percent) in the California Workforce Study (CWS) stated that they used pagers or cell phones on the job (Fligstein and Sharon 2002). Managers (65 percent) and professionals (44 percent) were most likely to use these devices. Among those who used these devices, 88 percent of managers and 68 percent of professionals reportedly used them for work after work hours. Compared to others in the CWS study, managers and professionals reportedly worked longer hours and were most likely to report that they had difficulty finding time for both family and work. The CWS study did not address how work and family time overlap. New technologies increase the possibilities for families to stay in contact during paid work (English-Lueck 2002), yet new technological practices also may facilitate exploitation: Studying teleworkers, Janet Salaff (2002) expresses concern that telework shifts burdens such as technical support from co-workers to families.

MERGERS OF HOME AND WORK IN A "JOB-SHARING" FAMILY

Marjaneh's family exemplifies how new technologies, management strategies, and gender relations are changing the possibilities for work collaborations within households. As a teenager, Marjaneh had helped out in her father's shop after her family emigrated to the United States. Similarly, Steve had done assembly work in the small side business that his father had run from the family garage. As family members switched from being shopkeepers to salaried professionals, they still worked together, but the nature of their collaborations changed. In line with Judith Stacey (1996), I described Marjaneh's family as "postmodern"—that is, a family that diverges from modern° ideals of separate spheres and from modern realities in which wives gave "invisible" help that supported the business and careers of their husbands. Marjaneh's family mixed feminist sensibilities, a superficially modern spatial divide (Steve drove to work; Marjaneh worked at home), and

modern: here, relating to the beginning of the period of the Industrial Revolution in the late eighteenth century.

a form of household labor (they collaborated on job tasks) that was almost pre-modern.° They were a *job-sharing family* as opposed to a shopkeeping family. The gender relations, management strategies, and communication technologies of postmodernity do not support an infinite array of family and work forms, but these forms are elastic and diverse.

pre-modern: relating to the period when most families engaged in farming or handicraft work rather than factory work.

From Shopkeeping to Job-Sharing

A decade before my study, Marjaneh and Steve had shared an apartment with Marjaneh's parents while the newlyweds worked as counter clerks at her father's hardware shop. The pace of the work had been slow, with plenty of time to buy coffee from a nearby café or read a newspaper. Marjaneh and Steve had just graduated from college, and they were waiting for responses to their resumes. As an undergraduate, Marjaneh started off majoring in the social sciences. After she met Steve, she began to take computer science courses. From chats with Steve and reading magazines, she believed that a high-tech career would be exciting and lucrative. Steve aided her to make the transition, assisting with her math homework. In exchange, Marjaneh helped Steve write papers for his courses.

After a few months at the shop of Marjaneh's father, the couple landed jobs as programmers at the same firm, and they got their own apartment. Marjaneh switched from programming to high-tech marketing. Although the couple no longer had the same employer, they helped each other with job tasks at home. Their educational and work histories had primed them for collaboration, and their shared technical expertise and industry knowledge were useful to each other. When they bought a home with Marjaneh's parents, their collaborations once again became intergenerational.

High-Tech Boom, Bust, and Revival

Between February and May 2000, I spent ten to fifteen hours per week observing Marjaneh's home life, and I interviewed Steve and Marjaneh (my main focus) before and after my four months of observations. To see a range of family activities, I varied the time of day and week of my visits. By chance, my observations began before the Iranian New Year in March and the high-tech downturn in April—events that affected their practices. After my observations in 2000, I kept in touch by phone, and I returned to their home for a few days each year between 2001 and 2005 to track changes.

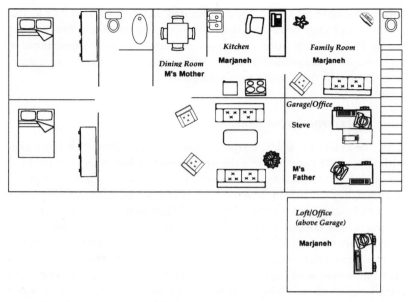

Spaces for Job Tasks in Marjaneh's Household, February 2000. Labeled areas indicate the family member who most often used room as a space to do job tasks.

Domestic Spaces as Job Cubicles

Before the high-tech downturn of April 2000, I made a diagram of the family's 15
use of domestic space for job tasks [see above]. Marjaneh telecommuted as a
high-tech marketing manager. Occasionally she had to make business trips
in and beyond the United States, but usually she worked from home. Her
main office was her loft, yet other rooms gradually filled with her files and
reports. When she first moved into her new home, Marjaneh had planned to
contain her work in her loft/office, but she said that she found it lonely. She
often worked with her laptop on the kitchen counter while watching TV and
talking to Steve and her parents.

Marjaneh had thought telecommuting would give her more control over
her day, but job demands increasingly dictated her use of household space
and her family interactions. Business calls interrupted chats with family
members and their viewing of TV shows in the evenings and on weekends.
When the phone rang, Marjaneh's dog would bark and she had to run from
the room or shush it. Also, she had to move away from the fountain in the
kitchen. Her father had placed a small stone fountain on the counter among

the flowers as a gift to Marjaneh. The water made splashing and tinkling noises. She said that she found the sound soothing, but she worried that callers might think that she was in the bathroom. In addition, she had to shush or escape from family members who called each other loudly or broke into laughter. Her parents sometimes seemed hurt or confused when she motioned for them to be quiet or to go away while she was on the phone, but she didn't feel that she had a choice. She also worried about awakening her family. She chose the loft as her office so she wouldn't disturb her family when she had to make calls at odd hours to the East Coast, Europe, or Asia.

Marjaneh had to constantly manage sounds. When she made business calls, she could be calling from anywhere—her home, her car, an airport, a regional office, a client's site, San Francisco, New York, London. . . . Not all of these places sounded "professional." A few times she took business calls in a local restaurant's parking lot. While her husband ate inside the noisy restaurant, she ran with her cell phone to the quiet of her car. When I began studying the family, Marjaneh did not have a cell phone—she was anxious about the possible brain cancer risks of holding a cell phone near her head. However, she got one after colleagues expressed surprise that she was not always accessible by phone. As a compromise, she bought a headset to distance the cell phone from her head.

Her husband, Steve, a software developer at a different firm, usually got his job done at his workplace. Both Marjaneh and her mother voiced concern that his long hours at his workplace were bad for his health, and they worried that it was dangerous for him to come home late at night. To pacify them, Steve sometimes used his garage/office for job tasks such as writing technical documentation. Marjaneh proofread his documentation (similar to their college days when she had helped with his papers). Occasionally at home he would get a call or email from a colleague in Silicon Valley or elsewhere about a problem with a program that his project team had written. Most of the time he would go to his workplace to deal with crises, but he increasingly dealt with crises from home, getting access to programs through a secure server.

Almost every night and weekend, Steve helped Marjaneh with her work reports. He spent at least ten hours each week on her projects, drawing upon his technical and industry knowledge. Marjaneh said that she often felt guilty asking him for help because he was tired and stressed from his own job. Steve helped Marjaneh to get her job done so that she could come to bed or watch TV. Marjaneh's mumblings that she could lose her job if she did not meet job demands also spurred his help. When they completed a project, he enjoyed her praise, and they often would go out to a restaurant to celebrate. However, when Marjaneh felt that Steve was not working quickly enough on her projects—or when Marjaneh had not proofread Steve's technical documentation—they would argue or not speak. Marjaneh noted that there were strong incentives for them to "make up" quickly whenever they had a falling out: They depended on each other's practical and emotional support to cope with work. Employer demands were displaced onto their personal relations, complicating their interactions.

While the job demands of Marjaneh and Steve often involved responding 20 to crises, the job demands of Marjaneh's parents were usually routine and contained within their workplaces. However, the older couple also did some work at home. Marjaneh's father, an engineer at a high-tech firm, shared the garage/office with Steve, engaging in various work activities (for example, searching the web to find needed information). A hardware engineer, Marjaneh's father served as technical support for the family, fixing their computers and peripherals. This support was useful for Marjaneh, who had difficulty getting timely technical support from her employer.

Marjaneh's mother, a department store manager, used the dining room table as a workspace a couple of times each week for a few hours to fill out paperwork by hand. She often asked Marjaneh to double-check her calculations or to help filling out forms. Unlike Marjaneh's erratic job demands and requests for help with work, her mother's work was predictable. At the end of each month and around certain holidays, she had more paperwork, and thus she brought more work home and desired more help.

The bathrooms were motivational retreats for Marjaneh and Steve, stocked with business journals that saluted the "dot-com revolution." When their energies flagged, Marjaneh and Steve reminded each other about the success stories they had read. In an ethnography of a high-tech firm, Gideon Kunda (1992) describes how senior managers use meetings to make ideological points and inculcate corporate culture. Business journals served a similar function within Marjaneh and Steve's home, but these journals fostered allegiance to high-tech business culture, not to a specific firm.

Proximity facilitated their collaborations. While Marjaneh's mother did paperwork at the dining table, Marjaneh might go to the kitchen and pour herself a cup of tea; her mother would call out for Marjaneh to double-check her calculations. And while Steve and Marjaneh watched TV, Marjaneh might get a business call; Steve would ask about the call and get drawn into giving help. Or while Steve and his father-in-law sat in the garage/office, his father-in-law might ask Steve a work question.

Like Steve and Marjaneh, many other couples today share work space at home.

On Saturdays, everyone in the house often was engaged in paid work or family support of paid work. While Marjaneh and her family worked on their own jobs or helped each other with work, Latina immigrants—a mother and a daughter—helped each other to clean the house. The "hired help" enabled Marjaneh's family to devote more of their time to their jobs. Marjaneh served as a kind of office manager. She would get up from her desk and move from loft to family room, family room to garage, garage to living room, directing the house cleaners . . . checking up on her husband's progress doing research for her . . . seeking out her father if she had a computer problem . . . helping her mother with paperwork from her job.

Throughout the week, Steve did much of the cooking. Praised as the fam- 25 ily "chef," he had honed his skills by watching cooking shows and buying cookbooks. On the weekends he prepared and froze meals for the week. The family also often ate at restaurants and bought fast food. Marjaneh rarely cooked. Although she was at home all day, she did not want to be viewed as a housewife. Since the days when they were students, Steve had agreed that placing her in that role would be sexist and unfair, so he had accepted cooking as his chore.

The family's labor divisions defied conventions of the breadwinner husband and the homemaker wife, yet their use of domestic space was to some extent gendered. Steve and his father-in-law never used the kitchen or dining areas for their job tasks, and Marjaneh and her mother rarely used the garage. Marjaneh found the garage cold and gloomy. Her father and husband left the cases off their computers after tinkering on them, exposing the metal and wire "innards" (as Marjaneh called them). Ripped-out innards were scattered on the floors, desks, and shelves. The innards made Marjaneh uncomfortable. Perhaps there are gendered computing aesthetics, influenced by cultural taboos against women tinkering with machines (Turkle 1995).

These gendered spaces made it more likely that Marjaneh would be drawn into helping her mother, and Steve would be drawn into collaborations with his father-in-law. Intergenerational exchanges about the nuts-and-bolts of computer hardware flowed between Marjaneh's father and Steve rather than between father and daughter. Steve became back-up technical support for the family, tinkering on their machines. . . .

CONCLUSION

plethora: a large number.

Often when one listens to researchers discuss the effects of paid work on family life, one gets the impression that work time limits family time. Researchers should pay more attention to the plethora° of family and work forms. While some families "juggle" home and work, others combine spheres. In this chapter I have shown how transformations in gender relations, management strategies, and technological practices enable some professionals to merge work and home in quasi-entrepreneurial ways that recall pre-industrial agrarian households and modern shopkeeping families. This merger can have positive influences on family togetherness and interdependence—separate spheres are not necessarily the most desirable family and work forms.

I do not mean to suggest that merging home and work has no downsides. For Marjaneh and Steve, combining home and work had mixed consequences. On the one hand, working on job tasks at home increased their family cohesion. On the other hand, this merger reduced the degree to which their home served as a refuge from job pressures. Marjaneh and Steve were exhausted by long work hours at their home, and they got into fights over their work collaborations. Mergers of home and work did not reduce their time together, but these mergers restricted the time that they had for preserving cultural calendars, entertaining guests, and relaxing with each other. Similar to the old middle class of shopkeepers, they collaborated to meet heavy job demands. Unlike shopkeeping families, they faced erratic demands that were driven by global processes. These global processes were "sped up" and made more invasive by the use of innovative communication technologies in a "new economy."

As Steve observed, job demands *limited the control* that they had over the 30 time and space of family life; family time was not so much cut as *depersonalized*. In the process, there was the danger (as Marjaneh suggested) that they might become strangers to that part of themselves and each other that was unrelated to the demands of work in a 24-7 global economy. Marjaneh and Steve "chose" to engage in work collaborations, yet their work practices were structured by employer expectations and work cultures that pushed them to be continuously connected to 24-7 work flows. They did not perceive many options. If they wished to hold onto their insecure yet lucrative jobs, their "choice" seemed to be between long work hours together or apart.

AFTERWORD

Identities and backgrounds matter in ethnographic research (as in any social interaction), but the subsets of our identities and experiences that matter change from situation to situation, and they are not always obvious.

This ethnography would have been different if I had shared the same ethnic background as Marjaneh and her parents. If I were a native Farsi speaker (instead of someone who had acquired a toddler-level grasp of the language from a workbook and tapes), I would have been better able to follow their conversations when they mixed English with Farsi. If I had been born in Iran and made a similar journey to the United States (instead of being someone who had merely read about Iran and its immigrants), I would have had a richer, felt understanding of the meanings of time, space, and sociality for them. Indeed, if my focus of study were the older couple instead of Marjaneh and Steve (who did not speak Farsi to each other), I would not have undertaken this project.

Yet I believe that one can make useful sociological observations about people even if one does not share their ethnicity. Born and raised in South L.A., I am an African American ethnographer who sometimes studies people with whom I seem to have little in common. Years ago, I acquired my taste for ethnography in a high school program that encouraged students to use the entire L.A. metropolis as a classroom—not just the region's many museums and libraries but also its diverse streets and people. The program helped me to see that people and places that seem very insular and strange at first glance often have interesting links to or similarities with familiar people and places.

Once while I was walking down Venice Boulevard carrying out some independent study or another for this high school project (I dimly remember I wanted to map changes in people and shops from working-class Arlington Boulevard down to bohemian Venice Beach), a friend from my neighborhood (who was also in the program) pulled up to the curb: She was on her way to interview the Hare Krishna. Did I want to come along? I said "Sure" and hopped in the car. The Hare Krishna temple was just a few blocks away. If memory serves, the young guy whom we met was named Mario Karma (Chicano? Italian?); he had grown up in L.A.'s urban core, and he mentioned various places that we knew. As he gave us a tour, I was struck by how familiar things seemed. As a child, I had been taken to Catholic and Pentecostal churches, and the sights, sounds, and smells of the Hare Krishna temple reminded me of these experiences: The incense, the statues, the chants (Catholic), the tambourines and ecstatic dancing (Pentecostal). I do not mean to suggest anything as saccharine as "people are the same wherever you go"—it is unwise to ignore the ways in which the interests and beliefs of groups clash with each other—yet the forms by which divergent groups express themselves around and through their bodies often have interesting convergences. These convergences enable a level of empathy that facilitates the interpretation of experiences.

As a teenager, I simply wanted to document diverse forms or ways of being in the world. Today, as a sociologist, I am interested in how and why particular forms—enabled by societal structures and global developments—emerge at particular historical moments among certain types of people in specific places. In the case of Marjaneh and Steve, I traced the ways in which their work form was enabled and structured by social, economic, and technological transformations. I strongly empathized with them. At the time of my study, I was a graduate student. Although different processes, relations, and ideologies structure my 24-7 work demands, I too longed for time to sleep.

NOTES

This research was made possible by a predoctoral fellowship from the UC Berkeley Center on Working Families, funded by the Alfred P. Sloan Foundation's program in Workplace, Workforce and Working Families.

1. Names and other identifying information have been altered to preserve confidentiality.

References

Arthur, Michael B., and Denise M. Rousseau, eds, 1996. *The boundaryless career: A new employment principle for a new employment era.* New York: Oxford University Press.

Barley, Stephen R., and Gideon Kunda. 2004. *Gurus, hired guns, and warm bodies: Itinerant experts in a knowledge economy.* Princeton, NJ: Princeton University Press.

Benner, Chris. 2002. *Work in the new economy: Flexible labor markets in Silicon Valley.* Cambridge, MA: Blackwell.

Castells, Manuel. 1996. *The rise of the network society.* Cambridge, MA: Blackwell.

English-Lueck, Jan A. 2002. *Cultures@SiliconValley.* Stanford, CA: Stanford University Press.

Fallows, Deborah. 2002. *Email at work.* Washington, DC: Pew Internet and American Life Project.

Fligstein, Neil, and Ofer Sharone. 2002. *Work in the postindustrial economy of California.* Berkeley, CA: Institute for Labor and Employment, University of California.

Galison, Peter, and Bruce Hevly, eds. 1992. *Big science: The growth of large scale research.* Stanford, CA: Stanford University Press.

Hochschild, Arlie. 1989. *The second shift.* New York: Viking.

———. 1997. *The time bind: When work becomes home and home becomes work.* New York: Metropolitan Books.

Kanter, Rosabeth M. 1977. *Men and women of the corporation.* New York: Basic Books.

Kunda, Gideon. 1992. *Engineering culture: Control and commitment in a high-tech corporation.* Philadelphia: Temple University Press.

Mokyr, Joel. 2001. "The rise and fall of the factory system: technology, firms, and households since the Industrial Revolution." www.faculty.econ.northwestern.edu/faculty/mokyr/pittsburgh.PDF

National Science Foundation. 2000. "Women as a percentage of all bachelor's degree recipients, by field: 1966–1996." *In Women, minorities, and persons with disabilities in science and engineering: 2000.* Arlington, VA: National Science Foundation (NSF 00-327).

Noble, David F. 1977. *America by design: Science, technology, and the rise of corporate capitalism.* Oxford: Oxford University Press.

Ó Riáin, Seán. 2000. "Net-working for a living: Irish software developers in the global workplace." In *Global Ethnography,* ed. Michael Burawoy, Joseph A. Blum, Sheba George, Zsuzsa Gille, Millie Thayer, Teresa Gowan, Lynne Haney, Maren Klawiter, Steve H. Lopez, and Seán Ó Riáin, 175–202. Berkeley, CA: University of California Press.

Papanek, Hanna. 1973. "Men, women, and work: Reflections on the two-person career." *American Journal of Sociology* 78(4): 852–72.

Perlow, Leslie A. 1997. *Finding time: How corporations, individuals, and families can benefit from new work practices.* Ithaca, NY: Cornell University Press.

Pycior, Helena M., Nancy G. Slack, and Pnina G. Abir-Am, eds. 1996. *Creative couples in the sciences.* New Brunswick, NJ: Rutgers University Press.

Ruskin, John. [1865] 1998. *Sesame and lilies.* www.gutenberg.org/etext/1293

Salaff, Janet W. 2002. "Where home is the office: The new form of flexible work." In *The internet in everyday life*, ed. Barry Wellman and Caroline Haythornwaite, 464–95. Oxford: Blackwell.

Saxenian, Annalee. 1994. *Regional advantage: Culture and competition in Silicon Valley and Route 129.* Cambridge, MA: Harvard University Press.

———. 1996. Beyond boundaries: Open labor markets and learning in Silicon Valley. In *The boundaryless career: A new employment principle for a new organizational era*, ed. Michael B. Arthur and Denise M. Rousseau, 23–39. New York: Oxford University Press.

Scanzoni, John, Karen Polonko, Jay D. Teachman, and Linda Thompson. 1989. *The sexual bond: rethinking families and close relationships.* Newbury Park, CA: Sage.

Segalen, Martine. 1996. "The Industrial Revolution: From proletariat to bourgeoisie." In *A history of the family, volume II: The impact of modernity*, ed. Andre Burguiere, Christiane Klapisch-Zuber, Martine Segalen, and Francoise Zonabend, 377–415. Cambridge, MA: Harvard University Press.

Smith, Dorothy. 1987. "Women's inequality in the family." In *Families and work*, ed. Naomi Gerstel and Harriet Engle Gross, 23–54. Philadelphia: Temple University Press.

Stacey, Judith. 1996. *In the name of the family: Rethinking family values in the postmodern age.* Boston: Beacon Press.

Tilly, Louise, and Jason Scott, 1989. *Women, work, and family.* New York: Routledge.

Turkle, Sherry. 1995. *Life on the screen: Identity in the age of the internet.* New York: Simon & Schuster.

Winder, Gordon. 1995. "Before the corporation and mass production: the licensing regime in the manufacture of North American harvesting machinery, 1830–1910." *Annals of the Association of American Geographers* 85(3): 521–52.

Zussman, Robert. 1987. "Work and family in the new middle class." In *Families and work*, ed. Naomi Gerstel and Harriet Engle Gross, 338–46. Philadelphia: Temple University Press.

RESPOND

1. The opening paragraph of this study explains that Alesia Montgomery is interested in the "mergers of paid work and family life." Rather than relying on questionnaires, surveys, or even interviews alone, she uses ethnography—prolonged participant observation where the researcher in some sense becomes part of the lives of those studied. What kinds

of evidence might such observation yield? What benefits might there be to studying a specific case in detail? What limitations?

2. How does the review of earlier studies about the gendered nature of work and family life provide necessary background for this study? How does it create a context for this study? Was this information new to you?

3. One of Montgomery's concerns is how technological advances are shaping contemporary life. How is this concern manifested in her report of Marjaneh and Steve's life? In what ways is this topic an organizing principle of her discussion?

4. Ethnographers are generally concerned with issues of space and the ways that the use of space shapes human interaction. How do we see this concern reflected in Montgomery's analysis? What role does the figure on p. 1014 play in Montgomery's description and analysis? Why is it important to her argument?

5. On first reading an ethnographic study, students who are not familiar with the genre sometimes claim that no data are presented. How might Montgomery respond? In other words, for an ethnographer, what counts as data?

6. Ethnographers generally are not interested in providing simple or simplistic descriptions of the phenomena that they study, and one of the goals of ethnography is often to help us, in the words of anthropologist Clifford Geertz, "see . . . ourselves among others"—that is, to see our own lives in new ways and to appreciate the ways that they are similar to and different from the lives of others. Reflect on the links between home and work in your own life and the life of your family. Is your home "a shelter" (as Ruskin defined "home") or something else? How have the technological developments of the past few decades shaped your or your family's life? How have they influenced the relationships among family, work, and home? Have these changes been related to gender in any way? **Write an essay** in which you explore these issues. To prepare for this task, make notes about the details of your own life for a few days—for example, your schedule, the technology that you use, and the number of times that you use technology. If you are in your teens or twenties, you may wish to interview some people who are over fifty to discover their perspectives on how technology continues to change the merger of family life and paid work.

We close this chapter with two related texts by Stewart D. Friedman, an award-winning teacher who is founding director of the Leadership Program and the Work/Life Integration Project at the Wharton School of the University of Pennsylvania. (Wharton was founded in 1881 as the first U.S. college-affiliated school of business.) Much of Friedman's research and publishing focuses on how people integrate work into their lives. The first text is a transcript of a short video that appears on Amazon.com's Web site selling Friedman's 2008 book, *Total Leadership: Be a Better Leader, Have a Richer Life*. For Friedman, *total leadership* is a vision of leadership that is informed by a person's core values, which are reflected in all aspects of his or her life. It contrasts with notions of leadership that focus only on the workplace. Such a redefinition of leadership is currently going on at many business schools across the United States and around the world. (Information on Friedman's approach, including training workshops and testimonials from former participants, can be found at http://www.totalleadership.org.)

The second text is a chapter from Friedman's book. Like much writing for members of the professional classes, it assumes an educated reader whose job includes supervising other people. It likewise assumes that the reader wants to do a better job of supervising than she or he currently is able to do. Although this selection is based on research in management, business, and psychology, it is not written like a textbook that presents a great deal of detailed information. In some ways, its frequent exercises and questions to reflect on make it seem like a self-help book. Finally, it makes an argument that is distinct from the arguments of other similar books: the writer hopes to sell books and likely tickets to training workshops. As you watch the video, study the transcript, read the chapter, and do the exercises, reflect on the many things that Friedman has mastered about how to construct effective arguments. At the same time, reflect on what you're working for and the likelihood that it will help you to be a better leader and have a richer life.

The Fallacy of "Work–Life Balance"

STEWART D. FRIEDMAN

Transcript of the Video on Amazon.com for the Book *Total Leadership*

http://www.amazon.com/gp/mpd/permalink/m39ac1ujq5dhud

Harvard Business Publishing
Total Leadership: Be a Better Leader, Have a Richer Life

Stewart D. Friedman, Author

A lot of people talk about work-life balance, many more people today than when I first started addressing this issue twenty years ago when my first son was born. And it's become a very present issue in many different sectors of

Compare Friedman's short video presentation with his written chapter. In what ways does the presentation, as an argument to be heard, differ from the written chapter? For more on oral arguments, see Chapter 15.

LINK TO P. 468

our society and abroad. And there's a lot of important reasons for that. But balance is the wrong metaphor. Balance is the wrong metaphor because it implies tradeoffs. It implies that you've got to give up one part of your life to have success in another part. And what I want to encourage people to do is to see the possibility of what I call "four-way wins," which requires that you use leadership to better integrate the different parts of your life, all four: work, home, community, and self.

Please email feedback to:
video@harvardbusiness.org
Harvard Business Publishing is an affiliate of Harvard Business School

Take the Four-Way View

STEWART D. FRIEDMAN

core values: the values that you hold "most dear and are willing to strive or even fight for." In an earlier chapter of his book, Friedman asks his readers to complete an exercise in which they come up with a list of five to nine core values and to explain the importance of each in one to two sentences. To get them started, he provides a list of forty-two values (such as "achievement, advancement, adventure, aesthetics, affluence, authority") along with short definitions, all based on the work of other researchers.

Kerry (Tanaka): a person that Friedman discusses as an example in an earlier chapter.

Now that you've thought about your core values° and your vision of the kind of world you want to create, we're ready to go deeper into what it means for you to act with authenticity by exploring the relative importance of the four domains of your life, the attention you give them, whether the goals you pursue in each one are in sync with the others, and how satisfied you are with how things are going, in each area and altogether. Like Kerry,° Lim Chang did all this too.

Lim's five-foot-ten-inch body barely contains his infectious energy. His jet-black hair contrasts sharply with the pearly-white teeth that shine brightly through his smile. Lim is the "rah-rah" guy on the soccer team who is always screaming to pump up his teammates. The son of a physician father and a homemaker mother, Lim, thirty-four, and his wife have a two-year-old son and another on the way. From offices in Orange County, he and the dozen people directly reporting to him manage West Coast operations of a national retail design firm. Although he works fifty-five to sixty hours each week, he makes it a point not to work on weekends.

He runs marathons for fun, though when I first met him, Lim was finding it quite difficult to keep up his exercise regimen. The issues that motivated his interest in my Total Leadership course were not unlike those many people confront. He was having a hard time achieving what at first he called "balance" between the different areas of his life. Here's what he wrote about his early efforts in the program, about two years after having completed it:

> One of the exercises in the initial push to clarify what was important was a chart that showed the level of importance of each of my four life domains and the time I was devoting to each. It became clear that I was paying a disproportionate amount of attention to my career and that I wasn't spending nearly enough time on developing my mind, body, and spirit.
>
> But it wasn't just about how I was spending my time, as I saw when I drew four circles representing what I really cared about in each of the four domains. I asked myself, did the circles line up as they do in the center of a tree, or were they disconnected, like random puddles all over the place? Was I being the person (the strong, centered "tree") I really wanted to be? The short answer: no. This made me feel uncomfortable.
>
> I rated how happy I was with the different aspects of my life, and I was surprised. If someone had simply asked me how satisfied I was in each

domain, the answers would not have matched that chart. By assessing the importance, time, and energy I gave to each domain, and the give-and-take among them, I was able to more realistically evaluate my overall satisfaction. It turned out that I was much more satisfied with work and family than with my community and self—that was not my intuition going into the exercise.

I started asking . . . What changes could I make to pay more attention to what really mattered to me—and less to what didn't? What was it that I was doing at work and at home that made me feel good about how things were going there? Was it that my behavior at work and at home was more consistent with my core values? What would people at work and home say made me most successful? If I could answer these questions, I might find new ways of using what I already knew about producing satisfaction at work and at home to improve my community and self areas.

Just as Lim did, in this chapter you're going to learn to take the four-way view. By looking closely at the different domains of your life—work, home, community, and self—you'll clarify what's important to you and see your life from a fresh perspective. You'll also begin to explore what it means for you to act with integrity by recognizing the whole person.

The exercises you'll do in this chapter will help you to discover whether 5 you're being real: are you paying attention to what you care about most, acting in ways that are consistent with the person you want to be, going after goals that matter, and achieving happiness in all the parts as well in your life as a whole?

DEFINE YOUR DOMAINS

Start by defining your four domains. This is a subjective process, so you must define your domains in whatever way makes the most sense for you. For most people, the work domain is your job: what you do for a living or, if you're between jobs, what you're aiming to do next. If you're in school, whether or not you have a job as well, then school is part of your work domain. To fully grasp what your work domain comprises, think beyond just the hours you sit in your cubicle, office, or whatever your work space is, and consider the wide array of things you do as part of your career. This might include taking classes, traveling, participating in trade associations, talking to mentors about your career, or doing research on future entrepreneurial opportunities.

Then there's the home, or family, domain. Again, it's a subjective judgment you'll make here. This domain can include the people (or animals) you live with, your family of origin (parents, siblings, and others), or your family of creation (spouse, significant other, children, and others).

Likewise, the net you cast around your community or society domain can be as wide as you like, including friends, neighbors, social groups, religious institutions, charitable activities, political committees, membership in non-profit organizations, or anything that bears on your impact on the world beyond your work and your family.

Finally, there is the domain of yourself. This includes your emotional health, intellectual knowledge, physical health, leisure, and spiritual life.

THE FOUR-WAY ATTENTION CHART

The next step in understanding your four life domains is to examine your 10 choices about the focus of your attention to them in light of their relative importance to you. Completing the four-way attention chart fills in an essential part of the picture of how things stand today. It shows how you manage the allocation of your time and energy—the amount of attention you pay to the various people and projects in your life—and so helps you assess whether you're actually doing what you care about doing.

This chart doesn't, however, address the other part of the picture: whether or not your actions and your goals for each domain—the how and the why—are in harmony with the others. We'll explore that later in this chapter. Together, these two assessments give a full picture of whether you're demonstrating authenticity and being real in all domains of your life. And painting it is a crucial step forward in your thinking about the experiments you might try to improve your satisfaction and performance in all domains.

Keep in mind, as you do this exercise, that your subjective judgment is all that matters here. For instance, your involvement in community and society is whatever this means to you, and not what others want of you. So it may be about giving money to charity, helping your friends, cleaning up your neighborhood, or getting involved in targeted campaigns to make the world a better place. And remember that this chart indicates only how you see things now. When you complete this chart again, after your experiments, your numbers will probably be different, if you're like most people who've done this. As you progress through the book—as you learn more about how to demonstrate authenticity, integrity, and creativity—the relationships among work, home, community, and self will change.

Victor (Gardener): a person that Friedman discusses as an example in an earlier chapter.

Victor's° Four-Way Attention Chart

Victor assessed the importance of the four major areas of his life by assigning these percentages in the first column: 35, 35, 10, and 20. At the same time

The Four-Way Attention Chart

One way of being real is to grasp the connection between the importance of each part of your life and what you actually pay attention to every day. The chart below is another window through which to see what's important to you. In the first column, consider the relative importance of each major area of your life *today*. Assign a percentage to each and make sure they add up to 100. If you place as much importance on work/career/school as you do on the other three areas of your life combined, put "50%" in that cell on the chart. If, as another example, all four domains are of equal importance to you, then put "25%" in each cell of the first column.

In the second column, consider how much time and energy you actually focus on each domain in a typical week. Assign a percentage to each. Make sure these numbers, too, add up to 100.

Domain	Importance	Focus of time and energy
Work/Career/School	%	%
Home/Family	%	%
Community/Society	%	%
Self: mind, body, spirit	%	%
	100%	100%

After you've completed the chart, write notes in response to the following questions:

1. What are the consequences of the current choices you make about your focus of time and energy spent at work, at home, in the community, and for yourself?

2. As you look at these eight numbers, are there any adjustments you'd like to make—either in what's important or in where you focus your attention—to change any of these numbers?

3. What would it take to actually make these adjustments in your life?

he started the Total Leadership program, Victor's work domain included being an IT director in a major bank *and* being a student in a full-time executive MBA program that convened for classes every other weekend and for longer stretches in the summer. This part, he observed, was equal in weight to his family domain, which comprised his wife, two children, and parents. His community domain, he noted, comprised a few friends and just a bit more. Of the four domains, he was unapologetic about this being the least important to him. Finally, his interest in his own personal fulfillment was less important to him than his work and his family, but more important than his involvement in community and society.

Victor then distributed percentages to indicate how much time and energy he actually spent in each area, in a typical week, in the second column: 65, 20, 5, and 10. In a demonstration of an obvious mismatch—which most people report when they do this exercise—he overemphasized work compared with the other domains. Everyone's chart is unique, of course. But what typically transpires over the course of the Total Leadership program is a noticeable move toward a closer fit between what's important and where you devote your attention. Here's some of what Victor said about his four-way attention chart:

What I care about and what I do with my time are not very well aligned. The mismatch with my family really bothers me. I make an effort to spend time at either end of the day to be around our kids by taking them to school, or just trying to get home before they go to bed, but our interactions aren't going that well at the moment—probably because I'm so preoccupied with work and school. My wife's started to refer to herself as a "single mom."

I just don't care much about my community domain right now. I try to keep up with my friends and do a small amount of volunteering and charitable giving. It's all I can do. And as for my self domain, I'm probably in the worst physical and spiritual shape ever. But I feel that I need to defer doing anything about this right now.

I'm just trying to do everything—and succeeding at little. It's imperative that I find ways of having the different parts of my life create more positive impact on each other. Otherwise, I don't see how I can keep dissatisfaction in one area of my life from spilling over into other areas.

The self-awareness Victor developed through this exercise was an important step. By thinking about his responses to his four-way attention chart, Victor started asking new questions about where he might find opportunities for constructive change in how he wove together his work and the rest of his life. Was there a way, for example, for him to make adjustments that would make his wife feel less like a "single mom" that would, at the same time, inspire him to bring greater enthusiasm to his work? Was it possible for him to give more attention to improving his physical well-being and, in doing so, produce benefits not only for his health but also for his employer, his family, and his community? [15]

These questions helped him to start thinking about some changes. But there was more to do still in finding gaps between the current state of things and what he really wanted in his life.

Your Four Circles

Once you have completed your four-way attention chart, you're ready to draw a graphical representation of the four domains that will help you perceive whether or not they are in harmony. The attention chart is especially useful for getting you to look squarely at the issue of your choices about the allocation of your attention—your time and energy. Drawing the four circles asks you to consider a different question: are you the same person wherever you go?

Here, it's not a matter of how much attention you're devoting to the different parts of your life but, rather, how the interests you are serving in one domain relate to your interests in the other domains. Are you being the person you want to be, no matter where you are in life?

The Four Circles

Are the four domains of your life compatible or in conflict? Before you draw anything, there are two choices to make as you think about the pattern of your four circles.

- **Consider size.** The first choice you've already made; that is, the *size* of the circles. The size of each circle corresponds to the importance you assigned to it in the first column of the four-way attention chart. If, for example, "Work" was 30 percent and "Home" was 40 percent, then the "Home" circle would be about one-third bigger than the "Work" circle. In this case, work is less important than home.

- **Think about relative location.** The second choice is each circle's *location in relation to the others*: do they overlap or are they separate? Where you place your four circles, how much they overlap represents your best estimate of how compatible or incompatible the domains are with each other. Complete *harmony* between any two domains—which exists when the aims in one domain, and your way of achieving them, fit perfectly with the other domain—would be represented by complete overlap of the two representative circles. Complete incompatibility, or *conflict*, between any two domains—when your actions and their results in one are antagonistic to the other—would be shown by representative circles that have no overlap at all.

Now you are ready to draw your circles. Take a piece of paper, or find a digital file, or go to www.totalleadership.org, and draw four circles, each representing one of the four domains: work, home, community, and self. Write the name of each domain in or around the corresponding circle.

Begin to write down your thoughts. One way to think about achieving greater authenticity is to imagine what you would have to do to have a life illustrated by four completely overlapping circles. Keep in mind that few people have completely overlapping circles; this is an image to aim for. What are your ideas for how you might pursue goals in such a way as to achieve greater overlap, or compatibility, and to reduce conflict among domains?

We'll use your four circles as another tool for gaining a deeper understanding of what's important to you in the different roles you play in life, how they affect each other, and where there are gaps between domains that you can close.

Imagine the Perfect Center of a Tree

Complete overlap of all four domains is, of course, extraordinarily rare. It's [20] hard to conceive of a real life in which the goals you seek and the way you act in all aspects of your life are in pure harmony. The best examples might be those of great religious leaders—the likes of Buddha, Christ, Mohammed, the Dalai Lama, and Moses. In the lives of these exemplars, the purposes pursued by the private person were essentially the same as those sought in the context of their work, family, and society.

But since you're human, not divine, don't worry if your four circles don't line up exactly. Indeed, if you drew your circles to look like the perfect center of a strong tree's trunk, with all four domains concentric around a common core, then please return this book immediately and contact me to arrange an interview! Consider that complete incompatibility between any two domains—circles that have no common area at all—is not uncommon. There is almost always some conflict, in the real world, between who you are in one part of your life and who you are in the other parts.

It's useful to identify areas of compatibility, as well as of discord, among life domains, for this helps you to see the harmony that already exists, and so give you ideas for expanding it. You'll start to ask, "If I can do it here, why not there . . . and there?"

This picture serves as an instrument to help you think about the relationships among the different parts of your life. The center of a tree is an ideal to strive for, and the contrast between it and your current picture, the one you just drew, can lead you to new ideas for taking action to increase your authenticity. The closer you can get to entirely overlapping domains, in other words, the more likely you're being the person you want to be, wherever you are and in whatever role you're in at that moment.

Learning from the Four Circles

We read what Victor thought about when he examined his responses to the four-way attention chart. Now lets look at how he drew his four circles, shown in figure 3-1.

This image painfully revealed to Victor that there was no overlap whatso- [25] ever between his work and family domains.

Figure 3-1. Victor's four circles

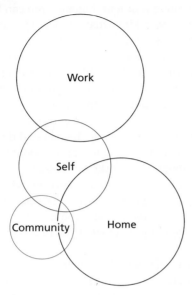

Work is pretty much out there on its own. There is some overlap with my self domain, as I get a good feeling about my self from having a successful working life. But that's pretty much it. I find this rather distressing! And there is not much overlap between my self and family domains at the moment. I really must do something about this.

What Victor realized when analyzing the picture he drew of his four circles is that, among other things, the person he is at work—the goals and interests he pursues as an IT director at an investment bank—is entirely different from the father and husband he wants to be at home. In Victor's leadership vision, parts of which you read in chapter 2, he wrote about having his children engaged in his work and also about applying skills he developed teaching his children music to his managerial responsibilities at work. There was some overlap between work and home domains in that leadership vision, but there were none that he could see in his current life circumstances. What Victor learned was discouraging to him, but it was a wake-up call, a seed of transformation. Already, Victor had clarified what's important to him. He began to create new insights about possible four-way wins.

One goal of the Total Leadership process is to create change in order to produce harmony among your four domains. You can learn, in other words, from your four circles by asking what you would have to do to have them overlapping. You might start by looking, for example, at your work. Would you have to change your career entirely to bring it closer to the person you are in your family? Or, instead, would you have to change how you think about what you do at work as it relates to your family, your role in society, and your mind, body, and spirit? Another way to approach this issue is to ask about the purpose of your career: is it to earn money to keep you and your loved ones fed and sheltered, to enjoy the material things in life, or is there something about it that makes you feel proud about the impact you're having on the world through your work? And if so, how does this feeling affect how your friends and family see you? Further, what would you have to change to make this feeling grow and be more a part of your everyday experience of your work and career? Would you have to *act* differently, or would you have to *think* differently about what you're accomplishing through your work?

Now let's consider questions about your home and family. What changes would you have to make to bring this part of your life into harmony with the other parts? Let's say you're a student just about to graduate college, for example. Would you have to change the level of dependence you now have on your parents? If so, how might you do this in a way that would be good for them and for you? Or let's say you're living in an intimate relationship with someone who has different values from yours and doesn't support the role you're playing in society. Should you end the relationship? Less drastically, perhaps, is there a way to change how she sees this other part of your life so that she becomes more supportive of it?

Pondering such questions as you look at your four circles generates ideas for specific things you might do to achieve greater compatibility and less conflict.

Roxanne's drawing of her four circles (see figure 3-2) was quite different from Victor's.

Even though there is no overlap between Roxanne's self and work domains—in other words, her professional life just isn't in sync with what she wants for her self in promoting a healthy mind, body, and spirit—there is quite a lot of overlap otherwise. For instance, through her roles as a mother and as a business professional, she feels she's making valuable contributions to society in raising her children and in selling chemical products that improve health care.

Figure 3-2. Roxanne's four circles

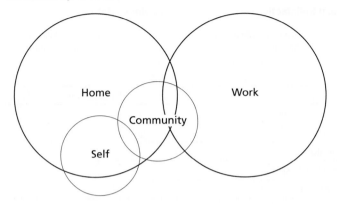

In studying her four circles, Roxanne began to have some thoughts about things she could do to produce even greater overlap.

> I tend to work at home on the weekends, mainly because, I'm embarrassed to admit, I've just not been creative enough to find something more engaging to do with my family that's good for all of us. I guess I've been driven by the belief that all my investments in work will free up my time to do other things later—and it's always *later*—when something more important is planned for our family.
>
> Maybe I can plan some things to do now with my family—like golf, tennis, swimming—that are also things that I want to do for myself. Or I can plan family activities that support what I'd like to be doing for our local community. Or I can become involved with already existing work activities that support the community, such as the United Way.

Just as it was for Roxanne, the picture you draw of your four circles is another tool for stimulating your thinking about how *you* might create better harmony among your life domains. But we're not quite done with the four-way view of your life's domains.

DOMAIN SATISFACTION:
YOUR FOUR-WAY HAPPINESS RATING

Now assess whether or not you're satisfied with each domain, and with your life as a whole. In other words, are you happy with how things are going?

Domain Satisfaction—The Four-Way Happiness Rating	
Indicate how satisfied you are presently with how things are going in each domain, and for your life as a whole, by writing a number from 1 to 10, where 1 = not satisfied and 10 = fully satisfied, in the appropriate column.	
Domain	**Satisfaction**
Work/Career/School	
Home/Family	
Community/Society	
Self: mind, body, spirit	
Life as a whole	

JUST A MATTER OF TIME?

So what is it about the relationship among the four domains that affects whether you feel satisfied? How you spend your time matters, of course. But, it turns out that, surprising as it might seem, managing your time is *not* the major factor. In a study described in *Work and Family—Allies or Enemies?* Jeff Greenhaus and I found that while the "time bind" so often cited in the literature on work/family conflict is no doubt very real, there is a more subtle and pervasive problem that reduces satisfaction in the different domains of life: psychological interference between them.[1] That's when your mind is pulled to somewhere other than where your body is. This happens to all of us. There may even be times when you've been reading this book and your eyes are on the page but your mind has drifted off. You aren't focused. Put differently, there are times when you might be physically present but psychologically absent—something people can usually tell because it affects your ability to connect with them.

If you reduce psychological interference, you increase your ability to focus on *what* matters *when* it matters, and you minimize the destructive impact conflicts can cause between, for instance, work and family. A main premise of this book is that it takes leadership skill to manage the boundaries between the different areas of your life—not just the physical boundaries of time and space, but the psychological boundaries of focus and attention—and to integrate them well for mutual gain.

Being real by demonstrating authenticity is a necessary first step. You must assess the relationship between what's important and where you devote your time. But you must also understand the implications of what your four circles mean to you. André, the married father of two young children and product manager for a global software developer, had this to say about what he learned from his analysis of the relationships among his four domains:

> When I first thought about creating the four circles, I realized that I had been looking at my life domains as separate wedges of a pie rather than as circles that could overlap. In other words, I was viewing my life—and its different parts—as a zero-sum game where to give to one part, I had to take from somewhere else. And where did it get me? When I took actions to make things better in one domain, it always meant decreasing my satisfaction in another domain.
>
> I believe this is why I find it so difficult to be fully engaged in the different domains. So often, I just feel as if I'm being pulled in different directions. When I try to prioritize things, I end up failing to meet expectations and do what people legitimately expect of me. That makes me dissatisfied.
>
> Looking at the domains this way has helped me realize that I have to change my thought process and find new ways to integrate the different areas of my life. They do overlap, and they need to overlap. They're not separate pieces of the pie.

Is it possible to have your pie and eat it too? The evidence I've seen convinces me that it is—certainly more so than most people believe. Getting there means taking steps to ensure that the goals you're pursuing in each domain of your life are mutually enriching *and* consistent with your core values and aspirations. Does this mean you need to change how you spend your time? Probably, and it might also mean change in how you think about what you're doing with the time you're spending.

Clarifying what's important enhances your sense of authenticity, of being who you want to be. You can take control and create for yourself a life where you do not always have to trade success and satisfaction in one domain for success and satisfaction in another.

When you've clarified what's important to you, you become more of a 40 leader who acts with authenticity, whose values and actions are aligned. When you lead with authenticity, it's easier to get support from the important people in your life. This book is not about striking a balance between work and the rest of life. It is about identifying your values—what's important to you—and making them come alive in your everyday actions at work, at home, in the community, and for your self.

Having done all this soul searching, looking within, you'll now look outward in the next steps on this journey.

Pause and Reflect on Your Four-Way View

Here are things to keep in mind as you synthesize what you've done in chapter 3 before moving on to chapter 4. Read through your responses to the exercises in this chapter. Consider the following questions. Write about them and then, if possible, talk about them with your coach.

1. What are the main ideas you take away from what you've just read?

2. What is the biggest disconnect in the relationship among your four domains?

3. What changes might you make to bring the four domains of your life into greater harmony?

4. How would such changes affect your happiness ratings?

NOTE

1. Stewart D. Friedman and Jeffrey H. Greenhaus, *Work and Family—Allies or Enemies? What Happens When Business Professionals Confront Life Choices* (New York: Oxford University Press, 2000).

RESPOND •

1. What argument is Stewart D. Friedman making in the video that is excerpted on the Amazon.com Web site? In what ways is it a definitional argument? (In addition to the features of definitional argument discussed in Chapter 9, note that a common strategy in a definitional argument is saying what something is *not*, as Friedman does here.) How is ethos created in this short video? (Consider not only what is said but also how it is packaged.)

2. Focus on the structure of the chapter from *Total Leadership*. (You may wish to list the titles of the sections and exercises in the order in which they occur to help you analyze the chapter's structure.) To what extent and in what ways is this chapter organized according to the principles of stasis theory (which are discussed in Chapter 1) or the categories of argument that are presented in the text (arguments of fact, arguments of definition, arguments of evaluation, causal arguments, and proposals)? Why is such an organization appropriate, given Friedman's goals?

3. How does Friedman use the extended examples of Victor and Roxanne to advance his argument? Would his argument be less effective without these examples? Why? What specific roles do they play in the argument?

4. What role do the activities in the chapter play in Friedman's argument? What did you learn from doing them, for example? (If you didn't complete them, do so now.) How are these activities indicated in the text? How effective is the layout of the text in this regard? What roles do Figures 3-1 and 3-2 play in Friedman's argument? What are the benefits of including two such figures, rather than simply relying on one?

5. What are you working for? Using the tools that Friedman provides in this chapter, **write an essay** in which you discuss your own efforts to understand the life that you seek, balancing commitments to work, home, community, and self. This essay may draw on any of the categories of argument that are presented in the text. You may wish to use a chart illustrating your four circles. In writing, you may draw on other readings in this chapter, other reading that you have done on this topic, and thoughts that you've had about these issues.

GLOSSARY

academic argument writing that is addressed to an audience well informed about the topic, that aims to convey a clear and compelling point in a somewhat formal style, and that follows agreed-upon conventions of usage, punctuation, and formats.

accidental condition in a definition, an element that helps to explain what's being defined but isn't essential to it. An accidental condition in defining a bird might be "ability to fly" because most, but not all, birds can fly. (See also *essential condition* and *sufficient condition*.)

ad hominem **argument** a fallacy of argument in which a writer's claim is answered by irrelevant attacks on his or her character.

analogy an extended comparison between something unfamiliar and something more familiar for the purpose of illuminating or dramatizing the unfamiliar. An analogy might, say, compare nuclear fission (less familiar) to a pool player's opening break (more familiar).

anaphora a figure of speech involving repetition, particularly of the same word at the beginning of several clauses.

antithesis the use of parallel structures to call attention to contrasts or opposites, as in *Some like it hot; some like it cold.*

antonomasia use of a title, epithet, or description in place of a name, as in *Your Honor* for *Judge.*

argument (1) a spoken, written, or visual text that expresses a point of view; (2) the use of evidence and reason to discover some version of the truth, as distinct from *persuasion*, the attempt to change someone else's point of view.

artistic appeal support for an argument that a writer creates based on principles of reason and shared knowledge rather than on facts and evidence. (See also *inartistic appeal*.)

assumption a belief regarded as true, upon which other claims are based.

assumption, cultural a belief regarded as true or commonsensical within a particular culture, such as the belief in individual freedom in American culture.

audience the person or persons to whom an argument is directed.

authority the quality conveyed by a writer who is knowledgeable about his or her subject and confident in that knowledge.

background the information a writer provides to create the context for an argument.

backing in Toulmin argument, the evidence provided to support a *warrant*.

bandwagon appeal a fallacy of argument in which a course of action is recommended on the grounds that everyone else is following it.

begging the question a fallacy of argument in which a claim is based on the very grounds that are in doubt or dispute: *Rita can't be the bicycle thief; she's never stolen anything.*

causal argument an argument that seeks to explain the effect(s) of a cause, the cause(s) of an effect, or a causal chain in which A causes B, B causes C, C causes D, and so on.

ceremonial argument an argument that deals with current values and addresses questions of praise and blame. Also called *epideictic*, ceremonial arguments include eulogies and graduation speeches.

character, appeal based on a strategy in which a writer presents an authoritative or credible self-image to convince an audience to accept a claim.

claim a statement that asserts a belief or truth. In arguments, most claims require supporting evidence. The claim is a key component in *Toulmin argument*.

classical oration a highly structured form of an argument developed in ancient Greece and Rome to defend or refute a thesis. The oration evolved to include six parts—*exordium, narratio, partitio, confirmatio, refutatio,* and *peroratio.*

confirmatio the fourth part of a classical oration, in which a speaker or writer offers evidence for the claim.

connotation the suggestions or associations that surround most words and extend beyond their literal meaning, creating associational effects. *Slender* and *skinny* have similar meanings, for example, but carry different connotations, the former more positive than the latter.

context the entire situation in which a piece of writing takes place, including the writer's purpose(s) for writing; the intended audience; the time and place of writing; the institutional, social, personal, and other influences on the piece of writing; the material conditions of writing (whether it's, for instance, online or on paper, in handwriting or print); and the writer's attitude toward the subject and the audience.

conviction the belief that a claim or course of action is true or reasonable. In a proposal argument, a writer must move an audience beyond conviction to action.

credibility an impression of integrity, honesty, and trustworthiness conveyed by a writer in an argument.

criterion in evaluative arguments, the standard by which something is measured to determine its quality or value.

definition, argument of an argument in which the claim specifies that something does or doesn't meet the conditions or features set forth in a definition: *Pluto is not a major planet.*

deliberative argument an argument that deals with action to be taken in the future, focusing on matters of policy. Deliberative arguments include parliamentary debates and campaign platforms.

delivery the presentation of a spoken argument.

dogmatism a fallacy of argument in which a claim is supported on the grounds that it's the only conclusion acceptable within a given community.

either-or choice a fallacy of argument in which a complicated issue is misrepresented as offering only two possible alternatives, one of which is often made to seem vastly preferable to the other.

emotional appeal a strategy in which a writer tries to generate specific emotions (such as fear, envy, anger, or pity) in an audience to dispose it to accept a claim.

enthymeme in Toulmin argument, a statement that links a claim to a supporting reason: *The bank will fail* (claim) *because it has lost the support of its largest investors* (reason). In classical rhetoric, an enthymeme is a *syllogism* with one term understood but not stated: *Socrates is mortal because he is a human being.* (The understood term is: *All human beings are mortal.*)

epideictic argument see *ceremonial argument.*

equivocation a fallacy of argument in which a lie is given the appearance of truth, or in which the truth is misrepresented in deceptive language.

essential condition in a definition, an element that must be part of the definition but, by itself, isn't enough to define the term. An essential condition in defining a bird might be "winged": all birds have wings, yet wings alone don't define a bird since some insects and mammals also have wings. (See also *accidental condition* and *sufficient condition.*)

ethical appeal see *character, appeal based on,* and *ethos.*

ethnographic observation a form of field research involving close and extended observation of a group, event, or phenomenon; careful and detailed note-taking during the observation; analysis of the notes; and interpretation of that analysis.

ethos the self-image a writer creates to define a relationship with readers. In arguments, most writers try to establish an ethos that suggests authority and credibility.

evaluation, argument of an argument in which the claim specifies that something does or doesn't meet established criteria: *The Nikon D3X is the most sophisticated digital SLR camera currently available.*

evidence material offered to support an argument. See *artistic appeal* and *inartistic appeal.*

example, definition by a definition that operates by identifying individual examples of what's being defined: *sports car—Corvette, Viper, Miata, Boxster.*

exordium the first part of a classical oration, in which a speaker or writer tries to win the attention and goodwill of an audience while introducing a subject.

experimental evidence evidence gathered through experimentation; often evidence that can be quantified (for example, a survey of students before and after an election might yield statistical evidence about changes in their attitudes toward the candidates). Experimental evidence is frequently crucial to scientific arguments.

fact, argument of an argument in which the claim can be proved or disproved with specific evidence or testimony: *The winter of 1998 was the warmest on record for the United States.*

fallacy of argument a flaw in the structure of an argument that renders its conclusion invalid or suspect. See ad hominem *argument, bandwagon appeal, begging the question, dogmatism, either-or choice, equivocation, false authority, faulty analogy, faulty causality, hasty generalization, non sequitur, scare tactic, sentimental appeal, slippery slope,* and *straw man.*

false authority a fallacy of argument in which a claim is based on the expertise of someone who lacks appropriate credentials.

faulty analogy a fallacy of argument in which a comparison between two objects or concepts is inaccurate or inconsequential.

faulty causality a fallacy of argument making the unwarranted assumption that because one event follows another, the first event causes the second. Also called *post hoc, ergo propter hoc,* faulty causality forms the basis of many superstitions.

firsthand evidence data—including surveys, observations, personal interviews, etc.—collected and personally examined by the writer. (See also *secondhand evidence.*)

flashpoint see *fallacy of argument.*

forensic argument an argument that deals with actions that have occurred in the past. Sometimes called judicial arguments, forensic arguments include legal cases involving judgments of guilt or innocence.

formal definition a definition that identifies something first by the general class to which it belongs *(genus)* and then by the characteristics that distinguish it from other members of that class *(species)*: *Baseball is a game* (genus) *played on a diamond by opposing teams of nine players who score runs by circling bases after striking a ball with a bat* (species).

genus in a definition, the general class to which an object or concept belongs: *baseball is a* sport; *green is a* color.

grounds in Toulmin argument, the evidence provided to support a claim and reason—that is, an *enthymeme.*

hard evidence support for an argument using facts, statistics, testimony, or other evidence the writer finds.

hasty generalization a fallacy of argument in which an inference is drawn from insufficient data.

hyperbole use of overstatement for special effect.

hypothesis an expectation for the findings of one's research or the conclusion to one's argument.

Hypotheses must be tested against evidence, opposing arguments, and so on.

immediate reason the cause that leads directly to an effect, such as an automobile accident that results in an injury to the driver. (See also *necessary reason* and *sufficient reason.*)

inartistic appeal support for an argument using facts, statistics, eyewitness testimony, or other evidence the writer finds rather than creates. (See also *artistic appeal.*)

intended readers the actual, real-life people whom a writer consciously wants to address in a piece of writing.

invention the process of finding and creating arguments to support a claim.

inverted word order moving grammatical elements of a sentence out of their usual order (subject-verb-object/complement) for special effect, as in *Tired I was; sleepy I was not.*

invitational argument a term used by Sonja Foss to describe arguments that are aimed not at vanquishing an opponent but at inviting others to collaborate in exploring mutually satisfying ways to solve problems.

invoked readers the readers directly addressed or implied in a text, which may include some that the writer didn't consciously intend to reach. An argument that refers to *those who have experienced a major trauma,* for example, invokes all readers who have undergone this experience.

irony use of language that suggests a meaning in contrast to the literal meaning of the words.

line of argument a strategy or approach used in an argument. Argumentative strategies include appeals to the heart (emotional appeals), to character (ethical appeals), and to facts and reason (logical appeals).

logical appeal a strategy in which a writer uses facts, evidence, and reason to make audience members accept a claim.

metaphor a figure of speech that makes a comparison, as in *The ship was a beacon of hope.*

narratio the second part of a classical oration, in which a speaker or writer presents the facts of a case.

necessary reason a cause that must be present for an effect to occur; for example, infection with a particular virus is a necessary reason for the development of AIDS. (See also *immediate reason* and *sufficient reason.*)

non sequitur a fallacy of argument in which claims, reasons, or warrants fail to connect logically; one point doesn't follow from another: *If you're really my friend, you'll lend me five hundred dollars.*

operational definition a definition that identifies an object by what it does or by the conditions that create it: *A line is the shortest distance between two points.*

parallelism use of similar grammatical structures or forms for pleasing effect: *in the classroom, on the playground, and at the mall.*

partitio the third part of a classical oration, in which a speaker or writer divides up the subject and explains what the claim will be.

pathos, appeal to see *emotional appeal.*

peroratio the sixth and final part of a classical oration, in which a speaker or writer summarizes the case and moves the audience to action.

persuasion the act of seeking to change someone else's point of view.

precedents actions or decisions in the past that have established a pattern or model for subsequent actions. Precedents are particularly important in legal cases.

premise a statement or position regarded as true and upon which other claims are based.

propaganda an argument advancing a point of view without regard to reason, fairness, or truth.

proposal argument an argument in which a claim is made in favor of or opposing a specific course of action: *Sport-utility vehicles should have to meet the same fuel economy standards as passenger cars.*

purpose the goal of an argument. Purposes include entertaining, informing, convincing, exploring, and deciding, among others.

qualifiers words or phrases that limit the scope of a claim: *usually; in a few cases; under these circumstances.*

qualitative argument an argument of evaluation that relies on nonnumerical criteria supported by reason, tradition, precedent, or logic.

quantitative argument an argument of evaluation that relies on criteria that can be measured, counted, or demonstrated objectively.

reason in writing, a statement that expands a claim by offering evidence to support it. The reason may be a statement of fact or another claim. In *Toulmin argument,* a *reason* is attached to a *claim* by a *warrant,* a statement that establishes the logical connection between claim and supporting reason.

rebuttal an answer that challenges or refutes a specific claim or charge. Rebuttals may also be offered by writers who anticipate objections to the claims or evidence they offer.

rebuttal, conditions of in Toulmin argument, potential objections to an argument. Writers need to anticipate such conditions in shaping their arguments.

refutatio the fifth part of a classical oration, in which a speaker or writer acknowledges and refutes opposing claims or evidence.

reversed structures a figure of speech that involves the inversion of clauses: *What is good in your writing is not original; what is original is not good.*

rhetoric the art of persuasion. Western rhetoric originated in ancient Greece as a discipline to prepare citizens for arguing cases in court.

rhetorical analysis an examination of how well the components of an argument work together to persuade or move an audience.

rhetorical questions questions posed to raise an issue or create an effect rather than to get a response: *You may well wonder, "What's in a name?"*

Rogerian argument an approach to argumentation based on the principle, articulated by psychotherapist Carl Rogers, that audiences respond best when they don't feel threatened. Rogerian argument stresses trust and urges those who disagree to find common ground.

scare tactic a fallacy of argument presenting an issue in terms of exaggerated threats or dangers.

scheme a figure of speech that involves a special arrangement of words, such as inversion.

secondhand evidence any information taken from outside sources, including library research and online sources. (See also *firsthand evidence.*)

sentimental appeal a fallacy of argument in which an appeal is based on excessive emotion.

simile a comparison that uses *like* or *as*: *My love is like a red, red rose* or *I wandered lonely as a cloud.*

slippery slope a fallacy of argument exaggerating the possibility that a relatively inconsequential action or choice today will have serious adverse consequences in the future.

species in a definition, the particular features that distinguish one member of a *genus* from another: *Baseball is a sport* (genus) *played on a diamond by teams of nine players* (species).

spin a kind of political advocacy that makes any fact or event, however unfavorable, serve a political purpose.

stance the writer's attitude toward the topic and the audience.

stasis theory in classical rhetoric, a method for coming up with appropriate arguments by determining the nature of a given situation: *a question of fact; of definition; of quality; or of policy.*

straw man a fallacy of argument in which an opponent's position is misrepresented as being more extreme than it actually is, so that it's easier to refute.

sufficient condition in a definition, an element or set of elements adequate to define a term. A sufficient condition in defining God, for example, might be "supreme being" or "first cause." No other conditions are necessary, though many might be made. (See also *accidental condition* and *essential condition.*)

sufficient reason a cause that alone is enough to produce a particular effect; for example, a particular level of smoke in the air will set off a smoke alarm. (See also *immediate reason* and *necessary reason.*)

syllogism in formal logic, a structure of deductive logic in which correctly formed major and minor premises lead to a necessary conclusion:

Major premise All human beings are mortal.

Minor premise Socrates is a human being.

Conclusion Socrates is mortal.

testimony a personal experience or observation used to support an argument.

thesis a sentence that succinctly states a writer's main point.

Toulmin argument a method of informal logic first described by Stephen Toulmin in *The Uses of Argument* (1958). Toulmin argument describes the key components of an argument as the *claim*, *reason*, *warrant*, *backing*, and *grounds*.

trope a figure of speech that involves a change in the usual meaning or signification of words, such as *metaphor*, *simile*, and *analogy*.

understatement a figure of speech that makes a weaker statement than a situation seems to call for. It can lead to powerful or to humorous effects.

values, appeal to a strategy in which a writer invokes shared principles and traditions of a society as a reason for accepting a claim.

warrant in *Toulmin argument*, the statement (expressed or implied) that establishes the logical connection between a claim and its supporting reason.

Claim	Don't eat that mushroom;
Reason	it's poisonous.
Warrant	What is poisonous should not be eaten.

ACKNOWLEDGMENTS

Chapter-Opening Art

Part 1 (left to right): © Brandon D. Cole/Corbis; AP Photo/Alex Brandon; AP Photo/ Office de Tourisme de Chartres; Desmond Kwande/AFP/Getty Images; AP Photo/Seth Wenig.

Part 2 (left to right): Imaginechina via AP Images; © Warner Bros./Courtesy Everett Collection; Courtesy of Reuben H. Fleet Science Center; AP Photo/PA, Fiona Hanson; © Foodcollection/age footstock.

Part 3 (left to right): © Peter Foley/Pool/epa/Corbis; Louisa Gouliamaki/AFP/ Getty Images; AP Photo/Alex Brandon; © Carlos Barria/Reuters/Corbis; Fox Broadcasting/Photofest © & ™ Fox.

Part 4 (left to right): Phil Cole/Getty Images; Juan Castillo/AFP/Getty Images; Fabrizio Costantini/The New York Times/Redux; © Tim Greyhavens/IPNstock .com; AP Photo/Ron Frehm.

Part 5 (left to right): © A. Ramey/PhotoEdit; (foreground) © Bettmann/Corbis; (background) Luis Acosta/Getty Images; © Ric Ergenbright/Corbis; © Richard A. Brooks/AFP/Getty Images; © Bob Sacha/Corbis.

Text

Marjorie Agosín. "Always Living in Spanish" and "English." Originally appeared in *Poets & Writers* in 1999. "English" translated by Monica Bruno. Reprinted with permission.

Sandy Baum and Jennifer Ma. "Education Pays: The Benefits of Higher Education for Individuals and Society, 2007." Copyright © 2007 the College Board. www.collegeboard.com. Reproduced with permission.

Anne E. Becker. "Abstract, Discussion, and Conclusions of Television, Disordered Eating, and Young Women in Fiji: Negotiating Body Image and Identity during Rapid Social Change." Originally published in *Culture, Medicine and Psychiatry*, December 1, 2004 issue, vol. 28, No. 4, pp. 433–437. Copyright © 2004 by Ovid Technologies, Inc. All rights reserved. Ovid® is a registered trademark of Ovid Technologies, Inc. and cannot be reproduced without permission. Reprinted with permission in the format Textbook via Copyright Clearance Center.

Daniel Ben-Ami. Excerpt from "Why People Hate Fat Americans." From *Spiked* (the London-based independent online publication), September 9, 2005. Copyright © *spiked* 2000–2009. All rights reserved. Reprinted by permission. www.spiked-online.com.

Michael Benson. "Send It Somewhere Special." From *The Washington Post*, Outlook section, July 13, 2008 issue. Copyright © 2008 by Washington Post Writers Group. Reproduced with permission of Washington Post Writers Group in the format Textbook by Copyright Clearance Center.

Richard Bernstein. "The Days After: A View from Abroad." From *The New York Times*, New York Times Blog Section, September 4, 2005 issue. Copyright © 2005 The New York Times. All rights reserved. Used by permission and protected by the Copyright Laws of the United States. The printing, copying, redistribution, or

Mark Bittman. "Why Take Food Seriously?" Originally titled, "The Way We Live Now: 10-12-08: Why Take Food Seriously?" from *The New York Times*, Magazine Section, October 12, 2008 issue, page 13. Copyright © 2008 The New York Times. All rights reserved. Used by permission and protected by the Copyright Laws of the United States. The printing, copying, redistribution, or retransmission of the material without express written permission is prohibited. www.nytimes.com.

Charles M. Blow. "A Profile of Online Profiles." From *The New York Times*, New York Times Blog Section, September 9, 2008 issue. Copyright © 2008 The New York Times. All rights reserved. Used by permission and protected by the Copyright Laws of the United States. The printing, copying, redistribution, or retransmission of the material without express written permission is prohibited. www.nytimes.com.

Derek Bok. "Protecting Freedom of Expression at Harvard." Originally published in *The Boston Globe*, May 25, 1991. Copyright © 1991. Reprinted by permission of the author.

danah m. boyd and Nicole B. Ellison. "Social Network Sites: Definition, History, and Scholarship." From the *Journal of Computer-Mediated Communication*, 13(1), article 11. http://jcmc.indiana.edu/vol13/issue1. Copyright © 2007 Journal of Computer-Mediated Communication. Reprinted with permission of Blackwell Publishing Ltd.

David Brower. Excerpts from "Let the River Run Through It." From *Sierra Magazine* (March/April 1997) by The New York Times Company. Reprinted with permission.

Michelle Bryant. "Selling Safe Sex in Public Schools." From *Life & Letters: A Publication of the College of Liberal Arts of the University of Texas at Austin*, Volume 4, Issue 2, Fall 2005. Reprinted with the permission of The University of Texas at Austin.

Lan Cao. Excerpt (pages 32–39) from *Monkey Bridge* by Lan Cao. Copyright © 1997 by Lan Cao. Used by permission of Viking Penguin, a division of Penguin Group (USA) Inc.

Colin A. Carter and Henry I. Miller. "The Hidden Costs of Corn-Based Ethanol." Opening of the article from *The Christian Science Monitor*, May 21, 2007 edition. Copyright © 2007 The Christian Science Monitor. Reprinted by permission of the publisher. All rights reserved.

"Character and the Primaries" chart. From Journalism.org, May 29, 2008, and the Project for Excellence in Journalism of the Pew Research Center. Copyright © 2008–2009 Project for Excellence in Journalism. Reprinted by permission.

Sandra Cisneros. Excerpt from "Bien Pretty." From *Woman Hollering Creek*. Copyright © 1991 Sandra Cisneros. Published by Vintage Books, a division of Random House, Inc., and originally in hardcover by Random House, Inc. By permission of Susan Bergholz Literary Services, New York, NY, and Lamy, NM. All rights reserved.

Patricia Cohen. "Professors' Liberalism Contagious? Maybe Not." From *The New York Times*, National Section, November 3, 2008. Copyright © 2008 The New York Times. All rights reserved. Used by permission and protected by the Copyright

Laws of the United States. The printing, copying, redistribution, or retransmission of the material without express written permission is prohibited. www.nytimes.com.

Randy Cohen, the Ethicist. "Between the Sexes." Originally published in *The New York Times*, October 27, 2002. Copyright © 2002 Randy Cohen. Reprinted with permission of the author. Includes "Letters in Response to Cohen's Advice" from Cara Weinstein Rosenthal, Helen Pogrin, Robert M. Gottesman, Eve Landy, Paul Berman, Margaret Ross.

David Cole. "What to Do about Torturers." Excerpt from David Cole's review of *Torture Team: Rumsfeld's Memo and the Betrayal of American Values* by Philippe Sands, published in *The New York Review of Books*, January 15, 2009 issue, volume 56, No. 1. Copyright © 2009 The New York Review of Books. Reprinted by permission of the publisher.

Mark Coleman. "Review of *Bottlemania: How Water Went on Sale and Why We Bought It*." From *Los Angeles Times*, June 1, 2008. Copyright © 2008 Los Angeles Times. Reprinted with permission.

Neal Conan. "Is Creating a Fake Online Profile a Criminal Act?" From Neal Conan's *Talk of the Nation* @ www.npr.org, December 4, 2008. Copyright © 2008. Reprinted by permission.

Cook's Country Magazine. "Ready-to-Bake Chocolate Chip Cookies." From the April 2005 issue of *Cook's Country Magazine* and the January 1996 issue of *Cook's Illustrated Magazine*. Copyright © 2005 Cooks Country Magazine. Copyright © 1996 Cook's Illustrated Magazine. Illustrations for "Thick and Chewy Chocolate Chip Cookies" provided by America's Test Kitchen. Copyright © 2009 America's Test Kitchen. Reprinted by permission. All rights reserved. www.americastestkitchen.com.

Cook's Illustrated Web site. Criteria of a good veggie burger from *Cook's Illustrated* online publication. Copyright © 2009 America's Test Kitchen. Reprinted by permission. All rights reserved. www.cooksillustrated.com.

N'Gai Croal. "You Don't Have to Be a Nerd." Excerpt from *Newsweek*, August 18–25, 2008 issue. Copyright © 2008 Newsweek. All rights reserved. Used by permission and protected by the Copyright Laws of the United States. The printing, copying, redistribution, or retransmission of the material without express written permission is prohibited.

Craig R. Dean. Excerpt from "Legalize Gay Marriage." From *The New York Times*, September 28, 1991 issue. Copyright © 1991 The New York Times. All rights reserved. Used by permission and protected by the Copyright Laws of the United States. The printing, copying, redistribution, or retransmission of the material without express written permission is prohibited.

Alan M. Dershowitz. "Testing Speech Codes." From *The Boston Globe Index* (2002). Reprinted by permission of the author.

Sam Dillon. "Evictions at Sorority Raise Issue of Bias." From *The New York Times*, National Section, February 25, 2007 issue, page 17. Copyright ©2007 The New York Times. All rights reserved. Used by permission and protected by the Copyright Laws of the United States. The printing, copying, redistribution, or retransmission of the material without express written permission is prohibited. www.nytimes.com.

William M. Gray and Philip J. Klotzback. Excerpt from "Forecast of Atlantic Hurricane Activity for September and October, 2005 and Seasonal Update Through August." Originally posted on http://hurricane.stmos.colostate.edu/forecasts/2005/sept2005, September 2, 2005. Reprinted with the permission of Dr. William M. Gray, Department of Atmospheric Science, Colorado State University.

Lisa Hardin. "Cultural Stress Linked to Suicide." Originally published in *The Stanford Daily*, May 31, 2007. Copyright © 2007 The Stanford Daily, Inc. All rights reserved. Reprinted with permission.

Heather Havenstein. "One in Five Employers Uses Social Networks in Hiring Process." First published in *Computerworld*, September 15, 2008. Copyright © 2008. Reprinted by permission.

Virginia Heffernan. "Kanye on Keyboards." From *The New York Times Magazine*, August 10, 2008 issue. Copyright © 2008 The New York Times. All rights reserved. Used by permission and protected by the Copyright Laws of the United States. The printing, copying, redistribution, or retransmission of the material without express written permission is prohibited.

Jess Henig and Lori Robertson. "What Is a Civil Union?" Originally published on FactCheck.org. Reprinted by permission.

Tom Hodgkinson. "With Friends Like These." Originally from *The Guardian*, January 14, 2008 issue. Copyright © 2008 Guardian News & Media Ltd, 2008. Reprinted by permission of Guardian News & Media Limited.

David Horowitz. "In Defense of Intellectual Diversity." First published in *The Chronicle of Higher Education*, 2004. Reprinted by permission of the author.

Langston Hughes. "Harlem (2)" ["What happens to a dream deferred..."], from *The Collected Poems of Langston Hughes* by Langston Hughes, edited by Arnold Rampersad with David Roessel, Associate Editor. Copyright © 1994 by the Estate of Langston Hughes. Used by permission of Alfred A. Knopf, a division of Random House, Inc.

Charles Isherwood. "The View From Uptown: American Dreaming to a Latin Beat." From *The New York Times*, March 10, 2008 issue. Copyright © 2008 The New York Times. All rights reserved. Used by permission and protected by the Copyright Laws of the United States. The printing, copying, redistribution, or retransmission of the material without express written permission is prohibited.

Mizuko Ito. Excerpts from "Executive Summary: Living and Learning with New Media: Summary of Findings from the Digital Youth Project." Copyright © 2008. Reprinted by permission.

Penn Jillette. "There Is No God." From the book *This I Believe: The Personal Philosophies of Remarkable Men and Women*, edited by Jay Allison and Dan Gediman. Copyright © 2005 by Penn Jillette. Copyright © 2006 by This I Believe, Inc. Reprinted by arrangement with Henry Holt and Company, LLC.

Sarah Karnasiewicz. "The Campus Crusade for Guys." First published in February 2005 on Salon.com.

Solomon H. Katz. "The World Food Crisis: An Overview of the Causes and Consequences." First published in *Anthropology News*, October 2008. Copyright © 2008 American Anthropological Association. Reprinted with permission of the publisher. www.aaanet.org.

Melanie Springer Mock. "Separation of Church and State: A War on Christmas and Other Misguided Notions." From *The Oregonian*, December 2008. Reprinted by permission of the author.

Alesia Montgomery. "Kitchen Conferences and Garage Cubicles: The Merger of Home and Work in the 24/7 Global Economy." Originally published in *The Changing Landscape of Work and Family in the American Middle Class: Reports from the Field*, edited by Elizabeth Rudd and Lara Descartes. Copyright © 2008. Reprinted by permission of Rowman and Littlefield.

Barbara Munson. "Common Themes and Questions about the Use of 'Indian' Logos." Reprinted by permission of the author.

Charles Murray. "Should the Obama Generation Drop Out?" From *The New York Times*, Op-Ed Section, December 28, 2008 issue, page 9. Copyright © 2008 The New York Times. All rights reserved. Used by permission and protected by the Copyright Laws of the United States. The printing, copying, redistribution, or retransmission of the material without express written permission is prohibited. www.nytimes.com. Letters to the Editor responses from: Jeff Adler, Michael Dedina, Lillian Hoodes, and Sandra Sherman. December 28, 2008. Reprinted with permission.

Cathy Newman. Excerpt from "Why Are We So Fat?" From *National Geographic* magazine, August 2004. Copyright © Cathy Newman/National Geographic Image Collection. Reprinted with permission of National Geographic Society.

Michael Osofsky. Excerpt from "The Psychological Experience of Security Officers Who Work with Executions." From *Stanford Undergraduate Research Journal* (May 2002). Reprinted with permission of the author in the format Textbook via Copyright Clearance Center.

Edward F. Palm. "The Veterans Are Coming! The Veterans Are Coming!" First published in *Inside Higher Education*, September 2008. Reprinted by permission of the author. www.insidehighered.com.

Eboo Patel. "We Are Each Other's Business." Copyright © 2005 by Eboo Patel. From *This I Believe: The Personal Philosophies of Remarkable Men and Women*, edited by Jay Allison and Dan Gediman. Copyright © 2006 by This I Believe, Inc. Reprinted by arrangement with Henry Holt and Company, LLC.

Lynn Peril. Excerpt from "Introduction." From *Pink Think: Becoming a Woman in Many Uneasy Lessons*, by Lynn Peril. Copyright © 2002 by Lynn Peril. Used by permission of W.W. Norton & Company.

Pew Global Attitudes Project. "When It Comes to Religion, the United States Is an Outlier." Adapted from "Unfavorable Views of Jews and Muslims on the Increase in Europe," September 17, 2008, Pew Global Attitudes Project, a Project of the Pew Research Center. Reprinted by permission.

Mark Pytlik. Excerpt from review of M.I.A.'s album, *Kala*. From Pitchforkmedia.com. Reprinted by permission of Pitchfork Media, Inc. All rights reserved. www.pitchforkmedia.com/article/record_review/44983-kala.

Mariam Rahmani. "Wearing a Head Scarf Is My Choice as a Muslim." From the *Austin American-Statesman*, July 1, 2005, pp. 1–3. Copyright © 2005 Mariam Rahmani. Reprinted by permission of Austin American-Statesman, in the format Textbook via Copyright Clearance Center.

Illustrations

p. 300: © Cho Taussig/Courtesy Everett Collection; p. 301: Jim Dyson/Getty Images; p. 313: Courtesy of Jack Chung; p. 321: Jeff Gentner/Getty Images; p. 327: Linda Nylind/Guardian News & Media Ltd 2007; p. 333: AP Photo/Paul Sakuma; p. 337: Karen Kasmauski/National Geographic/Getty Images; p. 345: Courtesy of Helen Garvy and Shire Press and Films; p. 346: Photo courtesy IISD/Earth Negotiations Bulletin; p. 349: AP Photo/Matt Slocum; p. 351: Courtesy of the Everett Collection; p. 355: (t) Peter McDonald, Australian Demographic and Social Research Institute, The Australian National University; p. 369: Dani Cardona/Reuters/Corbis; p. 375: Lester Lefkowitz/Getty Images; p. 376: (t) From *Grand Canyon Adventure: River at Risk*, courtesy MacGillivray Freeman Films; (b) Kevin Moloney/The New York Times/Redux; p. 377: AP Photo/Paul Sakuma; p. 379: Ethan Miller/Getty Images; p. 380: Ron Sanford/Photo Researchers; p. 385: AP Photo/Mary Altaffer; p. 388: AP Photo/PA, Fiona Hanson; p. 390: Courtesy of Xanadu Meadowlands; p. 391: AP Photo/Mike Derer; p. 399: Courtesy of Manasi Deshpande; p. 420: (tl) Picturenet/Veer; (tr) DesignPics Inc., Index Stock/Photolibrary; (b) Collage Photography/Veer; p. 423: Warner Brothers/Photofest; p. 428: Henny Rae Abrams/Getty Images; p. 436: © Peter Foley/Pool/epa/Corbis; p. 440: AP Photo/Milk Processors of America; p. 443: Courtesy The White House; p. 444: © Bettmann/Corbis; Mick Roessler/Photolibrary; p. 445: National Postal Museum; p. 447: Courtesy of the Campaign for Tobacco-Free Kids; p. 448: © Rob Bluey; p. 449: National Portrait Gallery, Smithsonian Institution/Art Resource, NY; p. 450: © Carlos Barria/Reuters/Corbis; p. 451: United Colors of Benetton/Photo by James Mollison; p. 453: NASA; p. 454: Louisa Gouliamaki/AFP/Getty Images; p. 455: AP Photo/Elise Amendola; p. 456: (l) AP Photo/Alex Brandon; (m) Courtesy McDonalds; (r) Louisiana Office of Tourism; p. 459: Ron Kimball Stock; p. 461: Mary Kate Denny/Photo Edit; p. 462: U.S. Census Bureau; p. 464: National Portrait Gallery London; p. 469: (l) U.S. Department of Agriculture; (t) http://www.dailykos.com; (br) Comstock/Punchstock; p. 472: AP/Wide World Photos; p. 474: Fox Broadcasting/Photofest © & ™ Fox; p. 478–482: © Frank Miller; p. 488: Courtesy of Gawker Media; p. 498: Kanye West/Mascotte Holdings, LLC.; p. 502: AP Photo/Mark Humphrey; p. 505: Ryan Collerd/The NY Times/Redux; p. 506–507: Human Rights Watch; p. 512: AP Photo/Ron Frehm; p. 519: Office of National Drug Control Policy; p. 521: © Tim Greyhavens/IPNstock.com; p. 527: Courtesy of Google, Inc. Reprinted with permission; p. 531: (t) Al Messerschmidt/Getty Images; (b) V.J. Lovero/Sports Illustrated/Getty Images; p. 538: Phil Cole/Getty Images; p. 540: Courtesy www.adbusters.org; p. 545: (l) Gene Hunt/Flickr; (m) andi licious/Flickr; (r) pedist/Flickr; p. 551: AP Photo/Reed Saxon; p. 553: (l) Printed with permission from *Popular Science* ® Bonnier Corporation. Copyright 2009. All rights reserved. (r) Reprinted with permission from *American Journal of Physics*, vol. 6, no. 7, July 2008. American Association of Physics Teachers; p. 558: (t) (m) Courtesy of www.mediamatters.org; (b) U.S. Department of State; p. 560: Juan Castillo/AFP/Getty Images; p. 564: Fabrizio Costantini/The New York Times/Redux; p. 586: Slate.com. Reprinted with permission; p. 603: © Andrew Hancock; p. 605: © Andrew Hancock; p. 609: © AP Photo/Reed Saxon; p. 610: © Thomas Cockrem/Alamy; p. 614: © MAPS.com/Corbis; p. 617: © HBO / Courtesy: Everett Collection/photo: Keith Bernstein; p. 621: © WWD/Condé Nast/Corbis; p. 622: Advertisement reprinted courtesy of Kenneth Cole; p. 624: © ALLARM; p. 626: © A. Ramey/PhotoEdit; p. 628: © Macduff Everton/Corbis; p. 633: © Phil Sears; p. 634: © Phil Sears; p. 636: © Eric Charbonneau/WireImage/Getty Images; p. 637: (t) © StockImages/Alamy; (b) © Bettmann/Corbis;

p. 638: © Roger L. Wollenberg/UPI/Landov; p. 641: © Phil Cole/Getty Images; p. 642: © AP Photo; p. 643: (l) Film still from The Miracle Worker/Courtesy Everett Collection; (r) © Robert Pitts/Landov; p. 644: Mary Evans Picture Library/Everett Collection; p. 650: © Lynn Johnson/Aurora/Getty Images; p.656: © AP Photo/G. Patterson; p. 657: danah boyd and Nicole Ellison (2007, October). "Social Network Sites: Definition, History, and Scholarship." Journal of Computer-Mediated Communication, 13(1), article 11.; p. 658: © Landov; p. 660: © C. Lyttle/zefa/Corbis; p. 661: © AP Photo/Evan Agostini; p. 662: © Hector Amezcua/Sacramento Bee/MCT/ Landov; p. 666: Used with permission of Inc. magazine Copyright © 2009. All rights reserved; p. 670: Courtesy Office of the Privacy Commissioner of Canada; p. 674: Photo by Todd Ganci/TGANCI.com; p. 677: © AP Photo/N. Harnik; p. 678: © Geert Allegaert; p. 682: Screenshot reprinted courtesy of the MacArthur Foundation/ macfound.org; p. 688: © Richard A. Brooks/AFP/Getty Images; p. 690: Besiege 3 © 2001–2009 Square Enix Holdings Co., Ltd. All Rights Reserved; p. 692: Screen capture by Dilan Mahendran, 2006. Used by permission; p. 695: © Jolene Kernick; p. 699: © Sheldon Smith/Arizona Daily Wildcat; p. 700: © Ted Soqui/Corbis; p. 701: © AP Photo/Tom Gannam; p. 708: (t) © Michael Golding/The Orange County Register/Zuma; (b) © AP Photo/Orlin Wagner; p. 721: Cindy Charles/Photo Edit, Inc.; p. 725–737: U.S. Census Bureau; p. 739: U.S. Census Bureau, Public Information Office (PIO); p. 744: © Ric Ergenbright/Corbis; p. 747: © Roger Viollet/The Image Works; p. 748: © Bettmann/Corbis; p. 757: © David Wells/The Image Works; p. 765: © Jim McHugh; p. 770: National Institute of Mental Health; p. 771: Agency for Healthcare Research and Quality; p. 779: (t) Rob Melnychuk/Getty Images; (b) © The New York Times; p. 780: George Rose/Getty Images; p. 781: Getty Images; p. 786: © Eleanor Bentall/Corbis; p. 787: Daniel Pepper/Getty Images; p. 796: Luis Acosta/Getty Images; p. 800: Chris Polk/Getty Images; p. 804: © The New Yorker Collection 2003 Alex Gregory from cartoonbank.com. All Rights Reserved; p. 806– 815: Knetchtel, John, ed. Food: Alphabet City Magazine 12, pp. 198–207, © 2007 Massachusetts Institute of Technology & Alphabet City Inc., by permission of The MIT Press and Claire Ironside; p. 806: "The Big Apple, Colborne, Ontario" photograph by Adrian Black; p. 807: "The Orange Julep, Montreal, Quebec" photograph by Adrian Black; p. 817: Dan Kitwood/Getty Images; p. 832: Jon Furniss/Getty Images; p. 838: Romeo Gacad/Getty Images; p. 841: © The New York Times; p. 845: © Ned Frisk/Corbis; p. 852–856: "Pew Global Attitudes Project, Unfavorable Views of Jews and Muslims on the Increase in Europe." 2008; p. 860: (tl) Jacob Silberberg/Getty Images; (tr) © The New York Times; (bl) © Punit Paranjpe/Reuters/Corbis; (br) © The New York Times; p. 861: (tl) © The New York Times; (tr) AP Images/Dita Alangkara; (bl) © The New York Times; (br) Paulo Fridman; p. 866: Sang Yun; p. 867: (l) © Corbis; (r) Joel Robine/Getty Images; p. 872: David Livingston/Getty Images; p. 873: Michael Newman/PhotoEdit; p. 875: Robert Maass; p. 878: Alex Wong/Getty Images; p. 879: Vernon Merritt III/Getty Images; p. 882: © Tim Wright/Corbis; p. 885: © Jonathan Blair/Corbis; p. 886: The Art Archive/Musée du Louvre Paris/Gianni Dagli Orti; p. 889: © Jerome Sessin/In Visu/Corbis; p. 897: Printed by permission of the Norman Rockwell Family Agency. Copyright © 1943 Norman Rockwell Family Entities. Collection of the Norman Rockwell Museum, Stockbridge, Massachusetts; p. 898: © Bettmann/Corbis; p. 903: Used with permission of Student Artist, Joseph Wagner, and Department of Residence Life, Western Washington University; p. 904: Used with permission of Student Artist, Stephanie Heyman, and Department of

Residence Life, Western Washington University; p. 905: Used with permission of Student Artist, Melanie Frost, and Department of Residence Life, Western Washington University; p. 906: Used with permission of Student Artist, Hannah Leimback, and Department of Residence Life, Western Washington University; p. 907: Used with permission of Student Artist, Megan Stampfli, and Department of Residence Life, Western Washington University; p. 909: By permission of Salon .com; p. 917: Mike Lester; p. 918: Dennis Draughon; p. 919: By permission of Mike Thompson and Creators Syndicate, Inc.; p. 920: (t) Signe Wilkinson, Cartoonist Group; (b) Dean Camp; p. 929: Warner Bros./The Kobal Collection/Alex Bailey; p. 934: © Reuters/Corbis; p. 938: Bachrach/Getty Images; p. 950: © Chuck Savage/ Corbis; p. 955: Mark Kauffman/Getty Images; p. 957: © Bettman/Corbis; p. 961: Hulton Archive/Getty Images; p. 964: (t) A. S. Alexander Collection of Ernest Hemingway. Department of Rare Books and Special Collections. Princeton University Library; (b) Paramount/The Kobal Collection; p. 972–974: "Dr. Monica Mayer" by Spencer Wilkinson, Jr., "Ken Kobus" by Ron Baraff, from *Listening is an Act of Love*, edited by David Isay, copyright © 2007 by Sound Portraits Productions, Inc. Used by permission of The Penguin Press, a division of Penguin Group (USA) Inc.; p. 978: © The New York Times; p. 979: Michelle V. Agnis/The New York Times/Redux; p. 987: Bureau of Labor Statistics; p. 1009: © Bob Sacha/Corbis; p. 1014: From *The Changing Landscapes of Work and Family in the American Middle Class: Reports from the Field*, edited by Elizabeth Rudd and Lara Descartes, 2008, Lexington Books. Reprinted with permission of the publisher; p. 1017: © Bill Varie/Somos Images/Corbis; p. 1025: Harvard Business School Publishing.

INDEX